Current Law

STATUTES

1997

VOLUME ONE

AUSTRALIA
LBC Information Services
Sydney

CANADA AND USA
Carswell
Toronto

NEW ZEALAND
Brooker's
Auckland

SINGAPORE AND MALAYSIA
Thomson Information (S.E. Asia)
Singapore

Current Law

STATUTES

1997

VOLUME ONE

SWEET & MAXWELL EDITORIAL TEAM

SHIRLEY ARCHER   PENNY DICKMAN
MELANIE BHAGAT   RACHAEL LOCKLEY
HANNAH CASEY   CERI PICKERING
FIONA CLEAVELEY   JANICE SAYER
MELISSA TEMPLE

W. GREEN EDITORIAL TEAM

STEPHEN HARVEY   PETER NICHOLSON

LONDON

SWEET & MAXWELL

EDINBURGH

W. GREEN

1997

Published by
SWEET & MAXWELL LIMITED
of 100 Avenue Road, London,
and W. GREEN LIMITED
of Alva Street, Edinburgh,
Typeset by MFK Information Services Limited, Hitchin, Herts.
and printed in Great Britain
by The Bath Press,
Bath, Avon.

ISBN This Volume only : 0 421 62860 X
As a set   : 0 421 62890 1

CONTENTS

CHRONOLOGICAL TABLE

VOLUME ONE

Annotators' names are in italic

VOLUME ONE

*c.*1. Horserace Totalisator Board Act 1997
  2. Land Registration Act 1997
     Professor Phillip H. Kenny, Head of School of Law, University of Northumbria at Newcastle
  3. Sea Fisheries (Shellfish) (Amendment) Act 1997
  4. Telecommunications (Fraud) Act 1997
     Richard Briggs, Head of Telecoms Group, Tucker Turner Kingsley Wood & Co. Solicitors
  5. Firearms (Amendment) Act 1997
     Peter J. Clarke, B.C.L., M.A., Barrister, Fellow and Tutor in Law, Jesus College, Oxford
  6. Local Government (Gaelic Names) (Scotland) Act 1997
  7. Northern Ireland Arms Decommissioning Act 1997
     Gary Scanlan and Sarah Gale, City University
  8. Town and Country Planning (Scotland) Act 1997
     David Bartos, LL.B. (Hons.), Advocate; David Cobb, LL.B. (Hons.), Advocate; Andrew F. Stewart, LL.B. (Hons.), Advocate; Jacqueline Williamson, LL.B. (Hons.), LL.M., Advocate, Barrister of the Inner Temple
  9. Planning (Listed Buildings and Conservation Areas) (Scotland) Act 1997
     Jacqueline Williamson, LL.B. (Hons.), LL.M., Advocate, Barrister of the Inner Temple
 10. Planning (Hazardous Substances) (Scotland) Act 1997
     Donald A. Reid, Morton Fraser Partnership, Edinburgh
 11. Planning (Consequential Provisions) (Scotland) Act 1997

ALPHABETICAL INDEX OF SHORT TITLES

STATUTES 1997

(References are to chapter numbers of 1997)

HORSERACE TOTALISATOR BOARD
ACT 1997

(1997 c.1)

An Act to confer power on the Horserace Totalisator Board to receive or negotiate bets made otherwise than by way of pool betting.

[27th February 1997]

PARLIAMENTARY DEBATES
    Hansard, H.L. Vol. 575, cols. 22, 710; Vol. 576, cols. 381, 589, 940. H.C. Vol. 287, col. 586; Vol. 289, col. 1247.

INTRODUCTION
    This Act amends s.1 of the Horserace Totalisator Board and Betting Levy Boards Act 1972 to confer new corporate powers for the Horserace Totalisator Board to receive or negotiate bets made otherwise than by way of pool betting except bets on the outcome of the National Lottery.

New corporate powers for the Horserace Totalisator Board

1.—(1) Section 1 of the Horserace Totalisator and Betting Levy Boards Act 1972 shall be amended as follows.

(2) For subsection (1)(b) there shall be substituted—

"(b) by way of business to receive or negotiate bets on any event made otherwise than by way of pool betting, except bets on the outcome of any lottery forming part of the National Lottery for the purposes of Part I of the National Lottery etc. Act 1993.".

(3) In subsection (2) the words "or (b)" shall be omitted.

Short title and extent

2.—(1) This Act may be cited as the Horserace Totalisator Board Act 1997.

(2) This Act does not extend to Northern Ireland.

INDEX

References are to sections

LAND REGISTRATION ACT 1997*

(1997 C. 2)

An Act to amend the Land Registration Act 1925.   [27th February 1997]

PARLIAMENTARY DEBATES
   Hansard, H.L. Vol. 575, cols. 731, 1159; Vol. 576, cols. 794, 1189. H.C. Vol. 289, col. 1316.

INTRODUCTION AND GENERAL NOTE
   This Act is the direct offspring of a Law Commission Report—*Transfer of Land: Land Registration* (Law Com. No. 235). For once, the whimsicalities of the parliamentary draftsperson have not come between the Law Commission and the effect intended.
   Sections 1 and 3 are concerned with accelerating the process of Land Registration. Section 1 makes a very major change by extending the range of events which lead to compulsory first registration of title. Gifts, dispositions by personal representatives and certain mortgages are brought within the scope of compulsory first registration. This may well cause problems for the inattentive conveyancer who overlooks the need for compulsory registration on the occasion of a routine transaction such as an assent or first mortgage.
   In these cases the effect of this Act will be watched with considerable interest because of the re-shaping (by amendments to the Land Registration Act 1925 (c. 21) (LRA 1925)) of the effect of non-registration. Section 123 of the LRA 1925 has (with no resolution by the courts) posed since 1925 an academic conundrum. The effect of failure to register in the specified time is there stated to be that the transaction becomes "void so far as regards the grant or conveyance of the legal estate". The meaning of this formula has never been before the courts. This is largely because perfectly properly the Land Registry has never refused a request for late registration. It is stated quite firmly in Ruoff and Roper, the sacred text of the registered land practitioner, that such an application for registration will never be refused and that will remain as true after this new Act as before. However, problems as to the effect of non-registration may well arise in the future because of the range of transactions affected by compulsory registration which will be handled by only a single solicitor—there being none of the checks which arise from the involvement of a solicitor acting for both purchaser and vendor. These possible problems are returned to below.
   Section 2 deals with a change to the rules for indemnifying persons as a result of error or omission in a registered title (see Law Commission's *Third Report on Land Registration* (Law Comm No 158).

---

* Annotations by Professor Phillip H. Kenny, Head of School of Law, University of Northumbria at Newcastle.

The reforms made by this Act are uncontroversial. The only criticism is the method of reform. Two sections of the LRA 1925 are amended and a new section (s.123A) inserted. Amongst property lawyers it is probably accepted that the LRA 1925 is the worst drafted piece of the 1925 legislation. Possibly it is the worst drafted piece of significant property legislation since the Prescription Act 1832 (c. 71) which itself is so oddly drafted that it reads like a freehand draft. It is a pity that the long awaited re-write of the Land Registration Act has not yet occurred. In any event developments in the computerised transmission of information will do more than legislation to usher in a new millennium of property ownership. The acid test of the rewrite that is long awaited is whether it will permit the speed and simplicity of dealing with real property that the computer age renders possible. The 1925 legislation has (whether regrettably or not) always been redolent of the world before the typewriter—how far into the future is the Law Commission prepared "*to boldly go*". The present Act is only the tiniest of steps forward.

Registration

Compulsory first registration

1. The following sections shall be substituted for section 123 of the Land Registration Act 1925—

"Compulsory registration: dispositions to which requirement to register applies

123.—(1) The requirement of compulsory registration applies in relation to the following dispositions of unregistered land—

    (a) any qualifying conveyance of the freehold estate;

    (b) any qualifying grant of a term of years absolute of more than 21 years from the date of the grant;

    (c) any qualifying assignment of a term of years absolute which on the date of the assignment has more than 21 years to run; and

    (d) any disposition effected by an assent (including a vesting assent) or by a vesting deed which is a disposition of—

        (i) the freehold estate, or

        (ii) a term of years absolute on which the date of the disposition has more than 21 years to run.

(2) The requirement of compulsory registration also applies in relation to any disposition by the estate owner of unregistered land which is a legal mortgage of—

    (a) the freehold estate, or

    (b) a term of years absolute which on the date of the mortgage has more than 21 years to run,

where, on its creation, the mortgage takes effect as a mortgage to be protected by the deposit of documents relating to that estate or term of years, and ranks in priority ahead of all other mortgages (if any) then affecting that estates or term of years.

(3) Without prejudice to the power to make an order under subsection (4) below, nothing in this section or section 123A of this Act has the effect of requiring the registration of title to—

    (a) an incorporeal hereditament;

    (b) mines and minerals apart from the surface; or

    (c) corporeal hereditaments which are part of a manor and included in the sale of a manor as such.

(4) The Lord Chancellor may by order—

    (a) amend this section so as to add to the dispositions in relation to which the requirement of compulsory registration applies any such disposition of, or otherwise affecting, a legal estate in unregistered land as is specified in the order; and

    (b) make such consequential amendments of any provision of, or having effect under, any Act as he thinks appropriate.

(5) Any order under subsection (4) above shall be made by statutory instrument subject to annulment in pursuance of a resolution of either House of Parliament.

(6) For the purposes of this section—

   (a) a conveyance, grant or assignment is a "qualifying" conveyance, grant or assignment if it is made—

      (i) for valuable or other consideration,

      (ii) by way of gift, or

      (iii) in pursuance of an order of any court;

   (b) a conveyance, grant or assignment of property with a negative value is to be regarded (without prejudice to the generality of paragraph (a)(i) above) as made for valuable or other consideration; and

   (c) "assignment" does not include an assignment or surrender of a lease to the owner of the immediate reversion where the term is to merge in that reversion.

Compulsory registration: effect of requirement to register

123A.—(1) This section applies to any disposition which, by virtue of any provision of section 123 of this Act, is one in relation to which the requirement of compulsory registration applies.

(2) Where any such disposition is effected, then—

   (a) if it is a disposition falling within section 123(1), the person who under the disposition is entitled to the legal estate transferred or created by it, or

   (b) if it is a disposition falling within section 123(2), the estate owner of the legal estate charged by the mortgage, or

   (c) (in either case) that person's successor in title or assign,

must before the end of the applicable period apply to the registrar to be registered (or alternatively, where he is not a person in a fiduciary position, to have any nominee registered) as the first proprietor of that estate.

(3) In this section "the applicable period" means in the first instance the period of two months beginning with the date of the disposition, but—

   (a) the registrar may, if satisfied on the application of any interested person that there is good reason for doing so, make an order extending or further extending that period; and

   (b) if he does so "the applicable period" means that period as for the time being extended under this subsection.

(4) Pending compliance with subsection (2) above the disposition shall operate to transfer or grant a legal estate, or (as the case may be) create a legal mortgage, in accordance with its terms.

(5) If subsection (2) above is not complied with, the disposition shall at the end of the applicable period become void as regards any such transfer, grant or creation of a legal estate; and—

   (a) if it is a disposition purporting to transfer a legal estate, the title to that estate shall thereupon revert to the transferor who shall hold that estate on a bare trust for the transferee;

   (b) if it is a disposition purporting to grant a legal estate or create a legal mortgage, the disposition shall thereupon take effect as if it were a contract to grant or create that estate or mortgage made for valuable consideration (whether or not it was so made or satisfies any of the formal requirements of such a contract).

(6) If an order extending the applicable period under subsection (3) above is made at a time when the disposition has become void in accordance with subsection (5) above, then as from the making of the order—

   (a) subsection (5) shall cease to apply to the disposition, and

   (b) subsection (4) above shall apply to it instead,

and similarly in the case of any further order so made.

(7) If any disposition is subsequently effected by way of replacement for a disposition which has become void in accordance with subsection (5) above, the requirement of compulsory registration shall apply in relation to it under section 123 in the same way as it applied in relation to the void disposition, and the provisions of this section shall have effect accordingly.

(8) Except to the extent to which the parties to any such replacement disposition agree otherwise, the transferee or grantee (as the case may be) shall—

(a) bear all the proper costs of and incidental to the disposition, and
(b) indemnify the transferor or grantor (as the case may be) in respect of any other liability reasonably incurred by him in consequence of the failure to comply with subsection (2) above.

(9) Where any such replacement disposition is a mortgage falling within section 123(2) of this Act, subsection (8) above shall apply as if the reference to the grantee were a reference to the mortgagor and the reference to the grantor were a reference to the mortgagee.

(10) Rules under this Act may make provision—

(a) applying to provisions of this Act to any dealings which take place between—
  (i) the date of any disposition to which this section applies, and
  (ii) the date of the application for first registration,
  as if the dealings had taken place after the date of the registration, and for the registration to be effective as of the date of the application.
(b) enabling the mortgagee under any mortgage falling within section 123(2) of this Act to require the legal estate charged by the mortgage to be registered whether or not the mortgagor consents."

GENERAL NOTE

This replaces s.123 of the Land Registration Act 1925 with a new s.123 and a new s.123A. It is best to look at each separately.

GENERAL NOTE TO NEW S.123 AS SUBSTITUTED

This section declares which transactions lead to compulsory registration. This is best dealt with by a simple table.

TRANSACTIONS REQUIRING/NOT REQUIRING COMPULSORY REGISTRATION

REGISTRATION REQUIRED	REGISTRATION NOT REQUIRED
Conveyance on sale	Mortgage other than a first mortgage secured by deposit of title deeds
Exchange with equality money	
Conveyance in return for the allotment or transfer of shares in a company	Partition
	Assent or appropriation
Conveyance in consideration of a rent-charge or annuity	Conveyance of the interest of an equitable tenant in common or of the legal estate "on the occasion of the purchase or release of a share in the proceeds of all or other beneficial interest" (Ruoff & Roper, *The Law and Practice of Registered Conveyancing* (1986, 5th ed., p. 176)
Compulsory purchase by deed poll	
Compulsory acquisition of a secure tenancy under the Housing Act 1985 (c. 68)	
A purchase under Pt. IV of the Housing Act 1988 (c. 50) (see s.108 and Sched. 12)	Conveyance of an interest which will immediately be merged in a superior registered estate or otherwise determined (LRR r.207)
Leasehold Transactions	

REGISTRATION REQUIRED	REGISTRATION NOT REQUIRED
Surrender of a lease for money consideration which does not result in an immediate merger	An assignment or a surrender of a lease to the owner of the immediate reversion and containing a declaration of merger (LRA 1925, s.123)
An assignment on sale of leasehold land held for a term of years absolute having more than 21 years to run from date of delivery of the assignment*	A conveyance of an equity of Redemption if the consideration is a covenant by purchaser to pay what is owing (*Simpson v. Connolly* [1953] 1 W.L.R. 911).
A grant of a term of years absolute of not more than 21 years from the date of delivery of the grant*	Enfranchisement or extinguishment of manorial incidents (LRA 1925, s.123(3))*
AS A RESULT OF 1997 ACT	Compulsory purchase by a general vesting declaration
Gift†	Souvenir Land Schemes (Land Registration (Souvenir Land) Rules 1972)
Voluntary Settlement†	
First mortgage secured by deposit of Title Deeds†	
Assent†	
Vesting Assent†	
Exchange with no Equality Money†	
An agreement to extinguish an existing debt if land is transferred†	
A conveyance in pursuance of an Order of the Court†	

* Amended by the LRA 1986 (c. 26), s.2.

† Registration is required in these cases if the transaction is with the freehold or a leasehold interest with more than 21 years to run.

Subs. (1)

The above table illustrates the effect of this subsection on the new 'triggers' for compulsory registration. The only areas which may be expected to cause any excitement are the following:
  (i) Conceivably there are some gifts of land which are prepared by laypersons who will be unaware of the requirement for registration;
  (ii) Assents and Vesting Assents are presumably invariably prepared in the office of a solicitor or licensed conveyancer. There is no requirement for compulsory registration as a result of death. The land can remain vested in the personal representatives as such. If it is to be sold this is likely to be the cheaper method of dealing with the estate. The personal representatives may, as they always have been able to, sell as personal representatives without the need for a compulsory registration. Even if a sale is not imminent there is no need for an assent if a sale is to come eventually. The personal representatives' title is not impeachable on the ground that time has elapsed since the grant. An assent is needed only where the personal representatives intend to deal with the land in some way other than a sale.
  (iii) The length of the lease (over 21 years) is tested at the date of the event giving rise to registration. It does not matter that it is shorter than the requisite length by the time of registration (see Sched. 1, para. 1(1)).
  (iv) Where the lease giving rise to registration is one by a charity then certain prescribed statements are required in the mortgage and in the case of a non-exempt charity a restriction is automatically entered on the register (see Sched. 1, para. 6). The form of these will be prescribed by an order under the Charities Act 1993 (c. 10).

Subs. (2)

This will seem to conveyancers a novel and irritating requirement. The need for first registration on the occasion of a first legal mortgage will be in many cases an expensive nuisance. For example, a property holding company owning thousands of titles might decide to remortgage its assets. This will now raise the possibility of an expensive first registration of many titles. In another example, a bank may take a legal charge using its own standard form—here there is often informality in the procedures used and the bank may overlook the need for a first registration.

Subs. (3)

This repeats the clear provisions to the same effect in LRA 1925 and will cause neither surprise nor problems.

Subss. (4), (5)

This permits new 'triggers' for first registration to be added. It does not allow the introduction of compulsory registration other than following a disposition. Thus, primary legislation will one day be necessary if stubborn pockets of unregistered land which have not changed hands are to be registered. But why pass such pointless legislation?

Subs. (6)

This subsection clarifies the meaning of qualifying conveyances. It contains little that will confuse or surprise. It is worth noting that:
— (6)(a)(i) includes exchanges,
— 6(a)(ii) 'gift' includes any settlement or resettlement where the legal estate changes hands,
— 6(b) repeats material in the former s.123(3).

New s.123A as inserted

This is a novel provision which does contain the potential for conveyancing disaster. It provides for who must effect a compulsory registration and a new set of rules governing the failure to make such an application. The long standing rule that compulsory registration must be effected within two months of the disposition giving rise to compulsory registration is unaffected. Similarly the mechanics of compulsory registration remain the same with the important caveat from the Land Registry's point of view that an application for compulsory registration will no longer be preceded, necessarily, by investigation of title by a solicitor. Before preparing deeds of assent and gifts some thought will doubtless be given in future to the question of what evidence will have to be produced to the Land Registry.

Subs. (1)

It will be noted that by virtue of Sched. 1, para. 4, s.123A applies also to cases of compulsory registration following exercise of the right to buy or to purchase a lease under the Housing Act 1985.

Subs. (2)

This subsection specifies who must apply for compulsory registration. The difficult case is sub-para. (b). This is concerned with compulsory registration following mortgages of unregistered land. Compulsory registration must be affected by 'the estate owner of the legal estate charged by the mortgage'. Where a mortgage is completed by a solicitor or licensed conveyancer this requirement will cause no problem. The person completing the mortgage on behalf of the lender will complete the registration on behalf of the borrower. The charge certificate will be returned to the lender's solicitor and thence to the lender for safe keeping.

However, there are many cases where legal mortgages are granted to banks and other lenders with less formality than is required by traditional conveyancing practice. Here it is inevitable that from time to time the need for compulsory registration will be overlooked.

Subs. (3)

The Land Registry has never refused an application for late registration and it can be assumed it never will as the purpose of the Land Registry is to achieve registration not to prevent it.

Subss. (4), (5)

These subsections represent a welcome change. Under the former s.123 the effect of non registration has always been a mystery. The new provisions are clearly drafted. Under subs. (4) the legal estate or title passes pending a timely application for first registration. Subsection (5) deals with the more problematical period where the time for compulsory registration has passed. The two cases dealt with in (5)(a) and (5)(b) need to be examined separately.

Subs. (5)(a)

Once the period for registration passes then the transferor holds the legal estate on trust for the transferee. This will, of course, be a trust of land under the Trusts of Land and Appointment of Trustees Act 1996 (c. 47) (TLATA 1996). The transferor will have the extensive powers of management conferred by that Act. Should the transferor dispose of the land to a fresh purchaser he may do so in two ways:

(i) He may produce the entire title including evidence of the transfer to the original transferee. This will show he owns the legal estate on a trust of land and has power to dispose of the land. Providing he does this by an overreaching conveyance, the former transferee's interest in land becomes simply an interest in the proceeds of sale. The fact that the new purchaser is aware of the whole situation is of no consequence. This seems to be the effect of a bare trust being brought within the overreaching framework of the LPA 1925 by s.1, TLATA 1996. A purchaser from the trustees is further protected by s.16, TLATA 1996. This has no application to registered land (s.16(7)) but the land in this case is not registered yet. A purchaser from the transferor cannot rely upon s.16 if he has *actual notice* of breach of a rule of law or equity by the trustees. It would seem from the wording of s.16(1) that *actual notice* that the transferor/trustees have not consulted the original transferee about the new sale cannot be a ground of impeaching the sale. (Section 16(2) refers to the relevance of actual notice and s.16(1) does not). However, in this case the statute is being used as an instrument of fraud effectively by the transferor/trustees and the new purchaser. There must be a realistic chance of the new transfer being set aside on this ground.

(ii) The original transferor may conceal (or in time forget about) the disposition to the transferee and sell the property relying on his original title. In this case there will still be a trust of land. However, providing the new purchaser is ignorant of this he will take entirely free of the trust as he will be a bona fide purchaser for value without notice.

A further point on subs. (5) is the position of land charges created in the conveyance which leads to first registration. Section 14(3) of the Land Charges Act 1972 (c. 61) provides that these cannot be registered as land charges. If the transferees' title is eventually registered they will be given effect to on the newly created register of title.

Subs. (6)

Once the time for registration has passed then the disposition leading to registration becomes void under subs. (5). However, when the Registrar makes an order allowing a further period then that disposition ceases to be void. It may occasionally occur in practice that a purchaser who has failed to register within the time period may try to sell the property. In *Pinekerry v. Needs (Kenneth) (Contractors)* (1992) 64 P. & C.R. 245 the court held that the new purchaser could not be forced to accept such a title (relying upon *Oakcacre v. Claire Cleaners (Holdings)* [1982] Ch. 197 and *Pips (Leisure Productions) v. Walton* (1982) 43 P. & C.R. 415). This should not be so under the new s.123A. The seller under s.123A(5) will hold on a bare trust for the first purchaser. The first purchaser, is therefore, in a position to be able to force the seller to complete and can, therefore, make out a good title. This basic principle is illustrated by *Re Baker and Selmons's Contract* [1907] 1 Ch. 238 where Swinfen Eady J. explained that the seller's title was good where the legal estate was vested in "a person bound to convey at their request" (p. 243). In *Pinekerry*, Scott L.J. adverted to the possibility that the seller there could have sought or demanded that the seller to it convey to the new purchaser (p. 254). This is made clearer in the newly written s.123A by the express provision that the original seller hold on a "bare trust" for its purchaser.

Indemnity

Indemnity for errors or omissions in the register

2. The following sections shall be substituted for section 83 of the Land Registration Act 1925—

"Indemnity for errors or omissions in the register

83.—(1) Where the register is rectified under this Act, then, subject to the provisions of this Act—

(a) any person suffering loss by reason of the rectification shall be entitled to be indemnified; and

(b) if, notwithstanding the rectification, the person in whose favour the register is rectified suffers loss by reason of an error or omission in the register in respect of which it is so rectified, he also shall be entitled to be indemnified.

(2) Where an error or omission has occurred in the register, but the register is not rectified, any person suffering loss by reason of the error

or omission shall, subject to the provisions of this Act, be entitled to be indemnified.

(3) Where any person suffers loss by reason of the loss or destruction of any document lodged at the registry for inspection or safe custody or by reason of an error in any official search, he shall be entitled to be indemnified under this Act.

(4) Subject to the following provisions of this section, a proprietor of any registered land or charge claiming in good faith under a forged disposition shall, where the register is rectified, be deemed to have suffered loss by reason of such rectification and shall be entitled to be indemnified under this Act.

(5) No indemnity shall be payable under this Act—

(a) on account of any loss suffered by a claimant wholly or partly as a result of his own fraud or wholly as a result of his own lack of proper care;

(b) on account of any mines or minerals, or the existence of any right to work or get mines or minerals, unless it is noted on the register that the mines or minerals are included in the title; or

(c) on account of any costs or expenses (of whatever nature) incurred without the consent of the registrar, unless—

(i) by reason of urgency it was not practicable to apply for the registrar's consent before they were incurred, and

(ii) the register subsequently approves them for the purposes of this paragraph.

(6) Where any loss suffered by a claimant is suffered partly as a result of his own lack of proper care, any indemnity payable to him shall be reduced to such extent as is just and equitable having regard to his share in the responsibility for the loss.

(7) For the purposes of subsections (5)(a) and (6) above, any fraud or lack of proper care on the part of a person from whom the claimant derives title (otherwise than under a disposition for valuable consideration which is registered or protected on the register) shall be treated as if it were fraud or lack of proper care on the part of the claimant (and the reference in subsection (6) to the claimant's share in the responsibility for the loss shall be construed accordingly).

(8) Where an indemnity is paid in respect of the loss of an estate or interest in or charge on land, the amount so paid shall not exceed—

(a) where the register is not rectified, the value of the estate, interest charge at the time when the error or omission which caused the loss was made;

(b) where the register is rectified, the value (if there had been no rectification) of the estate, interest or charge, immediately before the time of rectification.

(9) Subject to subsection (5)(c) above, as restricted by section 2(2) of the Land Registration and Land Charges Act 1971—

(a) an indemnity under any provision of this Act shall include such amount, if any, as may be reasonable in respect of any costs or expenses properly incurred by the claimant in relation to the matter; and

(b) a claimant for an indemnity under any such provision shall be entitled to an indemnity thereunder of such amount, if any, as may be reasonable in respect of any such costs or expenses, notwithstanding that no other indemnity money is payable thereunder.

(10) Where indemnity is paid to a claimant in respect of any loss, the registrar, on behalf of the Crown, shall be entitled—

(a) to recover the amount paid from any person who caused or substantially contributed to the loss by his fraud; or

(b) for the purpose of recovering the amount paid, to enforce—
    (i) any right of action (of whatever nature and however arising) which the claimant would have been entitled to enforce had the indemnity not been paid, and
    (ii) where the register has been rectified, any right of action (of whatever nature and however arising) which the person in whose favour the register has been rectified would have been entitled to enforce had it not been rectified.

(11) Subsection (10) above does not prejudice any other rights of recovery which by virtue of any enactment are exercisable by the registrar where he has made a payment of indemnity.

(12) A liability to pay indemnity under this Act shall be deemed to be a simple contract debt; and for the purposes of the Limitation Act 1980, the cause of action shall be deemed to arise at the time when the claimant knows, or but for his own default might have known, of the existence of his claim.

(13) This section applies to the Crown in like manner as it applies to a private person."

GENERAL NOTE

This introduces a new s.83 to the Land Registration Act 1925.

The new s.83 is derived from the Law Commission's *Third Report on Land Registration* (Law Com No 158). It is drafted to include some new provisions and some of the former subsections of s.83. The following table may be of help to the reader.

New Provision	*Former Provision*
s.83(1)(a)	s.83(1)
s.83(1)(b)	none
s.83(2)	s.83(2)
s.83(3)	s.83(3)
s.83(4)	s.83(4)
s.83(5)	This is new except that s.83(5)(b) is a re-enactment of the former s.83(5)(b)
s.83(6)	This amends s.83(6) by introducing contributing negligence
s.83(7)	s.83(5)(a)
s.83(8)(a)	s.83(6)(a)
s.83(8)(b)	s.83(6)(b)
s.83(9)	s.83(8)(a)
s.83(10)	s.83(9) but this is substantially new
s.83(11)	none—this is substantially new
s.83(12)	s.83(11)
s.83(13)	s.83(12)

s.83(1)

This retains the basic position that a person suffering loss by reason of rectification is entitled to an indemnity. Subsection (1)(b) introduces a new rule to correct a small lacuna in the former s.83. A person might obtain rectification but still suffer loss. An example of this appears in the case of *Freer v. Unwins* [1976] 1 All E.R. 634. A freehold title was rectified to include notice of a restrictive covenant. The plaintiff who obtained this rectification was the owner of land which claimed the benefit of the restrictive covenant. However, the court held that the rectification could not affect the holder of a leasehold title granted before the date of the rectification. The Law Commission view was that *Freer v. Unwins* was incorrect (Law Com No. 158, para. 3.8) whether that is so or not the law is now clear. A person who obtains rectification but still suffers loss may now obtain an indemnity.

s.83(5)

The significant change made by this subsection is to introduce an element of "contributory negligence" into indemnity claims. How this is to be given effect to is explained in the following subsection.

subs. (c)

This is a slightly different wording from the previous position. It makes it clear that *expenses* of investigating or trying to resolve a problem without incurring court *costs* can be refused by the Registrar. This slight widening against the claimant is balanced by an exception for costs and expenses incurred as a matter of urgency. Given the ease of communication with the Land Registry it will rarely be sensible to incur significant expenses without raising the issue with it.

subs. (6)

The concept of a contribution to the loss being measured on 'just and equitable' grounds is one with which lawyers are familiar. The wording is modelled very closely on s.1(1) of the Law Reform (Contributory Negligence) Act 1945 (c. 28). The degree of blameworthiness of the claimant and the extent to which it is the cause of the loss must both be taken into account. A passage from Winfield on Tort (14 ed., p. 187) sums up the Court's approach most cogently:

> "The result is, therefore, that there is no single principle for the apportionment of damages in cases of contributing negligence, and certainly no mathematical approach is possible. No doubt the extent of the plaintiff's lack of care [for his own safety] must be a major factor in all cases, but the court is directed by the statute to do what is 'just and equitable'. The matter is thus one for the discretion of the court, and though the discretion must be exercised judicially, it is both unnecessary and undesirable that the exercise of the discretion be fettered by rigid rules requiring the court to take some aspects of the given case into account and to reject others."

subs. (7)

This subsection is a replacement of s.83(5)(a).

subss. (10), (11)

This is substantially wider than the right of recourse given to the Land Registry under the former s.83(a). It gives a comprehensive right to be subrogated to claims of the claimant to recover the loss. It also gives a comprehensive right to be subrogated to claims which the person in whose favour a title is rectified would have had. Persons facing this possibility may be able to take comfort in the following statement from Lord Browne Wilkinson (*Hansard*, November 18, 1996, H.L. Vol. 575, col. 1159 at 1162)—". . . the Land Registry exercises such rights of recourse sparingly; in practice, only in such cases where there has been fraud or negligence. I further understand that it is not intended to change that practice".

subs. (12)

This subsection, unlike the previous s.83(11) provides one simple rule for limitation.

Fees

Registration fees

3. The following subsections shall be substituted for section (3) of section 145 of the Land Registration Act 1925 (registration fees)—

> "(3) Notwithstanding the provisions of subsection (1)(a) to (c) above, an order under this section may provide for reduced fees to be charged on the first registration of title to freehold or leasehold land in cases where such registration is not effected on an application made in pursuance of section 123A(2) of this Act.
>
> (3A) An order under this section may make different provision for different cases, and may in particular provide that no fees are payable in certain cases."

GENERAL NOTE

This replaces s.145(3) of the LRA 1925 with two new subsections. The simple purpose of this is to allow a flexible regime for fees chargeable for voluntary registration. Very large estates may face substantial fees when (*e.g.* on the occasion of a fresh vesting assent) they become subject to compulsory registration. Can money be saved by effecting a voluntary registration? This will need to be watched from time to time as will the possibility of effecting a "deal" with the Land Registry in order to take the opportunity of voluntary registration to tidy up the title to a large estate.

Supplementary

Consequential amendments and repeals

4.—(1) The enactments specified in Schedule 1 are amended in accordance with that Schedule, the amendments being consequential on the provisions of this Act.

(2) The enactments specified in Schedule 2 are repealed to the extent specified.

Short title, commencement and extent

5.—(1) This Act may be cited as the Land Registration Act 1997.

(2) The following provisions, namely—

(a) section 1,

(b) Part I of Schedule 1 and section 4(1) so far as relating thereto, and

(c) Part I of Schedule 2 and section 4(2) so far as relating thereto,

come into force on such day as the Lord Chancellor may appoint by order made by statutory instrument; and different days may be so appointed for different purposes.

(3) Otherwise this Act comes into force at the end of the period of two months beginning with the day on which it is passed.

(4) The provisions substituted by section 1 apply only in relation to dispositions made after the commencement of those provisions.

(5) The new section 83 substituted by section 2 applies in relation to any claim for indemnity made before the commencement of section 2 which has not been settled by agreement or finally determined by that time, as well as in relation to claims for indemnity made thereafter; but subsection (5)(c) of the new section 83 applies only to costs and expenses incurred in respect of proceedings, negotiations or other matters begun after the commencement of section 2.

(6) An order under subsection (2) above may contain such transitional provisions and savings as the Lord Chancellor considers appropriate in connection with the order.

(7) This Act extends to England and Wales only.

GENERAL NOTE

All provisions except s.1 come into force on April 27, 1997 (subs. (2)). The expected commencement date for s.1 is January 1, 1998.

SCHEDULES

SCHEDULE 1

CONSEQUENTIAL AMENDMENTS

PART I

AMENDMENTS CONSEQUENTIAL ON SECTION 1

LAND REGISTRATION ACT 1925 (C. 21)

1.—(1) In section 8 (application for registration of leasehold land) for subsection (1A) substitute—

"(1A) An application for registration in respect of leasehold land held under a lease in relation to the grant or assignment of which section 123A of this Act applies may be made within the applicable period within the meaning of section 123A, notwithstanding that by the date of the application the unexpired term of the lease is not more than twenty-one years."

(2) In section 69(3) (effect of registration on the legal estate), for "land in a compulsory area after the commencement of this Act" substitute "any land".

(3) In section 81(1) (power to remove land from the register)—

(a) for the words from the beginning to "in every case where" substitute "Where"; and

(b) for "the land (including an undivided share)" substitute "the undivided share".

LAND REGISTRATION AND LAND CHARGES ACT 1971 (C. 54)

2. In section 4 (souvenir land), in subsection (1)(d), for the words from "section 123" onwards substitute "sections 123 and 123A of that Act (compulsory registration);".

LAND CHARGES ACT 1972 (C. 61)

3. In section 14(3) (exclusion of matters affecting registered land or created by instruments necessitating registration of land), for the words from "section 123" to "is compulsory)" substitute "section 123A of the Land Registration Act 1925 (compulsory registration: effect of requirement to register)".

HOUSING ACT 1985 (C. 68)

4.—(1) In section 154 (registration of title), for subsection (1) substitute—

"(1) Where on the grant of a lease in pursuance of this Part the landlord's title to the dwelling-house is not registered, section 123A of the Land Registration Act 1925 (compulsory registration: effect of requirement to register) shall apply in relation to the grant of the lease whether or not it is granted for a term of more than 21 years."

(2) Where—

(a) after the coming into force of sub-paragraph (1) there is a conveyance falling within section 154(1)(b) as originally enacted (conveyance of freehold in pursuance of right mentioned in paragraph 2(1) or 8(1) of Schedule 8 to the Act in respect of shared ownership lease), and

(b) the landlord's title is not registered,

section 123A of the Land Registration Act 1925 (compulsory registration: effect of requirement to register) shall apply in relation to the conveyance (whether or not it would so apply apart from this sub-paragraph).

5.—(1) Paragraph 2 of Schedule 9A (land registration etc. where right to buy preserved) shall be amended as follows.

(2) For sub-paragraph (1) substitute—

"(1) Where on a qualifying disposal which takes the form of the grant or assignment of a lease the disponor's title to the dwelling-house is not registered, section 123A of the Land Registration Act 1925 (compulsory registration: effect of requirement to register) shall apply in relation to the disposal whether or not—

(a) (in the case of the grant of a lease) the lease is granted for a term of more than 21 years; or

(b) (in the case of an assignment) the lease is a lease for a term of which more than 21 years are unexpired."

(3) In sub-paragraph (2), for "In such a case" substitute "Where on a qualifying disposal the disponsor's title to the dwelling-house is not registered,".

CHARITIES ACT 1993 (C. 10)

6.—(1) In section 37(7)(b) (supplementary provisions relating to dispositions), for "to which section 123(1)" substitute "in relation to which section 123A".

(2) After subsection (1) of section 39 (supplementary provisions relating to mortgaging) insert—

"(1A) Where any such mortgage will be one falling within section 123(2) of the Land Registration Act 1925—

(a) the statement required by subsection (1) above shall be in such form as may be prescribed; and

(b) if the charity is not an exempt charity, the mortgage shall also contain a statement, in such form as may be prescribed, that the restrictions on disposition imposed by sections 36 above apply to the land (subject to subsection (9) of that section).

(1B) Where—

(a) an application is duly made for registration of a person's title to land in connection with such a mortgage as is mentioned in subsection (1A) above, and

(b) the mortgage contains statements complying with subsections (1) and (1A) above, and

(c) the charity is not an exempt charity,

the registrar shall enter in the register, in respect of the land, a restriction in such form as may be prescribed; and section 37(9) above shall apply in relation to any such restriction as it applies in relation to one entered in pursuance of section 37(8)."

(3) In section 39(6), for the words from ""prescribed"" onwards substitute—

"and subsections (1) to (1B) above shall be construed as one with the Land Registration Act 1925."

AGRICULTURE ACT 1993 (C. 37)

7.—(1) For paragraph 53(3) of Schedule 2 (provisions relating to carrying out of approved scheme of reorganisation) substitute—

"(3) The Chief Land Registrar may, if satisfied on the application of any interested person that there is good reason for doing so, make an order extending or further extending the period mentioned in sub-paragraph (2); and if he does so at a time when that sub-paragraph has operated to negative the transfer effected by section 11 above, it shall be taken not to have so operated."

(2) In paragraph 53(4) of Schedule 2—

(a) for "section 123(2)" substitute "section 123A(10)(a)"; and

(b) for "section 123" substitute "section 123A".

(3) For paragraph 14(3) of Schedule 4 (provisions relating to carrying out of approved transfer scheme) substitute—

"(3) The Chief Land Registrar may, if satisfied on the application of any interested person that there is good reason for doing so, make an order extending or further extending the period mentioned in sub-paragraph (2); and if he does so at a time when that sub-paragraph has operated to negative the transfer effected by section 35 above, it shall be taken not to have so operated."

(4) In paragraph 14(4) of Schedule 4—

(a) for "section 123(2)" substitute "section 123A(10)(a)"; and

(b) for "section 123" substitute "section 123A".

PART II

AMENDMENTS CONSEQUENTIAL ON SECTION 2

LAND REGISTRATION ACT 1986 (C. 26)

8. In section 5 (abolition of the Minor Interests Index)—

(a) in subsection (3), for "section 83(6)(a)" substitute "section 83(8)(a)"; and

(b) in subsection (4), for "section 83(10)" substitute "section 83(10)(b)(i)".

Section 4(2)   SCHEDULE 2

REPEALS

PART I

REPEALS CONSEQUENTIAL ON SECTION 1

Chapter	Short title	Extent of repeal
1925 c. 21.	Land Registration Act 1925.	Section 120.
1963 c. 33.	London Government Act 1963.	Section 80.
1965 c. 64.	Commons Registration Act 1965.	Section 12(a).
1985 c. 68.	Housing Act 1985.	In Schedule 20, paragraph 17(1).
1986 c. 26.	Land Registration Act 1986.	Section 2(1) to (3) and (5).
1988 c. 50.	Housing Act 1988.	Section 81(9)(a). Section 133(8)(a).
1989 c. 42.	Local Government and Housing Act 1989.	Section 173(8)(a).

PART II

REPEALS CONSEQUENTIAL ON SECTION 2

Chapter	Short title	Extent of repeal
1971 c. 54.	Land Registration and Land Charges Act 1971.	Section 2(4). Section 3. In section 15(5), "3".
1980 c. 58.	Limitation Act 1980.	In Schedule 3, paragraph 1.

INDEX

**References in roman type are to sections and Schedules of this Act:
those in italic are to sections of the 1925 Act, as amended**

SEA FISHERIES (SHELLFISH) (AMENDMENT) ACT 1997

(1997 c. 3)

An Act to make provision for fisheries for lobsters and other crustaceans.

[27th February 1997]

PARLIAMENTARY DEBATES
   Hansard, H.L. Vol. 576, col. 586; Vol 577, cols. 82, 1251, 1769. H.C. Vol. 290, col. 592.

INTRODUCTION
   This short Act simply inserts two words into s.1(1) of the Sea Fisheries (Shellfish) Act 1967 to extend the Secretary of State's power to make orders as to fisheries for lobsters and other crustaceans.

Power to make orders as to fisheries for lobsters and other crustaceans

1.—(1) Section 1(1) of the Sea Fisheries (Shellfish) Act 1967 (which enables the Secretary of State to make orders as to fisheries for shellfish) is amended as follows.
   (2) After "clams" there is inserted, "lobsters".
   (3) After "molluscs" there is inserted "or crustaceans".

Short title and extent

2.—(1) This Act may be cited as the Sea Fisheries (Shellfish) (Amendment) Act 1997.
   (2) This Act does not extend to Northern Ireland.

INDEX

References are to sections

TELECOMMUNICATIONS (FRAUD) ACT 1997*

(1997 c. 4)

An Act to amend the Telecommunications Act 1984 to make further provision for the prevention of fraud in connection with use of a telecommunication system. [27th February 1997]

PARLIAMENTARY DEBATES
Hansard, H.C. Vol. 285, col. 994; Vol. 287, col. 579. H.L. Vol. 576, col. 1275; Vol. 577, col. 943; Vol. 578, cols. 11, 458. The Bill had all party support and passed into law without amendment.

ABBREVIATIONS
"the 1984 Act": the Telecommunications Act 1984 (c. 12) (see s.3(2)).
"PACE": the Police and Criminal Evidence Act 1984 (c. 60).

COMMENCEMENT
The Act comes into force on April 27, 1997 (s.3(3)).

INTRODUCTION AND GENERAL NOTE
The Act gives effect to recommendations made in a joint industry and government study group on mobile phone fraud and crime reported to parliament in a written answer on October 24, 1995 (*Hansard*, col. 547). For some time it had been recognised that Telecoms fraud was a fast growing crime, often linked in to other crimes such as breaking in to cars and drugs, yet legislation did not give the police adequate power to fight it.

Both the new offences which are introduced require dishonesty, so the Act only targets fraudsters.

Since the law was blamed for failing to keep pace with technology, it is not surprising that the draftsman has attempted to draft in the widest possible way so this Act does not become outdated by technological advance. The Telecommunications Industry is at the heart of the emerging Information Society. Failure to enact effective further legislation would have risked destabilising the industry or meant the cost of fraud was passed on to the ordinary man in the street.

Section 1 creates two new offences in connection with obtaining a service provided by a telecommunications system. A person is guilty of the first offence if he has in his custody or under his control anything which he intends to use to obtain a service dishonestly or which he intends dishonestly to allow others to do so. He will also be guilty of the offence if he intends to use the thing or allow others to use it for a purpose connected with the dishonest obtaining of a telecommunications service (s.1).

A person is guilty of the second offence if he supplies or offers to supply anything knowing or believing the person to whom it is supplied or offered intends to use it to obtain a service dishonestly or dishonestly to allow others to use it to obtain a service. He will also be guilty of the offence if he knows or believes that the person to whom the thing is supplied or offered intends to use it or allow others to use it for a purpose connected with the dishonest obtaining of service (s.1).

The penalty on conviction on indictment is five years in prison or a fine or both, *i.e.* making the offences arrestable offences.

Section 2 increases the maximum sentence on conviction on indictment of the 1984 Act offence of dishonestly obtaining a telecommunications service with intent to avoid payment to five years *i.e.* now an arrestable offence.

Since the industry pressed for this Act, prosecutions can be expected to follow quite quickly after the Act comes into force.

The new offences should enable police to target and arrest the users of *scanners* (which identify the telephone number and ESN of legitimate mobile phones so they can be *cloned*). Cloning technology itself is rapidly evolving and the Act will no doubt be used to stamp out the fraudulent use of *dongles* (used to re-program and change the identity of stolen phones; when the stolen *clone* is programmed with the identity of a legitimate phone, it is the legitimate owner who ends up being billed). The Act is also apt to deal with "*grabbers*" (devices used to trigger a mobile phone and cause it to transmit information to create a clone of it), "*tumblers*" and "*magic*

---

* Annotations by Richard Briggs, Head of Telecoms Group, Tucker Turner Kingsley Wood & Co., 18 Bedford Row, London WC1R 4EB.

phones" (which not only grab the identity of nearby telephones but actually use them to make cloned calls).

The Government supported the Act as "a major deterrent to the increasing number of criminals who regard telecommunications fraud as an easy, relatively risk-free and highly profitable activity. It will hit the criminals where it hurts and be of major benefit to the police" (*per* Mr Ian Taylor, Minister for Science and Technology: *Hansard*, H.C. Vol. 287, col. 583).

Hopefully the courts will construe the Act accordingly, *i.e.* in the widest fashion according to its plain words. Not merely will fraudsters be looking at the application of the Act, but other countries (such as Ireland and Malaysia) are interested in seeing how it works.

The Act is intentionally drafted widely enough to follow through to charge the "Mr Bigs" behind *fraudulent call selling*. Although early prosecutions under the Act may focus on the mobile phone sector because it has identified the problem, the Act is equally available to combat types of fraud perpetrated on fixed network operators. The Act may be used to combat *dial through fraud* committed by hacking into a customer's PABX enabling the fraudster to make international calls billed to the legitimate customer. The Act also has a part to play in combating "*teeing in*" or "*clip-on fraud*". (At the expense of the ordinary residential customer, fraudsters use features such as call diversion and three way calling to sell calls to international destinations at less than the prices charged by the operator.) The Act will bite on the fraudster when he uses equipment to make a connection through the junction box in the street and tampers with the operator's network.

Possession or supply of anything for fraudulent purpose in connection with use of telecommunication system

1. In the 1984 Act, after section 42 there shall be inserted—

"Possession or supply of anything for fraudulent purpose in connection with use of telecommunication system

42A.—(1) Subsection (2) below applies if a person has in his custody or under his control anything which may be used for the purpose of obtaining, or for a purpose connected with the obtaining of, a service to which section 42(1) above applies.

(2) If the person intends—
   (a) to use the thing—
        (i) to obtain such a service dishonestly, or
        (ii) for a purpose connected with the dishonest obtaining of such a service,
   (b) dishonestly to allow the thing to be used to obtain such a service, or
   (c) to allow the thing to be used for a purpose connected with the dishonest obtaining of such a service,
he shall be guilty of an offence.

(3) Subsection (4) below applies if a person supplies or offers to supply anything which may be used for the purpose of obtaining, or for a purpose connected with the obtaining of, a service to which section 42(1) above applies.

(4) If the person supplying or offering to supply the thing knows or believes that the person to whom it is supplied or offered intends or intends if it is supplied to him—
   (a) to use it—
        (i) to obtain such a service dishonestly, or
        (ii) for a purpose connected with the dishonest obtaining of such a service,
   (b) dishonestly to allow it to be used to obtain such a service, or
   (c) to allow it to be used for a purpose connected with the dishonest obtaining of such a service,
he shall be guilty of an offence.

(5) A person guilty of an offence under this section shall be liable—
   (a) on summary conviction, to imprisonment for a term not exceeding six months or to a fine not exceeding the statutory maximum or to both, and

   (b) on conviction on indictment, to imprisonment for a term not exceeding five years or to a fine or to both.

   (6) In this section, references to use of a thing include, in the case of a thing which is used to record any data, use of any of the data."

GENERAL NOTE

   This section inserts a new s.42A into the 1984 Act which creates the two new offences. The first pre-requisite for each offence is dishonesty. Secondly the accused must have in his custody or under his control "anything" which may be used for obtaining "a service to which section 42(1) of the 1984 Act applies" namely any service provided by a "Telecommunications System" (defined in s.4(1) and (2) of the 1984 Act) the running of which is authorised by a licence granted under s.7 of the 1984 Act except for fraudulent receiving of broadcast or cable programmes which have their own offences under s.297 of the Copyright Designs and Patent Act 1988 (c. 48).

   The "thing" in s.42A(2) and (4) refers back to "anything" in s.42A(1). Most "things" will be physically seen and handled, but note subs. (6) which *includes use of data*. "Data" bears its ordinary meaning, which today is clearly understood. The draftsman therefore does not attempt a definition in this Act which is in accordance with the Law Commission Report on Computer Misuse (Cm 819; Law Com No. 186, Pt. III, para. 3.30), that a technical definition is undesirable in the context of a criminal offence. Accordingly, there was no statutory definition of data in the Computer Misuse Act 1990 (c. 18).

   "*Subscription fraud*" was mentioned in the House of Lords debate (applying for a telephone service using a fictitious identity. When the telephone bill arrives, the fraudster has disappeared). An individual *subscription fraudster* when caught could be prosecuted under s.42(1). It is possible that new s.42A(2) could be used to prosecute a dishonest dealer or service provider who used a database or telephone system to get a customer connected believing that he would commence a subscription fraud. Such an offence may, however, be better prosecuted under aiding and abetting the fraud itself.

   Section 42A(4) creates the offence of supplying or offering to supply believing that the person to whom it is supplied or offered intends to use it to obtain a service dishonestly or dishonestly to allow others to obtain a service.

   Section 42A(4)(c) creates an offence if he knows or believes that the person to whom the thing is supplied or offered intends to use it or to allow others to use it for a purpose connected with the dishonest obtaining of such a service. Thus the Act may be used to prosecute the "Mr Bigs" making the real money through telephone fraud.

   "The statutory maximum" sum (s.42A(5)(a)) prescribed by s.32 of the Magistrates' Courts Act 1980 (c. 43) is currently £5,000, but is capable of being increased under s.143 of that Act.

   By subs. (5)(b) the new offences are arrestable offences under s.24(1)(b) of the Police and Criminal Evidence Act 1984 (c. 60). Thus the police are given powers of entry for the purpose of arrest (PACE, s.17(1)(b)), powers of entry and search after arrest (PACE, s.18) and general powers of seizure (PACE, s.19).

   Presumably "*dishonestly*" will bear the same meaning as under the Theft Act 1968 (c. 60), see *R. v. Feely* [1973] 1 All ER 341, C.A., which held that "dishonesty" is a question of fact to be decided by the jury.

Increased penalty for fraudulent use of telecommunication system

   2.—(1) In section 42(1)(b) of the 1984 Act (penalty on conviction on indictment for fraudulent use of telecommunication system), for "two years" there shall be substituted "five years".

   (2) Subsection (1) above does not apply to an offence committed before this Act comes into force.

GENERAL NOTE

   From April 27, 1997 (s.3(3)), the offence of dishonestly obtaining a telecom service (see commentary under s.1, "a service to which s.42(1) applies") is an arrestable offence. (See commentary under s.1).

Short title, interpretation, commencement and extent

   3.—(1) This Act may be cited as the Telecommunications (Fraud) Act 1997.

   (2) In this Act "the 1984 Act" means the Telecommunications Act 1984.

(3) This Act shall come into force at the end of the period of two months beginning with the day on which it is passed.

(4) This Act extends to Northern Ireland.

GENERAL NOTE

The Act was passed on February 27, 1997 and comes in force on April 27, 1997 by virtue of subs. (3).

The Act extends to Northern Ireland (subs. (4)).

INDEX

References are to sections

FIREARMS (AMENDMENT) ACT 1997*

(1997 c. 5)

ARRANGEMENT OF SECTIONS

PART I

PROHIBITION OF WEAPONS AND AMMUNITION AND CONTROL OF SMALL-CALIBRE PISTOLS

*Annotations by Peter J. Clarke, B.C.L., M.A., Barrister, Fellow and Tutor in Law, Jesus College, Oxford.

An Act to amend the Firearms Acts 1968 to 1992; to make provision in relation to the licensing and regulation of pistol clubs; to make further provision for regulating the possession of, and transactions relating to, firearms and ammunition; and for connected purposes.

[27th February 1997]

PARLIAMENTARY DEBATES
    Hansard, H.C. Vol. 284, col. 794; Vol. 285, cols. 173, 698, 859; Vol. 286, cols. 1046, 1048; Vol. 290, cols. 747, 764. H.L. Vol. 576, cols. 794, 1288, 1312; Vol. 577, cols. 280, 293, 356, 561, 643, 1535, 1619; Vol. 578, cols. 123, 786.

INTRODUCTION AND GENERAL NOTE
    The Firearms (Amendment) Act 1997 (c.5) was passed as a response to the Dunblane tragedy of March 13, 1996 in which 16 schoolchildren and one of their teachers were killed by Thomas Hamilton. Hamilton used a handgun, which he held legitimately under the terms of a firearms certificate granted by the appropriate police authority.
    The Act (which had a stormy passage through both the House of Lords and the House of Commons) makes certain changes to the law:

  (i) Small firearms (*i.e.* weapons with a barrel length of less than 30 cm, or are less than 60 cm in length overall) become prohibited weapons; there is a range of exceptions. [ss.1–10].

  (ii) Small-calibre pistols (*i.e.* pistols chambered for .22 or smaller rim-fire cartridges and certain air pistols of similar calibre) are subject to special controls and new offences are created. [ss.11–18].

  (iii) Transitional arrangements for small-calibre pistols are made. [s.14 and Sched. 1].

  (iv) Provision is made for the licensing of pistol clubs and their premises, and for the regulation of these clubs. [ss.19–30].

  (v) Amendments to the law on transfers of firearms and shot guns and the notification requirements of transfer, deactivation of firearms and shot guns are made. [ss.31–37].

  (vi) Changes to the provisions concerning applications for certificates for firearms and shot guns are made. [ss.37 and 38].

  (vii) The law relating to the grant and revocation of firearms certificates is amended. [ss.38 and 40].

  (viii) A central register of applicants for and grantees of a firearm or shot gun certificate is established. [s.39].

  (ix) The system of appeals from decisions of chief officers of police is amended. [s.41].

  (x) There are other miscellaneous amendments. [ss.40 and 42 to 48 and Sched. 2].

This Act is one of a series of Acts passed in the last 15 years on the subject of firearms and matters related thereto. Some Acts were legislative responses to tragedies—or potential tragedies—involving firearms. Thus, the Firearms Act 1982 (c.31) was passed as a result of an attempt to shoot at a member of the Royal Family in the Mall; the Firearms (Amendment) Act 1988 (c.45) was passed as a result of the Hungerford tragedy when Michael Ryan ran amok with an automatic weapon. By way of contrast, the Firearms (Amendment) Act 1992 (c.31) and the Firearms (Amendment) Act 1994 (c.31) were passed to deal with comparatively minor particular, but perceived, defects in the legislation.

The Firearms Act 1997 is a direct result of the Dunblane tragedy. Lord Cullen conducted an Inquiry into the shooting; the recommendations of his Report that required legislation were intended to be contained in the FAA 1997: *Hansard*, H.C. Vol. 285, col. 174 (Mr. Michael Howard, Home Secretary), though this intention was queried at many points in the debates.

Many of the sections in these Acts contain amendments to the Firearms Act 1968 (c.27) and subsequent Acts, and the Firearms Act 1968 has now been so heavily amended and added to (not only by statute but by statutory instrument) that a new, consolidating, Act would be of great value.

One aspect of the Firearms (Amendment) Act 1988 (c.45) was the establishment of the Firearms Consultative Committee. This body has produced annual reports which provide useful information about the problems that have arisen within the shooting community, in connection with the application of the firearms legislation by the police, and in the interpretation of the legislation by the courts. Some, but not many, of its recommendations have been enacted.

The Firearms (Amendment) Act 1997 and the Firearms Acts 1968 to 1992 may be read together as the Firearms Act 1968 to 1997.

COMMENCEMENT

The changes introduced by the Act are to come into effect on such day as the Secretary of State may by statutory instrument appoint: s.53(3). Different days may be appointed for different sections and different areas (*ibid.*). Transitional provisions and savings may be included: s.53(4). Under s.51 the Secretary of State has the power to make transitional and consequential provisions: see note on that section, below. This power must be exercised by statutory instrument subject to the negative resolution procedure and may be used to modify any provision in the Firearms Act 1997 or in any other Act.

EXTENT

The Act does not extend to Northern Ireland: s.53(5).

ABBREVIATIONS

"Clarke & Ellis"	: Clarke & Ellis, *The Law Relating to Firearms* (Butterworths, 1981).
"FA 1968"	: Firearms Act 1968 (c.27).
"FA 1982"	: Firearms Act 1982 (c.31).
"FAA 1988"	: Firearms (Amendment) Act 1988 (c.45).
"FAA 1992"	: Firearms (Amendment) Act 1992 (c.31).
"FAA 1994"	: Firearms (Amendment) Act 1994 (c.31).
"FAA 1997"	: Firearms (Amendment) Act 1997 (c.5).
"FCC"	: Firearms Consultative Committee.

PART I

PROHIBITION OF WEAPONS AND AMMUNITION AND CONTROL OF
SMALL-CALIBRE PISTOLS

General prohibition of small firearms etc.

Extension of s.5 of the 1968 Act to prohibit certain small firearms etc.

1.—(1) Section 5 of the Firearms Act 1968 (referred to in this Act as "the 1968 Act") shall have effect with the following amendments.

(2) In subsection (1) (which describes weapons which are prohibited by section 5), after paragraph (ab) there shall be inserted the following paragraph—

"(aba) any firearm which either has a barrel less than 30 centimetres in length or is less than 60 centimetres in length overall, other than an air weapon, a small-calibre pistol, a muzzle-loading gun or a firearm designed as signalling apparatus;".

(3) In paragraph (ab) (self-loading or pump-action rifles) of that subsection, for the word "rifle" there shall be substituted the words "rifled gun".

(4) In paragraph (ac) (self-loading and pump-action smooth-bore guns) after the word "not" there shall be inserted the words "an air weapon or".

(5) In paragraph (ad) (smooth-bore revolver guns), for the words from "loaded" to the end there shall be substituted the words "a muzzle-loading gun".

(6) After subsection (7) there shall be inserted the following subsections—

"(8) For the purposes of subsection (1)(aba) and (ac) above, any detachable, folding, retractable or other movable butt-stock shall be disregarded in measuring the length of any firearm.

(9) Any reference in this section to a muzzle-loading gun is a reference to a gun which is designed to be loaded at the muzzle end of the barrel or chamber with a loose charge and a separate ball (or other missile)."

(7) The general prohibition by section 5 of the 1968 Act of firearms falling within subsection (1)(aba) of that section is subject to the special exemptions in sections 2 to 8 below.

(8) In sections 2 to 8 below any reference to a firearm certificate shall include a reference to a visitor's firearm permit.

(9) In section 57 of the 1968 Act (interpretation), after subsection (1) there shall be inserted the following subsection—

"(1A) In this Act "small-calibre pistol" means—

(a) a pistol chambered for .22 or smaller rim-fire cartridges; or

(b) an air pistol to which section 1 of this Act applies and which is designed to fire .22 or smaller diameter ammunition."

DEFINITIONS

"air weapon": FA 1968, s.1(3)(b) and s.57(1), applied to FAA 1997 by FAA 1997, s.50(2); and see FAA 1997, s.48.

"firearm": FA 1968, s.57(1) applied to FAA 1997 by FAA 1997, s.50(2).

"firearm certificate": FA 1968, s.57(4) applied to FAA 1997 by FAA 1997, s.50(2).

"muzzle-loading gun": see FAA 1968, s.5(9) as added by FAA 1997, s.1(6).

"pump-action": FA 1968, s.57(2) added by FAA 1988, s.21 applied to FAA 1997 by FAA 1997, s.50(2).

"small-calibre pistol": FAA 1968, s.57(1A), as substituted by FAA 1997, s.1(9).

GENERAL NOTE

This is one of the central parts of the Act; small calibre handguns are placed within the category of "prohibited weapons" within s.5. This latter section requires the authority of the

Secretary of State for the possession, purchase, acquisition, manufacture, sale or transfer of prohibited weapons or ammunition, and was substantially amended—and its scope extended—by the FAA 1988. Section 1 of the 1997 Act extends the definition still further. The Cullen Report recommended that single-shot hand guns could continue to be kept at home; the same recommendation applied to multi-shot hand guns, if they could be disabled. On this point, however, the Government announced their intention of drawing a distinction which Lord Cullen did not draw, between low-calibre and high-calibre weapons. (See note to subs. (9) and s.11, below). This compromise was the subject of much debate in both the Lords and the Commons; like any compromise, it was criticised as unjustified and/or unworkable. The possession of small-calibre hand guns (see s.1(9)) is still permitted at the premises of licensed pistol clubs and in certain other very limited cases; as Lord Cullen pointed out (*Report*, para.9.113), "I do not consider that the banning of handguns for target shooting or the banning of shooting clubs would be justified." There is also a useful discussion on the use of hand guns in the Third Annual Report of the FCC, Chap. 6.

The functions of the Defence Council (referred to in the FA 1968) were transferred to the Secretary of State by the Transfer of Functions (Prohibited Weapons) Order 1968 (S.I. 1968 No. 1200).

The concept of "possession" is one that has caused great difficulties, not only in the law relating to firearms, but elsewhere: see Smith & Hogan, *Criminal Law*, 7th ed. pp. 109–113, and Clarke & Ellis, pp. 4–9. Recent cases on the Firearms Act indicating the problem of possession are *R. v. Waller* [1991] Crim. L.R. 381, *R. v. Steele* [1993] Crim. L.R. 298, *Davis v. Buchanan*, 1994 S.C.C.R. 369 and *Smith v. H.M. Advocate*, 1996 S.C.C.R. 49 (and see *R. v. Vann and Davis* [1996] Crim. L.R. 52, *R. v. Calan Harrison* [1996] 1 Cr.App.R. 138 (on FA 1968, s.19)). Possession can include "proprietary possession" and "custodial possession" see *Hall v. Cotton and Treadwell* (1986) 83 Cr.App.R. 257 and *Sullivan v. Caithness (Earl)* (1975) 62 Cr.App.R. 105. Note also *L. v. DPP* [1996] 2 Cr.App.R. 501 at 517, *per* Otton L.J:

"[s.5 was] a statutory offence of possession and did not require proof of mens rea. Moreover the act of possessing a weapon was either wrong or innocent."

The offence of possession of a prohibited weapon under s.5, by analogy with FAA 1968, s.1, is an absolute offence: *Woodage v. Moss* [1974] 1 W.L.R. 411, *R. v. Howells* [1977] Q.B. 614, *R. v. Hussain* [1981] 1 W.L.R. 416 (irrelevant whether D knew that what he possessed was a firearm) (cases on s.1); *R. v. Bradish* (1990) 90 Cr.App.R. 271 (on s.5); Clarke & Ellis pp. 1 to 3.

The defence of necessity is available where the facts establish duress of circumstances to someone who acquires a weapon prohibited under FA 1968, s.5: *R. v. Pommell (Fitzroy Derek)* [1995] 2 Cr.App.R. 607 (*cf. DPP v. Bell (Derek)* [1992] RTR 335). However, D must desist from committing the crime as soon as he reasonably can: Smith & Hogan, *Criminal Law* 7th ed. p. 259, approved in *Pommell*: see at p. 615E, *per* Kennedy L.J. In *R. v. Wilson (Maxim)* [1989] Crim.L.R. 901 (a case on the possession of ammunition under FA 1968, s.11(3)) the court left open the question whether there was a defence of *locus poenitentiae* (the issue did not arise on the facts: Sir John Smith argued ([1989] Crim. L.R. at 902 to 903) that such a defence should be available; and this is certainly in accordance (by analogy) with the general principle in *Burns v. Nowell* (1880) 5 Q.B.D. 444 at 454:

"before a continuous act or proceeding, not originally lawful, can be treated as unlawful by reason of passing of an Act of Parliament by which in terms it is made so, a reasonable time must be allowed for discontinuance".

The term "firearm" is widely construed: see Clarke & Ellis pp.10 to 17; for example, in *Boyd v. McGlennan*, 1994 S.L.T. 1148, a speargun propelled by a rubber band was a "firearm"; it was irrelevant that there was neither explosion nor detonation, nor even a continuous barrel. *Cf. Bryson v. Gamage* [1907] 2 K.B. 630 (a case on the Pistols Act 1903 (c.18), where the weapon in question was considered to be "a mere toy" and thus outside the legislation): *quaere* whether this decision would be followed today.

Whether a weapon is within s.5 is to be determined by the kind of firearm it is, rather than by the description of an individual weapon: *R. v. Pannell* (1983) 76 Cr.App.R. 53, *R. v. Clarke (Frederick)* [1986] 1 W.L.R. 209; *Jessop v. Stevenson*, 1988 S.L.T. 223. The view of Taylor J. in *R. v. Jobling* [1981] Crim.L.R. 625 that whether a weapon is prohibited under s.5 is to be determined at the time the accused has it with him must now be read in the context of the cases referred to in the previous sentence.

Moreover, a prohibited weapon includes its component parts: see FA 1968, s.57(1)(b): *Clarke (Frederick)* above. The phrase "component parts" itself has been widely defined: see *R. v. Freeman* [1970] 1 W.L.R. 788, *Cafferata v. Wilson* [1936] 2 All E.R. 149, *Muir v. Cassidy*, 1953 S.L.T. (Sh. Ct.) 4, considered in Clarke & Ellis pp. 19 to 21. However, these latter cases have been heavily criticised and not followed by the High Court of Justiciary in *Kelly v. McKinnon*, 1983 S.L.T. 9, where it was emphasised that what mattered was whether the weapon was capable of being converted: in that case a .45 Colt revolver and a starting pistol which had been altered so that they could not fire, but which could easily be altered again so that they could be fired, were both firearms.

"The part [must be] identified as a component of a lethal barreled weapon ... a component part of something which is not a lethal weapon cannot, by itself, be a firearm, and it is nothing to the point that parts of that which is not a lethal weapon could be stripped therefrom and used in the construction of something which, when completed, would become a lethal weapon." (at 11, *per* the Lord Justice-General (Lord Emslie)).

The FCC recommended, in its Third Annual Report that "component parts" should be redefined so as to clearly limit the definition to pressure-bearing parts only. This proposal has not been adopted.

Nevertheless, a weapon may cease to be within s.5 if it is damaged or altered, or by the removal of so many components that it is no longer a "weapon": *Clarke (Frederick)* [1986] 1 W.L.R. at 253 to 254 *per* French J. This, of course, may be a difficult question of fact. It is not clear whether the broad definition of "component parts" would apply, or whether the approach in *Kelly v. McKinnon* would be adopted; the fact that French J. referred to the question of component parts in the subsequent paragraphs in his judgment may indicate that he favoured the approach in *Kelly v. McKinnon;* otherwise a conviction could have been justified on different grounds. The law relating to component parts of ammunition may, it appears, be similar: see *R. v. Stubbings* [1990] Crim.L.R. 811. (And see the general note to s.9, below). *Cf.* Greenwood, *Firearms Control*, p. 187.

Subs. (2)

Paragraph (aba) brings into the category of prohibited weapons any firearm which satisfies one of two criteria. Either it must have a barrel of less than 30 cm (the length of the barrel being measured from the muzzle to the point at which the charge is exploded on firing: FA 1968, s.57(6)(a)) or it must have an overall length of 60 cm. The term "length" is not defined in the context of a firearm (*cf.* the definition of the length of a barrel, above); the matter (subject to subs. (7)) is a question of fact. The added subs. (7) requires flexible butt-stocks to be disregarded in calculating the length. Muzzle-loading guns are described in the amended FA 1968, s.5, as added by FAA 1997, s.1(6). There is no definition of signalling apparatus: but see FA 1968, s.13 (Clarke & Ellis, pp. 59–61). However FAA 1997, s.1(2) requires that the firearm be designed as signalling apparatus; that requirement is not present in s.13.

Subs. (3)

This amends the amendment to the list of prohibited weapons made by the FAA 1988. The reason for the adoption of the term "rifled gun" instead of "rifle" is presumably to prevent any argument as to what is or is not a "rifle" *i.e.* whether the term "rifle" included a small hand gun with rifling. (*Cf.* FAA 1997, s.4(2) where a "shot pistol" was defined as a "smooth-bored gun.") According to FA 1968, s.57(4) (as amended by FAA 1988, s.25(2)) "rifle" includes "carbine". "Carbine" is not itself defined; the Oxford English Dictionary defines "carbine" as "a kind of firearm shorter than a musket", and cites the first use of the word as being in 1605. What the amendment presumably refers to, however, is a "rifled carbine" (Greener *Gunnery*, published 1858): *sed quaere.*

Subs. (4)

This excludes air weapons from the category of self-loading or pump-action smooth-bore guns that otherwise would be prohibited weapons. In *R. v. Thorpe* [1987] 1 W.L.R. 383 it was conceded that CO_2 was not "air" and therefore a weapon powered by CO_2 which discharged lead pellets was not an "air weapon". Likewise in *Peat v. Lees,* 1994 S.L.T. 400 a weapon powered by CO_2 could be within s.5, even though it might not be a lethal barreled weapon: CO_2 powered paintball guns converted to be fired by compressed air retained their prohibited status by virtue of FAA 1988, s.7(1). The status of a paintball gun designed to be fired by means of compressed air was left unclear: and this point may still be unclear after the amendment made by subs. (4), though it is submitted that the purpose of the amendment was to treat all paintball guns in the same way. This has been achieved by amending the definition of air weapons by FAA 1997, s.48 to include weapons powered by compressed CO_2. This amendment was added at the Report stage in the Commons: *Hansard,* H.C. Vol. 286, col. 1129. See also FCC Fourth Annual Report, paras. 7.25 to 7.28.

Subsections (4) and (5) refer to "smooth-bore guns": the term is not defined. By way of analogy, *R. v. Hucklebridge* [1980] 1 W.L.R. 1284 (following the dissenting judgment of Lord Widgery C.J. in *Creaser v. Tunnicliffe* [1977] 1 W.L.R. 1493), treats a rifle from which the rifling has been removed as a shotgun; thus a rifled gun from which the rifling had been removed could be a smooth-bore gun. Given that it would, presumably, be at least difficult—if not impossible—to re-rifle a weapon, the distinction between the approach to boring out the rifling of a weapon and the alteration of the nature of a repeating weapon to a single-shot weapon may be justified, though, following *Clarke (Frederick)* [1986] 1 W.L.R. 209, the matter could now fall for reconsideration by the courts.

Subs. (6)

This adds two new subsections to FA 1968, s.1.

The new subs. (8) applies to s.5(1)(aba) [above] and also to s.5(1)(ac)—the paragraph dealing with self-loading or pump-action smooth-bore guns. The test is, *inter alia,* whether the butt-stock is "detachable"; it does not matter whether it is readily or easily detachable, and it appears not to matter that the firearm, after the butt-stock has been detached, could only be used in a test rig: see *Hansard,* H.C. Vol. 285, col. 979 (Sir Jerry Wiggin; Miss A Widdecombe, Minister of State, Home Office). As a consequence the final words of the existing FA 1968, s.5(1)(ac) are repealed: see FAA 1997, Sched. 3.

The new subs. (9) defines a muzzle-loading gun for the purposes of the section—in reality the new s.5(1)(aba); the definition is clearly intended to apply to either old or modern reproduction weapons which are used in battle re-enactments, or for the sport of black-powder shooting (see Mr Michael Howard, the Home Secretary, in the Second Reading in the Commons, *Hansard,* H.C. Vol. 285, col. 186; Miss A Widdecombe, Minister of State, Home Office, in the Committee stage in the House of Commons, *Hansard,* H.C. Vol. 285, cols. 793 to 795). The new subsection was added in the Committee stage in the House of Commons: *Hansard,* H.C. Vol. 285, col. 797.

Subs. (7)

This provides that there are a number of specific exceptions where the treatment of handguns as prohibited weapons shall not apply, though a firearms certificate is necessary. The exemptions do not apply to other categories of prohibited weapon.

Subs. (8)

This provides the specific exceptions in subs. (7) apply not only where a firearm certificate is held, but where a visitor's firearm permit is held.

Subs. (9)

This is the crucial definition, which was much fought over in Parliament. It was argued, in particular, that target-shooting events at, for example, the Commonwealth Games, involved using weapons with a larger calibre; and that therefore the definition was too restrictive. The Government's answer to this point was simple: the Secretary of State could give permission for such weapons to be used at the Commonwealth Games to be held in Britain in 2002; however, the British team would not be able to participate in that event, through lack of practice (*per* Miss A Widdecombe, Minister of State, Home Office, *Hansard*, H.C. Vol. 285, col. 253).

The Cullen Report (p. 117), however, quotes the British Shooting Sports Council as stating that a .22 cartridge can be as lethal as a 9 mm cartridge in certain circumstances, and that it was possible to fire a greater number of controlled and carefully aimed shots in a specific time with rim-fire cartridges than was possible with centrefire. A rim-fire cartridge is one where "the priming compound is held in the hollow base flange or rim." (Brian J. Heard, *Handbook of Firearms and Ballistics*, p. 16).

Apart from the situations covered in ss.2 to 8, possession of larger-calibre pistols now constitutes the offence of possessing a prohibited weapon. Possession of larger-calibre air pistols to which s.1, FA 1968 applies also constitutes the offence.

Special exemptions from prohibition of small firearms

Slaughtering instruments

2. The authority of the Secretary of State is not required by virtue of subsection (1)(aba) of section 5 of the 1968 Act—

    (a) for a person to have in his possession, or to purchase or acquire, or to sell or transfer, a slaughtering instrument if he is authorised by a firearm certificate to have the instrument in his possession, or to purchase or acquire it;

    (b) for a person to have a slaughtering instrument in his possession if he is entitled, under section 10 of the 1968 Act, to have it in his possession without a firearm certificate.

"acquire": FA 1968, s.57(4) applied to FAA 1997 by FAA 1997, s.50(2).
"firearm certificate": FA 1968, s.57(4)(a) applied to FAA 1997 by FAA 1997, s.50(2).
"transfer": FA 1968, s.57(4) applied to FAA 1997 by FAA 1997, s.50(2).

GENERAL NOTE
Section 10 of the FA 1968 (as amended by the Slaughterhouses Act 1974 (c.3), s.46, and Sched. 3, para. 5, and subsequently by the Welfare of Animals (Slaughter or Killing) Regulations 1995 (S.I. 1995 No. 731)) allows slaughtermen licensed under the Slaughterhouses Acts 1954 to 1974 to continue using slaughtering instruments as part of their normal duties. Section 2 of the FAA 1997 allows this practice to continue. The Secretary of State is, for England and Wales, the Home Secretary; for Scotland, the Secretary of State for Scotland.

Para. (a)
Hand guns which are used for slaughtering may be possessed, purchased, acquired, sold or transferred, if the holder of the firearm certificate allows the possession, etc. "Sale" does not include "agreement to sell": Sale of Goods Act 1979 (c.54), s.2(4)(5).

Para. (b)
Possession of a hand-gun, even if it would otherwise be a prohibited weapon under s.5(1)(aba) by a licensed slaughterman in a slaughterhouse continues *not* to be an offence even without a firearms certificate or the authority of the Secretary of State.

Firearms used for humane killing of animals

3. The authority of the Secretary of State is not required by virtue of sub-section (1)(aba) of section 5 of the 1968 Act for a person to have in his possession, or to purchase or acquire, or to sell or transfer, a firearm if he is authorised by a firearm certificate to have the firearm in his possession, or to purchase or acquire it, subject to a condition that it is only for use in connection with the humane killing of animals.

DEFINITIONS
"acquire": FA 1968, s.57(4) applied to FAA 1997 by FAA 1997, s.50(2).
"firearm": FA 1968, s.57(4) applied to FAA 1997 by FAA 1997, s.50(2).
"firearm certificate": FA 1968, s.57(4) applied to FAA 1997 by FAA 1997, s.50(2).
"transfer": FA 1968, s.57(4) applied to FAA 1997 by FAA 1997, s.50(2).

GENERAL NOTE
This section is particularly applicable, for example, to veterinary surgeons, to RSPCA officials, and to hunt servants. The section, however is not so limited in its terms: the determining factor is the condition on the firearm certificate. The Government accepted that the alternatives available for the humane killing of animals, such as rifles, shot guns and tranquiliser darts, could not always be effective (*per* Miss A Widdecombe, Minister of State, Home Office, *Hansard,* H.C. Vol. 285, col. 860, and see the Wild Mammals (Protection) Act 1996 (c.3)).

Shot pistols used for shooting vermin

4.—(1) The authority of the Secretary of State is not required by virtue of subsection (1)(aba) of section 5 of the 1968 Act for a person to have in his possession, or to purchase or acquire, or to sell or transfer, a shot pistol if he is authorised by a firearm certificate to have the shot pistol in his possession, or to purchase or acquire it, subject to a condition that it is only for use in connection with the shooting of vermin.

(2) For the purposes of this section, "shot pistol" means a smooth-bored gun which is chambered for .410 cartridges or 9mm rim-fire cartridges.

DEFINITIONS
"acquire": FA 1968, s.57(4) applied to FAA 1997 by FAA 1997, s.50(2).
"firearm certificate": FA 1968, s.57(4) applied to FAA 1997 by FAA 1997, s.50(2).

"shot pistol": subs. (2).
"transfer": FA 1968, s.57(4) applied to FAA 1997 by FAA 1997, s.50(2).

GENERAL NOTE
This section is particularly applicable to gamekeepers, but the section is not limited to them: its applicability depends on the terms of the firearm certificate. According to Baroness Blatch, Minister of State, Home Office;
"a shot pistol is a smooth bore pistol which is chambered for .410 cartridges and specifically designed for vermin control inside barns and outbuildings. The relatively low power of the small shot cartridges minimises the damage to the fabric of the buildings". (*Hansard*, H.L. Vol. 577, col. 325).
The term "vermin" is not defined. The Oxford English Dictionary defines it as "animals of a noxious or objectionable kind ... now almost entirely restricted to those animals or birds which prey upon preserved game or crops, etc." This section was added at the Committee stage in the House of Lords: *Hansard,* H.L. Vol. 577, col. 325.

Races at athletic meetings

5. The authority of the Secretary of State is not required by virtue of sub-section (1)(aba) of section 5 of the 1968 Act—
- (a) for a person to have a firearm in his possession at an athletic meeting for the purpose of starting races at that meeting; or
- (b) for a person to have in his possession, or to purchase or acquire, or to sell or transfer, a firearm if he is authorised by a firearm certificate to have the firearm in his possession, or to purchase or acquire it, subject to a condition that it is only for use in connection with starting races at athletic meetings.

DEFINITIONS
"acquire": FA 1968, s.57(4) applied to FAA 1997 by FAA 1997, s.50(2).
"firearm": FA 1968, s.57(4) applied to FAA 1997 by FAA 1997, s.50(2).
"firearm certificate": FA 1968, s.57(4) applied to FAA 1997 by FAA 1997, s.50(2).
"transfer": FA 1968, s.57(4) applied to FAA 1997 by FAA 1997, s.50(2).

GENERAL NOTE
Although it might be thought that small-calibre starting pistols would be sufficient for the purposes of starting races, that is not so. According to Miss A Widdecombe (Minister of State, Home Office) in the House of Commons (*Hansard,* H.C. Vol. 285, col. 860 to 861) major athletics meetings require a starting gun with a loud bang and a highly visible flash, to ensure accuracy of timing. The term "athletic meeting" is used in FA 1968, s.11(2); it is not defined, but presumably includes any meeting, whether amateur or professional, at which athletic activities take place, whether as the sole or as the joint purpose of the gathering. The phrase "for the purpose of starting races at the meeting" might lead to difficulties: it is clear that a person about to start a race, or starting a race, is protected, but what of a person who has started the last race and still has the firearm in his possession? What of the starter who finds that the last race has been suddenly cancelled? Given the interpretation that the courts have placed on s.1, making it an absolute offence (see general note to s.1(2) above) a strict construction is likely. In the debates in the House of Lords, Baroness Blatch, (Minister of State, Home Office) stated (*Hansard*, H.L. Vol. 577, col. 323) that the section was confined absolutely to British Athletic Federation starters. It is unclear what is the basis for this alleged restriction on the interpretation of the section.
An attempt to exempt equipment for ships and aircraft from the legislation did not succeed: *Hansard*, H.L. Vol. 577, cols. 322 to 323.

Trophies of war

6. The authority of the Secretary of State is not required by virtue of sub-section (1)(aba) of section 5 of the 1968 Act for a person to have in his possession a firearm which was acquired as a trophy of war before 1st January 1946 if he is authorised by a firearm certificate to have it in his possession.

DEFINITIONS
"firearm": FA 1968, s.57(4) applied to FAA 1997 by FAA 1997, s.50(2).
"firearm certificate": FA 1968, s.57(4) applied to FAA 1997 by FAA 1997, s.50(2).

GENERAL NOTE
What matters is that the firearm was acquired by someone as a trophy of war before January 1, 1946, rather than that the present holder so acquired it. The original Bill referred to possession by the "original holder"; a compromise was suggested whereby someone could "inherit" such a weapon. In the debates in the House of Lords, Baroness Blatch, Minister of State, Home Office, stated (*Hansard*, H.L. Vol. 577, col. 324) that the legislation allowed spouses and other family members to inherit. There appears to be no such restriction in the legislation. Likewise, there is no requirement that the possessor has received the weapon on the death of the original possessor; indeed, it appears from the language of the section that the weapon could have been purchased.

The year 1946 was clearly chosen so as to allow weapons from both World Wars or before to continue to be covered by a firearm certificate, rather than to be brought into the category of prohibited weapons. A chief officer of police will continue to be able to specify conditions for the holding of such a weapon: FA 1968, s.27(2). The age of the weapon does not matter; and some such weapons might therefore be an antique possessed as a curiosity or ornament within FA 1968, s.58(2), even though s.6, unlike s.7, below, does not specifically preserve the effect of that section.

Weapons from later wars or insurrections that are prohibited weapons are within the amended FA 1968, s.5(1)(aba). There may well be an overlap with the exception in s.7 below.

Firearms of historic interest

7.—(1) The authority of the Secretary of State is not required by virtue of subsection (1)(aba) of section 5 of the 1968 Act for a person to have in his possession, or to purchase or acquire, or to sell or transfer, a firearm which—
(a) was manufactured before 1st January 1919; and
(b) is of a description specified under subsection (2) below,
if he is authorised by a firearm certificate to have the firearm in his possession, or to purchase or acquire it, subject to a condition that he does so only for the purpose of its being kept or exhibited as part of a collection.

(2) The Secretary of State may by order made by statutory instrument specify a description of firearm for the purposes of subsection (1) above if it appears to him that—
(a) firearms of that description were manufactured before 1st January 1919; and
(b) ammunition for firearms of that type is not readily available.

(3) The authority of the Secretary of State is not required by virtue of subsection (1)(aba) of section 5 of the 1968 Act for a person to have in his possession, or to purchase or acquire, or to sell or transfer, a firearm which—
(a) is of particular rarity, aesthetic quality or technical interest, or
(b) is of historical importance,
if he is authorised by a firearm certificate to have the firearm in his possession subject to a condition requiring it to be kept and used only at a place designated for the purposes of this subsection by the Secretary of State.

(4) This section has effect without prejudice to section 58(2) of the 1968 Act (antique firearms).

DEFINITIONS
"acquire": FA 1968, s.57(4) applied to FAA 1997 by FAA 1997, s.50(2).
"ammunition": FA 1968, s.57(4) applied to FAA 1997 by FAA 1997, s.50(2).
"firearm": FA 1968, s.57(4) applied to FAA 1997 by FAA 1997, s.50(2).
"firearm certificate": FA 1968, s.57(4) applied to FAA 1997 by FAA 1997, s.50(2).
"transfer": FA 1968, s.57(4) applied to FAA 1997 by FAA 1997, s.50(2).

GENERAL NOTE
This section enables the holder of a firearm certificate to hold what would otherwise be prohibited weapons under the amended FA 1968, s.5(1)(aba) as part of a collection, provided;
(i) the weapon was manufactured before January 1, 1919;
(ii) the Home Secretary has made a statutory instrument that weapons of that description were manufactured before that date; and that ammunition for firearms of that type is not readily available.

The operation of this section will depend on the statutory instruments made under it. The difficulty is that many weapons were of a description manufactured before 1919, and were in production after that date: a well-known example is the Browning designed, .45 Colt Government Model, introduced in 1911 and standard military issue in the U.S.A. for more than 70 years. Even if a weapon ceased to be produced before 1919, ammunition for it may well be readily available. An example much discussed in the Parliamentary debates was Winston Churchill's 7.63mm calibre Mauser pistol, which he credited with saving his life at the Battle of Omdurman in 1898.

It is not stated who is to determine the matters in s.7(3)(a); presumably this is a matter of fact. If a chief officer of police refuses to grant a firearm certificate for such a weapon, the matter will be considered by a court on appeal.

Weapons and ammunition used for treating animals

Weapons and ammunition used for treating animals

8. The authority of the Secretary of State is not required by virtue of subsection (1)(aba), (b) or (c) of section 5 of the 1968 Act for a person to have in his possession, or to purchase or acquire, or to sell or transfer, any firearm, weapon or ammunition designed or adapted for the purpose of tranquillising or otherwise treating any animal, if he is authorised by a firearm certificate to possess, or to purchase or acquire, the firearm, weapon or ammunition subject to a condition restricting its use to use in connection with the treatment of animals.

DEFINITIONS
"acquire": FA 1968, s.57(4) applied to FAA 1997 by FAA 1997, s.50(2).
"ammunition": FA 1968, s.57(4) applied to FAA 1997 by FAA 1997, s.50(2).
"firearm": FA 1968, s.57(4) applied to FAA 1997 by FAA 1997, s.50(2).
"firearm certificate": FA 1968, s.57(4) applied to FAA 1997 by FAA 1997, s.50(2).
"transfer": FA 1968, s.57(4) applied to FAA 1997 by FAA 1997, s.50(2).

GENERAL NOTE
This section prevents what was perceived as an anomaly from arising: were it not for this section certain weapons used by veterinary surgeons which fired, for example, tranquiliser darts, would have been prohibited weapons within FA 1968, s.5. If a large-calibre handgun is needed for treating an animal, then the weapon or its ammunition is not a "prohibited weapon" within the meaning of s.5, although a firearms certificate still needs to be held. The weapon or ammunition must be designed or adapted for the purpose, and there must be a condition restricting the weapon or ammunition's use in connection with the treatment of animals. Unlike ss.2 to 7 of the FAA 1997, this exemption applies not only to prohibited weapons under s.5(1)(aba), but also to weapons and ammunition under s.5(1)(b) [weapons designed, etc. to discharge a noxious thing] and s.5(1)(c) [ammunition containing, etc. such noxious things].

The phrase "designed and adapted" was considered in *R. v. Formosa and Upton* [1991] 1 All ER 131 (a case on FA 1968, s.5(1)(b)). The word "adapted" was to be given a narrower meaning than might otherwise have been the case because it was joined with the word "designed". It indicated some physical alteration that made it fit for the use in question: thus a washing-up liquid bottle filled with acid would not be "adapted".

This section was added in the Third Reading in the House of Lords: *Hansard,* H.L. Vol. 578, col. 135.

Prohibited ammunition: expanding ammunition and missiles for expanding ammunition

General prohibition of expanding ammunition etc.

9. In section 5(1A) of the 1968 Act (weapons and ammunition subject to general prohibition), for paragraph (f) there shall be substituted the following paragraph—

"(f) any ammunition which incorporates a missile designed or adapted to expand on impact;".

DEFINITIONS
"ammunition": FA 1968, s.57(4) applied to FAA 1997 by FAA 1997, s.50(2).

GENERAL NOTE

Section 5(1A) of the FA 1968 was added by the Firearms Act (Amendment) Regulations 1992 (S.I. 1992 No. 2823), made under the authority of FAA 1988, s.1(4). It included within s.5:

"any ammunition which is designed to be used with a pistol and incorporates a missile designed or adapted to explode on impact".

The amendment in the 1997 Act removes the words after "ammunition", "which is designed to be used with a pistol and". The scope of the paragraph therefore applies to all such ammunition, irrespective of the weapon from which it is designed to be fired.

"Ammunition" is widely defined: see Clarke & Ellis pp. 22 to 24. For example, a flare to be used in a flare-launcher was assumed to be ammunition in *R. v. Singh* [1989] Crim. L.R. 724. A dart or spear may, it is assumed, be ammunition if it can be discharged from a firearm: *see Boyd v. McGlennan*, 1994 S.L.T. 1148, though *cf. Bryson v. Gamage* [1907] 2 K.B. 670, ("toy"). In *R. v. Stubbings* [1990] Crim. L.R. 811 it was argued that cartridge cases, primed, but not loaded, were not ammunition. The court held that they were: they were a necessary component of ammunition; a cartridge containing primer is capable of producing an explosive effect when the trigger is pressed. Sir John Smith asks in commenting on *R. v. Stubbings* [1990] Crim. L.R. at 812:

"[w]hat is the essential quality which ammunition possesses? It appears to be the capacity to produce an explosive effect, even a small one, when the firearm is operated. Thus, empty cartridge cases are not ammunition".

Expanding ammunition etc.: exemptions from prohibition

10.—(1) Section 5A of the 1968 Act (exemptions from requirement of authority under section 5) shall be amended as follows.

(2) In subsection (4) (shooting of animals)—

(a) after the word "acquire", in the first place it appears, there shall be inserted the words ", or to sell or transfer,"; and

(b) for paragraphs (a) and (b) there shall be substituted the following paragraphs—

"(a) he is authorised by a firearm certificate or visitor's firearm permit to possess, or purchase or acquire, any expanding ammunition; and

(b) the certificate or permit is subject to a condition restricting the use of any expanding ammunition to use in connection with any one or more of the following, namely—

(i) the lawful shooting of deer;

(ii) the shooting of vermin or, in the course of carrying on activities in connection with the management of any estate, other wildlife;

(iii) the humane killing of animals;

(iv) the shooting of animals for the protection of other animals or humans.".

(3) For subsection (7) (firearms dealers) there shall be substituted the following subsection—

"(7) The authority of the Secretary of State shall not be required by virtue of subsection (1A) of section 5 of this Act for a person carrying on the business of a firearms dealer, or any servant of his, to have in his possession, or to purchase, acquire, sell or transfer, any expanding ammunition or the missile for any such ammunition in the ordinary course of that business.".

DEFINITIONS

"acquire": FA 1968, s.57(4) applied to FAA 1997 by FAA 1997, s.50(2).
"ammunition": FA 1968, s.57(4) applied to FAA 1997 by FAA 1997, s.50(2).
"firearm": FA 1968, s.57(4), applied to FAA 1997 by FAA 1997, s.50(2).
"firearm certificate": FA 1968, s.57(4) applied to FAA 1997 by FAA 1997, s.50(2).

"firearms dealer": FA 1968, s.57(4) applied to FAA 1997 by FAA 1997, s.50(2).
"transfer": FA 1968, s.57(4) applied to FAA 1997 by FAA 1997, s.50(2).

GENERAL NOTE

Section 5A of the FA 1968 was added by the Firearms Act (Amendment) Regulations 1992 (S.I. 1992 No. 2823), made under the authority of FAA 1988, s.1(4) and provides exemption from the need to obtain the authority of the Secretary of State under the added FA 1968, s.5(1A).

Section 5(1A) of the FA 1968 was added by the Firearms Act (Amendment) Regulations 1992 (S.I. 1992 No. 2823), made under the authority of FAA 1988, s.1(4).

The general exemption of expanding ammunition in connection with the shooting of animals was necessary on humanitarian grounds: Earl Balfour, *Hansard,* H.L. Vol. 577, col. 615.

Subs. (2)

This amends FA 1968, s.5A(4) so as to exempt not only the acquisition, but also sale or transfer of the ammunition previously exempt under s.5A(4).

Para. (b)

The substituted s.5(4)(a) removes the restriction that such ammunition has to be designed for use with a pistol; and also allows authorisation to be by a visitor's permit as well as by a certificate. There is also now a specific reference to expanding ammunition. The substituted para. (b) removes the requirement that the certificate (or permit) should contain a condition prohibiting the use of expanding ammunition for purposes not authorised by the European weapons directive [Directive 91/477/EEC—the directive on the control of the acquisition and possession of weapons].

The phrase "in connection with" replaces "in or in connection with" (the first two words were considered to be otiose); and the phrase is designed to ensure that the expanding ammunition can be used to "zero" or test the weapon for accuracy. As Baroness Blatch, Minister of State, Home Office, stated, (*Hansard,* H.L. Vol. 577, col. 616),

> "The Bill has been carefully designed to cover not only the actual use but also the preparatory steps that may have to be followed to ensure that the certificate holder is able to shoot the animal humanely. That includes allowing the certificate holder to zero or adjust the gun sights, as well as general testing and practice."

Expanding ammunition may be necessary to kill animals which pose a threat to human safety, and other animals such as foxes or hares which are specifically killed in connection with the management of an estate. Concern was expressed about agricultural tenants who are normally responsible for pest control on their holdings and enjoy statutory rights to control hares and rabbits under the Ground Game Act 1880 (c.47). Baroness Blatch, Minister of State, Home Office, stated (*Hansard,* H.L. Vol. 577, col. 616), that "management of an estate" is sufficiently broad to include "all manner of legal forms of occupation and management of land". The term "vermin" is not defined in the Act; for a definition see note to s.4. "Wildlife" is likewise undefined; the Oxford English Dictionary defines the term as "the native fauna and flora of a particular region". With respect, the word "native" may cause difficulty: is a muntjac deer—assuming it is not vermin—wildlife? What of, for example, Canada geese that winter here, or swallows that spend their summers here? See also the Wild Mammals (Protection) Act 1996 (c.3).

Subs. (3)

Consequent upon the amendment to FA 1968, s.5A, this removes the restrictions in the former FA 1968, s.5A(7): a firearms dealer or his servant may deal in expanding ammunition.

There are consequential amendments to FA 1968, s.5A: references to weapons being "designed to be used with a pistol" in subss. (4) and (8) are repealed: see FAA 1997, Sched. 3.

Provisions relating to the control of small-calibre pistols

Having small-calibre pistol outside licensed pistol club

11.—(1) After section 19 of the 1968 Act (carrying firearm in a public place) there shall be inserted the following section—

"Having small-calibre pistol outside premises of licensed pistol club

19A.—(1) It is an offence for any person to have a small-calibre pistol with him outside licensed premises of a licensed pistol club.

(2) It is not an offence for a person to have with him a small-calibre pistol if—

    (a) he is permitted by virtue of any provision of this Act to have the pistol in his possession without holding a firearm certificate or a visitor's firearm permit;

    (b) he is authorised to have the pistol with him by virtue of a permit granted under section 13 of the Firearms (Amendment) Act 1997; or

    (c) he is authorised to have the pistol in his possession by virtue of a firearm certificate or visitor's firearm permit which is not subject to a condition requiring it to be kept at a licensed pistol club.

(3) In this section "licensed pistol club" means a pistol club which is licensed under Part II of the Firearms (Amendment) Act 1997 and "licensed premises" has the meaning given in section 19 of that Act."

(2) In Part I of Schedule 6 to the 1968 Act (prosecution and punishment of offences), after the entry for section 19 there shall be inserted the following entry—

| "Section 19A. | Having small-calibre pistol outside premises of licensed pistol club. | (a) Summary | 6 months or a fine of the statutory maximum; or both. | — |
| | | (b) On indictment | 10 years or a fine; or both." | — |

DEFINITIONS

"firearm certificate": FA 1968, s.57(4) applied to FAA 1997 by FAA 1997, s.50(2).
"licensed premises": s.19.

GENERAL NOTE

This section proves a new offence of having a small-calibre pistol outside the licensed premises of a gun club. This was at the heart of the legislative reform. Many Members of Parliament wished to ban hand-guns altogether; others, however, wished to allow the possession of some—if not all—handguns to continue to be held under a firearm certificate. What has emerged is a compromise: it will be now rare for small-calibre pistols to be found outside the premises of licensed pistol clubs. The new Labour Government announced on May 10, 1997 that it will introduce legislation banning all handguns.

Subs. (1)

The word "outside" is not defined; the clear intention of the section is that any removal of the pistol from the licensed premises will be an offence.

The phrase "to have with him" is used in FA 1968, ss.18, 19, 20, 22(3)(4)(5). The phrase is to be contrasted with "possess" see *R. v. Kelt* [1977] 3 All ER 1099, where the issue was said to be one of fact, but there was a need for "a very close physical link, and a degree of immediate control". In *R. v. Pawlicki* [1992] 1 W.L.R. 827 (on FA 1968, s.18) it was emphasised that,

"a man who leaves a shotgun at home while he proceeds to the next town to rob a bank is still in possession of the shot gun, but does not have it with him when he commits the robbery at the bank" (at 831C *per* Steyn L.J.).

The emphasis was on "accessibility" [1992] 1 W.L.R. at 832B *per* Steyn L.J.

The cases of *Kelt* and *Pawlicki* were, of course, decided under a different section; and the context of the substituted s.19A would suggest, if anything, a stricter interpretation.

Subs. (2)

Paragraph (a) preserves the exceptions under the FAA 1997 where a person need not have a firearms certificate to have a small-calibre pistol, *i.e.* one defined under the added FA 1968, s.57(1A) (see note on s.1(9), above).

Paragraph (b) specifically cross refers to s.13 [chief officer of police may grant a permit for a small-calibre pistol to be taken outside the licensed premises for any "proper purpose".]

Paragraph (c) is self-explanatory.

Firearm certificates for small-calibre pistols: special conditions

12.—(1) If a chief officer of police is satisfied, on an application for the grant or renewal of a firearm certificate in respect of a small-calibre pistol, that the applicant's only reason for having the pistol in his possession is to use it for target shooting, any certificate which may be granted to the applicant or, as the case may be, renewed shall be held subject to the following conditions (in addition to any other conditions), namely—

(a) the pistol is only to be used for target shooting;

(b) the holder must be a member of a licensed pistol club specified in the certificate;

(c) the pistol must be kept at licensed premises of that club which are so specified.

(2) A person who commits an offence under section 1(2) of the 1968 Act by failing to comply with any of the conditions specified in subsection (1) above shall be treated for the purposes of provisions of that Act relating to the punishment of offences as committing that offence in an aggravated form.

(3) Any firearm certificate in force immediately before the day on which this section comes into force which—

(a) relates to a small-calibre pistol; and

(b) is subject to the condition that the pistol is only to be used on an approved range;

shall be treated on and after that day as being held subject to a condition requiring the pistol to be kept at licensed premises of a licensed pistol club.

(4) Subsections (1) and (3) above apply in relation to a visitor's firearm permit as they apply to a firearm certificate.

(5) A holder of a visitor's firearm permit who commits an offence under section 17(10)(b) of the Firearms (Amendment) Act 1988 (in this Act referred to as "the 1988 Act") by failing to comply with any condition mentioned in subsection (1) or (3) above is punishable—

(a) on conviction on indictment, with imprisonment for a term not exceeding seven years or a fine or both; and

(b) on summary conviction, to imprisonment for a term not exceeding six months or a fine not exceeding the statutory maximum or both.

DEFINITIONS

"firearm certificate": FA 1968, s.57(4) applied to FAA 1997 by FAA 1997, s.50(2).

"licensed pistol club" : FA 1968, s.19A as added by FAA 1997, s.11(1).

"licensed premises": s.19.

"small-calibre pistol": FA 1968, s.57(1A) added by FAA 1997, s.1(9).

GENERAL NOTE

This section provides that if the *only* reason for the certificate-holder to have the pistol is for use in target shooting, the three conditions in subs. (1) *must* be included in the certificate—in addition to any other conditions that may be imposed. "Target shooting" is not defined; targets may take a variety of forms. The customary target is the circular "bulls-eye" target; but humanoid targets are also used; and it could be argued that shooting at live animals released for the purpose could also be shooting at "targets". In view of the purpose for which the legislation was passed, however, it is to be expected that the courts will construe the phrase narrowly.

The phrase "is satisfied" is used in the FA 1968 (*e.g.* s.27). There was diverging authority on whether the test for determining the chief officer of police's "satisfaction" is subjective or objective. Moreover, a difference was emerging between the English and Scots cases as to how a court, on appeal from a decision of a chief officer of police, was entitled to act. In *Rodenhurst v. Chief Constable, Grampian Police* (1992) S.L.T. 104, it was held that a sheriff hearing an appeal from a chief constable was acting judicially; this was followed in *Grieve v. Chief Constable, Lothian and Borders Police,* 1993 S.L.T. (Sh.Ct.) 6. This differed from the approach in England (see *Kavanagh v. Chief Constable of Devon and Cornwall* [1974] Q.B. 624) and from a previous decision of the Court of Session (see *Kaye v. Hunter,* 1958 S.C. 208). According to Lord Ross, the Lord Justice-Clerk, in *Rodenhurst,* it was wrong to say that a sheriff could only interfere provided that a discretion conferred by the statute had not been reasonably exercised: there was a *lis* which was subject to review. The new FA 1968, s.44 (substituted by FAA 1997, s.41) provides that any appeal from a chief officer of police to the Crown Court (in England) or to the sheriff (in Scotland) shall be on the merits. See the general note to s.41, below.

"Chief officer of police" is defined by the Police and Magistrates' Court Act 1994 (c.29), s.49, Sched.5, Pt. I, para.15 (to be replaced in identical form by the Police Act 1996 (c.16), s.101(1)) as "a chief constable, the Commissioner of Police for the Metropolis, or the Commissioner of the City of London Police".

Subs. (2)

The reference to "aggravated" is in FA 1968, s.1. The penalty for such aggravated offences is greater: see FA 1968, Sched.6.

Subs. (5)

FAA 1988, s.17(10)(b) provides that if the holder of a visitor's permit fails to comply with a condition subject to which the permit is given he commits an offence; FAA 1997, s.12(5)(a) provides a much heavier penalty than that imposed by the original subsection.

Permits to have small-calibre pistols outside licensed pistol clubs

13.—(1) A person whose firearm certificate for a small-calibre pistol is held subject to a condition that the pistol must be kept at licensed premises of a licensed pistol club may make an application in the prescribed form to the chief officer of police for the area in which he resides for a permit under this section authorising a person specified in the permit to have the pistol in his possession outside those premises for any proper purpose.

(2) A permit under this section shall not, unless the circumstances appear to the chief officer of police to be exceptional, authorise any holder of a firearm certificate which relates to the pistol to have the pistol with him in any place other than the licensed premises of a licensed pistol club or the premises at which a designated target shooting competition specified in the permit is being held.

(3) A proper purpose for having a small-calibre pistol outside the licensed premises at which it is required to be kept may be any of the following, namely—

   (a) conveying the pistol to those premises following—

      (i) the release of the pistol from police custody under Schedule 1 to this Act;

      (ii) the purchase or acquisition of the pistol; or

      (iii) a change in the licensed premises at which the pistol is required to be kept;

   (b) having the pistol repaired or maintained by a registered firearms dealer;

   (c) enabling the pistol to be used at a designated target shooting competition;

   (d) selling or otherwise disposing of the pistol; or

   (e) any other purpose which appears to the chief officer of police to be proper in all the circumstances.

(4) Where a person makes an application under subsection (1) above in relation to a pistol, the chief officer of police may, if he thinks fit, grant a permit in the prescribed form; and any such permit—

   (a) shall specify the purpose for which it is granted and the name of any person who is authorised by the permit to have the pistol in his possession; and

   (b) shall be granted subject to such conditions as the chief officer of police thinks necessary to secure that such possession will not endanger the public safety or the peace;

and any conditions may include a time by which the pistol must be taken or returned to the licensed premises specified in the applicant's firearm certificate.

(5) It is an offence—

   (a) for a person to fail to comply with any condition contained in a permit under this section which authorises him to have a small-calibre pistol in his possession; or

(b) for a person knowingly or recklessly to make any statement which is false in a material particular for the purpose of procuring (whether for himself or another) the grant of a permit under this section.

(6) In proceedings against any person for an offence under subsection (5)(a) above, it shall be a defence for him to prove that he took all reasonable precautions and exercised all due diligence to avoid the commission of the offence.

(7) An offence under subsection (5) above shall be punishable on summary conviction with imprisonment for a term not exceeding six months or a fine not exceeding level 5 on the standard scale or both.

(8) Where any person authorised by a permit under this section to be in possession of a small-calibre pistol outside the licensed premises of a licensed pistol club has the pistol in his possession outside those premises for a purpose authorised by the permit—

(a) he shall not be guilty of an offence under section 19A of the 1968 Act; and

(b) his possession of the pistol outside those premises shall not without more be regarded as a failure to comply with the conditions to which any firearm certificate relating to the pistol is subject.

(9) The Secretary of State may by order designate such target shooting competitions as he thinks fit for the purposes of this section.

(10) This section applies to a person holding a visitor's firearm permit relating to a small-calibre pistol as it applies to a person holding a firearm certificate, except that any application for a permit under this section by the holder of a visitor's firearm permit shall be made to the chief officer of police who granted the visitor's firearm permit.

DEFINITIONS

"firearm certificate": FA 1968, s.57(4)(a) applied to FAA 1997 by FAA 1997, s.50(2).
"firearms dealer": FA 1968, s.57(4) applied to FAA 1997 by FAA 1997, s.50(2).
"licensed pistol club": FA 1968, s.19A as added by FAA 1997, s.11(1).
"licensed premises": s.19(2).
"small-calibre pistol": FA 1968, s.57(1A) added by FAA 1997, s.1(9).

GENERAL NOTE

Subs. (1)

This subsection allows the holder of a firearm certificate for a small-calibre pistol to apply to a chief officer of police for *anyone* (including—in extremely rare cases—the certificate-holder himself) to take the weapon outside the premises of the licensed club. The police are given a very broad discretion; they will need to be satisfied both that there is a good reason for moving the pistol from one place to another, and that the person who is moving the pistol is a proper person to move it.

Subs. (2)

This emphasises that the circumstances must appear to be exceptional before the permit will allow the holder of the permit to have the pistol with him at any place other than the licensed club or the place where the competition is to take place. Indeed, Baroness Blatch, Minister of State, Home Office, stated that "unless there were wholly exceptional circumstances, transport should be by a third party" (*Hansard*, H.L. Vol. 577, col. 358). Third parties might be accredited members of pistol clubs, or contractors; and it was envisaged that not even the members of the National squad would be able to carry their pistols with them.

Subs. (3)

The "proper purposes" are stated in this subsection; it is not stated in terms in subs. (1) that these are the only purposes, and to that extent the section is unclear. However, given that s.13(3)(e) refers to "any other purpose which appears to be ... proper in all the circumstances" the matter may not cause a difficulty. The Secretary of State may by order designate target shooting competitions for the purposes of the section: see subs. (9). The implication is that other target shooting competitions will not be designated, and thus that no permit will be given. There is a possible, small, exception under subs. 3(e): if a chief officer of police regards the circumstances as exceptional (s.13(2)) and he is prepared to certify that there is a "proper . . . purpose" under s.13(3), particularly under para. (e), then the pistol may be taken outside the licensed premises. It may be confidently predicted that such cases will be extremely rare.

The phrase "selling or otherwise disposing" is not defined. The word "transfer" was not used; presumably the definition of "transfer", which includes hiring, was considered too wide: the phrase used in para. (d) is presumably meant to include an out and out disposal.

Subs. (4)

There is a reference to a "prescribed form". By implication the chief officer of police cannot grant the permit in any other form; no new forms have yet been prescribed. There are, of course, existing prescribed forms.

A permit shall be granted subject to conditions so as not to endanger public safety or the peace: on the meaning of that phrase, see general note on s.38 below.

Subs. (5)

The phrase "knowingly or recklessly makes a statement false in any material particular" is worthy of note: "knowingly" is normally linked to belief of a fact, whereas "recklessly" relates to the mental element of the perpetrator. Presumably the sense of the phrase is "making a statement, knowing or being reckless as to whether it is false". The word "reckless" itself has caused serious difficulties in interpretation since *R. v. Caldwell* [1982] A.C. 341. Although Lord Roskill stated in *R. v. Seymour* [1983] 2 All ER 1058 at 1064 that "reckless" should be interpreted in the *Caldwell* sense unless Parliament "has otherwise ordained", this has not happened: see *e.g. R. v. Satnam; R. v. Kewal* (1984) 78 Cr.App.R. 149. In that case (one of rape) the issue was one of foreseeability, not of consequences, but of the state of mind of the victim. [And see generally, Smith & Hogan, *Criminal Law*, 7th ed. pp. 60 to 73]. The analogy with the form of words used in subs. (5) is at least arguable; thus if a defendant did not think at all about whether the statement in it was false, that would excuse him. On the other hand, the form-filling exercise required for obtaining a permit would be such that the issue of truth or falsehood of any statement should be in the forefront of his mind—and if a defendant said that he was not considering whether what he wrote was true or otherwise, it is extremely unlikely that he would be believed.

Subs. (6)

This provides the "due diligence" defence to subs. (5)(a)—though not to subs. (5)(b).

Subs. (8)

The phrase "without more" in para. (b) provides a clear hint that there may be other ways in which the permit-holder may be failing to comply with the conditions in the certificate under which the pistol is held. Conditions relating to security are an obvious example.

Subs. (10)

This emphasises that the application for a permit under s.13 must be to the chief officer of police who granted the visitor's permit, irrespective of where the visitor now is. A sponsor in England or Scotland is responsible for arranging for a permit to be issued: if there is no permit, the pistol may be seized by Customs and Excise on its arrival. Visitors' permits are governed by FAA 1988, s.17. It appears to be envisaged that the visitor's permit will allow the visitor to have the weapon at the pistol club; the import and conveyance of the weapon will be by police permit.

Transitional arrangements for certain small-calibre pistols

14. Schedule 1 (which enables a small-calibre pistol to be delivered to a police station and held in police custody for a limited period after section 11 above comes into force) shall have effect.

GENERAL NOTE

See General Note to Sched. 1 below.

Surrender of firearms, etc. and compensation

Surrender of prohibited small firearms and ammunition

15.—(1) The Secretary of State may make such arrangements as he thinks fit to secure the orderly surrender at designated police stations of firearms or ammunition the possession of which will become or has become unlawful by virtue of section 1 or 9 above.

(2) The chief officer of police for any area may designate any police station in his area as being suitable for the receipt of surrendered firearms or ammunition or surrendered firearms or ammunition of any description.

DEFINITIONS
"ammunition": FA 1968, s.57(4) applied to FAA 1997 by FAA 1997, s.50(2).
"firearm": FA 1968, s.57(4) applied to FAA 1997 by FAA 1997, s.50(2).

GENERAL NOTE
The arrangements for the surrender of newly-prohibited hand-guns are at the Secretary of State's discretion. It is for each chief officer of police to designate, at his discretion, police stations where weapons or ammunition may be received. It is arguable that he may designate different police stations for different descriptions of firearms or ammunition. The original Bill provided only for the surrender of firearms; the reference to ammunition was added in the Third Reading in the House of Lords: *Hansard,* H.L. Vol. 286, col. 1157.

Payments in respect of prohibited small firearms and ammunition

16.—(1) The Secretary of State shall, in accordance with a scheme made by him, make payments in respect of firearms and ammunition surrendered at designated police stations in accordance with the arrangements made by him under section 15 above.

(2) A scheme under subsection (1) above shall provide only for the making of payments to persons making claims for such payments in respect of firearms or ammunition—
  (a) which they had, and were entitled to have in their possession on or immediately before 16th October 1996 by virtue of firearm certificates held by them or by virtue of their being registered firearms dealers; or
  (b) which on or before that date they had contracted to acquire and were entitled to have in their possession after that date by virtue of such certificates held by them or by virtue of their being registered firearms dealers,
and their possession of which will become, or has become, unlawful by virtue of section 1(2) or 9 above.

(3) A scheme under subsection (1) above may—
  (a) restrict eligibility for receipt of payments to claims made in respect of firearms or ammunition surrendered within a period specified in the scheme;
  (b) provide for the procedure to be followed (including any time within which claims must be made and the provision of information) in respect of claims under the scheme and for the determination of such claims;
  (c) make different provision for different descriptions of firearm or ammunition or for different descriptions of claimant.

DEFINITIONS
"ammunition": FA 1968, s.57(4) applied to FAA 1997 by FAA 1997, s.50(2).
"firearm": FA 1968, s.57(4) applied to FAA 1997 by FAA 1997, s.50(2).
"firearm certificate": FA 1968, s.57(4) applied to FAA 1997 by FAA 1997, s.50(2).
"firearms dealer": FA 1968, s.57(4) applied to FAA 1997 by FAA 1997, s.50(2).

GENERAL NOTE
The extent of any scheme, its details, and the amount of compensation to be paid were the subject of much debate in Parliament; and the scheme adopted is much less generous than some would have wished.
Under the section, the Secretary of State has an obligation to make a scheme for compensation; this applies to those who held (or who had contracted to buy) firearms or ammunition possession of which would be unlawful and either,
  (a) they were entitled to hold those items under a firearms certificate; or
  (b) they were registered firearms dealers.
Ammunition includes expanding ammunition: s.9.

Details of how the scheme might operate were provided by Mr Michael Howard, the Home Secretary, in the Debate on the Third Reading in the House of Commons: *Hansard*, H.C. Vol. 286, cols. 1102 to 1103, and by Baroness Blatch, Minister of State, Home Office, in the Committee stage in the House of Lords: *Hansard,* Vol. 577, col. 575. There might be different schemes for firearms dealers and for individuals. The government proposals for compensation would work on the basis of a fair market value: the holder of a weapon would be given the choice of accepting:

(a) a flat rate per weapon;
(b) a value based on a list of values produced after discussion with the British Shooting Sports Council;
(c) in cases where a firearm was not within (b) or where the owner disputed the valuation, the holder could obtain his own valuation, and if this was not accepted, there would be recourse to independent valuation.

It was estimated that "a ballpark figure" for compensation might be £150m: Baroness Blatch, Minister of State, Home Office, *Hansard*, H.L. Vol. 577, col. 581.

It should also be noted that where small-calibre pistols are surrendered, or are treated as having been surrendered, the Secretary of State may make such payments to the previous holders as he thinks appropriate: s.14 and Sched. 1, para. 10.

Payments in respect of ancillary equipment

17.—(1) The Secretary of State shall, in accordance with any scheme which may be made by him, make payments in respect of ancillary equipment of any description specified in the scheme.

(2) For the purposes of subsection (1) above "ancillary equipment" means equipment, other than prohibited ammunition, which—

(a) is designed or adapted for use in connection with firearms prohibited by virtue of section 1(2) above; and
(b) has no practicable use in connection with any firearm which is not a prohibited weapon.

(3) A scheme under subsection (1) above shall provide only for the making of payments to persons making claims for such payments in respect of ancillary equipment—

(a) which they had in their possession on 16th October 1996; or
(b) which they had in their possession after that date, having purchased it by virtue of a contract entered into before that date.

(4) No payment shall be made under a scheme under subsection (1) above in relation to any ammunition unless its possession or, as the case may be, purchase by any person claiming a payment in respect of it was, at all material times, lawful by virtue of a firearm certificate held by him or by virtue of his being a registered firearms dealer.

(5) A scheme under subsection (1) above may require, as a condition of eligibility for receipt of payments under the scheme in respect of any equipment—

(a) the surrender (whether to the police or any other person) of that equipment in accordance with the scheme within a period specified by the scheme; or
(b) the disposal of that equipment by way of sale within a period so specified; or
(c) either such surrender or such disposal of the equipment within a period so specified.

(6) A scheme under subsection (1) above may—

(a) provide for the procedure to be followed (including any time within which claims must be made and the provision of information) in respect of claims under the scheme and for the determination of such claims;
(b) make different provision for different descriptions of equipment or for different descriptions of claimant.

DEFINITIONS
"ancillary equipment": subs. (2).
"firearm": FA 1968, s.57(4) applied to FAA 1997 by FAA 1997, s.50(2).
"firearm certificate": FA 1968, s.57(4) applied to FAA 1997 by FAA 1997, s.50(2).
"firearms dealer": FA 1968, s.57(4) applied to FAA 1997 by FAA 1997, s.50(2).

GENERAL NOTE
Payments in respect of ancillary equipment may be made under any scheme made by the Secretary of State; but this only applies to ancillary equipment which has no practical use in connection with a non-prohibited firearm. Examples might include reloading equipment for cartridges and specialised holders.
See also the General Note to s.16 above.

Parliamentary control of compensation schemes

18.—(1) Before making a compensation scheme the Secretary of State shall lay a draft of it before Parliament.

(2) The Secretary of State shall not make the scheme unless the draft has been approved by resolution of each House.

(3) This section applies to any alteration to the scheme as it applies to a compensation scheme.

(4) In this section "compensation scheme" means a scheme under section 16 or 17 above.

DEFINITIONS
"compensation scheme": subs. (4).

GENERAL NOTE
There was much debate in Parliament about the scope and nature of compensation. Attempts were made to provide for compensation to clubs that might cease to exist and which (for example) had invested heavily in their premises; likewise, there might be consequential losses to those who had to give up weapons. Notwithstanding amendments made by the House of Lords, the attitude of the Government appears to be a restrictive one, and when the schemes are unveiled, it is likely that they will be comparatively limited. See also the General Note to s.16 above.

PART II

LICENSED PISTOL CLUBS

Preliminary

Purpose of Part II

19.—(1) This Part provides for the licensing of pistol clubs and their premises and for the regulation of licensed pistol clubs.

(2) In this Act—

"licence" means a licence granted under section 21 below in respect of a pistol club and any premises of that club; and "licensed pistol club" shall be construed accordingly.

"licensed premises", in relation to a licensed pistol club, means any premises which are specified in the club's licence as being premises which may be used for the purpose of storing or using small-calibre pistols.

DEFINITIONS
"licensed pistol club": FA 1968, s.19A as added by FAA 1997, s.11(1).
"licensed premises": s.19(2).
"small-calibre pistol": FA 1968, s.57(1A) added by FAA 1997, s.1(9).

GENERAL NOTE
This section, and the rest of Pt. II, are a working out of the compromise whereby certain small-calibre pistols may be held legally, provided that they are (in essence) kept by licensed clubs at premises licensed under the Act. Given that a significant minority in the House of Commons wished to ban handguns altogether, the compromise is one that does not favour the holder

of a small-calibre pistol; and the restrictions are considerable. "Licensed premises" need not be the club-house; they could, for example, be the premises of a registered firearms dealer: Lord Mackay of Drumadoon, Lord Advocate, in the Committee stage in the House of Lords: *Hansard*, H.L. Vol. 577, col. 596.

"Premises" is defined in FA 1968, s.57(4) as including land.

No pistol club to operate without a licence

20.—(1) No club shall allow any small-calibre pistol to be stored or used on any of its club premises in connection with target shooting, unless the club is a licensed pistol club.

(2) No licensed pistol club shall allow a small-calibre pistol to be stored or used on any of its club premises by any holder of a firearm certificate or visitor's firearm permit subject to a condition that it is only to be used for target shooting, unless—

(a) the certificate or permit holder is a member of that club;

(b) the premises are specified in the club's licence as premises at which small-calibre pistols may be stored and used;

(c) the premises are specified in the certificate or permit as the place where the pistol is to be kept.

(3) Subsection (2) above does not apply to—

(a) the storage on licensed premises of a licensed pistol club of a small-calibre pistol purchased or acquired by the responsible officer of that club for use only by members of the club in connection with target shooting;

(b) the use on licensed premises of a licensed pistol club of a small-calibre pistol by a member of the club who is permitted to have it in his possession by virtue of section 27(3) below; or

(c) the use of a pistol on the licensed premises of a licensed pistol club if the person using the pistol is authorised by a permit under section 13 above to have the pistol with him on those premises.

(4) If a small-calibre pistol is stored or used in contravention of subsection (1) or (2) above, the persons or any of the persons responsible for the management of the club commit an offence punishable on summary conviction with imprisonment for a term not exceeding six months or a fine not exceeding level 5 on the standard scale or both.

(5) In proceedings against any person for an offence under subsection (4) above, it shall be a defence for him to prove that he took all reasonable precautions and exercised all due diligence to avoid the commission of the offence.

(6) In this section "club premises" means premises which are occupied by and habitually used for the purposes of the club.

DEFINITIONS

"acquired": FA 1968, s.57(4) applied to FAA 1997 by FAA 1997, s.50(2).
"club premises": subs. (6).
"firearm certificate": FA 1968, s.57(4) applied to FAA 1997 by FAA 1997, s.50(2).
"licence": s.19(2).
"licensed pistol club": FA 1968, s.19A as added by FAA 1997, s.11(1).
"licensed premises": s.19(2).
"small-calibre pistol": FA 1968, s.57(1A) added by FAA 1997, s.1(9).

GENERAL NOTE

This relates to both storage and use of small-calibre pistols in connection with target-shooting. Small-calibre pistols which are legitimately held otherwise than for target-shooting, for example under FAA 1997, ss.2 to 8, are not subject to these restrictions. If the pistol is only to be used for target shooting, the strict terms of subs. (2) must be followed, subject to the exceptions in subs. (3). Subsection (3)(a) allows small-calibre pistols to be stored as long as they are used only by members of the club in connection with target shooting.

FAA s.27(3) (itself subject to subss. (4) and (5)) allows a member of a licensed pistol club to use a small-calibre pistol for not more than 28 days without holding a firearms certificate: the intention of the subsection is to allow an individual interested in a particular weapon to use that weapon—provided he is a member of the club—for a "trial period".

FAA 1997, s.13 above, deals with the situation where a permit has been granted for the pistol to be held elsewhere than at the licensed premises at which it is required, under the terms of the firearm certificate, to be held. Thus, a member of club A may be allowed, by permit, to use his weapon at Club B.

Subss. (4) and (5)

The section is potentially wide, notwithstanding the availability of the "due diligence" defence: *cf.* s.13(6) above. The phrase "persons responsible for the management of the club" is not a term of art and is not defined. Thus, the Committee of a club, its officers, the trustees who own or lease the club premises could all be—if the facts merit it—"persons responsible". Indeed, an ordinary member—especially if he himself takes on responsibilities—might also be within the subsection. The phrase "persons responsible for the management of the club" is presumably meant to be wider than "responsible officer": see s.21(7).

Grant, variation, and revocation of licences

Grant of licences

21.—(1) The Secretary of State may, if he thinks fit, on the application in the prescribed form of an officer of a club who has been nominated for the purpose, grant a licence in respect of that club and such club premises as are specified in the licence.

(2) The application shall specify the club premises (or if two or more separate premises, each of them) in respect of which a licence is sought, being premises where storage of small-calibre pistols on behalf of members of the club, or the use of such pistols by members for target shooting, will be permitted by the licence.

(3) A licence shall specify the club premises on which small-calibre pistols may be stored or used and may limit the uses which may be made of the premises so specified or any part of them.

(4) A licence may include limitations excluding or restricting the application of section 27(3) below to members of the club.

(5) A licence shall be granted to the officer of the club who made the application on behalf of the club.

(6) There shall be payable on the grant or renewal of a licence a fee of £150.

This subsection shall be included in the provisions which may be amended by an order under section 43 of the 1968 Act.

(7) In this Part "the responsible officer", in relation to a licensed pistol club, means the officer of the club to whom the licence was granted or who has since become the responsible officer by virtue of a variation of the terms of the licence.

DEFINITIONS

"licence": s.19(2).
"responsible officer": subs. (7).
"small-calibre pistol": FA 1968, s.57(1A) added by FAA 1997, s.1(9).

GENERAL NOTE

The reference to a nominated officer presumably implies that the nomination is by the club. Given the difficulties that may arise with the constitution and organisation of clubs, there should be a clear statement, either in the constitution, or by a vote at a properly called general meeting, indicating who the nominated officer is and what the nominated officer can do. The "responsible officer" will hold the certificate. The emphasis of the section is on the premises and on the restrictions that may be placed on their use—or on the use of certain parts of them. It is also provided that s.27(3), the "trial membership" subsection, may be excluded under the terms of the licence.

Criteria for grant of licence

22.—(1) The Secretary of State shall (without prejudice to all other relevant considerations) only grant a licence in respect of a club and any of its premises if, after consulting the chief officer of police for the area in which the premises are situated, he is satisfied that the arrangements for storing and using small-calibre pistols there are such that their storage and use will not endanger the public safety or the peace.

(2) The Secretary of State may publish such guidance as he considers appropriate for the purpose of informing persons seeking a licence of criteria that must be met by a club and its premises before any application for the grant of a licence in respect of that club and those premises will be considered.

DEFINITIONS
"licence": s.19(2).
"small-calibre pistol": FA 1968, s.57(1A) added by FAA 1997, s.1(9).

GENERAL NOTE
This is a peculiarly drafted section. The Secretary of State is required to consult the local chief officer of police before granting a licence. Such licence will only be granted if the chief officer is satisfied that the arrangements for the storage and use of small-calibre pistols is "safe". However, this is without prejudice to all other "relevant considerations". These are not stated—but it is difficult to see, if a chief officer of police states that he is not satisfied—and there are reasons for his dissatisfaction—that any other considerations will have sufficient weight to overtrump the chief officer's view. This construction, it is submitted, is supported by subs. (2). The Secretary of State may publish guidance concerning the criteria that must be met before any application will be *considered*. "Guidance" of course, is just that; but given that subs. (2) contemplates that there is a threshold to be crossed before even consideration can be given to the grant of a licence, let alone the granting of the licence itself, a club seeking approval will be in severe difficulties if the guidance (if issued) is not followed. Such guidance is very likely to include the suggestion that the police should be asked to comment on the proposed arrangements; and the guidance may well suggest that if such approval is not forthcoming, then consideration of granting a licence, let alone the grant of the licence itself will not occur. The language of the section was justified in the Committee stage in the House of Lords by Lord Mackay of Drumadoon, Lord Advocate: he stated that the Government accepted that criteria for security should be published and made familiar, "a common-sense administrative matter". (*Hansard*, H.L. Vol. 577, col. 603). With respect, that does not deal with the points on the language of the section considered above: either there is a requirement that must be fulfilled, or there should be guidance which is merely advisory. There will be considerable scope both for appeal and—perhaps—for judicial review.

Licence conditions

23.—(1) A licence shall be granted subject to such conditions specified in it as the Secretary of State thinks necessary for securing that the operation of the club, and the storage and use of small-calibre pistols on the premises specified in the licence, will not endanger the public safety or the peace.

(2) It is an offence for the persons or any of the persons responsible for the management of a licensed pistol club to fail to comply with any condition of the licence or, as the case may be, to fail to secure that any such condition is complied with.

(3) In proceedings against any person for an offence under subsection (2) above, it shall be a defence for him to prove that he took all reasonable precautions and exercised all due diligence to avoid the commission of the offence.

(4) An offence under subsection (2) above is punishable on summary conviction with imprisonment for a term not exceeding six months or a fine not exceeding level 5 on the standard scale or both.

DEFINITIONS
"licence": s.19(2).
"licensed pistol club": FA 1968, s.19A as added by FAA 1997, s.11(1).
"small-calibre pistol": FA 1968, s.57(1A) added by FAA 1997, s.1(9).

GENERAL NOTE
This section gives the Secretary of State extremely wide powers: *cf.* s.13(4)(b) and notes thereon, above.

Duration of licence and renewal

24.—(1) A licence shall (unless previously revoked) continue in force for six years from the date on which it is granted but shall be renewable for further periods of six years at a time.

The provisions of this Part shall apply to the renewal of a licence as they apply to a grant.

(2) The Secretary of State may by order amend subsection (1) above by substituting for any period mentioned in that subsection such longer or shorter period as may be specified in the order.

(3) An order under subsection (2) above reducing the period for which a licence may be granted or renewed shall only apply to licences granted or renewed after the date on which the order comes into force.

(4) The power to make an order under subsection (2) above is exercisable by statutory instrument subject to annulment in pursuance of a resolution of either House of Parliament.

DEFINITIONS
  "licence": s.19(2).

GENERAL NOTE
  This deals with the granting or renewal of club licences; the period of six years may only be shortened by Order so as to apply to licences granted or renewed after the Order is made. This change was added at the Report stage in the House of Commons: *Hansard*, H.C. Vol. 577, col. 1620.

Variation of licence

25.—(1) The Secretary of State may at any time, if he thinks fit (and whether on the application of the responsible officer or not) vary the terms and conditions of a licence granted in respect of a licensed pistol club, by notice in writing—

(a) to the responsible officer; or

(b) to the persons, or any of the persons, for the time being responsible for the management of the club.

(2) A notice varying a licence under subsection (1) above may require the person or persons notified to deliver up the licence to the Secretary of State within 21 days of the date of the notice for the purpose of having it amended in accordance with the variation; and it is an offence for a person so notified to fail to comply with a notice under this subsection.

(3) An offence under subsection (2) above is punishable on summary conviction with a fine not exceeding level 3 on the standard scale.

DEFINITIONS
  "licence": s.19(2).
  "licensed pistol club": FA 1968, s.19A as added by FAA 1997, s.11(1).
  "responsible officer": s.21(7).

GENERAL NOTE
  This section gives the Secretary of State an extremely wide discretion to vary the terms and conditions of club licence, whether or not an application has been made by the club. Presumably the Secretary of State can act at the instigation of others, for example, a chief officer of police.

Revocation of licence

26.—(1) The Secretary of State may at any time, if he thinks fit, revoke a licence by notice in writing—

(a) to the responsible officer of the club;

(b) to the persons, or any of the persons, for the time being responsible for the management of the club.

(2) Where a licence is revoked the Secretary of State shall by notice in writing—

    (a) require the person or persons notified to surrender the licence to him forthwith;

    (b) require the person or persons notified to deliver forthwith into the custody of the chief officer of police for the area in which the premises are situated any small-calibre pistols stored on the club premises;

    (c) require the responsible officer to surrender to him the register kept by him under section 28 below (or, if the register is kept by means of a computer, a copy of the information comprised in the register in a visible and legible form) within 21 days from the date of the notice.

(3) Where the licence of a licensed pistol club is revoked by the Secretary of State under subsection (1) above, notice shall be given to each member of the club holding a firearm certificate or visitor's firearm permit—

    (a) informing the member that the licence has been revoked; and

    (b) if the chief officer thinks fit, requiring the member to deliver up his firearm certificate or, as the case may be, his visitor's firearm permit within 21 days of the date of the notice, for the purpose of amending it.

(4) A notice under subsection (3) above to a member of a pistol club whose licence has been revoked shall be given by the chief officer of police who granted the certificate or permit to that member.

(5) The holder of a firearm certificate or a visitor's firearm permit granted in respect of a small-calibre pistol which is required by the certificate or permit to be kept at the licensed premises of a licensed pistol club shall not be guilty of any offence under this Act or the 1968 Act by reason only that the pistol continues to be kept at those premises after the licence has been revoked and before the pistol is delivered into police custody in accordance with a notice under subsection (2) above.

(6) A small-calibre pistol delivered into police custody by virtue of a notice under subsection (2) above shall not be released to any person except on the authority of the chief officer of police into whose custody it was delivered.

(7) The holder of a firearm certificate relating to the pistol, or any other person who may lawfully have the pistol in his possession, may apply in writing to the chief officer for the release of the pistol (whether to him or to a person nominated by him).

(8) When such an application is made the chief officer of police may require such written statements, from any person, as he considers necessary for the purpose of determining the application.

(9) A person who fails to comply with a notice under subsection (2) or (3) above commits an offence punishable on summary conviction with a fine not exceeding level 3 on the standard scale.

DEFINITIONS

    "firearm certificate": FA 1968, s.57(4) applied to FAA 1997 by FAA 1997, s.50(2).
    "licence": s.19.
    "licensed pistol club": FA 1968, s.19A as added by FAA 1997, s.11(1).
    "licensed premises": s.19(2).
    "responsible officer": s.21(7).
    "small-calibre pistol": FA 1968, s.57(1A) added by FAA 1997, s.1(9).

GENERAL NOTE

    This section sets out, in great detail, what is to happen on the revocation of a club licence. Once a club licence is revoked, the Secretary of State is obliged to require the immediate delivery of small-calibre pistols stored at the club premises to the appropriate chief officer of police. The word "deliver" was changed from "surrender" in the House of Lords, *Hansard,* H.L. Vol. 578, col. 137 (*per* Baroness Blatch, Minister of State, Home Office). It is envisaged that if a licence is revoked, the police would deliver the Secretary of State's notice to the club and the police would then be on the premises to take delivery of the weapons. Notwithstanding that, however, the word "deliver" is of too wide a meaning to be limited to that example; and unless the word is held to be sufficiently ambiguous to invoke the doctrine in *Pepper v. Hart* [1993] A.C. 593, there will be practical difficulties in the operation of the section. Thus if, for example, the firearm certificate holder has to transport the weapon to a police station, he would, in ordinary parlance, be "delivering" it.

The section was substantially amended in the House of Lords at the Report stage; and subss. (6), (7) and (8) were added in the Third Reading in the House of Lords, *Hansard,* H.L. Vol. 578, col. 156. The width of subs. (8) may be noted: any person may be required to give a written statement to the chief officer of police before he determines an application by a firearm certificate holder to have the pistol the subject of the certificate released to him.

Exemptions from s.1 of the 1968 Act relating to licensed pistol clubs

27.—(1) The responsible officer of a licensed pistol club may, without holding a firearm certificate, have a small-calibre pistol or ammunition in his possession on the licensed premises of that club.

(2) Any other officer or member of such a club may also, without holding a firearm certificate, be in possession of a small-calibre pistol or ammunition on those premises in any circumstances if the chief officer of police for the area in which the premises are situated has given his approval in writing for that person to have possession of small-calibre pistols or ammunition in such circumstances.

(3) Subject to subsections (4) and (5) below, a member of a licensed pistol club who has not previously held a firearm certificate in relation to a small-calibre pistol may, without holding a firearm certificate, have in his possession a small-calibre pistol and ammunition on licensed premises of that club when engaged in connection with target shooting under the supervision of an officer of the club.

(4) Subsection (3) above shall not apply to a person after the end of the period of 28 days beginning with the first day on which he has a small-calibre pistol in his possession by virtue of that subsection.

(5) The application of subsection (3) above to members of a licensed pistol club may be excluded or restricted in relation to the club by limitations contained in the licence.

DEFINITIONS

"ammunition": FA 1968, s.57(4) applied to FAA 1997 by FAA 1997, s.50(2).
"firearm certificate": FA 1968, s.57(4) applied to FAA 1997 by FAA 1997, s.50(2).
"licence": s.19.
"licensed pistol club": FA 1968, s.19A as added by FAA 1997, s.11(1).
"licensed premises": s.19(2).
"responsible officer": s.21(7).
"small-calibre pistol": FA 1968, s.57(1A) added by FAA 1997, s.1(9).

GENERAL NOTE

This section provides three useful exemptions from the requirement that the possessor of a small-calibre pistol on the licensed premises of a licensed club needs a firearm certificate. The first, unqualified, allows the responsible officer of a licensed club to possess such a weapon belonging to a club member without holding a separate firearms certificate. The second allows individual officers or members of the club to possess such weapons where the chief officer of police has given permission in writing; this would allow, for example, a range-conducting officer to be included in the certificate, if the chief officer of police allowed. The third exemption is considered under the note to subss. (3) and (4) below.

Subss. (3) and (4)

This provides for "trial use" of small-calibre pistols. Members of a club may, under supervision of a club officer, possess a weapon and ammunition for the purposes of target shooting for not more than 28 days (the time running from the day when there is first possession) after the first time the individual had the weapon or ammunition. This right is not automatic: the application of the subsection may be excluded or restricted by the terms of the club licence. The amendment itself had its genesis in the debates in the House of Lords; the present wording was added to the Bill on the House of Commons' consideration of the amendments made by the House of Lords: *Hansard,* H.C. Vol. 290, col. 821.

Pistol registers

Registers to be kept at licensed pistol clubs

28.—(1) The responsible officer of a licensed pistol club shall keep at the licensed premises of the club a register ("the pistol register") relating to the small-calibre pistols stored and used at those premises.

If two or more separate premises are licensed, a register shall be kept at each of those premises.

(2) The responsible officer shall enter or cause to be entered in the pistol register the following particulars in relation to each pistol stored at the licensed premises at which the register is kept, that is to say—

- (a) the name and address of the person (or if more than one each person) authorised by a firearm certificate or visitor's firearm permit to have the pistol in his possession;
- (b) a description of the pistol;
- (c) the date on which the pistol was first stored at the premises;
- (d) the date and time of any removal of the pistol from the premises (together with the date of issue of any permit under section 13 above authorising the removal and the police force which issued it);
- (e) the date and time of the return of the pistol after being removed;
- (f) any other particulars required to be entered in the register by regulations under section 29 below;

and any entry relating to the date on which a pistol was first stored at the premises, or its subsequent removal from or return to those premises, shall be made within twenty four hours of that event.

(3) The information recorded on a pistol register shall (unless the register is surrendered to the Secretary of State under section 26(2) above) be kept so that each entry made in it will be available for inspection for at least five years from the date on which it was made.

(4) It is an offence for the responsible officer—

- (a) to fail to comply with any requirement of this section;
- (b) knowingly or recklessly to make any entry in the pistol register which is false in any material particular.

(5) An offence under subsection (4) above is punishable on summary conviction with imprisonment for a term not exceeding six months or a fine not exceeding level 5 on the standard scale or both.

DEFINITIONS
   "firearm certificate": FA 1968, s.57(4) applied to FAA 1997 by FAA 1997, s.50(2).
   "licensed pistol club": FA 1968, s.19A as added by FAA 1997, s.11(1).
   "licensed premises": s.19(2).
   "responsible officer": s.21(7).
   "small-calibre pistol": FA 1968, s.57(1A) added by FAA 1997, s.1(9).
   "the pistol register": subs. (1).

GENERAL NOTE
   This section provides, in considerable detail, for the keeping of pistol registers at each licensed premises of the licensed club. In particular, any entry relating to the storage, removal, or return of a pistol must be made within 24 hours of the event in question.

Subs. (5)
   On "knowingly or recklessly", etc., see note to s.13(5), above.

Supplementary

Regulations

29.—(1) The Secretary of State may by regulations—
- (a) prescribe requirements in relation to licensed pistol clubs, the operation of such clubs and the licensed premises of such clubs;

(b) impose obligations on the responsible officer or the persons responsible for the management of a licensed pistol club;

(c) impose obligations on persons who are authorised under section 27(2) above to have a small-calibre pistol in their possession on licensed premises of licensed pistol clubs without holding firearm certificates.

(2) The regulations may provide for breach of any provision made under subsection (1)(b) or (c) above to be an offence punishable on summary conviction with—

(a) imprisonment for a term not exceeding six months or a fine not exceeding level 5 on the standard scale or both; or

(b) such lesser penalty as may be prescribed in the regulations.

(3) The regulations may provide that in any proceedings against a person for an offence under the regulations, it is a defence for him to prove that he took all reasonable precautions and exercised all due diligence to avoid the commission of the offence.

(4) The power to make regulations under this section shall be exercisable by statutory instrument which shall be subject to annulment in pursuance of a resolution of either House of Parliament.

DEFINITIONS
"firearm certificate": FA 1968, s.57(4) applied to FAA 1997 by FAA 1997, s.50(2).
"licensed pistol club": FA 1968, s.19A as added by FAA 1997, s.11(1).
"licensed premises": s.19(2).
"responsible officer": s.21(7).
"small-calibre pistol": FA 1968, s.57(1A) added by FAA 1997, s.1(9).

GENERAL NOTE
This section gives the Secretary of State very wide powers to make regulations, in particular to impose obligations on club offices and on those who are allowed small-calibre pistols without the need for a firearms certificate.

Powers of entry and inspection

30.—(1) A constable or civilian officer duly authorised in writing in that behalf by the chief officer of police for the area in which any licensed premises of a licensed pistol club are situated may, on producing if required his authority—

(a) enter those premises, and

(b) inspect those premises, and anything on them,

for the purpose of ascertaining whether the provisions of this Part, any regulations under section 29 above, and any limitations or conditions contained in the licence of the club are being complied with.

(2) The power of a constable or civilian officer under subsection (1) above to inspect anything on licensed premises includes power to require any information which is kept by means of a computer and is accessible from the premises to be made available for inspection in a visible and legible form.

(3) It is an offence for any person intentionally to obstruct a constable or civilian officer in the exercise of his powers under subsection (1) above.

(4) An offence under subsection (3) above is punishable on summary conviction with a fine not exceeding level 3 on the standard scale.

DEFINITIONS
"civilian officer": FA 1968, s.57(4) added by FAA 1997, s.43(2).
"licence": s.19.
"licensed pistol club": FA 1968, s.19A as added by FAA 1997, s.11(1).
"licensed premises": s.19(2).

GENERAL NOTE
Police officers and civilian officers are given power to enter licensed club premises and to inspect them and anything on them. This will ensure that clubs obey the conditions in their

licence, and that all the required information is available. See the previous provisions of Pt. II of the Act and regulations made by the Secretary of State made under s.29.

Penalty for false statements

31.—(1) It is an offence for a person knowingly or recklessly to make a statement false in any material particular for the purpose of procuring the grant, renewal or variation of a licence or the release of a small-calibre pistol from police custody under section 26 above.

(2) An offence under subsection (1) above is punishable on summary conviction with imprisonment for a term not exceeding six months or a fine not exceeding level 5 on the standard scale or both.

DEFINITIONS
"licence": s.19.
"small-calibre pistol": FA 1968, s.57(1A) added by FAA 1997, s.1(9).

GENERAL NOTE
On "knowingly or recklessly", etc., see general note to s.13(5), above.

PART III

REGULATION OF FIREARMS AND AMMUNITION

Transfers and other events relating to firearms and ammunition

Transfers of firearms etc. to be in person

32.—(1) This section applies where, in Great Britain—
(a) a firearm or ammunition to which section 1 of the 1968 Act applies is sold, let on hire, lent or given by any person, or
(b) a shot gun is sold, let on hire or given, or lent for a period of more than 72 hours by any person,
to another person who is neither a registered firearms dealer nor a person who is entitled to purchase or acquire the firearm or ammunition without holding a firearm or shot gun certificate or a visitor's firearm or shot gun permit.

(2) Where a transfer to which this section applies takes place—
(a) the transferee must produce to the transferor the certificate or permit entitling him to purchase or acquire the firearm or ammunition being transferred;
(b) the transferor must comply with any instructions contained in the certificate or permit produced by the transferee;
(c) the transferor must hand the firearm or ammunition to the transferee, and the transferee must receive it, in person.

(3) A failure by the transferor or transferee to comply with subsection (2) above shall be an offence.

DEFINITIONS
"acquire": FA 1968, s.57(4) applied to FAA 1997 by FAA 1997, s.50(2).
"ammunition": FA 1968, s.57(4) applied to FAA 1997 by FAA 1997, s.50(2).
"firearm": FA 1968, s.57(4) applied to FAA 1997 by FAA 1997, s.50(2).
"firearm certificate": FA 1968, s.57(4) applied to FAA 1997 by FAA 1997, s.50(2).
"firearms dealer": FA 1968, s.57(4) applied to FAA 1997 by FAA 1997, s.50(2).
"shot gun": FA 1968, s.57(4) applied to FAA 1997 by FAA 1997, s.50(2).
"shot gun certificate": FA 1968, s.57(4) applied to FAA 1997 by FAA 1997, s.50(2).
"transfer": FA 1968, s.57(4) applied to FAA 1997 by FAA 1997, s.50(2).

GENERAL NOTE
This section, of general import, provides that transfers of s.1 firearms and ammunition must be:
(i) in person,

(ii) to a transferee entitled to purchase or acquire the firearm, or to a registered firearms dealer, or to someone not required to hold a firearm certificate or visitor's permit.

There is a similar regime for shotguns, though shot gun cartridges (if within FA 1968, s.1(4)(a)) are not within the scope of this section; neither are the other items of ammunition referred to in FA 1968, s.1(4).

The difference between the two regimes is that sale and letting on hire are covered by both; loans of firearms and ammunition are caught by the section, whereas gratuitous loans of shotguns for more than 72 hours are not.

As a result of this section, all postal sales of firearms, shot-guns and ammunition (save for s.1(4) ammunition) are now banned.

Notification of transfers involving firearms

33.—(1) This section applies where in Great Britain—

(a) any firearm to which section 1 of the 1968 Act applies is sold, let on hire, lent or given;

(b) any shot gun is sold, let on hire or given, or lent for a period of more than 72 hours.

(2) Any party to a transfer to which this section applies who is the holder of a firearm or shot gun certificate or, as the case may be, a visitor's firearm or shot gun permit which relates to the firearm in question shall within seven days of the transfer give notice to the chief officer of police who granted his certificate or permit.

(3) A notice required by subsection (2) above shall—

(a) contain a description of the firearm in question (giving its identification number if any); and

(b) state the nature of the transaction and the name and address of the other party;

and any such notice shall be sent by registered post or the recorded delivery service.

(4) A failure by a party to a transaction to which this section applies to give the notice required by this section shall be an offence.

DEFINITIONS

"firearm": FA 1968, s.57(4) applied to FAA 1997 by FAA 1997, s.50(2).
"firearm certificate": FA 1968, s.57(4) applied to FAA 1997 by FAA 1997, s.50(2).
"shot gun": FA 1968, s.57(4) applied to FAA 1997 by FAA 1997, s.50(2).
"shot gun certificate": FA 1968, s.57(4) applied to FAA 1997 by FAA 1997, s.50(2).
"transfer": FA 1968, s.57(4) applied to FAA 1997 by FAA 1997, s.50(2).

GENERAL NOTE

This provides that details of any transfer of a weapon under s.32 (save for gratuitous loans of shot guns for less than 72 hours) must be notified to a chief officer of police within seven days.

This and s.32 provide a new code on the transfer of weapons; the short-term loan of shot guns is presumably exempt so that, for example, the gratuitous loan of a shot gun for a weekend's shooting is not subject to notification; this covers, for example, the case of the estate shot gun held by a gamekeeper whose employer allows a visitor to shoot with it over the weekend.

"Ammunition" is defined in FA 1968, s.57(2) as meaning "ammunition for any firearm and includes grenades, bombs and other like missiles, whether capable of use with a firearm or not, and also includes prohibited ammunition".

Notification of de-activation, destruction or loss of firearms etc.

34.—(1) Where, in Great Britain—

(a) a firearm to which a firearm or shot gun certificate relates; or

(b) a firearm to which a visitor's firearm or shot gun permit relates,

is de-activated, destroyed or lost (whether by theft or otherwise), the certificate holder who was last in possession of the firearm before that event shall within seven days of that event give notice of it to the chief officer of police who granted the certificate or permit.

(2) Where, in Great Britain, any ammunition to which section 1 of the 1968 Act applies, and a firearm certificate or a visitor's firearm permit relates, is

lost (whether by theft or otherwise), the certificate or permit holder who was last in possession of the ammunition before that event shall within seven days of the loss give notice of it to the chief officer of police who granted the certificate or permit.

(3) A notice required by this section shall—

(a) describe the firearm or ammunition in question (giving the identification number of the firearm if any);

(b) state the nature of the event;

and any such notice shall be sent by registered post or the recorded delivery service.

(4) A failure, without reasonable excuse, to give a notice required by this section shall be an offence.

(5) For the purposes of this section and section 35 below a firearm is de-activated if it would, by virtue of section 8 of the 1988 Act be presumed to be rendered incapable of discharging any shot, bullet or other missile.

DEFINITIONS

"ammunition": FA 1968, s.57(4) applied to FAA 1997 by FAA 1997, s.50(2).
"firearm": FA 1968, s.57(4) applied to FAA 1997 by FAA 1997, s.50(2).
"firearm certificate": FA 1968, s.57(4) applied to FAA 1997 by FAA 1997, s.50(2).
"shot gun": FA 1968, s.57(4) applied to FAA 1997 by FAA 1997, s.50(2).
"shot gun certificate": FA 1968, s.57(4) applied to FAA 1997 by FAA 1997, s.50(2).

GENERAL NOTE

The section provides that if a firearm, the subject of a firearm or shot-gun certificate, or of a visitor's permit, is deactivated, destroyed, or lost, the chief officer of police must be notified within seven days of the event. Loss includes theft. Section 34(4) provides a defence of reasonable excuse: if, for example, the certificate holder were abroad and were unaware that his premises had been burgled and a weapon stolen, he would have, it is assumed, a "reasonable excuse" for not informing the police. The degree of particularity required in specifying the "event" is not stated; presumably "the firearm was stolen from the secure cabinet in my house when I was on holiday" would be sufficient.

"Deactivation": under FAA 1988, s.8, a weapon is deactivated if marked and certified by the Master Wardens and Society of the Mystery of Gunmakers of the City of London or the guardians of the Birmingham proof house or the rifle range at Small Heath in Birmingham (see FA 1968, s.58(1)) or some other person approved by the Secretary of State; the deactivation must render a firearm incapable of discharging a missile.

Notification of events taking place outside Great Britain involving firearms etc.

35.—(1) Where, outside Great Britain, any firearm or shot gun is sold or otherwise disposed of by a transferor whose acquisition or purchase of the firearm or shot gun was authorised by a firearm certificate or shot gun certificate, the transferor shall within 14 days of the disposal give notice of it to the chief officer of police who granted his certificate.

(2) A failure to give a notice required by subsection (1) above shall be an offence.

(3) Where, outside Great Britain—

(a) a firearm to which a firearm or shot gun certificate relates is de-activated, destroyed or lost (whether by theft or otherwise); or

(b) any ammunition to which section 1 of the 1968 Act applies, and a firearm certificate relates, is lost (whether by theft or otherwise),

the certificate holder who was last in possession of the firearm or ammunition before that event shall within 14 days of the event give notice of it to the chief officer of police who granted the certificate.

(4) A failure, without reasonable excuse, to give a notice required by subsection (3) above shall be an offence.

(5) A notice required by this section shall—

(a) contain a description of the firearm or ammunition in question (including any identification number); and

(b) state the nature of the event and, in the case of a disposal, the name and address of the other party.

(6) A notice required by this section shall be sent within 14 days of the disposal or other event—

(a) if it is sent from a place in the United Kingdom, by registered post or by the recorded delivery service; and

(b) in any other case, in such manner as most closely corresponds to the use of registered post or the recorded delivery service.

DEFINITIONS
"firearm": FA 1968, s.57(4) applied to FAA 1997 by FAA 1997, s.50(2).
"firearm certificate": FA 1968, s.57(4) applied to FAA 1997 by FAA 1997, s.50(2).
"shot gun": FA 1968, s.57(4) applied to FAA 1997 by FAA 1997, s.50(2).
"shot gun certificate": FA 1968, s.57(4) applied to FAA 1997 by FAA 1997, s.50(2).

GENERAL NOTE
This covers similar situations to those in ss.33 and 34 where the act takes place outside Great Britain; 14 days are allowed for notice.

Penalty for offences under ss.32 to 35

36. An offence under section 32, 33, 34 or 35 above shall—

(a) if committed in relation to a transfer or other event involving a firearm or ammunition to which section 1 of the 1968 Act applies be punishable—

(i) on summary conviction with imprisonment for a term not exceeding six months or a fine not exceeding the statutory maximum or both;

(ii) on conviction on indictment with imprisonment for a term not exceeding five years or a fine or both;

(b) if committed in relation to a transfer or other event involving a shot gun be punishable on summary conviction with imprisonment for a term not exceeding six months or a fine not exceeding level 5 on the standard scale or both.

DEFINITIONS
"ammunition": FA 1968, s.57(4) applied to FAA 1997 by FAA 1997, s.50(2).
"firearm": FA 1968, s.57(4) applied to FAA 1997 by FAA 1997, s.50(2).
"transfer": FA 1968, s.57(4) applied to FAA 1997 by FAA 1997, s.50(2).

GENERAL NOTE
This section provides the penalties for offences under ss.32 to 35.

Firearm and shot gun certificates

Applications for certificates and referees

37. For section 26 of the 1968 Act there shall be substituted the following sections—

"Applications for firearm certificates
26A.—(1) An application for the grant of a firearm certificate shall be made in the prescribed form to the chief officer of police for the area in which the applicant resides and shall state such particulars as may be required by the form.

(2) Rules made by the Secretary of State under section 53 of this Act may require any application for a firearm certificate to be accompanied by up to four photographs of the applicant and by the names and addresses of two persons who have agreed to act as referees.

(3) The rules may require that, before considering an application for a firearm certificate, the chief officer of police has the following from each referee nominated by the applicant—

  (a) verification in the prescribed manner of—

        (i) any prescribed particulars; and

        (ii) the likeness to the applicant of the photographs submitted with the application;

  (b) a statement in the prescribed form to the effect that he knows of no reason why the applicant should not be permitted to possess a firearm; and

  (c) such other statements or information in connection with the application or the applicant as may be prescribed.

Applications for shot gun certificates

26B.—(1) An application for the grant of a shot gun certificate shall be made in the prescribed form to the chief officer of police for the area in which the applicant resides and shall state such particulars as may be required by the form.

(2) Rules made by the Secretary of State under section 53 of this Act may—

  (a) require any application for a certificate to be accompanied by up to four photographs of the applicant;

  (b) require the verification in the prescribed manner of any prescribed particulars and of the likeness of those photographs to the applicant;

  (c) require any application for a certificate to be accompanied by a statement by the person verifying the matters mentioned in paragraph (b) above to the effect that he knows of no reason why the applicant should not be permitted to possess a shot gun."

DEFINITIONS

"firearm": FA 1968, s.57(4) applied to FAA 1997 by FAA 1997, s.50(2).
"firearm certificate": FA 1968, s.57(4) applied to FAA 1997 by FAA 1997, s.50(2).
"shot gun": FA 1968, s.57(4) applied to FAA 1997 by FAA 1997, s.50(2).
"shot gun certificate": FA 1968, s.57(4) applied to FAA 1997 by FAA 1997, s.50(2).

GENERAL NOTE

This re-enacts, in substance, the previous law governing the granting of firearm certificates and shot gun certificates, save that (sensibly) the provisions are in two separate, substituted, sections. The provisions repeat the provisions of FA 1968, s.26 (as amended by FAA 1988, ss.9 and 10). The section specifies in considerable detail what may be included in the application form, but there is no requirement that these matters must be included. Likewise, there is nothing to say what, apart from this information, may or may not be included in the application form: in this respect the language of the substituted s.26A(3)(c) [application for a firearm certificate] has no equivalent in the language of the substituted s.26B [application for a shot gun certificate].

It is assumed that there will be new prescribed forms.

Grant of firearm certificates

38. For subsection (1) of section 27 of the 1968 Act (special provisions about the grant of firearms certificates) there shall be substituted the following subsection—

"(1) A firearm certificate shall be granted where the chief officer of police is satisfied—

  (a) that the applicant is fit to be entrusted with a firearm to which section 1 of this Act applies and is not a person prohibited by this Act from possessing such a firearm;

    (b) that he has a good reason for having in his possession, or for pur-
chasing or acquiring, the firearm or ammunition in respect of
which the application is made; and

    (c) that in all the circumstances the applicant can be permitted to
have the firearm or ammunition in his possession without danger
to the public safety or to the peace."

Definitions

  "acquire": FA 1968, s.57(4) applied to FAA 1997 by FAA 1997, s.50(2).
  "ammunition": FA 1968, s.57(4) applied to FAA 1997 by FAA 1997, s.50(2).
  "firearm": FA 1968, s.57(4) applied to FAA 1997 by FAA 1997, s.50(2).
  "firearm certificate": FA 1968, s.57(4)(a) applied to FAA 1997 by FAA 1997, s.50(2).

General Note

This section amends the previous law governing the grant of firearm certificates. The existing
s.27(1) stated that a firearm certificate should be granted, if the chief officer of police was satisfied that the applicant had a good reason for having the weapon, and could be permitted to have
the firearm in his possession without danger to the public safety or to the peace. There was,
however, this proviso:

    "a firearm certificate shall not be granted to a person whom the chief officer of police has
    reason to believe to be prohibited by this Act from possessing a firearm to which section 1 of
    this Act applies, or to be of intemperate habits or unsound mind, or to be for any reason
    unfitted to be entrusted with such a firearm".

The new section is less specific; the phrases "fit to be entrusted with a firearm" and "in all the
circumstances the applicant can be permitted" clearly allow considerable latitude.

The phrase "shall be granted where the chief officer of police is satisfied" remains: though
case-law on s.27 and its predecessors does not give the phrase "shall be granted" its natural
meaning: see *e.g. Todd v. Neilans,* 1940 S.L.T. (Sh.Ct.) 4, *Kaye v. Hunter,* 1958 S.C. 208 (though
see the disapproval of certain matters in the case in *Rodenhurst v. Chief Constable, Grampian
Police,* 1992 S.L.T. 104); and see Clarke & Ellis pp. 75 to 77 and the general note to s.13, above.

The reference to "prohibited by this Act" is repeated from the previous s.27(1) and related to
FA 1968, s.21(1) to (3) (as amended): in short, the provision covers those who have been sentenced or otherwise dealt with by the courts in certain ways. See Clarke & Ellis, pp. 94 to 96.

The phrase "danger to the public safety or to the peace" has been judicially considered; in the
earlier cases, the nature of the individual was considered: *Anderson v. Neilans,* 1940 S.L.T.
(Sh.Ct.) 14, as was the area: *Hughson v. Lerwick Police,* 1956 S.L.T. (Sh.Ct.) 18. In *Ackers v.
Taylor* [1974] 1 W.L.R. 405 the phrase was construed so as to include poaching without violence,
in *Luke v. Little,* 1980 S.L.T. (Sh.Ct.) 138, three offences of drunken driving were held to bring
the applicant within the phrase (and see *Chief Constable of Essex v. Germain, The Times,* 15
April 1991 and *Dabek v. Chief Constable of Devon and Cornwall* (1991) 155 J.P. 55). In *Spencer-
Stewart v. Chief Constable of Kent* (1989) 89 Cr.App.R. 307 the Divisional Court held that what
was material was the danger contemplated by the use of the weapon in question: bouts of drunk-
enness would make an individual dangerous. It was not true that any form of criminal behaviour
would be enough,

    "irrespective of whether it is likely to lead to the commission of a crime involving the use
    of a shotgun" (at 313, *per* Bingham L.J.).

See Clarke & Ellis, pp. 91 to 93.

Register of holders of shot gun and firearm certificates

    39.—(1) There shall be established a central register of all persons who
have applied for a firearm or shot gun certificate or to whom a firearm or shot
gun certificate has been granted or whose certificate has been renewed.

    (2) The register shall—

    (a) record a suitable identifying number for each person to whom a certifi-
cate is issued; and

    (b) be kept by means of a computer which provides access on-line to all
police forces.

Definitions

  "firearm certificate": FA 1968, s.57(4) applied to FAA 1997 by FAA 1997, s.50(2).
  "shot gun certificate": FA 1968, s.57(4) applied to FAA 1997 by FAA 1997, s.50(2).

GENERAL NOTE

This section provides, for the first time, for a central register of firearm and shotgun certificates; the register is to be computerised and accessible by all police forces. There was considerable discussion, during the Parliamentary debates, of the "Phoenix" computer. The aim of the system is to hold information about those who have had a firearm or shot gun certificate refused or revoked, as well as those who hold such certificates: Miss A Widdecombe, Minister of State, Home Office, *Hansard,* H.C. Vol. 290, col. 824. (Consideration of Lords' amendments).

Consideration was given to the establishment of a Central Firearms Board: the idea was rejected, principally because it would have involved a duplication of effort with the police.

Revocation of certificates

40. For section 30 (revocation of certificates) of the Firearms Act 1968 there shall be substituted the following sections—

"Revocation of firearm certificates

30A.—(1) A firearm certificate may be revoked by the chief officer of police for the area in which the holder resides on any of the grounds mentioned in subsections (2) to (5) below.

(2) The certificate may be revoked if the chief officer of police has reason to believe—

(a) that the holder is of intemperate habits or unsound mind or is otherwise unfitted to be entrusted with a firearm; or

(b) that the holder can no longer be permitted to have the firearm or ammunition to which the certificate relates in his possession without danger to the public safety or to the peace.

(3) The certificate may be revoked if the chief officer of police is satisfied that the holder is prohibited by this Act from possessing a firearm to which section 1 of this Act applies.

(4) The certificate may be revoked if the chief officer of police is satisfied that the holder no longer has a good reason for having in his possession, or for purchasing or acquiring, the firearm or ammunition which he is authorised by virtue of the certificate to have in his possession or to purchase or acquire.

(5) A firearm certificate may be revoked if the holder fails to comply with a notice under section 29(1) of this Act requiring him to deliver up the certificate.

(6) A person aggrieved by the revocation of a certificate under subsection (2), (3) or (4) of this section may in accordance with section 44 of this Act appeal against the revocation.

Partial revocation of firearm certificates

30B.—(1) The chief officer of police for the area in which the holder of a firearm certificate resides may partially revoke the certificate, that is to say, he may revoke the certificate in relation to any firearm or ammunition which the holder is authorised by virtue of the certificate to have in his possession or to purchase or acquire.

(2) A firearm certificate may be partially revoked only if the chief officer of police is satisfied that the holder no longer has a good reason for having in his possession, or for purchasing or acquiring, the firearm or ammunition to which the partial revocation relates.

(3) A person aggrieved by the partial revocation of a certificate may in accordance with section 44 of this Act appeal against the partial revocation.

Revocation of shot gun certificates

30C.—(1) A shot gun certificate may be revoked by the chief officer of police for the area in which the holder resides if he is satisfied that the holder is prohibited by this Act from possessing a shot gun or cannot be permitted to possess a shot gun without danger to the public safety or to the peace.

(2) A person aggrieved by the revocation of a shot gun certificate may in accordance with section 44 of this Act appeal against the revocation.

Revocation of certificates: supplementary

30D.—(1) Where a certificate is revoked under section 30A or 30C of this Act the chief officer of police shall by notice in writing require the holder to surrender the certificate.

(2) Where a certificate is partially revoked under section 30B of this Act the chief officer of police shall by notice in writing require the holder to deliver up the certificate for the purpose of amending it.

(3) It is an offence for the holder of a certificate to fail to comply with a notice under subsection (1) or (2) above within twenty-one days from the date of the notice.

(4) If an appeal is brought against a revocation or partial revocation—
  (a) this section shall not apply to that revocation or partial revocation unless the appeal is abandoned or dismissed; and
  (b) it shall then apply with the substitution, for the reference to the date of the notice, of a reference to the date on which the appeal was abandoned or dismissed.

(5) This section shall not apply in relation to—
  (a) the revocation of a firearm certificate on any ground mentioned in section 30A(2), (3) or (4) of this Act;
  (b) the revocation of a shot gun certificate,

if the chief officer of police serves a notice on the holder under section 12 of the Firearms Act 1988 requiring him to surrender forthwith his certificate and any firearms and ammunition in his possession by virtue of the certificate."

DEFINITIONS
  "ammunition": FA 1968, s.57(4) applied to FAA 1997 by FAA 1997, s.50(2).
  "firearm": FA 1968, s.57(4) applied to FAA 1997 by FAA 1997, s.50(2).
  "firearm certificate": FA 1968, s.57(4) applied to FAA 1997 by FAA 1997, s.50(2).
  "shot gun": FA 1968, s.57(4) applied to FAA 1997 by FAA 1997, s.50(2).
  "shot gun certificate": FA 1968, s.57(4) applied to FAA 1997 by FAA 1997, s.50(2).

GENERAL NOTE
  This section repeals and replaces the existing FA 1968, s.30 (which deals with the revocation of firearm certificates and shot gun certificates) with three separate sections, respectively dealing with the revocation of firearm certificates, partial revocation of firearm certificates, and revocation of shot gun certificates. The possibility of partial revocation of firearm certificates has been added; there is no equivalent provision for the partial revocation of shot gun certificates.

GENERAL NOTE ON SUBSTITUTED FA 1968, s.30A
Subs. (2)
  Subsection (2)(a) re-enacts part of the existing FA 1968, s.30(1). It preserves the language "of intemperate habits or of unsound mind", even though that language is now no longer part of the (substituted) FA 1968, s.27(1) (see general note to s.38, above). "Unsoundness of mind" appears to be wider than insanity within the *M'Naghten Rules* (1843) 10 Cl. & F. 200; in *Harrod v. Harrod* (1854) 1 K. & J. 4, unsoundness of mind was to be distinguished from dullness of intellect; in *Pilkington v. Gray* [1899] A.C. 401 mere eccentricity was held not to amount to unsoundness of mind.
  In *Milligan v. Chief Constable of Glasgow,* 1976 S.L.T. (Sh.Ct.) 53 it was implied that three convictions for breathalyser offences in just over three years indicated "intemperate habits", though there was an indication that if there were a two-year period thereafter free of such convictions the position might be different. See also *Luke v. Little,* 1980 S.L.T. (Sh. Ct.) 138.
  Subsection (2)(b) is new as far as the revocation of firearms certificates, but closely mirrors FA 1968, s.30(2) [revocation of shot gun certificates]. It also reflects the form of the new FA 1968,

s.27(1) (grant of certificate) substituted by FAA 1997, s.38, above. As to "danger to the public safety or to the peace", see general note on s.38, above.

Subs. (3)
   This provides that if a person is prohibited from possessing a s.1 firearm, there is discretion to revoke the certificate. It is perhaps surprising that this is not mandatory.

Subs. (4)
   Subsection (4) is new: it provides that if circumstances change, revocation may be justified on the ground that, had an application been made at the time that revocation is being considered, the application would have been refused.

Subs. (5)
   FA 1968, s.29(1) provides that a firearm certificate may be varied; a refusal to deliver it up for variation is a ground for revoking it altogether.

GENERAL NOTE ON SUBSTITUTED FA 1968, S.30B
   This provides for partial revocation; the only ground for such partial revocation is set out in subs. (2) and relates to the firearm or ammunition in question. The section is presumably directed at someone who has a number of weapons, one of which (in the view of the chief officer of police) the certificate-holder no longer has a justification for possessing.

GENERAL NOTE ON SUBSTITUTED FA 1968, S.30C
   This re-enacts FA 1968, s.30(2), and part of s.30(4).

GENERAL NOTE ON SUBSTITUTED FA 1968, S.30D
   This section deals with the implications of the substituted ss.30A, 30B and 30C.
   Section 30(4) provides that if there is an appeal against revocation or partial revocation, the revocation will be effective when the appeal is abandoned or dismissed. However, the effect of FAA 1988, s.12 is preserved in so far as revocations made under the substituted s.30D(5) are concerned: *i.e.* the chief officer of police may require the certificate, the weapon and ammunition the subject of the revocation to be surrendered forthwith.

Appeals

   41.—(1) For section 44 of the 1968 Act (appeals against police decisions) there shall be substituted the following section—

"Appeals against police decisions
      44.—(1) An appeal against a decision of a chief officer of police under section 28A, 29, 30A, 30B, 30C, 34, 36, 37 or 38 of this Act lies—
      (a) in England and Wales, to the Crown Court; and
      (b) in Scotland, to the sheriff.
      (2) An appeal shall be determined on the merits (and not by way of review).
      (3) The court or sheriff hearing an appeal may consider any evidence or other matter, whether or not it was available when the decision of the chief officer was taken.
      (4) In relation to an appeal specified in the first column of Part I of Schedule 5 to this Act, the third column shows the sheriff having jurisdiction to entertain the appeal.
      (5) In Schedule 5 to this Act—
      (a) Part II shall have effect in relation to appeals to the Crown Court; and
      (b) Part III shall have effect in relation to appeals to the sheriff."
   (2) In Schedule 5 to the 1968 Act (provisions as to appeals), after Part II there shall be inserted—

"PART III

APPEALS IN SCOTLAND

   1. An appeal to the sheriff shall be by way of summary application.
   2. An application shall be made within 21 days after the date on which

the appellant has received notice of the decision of the chief officer of police in respect of which the appeal is made.

3. On the hearing of the appeal the sheriff may either dismiss the appeal or give the chief officer of police such directions as he thinks fit as respects the certificate or register which is the subject of the appeal.

4. The decision of the sheriff on an appeal may be appealed only on a point of law."

GENERAL NOTE

The Cullen Report (para. 8.119) suggested that there should be a recognition of police discretion in the granting of certificates for weapons, and that there should be an appeal to a court of law, but that such appeal should be on specific, enumerated, grounds. However, as Lord Mackay of Drumadoon, the Lord Advocate, pointed out in the Debates in the House of Lords on the Third Reading of the Bill (*Hansard,* H.L. Vol. 578, cols. 161 to 164), this caused a problem. Under Art. 6 of the European Convention of Human Rights, there has to be an independent judicial determination when an individual's rights are being affected by a decision. The aim of the revised s.44 was to provide for an appeal on the merits, and this might well include consideration of material not available at the time the original decision was taken. Lord Mackay of Drumadoon stated that in making decisions, Chief Constables were not restricted in any way as to the information they could use—criminal convictions, information about aspects of an applicant's character were two examples that were cited; and it did not matter that such information might not be admissible in a court of law. Indeed, a Chief Constable was entitled to use information which he wished to remain anonymous, "to protect a registered informer or for some other sound operational reason". Lord Mackay of Drumadoon, however, accepted that a Chief Constable, on the hearing of an appeal against his decision, might not wish to place the material before the court—in which case it would hinder the chances of the decision appealed against being upheld.

After the decision of the Court of Session in *Rodenhurst v. Chief Constable, Grampian Police,* 1992 S.L.T. 104, there appeared to be emerging a distinction between the approaches adopted by the English and the Scottish courts. It was unclear whether the appeal was an administrative or a judicial appeal (at least in Scotland): see further the general note to s.12, above. It is now clear from s.44(2) that the appeal is to be dealt with on the merits; it is an appeal and not a review.

The decisions that can be appealed against are: (references are to FA 1968, as amended):

Section 28A (grant and renewal of certificates); substituted by FAA 1997, s.52.
Section 29 (variation of firearm certificate).
Section 30A (revocation of firearm certificate).
Section 30B (partial revocation of firearm certificate).
Section 30C (revocation of shot gun certificate).
Section 34 (refusal of registration as firearms dealer).
Section 36 (conditions as to registration of firearms dealer).
Section 37 (refusal to register a place of business of a registered firearms dealer).
Section 38 (removal of registered firearms dealer from the register).

Registered firearms dealers

Authorised dealing with firearms by registered firearms dealers

42.—(1) In section 8 of the 1968 Act (authorised dealing with firearms), after subsection (1) there shall be inserted the following subsection—

"(1A) Subsection (1) above applies to the possession, purchase or acquisition of a firearm or ammunition in the ordinary course of the business of a firearms dealer notwithstanding that the firearm or ammunition is in the possession of, or purchased or acquired by, the dealer or his servant at a place which is not a place of business of the dealer or which he has not registered as a place of business under section 33 or 37 of this Act."

(2) In section 33(3) of the 1968 Act (applications for registration as firearms dealer)—

(a) for the words from the beginning to "applicant" there shall be substituted the words "An applicant for registration as a firearms dealer";
(b) after the word "shall", in the second place it appears, there shall be inserted the words "(if he registers the applicant as a firearms dealer)".

DEFINITIONS

"acquire": FA 1968, s.57(4) applied to FAA 1997 by FAA 1997, s.50(2).
"ammunition": FA 1968, s.57(4) applied to FAA 1997 by FAA 1997, s.50(2).
"firearm": FA 1968, s.57(4) applied to FAA 1997 by FAA 1997, s.50(2).
"firearms dealer": FA 1968, s.57(4) applied to FAA 1997 by FAA 1997, s.50(2).

GENERAL NOTE

This adds a new subsection to FA 1968, s.8, and allows a registered firearms dealer to possess, etc. a firearm or ammunition even though such possession is not at the place of business of the dealer or is not at a registered place of business under the Act. Problems had arisen in one case where a dealer had acted in the course of his business and yet was in breach of the law: he had agreed the sale of a firearm and had delivered the firearm to the client at Bisley. As Bisley was not a registered place of business, an offence was committed. The decision in *R. v. Bull (Adrian William)* (1994) 99 Cr.App.R. 193 was discussed at several points in the Parliamentary debates. In *Bull,* the Court of Appeal held that the phrase "every place of business at which [the applicant] proposed to carry on business as a firearms dealer" should be given a wide construction; therefore the appellant, who had stored firearms in a barn which was not a registered place of business, committed an offence. FA 1968, s.33 required *every place of business* [italicised in the judgment] to be registered, and the exemption in FA 1968, s.8 applied to possession in the course of *that* business [italicised in the judgment] (see *Bull* at p. 202, *per* Cresswell J.).

As *Bull* shows, however, other offences may be committed where firearms are stored, for example under the Health and Safety legislation.

The section was added at the Report stage in the House of Lords (*Hansard,* Vol. 577, cols. 1659 to 1660; Lord Mackay of Drumadoon, the Lord Advocate, explained the problem as being that the dealer might possess weapons in places where he could not be expected to register: examples given were when delivering a firearm to a customer, purchasing a firearm at an auction, or examining a gun when visiting a client's home. It will be noted that none of the examples is close to the facts of *Bull*, where the dealer was storing weapons in a barn. Indeed, in the Debates, Lord Mackay of Drumadoon stated (*ibid.*) that the Government considered that on the facts of that case the barn should have been registered as a place of business; in other words the decision of the Court of Appeal in *Bull* was not to be reversed.

In this respect, the language of the section is a little peculiar. FA 1968, s.33 provides that an applicant for registration as a firearms dealer must provide particulars of every proposed place of business, and "except as provided in [the] Act", every such place of business must be registered. FA 1968, s.37 also provides for the registration of a new place of business. Therefore, the FA 1968 implies that every place of business of a firearms dealer must be registered. The force of the phrase "not a place of business of the dealer or which he has not registered as a place of business under [ss.33 or 37]" is thus unclear. Presumably it means that possession, etc. in the ordinary course of business will be an authorised dealing and thus protected by the new subs. (1A) unless the firearm or ammunition is at an unregistered place of business. The definition of a "place of business" is thus crucial: and *Bull* suggests a wide construction of that phrase.

Miscellaneous

Power of search with warrant

43.—(1) For section 46 of the 1968 Act (power of search with warrant), there shall be substituted the following section—

"Power of search with warrant

46.—(1) If a justice of the peace or, in Scotland, the sheriff, is satisfied by information on oath that there is reasonable ground for suspecting—

    (a) that an offence relevant for the purposes of this section has been, or being, or is about to be committed; or

    (b) that, in connection with a firearm or ammunition, there is a danger to the public safety or to the peace,

he may grant a warrant for any of the purposes mentioned in subsection (2) below.

(2) A warrant under this section may authorise a constable or civilian officer—

    (a) to enter at any time any premises or place named in the warrant, if necessary by force, and to search the premises or place and every person found there;

    (b) to seize and detain anything which he may find on the premises or place, or on any such person, in respect of which or in connection with which he has reasonable ground for suspecting—

        (i) that an offence relevant for the purposes of this section has been, is being or is about to be committed; or

        (ii) that in connection with a firearm, imitation firearm or ammunition there is a danger to the public safety or to the peace.

    (3) The power of a constable or civilian officer under subsection (2)(b) above to seize and detain anything found on any premises or place shall include power to require any information which is kept by means of a computer and is accessible from the premises or place to be produced in a form in which it is visible and legible and can be taken away.

    (4) The offences relevant for the purposes of this section are all offences under this Act except an offence under section 22(3) or an offence relating specifically to air weapons.

    (5) It is an offence for any person intentionally to obstruct a constable or civilian officer in the exercise of his powers under this section."

(2) In section 57(4) of the 1968 Act (interpretation) after the definition of "certificate" there shall be inserted the following definition—

" "civilian officer" means—

    (a) a person employed by a police authority or the Corporation of the City of London who is under the direction and control of a chief officer of police; or

    (b) a person employed under the Commissioner of Police for the Metropolis or the Receiver of the Metropolitan Police District who is not a constable and whose salary is paid out of the Metropolitan Police Fund."

(3) In Part I of Schedule 6 to the 1968 Act (prosecution and punishment of offences), after the entry for section 42A there shall be inserted the following entry—

"Section 46.	Obstructing constable or civilian officer in exercise of search powers.	Summary.	6 months or a fine of level 5 on the standard scale; or both."	—

DEFINITIONS

"ammunition": FA 1968, s.57(4) applied to FAA 1997 by FAA 1997, s.50(2).
"civilian officer": FA 1968, s.57(4), as added by FAA 1997, s.43(2).
"firearm": FA 1968, s.57(4) applied to FAA 1997 by FAA 1997, s.50(2).
"imitation firearm": FA 1968, s.57(4) applied to FAA 1997 by FAA 1997, s.50(2).
"premises": FA 1968, s.57(4) applied to FAA 1997 by FAA 1997, s.50(2).

GENERAL NOTE

This substitutes a new FA 1968, s.46, dealing with the power of search with warrant. Subsection (1)(a) is a re-enactment of part of section 46(1); para. 1(b) is new.

The authorisation of civilian officers is new; and under s.46(2)(b) the power to seize "anything" is much wider than the previous language "firearm or ammunition" and would include documents or, indeed, any evidential material whatsoever. Paragraph 2(b)(ii) is also new, and reflects para. 1(b), above. The specific reference to accessible information in computers is noteworthy: it was added in the Report stage in the House of Lords (*Hansard*, H.L. Vol. 577, col. 1661). Subsection (5) is also new: the word "intentionally" should be noted; this is in addition to the general offence of obstructing a constable in the execution of his duty. It is added for two reasons: first, because of the reference to "civilian officers" and second, because the punishment is greater (see the substituted s.46(3)) than it is for the offence of willfully obstructing a constable in the execution of his duty: Police Act 1996 (c.16), s.89(2) re-enacting Police Act 1964 (c.48), s.51(3) as amended. Punishment for the offence under FAA 1997, s.46 is six months imprisonment or a fine of level 5 on the standard scale or both; under the Police Act 1996, s.89(2) the punishment is one month's imprisonment, a fine of level 3 on the standard scale, or both.

Firearm certificates for certain firearms used for target shooting: special conditions

44.—(1) If a chief officer of police is satisfied, on an application for the grant or renewal of a firearm certificate in relation to any rifle or muzzle-loading pistol which is not a prohibited weapon, that the applicant's only reason for having it in his possession is to use it for target shooting, any certificate which may be granted to the applicant or, as the case may be, renewed shall be held subject to the following conditions (in addition to any other conditions), namely—

(a) the rifle or pistol is only to be used for target shooting; and

(b) the holder must be a member of an approved rifle club or, as the case may be, muzzle-loading pistol club specified in the certificate.

(2) In this section, "muzzle loading pistol" means a pistol designed to be loaded at the muzzle end of the barrel or chamber with a loose charge and a separate ball (or other missile).

DEFINITIONS

"firearm certificate": FA 1968, s.57(4)(a) applied to FAA 1997 by FAA 1997, s.50(2).

"muzzle-loading pistol": subs. (2).

"prohibited weapon": FA 1968, s.5(2) as amended applied to FAA 1997 by FAA 1997, s.50(2).

"rifle": FAA 1988, s.25(3) applied to FA 1968 by FAA 1988, s.25(1) and to FAA 1997 by FAA 1997, s.50(2).

GENERAL NOTE

Where a chief officer of police is satisfied that the applicant's only reason for possession of a rifle or a muzzle-loading pistol is for target shooting, any certificate *must*, on grant or renewal of the certificate, contain the conditions in subs. (1)(a) and (b). There is, of course, no requirement that a certificate be granted at all: and the weapon must be one that is not prohibited and thus is still within the scope of FA 1968, s.1.

The phrase "target-shooting" is considered in the General Note to s.12, above. For "approved rifle club" see general note to s.45, below.

Approved rifle clubs and muzzle-loading pistol clubs

45.—(1) For section 15 of the 1988 Act (rifle and pistol clubs) there shall be substituted the following section—

"Approved rifle clubs and muzzle-loading pistol clubs

15.—(1) Subject to subsection (4) below, a member of a rifle club approved by the Secretary of State may, without holding a firearm certificate, have in his possession a rifle and ammunition when engaged as a member of the club in connection with target shooting.

(2) Any rifle club may apply for approval, whether or not it is intended that any club members will, by virtue of subsection (1) above, have rifles or ammunition in their possession without holding firearm certificates.

(3) The Secretary of State may publish such guidance as he considers appropriate for the purpose of informing those seeking approval for a club of criteria that must be met before any application for such approval will be considered.

(4) The application of subsection (1) above to members of an approved rifle club may—

(a) be excluded in relation to the club, or

(b) be restricted to target shooting with specified types of rifle,

by limitations contained in the approval.

(5) An approval—

(a) may be granted subject to such conditions specified in it as the Secretary of State thinks fit;

(b) may at any time be varied or withdrawn by the Secretary of State; and

(c) shall (unless withdrawn) continue in force for six years from the date on which it is granted or last renewed.

(6) There shall be payable on the grant or renewal of an approval a fee of £84 but this subsection shall be included in the provisions which may be amended by an order under section 43 of the principal Act.

(7) A constable or civilian officer authorised in writing in that behalf may, on producing if required his authority, enter any premises occupied or used by an approved rifle club and inspect those premises, and anything on them, for the purpose of ascertaining whether the provisions of this section, and any limitations or conditions in the approval, are being complied with.

(8) The power of a constable or civilian officer under subsection (7) above to inspect anything on club premises shall include power to require any information which is kept by means of a computer and is accessible from the premises to be made available for inspection in a visible and legible form.

(9) It is an offence for a person intentionally to obstruct a constable or civilian officer in the exercise of his powers under subsection (7) above; and that offence shall be punishable on summary conviction with a fine not exceeding level 3 on the standard scale.

(10) In this section and section 15A below—

"approval", means an approval under this section; and "approved" shall be construed accordingly;

"civilian officer" has the same meaning as in the principal Act; and "rifle club" includes a miniature rifle club.

(11) This section applies in relation to a muzzle-loading pistol club and its members as it applies to a rifle club and its members with the substitution for any reference to a rifle of a reference to a muzzle-loading pistol.

(12) In subsection (11) above—

"muzzle-loading pistol club" means a club where muzzle-loading pistols are used for target shooting; and

"muzzle-loading pistol" means a pistol designed to be loaded at the muzzle end of the barrel or chamber with a loose charge and a separate ball (or other missile).".

(2) A club may be approved by the Secretary of State under section 15 of the 1988 Act and also licensed under this Act as a pistol club.

(3) Any approval of a rifle or miniature rifle club or muzzle-loading pistol club under section 15 of the 1988 Act which is in force immediately before the commencement of this section shall have effect as if it were an approval under section 15 of the 1988 Act as substituted by subsection (1) above.

DEFINITIONS

"ammunition": FA 1968, s.57(4) applied to FAA 1997 by FAA 1997, s.50(2).
"approval": FAA 1988, s.15(10) substituted by FAA 1997, s.46.
"civilian officer": FA 1968, s.57(4), as added by FAA 1997, s.43(2).
"firearm": FA 1968, s.57(4) applied to FAA 1997 by FAA 1997, s.50(2).
"firearm certificate": FA 1968, s.57(4) applied to FAA 1997 by FAA 1997, s.50(2).
"muzzle-loading pistol": FAA 1988, s.15(11) substituted by FAA 1997, s.45.
"muzzle loading pistol club": FAA 1988, s.15(11) substituted by FAA 1997, s.45.
"premises": FA 1968, s.57(4) applied to FAA 1997 by FAA 1997, s.50(2).
"rifle": FAA 1988, s.25(3) applied to FA 1968 by FAA 1988, s.25(1) and to FAA 1997 by FAA 1997, s.50(2).
"rifle club": FA 1988, s.15(11) substituted by FAA 1997, s.45.

GENERAL NOTE

This replaces FAA 1988, s.15, itself amending FA 1968, s.11(3). The substituted section is much longer and more complex than its predecessor, as well as being much more restrictive. As previously, the approval of the Secretary of State is necessary for approval of a rifle club. References to "pistol clubs" have gone, in accordance with one of the principal objects of the 1997 Act, though the position of "muzzle-loading pistol clubs" is preserved by the substituted subs. (11). The term "rifle club" now includes "miniature rifle club": subs. (10).

Subs. (1)
Subject to the general points above, this is in substance a re-enactment of FAA 1988, s.15(1). The phrase "in connection with" has replaced, "in, or in connection with". It was considered that the first two words of the former legislation added nothing. The phrase "target shooting" has replaced "target practice"; this makes clear, for example, that a competition which involves shooting at targets is covered, as distinct from practice for such competition. The phrase "target-shooting" is further considered in the General Note to s.12, above.

Subs. (2)
This allows a club to apply for approval as such, even though it is not intended that members without firearms certificates will use its facilities. This would give the club the opportunity at a later stage to allow new members to the sport to shoot.

Subs. (3)
This allows the Secretary of State to publish guidance to those seeking approval of a club of the criteria that *must* be met before an application is approved. This draconian language has been the subject of comment: see General Note on s.22 above.

Subs. (4)
Paragraph (a) is new; this means that a club may be "an approved rifle club", and yet its members may not be permitted to have in their possession rifles, muzzle-loading pistols, or ammunition without a firearms certificate. Paragraph (b) is a variation on the existing FAA 1988, s.15(2).

Subs. (7)
See general note to s.30(1), above.

Subs. (8)
This section was added at the Report stage in the House of Lords. See note to s.30(2), above.

Coterminous pistol club licences and rifle club approvals

46. After section 15 of the 1988 Act there shall be inserted the following section—

"Coterminous pistol club licences and rifle club approvals

15A.—(1) Where an application is made on behalf of a club which is approved under section 15 above for the grant or renewal of a pistol club licence, the officer of the club making the application may also apply for the club's approval to be withdrawn and replaced by a new approval taking effect on the same day as that on which the licence is granted or renewed.

(2) Where an application is made on behalf of a club which has a pistol club licence for the grant or renewal of approval under section 15 above, that approval may, if the club so requests, be granted or renewed for such period less than six years as will secure that it expires at the same time as the licence.

(3) The fee payable on the grant or renewal of an approval which—
(a) takes effect, whether by virtue of subsection (1) above or otherwise, at the same time as a pistol club licence granted or renewed in respect of that club, or
(b) is granted or renewed by virtue of subsection (2) above for a period less than six years,
shall be £21 instead of that specified in section 15(6) above.

This subsection shall be included in the provisions that may be amended by an order under section 43 of the principal Act.

(4) In this section "pistol club licence" means a licence under section 21 of the Firearms (Amendment) Act 1997.".

DEFINITIONS
"ammunition": FA 1968, s.57(4) applied to FAA 1997 by FAA 1997, s.50(2).
"approval": FAA 1988, s.15(10) substituted by FAA 1997, s.46.
"civilian officer": FA 1968, s.57(4), as added by FAA 1997, s.43(2).
"firearm": FA 1968, s.57(4) applied to FAA 1997 by FAA 1997, s.50(2).
"firearm certificate": FA 1968, s.57(4)(a) applied to FAA 1997 by FAA 1997, s.50(2).
"muzzle-loading pistol": FAA 1988, s.15(11) substituted by FAA 1997, s.45.
"muzzle loading pistol club": FAA 1988, s.15(11) substituted by FAA 1997, s.45.
"premises": FA 1968, s.57(4) applied to FAA 1997 by FAA 1997, s.50(2).
"rifle": FAA 1988, s.25(3) applied to FA 1968 by FAA 1988, s.25(1) and to FAA 1997 by FAA 1997, s.50(2).
"rifle club": FA 1988, s.15(11) substituted by FAA 1997, s.45.

GENERAL NOTE
This section, added at the Report stage in the House of Commons, allows a club to hold a coterminous pistol club licence and rifle club approval, with a considerably lower fee.

Museums eligible for a museums firearm licence

47. In the Schedule to the 1988 Act (firearms and ammunition in museums to which the Schedule applies)—
  (a) the existing provisions of paragraph 5 shall be numbered as sub-paragraph (1) of that paragraph;
  (b) after that sub-paragraph there shall be inserted the following sub-paragraphs—
    "(2) This Schedule also applies to any museum or similar institution in Great Britain which is of a description specified in an order made for the purposes of this sub-paragraph by the Secretary of State and whose collection includes or is to include firearms.
    (3) An order under sub-paragraph (2) above may specify any description of museum or similar institution which appears to the Secretary of State to have as its purpose, or one of its purposes, the preservation for the public benefit of a collection of historical, artistic or scientific interest.
    (4) The power to make an order under sub-paragraph (2) above shall be exercisable by statutory instrument.".

DEFINITIONS
"ammunition": FA 1968, s.57(4) applied to FAA 1997 by FAA 1997, s.50(2).
"firearm": FA 1968, s.57(4) applied to FAA 1997 by FAA 1997, s.50(2).

GENERAL NOTE
The FAA 1988, s.1 and Sched. 1 provided for museum firearms licences to be granted to certain museums, thus enabling museums to hold firearms and ammunition without a firearm certificate or a shot gun certificate; and, if the licence provided, to hold prohibited weapons without the authority of the Secretary of State. Paragraph 5 of that Schedule lists a number of museums, and the sub-paragraph added by FAA 1997, s.47 provides for a general addition of museums which have as a purpose (or the only purpose) of preservation for the public benefit, a collection of historical, artistic or scientific interest. Paragraph 5 required, however, that the museum or similar institution had to be maintained wholly or mainly out of money provided by Parliament or a local authority. This last requirement has now gone: the source of funding does not matter. Thus, for example, regimental museums funded principally from private donations may now be within the scope of the Schedule if the Secretary of State by statutory instrument so orders. Baroness Blatch, Minister of State, Home Office, in the debates in the House of Lords, stated that museums currently registered under the Museums and Galleries Commission were likely to be added to the Schedule, if they had the appropriate objects: *Hansard,* H.L. Vol. 577, col. 647.

Firearms powered by compressed carbon dioxide

48. Any reference to an air rifle, air pistol or air gun—

(a) in the Firearms Acts 1968 to 1997; or

(b) in the Firearms (Dangerous Air Weapons) Rules 1969 or the Firearms (Dangerous Air Weapons) (Scotland) Rules 1969,

shall include a reference to a rifle, pistol or gun powered by compressed carbon dioxide.

DEFINITIONS

"rifle": FAA 1988, s.25(3) applied to FA 1968 by FAA 1988, s.25(1) and to FAA 1997 by FAA 1997, s.50(2).

PART IV

FINAL PROVISIONS

Financial provisions

49.—(1) Any expenses incurred by the Secretary of State which are attributable to the provisions of this Act, and any sums required by him for making payments under this Act, shall be paid out of money provided by Parliament.

(2) Any fees received by the Secretary of State under section 21(6) above shall be paid into the Consolidated Fund.

Interpretation and supplementary provisions

50.—(1) In this Act—

"licence", "licensed pistol club" and "licensed premises" have the meanings given by section 19 above;

"small-calibre pistol" means—

(a) a pistol chambered for .22 or smaller rim-fire cartridges; or

(b) an air pistol to which section 1 of the 1968 Act applies and which is designed to fire .22 or smaller diameter ammunition;

"the 1968 Act" means the Firearms Act 1968;

"the 1988 Act" means the Firearms (Amendment) Act 1988.

(2) Any expression used in this Act which is also used in the 1968 Act or the 1988 Act has the same meaning as in that Act.

(3) Any reference in the 1968 Act to a person who is by virtue of that Act entitled to possess, purchase or acquire any weapon or ammunition without holding a certificate shall include a reference to a person who is so entitled by virtue of any provision of this Act.

(4) Sections 46, 51(4) and 52 of the 1968 Act (powers of search, time-limit for prosecutions and forfeiture and cancellation orders on conviction) shall apply also to offences under this Act.

(5) Sections 53 to 56 and section 58 of the 1968 Act (rules, Crown application, service of notices and savings) shall have effect as if this Act were contained in that Act.

(6) The provisions of this Act shall be treated as contained in the 1968 Act for the purposes of the Firearms Act 1982 (imitation firearms readily convertible into firearms to which section 1 of the 1968 Act applies).

DEFINITIONS

"acquire": FA 1968, s.57(4) applied to FAA 1997 by FAA 1997, s.50(2).

"ammunition": FA 1968, s.57(4) applied to FAA 1997 by FAA 1997, s.50(2).

"certificate": FA 1968, s.57(4)(a) applied to FAA 1997 by FAA 1997, s.50(2).

"firearm": FA 1968, s.57(4) applied to FAA 1997 by FAA 1997, s.50(2).

Subs. (4)

FA 1968, s.46 (as substituted by FAA 1997, s.43(1)) deals with the powers of search with a warrant;

FA 1968, s.51(4) allows certain summary proceedings to be begun within four years of the offence;

FA 1968, s.52 deals with forfeiture.

Subs. (6)

This subsection, which was added at the Report stage in the House of Commons (*Hansard*, H.C. Vol. 286, col. 1161) makes it clear that the provisions of the FAA 1997 are deemed to be in existence for the purposes of the operation of the FA 1982 (readily convertible imitation firearms).

Power to make transitional, consequential etc. provisions

51.—(1) The Secretary of State may by regulations make such transitional and consequential provisions and such savings as he considers necessary or expedient in preparation for, in connection with, or in consequence of—

(a) the coming into force of any provision of this Act; or

(b) the operation of any enactment repealed or amended by a provision of this Act during any period when the repeal or amendment is not wholly in force.

(2) Regulations under this section may make modifications of any enactment contained in this or in any other Act.

(3) The power to make regulations under subsection (2) above shall be exercisable by statutory instrument which shall be subject to annulment in pursuance of a resolution of either House of Parliament.

GENERAL NOTE

This section was the subject of very considerable debate in the House of Lords. It was suggested that the word "consequential", in particular, was capable of being given a very wide interpretation: thus, the banning of all handguns might be seen as a consequence of the FAA 1997. Baroness Blatch, Minister of State, Home Office, stated, on behalf of the Government that the object of the section was to deal with unforeseen anomalies and to be a safeguarding provision (*Hansard*, H.L. Vol. 578, col. 171 (Third Reading)). Similar statements were made in the House of Commons on behalf of the Government by Miss Ann Widdecombe (*Hansard*, H.C. Vol. 298, col. 828).

Minor and consequential amendments and repeals

52.—(1) Schedule 2 (minor and consequential amendments) shall have effect.

(2) The enactments mentioned in Schedule 3 (which include spent enactments) are repealed to the extent specified in the third column of that Schedule.

Short title, commencement and extent

53.—(1) This Act may be cited as the Firearms (Amendment) Act 1997.

(2) This Act and the Firearms Acts 1968 to 1992 may be cited together as the Firearms Acts 1968 to 1997.

(3) This Act shall come into force on such day as the Secretary of State may by order made by statutory instrument appoint; and different days may be appointed for different purposes and different areas.

(4) An order under subsection (3) above may contain such transitional provision and savings (whether or not involving the modification of any statutory provision) as appear to the Secretary of State to be necessary or expedient in connection with any provisions brought into force.

(5) This Act does not extend to Northern Ireland.

SCHEDULES

SCHEDULE 1

TRANSITIONAL ARRANGEMENTS FOR SMALL-CALIBRE PISTOLS

Preliminary

1. This Schedule applies to any person who—
(a) by virtue of a firearm certificate, has a small-calibre pistol belonging to him in his possession, or has contracted to acquire any such pistol, before the appointed day; and
(b) will, after the appointed day, be required to keep that pistol at licensed premises of a licensed club.

Delivery of pistols to police

2.—(1) A person to whom this Schedule applies may, at any time before the appointed day, deliver a small-calibre pistol ("the pistol") to any designated police station for safe keeping; and if he does so he shall also deliver up the firearm certificate in order that the delivery of the pistol may be recorded therein.

(2) Sub-paragraph (1) above applies to a pistol which a person has (before the appointed day) contracted to acquire if it is delivered to any designated police station as soon as reasonably practicable after it comes into his possession.

(3) The pistol shall be kept in police custody (whether at the designated police station or otherwise) until it is—
(a) released under paragraph 6 or 7 below;
(b) surrendered to the police before the end of the transitional period under paragraph 9(2) below;
(c) deemed to have been surrendered by virtue of paragraph 8 below.

Free renewal of firearm certificates

3.—(1) The delivery of the pistol into police custody does not affect the validity of any firearm certificate authorising the holder to have it in his possession.

(2) If a firearm certificate which authorises any person to have the pistol in his possession expires at a time when the pistol is in police custody, no fee shall be charged for the renewal of the certificate unless the renewed certificate also relates to another firearm, or ammunition for another firearm, which is not at that time in police custody.

(3) Where a firearm certificate is renewed by the police free of charge, and the pistol is released to the holder of that certificate under paragraph 6 or 7 below, he shall at that time pay any fee which, apart from this paragraph, he would have been charged on the renewal of his certificate.

Release of pistols in police custody

4. A small-calibre pistol being kept in police custody shall not be released to any person except on the authority of the chief officer of police for the area in which the designated police station to which it was delivered under paragraph 2 above is situated.

5.—(1) Any holder of a firearm certificate relating to the pistol, or any other person who may lawfully have the pistol in his possession, may apply in writing for the release of the pistol to the chief officer of police for the area in which the designated police station to which it was delivered under paragraph 2 above is situated.

(2) An application under sub-paragraph (1) above must be made at least four weeks before the end of the transitional period.

6. If the applicant for release is the person who delivered the pistol into police custody, the chief officer of police shall release the pistol if he is satisfied that the person receiving it—
(a) is authorised to convey the pistol to the licensed premises of a licensed pistol club by a permit under section 13 on behalf of a holder of a firearm certificate held subject to the conditions specified in section 12 and who—
(i) is a member of the licensed pistol club specified in the certificate;
(ii) has made arrangements for the pistol to be kept at the licensed premises of that club which are so specified,

(b) is the holder of a firearm certificate authorising him to have the pistol in his possession, but which is not subject to those conditions;

(c) is entitled to have the pistol in his possession without a firearm certificate.

7.—(1) Where a person other than the person who delivered the pistol into police custody applies for it to be released, the chief officer of police shall release the pistol only if he is satisfied—

(a) that the person who originally delivered the pistol into that custody has either disposed of any interest in it or certified that he is content for it to be delivered to the applicant; and

(b) that the person receiving the pistol is either a registered firearms dealer who has lawfully purchased or acquired the pistol and intends to have it in his possession in the ordinary course of his business or a person falling within paragraph 6(a), (b) or (c) above.

(2) Where an application is made as mentioned in sub-paragraph (1) above, the chief officer of police may require such written statements from the person who delivered the pistol into police custody and from the person applying for the release of the pistol as he considers necessary for the purpose of determining the application.

(3) It is an offence for any person knowingly or recklessly to make a statement which is false in any material particular for the purpose of procuring, whether for himself or for another person, the release of a pistol from police custody.

(4) An offence under sub-paragraph (3) above shall be punishable on summary conviction with imprisonment for a term not exceeding six months or a fine not exceeding level 5 on the standard scale or both.

Period of safe-keeping by police

8.—(1) If the pistol is not released before the end of the transitional period it shall be treated as if it had been surrendered to the police immediately after the end of that period.

(2) If an application for release of the pistol is made at least four weeks before the end of that period—

(a) the pistol shall not be deemed to have been surrendered under this paragraph while the application is being determined; and

(b) if the pistol is not released, it shall be deemed to have been so surrendered when the application is finally determined.

(3) Where a person is deemed to have surrendered the pistol under this paragraph, his firearm certificate shall be deemed to have expired so far as it relates to that pistol.

Voluntary surrender of pistols

9.—(1) A person to whom this Schedule applies may before the appointed day, surrender a small-calibre pistol belonging to him at any designated police station instead of keeping it at licensed premises of a licensed pistol club or delivering it into police custody.

(2) Where a small-calibre pistol has been delivered into police custody, the person who delivered it may (if it still belongs to him) surrender the pistol by giving notice that he is surrendering it to the chief officer of police for the area in which the designated police station to which he delivered it is situated.

10. The Secretary of State may make such payments, to such persons, as he may consider appropriate in respect of small-calibre pistols which are surrendered, or are treated as having been surrendered, by virtue of paragraph 8 or 9 above.

Supplementary

11. The chief officer of police shall not be obliged to make pistols delivered to him under paragraph 2 above available for inspection either by the certificate holder or by any other person.

12.—(1) In this Schedule—

"designated police station" means a police station designated by any chief officer of police for the purposes of this Schedule;

"police custody" means police custody under paragraph 2;

"the appointed day" means the day on which section 11 comes into force;

"the transitional period" means the period of one year beginning with the appointed day.

(2) The Secretary of State may by order amend the definition of the transitional period so as to substitute, for any period for the time being specified in that definition, such other period as may be specified by the order.

An order under this sub-paragraph may make different provisions for different purposes and different areas.

(3) The power to make an order under sub-paragraph (2) above shall be exercisable by statutory instrument which shall be subject to annulment in pursuance of a resolution of either House of Parliament.

GENERAL NOTE

The Schedule deals with the transitional period—one year from s.11 of the FAA 1997 coming into effect—during which small-calibre pistols are to be delivered to designated police stations. Under para. 9, such weapons may be voluntarily surrendered before the period begins. Compensation may be payable in respect of weapons that are surrendered, or are deemed to have been surrendered. Such payments are not made under the scheme to be set up by statutory instrument under ss.16 and 17. The payments under the Schedule were described as "gratuitous" (Baroness Blatch, Minister of State, Home Office in the Committee stage in the House of Lords, *Hansard,* H.L. Vol. 577, col. 576). The intention is that those who receive compensation under this scheme will be treated as favourably as those who surrender the prohibited higher-calibre guns. The transitional period of one year would give holders of weapons and accessories the opportunity to sell them abroad; therefore there was no need for special rules concerning export licences—the Department of Trade and Industry was said to be able to process an export licence within 10 days of the receipt of a completed application.

Section 52   SCHEDULE 2

CONSEQUENTIAL AND MINOR AMENDMENTS

Firearms Act 1968 (c.27)

1. The Firearms Act 1968 shall be amended as follows.

2.—(1) In section 3(5) (false statements with a view to purchasing or acquiring firearm etc.), for the words "makes any false statement" there shall be substituted the words "knowingly or recklessly makes a statement false in any material particular".

(2) In section 7(2), 9(3), 13(2) and 29(3) (all of which concern false statements), for the words "to make any statement which he knows to be false" there shall be substituted the words "knowingly or recklessly to make a statement false in any material particular".

(3) In section 39(1) (offences in connection with registration of dealers), for the words "makes any statement which he knows to be false" there shall be substituted the words "knowingly or recklessly makes a statement false in any material particular".

3. In section 11(3), 23(2) and 54(5) (all of which refer to use of firearms or ammunition for target practice), for the words "target practice", in each place where they occur, there shall be substituted the words "target shooting".

4.—(1) After section 28 there shall be inserted the following section—

"Certificates: supplementary

28A.—(1) A certificate shall, unless previously revoked or cancelled, continue in force for five years from the date when it was granted or last renewed, but shall be renewable for a further period of five years by the chief officer of police for the area in which the holder resides.

(2) The provisions of this Act apply to the renewal of a certificate as they apply to a grant; but, subject to the power of renewal conferred by this subsection, a certificate granted or last renewed in Northern Ireland shall not continue in force for a period longer than that for which it was so granted or last renewed.

(3) The Secretary of State may by order amend subsection (1) above so as to substitute for any reference to a period for the time being specified in that subsection a reference to such other period as may be specified in the order.

(4) An order made under subsection (3) above shall apply only to certificates granted or renewed after the date on which the order comes into force.

(5) The power to make orders under subsection (3) above shall be exercisable by statutory instrument which shall be subject to annulment in pursuance of a resolution of either House of Parliament.

(6) A person aggrieved by the refusal of a chief officer of police to grant or to renew a certificate under this Act may in accordance with section 44 of this Act appeal against the refusal.

(7) It is an offence for a person knowingly or recklessly to make any statement which is false in any material particular for the purpose of procuring (whether for himself or another) the grant or renewal of a certificate under this Act."

(2) In Part I of Schedule 6 (prosecution and punishment of offences), in the entry relating to section 26(5) (making of false statement in order to procure grant or renewal of certificate) for the words "Section 26(5)" there shall be substituted the words "Section 28A(7)".

5. In section 32 (exemption from fee for certificate in certain cases) for subsection (2) there shall be substituted the following subsections—

"(2) No fee shall be payable on the grant to a responsible officer of a rifle club, miniature rifle club or muzzle-loading pistol club which is approved under section 15 of the Firearms (Amendment) Act 1988 of a firearm certificate in respect of rifles, miniature rifles or muzzle-loading pistols, or ammunition, to be used solely for target shooting by the members of the club, or on the variation or renewal of a certificate so granted.

(2A) Subsection (2) above—
 (a) does not apply if the operation of subsection (1) of section 15 of the Firearms (Amendment) Act 1988 is excluded in relation to the club by a limitation in the approval; or
 (b) if the operation of subsection (1) of that section in relation to the club is limited by the approval to target shooting with specified types of rifles, miniature rifles or muzzle-loading pistols, only applies to a certificate in respect of rifles, miniature rifles or pistols of those types.

(2B) No fee shall be payable on the grant to a person acting in his capacity as the responsible officer of a licensed pistol club of a firearm certificate in respect of small-calibre pistols or ammunition to be used solely for target shooting by members of the club, or on the variation or renewal of a certificate so granted.".

6. In section 32A(4)(b) and 32C(7), for the words "section 4(2) of the Firearms (Amendment) Act 1988 (formalities on transfer of shot guns)" there shall be substituted the words "section 32(2)(b) of the Firearms (Amendment) Act 1997 (requirements relating to transfers of firearms)".

7. In section 38(8) (surrender of register of transactions by dealer) after the words "this Act" there shall be inserted "(or, if the register is kept by means of a computer, a copy of the information comprised in that register in a visible and legible form)".

8. In section 40 (compulsory register of transactions)—
 (a) in subsection (4)—
   (i) after the word "constable" (in both places it appears) there shall be inserted the words "or a civilian officer";
   (ii) after the words "the register" there shall be inserted the words "(or if the register is kept by means of a computer, a copy of the information comprised in that register in a visible and legible form);"; and
 (b) after that subsection there shall be inserted the following subsection—
   "(4A) Every person keeping a register in accordance with this section by means of a computer shall secure that the information comprised in the register can readily be pro-duced in a form in which it is visible and legible and can be taken away.".

9. In section 50 (special powers of arrest) for subsection (2) there shall be substituted the following—
   "(2) A constable may arrest without warrant any person whom he has reasonable cause to suspect to be committing an offence under section 4, 5, 18, 19, 19A, 20, 21 or 47(2) of this Act and, for the purpose of exercising the power conferred by this subsection, may enter any place.".

10. In section 54(1) (application of Parts I and II to the Crown) for the words "26 to 32" there shall be substituted the words "26A to 32".

11. In section 54(2)(b), for the words "section 26" there shall be substituted the words "section 26A".

12. In Schedule 5 (provisions as to appeals under section 44), in column 1 of Part I, in paragraph 1, for the words "26(4), 29(2) or 30(3)" there shall be substituted the words "28A(6), 29(2), 30A(6), 30B(3) or 30C(2)".

13. In Part I of Schedule 6 (prosecution and punishment of offences) to the 1968 Act, for the entry relating to section 1(2) (non-compliance with condition of firearm certificate) there shall be substituted the following entry—

| "Section 1(2). | Non-compliance with condition of firearm certificate. | (a) Summary | (i) where the offence is committed in an aggravated form within the meaning of section 12 of the Firearms (Amendment) Act 1997, 6 months or a fine of the statutory maximum; or both. (ii) in any other case, 6 months or a fine of level 5 on the standard scale; or both. | — |
| | | (b) On indictment | where the offence is committed in an aggravated form within the meaning of section 12 of the Firearms (Amendment) Act 1997, 7 years or a fine; or both." | — |

14. In Part I of Schedule 6 (prosecution and punishment of offences), in the entry relating to section 30(4) (failure to surrender certificate on revocation) for the words "Section 30(4)" there shall be substituted the words "Section 30D(3)".

Firearms (Amendment) Act 1988 (c. 45)

15. The Firearms (Amendment) Act 1988 shall be amended as follows.

16. In section 7(1) (conversion not to affect classification), for paragraph (a) there shall be substituted the following paragraph—

"(a) has at any time (whether before or after the passing of the Firearms (Amendment) Act 1997) been a weapon of a kind described in section 5(1) or (1A) of the principal Act (including any amendments to section 5(1) made under section 1(4) of this Act);".

17. In section 11(1) (co-terminous certificates) for the words "subsection (3), or in an order made under subsection (3A) of section 26" there shall be substituted the words "subsection (1), or in an order made under subsection (3) of section 28A".

18. In section 12 (revocation of certificates) in subsection (1), for the words "under section 30(1)(a) or (2)", there shall be substituted the words "under section 30A(2), (3) or (4) or 30C".

19. In section 17(10) and paragraph 4(1) of the Schedule, for the words "to make any statement which he knows to be false" there shall be substituted the words "knowingly or recklessly to make a statement false in any material particular".

20. In section 22(1)(c) (firearms consultative committee), for the words "the principal Act, the Firearms Act 1982 and this Act" there shall be substituted the words "the Firearms Acts 1968 to 1997".

GENERAL NOTE

This lists a considerable number of minor and consequential amendments.

Para. 2

For "knowingly or recklessly makes a statement false in any material particular" see general note to s.13(5), above.

Para. 3

See general note to s.12.

Para. 4

This provides an additional s.28A to the FA 1968. It provides for the duration of certificates—both firearm certificates and shot gun certificates—and re-enacts the amendments made by FAA 1992, s.1, allowing for the duration of certificates to be extended or curtailed; curtailment, however, cannot operate with respect to existing certificates. As a consequence, FAA 1992, s.1 is repealed: FAA 1997, Sched. 3.

Para. 5

This provides an additional exemption from fee for firearms certificates in connection with rifle clubs and muzzle-loading pistol clubs. The restrictions in s.32(2A) should be noted.

Para. 7
 This reflects the right of constables and civilian officers to have access to certain records produced or held on computers: see ss.30(2) and 43(3).

Para. 8
 This contains three, disparate, amendments. FA 1968, s.40 provides that those who, by way of trade or business, manufacture, sell or transfer firearms or ammunition, have to keep a register of such transactions. The first amendment to s.40(4) allows civilian officers to inspect records, etc. in the same way as constables can. The second amendment allows a copy of a computer produced register to be inspected. The new subs. (4A), however, requires that any person within s.40 who keeps a register by means of a computer must ensure that the information on the computer can readily be produced in a visible, legible and transportable form. How this will be interpreted is not clear. Much of the information on such registers could be of use to criminals as well as to the police; and a security-minded trader might well attempt to make such information difficult to access, save with certain stringent checks or safeguards. What if the individual with the appropriate passwords is away? Does this prevent the information being "readily" available?

Para. 9
 This amends the law relating to powers of arrest without warrant.
 The offences for which such arrest may now occur are:
　FA 1968, s.4 (conversion of weapons).
　FA 1968, s.5 (possession of prohibited weapons).
　FA 1968, s.18 (carrying firearm with criminal intent).
　FA 1968, s.19 (carrying firearm in a public place).
　FA 1968, s.19A (as added by FAA 1997, s.11) (having a small-calibre pistol outside the premises of a licensed pistol club).
　FA 1968, s.20 (trespassing with a firearm).
　FA 1968, s.21 (possession of firearm by convicted criminal).
　FA 1968, s.47(2) (failure to hand over firearm, etc. when requested to do so by a constable).
 Sections 4, 5 and 18 previously only gave a power of arrest without warrant in Scotland. Section 19A, by definition, is an offence that was previously not arrestable without warrant; the other sections are re-enactments of the previous legislation.

Para. 16
 This provides that the handguns made prohibited weapons by FAA 1997 are always regarded as having been prohibited weapons for the purposes of conversion; and conversion will not therefore affect their status as prohibited weapons, even though they were not prohibited weapons either when constructed or previously held.

Section 52　　　　　　　　　　SCHEDULE 3

REPEALS

Chapter	Short title	Extent of repeal
1968 c. 27.	Firearms Act 1968.	In section 5(1)(ac) the words "(excluding any detachable, folding, retractable or other moveable butt-stock)". In section 5A, in subsection (4) the words "which is designed to be used with a pistol" and in subsection (8) the words "is designed to be used with a pistol and". In section 23(2)(a), the words "in, or". Section 28(3). Section 42. In section 54(5)(b), the words "in, or". In Schedule 6, the entry relating to section 42.
1988 c. 45.	Firearms (Amendment) Act 1988.	Section 4. In section 9, the words from the beginning to "and". Section 10. In section 12(5), the words from the beginning to "subsection (1) above".
1992 c. 31.	Firearms (Amendment) Act 1992.	Section 1.

INDEX

References are to sections and Schedules

LOCAL GOVERNMENT (GAELIC NAMES) (SCOTLAND) ACT 1997

(1997 c.6)

An Act to enable local authorities in Scotland to take Gaelic names; and for connected purposes. [27th February 1997]

PARLIAMENTARY DEBATES

Hansard, H.C. Vol. 285, col. 995; Vol. 287, col. 586. H.L. Vol. 576, col. 1275; Vol. 578, cols. 458, 905.

INTRODUCTION

This Act inserts new subsection (1A) into s.23 of the Local Government (Scotland) Act 1973 to allow Scottish councils to change their name to 'Comhairle' with the addition of the name of their area. A council may do so where the name of the area is also changed into Gaelic, and where a resolution is passed in accordance with s.23(1) of the 1973 Act. This Act shall come into force on April 27, 1997 and extends only to Scotland.

Power of council to change name into Gaelic and vice-versa

1. In section 23 of the Local Government (Scotland) Act 1973 (change of name of local government area), there shall be inserted, after subsection (1), the following subsections—

"(1A) Where a council so change the name of their area into Gaelic, they may also, by a resolution passed in accordance with subsection (1) above and notwithstanding sections 2(3) and 3(1)(a) of the Local Government etc. (Scotland) Act 1994, decide that their name shall be "Comhairle" with the addition of the name of their area.

(1B) A council which have so changed their name into Gaelic may, by a resolution passed in accordance with subsection (1) above, change it back into English.".

Short title, commencement and extent

2.—(1) This Act may be cited as the Local Government (Gaelic Names) (Scotland) Act 1997.

(2) This Act shall come into force on the expiry of the period of two months beginning with the day on which it is passed.

(3) This Act extends to Scotland only.

INDEX

References are to sections

NORTHERN IRELAND ARMS DECOMMISSIONING ACT 1997*

(1997 c. 7)

An Act to make provision connected with Northern Ireland about the decommissioning of firearms, ammunition and explosives; and for connected purposes.   [27th February 1997]

PARLIAMENTARY DEBATES
    Hansard, H.C. Vol. 286, col. 571; Vol. 287, col. 22; Vol. 288, col. 470. H.L. Vol. 577, col. 1282; Vol. 578, cols. 622, 1041.

INTRODUCTION AND GENERAL NOTE
    In moving the second reading of the Northern Ireland Arms Decommissioning Bill, The Secretary of State for Northern Ireland, Sir Patrick Mayhew, outlined the background to, and the rationale behind the Bill as follows:
        "In a democracy, politics and violence do not mix. Arms and explosives, illegally held and illegally used for political purposes, have for long bedevilled the politics of Northern Ireland and, more importantly, the lives of its people. They have to be removed from the scene. It is tempting to say that they must be eradicated. It is true that the police services on both sides of the border will continue to root them out where they can . . . .
        Expressed briefly, the natural fear is that the armaments are held onto in order that one day they may be used. Otherwise, what is their purpose? If that were correct, it would not be compatible with the exclusive commitment to peaceful methods and to the democratic process that is rightly required of all who seek in this democracy to negotiate its future. If that is judged to be absent in any party, no matter that it be an elected one, others will not sit at the table with it.
        That is why armaments have to be removed. That much almost everyone is agreed on: it is the easy bit. It gets much harder when it is recognised that, illegal though it is to hold them, the yielding up of those armaments will be done either voluntarily or not at all. Therefore, to secure the best prospect of having them dealt with so that they are for ever put out of harm's way, it is necessary to put in place a more sophisticated scheme than many would like.
        I acknowledge that; but to those who bridle at the notion of helping terrorists to decide to get rid of their weapons, I offer this thought. A weapon which, in accordance with any such scheme, is taken out of commission can never kill in the future, as it may have killed in the past. A weapon which is retained in terrorist hands may well kill again, unless it is seized by the security forces before it can do so, which cannot be ensured.
        No scheme of any kind can be constructed without a downside. But the thought that I have offered is the justification for seeking to put a well-judged scheme in place. That is the view of the Government; and we are fortified in that view by the international body, set up by the British and Irish Governments, when it reported in January this year . . .
        This Bill is intended to reflect, and enable effect to be given to, the six principles underlying the detailed guidelines which Mitchell has provided in paragraphs 39 to 50 of the report. Those were that the decommissioning process should: first, suggest neither victory nor

---

* Annotations by Gary Scanlan and Sarah Gale of City University.

defeat; secondly, take place to the satisfaction of an independent commission; thirdly, result in the complete destruction of armaments in a manner that contributes to public safety; fourthly be fully verifiable; fifthly, not expose individuals to prosecution; and sixthly, be mutual." (*Hansard*, H.C. Vol. 287, No. 32, col. 22, December 9, 1996.)

The Secretary of State referred to an International Body chaired by Senator George Mitchell. This body worked in conjunction with Prime Minister Holkeri and General de Chastlain. The Body's remit was to provide an independent assessment of the decommissioning problem and to report on any arrangements which would facilitate the removal of illegal arms from the Irish political scene.

The Body published its report entitled "the Mitchell Report" on January 22, 1996. The Government's stance on decommissioning is based on this Report.

The Mitchell Report can be seen as falling into several parts. The first part examines the question of when decommissioning should take place, the second with how decommissioning can be undertaken and successfully completed. The Bill only addresses the second issue. Its principal purpose is to enable the Secretary of State to give effect to the Mitchell Report's recommendations as to how decommissioning should take place.

Decommissioning scheme

1.—(1) In this Act a "decommissioning scheme" is any scheme which—
 (a) is made by the Secretary of State to facilitate the decommissioning of firearms, ammunition and explosives in Northern Ireland, and.
 (b) includes provisions satisfying the requirements of sections 2 and 3 (whether or not it also includes other provisions).
 (2) Section 2 of the Documentary Evidence Act 1868 (mode of proving certain documents) shall apply to a decommissioning scheme.

GENERAL NOTE

This section defines the nature of the "decommissioning scheme". This scheme is to be set up by the Secretary of State to ensure the decommissioning of illegal firearms, ammunition and explosives in Northern Ireland. The scheme is meant to be administrative.

This section has been drafted in the simplest of terms so that all parties involved in the decommissioning process are entirely clear as to what is required. The wording of the section was intended to promote flexibility and to ensure that the Government could make, amend, withdraw or replace the scheme as quickly as possible and in the light of changing circumstances.

Duration of decommissioning scheme

2.—(1) A decommissioning scheme must identify a period during which firearms, ammunition and explosives may be dealt with in accordance with the scheme ("the amnesty period").
 (2) The amnesty period must end before—
 (a) the first anniversary of the day on which this Act is passed, or
 (b) such later day as the Secretary of State may by order from time to time appoint.
 (3) A day appointed by an order under subsection (2)(b) must not be—
 (a) more than twelve months after the day on which the order is made, or
 (b) more than five years after the day on which this Act is passed.
 (4) An order under subsection (2)(b) shall be made by statutory instrument; and no order shall be made unless a draft has been laid before, and approved by resolution of, each House of Parliament.

DEFINITIONS

"Amnesty period": ss.2(2) to (4).

GENERAL NOTE

This section requires that the amnesty period (see note to s.4 below) during which illegal firearms, ammunition and explosives may be dealt with in accordance with the decommissioning scheme made by the Secretary of State under the aegis of s.1 of the Act be specified in the scheme.

The section principally deals with the duration of the decommissioning scheme. In the first instance the amnesty period will end a year after the passing of the Act. However, there will be an option to extend the amnesty periods for up to 12 months. This option would need parliamentary approval and would be subject to a maximum of five years commencing from the date of the passing of the Act.

Methods of decommissioning

3.—(1) A decommissioning scheme must make provision for one or more of the following ways of dealing with firearms, ammunition and explosives (and may make provision for others)—
 (a) transfer to the Commission mentioned in section 7, or to a designated person, for destruction;
 (b) depositing for collection and destruction by the Commission or a designated person;
 (c) provision of information for the purpose of collection and destruction by the Commission or a designated person;
 (d) destruction by persons in unlawful possession.
 (2) In subsection (1) "designated person" means a person designated by the Secretary of State or, in the case of firearms, ammunition or explosives transferred or collected in the Republic of Ireland, a person designated by the Minister for Justice of the Republic.

DEFINITIONS
 "Designated person": s.3(2).

GENERAL NOTE
 This section requires that a decommissioning scheme under s.1 of the Act should deal with the decommissioning of illegal firearms, ammunition and explosives in one or more of the ways specified in the section, while allowing the decommissioning scheme to make provision for other methods of decommissioning. The methods of decommissioning specified in subs. (1) reflect the decommissioning methods identified in the Mitchell Report.

Amnesty

4.—(1) No proceedings shall be brought for an offence listed in the Schedule to this Act in respect of anything done in accordance with a decommissioning scheme.
 (2) The Secretary of State may by order add any offence or description of offence to, or remove any offence or description of offence from, the list in the Schedule to this Act.
 (3) An order under subsection (2)—
 (a) shall be made by statutory instrument, and
 (b) may include such transitional provisions as appear to the Secretary of State to be expedient.
 (4) No order shall be made under subsection (2) unless and draft has been laid before, and approved by resolution of, each House of Parliament.

GENERAL NOTE
 Section 4 and the Schedule to the Act give effect to the Mitchell Report's recommendations that:
 "… the decommissioning process should not expose individuals to prosecution".
 The section accordingly provides for an amnesty from prosecution for those who have committed the offences specified in the Schedule (generally offences of a possessory character). However, the amnesty only applies to persons acting within the ambit of the decommissioning scheme set out in s.1 of the Act.

Evidence

5.—(1) A decommissioned article, or information derived from it, shall not be admissible in evidence in criminal proceedings.

(2) Evidence of anything done, and of any information obtained, in accordance with a decommissioning scheme shall not be admissible in criminal proceedings.

(3) Subsections (1) and (2) shall not apply to the admission of evidence adduced in criminal proceedings on behalf of the accused.

(4) Subsection (1) shall not apply to proceedings for an offence alleged to have been committed by the use of, or in relation to, something which was a decommissioned article at the time when the offence is alleged to have been committed.

GENERAL NOTE

This section limits the use in evidence in any criminal proceedings of information obtained as a consequence of a decommissioning scheme carried out under s.1 of the Act. This section therefore gives effect to one of the central principles in the recommendations made by the Mitchell Report (see para. 8 of the Report). This section thus provides that a decommissioned article, be it a firearm, ammunition or an explosive, should not be admissible as evidence in criminal proceedings, nor should any evidence derived from that article be admissible in any subsequent criminal action.

The above limitation on the admissibility of evidence does not however apply to proceedings relating to any offence alleged to have been committed with an article that was decommissioned at the time when the relevant offence was committed, nor to evidence adduced on behalf of the accused in criminal proceedings.

Testing decommissioned articles

6.—(1) A person who has received a decommissioned article shall not carry out, or cause or permit anyone else to carry out, a test or procedure in relation to the article the purpose of which is—

    (a) to discover information about anything done with or in relation to any decommissioned article,

    (b) to discover who has been in contact with, or near to, any decommissioned article,

    (c) to discover where any decommissioned article was at any time (including the conditions under which it was kept),

    (d) to discover when any decommissioned article was in contact with, or near to, a particular person or when it was in a particular place or kept under particular conditions,

    (e) to discover when or where any decommissioned article was made, or

    (f) to discover the composition of any decommissioned article.

(2) Subsection (1)(f) does not prohibit a test or procedure the purpose of which is—

    (a) to determine whether an article is, or contains, an explosive or ammunition,

    (b) to determine the quantity of explosive or ammunition present, or

    (c) to determine whether an article can safely be moved or otherwise dealt with.

(3) Subsection (1) does not prohibit a test or procedure the purpose of which is to discover information in relation to a decommissioned article where the information—

    (a) is sought for the purposes of the investigation of an offence alleged to have been committed at a time after the article became a decommissioned article, and

    (b) does not concern the treatment of the article in accordance with a decommissioning scheme.

GENERAL NOTE

This section gives effect to the forensic testing recommendations in the Mitchell Report. Section 6 prevents certain types of tests and procedures taking place in relation to the decommissioned articles (firearms, ammunition or explosives). However, tests and procedures that are carried out in order to check the safety of the decommissioned articles or to verify them, are allowed. Similarly, decommissioned articles can be tested if the testing is in connection with the investigation of any offence alleged to have been committed after the article was decommissioned.

The Commission

7.—(1) In this section "the Commission" means an independent organisation established by an agreement, made in connection with the affairs of Northern Ireland between Her Majesty's Government in the United Kingdom and the Government of the Republic of Ireland, to facilitate the decommissioning of firearms, ammunition and explosives.

(2) The Secretary of State may by order—

(a) confer on the Commission the legal capacities of a body corporate;

(b) confer on the Commission, in such cases, to such extent and with such modifications as the order may specify, any of the privileges and immunities set out in Part I of Schedule 1 to the International Organisations Act 1968;

(c) confer on members and servants of the Commission and members of their families who form part of their households, in such cases, to such extent and with such modifications as the order may specify any of the privileges and immunities set out in Parts II, III and V of that Schedule;

(d) make provision about the waiver of privileges and immunities.

In this subsection "servants of the Commission" includes agents of, and persons carrying out work for or giving advice to, the Commission.

(3) An order under subsection (2)—

(a) may make different provision for different cases (including different provision for different persons);

(b) shall be made by statutory instrument which shall be subject to annulment in pursuance of a resolution of either House of Parliament.

(4) The Secretary of State may—

(a) make payments to the Commission or to members of the Commission;

(b) provide for the Commissions such premises and facilities, and the services of such staff, as he thinks appropriate.

(5) This section shall come into force on such day as the Secretary of State, after consulting the Minister for Justice of the Republic of Ireland, may by order made by statutory instrument appoint.

(6) This section shall cease to have effect at the end of such day as the Secretary of State, after consulting the Minister for Justice of the Republic of Ireland, may by order made by statutory instrument appoint; and an order under this subsection may include such transitional provisions as appear to the Secretary of State to be expedient.

GENERAL NOTE

This section makes provision for an independent Commission to be set up in accordance with the recommendations of the Mitchell Report. The remit of the Commission may extend to overseeing the decommissioning of firearms, ammunition and explosives. The Commission is to be established by an international agreement between the Governments of the U.K. and the Irish Republic. The Secretary of State for Northern Ireland is to be empowered to give the body corporate status. Its members, employees and their families (the immediate family that forms part of their households) could have the appropriate legal status, immunities and privileges commensurate with membership of this type of international body conferred upon them.

The Commission will be able to function independently in both the U.K. and in the Irish Republic. The eventual composition and size of the Commission will be dependent on its role in the decommissioning scheme. This section is drafted widely so as to enable the Commission to be set up in an advisory capacity before the decommissioning scheme gets under way. The Commission will be able to report to the U.K. Government and/or to the Government of the Irish Republic in its advisory capacity.

Arms in England and Wales and Scotland

8.—(1) This section applies to any scheme which—

(a) is made by the Secretary of State, for purposes relating to the affairs of Northern Ireland, to facilitate the decommissioning of firearms, ammunition and explosives in England and Wales or in Scotland, and

(b) includes provisions satisfying the requirement of sections 2 and 3 (whether or not it also includes other provisions).

(2) The Secretary of State may by order provide that a scheme to which this section applies shall be a decommissioning scheme for the purposes of this Act.

(3) In relation to a scheme which is a decommissioning scheme by virtue of subsection (2), the Schedule to this Act shall have effect with the substitution for any offence under the law of Northern Ireland of such similar offence under the law of England and Wales, or as the case may be of Scotland, as the Secretary of State may specify by order.

(4) An order under this section shall be made by statutory instrument; and no order shall be made unless a draft has been laid before, and approved by resolution of, each House of Parliament.

GENERAL NOTE

Section 8 makes provision for decommissioning schemes involving firearms, ammunition and explosives in England, Wales and Scotland. It allows the Secretary of State to determine whether a decommissioning scheme carried out in England, Wales or Scotland is to be regarded as satisfying the requirements of ss.2 and 3 of the Act. This is subject to the proviso that the relevant scheme relates to the affairs of Northern Ireland.

The rationale behind this section was explained by the Secretary of State for Northern Ireland, Sir Patrick Mayhew, as follows:

"I have introduced that [s.8] into the Bill [now the Act] in order to meet the understandable sensitivity of those who saw an entirely unintended possibility that somehow it was considered less important to bring people to justice in Northern Ireland than in England, Wales or in Scotland."

Expenses

9. Any expenses incurred by the Secretary of State in connection with a decommissioning scheme or under section 7(4) shall be paid out of money provided by Parliament.

Interpretation

10.—(1) In this Act—

"ammunition" means anything which is—

(a) ammunition within the meaning of the Firearms (Northern Ireland) Order 1981, or

(b) a component of such ammunition;

"decommissioned article" means—

(a) anything which has been transferred, deposited or collected in accordance with a decommissioning scheme,

(b) anything found on or in, or received with, something falling within paragraph (a), and

(c) a part of, or thing derived from, something falling within paragraph (a) or (b);

"destruction" includes making permanently inaccessible or permanently unusable;

"firearm" means anything which—
    (a) is a firearm within the meaning of the Firearms (Northern Ireland) Order 1981,
    (b) is an accessory to such a firearm,
    (c) is a weapon designed or adapted for the discharge of any thing, or
    (d) has the appearance of being one of the things described in paragraphs (a) to (c);
"explosive" means anything which is—
    (a) an explosive within the meaning of the Explosives Act 1875, or
    (b) an explosive substance within the meaning of the Explosive Substances Act 1883.

(2) In this Act, references to things done in accordance with a decommissioning scheme include references to things done in accordance with arrangements provided for by a scheme.

Short title and saving

11.—(1) This Act may be cited as the Northern Ireland Arms Decommissioning Act 1997.

(2) Nothing in this Act shall prejudice any power or discretion exercisable apart from this Act in relation to the institution or conduct of criminal proceedings.

Section 4(1)   SCHEDULE

OFFENCES COVERED BY THE AMNESTY

Explosives Act 1875

1. An offence of contravening any provision of the Explosives Act 1875 or any instrument under that Act.

Explosive Substances Act 1883

2. An offence under section 4 of the Explosive Substances Act 1883 (possession of explosive under suspicious circumstances, &c.).

Criminal Law Act (Northern Ireland) 1967

3. An offence under section 5 of the Criminal Law Act (Northern Ireland) 1967 (concealing offences, &c.).

Theft Act (Northern Ireland) 1969

4. An offence under section 1 or 21 of the Theft Act (Northern Ireland) 1969 (theft and handling stolen goods).

Explosives Act (Northern Ireland) 1970

5. An offence under any provision of the Explosives Act (Northern Ireland) 1970.

Health and Safety at Work (Northern Ireland) Order 1978

6. An offence under any provision of the Health and Safety at Work (Northern Ireland) Order 1978.

Customs and Excise Acts 1979

7. An offence under any provision of the Customs and Excise Act 1979 (within the meaning of the Customs and Excise Management Act 1979).

Firearms (Northern Ireland) Order 1981

8. An offence under any of the following provisions of the Firearms (Northern Ireland) Order 1981:
  (a) article 3(1) (possession, &c. of firearms or ammunition not authorised by firearm certificate);
  (b) article 4(1) and (2) (transactions with firearms and ammunition);
  (c) article 6(1), (1A) and (4) (prohibited firearms and ammunition);
  (d) article 7 (movement of firearms and ammunition);
  (e) article 18(2), in so far as it concerns possession of firearms or imitation firearms at the time of being arrested;
  (f) article 20(1) (carrying firearms in a public place);
  (g) article 21 (trespassing with firearms);
  (h) article 22(5) and (7) (possession of firearms by person previously convicted of crime, &c.);
  (i) article 23 (possession of firearms and ammunition in suspicious circumstances);
  (j) article 26 (acquisition and possession of firearms and ammunition by persons under 18);
  (k) article 43 (failure to comply with requirements relating to transactions in firearms, &c.).

Prevention of Terrorism (Temporary Provisions) Act 1989

9. An offence under either of the following provisions of the Prevention of Terrorism (Temporary Provisions) Act 1989—
  (a) section 10(1)(b) (making property available for the benefit of a proscribed organisation, &c.);
  (b) section 18 (failure to disclose information about acts of terrorism).

Northern Ireland (Emergency Provisions) Act 1996

10. An offence under any of the following provisions of the Northern Ireland (Emergency Provisions) Act 1996—
  (a) section 29 (directing terrorist organisation);
  (b) section 30(1)(c) (inviting persons to carry out orders on behalf of a proscribed organisation, &c.);
  (c) section 30(1)(d)(ii) or (iii) (meetings);
  (d) section 31 (displaying of support in public for proscribed organisation);
  (e) section 32 (possession of items intended for terrorist purposes);
  (f) section 35 (wearing of hoods, &c. in public place).

Inchoate offences

11. The offence of aiding, abetting, counselling, procuring or inciting the commission of an offence specified in this Schedule.

12. The offence of attempting or conspiring to commit an offence specified in this Schedule.

INDEX

References are to sections and the Schedule

TOWN AND COUNTRY PLANNING (SCOTLAND) ACT 1997*

(1997 c. 8)

[A Table showing the derivation of the provisions of this consolidation Act will be found at the end of the Act. The Table has no official status.]

ARRANGEMENT OF SECTIONS

PART I

ADMINISTRATION

PART II

DEVELOPMENT PLANS

Surveys

Structure plans

Local plans

Supplementary provisions

General

PART III

CONTROL OVER DEVELOPMENT

Meaning of development

Requirement for planning permission

---

* Annotations by David Bartos, LL.B. (Hons.), Advocate, David Cobb, LL.B. (Hons.), Advocate, Andrew F. Stewart, LL.B. (Hons.), Advocate, Jacqueline Williamson, LL.B. (Hons.), LL.M., Advocate, Barrister of the Inner Temple.

PART VII

SPECIAL CONTROLS

CHAPTER I

TREES

General duty of planning authorities as respects trees

Tree preservation orders

An Act to consolidate certain enactments relating to town and country planning in Scotland with amendments to give effect to recommendations of the Scottish Law Commission.   [27th February 1997]

PARLIAMENTARY DEBATES

    Hansard, H.L. Vol. 576, cols. 122, 586, 673; Vol. 577, cols. 559, 1082. H.C. Vol. 291, col. 195.

INTRODUCTION AND GENERAL NOTE

    The Town and Country Planning (Scotland) Act 1997 (c.8), is one of a package of four statutes to consolidate town and country law in Scotland. The others are the Planning (Listed Buildings and Conservation Areas) (Scotland) Act 1997 (c.9); the Planning (Hazardous Substances) (Scotland) Act 1997 (c.10) and the Planning (Consequential Provisions) (Scotland) Act 1997 (c.11). The Acts may be collectively known as the "planning Acts". The planning Acts came into force collectively on May 27, 1997. The previous legislation relating to town and country planning has been in desperate need of consolidation for some time. The principal Town and Country Planning (Scotland) Act 1972 (c.42) was the subject of numerous amendments over its 15 year existence. This resulted in a disparate and fragmented scheme of legislation which caused not inconsiderable difficulty to practitioners and others involved in the use and development of land.

    The purpose of the four statutes is to consolidate existing legislation on town and country planning and to give effect to recommendations of the Scottish Law Commission contained in Scot Law Com. No. 157. The Town and Country Planning (Scotland) Act 1997, is the principal and largest of the four statutes. It aims to completely restructure and clarify the previous legislation. In doing so, it has repealed a number of the previous statutes. They include the Town and Country Planning (Amendment) (Scotland) Act 1972 (c.42), the Town and Country Planning (Scotland) Act 1972 (c.52), and the Town and Country Planning (Scotland) Act 1977 (c.10) (see further Sched.1, Pt. 1 to the Planning (Consequential Provisions) (Scotland) Act 1977 (c.11), for details of all repeals, consequential amendments, transitional matters and savings). Effect is given to the recommendations by the Scottish Law Commission in the four statutes, however, those recommendations relate to minor anomalies and inconsistencies in the previous legislation. They do not involve substantial amendments to the existing planning regime.

Consideration of the planning Acts is restricted in these annotations to the Town and Country Planning (Scotland) Act 1997. The parts are set out with an emphasis on those sections likely to be of most interest.

Pt. I—Administration

This Part consolidates the previous disparate provisions relating to the administration of planning law into ss.1, 2 and 3 of the 1997 Act.

Pt. II—Development Plans

Sections 4 to 25 essentially restructure the previous provisions relating to structure and local plans in the 1972 Act. In particular, s.5 of the Act re-enacts s.4A of the 1972 Act which was introduced by s.33 of the Local Government etc. (Scotland) Act 1994. Section 5 empowers the Secretary of State, by order, to designate areas in respect of which planning authorities must prepare structure plans. This power was created as a result of the abolition of regional councils to whom the preparation of structure plans had been previously allocated. Section 6 makes provision for those structure plans in existence prior to the local government reorganisation, to remain extant. The status of development plans when making determinations under the planning Acts is unchanged—see s.25.

Pt. III—Control Over Development

Sections 26 to 75 restructure and reproduce the previous Pt. III of the 1972 Act on general planning control. Sections 26 to 29 deal with the meaning of development and the requirement for planning permission. It is interesting that in s.29(1), Parliament has seen fit to place an emphasis upon four general circumstances in which planning permission may be granted. Section 29(1) does not however seek to place a limit upon the granting of planning permission. Deemed planning permission is expressly preserved in subs. (2). Further, subs. (3) provides that s.29 is without prejudice to the other provisions of this Act which provide for the grant of planning permission.

Section 47(5) gives effect to the first of the Scottish Law Commission recommendations. The 1972 Act contained a number of anomalies in respect of appeals against a failure by the planning authority to take a decision. For example s.214(1) of the 1972 Act provided that certain applications and appeals by statutory undertakers should be determined by the Secretary of State and the appropriate Minister. Subsection (1)(b) applies this provision to appeals made to the Secretary of State under Pt. III from a *decision* on an application for planning permission. No express provision existed for appeals by statutory undertakers where the planning authority had not taken a decision. Section 47(5) seeks to cure this anomaly by providing that in relation to such appeals, the planning authority shall be deemed to have decided to refuse the planning application in question.

The provision relating to planning agreements is contained in s.75 of the 1997 Act. The recent House of Lords decision in *Tesco Stores v. Secretary of State for the Environment* 1995 1 W.L.R. 759 sought to clarify the status of the English equivalent of planning agreements in planning decisions. According to their Lordships, the test to be applied in determining whether a planning agreement is a material consideration is whether it has that connection with the proposed development which is not *de minimis*. If a connection can be established, the planning authority must have regard to it. However, the amount of weight to be given to planning agreement is a matter for the decision maker, subject only to the need to have regard to established planning policies and not to act unreasonably in the Wednesbury sense. Subsection (5) makes it clear that a planning agreement cannot be construed as fettering the statutory powers or duties of a Minister or planning authority under this Act, provided that those powers are properly exercised.

Sections 63(4), 139(4) and 142(4) of the 1997 Act were enacted to give effect to the Scottish Law Commission's recommendation to subject the issue of completion notices, enforcement notices and stop notices by the Secretary of State, to the same planning regime as those issued by a planning authority.

Pt. IV—Compensation for Effects of Certain Orders, Notices, etc.

Sections 76 to 86 deal with the entitlement and assessment of compensation for revocation and modification of planning permission. In particular, s.86 provides for claims to be referred to the Lands Tribunal in the event of disputes, except as may be otherwise provided by any regulations made under this Act.

Pt. V—Rights of Owners to Require Purchase of Interests
This Part is divided into two chapters: Chap. 1 relates to interests affected by planning decisions or orders; Chap. 2 is concerned with interests which are affected by planning proposals—blighted land. Both chapters contain detailed provisions on the service of notices requiring the recipient to compulsorily acquire the land specified in the notice and/or pay compensation. Reference might also be made to Sched. 14 which forms an integral part of Chap. 2 in relation to blighted land.

Pt. VI—Enforcement
Sections 123 to 158 are concerned with the enforcement of planning controls. The Scottish Law Commission recommended a number of amendments to clarify existing minor anomalies in the 1972 Act which were subsequently adopted in the 1997 Act (see Recommendations 9, 10 and 11 of Scot Law Com. No. 157).

Pt. VII—Special Controls
Sections 159 to 187 encompass three individual chapters: Trees, Neighbourhood Development and Advertisements. The separation of these chapters from Pt. VI on Enforcement is a recognition of the peculiar considerations which may arise in relation to these controls.

Pt. VIII—Acquisition of Land for Planning Purposes, Etc.
Sections 188 to 201 are concerned with the acquisition and compulsory acquisition of land. This Part represents a consolidation of the previous legislation relating to this area of law. Other than a minor amendment by the Scottish Law Commission in s.191—disposal of land held for planning purposes (see Recommendation 11), the previous planning regime remains intact.

Pt. IX—Roads, Footpaths and Rights of Way
Sections 202 to 213 represent a significant consolidation of the previous provisions on roads, footpaths and rights of way. This Part should be read in conjunction with Sched. 16 which sets out the statutory procedure for the making or confirmation of orders relating to roads and rights of way.

Pt. X—Statutory Undertakers
Sections 214 to 236 are concerned with the application of planning provisions to statutory undertakers. It is interesting that the privatised railway operators appear to have retained their statutory undertaker status without modification.

Pt. XI—Validity
Sections 237 to 241 are concerned with the validity of and proceedings for questioning the validity of development plans, certain orders, schemes and directions. It is notable that no attempt has been made to define the term "persons aggrieved". This will remain a matter for the courts. The statutory grounds of appeal remain unchanged. The time-limit for challenges to the validity of certain orders, decisions and directions in s.239(3) has been slightly modified to include a reference to those orders or decisions which take effect without confirmation. In those circumstances, an application must be made within six weeks from the date on which the action was taken.

Pt. XII—Crown Land
Sections 242 to 251 replicate previous provisions of the 1972 Act and the Town and Country Planning Act 1984.

Pt. XIII—Financial Provisions
Sections 252 to 261 contain various financial provisions, for example the payment of fees for planning applications. These provisions should also be read in conjunction with the relevant provisions pertaining to the entitlement to compensation.

Pt. XIV—Miscellaneous and General Provisions
Sections 262 to 278 cover a wide variety of matters. Section 264 on natural heritage areas contains a slight variation on the weight to be given to a designating site. Subsection (2) now requires that "special attention" be paid to a natural heritage area. This amendment was inserted into the 1972 Act by the Natural Heritage (Scotland) Act 1991 (c.28), which previously mentioned that a "regard" was to be had to natural heritage areas.

Sched. 1—Old Development Plans
Schedule 1 contains the definition of old development plans. It also provides a transitional arrangement for the continuation in force of old development plans which were in force immediately before this Act came into force.

Sched. 2—Exemptions from Planning Permission for Certain Land Uses in 1948
Schedule 2 contains exemptions from planning permission for certain purposes which were in use between July 1, 1948 and December 8, 1969.

Sched. 3—Conditions Relating to Mineral Workings
Schedule 3 makes provision for the conditions to be imposed in relation to mineral workings. Part II of Sched. 3 also empowers a planning authority to impose such aftercare conditions following the revocation or modification of the planning permission as the planning authority may think fit.

Sched. 4—Determination of Certain Appeals by Persons Appointed by the Secretary of State
Schedule 4 establishes the framework within which the Secretary of State may, by regulations prescribe those classes of appeals which are to be determined by a person appointed by the Secretary of State on his behalf.

Sched. 5—Simplified Planning Zones
Schedule 5 establishes the statutory framework for the designations of simplified planning zones.

Sched. 6—Planning Inquiry Commissions
Schedule 6 provides the framework within which the Secretary of State may refer matters of public interest to a planning inquiry commission. To date, no planning inquiry commission has ever been established—see statement of the Rt. Hon. Peter Shore M.P. published at [1978] J.P.L. 731.

Sched. 7—Joint Planning Inquiry Commissions
Schedule 7 establishes the framework for the constitution and powers of joint planning inquiry commissions.

Sched. 8—Old Mineral Workings and Permissions
Schedule 8 empowers a planning authority, by order, to require the discontinuance or prohibit the resumption of mineral workings. The planning authority is also empowered to impose after-care conditions in respect of such workings. Provision is also made for the registration of old mineral permissions granted under the Interim Development Orders post-1943.

Sched. 9—Review of Old Mining Permissions
Schedule 9 imposes a duty upon planning authorities to compile a list of mineral sites in their area. This first list may only contain those sites which are either active Phase I or II sites or dormant sites. A second list must also be prepared consisting only of active Phase II sites. These lists must be advertised.

Sched. 10—Periodic Review of Mineral Planning Permissions
Schedule 10 requires the planning authority to carry out periodic reviews of mineral permissions relating to a mining site in their area.

Sched. 11—Development Not Constituting New Development
Schedule 11 lists those works which are not to be regarded as new development.

Sched. 12—Condition Treated as Applicable to Rebuilding and Alterations
Schedule 12 specifies the condition which is to be treated as rebuilding or an alteration.

Sched. 13—Regulations as to Compensation in Respect of Orders relating to Mineral Workings
Schedule 13 empowers the Secretary of State, by regulations, to modify those provisions relating to compensation. The rationale behind this provision is to allow an alteration of the assessment or rate of compensation, to be made by the Secretary of State without the need for amendment of the primary legislation itself. Regulations are only effective if they are approved by both Houses of Parliament. Thus, Parliament retains a degree of control.

Sched. 14—Blighted Land
Schedule 14 contains provisions relating to land blight.

Sched. 15—General Vesting Declarations
Schedule 15 contains provisions relating to vesting declarations.

Sched. 16—Procedure for Making and Confirming Orders Relating to Roads and Rights of Way
The detailed procedures for the making of these Orders are contained within this Schedule.

Sched. 17—Enforcement as Respects War-Time Breaches by the Crown of Planning Control
Schedule 17 is concerned with applications to the Secretary of State for a compliance determination in respect of works carried out on land during the war period.

Sched. 18—Provisions of this Act Referred to in ss.261 to 263
Schedule 18 lists the provisions of this Act relevant to the expenses of and borrowing by local authorities (s.261); the power to modify the Act in relation to minerals (s.262); the application of certain provisions to planning authorities (s.263).

ABBREVIATIONS

"CAA"	: Civil Aviation Authority.
"the Carnwath Report"	: *Enforcing Planning Control*, HMSO, February 1989 by Robert Carnwath Q.C.
"CPO"	: compulsory purchase orders.
"FDA"	: Forestry Dedication Agreement.
"GDPO"	: Town and Country Planning (General Development Procedure) (Scotland) Order 1992 (S.I. 1992 No. 224, as amended by S.I. 1992 No. 2083, S.I. 1994 No. 2585, S.I. 1994 No. 3293, S.I. 1996 No. 467).
"GPDO"	: Town and Country Planning (General Permitted Development) (Scotland) Order 1992 (S.I. 1992 No. 223, as amended by S.I. 1992 No. 1078, S.I. 1992 No. 2084, S.I. 1993 No. 1036, S.I. 1994 No. 1442, S.I. 1994 No. 329, S.I. 1996 No. 3023).
"GVD"	: General Vesting Declaration.
"Lands Clauses Acts"	: Lands Clauses Consolidation (Scotland) Act 1845 (c.19) and the Land Clauses Consolidation Acts Amendment Act 1860 (c.106) and the Acts made under them.
"N.S.A.D."	: National Scenic Area Designations.
"PAN"	: Planning Advice Note.
"PFI"	: Private Finance Initiative.
"PLI"	: Public Local Inquiry.
"Plans Regs."	: Town and Country Planning (Structure and Local Plans) (Scotland) Regulations 1983 (S.I. 1983 No. 1590).
"SLCR"	: Scottish Law Commission Report.
"SOIRU"	: Scottish Office Inquiry Reporters Unit.
"SPZs"	: simplified planning zones.
"TPO"	: Tree Preservation Order.
"1973 Act"	: Local Government (Scotland) Act 1973 (c.65).
"1975 Regulations"	: Town and Country Planning (Tree Preservation Order and Trees in Conservation Areas) (Scotland) Regulations 1975 (S.I. 1975 No. 1204).
"1981 Regulations"	: Town and Country Planning (Tree Preservation Order and Trees in Conservation Areas) (Scotland) Amendment Regulations 1981 (S.I. 1981 No. 1835).
"1984 Regulations"	: Town and Country Planning (Control of Advertisements) (Scotland) Regulations 1984 (S.I. 1984 No. 467).
"1992 Regulations"	: Town and Country Planning (Control of Advertisements) (Scotland) Amendment Regulations 1992 (S.I. 1992 No. 1763).

PART I

ADMINISTRATION

Planning authorities

1.—(1) The planning authority for the purposes of this Act shall be the local authority and the district of the planning authority shall be the area of the local authority.

(2) In any enactment or instrument made under or by virtue of an enactment, a reference to a planning authority shall, unless otherwise provided, or unless the contest otherwise requires, be construed as a reference to a local authority.

DEFINITIONS
"enactment": s.277(1).
"local authority": s.277(1).
"planning authority": ss.1(1), 277(1).

GENERAL NOTE
Subs. (1)

For the purpose of this or any other Act, regulation or development order made under this or any other Act, the "planning authority" is a council constituted under s.2 of the Local Government etc. (Scotland) Act 1994 (c.39). Each council under the 1994 Act is a planning authority. This contrasts with the position before April 1, 1996 when district councils within Borders, Dumfries and Galloway, and Highland Regions were not planning authorities.

Enterprise zones

2.—(1) An order under paragraph 5 of Schedule 32 to the Local Government, Planning and Land Act 1980 (designation of enterprise zone) may provide that the enterprise zone authority shall be the planning authority for the zone for such purposes of the planning Acts and in relation to such kinds of development as may be specified in the order.

(2) Without prejudice to the generality of paragraph 15(1) of that Schedule (modification of orders by the Secretary of State), an order under that paragraph may provide that the enterprise zone authority shall be the planning authority for the zone for different purposes of the planning Acts or in relation to different kinds of development.

(3) Where such provision as is mentioned in subsection (1) or (2) is made by an order designating an enterprise zone or, as the case may be, an order modifying such an order, while the zone subsists the enterprise zone authority shall be, to the extent mentioned in the order (as it has effect subject to any such modifications) and to the extent that it is not already, the planning authority for the zone in place of any authority who would otherwise be the planning authority for the zone.

(4) The Secretary of State may by regulations make transitional and supplementary provision in relation to a provision of an order under paragraph 5 of that Schedule made by virtue of subsection (1).

(5) Such regulations may modify any provision of the planning Acts or any instrument made under any of them or may apply any such enactment or instrument (with or without modification) in making such transitional or supplementary provision.

DEFINITIONS
"development": ss.26, 277(1).
"planning Acts": s.277(1).
"planning authority": ss.1(1), 277(1).

GENERAL NOTE
Subs. (1)
An "enterprise zone" is an area of land where an enterprise zone scheme has granted planning permission for specific development or specific classes of development: Local Government, Planning and Land Act 1980 (c.65), s.179 and Sched. 32, para. 17. In addition, most non-residential land within an enterprise zone is free from rates: 1980 Act, s.179 and Sched. 32, para. 33.
    See also general note to s.55.
    "*enterprise zone authority*": This is the planning authority which exercises planning functions for an enterprise zone.

Urban development areas

3.—(1) Where an order is made under subsection (6) of section 149 of the Local Government, Planning and Land Act 1980 (urban development corporation as planning authority), the urban development corporation specified in the order shall be the planning authority for such area as may be so specified in place of any authority who would otherwise be the planning authority for that area in relation to such kinds of development as may be so specified.
    (2) Where an order under subsection (8)(a) of that section confers any functions on an urban development corporation in relation to any area the corporation shall have those functions in place of any authority (except the Secretary of State) who would otherwise have them in that area.

DEFINITIONS
    "development": ss.26, 277(1).
    "planning authority": ss.1(1), 277(1).

GENERAL NOTE
Subs. (1)
"*order under s.149(6) of the Local Government, Planning and Land Act 1980*": This is an order by the Secretary of State providing that in an urban development area the planning authority shall be the urban development corporation. The order under s.149(6) may exclude the transfer of certain planning functions to the urban development corporation.

PART II

DEVELOPMENT PLANS

Surveys

Survey of planning districts

4.—(1) It shall be the duty of the planning authority to keep under review the matters which may be expected to affect the development of their district or the planning of its development.
    (2) A planning authority may, if they think fit, institute a survey, examining the matters referred to in subsection (1), of the whole or any part of their district, and references in subsection (3) to the district of a planning authority shall be construed as including any part of that district which is the subject of a survey under this subsection.
    (3) Without prejudice to the generality of subsections (1) and (2), the matters to be kept under review and examined under those subsections shall include—
    (a) the principal physical and economic characteristics of the district of the authority (including the principal purposes for which land is used) and, so far as they may be expected to affect that district, of any neighbouring districts;
    (b) the size, composition and distribution of the population of that district (whether resident or otherwise);

(c) without prejudice to paragraph (a), the communications, transport system and traffic of that district and, so far as they may be expected to affect that district, of any neighbouring districts;

(d) any considerations not mentioned in paragraphs (a), (b) or (c) which may be expected to affect any matters so mentioned;

(e) such other matters as may be prescribed;

(f) any changes already projected in any of the matters mentioned in any of the previous paragraphs and the effect which those changes are likely to have on the development of that district or the planning of such development.

(4) A planning authority shall, for the purpose of discharging their functions under this section of keeping under review and examining any matters relating to the district of another planning authority, consult that other authority about those matters.

DEFINITIONS
"development": ss.26, 277(1).
"functions": s.277(1).
"planning authority": ss.1(1), 277(1).
"prescribed": s.277(1).
"use": s.277(1).

GENERAL NOTE
Subss. (1), (2)
For government guidance see PAN 49, paras. 14 to 16.

Subs. (3)
For physical characteristics see PAN 3 (The Countryside), PAN 13 (Planning and Geology). For economic characteristics see PAN 1 (Agriculture), PAN 13 (Forestry), PAN 5 (Sport, Outdoor Recreation and Tourism), PAN 12 (Fishing), and PAN 42 (Golf Courses).
For size, distribution and composition of population see PAN 8.

Designation of structure plan areas

5.—(1) The Secretary of State may by order designate areas ("structure plan areas") in respect of which planning authorities are to prepare structure plans.

(2) The district of every planning authority in Scotland shall be included in a structure plan area.

(3) A structure plan area may extend to the district of more than one planning authority, and may extend to only part of the district of a planning authority.

(4) Where a structure plan area extends to the district of more than one planning authority, the planning authorities concerned shall jointly carry out the functions conferred upon them under sections 4 and 6 to 9 in accordance with such arrangements as they may agree for that purpose under sections 56 (discharge of functions by local authorities), 57 (appointment of committees) and 58 (expenses of joint committees) of the Local Government (Scotland) Act 1973.

DEFINITIONS
"functions": s.277(1).
"planning authority": ss.1(1), 277(1).

GENERAL NOTE
Origin of section: This section re-enacts s.4A of the 1972 Act which was introduced by s.33 of the Local Government, etc. (Scotland) Act 1994 (c.39) as part of local government reorganization. The section was necessary because of the abolition of regional councils to whom the preparation

of structure plans had been allocated by s.172 and Sched. 22 of the Local Government (Scotland) Act 1973 (c.65).

Subs. (1)

The importance of the structure plan is that, once approved by the Secretary of State, it forms the dominant half of the development plan which applies to any area of land: s.24(1). The other half of the development plan, namely the local plan, must conform generally to the structure plan in force for the time being: s.11(5)(b). For the importance of the development plan in the development of land see ss.24 and 25.

The system of structure and local plans was introduced by the Town and Country (Scotland) Act 1969 (c.30) following recommendations by the Ministers' Planning Advisory Group in "*The Future of Development Plans*" (H.M.S.O., 1965). It followed dissatisfaction with the unitary development plans required by the 1947 Act.

Structure plan areas are:

Shetland Islands	Highland
Orkney Islands	Aberdeen and Aberdeenshire (J)
Western Isles	Dundee and Angus (J)
Argyll and Bute	Perthshire and Kinross
Glasgow and Clyde Valley (J)	Fife
Ayrshire (J)	Stirling and Clackmannan (J)
Dumfries and Galloway	Falkirk
Scottish Borders	Edinburgh and the Lothians (J)
Moray	

(Designation of Structure Plan Areas (Scotland) Order 1995 (S.I. 1995 No.3002)).

Subs. (4)

The planning authorities with districts in the structure plan areas marked (J) in the above table will have to carry out their functions jointly with other authorities whose districts lie in the same structure plan area. They may delegate their structure planning functions to a joint committee or to one of their officers: 1973 Act, s.56. A joint committee may include persons who are not members of either authority: 1973 Act, s.57(3). Planning authorities must agree on the paying of expenses incurred by a joint committee failing which the Secretary of State will determine liability: 1973 Act, s.58. If planning authorities or their joint committee are unable to agree on a joint structure plan, each authority may include alternative proposals in the proposed plan: s.6(4) and see also Secretary of State's default power in s.6.

Structure plans

Structure plans: continuity of old and preparation of new plans

6.—(1) Each structure plan approved by the Secretary of State under the 1972 Act with respect to the district of a planning authority which is in operation immediately before the commencement of this Act shall continue in force after its commencement (subject to any alterations then in operation and to the following provisions of this Part).

(2) Where, as a result of the making of an order under section 5, the area in respect of which a planning authority are obliged (whether acting alone or jointly with another authority or authorities) to prepare a structure plan is different from the area in respect of which a structure plan is for the time being in force, they shall prepare and submit to the Secretary of State for his approval a structure plan for their district complying with the provisions of section 7(1), together with a copy of the report of any survey which they have carried out under section 4(2).

(3) The Secretary of State may direct a planning authority to carry out their duty under subsection (2) within a specified period from the direction, and any planning authority to whom such a direction is made shall comply with it.

(4) Where a structure plan area extends to the district of more than one planning authority, and the authorities concerned are unable to agree on a joint structure plan for that area, then, without prejudice to the Secretary of State's powers under section 22 of this Act and section 62B (power of Sec-

retary of State to establish joint boards) of the Local Government (Scotland) Act 1973, each authority concerned may include in the plan submitted to the Secretary of State alternative proposals in respect of particular matters.

(5) Where authorities submit alternative proposals under subsection (4), such proposals shall be accompanied by a statement of the reasoning behind the proposals.

(6) The planning authority shall send with the structure plan submitted by them under this section a report of the results of their review of the relevant matters under section 4 together with any other information on which the proposals are based.

(7) A copy report submitted under subsection (2) shall include an estimate of any changes likely to occur, during such period as the planning authority consider appropriate, in the matters mentioned in section 4(3).

(8) Before submitting a structure plan under this section, the planning authority shall consult any other planning authority who are likely to be affected by the plan.

DEFINITIONS
   "planning authority": ss.1(1), 277(1).
   "1972 Act; the": s.277(1).

GENERAL NOTE
Subs. (1)
   This provides that the pre-reorganization structure plans are to remain in force until they are replaced. The extent to which it is competent for new authorities to alter those plans is unclear.
   "Immediately before the commencement of this Act" is May 26, 1997.

Subs. (2)
   For structure plan areas see the general note to s.5. The Designation of Structure Plan Areas (Scotland) Order 1995 (S.I. 1995 No.3002) designated the following new structure plan areas:
   From the old Strathclyde area:
      Argyll and Bute,
      Glasgow and Clyde Valley,
      Ayrshire

   From the old Grampian area:
      Moray,
      Aberdeen and Aberdeenshire

   From the old Tayside area:
      Perthshire and Kinross,
      Dundee and Angus

   From the old Central area:
      Stirling and Clackmannan,
      Falkirk
   These structure plans must comply with the format laid down by s.7(1). They will be brand new plans rather than replacement plans: s.6(2).

Subs. (4)
   The Secretary of State may—
   (a) under s.22 of the 1973 Act,
      (i) direct the planning authority(ies) to prepare, submit, or adopt a structure or local plan;
      (ii) prepare or make or alter or replace a structure or local plan;
      (iii) authorize any planning authority with an interest in the proper planning of the defaulting authority's district to prepare, make, alter or replace a structure plan;
      (iv) require the defaulting authority to repay his expenses or pay the certified expenses of the other authority which was incurred in doing what the defaulting authority should have done;
   (b) under s.62B of the 1973 Act,
   where local authorities have failed to operate satisfactory arrangements for the joint discharge of their functions, establish a joint board to carry out those functions. A joint board differs from

a joint committee in that it is a corporate body separate from the local authorities. The Secretary of State decides the membership, and may include persons not nominated by the planning authorities.

Form and content of structure plans

7.—(1) The structure plan for any district shall be a written statement—

(a) formulating the planning authority's policy and general proposals in respect of the development and other use of land in that district (including measures for the conservation of the natural beauty and amenity of the land, the improvement of the physical environment and the management of traffic).

(b) stating the relationship of those proposals to general proposals for the development and other use of land in neighbouring districts which may be expected to affect that district, and

(c) containing such other matters as may be prescribed.

(2) In formulating their policy and general proposals under subsection (1)(a), the planning authority shall secure that the policy and proposals are justified by the results of the survey under section 4(1) of the 1972 Act, any fresh survey under section 4(2) of that Act or any survey instituted by them under section 4 of this Act and by any other information which they may obtain and shall have regard—

(a) to current policies with respect to the economic planning and development of the region as a whole, and

(b) to the resources likely to be available for the carrying out of the proposals of the structure plan.

(3) A structure plan for any district shall contain or be accompanied by such diagrams, illustrations and descriptive matter as the planning authority think appropriate for the purpose of explaining or illustrating the proposals in the plan, or as may be prescribed, and any such diagrams, illustrations and descriptive matter shall be treated as forming part of the plan.

DEFINITIONS

"development": ss.26, 277(1).
"land": s.277(1).
"planning authority": s.277(1).
"prescribed": s.277(1).
"use": s.277(1).

GENERAL NOTE

Subss. (1), (3)

The written statement must have a title, including the name(s) of the planning authority(ies) responsible for it: Town and Country Planning (Structure and Local Plans) (Scotland) Regulations 1983 (S.I. 1983 No.1590) (the "Plans Regs"), reg. 5.

The written statement should cover the matters in paras. (a) and (b) and as prescribed in reg. 7 of the Plans Regs. The policies and general proposals should be justified and set apart from the other contents of the plan: Plans Regs, reg. 6. For government guidance, see PAN 37, paras. 34 to 43.

The plan must also contain a non-map based "key diagram" (which may be inset to the main text) showing so far as practicable the written policies and general proposals: Plans Regs., reg. 9.

For interpretation of structure plan see the general note to s.25.

Subs. (2)

This subsection lays down how a planning authority is to formulate structure plan proposals.

Publicity in connection with structure plans

8.—(1) When preparing a structure plan for their district and before finally determining its content for submission to the Secretary of State, the planning authority shall take such steps as will in their opinion secure—

(a) that adequate publicity is given in their district to the report of the survey under section 4 of this Act and to the matters which they propose to include in the plan,

(b) that persons who may be expected to desire an opportunity of making representations to the authority with respect to those matters are made aware that they are entitled to an opportunity of doing so, and

(c) that such persons are given an adequate opportunity of making such representations.

(2) The authority shall consider any representations made to them within the prescribed period.

(3) Where authorities submit alternative proposals in relation to particular matters to the Secretary of State under section 6(4), their duty under subsection (1) is to secure that adequate publicity is given in each of their districts to all the matters which either or any of them propose to include in the plan.

(4) Not later than the submission of a structure plan to the Secretary of State, the planning authority shall make copies of the plan as submitted to the Secretary of State available for inspection at their office and at such other places as may be prescribed.

(5) Each copy of the plan shall be accompanied by a statement of the time within which objections to the plan may be made to the Secretary of State.

(6) A structure plan submitted by the planning authority to the Secretary of State for his approval shall be accompanied by a statement containing such particulars, if any, as may be prescribed—

(a) of the steps which the authority have taken to comply with subsection (1), and

(b) of the authority's consultations with, and consideration of the views of, other persons with respect to those matters.

(7) If after considering the statement submitted with, and the matters included in, the structure plan and any other information provided by the planning authority, the Secretary of State is satisfied that the purposes of paragraphs (a) to (c) of subsection (1) have been adequately achieved by the steps taken by the authority in compliance with that subsection. he shall proceed to consider whether to approve the plan.

(8) If the Secretary of State is not satisfied as mentioned in subsection (7), he shall return the plan to the authority and direct them—

(a) to take such further action as he may specify in order better to achieve those purposes, and

(b) after doing so, to resubmit the plan with such modifications, if any, as they then consider appropriate and, if so required by the direction, to do so within a specified period.

(9) Where the Secretary of State returns the plan to the planning authority under subsection (8), he shall—

(a) inform the authority of his reasons for doing so, and

(b) if any person has made an objection to the plan to him, also inform that person that he has returned the plan.

(10) A planning authority who are given directions by the Secretary of State under subsection (8) shall immediately withdraw the copies of the plans made available tor inspection as required by subsection (4).

(11) Subsections (4) to (10) shall apply, with the necessary modifications, in relation to a structure plan resubmitted to the Secretary of State in accordance with directions given by him under subsection (8) as they apply in relation to the plan as originally submitted.

DEFINITIONS
   "planning authority": ss.1(1), 277(1).
   "prescribed": s.277(1).

GENERAL NOTE
Subs. (1)
    This section applies to the submission of the first structure plan. It will therefore apply to the new structure plans for the areas listed in the general note to s.6. As the other areas (and plans) remain unchanged, they will be amended or replaced with the similar procedure in s.9.
    "person" includes a body of persons corporate or unincorporate: Interpretation Act 1978 (c.30), s.5 and Sched. 1.

Subs. (2)
    The prescribed period is one, not less than four weeks, specified by the planning authority in publicizing their survey report and structure plan proposals: Plans Regs, reg. 3.

Subs. (6)
    The statement should contain a brief account of how the planning authority complied with s.8(1) (publicity): Plans Regs, reg. 12.
    If the plan is for an area covered by more than one authority, it may contain alternative proposals from each authority: s.6(4). If it does, each alternative must be accompanied by a statement of the reasoning behind it: s.6(5).

Subss. (8), (9)
    On receipt of the plan and direction, the planning authority(ies) must comply with the advertisement requirements of reg. 14 of the Plans Regs.

Subs. (11)
    In addition to the matters specified in the original statement for submission, when re-submitting, the planning authority must comply with regs. 15 and 20 of the Plans Regs.

Alteration and replacement of structure plans

    9.—(1) A planning authority—
    (a) may at any time submit to the Secretary of State proposals for such alterations to or repeal and replacement of the structure plan for their district as appear to them to be expedient, and
    (b) shall, if so directed by the Secretary of State, submit to him within a period specified in the direction proposals for such alterations to or repeal and replacement of the plan as the Secretary of State may direct.
    (2) Such proposals may relate to the whole or to part of the district to which the plan relates.
    (3) The planning authority shall send with the proposals submitted by them under this section a report of the results of their review of the relevant matters under section 4 together with any other information on which the proposals are based, and subsections (4) and (5) of section 8 shall apply, with any necessary modifications, in relation to the proposals as they apply in relation to a structure plan.
    (4) Before a planning authority submit proposals under this section they shall—
    (a) consult every other planning authority who are likely to be affected by the proposals,
    (b) give such publicity (if any) to, and undertake such other consultation (if any) about, the proposals as they think fit, and
    (c) consider any representations timeously made to them about the proposals.
    (5) The planning authority shall send with any proposals submitted by them under this section a statement of the steps they have taken to comply with subsection (4) and, if they have not publicised or have not consulted under that subsection, the statement shall explain the absence of such publicity or as the case may be consultation.
    (6) If the Secretary of State is not satisfied with the steps taken by the planning authority to comply with subsection (4), or as the case may be if he is not satisfied with the terms of any explanation provided by them under sub-

section (5), he may return the proposals to the authority, and may direct them—

(a) to take such steps or further steps as he may specify, and

(b) after they have done so, to resubmit the proposals with such modification, if any, as they consider appropriate.

(7) Where, under subsection (6), the Secretary of State returns proposals, he shall—

(a) inform the authority of his reasons for doing so, and

(b) if any person has made to him an objection to the proposals, inform that person that he has returned the proposals.

(8) A planning authority who are given directions under subsection (6) shall immediately withdraw the copies which have, under section 8(4) (as applied by subsection (3)) been made available for inspection.

(9) Section 8(4) and (5) and subsections (4) to (8) of this section shall apply, in relation to proposals resubmitted in accordance with directions given under subsection (6), as they apply in relation to proposals submitted under subsection (1).

DEFINITIONS
"planning authority": ss.1(1), 277(1).

GENERAL NOTE
Subs. (1)
A structure plan has no statutory lifespan. It should aim to provide a framework for development for about 10 years: See PAN 37, paras. 20 and 21. This section is similar to s.8.

Subs. (5)
See also reg. 21 of the Plans Regs.

Subss. (6) to (9)
See also *Glasgow for the People v. Secretary of State for Scotland,* 1993 S.C.L.R. 775.

Approval or rejection of structure plans and proposals for alteration or replacement

10.—(1) The Secretary of State may, after considering a relevant proposal, either approve it (in whole or in part and with or without modifications or reservations) or reject it.

(2) In this section, "relevant proposal" means—

(a) a structure plan (including any alternative proposals included in the plan by virtue of section 6(4)), or

(b) a proposal for the alteration or repeal and replacement of a structure plan,

submitted (or resubmitted) to the Secretary of State.

(3) In considering a relevant proposal the Secretary of State may take into account any matters which he thinks are relevant, whether or not they were taken into account in the proposal as submitted to him.

(4) Where on considering a relevant proposal the Secretary of State does not determine then to reject it, he shall, before determining whether or not to approve it—

(a) consider any objections to the proposal, so far as they are made in accordance with regulations, and

(b) if, but only if, it appears to him that an examination in public should be held of any matter affecting his consideration of the proposal, cause a person or persons, appointed by him for the purpose, to hold such an examination.

(5) The Secretary of State may make regulations with respect to the procedure to be followed at any examination under subsection (4).

(6) The Secretary of State need not secure to any planning authority or other person a right to be heard at any such examination and, subject to sub-

section (7), only such bodies and persons as he may before or during the course of the examination invite to do so may take part in it.

(7) The person or persons holding the examination may before or during the course of the examination invite additional bodies or persons to take part in it if it appears to him or them desirable to do so.

(8) An examination under subsection (4)(b) shall constitute a statutory inquiry for the purposes of section 1(1)(c) of the Tribunals and Inquiries Act 1992, but shall not constitute such an inquiry for any other purpose of that Act.

(9) On considering a relevant proposal the Secretary of State may consult, or consider the views of, any planning authority or other person, but shall not be under any obligation to do so.

(10) On exercising his powers under subsection (1) in relation to a relevant proposal, the Secretary of State shall give such statement as he considers appropriate of the reasons governing his decision.

DEFINITIONS
"planning authority": ss.1(1), 277(1).
"relevant proposal": s.10(2).

GENERAL NOTE
Subs. (1)
For what the Secretary of State must do before approving or rejecting a proposal see subss. (3) and (4).

Subss. (4), (5)
The objections referred to in para. (a) are those made to the structure plan proposals: See the general note to s.8.

"examination in public"—Where the Secretary of State decides to hold an examination in public he must advertise a notice of that intention in the Edinburgh Gazette and for two consecutive weeks in at least one local newspaper circulating in the locality covered by the structure plan: Plans Regs. reg. 17. There are no rules of procedure but there is a Code of Practice issued in Scottish Office Circular 6/1985.
Where the Secretary of State proposes to approve a structure plan with modifications he must comply with the publicity and objection provisions in reg. 18 of the Plans Regs: See *Central Regional Council v. Secretary of State for Scotland*, 1991 S.L.T. 702.

Subs. (8)
This simply requires the Council on Tribunals (the tribunals ombudsman) to consider a report on any matters relating to the administrative procedures of an examination in public. It does not enable the Lord Advocate to make statutory rules for the conduct of the examination. *cf.* s.15 (for local plan inquiries).

Local plans

Preparation of local plans

11.—(1) Every planning authority shall prepare local plans for all parts of their district, and two or more planning authorities may prepare a joint local plan extending to parts of each of their districts.

(2) It shall be the duty of the planning authority—

(a) for the purpose of preparing a local plan, to institute a survey of their district or any part of it, in so far as not already done, taking into account the matters which the authority think necessary for the formulation of their proposals, and

(b) to keep those matters under review during and after the preparation of the local plan.

(3) A local plan shall consist of—

(a) a written statement formulating in such detail as the planning authority think appropriate the authority's proposals for the development and other use of land in that part of their district or for any description of development or other use of such land including in either case such measures as the planning authority think fit for the conservation of the natural beauty and amenity of the land, the improvement of the physical environment and the management of traffic,

(b) a map showing those proposals, and

(c) such diagrams, illustrations and descriptive matter as the planning authority think appropriate to explain or illustrate those proposals, or as may be prescribed,

and shall contain such matters as may be prescribed.

(4) Different local plans may be prepared for different purposes for the same part of any district.

(5) In formulating their proposals in a local plan the planning authority—

(a) shall have regard to any information and any other considerations which appear to them to be relevant or which may be prescribed, and

(b) shall secure that the local plan conforms generally to the structure plan, as it stands for the time being, whether or not it has been approved by the Secretary of State.

(6) Where an area is indicated as an action area in a structure plan which has been approved by the Secretary of State, the planning authority shall (if they have not already done so), as soon as practicable after the approval of the plan, prepare a local plan for that area.

DEFINITIONS
"land": s.277(1).
"planning authority": ss.1(1), 277(1).
"prescribed": s.277(1).
"use": s.277(1).

GENERAL NOTE
Subs. (1)
The local plan, once adopted by the planning authority or approved by the Secretary of State forms one half of the development plan which applies to an area of land: s.14(1). The other half is the structure plan to which the local plan must generally conform: s.11(5)(b).

Subs. (3)
A local plan must contain—
(a) a title with
(i) a name ending with the words "local plan"; or "action area local plan";
(ii) an indication of the geographical real covered by the plan;
(b) a statement of which planning authority prepared it;
(c) a written statement of—
(i) the authority's proposals for land use in the area with a reasoned justification for them;
(ii) the matters prescribed by reg. 25 of the Plans Regs;
(d) a map ("proposals map") based on an Ordnance Survey map with national grid lines and numbers with a scale and legend showing the proposals, possibly with smaller unit maps: See Plans Regs. regs. 22 to 27.
Each document on the plan must have (a) and (b) on it: Plans Regs. reg. 22(3).
For government guidance on the form of local plans see annex 2 to PAN 49. For interpretation of "local plan" see the general note to s.25.

Publicity and consultation

12.—(1) Subject to subsection (6), a planning authority who propose to prepare, alter, repeal or replace a local plan shall take such steps as will in their opinion secure—

(a) that adequate publicity is given in their district to any relevant matter arising out of a survey of the district or part of the district carried out under section 4 or 11 and to the proposals,

(b) that persons who may be expected to wish to make representations to the authority about the proposals are made aware that they are entitled to do so, and

(c) that such persons are given an adequate opportunity of making such representations.

(2) The planning authority shall consider any representations made to them within the prescribed period.

(3) Having prepared the local plan or, as the case may be, the proposals for alteration, repeal or replacement, the planning authority shall before adopting the plan or proposals or submitting it or them for approval under section 18—

(a) make copies available for inspection at their office and at such other places as appear to them to be appropriate, and

(b) send a copy to the Secretary of State.

(4) Each copy made available for inspection under subsection (3) shall be accompanied by a statement of the time within which objections may be made to the authority.

(5) The copy of the plan or proposals sent to the Secretary of State, or made available for inspection, under subsection (3) shall be accompanied by a statement containing such particulars, if any, as may be prescribed—

(a) of the steps which the authority have taken to comply with subsection (1), and

(b) of the authority's consultations with, and their consideration of the views of, other persons.

(6) If the planning authority propose to alter a local plan and do not consider it appropriate to take the steps referred to in subsection (1), they may instead include, with the copies of those proposals made available for inspection under subsection (3) and with the copy sent to the Secretary of State, a statement of their reasons for not doing so.

DEFINITIONS
    "planning authority": ss.1(1), 277(1).
    "prescribed": s.277(1).

GENERAL NOTE
Subs. (1)
    "Preparation" appears to involve the creation of the first local plan for an area. Most of Scotland is now covered by local plans. This means that this section will usually apply to "alterations, repeal or replacement" of existing local plans. This note is written from the viewpoint of alteration.
    For the duties to formulate alterations see the general note to s.13.
    For the meaning of "person" see the general note to s.8.

Subs. (2)
    This is a period not less than four weeks, specified by the planning authority in publicising their survey report and local plan proposals: Plan Regs, reg. 3.

Subs. (5)
    The statement should containing a brief account of the matters in paras. (a) and (b): Plan Regs, reg. 12.

Alteration of local plans

13.—(1) A planning authority shall keep under review any local plan adopted by them, or approved by the Secretary of State, and may at any time make proposals for the alteration, repeal or replacement of that plan.

(2) In complying with subsection (1) the planning authority—

(a) shall have regard to any information and any other considerations which appear to them to be relevant or which may be prescribed, and

(b) shall secure that any proposals conform generally to the structure plan as it stands for the time being, whether or not it has been approved by the Secretary of State.

(3) Any such proposals may include proposals for the repeal of two or more local plans and their replacement with one local plan.

(4) Where a local plan has been approved by the Secretary of State the planning authority shall not make such proposals in relation to that plan without his consent.

DEFINITIONS
"planning authority": ss.1(1), 277(1).

GENERAL NOTE
Subs. (1)
Once a local plan has come into force a planning authority must keep it under review: s.13(1). As with structure plans, local plans do not have a fixed statutory lifespan. Current government advice recommends that they should provide some certainty over a minimum five year period: PAN 49, para. 62. For government advice on monitoring and review see PAN 49, paras. 14 to 16. For situations where alteration or replacement may be necessary see PAN 49, para. 18.

Subs. (2)
It is quite unclear when a structure plan "stands for the time being". One may surmise that it is when it has been submitted to the Secretary of State but not yet approved.

Subs. (3)
This may be attractive for new planning authorities which encompass the districts of more than one pre-reorganization authority.

Subs. (4)
This means that if the Secretary of State has called in a proposed local plan under s.18, and had to approve it, any alteration to it must also have his consent.

Power of Secretary of State to direct making of local plan etc.

14.—(1) Subject to the provisions of this section the Secretary of State may direct a planning authority to prepare—

(a) a local plan for their district or part of it;

(b) proposals for the alteration, repeal or replacement of a local plan adopted by them or approved by him.

(2) The Secretary of State may so direct only before he approves the structure plan for the district in question.

(3) A direction under subsection (1) shall specify the nature of the plan or, as the case may be, the proposals required.

(4) Before giving such a direction, the Secretary of State shall consult the planning authority about it.

(5) The planning authority shall comply with the direction as soon as practicable and shall take steps for the adoption of the local plan or, as the case may be, the alteration, repeal or replacement of it.

DEFINITIONS
"planning authority": ss.2(1), 277(1).

Objections: local inquiry or other hearing

15.—(1) The planning authority may cause a local inquiry or other hearing to be held for the purpose of considering objections to a local plan or to proposals for the alteration, repeal or replacement of a local plan prepared by them.

(2) If an objector so requires, the planning authority shall cause such a local inquiry or other hearing to be held in the case of objections made in accordance with regulations.

(3) A local inquiry or other hearing under this section shall be held by a person appointed by the Secretary of State or, in such cases as may be prescribed, by the authority themselves.

(4) Regulations may—

(a) make provision with respect to the appointment and qualifications for appointment of persons to hold a local inquiry or other hearing;

(b) include provision enabling the Secretary of State to direct a planning authority to appoint a particular person, or one of a specified list or class of persons;

(c) make provision with respect to the allowances of the person appointed.

(5) Subsections (4) to (8) of section 265 apply to an inquiry held under this section.

(6) The Tribunals and Inquiries Act 1992 shall apply to a local inquiry or other hearing held under this section as it applies to a statutory inquiry held by the Secretary of State, but as if in section 10(1) of that Act (statement of reasons for decisions) the reference to any decision taken by the Secretary of State were a reference to a decision taken by a local authority.

DEFINITIONS
"local authority": s.277(1).
"planning authority": s.277(1).

GENERAL NOTE
Subss. (1) and (2)

Where any objector has objected to a proposal to alter or replace the local plan, the planning authority must, if the objector requires, call a local inquiry or other hearing, for the purpose of considering the objection. In addition, the planning authority may, if it wishes, call a local inquiry for the purpose of considering proposals to alter or replace the local plan.

Local Plan Inquiry Practice: It is beyond the scope of this note to give a detailed description of practice. The salient features are as follows:

(a) Person holding the inquiry—where the inquiry is to consider an objection the planning authority must appoint a person from the Secretary of State's list: Plans Reg. 33(1) and see SODD Circular 1/1996. The list will usually contain civil servants from the Scottish Office Inquiry Reporters Unit ("SOIRU"). Where the planning authority does not choose such a person, the Secretary of State will do so (again from SOIRU).

(b) Renumeration of appointed person—the person, or if he is a civil servant, the Secretary of State, is entitled to renumeration at a fixed rate (see s.16) and allowance as the planning authority thinks fit (subject to the direction of the Secretary of State), reg. 33(2).

(c) Plan Regs—there are no rules but the Secretary of State has issued a code of practice contained in SODD Circular 32/1996. Both citation of witness and evidence on oath are competent: ss.15(5) and 265(4) to (8).

Costs of local inquiry or other hearing

16.—(1) The planning authority shall—

(a) where a person appointed under or by virtue of section 15 to hold a local inquiry or other hearing is in the public service of the Crown, pay the Secretary of State, and

(b) in any other case, pay the person so appointed,

a sum, determined in accordance with regulations under subsection (2), in respect of the performance by the person so appointed of his functions in relation to the inquiry or hearing (whether or not it takes place).

(2) Regulations may make provision with respect to the determination of the sum referred to in subsection (1) and may in particular prescribe, in relation to any class of person appointed under or by virtue of section 15, a standard daily amount applicable in respect of each day on which a person of that class is engaged in holding, or in work connected with, the inquiry or hearing.

(3) Without prejudice to the generality of subsection (2), the Secretary of State may, in prescribing by virtue of that subsection a standard daily amount for any class of person—

(a) where the persons of that class are in the public service of the Crown, have regard to the general staff costs and overheads of his department, and

(b) in any other case, have regard to the general administrative costs incurred by persons of that class in connection with the performance by them of their functions in relation to such inquiries and hearings.

DEFINITIONS
"planning authority": ss.1(3), 277(1).

GENERAL NOTE
Subs. (1)
The planning authority must pay a person appointed after March 31, 1996 £275 for each day he holds or does work connected with the inquiry: Town and Country Planning (Courts of Inquiries etc.) (Standard Daily Account) Regulations 1996 (S.I. 1996 No.493).

Adoption of proposals

17.—(1) After the expiry of the period for making objections to a local plan or, as the case may be, proposals for the alteration, repeal or replacement of a local plan or, if such objections were duly made within that period, after considering the objections so made, the planning authority may, subject to this section and to section 18, by resolution adopt the plan or the proposals.

(2) The planning authority may adopt the plan or the proposals as originally prepared or as modified so as to take account of—

(a) any such objections as are mentioned in subsection (1) whether or not they have been the subject of a local inquiry or other hearing,

(b) any matters arising out of such objections, or

(c) any minor drafting or technical matters.

(3) Where the Secretary of State has, under section 10, approved a structure plan for any area the planning authority shall not adopt any plan or proposals which do not conform to that structure plan.

(4) After copies of the plan or proposals have been sent to the Secretary of State and before the plan or proposals have been adopted by the planning authority, the Secretary of State may, if it appears to him that the plan or proposals are unsatisfactory, and without prejudice to his power to make a direction under section 18(1), direct the authority to consider modifying the plan or proposals in such respects as are indicated in the direction.

(5) A planning authority to whom such a direction is given shall not adopt the plan or proposals unless they satisfy the Secretary of State that they have made the modifications necessary to conform with the direction or the direction is withdrawn.

DEFINITIONS
"planning authority": ss.1(1), 277(1).

GENERAL NOTE
Subs. (1)
After considering any competent objections of the draft plan and provided the Secretary of State has not (a) directed modifications or proposals for modifications (s.17(4)) nor (b) directed that the draft plan be submitted to him for approval (*i.e.* "called in") (s.18(1)), the planning authority may by a resolution adopt the draft plan.

If the Secretary of State calls in the draft local plan, the plan must be approved by him before it can take effect: s.18(1).

Where the Secretary of State directs modification the planning authority must first satisfy the Secretary of State that they have made the necessary modifications before adopting the plan (s.17(5)).

Calling in of plan or proposals for approval by Secretary of State

18.—(1) After a copy of a local plan or of proposals for the alteration, repeal or replacement of a local plan has been sent to the Secretary of State and before the plan or proposals have been adopted by the planning authority, the Secretary of State may direct that the plan or proposals shall be submitted to him for his approval.

(2) If the Secretary of State gives a direction under subsection (1)—
  (a) the authority shall submit the plan or proposals to him,
  (b) the authority shall not hold a local inquiry or other hearing in respect of the plan or proposals under section 15, and
  (c) the plan or proposals shall not have effect unless approved by the Secretary of State.

DEFINITIONS
"planning authority": ss.1(1), 277(1).

GENERAL NOTE
Subs. (1)
The Secretary of State's direction that a planning authority submit the plan to him for his approval is commonly referred to as "calling in".

The section does not specify the grounds for calling in but generally it will be where the proposed local plan clashes with a government policy guideline: See *e.g. R. v. Secretary of State for the Environment ex p. Southwark London Borough Council* (1987) 54 P. & C.R. 226.

The Secretary of State has no duty to consult anyone before calling in the proposed plan: *R. v. Secretary of State for the Environment ex p. Southwark London Borough Council* (above).

Approval of plan of proposals by Secretary of State

19.—(1) The Secretary of State may, after considering a plan or proposals submitted to him under section 18, either approve (in whole or in part and with or without modifications or reservations) or reject the plan or proposals.

(2) In considering the plan or proposals the Secretary of State may take into account any matters he thinks are relevant, whether or not they were taken into account in the plan or proposals as submitted to him.

(3) Where on considering the plan or proposals the Secretary of State does not determine then to reject it or them, he shall before determining whether or not to approve it or them—
  (a) consider any objections to the plan or proposals so far as made in accordance with regulations,
  (b) give any person who made such an objection and has not withdrawn it an opportunity of appearing before and being heard by a person appointed by him for the purpose, and
  (c) if a local inquiry or other hearing is held, also give such an opportunity to the planning authority and such other persons as he thinks fit,
but if a local inquiry or other hearing into the objections has already been held by the authority he need not cause any other inquiry or hearing to be held.

(4) In considering the plan or proposals the Secretary of State may consult or consider the views of any planning authority or any other person; but he need not do so, or give an opportunity for the making of representations or objections, or cause a local inquiry or other hearing to be held, unless required to do so by subsection (3).

DEFINITIONS
"local inquiry": s.265.
"planning authority": ss.1(1), 277(1).

GENERAL NOTE
Subss. (1) to (4)
Subsections (2) to (4) are a comprehensive code of procedure for the Secretary of State in

deciding a local plan proposal: *R. v. Secretary of State for the Environment ex p. Southwark London Borough Council* (1984) 54 P. & C.R. 266, 235 *per* Lloyd L.J. Where the Secretary of State is minded to reject the proposals outright he need not consult with anyone. In any other case he must carry out the consultation required by subs. (3): *R. v. Secretary of State for the Environment ex p. Southwark London Borough Council* (above).

Supplementary provisions

Disregarding of representations with respect to development authorised by or under other enactments

20. Notwithstanding anything in the previous provisions of this Part, neither the Secretary of State nor a planning authority need consider representations or objections with respect to a structure plan, a local plan or any proposal to alter, repeal or replace any such plan if it appears to the Secretary of State or the authority, as the case may be, that those representations or objections are in substance representations or objections with respect to things done or proposed to be done in pursuance of—

   (a) an order or scheme under section 5, 7, 9 or 12 of the Roads (Scotland) Act 1984 (trunk road orders, special road schemes and orders for other public roads);

   (b) an order under section 1 of the New Towns Act 1946 or section 1 of the New Towns (Scotland) Act 1968 (designation of sites of new towns).

DEFINITIONS
  "planning authority": ss.1(1), 277(1).

Power of Secretary of State to make regulations as to structure and local plans

21.—(1) Without prejudice to the previous provisions of this Part, the Secretary of State may make regulations with respect to—

   (a) the form and content of structure and local plans, and

   (b) the procedure to be followed in connection with their preparation, submission, withdrawal, approval adoption, making, alteration, modification, repeal and replacement.

(2) In particular any such regulations may—

   (a) provide for the publicity to be given to the report of any survey carried out by a planning authority under section 4;

   (b) provide for the notice to be given of, or the publicity to be given to—

      (i) matters included or proposed to be included in any such plan,

      (ii) the approval, adoption or making of any such plan or any alteration, modification, repeal or replacement of it, or

      (iii) any other prescribed procedural step,

   and for publicity to be given to the procedure to be followed as mentioned in subsection (1)(b);

   (c) make provision with respect to the making and consideration of representations with respect to matters to be included in, or objections to, any such plan or proposals for its alteration, modification, repeal or replacement;

   (d) without prejudice to paragraph (b), provide for notice to be given to particular persons of the approval, adoption, alteration or modification of any plan, if they have objected to the plan and have notified the planning authority of their wish to receive notice, subject (if the regulations so provide) to the payment of a reasonable charge for receiving it;

   (e) require or authorise a planning authority to consult, or consider the views of, other persons before taking any prescribed procedural step;

   (f) require a planning authority, in such cases as may be prescribed or in such particular cases as the Secretary of State may direct, to provide persons on request by them with copies of any plan or document which has been made public for the purpose mentioned in section 8(1)(a) or 12(1)(a) or has been made available for inspection under section 8(4) or 12(3), subject (if the regulations so provide) to the payment of a reasonable charge;

(g) provide for the publication and inspection of any structure plan or local plan which has been approved, adopted or made, or any document approved, adopted or made altering, repealing or replacing any such plan, and for copies of any such plan or document to be made available on sale.

(3) Such regulations may extend throughout Scotland or to specified areas only and may make different provisions for different cases.

(4) Subject to the previous provisions of this Part and to any such regulations, the Secretary of State may give directions to any planning authority, or to planning authorities generally—

(a) for formulating the procedure for the carrying out of their functions under this Part;

(b) for requiring them to give him such information as he may require for carrying out any of his functions under this Part.

(5) Subject to section 237, a structure plan or local plan or any alteration, repeal or replacement thereof shall become operative on a date appointed for the purpose in the relevant notice of approval, resolution of adoption or notice of the making, alteration, repeal or replacement of the plan.

DEFINITIONS
"planning authority": ss.1(1), 277(1).
"prescribed": s.277(1).

GENERAL NOTE
Subs. (2)
para. (f)
"*purpose mentioned in ss.8(1)(a) or 12(1)(a)*": This drafting is odd as neither provision mentions a purpose. Sections 8(1)(c) and 12(1)(c) do mention the purpose of giving adequate opportunity to persons to make representation.
"*person*": See the general note to s.8.

para. (g)
Availability for inspection under ss.8(4) and 12(3): These provisions require a planning authority to allow inspection of a structure or local plan before submission to the Secretary of State, or for a local plan, adoption by the authority.
Availability of inspection of local or structure plans in force: A planning authority must comply with reg. 43 of the Plan Regulations.
Sale of Copy Operative or draft local or structure plan: See reg. 44 of the Plan Regulations.

Subs. (5)
Operation of structure or local plan: It comes into operation (force or effect) on the date specified in the Secretary of State's notice of approval or in the planning authority's resolution of adoption.
Appeal against structure or local plan: See ss.237 and 238.

Default powers of Secretary of State

22.—(1) Where, by virtue of any of the previous provisions of this Part, any structure or local plan is, or proposals for the alteration, repeal or replacement of such a plan are, required to be prepared or submitted to the Secretary of State, or steps are required to be taken for the adoption of any such plan or proposals, then—

(a) if at any time the Secretary of State is satisfied that the planning authority are not taking the steps necessary to enable them to submit or adopt such a plan or proposals within a reasonable period, or

(b) in a case where a period is specified for the submission or adoption of any such plan or proposals, if no such plan or proposals have been submitted or adopted within that period,

the Secretary of State may direct the planning authority to carry out their functions in relation to the matters mentioned in this subsection and may specify in the direction the factors to be taken into account or objectives to be achieved by the planning authority in so doing, or the Secretary of State may carry out a survey in accordance with the provisions of section 4 or prepare and make a structure plan or local plan or, as the case may be, alter, repeal or replace it, as he thinks fit.

(2) Where under subsection (1) the Secretary of State has power to do anything which should have been done by a planning authority ("the defaulting authority"), he may, if he thinks fit, authorise any other planning authority who appear to him to have an interest in the proper planning of the district of the defaulting authority to do it.

(3) Where under subsection (1) the Secretary of State has power to do anything which should have been done by a planning authority acting jointly with another planning authority or authorities, he may, if he thinks fit, authorise one of those authorities to do that thing on behalf of both or all of them.

(4) The previous provisions of this Part shall, so far as applicable, apply with any necessary modifications in relation to the doing of anything under this section by the Secretary of State or an authority other than the defaulting authority and the thing so done.

(5) The defaulting authority—
(a) shall on demand repay to the Secretary of State so much of any expenses incurred by him in connection with the doing of anything which should have been done by them as he certifies to have been incurred in the performance of their functions, and
(b) shall repay to any other authority who do under this section anything which should have been done by the defaulting authority, any expenses certified by the Secretary of State to have been reasonably incurred by that other authority in connection with the doing of that thing.

DEFINITIONS
"planning authority": ss.1(1), 277(1).

GENERAL NOTE
Subs. (1)
The "previous provisions of this part" are ss.4 to 21.

Reviews of plans in enterprise zones

23.—(1) As soon as practicable after an order has been made under paragraph 5 of Schedule 32 to the Local Government, Planning and Land Act 1980 (designation of enterprise zone scheme) or a notification has been given under paragraph 11 of that Schedule (modification of such a scheme), any planning authority for an area in which the enterprise zone is wholly or partly situated shall review—
(a) any structure plan for their area or for part of it which relates to the whole or part of the zone in the light of the provisions of the scheme or modified scheme, and
(b) any local plan which relates to any land situated in the zone.
(2) A planning authority shall—
(a) submit to the Secretary of State proposals for any alterations to a structure plan which they consider necessary to take account of the scheme or the modified scheme, and
(b) make proposals for any alterations to such a local plan as is mentioned in subsection (1)(b) which they consider necessary to take account of

the scheme or modified scheme, or for the repeal or replacement of any of those plans whose repeal or replacement they consider necessary for that purpose.

DEFINITIONS
"land": s.277(1).
"planning authority": ss.1(1), 277(1).

GENERAL NOTE
Subs. (1)
See general note to s.1.

Meaning of "development plan"

24.—(1) For the purposes of this Act, any other town and country planning and the Land Compensation (Scotland) Act 1963, the development plan for any area (whether the whole or part of the district of a planning authority) shall be taken as consisting of—
  (a) the provisions of the structure plan for the time being in force for that district or the relevant part of that district, together with the Secretary of State's notice of approval of the plan,
  (b) any alterations to that plan, together with the Secretary of State's notices of approval of them,
  (c) any provisions of a local plan for the time being applicable to the area, together with a copy of the authority's resolution of adoption or, as the case may be, the Secretary of State's notice of approval of the local plan, and
  (d) any alterations to that local plan, together with a copy of the authority's resolutions of adoption or, as the case may be, the Secretary of State's notices of approval of them.
  (2) References in subsection (1) to the provisions of any plan, notices of approval, alterations and resolutions of adoption shall, in relation to an area forming part of the district to which they are applicable, be respectively construed as references to so much of those provisions, notices, alterations and resolutions as is applicable to the area.
  (3) References in subsections (1) and (2) to notices of approval shall in relation to any plan or alteration made by the Secretary of State under section 22 be construed as references to notices of the making of the plan or alteration.
  (4) This section has effect subject to Schedule 1 (old development plans).
  (5) For the avoidance of doubt it is provided that, notwithstanding—
  (a) any changes made to local government areas by the Local Government etc. (Scotland) Act 1994, and
  (b) any alterations to structure plan areas made by orders under section 5, the structure plans and local plans made prior to the coming into force of the provisions mentioned in paragraphs (a) and (b) shall remain in force until replaced by new plans made under or by virtue of those provisions.
  (6) Any reference in the Land Compensation (Scotland) Act 1963 to an area defined in a current development plan as an area of comprehensive development shall be construed as a reference to an action area for which a local plan is in force or, as the case may be, to a comprehensive development area.

DEFINITIONS
"enactment": s.277(1).
"planning authority": ss.1(1), 277(1).

GENERAL NOTE
Subs. (1)
Except in the rare situation where an "old development plan" is still in force, a development

plan comprises the items listed in this subsection. An unapproved or unadopted proposal for amendment of a structure or local plan is not part of the "development plan": *Falkirk District Council v. Secretary of State for Scotland*, 1991 S.L.T. 553. It may nevertheless, in appropriate circumstances, be a material consideration in granting or refusing an application for planning permission: *Glasgow District Council, City of v. Secretary of State for Scotland*, 1992 S.C.L.R. 453.

Interpretation of development plan: See general note to s.25.

Subs. (3)

If a planning authority does not submit a structure or local plan or any amendment of them within either a specified or a reasonable period the Secretary of State may make plan or amendment instead: s.22(1). In that case there is obviously no need for the Secretary of State to approve his plan or amendment.

Subs. (4)

"Old development plans" are plans which were made before May 16, 1977 (or in Orkney before April 1, 1977) and which were in force on May 15, 1977: Sched. 1, para. 1; 1972 Act, Sched. 5, para. 2; and Town and Country Planning (Development Plans) (Scotland) Order 1977 (S.I. 1977 No. 794). They were unitary plans which had been made by the pre-1975 local authorities under the 1947 Act.

In simple terms Sched. 1 provides that the old development plan remains in force where land is not covered by both a structure and local plan. As structure plans now cover the whole of Scotland only in areas where there is no local plan does the old development plan remain part of the "development plan". In those exceptional areas the street authorization map of the old plan is deemed to be the local plan, and whenever the structure plan conflicts with the old plan, the provision which is most favorable to the granting of planning permission is part of the "development plan".

General

Status of development plans

25. Where, in making any determination under the planning Acts, regard is to be had to the development plan, the determination shall be made in accordance with the plan unless material considerations indicate otherwise.

DEFINITIONS
"development plan": ss.24(2), 277(1).
"planning Acts": s.277(1).

GENERAL NOTE
Origin: This section was added as a government amendment to the 1991 Planning and Corporation Bill in the final stages of the House of Commons. In introducing the clause to become this section, the responsible minister, Sir George Young stated,

"[the terms of this section] would make clear to planning authorities and others how to go about making the decision. If the development plan has something to say on a particular application, the starting point would be that the plan should be followed unless the weight of the other considerations tell against it. In other words there would be a presumption in favour of the development plan. But it would still allow appropriate weight to be given to all other material considerations.

One material consideration would, of course be the extent to which the development plan was up to date. Clearly, if the development plan is to carry its full weight it needs to be up to date and consistent with national and regional policies as well as relevant to the proposal in question." (*Hansard*, H.C., Vol. 193, cols. 311–12).

"*determination under the Planning Acts*": The section applies to every decision-maker where he or it has to have "regard to the development plan" before making the decision.

"*in accordance with the plan*": The decision-maker should look first whether the proposal is in accordance with the plan. If it is not, he should consider whether there are material considerations which indicate a departure from the plan: *Houghton v. Secretary of State for Environment* (1995) 70 P. & C.R. 178, 183 *per* M. Spence Q.C.

The plan is the most is the most up to date approved structure plan read together with the most up to date adopted or approved local plan: s.24. Where the development plan is silent on the issue to be decided, there may be difficulty in applying s.25.

In interpreting the plan where there is a conflict between the written statement and a diagram or other document the former prevails: Plans Regs. regs. 10 and 27. The interpretation of the development plan is an issue of fact for the decision-maker: *Cooper* (1995) P. & C.R. 529.

PART III

CONTROL OVER DEVELOPMENT

Meaning of development

Meaning of "development"

26.—(1) Subject to the following provisions of this section, in this Act, except where the context otherwise requires, "development" means the carrying out of building, engineering, mining or other operations in, on, over or under land, or the making of any material change in the use of any buildings or other land.

(2) The following operations or uses of land shall not be taken for the purposes of this Act to involve development of the land—

(a) the carrying out of works for the maintenance, improvement or other alteration of any building being works which—
  (i) affect only the interior of the building, or
  (ii) do not materially affect the external appearance of the building,
  and are not works for making good war damage within the meaning of the War Damage Act 1943 or works begun after 7th December, 1969 for the alteration of a building by providing additional space in it underground;

(b) the carrying out by a local roads authority on land within the boundaries of a road of any works required for the maintenance or improvement of the road;

(c) the carrying out by a local authority or statutory undertakers of any works for the purpose of inspecting, repairing or renewing any sewers, mains, pipes, cables or other apparatus, including the breaking open of any road or other land for that purpose;

(d) the use of any buildings or other land within the curtilage of a dwellinghouse for any purpose incidental to the enjoyment of the dwellinghouse as such;

(e) the use of any land for the purposes of agriculture or forestry (including afforestation) and the use for any of those purposes of any building occupied together with land so used;

(f) in the case of buildings or other land which are used for a purpose of any class specified in an order made by the Secretary of State under this section, the use of the buildings or other land or, subject to the provisions of the order, of any part of the buildings or the other land, for any other purpose of the same class;

(g) the demolition of any description of building specified in a direction given by the Secretary of State to planning authorities generally or to a particular planning authority.

(3) For the avoidance of doubt it is hereby declared that for the purposes of this section—

(a) the use as two or more separate dwellinghouses of any building previously used as a single dwellinghouse involves a material change in the use of the building and of each part of it which is so used;

(b) the deposit of refuse or waste materials on land involves a material change in its use, notwithstanding that the land is comprised in a site already used for that purpose, if—

(i) the superficial area of the deposit is extended, or

(ii) the height of the deposit is extended and exceeds the level of the land adjoining the site.

(4) For the purposes of this Act building operations include—

(a) demolition of buildings,

(b) rebuilding,

(c) structural alterations of or additions to buildings, and

(d) other operations normally undertaken by a person carrying on business as a builder.

(5) For the purposes of this Act mining operations include—

(a) the removal of material of any description—

(i) from a mineral-working deposit,

(ii) from a deposit of pulverised fuel ash or other furnace ash or clinker, or

(iii) from a deposit of iron, steel or other metallic slags, and

(b) the extraction of minerals from a disused railway embankment.

(6) Where the placing or assembly of any tank in any part of any inland waters for the purpose of fish farming there would not, apart from this subsection, involve development of the land below, this Act shall have effect as if the tank resulted from carrying out engineering operations over that land; and in this subsection—

"fish farming" means the breeding, rearing or keeping of fish or shellfish (which includes any kind of crustacean or mollusc);

"inland waters" means waters which do not form part of the sea or of any creek, bay or estuary or of any river as far as the tide flows; and

"tank" includes any cage and any other structure for use in fish farming.

(7) Without prejudice to any regulations under this Act relating to the control of advertisements, the use for the display of advertisements of any external part of a building which is not normally used for that purpose shall be treated for the purposes of this section as involving a material change in the use of that part of the building.

DEFINITIONS

"advertisement": s.277(1).

"agriculture": s.277(1).

"building": s.277(1).

"building operations": subs. (4), s.277(1).

"engineering operation": s.277(1).

"improvement": s.277(1).

"land": s.277(1).

"local roads authority": s.277(1).

"mineral-working deposit": s.277(1).

"minerals": s.277(1).

"mining operations": subs. (5), s.277(1).

"road": s.277(1).

"statutory undertaker": ss.214, 277(1).

"use": s.277(1).

GENERAL NOTE

Subss. (1) to (7)

From July 1, 1947, when the Town and Country Planning (Scotland) Act 1947 (c.53) came into force, a landowner's right to develop his land was taken away and given to the planning authority and, ultimately, to the Secretary of State. This section is crucial since it defines the extent of the right which was nationalized.

The current definition of "development" is derived from the original definition in s.10(2) of the 1947 Act. The major changes to the 1947 definition have been:

(a) the definition of "mining operations" in subs. (5) (by the Town and Country Planning (Minerals) Act 1981 (c.36), s.19), from January 1, 1988;

(b) the substitution of "road" for the former "highway" in subs. (2) (by the Roads (Scotland) Act 1984 (c.54), Sched. 9, para. 70), from January 1, 1985;

(c) the extension of the Use Classes Order to changes in use of parts of a planning unit (by the Housing and Planning Act 1986 (c.63), Sched. 11, para. 29), from January 7, 1987;

(d) the extension of "building operations" to include demolition and allowing the Secretary of State to exclude categories of demolition (by the Planning and Compensation Act 1991 (c.34), s.41) from February 3, 1995.

Duality of development: "Development" has two forms. They are (A) operational development; and (B) change of use development.

(A) Operational development

There are four types of operational development.

(1) Building operations—A "building" includes any structure or erection but not plant or machinery comprised in it: s.277(1) and see general note above.

Clearly building operations include the construction of buildings. From February 3, 1995, they undoubtedly include the demolition (subject to the Secretary of State's exclusions) of buildings, rebuilding, structural alteration or addition to buildings and other operations normally done by a person carrying on business as a builder: s.26(4). Before that date it was unclear whether demolition was a building or engineering operation: See *Coleshill & District Investment Co. v. Minister of Housing and Local Government* [1969] 1 W.L.R. 746, and *Glasgow District Council, City of v. Secretary of State for Scotland*, 1980 S.C. 150. In *Glasgow District Council*, the Second Division held, (*obiter*) that the demolition of floors of a tenement and the re-roofing of the remaining part was a building operation.

Building operations do not include:

(a) operations for the maintenance, improvement or alteration of a building which do not materially affect its external appearance (subs. (2)(a)), nor

(b) the demolition of a description of building specified in the Town and Country Planning (Demolition which is not development) (Scotland) Direction 1995 (attached to Scottish Office Circular 15/1995) (subs. (2)(g)).

They have been held not to include the fitting of rough corrugated canopies on to caravans: *Britt v. Buckingham County Council* (1963) 14 P. & C.R. 318.

(2) Engineering operations—these are operations of a kind usually undertaken by or calling for the skills of an engineer: *Fayrewood Fish Farms v. Secretary of State for the Environment* [1984] J.P.L. 267. The larger the physical task is the more likely it is to be an "engineering operation": *Coleshill and District Investment Co.* (above), at 756D *per* Lord Morris of Borth-y-Gest and 756D–F *per* Lord Pearson.

They include the placing or assembly of a cage or structure used in fish farming in any part of inland waters: subs. (6).

Engineering operations do not include:

(a) the carrying out by a local authority of maintenance or improvement works on any road (as defined in the Roads (Scotland) Act 1984), nor

(b) the carrying out by a local authority or statutory undertaker of works for the inspection, repair or renewal of any sewer, main, pipe, cable or other apparatus.

(3) Mining operations—these include the activities described in subs. (5).

(4) Other operations—the reference to "other operations" is something of a mystery since various courts have been unable to find a *genus* between building, engineering, and mining operations: *Ross v. Aberdeen County Council*, 1953 S.L.T. (Sh. Ct.) 65, 66 *per* Sheriff Hamilton; and *Coleshill & District Investment Co.* (above), 764F *per* Lord Wilberforce.

(B) Change of Use development

This is considerably more difficult to identify. The easiest starting point is that certain changes in use are automatically development. These are:

(a) change of use of a building from a single dwellinghouse to two or more separate dwellinghouses;

(b) deposit of refuse or waste materials on any area of land not previously deposited on;

(c) deposit of refuse or waste materials on an area of land previously deposited on which raises the height of the deposit above the level of the land adjoining the site: See *Alexandra Transport Co. v. Secretary of State for Scotland*, 1974 S.L.T. 81;

(d) use of the outside of a building for the display of advertisements when it is not normally used for that purpose: subs. (7).

Certain changes in use are automatically not development:

(a) change in the use of the land or buildings within the "curtilage" of a dwellinghouse for any purpose incidental to its use as such;

(b) change in the use of land to agricultural or forestry purposes including use of buildings occupied with that land for those purposes;

(c) change in the use of land for a purpose which is grouped with existing use in the same class as defined in the Use Classes (Scotland) Order 1989 (S.I. 1989 No.147, amended by S.I. 1993 No.1028): See *Percy (G.) Trentham v. Gloucestershire County Council* [1966] 1 W.L.R. 506.

A "forestry purpose" includes the storage of timber on a plot of land about 1.5 km from the forest where it was cut: *Farleyer Estate v. Secretary of State for Scotland*, 1992 S.C. 202.

If the change in use is not one of the above, one must assess whether it is a material change in the use of land. To do this one must:

(a) identify the extent of the land or building against which the materiality of the change is to be judged ("the planning unit"); and

(b) for that unit compare the existing use with the proposed use: *Alexandra Transport Co.* (above), 84 *per* Lord Milligan.

The planning unit will be the whole site occupied by the person wishing to make a change in use of it or a part of it, except where the site has two or more physically distinct areas which are used for different main purposes: *Burdle v. Secretary of State for the Environment* [1972] 1 W.L.R. 1207, 1212C–1213A *per* Bridge J.

Rarely, if ever, will one room of a dwellinghouse be seen as a separate planning unit: *Wood* [1977] 1 W.L.R. 707, 712.

Intensification of the existing use may be a material change in use. So use of a site to station four caravans when it previously had one was held to be a material change in use: *James v. Minister of Housing and Local Government* [1966] 1 W.L.R. 135.

Time when development begun

27.—(1) Subject to the following provisions of this section, for the purposes of this Act development of land shall be taken to be initiated—

(a) if the development consists of the carrying out of operations, at the time when those operations are begun;

(b) if the development consists of a change in use, at the time when the new use is instituted;

(c) if the development consists both of the carrying out of operations and of a change in use, at the earlier of the times mentioned in paragraphs (a) and (b).

(2) For the purposes of the provisions of this Part mentioned in subsection (3) development shall be taken to be begun on the earliest date on which any material operation comprised in the development begins to be carried out.

(3) The provisions referred to in subsection (2) are sections 52(2), 53(6), 54(4), 58, 59 and 61.

(4) In subsection (2) "material operation" means—

(a) any work of construction in the course of the erection of a building,

(b) any work of demolition of a building,

(c) the digging of a trench which is to contain the foundations, or part of the foundations, of a building,

(d) the laying of any underground main or pipe to the foundations, or part of the foundations, of a building or to any such trench as is mentioned in paragraph (c),

(e) any operation in the course of laying out or constructing a road or part of a road, or

(f) any change in the use of any land which constitutes material development.

(5) In subsection (4)(f) "material development" means any development other than—

(a) development for which planning permission is granted by a general development order for the time being in force and which is carried out so as to comply with any condition or limitation subject to which planning permission is so granted,

(b) development of a class specified in paragraph 1 or 2 of Schedule 11, and
(c) development of any class prescribed for the purposes of this subsection.

(6) In subsection (5) "general development order" means a development order (within the meaning of section 30(2)) made as a general order applicable (subject to such exceptions as may be specified in it) to all land in Scotland.

DEFINITIONS
"building": s.277(1).
"development": ss.26, 277(1).
"development order": ss.30, 277(1).
"erection": s.277(1).
"general development order": subs. (6).
"initiated": subs. (1), s.277(6).
"land": s.277(1).
"material development": subs. (5).
"material operation": subs. (4).
"planning permission": s.277(1).
"road": s.277(1).
"use": s.277(1).

GENERAL NOTE
Subs. (1)
This is relevant for s.81(6) (recoverable compensation).

Subss. (2) to (4)
When development is "begun" is relevant for satisfying the time limits which prevent the expiry of the planning permission. Sections 52(2), 53(6), and 54(4) relate to the expiry planning permission granted by a simplified planning zone. Sections 58 and 59 relate to the expiry of planning permission granted by a planning authority (or the Secretary of State or a reporter) on an application to it. Section 61 relates to completion of development notices.

Very little need be done to "begin" development: See *Malvern Hills District Council v. Secretary of State for the Environment* (1983) 46 P. & C.R. 58 *per* Eveleigh L.J. That said, the work in a "material operation" must be genuinely done for the purpose of carrying out the permitted development. See also *Platt (Daniel) v. Secretary of State for the Environment* [1996] E.G.C.S. 113; and *Age Crest v. Gwynedd County Council* [1996] E.G.C.S. 115.

Building operation may be "begun" even where the developer has failed to comply with his duty to obtain a building warrant under the Building (Scotland) Act 1959 (c.24), and the Building (Scotland) Act 1970 (c.38): *Glasgow District Council, City of v. Secretary of State for Scotland (No. 2)*, 1993 S.L.T. 268.

Requirement for planning permission

Development requiring planning permission

28.—(1) Subject to the following provisions of this section, planning permission is required for the carrying out of any development of land.

(2) Where planning permission to develop land has been granted for a limited period, planning permission is not required for the resumption, at the end of that period, of its use for the purpose for which it was normally used before the permission was granted.

(3) Where by a development order planning permission to develop land has been granted subject to limitations, planning permission is not required for the use of that land which (apart from its use in accordance with that permission) is its normal use.

(4) Where an enforcement notice has been served in respect of any development of land, planning permission is not required for the use of that land

for the purpose for which (in accordance with the provisions of this Part) it could lawfully have been used if that development had not been carried out.

(5) In determining for the purposes of subsections (2) and (3) what is or was the normal use of land, no account shall be taken of any use begun in contravention of this Part or of previous planning control.

(6) For the purposes of this section a use of land shall be taken to have been begun in contravention of previous planning control if it was begun in contravention of Part II of the 1947 Act or Part III of the 1972 Act.

(7) Subsection (1) has effect subject to Schedule 2 (which contains exemptions for certain uses of land on 1st July 1948).

DEFINITIONS
  "development": ss.26, 277(1).
  "development order": ss.30, 277(1).
  "enforcement notice": ss.127, 277(1).
  "land": s.277(1).
  "planning permission": s.277(1).
  "planning permission granted for a limited period": ss.41(3), 277(1).
  "use": s.277(1).

GENERAL NOTE
Subs. (1)
  This section imposes a general duty to obtain planning permission before carrying out any development. The duty does not apply where a local authority or other statutory regulatory body requires an owner or occupier to "develop" land or buildings for the purposes of public safety: *Glasgow District Council, City of v. Secretary of State for Scotland*, 1980 S.C. 150 (no planning permission necessary to partly demolish a tenement in compliance with a demolition order under the Building (Scotland) Acts).

Subs. (2)
  The grant for a limited period is imposed by a condition attached to the permission in terms of s.41(1)(b).

Subs. (5)
  This "Part" is ss.26 to 75.

Subs. (7)
  Schedule 2 clarifies the lawfulness of certain material changes of use from July 1, 1948 to December 7, 1969.

Granting of planning permission: general

29.—(1) Planning permission may be granted—
  (a) by a development order,
  (b) by the planning authority (or, where this Part so provides, by the Secretary of State) on application to the authority in accordance with regulations or a development order,
  (c) on the adoption or approval of a simplified planning zone scheme or alterations to such a scheme in accordance with section 49 or, as the case may be, section 53, or
  (d) on the designation of an enterprise zone or the approval of a modified scheme under Schedule 32 to the Local Government Planning and Land Act 1980 in accordance with section 55 of this Act.

(2) Planning permission may also be deemed to be granted under section 57 (development with government authorisation).

(3) This section is without prejudice to any other provisions of this Act providing for the granting of permission.

DEFINITIONS
  "development": ss.26, 277(1).
  "development order": ss.30, 277(1).
  "enforcement notice": ss.127, 277(1).

"land": s.277(1).
"planning authority": ss.1(1), 277(1).
"planning permission": s.277(1).
"simplified planning zone": ss.49, 277(1).

GENERAL NOTE
Subs. (1)
    In popular parlance, the term "planning permission" is often restricted to a permission granted by a planning authority on an application made to it, or the Secretary of State or a reporter on appeal. This section makes it clear that it is only one of four types of planning permission.

Subs. (2)
    Aside from the four types of planning permission there are at least two types of "deemed" planning permission. The most obvious is when a local authority seeks to develop its own land: See s.263. There is also the one mentioned in s.57.

Development orders

Development orders: general

30.—(1) The Secretary of State shall by regulations or by order provide for the granting of planning permission.
    (2) An order under this section (in this Act referred to as a "development order") may itself grant planning permission for development specified in the order, or for development of any class so specified, and may be made either—
  (a) as a general order applicable, except so far as it otherwise provides, to all land, but which may make different provision with respect to different descriptions of land, or
  (b) as a special order applicable only to such land or descriptions of land as may be specified in the order.
    (3) In respect of development for which planning permission is not granted by a development order, regulations or an order may provide for the granting of planning permission by the planning authority (or, where this Part so provides, by the Secretary of State) on an application made to the planning authority in accordance with the regulations or the order.

DEFINITIONS
    "development order": subs. (2), s.277(1).
    "development plan": ss.24, 277(1).
    "land": s.277(1).
    "planning authority": ss.1(1), 277(1).

GENERAL NOTE
Subss. (1) and (2)
    The most recent development order is the Town and Country Planning (General Permitted Development) (Scotland) Order 1992 (S.I. 1992 No.223, as amended by S.I. 1992 No.1078, S.I. 1992 No.2084, S.I. 1993 No.1036, S.I. 1994 No.1442, S.I. 1994 No.329, and S.I. 1996 No.3023) ("GPDO").
    Like all delegated legislation under the 1972 Act, it continues to have effect as if it had been enacted under the corresponding section of this Act: Interpretation Act 1978 (c.30), s.17(2) and Planning (Consequential Provisions) (Scotland) Act 1997 (c.11), s.2(2).
    It came into force on March 13, 1992. For development over most of the 1980s the Town and Country Planning (General Development) (Scotland) Order 1981 (S.I. 1981 No.830, as amended by S.I. 1984 No.237, S.I. 1985 No.2007, S.I. 1988 No.1249, S.I. 1990 No.508) still applies.
    The GPDO is an automatic grant of planning permission for the classes of development stated within it. That said, it does not have the effect of making the activities classed "development" within the definition in s.26. This is because that would be to use subordinate legislation to interpret primary legislation, which is contrary to principle. The GPDO does not grant permission contrary to any condition imposed by planning permission granted on application: GPDO, art. 3(4).
    The GPDO grants planning permission for 71 separate classes of development which are grouped in 24 parts: GPDO, art. 3 and Sched. The parts are:

1. Development within the curtilage of a dwellinghouse,
2. Sundry minor operations,
3. Changes of use,
4. Temporary buildings and uses,
5. Caravan sites,
6. Agricultural buildings and operations,
7. Forestry buildings and operations,
8. Industrial and warehouse use,
9. Repairs to private roads and ways,
10. Repairs to services,
11. Development under local or private Acts or Orders,
12. Development by local authorities,
13. Development by statutory undertakers,
14. Aviation development,
15. Mineral exploration,
16. Development ancillary to mining operations,
17. Coal authority and licensee mining development,
18. Waste tipping at a mine,
19. Removal of material from mineral working deposits,
20. Development by telecommunications code-systems operators,
21. Others,
22. Development at amusement parks,
23. Demolition of buildings,
24. Toll road facilities.

Permission granted by development order

31.—(1) Planning permission granted by a development order may be granted either unconditionally or subject to such conditions or limitations as may be specified in the order.

(2) Without prejudice to the generality of subsection (1), where planning permission is granted by a development order for the erection, extension or alteration of any buildings, the order may require the approval of the planning authority to be obtained with respect to the design or external appearance of the buildings.

(3) Without prejudice to the generality of subsection (1), where planning permission is granted by a development order for development of a specified class, the order may enable the Secretary of State or the planning authority to direct that the permission shall not apply either—

(a) in relation to development in a particular area, or

(b) in relation to any particular development.

(4) Any provision of a development order by which permission is granted for the use of land for any purpose on a limited number of days in a period specified in that provision shall (without prejudice to the generality of references in this Act to limitations) be taken to be a provision granting permission for the use of land for any purpose subject to the limitation that the land shall not be used for any one purpose in pursuance of that provision on more than that number of days in that period.

(5) For the purpose of enabling development to be carried out in accordance with planning permission, or otherwise for the purpose of promoting proper development in accordance with the development plan, a development order may direct that any enactment passed before 13th August 1947, or any regulations, orders or byelaws made at any time under any such enactment—

(a) shall not apply to any development specified in the order, or

(b) shall apply to it subject to such modifications as may be so specified.

GENERAL NOTE
Subs. (3)

The Secretary of State has provided for the exclusion of development order planning permission by providing that if he or the planning authority are satisfied that:

(a) any class of development permitted by the order (except classes 54 and 56); or

(b) any particular development which is covered by the classes should not be carried out in any geographical area, it,

[he or it may direct that the development order planning permission will not apply to the class of or the development in question in that area: GPDO, art. 4(1)].

Such directions are often referred to as "art. 4 directions". Certain art. 4 directions by a planning authority require the approval of the Secretary of State before they can come into force.

Applications for planning permission

Form and content of applications for planning permission

32. Any application to a planning authority for planning permission—
(a) shall be made in such manner as may be prescribed by regulations or by a development order, and
(b) shall include such particulars and be verified by such evidence as may be required by the regulations or the development order or by directions given by the planning authority under the regulations or order.

DEFINITIONS
"development order": ss.30, 277(1).
"planning authority": ss.1(1), 277(1).
"planning permission": s.277(1).

GENERAL NOTE
Form and content of application for planning permission: See arts. 3 to 5 of the GDPO.

On the application form the applicant should clearly describe the proposed development so that the nature of the proposal is clear to and does not mislead any member of the public. If the applicant does not do this he risks obtaining planning permission for only part of his proposed development: See *Cumming v. Secretary of State for Scotland*, 1992 S.C. 463.

Regulations or development order: For enactment procedure see s.275.

Planning permission for development already carried out

33.—(1) On an application made to a planning authority, the planning permission which may be granted includes planning permission for development carried out before the date of the application.
(2) Subsection (1) applies to development carried out—
(a) without planning permission,
(b) in accordance with planning permission granted for a limited period, or
(c) without complying with some condition subject to which planning permission was granted.
(3) Planning permission for such development may be granted so as to have effect from—
(a) the date on which the development was carried out, or
(b) if it was carried out in accordance with planning permission granted for a limited period, the end of that period.

DEFINITIONS
"planning authority": ss.1(1), 277(1).
"planning permission": s.277(1).
"planning permission granted for a limited period": ss.41(3), 277(1).

GENERAL NOTE
Origin of section: It was introduced by Sched. 13, para. 8 of the Planning and Compensation Act 1991 (c.34).

Publicity for applications

Publication of notices of applications

34.—(1) Subject to subsection (2), regulations or a development order may provide, either in relation to applications generally or in relation to applications of a class or classes prescribed in the regulations or order, that—

  (a) any such application shall have been notified to such persons or classes of person, and in such manner, as may be so prescribed;

  (b) any such application shall have been advertised, either in a local newspaper or on the land to which the application relates, or both, in such a manner and for such a period or on such a number of occasions as may be so prescribed;

  (c) any newspaper advertisement required by virtue of paragraph (b) shall be placed by the planning authority to whom the application is made;

  (d) the planning authority may recover from the applicant the cost incurred by them in arranging any such advertisement;

  (e) any such application shall be accompanied by such certificates as to compliance with the requirements of provisions made under paragraphs (a) and (b) as may be so prescribed;

  (f) the applicant shall furnish, at such time and to such persons as may be so prescribed, such information with respect to the application as may be so prescribed;

  (g) no such application shall be entertained unless such further conditions as to payment as may be so prescribed have been complied with;

  (h) no such application shall be determined until after the expiry of any period which may be so prescribed.

(2) The applications mentioned in subsection (1) are—

  (a) applications for planning permission,

  (b) applications for an approval required by a development order, and

  (c) applications for any consent, agreement or approval required by a condition imposed on a grant of planning permission.

(3) If any person knowingly or recklessly—

  (a) issues a notification,

  (b) makes advertisement (other than newspaper advertisement), or

  (c) supplies a certificate,

which purports to comply with provisions made under subsection (1) but which contains a statement which is false or misleading in a material particular, he shall be guilty of an offence.

(4) A person guilty of an offence under this section shall be liable on summary conviction to a fine not exceeding level 3 on the standard scale.

(5) A planning authority shall not entertain any application for planning permission unless any requirements imposed by virtue of this section have been satisfied.

(6) Proceedings for an offence under this section may be brought at any time within the period of 2 years following the commission of the offence.

DEFINITIONS
  "development order": ss.30, 277(1).
  "land": s.277(1).
  "planning authority": ss.1(1), 277(1).
  "planning permission": s.277(1).
  "prescribed": s.277(1).

GENERAL NOTE
Origin of section: This section was introduced by s.1 of and Sched. 13, para. 6 to the Planning and Compensation Act 1991. It replaced the detailed provisions for publicity of applications with an

enabling power to the Secretary of State to make regulations or a development order requiring the applicant and planning authority carry out certain notification and confirmation of notification procedures.

Subs. (1)
The Secretary of State has made a development order in the form of the GDPO. For neighbour notification see the complex provisions in art. 9 of the GDPO.

Notice etc. of applications to owners and agricultural tenants

35.—(1) Regulations or a development order shall make provision—
(a) as to the notice of any application for planning permission to be given to any person (other than the applicant) who at the beginning of the period of 21 days ending with the date of the application was—
    (i) the owner of, or
    (ii) the tenant of any agricultural holding any part of which was comprised in,
any of the land to which the application relates, and
(b) requiring any applicant for such permission to issue a certificate as to the interests in the land to which the application relates or the purpose for which it is used,
and provide for publicising such applications and for the form, content and service of such notices and certificates.

(2) The regulations or order may require an applicant for planning permission to certify, in such form as may be prescribed by the regulations or the order, or to provide evidence, that any requirements of the regulations or the order have been satisfied.

(3) Regulations or an order making any provision by virtue of this section may make different provision for different cases or different classes of development.

(4) A planning authority shall not entertain any application for planning permission unless any requirements imposed by virtue of this section have been satisfied.

(5) If any person—
(a) issues a certificate which purports to comply with any requirement imposed by virtue of this section and contains a statement which he knows to be false or misleading in a material particular, or
(b) recklessly issues a certificate which purports to comply with any such requirement and contains a statement which is false or misleading in a material particular,
he shall be guilty of an offence.

(6) A person guilty of an offence under this section shall be liable on summary conviction to a fine not exceeding level 5 on the standard scale.

(7) In this section—
"agricultural holding" has the same meaning as in the Agricultural Holdings (Scotland) Act 1991; and
"owner" in relation to any land means any person who—
    (a) under the Lands Clauses Acts would be enabled to sell and convey the land to the promoters of an undertaking and includes any person entitled to possession of the land as lessee under a lease the unexpired period of which is not less than 7 years, or
    (b) in the case of such applications as may be prescribed by regulations or by a development order, is entitled to an interest in any mineral so prescribed,
and the reference to the interests in the land to which an application for planning permission relates includes any interest in any mineral in, on or under the land.

(8) Proceedings for an offence under this section may be brought at any time within the period of 2 years following the commission of the offence.

DEFINITIONS
   "agricultural holding": s.35(7).
   "development": ss.26, 277(1).
   "development order": ss.30, 277(1).
   "land": s.277(1).
   "owner": subs. (7).

GENERAL NOTE
Origin of section: It was introduced by the Planning and Compensation Act 1991, s.46(1). It followed the Scottish Development Department consultation paper *"Efficient Planning"* (July 1989) which pointed out that the then procedures, partly in primary and partly in delegated legislation were confusing.

Subs. (1)
   See GDPO, art. 8 and Sched. 3. A certificate signed by the applicant with an error in stating the owner of the land is still a "certificate" for the purposes of this subsection and art. 8 and Sched. 3: *R. v. Bradford-on-Avon Urban District Council ex p. Boulton* [1964] 1 W.L.R. 1136.

Subs. (4)
   If a planning authority entertains an application for planning permission when any require-ments imposed by art. 8 of and Sched. 3 to the GDPO have not been satisfied, then if the failure was not a deliberate or unauthorised (fraudulent) act intended to deceive the authority and the authority had no reason to suspect the failure, the authority's decision will be voidable: *Pollock v. Secretary of State for Scotland,* 1993 S.L.T. 1173, 1177G *per* Lord Cameron of Lochbroom, and see *Lochore v. Moray District Council,* 1992 S.L.T. 16.
   Where the authority's decision is voidable, the court has a discretion whether to annul the decision. For a decision which was annulled see *Main v. Swansea City Council* (1984) 49 P. & C.R. 26.

Subs. (5)
   For what amounts to "recklessly" see *Allan v. Patterson,* 1980 S.L.T. 77.

Subs. (7)
   An "Agricultural holding" is the aggregate of land used for agriculture for trade or business (and other land designated by the Secretary of State as such) comprised in a lease where the tenant is not in any office, appointment or employment under the landlord: Agricultural Hold-ings (Scotland) Act 1991 (c.55), s.1.
   The "Lands Clauses Acts" are the Land Clauses Consolidation (Scotland) Act 1845 (c.19) and the Land Clauses Consolidation Acts Amendment Act 1860 (c.106) and the Acts made under them: Interpretation Act 1978 (c.30), s.5 and Sched. 1.

Registers of applications etc.

   36.—(1) Every planning authority shall keep, in such manner as may be prescribed by regulations or a development order, a register containing such information as may be so prescribed with respect to—
   (a) applications for planning permission and for approval required by the regulations or order made to that authority,
   (b) the manner in which such applications have been dealt with, and
   (c) simplified planning zone schemes relating to zones in the authority's area.
   (2) The regulations or the order may make provision for the register to be kept in two or more parts, each part containing such information relating to applications mentioned in subsection (1)(a) as may be prescribed by the regulations or order.
   (3) The regulations or the order may also make provision—
   (a) for a specified part of the register to contain copies of applications and of any plans or drawings submitted with them, and
   (b) for the entry relating to any application, and everything relating to it, to be removed from that part of the register when the application (including any appeal arising out of it) has been finally disposed of (without prejudice to the inclusion of any different entry relating to it in another part of the register).

(4) Every register kept under this section shall be available for inspection by the public at all reasonable hours.

DEFINITIONS
"planning authority": ss.1(1), 277(1).
"simplified planning zone scheme": s.277(1).

GENERAL NOTE
Subs. (1)
See GPDO, art. 10 and Sched. 5.

Subs. (2)
The Register of Applications is indeed in two parts. In simple terms Pt. I contains copies of applications which have not been finally disposed of, together with related documents. Part II contains lists of information relating to all applications for planning permission, including those which have been disposed of. See GDPO, Sched. 5.

Subs. (3)
See GDPO, Sched. 5.

Subs. (4)
This subsection does not entitle a planning authority to charge a natural person a fee for inspection of the register: *Stirrat Park Hogg v. Dumbarton District Council*, 1996 S.L.T. 1113.

Determination of applications

Determination of applications: general considerations

37.—(1) Where an application is made to a planning authority for planning permission—
    (a) subject to sections 58 and 59, they may grant planning permission, either unconditionally or subject to such conditions as they think fit, or
    (b) they may refuse planning permission.
(2) In dealing with such an application the authority shall have regard to the provisions of the development plan, so far as material to the application, and to any other material considerations.
(3) Subsection (1) has effect subject to sections 34 and 35 and to the following provisions of this Act, and to sections 59(1), 60 and 65 of the Planning (Listed Buildings and Conservation Areas) (Scotland) Act 1997.
(4) The date of the grant or refusal of—
    (a) planning permission,
    (b) an approval required by a development order, or
    (c) any consent, agreement or approval required by a condition imposed on the grant of planning permission,
shall be the date on which the planning authority's decision bears to have been signed on behalf of the authority.

DEFINITIONS
"development order": ss.30, 277(1).
"development plan": ss.24, 277(1).
"planning authority": ss.1(1), 277(1).

GENERAL NOTE
Subs. (1)
"*subject to sections 58 and 59*": Section 58 imposes a presumed condition that the development must be begun not later than five years from the date of the granting of the planning permission. Section 59 imposes presumed conditions on grants of outline planning permission (*e.g.* time limits for approval of reserved matters).

"*subject to such conditions as they think fit*"—Despite the wide terms of this power, it is not unlimited. First, a condition in a planning permission is a provision which in some way qualifies or restricts the starting or extent of the permitted development. Thus mere narrative of the reasons for permitting the development, even if it is labelled a "condition", can not be a condition: *Lowe (David) & Sons v. Musselburgh Town Council*, 1973 S.C. 130, 142 *per* Lord President Emslie.

Secondly, the condition must:

(a) be unambiguous, intelligible (*Lowe (David) & Sons* (above));
(b) be for a planning rather than an ulterior purpose;
(c) fairly and reasonably relate to the permitted development;
(d) be not so unreasonable that no reasonable planning authority would have imposed it (*Grampian Regional Council v. Secretary of State for Scotland*, 1984 S.C. (H.L.) 58, 66 *per* Lord Keith of Kinkel).

(a) Unambiguous and intelligible

Where a condition is meaningless or absurd it is *ultra vires* the imposer of the condition and, if appealed to the court, will be quashed: *Eastwood District Council v. Secretary of State*, 1994 S.L.T. 38. In such a case the court may remit the condition back to the Secretary of State.

(b) For a planning rather than ulterior purpose

A planning purpose is one which relates to the character of the use of the land: *Westminster City Council v. Great Portland Street Estates* [1985] A.C. 661, 670D *per* Lord Scarman. Exceptionally, the personal circumstances of an occupier unrelated to the use of the land may be considered: *Westminster City Council* (above), 670E to G *per* Lord Scarman. Thus a planning condition may restrict the employment of a future occupier of a house to be erected: *Fawcett Properties v. Buckingham County Council* [1961] A.C. 636.

(c) Fairly and reasonably relate to the permitted development

Each development must be looked at individually. That said, in recent years the concept has been applied flexibly to include a wide range of off-site infrastructure provision: *e.g. R. v. Plymouth City Council, ex p. South Devon Co-operative Society* (1993) 67 P. & C.R. 78, *Tesco Stores v. Secretary of State for the Environment* [1995] 2 All E.R. 636.

(d) Not be wholly unreasonable

A planning authority may impose a condition which an applicant can not fulfill without the consent of a third party: *Grampian Regional Council* (above) (condition that a road be closed). Such a condition may be imposed even where it appears to have no reasonable prospects of fulfilment: *Strathclyde Regional Council v. Secretary of State for Scotland*, 1996 S.C. 165, 177A *per* Second Division.

A condition that an applicant build a road to serve development not in the application may be wholly unreasonable: *Hall & Co. v. Shoreham-by-Sea U.D.C.* [1964] 1 W.L.R. 240.

Scottish Office Circular 8/1986 contains guidance on the imposition of conditions but it does not lay down rules of law on the validity of a condition: *Strathclyde Regional Council* (above), 176E. At the back of the circular there are style conditions, but again these are not guaranteed to be beyond challenge.

For severability of valid conditions from invalid conditions see *North East Fife District Council v. Secretary of State for Scotland*, 1992 S.L.T. 373.

Subs. (2)

The 1947 Act nationalized a landowner's development rights. Unfortunately, where the Act left the landowner having to apply to the planning authority for permission to develop his land, it gave no clear indication, of what he would have to do to obtain it. Equally, the Act gave no clear indication to the planning authority on when it should grant the permission. Until recently, subs. (2) was the only help which the Act gave to both parties. This changed when what is now s.25 came into force. Subsection (2) does not sit easily with s.25. In effect subs. (2) has been largely amended to read, for practical purposes,

"In dealing with such an application, the authority shall determine it in accordance with the development plan unless other material considerations indicate otherwise."

In addition, a planning authority can not grant planning permission for a development which is likely to have a significant effect (either alone or in combination with other plans or projects) on a "European Site" and which is not directly connected with or necessary to the management of the site: Conservation (Natural Habitats, etc.) Regulations 1994 (S.I. 1994 No.2716), reg. 65. A "European Site" is defined in those regulations.

A planning authority can not bind itself by contract to exclude any material consideration: *Stringer v. Minister of Housing and Local Government* [1970] 1 W.L.R. 1281, 1290 *per* Cooke J.

"*material considerations*": These have never been defined in a statute. "Material" means "relevant": *Tesco Stores* (above) at 642b *per* Lord Keith of Kinkel. Case law has established that the following *may* be material considerations in specific cases. The materiality of any one consideration will however vary from case to case. The following is a list of some considerations for general guidance. They are not in any order of importance.

   (i) The development plan—Until s.25 came into force, the development plan was merely one of the material considerations, although it had to be looked at in every case: *Simpson v. Edinburgh Corporation*, 1960 S.C. 313. For the effect of s.25 on the development plan see the general note to s.25

   (ii) a "finalised" but unadopted plan

   (iii) Ministerial circulars

   (iv) Ministerial national planning policy guidelines

   (v) continuing need for existing use

   (vi) developer's private business interests

   (vii) precedent for similar development of neighbouring sites

   (viii) availability of alternative sites

   (ix) environmental impact assessment

   (x) nature conservation designation of site

   (xi) building conservation designation (listing) of site

   (xii) hazardous development

   (xiii) impact on use of nearby land (*e.g.* roads, runways, etc.)

   (xiv) visual impact of development.

Subs. (3)

This suggests that a planning authority has no power at all to decide an application for planning permission unless the GDPO requirements of ss.34 and 35, and the remaining sections of the Act, and ss.59(1), 60, and 65 of the Planning (Listed Buildings and Conservation Areas) (Scotland) Act 1997 have been complied with.

It appears to tie in with ss.34(5) and 35(4), and see general notes to these sections.

Consultations in connection with determination of applications

38.—(1) In determining any application to which section 34(1) applies, the planning authority shall take into account any representations relating to that application which are received by them before the expiry of any period prescribed under subsection (1)(h) of that section.

(2) Where an application for planning permission is accompanied by such a certificate as is mentioned in section 35(1)(b), regulations or a development order may—

  (a) provide that a planning authority shall not determine an application for planning permission before the end of such period as may be prescribed;

  (b) require a planning authority—

     (i) to take into account in determining such an application such representations, made within such period, as may be prescribed, and

     (ii) to give to any person whose representations have been taken into account such notice as may be prescribed of their decision.

(3) Regulations or a development order making any provision by virtue of this section may make different provision for different cases or different classes of development.

(4) Before a planning authority grant planning permission for the use of land as a caravan site they shall, unless they are also the authority with power to issue a site licence for that land, consult the local authority with that power.

(5) In this section "site licence" means a licence under Part 1 of the Caravan Sites and Control of Development Act 1960 authorising the use of land as a caravan site.

DEFINITIONS

   "caravan site": s.277(1).

   "planning authority": ss.1(1), 277(1).

   "land": s.277(1).

   "prescribed": s.277(1).

   "site licence": s.38(5).

GENERAL NOTE
Subs. (1)

Section 34(1) applies to (a) applications for planning permission; (b) applications for approval required by a development order; (c) applications for consent or approval required by a planning condition: s.34(2).

For the period prescribed under s.34(1)(h) see GDPO, art. 14.

Subs. (2)

"*certificate mentioned in section 35(1)(b)*": this is the certificate of ownership which an applicant who is not an owner has to obtain. See the general note to s.35.

Power of planning authority to decline to determine applications

39.—(1) A planning authority may decline to determine an application for planning permission for the development of any land if—

 (a) within the period of 2 years ending with the date on which the application is received, the Secretary of State has refused a similar application referred to him under section 46 or has dismissed an appeal against the refusal of a similar application, and

 (b) in the opinion of the authority there has been no significant change since the refusal or, as the case may be, dismissal mentioned in paragraph (a) in the development plan, so far as material to the application, or in any other material considerations.

(2) For the purposes of this section an application for planning permission for the development of any land shall be taken to be similar to a later application only if the development and the land to which the applications relate are in the opinion of the planning authority the same or substantially the same.

(3) The reference in subsection (1)(a) to an appeal against the refusal of an application includes an appeal under section 47(2) in respect of an application.

DEFINITIONS
   "development": ss.26, 277(1).
   "development plan": ss.24, 277(1).
   "land": s.277(1).
   "planning authority": ss.1(1), 277(1).

GENERAL NOTE
Subs. (1)

The purpose of this section is to prevent developers from grinding down planning authorities by repeated applications. It is however important to note that it only comes into play when the earlier refusal of the application was ultimately by the Secretary of State. If the planning authority refused the earlier application but the applicant did not appeal, he may instantly present a fresh application which the authority may not decline to consider.

A referral to the Secretary of State under s.46(1) is commonly referred to as a "calling in". A "similar application" is defined in subs. (2).

Before a planning authority may decline to decide an application for planning permission,

 (a) the application must be similar to an earlier application which, within two years before receipt of the application, was refused by the Secretary of State after call in or dismissed by him on appeal; and

 (b) the development plan and any other material considerations considered in the earlier application have not changed significantly since the date of refusal or dismissal.

For what is meant by "similarity" see below.

Subs. (2)

In short this subsection states that "similar" means "the same or substantially the same". Usually there will be some difference between the applications. What then does "substantially the same" mean? In answering the question, the planning authority must look to all the considerations including physical and other changes between the development first proposed and the development later proposed and whether the same planning considerations apply: *Noble Organization (The) v. Falkirk District Council*, 1993 S.C. 221, 230D–E *per* Extra Division.

Subs. (3)
An appeal under s.47(2) is an appeal against the planning authority's failure to intimate to the applicant (a) their decision on the application, (b) their declinature to consider the application, or (c) the Secretary of State's calling in of the application: ss.39(3) and 47(2).

Assessment of environmental effects

40.—(1) The Secretary of State may by regulations make provision about the consideration to be given, before planning permission for development of any class specified in the regulations is granted, to the likely environmental effects of the proposed development.

(2) The regulations—
(a) may make the same provision as, or provision similar or corresponding to, any provision made, for the purposes of any Community obligation of the United Kingdom about the assessment of the likely effects of development on the environment, under section 2(2) of the European Communities Act 1972, and
(b) may make different provisions for different classes of development.

(3) Where a draft of regulations made in exercise both of the power conferred by this section and the power conferred by section 2(2) of the European Communities Act 1972 is approved by resolution of each House of Parliament, no statutory instrument containing such regulations shall be subject to annulment by virtue of section 275(3).

DEFINITIONS
"development": ss.26, 277(1).

GENERAL NOTE
Origin of section: This was introduced by s.48 of the Planning and Compensation Act 1991 (c.34). The purpose was to enable ministers to extend the categories of development for which an applicant for planning permission has to obtain an environmental statement on the likely significant effect of the development on the physical, natural, and human environment. The categories of development remain imposed by the Environmental Assessment (Scotland) Regulations 1988 (S.I. 1988 No.1221) which implement Council Directive 85/337/EEC.

Subs. (2)
A "Community obligation" is an obligation created by or under the treaties listed in s.1(2) of the European Communities Act 1972 (c.68): Interpretation Act 1978, s.5, and Sched. 1; and European Communities Act 1972, s.1(2) and Sched. 1.
The "United Kingdom" is Great Britain and Northern Ireland: Interpretation Act 1978, s.5 and Sched. 1. The Act of Union 1707 provides that Great Britain includes Scotland.
Section 2(2) of the European Communities Act 1972 is a general enabling provision which enables Her Majesty by Order in Council, and a minister designated by Order in Council, to implement a U.K. obligation under the treaties or an E.C. directive, by U.K. subordinate legislation. It is frequently used.

Subs. (3)
As the U.K. can not refuse to make law to implement an E.C. directive, Parliament has no veto over subordinate legislation for that purpose. For regulations made under this section or s.2(2) of the European Communities Act 1972, the provision for annulment under s.275 is therefore irrelevant.

Conditional grant of planning permission

41.—(1) Without prejudice to the generality of section 37(1) to (3), conditions may be imposed on the grant of planning permission under that section—
(a) for regulating the development or use of any land under the control of the applicant (whether or not it is land in respect of which the application was made) or requiring the carrying out of works on any such land, so far as appears to the planning authority to be expedient for the

purposes of or in connection with the development authorised by the permission;
  (b) for requiring the removal of any buildings or works authorised by the permission, or the discontinuance of any use of land so authorised, at the end of a specified period, and the carrying out of any works required for the reinstatement of land at the end of that period.
  (2) Conditions may not be imposed by a planning authority under subsection (1)(a) for regulating the development or use of any land within the area of another planning authority except with the consent of that authority.
  (3) Subject to paragraph 1(6)(a) of Schedule 3, a planning permission which is granted subject to such a condition as is mentioned in subsection (1)(b) is in this Act referred to as "planning permission granted for a limited period".
  (4) Where—
  (a) planning permission is granted for development consisting of or including the carrying out of building or other operations subject to a condition that the operations shall be commenced not later than a time specified in the condition, and
  (b) any building or other operations are commenced after the time so specified,
the commencement and carrying out of those operations do not constitute development for which that permission was granted.
  (5) Subsection (4)(a) does not apply to a condition attached to the planning permission by or under section 58 or 59.
  (6) Part I of Schedule 3 shall have effect for the purpose of making special provision with respect to the conditions which may be imposed on the grant of planning permission for development consisting of the winning and working of minerals.

DEFINITIONS
  "buildings or works": s.277(1).
  "development": ss.26, 277(1).
  "land": s.277(1).
  "minerals": s.277(1).
  "planning authority": ss.1(1), 277(1).
  "use": s.277(1).

GENERAL NOTE
Subs. (4)
  This subsection does not apply—
  (a) to the five (or greater or lesser) year commencement for development condition imposed by or under s.58, nor
  (b) to the conditions attached to outline permission imposed by or under s.59: s.41(5).

Subs. (6)
  Except where a planning authority specifies a longer or shorter period, a grant after February 21, 1982 of planning permission for (a) the winning and working of minerals; or (b) involving the depositing of mineral waste is automatically subject to a condition that the winning, working, or depositing must cease no later than 60 years beginning with the date of the permission: Sched. 3, para. 1. A grant of permission before February 22, 1982 has to cease no later than February 21, 2042: Sched. 3, para. 1(3).
  When granting such permission the planning authority may also impose conditions requiring the restoration of the site with soil or soil-making material (a "restoration condition") and the bringing of the restored site to a required standard for agriculture, forestry, or amenity (an "aftercare condition"): See Sched. 3, paras. 1 to 6.

Determination of applications to develop land without compliance with conditions previously attached

  42.—(1) This section applies, subject to subsection (4), to applications for planning permission for the development of land without complying with conditions subject to which a previous planning permission was granted.

(2) On such an application the planning authority shall consider only the question of the conditions subject to which planning permission should be granted, and—

    (a) if they decide that planning permission should be granted subject to conditions differing from those subject to which the previous permission was granted, or that it should be granted unconditionally, they shall grant planning permission accordingly;

    (b) if they decide that planning permission should be granted subject to the same conditions as those subject to which the previous permission was granted, they shall refuse the application.

(3) Special provision may be made with respect to such applications—

    (a) by regulations under section 32 as regards the form and content of the application, and

    (b) by a development order as regards the procedure to be followed in connection with the application.

(4) This section does not apply if the previous permission was granted subject to a condition as to the time within which the development to which it related was to be begun, and that time has expired without the development having been begun.

DEFINITIONS
"development": ss.26, 277(1).
"development order": ss.30, 277(1).
"land": s.277(1).
"planning authority": ss.1(1), 277(1).
"planning permission": s.277(1).
"use": s.277(1).

GENERAL NOTE
Subs. (1)
    Despite the oblique wording, the purpose of this section is to enable the recipients of conditional planning permission to apply to the planning authority to change the conditions. It was introduced by s.53 of and Sched. 11, para. 31 to the Housing and Planning Act 1986 (c.63).

Subs. (2)
    An application has to be in writing and to give sufficient information to enable the planning authority to identify the grant whose condition the applicant wishes to have varied: GPDO, art. 5(2).

    For a list of circumstances when the application can by made see *Allied London Property Investment v. Secretary of State for the Environment* (1996) 72 P. & C.R. 327, 332. Despite the apparent power to grant unconditional permission, the planning authority has no power to derogate from the conditions of time limits imposed by ss.58 and 59: *R. v. Secretary of State for the Environment ex p. Corby Borough Council* [1994] 1 P.L.R. 38, and *R. v. London Docklands Development Corporation* (1996) 73 P. & C.R. 199. "Conditions" which may be changed include the reserved matters in an outline permission even where the applicant has failed to bring any application for approval of those matters within the time limit imposed by s.59.

Directions etc. as to method of dealing with applications

    43.—(1) Provision may be made by regulations or a development order for regulating the manner in which applications for planning permission to develop land are to be dealt with by planning authorities, and in particular—

    (a) for enabling the Secretary of State to give directions restricting the grant of planning permission by the planning authority, either indefinitely or during such period as may be specified in the directions, in respect of any such development, or in respect of development of any such class, as may be so specified;

    (b) for authorising the planning authority, in such cases and subject to such conditions as may be prescribed by the regulations or the order, or by directions given by the Secretary of State under the regulations or the order, to grant planning permission for development which does not accord with the provisions of the development plan;

(c) for requiring the planning authority, before granting or refusing planning permission for any development, to consult such authorities or persons as may be prescribed by the regulations or the order or by directions given by the Secretary of State under the regulations or the order;

(d) for requiring the planning authority to give to any applicant for planning permission, within such time as may be prescribed by the regulations or the order, such notice as may be so prescribed as to the manner in which his application has been dealt with;

(e) for requiring the planning authority to give any applicant for any consent, agreement or approval required by a condition imposed on a grant of planning permission notice of their decision on his application, within such time as may be so prescribed;

(f) for requiring the planning authority to give to the Secretary of State and to such other persons as may be prescribed by or under the regulations or the order, such information as may be so prescribed with respect to applications for planning permission made to the authority, including information as to the manner in which any such application has been dealt with.

(2) Paragraphs (d) and (f) of subsection (1) shall apply in relation to applications for an approval required by regulations under this Act or a development order as they apply in relation to applications for planning permission.

DEFINITIONS
 "development order": ss.30, 277(1).
 "land": s.277(1).
 "planning authorities": ss.1(1), 277(1).

GENERAL NOTE
Subs. (1)
 See the GPDO.

Effect of planning permission

44.—(1) Without prejudice to the provisions of this Part as to the duration, revocation or modification of planning permission, any grant of planning permission to develop land shall (except in so far as the permission otherwise provides) enure for the benefit of the land and of all persons for the time being interested in it.

(2) Where planning permission is granted for the erection of a building, the grant of permission may specify the purposes for which the building may be used.

(3) If no purpose is so specified, the permission shall be construed as including permission to use the building for the purpose for which it is designed.

DEFINITIONS
 "building": s.277(1).
 "erection": s.277(1).
 "land": s.277(1).
 "planning permission": s.277(1).
 "use": s.277(1).

GENERAL NOTE
Subs. (1)
 Except where it states otherwise, the development right contained in the planning permission runs with the land to which it relates. So, one owner may obtain outline permission and then transfer ownership to another owner who may apply for the approval of the reserved matters in

the permission: See *e.g. Inverclyde District Council v. Secretary of State for Scotland*, 1982 S.C. 64 (H.L.).

A deemed planning permission obtained by a planning authority to develop its own land enures only for the benefit of the authority and not for the benefit of the land: Town and Country Planning (Development by Planning Authorities) Regulations 1981 (S.I. 1981 No. 829), reg. 7.

Abandonment and prescription of planning permission: Provided the development right is capable of being implemented according to its terms, it can not be abandoned: *Pioneer Aggregates (U.K.) v. Secretary of State for the Environment* [1985] A.C. 132. The sub-division of the land to which a permission relates, or the change of its physical features may render it incapable of being implemented and abandoned.

The reasoning behind the *Pioneer Aggregates* case was that since the Town and Country Planning Act is a special code for development, the ordinary private law rules relating to abandonment of rights do not apply. Although there are no reported cases on whether the right under planning permission prescribes under the Prescription and Limitation (Scotland) Act 1973 (c.52), the reasoning in *Pioneer Aggregates* suggests that the 1973 Act does not make planning permission prescribe.

"persons": see the General Note to s.8.

Subs. (2)
The grant may specify the purpose for the building by simply having an adjective in front of the word "building". Thus a grant allowing erection of an "agricultural cottage" was held to specify that it had to be used by an agricultural worker: *Wilson v. West Sussex County Council* [1963] 2 Q.B. 764.

Subs. (3)
The "purpose for which it is designed" includes purposes ancillary or incidental to the purpose of design: *Peake v. Secretary of State for Wales* (1971) 22 P. & C.R. 889, 893. Equally, where a "building" as defined in the Act, is attached to a larger building, the building may still be used for the existing use of the main building: *Wood v. Secretary of State for the Environment* [1973] 1 W.L.R. 707, 713A *per* Widgery L.J.

Duty to draw attention to certain provisions for benefit of disabled

45.—(1) This section applies to the grant by the planning authority of an application for planning permission in respect of any building or premises in relation to which a duty is imposed by any of sections 4, 5 and 7 to 8A of the Chronically Sick and Disabled Persons Act 1970 (facilities at premises open to the public to include, where reasonable and practicable; provision for the needs of the disabled etc.).

(2) The planning authority shall, when granting the planning permission, draw the attention of the person to whom the permission is granted to the section or sections in question.

DEFINITIONS
"building": s.277(1).
"planning authority": ss.1(1), 277(1).
"planning permission": s.277(1).

GENERAL NOTE
Subs. (1)
The use of the words "in respect of" suggest that this section applies to user development as well as operational development.

The building or premises affected are:
  (a) those to which the public are to be admitted whether or not on payment;
  (b) university buildings including halls;
  (c) university colleges;
  (d) central institutions;
  (e) schools;
  (f) offices, shops, or railway premises to which the Offices, Shops and Railway Premises Act 1963 (c.41) applied before its recent repeal;
  (g) factories as defined in s.175 of the Factories Act 1961 (c.34) where persons are employed to work.

Secretary of State's powers in relation to planning applications and decisions

Call-in of applications by Secretary of State

46.—(1) The Secretary of State may give directions requiring any such applications as are mentioned in section 34(2) to be referred to him instead of being dealt with by planning authorities.

(2) A direction under this section—

(a) may be given either to a particular planning authority or to planning authorities generally, and

(b) may relate either to a particular application or to applications of a class specified in the direction.

(3) Any application in respect of which a direction under this section has effect shall be referred to the Secretary of State.

(4) Subject to subsection (5), where an application is referred to the Secretary of State under this section—

(a) sections 33, 37(1) to (3), 38(1) to (3), 41(1) and (2) and 42 and paragraphs 2 to 6 of Schedule 3 shall apply, with any necessary modifications, as they apply to an application which falls to be determined by the planning authority, and

(b) regulations or a development order may apply, with or without modifications, to an application so referred any requirements imposed by the regulations or order by virtue of section 34 or 35.

(5) Before determining an application referred to him under this section, the Secretary of State shall, if either the applicant or the planning authority so wish, give to each of them an opportunity of appearing before, and being heard by, a person appointed by the Secretary of State for the purpose.

(6) Subsection (5) does not apply to an application for planning permission referred to a Planning Inquiry Commission under section 69.

(7) The decision of the Secretary of State on any application referred to him under this section shall be final.

DEFINITIONS

"development order": ss.30, 277(1).
"planning authority": ss.1(1), 277(1).
"planning permission": s.277(1).

GENERAL NOTE

Subs. (1)

The giving of a direction requiring a referral by the planning authority is commonly referred to as a "calling in". The following applications may be called in:

(a) application for planning permission;

(b) application for approval required by a development order;

(c) application for any consent, agreement, or approval required by a condition imposed on a grant of planning permission.

"may give directions"—In deciding whether to call in an application the Secretary of State must not concern himself with the merits of the application: *Lakin v. Secretary of State for Scotland*, 1988 S.L.T. 780, 791L *per* L.C.J. Ross, and 799F *per* Mayfield L.J. Usually the Secretary of State will consider whether the application raises issues which have a significance beyond the district of the planning authority *e.g.* it may affect the district of another planning authority or raise "national issues".

Subs. (4)

This places the Secretary of State in the shoes of the planning authority.

Subs. (5)

The applicant or the planning authority are entitled to appear and be heard by a person appointed by the Secretary of State. In practice this person will be a civil servant from the Scottish Office Inquiry Reporters Unit ("SOIRU") known as a reporter.

Subs. (7)

In many ways the position of the called in application is the same as an application which has been appealed to the Secretary of State. One of these is that the Secretary of State's decision is final, subject to an application to the Court of Session under s.239.

Right to appeal against planning decisions and failure to take such decisions

47.—(1) Where a planning authority—

(a) refuse an application for planning permission or grant it subject to conditions,

(b) refuse an application for any consent, agreement or approval of that authority required by a condition imposed on a grant of planning permission or grant it subject to conditions, or

(c) refuse an application for any approval of that authority required under a development order or grant it subject to conditions,

the applicant may appeal to the Secretary of State.

(2) A person who has made such an application may also appeal to the Secretary of State if the planning authority have not given to the applicant—

(a) notice of their decision the application,

(b) notice that they have exercised their power under section 39 to decline to determine the application, or

(c) notice that the application has been referred to the Secretary of State in accordance with directions given under section 46,

within such period as may be prescribed by regulations or a development order or within such extended period as may at any time be agreed upon in writing between the applicant and the authority.

(3) Any appeal under this section shall be made by notice served within such time and in such manner as may be prescribed by regulations or a development order.

(4) The time prescribed for the service of such a notice must not be less than—

(a) 28 days from the date of the notification of the decision, or

(b) in the case of an appeal under subsection (2), 28 days from the end of the period prescribed as mentioned in subsection (2) or, as the case may be, the extended period mentioned in that subsection.

(5) For the purposes of the application of sections 48(1) and 218(1)(b) and paragraph 2(2)(c) of Schedule 16 in relation to an appeal under subsection (2), the authority shall be deemed to have decided to refuse the application in question.

Definitions

"development": ss.26, 277(1).
"development order": ss.30, 277(1).
"planning authority": ss.1(1), 277(1).
"planning permission": s.277(1).
"prescribed": s.277(1).

General Note

Subs. (2)

The period prescribed is two months from—

(a) the date when the application and any certificates required by the Act were lodged with the planning authority; or

(b) if the applicant has to pay a fee or the cost of advertisement of the application in a newspaper, the date when the applicant has completed lodging the application, the requisite certificates with and paid the fee or cost to the planning authority: GDPO, art. 14(2) and (3).

Subs. (3)

The applicant must give notice of appeal on a form obtained from the Secretary of State: GDPO, art. 23(4).

The form and its enclosures—On the form the applicant should state his grounds of appeal: GDPO, art. 23(4). The form should be accompanied by—
 (1) (a) the application;
   (b) the documents submitted with it;
   (c) any notice of decision or determination appealed against; and
   (d) all other relevant correspondence with the planning authority;
 (2) the certificate under s.35(1) (as to the interests in the land, etc.); and
 (3) a statement whether the applicant wishes the appeal to be determined on the basis of written submissions without the holding of a public inquiry.

Methods of service are—
  (a) by personal delivery;
  (b) in a prepaid registered letter or by recorded delivery addressed to the Secretary of State for Scotland; or the principal office of the planning authority: See s.271.

Subs. (4)
 The applicant must (a) within six months of the decision or determination, or (b) within six months of the expiry of the prescribed (see above) period for the planning authority to give notice of its decision, serve—
  (i) the notice of appeal and its enclosures on the Secretary of State; and
  (ii) a copy of the notice of appeal on the planning authority.

Subs. (5)
 This provision enables the Secretary of State to decide an application which has been appealed because the planning authority have failed to make a timeous decision.

Determination of appeals

 48.—(1) On an appeal under section 47 the Secretary of State may—
 (a) allow or dismiss the appeal, or
 (b) reverse or vary any part of the decision of the planning authority (whether the appeal relates to that part of it or not),
and may deal with the application as if it had been made to him in the first instance.
 (2) Before determining the appeal the Secretary of State shall, if either the appellant or the planning authority so wish, give each of them an opportunity of appearing before and being heard by a person appointed by the Secretary of State for the purpose.
 (3) If the Secretary of State proposes to reverse or vary any part of the decision of the planning authority to which the appeal does not relate, he shall give notice of his intention to the planning authority and to the appellant and shall give each of them an opportunity of making representations about his proposals.
 (4) Subsection (2) does not apply to an appeal referred to—
 (a) a Planning Inquiry Commission under section 69, or
 (b) a Joint Planning Inquiry Commission under section 70.
 (5) Subject to subsection (2), in relation to an appeal to the Secretary of State under section 47—
 (a) sections 33, 37(1) to (3), 38(1) to (3), 41(1) and (2) and 42 and Part I of Schedule 3 shall apply, with any necessary modifications, as they apply in relation to an application for planning permission which falls to be determined by the planning authority, and
 (b) regulations or a development order may apply, with or without modifications, to such an appeal any requirements imposed by the regulations or order by virtue of section 34 or 35.
 (6) The decision of the Secretary of State on such an appeal shall be final.
 (7) If, before or during the determination of such an appeal in respect of an application for planning permission to develop land, the Secretary of State forms the opinion that, having regard to the provisions of sections 37 and

41(1) and (2), any regulations made under this Act in that regard and of any development order and any directions given under such regulations or order, planning permission for that development—

(a) could not have been granted by the planning authority, or

(b) could not have been granted otherwise than subject to the conditions imposed,

he may decline to determine the appeal or to proceed with the determination.

(8) If at any time before or during the determination of an appeal under section 47 it appears to the Secretary of State that the appellant is responsible for undue delay in the progress of the appeal, he may—

(a) give the appellant notice that the appeal will be dismissed unless the appellant takes, within the period specified in the notice, such steps as are specified in the notice for the expedition of the appeal, and

(b) if the appellant fails to take those steps within that period, dismiss the appeal accordingly.

(9) Schedule 4 applies to appeals under section 47, including appeals under that section as applied by or under any other provision of this Act.

DEFINITIONS

"development": ss.26, 277(1).

"development order": ss.30, 277(1).

"land": s.277(1).

"planning authority": ss.1(1), 277(1).

"planning permission": s.277(1).

GENERAL NOTE

Subss. (1) and (9)

Appeals may be determined by either the Secretary of State himself or by a person appointed by him (known as a "reporter"). This is the effect of Sched. 4, para. 1 which has enabled the Secretary of State to make the Town and Country Planning (Determination of Appeals by Appointed Persons) (Prescribed Classes) Regulations 1987 (S.I. 1987 No.1531); Sched. 4, para. 1. Under these regulations the Secretary of State has delegated the determination of, subject to one exception, all appeals under s.47 to reporters: 1987 Regs, reg. 3 and Sched. 1. The exception covers appeals by statutory undertakers (as defined in the regulations) in relation to land specified in s.218(2); 1987 Regs, reg. 4 and Sched. 2.

The Secretary of State, may reclaim jurisdiction to determine a specific appeal or a class of appeals; Sched. 4, paras. 1(2) and 3(1).

Most appeals are thus decided by the reporters, although formally their decisions are treated as being of the Secretary of State; Sched. 4, para. 2(6). Today, reporters are full time civil servants who are members of the Scottish Office Inquiry Reporters Unit ("SOIRU"), although there is no statutory requirement that they be so. Indeed at one time part-time reporters were not infrequent and included advocates.

Subsections 1, 3, 5, and 8 apply to reporters as they do to the Secretary of State: Sched. 4, para. 2(1)(a).

Subs. (2)

This applies only to appeals decided by the Secretary of State. It gives the planning authority and the applicant a right "to appear and be heard" by a person appointed by the Secretary of State (*i.e.* a reporter). The right does not have to be exercised, and the appeal may be determined by written submissions instead. Over 80 per cent of appeals are decided on written submissions. The principal factors in favour of written submissions are cost and speed. The principal factors against are lack of the chance to discuss and present complex and important issues, inability to lead persuasive oral evidence and to cross-examine contrary evidence; and a statistically lower success rate.

Where a party has opted for a hearing and a local inquiry has been called, and all parties and the Secretary of State agree, the appeal may be dealt with by written submissions: Town and Country Planning (Written Submissions Procedure) (Scotland) Regulations 1990, reg. 3(2). Where a party changes its position in this way it should beware the possibility of being found liable in expenses.

It is understood that new rules for local inquiries have been made and will soon come into force. A detailed discussion of the existing rules is therefore inappropriate.

Simplified planning zones

Simplified planning zones

49.—(1) A simplified planning zone is an area in respect of which a simplified planning zone scheme is in force.

(2) The adoption or approval of a simplified planning zone scheme has effect to grant in relation to the zone, or any part of it specified in the scheme, planning permission—

(a) for development specified in the scheme, or

(b) for development of any class so specified.

(3) Planning permission under a simplified planning zone scheme may be unconditional or subject to such conditions, limitations or exceptions as may be specified in the scheme.

DEFINITIONS

"development": ss.26, 277(1).
"planning permission": s.277(1).
"simplified planning zone": ss.49(1), 277(1).

GENERAL NOTE

Origin: This section and ss.50 to 54 were introduced by the Housing and Planning Act 1986 (c.63). They introduced the automatic granting of planning permission by planning authority designated development order known as a "simplified planning zone scheme". The origin and purpose of simplified planning zones ("SPZs") was noted by Lord Skelmersdale in the committee stage of the Bill in the House of Lords (*Hansard*, H.L., Vol. 480, cols. 533 to 534):

"Whatever SPZs may be, I can not agree with the noble Lord that they are anything to do with enterprise zones. I agree when he says that their initial conception is a result of enterprise zones, but they are significantly different. What exactly are they? I hope that it will help the committee when I say that I have come to see them as local general development orders made by planning authorities, taking into account the particular circumstances of their areas or part of their areas."

Subs. (1)

Certain environmentally sensitive land may not be covered by an SPZ: see s.54. In addition, an SPZ scheme can not grant planning permission for a development which is likely to have a significant effect (either alone or in combination with other plans or projects) on a "European Site" and which is not directly connected with or necessary to the management of the Site: Conservation (Natural Habitats, etc.) Regulations 1994 (S.I. 1994 No.2716), reg. 65. A "European Site" is defined in those regulations. This prohibition applies to development begun both before and after November 9, 1994 when the regulations came into force. There is compensation for developers who did not manage to complete their development before that date.

Subs. (2)

The SPZ must specify—

(a) the development or classes of development for which it grants permission;

(b) the land covered by that development;

(c) any conditions, limitations, or exceptions subject to which permission is granted; and

(d) any other matters which may be prescribed by the Secretary of State's regulations: Sched. 5, para. 1(2).

The format of the SPZ is laid down in Sched. 5, para. 1(1) and in reg. 6 of the Town and Country Planning (Simplified Planning Zone) (Scotland) Regulations 1995 (S.I. 1995 No.2043) (the "SPZ" regs.).

An SPZ ceases to have effect 10 years after the date of its adoption or approval: s.52(1).

Subs. (3)

For use of SPZ to grant limited or conditional planning permission see s.51.

Making of simplified planning zone schemes

50.—(1) Every planning authority shall consider, as soon as practical after 1st October 1987, the question for which part or parts of their district a simplified planning zone scheme is desirable, and then shall keep that question under review.

(2) If as a result of their original consideration or of any such review a planning authority decide that it is desirable to prepare a scheme for any part of their district they shall do so; and a planning authority may at any time decide—

(a) to make a simplified planning zone scheme,

(b) to alter a scheme adopted by them, or

(c) with the consent of the Secretary of State, to alter a scheme approved by him.

(3) Schedule 5 has effect with respect to the making and alteration of simplified planning zone schemes and other related matters.

DEFINITIONS
"planning authority": ss.1(1), 277(1).
"simplified planning zone": ss.49, 277(1).

GENERAL NOTE
Subs. (1)
For government guidance to planning authorities on SPZs see Scottish Office Circular 18/1995.

Subs. (2)
The planning authority may make a scheme—
(a) on its own initiative; or
(b) in compliance with a direction to do so by the Secretary of State following the request by a private person for a new scheme or the alteration or substitution of an existing scheme: Sched. 5, para. 2 and see also para. 11.

Simplified planning zone schemes: conditions and limitations on planning permission

51.—(1) The conditions and limitations on planning permission which may be specified in a simplified planning zone scheme may include—

(a) conditions or limitations in respect of all development permitted by the scheme or in respect of particular descriptions of development so permitted, and

(b) conditions or limitations requiring the consent, agreement or approval of the planning authority in relation to particular descriptions of permitted development.

(2) Different conditions or limitations may be specified for different cases or classes of case.

(3) Nothing in a simplified planning zone scheme shall affect the right of any person—

(a) to do anything not amounting to development, or

(b) to carry out development for which planning permission is not required or for which permission has been granted otherwise than by the scheme.

(4) No limitation or restriction subject to which permission has been granted otherwise than under the scheme shall affect the right of any person to carry out development for which permission has been granted under the scheme.

DEFINITIONS
"development": ss.26, 277(1).
"planning authority": ss.1(1), 277(1).
"planning permission": s.277(1).
"simplified planning zone": ss.49(1), 277(1).

GENERAL NOTE
Subs. (4)
Planning permission granted by an SPZ is unaffected by conditions or limitations attached to other forms of planning permission (*e.g.* grant by an authority on application, grant by development order).

Duration of simplified planning zone scheme

52.—(1) A simplified planning zone scheme shall take effect on the date of its adoption or approval and shall cease to have effect at the end of the period of 10 years beginning with that date.

(2) When the scheme ceases to have effect planning permission under it shall also cease to have effect except in a case where the development authorised by it has been begun.

DEFINITIONS
    "development": ss.26, 277(1).
    "planning permission": s.277(1).
    "simplified planning zone": ss.49(1), 277(1).

GENERAL NOTE
Subs. (2)
    For when development is "begun" see s.27.

Alteration of simplified planning zone scheme

53.—(1) This section applies where alterations to a simplified planning zone scheme are adopted or approved.

(2) The adoption or approval of alterations providing for the inclusion of land in the simplified planning zone has effect to grant in relation to that land, or such part of it as is specified in the scheme, planning permission for development so specified or of any class so specified.

(3) The adoption or approval of alterations providing for the grant of planning permission has effect to grant such permission in relation to the simplified planning zone, or such part of it as is specified in the scheme, for development so specified or development of any class so specified.

(4) The adoption or approval of alterations providing for the withdrawal or relaxation of conditions, limitations or restrictions to which planning permission under the scheme is subject has effect to withdraw or relax the conditions, limitations or restrictions immediately.

(5) The adoption or approval of alterations providing for—

(a) the exclusion of land from the simplified planning zone,

(b) the withdrawal of planning permission, or

(c) the imposition of new or more stringent conditions, limitations or restrictions to which planning permission under the scheme is subject,

has effect to withdraw permission, or to impose the conditions, limitations or restrictions, with effect from the end of the period of 12 months beginning with the date of the adoption or approval.

(6) The adoption or approval of alterations to a scheme does not affect planning permission under the scheme in any case where the development authorised by it has been begun.

DEFINITIONS
    "development": ss.26, 277(1).
    "land": s.277(1).
    "planning permission": s.277(1).
    "simplified planning zone": ss.49(1), 277(1).

GENERAL NOTE
Subs. (1)
    For restrictions on alteration see General Note to s.49.

Subs. (6)
    For when development is "begun" see s.27.

Exclusion of certain descriptions of land or development

54.—(1) The following descriptions of land may not be included in a simplified planning zone—

    (a) land in a conservation area;
    (b) land in a National Scenic Area;
    (c) land identified in the development plan for the area as part of a green belt;
    (d) land in respect of which a notification or order is in force under section 28 or 29 of the Wildlife and Countryside Act 1981 (areas of special scientific interest).

    (2) Where land included in a simplified planning zone becomes land of a description mentioned in subsection (1), that subsection does not have effect to exclude it from the zone.

    (3) The Secretary of State may by order provide that no simplified planning zone scheme shall have effect to grant planning permission—
    (a) in relation to an area of land specified in the order or to areas of land of a description so specified, or
    (b) for development of a description specified in the order.

    (4) An order under subsection (3) has effect to withdraw such planning permission under a simplified planning zone scheme already in force with effect from the date on which the order comes into force, except in a case where the development authorised by the permission has been begun.

DEFINITIONS
    "conservation area": s.277(1).
    "development": ss.26, 277(1).
    "development plan": ss.24, 277(1).
    "land": s.277(1).
    "planning permission": s.277(1).
    "simplified planning zone": ss.49(1), 277(1).

GENERAL NOTE
Subs. (1)
    A "National Scenic Area" is an area of outstanding scenic value and beauty in a national context designated by the Secretary of State in a direction made between January 6, 1987 and April 1, 1992. From April 1, 1992 no new National Scenic Areas may be made: Natural Heritage (Scotland) Act 1991 (c.28), s.6. Every planning authority should have a register of National Scenic Areas: 1972 Act, s.262C(3) (in force between those dates).

Subs. (2)
    This means that the designation of one of the sites mentioned above can not withdraw the planning permission granted by the SPZ.

Subs. (3)
    No SPZ scheme may grant planning permission for:
    (a) developments listed in Sched. 1 to the Environmental Assessment Regulations 1988;
    (b) developments listed in Sched. 2 to those regulations where they would be likely to have significant effects on the environment by virtue of, *inter alia,* their nature or size: Town and Country Planning (Simplified Planning Zone) (Scotland) Order 1995 (S.I. 1995 No.2044).
    The order must be in a statutory instrument which is subject to annulment in pursuance of a resolution of either House of Parliament: s.275(4) and (5).

Enterprise zone schemes

Planning permission for development in enterprise zones

    55.—(1) An order designating an enterprise zone under Schedule 32 to the Local Government, Planning and Land Act 1980 shall (without more) have effect on the date on which the order designating the zone takes effect to grant planning permission for development specified in the scheme or for development of any class so specified.

    (2) The approval of a modified scheme under paragraph 11 of that Schedule shall (without more) have effect on the date on which the modifications

take effect to grant planning permission for development specified in the modified scheme or for development of any class so specified.

(3) Planning permission so granted shall be subject to such conditions or limitations as may be specified in the scheme or modified scheme or, if none are specified, shall be unconditional.

(4) Subject to subsection (5), where planning permission is so granted for any development or class of development the enterprise zone authority may direct that the permission shall not apply in relation to—

(a) a specified development,

(b) a specified class of development, or

(c) a specified class of development in a specified area within the enterprise zone.

(5) An enterprise zone authority shall not give a direction under subsection (4) unless—

(a) they have submitted it to the Secretary of State, and

(b) he has notified them that he approves of their giving it.

(6) If the scheme or the modified scheme specifies, in relation to any development it permits, matters which will require approval by the enterprise zone authority, the permission shall have effect accordingly.

(7) The Secretary of State may by regulations make provision as to—

(a) the procedure for giving a direction under subsection (4), and

(b) the method and procedure relating to the approval of matters specified in a scheme or modified scheme as mentioned in subsection (6).

(8) Such regulations may modify any provision of the planning Acts or any instrument made under them or may apply any such provision or instrument (with or without modification) in making any such provision as is mentioned in subsection (7).

(9) Nothing in this section prevents planning permission being granted in relation to land in an enterprise zone otherwise than by virtue of this section (whether the permission is granted in pursuance of an application made under this Part or by a development order).

(10) Nothing in this section prejudices the right of any person to carry out development apart from this section.

DEFINITIONS

"development": ss.26, 277(1).

"development order": ss.30, 277(1).

"enterprise zone scheme": ss.55, 277(1).

"land": s.277(1).

"planning permission": s.277(1).

GENERAL NOTE

Subs. (1)

The order is similar to the GPDO. It is made by the Secretary of State in the form of a statutory instrument: Local Government, Planning and Land Act 1980 (c.65), Sched. 32, para. 5(3). The order will state when it, and the grant of planning permission, takes effect. See, further, 1980 Act, Sched. 32, para. 5.

An enterprise zone ceases to have effect on the date specified in the order: 1980 Act, Sched. 32, para. 5.

In addition, an enterprise zone scheme can not grant planning permission for a development which is likely to have a significant effect (either alone or in combination with other plans or projects) on a "European Site" and which is not directly connected with or necessary to the management of the site: Conservation (Natural Habitats, etc.) Regulations 1994 (S.I. 1994 No.2716), reg. 65. A "European Site" is defined in those regulations. This prohibition applies to development begun both before and after November 9, 1994 when the regulations came into force. There is compensation for developers who did not manage to complete their development before that date.

Subs. (2)

Although the enterprise zone order is a statutory instrument, the Secretary of State may, after preliminary requirements have been satisfied, modify the order by an unpublished notification to the enterprise zone authority: 1980 Act, Sched. 32, para.11(1). The modification takes effect on the date specified in the Secretary of State's notification.

Subs. (3)
   Cf. s.31(1).

Subs. (4)
   This is similar to s.31(3) except that only the enterprise zone authority, and not the Secretary of State, may direct that the planning permission granted by the zone order shall not apply. The similarity with art. 4 of the GPDO is that the authority needs the prior notified approval of the Secretary of State before it withdraws the permission: s.55(5).

Subs. (9)
   This means, for example, if an enterprise zone scheme gives conditional planning permission for a development, and a development order or an SPZ gives unconditional planning permission, the developer can rely on the unconditional permission. This is confirmed by the terms of subs. (10).

Effect on planning permission of modification or termination of scheme

   56.—(1) Modifications to an enterprise zone scheme do not affect planning permission under the scheme in any case where the development authorised by it has been begun before the modifications take effect.
   (2) When an area ceases to be an enterprise zone, planning permission under the scheme shall cease to have effect except in a case where the development authorised by it has been begun.

DEFINITIONS
   "development": ss.26, 277(1).
   "enterprise zone scheme": ss.55, 277(1).
   "planning permission": s.277(1).

GENERAL NOTE
Subs. (1)
   For when development "begins" see s.27.

Subs. (2)
   An area ceases to be an enterprise zone on the date specified in the order: See General Note to s.55(1). For when development "begins" see s.27.

Deemed planning permission

Development with government authorisation

   57.—(1) Where the authorisation of a government department is required by virtue of an enactment in respect of development to be carried out by a local authority, or by statutory undertakers who are not a local authority, that department may, on granting that authorisation, direct that planning permission for that development shall be deemed to be granted, subject to such conditions (if any) as may be specified in the direction.
   (2) On granting a consent under section 36 or 37 of the Electricity Act 1989 in respect of any operation or change of use that constitutes development, the Secretary of State may direct that planning permission for that development and any ancillary development shall be deemed to be granted, subject to such conditions (if any) as may be specified in the direction.
   (3) The provisions of this Act (except Part XI) shall apply in relation to any planning permission deemed to be granted by virtue of a direction under this section as if it had been granted by the Secretary of State on an application referred to him under section 46.
   (4) For the purposes of this section development is authorised by a government department if—
   (a) any consent, authority or approval to or for the development is granted by the department in pursuance of an enactment,

(b) a compulsory purchase order is confirmed by the department authorising the purchase of land for the purpose of the development,

(c) consent is granted by the department to the appropriation of land for the purpose of the development or the acquisition of land by agreement for that purpose,

(d) authority is given by the department—

(i) for the borrowing of money for the purpose of the development, or

(ii) for the application for that purpose of any money not otherwise so applicable, or

(e) any undertaking is given by the department to pay a grant in respect of the development in accordance with an enactment authorising the payment of such grants,

and references in this section to the authorisation of a government department shall be construed accordingly.

(5) In subsection (2) "ancillary development", in relation to development consisting of the extension of a generating station, does not include any development which is not directly related to the generation of electricity by that station; and in this subsection "extension" and"generating station" have the same meanings as in Part I of the Electricity Act 1989.

DEFINITIONS
"ancillary development": subs. (5).
"development": ss.1(1), 277(1).
"enactment": s.277(1).
"extension": subs. (5).
"generating station": subs. (5).
"government department": s.277(1).
"land": s.277(1).
"local authority": s.277(1).
"planning permission": s.277(1).
"statutory undertakers": s.214(1).
"use": s.277(1).

GENERAL NOTE
Subs. (1)
    This section allows any Minister to grant deemed planning permission for a development which requires his authorisation and which he "authorises". "Authorisation" is defined in subs. (4).
    An example of an enactment which requires authorisation is the Pipelines Act 1962 (c.58), s.5. The Minister's power to grant deemed planning permission is restricted by:

(a) Conservation (Natural Habitats etc.) Regulations 1994, reg. 54,
(b) Electricity and Pipe Line Works (Assessment of Environmental Effects) Regulations 1990 (S.I. 1990 No.4420).

Subss. (2) and (5)
    This is a consent to the installation of an electricity line (exceeding 20 kV) above ground.
    In Pt. I of the Electricity Act 1989 (c.29),

"generating station" means "in relation to a generating station wholly or mainly driven by water, includes all structures and works for holding or channelling water for a purpose directly related to the generation of electricity by that station".

"extension" includes "in relation to a generating station the use by the person operating the station of any land (wherever) situated for a purpose directly related to the generation of electricity by that station.

Subs. (3)
    Part XI provides, *inter alia*, for an appeal to the Court of Session. A challenge to a deemed planning permission under this section must thus be made by judicial review.

Duration of planning permission

General condition limiting duration of planning permission

58.—(1) Subject to the provisions of this section, every planning permission granted or deemed to be granted shall be granted or, as the case may be, be deemed to be granted subject to the condition that the development to which it relates must be begun not later than the expiration of—
  (a) 5 years beginning with the date on which the permission is granted or, as the case may be, deemed to be granted, or
  (b) such other period (whether longer or shorter) beginning with that date as the authority concerned with the terms of the planning permission may direct.
  (2) The period mentioned in subsection (1)(b) shall be a period which the authority consider appropriate having regard to the provisions of the development plan and to any other material considerations.
  (3) If planning permission is granted without the condition required by subsection (1), it shall be deemed to have been granted subject to the condition that the development to which it relates must be begun not later than the expiration of 5 years beginning with the date of the grant.
  (4) Nothing in this section applies to—
  (a) any planning permission granted by a development order,
  (b) any planning permission for any development carried out before the grant of planning permission,
  (c) any planning permission granted for a limited period,
  (d) any planning permission for development consisting of the winning and working of minerals or involving the depositing of mineral waste which is granted (or deemed to be granted) subject to a condition that the development to which it relates must be begun before the expiration of a specified period after—
        (i) the completion of other development consisting of the winning and working of minerals already being carried out by the applicant for the planning permission, or
        (ii) the cessation of depositing of mineral waste already being carried out by the applicant for the planning permission,
  (e) any planning permission granted by an enterprise zone scheme,
  (f) any planning permission granted by a simplified planning zone scheme, or
  (g) any outline planning permission, within the meaning of section 59.

DEFINITIONS
  "authority": s.60(1).
  "development plan": ss.24, 277(1).
  "enterprise zone scheme": ss.55, 277(1).
  "land": s.277(1).
  "minerals": s.277(1).
  "outline planning permission": s.59(1).
  "planning permission": s.277(1).
  "planning permission granted for a limited period": s.277(1).
  "simplified planning zone": ss.49, 277(1).
  "use": s.277(1).

GENERAL NOTE
Origin: The 1947 Act did not contain a statutory implied condition that the permitted development should begin within a specified period. Planning authorities were free to impose express time limit conditions: *Kent County Council v. Kingsway Investments (Kent)* [1971] A.C. 72. This section was introduced originally by the Town and Country (Scotland) Act 1969 (c.30) and came into force for permissions granted after 1969.

Pre-December 8, 1969 permissions—The 1969 Act gave, for those permissions covering development not begun before January 1, 1969, a statutory implied condition of commencement within five years from December 8, 1969: see 1972 Act, Sched. 22, para. 15.

Subss. (1), (2) and (4)
There is no time limit to begin—
(a) development permitted automatically (*e.g.* by the GPDO, an SPZ, an enterprise zone scheme),
(b) subject to Sched. 3, para. 1(6)(a) development described in s.41(1)(b), or
(c) mineral working or mineral waste depositing described in subs. (4)(d).
For time limits for outline planning permission see s.59(2)(b).
For when development begins see s.27. Development not begun within the five year or alternative period is no longer covered by the permission: s.60(4)(a).
In directing an alternative period the planning authority, Secretary of State, or reporter must do so in accordance with the development plan unless material considerations indicate otherwise: ss.60(1), 58(2) and 25.

Outline planning permission

59.—(1) In this section "outline planning permission" means planning permission granted, in accordance with the provisions of regulations or a development order, with the reservation for subsequent approval by the planning authority or the Secretary of State of matters not particularised in the application ("reserved matters").

(2) Subject to the provisions of this section, where outline planning permission is granted for development consisting of or including the carrying out of building or other operations, it shall be granted subject to conditions to the effect—
(a) that, in the case of any reserved matter, application for approval must be made before—
(i) the expiration of 3 years from the date of the grant of outline planning permission,
(ii) the expiration of 6 months from the date on which an earlier application for such approval was refused, or
(iii) the expiration of 6 months from the date on which an appeal against such refusal was dismissed,
whichever is the latest, and
(b) that the development to which the permission relates must be begun not later than—
(i) the expiration of 5 years from the date of the grant of outline planning permission, or
(ii) if later, the expiration of 2 years from the final approval of the reserved matters or, in the case of approval on different dates, the final approval of the last such matter to be approved.

(3) Only one application for approval may be made in a case to which subsection (2)(a) applies after the expiration of the 3 year period mentioned in subsection (2)(a)(i).

(4) If outline planning permission is granted without the conditions required by subsection (2), it shall be deemed to have been granted subject to those conditions.

(5) The authority concerned with the terms of an outline planning permission may in applying subsection (2) substitute, or direct that there be substituted, for the periods of 3 years, 5 years and 2 years referred to in that subsection such other periods respectively (whether longer or shorter) as they consider appropriate.

(6) The authority may also specify, or direct that there be specified, separate periods under subsection (2)(a) in relation to separate parts of the devel-

opment to which the planning permission relates; and, if they do so, the condition required by subsection (2)(b) shall then be framed correspondingly by reference to those parts, instead of by reference to the development as a whole.

(7) In considering whether to exercise their powers under subsections (5) and (6), the authority shall have regard to the provisions of the development plan and to any other material considerations.

DEFINITIONS
    "authority": s.60(1).
    "building": s.277(1).
    "development": ss.26, 277(1).
    "development order": ss.30(2), 277(1).
    "development plan": ss.24, 277(1).
    "final approval": s.60(2).
    "outline planning permission": s.59(1).
    "planning authority": s.277(1).
    "planning permission": s.277(1).
    "reserved matters": s.59(1).

GENERAL NOTE
Subs. (1)
    Outline planning permission may be granted by a planning authority on application to it or by the Secretary of State in a development order.

Subs. (2)
    This imposes two statutory implied conditions on the grant of outline planning permission. The first condition imposes a time limit on the application for the approval of the reserved matters. The second condition imposes a time limit within which the development must be begun.

    "*application for approval [of reserved matters]*"—For form see GDPO, art. 6. An application for ordinary planning permission to carry out development similar to that already permitted in outline may be construed as an application for approval of a reserved matter: *Inverclyde District Council v. Secretary of State for Scotland*, 1982 S.C. (H.L.) 64 and see *Cardiff v. Secretary of State for Wales* (1971) 22 P. & C.R. 718.
    Time limit for application for approval of reserved matters—The planning authority may impose an express time limit which over-rides the statutory implied time limit: s.59(5). They may also specify express limits for different parts of the development: s.59(6). These express time limits must be in accordance with the development plan unless material considerations indicate otherwise: ss.59(7) and 25 and see the General Note to s.25.
    Before the expiry of the three (or other) years from the grant of the outline permission, the applicant may apply more than once for approval of different proposals for the same reserved matters: *Hunterston Development Co. v. Secretary of State for Scotland*, 1991 S.C. 407. After the expiry of that time limit, the applicant may not apply unless an application for approval or appeal from its refusal, still had to be disposed of. If the application or appeal is disposed of after the expiry of the time limit, he may, within six months of the refusal or if appealed, the dismissal of the appeal, make one last fresh application: s.59(2)(a)(ii) and (iii) and (3).
    Time limit within which development must be begun—For when a development "begins" see s.27. The development must be begun by whichever is the later of—
    (a) the expiry of five years from the date of the grant; or
    (b) the expiry of two years from the final approval of the last reserved matter to be approved.

Provisions supplementary to sections 58 and 59

    60.—(1) The authority referred to in section 58(1)(b) and 59(5) is—
    (a) the planning authority or the Secretary of State, in the case of planning permission granted by them,
    (b) in the case of planning permission deemed to be granted under section 57(1), the department on whose direction planning permission is deemed to be granted,
    (c) in the case of planning permission deemed to be granted under section 57(2), the Secretary of State, and

(d) in the case of planning permission granted on an appeal determined under paragraph 1 or 5 of Schedule 4 by a person appointed by the Secretary of State to determine the appeal, that person.

(2) For the purposes of section 59, a reserved matter shall be treated as finally approved—

(a) when an application for approval is granted, or

(b) in a case where the application is made to the planning authority and on an appeal to the Secretary of State against the authority's decision on the application the Secretary of State or a person mentioned in subsection (1)(d) grants the approval, when the appeal is determined.

(3) Where a planning authority grant planning permission, the fact that any of the conditions of the permission are required by the provisions of section 58 or 59 to be imposed, or are deemed by those provisions to be imposed, shall not prevent the conditions being the subject of an appeal under section 47 against the decision of the authority.

(4) In the case of planning permission (whether outline or other) which has conditions attached to it by or under section 58 or 59—

(a) development carried out after the date by which the conditions require it to be carried out shall be treated as not authorised by the permission, and

(b) an application for approval of a reserved matter, if it is made after the date by which the conditions require it to be made, shall be treated as not made in accordance with the terms of the permission.

DEFINITIONS
"development": ss.26, 277(1).
"planning authority": ss.1(1), 277(1).
"planning permission": s.277(1).

GENERAL NOTE
This is simply a consequential provisions section for ss.58 and 59.

Termination of planning permission by reference to time limit: completion notices

61.—(1) This section applies where—

(a) by virtue of section 58 or 59, a planning permission is subject to a condition that the development to which the permission relates must be begun before the expiration of a particular period, that development has been begun within that period, but that period has elapsed without the development having been completed,

(b) development has been begun in accordance with planning permission under a simplified planning zone scheme but has not been completed by the time the area ceases to be a simplified planning zone, or

(c) development has been begun in accordance with planning permission under an enterprise zone scheme but has not been completed by the time the area ceases to be an enterprise zone.

(2) If the planning authority are of the opinion that the development will not be completed within a reasonable period, they may serve a notice ("a completion notice") stating that the planning permission will cease to have effect at the expiration of a further period specified in the notice.

(3) The period so specified must not be less than 12 months after the notice takes effect.

(4) A completion notice shall be served—

(a) on the owner of the land,

(b) on the occupier of the land, and

(c) on any other person who in the opinion of the planning authority will be affected by the notice.

(5) The planning authority may withdraw a completion notice at any time before the expiration of the period specified in it as the period at the expiration of which the planning permission is to cease to have effect.

(6) If they do so they shall immediately give notice of the withdrawal to every person who was served with the completion notice.

DEFINITIONS
"completion notice": s.61(2).
"development": ss.26, 277(1).
"enterprise zone": ss.55, 277(1).
"land": s.277(1).
"owner": s.277(1).
"planning authority": ss.1(1), 277(1).
"simplified planning zone": ss.49, 277(1).

GENERAL NOTE
Subs. (1)
This section applies to—
(a) all (application or development order based) planning permissions granted after December 7, 1969 where the permitted development has begun but not finished within an applicable time limit for commencement,
(b) all SPZ based planning permissions not finished by the expiry of the SPZ,
(c) all enterprise zone based permissions not finished by the expiry of the enterprise zone scheme.

Subs. (2)
For service see s.271.

Subs. (3)
The notice takes effect on being confirmed by the Secretary of State: s.62(1). It follows that the notice should specify the period as "[x months, weeks, or days] after the confirmation of this notice by the Secretary of State".

Subs. (6)
It is unclear whether the planning authority have to serve the notice of withdrawal.

Effect of completion notice

62.—(1) A completion notice shall not take effect unless and until it is confirmed by the Secretary of State.

(2) In confirming a completion notice the Secretary of State may substitute some longer period for that specified in the notice as the period at the expiration of which the planning permission is to cease to have effect.

(3) If, within such period as may be specified in a completion notice (which must not be less than 28 days from its service) any person on whom the notice is served so requires, the Secretary of State, before confirming the notice, shall give him and the planning authority an opportunity of appearing before and being heard by a person appointed by the Secretary of State for the purpose.

(4) If a completion notice takes effect, the planning permission referred to in it shall become invalid at the expiration of the period specified in the notice (whether the original period specified under section 61(2) or a longer period substituted by the Secretary of State under subsection (2)).

(5) Subsection (4) shall not affect any permission so far as development carried out under it before the end of the period mentioned in that subsection is concerned.

DEFINITIONS
"completion notice": s.61(2).
"development": ss.26, 277(1).
"planning authority": ss.1(1), 277(1).
"planning permission": s.277(1).

Subs. (1)

The Secretary of State may not confirm the notice before the expiry of 28 days from the date of service: s.62(3).

Subs. (3)

The persons on whom a completion notice is served are—

  (a) the owner of the land,

  (b) the occupier of the land,

  (c) any other person who the planning authority thought would be affected by the notice: s.61(4).

Power of Secretary of State to serve completion notice

63.—(1) If it appears to the Secretary of State that it is expedient that a completion notice should be served in respect of any land, he may himself serve such a notice under section 61.

(2) A completion notice served by the Secretary of State shall have the same effect as if it had been served by the planning authority.

(3) The Secretary of State shall not serve such a notice without consulting the planning authority.

(4) The provisions of this Act relating to completion notices apply, so far as relevant, to a completion notice served by the Secretary of State as they apply to a completion notice served by a planning authority, but with the substitution for any reference in those provisions to the planning authority of a reference to the Secretary of State, and any other necessary modifications.

DEFINITIONS

  "completion notice": s.61(2).

  "land": s.277(1).

  "planning authority": ss.1(1), 277(1).

GENERAL NOTE

Subs. (4)

This was inserted into the Act on the recommendation of the Scottish Law Commission in their "*Report on the consolidation of certain enactments relating to Town and Country Planning in Scotland*" No.157 of November 1996 (Cmnd. 3644). Section 62(3) suggests that the Secretary of State must confirm his own notice before it comes into effect. See further General Notes to ss.61 and 62.

Variation, revocation and modification of planning permission

Power to vary planning permission

64. Notwithstanding any other provision of this Part, a planning authority may, at the request of the grantee or a person acting with his consent, vary any planning permission granted by them, if it appears to them that the variation sought is not material.

DEFINITIONS

  "planning authority": ss.1(1), 277(1).

  "planning permission": s.277(1).

GENERAL NOTE

"*at the request of the grantee or a person acting with his consent*": This suggests that, despite the fact that planning permission usually runs with the land, the right to request a minor variation lies with the original recipient of the planning permission or a person with his consent.

Power to revoke or modify planning permission

65.—(1) If it appears to the planning authority that it is expedient to revoke or modify any permission to develop land granted on an application made under this Part, the authority may by order revoke or modify the permission to such extent as they consider expedient.

(2) In exercising their functions under subsection (1) the authority shall have regard to the development plan and to any other material considerations.

(3) The power conferred by this section may be exercised—

(a) where the permission relates to the carrying out of building or other operations, at any time before those operations have been completed;

(b) where the permission relates to a change of the use of any land, at any time before the change has taken place.

(4) The revocation or modification of permission for the carrying out of building or other operations shall not affect so much of those operations as has previously been carried out.

(5) Part II of Schedule 3 shall have effect for the purpose of making special provision with respect to the conditions which may be imposed by an order under this section revoking or modifying permission for development consisting of the winning and working of minerals or involving the depositing of refuse or waste materials.

DEFINITIONS

"building": s.277(1).
"development": ss.26, 277(1).
"development plan": ss.24, 277(1).
"functions": s.277(1).
"land": s.277(1).
"minerals": s.277(1).
"planning authority": ss.1(1), 277(1).
"planning permission": s.277(1).
"use": s.277(1).

GENERAL NOTE
Subs. (1)
This "Part" is ss.26 to 75.

Subs. (2)
See s.25.

Subs. (3)
The power to revoke or modify is exercised by a planning authority when it makes the order of revocation or modification: *Caledonian Terminal Investments v. Edinburgh Corporation*, 1970 S.C. 272.

A change of use takes place when the new, permitted use begins: *Caledonian Terminal Investments* (above).

The revocation or modification order takes effect only on (a) confirmation by the Secretary of State (s.66(1)) or (b) if s.67 applies, on the expiry of a period of not less than 28 days from the advertisement of the order.

Subs. (4)
"Previously carried out" appears to refer to the period before the planning authority made the order. The order, if confirmed, may therefore affect operations carried out between the date of the order and the date of its confirmation by the Secretary of State.

Subs. (5)
An order modifying a permission for the winning or working of minerals or involving the depositing of refuse or waste materials, may impose the aftercare and restoration conditions referred to in Sched. 3.

Procedure for section 65 orders: opposed cases

66.—(1) Except as provided in section 67, an order under section 65 shall not take effect unless it is confirmed by the Secretary of State.

(2) Where a planning authority submit such an order to the Secretary of State for confirmation, they shall serve notice on—

(a) the owner of the land affected,

(b) the lessee and the occupier of the land affected, and

(c) any other person who in their opinion will be affected by the order.

(3) The notice shall specify the period within which any person on whom it is served may require the Secretary of State to give him an opportunity of appearing before, and being heard by, a person appointed by the Secretary of State for the purpose.

(4) If within that period such a person so requires, the Secretary of State shall, before he confirms the order, give such an opportunity both to that person and to the planning authority.

(5) The period referred to in subsection (3) must not be less than 28 days from the service of the notice.

(6) The Secretary of State may confirm an order submitted to him under this section without modification or subject to such modifications as he considers expedient.

DEFINITIONS
  "land": s.277(1).
  "owner": s.277(1).
  "planning authority": ss.1(1), 277(1).

GENERAL NOTE
Subs. (1)
  Section 67 provides an alternative confirmation procedure for revocation and modification orders. It can be used where the owner, tenant, and occupier of the land, and all other persons whom the authority thinks may be affected by the order have notified in writing to it that they do not object to the order: s.67(1).

Subs. (2)
  For service see s.271. For the meaning of "person" see General Note to s.8.

Procedure for section 65 orders: unopposed cases

67.—(1) This section applies where—

(a) the planning authority have made an order under section 65, and

(b) the owner, the lessee and the occupier of the land and all persons who in the authority's opinion will be affected by the order have notified the authority in writing that they do not object to it.

(2) Where this section applies, instead of submitting the order to the Secretary of State for confirmation the authority shall advertise in the prescribed manner the fact that the order has been made, and the advertisement must specify—

(a) subject to subsection (4), the period within which persons affected by the order may give notice to the Secretary of State that they wish to have an opportunity of appearing before, and being heard by, a person appointed by the Secretary of State for the purpose, and

(b) subject to subsection (5), the period at the expiration of which, if no such notice is given to the Secretary of State, the order may take effect by virtue of this section without being confirmed by the Secretary of State.

(3) The authority shall also serve notice to the same effect on the persons mentioned in subsection (1)(b).

(4) The period referred to in subsection (2)(a) must not be less than 28 days from the date the advertisement first appears.

(5) The period referred to in subsection (2)(b) must not be less than 14 days from the expiration of the period referred to in subsection (2)(a).

(6) The authority shall send a copy of any advertisement published under subsection (2) to the Secretary of State not more than 3 days after the publication.

(7) If—

(a) no person claiming to be affected by the order has given notice to the Secretary of State under subsection (2)(a) within the period referred to in that subsection, and

(b) the Secretary of State has not directed within that period that the order be submitted to him for confirmation,

the order shall take effect at the expiry of the period referred to in subsection (2)(b), without being confirmed by the Secretary of State as required by section 66(1).

(8) This section does not apply to—

(a) an order revoking or modifying a planning permission granted or deemed to have been granted by the Secretary of State under this Part or Part VI, or

(b) an order modifying any conditions to which a planning permission is subject by virtue of section 58 or 59.

DEFINITIONS

"land": s.277(1).
"owner": s.277(1).
"planning authority": ss.1(1), 277(1).
"planning permission": s.277(1).
"prescribed": s.277(1).

GENERAL NOTE

Subss. (1) and (8)

This method of confirmation does not apply to revocations or modifications of permissions granted by the Secretary of State or a reporter, nor to commencement time limit conditions.

For meaning of "person" see General Note to s.8.

Subs. (2)

The advertisement should be in Form 1 of Sched. 2 to the Town and Country Planning (General) (Scotland) Regulations 1976 (S.I. 1976 No.2022).

Subs. (3)

The notice should be in Form 2 of Sched. 2 to the above 1976 regulations. For service see s.271.

Revocation and modification of planning permission by the Secretary of State

68.—(1) If it appears to the Secretary of State that it is expedient that an order should be made under section 65, he may himself make such an order.

(2) Such an order made by the Secretary of State shall have the same effect as if it had been made by the planning authority and confirmed by the Secretary of State.

(3) The Secretary of State shall not make such an order without consulting the planning authority.

(4) Where the Secretary of State proposes to make such an order he shall serve notice on the planning authority.

(5) The notice shall specify the period (which must not be less than 28 days from the date of its service) within which the authority may require an opportunity of appearing before and being heard by a person appointed by the Secretary of State for the purpose.

(6) If within that period the authority so require, the Secretary of State shall, before making the order, give the authority such an opportunity.

(7) The provisions of this Part and of any regulations made under this Act with respect to the procedure to be followed in connection with the submission by the planning authority of any order under section 65, its confirmation by the Secretary of State and the service of copies of it as confirmed shall have effect, subject to any necessary modifications, in relation to any proposal by the Secretary of State to make such an order by virtue of subsection (1), its making by him and the service of copies of it.

(8) Part II of Schedule 3 shall have effect in relation to orders made by the Secretary of State by virtue of subsection (1) as it has effect in relation to orders made by the planning authority under section 65.

DEFINITIONS
"planning authority": ss.1(1), 277(1).
"planning permission": s.277(1).

GENERAL NOTE
Subs. (1)
An "order under s.65" is an order revoking or modifying a planning permission granted on an application.

Subs. (2)
This means that the order takes effect when the Secretary of State makes it.

Subs. (4)
For service see s.271.

Subs. (5)
The person appointed will usually be a reporter from SOIRU. See the General Note to s.48.

Subs. (7)
Presumably this refers to ss.66(2) and (3) and 67.

Subs. (8)
An order modifying a permission for the winning or working of minerals or involving the depositing of refuse or waste materials, may impose the aftercare and restoration conditions referred to in Sched. 3.

References to Planning Inquiry Commissions

Power to refer certain planning questions to Planning Inquiry Commission

69.—(1) The Secretary of State may constitute a Planning Inquiry Commission to inquire into and report on any matter referred to them under subsection (2) in the circumstances mentioned in subsection (3).

(2) The matters that may be referred to a Planning Inquiry Commission are—

(a) an application for planning permission which the Secretary of State has under section 46 directed to be referred to him instead of being dealt with by a planning authority;

(b) an appeal under section 47 (including that section as applied by or under any other provision of this Act);

(c) a proposal that a government department should give a direction under section 57(1) that planning permission shall be deemed to be granted for development by a local authority or by statutory undertakers which is required by any enactment to be authorised by that department;

(d) a proposal that development should be carried out by or on behalf of a government department.

(3) Any of those matters may be referred to a Planning Inquiry Commission under this section if it appears expedient to the responsible Minister or Ministers that the question whether the proposed development should be permitted to be carried out should be the subject of a special inquiry on either or both of the following grounds—

(a) that there are considerations of national or regional importance which are relevant to the determination of that question and require evaluation, but a proper evaluation of them cannot be made unless there is a special inquiry for the purpose;

(b) that the technical or scientific aspects of the proposed development are of so unfamiliar a character as to jeopardise a proper determination of that question unless there is a special inquiry for the purpose.

(4) Schedule 6, which contains further provisions as to Planning Inquiry Commissions, and as to the meaning of "the responsible Minister or Ministers" in subsection (3) and in that Schedule, shall have effect.

Definitions
"development": ss.26, 277(1).
"development plan": ss.24, 277(1).
"enactment": s.277(1).
"functions": s.277(1).
"government department": s.277(1).
"land": s.277(1).
"local authority": s.277(1).
"planning authority": ss.1(1), 277(1).
"Minister": s.277(1).
"planning permission": s.277(1).
"the responsible Minister or Ministers": s.277(1).
"statutory undertakers": s.214.

General Note
Subs. (1)
    This section, s.70 and Scheds. 6 and 7 were introduced by ss.61 to 66 of the Town and Country (Scotland) Act 1969 (c.30). For the background to the introduction of the planning inquiry commission see L. Edwards and J. Rowan Robinson, *"Whatever Happened to the Planning Inquiry Commission?"* [1980] J.P.L. 307.
    No planning inquiry commission has ever been constituted. For the reasons why see the statement of The Rt. Hon. Peter Shore M.P. the then Secretary of State for the Environment, published at [1978] J.P.L. 731.

Power to refer certain planning questions to Joint Planning Inquiry Commission

70.—(1) The Ministers may constitute a Joint Planning Inquiry Commission to inquire into and report on any matter referred to them under subsection (2).

(2) The matters that may be referred to a Joint Planning Inquiry Commission are the matters which may, under section 101 of the Town and Country Planning Act 1990 or section 69 of this Act, be referred to a Planning Inquiry Commission but which appear to the Ministers to involve considerations affecting both Scotland and England.

(3) In subsections (1) and (2) "the Ministers" means the Secretaries of State for the time being having general responsibility in planning matters in relation to Scotland and in relation to England acting jointly.

(4) Schedule 7, which contains further provisions as to Joint Planning Inquiry Commissions, shall have effect.

Definitions
"Ministers": s.277(1).

Other controls over development

Orders requiring discontinuance of use or alteration or removal of buildings or works

71.—(1) If, having regard to the development plan and to any other material considerations, it appears to a planning authority that it is expedient in the interests of the proper planning of their area (including the interests of amenity)—

 (a) that any use of land should be discontinued or that any conditions should be imposed on the continuance of a use of land, or

 (b) that any buildings or works should be altered or removed,

they may by order—

 (i) require the discontinuance of that use, or

 (ii) impose such conditions as may be specified in the order on the continuance of it, or

 (iii) require such steps as may be so specified to be taken for the alteration or removal of the buildings or works,

as the case may be.

(2) An order under this section may grant planning permission for any development of the land to which the order relates, subject to such conditions as may be specified in the order.

(3) Section 65 shall apply in relation to any planning permission granted by an order under this section as it applies in relation to planning permission granted by the planning authority on an application made under this Part.

(4) The planning permission which may be granted by an order under this section includes planning permission, subject to such conditions as may be specified in the order, for development carried out before the date on which the order was submitted to the Secretary of State under this section.

(5) Planning permission for such development may be granted so as to have effect from—

 (a) the date on which the development was carried out, or

 (b) if it was carried out in accordance with planning permission granted for a limited period, the end of that period.

(6) Where the requirements of an order under this section will involve the displacement of persons residing in any premises, it shall be the duty of the planning authority, in so far as there is no other residential accommodation suitable to the reasonable requirements of those persons available on reasonable terms, to secure the provision of such accommodation in advance of the displacement.

(7) In the case of planning permission granted by an order under this section, the authority referred to in sections 58(1)(b) and 59(5) is the planning authority making the order.

(8) The previous provisions of this section do not apply to the use of any land for development consisting of the winning or working of minerals or involving the deposit of refuse or waste materials except as provided in Schedule 8, and in that Schedule—

 (a) Part I shall have effect for the purpose of making provision as respects land which is or has been so used, and

 (b) Part II shall have effect as respects the registration of old mining provisions.

DEFINITIONS

 "building": s.277(1).
 "building or works": s.277(1).
 "development": ss.26, 277(1).
 "development plan": ss.24, 277(1).
 "land": s.277(1).
 "minerals": s.277(1).
 "planning authority": s.277(1).
 "planning permission": s.277(1).
 "planning permission granted for a limited period": ss.41(3), 277(1).
 "use": s.277(1).

GENERAL NOTE
Subss. (1) and (8)
This section does not apply to land used for the winning or working of minerals or involving the deposit of refuse or waste materials: subs. (8). There is a separate regime for such land, which however has some common features, in Sched. 8.

The "interests of amenity" include future amenity as well as existing amenity: *Re Lamplugh* (1967) 19 P. & C.R. 125. The grounds for an order in paras. (a) and (b) are independent options: *Re Lamplugh* (above).

A discontinuance order takes effect on confirmation by the Secretary of State: s.103(1).

Subss. (2) and (3)
See ss.25 and 37. If the planning authority wish to grant planning permission they must do so in accordance with the development plan unless material considerations indicate otherwise.

Subs. (6)
"Reasonable suitable residential accommodation" may involve temporary bed and breakfast accommodation pending discussion of permanent accommodation: *R. v. East Hertfordshire District Council ex p. Smith*, "The Times", January 25, 1990.

Confirmation by Secretary of State of section 71 orders

72.—(1) An order under section 71 shall not take effect unless it is confirmed by the Secretary of State, either without modification or subject to such modifications as he considers expedient.

(2) Where a planning authority submit an order to the Secretary of State for his confirmation under this section, they shall serve notice—

   (a) on the owner of the land affected,

   (b) on the lessee and the occupier of that land, and

   (c) on any other person who in their opinion will be affected by the order.

(3) The notice shall specify the period (which must not be less than 28 days from the date of its service) within which any person on whom it is served may require the Secretary of State to give him an opportunity of appearing before and being heard by a person appointed by the Secretary of State for the purpose.

(4) If within that period such a person so requires, the Secretary of State shall, before confirming the order, give such an opportunity both to that person and to the planning authority.

(5) Where an order under section 71 has been confirmed by the Secretary of State, the planning authority shall serve a copy of the order on the owner, the lessee and occupier of the land to which the order relates.

DEFINITIONS
   "land": s.277(1).
   "owner": s.277(1).
   "planning authority": ss.1(1), 277(1).
   "planning permission": s.277(1).

GENERAL NOTE
Subs. (1)
This section is very similar to s.66 for revocation or modification orders.

Subss. (2), (3), and (5)
   For "service" see s.271.

Power of the Secretary of State to make section 71 orders

73.—(1) If it appears to the Secretary of State that it is expedient that an order should be made under section 71, he may himself make such an order.

(2) Such an order made by the Secretary of State shall have the same effect as if it had been made by the planning authority and confirmed by the Secretary of State.

(3) The Secretary of State shall not make such an order without consulting the planning authority.

(4) Where the Secretary of State proposes to make such an order he shall serve notice on the planning authority.

(5) The notice shall specify the period (which must not be less than 28 days from the date of its service) within which the authority may require the Secretary of State to give them an opportunity of appearing before and being heard by a person appointed by the Secretary of State for the purpose.

(6) If within that period the authority so require, the Secretary of State shall, before making the order, give the authority such an opportunity.

(7) The provisions of this Part and of any regulations made under this Act with respect to the procedure to be followed in connection with the submission by the planning authority of any order under section 71, its confirmation by the Secretary of State and the service of copies of it as confirmed shall have effect, subject to any necessary modifications, in relation to any proposal by the Secretary of State to make such an order by virtue of subsection (1), its making by him and the service of copies of it.

DEFINITIONS
"planning authority": ss.1(1), 277(1).

GENERAL NOTE
Subss. (4), (7), and (8)
For "service" see s.271.

Review of mineral planning permissions

74.—(1) Schedule 9 (which makes provision as respects the review of old mineral planning permissions) and Schedule 10 (which makes provision as respects the periodic review of mineral planning permissions) shall have effect.

(2) Without prejudice to the generality of sections 30 and 31, a development order may make, in relation to any planning permission which is granted by a development order for minerals development, provision similar to any provision made by Schedule 9 or 10.

(3) In this section and those Schedules "minerals development" means development consisting of the winning and working of minerals, or involving the depositing of mineral waste.

DEFINITIONS
"development": ss.26, 277(1).
"minerals": s.277(1).
"mineral development": subs. (3).

Agreements regulating development or use of land

75.—(1) A planning authority may enter into an agreement with any person interested in land in their district (in so far as the interest of that person enables him to bind the land) for the purpose of restricting or regulating the development or use of the land, either permanently or during such period as may be prescribed by the agreement.

(2) Any such agreement may contain such incidental and consequential provisions (including financial ones) as appear to the planning authority to be necessary or expedient for the purposes of the agreement.

(3) An agreement made under this section with any person interested in land may, if the agreement has been recorded in the appropriate Register of Sasines or, as the case may be, registered in the Land Register of Scotland, be enforceable at the instance of the planning authority against persons deriving title to the land from the person with whom the agreement was entered into.

(4) No such agreement shall at any time be enforceable against a third party who has in good faith and for value acquired right (whether completed by infeftment or not) to the land prior to the agreement being recorded or registered or against any person deriving title from such third party.

(5) Nothing in this section or in any agreement made under it shall be construed—

(a) as restricting the exercise, in relation to land which is the subject of any such agreement, of any powers exercisable by any Minister or authority under this Act so long as those powers are exercised in accordance with the provisions of the development plan, or in accordance with any directions which may have been given by the Secretary of State as to the provisions to be included in such a plan, or

(b) as requiring the exercise of any such powers otherwise than as mentioned in paragraph (a).

DEFINITIONS
"development": ss.1(1), 277(1).
"development plan": ss.24, 277(1).
"land": s.277(1).
"Minister": s.277(1).
"prescribed": s.277(1).
"use": s.277(1).

GENERAL NOTE
Subss. (1) to (3)
The previous sections of this Part provide for compulsory restriction of development. In contrast this section provides for voluntary restriction or regulation of development. "Agreement" implies voluntary consent. This section simply enables planning authorities to enter into agreements with landowners which under the general law of contract they can already do between themselves. A "section 75 agreement" is thus a normal contract, with the added specialities in the section. It is very similar to the real burdens on land imposed by a feu disposition or a deed of conditions. It can in fact be seen as a statutory deed of conditions.

The specialities are as follows—

(a) the land, structure, or erection to be burdened must be within the area of the planning authority,

(b) the landowner must be infeft in the land, structure or erection,

(c) the agreement must be for the purpose of restricting or regulating the development (as defined in s.26) or use of the land,

(d) the restriction or regulation may be permanent or may last during such period prescribed in the agreement,

(e) the agreement may contain such incidental and consequential provisions (including provisions of a financial character) as appear to the planning authority to be necessary or expedient for the purpose of the agreement,

(f) if the agreement is registered in the General Register of Sasines or Land Register of Scotland, the owner's duties will (with the exception noted in subs. (4)) run with the land and be enforceable by the planning authority against the successors of the owner.

With regard to (b), the requirement of infeftment appears to be implicit in the requirement of the person to have an interest enabling him to "bind the land".

With regard to (c), this suggests that the regulation is restricted to what happens on the land rather than off it.

With regard to (d) prescription appears to have been excluded. Possibly through an oversight, the Lands Tribunal for Scotland, unlike its equivalent body in England and Wales, does not have jurisdiction to discharge a s.75 restriction: Conveyancing and Feudal Reform (Scotland) Act 1970 (c.35), s.1. It is even unclear whether a planning authority can unilaterally discharge a s.75 restriction. Common sense suggests that it should.

A planning authority is not entitled to make the grant of planning permission dependent on the applicant entering into a s.75 agreement which has no more than a minimal connection with the proposed development: *Tesco Stores Limited v. Secretary of State for the Environment* [1995] 2 All E.R. 636 at 647, *per* Lord Keith of Kinkel. This is because such a situation would amount to the planning authority selling and the developer buying planning permission, with the s.75 owner's duties as the price. Given that public policy background, it may be arguable that a s.75 agreement entered into against that background, is void as a *pactum illicitum*.

Subs. (5)
This is a puzzling section: See *Windsor and Maidenhead Royal Borough v. Brandrose Investments* [1983] 1 W.L.R. 509.

PART IV

COMPENSATION FOR EFFECTS OF CERTAIN ORDERS, NOTICES ETC.

Compensation for revocation or modification of planning permission

Compensation where planning permission revoked or modified

76.—(1) Where planning permission is revoked or modified by an order under section 65, then if, on a claim made to the planning authority within the prescribed time and in the prescribed manner, it is shown that a person interested in the land—

(a) has incurred expenditure in carrying out work which is rendered abortive by the revocation or modification, or

(b) has otherwise sustained loss or damage which is directly attributable to the revocation or modification,

the planning authority shall pay that person compensation in respect of that expenditure, loss or damage.

(2) For the purposes of this section, any expenditure incurred in the preparation of plans for the purposes of any work, or upon other similar matters preparatory to it, shall be taken to be included in the expenditure incurred in carrying out that work.

(3) Subject to subsection (2), no compensation shall be paid under this section in respect of—

(a) any work carried out before the grant of the permission which is revoked or modified, or

(b) any other loss or damage arising out of anything done or omitted to be done before the grant of that permission (other than loss or damage consisting of depreciation of the value of an interest in land).

(4) In calculating for the purposes of this section the amount of any loss or damage consisting of depreciation of the value of an interest in land, it shall be assumed that planning permission would be granted—

(a) subject to the condition set out in Schedule 12, for any development of a class specified in paragraph 1 of Schedule 11;

(b) for any development of a class specified in paragraph 2 of Schedule 11.

(5) In this Part any reference to an order under section 65 includes a reference to an order under the provisions of that section as applied by section 71(3) and paragraph 1(2) of Schedule 8.

DEFINITIONS
   "development": ss.26, 277(1).
   "land": s.277(1).
   "planning authority": ss.1, 277(1).
   "planning permission": s.277(1).
   "prescribed": s.277(1).

GENERAL NOTE

This section provides for compensation to be payable if planning permission which has been granted is later modified or revoked under s.65. Further examples of compensation for the withdrawal of the rights contained in a planning permission are found in s.77 (compensation for withdrawal of permission formerly granted by a development order) and s.83 (compensation for discontinuance orders). For special provisions as to compensation in relation to minerals see s.84.

The two heads of compensation under this section are as follows:

(a) abortive expenditure (subs. (1)(a)) incurred after the grant of the permission (subs. (3)), including that on preparatory matters such as the preparation of plans (subs. (2)); and

(b) other loss or damage directly attributable to the modification or revocation, arising out of anything done after the grant of the permission (subs. (3)), or arising beforehand in respect of compensation for depreciation (subs. (3)). This may include, for example:

   (i) depreciation (see note below to subs. (4))

   (ii) future business profits (*Hobbs (Quarries) v. Somerset County Council* (1975) 30 P. & C.R. 286; *Hanford v. Oxfordshire County Council* (1952) 2 P. & C.R. 286, L.T.).

Subs. (4)

In calculating compensation for depreciation, it is assumed that planning permission would be granted for the following :

    (a) rebuilding a building in existence before July 1, 1948 or other prescribed date, provided the cubic content of the original building is not substantially exceeded (Sched. 11, para. 1(1)(a) and (b) and Sched. 12);

    (b) works to the interior of a building, or not materially affecting the external appearance, provided the cubic content of the original building is not substantially exceeded (Sched. 11, para. 1(1)(c));

    (c) sub-division of use of a dwellinghouse (Sched. 11, para. 1(2)).

The English equivalent of subs. (4) is to be applied literally (*Colley v. Canterbury City Council* [1993] 1 All E.R. 591 (H.L.)).

In relation to the assessment of compensation under this section, the value of any interest may be a minus quantity (s.87(2)).

"*Prescribed*": see The Town and Country Planning (General) (Scotland) Regulations 1976 (S.I. 1976 No. 2022) reg. 4.

Compensation for refusal or conditional grant of planning permission formerly granted by development order

77.—(1) Where—

    (a) planning permission granted by a development order is withdrawn (whether by the revocation or amendment of the order or by the issue of directions under powers conferred by the order), and

    (b) on an application made under Part III planning permission for development formerly permitted by that order is refused or is granted subject to conditions other than those imposed by that order,

section 76 shall apply as if the planning permission granted by the development order—

        (i) had been granted by the planning authority under Part III, and

        (ii) had been revoked or modified by an order under section 65.

(2) Where planning permission granted by a development order is withdrawn by revocation or amendment of the order, this section applies only if the application referred to in subsection (1)(b) is made before the end of the period of 12 months beginning with the date on which the revocation or amendment came into operation.

(3) This section does not apply in relation to planning permission for the development of operational land of statutory undertakers.

(4) Regulations may provide that subsection (1) shall not apply where planning permission granted by a development order for demolition of buildings or any description of buildings is withdrawn by the issue of directions under powers conferred by the order.

DEFINITIONS

    "building": s.277(1).

    "development": ss.26, 277(1).

    "development order": ss.30, 277(1).

    "operational land": ss.215, 277(1).

    "planning authority": ss.1, 277(1).

    "planning permission": s.277(1).

    "statutory undertakers": ss.214, 277(1).

GENERAL NOTE

This section extends the compensation provisions of s.66 to apply to withdrawal of planning permission granted by a development order (subs. (1)). The section applies where an application for planning permission which would have been permitted under the order is made within 12 months of the withdrawal (subs. (2)) and subsequently refused or granted subject to conditions other than those imposed in the order (subs. (1)).

Subs. (3)

The section does not apply in respect of the operational land of statutory undertakers. For the compensation rights of statutory undertakers see ss.232 to 235.

Subs. (4)

The purpose of this subsection is to ensure that authorities are not being discouraged from proper use of art. 4 directions by fear of compensation liability. The Secretary of State may by regulations disapply the right to compensation under this section in respect of a withdrawal by an art. 4 direction of demolition permission by an art. 4 direction. See the Town and Country Planning (General Permitted Development) (Scotland) Order 1992 (S.I. 1992 No. 223) (as amended), art. 4.

Apportionment of compensation for depreciation

78.—(1) Where compensation which becomes payable under section 76 includes compensation for depreciation of an amount exceeding £20, the planning authority—

(a) if it appears to them to be practicable to do so, shall apportion the amount of the compensation for depreciation between different parts of the land to which the claim for that compensation relates, and

(b) shall give particulars of any such apportionment to the claimant and to any other person entitled to an interest in land which appears to the authority to be substantially affected by the apportionment.

(2) In carrying out an apportionment under subsection (1)(a), the planning authority shall—

(a) divide the land into parts, and

(b) distribute the compensation for depreciation between those parts, according to the way in which different parts of the land appear to the authority to be differently affected by the order or, in a case falling within section 77, the relevant planning decision, in consequence of which the compensation is payable.

(3) Regulations shall make provision—

(a) for enabling the claimant or any other person to whom notice of the planning authority's apportionment has been given in accordance with subsection (1), or who establishes that he is entitled to an interest in land which is substantially affected by such an apportionment, if he wishes to dispute the apportionment, to require it to be referred to the Lands Tribunal,

(b) for enabling the claimant and any other person mentioned in paragraph (a) to be heard by the Tribunal on any reference under this section of that apportionment, and

(c) for requiring the Tribunal, on any such reference, either to confirm or vary the apportionment and to notify the parties of the decision.

(4) On a reference to the Lands Tribunal by virtue of subsection (3), subsections (1) and (2), so far as they relate to the making of an apportionment, shall apply with the substitution, for references to the planning authority, of references to the Lands Tribunal.

(5) In this section—

"compensation for depreciation" means so much of any compensation payable under section 76 as is payable in respect of loss or damage consisting of depreciation of the value of an interest in land, and

"relevant planning decision" means the planning decision by which planning permission is refused, or is granted subject to conditions other than those previously imposed by the development order.

DEFINITIONS

"compensation for depreciation": subs. (5).
"development": ss.26, 277(1).
"development order": ss.30, 277(1).
"land": s.277(1).

"Lands Tribunal": s.277(1).
"planning authority": ss.1, 277(1).
"planning decision": s.277(1).
"planning permission": s.277(1).
"relevant planning decision": subs. (5).

GENERAL NOTE
This section provides that where the compensation under s.76 includes compensation for depreciation of an amount exceeding £20, the planning authority must, where practicable, apportion the compensation for depreciation between different parts of the land (subs. (1)). A compensation notice is recorded in the Register of Sasines or registered in the Land Register and sent to the Secretary of State (s.79), and no further development can be carried out until the compensation is paid or secured to the satisfaction of the Secretary of State (s.80).

Any person notified of the apportionment or whose interest in land is substantially affected by it may appeal to the Lands Tribunal.

"*Prescribed*": see The Town and Country Planning (General) (Scotland) Regulations 1976 (S.I. 1976 No. 2022), reg. 4.

Registration of compensation for depreciation

79.—(1) Where compensation which becomes payable under section 76 includes compensation for depreciation of an amount exceeding £20, the planning authority shall—

    (a) have a notice in the prescribed form stating that such compensation has become payable, specifying the land to which the compensation relates, the amount of the compensation for depreciation and any apportionment of it under section 78, recorded in the appropriate Register of Sasines or registered in the Land Register of Scotland, and

    (b) send a copy of the notice to the Secretary of State.

(2) In relation to compensation for depreciation specified in a notice recorded or, as the case may be, registered under subsection (1), references in this Part to so much of the compensation as is attributable to a part of the land to which the notice relates shall be construed in accordance with the following provisions, that is to say—

    (a) if the notice does not include an apportionment under section 78, the amount of the compensation shall be treated as distributed rateably according to area over the land to which the notice relates;

    (b) if the notice includes such an apportionment, the compensation shall be treated as distributed in accordance with that apportionment as between the different parts of the land by reference to which the apportionment is made; and so much of the compensation as, in accordance with the apportionment, is attributed to a part of the land shall be treated as distributed rateably according to area over that part of the land.

DEFINITIONS
"compensation for depreciation": s.79(1).
"land": s.277(1).

GENERAL NOTE
See commentary to s.78.

Recovery of compensation on subsequent development

80.—(1) No person shall carry out any development to which this section applies, on land in respect of which a notice (in this Part referred to as a "compensation notice") is recorded or, as the case may be, registered under section 79(1), until such amount, if any, as is recoverable under this section in respect of the compensation specified in the notice has been paid or secured to the satisfaction of the Secretary of State.

(2) Subject to the following provisions of this section, this section applies to any development—

(a) which is development of a residential, commercial or industrial character and consists wholly or mainly of the construction of houses, flats, shop or office premises, or industrial buildings (including warehouses), or any combination thereof,

(b) which consists in the winning and working of minerals, or

(c) to which, having regard to the probable value of the development, it is in the opinion of the Secretary of State reasonable that this section should apply.

(3) This section shall not apply to any development by virtue of subsection (2)(c) if, on an application made to him for the purpose, the Secretary of State has certified that, having regard to the probable value of the development, it is not in his opinion reasonable that this section should apply to it.

(4) Where the compensation specified in the compensation notice became payable in respect of the imposition of conditions on the granting of permission to develop land, this section shall not apply to the development for which that permission was granted.

(5) This section does not apply to any development—

(a) of a class specified in paragraph 1 of Schedule 11 which is carried out in accordance with the condition set out in Schedule 12, or

(b) of a class specified in paragraph 2 of Schedule 11.

(6) This section does not apply in a case where the compensation under section 76 specified in a compensation notice became payable in respect of an order modifying planning permission, and the development is in accordance with that permission as modified by that order.

DEFINITIONS
"building": s.277(1).
"compensation notice": subs. (1).
"develop": ss.26, 277(1).
"development": ss.26, 277(1).
"land": s.277(1).
"winning and working of minerals": s.277(1).

GENERAL NOTE
See commentary to s.78.

Subs. (5)
This section does not apply to:

(a) rebuilding a building in existence before July 1, 1948 or other prescribed date, provided the cubic content of the original building is not substantially exceeded (Sched. 11, para. 1(1)(a) and (b) and Sched. 12);

(b) works to the interior of a building, or not materially affecting the external appearance, provided the cubic content of the original building is not substantially exceeded (Sched. 11, para. 1(1)(c) and Sched. 12);

(c) sub-division of use of a dwellinghouse (Sched. 11, para. 1(2)).

Amount recoverable, and provisions for payment or remission

81.—(1) Subject to the following provisions of this section, the amount recoverable under section 80 in respect of the compensation specified in a compensation notice—

(a) if the land on which the development is to be carried out (in this subsection referred to as "the development area") is identical with, or includes (with other land) the whole of, the land comprised in the compensation notice, shall be the amount of compensation specified in that notice;

(b) if the development area forms part of the land comprised in the compensation notice, or includes part of that land together with other land not comprised in that notice, shall be so much of the amount of the compensation specified in that notice as is attributable to land comprised in that notice and falling within the development area.

(2) Where, in the case of any land in respect of which a compensation notice has been recorded or registered, the Secretary of State is satisfied, having regard to the probable value of any proper development of that land, that no such development is likely to be carried out unless he exercises his powers under this subsection, he may, in the case of any particular development, remit the whole or any part of any amount otherwise recoverable under section 80.

(3) Where, in connection with the development of any land, an amount becomes recoverable under section 80 in respect of the compensation specified in a compensation notice, then, except where, and to the extent that, payment of that amount has been remitted under subsection (2) above, no amount shall be recoverable under section 80 in respect of that compensation, in so far as it is attributable to that land, in connection with any subsequent development thereof.

(4) No amount shall be recoverable under section 80 in respect of any compensation by reference to which a sum has become recoverable by the Secretary of State under section 257.

(5) An amount recoverable under section 80 in respect of any compensation—

(a) shall be payable to the Secretary of State,

(b) shall be so payable either as a single capital payment or as a series of instalments of capital and interest combined, or as a series of other annual or periodical payments, of such amounts, and payable at such times, as the Secretary of State may direct, after taking into account any representations made by the person by whom the development is to be carried out, and

(c) except where the amount is payable as a single capital payment, shall be secured by that person to the satisfaction of the Secretary of State (whether by heritable or other security, personal bond or otherwise).

(6) If any person initiates any development to which section 80 applies in contravention of subsection (1) of that section, the Secretary of State may serve a notice on him specifying the amount appearing to the Secretary of State to be the amount recoverable under that section in respect of the compensation in question, and requiring him to pay that amount to the Secretary of State within such period, not being less than 3 months after the service of the notice, as may be specified in the notice.

(7) Where, after a compensation notice in respect of any land has been recorded or, as the case may be, registered—

(a) any amount recoverable under this section in respect of the compensation specified in the notice, or any part of such amount, has been paid to the Secretary of State, or

(b) circumstances arise under which by virtue of any provision of this Act no amount is so recoverable in respect of the land specified in the notice or any part of that land,

the Secretary of State shall cause to be recorded in the appropriate Register of Sasines or, as the case may be, registered in the Land Register of Scotland, a notice of that fact, specifying the land to which such fact relates and, in the case of any notice of the fact that part only of such amount has been so paid, stating whether the balance has been secured to the satisfaction of the Secretary of State or has been remitted by him under subsection (2) of this section, and shall send a copy of it to the planning authority.

DEFINITIONS
  "compensation notice": s.80(1).
  "development": ss.26, 277(1).
  "development area": subs. (1)(a).
  "land": s.277(1).

GENERAL NOTE
This section sets out the calculation of the sum recoverable under s.80 by way of compensation, and the procedures for payment, or as the case may be, remission of that sum.

Subs. (4)
Section 257 sets out circumstances in which the Secretary of State may recover compensation from an authority acquiring an interest in land by compulsory or other purchase.

Provisions for payment or remission of amount recoverable under section 80

82.—(1) Subject to subsection (2), any sum recovered by the Secretary of State under section 80 shall be paid to the planning authority who paid the compensation to which that sum relates.

(2) Subject to subsection (3), in paying any such sum to the planning authority, the Secretary of State shall deduct from it the amount of any grant paid by him under Part XIII in respect of that compensation.

(3) If the sum recovered by the Secretary of State under section 80—

(a) is an instalment of the total sum recoverable, or

(b) is recovered by reference to development of part of the land in respect of which the compensation was payable,

any deduction to be made under subsection (2) shall be a deduction of such amount as the Secretary of State may determine to be the proper proportion of the amount referred to in that subsection.

DEFINITIONS
"development": ss.26, 277(1).
"planning authority": ss.1, 277(1).
"land": s.277(1).

GENERAL NOTE
Any amount recovered under s.80 is paid to the planning authority, after deduction of any relevant grant.

Compensation in respect of orders under section 71 etc.

83.—(1) this section shall have effect where an order is made under section 71 or paragraph 1 of Schedule 8—

(a) requiring a use of land to be discontinued,

(b) imposing conditions on the continuance of it, or

(c) requiring any buildings or works on land or, in the case of an order under paragraph 1 of Schedule 8, any plant or machinery to be altered or removed.

(2) If, on a claim made to the planning authority within the prescribed time and in the prescribed manner, it is shown that any person has suffered damage in consequence of the order—

(a) by depreciation of the value of an interest to which he is entitled in the land, or

(b) by being disturbed in his enjoyment of the land,

that authority shall pay to that person compensation in respect of that damage.

(3) Without prejudice to subsection (2), any person who carries out any works in compliance with the order shall be entitled, on a claim made as mentioned in that subsection, to recover from the planning authority compensation in respect of any expenses reasonably incurred by him in that behalf.

(4) Any compensation payable to a person under this section by virtue of such an order as is mentioned in subsection (1) shall be reduced by the value

to him of any timber, apparatus or other materials removed for the purpose of complying with the order.

DEFINITIONS
"building": s.277(1).
"building or works": s.277(1).
"land": s.277(1).
"planning authority": ss.1, 277(1).
"use": s.277(1).

GENERAL NOTE
This section provides for the payment of compensation in respect of a discontinuance order.
In accordance with Recommendation 3 of the Scottish Law Commission Report ("SLCR"), compensation is now available in respect of orders requiring plant and machinery to be removed (subs. (1)(c)).
There are three heads of compensation:
(a) depreciation of the value of an interest in land. The person entitled to the interest in land may claim under this head;
(b) disturbance in the enjoyment of land. Any person may claim under this head;
(c) expenses reasonably incurred in carrying out works in compliance with the discontinuance order.

Subs. (4)
This subsection provides for the mitigation of the claimant's loss by providing that any compensation is reduced by the value to the claimant of materials removed for the purpose of complying with the discontinuance order.
"*Prescribed*": see the Town and Country Planning (General) (Scotland) Regulations 1976 (S.I. 1976 No. 2022).

Special basis for compensation in respect of certain orders affecting mineral working

84. Schedule 13 shall have effect for the purpose of making special provision as respects the payment of compensation in certain circumstances where an order under section 65 modifies planning permission for development consisting of the winning and working of minerals or an order is made under paragraph 1, 3, 5 or 6 of Schedule 8.

DEFINITIONS
"development": ss.26, 277(1).
"planning permission": s.277(1).
"prescribed": s.277(1).
"winning and working of minerals": s.277(1).

GENERAL NOTE
Schedule 13 empowers the Secretary of State to make by statutory instrument special provision for compensation in respect of minerals. Such compensation is governed by the Town and Country Planning (Compensation for Restrictions on Mineral Workings) (Scotland) Regulations 1981 as amended (S.I. 1987 No. 433).

Power to make provision for determination of claims

85.—(1) Regulations shall make provision—
(a) for requiring claims for compensation to be determined by the Secretary of State in such manner as may be prescribed;
(b) for regulating the practice and procedure to be followed in connection with the determination of such claims;
(c) for requiring the Secretary of State on determining any such claim—
(i) to give notice of his determination to the claimant and to any other person who has made and not withdrawn a claim for compensation in respect of the same planning decision, and
(ii) if his determination includes an apportionment, to give particulars of the apportionment to any other person entitled to an

interest in land appearing to the Secretary of State to be an interest substantially affected by the apportionment;

    (d) for requiring the Secretary of State to pay any compensation determined under this section to the person entitled to it.

(2) Subject to subsection (3), provision shall be made by such regulations—

    (a) for enabling the claimant or any other person to whom notice of the Secretary of State's determination has been given in accordance with subsection (1), if he wishes to dispute the determination, to require it to be referred to the Lands Tribunal;

    (b) for enabling the claimant and any other person to whom particulars of an apportionment included in that determination have been so given, or who establishes that he is entitled to an interest in land which is substantially affected by such an apportionment, if he wishes to dispute the apportionment, to require it to be referred to the Lands Tribunal;

    (c) for enabling the claimant and every other person to whom notice of any determination or apportionment has been given as mentioned in paragraph (a) or (b) to be heard by the Tribunal on any reference under this section of that determination or, as the case may be, of that apportionment; and

    (d) for requiring the Tribunal, on any such reference, either to confirm or to vary the Secretary of State's determination or the apportionment, as the case may be, and to notify the parties of the decision of the Tribunal.

(3) Where on a reference to the Lands Tribunal under this section it is shown that an apportionment—

    (a) relates wholly or partly to the same matters as a previous apportionment, and

    (b) is consistent with that previous apportionment in so far as it relates to those matters,

the Tribunal shall not vary the apportionment in such a way as to be inconsistent with the previous apportionment in so far as it relates to those matters.

DEFINITIONS
    "Lands Tribunal": s.277(1).
    "planning decision": s.277(1).

GENERAL NOTE
    This section empowers the Secretary of State to prescribe by statutory instrument the procedures of a compensation claim, and provides for an appeal to the Lands Tribunal.

Lands Tribunal to determine claims if not otherwise provided

86.—(1) Except in so far as may be otherwise provided by any regulations made under this Act, any question of disputed compensation under this Part shall be referred to and determined by the Lands Tribunal.

(2) In relation to the determination of any such question, the provisions of sections 9 and 11 of the Land Compensation (Scotland) Act 1963 shall apply, subject to any necessary modifications and to the provisions of any regulations made under this Act.

DEFINITIONS
    "Lands Tribunal": s.277(1).

GENERAL NOTE
Subs. (1)
    Any questions of disputed compensation are to be referred to and determined by the Lands Tribunal.

Subs. (2)

Section 9 of the Land Compensation (Scotland) Act 1963 (c.51) deals with procedure before the Lands Tribunal and s.11 deals with awards of expenses by the Lands Tribunal.

Supplementary provisions

General provisions as to compensation for depreciation under this Part

87.—(1) For the purpose of assessing any compensation to which this section applies, the rules set out in section 12 of the Land Compensation (Scotland) Act 1963 shall, so far as applicable and subject to any necessary modifications, have effect as they have effect for the purpose of assessing compensation for the compulsory acquisition of an interest in land.

(2) This section applies to any compensation which, under the provisions of this Part, is payable in respect of depreciation of the value of an interest in land.

(3) In relation to the assessment of compensation payable under section 76, the value of any interest may be a minus quantity.

(4) Where an interest in land is subject to a heritable security—

  (a) any compensation to which this section applies, which is payable in respect of depreciation of the value of that interest, shall be assessed as if the interest were not subject to the security;

  (b) a claim for any such compensation may be made by any creditor in a heritable security over the interest, but without prejudice to the making of a claim by the person entitled to the interest;

  (c) no compensation to which this section applies shall be payable in respect of the interest of the creditor in the heritable security (as distinct from the interest which is subject to the security); and

  (d) any compensation to which this section applies which is payable in respect of the interest which is subject to the heritable security shall be paid to the creditor in the security, or, if there is more than one such creditor, to the creditor whose security ranks first, and shall in either case be applied by him as if it were proceeds of sale by him under the powers competent to creditors in heritable securities.

Definitions

"heritable security": s.277(1).
"land": s.277(1).

General Note

This section sets out the method of assessment of compensation for depreciation.

Subs. (1)

The rules for assessing compensation set out in s.12 of the Land Compensation (Scotland) Act 1963 apply *mutatis mutandis* to the assessment of compensation in respect of depreciation.

Subs. (4)

Where there is a heritable security over property, the holder of the security may claim compensation in respect of the property but may not do so in respect of the security. The security holder must apply the compensation in the same way as the proceeds of a sale under the security.

Part V

Rights of Owners etc. to Require Purchase of Interests

Chapter I

Interests Affected by Planning Decisions or Orders

Service of purchase notices

Circumstances in which purchase notices may be served

88.—(1) This section applies where—

(a) on an application for planning permission to develop any land, permission is refused or is granted subject to conditions,

(b) by an order under section 65 planning permission in respect of any land is revoked, or is modified by the imposition of conditions, or

(c) an order is made under section 71 or paragraph 1 of Schedule 8 in respect of any land.

(2) If—

(a) in the case mentioned in subsection (1)(a) or (b), any owner or lessee of the land claims that the conditions mentioned in subsection (3) are satisfied with respect to it, or

(b) in the case mentioned in subsection (1)(c), any person entitled to an interest in land in respect of which the order is made claims that the conditions mentioned in subsection (4) are satisfied with respect to it,

he may, within the prescribed time and in the prescribed manner, serve on the planning authority in whose district the land is situated a notice (in this Act referred to as "a purchase notice") requiring that authority to purchase his interest in the land in accordance with this Chapter.

(3) The conditions mentioned in subsection (2)(a) are—

(a) that the land has become incapable of reasonably beneficial use in its existing state,

(b) in a case where planning permission was granted subject to conditions or was modified by the imposition of conditions, that the land cannot be rendered capable of reasonably beneficial use by the carrying out of the permitted development in accordance with those conditions, and

(c) in any case, that the land cannot be rendered capable of reasonably beneficial use by the carrying out of any other development for which planning permission has been granted or for which the planning authority or the Secretary of State has undertaken to grant planning permission.

(4) The conditions mentioned in subsection (2)(b) are—

(a) that by reason of the order the land is incapable of reasonably beneficial use in its existing state, and

(b) that it cannot be rendered capable of reasonably beneficial use by the carrying out of any development for which planning permission has been granted, whether by that order or otherwise.

(5) For the purposes of subsection (1)(a) and any claim arising in the circumstances mentioned in that subsection, the conditions referred to in sections 58 and 59 shall be disregarded.

(6) A person on whom a repairs notice has been served under section 43 of the Planning (Listed Buildings and Conservation Areas) (Scotland) Act 1997 shall not be entitled to serve a purchase notice in the circumstances mentioned in subsection (1)(a) in respect of the building in question—

(a) until the expiration of 3 months beginning with the date of the service of the repairs notice, and

(b) if during that period the compulsory acquisition of the building is begun in the exercise of powers under section 42 of that Act, unless and until the compulsory acquisition is discontinued.

(7) For the purposes of subsection (6) a compulsory acquisition—

(a) is started when the notice required by paragraph 3(b) of Schedule 1 to the Acquisition of Land (Authorisation Procedure) (Scotland) Act 1947 is served, and

(b) is discontinued—

    (i) in the case of acquisition by the Secretary of State, when he decides not to make the compulsory purchase order, and

    (ii) in any other case, when the order is withdrawn or the Secretary of State decides not to confirm it.

(8) No purchase notice shall be served in respect of an interest in land while the land is incapable of reasonably beneficial use by reason only of such an order as is mentioned in subsection (1)(c), except by virtue of a claim under subsection (2)(b).

DEFINITIONS
"building": s.277(1).
"compulsory acquisition": s.277(1).
"development": ss.26, 277(1).
"land": s.277(1).
"lessee": s.99(2).
"owner": ss.99(2), 277(1).
"planning permission": s.277(1).
"purchase notice": ss.88, 277(1).
"use": s.277(1).

GENERAL NOTE
Where a planning decision renders land incapable of reasonably beneficial use, this and the following sections provide a mechanism for an owner or other interested party to have the planning authority compulsorily acquire the land and pay compensation. If the authority is prepared to do so voluntarily by agreement, it will not in practice be necessary for the owner or other interested party to resort to this mechanism. The mechanism is triggered by the service by the owner or other interested party of a purchase notice.

Land in respect of which a purchase notice may be served—
(a) The purchase notice must relate to the whole of the land to the extent covered by the planning permission in question (*Cook and Woodham v. Winchester City Council* (1994) 69 P. & C.R. 99).
(b) Crown land may not be the subject of a purchase notice unless the authority has refused an offer to sell the land to it (s.244(2)).
(c) Special procedures in relation to amenity land are set out in s.93.

"Reasonably beneficial use". In determining whether land is incapable of reasonably beneficial use no account is to be taken of any prospective development other than (s.89):
    (i) rebuilding a building in existence before July 1, 1948 or other prescribed date, provided the cubic content of the original building is not substantially exceeded (Sched. 11, para. 1(1)(a) and (b));
    (ii) works to the interior of a building, or not materially affecting the external appearance, provided the cubic content of the original building is not substantially exceeded (Sched. 11, para. 1(1)(c));
    (iii) sub-division of use of a dwellinghouse (Sched. 11, para. 1(2)).

Preconditions for service of purchase notice relating to planning permission decisions. An owner or lessee of land may serve a purchase notice (subs. (2)(a)) where an application for planning permission is:
    (i) refused (subs. (1)(a)). There must be an actual refusal: deemed refusal under s.47 by failure to notify the applicant is not sufficient;
    (ii) granted subject to conditions (subs. (1)(a)). This ground is not available in respect of conditions limiting the duration of planning permission under s.58 nor conditions relating to outline planning permission under s.59 (subs. (5)); or
    (iii) revoked or modified (subs. (1)(b)).

There are three grounds for service of the notice:
- (i) that the land has become incapable of reasonably beneficial use in its existing state (subs. (3)(a));
- (ii) that the land cannot be rendered capable of reasonably beneficial use by carrying out permitted development in accordance with any conditions of the planning permission (subs. (3)(b)); and
- (iii) that the land cannot be rendered capable of reasonably beneficial use by carrying out any other development which has been, or has undertaken to be, granted (subs. (3)(c)).

There are restrictions on the right of persons on whom a repair notice have been served under s.43 of the Planning (Listed Buildings and Conservation Areas) (Scotland) Act 1997 (c.10) to serve a purchase notice in respect of the refusal of planning permission or grant subject to condition. Such persons may not serve a purchase notice during the period of three months after service of the repair notice, nor during the subsistence of any compulsory acquisition commenced during that period (subss. (6) and (7)).

All of the owners of the relevant land must serve the notice (*Smart & Courtenay Dale v. Dover Rural District Council* (1972) 23 P. & C.R. 408).

Preconditions for service of purchase notice relating to discontinuance or removal decisions. Any person entitled to an interest in land may serve a purchase notice (subs. (2)(b)) where an order is made requiring discontinuance of use or alteration or removal of buildings or works under s.71, or, in relation to minerals, under Sched. 8, para. 1 (subs. (1)(c)). A purchase notice in respect of such a discontinuance or removal order can not be served except by virtue of a claim under subs. (2)(b) (subs. (8)).

There are two grounds for service of the notice:
- (i) that by reason of the order the land is incapable of reasonably beneficial use in its existing state (subs. (4)(a));
- (ii) that it cannot be rendered capable of reasonably beneficial use by carrying any development for which planning permission has been granted (subs. (4)(b)).

Circumstances in which land incapable of reasonably beneficial use

89. Where, for the purpose of determining whether the conditions specified in section 88(3) or (4) are satisfied in relation to any land, any question arises as to what is or would in any particular circumstances be a reasonably beneficial use of that land, then, in determining that question for that purpose, no account shall be taken of any prospective development other than any development specified in paragraph 1 or 2 of Schedule 11.

DEFINITIONS
"development": ss.26, 277(1).
"land": s.277(1).

GENERAL NOTE
See commentary to s.88.

Duties of authorities on service of purchase notice

Action by planning authority on whom purchase notice is served

90.—(1) The planning authority on whom a purchase notice is served shall serve on the owner or lessee by whom the purchase notice was served a notice (a "response notice") stating—
- (a) that the planning authority are willing to comply with the purchase notice,
- (b) that another local authority or statutory undertakers specified in the response notice have agreed to comply with it in their place, or
- (c) that for reasons so specified the planning authority are not willing to comply with the purchase notice and have not found any other local authority or statutory undertakers who will agree to comply with it in their place, and that they have sent the Secretary of State a copy of the purchase notice and of the response notice.

(2) A response notice must be served before the end of the period of 3 months beginning with the date of service of the purchase notice.

(3) Where the planning authority on whom a purchase notice is served by an owner or lessee have served a response notice on him in accordance with subsection (1)(a) or (b), the planning authority or, as the case may be, the other local authority or statutory undertakers specified in the response notice shall be deemed—

    (a) to be authorised to acquire the interest of the owner or lessee compulsorily in accordance with the relevant provisions, and

    (b) to have served a notice to treat in respect of it on the date of service of the response notice.

(4) Where the planning authority propose to serve such a response notice as is mentioned in subsection (1)(c), they must first send the Secretary of State a copy—

    (a) of the proposed response notice, and

    (b) of the purchase notice.

(5) Where the planning authority on whom a purchase notice is served by an owner or lessee do not serve a response notice on him before the end of the period mentioned in subsection (2)—

    (a) the purchase notice shall be deemed to be confirmed at the end of that period, and

    (b) subsection (3) shall apply as if the authority had served a response notice on him on the last day of that period.

(6) A notice to treat which is deemed to have been served by virtue of subsection (3)(b) or (5)(b) may not be withdrawn under section 39 of the Land Compensation (Scotland) Act 1963.

DEFINITIONS

"lessee": s.99(2).
"local authority": s.277(1).
"owner": ss.99(2), 277(1).
"planning authority": ss.1, 277(1).
"purchase notice": ss.88, 277(1).
"the relevant provisions": s.99.
"response notice": subs. (1).
"statutory undertakers": ss.99, 214, 277(1).

GENERAL NOTE

A planning authority on whom a purchase notice is served must serve a response notice (subs. (1)) within three months (subs. (2)), which failing the purchase notice is deemed to be confirmed at the end of that period (subs. (5)). If the response notice states that the planning authority or other local authority or statutory undertaker are willing to comply with the notice (subs. (1)(a) and (b)), the relevant authority or undertaker is authorised to compulsorily purchase the land (subs. (3)).

If the planning authority is not willing to comply, and has not found any other local authority or statutory undertaking who is so willing, the response notice must give reasons and state that the purchase and response notices have been sent to the Secretary of State (subs. (1)(c)). A draft of the response notice must previously have been sent to the Secretary of State (subs. (4)).

Procedure on reference to purchase notice to Secretary of State

91.—(1) Where a copy of a purchase notice is sent to the Secretary of State under section 90(4), he shall consider whether to confirm the notice or to take other action under section 92 in respect of it.

(2) Before confirming a purchase notice or taking such other action, the Secretary of State shall give notice of his proposed action—

    (a) to the person who served the purchase notice,

    (b) to the planning authority on whom it was served, and

    (c) if the Secretary of State proposes to substitute any other local authority or statutory undertakers for the planning authority on whom the notice was served, to them.

(3) A notice under subsection (2) shall specify the period (which must not be less than 28 days from its service) within which any of the persons, author-

ities or statutory undertakers on whom it is served may require the Secretary of State to give them an opportunity of appearing before, and being heard by, a person appointed by the Secretary of State for the purpose.

(4) If within that period any of those persons, authorities or statutory undertakers so require, the Secretary of State shall, before he confirms the purchase notice or takes any other action under section 92 in respect of it, give each of them such an opportunity.

(5) If, after any of those persons, authorities or statutory undertakers have appeared before and been heard by the appointed person, or the persons, authorities and undertakers concerned have agreed to dispense with a hearing, it appears to the Secretary of State to be expedient to take action under section 92 otherwise than in accordance with the notice given by him, the Secretary of State may take that action accordingly.

DEFINITIONS
  "local authority": s.277(1).
  "planning authority": ss.1, 277(1).
  "purchase notice": ss.88, 277(1).
  "statutory undertakers": ss.99, 214, 277(1).

GENERAL NOTE
  Where the authority is unwilling to comply with a purchase notice, on receipt of the draft response notice the Secretary of State must form a preliminary view as to what action he proposes to take under s.93 (subs. (1)), and notify that view to interested parties (subs. (2)), who have an opportunity to make representations (subss. (3) and (4)).

Action by Secretary of State in relation to purchase notice

92.—(1) Subject to the following provisions of this section and to section 93(3), if the Secretary of State is satisfied that the conditions specified in subsection (3) or, as the case may be, subsection (4) of section 88 are satisfied in relation to a purchase notice, he shall confirm the notice.

(2) If it appears to the Secretary of State to be expedient to do so, he may, instead of confirming the purchase notice—

(a) in the case of a notice served on account of the refusal of planning permission, grant planning permission for the development in question;

(b) in the case of a notice served on account of planning permission for development being granted subject to conditions, revoke or amend those conditions so far as appears to him to be required in order to enable the land to be rendered capable of reasonably beneficial use by the carrying out of that development;

(c) in the case of a notice served on account of the revocation of planning permission by an order under section 65, cancel the order;

(d) in the case of a notice served on account of the modification of planning permission by such an order by the imposition of conditions, revoke or amend those conditions so far as appears to him to be required in order to enable the land to be rendered capable of reasonably beneficial use by the carrying out of the development in respect of which the permission was granted; or

(e) in the case of a notice served on account of the making of an order under section 71 or paragraph 1 of Schedule 8, revoke the order or, as the case may be, amend the order so far as appears to him to be required in order to prevent the land from being rendered incapable of reasonably beneficial use by the order.

(3) If it appears to the Secretary of State that the land, or any part of the land, to which the purchase notice relates could be rendered capable of reasonably beneficial use within a reasonable time by the carrying out of any other development for which planning permission ought to be granted, he may, instead of confirming the purchase notice or, as the case may be, of

confirming it so far as it relates to that part of the land, direct that, if an application for planning permission for that development is made, it must be granted.

(4) If it appears to the Secretary of State to be expedient that another local authority or statutory undertakers should acquire the interest of the owner or lessee for the purpose of any of their functions, he may, if he confirms the notice, modify it, in relation to either the whole or any part of the land to which the purchase notice relates, by substituting another local authority or statutory undertakers for the planning authority on whom the notice was served.

(5) Any reference in section 91 to the taking of action by the Secretary of State under this section includes a reference to the taking by him of a decision not to confirm the purchase notice either on the grounds that any of the conditions referred to in subsection (1) are not satisfied or by virtue of section 93.

DEFINITIONS
  "development": ss.26, 277(1).
  "land": s.277(1).
  "local authority": s.277(1).
  "planning authority": ss.1, 277(1).
  "planning permission": s.277(1).
  "purchase notice": ss.88, 277(1).
  "statutory undertakers": ss.99, 214, 277(1).
  "use": s.277(1).

GENERAL NOTE
  If the Secretary of State is satisfied that the land is incapable of reasonably beneficial use, he may:
    (i)   confirm the purchase order (subs. (1));
    (ii) grant planning permission (subs. (2)(a));
    (iii) revoke or amend conditions (subs. (2)(b) and (d));
    (iv) cancel a revocation of planning permission (subs. (2)(c));
    (v)   revoke or amend an order requiring discontinuance of use or alteration or removal of buildings or works under s.71, or, in relation to minerals, under Sched. 8, para. 1 (subs. (2)(e));
    (vi) direct that if a planning permission application is made it must be granted (subs. (3));
    (vii) modify the purchase notice by substituting another local authority or statutory undertakers (subs. (4)).
  Drafting errors in previous planning legislation have been corrected in this section in accordance with Recommendation 4.1 of the SLCR.

Power to refuse to confirm purchase notice where land has restricted use by virtue of previous planning permission

93.—(1) This section applies where a purchase notice is served in respect of land which consists in whole or in part of land which has a restricted use by virtue of an existing planning permission.

(2) For the purposes of this section, land is to be treated as having a restricted use by virtue of an existing planning permission if it is part of a larger area in respect of which planning permission has previously been granted (and has not been revoked) and either—

   (a) it remains a condition of the planning permission (however expressed) that that part shall remain undeveloped or be preserved or laid out in a particular way as amenity land in relation to the remainder, or

   (b) the planning permission was granted on an application which contemplated (expressly or by necessary implication) that the part should not be comprised in the development for which planning permission was sought, or should be preserved or laid out as mentioned in paragraph (a).

(3) Where a copy of the purchase notice is sent to the Secretary of State under section 90(4), although satisfied that the land has become incapable of

reasonably beneficial use in its existing state, he need not confirm the notice under section 92(1) if it appears to him that the land having a restricted use by virtue of an existing planning permission ought, in accordance with that permission, to remain undeveloped or, as the case may be, remain or be preserved or laid out as amenity land in relation to the remainder of the large area for which that planning permission was granted.

<small>Definitions</small>
 "development": ss.26, 277(1).
 "land": s.277(1).
 "planning permission": s.277(1).
 "purchase notice": ss.88, 277(1).
 "restricted use": subs. (2).
 "use": s.277(1).

<small>General Note</small>
 The words *"shall remain undeveloped"* mean that no development may take place and are not restricted to land remaining undeveloped for amenity purposes (*Strathclyde Regional Council v. Secretary of State for Scotland*, 1987 S.L.T. 724 (Second Division)).
 Drafting errors in previous planning legislation have been corrected in this section in accordance with Recommendations 4.2 and 5 of the SLCR.

Effect of Secretary of State's action in relation to purchase notice

94.—(1) Where the Secretary of State confirms a purchase notice—
 (a) the planning authority on whom the purchase notice was served, or
 (b) if under section 92(4) the Secretary of State modified the purchase notice by substituting another local authority or statutory undertakers for that planning authority, that other authority or those undertakers,
shall be deemed to be authorised to acquire the interest of the owner or lessee compulsorily in accordance with the relevant provisions, and to have served a notice to treat in respect of it on such date as the Secretary of State may direct.
 (2) If, before the end of the relevant period, the Secretary of State has neither—
 (a) confirmed the purchase notice, nor
 (b) taken any such action in respect of it as is mentioned in section 92(2) or (3), nor
 (c) notified the owner or lessee by whom the notice was served that he does not propose to confirm the notice,
the notice shall be deemed to be confirmed at the end of that period, and the authority on whom the notice was served shall be deemed to be authorised as mentioned in subsection (1) and to have served a notice to treat in respect of the owner's interest at the end of that period.
 (3) Subject to subsection (4), for the purposes of subsection (2) the relevant period is the period of 6 months beginning with the date on which a copy of the purchase notice was sent to the Secretary of State.
 (4) The relevant period does not run if the Secretary of State has before him at the same time both—
 (a) a copy of the purchase notice sent to him under section 90(4), and
 (b) a notice of appeal under section 47, 130 or 154 of this Act or under section 18 or 35 of the Planning (Listed Buildings and Conservation Areas) (Scotland) Act 1997 (appeals against refusal of listed building consent, etc. and appeals against listed building enforcement notices) or under section 19 of the Planning (Hazardous Substances) (Scotland) Act 1997 (appeals against decisions and failure to take decisions relating to hazardous substances) relating to any of the land to which the purchase notice relates.
 (5) Where—

(a) the Secretary of State has notified the owner or lessee by whom a purchase notice has been served of a decision on his part to confirm, or not to confirm, the notice, and

(b) that decision is quashed under Part XI,

the purchase notice shall be treated as cancelled, but the owner or lessee may serve a further purchase notice in its place.

(6) The reference in subsection (5) to a decision to confirm, or not to confirm, the purchase notice includes—

(a) any decision not to confirm the notice in respect of any part of the land to which it relates, and

(b) any decision to grant any permission, or give any direction, instead of confirming the notice, in respect of any part (or the whole) of the land to which it relates.

(7) For the purposes of determining whether a further purchase notice under subsection (5) was served within the period prescribed for the service of purchase notices, the planning decision in consequence of which the notice was served shall be treated as having been made on the date on which the decision of the Secretary of State was quashed.

(8) A notice to treat which is deemed to have been served by virtue of subsection (1) or (2) may not be withdrawn under section 39 of the Land Compensation (Scotland) Act 1963.

DEFINITIONS
"land": s.277(1).
"lessee": s.99(2).
"local authority": s.277(1).
"owner": ss.99(2), 277(1).
"planning authority": ss.1, 277(1).
"planning decision": s.277(1).
"purchase notice": ss.88, 277(1).
"the relevant period": s.94.
"statutory undertakers": ss.99, 214, 277(1).

GENERAL NOTE
Where the Secretary of State confirms the purchase notice the relevant authority or statutory undertaker is authorised to compulsorily purchase the land (subs. (1)). Failure of the Secretary of State to act within six months amounts to a deemed confirmation (subss. (2) and (3)), unless an appeal is pending (subs. (4)).

Thereafter, the compulsory purchase proceeds in the normal way, except that the deemed notice to treat may not be withdrawn (subs. (8)). If the Secretary of State's decision is quashed under Pt. XI of the Act, a fresh purchase notice may be served (subss. (5), (6) and (7)).

Compensation

Special provisions as to compensation where purchase notice served

95.—(1) Where compensation is payable by virtue of section 76 in respect of expenditure incurred in carrying out any work on land, any compensation payable in respect of the acquisition of an interest in the land in pursuance of a purchase notice shall be reduced by an amount equal to the value of those works.

(2) Where—

(a) the Secretary of State directs under section 92(3) that, if an application for it is made, planning permission must be granted for the development of any land, and

(b) on a claim made to the planning authority within the prescribed time and in the prescribed manner, it is shown that the permitted development value of the interest in that land in respect of which the purchase notice was served is less than its Schedule 11 value,

the planning authority shall pay the person entitled to that interest compensation of an amount equal to the difference.

(3) If the planning permission mentioned in subsection (2)(a) would be granted subject to conditions for regulating the design or external appearance, or the size or height of buildings, or for regulating the number of buildings to be erected on the land, the Secretary of State may direct that in assessing any compensation payable under subsection (2) those conditions must be disregarded, either altogether or to such extent as may be specified in the direction.

(4) The Secretary of State may give a direction under subsection (3) only if it appears to him to be reasonable to do so having regard to the local circumstances.

(5) Sections 86 and 87 shall have effect in relation to compensation under subsection (2) as they have effect in relation to compensation to which those sections apply.

(6) In this section—

"permitted development value", in relation to an interest in land in respect of which a direction is given under section 92(3), means the value of that interest calculated with regard to that direction, but on the assumption that no planning permission would be granted otherwise than in accordance with that direction, and

"Schedule 11 value", in relation to such an interest, means the value of that interest calculated on the assumption that planning permission would be granted—

(a) subject to the conditions set out in Schedule 12, for any development of a class specified in paragraph 1 of Schedule 11, and

(b) for any development of a class specified in paragraph 2 of Schedule 11.

(7) Where a purchase notice in respect of an interest in land is served in consequence of an order under section 71 or paragraph 1 of Schedule 8, then if—

(a) that interest is acquired in accordance with this Chapter, or

(b) compensation is payable in respect of that interest under subsection (2),

no compensation shall be payable in respect of that order under section 83.

DEFINITIONS
"building": s.277(1).
"development": ss.26, 277(1).
"land": s.277(1).
"permitted development value": subs. (6).
"planning authority": ss.1, 277(1).
"planning permission": s.277(1).
"prescribed": s.277(1).
"purchase notice": ss.88, 277(1).
"Schedule 11 value": subs. (6).

GENERAL NOTE
Subs. (1)
This subsection prevents double compensation by providing that the compensation payable in respect of the purchase of land is reduced by any compensation payable for works on that land.

Subss. (2) to (6)
These subsections provide for compensation where the Secretary of State deals with the purchase notice by directing that if planning permission is applied for it must be granted. The amount of the compensation is the shortfall between the compensation which would have been due had the purchase notice been complied with, and the value of the land with said planning permission.

Subs. (7)
This subsection prevents double compensation by providing that if compensation is payable in respect of the purchase of land, no compensation is payable for an order requiring discontinuance of use or alteration or removal of building or works on that land.

Special provisions for requiring purchase of whole of partially affected agricultural unit

Counter-notice requiring purchase of remainder of agricultural unit

96.—(1) This section applies where—

(a) an acquiring authority is deemed under this Chapter to have served notice to treat in respect of any agricultural land on a person ("the claimant") who has a greater interest in the land than as tenant for a year or from year to year (whether or not he is in occupation of the land), and

(b) the claimant has such an interest in other agricultural land ("the unaffected area") comprised in the same agricultural unit as that to which the notice relates.

(2) Where this section applies the claimant may serve on the acquiring authority a counter-notice—

(a) claiming that the unaffected area is not reasonably capable of being farmed, either by itself or in conjunction with other relevant land, as a separate agricultural unit, and

(b) requiring the acquiring authority to purchase his interest in the whole of the unaffected area.

(3) Subject to subsection (4), "other relevant land" in subsection (2) means—

(a) land which is comprised in the same agricultural unit as the land to which the notice to treat relates and in which the claimant does not have such an interest as is mentioned in subsection (1), and

(b) land which is comprised in any other agricultural unit occupied by the claimant on the date on which the notice to treat is deemed to have been served and in respect of which he is then entitled to a greater interest than as tenant for a year or from year to year.

(4) Where a notice to treat has been served or is deemed under this Chapter or Schedule 15 to have been served in respect of any of the unaffected area or in respect of other relevant land as defined in subsection (3), then, unless and until the notice to treat is withdrawn, this section and section 97 shall have effect as if that land did not form part of the unaffected land or, as the case may be, did not constitute other relevant land.

(5) Where a counter-notice is served under subsection (2) the claimant shall also serve a copy of it on any other person who has an interest in the unaffected area (but failure to comply with this subsection shall not invalidate the counter-notice).

(6) A counter-notice under subsection (2) and any copy of that notice required to be served under subsection (5) must be served within the period of 2 months beginning with the date on which the notice to treat is deemed to have been served.

(7) This section is without prejudice to the rights conferred by sections 91 and 92 of the Lands Clauses Consolidation (Scotland) Act 1845 (provisions as to divided land).

DEFINITIONS

"acquiring authority": ss.98(2), 277(1).
"agricultural land": s.98(2).
"agricultural unit": ss.98(2) and 122(1).
"claimant": subs. (1)(a).
"land": s.277(1).
"other relevant land": subs. (3).
"unaffected area": subs. (1)(b).

GENERAL NOTE

This section makes special provision to allow a claimant to require the acquisition of the whole of an agricultural unit, part of which is the subject of a purchase notice. Such provision is without prejudice to the general provisions on compulsory purchase of divided land contained in ss.91 and 92 of the Lands Clauses Consolidation (Scotland) Act 1845 (c.19).

A counter-notice must be served on the acquiring authority within two months after the purchase notice has been confirmed (subss. (1), (6)). It can be served by any person who has an interest greater than a tenancy for a year (or for year to year) in the land subject to the purchase notice (the "affected land") and the remainder of the unit (the "unaffected land") (subs. (1)). A copy should be served on any other person having an interest in the affected area, but failure to do so will not invalidate the counter-notice (subs. (5)).

The counter-notice must claim that the unaffected area is not reasonably capable of being farmed as a separate agricultural unit either—

    (a) on its own; or

    (b) in conjunction with another part of the same unit in which the claimant does not have an interest greater than a tenancy for a year (or for year to year); or

    (c) in conjunction with another unit in which the claimant does have such an interest (subss. (2)(a) and (3)).

Further, the counter-notice must require the authority to purchase the unaffected land (subs. (2)(b)).

Effect of counter-notice under section 96

97.—(1) If the acquiring authority do not within the period of 2 months beginning with the date of service of a counter-notice under section 96 agree in writing to accept the counter-notice as valid, the claimant or the authority may, within 2 months after the end of that period, refer it to the Lands Tribunal.

(2) On such a reference the Lands Tribunal shall determine whether the claim in the counter-notice is justified and declare the counter-notice valid or invalid accordingly.

(3) Where a counter-notice is accepted as valid under subsection (1) or declared to be valid under subsection (2), the acquiring authority shall be deemed—

    (a) to be authorised to acquire compulsorily the interest of the claimant in the land to which the requirement in the counter-notice relates under the same provision of this Chapter as they are authorised to acquire the other land in the agricultural unit in question, and

    (b) to have served a notice to treat in respect of that land on the date on which notice to treat is deemed to have been served under that provision.

(4) A claimant may withdraw a counter-notice at any time before the compensation payable in respect of a compulsory acquisition in pursuance of the counter-notice has been determined by the Lands Tribunal or at any time before the end of 6 weeks beginning with the date on which it is determined.

(5) Where a counter-notice is withdrawn by virtue of subsection (4) any notice to treat deemed to have been served in consequence of it shall be deemed to have been withdrawn.

(6) Without prejudice to subsection (5), a notice to treat deemed to have been served by virtue of this section may not be withdrawn under section 39 of the Land Compensation (Scotland) Act 1963.

(7) The compensation payable in respect of the acquisition of an interest in land in pursuance of a notice to treat deemed to have been served by virtue of this section shall be assessed on the assumptions mentioned in section 5(2), (3) and (4) of the Land Compensation (Scotland) Act 1973.

(8) Where by virtue of this section the acquiring authority become or will become entitled to a lease of any land but not to the interest of the lessor—

    (a) the authority shall offer to renounce the lease to the lessor on such terms as the authority consider reasonable,

    (b) the question of what is reasonable may be referred to the Lands Tribunal by the authority or the lessor and, if at the expiration of the period of 3 months after the date of the offer mentioned in paragraph (a) the authority and the lessor have not agreed on the question and

that question has not been referred to the Tribunal by the lessor, it shall be so referred by the authority, and
(c) if that question is referred to the Tribunal, the lessor shall be deemed—
    (i) to have accepted the renunciation of the lease at the expiry of one month after the date of the determination of the Tribunal or on such other date as the Tribunal may direct, and
    (ii) to have agreed with the authority on the terms of surrender which the Tribunal has held to be reasonable.
(9) For the purposes of subsection (8) any terms as to renunciation contained in the lease shall be disregarded.
(10) Where the lessor—
(a) refuses to accept any sum payable to him by virtue of subsection (8), or
(b) refuses or fails to make out his title to the satisfaction of the acquiring authority,
they may pay into the bank within the meaning of section 3 of the Lands Clauses Consolidation (Scotland) Act 1845 any such sum payable to the lessor and sections 75, 76, 77 and 79 of that Act shall apply to that sum with the necessary modifications.
(11) Where an acquiring authority who become entitled to the lease of any land as mentioned in subsection (8) are a body incorporated by or under any enactment, the corporate powers of the authority shall, if they would not otherwise do so, include the power to farm that land.

DEFINITIONS
    "acquiring authority": ss.98(2), 277(1).
    "agricultural unit": ss.98(2), 122(1).
    "claimant": s.96(1)(a).
    "compulsory acquisition": s.277(1).
    "land": s.277(1).
    "Lands Tribunal": s.277(1).
    "lease": s.277(1).

GENERAL NOTE
    If the authority does not accept the counter-notice within two months, there is an appeal to the Lands Tribunal (subss. (1) and (2)).
    Acceptance of the counter-notice triggers compulsory acquisition procedures (subs. (3)). The authority may not withdraw (subs. (6)), but the claimant may do so before the expiry of six weeks from a determination of the Lands Tribunal (subs. (5)).
    Compensation is payable in accordance with s.5(2), (3) and (4) of the Land Compensation (Scotland) Act 1963 (c.51) (subs. (6)).
    An authority which acquires a tenant's interest may renounce that interest to the landlord on reasonable terms (subs. (8)) and without regard to the renunciation provisions of the lease (subs. (9)). There is provision for the matter to be referred to the Lands Tribunal (subs. (8)). The refusal of a landlord to co-operate will not stand in the way of the renunciation as the procedures in s.5(2), (3) and (4) of the Lands Clauses Consolidation (Scotland) Act 1845 may be used (subs. (10)). These procedures provide for the transfer of title by execution of a notarial instrument on deposit of the sum payable.

Provisions supplemental to sections 96 and 97

98.—(1) Sections 96 and 97 apply in relation to the acquisition of interests in land by government departments which possess compulsory purchase powers as they apply in relation to the acquisition of interests in land by authorities who are not government departments.
(2) In sections 96 and 97—
    "acquiring authority" has the same meaning as in the Land Compensation (Scotland) Act 1963;
    "agricultural" and "agricultural land" have the meaning given in section 86 of the Agriculture (Scotland) Act 1948 and references to the

farming of land include references to the carrying on in relation to the land of any agricultural activities;

"agricultural unit" has the meaning given in section 122(1); and

"government departments which possess compulsory purchase powers" means government departments being authorities possessing compulsory purchase powers within the meaning of the Land Compensation (Scotland) Act 1963.

DEFINITIONS
"government departments which possess compulsory purchase powers": subs. (2).
"land": s.277(1).

Supplemental

Interpretation of Chapter I

99.—(1) In this Chapter—

"the relevant provisions" means—

      (a) the provisions of Part VIII, or

      (b) in the case of statutory undertakers, any statutory provision (however expressed) under which they have power, or may be authorised, to purchase land compulsorily for the purposes of their undertaking; and

"statutory undertakers" includes public telecommunications operators.

(2) In the case of a purchase notice served by such a person as is mentioned in subsection (2)(b) of section 88, references in this Chapter to the owner or lessee of the land include references to that person unless the context otherwise requires.

GENERAL NOTE
Drafting errors in previous planning legislation have been corrected in this section in accordance with Recommendation 4.3 of the SLCR.

CHAPTER II

INTERESTS AFFECTED BY PLANNING PROPOSALS: BLIGHT

Preliminary

Scope of Chapter II

100.—(1) This Chapter shall have effect in relation to land falling within any paragraph of Schedule 14 (land affected by planning proposals of public authorities etc.); and in this Chapter such land is referred to as "blighted land".

(2) Subject to the provisions of sections 112 and 113, an interest qualifies for protection under this Chapter if—

      (a) it is an interest in a hereditament or part of a hereditament and on the relevant date it satisfies one of the conditions mentioned in subsection (3), or

      (b) it is an interest in an agricultural unit or part of an agricultural unit and on the relevant date it is the interest of an owner-occupier of the unit;

and in this Chapter such an interest is referred to as "a qualifying interest".

(3) The conditions mentioned in subsection (2)(a) are—

      (a) that the annual value of the hereditament does not exceed such amount as may be prescribed for the purposes of this paragraph by an order made by the Secretary of State, and the interest is the interest of an owner-occupier of the hereditament, or

(b) that the interest is the interest of a resident owner-occupier of the hereditament.

(4) The Secretary of State may by regulations substitute for any reference in this Chapter to "annual value" or "hereditament" such other reference as he may consider appropriate; and such regulations may make such supplemental or consequential amendments of this Act or any other enactment whether passed before or after this Act as the Secretary of State thinks fit.

(5) In this section "the relevant date", in relation to an interest, means the date of service of a notice under section 101 in respect of it.

(6) In this Chapter "blight notice" means a notice served under section 101.

DEFINITIONS
"agricultural": s.277(1).
"agricultural unit": s.122(1).
"annual value": ss.122(1), 122(4).
"blight notice": subs. (6) and s.122(1).
"blighted land": s.100.
"hereditament": s.122(1), (3) and (4).
"land": s.277(1).
"owner": s.277(1).
"owner-occupier": ss.115, 119.
"prescribed": s.277(1).
"a qualifying interest": subs. (2).
"relevant date": subs. (5).

GENERAL NOTE
This chapter provides a mechanism whereby the owner of land or other interested party affected by a proposed public work may require the acquisition of the land by the appropriate authority. If the authority is prepared to do so voluntarily by agreement, it will not in practice be necessary for the owner or other interested party to resort to this mechanism. The mechanism is triggered by the service by the owner or other interested party of a blight notice.

"Blighted land". Blight notice procedure is available in respect of "blighted land" which is defined in Sched. 14. The definition falls under five headings:

(1) Land allocated for public authorities in development plans (Sched. 13, paras. 1–4).
The following are "blighted land" under this heading:
–land indicated in a structure or local plan as land which may be required for the purposes of:
   (i) the functions of a government department, local authority or statutory undertakers; or
   (ii) the establishment or running by a public telecommunications operator of a telecommunications system (paras. 1(a) and 2);
–land indicated in a structure plan as land which may be included in an action area (para. 1(b));
–land which is shown in an approved plan (other than a development plan) as land which may be required for the functions of a government department, local authority or statutory undertakers (para. 3); and
–land which a planning authority has resolved to, or been directed by the Secretary of State to, safeguard for development for the functions of a government department, local authority or statutory undertakers (para. 4)).
The definitions extend in certain circumstances beyond approved plans to proposed plans which are in the process of being adopted (paras. 1(4) and 2(2)).
(2) New towns and urban development areas.
The following are "blighted land" under this heading:
   (i) the site of a proposed new town (paras. 5 and 6); and
   (ii) an area designated or intended to be designated as an urban development area (para. 7).
(3) Housing action areas.
The following are "blighted land" under this heading:
   (i) a housing action area (para. 8); and
   (ii) an area surrounded by or adjoining a housing action area (para. 9).

(4) Roads.

The following are "blighted land" under this heading:

    (i) land indicated in a development plan as on which a road is to be constructed, altered or improved (para. 10);

    (ii) land in relation to which an order or scheme indicates that a compulsory acquisition power may become exercisable in respect of the construction, alteration or improvement of a road (para. 11);

    (iii) land indicated in a plan approved by a local authority as on which a road is to be constructed, altered or improved (para. 12); and

    (iv) land on which the Secretary of State has given notice that he proposes to construct, alter or improve a road (para. 13);

(5) Compulsory purchase.

The following are "blighted land" under this heading:

    (i) land in respect of which compulsory purchase has been authorised (paras. 14 and 15(1)); and

    (ii) land in respect of which compulsory purchase has been proposed in a draft order (para. 16).

"*Qualifying interest*". The interests which qualify for protection in respect of planning blight are as follows:

(1) the interest of an owner-occupier in a hereditament whose annual value (*i.e.* in most cases its rateable value) does not exceed a prescribed amount (subss. (2)(a) and 3(a)). The amount currently prescribed is £21,500 (Town and Country Planning (Limit of Annual Value) (Scotland) Order 1995 (S.I. 1995 No. 3048)). The intention behind these provisions is to make the protection available to small businesses. A hereditament is land other than agricultural land forming a single entry on the valuation roll (subs. 122(1), (2) and (3)). The whole property, or a substantial part thereof, must have been occupied by the owner:

–for the six months prior to the service of the notice, or

–where the property was unoccupied within a year prior to such service, for the six months prior to cessation of occupation (s.119(1)).

(2) the interest of a resident owner-occupier of a private dwelling (subss. 2(a) and 3(b)).

The whole property, or a substantial part thereof, must have been occupied by an individual:

–for the six months prior to the service of the notice, or

–where the property was unoccupied within a year prior to such service, for the six months prior to cessation of occupation (s.119(3)).

(3) the interest of an owner-occupier in an agricultural unit (subs. (2)(b)). An agricultural unit is land occupied as a unit for agricultural purposes, including any dwellinghouse or other building occupied by the same person for the purpose of farming the land (s.122(1)). The whole unit must have been occupied by the owner:

–for the six months prior to the service of the notice, or

–for a six months period ending not more than 12 months before that date (s.119(2)).

For examples of cases on "occupation" see *Minister of Transport v. Holland* (1962) 14 P. & C.R. 259 and *Garbett v. Hartlepool Borough Council* (1975) 30 P. & C.R. 517. Occupation by a partnership is not occupation by its partners individually (s.115).

The personal successors (s.112) and heritable creditors (s.113) of a person having a qualifying interest are entitled to serve blight notices.

Blight notices

Notice requiring purchase of blighted land

101.—(1) Where the whole or part of a hereditament or agricultural unit is comprised in blighted land and a person claims that—

    (a) he is entitled to a qualifying interest in that hereditament or unit,

    (b) he has made reasonable endeavours to sell that interest or the land falls within paragraph 14 or 15 of Schedule 14 and the powers of compulsory acquisition remain exercisable, and

    (c) in consequence of the fact that the hereditament or unit or a part of it was, or was likely to be, comprised in blighted land, he has been unable to sell that interest except at a price substantially lower than that for which it might reasonably have been expected to sell if no part of the hereditament or unit were, or were likely to be, comprised in such land,

he may serve on the appropriate authority a notice in the prescribed form requiring that authority to purchase that interest to the extent specified in, and otherwise in accordance with, this Chapter.

(2) Subject to subsection (3), subsection (1) shall apply in relation to an interest in part of a hereditament or unit as it applies in relation to an interest in the whole of a hereditament or unit.

(3) Subsection (2) shall not enable any person—

(a) if he is entitled to an interest in the whole of a hereditament or agricultural unit, to make any claim or serve any notice under this section in respect of his interest in part of a hereditament or unit, or

(b) if he is entitled to an interest only in part of a hereditament or agricultural unit, to make or serve any such claim or notice in respect of his interest in less than the whole of that part.

(4) In this Chapter—

(a) subject to section 112(1), "the claimant", in relation to a blight notice, means the person who served that notice, and

(b) any reference to the interest of the claimant, in relation to a blight notice, is a reference to the interest which the notice requires the appropriate authority to purchase as mentioned in subsection (1).

(5) Where the claimant is a crofter or cottar, this section shall have effect as if—

(a) in subsection (1)(b) for the word "sell" there were substituted the word "assign",

(b) in subsection (1)(c) for the words from "sell that interest" to "to sell" there were substituted the words "assign his interest except at a price substantially lower than that for which he might reasonably have been expected to assign it", and

(c) in subsections (1) and (4) for the word "purchase" there were substituted the words "take possession of".

DEFINITIONS
"agricultural": s.277(1).
"agricultural unit": s.122(1).
"appropriate authority": s.120.
"blight notice": ss.100(6), 122(1).
"blighted land": s.100.
"claimant": subs. (4), s.122(1).
"compulsory acquisition": s.277(1).
"conservation area": s.277(1).
"cottar": s.122(1).
"crofter": s.122(1).
"hereditament": s.122(1), (3) and (4).
"land": s.277(1).
"qualifying interest": s.100(2).

GENERAL NOTE
Subs. (1)
The pre-conditions for service of a blight notice are that the claimant:
(a) is entitled to a qualifying interest;
(b) has made reasonable endeavours to sell. This precondition does not apply to land blighted on grounds relating to compulsory purchase where the powers of compulsory acquisition remain exercisable; and
(c) as a result of the blight has been unable to sell except at a substantially reduced price.
"*Prescribed form*": see The Town and Country Planning (General) (Scotland) Regulations 1976 (S.I. 1976 No. 2022) reg. 3 and Sched. 1.

Subs. (3)

The claim must be in respect of the claimant's entire interest in the relevant hereditament or agricultural unit. Nevertheless, the authority may proceed to acquire only part of the property (s.102(4)(c)).

Subs. (5)

Drafting errors in previous planning legislation have been corrected in this subsection in accordance with Recommendation 6 of the SLCR.

No notice can be served under this section if a notice under s.112 (blight notices by personal representatives) or s.113 (blight notices by heritable creditor) is outstanding (s.114).

Counter-notice objecting to blight notice

102.—(1) Where a blight notice has been served in respect of a hereditament or an agricultural unit, the appropriate authority may serve on the claimant a counter-notice in the prescribed form objecting to the notice.

(2) A counter-notice under subsection (1) may be served at any time before the end of the period of 2 months beginning with the date of service of the blight notice.

(3) Such a counter-notice shall specify the grounds on which the appropriate authority object to the blight notice (being one or more of the grounds specified in subsection (4) or, as relevant, in section 110(1), 112(5) or 113(5)).

(4) Subject to the following provisions of this section, the grounds on which objection may be made in a counter-notice to a notice served under section 101 are—

    (a) that no part of the hereditament or agricultural unit to which the notice relates is comprised in blighted land;

    (b) that the appropriate authority (unless compelled to do so by virtue of this Chapter) do not propose to acquire any part of the hereditament, or in the case of an agricultural unit any part of the affected area, in the exercise of any relevant powers;

    (c) that the appropriate authority propose in the exercise of relevant powers to acquire a part of the hereditament or, in the case of an agricultural unit, a part of the affected area specified in the counter-notice, but (unless compelled to do so by virtue of this Chapter) do not propose to acquire any other part of that hereditament or area in the exercise of any such powers;

    (d) in the case of land falling within paragraph 1 or 10 but not 11, 12 or 13 of Schedule 14, that the appropriate authority (unless compelled to do so by virtue of this Chapter) do not propose to acquire in the exercise of any relevant powers any part of the hereditament or, in the case of an agricultural unit, any part of the affected area during the period of 15 years from the date of the counter-notice or such longer period from that date as may be specified in the counter-notice;

    (e) that, on the date of service of the notice under section 101, the claimant was not entitled to an interest in any part of the hereditament or agricultural unit to which the notice relates;

    (f) that (for reasons specified in the counter-notice) the interest of the claimant is not a qualifying interest;

    (g) that the conditions specified in paragraphs (b) and (c) of section 101(1) are not fulfilled.

(5) Where the appropriate enactment confers power to acquire rights over land, subsection (4) shall have effect as if—

    (a) in paragraph (b) after the word "acquire" there were inserted the words "or to acquire any rights in or over",

    (b) in paragraph (c) for the words "do not propose to acquire" there were substituted the words "propose neither to acquire, nor to acquire any right in or over", and

(c) in paragraph (d) after the words "affected area" there were inserted "or to acquire any right in or over any part of it".

(6) An objection may not be made on the grounds mentioned in paragraph (d) of subsection (4) if it may be made on the grounds mentioned in paragraph (b) of that subsection.

(7) An objection may not be made on the grounds mentioned in paragraphs (b) or (c) of subsection (4) in a counter-notice to a blight notice served by virtue of paragraphs 8 or 9 of Schedule 14.

(8) In this section, "relevant powers", in relation to blighted land falling within any paragraph of Schedule 14, means any powers under which the appropriate authority are or could be authorised—

(a) to acquire that land or any rights in or over it compulsorily as being land falling within such paragraph, or

(b) to acquire that land or any rights in or over it compulsorily for any of the relevant purposes;

and "the relevant purposes", in relation to any such land, means the purposes for which, in accordance with the circumstances by virtue of which that land falls within the paragraph in question, it is liable to be acquired or is indicated as being proposed to be acquired.

DEFINITIONS

"agricultural": s.277(1).
"agricultural unit": s.122(1).
"appropriate authority": s.120.
"blight notice": ss.100(6), 122(1).
"blighted land": s.100.
"the claimant": ss.101(4), 122(1).
"hereditament": s.122(1), (3) and (4).
"land": s.277(1).
"a qualifying interest": s.100(2).
"relevant powers": subs. (8).
"relevant purposes": subs. (8).

GENERAL NOTE

The authority may serve a counter-notice within two months of the date of service of the blight notice (subss. (1) and (2)). If they fail to do so they are deemed to be authorised to acquire compulsorily the claimant's interest and to have served a notice to treat (s.105). If the authority claims that the blight notice should have been served not on them but on another authority, they may not serve a counter-notice on that ground but instead should refer the matter to the Secretary of State under s.120(2), in which case the two month period will not begin to run until the Secretary of State's determination (s.120(3)(a)).

The counter-notice must specify one of the following grounds of objection (subs. (3)), which apply *mutatis mutandis* to the acquisition of rights in or over land (subs. (5)):

(a) that no part of the land to which the notice relates is comprised in blighted land (subs. (4)(a));

(b) that the authority do not propose to acquire any part of the land (subs. (4)(b));

(c) that the authority propose to acquire part only of the land specified in the notice (subs. (4)(c)). Where the blight notice is in respect of an agricultural unit only part of which is blighted, the counter-notice may not specify ground (c) unless it also specifies ground (g) below (s.110(2)). Objection by the authority on ground (c) does not affect the owner's right under compulsory purchase procedures to require the authority to purchase the whole of a hereditament or of the affected part of an agricultural unit (s.117);

(d) in the case of land falling within Sched. 14, para. 1 (land allocated for public functions in structure plan, etc.) or 10 (land indicated in a development plan as on which a road is to be constructed, altered or improved) but not 11, 12 or 13 (other land relating to roads), that the authority do not propose to make the acquisition for fifteen or more years (subs. (4)(d));

(e) that on the date of service of the blight notice, the claimant was not entitled to an interest in the land to which it relates (subs. (4)(e));

(f) that the claimant has not made reasonable efforts to sell his interest, or has been able to sell otherwise than at a reduced price (subs. (4)(f));

(g) where the blight notice is in respect of an agricultural unit only part of which is blighted, that the claim made in the blight notice as to the unreasonableness of farming the unaffected area is not justified (s.110(1)).

For special provisions as to the grounds to be contained in a counter-notice to a blight notice served by personal representatives and heritable creditors see ss.112(5) and 113(5).

For provisions as to how the grounds listed above are to be dealt with by the Lands Tribunal see s.104.

The authority may not raise any objection other than those listed above, nor object otherwise than by counter-notice (*Essex County Council v. Essex Incorporated Congregational Church Union* [1963] A.C. 808, H.L.; *Burn v. North Yorkshire County Council* (1991) 63 P. & C.R. 81).

A counter-notice may not be amended after service (*McGinigle v. Renfrew District Council*, 1992 S.L.T. (Lands Tr.) 97).

"*Prescribed form*": see the Town and Country Planning (General) (Scotland) Regulations 1976 (S.I. 1976 No. 2022) reg. 3 and Sched. 1.

Further counter-notice where certain proposals have come into force

103.—(1) Where—
(a) an appropriate authority have served a counter-notice objecting to a blight notice in respect of any land falling within—
    (i) paragraph 1 of Schedule 14 by virtue of paragraph 1(4),
    (ii) paragraph 2 of that Schedule by virtue of paragraph 2(2), or
    (iii) paragraph 11 of that Schedule, and
(b) the relevant plan or alterations or, as the case may be, the relevant order or scheme comes into force (whether in its original form or with modifications),
the appropriate authority may serve on the claimant, in substitution for the counter-notice already served, a further counter-notice specifying different grounds of objection.

(2) Such a further counter-notice shall not be served—
(a) at any time after the end of the period of 2 months beginning with the date on which the relevant plan or alterations or, as the case may be, the relevant order or scheme come into force, or
(b) if the objection in the counter-notice already served has been withdrawn or the Lands Tribunal has already determined whether or not to uphold that objection.

DEFINITIONS
"appropriate authority": s.120.
"blight notice": ss.100(6), 122(1).
"claimant": ss.101(4), 122(1).

GENERAL NOTE
If the blight notice is based on a draft plan or scheme, the authority may serve a further counter-notice when the plan or scheme is finalised (subs. (1)), provided they do so within two months of the finalisation and the original counter-notice has not been withdrawn or determined by the Lands Tribunal (subs. (2)).

Reference of objection to Lands Tribunal: general

104.—(1) Where a counter-notice has been served under section 102 objecting to a blight notice, the claimant may require the objection to be referred to the Lands Tribunal.

(2) Such a reference may be required under subsection (1) at any time before the end of the period of 2 months beginning with the date of service of the counter-notice.

(3) On any such reference, if the objection is not withdrawn, the Lands Tribunal shall consider—

(a) the matters set out in the notice served by the claimant, and

(b) the grounds of the objection specified in the counter-notice,

and, subject to subsection (4), unless it is shown to the satisfaction of the Tribunal that the objection is not well-founded, the Tribunal shall uphold the objection.

(4) An objection on the grounds mentioned in section 102(4)(b), (c) or (d) shall not be upheld by the Tribunal unless it is shown to the satisfaction of the Tribunal that the objection is well-founded.

(5) If the Tribunal determines not to uphold the objection, the Tribunal shall declare that the notice to which the counter-notice relates is a valid notice.

(6) If the Tribunal upholds the objection, but only on the grounds mentioned in section 102(4)(c), the Tribunal shall declare that the notice is a valid notice in relation to the part of the hereditament, or in the case of an agricultural unit the part of the affected area, specified in the counter-notice as being the part which the appropriate authority propose to acquire as mentioned in that notice, but not in relation to any other part of the hereditament or affected area.

(7) In a case falling within subsection (5) or (6), the Tribunal shall give directions specifying the date on which notice to treat (as mentioned in section 105) or, in a case where the claimant is a crofter or cottar, notice of entry (as mentioned in that section) is to be deemed to have been served.

(8) This section shall have effect in relation to a further counter-notice served by virtue of section 103(1) as it has effect in relation to the counter-notice for which it is substituted.

DEFINITIONS
"agricultural": s.277(1).
"agricultural unit": s.122(1).
"appropriate authority": s.120.
"blight notice": ss.100(6), 122(1).
"claimant": ss.101(4), 122(1).
"cottar": s.122(1).
"crofter": s.122(1).
"Lands Tribunal": s.277(1).

GENERAL NOTE

Where a counter-notice (or further counter-notice: subs. (8)) has been served, a claimant who wishes to insist on the blight notice has two months to refer the objection to the Lands Tribunal (subs. (1)).

Generally the onus is on the claimant to show that the objection is not well founded (subs. (3); *Malcolm Campbell v. Glasgow Corporation*, 1972 S.L.T. (Lands Tr.) 8), but the onus is on the authority if their objection is on the following grounds (subs. (4)), all of which relate to the intention of the authority:

–that the authority do not propose to acquire any part of the land (s.102(4)(b));

–that the authority propose to acquire part only of the land specified in the notice (s.102(4)(c)); or

— in the case of land falling within Sched. 14, paras. 1 (land allocated for public functions in structure plan, etc.) or 10 (land indicated in a development plan as on which a road is to be constructed, altered or improved) but not 11, 12 or 13 (other land relating to roads), that the authority do not propose to make the acquisition for fifteen or more years (s.102(4)(d)).

If the Tribunal does not uphold the objection it declares the blight notice a valid notice (subs. (5)). If the Tribunal upholds an objection based on the ground that the authority proposes to acquire only part of the land specified in the blight notice, it declares the notice valid only in relation to the part to be acquired (subs. (6)). In either case, the Tribunal specifies the date on which the notice to treat is deemed to have been served (subs. (7)), and the authority is deemed to be authorised to compulsorily acquire the land (s.105(2)).

For special provisions under which the authority may be compelled to acquire the whole of a partially affected agricultural unit see s.109.

The upholding by the Tribunal of an objection to the purchase of part of the land specified in the blight notice does not affect the owner's right under compulsory purchase procedures to require the authority to purchase the whole of a hereditament or of the affected part of an agricultural unit (s.117).

Drafting errors in previous planning legislation have been corrected in this section in accordance with Recommendation 6 of the SLCR.

Effect of valid blight notice

105.—(1) Subsection (2) applies where a blight notice has been served and either—

  (a) no counter-notice objecting to that notice is served in accordance with this Chapter, or

  (b) where such a counter-notice has been served, the objection is withdrawn or, on a reference to the Lands Tribunal, is not upheld by the Tribunal.

(2) Where this subsection applies, the appropriate authority shall be deemed—

  (a) to be authorised to acquire compulsorily under the appropriate enactment the interest of the claimant in the hereditament, or in the case of an agricultural unit the interest of the claimant in so far as it subsists in the affected area, and

  (b) to have served a notice to treat in respect of it on the date mentioned in subsection (3).

(3) The date referred to in subsection (2)—

  (a) in a case where, on a reference to the Lands Tribunal, the Tribunal determines not to uphold the objection, is the date specified in directions given by the Tribunal in accordance with section 104(7), and

  (b) in any other case, is the date on which the period of 2 months beginning with the date of service of the blight notice comes to an end.

(4) Subsection (5) applies where the appropriate authority have served a counter-notice objecting to a blight notice on the grounds mentioned in section 102(4)(c) and either—

  (a) the claimant, without referring that objection to the Lands Tribunal, and before the time for so referring it has expired—

      (i) gives notice to the appropriate authority that he accepts the proposal of the authority to acquire the part of the hereditament or affected area specified in the counter-notice, and

      (ii) withdraws his claim as to the remainder of that hereditament or area, or

  (b) on a reference to the Lands Tribunal, the Tribunal makes a declaration in accordance with section 104(6) in respect of that part of the hereditament or affected area.

(5) Where this subsection applies, the appropriate authority shall be deemed—

  (a) to be authorised to acquire compulsorily under the appropriate enactment the interest of the claimant in so far as it subsists in the part of the hereditament or affected area specified in the counter-notice (but not in so far as it subsists in any other part of that hereditament or area), and

  (b) to have served a notice to treat in respect of it on the date mentioned in subsection (6).

(6) The date referred to in subsection (5)—

  (a) in a case falling within paragraph (a) of subsection (4), is the date on which notice is given in accordance with that paragraph, and

  (b) in a case falling within paragraph (b) of that subsection, is the date specified in directions given by the Lands Tribunal in accordance with section 104(7).

(7) Where the claimant is a crofter or cottar, this section applies as if in subsections (2) and (5) for the words from "acquire" to "in respect of it" there were substituted the words "require the crofter or cottar to give up

possession of the land occupied by him and to have served a notice of entry in respect thereof under paragraph 3 of Schedule 2 to the Acquisition of Land (Authorisation Procedure) (Scotland) Act 1947".

DEFINITIONS
  "agricultural": s.277(1).
  "agricultural unit": s.122(1).
  "appropriate authority": s.120.
  "appropriate enactment": s.121.
  "blight notice": ss.100(6), 122(1).
  "claimant": ss.101(4), 122(1).
  "cottar": s.122(1).
  "crofter": s.122(1).
  "hereditament": s.122(1), (3) and (4).
  "Lands Tribunal": s.277(1).

GENERAL NOTE
    A blight notice is a valid blight notice if no counter-notice is served by the authority within two months, or the objection to any counter-notice is withdrawn by the authority or not upheld by the Lands Tribunal (subs. (1)). The blight notice is implemented through normal compulsory purchase procedure, with the authority being deemed to serve a notice to treat on the expiry of the two months or the date specified by the Tribunal (subs. (2)) as the case may be.
    Where only part of the land is specified in the blight notice, similar procedures apply (subss. (4) to (6)), with the authority being deemed to serve a notice to treat on the acceptance by the claimant of the part acquisition, or on the date specified by the Tribunal (subs. (6)) as the case may be. The owner's right under compulsory purchase procedures to require the authority to purchase the whole of a hereditament or of the affected part of an agricultural unit is not affected (s.117).
    Drafting errors in previous planning legislation have been corrected in this section in accordance with Recommendation 6 of the SLCR.

Effect on powers of compulsory acquisition of counter-notice disclaiming intention to acquire

106.—(1) Subsection (2) shall have effect where the grounds of objection specified in a counter-notice served under section 102 consist of or include the grounds mentioned in paragraph (b) or (d) of subsection (4) of that section and either—

  (a) the objection on the grounds mentioned in that paragraph is referred to and upheld by the Lands Tribunal, or

  (b) the time for referring that objection to the Lands Tribunal expires without its having been so referred.

(2) If—

  (a) a compulsory purchase order has been made under the appropriate enactment in respect of land which consists of or includes the whole or part of the hereditament or agricultural unit to which the counter-notice relates, or

  (b) the land in question falls within paragraph 14 of Schedule 14,

any power conferred by that order or, as the case may be, by special enactment for the compulsory acquisition of the interest of the claimant in the hereditament or agricultural unit or any part of it shall cease to have effect.

(3) Subsection (4) shall have effect where the grounds of objection specified in a counter-notice under section 102 consist of or include the grounds mentioned in paragraph (c) of subsection (4) of that section and either—

  (a) the objection on the grounds mentioned in that paragraph is referred to and upheld by the Lands Tribunal, or

  (b) the time for referring that objection to the Lands Tribunal expires without its having been so referred;

and in subsection (4) any reference to "the part of the hereditament or affected area not required" is a reference to the whole of that hereditament or area except the part specified in the counter-notice as being the part which the appropriate authority propose to acquire as mentioned in the counter-notice.

(4) If—

(a) a compulsory purchase order has been made under the appropriate enactment in respect of land which consists of or includes any of the part of the hereditament or affected area not required, or

(b) the land in question falls within paragraph 14 of Schedule 14,

any power conferred by that order or, as the case may be, by the special enactment for the compulsory acquisition of the interest of the claimant in any land comprised in the part of the hereditament or affected area not required shall cease to have effect.

(5) Where the claimant is a crofter or cottar, this section shall have effect as if in subsections (2) and (4) for the words from "or, as the case may be, by" to "claimant in" there were substituted the words "to require the crofter or collar to give up possession of".

DEFINITIONS
   "agricultural": s.277(1).
   "agricultural unit": s.122(1).
   "appropriate enactment": s.121.
   "claimant": ss.101(4), 122(1).
   "compulsory acquisition": s.277(1).
   "cottar": s.122(1).
   "crofter": s.122(1).
   "hereditament": s.122(1), (3) and (4).
   "land": s.277(1).
   "Lands Tribunal": s.277(1).
   "special enactment": s.122(1).
   "the part of the hereditament or affected area not required": subs. (3).

GENERAL NOTE
   This section provides that if the authority states in its counter-notice that it has no intention to acquire land, any compulsory purchase powers over that land cease to have effect.
   The owner's right under compulsory purchase procedures to require the authority to purchase the whole of a hereditament or of the affected part of an agricultural unit is not affected (s.117).
   Drafting errors in previous planning legislation have been corrected in this section in accordance with Recommendation 6 of the SLCR.

Withdrawal of blight notice

107.—(1) Subject to subsection (3), the claimant may withdraw a blight notice at any time before the compensation payable in respect of a compulsory acquisition in pursuance of the notice has been determined by the Lands Tribunal or, if there has been such a determination, at any time before the end of the period of 6 weeks beginning with the date of the determination.

(2) Where a blight notice is withdrawn by virtue of subsection (1) any notice to treat deemed to have been served in consequence of it shall be deemed to have been withdrawn.

(3) A claimant shall not be entitled by virtue of subsection (1) to withdraw a notice after the appropriate authority have exercised a right of entering and taking possession of land in pursuance of a notice to treat deemed to have been served in consequence of that notice.

(4) No compensation shall be payable in respect of the withdrawal of a notice to treat which is deemed to have been withdrawn by virtue of subsection (2).

DEFINITIONS
   "appropriate authority": s.120.
   "blight notice": ss.100(6), 122(1).
   "claimant": ss.101(4), 122(1).

"compulsory acquisition": s.277(1).
"land": s.277(1).
"Lands Tribunal": s.277(1).

GENERAL NOTE
A claimant may withdraw a blight notice at any time until six weeks after determination of compensation by the Lands Tribunal (subs. (1)), provided that he may not do so after the authority has taken entry (subs. (3)).

Compensation

Special provisions as to compensation for acquisition in pursuance of blight notice

108.—(1) Where—
(a) an interest in land is acquired in pursuance of a blight notice, and
(b) the interest is one in respect of which a compulsory purchase order is in force under section 1 of the Acquisition of Land (Authorisation Procedure) (Scotland) Act 1947, as applied by section 42 of the Planning (Listed Buildings and Conservation Areas) (Scotland) Act 1997, containing a direction for minimum compensation under section 45 of that Act of 1997,

the compensation payable for the acquisition shall be assessed in accordance with that direction and as if the notice to treat deemed to have been served in respect of the interest under section 105 had been served in pursuance of the compulsory purchase order.

(2) Where—
(a) an interest in land is acquired in pursuance of a blight notice, and
(b) the interest is one in respect of which a compulsory purchase order is in force under section 1 of the said Act of 1947 as applied by paragraph 5 of Schedule 8 to the Housing (Scotland) Act 1987 (acquisition of land for housing action areas),

the compensation payable for the acquisition shall be assessed in accordance with paragraph 12(2) and (3) of that Schedule and as if the notice to treat deemed to have been served in respect of the interest under section 105 had been served in pursuance of the compulsory purchase order.

(3) The compensation payable in respect of the acquisition by virtue of section 111 of an interest in land comprised in—
(a) the unaffected area of an agricultural unit, or
(b) if the appropriate authority have served a counter-notice objecting to the blight notice on the grounds mentioned in section 102(4)(c), so much of the affected area of the unit as is not specified in the counter-notice,

shall be assessed on the assumptions mentioned in section 5(2), (3) and (4) of the Land Compensation (Scotland) Act 1973.

(4) In subsection (3) the reference to "the appropriate authority" shall be construed as if the unaffected area of an agricultural unit were part of the affected area.

DEFINITIONS
"agricultural": s.277(1).
"agricultural unit": s.122(1).
"appropriate authority": s.120.
"blight notice": ss.100(6), 122(1).
"blighted land": s.100.

GENERAL NOTE
Subss. (1) and (2)
The compensation payable pursuant to a blight notice is no more than would be paid under ordinary compulsory acquisition procedures in the case of:
–listed buildings in disrepair (subs. (1)); and
–slum clearance (subs. (2)).

Special provisions for requiring purchase of whole of partially affected agricultural units

Inclusion in blight notice of requirement to purchase part of agricultural unit unaffected by blight

109.—(1) This section applies where—

(a) a blight notice is served in respect of an interest in the whole or part of an agricultural unit, and

(b) on the date of service that unit or part contains land ("the unaffected area") which is not blighted land as well as land ("the affected area") which is such land.

(2) Where this section applies the claimant may include in the blight notice—

(a) a claim that the unaffected area is not reasonably capable of being farmed, either by itself or in conjunction with other relevant land, as a separate agricultural unit, and

(b) a requirement that the appropriate authority shall purchase his interest in the whole of the unit or, as the case may be, in the whole of the part of it to which the notice relates.

(3) Subject to section 110(4), "other relevant land" in subsection (2) means—

(a) if the blight notice is served only in respect of part of the land comprised in the agricultural unit, the remainder of it, and

(b) land which is comprised in any other agricultural unit occupied by the claimant on the date of service and in respect of which he is then entitled to an owner's interest as defined in section 119(4).

(4) Where a blight notice to which this section applies is served by a crofter or cottar, subsection (2) shall have effect as if for paragraph (b) there were substituted the following paragraph—

> "(b) a requirement that the appropriate authority shall take possession of the whole of the unit or, as the case may be, the whole of the part of it to which the notice relates."

DEFINITIONS

"agricultural": s.277(1).
"agricultural unit": s.122(1).
"affected area": subs. (1)(b), s.122(1).
"blight notice": ss.100(6), 122(1).
"the claimant": ss.101(4), 122(1).
"cottar": s.122(1).
"crofter": s.122(1).
"land": s.277(1).
"winning and working of minerals": s.277(1).

GENERAL NOTE

Where only part of an agricultural unit is blighted land, the claimant may in the blight notice require the authority to purchase unblighted land which is not reasonably capable of being farmed, either by itself or in conjunction with other relevant land (subss. (1) and (2)). "Other relevant land" is defined in subs. (3) as the remainder of the unit, or other land owned by the claimant or over which he has a lease with not less than three years still to run or in respect of which he is a crofter or cottar. Where the authority has indicated in a counter-notice that it intends to buy part only of the land specified in a blight notice, "other relevant land" includes the remainder of the specified land (s.110(4)).

The authority may include in its counter-notice an objection on the ground that the claim that the unblighted land is not reasonably capable of being farmed is not justified (s.110(1)). See the commentary to s.102.

If the Lands Tribunal takes the view that the unblighted land is reasonably capable of being farmed, it may nevertheless uphold the blight notice in respect of the blighted land (s.110(4)).

Drafting errors in previous planning legislation have been corrected in this section in accordance with Recommendation 6 of the SLCR.

Objection to section 109 notice

110.—(1) The grounds on which objection may be made in a counter-notice to a blight notice served by virtue of section 109 shall include the ground that the claim made in the notice is not justified.

(2) Objection shall not be made to a blight notice served by virtue of section 109 on the grounds mentioned in section 102(4)(c) unless it is also made on the grounds mentioned in subsection (1).

(3) The Lands Tribunal shall not uphold an objection to a notice served by virtue of section 109 on the grounds mentioned in section 102(4)(c) unless it also upholds the objection on the grounds mentioned in subsection (1).

(4) Where objection is made to a blight notice served by virtue of section 109 on the ground mentioned in subsection (1) and also on those mentioned in section 102(4)(c), the Lands Tribunal, in determining whether or not to uphold the objection, shall treat that part of the affected area which is not specified in the counter-notice as included in "other relevant land" as defined in section 109(3).

(5) If the Lands Tribunal upholds an objection but only on the ground mentioned in subsection (1), the Tribunal shall declare that the blight notice is a valid notice in relation to the affected area but not in relation to the unaffected area.

(6) If the Lands Tribunal upholds an objection both on the ground mentioned in subsection (1) and on the grounds mentioned in section 102(4)(c) (but not on any other grounds) the Tribunal shall declare that the blight notice is a valid notice in relation to the part of the affected area specified in the counter-notice as being the part which the appropriate authority propose to acquire as mentioned in that notice but not in relation to any other part of the affected area or in relation to the unaffected area.

(7) In a case falling within subsection (5) or (6), the Lands Tribunal shall give directions specifying a date on which notice to treat (as mentioned in sections 105 and 111) is to be deemed to have been served.

(8) Section 104(6) shall not apply to any blight notice served by virtue of section 109.

DEFINITIONS
"affected area": ss.109(1)(b), 122(1).
"blight notice": ss.100(6), 122(1).
"Lands Tribunal": s.277(1).

GENERAL NOTE
See commentary to s.109.

Effect of section 109 notice

111.—(1) In relation to a blight notice served by virtue of section 109—
(a) subsection (2) of section 105 shall have effect as if for the words "or in the case of an agricultural unit the interest of the claimant in so far as it subsists in the affected area" there were substituted the words "or agricultural unit", and
(b) subsections (4) and (5) of that section shall not apply.
(2) Where the appropriate authority have served a counter-notice objecting to a blight notice on the grounds mentioned in section 110(1), then if either—
(a) the claimant, without referring that objection to the Lands Tribunal and before the time for so referring it has expired, gives notice to the appropriate authority that he withdraws his claim as to the unaffected area, or

(b) on a reference to the Tribunal, the Tribunal makes a declaration in accordance with section 110(5),

the appropriate authority shall be deemed to be authorised to acquire compulsorily under the appropriate enactment the interest of the claimant in so far as it subsists in the affected area (but not in so far as it subsists in the unaffected area), and to have served a notice to treat in respect of it on the date mentioned in subsection (3).

(3) The date referred to in subsection (2)—

(a) in a case falling within paragraph (a) of that subsection, is the date on which notice is given in accordance with that paragraph, and

(b) in a case falling within paragraph (b) of that subsection, is the date specified in directions given by the Tribunal in accordance with section 110(7).

(4) Where the appropriate authority have served a counter-notice objecting to a blight notice on the grounds mentioned in section 110(1) and also on the grounds mentioned in section 102(4)(c), then if either—

(a) the claimant, without referring that objection to the Lands Tribunal and before the time for so referring it has expired—

(i) gives notice to the appropriate authority that he accepts the proposal of the authority to acquire the part of the affected area specified in the counter-notice, and

(ii) withdraws his claim as to the remainder of that area and as to the unaffected area, or

(b) on a reference to the Tribunal, the Tribunal makes a declaration in accordance with section 110(6) in respect of that part of the affected area,

the appropriate authority shall be deemed to be authorised to acquire compulsorily under the appropriate enactment the interest of the claimant in so far as it subsists in the part of the affected area specified in the counter-notice (but not in so far as it subsists in any other part of that area or in the unaffected area) and to have served a notice to treat in respect of it on the date mentioned in subsection (5).

(5) The date referred to in subsection (4)—

(a) in a case falling within paragraph (a) of that subsection, is the date on which notice is given in accordance with that paragraph, and

(b) in a case falling within paragraph (b) of that subsection, is the date specified in directions given by the Tribunal in accordance with section 110(7).

(6) In relation to a blight notice served by virtue of section 109 references to "the appropriate authority" and "the appropriate enactment" shall be construed as if the unaffected area of an agricultural unit were part of the affected area.

(7) Where the claimant is a crofter or cottar this section shall have effect as if—

(a) in subsections (2) and (4), for the words from "acquire compulsorily" to "interest" and for the words "to treat in respect of it" there were substituted respectively the words "take possession compulsorily of the land" and the words "of entry in respect of that land under paragraph 3 of Schedule 2 to the Acquisition of Land (Authorisation Procedure) (Scotland) Act 1947", and

(b) in subsection (4)(a)(i), for the word "acquire" there were substituted the words "take possession of".

DEFINITIONS
"agricultural": s.277(1).
"agricultural unit": s.122(1).
"appropriate authority": subs. (6), s.120.
"appropriate enactment": subs. (6), s.121.

"blight notice": ss.100(6), 122(1).
"claimant": ss.101(4), 122(1).
"cottar": s.122(1).
"crofter": s.122(1).
"Lands Tribunal": s.277(1).

GENERAL NOTE
   This section makes consequential amendments to the provisions of the Act dealing generally with blight notices in order that they may accommodate the special circumstances of blight notices served under s.109.

Successors, heritable creditors and partnerships

Powers of successors in respect of blight notice

   112.—(1) In relation to any time after the death of a person who has served a blight notice, sections 102(1), 103(1), 104(1), 105(4) and (5), 107(1) and 111(2) and (4) shall apply as if any reference in them to the claimant were a reference to the person who, on the claimant's death, has succeeded to his interest in the hereditament or agricultural unit in question.
   (2) Where the whole or part of a hereditament or agricultural unit is comprised in blighted land and a person claims that—
   (a) he is the personal representative of a person ("the deceased") who at the date of his death was entitled to an interest in that hereditament or unit,
   (b) the interest was one which would have been a qualifying interest if a notice under section 101 had been served in respect of it on that date,
   (c) he has made reasonable endeavours to sell that interest,
   (d) in consequence of the fact that the hereditament or unit or a part of it was, or was likely to be, comprised in blighted land, he has been unable to sell that interest except at a price substantially lower than that for which it might reasonably have been expected to sell if no part of the hereditament or unit were, or were likely to be, comprised in such land, and
   (e) one or more individuals are (to the exclusion of any body corporate) beneficially entitled to that interest,
he may serve on the appropriate authority a notice in the prescribed form requiring that authority to purchase that interest to the extent specified in, and otherwise in accordance with, this Chapter.
   (3) Subject to subsection (4), subsection (2) shall apply in relation to an interest in part of a hereditament or agricultural unit as it applies in relation to an interest in the whole of a hereditament or agricultural unit.
   (4) Subsection (3) shall not enable any person—
   (a) if the deceased was entitled to an interest in the whole of a hereditament or agricultural unit, to make any claim or serve any notice under this section in respect of the deceased's interest in part of the hereditament or unit, or
   (b) if the deceased was entitled to an interest only in part of the hereditament or agricultural unit, to make or serve any such claim or notice in respect of the deceased's interest in less than the whole of that part.
   (5) Subject to sections 102(6) and (7) and 110(2) and (3), the grounds on which objection may be made in a counter-notice under section 102 to a notice under this section are those specified in paragraphs (a) to (c) of subsection (4) of that section and, in a case to which it applies, the grounds specified in paragraph (d) of that subsection and also the following grounds—
   (a) that the claimant is not the personal representative of the deceased or that, on the date of the deceased's death, the deceased was not entitled to an interest in any part of the hereditament or agricultural unit to which the notice relates;

(b) that (for reasons specified in the counter-notice) the interest of the deceased is not such as is specified in subsection (2)(b);
(c) that the conditions specified in subsection (2)(c), (d) or (e) are not satisfied.

DEFINITIONS
    "agricultural unit": s.122(1).
    "appropriate authority": s.120.
    "blighted land": s.100.
    "claimant": ss.101(4), 122(1).
    "deceased": subs. (2)(a).
    "hereditament": s.122(1), (3) and (4).
    "qualifying interest": s.100(2).

GENERAL NOTE
    This section provides that where a person who is entitled to serve a blight notice dies, the notice may be sent by his personal representatives. In these circumstances, the grounds on which the authority may object by way of counter-notice are similar *mutatis mutandis* to the grounds on which they would have been entitled to object to a blight notice served by the deceased, and in addition they may object on the grounds that:
    –the claimant is not the personal representative of the deceased (subs. (5)(a));
    –no individuals are beneficially entitled to the interest (subs. (5)(c)).
    Drafting errors in previous planning legislation have been corrected in this section in accordance with Recommendations 7 and 8.1 of the SLCR.
    No notice can be served under this section if a notice under s.101 (blight notices by owner, etc.) or s.113 (blight notices by heritable creditor) is outstanding (s.114).

"*Prescribed form*": see the Town and Country Planning (General) (Scotland) Regulations 1976 (S.I. 1976 No. 2022), reg. 3 and Sched. 1.

Power of heritable creditor to serve blight notice

    113.—(1) Where the whole or part of a hereditament or agricultural unit is comprised in blighted land and a person claims that—
(a) he is entitled as heritable creditor (by virtue of a power which has become exercisable) to sell an interest in the hereditament or unit, giving immediate vacant possession of the land,
(b) he has made reasonable endeavours to sell that interest or the land falls within paragraph 14 or 15 of Schedule 14 and the powers of compulsory acquisition remain exercisable, and
(c) in consequence of the fact that the hereditament or unit or a part of it was, or was likely to be, comprised in blighted land, he has been unable to sell that interest except at a price substantially lower than that for which it might reasonably have been expected to sell if no part of the hereditament or unit were, or were likely to be, comprised in such land,
then, subject to the provisions of this section, he may serve on the appropriate authority a notice in the prescribed form requiring that authority to purchase that interest to the extent specified in, and otherwise in accordance with, this Chapter.
    (2) Subject to subsection (3), subsection (1) shall apply in relation to an interest in part of a hereditament or agricultural unit as it applies in relation to an interest in the whole of a hereditament or agricultural unit.
    (3) Subsection (2) shall not enable a person—
(a) if his interest as heritable creditor is in the whole of a hereditament or agricultural unit, to make any claim or serve any notice under this section in respect of any interest in part of the hereditament or agricultural unit, or
(b) if his interest as heritable creditor is only in part of a hereditament or agricultural unit, to make or serve any such notice or claim in respect of any interest in less than the whole of that part.

(4) Notice under this section shall not be served unless the interest which the heritable creditor claims he has the power to sell—

   (a) could be the subject of a notice under section 101 served by the person entitled to it on the date of service of the notice under this section, or

   (b) could have been the subject of such a notice served by that person on a date not more than 6 months before the date of service of the notice under this section.

(5) Subject to sections 102(6) and (7) and 110(2) and (3), the grounds on which objection may be made in a counter-notice under section 102 to a notice under this section are those specified in paragraphs (a) to (c) of subsection (4) of that section and, in a case to which it applies, the grounds specified in paragraph (d) of that subsection and also the following grounds—

   (a) that, on the date of service of the notice under this section, the claimant had no interest as heritable creditor in any part of the hereditament or agricultural unit to which the notice relates;

   (b) that (for reasons specified in the counter-notice) the claimant had not on that date the power referred to in subsection (1)(a);

   (c) that the conditions specified in subsection (1)(b) and (c) are not fulfilled;

   (d) that (for reasons specified in the counter-notice) neither of the conditions specified in subsection (4) was, on the date of service of the notice under this section, satisfied with regard to the interest referred to in that subsection.

DEFINITIONS

"agricultural": s.277(1).
"agricultural unit": s.122(1).
"appropriate authority": s.120.
"blighted land": s.100.
"hereditament": s.122(1), (3) and (4).
"heritable creditor": s.277(1).

GENERAL NOTE

This section provides that a blight notice may be sent by a heritable creditor whose power of sale has become exercisable. In these circumstances, the grounds on which the authority may object by way of counter-notice are similar *mutatis mutandis* to the grounds on which they would have been entitled to object to a blight notice served by the deceased, and in addition they may object on the grounds that:

–the claimant had no interest as heritable creditor at the date of service of the notice (subs. (5)(a));

–the claimant had not at that date an exercisable power of sale (subs. (5)(b)); or

–the debtor would not have been entitled to serve a blight notice on or within six months prior to that date (subs. (5)(d)).

Drafting errors in previous planning legislation have been corrected in this section in accordance with Recommendation 8.2 of the SLCR.

No notice can be served under this section if a notice under s.101 (blight notices by owner, etc.) or s.112 (blight notices by personal representatives) is outstanding (s.114).

"*Prescribed form*": see the Town and Country Planning (General) (Scotland) Regulations 1976 (S.I. 1976 No. 2022), reg. 3 and Sched. 1.

Prohibition on service of simultaneous notices under sections 101, 112 and 113

114.—(1) No notice shall be served under section 101 or 112 in respect of a hereditament or agricultural unit, or any part of it, at a time when a notice already served under section 113 is outstanding with respect to it, and no notice shall be served under section 113 at a time when a notice already served under section 101 or 112 is outstanding with respect to the relevant hereditament, agricultural unit or part.

(2) For the purposes of subsection (1), a notice shall be treated as outstanding with respect to a hereditament, agricultural unit or part—

(a) until it is withdrawn in relation to the hereditament, agricultural unit or part, or

(b) in a case where an objection to the notice has been made by a counter-notice under section 102, until either—

(i) the period of 2 months specified in section 104 elapses without the claimant having required the objection to be referred to the Lands Tribunal under that section, or

(ii) the objection, having been so referred, is upheld by the Tribunal with respect to the hereditament, agricultural unit or part.

DEFINITIONS
"agricultural": s.277(1).
"agricultural unit": s.122(1).
"claimant": ss.101(4), 122(1).
"hereditament": s.122(1), (3) and (4).
"Lands Tribunal": s.277(1).

GENERAL NOTE
No notice can be served under s.101 (blight notices by owner, etc.), s.112 (blight notices by personal representatives) or s.113 (blight notices by heritable creditor) if a notice under another of these sections is outstanding.

Special provisions as to partnerships

115.—(1) This section shall have effect for the purposes of the application of this Chapter to a hereditament or agricultural unit occupied for the purposes of a partnership firm.

(2) Occupation for the purposes of the firm shall be treated as occupation by the firm, and not as occupation by any one or more of the partners individually, and the definitions of "owner-occupier" in section 119(1) and (2) shall apply in relation to the firm accordingly.

(3) If, after the service by the firm of a blight notice, any change occurs (whether by death or otherwise) in the constitution of the firm, any proceedings, rights or obligations consequential upon that notice may be carried on or exercised by or against, or, as the case may be, shall be incumbent upon, the partners for the time being constituting the firm.

(4) Nothing in this Chapter shall be construed as indicating an intention to exclude the operation of the definition of "person" in Schedule 1 to the Interpretation Act 1978 (by which, unless the contrary intention appears, "person" includes any body of persons corporate or unincorporate) in relation to any provision of this Chapter.

(5) Subsection (2) shall not affect the definition of "resident owner-occupier" in section 119(3).

DEFINITIONS
"agricultural": s.277(1).
"agricultural unit": s.122(1).
"blight notice": ss.100(6), 122(1).
"hereditament": s.122(1), (3) and (4).
"owner-occupier": subs. (2), s.119.

GENERAL NOTE
This section makes special provision in respect of partnerships. In Scots law a partnership has separate legal personality. Occupation by the partnership is not treated as occupation by the partners individually (subs. (2)). If the constitution of a partnership changes after service of a blight notice, matters proceed as if there had been no change (subs. (4)).

Miscellaneous and supplementary provisions

Power of Secretary of State to acquire land affected by orders relating to new towns etc. where blight notice served

116.—(1) Where a blight notice has been served in respect of land falling within paragraph 5, 6 or 7 of Schedule 14, then until such time as a development corporation is established for the new town or, as the case may be, an urban development corporation is established for the urban development area the Secretary of State shall have power to acquire compulsorily any interest in the land in pursuance of the blight notice served by virtue of the paragraph that applies.

(2) Where the Secretary of State acquires an interest under subsection (1), then—

(a) if the land is or becomes land within paragraph 6 or, as the case may be, paragraph 7(b) of Schedule 14, the interest shall be transferred by him to the development corporation established for the new town or, as the case may be, the urban development corporation established for the urban development area, and

(b) in any other case, the interest may be disposed of by him in such manner as he thinks fit.

(3) The Land Compensation (Scotland) Act 1963 shall have effect in relation to the compensation payable in respect of the acquisition of an interest by the Secretary of State under subsection (1) as if—

(a) the acquisition were by a development corporation under the New Towns (Scotland) Act 1968 or, as the case may be, by an urban development corporation under Part XVI of the Local Government, Planning and Land Act 1980,

(b) in the case of land within paragraph 5 of Schedule 14, the land formed part of an area designated as the site of a new town by an order which has come into operation under section 1 of the New Towns (Scotland) Act 1968, and

(c) in the case of land within paragraph 7(a) of Schedule 14, the land formed part of an area designated as an urban development area by an order under section 134 of the Local Government, Planning and Land Act 1980 which has come into operation.

(4) Where a blight notice to which subsection (1) relates has been served by a crofter or cottar the preceding subsections shall have effect as if there were substituted—

(a) in subsection (1), for the words "acquire compulsorily any interest in the land" the words "take possession of any land occupied by the crofter or cottar",

(b) in subsection (2), for the words "acquires an interest" and "interest" the words "takes possession" and "possession" respectively, and

(c) in subsection (3), for the words from "acquisition of" to "acquisition were" the words "taking of possession of land by the Secretary of State under subsection (1) as if the taking of possession were".

DEFINITIONS
"blight notice": ss.100(6), 122(1).
"cottar": s.122(1).
"crofter": s.122(1).
"land": s.277(1).
"urban development area": s.277(1).
"urban development corporation": s.277(1).

GENERAL NOTE
Where land is blighted on the ground of being:
–the site of a proposed new town (Sched. 14, paras. 5 and 6); or

–an area designated or intended to be designated as an urban development area (Sched. 14, para. 7),

this section gives power to acquire land specified in a blight notice to the Secretary of State until such time as the relevant development corporation is established. In these circumstances the Secretary of State is "the appropriate authority" (s.120(4)).

Saving for claimant's right to sell whole hereditament, etc.

117.—(1) The provisions of sections 102(4)(c), 104(6), 105(4) and (5) and 106(3) and (4) relating to hereditaments shall not affect—

(a) the right of a claimant under section 90 of the Lands Clauses Consolidation (Scotland) Act 1845 to sell the whole of the hereditament or, in the case of an agricultural unit, the whole of the affected area, which he has required the authority to purchase, or

(b) the right of a claimant under paragraph 4 of Schedule 2 to the Acquisition of Land (Authorisation Procedure) (Scotland) Act 1947 to sell (unless the Lands Tribunal otherwise determines) the whole of the hereditament or, as the case may be, affected area which he has required that authority to purchase.

(2) In consequence of subsection (1)(b), in determining whether or not to uphold an objection relating to a hereditament on the grounds mentioned in section 102(4)(c), the Lands Tribunal shall consider (in addition to the other matters which they are required to consider) whether—

(a) in the case of a house, building or factory, the part proposed to be acquired can be taken without material detriment to the house, building or factory, or

(b) in the case of a park or garden belonging to a house, the part proposed to be acquired can be taken without seriously affecting the amenity or convenience of the house.

DEFINITIONS
"agricultural": s.277(1).
"agricultural unit": s.122(1).
"appropriate authority": s.120.
"building": s.277(1).
"claimant": ss.101(4), 122(1).
"hereditament": s.122(1), (3) and (4).
"Lands Tribunal": s.277(1).

GENERAL NOTE
This section preserves and applies to blight notice procedures the owner's right under compulsory purchase procedures to require the authority to purchase the whole of a hereditament or of the affected part of an agricultural unit.

No withdrawal of constructive notice to treat

118. Without prejudice to the provisions of section 107(1) and (7), a notice to treat which is deemed to have been served by virtue of this Chapter may not be withdrawn under section 39 of the Land Compensation (Scotland) Act 1963.

GENERAL NOTE
In normal compulsory purchase procedures the notice to treat may be withdrawn under s.39 of the Land Compensation (Scotland) Act 1963. This section provides that in compulsory purchase procedures following on from a blight notice, the deemed notice to treat may not be withdrawn by the authority. It is deemed to be withdrawn by the claimant if the claimant withdraws the blight notice (s.107(2)).

Meaning of "owner-occupier" and "resident owner-occupier"

119.—(1) Subject to the following provisions of this section, in this Chapter "owner-occupier", in relation to a hereditament, means—

(a) a person who occupies the whole or a substantial part of the hereditament in right of an owner's interest in it, and has so occupied the hereditament or that part of it during the whole of the period of 6 months ending with the date of service, or

(b) if the whole or a substantial part of the hereditament was unoccupied for a period of not more than 12 months ending with that date, a person who so occupied the hereditament or, as the case may be, that part of it during the whole of a period of 6 months ending immediately before the period when it was not occupied.

(2) Subject to the following provisions of this section, in this Chapter "owner-occupier", in relation to an agricultural unit, means a person who—

(a) occupies the whole of that unit and has occupied it during the whole of the period of 6 months ending with the date of service, or

(b) occupied the whole of that unit during the whole of a period of 6 months ending not more than 12 months before the date of service,

and, at all times material for the purposes of paragraph (a) or, as the case may be, paragraph (b), has been entitled to an owner's interest in the whole or part of that unit.

(3) In this Chapter "resident owner-occupier", in relation to a hereditament, means—

(a) an individual who occupies the whole or a substantial part of the hereditament as a private dwelling in right of an owner's interest in it, and has so occupied the hereditament or, as the case may be, that part during the whole of the period of 6 months ending with the date of service, or

(b) if the whole or a substantial part of the hereditament was unoccupied for a period of not more than 12 months ending with that date, an individual who so occupied the hereditament or, as the case may be, that part during the whole of a period of 6 months ending immediately before the period when it was not occupied.

(4) In this section—

"owner's interest", in relation to a hereditament or agricultural unit, or part of it, includes the interest of—

(a) the lessee under a lease of it not less than 3 years of which remain unexpired on the date of service, and

(b) a crofter or cottar; and

"date of service", in relation to a hereditament or agricultural unit, means the date of service of a notice in respect of it under section 101.

<small>DEFINITIONS</small>
"agricultural": s.277(1).
"agricultural unit": s.122(1).
"blight notice": ss.100(6), 122(1).
"date of service": subs. (4), s.122(5).
"hereditament": s.122(1), (3) and (4).
"owner's interest": subs. (4).

<small>GENERAL NOTE</small>
This section contains definitions necessary to establish under ss.100 and 101 whether a person is entitled to serve a blight notice.

Drafting errors in previous planning legislation have been corrected in this section in accordance with Recommendation 6 of the SLCR.

"Appropriate authority" for purposes of Chapter II

120.—(1) Subject to the following provisions of this section, in this Chapter "the appropriate authority", in relation to any land, means the government department, local authority or other body or person by whom, in accordance with the circumstances by virtue of which the land falls within any paragraph of Schedule 14, the land is liable to be acquired or is indicated as being proposed to be acquired or, as the case may be, any right over the land is proposed to be acquired.

(2) If any question arises—

(a) whether the appropriate authority in relation to any land for the purposes of this Chapter is the Secretary of State or a local roads authority,

(b) which of two or more local roads authorities is the appropriate authority in relation to any land for those purposes, or

(c) which of two or more local authorities is the appropriate authority in relation to any land for those purposes,

that question shall be referred to the Secretary of State, whose decision shall be final.

(3) If any question arises as to which authority is the appropriate authority for the purposes of this Chapter—

(a) section 102(2) shall have effect as if the reference to the date of service of the blight notice were a reference to that date or, if it is later, the date on which that question is determined,

(b) section 113(4)(b) shall apply with the substitution for the period of 6 months of a reference to that period extended by so long as it takes to obtain a determination of the question, and

(c) section 119(1)(b), (2)(b) and (3)(b) shall apply with the substitution for the reference to 12 months before the date of service of a reference to that period extended by so long as it takes to obtain a determination of the question.

(4) In relation to land falling within paragraph 5, 6 or 7 of Schedule 14, until such time as a development corporation is established for the new town or, as the case may be, an urban development corporation is established for the urban development area, this Chapter shall have effect as if "the appropriate authority" were the Secretary of State.

DEFINITIONS

"government department": s.277(1).
"land": s.277(1).
"local authority": s.277(1).
"local roads authority": s.277(1).
"urban development area": s.277(1).
"urban development corporation": s.277(1).

GENERAL NOTE

This section identifies the "appropriate authority" for the purposes of Chap. II. Any questions as to which of two or more authorities is the "appropriate authority" are to be settled by the Secretary of State (subs. (2)).

Subs. (4)

Where land is blighted on the ground of being:
–the site of a proposed new town (Sched. 14, paras. 5 and 6); and
–an area designated or intended to be designated as an urban development area (Sched. 14, para. 7),
the Secretary of State is "the appropriate authority". In these circumstances, until such time as the relevant development corporation is established, s.116 gives the Secretary of State power to acquire land specified in a blight notice.

"Appropriate enactment" for purposes of Chapter II

121.—(1) Subject to the following provisions of this section, in this Chapter "the appropriate enactment", in relation to land falling within any paragraph of Schedule 14, means the enactment which provides for the compulsory acquisition of land as being land falling within that paragraph.

(2) In relation to land falling within paragraph 2 of that Schedule, an enactment shall for the purposes of subsection (1) be taken to be an enactment

which provides for the compulsory acquisition of land as being land falling within that paragraph if—

(a) the enactment provides for the compulsory acquisition of land for the purposes of the functions which are indicated in the development plan as being the functions for the purposes of which the land is allocated or is proposed to be developed, or

(b) where no particular functions are so indicated in the development plan, the enactment provides for the compulsory acquisition of land for the purposes of any of the functions of the government department, local authority or other body for the purposes of whose functions the land is allocated or is defined as the site of proposed development.

(3) In relation to land falling within paragraph 2 of that Schedule by virtue of paragraph 2(2), "the appropriate enactment" shall be determined in accordance with subsection (2) as if references in that subsection to the development plan were references to any such plan, proposal or modifications as are mentioned in paragraph 2(2)(a), (b) or (c).

(4) In relation to land falling within paragraph 3 or 4 of that Schedule, "the appropriate enactment" shall be determined in accordance with subsection (2) as if references in that subsection to the development plan were references to the resolution or direction in question.

(5) In relation to land falling within paragraph 5, 6 or 7 of that Schedule, until such time as a development corporation is established for the new town or, as the case may be, an urban development corporation is established for the urban development area, this Chapter shall have effect as if "the appropriate enactment" were section 116(1).

(6) In relation to land falling within paragraph 8 or 9 of that Schedule, "the appropriate enactment" means Part IV of the Housing (Scotland) Act 1987.

(7) In relation to land falling within paragraph 15 of that Schedule by virtue of paragraph 15(2), "the appropriate enactment" means the enactment which would provide for the compulsory acquisition of the land or of the rights over the land if the relevant compulsory purchase order were confirmed or made.

(8) Where, in accordance with the circumstances by virtue of which any land falls within any paragraph of that Schedule, it is indicated that the land is proposed to be acquired for roads purposes, any enactment under which a roads authority are or (subject to the fulfilment of the relevant conditions) could be authorised to acquire that land compulsorily for roads purposes shall, for the purposes of subsection (1), be taken to be an enactment providing for the compulsory acquisition of that land as being land falling within that paragraph.

(9) In subsection (8) the reference to the fulfilment of the relevant conditions is a reference to such one or more of the following as are applicable to the circumstances in question—

(a) the coming into operation of any requisite order or scheme under the provisions of the Roads (Scotland) Act 1984;

(b) the making or approval of any requisite plans.

(10) If, apart from this subsection, two or more enactments would be the appropriate enactment in relation to any land for the purposes of this Chapter, the appropriate enactment for those purposes shall be taken to be that one of those enactments under which, in the circumstances in question, it is most likely that (apart from this Chapter) the land would have been acquired by the appropriate authority.

(11) If any question arises as to which enactment is the appropriate enactment in relation to any land for the purposes of this Chapter, that question shall be referred—

(a) where the appropriate authority are a government department, to the Minister in charge of that department,

(b) where the appropriate authority are statutory undertakers, to the appropriate Minister, and

(c) in any other case, to the Secretary of State,

and the decision of the Minister or, as the case may be, the Secretary of State shall be final.

DEFINITIONS

   "compulsory acquisition": s.277(1).
   "development": ss.26, 277(1).
   "development plan": ss.24, 277(1).
   "functions": s.277(1).
   "government department": s.277(1).
   "land": s.277(1).
   "local authority": s.277(1).
   "statutory undertakers": ss.214, 277(1).
   "urban development area": s.277(1).
   "urban development corporation": s.277(1).

GENERAL NOTE

   This section identifies the "appropriate enactment" for the purposes of Chap. II. Any questions as to which enactment is the "appropriate enactment" are to be settled by, depending on the circumstances, a Minister or the Secretary of State (subs. (11)).

General interpretation of Chapter II

122.—(1) Subject to the following provisions of this section, in this Chapter—

   "the affected area", in relation to an agricultural unit, means so much of that unit as, on the date of service, consists of land falling within any paragraph of Schedule 14;

   "agricultural unit" means land which is occupied as a unit for agricultural purposes, including any dwellinghouse or other building occupied by the same person for the purpose of farming the land;

   "annual value", in relation to a hereditament, means the value which, on the date of service, is shown in the valuation roll as the rateable value of the hereditament, except that, where the rateable value differs from the net annual value, it means the value which on that date is shown in the valuation roll as the net annual value of it;

   "blight notice" has the meaning given in section 100(6);

   "the claimant" has the meaning given in section 101(4);

   "cottar" has the meaning given in section 12(5) of the Crofters (Scotland) Act 1993;

   "crofter" has the meaning given in section 3(3) of that Act;

   "hereditament" means the aggregate of the lands and heritages (not being agricultural lands and heritages within the meaning of section 7 of the Valuation and Rating (Scotland) Act 1956) which form the subject of a single entry in the valuation roll for the time being in force for a valuation area;

   "special enactment" means a local enactment, or a provision contained in an Act other than a local or private Act, which is a local enactment or provision authorising the compulsory acquisition of land specifically identified in it; and in this definition "local enactment" means a local or private Act, or an order confirmed by Parliament or brought into operation in accordance with special parliamentary procedure.

(2) Where any land is on the boundary between two or more valuation areas, and accordingly—

   (a) different parts of that land form the subject of single entries in the valuation rolls for the time being in force for those areas respectively, but

(b) if the whole of that land had been in one of those areas, it would have formed the subject of a single entry in the valuation roll for that area, the whole of that land shall be treated, for the purposes of the definition of "hereditament" in subsection (1) of this section, as if it formed the subject of a single entry in the valuation roll for a valuation area.

(3) Land which forms the subject of an entry in the valuation roll by reason only that it is land over which any sporting rights are exercisable, or that it is land over which a right of exhibiting advertisements is let out or reserved, shall not be taken to be a hereditament within that definition.

(4) Where, in accordance with subsection (2), land of which different parts form the subject of single entries in the valuation rolls for the time being in force for two or more valuation areas is treated as if it formed the subject of a single entry in the valuation roll for a valuation area, the definition of "annual value" in subsection (1) shall apply as if any reference in that definition to a value shown in the valuation roll were a reference to the aggregate of the values shown (as rateable values or as net annual values, as the case may be) in those valuation rolls in relation to the different parts of that land.

(5) In this section "date of service" has the same meaning as in section 119.

PART VI

ENFORCEMENT

Application

Expressions used in connection with enforcement

123.—(1) For the purposes of this Act—
(a) carrying out development without the required planning permission, or
(b) failing to comply with any condition or limitation subject to which planning permission has been granted,
constitutes a breach of planning control.

(2) For the purposes of this Act—
(a) the issue of an enforcement notice, or
(b) the service of a breach of condition notice,
under this Part constitutes taking enforcement action.

(3) In this Part "planning permission" includes planning permission under Part III of the 1947 Act and Part III of the 1972 Act.

DEFINITIONS
"breach of condition notice": ss.145, 277(1).
"breach of planning control": ss.123, 277(1).
"development": ss.26, 277(1).
"development order": ss.30, 277(1).
"enforcement notice": ss.127, 277(1).
"planning permission": subs. (3), s.277(1).

GENERAL NOTE
The main methods of enforcement are the service of an enforcement notice or a breach of condition notice. These methods comprise "taking enforcement action" (subs. (2)), and may be supplemented where appropriate by a stop notice (s.140) or interdict (s.146).
Enforcement action may be taken under the Act where there is a breach of planning control, which is defined in subs. (1) as one of two situations:
(a) carrying out development without the required planning permission; or
(b) failing to comply with any condition or limitation of the planning permission.

In either case the action can be taken whether the planning permission was granted under this or previous Planning Acts (subs. (3)).

The enforcement notice must state which of the two situations applies (s.128(1)(b)).

Enforcement action can be taken in respect of a limitation only if the limitation is contained within the deed itself or is a condition (*Peacock Homes v. Secretary of State for the Environment* [1994] J.P.L. 729).

Further provision as to enforcement notices is made in the Enforcement of Control (No. 2) (Scotland) Regulations 1992 (S.I. 1992 No. 2086).

Time limits

124.—(1) Where there has been a breach of planning control consisting in the carrying out without planning permission of building, engineering, mining or other operations in, on, over or under land, no enforcement action may be taken after the end of the period of 4 years beginning with the date on which the operations were substantially completed.

(2) Where there has been a breach of planning control consisting in the change of use of any building to use as a single dwellinghouse, no enforcement action may be taken after the end of the period of 4 years beginning with the date of the breach.

(3) In the case of any other breach of planning control, no enforcement action may be taken after the end of the period of 10 years beginning with the date of the breach.

(4) Subsections (1) to (3) do not prevent—

(a) the service of a breach of condition notice in respect of any breach of planning control if an enforcement notice in respect of the breach is in effect, or

(b) taking further enforcement action in respect of any breach of planning control if, during the period of 4 years ending with that action being taken, the planning authority have taken or purported to take enforcement action in respect of that breach.

DEFINITIONS

"breach of condition notice": ss.145, 277(1).
"breach of planning control": ss.123, 277(1).
"building": s.277(1).
"enforcement action": s.123(2).
"enforcement notice": ss.127, 277(1).
"land": s.277(1).
"mining operations": ss.26, 277(1).
"planning authority": ss.1, 277(1).
"planning permission": ss.123(3), 277(1).

GENERAL NOTE

General rule. This section provides for immunity from the taking of enforcement action after a specified period of time. The period is ascertained as follows:

–in the case of building, engineering mining or other operations carried on without planning permission, four years from the date on which the operations were "substantially completed" (s.124(1)). Accordingly, elements carried out prior to the four year period can be enforced if the operation continues into the four year period. Whether any given actings are elements of an operation or a separate operation is a matter of fact and degree (*Worthy Fuel Injection v. Secretary of State for the Environment and Southampton City Council* [1983] J.P.L. 173);

–in the case of change of use to a single dwelling house, four years beginning on the date of breach (s.124(2)). This period also applies to residential sub-divisions (*Van Dyck v. Secretary of State for the Environment* [1993] J.P.L. 565);

–in any other case, 10 years beginning on the date of breach (s.124(3)). Given that changes of use are often gradual, there can be difficulties of proof in establishing the date of breach: the only effective test is to compare the use 10 years previously with the current use and determine whether there has been any material change (*Cheshire County Council v. Secretary of State for the Environment* (1971) 222 EG 35).

Exceptions. Enforcement action can be taken outwith the above periods as follows:

–where an enforcement notice is already in effect (subs. (4)(a));
–where prior enforcement action has been taken within the previous four years (subs. (4)(b)). This can be done even if there was an error or defect in the original enforcement notice so long as the purpose of the original notice is the same as the purpose of the second notice (*Barn Properties v. Secretary of State for Scotland*, 1996 S.L.T. 964). The prior action must have been taken timeously (*William Boyer (Transport) v. Secretary of State for the Environment, The Times*, February 7, 1996; and
–where a change of use is enforced against, any incidental operations forming an integral part of such change of use can be enforced against outwith the limitation period (*Murfitt v. Secretary of State for the Environment*, [1980] J.P.L. 598; *Perkins v. Secretary of State for the Environment* [1981] J.P.L. 755; *Somak Travel v. Secretary of State for the Environment* (1988) 55 P. & C.R. 250; *Pope v. Secretary of State for the Environment* [1991] EGCS 112).

Planning contravention notices

Power to require information about activities on land

125.—(1) Where it appears to the planning authority that there may have been a breach of planning control in respect of any land, they may serve notice to that effect (referred to in this Act as a "planning contravention notice") on any person who—

(a) is the owner or occupier of the land or has any other interests in it, or
(b) is carrying out operations on the land or is using it for any purpose.

(2) A planning contravention notice may require the person on whom it is served to give such information as to—

(a) any operations being carried out on the land, any use of the land and any other activities being carried out on the land, and
(b) any matter relating to the conditions or limitations subject to which any planning permission in respect of the land has been granted,

as may be specified in the notice.

(3) Without prejudice to the generality of subsection (2), the notice may require the person on whom it is served, so far as he is able—

(a) to state whether or not the land is being used for any purpose specified in the notice or any operations or activities specified in the notice are being or have been carried out on the land;
(b) to state when any use, operations or activities began;
(c) to give the name and address of any person known to him to use or have used the land for any purpose or to be carrying out, or have carried out, any operations or activities on the land;
(d) to give any information he holds as to any planning permission for any use or operations or any reason for planning permission not being required for any use or operation;
(e) to state the nature of his interest (if any) in the land and the name and address of any other person known to him to have an interest in the land.

(4) A planning contravention notice may give notice of a time and place at which—

(a) any offer which the person on whom the notice is served may wish to make to apply for planning permission, to refrain from carrying out any operations or activities or to undertake remedial works, and
(b) any representations which he may wish to make about the notice,

will be considered by the authority, and the authority shall give him an opportunity to make in person any such offer or representations at that time and place.

(5) A planning contravention notice must inform the person on whom it is served—

(a) of the likely consequences of his failing to respond to the notice and, in particular, that enforcement action may be taken, and
(b) of the effect of section 143(6).

(6) Any requirement of a planning contravention notice shall be complied with by giving information in writing to the planning authority.

(7) The service of a planning contravention notice does not affect any other power exercisable in respect of any breach of planning control.

(8) In this section references to operations or activities on land include operations or activities in, under or over the land.

DEFINITIONS
"breach of planning control": ss.123, 277(1).
"disposal": s.277(1).
"enforcement action": s.123(2).
"land": s.277(1).
"owner": s.277(1).
"planning authority": ss.1, 277(1).
"planning permission": ss.123(3), 277(1).
"use": s.277(1).

GENERAL NOTE
The purpose of a planning contravention notice is to act as a formal warning of the prospect of an enforcement or stop notice and to enable the authority to obtain more information. The service of the notice may therefore encourage negotiations between the authority and the person thought to be in breach, while at the same time furnishing the authority with the information required to proceed with enforcement action should agreement not be reached.

Negotiations are further encouraged by subs. (4), in terms of which the authority may offer a "time and place meeting at which the recipient of the notice may make an offer and representations".

A planning authority may serve a planning contravention notice where it appears to it that there may have been a breach of planning control (subs. (1)). It may not do so where there is no suggestion of such breach (*R. v. Teignbridge District Council, ex p. Teignmouth Quay Co.* [1994] EGCS 203).

The notice must warn the recipient (subs. (5)):
–of the likely consequences if failure to respond, including that enforcement action might be taken; and
–of the effect of s.143(5), that is, that his right to compensation in the event of a stop notice being served will be affected by failure to provide the requested information.

There are also criminal sanctions for non-compliance with the notice: see s.126.

Penalties for non-compliance with planning contravention notice

126.—(1) If at any time after the end of the period of 21 days beginning with the day on which a planning contravention notice has been served on any person, he has not complied with any requirement of the notice, he shall be guilty of an offence.

(2) An offence under subsection (1) may be charged by reference to any day or longer period of time and a person may be convicted of a second or subsequent offence under that subsection by reference to any period of time following the preceding conviction for such an offence.

(3) It shall be a defence for a person charged with an offence under subsection (1) to prove that he had a reasonable excuse for failing to comply with the requirement.

(4) A person guilty of an offence under subsection (1) shall be liable on summary conviction to a fine not exceeding level 3 on the standard scale.

(5) If any person—
 (a) makes any statement purporting to comply with a requirement of a planning contravention notice which he knows to be false or misleading in a material particular, or
 (b) recklessly makes such a statement which is false or misleading in a material particular,
he shall be guilty of an offence.

(6) A person guilty of an offence under subsection (5) shall be liable on summary conviction to a fine not exceeding level 5 on the standard scale.

DEFINITIONS
  "development": ss.26, 277(1).
  "planning contravention notice": ss.125, 277(1).

GENERAL NOTE
  This section makes it a criminal offence to fail, without reasonable excuse, to comply with a planning contravention notice within 21 days, or to knowingly or recklessly make a false or misleading statement purporting to comply with a requirement of such a notice.

Enforcement notices

Issue of enforcement notice

127.—(1) The planning authority may issue a notice (in this Act referred to as an "enforcement notice") where it appears to them—
  (a) that there has been a breach of planning control, and
  (b) that it is expedient to issue the notice, having regard to the provisions of the development plan and to any other material considerations.
  (2) A copy of an enforcement notice shall be served—
  (a) on the owner and on the occupier of the land to which it relates, and
  (b) on any other person having an interest in the land, being an interest which, in the opinion of the authority, is materially affected by the notice.
  (3) The service of the notice shall take place—
  (a) not more than 28 days after its date of issue, and
  (b) not less than 28 days before the date specified in it as the date on which it is to take effect.

DEFINITIONS
  "breach of planning control": ss.123, 277(1).
  "development": ss.26, 277(1).
  "development plan": ss.24, 277(1).
  "land": s.277(1).
  "owner": s.277(1).
  "planning authority": ss.1, 277(1).

GENERAL NOTE
  This section sets out the circumstances in which a planning authority may issue an enforcement notice (subs. (1)) and the persons on whom it must serve the notice (subs. (2)). In addition it provides for timelimits: the notice must be served not more than 28 days after its issue and not less than 28 days before it takes effect (subs. (3)).
  Failure to serve the notice properly may render it a nullity (*Gill v. Clydebank District Council*, 1983 S.C. 76; *Martin v. Bearsden and Milngavie District Council*, 1987 S.C. 80); *R. v. Greenwich London Borough Council ex p. Patel* (1985) 51 P. & C.R. 282).

Contents and effect of notice

128.—(1) An enforcement notice shall state—
  (a) the matters which appear to the planning authority to constitute the breach of planning control, and
  (b) the paragraph of section 123(1) within which, in the opinion of the authority, the breach falls.
  (2) A notice complies with subsection (1)(a) if it enables any person on whom a copy of it is served to know what those matters are.
  (3) An enforcement notice shall specify the steps which the authority require to be taken, or the activities which the authority require to cease, in order to achieve, wholly or partly, any of the following purposes.
  (4) Those purposes are—
  (a) remedying the breach by making any development comply with the terms (including conditions and limitations) of any planning permission which has been granted in respect of the land by discontinuing

any use of the land or by restoring the land to its condition before the breach took place; or

(b) remedying any injury to amenity which has been caused by the breach.

(5) An enforcement notice may, for example, require—

(a) the alteration or removal of any buildings or works,

(b) the carrying out of any building or other operations,

(c) any activity on the land not to be carried on except to the extent specified in the notice, or

(d) the contour of a deposit of refuse or waste materials on land to be modified by altering the gradient or gradients of its sides.

(6) An enforcement notice issued in respect of a breach of planning control consisting of demolition of a building may require the construction of a building (in this section referred to as a "replacement building") which, subject to subsection (7), is as similar as possible to the demolished building.

(7) A replacement building—

(a) must comply with any requirement imposed by or under any enactment applicable to the construction of buildings,

(b) may differ from the demolished building in any respect which, if the demolished building had been altered in that respect, would not have constituted a breach of planning control, and

(c) must comply with any regulations made for the purposes of this subsection (including regulations modifying paragraphs (a) and (b) of this subsection).

(8) An enforcement notice shall specify the date on which it is to take effect and, subject to section 131(3), shall take effect on that date.

(9) An enforcement notice shall specify the period for compliance with the notice at the end of which any steps are required to have been taken or any activities are required to have ceased, and may specify different periods for different steps or activities.

(10) Where different periods apply to different steps or activities, references in this Part to the period for compliance with an enforcement notice, in relation to any step or activity, are to the period at the end of which the step is required to have been taken or the activity is required to have ceased.

(11) An enforcement notice shall specify such additional matters as may be prescribed.

(12) Regulations may require every copy of an enforcement notice served under section 127 to be accompanied by an explanatory note giving prescribed information as to the right of appeal under section 130.

(13) Where—

(a) an enforcement notice in respect of any breach of planning control could have required any buildings or works to be removed or any activity to cease, but does not do so, and

(b) all the requirements of the notice have been complied with,

then, so far as the notice did not so require, planning permission shall be treated as having been granted under section 33 in respect of development consisting of the construction of the buildings or works or, as the case may be, the carrying out of the activities.

(14) Where—

(a) an enforcement notice requires the construction of a replacement building, and

(b) all the requirements of the notice with respect to that construction have been complied with,

planning permission shall be treated as having been granted under section 33 in respect of development consisting of that construction.

DEFINITIONS
"breach of planning control": ss.123, 277(1).
"building": s.277(1).

"building or works": s.277(1).
"building operations": ss.26, 277(1).
"depositing of refuse or waste materials": s.277(1).
"development": ss.26, 277(1).
"development plan": ss.24, 277(1).
"enforcement notice": ss.127, 277(1).
"land": s.277(1).
"planning authority": ss.1, 277(1).
"replacement building": subs. (6).

GENERAL NOTE
This section provides for the contents of the enforcement notice as follows. Further details of the contents of an enforcement notice are prescribed in Enforcement of Control (No. 2) (Scotland) Regulations 1992 (S.I. 1992 No. 2086), regs. 3 and 4.

Information relating to the breach. The notice must contain the matters which appear to the planning authority to constitute the breach of planning control (subs. (1)(a)), and the paragraph of s.123(1) in which in their opinion the breach falls (subs. (1)(b)).

In order to prevent a notice being successfully challenged on an overly strict view of the amount of specification required of these matters, the obligation is to "state", not specify, and subs. (2) provides that it is sufficient for the notice to give sufficient details of such matters to enable the recipient to know what the matters are.

Steps required. The notice must specify the steps which the authority require to be taken, or activities which they require to be ceased (subs. (3)). The obligation to "specify" is higher than that to "state" under subs. (1). A notice lacking in specification is a nullity (*e.g. Metallic Protectives v. Secretary of State for the Environment* [1976] J.P.L. 166).

The steps must be wholly or partly in order to achieve the purposes set out in subs. (4). These purposes are to remedy the breach (subs. (4)(a)) or any injury caused by the breach (subs. (4)(b)). Examples are set out in subs. (5). "Under-enforcement" is permitted, and so long as the notice is complied with, planning permission is deemed to be granted (subs. (14)).

Further, where the notice is issued in respect of a breach of planning control consisting of demolition of a building, the notice may require construction of a replacement building (subs. (6)). The unauthorised demolition of a building may be the subject of an enforcement notice as demolition falls within the definition of "building or works" (s.277(1)). The authority must comply with the law regarding construction of buildings (subs. (7)(a)). There is provision for under-enforcement: the authority may under-enforce by permitting the replacement to differ from the demolished building (subs. (7)(b)), and so long as the replacement building is constructed in compliance with the notice, planning permission is deemed to be granted (subs. (14)).

Effective date. The notice takes effect from a date which must be specified in it (subs. (8)).

There must also be specified in the notice a date for compliance, or different dates for compliance with different steps or activities (subs. (9), (10)).

Variation and withdrawal of enforcement notice

129.—(1) The planning authority may—
(a) withdraw an enforcement notice issued by them, or
(b) waive or relax any requirement of such a notice and, in particular, may extend any period specified in accordance with section 128(9).

(2) The powers conferred by subsection (1) may be exercised whether or not the notice has taken effect.

(3) The planning authority shall, immediately after exercising the powers conferred by subsection (1), give notice of the exercise to every person who has been served with a copy of the enforcement notice or would, if the notice were reissued, be served with a copy of it.

(4) The withdrawal of an enforcement notice does not affect the power of the planning authority to issue a further enforcement notice.

DEFINITIONS
"enforcement notice": ss.127, 277(1).
"planning authority": ss.1, 277(1).

GENERAL NOTE
The planning authority has a discretion to withdraw, waive or relax an enforcement notice (subs. (1)), whether or not the notice has taken effect (subs. (2)). Accordingly, old notices no longer of relevance can be cleared off the enforcement register.

Notice of the exercise of such discretion must be given to the persons specified in subs. (3).

The planning authority may in appropriate circumstances issue a fresh enforcement notice (subs. (4)).

Appeal against enforcement notice

130.—(1) A person on whom an enforcement notice is served or any other person having an interest in the land may, at any time before the date specified in the notice as the date on which it is to take effect, appeal to the Secretary of State against the notice on any of the following grounds—

   (a) that, in respect of any breach of planning control which may be constituted by the matters stated in the notice, planning permission ought to be granted or, as the case may be, the condition or limitation concerned ought to be discharged;

   (b) that those matters have not occurred;

   (c) that those matters (if they occurred) do not constitute a breach of planning control;

   (d) that, at the date when the notice was issued, no enforcement action could be taken in respect of any breach of planning control which may be constituted by those matters;

   (e) that copies of the enforcement notice were not served as required by section 127;

   (f) that the steps required by the notice to be taken, or the activities required by the notice to cease, exceed what is necessary to remedy any breach of planning control which may be constituted by those matters or, as the case may be, to remedy any injury to amenity which has been caused by any such breach;

   (g) that any period specified in the notice in accordance with section 128(9) falls short of what should reasonably be allowed.

(2) An appeal under this section shall be made either—

   (a) by giving written notice of the appeal to the Secretary of State before the date specified in the enforcement notice as the date on which it is to take effect, or

   (b) by sending such notice to him in a properly addressed and prepaid letter posted to him at such time that, in the ordinary course of post, it would be delivered to him before that date.

(3) A person who gives notice under subsection (2) shall submit to the Secretary of State, either when giving the notice or within the prescribed time, a statement in writing—

   (a) specifying the grounds on which he is appealing against the enforcement notice, and

   (b) giving such further information as may be prescribed.

DEFINITIONS
   "breach of planning control": ss.123, 277(1).
   "enforcement notice": ss.127, 277(1).
   "planning permission": ss.123(3), 277(1).

GENERAL NOTE
   Any person on whom an enforcement notice is served, or having an interest in the land, may appeal to the Secretary of State under this section. During the appeal process the enforcement notice is of no effect (s.131(3)).

Grounds of appeal. The recipient of an enforcement notice may appeal against it only on the specific and limited grounds set out in subs. (1) (*Tarn v. Secretary of State for Scotland* (First Division) February 11, 1997, unreported).

   The grounds of appeal are as follows:

(a) planning permission ought to be granted.

An appeal which is brought under this ground will lapse unless the requisite fee is paid time-ously (s.133(8));

(b) the matters set out in the enforcement notice have not occurred;

(c) those matters did not constitute a breach of planning control;

(d) no enforcement action could be taken as at the date of issue of the enforcement notice;

(e) copies of the notice were not served in accordance with s.127. However, the Secretary of State may disregard failure to serve the enforcement notice on any person if neither that person or the appellant were substantially prejudiced thereby (s.132(4));

(f) the steps, or cessation of activities, required by the notice exceed what is necessary to remedy the breach;

(g) the period for compliance is unreasonably short.

Procedure. The appeal must be made in writing and given, or posted to arrive in the ordinary course of post, before the effective date set out in the enforcement notice (subs. (2)). The time-limit is strict and late appeals cannot be heard (*Howard v. Secretary of State for the Environment* [1975] Q.B. 235; *R. v. Secretary of State for the Environment ex p. J.B.I. Financial Consultants* [1989] J.P.L. 365).

Further provision as to appeals is made in Enforcement of Control (No. 2) (Scotland) Regulations 1992 (S.I. 1992 No. 2086), regs. 5 and 6.

Appeals: supplementary provisions

131.—(1) The Secretary of State may by regulations prescribe the procedure which is to be followed on appeals under section 130 and, in particular, but without prejudice to the generality of the foregoing provisions of this subsection, in so prescribing may—

(a) specify the matters on which information is to be given in a statement under section 130(3);

(b) require the planning authority to submit, within such time as may be specified, a statement indicating the submissions which they propose to put forward on the appeal;

(c) specify the matters to be included in such a statement;

(d) require the authority or the appellant to give such notice of an appeal as may be specified to such persons as may be specified;

(e) require the authority to send to the Secretary of State, within such period from the date of the bringing of the appeal as may be specified, a copy of the enforcement notice and a list of the persons served with copies of it.

(2) Subject to section 132(3), the Secretary of State shall, if either the appellant or the planning authority so desire, give each of them an opportunity of appearing before and being heard by a person appointed by the Secretary of State for the purpose.

(3) Where an appeal is brought under section 130 the enforcement notice shall be of no effect pending the final determination or the withdrawal of the appeal.

(4) Schedule 4 applies to appeals under section 130, including appeals under that section as applied by regulations under any other provisions of this Act.

DEFINITIONS

"enforcement notice": ss.127, 277(1).

"open space": s.277(1).

"planning authority": ss.1, 277(1).

"prescribed": s.277(1).

GENERAL NOTE

"*Regulations*": see Enforcement of Control (No. 2) (Scotland) Regulations 1992 (S.I. 1992 No. 2086).

Further provisions as to procedure are set out in Sched. 4 (subs. (4)).

Provided the appellant or the authority follow procedures correctly (s.132(2)), they have a right to appear and be heard (subs. (2)).

General provisions relating to determination of appeals

132.—(1) On the determination of an appeal under section 130, the Secretary of State shall give directions for giving effect to the determination, including, where appropriate, directions for quashing the enforcement notice.

(2) On such an appeal the Secretary of State may—

(a) correct any defect, error or misdescription in the enforcement notice, or

(b) vary the terms of the enforcement notice,

if he is satisfied that the correction or variation will not cause injustice to the appellant or the planning authority.

(3) The Secretary of State may—

(a) dismiss an appeal if the appellant fails to comply with section 130(3) within the prescribed time, and

(b) allow an appeal and quash the enforcement notice if the planning authority fail to comply with any requirement imposed by virtue of paragraph (b), (c) or (e) of section 131(1).

(4) Where it would otherwise be a ground for determining an appeal in favour of the appellant that a person required by section 127(2) to be served with a copy of the enforcement notice was not served, the Secretary of State may disregard that fact if neither the appellant nor that person has been substantially prejudiced by the failure to serve him.

DEFINITIONS
"enforcement notice": ss.127, 277(1).

GENERAL NOTE
The Secretary of State has power to quash the enforcement notice (subs. (1)). He also has power to correct or vary it, so long as injustice is not caused to the appellant or planning authority (subs. (2)). The power to vary may be used, for example, to correct a defective notice (*Barn Properties v. Secretary of State for Scotland*, 1996 S.L.T. 964 (Extra Division)) or where the steps specified in the notice go beyond what is necessary to remedy the breach of control (*Mansi v. Elstree Rural District Council* (1964) 16 P. & C.R. 153; *South Ribble Borough Council v. Secretary of State for the Environment* [1991] 1 P.L.R. 29).

He may dismiss or allow the appeal if the relevant parties fail to follow certain procedures (subs. (4)).

Grant or modification of planning permission on appeal against enforcement notice

133.—(1) On the determination of an appeal under section 130, the Secretary of State may—

(a) grant planning permission in respect of any of the matters stated in the enforcement notice as constituting a breach of planning control or any of those matters so far as relating to part of the land to which the notice relates,

(b) discharge any condition or limitation subject to which planning permission was granted,

(c) grant planning permission for such other development on the land to which the enforcement notice relates as appears to him to be appropriate, and

(d) determine whether on the date on which the appeal was made, any existing use of the land was lawful, any operations which had been carried out in, on, over or under the land were lawful or any matter constituting a failure to comply with any condition or limitation subject to which the permission was granted was lawful and, if so, issue a certificate under section 150.

(2) The provisions of sections 150 to 153 mentioned in subsection (3) shall apply for the purposes of subsection (1)(d) as they apply for the purposes of section 150, but as if—

(a) any reference to an application for a certificate were a reference to the appeal and any reference to the date of such an application were a reference to the date on which the appeal is made, and

(b) references to the planning authority were references to the Secretary of State.

(3) Those provisions are sections 150(5) to (7), 152(4) (so far as it relates to the form of the certificate), (6) and (7) and 153.

(4) In considering whether to grant planning permission under subsection (1), the Secretary of State shall have regard to the provisions of the development plan, so far as material to the subject matter of the enforcement notice, and to any other material considerations.

(5) The planning permission which may be granted under subsection (1) is any planning permission which might be granted on an application under Part III.

(6) Where the Secretary of State discharges a condition or limitation under subsection (1), he may substitute for it any other condition or limitation.

(7) Where an appeal against an enforcement notice is brought under section 130, the appellant shall be deemed to have made an application for planning permission in respect of the matters stated in the enforcement notice as constituting a breach of planning control.

(8) Where—

(a) the statement under section 130(3) specifies the ground mentioned in subsection (1)(a) of that section,

(b) any fee is payable under regulations made by virtue of section 252 in respect of the application deemed to be made by virtue of the appeal, and

(c) the Secretary of State gives notice in writing to the appellant specifying the period within which the fee must be paid,

then, if that fee is not paid within that period, the appeal, so far as brought on that ground, and the application shall lapse at the end of that period.

(9) Any planning permission granted under subsection (1) on an appeal shall be treated as granted on the application deemed to have been made by the appellant.

(10) In relation to a grant of planning permission or a determination under subsection (1) the Secretary of State's decision shall be final.

(11) For the purposes of section 36 the decision shall be treated as having been given by the Secretary of State in dealing with an application for planning permission made to the planning authority.

DEFINITIONS

"breach of planning control": ss.123, 277(1).
"development plan": ss.24, 277(1).
"enforcement notice": ss.127, 277(1).
"land": s.277(1).
"planning authority": ss.1, 277(1).
"planning permission": ss.123(3), 277(1).

GENERAL NOTE

In determining an appeal the Secretary of State may, rather than uphold the enforcement notice, regularise the development by:

–granting planning permission (subs. (1)(a)). However in granting permission he must have regard to the development plan (subs. (4)). By bringing an appeal the appellant is deemed to have made an application for planning permission (subs. (7)) and the permission is deemed to have been granted under that application (subs. (9));

–discharging or any conditions or limitations on the existing permission (subs. (1)(b));

–substituting other conditions or limitations therefor (subs. (5)). The Secretary of State must give the parties an opportunity to express their views on the proposed substitutes (*Dunfermline District Council v. Secretary of State for Scotland*, 1996 S.L.T. 89); or

–determining that the use was lawful and issuing a certificate under s.150 (subs. (1)(c)).

The Secretary of State's decision is final (subs. (10)).

Validity of enforcement notices

134. The validity of an enforcement notice shall not be questioned in any proceedings whatsoever on any of the grounds specified in section 130(1)(b) to (e) except by appeal under that section.

<small>DEFINITIONS</small>
"enforcement notice": ss.127, 277(1).

<small>GENERAL NOTE</small>
Challenges in respect of the grounds specified in s.130(1)(b) to (e) can be made only by appeal under s.130.

Execution and cost of works required by enforcement notice

135.—(1) If any steps which are required by an enforcement notice to be taken have not been taken within the compliance period, the planning authority may—

(a) enter the land and take those steps, and

(b) recover from the person who is then the owner or lessee of the land any expenses reasonably incurred by them in doing so.

(2) If that person did not appeal to the Secretary of State although entitled to do so, he shall not be entitled to dispute the validity of the action taken by the planning authority under subsection (1) in accordance with the enforcement notice.

(3) In computing the amount of the expenses which may be recovered by them under subsection (1), a planning authority may include in that amount such proportion of their administrative expenses as seems to them to be appropriate.

(4) Where a copy of an enforcement notice has been served in respect of any breach of planning control—

(a) any expenses incurred by the owner, lessee or occupier of any land for the purpose of complying with the notice, and

(b) any sums paid by the owner or lessee of any land under subsection (1) in respect of expenses incurred by the planning authority in taking steps required by such a notice to be taken,

shall be recoverable from the person by whom the breach of planning control was committed.

(5) If on a complaint by the owner of any land it appears to the sheriff that the occupier of the land is preventing the owner from carrying out work required to be carried out by an enforcement notice, the sheriff may by warrant authorise the owner to go on to the land and carry out that work.

(6) A planning authority taking steps under subsection (1) may sell any materials removed by them from the land unless those materials are claimed by the owner within 3 days of their removal.

(7) After any such sale the planning authority shall pay the proceeds to the owner less the expenses recoverable by them from him.

(8) Where a planning authority seek, under subsection (1), to recover any expenses from a person on the basis that he is the owner of any land, and such person proves that—

(a) he is receiving the rent in respect of that land merely as trustee, tutor, curator, factor or agent of some other person, and

(b) he has not, and since the date of the service on him of the demand for payment has not had, in his hands on behalf of that other person sufficient money to discharge the whole demand of the authority,

his liability shall be limited to the total amount of the money which he has or has had in his hands on behalf of that other person.

(9) A planning authority who by reason of subsection (8) have not recovered the whole of any such expenses from a trustee, tutor, curator, fac-

tor or agent may recover any unpaid balance from the person on whose behalf the rent is received.

(10) Any person who wilfully obstructs a person acting in the exercise of powers under subsection (1) shall be guilty of an offence and liable on summary conviction to a fine not exceeding level 3 on the standard scale.

(11) In this section and in sections 136, 140 and 141 any reference to the compliance period, in relation to an enforcement notice, is a reference to the period specified in the notice for compliance with it or such extended period as the planning authority may allow for compliance with it.

DEFINITIONS
"breach of planning control": ss.123, 277(1).
"enforcement notice": ss.127, 277(1).
"land": s.277(1).
"owner": s.277(1).
"planning authority": ss.1, 277(1).

GENERAL NOTE
This section allows the planning authority to ensure that the steps set out in the enforcement notice are complied with by itself entering the land and taking the steps (subs. (1)(a)), and recovering the expenses (subs. (1)(b)), including the authority's administration expenses (subs. (3)).

It is a criminal offence to wilfully obstruct such action (subs. (10)). Provision is made for the authority selling any materials removed and accounting to the owner for the proceeds (subss. (6) and (7)).

An owner of land who is being prevented by the occupier from carrying out work required by an enforcement notice may apply to the sheriff for authority to enter the land and carry out the work (subs. (5)).

The liability of trustees, agents, etc. to the authority is limited to the amount of the trust, etc. funds which they have or had in their hands (subs. (8)).

Subs. (11)
This subsection implements Recommendation 9 of the SLCR by providing for the compliance period in respect of each of ss.136, 140 and 141 to be the same.

Offence where enforcement notice not complied with

136.—(1) Where, at any time after the end of the compliance period in respect of an enforcement notice, any step required by the notice to be taken has not been taken or any activity required by the notice to cease is being carried on, the person who is then the owner of the land is in breach of the notice.

(2) Where the owner of the land is in breach of the notice he shall be guilty of an offence.

(3) In proceedings against any person for an offence under subsection (2), it shall be a defence for him to show that he did everything he could be expected to do to secure compliance with the notice.

(4) A person who has control of or an interest in the land to which an enforcement notice relates (other than the owner) must not carry on any activity which is required by the notice to cease or cause or permit such an activity to be carried on.

(5) A person who, at any time after the end of the period for compliance with the notice, contravenes subsection (4) shall be guilty of an offence.

(6) An offence under subsection (2) or (5) may be charged by reference to any day or longer period of time and a person may be convicted of a second or subsequent offence under the subsection in question by reference to any period of time following the preceding conviction for such an offence.

(7) Where—

(a) a person charged with an offence under this section has not been served with a copy of the enforcement notice, and

(b) the notice is not contained in the appropriate register kept under section 147,

it shall be a defence for him to show that he was not aware of the existence of the notice.

(8) A person guilty of an offence under this section shall be liable—
(a) on summary conviction, to a fine not exceeding £20,000, and
(b) on conviction on indictment, to a fine.

(9) In determining the amount of any fine to be imposed on a person convicted of an offence under this section, the court shall in particular have regard to any financial benefit which has accrued or appears likely to accrue to him in consequence of the offence.

DEFINITIONS
"enforcement notice": ss.127, 277(1).
"land": s.277(1).
"owner": s.277(1).

GENERAL NOTE
This section provides criminal offences for breach of the enforcement notice. In order to act as a deterrent, the penalties are severe.

The offences may be charged by reference to a particular length of time, and further charges can be brought for subsequent periods (subs. (6)).

Offence by owner of land. If at any time after the end of the compliance period set out in the enforcement notice, any step or cessation required by the notice has not been complied with, the owner is guilty of an offence (subss. (1) and (2)).

Defences of owner. Two defences are open to the owner:
–that he did everything he could be expected to do to comply with the notice (subs. (3)). It has been held in England that this defence is not open to an owner who had the power to comply with the notice without assistance from others (*R. v. Beard, The Independent,* July 1, 1996);
–that he was not aware of the existence of a notice which was neither served on him nor contained in the appropriate register (subs. (7)).

Offence by controller of land. If at any time after the end of the compliance period set out in the enforcement notice, any person (not the owner) in control of the land or an interest in the land, who carries on or causes or permits to carry on any activity which is required by the notice to cease is guilty of an offence (subss. (4) and (5)).

Defence of controller. That he was not aware of the existence of a notice which was neither served on him nor contained in the appropriate register (subs. (7)).

Penalties. On conviction a person is liable to a substantial fine: a maximum of £20,000 on summary conviction and unlimited on indictment (subs. (8)). In determining the amount of the fine the court has regard to the financial benefit accruing in consequence of the offence (subs. (9)).

Effect of planning permission etc. on enforcement or breach of condition notice

137.—(1) Where, after the service of—
(a) a copy of an enforcement notice, or
(b) a breach of condition notice,
planning permission is granted for any development carried out before the grant of that permission, the notice shall cease to have effect so far as inconsistent with that permission.

(2) Where, after a breach of condition notice has been served, any condition to which the notice relates is discharged, the notice shall cease to have effect so far as it requires any person to secure compliance with the condition in question.

(3) The fact that an enforcement notice or breach of condition notice has wholly or partly ceased to have effect by virtue of this section shall not affect the liability of any person for an offence in respect of a previous failure to comply, or secure compliance, with the notice.

DEFINITIONS
   "breach of condition notice": ss.145, 277(1).
   "development": ss.26, 277(1).
   "enforcement notice": ss.127, 277(1).

GENERAL NOTE
   The Secretary of State has power to grant planning permission in determining an appeal. If he does so, the notice ceases to have effect as far as inconsistent with the provision (subs. (1)). The notice remains otherwise in force (*e.g. Havering London Borough v. Secretary of State for the Environment* [1983] J.P.L. 240).
   Similar provision is made by subs. (2) in respect of the Secretary of State's power to discharge a condition.
   Subsection (3) provides that subss. (1) and (2) do not have retrospective effect in respect of failure to comply with the notice.

Enforcement notice to have effect against subsequent development

138.—(1) Compliance with an enforcement notice, whether in respect of—
   (a) the removal or alteration of any building or works,
   (b) the discontinuance of any use of land, or
   (c) any other requirements contained in the notice,
shall not discharge the notice.
   (2) Without prejudice to subsection (1), any provision of an enforcement notice requiring a use of land to be discontinued shall operate as a requirement that it shall be discontinued permanently, to the extent that it is in contravention of Part III; and accordingly the resumption of that use at any time after it has been discontinued in compliance with the enforcement notice shall to that extent be in contravention of the enforcement notice.
   (3) Without prejudice to subsection (1), if any development is carried out on land by way of reinstating or restoring buildings or works which have been removed or altered in compliance with an enforcement notice, the notice shall, notwithstanding that its terms are not apt for the purpose, be deemed to apply in relation to the buildings or works as reinstated or restored as it applied in relation to the buildings or works before they were removed or altered.
   (4) A person who, without the grant of planning permission in that behalf, carries out any development on land by way of reinstating or restoring buildings or works which have been removed or altered in compliance with an enforcement notice shall be guilty of an offence, and shall be liable on summary conviction to a fine not exceeding level 5 on the standard scale.

DEFINITIONS
   "building": s.277(1).
   "building or works": s.277(1).
   "development": s.277(1) and s.26.
   "enforcement notice": s.277(1) and s.127.
   "land": s.277(1).
   "use": s.277(1).

GENERAL NOTE
   An enforcement notice remains in effect notwithstanding that it is complied with (subs. (1)). If compliance subsequently ceases, the notice is contravened (subss. (2) and (3)), and a criminal offence is committed (subs. (4)).

Power of Secretary of State to serve enforcement notice

139.—(1) If it appears to the Secretary of State that it is expedient that an enforcement notice should be served in respect of any land, he may himself serve such a notice under section 127.

(2) An enforcement notice served by the Secretary of State shall have the same effect as if it had been served by the planning authority.

(3) The Secretary of State shall not serve such a notice without consulting the planning authority.

(4) The provisions of this Act relating to enforcement notices apply, so far as relevant, to an enforcement notice served by the Secretary of State as they apply to an enforcement notice served by a planning authority, but with the substitution for any reference to the planning authority of a reference to the Secretary of State, and any other necessary modifications.

DEFINITIONS
"enforcement notice": ss.127, 277(1).
"land": s.277(1).
"planning authority": ss.1, 277(1).

GENERAL NOTE
This section provides for the service of an enforcement notice by the Secretary of State himself, after consulting with the planning authority. In accordance with recommendation 2 of SLCR, subs. (4) applies the same general regime to enforcement notices served by the Secretary of State as applies to those served by the planning authority.

Stop notices

Stop notices

140.—(1) Where the planning authority consider it expedient that any relevant activity should cease before the expiry of the compliance period in respect of an enforcement notice, they may, when they serve the copy of the enforcement notice or afterwards, serve a notice (in this Act referred to as a "stop notice") prohibiting the carrying out of that activity on the land to which the enforcement notice relates, or any part of that land specified in the stop notice.

(2) In this section, "relevant activity" means any activity specified in the enforcement notice as an activity which the planning authority require to cease and any activity carried out as part of that activity or associated with that activity.

(3) A stop notice may not be served where the enforcement notice has taken effect.

(4) A stop notice shall not prohibit the use of any building as a dwellinghouse.

(5) A stop notice shall not prohibit the carrying out of any activity if the activity has been carried out (whether continuously or not) for a period of more than 4 years ending with the service of the notice; and for the purposes of this subsection no account is to be taken of any period during which the activity was authorised by planning permission.

(6) Subsection (5) does not prevent a stop notice prohibiting any activity consisting of, or incidental to, building, engineering, mining or other operations or the deposit of refuse or waste materials.

(7) A stop notice shall specify the date when it is to come into effect, and that date—

    (a) must not be earlier than 3 days after the date when the notice is served, unless the planning authority consider that there are special reasons for specifying an earlier date and a statement of those reasons is served with the stop notice, and

    (b) must not be later than 28 days from the date when the notice is first served on any person.

(8) A stop notice may be served by the planning authority on any person who appears to them to have an interest in the land or to be engaged in the relevant activity specified in the enforcement notice.

(9) The planning authority may at any time withdraw a stop notice (without prejudice to their power to serve another) by notice which shall be—
(a) served on all persons who were served with the stop notice, and
(b) publicised by displaying it for 7 days in place of all or any relative site notices.

DEFINITIONS
"building": s.277(1).
"building operations": ss.26, 277(1).
"depositing of refuse or waste materials": s.277(1).
"enforcement notice": ss.127, 277(1).
"engineering operations": s.277(1).
"planning authority": ss.1, 277(1).
"relevant activity": subs. (2)
"stop notice": subs. (1), s.277(1).

GENERAL NOTE
There must be a gap of not less than 28 days between an enforcement notice being served and taking effect (s.127(3)). If the authority want to achieve a more immediate ban on activities specified in the enforcement notice, they may serve a stop notice. At the expiry of the compliance period specified in the enforcement notice, the stop notice is superseded by the enforcement notice and ceases to have effect (s.141(b)). The stop notice is parasitic on the enforcement notice. Accordingly it falls if the enforcement notice is withdrawn or quashed (s.141(a)) or varied so as to no longer be applicable (s.141(2)), and lack of specification in the stop notice may be cured by reference to adequate specification in the enforcement notice (*Bristol Stadium v. Brown* [1980] J.P.L. 107).

Service of stop notices. The authority may serve a stop notice when they serve the enforcement notice, or afterwards (subs. (1)). The stop notice prohibits the carrying on of "relevant activity" over all or part of the land to which the enforcement notice relates (subs. (1)). "Relevant activity" is defined in subs. (2) as any activity specified in the enforcement notice as one which the authority requires to cease, or associated activities.
A stop notice may be served on any person who appears to have an interest in the land or be engaged in the relevant activity (subs. (8)).
A defect in service will be cured if it is shown that the planning authority took all reasonably practicable steps to effect proper service (s.141(4)).
The stop notice may be publicised by displaying a site notice on the relevant land (s.141(2)).
The authority has discretion as to whether to serve a stop notice. They are entitled to do so if they consider it expedient that the activity should cease before the expiry of the compliance period set out in the enforcement notice (subs. (1)).

Restrictions on the use of stop notices. A stop notice may not:
–be served where the enforcement notice has taken effect (subs. (3));
–prohibit the use of a building as a dwelling house (subs. (4)); nor
–prohibit an activity which has been carried out without planning permission for an aggregate period of more than four years (subs. (5)). Accordingly, any period for which the activity was covered by a limited period permission will not count towards the four years. This restriction applies only to uses, as it does not apply in respect of building, engineering, mining or other operations or the deposit of refuse or waste (subs. (6)).

Effective date. The stop notice comes into effect on a date not later than 28 days and generally not earlier than three days after service (subs. (7)). However it can come into effect earlier than three days if there are special reasons, in which case a statement of these reasons must be served with the stop notice (subs. (7)(a)).
The effective date must be stated in the stop notice (subs. (7)).

Withdrawal of stop notices. The authority may withdraw a stop notice (subs. (9)). If they do so, they remain entitled to serve a fresh stop notice (subs. (9)).
A notice withdrawing a stop notice must be served on the persons on whom the stop notice was served, and displayed for seven days in place of the relevant site notices (subs. (9)).
The withdrawal takes effect on the service of the notice of withdrawal (s.141(1)(c)).

Challenge to issue of stop notice. The court will not interdict an authority from issuing an *intra vires* stop notice, and any challenge to such a notice must proceed by way of a challenge to the related enforcement notice under s.130 (*Central Regional Council v. Clackmannan District Council*, 1983 S.L.T. 660; *Earl Car Sales (Edinburgh) v. City of Edinburgh District Council*, 1984 S.L.T. 8).

Stop notices: supplementary provisions

141.—(1) A stop notice shall cease to have effect when—

(a) the enforcement notice to which it relates is withdrawn or quashed,

(b) the compliance period specified under section 128(9) expires, or

(c) notice of the withdrawal of the stop notice is served under section 140(9),

whichever occurs first.

(2) Where the enforcement notice to which a stop notice relates is varied so that it no longer relates to any relevant activity, the stop notice shall cease to have effect in relation to that activity.

(3) Where a stop notice has been served in respect of any land, the planning authority may publicise it by displaying on the land a notice (in this section and section 144 referred to as a "site notice")—

(a) stating that a stop notice has been served on a particular person or persons,

(b) indicating its requirements, and

(c) stating that any person contravening it may be prosecuted for an offence under section 144.

(4) A stop notice shall not be invalid by reason that a copy of the enforcement notice to which it relates was not served as required by section 127 if it is shown that the planning authority took all such steps as were reasonably practicable to effect proper service.

DEFINITIONS
"enforcement notice": ss.127, 277(1).
"land": s.277(1).
"site notice": subs. (3).
"stop notice": ss.140, 277(1).

GENERAL NOTE
See commentary to s.140.

Power of the Secretary of State to serve stop notice

142.—(1) If it appears to the Secretary of State that it is expedient that a stop notice should be served in respect of any land, he may himself serve such a notice under section 140.

(2) A stop notice served by the Secretary of State shall have the same effect as if it had been served by the planning authority.

(3) The Secretary of State shall not serve such a notice without consulting the planning authority.

(4) The provisions of this Act relating to stop notices apply, so far as relevant, to a stop notice served by the Secretary of State as they apply to a stop notice served by a planning authority, but with the substitution for any reference to the planning authority of a reference to the Secretary of State, and any other necessary modifications.

DEFINITIONS
"land": s.277(1).
"planning authority": ss.1, 277(1).
"stop notice": ss.140, 277(1).

GENERAL NOTE
This section provides for the service of a stop notice by the Secretary of State himself, after consulting with the planning authority.

In accordance with recommendation 2 of the SLCR, subs. (4) applies the same general regime to stop notices served by the Secretary of State as applies to those served by the planning authority.

Compensation for loss due to stop notice

143.—(1) Subject to the provisions of this section, where a stop notice under section 140 ceases to have effect a person who, when the stop notice is first served, has an interest, whether as owner or occupier or otherwise, in the land to which the notice relates shall be entitled to be compensated by the planning authority in respect of any loss or damage directly attributable to the prohibition contained in the notice or, in a case within subsection (1)(b), the prohibition of such of the activities prohibited by the stop notice as cease to be relevant activities.

(2) For the purposes of this section a stop notice ceases to have effect when—

(a) the enforcement notice is quashed on grounds other than those mentioned in paragraph (a) of section 130(1),

(b) the enforcement notice is varied (otherwise than on the grounds mentioned in that paragraph) so that any activity the carrying out of which is prohibited by the stop notice ceases to be a relevant activity within the meaning of section 140(2),

(c) the enforcement notice is withdrawn by the planning authority otherwise than in consequence of the grant by them of planning permission for the development to which the notice relates, or

(d) the stop notice is withdrawn.

(3) A claim for compensation under this section shall be made to the planning authority within the prescribed time and in the prescribed manner.

(4) The loss or damage in respect of which compensation is payable under this section in respect of a prohibition shall include any sum payable in respect of a breach of contract caused by the taking of action necessary to comply with the prohibition.

(5) No compensation is payable under this section—

(a) in respect of the prohibition in a stop notice of any activity which, at any time when the notice is in force, constitutes or contributes to a breach of planning control, or

(b) in the case of a claimant who was required to provide information under section 125, 126 or 272 in respect of any loss or damage suffered by him which could have been avoided if he had provided the information or had otherwise co-operated with the planning authority when responding to the notice.

(6) Except in so far as may be otherwise provided by any regulations made under this Act, any question of disputed compensation under this Part shall be referred to and determined by the Lands Tribunal.

(7) In relation to the determination of any such question, the provisions of sections 9 and 11 of the Land Compensation (Scotland) Act 1963 shall apply subject to any necessary modifications and to the provisions of any regulations made under this Act.

DEFINITIONS
"breach of planning control": ss.123, 277(1).
"enforcement notice": ss.127, 277(1).
"Lands Tribunal": s.277(1).
"owner": s.277(1).
"planning authority": ss.1, 277(1).
"prescribed": s.277(1).
"relevant activity": s.140(2)
"stop notice": ss.140, 277(1).

GENERAL NOTE
    This section provides for the person on whom a stop notice is served to be compensated by the planning authority for certain loss or damage due to the stop notice.

Right to compensation. The persons who may be entitled to compensation are those who had an interest in the land when the stop notice was first served (subs. (1)).
    Their right arises when the stop notice ceases to have effect (subs. (1)), that is:
    –the stop notice is quashed on a factual or procedural ground (subs. (2)(a));
    –the stop notice is varied on a factual or procedural ground (subs. (2)(b));
    –the enforcement notice is withdrawn, other than in consequence of grant of planning permission (subs. (2)(c));
    –the stop notice is withdrawn (subs. (2)(d)).
    No compensation is payable:
    –in respect of activity in breach of planning control (subs. (5)(a)); nor
    –where the claimant has contributed to the loss by failing to provide information or cooperate in response to a planning contravention notice or a request for information under s.272 (subs. (5)).

Amount of compensation. The compensation is for loss or damage "directly attributable" to the prohibition (subs. (1)), including any sum payable in respect of breach of contract (subs. (4)). For examples of the heads of compensation which have been allowed, see *Sample (J) (Warkworth) v. Alnwick District Council,* 271 (1984) E.G. 204, *Graysmark v. South Hams District Council* [1989] 3 E.G. 75, and *Robert Barnes and Co. v. Malvern Hills District Council* (1985) 274 E.G. 733.

Procedure. "Prescribed time" "prescribed manner": see *the Town and Country Planning (General) (Scotland) Regulations 1976* (S.I. 1976 No.2022), reg. 4.
    Disputes are referred to the Lands Tribunal (subss. (6) and (7)).

Penalties for contravention of stop notice

144.—(1) If any person contravenes a stop notice after a site notice has been displayed or the stop notice has been served on him he shall be guilty of an offence.
    (2) An offence under this section may be charged by reference to any day or longer period of time and a person may be convicted of a second or subsequent offence under this section by reference to any period of time following the preceding conviction for such an offence.
    (3) It shall be a defence in any proceedings under subsection (1) that—
    (a) the stop notice was not served on the accused, and
    (b) he had no reasonable cause to believe that the activity was prohibited by the stop notice.
    (4) References in this section to contravening a stop notice include causing or permitting its contravention.
    (5) A person guilty of an offence under this section shall be liable—
    (a) on summary conviction, to a fine not exceeding £20,000, and
    (b) on conviction on indictment, to a fine.
    (6) In determining the amount of any fine to be imposed on a person convicted of an offence under this section, the court shall in particular have regard to any financial benefit which has accrued or appears likely to accrue to him in consequence of the offence.

DEFINITIONS
    "site notice": s.141(3).
    "stop notice": ss.140, 277(1).

GENERAL NOTE
    This section provides a criminal offence for contravention of the stop notice. In order to act as a deterrent, the penalties are severe.

The offence may be charged by reference to a particular length of time, and further charges can be brought for subsequent periods (subs. (2)).

Offence. A person who contravenes a stop notice after it has been served on him or a site notice has been displayed is guilty of an offence (subs. (1)).

Defence. Two defences are open:
  –that the notice was not served on him (subs. (3)(a));
  –that he had no reasonable cause to believe the activity was prohibited by the stop notice (subs. (3)(b)).

Penalties. On conviction a person is liable to a substantial fine: a maximum of £20,000 on summary conviction and unlimited on indictment (subs. (5)). In determining the amount of the fine the court has regard to the financial benefit accruing in consequence of the offence (subs. (6)).

Breach of condition notices

Enforcement of conditions

145.—(1) This section applies where planning permission for carrying out any development has been granted subject to conditions.

(2) The planning authority may, if any of the conditions is not complied with, serve a notice (in this Act referred to as a "breach of condition notice") on—
  (a) any person who is carrying out or has carried out the development, or
  (b) any person having control of the land,
requiring him to secure compliance with such of the conditions as are specified in the notice.

(3) References in this section to the person responsible are to the person on whom the breach of condition notice has been served.

(4) The conditions which may be specified in a notice served by virtue of subsection (2)(b) are any of the conditions regulating the use of the land.

(5) A breach of condition notice shall specify the steps which the authority consider ought to be taken, or the activities which the authority consider ought to cease, to secure compliance with the conditions specified in the notice.

(6) The authority may by notice served on the person responsible withdraw the breach of condition notice, but its withdrawal shall not affect the power to serve on him a further breach of condition notice in respect of the conditions specified in the earlier notice or any other conditions.

(7) The period allowed for compliance with the notice is—
  (a) such period of not less than 28 days beginning with the date of service of the notice as may be specified in the notice, or
  (b) that period as extended by a further notice served by the planning authority on the person responsible.

(8) If, at any time after the end of the period allowed for compliance with the notice—
  (a) any of the conditions specified in the notice is not complied with, and
  (b) the steps specified in the notice have not been taken or, as the case may be, the activities specified in the notice have not ceased,
the person responsible is in breach of the notice.

(9) If the person responsible is in breach of the notice he shall be guilty of an offence.

(10) An offence under subsection (9) may be charged by reference to any day or longer period of time and a person may be convicted of a second or subsequent offence under that subsection by reference to any period of time following the preceding conviction for such an offence.

(11) It shall be a defence for a person charged with an offence under subsection (9) to prove—
  (a) that he took all reasonable measures to secure compliance with the conditions specified in the notice, or
  (b) where the notice was served on him by virtue of subsection (2)(b), that he no longer had control of the land.

(12) A person who is guilty of an offence under subsection (9) shall be liable on summary conviction to a fine not exceeding level 3 on the standard scale.

(13) In this section—
  (a) "conditions" includes limitations; and
  (b) references to carrying out any development include causing or permitting another to do so.

DEFINITIONS
  "breach of condition notice": subs. (2).
  "carrying out any development": subs. (13)(b).
  "conditions": subs. (13)(a).
  "planning authority": ss.1, 277(1).
  "planning permission": ss.123(3), 277(1).

GENERAL NOTE
  The procedures relating to breach of condition notices are designed to allow action to be taken simply and quickly against any breach of planning permission without having resort to the enforcement notice procedure, which in addition to being slow could be counterproductive in that it could halt activity rather than merely ensure compliance with a condition.
  The section applies to limitations as well as conditions (subs. (13)(a)), and to those causing and permitting development as well as those carrying it on (subs. (13)(b)).

Service of breach of condition notice. Where planning permission has been granted subject to conditions, the planning authority may serve a breach of condition notice on the person carrying on or who carried on the development or having control of the land (subss. (1) and (2)).
  The notice requires the recipient to secure compliance with the conditions specified therein (subs. (2)), and must specify the steps to be taken or activities which must cease (subs. (5)).

Withdrawal. The authority may withdraw breach of condition notice by notice, but may at a later date serve a fresh breach of condition notice (subs. (6)).

Offence. It is a criminal offence to fail, to comply with a planning contravention notice within the period of 21 days from service or such further period as may be allowed by the authority by further notice (subss. (7), (8) and (9)).
  There are two defences:
  –that the person took all reasonable steps to secure compliance (subs. (11)(a)); and
  –that he no longer had control of the land (subs. (11)(b)).

Interdicts

Interdicts restraining breaches of planning control

146.—(1) Whether or not they have exercised or propose to exercise any of their other powers under this Act, a planning authority may seek to restrain or prevent any actual or apprehended breach of any of the controls provided for by or under this Act by means of an application for interdict.

(2) On an application under subsection (1) the court may grant such interdict as it thinks appropriate for the purpose of restraining or preventing the breach.

(3) In this section "the court" means the Court of Session or the sheriff.

DEFINITIONS
  "breach of planning control": ss.123, 277(1).
  "court": subs. (3).
  "planning authority": ss.1, 277(1).

This section provides that the planning authority may seek to restrain or prevent by interdict in the Court of Session or Sheriff Court any actual or apprehended breach of the controls set out in the Act.

The forerunner of this section was introduced by the Planning and Compensation Act 1991, s.35, to overcome doubts as to the competency of such an interdict at common law.

Registers

Register of enforcement, breach of condition and stop notices

147.—(1) Every planning authority shall, with respect to enforcement notices, breach of condition notices and stop notices which have been served in relation to land in their district, keep a register—

(a)   in such manner, and

(b)   containing such information,

as may be prescribed; and there may also be prescribed circumstances in which an entry in the register shall be deleted.

(2) Every register kept under this section shall be available for inspection by the public at all reasonable hours.

DEFINITIONS

"breach of condition notice": ss.145, 277(1).

"enforcement notice": ss.127, 277(1).

"planning authority": ss.1, 277(1).

"prescribed": s.277(1).

"stop notice": ss.140, 277(1).

GENERAL NOTE

This section obliges the planning authority to maintain a public register of enforcement, breach of condition and stop notices.

"Prescribed": Enforcement of Control (No. 2) (Scotland) Regulations 1992 (S.I. 1992 No.2086), reg. 7.

Enforcement of orders for discontinuance of use, etc.

Penalties for contravention of orders under section 71 and Schedule 8

148.—(1) Any person who without planning permission—

(a)   uses land, or causes or permits land to be used—

(i) for any purpose for which an order under section 71 or paragraph 1 of Schedule 8 has required that its use shall be discontinued, or

(ii) in contravention of any condition imposed by such an order by virtue of subsection (1) of that section or, as the case may be, sub-paragraph (1) of that paragraph,

(b)   resumes, or causes or permits to be resumed, development consisting of the winning and working of minerals or involving the depositing of mineral waste the resumption of which an order under paragraph 3 of that Schedule has prohibited, or

(c)   contravenes, or causes or permits to be contravened, any such requirement as is specified in sub-paragraph (3) or (4) of that paragraph,

shall be guilty of an offence.

(2) Any person who contravenes any requirement of a suspension order or a supplementary suspension order under paragraph 5 or 6 of Schedule 8 or who causes or permits any requirement of such an order to be contravened shall be guilty of an offence.

(3) Any person guilty of an offence under this section shall be liable—

(a)   on summary conviction, to a fine not exceeding the statutory maximum, and

(b) on conviction on indictment, to a fine.

(4) It shall be a defence for a person charged with an offence under this section to prove that he took all reasonable measures and exercised all due diligence to avoid commission of the offence by himself or by any person under his control.

(5) If in any case the defence provided by subsection (4) involves an allegation that the commission of the offence was due to the act or default of another person or due to reliance on information supplied by another person, the person charged shall not, without the leave of the court, be entitled to rely on the defence unless, within a period ending 7 clear days before the hearing, he has served on the prosecutor a notice in writing giving such information identifying or assisting in the identification of the other person as was then in his possession.

DEFINITIONS
  "depositing of mineral waste": s.277(1).
  "development": ss.26, 277(1).
  "land": s.277(1).
  "minerals": s.277(1).
  "planning permission": ss.123(3), 277(1).
  "use": s.277(1).
  "winning and working of minerals": s.277(1).

GENERAL NOTE
Offences. This section provides for the criminal enforcement of:
  –discontinuance orders under s.71 and mineral discontinuance orders under Sched. 8, para. 1
    (subs. (1)(a));
  –mineral prohibition orders under Sched. 8, para. 3 (subs. (1)(b)); and
  –suspension and supplementary suspension orders under Sched. 8 para. (5) or (6) (subs. (2)).

Defences. It is a defence to the above offences to prove that the accused took all reasonable steps and exercised all due diligence to avoid commission of the offence by himself or any person under his control (subs. (4)).

Seven days notice must be given to the prosecutor of any such defence based on the acting of a third party (subs. (5)).

Enforcement of orders under section 71 and Schedule 8

149.—(1) This section applies where—
  (a) any step required by an order under section 71 or paragraph 1 of Schedule 8 to be taken for the alteration or removal of any buildings or works or any plant or machinery,
  (b) any step required by an order under paragraph 3 of that Schedule to be taken—
        (i) for the alteration or removal of plant or machinery, or
        (ii) for the removal or alleviation of any injury to amenity, or
  (c) any step for the protection of the environment required to be taken by a suspension order or a supplementary suspension order under paragraph 5 or 6 of that Schedule,
has not been taken within the period specified in the order or within such extended period as the planning authority may allow.

(2) Where this section applies the planning authority may enter the land and take the required step and may recover from the person who is then the owner of the land any expenses reasonably incurred by them in doing so.

(3) A planning authority taking any step under subsection (1) may sell any materials removed by them from any land unless those materials are claimed by the owner within 3 days of their removal by the planning authority.

(4) Where such materials have been sold the planning authority shall pay the owner the net proceeds of the sale after deducting any expenses recoverable by them from him.

DEFINITIONS
"building": s.277(1).
"building or works": s.277(1).
"land": s.277(1).
"owner": s.277(1).
"planning authority": ss.1, 277(1).

GENERAL NOTE
This section empowers the planning authority to enter land, take steps and recover expenses in the enforcement of:
–discontinuance orders under s.71 and mineral discontinuance orders under Sched. 8, para. 1 (subs. (1)(a));
–mineral prohibition orders under Sched. 8, para. 3 (subs. (1)(b)); and
–suspension and supplementary suspension orders under Sched. 8, para. (5) or (6) (subs. (1(c)).
Provision is made for the authority selling any materials removed and accounting to the owner for the proceeds (subss. (3) and (4)).

Certificate of lawful use or development

Certificate of lawfulness of existing use or development

150.—(1) If any person wishes to ascertain whether—
(a) any existing use of buildings or other land is lawful,
(b) any operations which have been carried out in, on, over or under land are lawful, or
(c) any other matter constituting a failure to comply with any condition or limitation subject to which planning permission has been granted is lawful,
he may make an application for the purpose to the planning authority specifying the land and describing the use, operations or other matter.

(2) For the purposes of this Act, uses and operations are lawful at any time if—
(a) no enforcement action may then be taken in respect of them (whether because they did not involve development or require planning permission or because the time for enforcement action has expired or for any other reason), and
(b) they do not constitute a contravention of any of the requirements of any enforcement notice then in force.

(3) For the purposes of this Act, any matter constituting a failure to comply with any condition or limitation subject to which planning permission has been granted is lawful at any time if—
(a) the time for taking enforcement action in respect of the failure has then expired, and
(b) it does not constitute a contravention of any of the requirements of any enforcement notice or breach of condition notice then in force.

(4) If, on an application under this section, the planning authority are provided with information satisfying them of the lawfulness at the time of the application of the use, operations or other matter described in the application, or that description as modified by the planning authority or a description substituted by them, they shall issue a certificate to that effect; and in any other case they shall refuse the application.

(5) A certificate under this section shall—
(a) specify the land to which it relates,
(b) describe the use, operations or other matter in question (in the case of any use falling within one of the classes specified in an order under section 26(2)(f), identifying it by reference to that class),
(c) give the reasons for determining the use, operations or other thing to be lawful, and
(d) specify the date of the application for the certificate.

(6) The lawfulness of any use, operations or other matter for which a certificate is in force under this section shall be conclusively presumed.

(7) A certificate under this section in respect of any use shall also have effect, for the purposes of the following enactments, as if it were a grant of planning permission—

(a) section 3(3) of the Caravan Sites and Control of Development Act 1960,

(b) section 5(2) of the Control of Pollution Act 1974, and

(c) section 36(2)(a) of the Environmental Protection Act 1990.

DEFINITIONS

"building": s.277(1).
"enforcement action": s.123(2).
"land": s.277(1).
"open space": s.277(1).
"planning authority": ss.1, 277(1).
"use": s.277(1).

GENERAL NOTE

This section provides a mechanism whereby any person can ascertain the lawfulness of any existing use or development by applying for a certificate of lawful use. A similar procedure in respect of proposed uses is provided by s.151.

Application for certificate. Any person may apply for a certificate, not only the owner or occupier (subs. (1)).

The purpose of the application is to ascertain whether the use or development is lawful in one of three respects (subs. (1)). Lawful means that no enforcement action may be taken, and that any current enforcement or breach of condition notice is not contravened (subs. (2)).

The three respects are :

–any existing use of buildings or land is lawful (subs. (1)(a));

–any operations which have been carried out are lawful (subs. (1)(b)); or

–in respect of a failure to comply with a condition or limitation, the time for taking enforcement action has expired and any current enforcement or breach of condition notice is not contravened (subs. (1)(c)).

For the procedures for application see the Town and Country Planning (General Development Procedure (Scotland) Order 1992 (S.I. 1992 No.224), regs. 26–8.

Certificate. The authority are obliged to issue a certificate if they are satisfied as to the lawfulness of the use or operations at the time of the application (subs. (4)). The certificate is conclusive (subs. (6)), and has effect in respect of certain other statutes as if it were a grant of planning permission (subs. (7)). It must contain details of the land, the use or operations, the reasons for determining that they are lawful and the date of the application (subs. (5)).

Certificate of lawfulness of proposed use or development

151.—(1) If any person wishes to ascertain whether—

(a) any proposed use of buildings or other land, or

(b) any operations proposed to be carried out in, on, over or under land,

would be lawful, he may make an application for the purpose to the planning authority specifying the land and describing the use or operations in question.

(2) If, on an application under this section, the planning authority are provided with information satisfying them that the use or operations described in the application would be lawful if instituted or begun at the time of the application they shall issue a certificate to that effect; and in any other case they shall refuse the application.

(3) A certificate under this section shall—

(a) specify the land to which it relates,

(b) describe the use or operations in question (in the case of any use falling within one of the classes specified in an order under section 26(2)(f), identifying it by reference to that class),

(c) give the reasons for determining the use or operations to be lawful, and

(d) specify the date of the application for the certificate.

(4) There shall be an irrefutable presumption as to the lawfulness of any use or operations for which a certificate is in force under this section unless there is a material change, before the use is instituted or the operations are begun, in any of the matters relevant to determining such lawfulness.

DEFINITIONS
"land": s.277(1).
"planning authority": ss.1, 277(1).
"use": s.277(1).

GENERAL NOTE
   This section provides a mechanism whereby any person can ascertain the lawfulness of any proposed use or development by applying for a certificate of lawful use. A similar procedure in respect of existing use or development is provided by s.150.

Application for certificate. Any person may apply for a certificate, not only the owner or occupier (subs. (1)).
   For the procedures for application see the Town and Country Planning (General Development Procedure (Scotland) Order 1992 (S.I. 1992 No.224), regs. 26–8.

Certificate. The authority are obliged to issue a certificate if they are satisfied as to the lawfulness of the use or operations at the time of the application (subs. (2)). The certificate gives rise to an irrefutable presumption that the use or operations are lawful, unless there is a material change before commencement of the use or operations (subs (4)). It must contain details of the land, the use or operations, the reasons for determining that they are lawful and the date of the application (subs. (3)).

Certificates under sections 150 and 151: supplementary provisions

   152.—(1) An application for a certificate under section 150 or 151 shall be made in such manner as may be prescribed by regulations or a development order and shall include such particulars, and be verified by such evidence, as may be required by such regulations or such an order or by any directions given under such regulations or such an order or by the planning authority.

   (2) Provision may be made by such regulations or a development order for regulating the manner in which applications for certificates under those sections are to be dealt with by planning authorities.

   (3) In particular, such regulations or such an order may provide for requiring the authority—

   (a) to give to any applicant within such time as may be prescribed by the regulations or the order such notice as may be so prescribed as to the manner in which his application has been dealt with, and

   (b) to give to the Secretary of State and to such other persons as may be prescribed by or under the regulations or the order, such information as may be so prescribed with respect to such applications made to the authority, including information as to the manner in which any application has been dealt with.

   (4) A certificate under section 150 or 151 may be issued—

   (a) for the whole or part of the land specified in the application, and

   (b) where the application specifies two or more uses, operations or other things, for all of them or some one or more of them,

and shall be in such form as may be prescribed by such regulations or a development order.

   (5) A certificate under section 150 or 151 shall not affect any matter constituting a failure to comply with any condition or limitation subject to which

planning permission has been granted unless that matter is described in the certificate.

(6) In section 36 references to applications for planning permission shall include references to applications for certificates under section 150 or 151.

(7) A planning authority may revoke a certificate under section 150 or 151 if, on the application for the certificate—

(a) a statement was made or document used which was false in a material particular, or

(b) any material information was withheld.

(8) Provision may be made by such regulations or a development order for regulating the manner in which certificates may be revoked and the notice to be given of such revocation.

DEFINITIONS
    "acquiring authority": s.277(1).
    "development order": ss.30, 277(1).
    "land": s.277(1).
    "planning authority": ss.1, 277(1).
    "planning permission": ss.123(3), 277(1).
    "prescribed": s.277(1).
    "use": s.277(1).

GENERAL NOTE
"*Prescribed*": the Town and Country Planning (General Development Procedure (Scotland) Order 1992 (S.I. 1992 No.224), regs. 26-9.

Offences

153.—(1) If any person, for the purpose of procuring a particular decision on an application (whether by himself or another) for the issue of a certificate under section 150 or 151 of this Act—

(a) knowingly or recklessly makes a statement which is false or misleading in a material particular,

(b) with intent to deceive, uses any document which is false or misleading in a material particular, or

(c) with intent to deceive, withholds any material information,

he shall be guilty of an offence.

(2) A person guilty of an offence under subsection (1) shall be liable—

(a) on summary conviction, to a fine not exceeding the statutory maximum, and

(b) on conviction on indictment, to imprisonment for a term not exceeding 2 years. or a fine, or both.

GENERAL NOTE
This section provides that it is an offence for any person (not just the applicant) to give false or misleading statements or documents, or withhold information, for the purposes of procuring a decision on an application for a certificate of existing or proposed lawful use or development.

Appeals against refusal or failure to give decision on application

154.—(1) Where an application is made to a planning authority for a certificate under section 150 or 151 and—

(a) the application is refused or is refused in part, or

(b) the planning authority do not give notice to the applicant of their decision on the application within such period as may be prescribed by regulations or a development order or within such extended period as may at any time be agreed in writing by the applicant and the authority,

the applicant may appeal to the Secretary of State.

(2) An appeal under subsection (1) shall be by notice given within such period (not being less than 28 days) as may be prescribed by regulations or a development order.

(3) On any such appeal, if and so far as the Secretary of State is satisfied—

(a) in the case of an appeal under subsection (1)(a), that the authority's refusal is not well-founded, or

(b) in the case of an appeal under subsection (1)(b), that, if the planning authority had refused the application, their refusal would not have been well-founded,

he shall grant the appellant a certificate under section 150 or 151 accordingly or, in the case of a refusal in part, modify the certificate granted by the authority on the application.

(4) If and so far as the Secretary of State is satisfied that the authority's refusal is or, as the case may be, would have been well-founded, he shall dismiss the appeal.

(5) Schedule 4 applies to appeals under this section.

DEFINITIONS
   "development order": ss.30, 277(1).
   "planning authority": ss.1, 277(1).
   "prescribed": s.277(1).

GENERAL NOTE
   This section provides for an appeal to the Secretary of State against refusal of the application in whole or part or failure of the authority to notify the applicant of their decision timeously (subs. (1)).
   The Secretary of State must give the parties, if they so wish, an opportunity appear and be heard (s.155).
   The Secretary of State may grant or modify a certificate or dismiss the appeal (subss. (3) and (4)). He must notify the authority of any grant of certificate (s.155).
   Drafting errors in previous planning legislation have been corrected in this section in accordance with Recommendations 10.1 and 10.2 of the SLCR.

Further provisions as to appeals to the Secretary of State

155.—(1) Before determining an appeal under section 154(1), the Secretary of State shall, if either the appellant or the planning authority so wish, give each of them an opportunity of appearing before, and being heard by, a person appointed by the Secretary of State for the purpose.

(2) Where the Secretary of State or a person appointed by him under Schedule 4 to determine an appeal grants a certificate under section 150 or 151, the Secretary of State or that person shall give notice to the planning authority of that fact.

DEFINITIONS
   "planning authority": ss.1, 277(1).

GENERAL NOTE
   See commentary to s.154.

Rights of entry for enforcement purposes

Right to enter without warrant

156.—(1) Any person duly authorised in writing by a planning authority may at any reasonable hour enter any land—

(a) to ascertain whether there is or has been any breach of planning control on the land or any other land;

(b) to determine whether any of the powers conferred on a planning authority by sections 127 to 138, 140, 141, 144, 145 and 147 to 155 should be exercised in relation to the land or any other land;

(c) to determine how any such power should be exercised in relation to the land or any other land;

(d) to ascertain whether there has been compliance with any requirement imposed as a result of any such power having been exercised in relation to the land or any other land,

if there are reasonable grounds for entering for the purpose in question.

(2) Any person duly authorised in writing by the Secretary of State may at any reasonable hour enter any land to determine whether an enforcement notice should be issued in relation to the land or any other land, if there are reasonable grounds for entering for that purpose.

(3) The Secretary of State shall not so authorise any person without consulting the planning authority.

(4) Admission to any building used as a dwellinghouse shall not be demanded as of right by virtue of subsection (1) or (2) unless 24 hours' notice of the intended entry has been given to the occupier of the building.

DEFINITIONS
"breach of planning control": ss.123, 277(1).
"enforcement notice": ss.127, 277(1).
"land": s.277(1).
"planning authority": ss.1, 277(1).

GENERAL NOTE
Rights of entry for enforcement purposes may be granted by the planning authority (subs. (1)), the Secretary of State (subs. (2)) and the sheriff (s.157), as follows.

The planning authority may authorise entry if it has reasonable grounds for doing so for the purposes of:
–ascertaining if there has been a breach of control (subs. (1)(a));
–determining whether and how enforcement powers should be used (subss. (1)(b) and (c)); or
–ascertaining whether any enforcement procedure had been complied with (subs. (1)(d)).
The entry must be at a reasonable hour (subs. (1)), and 24 hours' notice must be given of entry to a dwelling-house (subs. (4)).

The Secretary of State may authorise entry if he has reasonable grounds for doing so for the purposes of determining whether an enforcement notice should be issued.
The entry must be at a reasonable hour (subs. (1)), and 24 hours' notice must be given of entry to a dwelling-house (subs. (4)).

The sheriff may by warrant authorise entry if BOTH
he has reasonable grounds for doing so for the purposes of:
–ascertaining if there has been a breach of control ;
–determining whether and how enforcement powers should be used ;
–ascertaining whether any enforcement procedure had been complied with; or
–of determining whether an enforcement notice should be issued
AND
admission has been, or it is reasonably apprehended will be, refused, or there is urgency (s.157).
Only one entry is permitted under the warrant and it must take place within a month and at a reasonable hour except in cases of urgency (s.157(3)).
It is an offence to obstruct the exercise of a right of entry (s.158(2)).
The authorised person may take with him other necessary persons (s.158(1)(b)). Before entry he must state his purpose and if required prove his authority (s.158(1)(a)); after entry he must leave the premises as secure as he found it (s.158(1)(c)).
A planning authority or Secretary of State who authorises entry is responsible for compensating for any loss or damage suffered in exercise of such a right (s.158(3)). It is an offence to use any manufacturing or trade information obtained in the course of any authorised entry (s.158(5)).

Right to enter under warrant

157.—(1) If the sheriff is satisfied—

(a) that there are reasonable grounds for entering any land for any of the purposes mentioned in section 156(1) or (2), and

(b) that—
>   (i) admission to the land has been refused, or a refusal is reasonably apprehended, or
>   (ii) the case is one of urgency,

he may issue a warrant authorising any person duly authorised in writing to enter the land.

(2) For the purposes of subsection (1)(b)(i) admission to land shall be regarded as having been refused if no reply is received to a request for admission within a reasonable period.

(3) A warrant authorises entry on one occasion only and that entry must be—
>   (a) within one month from the date of the issue of the warrant, and
>   (b) at a reasonable hour, unless the case is one of urgency.

DEFINITIONS
"breach of planning control": ss.123, 277(1).
"land": s.277(1).

GENERAL NOTE
See the commentary to s.156.

Rights of entry: supplementary provisions

158.—(1) A person authorised to enter any land in pursuance of a right of entry conferred under or by virtue of section 156 or 157 (referred to in this section as "a right of entry")—
>   (a) shall, if so required, produce evidence of his authority and state the purpose of his entry before so entering,
>   (b) may take with him such other persons as may be necessary, and
>   (c) on leaving the land shall, if the owner or occupier is not then present, leave it as effectively secured against trespassers as he found it.

(2) Any person who wilfully obstructs a person acting in the exercise of a right of entry shall be guilty of an offence and liable on summary conviction to a fine not exceeding level 3 on the standard scale.

(3) If any damage is caused to land or moveable property in the exercise of a right of entry, compensation may be recovered by any person suffering the damage from the authority who gave the written authority for the entry or, as the case may be, the Secretary of State.

(4) The provisions of section 86 shall apply in relation to compensation under subsection (3) as they apply in relation to compensation under Part IV.

(5) If any person who enters any land, in exercise of a right of entry discloses to any person any information obtained by him while on the land as to any manufacturing process or trade secret, he shall be guilty of an offence.

(6) Subsection (5) does not apply if the disclosure is made by a person in the course of performing his duty in connection with the purpose for which he was authorised to enter the land.

(7) A person who is guilty of an offence under subsection (5) shall be liable—
>   (a) on summary conviction to a fine not exceeding the statutory maximum, or
>   (b) on conviction on indictment to imprisonment for a term not exceeding 2 years or a fine or both.

DEFINITIONS
"land": s.277(1).
"owner": s.277(1).

PART VII

SPECIAL CONTROLS

GENERAL NOTE
Special Controls
Part VII of the Act is concerned with areas of planning Control which do not sit easily with the general regime of development Control and enforcement contained within Pts. III and VI. The areas in question relate to Tree Preservation Orders ("TPOs") (Chap. I), Waste Land Notices (Chap. II) and Advertisements (Chap. III).

In the case of the former, the opportunity has been taken to clarify which parts of the enforcement notice regime are properly applicable to the provisions contained in ss.168-170. In the case of the Town and Country Planning (Scotland) Act 1972 (c.52), it was sometimes a matter of applying judgment and common sense in order to determine which provisions could be excised or disregarded in relation to TPOs. Now, the relevant enforcement provisions are free-standing.

All of the areas of control contained in this Part relate to environmentally sensitive issues, with a particular emphasis on visual amenity. Two out of the three (TPOs and Advertisements) have their provisions specifically modified in relation to conservation areas. It will be apparent that in many cases, little exists in the way of case law in Scotland in relation to the interpretation of these provisions, but this may become less so as interest in the area of Environmental Law increases.

CHAPTER I

TREES

General duty of planning authorities as respects trees

Planning permission to include appropriate provision for preservation and planting of trees

159. It shall be the duty of the planning authority—

(a) to ensure, whenever it is appropriate, that in granting planning permission for any development adequate provision is made, by the imposition of conditions, for the preservation or planting of trees, and

(b) to make such orders under section 160 as appear to the authority to be necessary in connection with the grant of such permission, whether for giving effect to such conditions or otherwise.

DEFINITIONS
"development": ss.26, 277(1).
"planning authority": ss.1, 277(1).
"planning permission": Pt. II.

GENERAL NOTE
The development of sites in the country or within the policies of, for example, a mansion house set within its own grounds will frequently highlight a conflict between achievement of an economic development of the site and the amenity derived from the existence of mature belts of trees. (Occasionally single trees may be of an age and quality to merit specific attention.) Tree Preservation Orders (TPOs) were originally introduced by the Town and Country Planning (Scotland) Act 1932 (c.49), and widened in their effect by subsequent legislation (see for example, s.9 of the Town and Country Amenities Act 1974 (c.32)).

Since the passing of the Town and Country Planning (Scotland) Act 1947 (c.53), local planning authorities in Scotland have enjoyed responsibility under the planning legislation for consideration of protection of trees in the course of granting a planning permission, and for the making of Tree Preservation Orders, which are capable of entering the Land Register (Land Registration (Scotland) Act 1979 (c.33), ss.2(4)(c), 28(1)(e)) or the Register of Sasines (see s.161(2)). As such, these orders are capable of creating or burdening real rights. The former responsibility is a duty for the planning authority to apply in all circumstances, the latter is a matter for the authority's discretion, irrespective of whether it is exercised in conjunction with a specific planning proposal.

Interestingly, there is no definition of "tree" given in either the Act or the relevant subordinate legislation, and there are no reported decisions in Scotland. In England, there has been some difference in approach to the issue of definition of the term. (*cf. Kent County Council v. Batchelor* (1976) 33 P. & C.R. 185 and *Bullock v. Secretary of State for the Environment* (1980) 40 P. & C.R. 246).

Tree preservation orders

Power to make tree preservation orders

160.—(1) If it appears to a planning authority that it is expedient in the interests of amenity to make provision for the preservation of trees or woodlands in their district, they may for that purpose make an order with respect to such trees, groups of trees or woodlands as may be specified in the order.

(2) An order under subsection (1) is in this Act referred to as a "tree preservation order".

(3) A tree preservation order may, in particular, make provision—

(a) for prohibiting (subject to any exemptions for which provision may be made by the order) the cutting down, topping, lopping, uprooting, wilful damage or wilful destruction of trees except with the consent of the planning authority, and for enabling that authority to give their consent subject to conditions;

(b) for securing the replanting, in such manner as may be prescribed by or under the order, of any part of a woodland area which is felled in the course of forestry operations permitted by or under the order;

(c) for applying, in relation to any consent under the order, and to applications for such consent, any of the provisions of this Act mentioned in subsection (4), subject to such adaptations and modifications as may be specified in the order.

(4) The provisions referred to in subsection (3)(c) are—

(a) the provisions of Part III relating to planning permission and to applications for planning permission, except sections 32, 34, 35, 36(2) and (3), 38, 58 to 62, 69 and 70 and Schedules 6 and 7, and section 65 of the Planning (Listed Buildings and Conservation Areas) (Scotland) Act 1997,

(b) sections 88 to 92, 94 and 95 (except so far as they relate to purchase notices served in consequence of such orders as are mentioned in section 88(1)(b) or (c)), and

(c) section 263.

(5) A tree preservation order may be made so as to apply, in relation to trees to be planted pursuant to any such conditions as are mentioned in section 159(a), as from the time when those trees are planted.

(6) Without prejudice to any other exemptions for which provision may be made by a tree preservation order, nothing in such an order shall prohibit the uprooting, felling or lopping of trees if—

(a) it is urgently necessary in the interests of safety,

(b) it is necessary for the prevention or abatement of a nuisance, or

(c) it is in compliance with any obligation imposed by or under an Act of Parliament,

so long as, where paragraph (a) or (b) applies, notice in writing of the proposed operations is given to the planning authority as soon as practicable after the operations become necessary.

(7) This section shall have effect subject to—

(a) section 39(2) of the Housing and Planning Act 1986 (saving for effect of section 2(4) of the Opencast Coal Act 1958 on land affected by a tree preservation order despite its repeal), and

(b) section 15 of the Forestry Act 1967 (licences under that Act to fell trees comprised in a tree preservation order).

DEFINITIONS
"district": s.1(1).
"planning authority": ss.1, 277.
"purchase notices": s.88(2).
"tree preservation order": s.160(2).

GENERAL NOTE

Section 160 sets out the extent to which planning authorities enjoy a discretion (as opposed to the obligations arising in the circumstances specified in s.159) to make Tree Preservation Orders (TPOs) over land within their district. Such orders can be made "in the interests of amenity" of a part of the authority's district, and can range from the protection of individual trees (see below) to entire woodlands (subs. (1)). (Some guidance is also to be found in SDD Circulars 87/1975 and 31/1981.)

The general extent to which operations on trees are circumscribed once a TPO is in effect are set out in subs. (3), and in particular, the prohibited acts of "cutting down, topping, lopping, uprooting, wilful damage or wilful destruction" of trees protected by a TPO (subs. (3)(a)). None of these terms are defined in the Act.

It will be noted that even the lawful felling of trees subject to a TPO can be accompanied by a re-planting obligation in the circumstances described in subs. (3)(b). A regime similar to that applying to grants of planning permission under Pt. III (save for parts which are not germane to TPOs, or else are duplicated within Pt. VII) is established whereby planning authorities may grant consents to carry out operations on protected trees (subss. (3)(c),(4)).

Subsection (6) offers owners of land affected by TPOs latitude in the circumstances specified under subss. (a)–(c), whereby the process for obtaining consents can be avoided. Clearly, a tension will always exist between the proper discretion given to landowners to avoid the adverse consequences stemming from having a dangerous tree (or one which is a source of nuisance) on their land, and the scope available to the less scrupulous to circumvent the purpose of the TPO. One such situation relates to the effects of bad weather or sudden deterioration of the condition of trees.

As a contrast, an avenue of trees may well have its visual impact destroyed by the removal of a few key trees on spurious grounds. On the other hand, a severe gale overnight may require an instantaneous decision on the removal of a tree to avoid danger to passers-by. Whilst the planning authority requires to be notified of such operations as soon as practicable *after* the operations have taken place, the evidential difficulties of establishing that the subs. (6) grounds existed at the time are obvious.

It should be noted that specification in the TPO of the trees affected may be important in order to establish the extent of protection. While subs. (3)(b) also permits a TPO to require the replanting of lawfully felled trees (see also, s.167), the limitations of an Order in regard to replacement of trees planted after others have been removed with the consent of the planning authority were highlighted in the Sheriff Court case of *Brown v. Michael B. Cooper*, 1990 S.C.C.R. 675.

Form of and procedure applicable to orders

161.—(1) Subject to section 163 and 249, a tree preservation order shall not take effect until it is confirmed by the planning authority and the planning authority may confirm any such order either without modification or subject to such modifications as they consider expedient.

(2) As soon as a tree preservation order is confirmed, the planning authority shall record it in the appropriate Register of Sasines or, as the case may be, register it in the Land Register of Scotland.

(3) Provision may be made by regulations with respect to—
(a) the form of tree preservation orders, and
(b) the procedure to be followed in connection with the confirmation of such orders.

(4) Without prejudice to the generality of subsection (3), the regulations may make provision—

(a) that, before a tree preservation order is confirmed by the planning authority, notice of the making of the order shall be given to the owners, lessees and occupiers of land affected by the order and to such other persons, if any, as may be specified in the regulations,

(b) that objections and representations with respect to the order, if duly made in accordance with the regulations, shall be considered before the order is confirmed by the planning authority, and

(c) that copies of the order, when confirmed by the authority, shall be served on such persons as may be specified in the regulations.

DEFINITIONS
"Owners": s.277.
"planning authority": s.1, s.277.
"tree preservation order": s.160(2).

GENERAL NOTE

Except in two specific circumstances, (provisional TPOs (s.163) and prospective disposals of Crown land (s.249)), TPOs require to go through a normal process of publication, notification, objection and consideration of objections, and possible modification prior to being confirmed by the planning authority (subs. (1)). Only after confirmation is registration of the TPO in the Land or Sasine Registers competent (subs. (2)).

The process for achieving confirmation of a TPO is set out in the Town and Country Planning (Tree Preservation Order and Trees in Conservation Areas) (Scotland) Regulations 1975 (S.I. 1975 No.1204), as amended by the Town and Country Planning (Tree Preservation Order and Trees in Conservation Areas) (Scotland) Amendment Regulations 1981 (S.I. 1981 No.1835), and the Town and Country Planning (Tree Preservation Order and Trees in Conservation Areas) (Scotland) Amendment Regulations 1984 (S.I. 1984 No.329).

One obvious problem is that the process, even assuming that the planning authority can carry it out in the minimum time, can take several weeks to go through. From the standpoint of a potential purchaser of heritage, there is no provision for a notice of Intention to make a TPO to be entered in the registers, although as noted below, such notice must be served on the Keeper of the Registers. However, the intention to make a TPO may not show up on a Form 10 Report or on a Sasine Interim Report. It ought, however, to be disclosed on a local authority Property Enquiry Certificate.

The Regulations require service of notices of intention to make a TPO on:

(a) Owners, lessees and occupiers of the land affected by the Order.

(b) Any persons entitled to work minerals from the surface within that land.

(c) Any persons entitled to fell any trees affected by the order.

[Reg. 5(d), of the 1975 Regulations]

Separate provision is made for service of notice of intention on the Keeper of the Registers and the Conservator of Forests [Reg. 5(c)]. The notice must also be advertised, and made available for inspection locally [Regs. 5(a), (b), 1975 Regulations].

Since 1981, it has been a matter for the "planning authorities" (District Councils up to 1996) to determine the position where objections to proposed TPOs are received. Objections require to be submitted to the planning authority in writing within 28 days of service of the notice on "owners and lessees", or else publication of an advertisement locally. [Reg. 7(2), 1975 Regulations].

Where objections to the proposed Order are received, there is no obligation on a planning authority to hold a Public Local Inquiry ("PLI") on the TPO prior to confirmation. However, if a PLI is held, the report eventually produced must be "taken into consideration" by the planning authority in deciding whether to confirm the TPO [Reg. 8(2), 1975 Regulations, as amended].

Once confirmed, (and s.161(1) makes clear that confirmation of the Order can occur subject to modifications) the TPO requires to be either recorded in the Register of Sasines or entered in the Land Register (s.161(2) and Reg. 10, 1975 Regulations). In addition, intimation of the decision to confirm the TPO requires to be given to those persons on whom notice was initially served specifically [Reg. 9(a), 1975 Regulations, as amended]. Also, advertisement of the decision of the planning authority, and the publication of the confirmed Order for public inspection is required. [Reg. 9(b), 1975 Regulations, as amended].

The form of a TPO is set out in the Sched. to the 1975 Regulations. As is normal, it is necessary only to "substantially follow" the form prescribed, thereby allowing some latitude in drafting according to circumstances on the ground. In practice however, the periods required to elapse between the various stages by virtue of the 1975 Regulations mean that one cannot expect even the most assiduous of planning authorities using this procedure to be able to place a TPO on record in less than 42 days, and that only where no objections are received. (See note to s.163 below).

Orders affecting land where Forestry Commissioners interested

162.—(1) In relation to land in which the Forestry Commissioners have an interest, a tree preservation order may be made only if—

(a) there is not in force in respect of the land a plan of operations or other working plan approved by the Commissioners under a forestry dedication agreement, and

(b) the Commissioners consent to the making of the order.

(2) For the purposes of subsection (1), the Forestry Commissioners have an interest in land if—

(a) they have made a grant or loan under section 1 of the Forestry Act 1979 in respect of it, or

(b) there is a forestry dedication agreement in force in respect of it.

(3) A tree preservation order in respect of such land shall not have effect so as to prohibit, or to require any consent for, the cutting down of a tree in accordance with a plan of operations or other working plan approved by the Forestry Commissioners, and for the time being in force, under a forestry dedication agreement or under the conditions of a grant or loan made under section 1 of the Forestry Act 1979.

(4) In this section—

(a) "a forestry dedication agreement" means an agreement entered into with the Commissioners under section 5 of the Forestry Act 1967; and

(b) references to provisions of the Forestry Act 1967 and the Forestry Act 1979 include references to any corresponding provisions replaced by those provisions or by earlier corresponding provisions.

DEFINITIONS
"land": s.277(1).
"tree preservation order": s.160(2).

GENERAL NOTE
There is an evident scope for conflict between the respective statutory roles of planning authorities and the Forestry Commissioners in relation to trees. Whilst it is not simple to envisage this occurring in practice, the broad terms of s.160 could see a woodland managed or supported by the Forestry Commission falling within the ambit of a TPO.

To prevent such conflicts arising, consent of the Forestry Commissioners is required where a TPO is proposed over any land where a grant has already been paid to the landowner under s.1 of the Forestry Act 1979, or else a "forestry dedication agreement" (FDA) has been made between the landowner and the Forestry Commissioners, otherwise a TPO cannot be made (subs. (2)). (As to how the Forestry Commissioners grant such consent, see s.15 of the Forestry Act 1967 (c.10)). Also, if a "plan of operation" has been made under a FDA, a TPO cannot be made (subs. (1)). (See also SDD Circular 7/1984.)

The operation of a confirmed TPO will also be circumscribed where the Forestry Commissioners have approved a "plan of operation" in conjunction with a Grant or an FDA (subs. (3)). In effect, approval of a "plan of operation" by the Forestry Commissioners is a deemed consent to the cutting down of a tree, where such an operation falls within the management activities presaged by the plan.

Provisional tree preservation orders

163.—(1) If it appears to a planning authority that a tree preservation order proposed to be made by that authority should take effect immediately without previous confirmation, they may include in the order as made by them a direction that this section shall apply to the order.

(2) Notwithstanding section 161(1), an order which contains such a direction—

(a) shall take effect provisionally on such date as may be specified in it, and

(b) shall continue in force by virtue of this section until—

(i) the expiration of a period of 6 months beginning with the date on which the order was made, or

(ii) the date on which the order is confirmed,

whichever first occurs.

(3) Provision shall be made by regulations for securing that the notices to be given of the making of a tree preservation order containing a direction under this section shall include a statement of the effect of the direction.

DEFINITIONS

"planning authority": ss.1, 277.

"tree preservation order": s.160(2).

GENERAL NOTE

The delays inherent in the process of making a TPO have been noted in relation to the provisions of s.161. Whilst a landowner will be put on notice of the intention of the planning authority to make a TPO in pursuance of these powers, this alone will place him under no restrictions in relation to the trees prospectively subject to the TPO. Therefore, the purpose of making the TPO could well be defeated by the time the TPO is placed on record.

Thus, since the time of passing the Town and Country Planning (Scotland) Act 1947 (c.53) (when confirmation was a matter for the Secretary of State), Parliament has been alive to the irrevocable nature of felling trees intended for protection. In what is now s.163, powers are given to planning authorities to direct that a TPO is effective in relation to the trees referred to in the TPO for a maximum period of six months subsequent to the TPO being *made* by the planning authority (subs. 163(2)(a) and (b)), or else, until the TPO is confirmed (if earlier) (subs. (2)(b)(ii)).

Where such a Direction is made, the Order is generally referred to as a Provisional TPO. It will be apparent, therefore, that trees may enjoy protection under a Provisional TPO which does not necessarily subsist in the confirmed TPO, since the latter may be confirmed subject to modifications (s.161(1)).

If the planning authority follows this path, it must advise "owners, lessees and occupiers" of the effect of a Direction made under s.163, declaring a TPO to be (in the majority of cases) in effect from the date of its being made, when such persons are notified of the making of the TPO (subs. (3) and Reg. 5(d), 1975 Regulations). The date on which the Direction takes effect must be included within such notification [1975 Regulations, Sched., para. 15]. (Incidentally, no express requirement on planning authorities to include information with regard to a s.163 Direction having been made when advertising the making of the TPO is contained in the Act or the 1975 Regulations, but presumably, this would be carried out in practice).

Power for Secretary of State to make tree preservation orders

164.—(1) If it appears to the Secretary of State that it is expedient that a tree preservation order, or an order amending or revoking such an order, should be made, he may himself make such an order.

(2) Such an order made by the Secretary of State shall have the same effect as if it had been made by the planning authority and confirmed by them under this Chapter.

(3) The Secretary of State shall not make such an order without consulting the planning authority.

(4) The provisions of this Chapter and of any regulations made under it with respect to the procedure to be followed in connection with the making and confirmation of any order mentioned in subsection (1) and the service of copies of it as confirmed shall have effect, subject to any necessary modifications, in relation to any proposal by the Secretary of State to make such an order by virtue of subsection (1), its making by him and the service of copies of it.

DEFINITIONS

"planning authority": ss.1, 277.

GENERAL NOTE

Given the role of the Secretary of State as a planning authority in his own right, allied to his position of undertaking general oversight of the entire planning system, it is no surprise to find powers vested in him which both duplicate those of the planning authorities, and also grant express powers to modify and revoke TPOs. (It is, therefore, unclear whether the planning authorities themselves enjoy these latter powers, but reference to Reg. 5 of the 1975 Regulations implies that this may be the case).

By virtue of subs. (4), it seems that exercise of the Secretary of State's powers under this section requires to follow the procedure set out in ss.160–163, and also the applicable parts of the 1975 Regulations, as amended. One additional step provided is that of consulting with the relevant planning authority in all cases before the Secretary of State himself makes a TPO (subs. 164(3)). It seems that the point at which the Secretary of State "consults" is essentially a matter for his discretion.

Compensation for loss or damage caused by orders etc.

Compensation in respect of tree preservation orders

165.—(1) A tree preservation order may make provision for the payment by the planning authority, subject to such exceptions and conditions as may be specified in the order, of compensation in respect of loss or damage caused or incurred in consequence of—

(a) the refusal of any consent required under the order, or

(b) the grant of any such consent subject to conditions.

(2) Except in so far as may be otherwise provided by section 166(5), any tree preservation order or any regulations made under this Act, any question of disputed compensation under this section shall be referred to and determined by the Lands Tribunal.

(3) In relation to the determination of any such question, the provisions of sections 9 and 11 of the Land Compensation (Scotland) Act 1963 shall apply subject to any necessary modifications and to the provisions of any regulations made under this Act.

DEFINITIONS

"Lands Tribunal": s.277(1).
"planning authority": ss.1, 277.
"tree preservation order": s.160(2).

GENERAL NOTE

The gain in public amenity from the preservation of trees when secured via a TPO, may often require balancing with the consequences for a landowner as to the possibility of developing his land, or the value of any Timber interests thereby affected.

However, the making of a TPO does not, of itself, give rise to any claim for compensation. Subsection (1) makes clear that only where an application for Consent to carry out operations under s.160(3) has been refused, or has been granted subject to conditions, does a right to claim compensation arise, if such provision is made in the TPO. (Sched., art. 9, 1975 Regulations, as amended).

On the other hand, where a planning authority certify that a refusal of Consent relating to a tree, or else the imposition of conditions is required (a) in the interests of good forestry, or (b) that outwith woodlands, trees have an outstanding or special amenity value; no compensation is payable (*ibid.*).

Determination of compensation. Except in cases where a requirement of re-planting is involved, this is a matter for the Lands Tribunal, presumably applying normal principles, with the intention of taking account of injurious affection to the Claimant's land which would arise from the felling of the trees in question (*ibid.*, art. 10(b)) (*cf.* s.166(1)(a)). Incidentally, the terms "compensation" and "loss or damage" are not defined for the purposes of this section, and presumably are intended to be interpreted in the same manner as Lands Compensation Legislation.

It is a little unclear against whom a claim might lie against where the Secretary of State has exercised powers under s.164. However, claims for compensation must be made in writing within six months of the decision of the planning authority complained against (Sched., art. 11, 1975 Regulations, as amended).

Compensation in respect of requirement as to replanting of trees

166.—(1) This section applies where—

(a) a requirement is imposed by the planning authority or the Secretary of

State under a tree preservation order for securing the replanting of all or any part of a woodland area which is felled in the course of forestry operations permitted by or under the order, and

(b) the Forestry Commissioners decide not to make any grant or loan under section 1 of the Forestry Act 1979 in respect of the replanting by reason that the requirement frustrates the use of the woodland area for the growing of timber or other forest products for commercial purposes and in accordance with the rules or practice of good forestry.

(2) Where this section applies, the planning authority exercising functions under the tree preservation order shall be liable, on the making of a claim in accordance with this section, to pay compensation in respect of such loss or damage, if any, as is caused or incurred in consequence of compliance with the requirement.

(3) The Forestry Commissioners shall, at the request of the person under a duty to comply with such a requirement as is mentioned in subsection (1)(a), give a certificate stating—

(a) whether they have decided not to make such a grant or loan as is mentioned in subsection (1)(b), and

(b) if so, the grounds for their decision.

(4) A claim for compensation under this section must be served on the planning authority—

(a) within 12 months from the date on which the requirement was made, or

(b) where an application has been made to the Secretary of State for the determination of any question relating to the reasonableness of a requirement, within 12 months from the date of the determination of the Secretary of State,

but subject in either case to such extension of that period as the planning authority may allow.

(5) Any question of disputed compensation under this section shall be determined in accordance with section 70 of the Countryside (Scotland) Act 1967.

DEFINITIONS
"planning authority": ss.1, 277.
"tree preservation order": s.160(2).

GENERAL NOTE

This Section again highlights the potential for conflict between the statutory responsibilities of planning authorities and the Forestry Commissioners. The former may have a desire to see felled trees restored where a TPO has been in force over them (subs. (1)(a)), which runs opposite to the good husbandry role for their woodlands which rests with the latter.

This conflict is resolved by allowing the will of the Forestry Commissioners to prevail where they consider a requirement to re-plant to be detrimental to the use of the area affected for Forestry purposes, and withhold Grant under the Forestry Act 1979 (c.21) (subs. (1)(b)). Provision is made for certification to be given to this effect by the Forestry Commissioners (subs. (3)). A planning authority insisting on re-planting in these circumstances – and the reasonableness of such a requirement is, in any event, appealable to the Secretary of State in terms of s.169 – is liable to be required to compensate for "loss or damage" suffered by the landowner in complying with the re-planting obligation (subs. (2)).

The reference to the Countryside (Scotland) Act 1967 (c.86) (in subs. (5)) appears to envisage assessment of compensation being made on the basis of Depreciation of the value of the Claimant's interest in the land, as assessed by the Lands Tribunal. Such a figure may not, of course, be the same as the loss of Grant from the Forestry Commission. Claims for compensation must be made to the planning authority within 12 months of the decision of the planning authority (or else the Secretary of State if the matter is determined after Appeal) requiring re-planting to take place (subs. (4)(a) and (b)).

Consequences of tree removal etc.

Replacement of trees

167.—(1) If any tree in respect of which a tree preservation order is for the time being in force—

(a) is removed, uprooted or destroyed in contravention of the order, or

(b) except in the case of a tree to which the order applies as part of a wood-land, is removed, uprooted or destroyed or dies at a time when its felling or uprooting is authorised only by virtue of section 160(6)(a),

it shall be the duty of the owner of the land to plant another tree of an appropriate size and species at the same place as soon as he reasonably can.

(2) The duty imposed by subsection (1) does not apply to an owner if on application by him the planning authority dispense with it.

(3) In respect of trees in a woodland it shall be sufficient for the purposes of this section to replace the trees removed, uprooted or destroyed by planting the same number of trees—

(a) on or near the land on which the trees removed, uprooted or destroyed stood, or

(b) on such other land as may be agreed between the planning authority and the owner of the land,

and in such places as may be designated by the planning authority.

(4) In relation to any tree planted pursuant to this section, the relevant tree preservation order shall apply as it applied to the original tree.

(5) The duty imposed by subsection (1) on the owner of any land shall attach to the person who is from time to time the owner of the land.

DEFINITIONS
  "land": s.277(1).
  "owner" s.277(1).
  "planning authority": ss.1, 277.
  "tree preservation order": s.160(2).

GENERAL NOTE
    The general purpose of s.167 is to enshrine the general duty of a landowner to "replace" (that is, to provide a tree of a similar nature, age and quality) as opposed to re-planting a (new, young) tree where the original tree is (a) removed, uprooted or destroyed in breach of a TPO; or (b) similarly treated, or else dies, in the course of undertaking the protective or obligatory steps specified in s.160(6).
    In this case, the duty is to "plant another tree . . . in the same place", as soon as is reasonably possible (subs. (1)). Clearly, this obligation threatens a defaulting landowner with considerable expense, and obviously, the older or more rare the tree, the greater such expense is likely to be. Moreover, this duty can transmit to successor landowners (subs. (5)), and may be a matter to be prudently covered in missives where a property is being purchased which lies within fairly mature Woodlands. For land which is not part of a Woodland, a power to dispense with the s.167 obligation is vested in the planning authority (subs. (2)).
    For practical reasons, a different regime applies to trees removed from a Woodland in breach of a TPO, as constituted by subs. (3). Here, the overall damage which the Woodland could suffer by imposition of a requirement of strict replacement of the removed trees is recognised in a proviso originally inserted by s.2(3) of the Town and Country Planning (Amendment) Act 1985 (c.52). As a result, replacement of trees "on or near" the destroyed site, or even replacement on a different site altogether – if carried out in agreement with the planning authority – can constitute sufficient discharge of the s.167 duty (subs. (3)(a) and (b)).
    An important adjunct to this provision is the deeming of any replacement tree so planted to be the original tree comprised within the TPO (subs. (4)). It is essential, however, to establish a link between the original trees and their replacements where a Summary Complaint is raised alleging breach of the provisions of the TPO (*Brown v. Michael B. Cooper*, 1990 S.C.C.R. 675).

Enforcement of duties as to replacement of trees

168.—(1) If it appears to the planning authority that—

(a) the provisions of section 167, or

(b) any conditions of a consent given under a tree preservation order which require the replacement of trees,
are not complied with in the case of any tree or trees, the authority may serve on the owner of the land a notice requiring him, within such period as may be specified in the notice, to plant a tree or trees of such size and species as may be so specified.

(2) A notice under subsection (1) may be served by a planning authority only within 2 years from the date on which the failure to comply with those provisions or conditions came to the knowledge of the authority.

(3) A notice under subsection (1) shall specify a period at the end of which it is to take effect, being a period of not less than 28 days beginning with the date of service of the notice.

(4) The duty imposed by section 167(1) may only be enforced as provided by this section and not otherwise.

DEFINITIONS
"land": s.277(1).
"owner": s.277(1).
"planning authority": ss.1, 277.
"tree preservation order": s.160(2).

GENERAL NOTE
Section 168 applies a quasi-enforcement notice regime in relation to apprehended breaches of s.167 (Replacement of trees where a TPO is breached), or else a Consent given under a TPO, requiring a landowner to plant replacement Trees (s.160(3)(b) and (c)). The planning authority has two years subsequent to becoming aware of a breach of the above, to serve a notice requiring the landowner to undertake the necessary replacement planting as required by the authority (subss. (1) and (2)). (This regime is clearly applicable to a successor where s.167 applies. Is the same also true where obligations under a Consent are breached?) The requirement takes effect not less than 28 days after service of the notice (subs. (3)).

The enforcement regime is set out in ss.168-170, and it appears that breach of any of the requirements of notices served under this procedure cannot constitute a Criminal offence (see s.172).

Appeal against section 168 notice

169.—(1) A person on whom a notice under section 168(1) is served may appeal to the Secretary of State against the notice on any of the following grounds—
(a) that the provisions of section 167 or, as the case may be, the conditions mentioned in section 168(1)(b) are not applicable or have been complied with;
(b) that in all the circumstances of the case the duty imposed by section 167 should be dispensed with in relation to any tree;
(c) that the requirements of the notice are unreasonable in respect of the period or the size or species of trees specified in it;
(d) that the planting of a tree or trees in accordance with the notice is not required in the interests of amenity or would be contrary to the practice of good forestry;
(e) that the place on which the tree is or trees are required to be planted is unsuitable for that purpose.

(2) An appeal under subsection (1) may be made either by giving written notice to the Secretary of State before the end of the period specified in accordance with section 168(3), or by sending such notice to him in a properly addressed and prepaid letter posted to him at such time that, in the ordinary course of post, it would be delivered to him before the end of that period.

(3) A person who gives notice under subsection (2) shall submit to the Secretary of State, either when giving the notice or within such time as may be prescribed under subsection (4), a statement in writing—
(a) specifying the grounds on which he is appealing against the notice under section 168(1), and

(b) giving such further information as may be so prescribed.

(4) The Secretary of State may prescribe the procedure to be followed on appeals under this section, and (without prejudice to the generality of the foregoing provisions of this subsection) in so prescribing—

   (a) may specify the time within which an appellant is to submit a statement under subsection (3) and the matters on which information is to be given in such a statement;

   (b) may require the planning authority to submit, within such time as may be specified, a statement indicating the submissions which they propose to put forward on the appeal;

   (c) may specify the matters to be included in such a statement;

   (d) may require the authority or the appellant to give such notice of an appeal under this section as may be specified to such persons as may be specified;

   (e) may require the authority to send to the Secretary of State, within such period from the date of the bringing of the appeal as may be specified, a copy of the notice and a list of the persons on whom the notice has been served.

(5) The Secretary of State may—

   (a) dismiss an appeal if the appellant fails to comply with subsection (3) within the time prescribed under subsection (4)(a), and

   (b) allow an appeal and quash the notice under section 168(1) if the planning authority fail to comply with any requirement imposed by virtue of paragraph (b), (c) or (e) of subsection (4).

(6) Subject to subsection (5), the Secretary of State shall, if either the planning authority or the appellant so desire, afford to each of them an opportunity of appearing before, and being heard by, a person appointed by him for the purpose.

(7) Where such an appeal is brought, the notice under section 168(1) shall be of no effect pending the final determination or the withdrawal of the appeal.

(8) On such an appeal the Secretary of State may—

   (a) correct any defect, error or misdescription in the notice under section 168(1), or

   (b) vary its terms,

if he is satisfied that the correction or variation will not cause injustice to the appellant or the planning authority.

(9) On the determination of such an appeal the Secretary of State shall give directions for giving effect to the determination including, where appropriate, directions for quashing the notice under section 168(1).

(10) Schedule 4 applies to appeals under this section.

Definitions
"planning authority": ss.1, 277(1).

General Note
This Section essentially adopts the relevant parts of the enforcement notice Appeals procedure which were formerly part of the (heavily amended) s.85 of the 1972 Act, and applies these to circumstances where a notice has been served under s.168. In the process, any doubts as to which parts of the old section were applicable to breaches of the TPO enforcement regime have been removed.

Subs. (1)
Prior to the enactment of s.54 of the Planning and Compensation Act 1991 (c.34), appeals against what is now a s.168 notice required to be brought within the terms of the present subs. (1)(a),(c)–(e). Recognition that these provisions alone might oblige an Appellant, on a strict reading of the legislation, to carry out manifestly unjust operations seems to have led to the "catch-all" terms of sub-para. (b). It would seem possible to lodge an appeal citing more than one of the grounds of appeal specified in this subsection.

Subs. (2)

Appeals must be made to the Secretary of State in writing prior to the end of the period specified in the notice in terms of s.168(3). This period may close only 28 days after the notice has been served on the Appellant. (See note to s.161 above). An application is not made for appeal against an enforcement notice until it is received, where the relevant provisions require the application to be made within a certain time. (*Adam v. Secretary of State for Scotland*, 1988 S.L.T. 300). Thus far, the Secretary of State has not made any formal specification in terms of subs. (4).

Subs. (3)

Whilst the Secretary of State did not prescribed any period under the previous legislation (s.85(2B) and s.99(3), of the 1972 Act), for submitting a statement specifying the grounds of appeal, the most likely interpretation is that the nature of appeal and supporting grounds must be sent simultaneously. The Secretary of State has not made any further prescription of additional information requiring to be submitted with the appeal.

Subs. (4)

Again, no Regulations were made under the predecessor legislation in relation to the matters specified, and these powers appear to be held in reserve by the Secretary of State.

Subs. (5)

These provisions are intended to prevent the dilatory pursuit of the appeal from either side. Whilst this makes sense from the administrative point of view in any event, in this particular situation, the alleged harm to public amenity makes it imperative that matters do not drag on. Curiously, a failure to serve notice of the appeal on third parties does not expressly authorise the appeal to be dismissed.

Subs. (6)

This subsection leaves open the possibility of a s.169 appeal being dealt with by written submission alone. However, it is open to either party to insist on determination being made by a person appointed by the Secretary of State, following upon a hearing. Reference to the provisions of Sched. 4 implies that the Secretary of State is entitled to determine the appeal himself (Sched. 4, para. 3(1)).

Subs. (7)

This is a standard provision for preserving the status quo pending the determination of the Appeal.

Subs. (8)

The Secretary of State can effectively re-write the terms of a s.168 notice where to do so would avoid "injustice" to the parties. Whilst "injustice" is a nebulous concept in the abstract, the actual dispute may become better focused by a judicious use of the power.

It is probably incompetent to seek to raise a Petition for Judicial Review where the Secretary of State disregards a failure of Service. (*Gill v. Clydebank District Council*, 1983 S.C. 76). It is competent for a Reporter to vary the terms of an enforcement notice in order to delete an ultra vires requirement where satisfied that to do so would not cause injustice to the Appellant or to the planning authority (*Barn Properties v. Secretary of State for Scotland*, 1996 S.L.T. 964).

Subs. (9)

It seems the Secretary of State can also change the means by which a breach of s.167 should be remedied. Alternatively, he may declare the notice to be quashed, presumably on one or more of the grounds specified in subs. (1).

Execution and cost of works required by section 168 notice

170.—(1) If, within the period specified in a notice under section 168(1) for compliance with it, or within such extended period as the planning authority may allow, any trees which are required to be planted by a notice under that section have not been planted, the planning authority may—

(a) enter the land and plant those trees, and

(b) recover from the person who is then the owner or lessee of the land any expenses reasonably incurred by them in doing so.

(2) If the person mentioned in subsection (1)(b) was entitled to appeal to the Secretary of State but did not do so, he shall not be entitled in proceedings under that subsection to dispute the validity of the action taken in accordance with the notice by the planning authority.

(3) In computing the amount of the expenses which may be recovered by them under subsection (1), a planning authority may include in that amount such proportion of their administrative expenses as seems to them to be appropriate.

(4) Where a notice under section 168(1) has been served—

(a) any expenses incurred by the owner, lessee or occupier of any land for the purpose of complying with the notice, and

(b) any sums paid by the owner or lessee of any land under subsection (1) in respect of expenses incurred by the planning authority in planting trees required by such a notice to be planted,

shall be recoverable from the person responsible for the cutting down, destruction or removal of the original tree or trees.

(5) If on a complaint by the owner of any land it appears to the sheriff that the occupier of the land is preventing the owner from carrying out work required to be carried out by a notice under section 168(1), the sheriff may by warrant authorise the owner to go on to the land and carry out the work.

(6) A planning authority taking steps under subsection (1) may sell any materials removed by them from the land unless those materials are claimed by the owner within 3 days of their removal by the planning authority.

(7) Where such materials have been sold the planning authority shall pay the owner the proceeds of the sale after deducting any expenses recoverable by them from him.

(8) Where a planning authority seek under subsection (1) to recover any expenses from a person on the basis that he is the owner of any land, and such person proves that—

(a) he is receiving the rent in respect of that land merely as trustee, tutor, curator, factor or agent of some other person, and

(b) he has not, and since the date of the service on him of the demand for payment has not had, in his hands on behalf of that other person sufficient money to discharge the whole demand of the authority,

his liability shall be limited to the total amount of the money which he has or has had in his hands on behalf of that other person.

(9) A planning authority who by reason of subsection (8) have not recovered the whole of any such expenses from a trustee, tutor, curator, factor or agent may recover any unpaid balance from the person on whose behalf the rent is received.

(10) Any person who wilfully obstructs a person acting in the exercise of the power conferred by subsection (1) shall be guilty of an offence and liable on summary conviction to a fine not exceeding level 3 on the standard scale.

DEFINITIONS

"land": s.277(1).

"owner": s.277(1).

"planning authority": ss.1, 277(1).

GENERAL NOTE

It is a normal part of statutory enforcement procedures that the enforcing authority may themselves undertake works necessary to remedy a breach of control or default by a landowner, and subsequently seek redress from the landowner, or any such other persons as statute may fix with liability. The problem from the authority's point of view is that it may be faced with the immediate outlay of significant expenditure – often the reason the liable individual has not carried out the works in the first place – without certainty of recovery.

Even a cursory glance at s.170 shows that the trail to recovery of expenditure by the planning authority is not straightforward, and may involve pursuit of more than one person. A criminal sanction arises, however, where the planning authority is obstructed in the exercise of its powers. (see s.170(10), below).

Subs. (1)

It is clear enough that a s.168 notice can specify a period within which a breach is to be remedied (s.168(3)), and that failure to comply can result in s.170 being invoked. It is not clear how much time (if any), a "landowner or lessee" has from the determination of an unsuccessful s.169 appeal to comply with the original s.168 notice, before the provisions of s.170 can be triggered by the planning authority. Presumably, the intention is that the planning authority should exercise its discretion to allow the liable individual a reasonable time to acquire and transport the required trees (they may have taken steps to ascertain the position in this regard against future action by themselves) before acting under s.170.

It is a little confusing to see the expression "owner or lessee" appear here, given that lessees with more than three years of their lease to run fall within the definition of "owner" for the overall purposes of the Act (s.277(1)). Does this mean the intention is to catch under this section, anyone holding a lease, with however small a period until expiry?

Subs. (2)

It is important to appreciate that this provision is intended only to prevent late challenges to the validity of a s.168 notice, where the "owner or lessee" has failed to exercise rights under s.169. Any other defences which may be available (see, for example, s.170(8)) do not appear to be excluded. It seems that the word "person" in this context is all-embracing, and could include Crown properties (*Advocate (Lord) v. Strathclyde Regional Council and Dumbarton District Council*, 1988 S.L.T. 546).

Subs. (3)

Many planning authorities, in such situations, will charge administrative expenses on a flat rate or percentage of the other costs incurred in replacing the trees in question. It may not always be clear what proportion of their expenses they are considering to be "appropriate".

Subs. (4)

In essence, this subsection offers a right of relief in favour of the "owner, lessee or occupier" of land subject to a s.168 notice. Where the work required by the s.168 notice is not carried out by the planning authority then all three, in relation to the expenses incurred, or else the "Owner or lessee" in relation to sums paid out relative to the work, are entitled to seek recovery against the "person responsible" for the loss of the trees.

Whilst this is a potentially helpful protection to a landowner who suffers unauthorised felling of protected trees (assuming the "person responsible" can be identified), the position of, say, a timber-operative acting with the landowner's consent is potentially more perilous. Were a landowner to authorise the felling of protected trees knowingly, is it a defence to a payment action raised on foot of subs. (4) that the landowner did not tell his contractor, or else concealed, the fact that a TPO was in existence?

Subs. (5)

It is again normal procedure to provide for a warrant to be obtained to execute works required under a statutory notice, where execution of that work is being obstructed by the occupier of the affected land. It is perhaps more unusual outwith the Planning Acts to find the power to obtain the warrant vested in the hands of a private individual rather than the public authority. However, the owner (but not a lessee with an unexpired portion of less than three years (s.277(1))) can obtain such a warrant where he can aver that the "occupier" is preventing the execution of such works.

Subss. (6), (7)

This provision is parallel to the provisions of s.136 in relation to enforcement notices. "Materials" is not defined in any way, and would probably, receive a broad interpretation. In the current case, the most likely "material" to be removed might be the cut-up timber from the felled trees.

It is interesting to note that subs. (6) does not vest the "materials" in the planning authority, but merely authorises their sale. It appears from this and the following subsection that the planning authority is being placed in a position of Agent *ex statu* for the owner of the "materials". As such, some of the common law duties attaching to agents may also apply here, particularly with regard to the price obtained for the "materials".

It should also be borne in mind that the planning authority may well be acting for an unknown Principal were such a sale to take place. In either eventuality established by the subss. (6) and (7), proof of title to the materials is a further hurdle to be crossed.

Subss. (8), (9)

Subsection (8) is also the parallel of provisions in s.136. It is clearly inequitable that a person acting in any of the limited capacities specified in subs. (8) should incur a personal liability under the section. Similar considerations apply to the estate or the monies under that person's control, hence the additional provision in subs. (9) for repayment to be sought from the true beneficiary of the rents or other monies.

This alone may present the planning authority with a difficult process in recovering what may be a relatively small sum. It is also unclear how far back a sum of money which, say, a trustee "has had" in his hands can be traced back in order to establish the limit of his liability under subs. (8).

Subs. (10)

It will be noted that a Criminal Offence is established which arises from the obstruction of replacement work after a s.168 notice has been served. The Level of Fine payable was increased to Level 3 (£1,000) by virtue of the Planning and Compensation Act 1991 (c.34) (see also, *Enforcing Planning Control* HMSO, February 1989 by Robert Carnwath Q.C.).

Penalties for non-compliance with tree preservation order

171.—(1) If any person, in contravention of a tree preservation order—
(a) cuts down, uproots or wilfully destroys a tree, or
(b) wilfully damages, tops or lops a tree in such a manner as to be likely to destroy it,
he shall be guilty of an offence.

(2) A person guilty of an offence under subsection (1) shall be liable—
(a) on summary conviction to a fine not exceeding £20,000, and
(b) on conviction on indictment, to a fine.

(3) In determining the amount of any fine to be imposed on a person convicted of an offence under subsection (1), the court shall in particular have regard to any financial benefit which has accrued or appears likely to accrue to him in consequence of the offence.

(4) If any person contravenes the provisions of a tree preservation order otherwise than as mentioned in subsection (1), he shall be guilty of an offence and liable on summary conviction to a fine not exceeding level 4 on the standard scale.

DEFINITIONS
"tree preservation order": s.160(2).

GENERAL NOTE

Aside from the specific responsibilities of landowners and lessees described above, a criminal sanction applies to any person who wilfully carries out any of the acts mentioned in subs. (1), or otherwise contravenes the provisions of a TPO (subs. (4)).

In accordance with the Carnwath Report, the maximum level of fine (unlimited on indictment, £20,000 on summary complaint) for breach of subs. (1) has been set at a level intended to deter the commission of the offence. A somewhat lesser fine (Level 4 – £2,500) can be imposed for subs. (4) offences, which relate to less significant breaches of the provisions of a TPO.

The legislation has long recognised that breach of planning control and financial gain will be interlinked in some cases, hence the provisions of subs. (3), relating to the financial benefit accruing from commission of the offence. Prior to the Planning and Compensation Act 1991 (c.34), the "any financial benefit" test was applied only to conviction on indictment. With the increased maximum fine available for conviction under summary procedure, the test is now applied to all convictions for breach of subs. (1).

Nevertheless, substantial fines can be justified in order to prevent trees being felled with impunity. Difficulties in meeting the fine to be imposed are generally to be disregarded in passing sentence. (*White v. Hamilton*, 1987 S.C.C.R. 12.)

Trees in conservation areas

Preservation of trees in conservation areas

172.—(1) Subject to the provisions of this section and section 173, any person who, in relation to a tree to which this section applies, does any act which might by virtue of section 160(3)(a) be prohibited by a tree preservation order shall be guilty of an offence.

(2) Subject to section 173, this section applies to any tree in a conservation area in respect of which no tree preservation order is for the time being in force.

(3) It shall be a defence for a person charged with an offence under subsection (1) to prove—

   (a) that he served notice of his intention to do the act in question (with sufficient particulars to identify the tree) on the planning authority in whose area the tree is or was situated, and

   (b) that he did the act in question—

        (i) with the consent of the planning authority in whose area the tree is or was situated, or

        (ii) after the expiry of the period of 6 weeks from the date of the notice but before the expiry of the period of 2 years from that date.

(4) Section 171 shall apply to an offence under this section as it applies to a contravention of a tree preservation order.

DEFINITIONS
   "conservation area": s.277(1).
   "planning authority": ss.1, 277(1).
   "tree preservation order": s.160(2).

GENERAL NOTE
   Designation of a conservation area by a planning authority acts as a deemed TPO for the whole of that area, unless a TPO is already in force over part of the conservation area (subs. (2)). Accordingly, separate provision requires to be made for permitting acts otherwise requiring consent of the planning authority to be carried out, which would be of no import elsewhere unless a TPO was in effect.

   However, the initial premise of this section is that any act of cutting down, lopping, etc. of trees in a conservation area, without the consent of the planning authority constitutes an offence (subs. (1)). Where matters differ slightly from the normal TPO regime is that it is possible for the person intending to carry out the operations to furnish the planning authority with adequate notice of the operations intended to be carried out (see subs. (3)(a)).

   Provided that such work is carried out not less than six weeks after and within two years subsequent to such notification, a defence to any criminal prosecution exists (subs. (3)(b)(ii)). Similarly, a defence of consent on the part of the planning authority to the operations can be pled (subs. (3)(b)(i)), although since the planning authority is likely to be the party reporting an alleged offence to the Procurator Fiscal, this provision seems a little circular.

   Interestingly, a provision similar to s.160(6) is not made directly here for use in cases of emergency or nuisance. (See however s.173(4)). The same sanctions are applied on conviction of an offence under subs. (1) as for s.171 (subs. (4)).

Power to disapply section 172

173.—(1) The Secretary of State may by regulations direct that section 172 shall not apply in such cases as may be specified in the regulations.

(2) Without prejudice to the generality of subsection (1), the regulations may be framed so as to exempt from the application of that section cases defined by reference to all or any of the following matters—

   (a) acts of such descriptions or done in such circumstances or subject to such conditions as may be specified in the regulations;

   (b) trees in such conservation areas as may be so specified;

(c) trees of a size or species so specified; or

(d) trees belonging to persons or bodies of a description so specified.

(3) The regulations may, in relation to any matter by reference to which an exemption is conferred by them, make different provision for different circumstances.

(4) Regulations under subsection (1) may in particular, but without prejudice to the generality of that subsection, exempt from the application of section 172 cases exempted from section 160 by subsection (6) of that section.

DEFINITIONS
"conservation areas": s.277(1).

GENERAL NOTE
This provision gives the Secretary of State power to make Regulations lessening the effect of s.172 in all or some conservation areas, and to impose less strict regimes for certain acts, or trees or landowners. The provisions of s.160(6) (situations of emergency or nuisance) can also be given effect. The principal Regulations made under the predecessor legislation (s.59A of the1972 Act) are the Town and Country Planning (Tree Preservation and Trees in Conservation Areas) (Scotland) Regulations 1975 (S.I. 1975 No.1204), as amended by S.I. 1981 No.1385, S.I. 1984 No.329 (see above).

Essentially, these Regulations permit "uprooting, felling and lopping" of trees where urgently necessary in the interests of safety or for prevention of a nuisance. (1975 Regulations, Sched. 2, para. 3). It is necessary to give notice to the planning authority that such operations are taking place, once the need has arisen.

The cutting down of trees in connection with certain forestry operations, or where required by statute, and also acts by certain statutory undertakers enjoy deemed consent under the Regulations (*ibid.*, Sched. 2). Other works, including removal of trees of a diameter of less than 100 mm in order to promote the growth of other trees, also enjoy deemed consent (*ibid.*, Reg. 11).

Enforcement of controls as respects trees in conservation areas

174.—(1) If any tree to which section 172 applies—

(a) is removed, uprooted or destroyed in contravention of that section, or

(b) is removed, uprooted or destroyed or dies at a time when its cutting down or uprooting is authorised only by virtue of the provisions of such regulations under subsection (1) of section 173 as are mentioned in subsection (4) of that section,

it shall be the duty of the owner of the land to plant another tree of an appropriate size and species at the same place as soon as he reasonably can.

(2) The duty imposed by subsection (1) does not apply to an owner if on application by him the planning authority dispense with it.

(3) The duty imposed by subsection (1) on the owner of any land attaches to the person who is from time to time the owner of the land and may be enforced as provided by section 168 and not otherwise.

DEFINITIONS
"land": s.277(1).
"owner": s.277(1).
"planning authority": ss.1, 277(1).

GENERAL NOTE
This section imports the obligation of replacement of felled trees specified in s.167 where a TPO is in force, into the regime applicable to conservation areas (subs. (1)). The same provision for the planning authority to waive the obligation is made as for land subject to a TPO (subs. (2)).

Finally, the enforcement and appeal procedure contained in ss.168–170 is applied to the replacement obligation relative to conservation areas (subs. (3)).

Register of section 172 notices

175. It shall be the duty of a planning authority to compile and keep available for public inspection free of charge at all reasonable hours and at a convenient place a register containing such particulars as the Secretary of State may determine of notices under section 172 affecting trees in their district.

DEFINITIONS
  "district": s.1(1).
  "planning authority": ss.1, 277(1).

GENERAL NOTE
  The greater public interest presumed to apply to conservation areas has produced an obligation on planning authorities to record the occasions when notice to carry out operations under s.172 has been served on them. In this manner members of the public will be able to satisfy themselves that notice was, at least, given where they have noticed works to trees being carried out. The Register of such notices must be kept available for Public Inspection, free of charge (*cf.* s.181)

Rights of entry

Rights to enter without warrant

176.—(1) Any person duly authorised in writing by a planning authority may enter any land for the purpose of—
  (a) surveying it in connection with making or confirming a tree preservation order with respect to the land,
  (b) ascertaining whether an offence under section 171 or 172 has been committed on the land, or
  (c) determining whether a notice under section 168(1) should be served on the owner of the land,
if there are reasonable grounds for entering for the purpose in question.
  (2) Any person duly authorised in writing by the Secretary of State may enter any land for the purpose of surveying it in connection with making, amending or revoking a tree preservation order with respect to the land if there are reasonable grounds for entering for that purpose.
  (3) Any person who is duly authorised in writing by a planning authority may enter any land in connection with the exercise of any functions conferred on the authority by or under sections 159 to 163 and 167 to 170.
  (4) Any person who is an officer of the Valuation Office may enter any land for the purpose of surveying it, or estimating its value, in connection with a claim for compensation in respect of any land which is payable by the planning authority under section 165.
  (5) Any person who is duly authorised in writing by the Secretary of State may enter any land in connection with the exercise of any functions conferred on the Secretary of State by or under sections 160 to 162, 168(1) to (3), 169 and 170.
  (6) The Secretary of State shall not authorise any person as mentioned in subsection (2) without consulting the planning authority.
  (7) Admission shall not be demanded as of right—
  (a) by virtue of subsection (1) or (2) to any building used as a dwelling-house, or
  (b) by virtue of subsection (3), (4) or (5) to any land which is occupied, unless 24 hours' notice of the intended entry has been given to the occupier.
  (8) Any right to enter by virtue of this section shall be exercised at a reasonable hour.

DEFINITIONS
  "building": s.277(1).
  "land": s.277(1).
  "planning authority": ss.1, 27.
  "tree preservation order": s.160(2).
  "Valuation Office": s.277(1).

GENERAL NOTE

In keeping with the separation of provisions on enforcement procedures, the powers of entry of officials relative to TPOs have been re-enacted as a discrete part of the Act. Thus, any ambiguity or obscurity in construing these powers in their overall context should have been removed.

The powers now re-enacted were introduced by s.54 of the planning and compensation Act 1991, again in response to the Carnwath Report. It seems that the previous powers of entering for the purpose of "surveying" proved troublesome, as had the requirement of the old s.265 of the 1972 Act for the giving of 24 hours notice of entry to land. (See also SDD Circular 9/1992.)

Subss. (1), (2)

Accordingly, any person (not necessarily an officer of the planning authority *cf.* s.177(4)) duly authorised in writing by a planning authority may enter any land (subject to the restrictions imposed by subss. (7) and (8)), for the three purposes specified in subs. (1). These are:
  (a) surveying it in connection with the making or confirming of a TPO with respect to the land.
  (b) ascertaining whether an offence under ss.171 or 172 has been committed on the land.
  (c) determining whether a s.168 notice should be served with respect to the land.

The Secretary of State also enjoys similar power, but limited to the purpose of surveying relative to the making, amending and revoking of TPOs (subs. (2)), in reflection of his own powers under s.164.

As has been stated elsewhere, it may be a nice question for the courts to decide what the test is for a person who has been "duly authorised" under these subsections. The choice seems to lie between a general authorisation intended to be good on all occasions when the power is exercised, as against specific authorisation being required on each and every occasion entry is sought under this section.

In the case of officers of the planning authority or Secretary of State, this problem may be addressed by a properly worded delegation from the authority itself. However, it would seem unsafe to assume that a person external to the authority (for example, a Consultant Arboriculturalist) could enjoy a general authorisation.

The second difficulty is that all of the powers considered thus far require to be exercised where there are "reasonable grounds" for exercising the right of entry. What do these comprise? Is it a matter for the authorised person or for the authority itself to decide when "reasonable grounds" exist?

Subs. (3)

In relation to the powers relating to the making of TPOs (ss.159–163), and the related enforcement powers (ss.167–170), the planning authority can authorise any person to enter land without the need for "reasonable grounds". The power again has to be exercised subject to the restrictions imposed by subss. (7) and (8).

Subs. (4)

This enables any officer of the Valuation Office to enter land for the purposes of assessing compensation payable in the circumstances described in s.165. Once again the restriction imposed by subs. (7) and (8) are applicable.

Subss. (5), (6)

Aside from the power to carry out a survey granted by subs. (2), the Secretary of State is also permitted to authorise any person to enter land in relation to any powers conferred on the Secretary of State in relation to tree preservation (these are to be found in ss.160–162, s.168(1)–(3), ss.169–170)). For purposes related to any exercise of his powers under s.176(2), the Secretary of State must first consult the planning authority.

It is not clear whether this extends to consulting on the fact of the proposal to authorise entry, the identity of the person having the authorisation, or the existence of "reasonable grounds". Without any obvious reason, the Secretary of State has no obligation to consult with the planning authority when exercising his powers under subs. (5).

Subs. (7)

This provision represents the balance struck between the rights of landowners and occupiers of premises, (which one can surmise will be stringently protected by the courts) with the desire of Carnwath to create a workable enforcement regime.

Thus, 24 hours notice of entry requires to be given by the planning authority or Secretary of State under subss. (1) and (2) only where it is proposed to enter a "dwellinghouse" (a term which is not defined), in exercise of the power of entry. In essence, if entry to gardens, policies, etc. can be freely taken under this definition, the powers of the statutory authorities in relation to TPOs seem to be helpful.

It will rarely be necessary to enter a house in order to determine whether a breach of a TPO has taken place. It seems, therefore, that these powers will generally be invoked in cases of urgency.

By contrast, the subss. (3)–(5) powers may require a judgment to be made as to whether "land" (see s.277(1)) is "occupied", if entry without notice is to be contemplated. In most cases it will be safer to allow 24 hours notice to elapse to permit entry to be taken lawfully.

Both situations require any 24 hour notification to be "given" to the occupier of the house or land, presumably in one of the fashions specified in s.271. This ought to be straightforward in the case of entry to houses (subs. (7)(a)). However, it may be apparent that notice is required to allow entry to land which is manifestly in occupation (subs. (7)(b)), but that will not necessarily reveal the identity of the occupier.

Resort can, of course, be had from s.272 and what information can be gleaned from the Valuation Roll, but if the latter fails to yield an answer, some days may elapse before the s.272 notice is forthcoming. Until the identity of the occupier is discovered however, entry to the land cannot be taken under subss. (3)–(5).

Subs. (9)

This subsection applies in all of the instances where a right of entry is constituted under s.176. There is no guidance given as to what a "reasonable hour" is intended to comprehend. It would seem to have been simple enough for the draftsman to set a "no earlier than . . . no later than" gloss on the provisions, and also to give guidance on the position during weekends and Public Holidays. The absence of such does seem to imply a degree of latitude in timing, provided that the exercise is made in a reasonable fashion, having regard to all the circumstances at the time. Since trees are the subject of the protective regime, there may be a great difference between appearing on a person's land at 5.30 in the evening in December as opposed to July, when the likelihood of damage being carried out overnight is greater. However, the absence of the "in case of urgency" provision attaching to warrants (s.177(3)) in this case suggests that all exercises of powers under s.176 must be made at a "reasonable hour".

Right to enter under warrant

177.—(1) If the sheriff is satisfied—

(a) that there are reasonable grounds for entering any land for any of the purposes mentioned in section 176(1) or (2), and

(b) that—

    (i) admission to the land has been refused, or a refusal is reasonably apprehended, or

    (ii) the case is one of urgency,

he may issue a warrant authorising any person duly authorised in writing by a planning authority or, as the case may be, the Secretary of State to enter the land.

(2) For the purposes of subsection (1)(b)(i) of this section admission to land shall be regarded as having been refused if no reply is received to a request for admission within a reasonable period.

(3) A warrant authorises entry on one occasion only and that entry must be—

(a) within one month from the date of the issue of the warrant, and

(b) at a reasonable hour, unless the case is one of urgency.

DEFINITIONS

"land": s.277(1).
"planning authority": ss.1, 277(1).

GENERAL NOTE

It is again a standard part of statutory enforcement provisions that application for judicial warrant to enter land can be obtained by the statutory authority in order to perform its functions. Here, a Sheriff (presumably in response to a summary application) can grant authority to any person duly authorised by the planning authority or Secretary of State, to enter the land (subs. (1)).

Two points should be noted here; the first is that grounds must be established as existing under s.176(1) and (2) (subs. (1)(a)). Secondly, the warrant must be carefully framed and read so as to ensure that the chain of authority produced does not break down over the question of whether a person is "duly authorised". In these circumstances, issuing of specific authorisation of the person, incorporating reference to the warrant, may be advisable before the warrant is actually enforced.

Furthermore, once the first limb of the subs. (1) test has been satisfied, the Sheriff must be further satisfied:

(a) that admission to the land has been refused, or is reasonably apprehended or,

(b) that the matter is one of urgency (subs. (1)(b)).

There are well-established ways of meeting this requirement in ordinary circumstances, but it was recognised in the 1991 Act that a lacuna could arise if no response one way or another was received to a s.176(7) notice. Accordingly, subs. (2) provides a test whereby a refusal of admission is deemed to have been given where a "reasonable period" has elapsed after the giving of a "request for admission". (Presumably this is intended to include the giving of a s.176(7) notice).

Subs. (3)

A warrant obtained under s.177 does not, as in other cases, permit entry on foot of its terms to be taken freely. Indeed, the subsection offers considerable safeguards to landowners and occupiers.

First, a warrant will obtain entry to the land on only one occasion. As a warrant can only be obtained pursuant to surveying work proposed in terms of s.176(1) and (2), this seems to be a reasonable limit to the authority granted.

It will be a matter for the authority obtaining the warrant to make reasonable arrangements to undertake the survey in one visit. Presumably, where entry is refused by the occupier or landowner, the authority of the warrant is not exhausted.

Secondly, the warrant must be executed within one month of its issue. In many cases, entry may be agreed voluntarily once the warrant has been obtained, but it is important that the expiry date (one month after issue of the warrant) is not forgotten if the survey takes time to organise.

Thirdly, the "reasonable hour" test is qualified where "the case is one of urgency". It would seem to be a matter for the authority to establish reasons pointing to the necessity for taking entry outwith reasonable hours, to a level somewhat higher than mere convenience. Nevertheless, the scope for irreparable damage to be sustained by existing trees if protective measures are not taken is considerable, and will require use of this wider power on occasions.

Rights of entry: supplementary provisions

178.—(1) Any power conferred under or by virtue of section 176 or 177 to enter land (referred to in this section as "a right of entry") shall be construed as including power to take samples from any tree and samples of the soil.

(2) A person authorised to enter land in the exercise of a right of entry—

(a) shall, if so required, produce evidence of his authority and state the purpose of his entry before so entering,

(b) may take with him such other persons as may be necessary, and

(c) on leaving the land shall, if the owner or occupier is not then present, leave it as effectively secured against trespassers as he found it.

(3) Any person who wilfully obstructs a person acting in the exercise of a right of entry shall be guilty of an offence and liable on summary conviction to a fine not exceeding level 3 on the standard scale.

(4) If any damage is caused to land or moveable property in the exercise of a right of entry, compensation may be recovered by any person suffering the damage from the authority who gave the written authority for the entry or, as the case may be, the Secretary of State.

DEFINITIONS

"land": s.277(1).

"right of entry": s.178(1).

GENERAL NOTE

All of the powers comprised in this section were introduced by the 1991 Act as adjuncts to the enhanced enforcement procedures sought by Carnwath.

Subsection (1) allows the taking of samples from any tree or soil as an incident to a right of entry being exercised under ss.176 and 177. This will allow establishment of whether a tree is diseased or is being affected by substances in the soil.

Subsection (2) clarifies the rights and obligations of any persons exercising a "right of entry". It seems that provided that one person exercising the right is "duly authorised" (and shows that authority if required), it is unnecessary for others accompanying him to be separately authorised (subs. (2)(a) and (b)).

The obligation to secure land on departure (subs. (2)(c)) is sensible from a common-sense standpoint, particularly if areas with livestock are being surveyed. Nevertheless, scope for dispute and resort to the compensation provisions (subs. (4)) will inherently exist if entry is taken in the absence of the landowner or occupier, and damage to property is later alleged to have occurred.

The offence created by subs. (3) is an obvious corollary to other offences relating to the protection and enforcement process. The offence – which carries a lesser maximum fine (level 3—£1,000) than other offences – is one of obstructing a "right of entry", which applies to entry obtained with or without the benefit of a warrant.

Subsection (4) does not make entirely clear how compensation is to be determined, but presumably the principles operative under the Lands Compensation Legislation would be relevant here.

CHAPTER II

LAND ADVERSELY AFFECTING AMENITY OF NEIGHBOURHOOD

Land adversely affecting other land

GENERAL NOTE

The powers established by the next three sections relate to powers to issue what are colloquially referred to as "Waste Land notices". This is perhaps a succinct description of their purpose, notwithstanding the broader test set out in Statute, which is considered below.

There are two significant aspects to waste land notices which can be usefully appreciated; the first is that they do not require any breach of planning control to have occurred before action can be taken. In many instances, it may be the absence of "development" in the sense meant by s.26, which is causing a visual or environmental nuisance.

The second point is that action can be taken for the benefit of land outwith the area of the initiating planning authority for the benefit of land outwith its district. Thus, an abandoned waste tip may be, owing to location and prevailing winds, peripheral to the area of planning Authority A, but a major nuisance to the inhabitants of the area of planning Authority B.

Notice requiring proper maintenance of land

179.—(1) If it appears to a planning authority that the amenity of any part of their district, or an adjoining district, is adversely affected by the condition of any land in their district they may serve on the owner, lessee and occupier of the land a notice under this section requiring such steps for abating the adverse effect as may be specified in the notice to be taken within such period as may be so specified.

(2) Service under subsection (1) shall be effected by the service of a copy of the notice.

(3) Subject to section 180, a notice under this section shall take effect on such date as may be specified in the notice, being a date not less than 28 days after the latest service thereof under subsection (1).

(4) The planning authority may withdraw a notice under this section (without prejudice to their power to serve another) at any time before it takes effect; and if they so withdraw it, they shall forthwith give notice of the withdrawal to every person on whom the notice was served.

(5) No notice may be served under subsection (1) with reference to any building which is—

(a) a building which is the subject of a scheme or order under the enactments for the time being in force with respect to ancient monuments, or

(b) a building for the time being included in a list of monuments published by the Secretary of State under any such enactment.

(6) The provisions of section 135 shall, subject to any necessary modifications, apply in respect of a notice under this section as they apply in respect of an enforcement notice under section 127.

DEFINITIONS
"building": s.277(1).
"district": s.1(1).
"land": s.277(1).
"owner": s.277(1).
"planning authority": ss.1, 277(1).

GENERAL NOTE
Subs. (1)
This subsection sets out a broad test for establishing the grounds on which action can be taken. Clearly, a link must be established between the subjective test of "adverse effect" on "amenity" arising from the "condition" of the land in question (see, for example, *Lawrie v. Edinburgh Corporation*, 1953 S.L.T. (Sh. Ct.) 17 *and Stevenson v. Midlothian District Council*, 1983 S.L.T. 433). There is, therefore some scope for subjectivity in approach. (See para. 23 of Annex D to SDD Circular 6/1984).

The notice will advise the "owner, lessee or occupier" of a specific set of steps to be taken within a specified period which will "abate" the "adverse effect" of the "waste land".

Subs. (2)
The methods of effecting service of notices for the purposes of the Act are set out in s.271.

Subs. (3)
The various requirements made in any s.179 notice cannot be made effective, at the earliest, until 28 days after the latest date of service on an "owner, lessee or occupier". As a result, waste land notices are unlikely to be useful in preventing seriously injurious effects from continuing where these require to be dealt with as a result of the dangerous condition of land or other situations of emergency.

Clearly, the period specified in the notice for taking remedial "steps" (subs. (1)) will require to reflect the delay in the notice taking effect, and cannot specify the act requiring to be taken before the expiry of that period. Appeals against a waste land notice are considered in relation to s.180.

Subs. (4)
It will generally be hoped that resort to a waste land notice will be made only where attempts by the planning authority to engage the co-operation of the person having responsibility for the land have failed. Equally, up to the date of taking effect of the notice (which need not, of course, only be the minimum 28 days), the door to voluntary resolution of the problem is not closed.

Therefore, a waste land notice can be withdrawn by the planning authority at any time up to the time when it takes effect. On the basis that a notice may be withdrawn on the basis of a voluntary agreement to take "steps" which subsequently fails, previous withdrawal of a notice by the planning authority does not bar it from further service of a notice.

Notification of withdrawal of a waste land notice requires to be given to each person served with the original notice.

Subs. (5)
Specific exclusion from the regime relating to waste land notices is made in relation to buildings which fall within the scheme of Ancient Monuments. This exclusion applies from the point at which the building is listed (see s.1 of the Ancient Monuments and Archaeological Areas Act 1979). It seems that the land adjacent to a building excluded under this provision could fall within the ambit of a waste land notice, given the definition of "building" provided by s.277(1).

Subs. (6)
The provisions of s.135, relative to enforcement notices, empowering planning authorities to undertake works (s.135) required to secure compliance with a waste land notice and to recharge

expenses to the "owner or lessee" of the land concerned are applied here. In this regard, the commentary on the effect of the provisions and operation of s.135, are equally applicable in relation to waste land notices.

Appeal against notice under section 179

180.—(1) A person on whom a notice under section 179 is served, or any other person having an interest in the land to which the notice relates, may at any time before the date specified in the notice as the date on which it is to take effect appeal to the Secretary of State against the notice, on any of the following grounds—

(a) that neither the amenity of any part of the planning authority's district nor that of any adjoining district has been adversely affected;

(b) that the steps required by the notice to be taken exceed what is necessary to remedy any such adverse effect;

(c) that the specified period for compliance with the notice falls short of what should reasonably be allowed;

(d) that the condition of the land is attributable to, and such as results in the ordinary course of events from, a continuing lawful use of the land or from continuing lawful operations carried out thereon; or

(e) that the notice was served other than in accordance with section 179.

(2) An appeal under this section shall be made by notice in writing to the Secretary of State.

(3) The provisions of sections 130(3), 131(1) and (2) and 132(3) shall apply to appeals under this section as they apply to appeals under those sections.

(4) On an appeal under this section the Secretary of State—

(a) may correct any informality, defect or technical error in the notice if he is satisfied that it is not material, and

(b) may disregard the failure of the planning authority to serve the notice upon a person upon whom it should have been served, if it appears to him that neither that person nor the appellant has been substantially prejudiced by that failure.

(5) Where an appeal is brought under this section, the notice under section 179 shall be of no effect pending the final determination, or the withdrawal, of the appeal.

(6) In determining an appeal under this section the Secretary of State shall give such directions as seem to him appropriate; and these may include directions for quashing the notice or for varying its terms in favour of the appellant.

(7) Schedule 4 applies to appeals under this section.

DEFINITIONS
"land": s.277(1).
"planning authority": ss.1, 277(1).
"use": s.277(1).

GENERAL NOTE
Only when the Local Government and Planning (Scotland) Act 1982 (c.43) took effect was a provision for appeal against a waste land notice inserted as s.63A of the 1972 Act. Again, the procedure applicable to enforcement notice appeals is applied in part, and previous comments on those sections where mentioned in relation to subs. (3) should be referred to in this context.

Subs. (1)
Appeals must be made to the Secretary of State against a waste land notice prior to the notice taking effect on the date which is specified on the face of it. An application is not made for appeal against an enforcement notice until it is received, where the relevant provisions require the application to be made within a certain time. (*Adam v. Secretary of State for Scotland*, 1988 S.L.T. 300).

There are five grounds of appeal set out, all of which apparently could be used cumulatively. These are:

(a) Neither the amenity of the area of the planning authority nor that of any adjoining district has been "adversely affected".

It seems that both limbs of the test require to be satisfied. In most cases, the "adverse effect" will be confined solely to the area of the planning authority serving the notice. Here, it is with the first limb of the test which the appeal will be concerned.

Where the notice is served on the basis of "adverse effect" on two areas, or the area adjoining that of planning Authority A alone, it seems both limbs of the test would require to be satisfied. In the first instance, an appeal seems to fail unless the absence of "adverse effect" in both areas can be established. In the second instance, the appeal may only concern itself with the position in Area B.

(b) The steps required by the notice to remedy any "adverse effect" exceed what is necessary.

Here there is evident scope for disagreement about whether the notice asks its recipient to go beyond the minimum necessary to "abat[e]" the adverse effect" of the condition of the land. To go beyond this may, of course, accrue a public benefit, but may cause a landowner to incur unnecessary expense.

It is open to the Secretary of State to impose lesser obligations without quashing the notice (subs. (6)).

(c) The period specified for compliance with the notice falls short of what should reasonably be allowed.

Much the same considerations as in (b) require to be balanced in this regard. How quickly is it reasonably necessary for remedial works to be carried out to the land, bearing in mind that at least 28 days must elapse from the last date of service of the notice before it takes effect?

Again, a balance between the history of the site prior to the notice being served, and the expense of carrying out remedial works within a defined timescale (which may necessitate mobilisation of resources at premium rates) requires to be struck. Here also, the Secretary of State can impose a longer timescale without quashing the notice (subs. (6)).

(d) The condition of the land is attributable to the ordinary effects of a continuing lawful use of the land or continuing lawful operations thereon.

The essence of this ground is that the land in question has not been allowed to become waste land or to lie derelict. If this is the case, any "adverse [effect]" on amenity requires to be addressed by the use of the power. It seems to be incumbent, however, on the appellant to establish that a "use" (see s.277(1)) or "operation" was "continuing" at the time of making the appeal. This is a matter of fact for the Secretary of State to determine. It is not clear whether a resumption of activity objectively discontinued at the time of service of the notice, or else discontinued after the appeal was made, is sufficient to found a successful appeal.

(e) Failure to serve a notice in terms of s.179.

Reference has been made above to the service of notice provisions. The Secretary of State has powers, in any event, to excuse a failure in service on the grounds specified in s.180(4)(b). It is probably incompetent to seek to raise a petition for judicial review where the Secretary of State disregards a failure of service. (*Gill v. Clydebank District Council*, 1983 S.C. 76).

Subss. (2), (3)

This requires appeals against waste land notices to be made in writing to the Secretary of State. An application is not made for appeal against an enforcement notice until it is received, where the relevant provisions require the application to be made within a certain time. (*Adam v. Secretary of State for Scotland*, 1988 S.L.T. 300). Section 130(3) as applied here, requires the grounds of appeal to be specified as part of the appeal letter.

The procedure leading up to the determination of an appeal is set out in s.131(1), although no Regulations have yet been made in this respect. Essentially, the procedure requires the position of the planning authority to be set out in their submission in support of the waste land notice, and also to submit the notice itself together with details of the persons served with the notice.

As with appeals against s.168 notices, either party to the appeal can insist upon the appeal being determined by a person appointed by the Secretary of State (s.131(2)). This right applies unless the appeal is rejected, or else the notice is quashed for want of timeous intimation of matters to be requiring provided by one of the parties (s.132(3)). An attempt to obtain a declarator that the Secretary of State had no power to hear or to deal with an appeal against a waste land notice, and for the reduction thereof was described as being "entirely without merit" in *Stevenson v. Midlothian District Council*, 1983 S.L.T. 433.

Subs. (4)

This is a provision designed to ensure that an otherwise valid waste land notice does not fall to be quashed on appeal by virtue of an over-technical approach.

It is not unusual to allow the Secretary of State to waive any shortcoming in the notice itself which is not of a material nature (subs. (4)(a)). The subsection also recognises the possibility that "waste land" may have achieved that condition because a person with a recognised interest in it has not taken a recent interest in it, and cannot easily be traced. Thus, a failure to comply with the requirements of s.179(2) to carry out service on a person who is not the appellant can be waived where the Secretary of State is satisfied that neither the appellant nor the omitted person have suffered "substantial prejudice" from the failure.

It is probably incompetent to seek to raise a petition for judicial review where the Secretary of State disregards a failure of service. (*Gill v. Clydebank District Council*, 1983 S.C. 76).

Subs. (5)

As is normal in relation to the enforcement regime, a waste land notice has its effect suspended, pending the outcome of any appeal taken against its terms.

Subs. (6)

The Secretary of State is given wide powers to determine the outcome of an appeal, including the quashing of the notice. He can also vary the notice so as to impose lesser obligations only on the appellant. This is consistent with the ground of appeal provided by subs. 180(1)(b) and (c).

Subs. (7)

The reference to Sched. 4 amplifies for the purposes of appeals against waste land notices and analogous appeals what the procedure is where the Secretary of State determines that such appeals should be heard by a person appointed by him.

Register of notices under section 179

181.—(1) Every planning authority shall keep a register of notices under section 179 which have been served in relation to land in their district—

(a) in such manner, and

(b) containing such information,

as may be prescribed; and there may also be prescribed circumstances in which an entry in the register shall be deleted.

(2) Every register kept under subsection (1) shall be available for inspection by the public at all reasonable hours.

DEFINITIONS

"district": s.1(1).

"land": s.277(1).

"planning authority": ss.1, 277(1).

GENERAL NOTE

As is the case for similar notices, planning authorities are required to maintain a Register of Waste Land notices for public inspection. Withdrawals of notices, and appeals leading to the quashing of a notice will require removal of these notices from the Register.

Notwithstanding the absence of the words "free of charge" in this section (*cf.* s.175), it appears to be incompetent to seek to make a charge for inspection of the Register kept under this section. (*Stirrat Park Hogg v. Dumbarton District Council*, 1996 S.L.T. 1113).

CHAPTER III

ADVERTISEMENTS

Advertisement regulations

GENERAL NOTE

Some form of regulation over the erection and siting of advertisement hoardings, or the use of land for this purpose has existed since 1948. The provisions of the 1972 Act have been adopted unamended into the current legislation.

Regulations controlling display of advertisements

182.—(1) Regulations shall make provision for restricting or regulating the display of advertisements so far as appears to the Secretary of State to be expedient in the interests of amenity or public safety.

(2) Without prejudice to the generality of subsection (1), any such regulations may provide—

(a) for regulating the dimensions, appearance and position of advertisements which may be displayed, the sites on which advertisements may be displayed and the manner in which they are to be affixed to the land;

(b) for requiring the consent of the planning authority to be obtained for the display of advertisements, or of advertisements of any class specified in the regulations;

(c) for applying, in relation to any such consent and to applications for such consent, any of the provisions mentioned in subsection (3), subject to such adaptations and modifications as may be specified in the regulations;

(d) for the constitution, for the purposes of the regulations, of such advisory committees as may be prescribed by the regulations, and for determining the manner in which the expenses of any such committee are to be defrayed.

(3) The provisions referred to in subsection (2)(c) are—

(a) the provisions of Part III relating to planning permission and to applications for planning permission, except sections 32, 34, 35, 36(2) and (3), 38, 58 to 62, 69 and 70 and Schedules 6 and 7, and section 65 of the Planning (Listed Buildings and Conservation Areas) (Scotland) Act 1997,

(b) sections 88 to 92, 94 and 95 (except so far as they relate to purchase notices served in consequence of such orders as are mentioned in section 88(1)(b) or (c)), and

(c) section 263.

DEFINITIONS
"advertisement": s.277(1).
"land": s.277(1).
"planning permission": Pt. III, s.277(1).
"purchase notice": s.88.

GENERAL NOTE
The broad regulatory power of the Secretary of State is set out in subs. (1). Powers in respect of specific matters (considered below) are contained in subs. (2).

Four specific areas are identified for possible control in subs. (2), which are:

(a) Dimensions, appearance and position of advertisements, and sites for display and manner of fixing to land. (see Sched. 1 of the Town and Country Planning (Control of Advertisements) (Scotland) Regulations 1984 (S.I. 1984 No.467), as amended)).

(b) Consent of planning authority required for display of advertisements generally or in a conservation area (Regs. 5, 11 and Sched. 4 of the 1984 Regulations.

(c) Application of any provisions contained in Pt. III of the Act to the regime for advertisements (see also subs. (3)(a)).

(d) Constitution of Advisory Committees.

(Neither of the heads (c) or (d) have been utilised in the 1984 Regulations, with the exception of incorporating the provisions of Sched. 4, in relation to determination of appeals by persons appointed by the Secretary of State).

Regulations. The Regulations made in this regard are the Town and Country Planning (Control of Advertisements) (Scotland) Regulations 1984 (S.I. 1984 No.467). These were amended by the Town and Country Planning (Control of Advertisements) (Scotland) Amendment Regulations 1992 (S.I. 1992 No.1763),which widened slightly the definition of "advertisement". (See also "*Planning*", Neil Collar (W. Green and Sons) pp. 339–351 for a fuller exposition).

"*advertisement*": The Town and Country Planning (Control of Advertisements) (Scotland) Regulations 1984, as amended, define this term in the same terms as s.277(1).

Power to make different advertisement regulations for different areas

183.—(1) Regulations made under section 182 may make different provision with respect to different areas, and in particular may make special provision—

(a) with respect to conservation areas, and

(b) with respect to areas defined for the purposes of the regulations as areas of special control.

(2) An area may be defined as an area of special control if it is—

(a) a rural area, or

(b) an area which appears to the Secretary of State to require special protection on grounds of amenity.

(3) Without prejudice to the generality of subsection (1), the regulations may prohibit the display in an area of special control of all advertisements except advertisements of such classes (if any) as may be prescribed.

(4) Areas of special control for the purposes of the regulations may be defined by means of orders made or approved by the Secretary of State in accordance with the provisions of the regulations.

(5) Where the Secretary of State is authorised by the regulations to make or approve any such order as is mentioned in subsection (4), the regulations shall provide—

(a) for the publication of notice of the proposed order in such manner as may be prescribed,

(b) for the consideration of objections duly made to it, and

(c) for the holding of such inquiries or other hearings as may be prescribed,

before the order is made or approved.

(6) Nothing in this section or in any such regulations shall be construed as authorising the restricting or regulation of the display of any advertisement by reason only of the subject matter or wording of it.

DEFINITIONS
"advertisement": s.277(1).

GENERAL NOTE
The primary purpose of this section is to furnish the Secretary of State with the power to make Regulations over the location of advertisement hoardings in areas of special sensitivity such as conservation areas or areas of high amenity. The section also enables the Secretary of State to make Regulations regarding the process by which such areas are designated. It should be noted that it is the erection of the hoardings and not what advertisements appear on the hoardings which is subject to control. (subs. (6)).

This issue has been addressed in the 1984 Regulations, and in terms of Regs. 8 and 9 and Sched. 2 thereto, it is a matter for planning authorities to decide whether part of their district should be designated as an "area of special control". If so, a process of public notification followed by resolution (or otherwise) of objections, and eventual confirmation of designation as an area of special control by order of the Secretary of State is carried through in the manner specified in the Regulations.

Once such an order is in force, only advertisement hoardings enjoying deemed consent in terms of Sched. 4 (see below) and other prescribed advertisements (see Reg. 9) can lawfully continue on a permanent basis. No specific direction to planning authorities in exercising their powers of designation is given beyond that of acting in the "interests of amenity" [Reg. 8(4) of the 1984 Regulations].

"*conservation area*": See s.61 of the Planning (Listed Buildings and Conservation Areas) (Scotland) Act 1997 (c.9).

Planning permission not needed for advertisements complying with regulations

184. Where the display of advertisements in accordance with regulations made under section 182 involves development of land—

(a) planning permission for that development shall be deemed to be granted by virtue of this section, and

(b) no application shall be necessary for that development under Part III.

DEFINITIONS
"advertisement": s.277(1).
"land": s.277(1).
"planning permission": Pt. III.

GENERAL NOTE
    As indicated above, provision has been made in the 1984 Regulations for certain specified advertisements to enjoy a deemed planning consent. This arises in amplification of the provisions of this section, which makes clear that advertisements covered by the 1984 Regulations require no further planning permission to be obtained in terms of Pt. III (subs. (b)). However, the erection of canopies which themselves contain advertising material does not convert the canopies into advertisements that can benefit from the deemed planning consent *(Glasgow District Council, City of v. Secretary of State for Scotland*, 1989 S.L.T. 256).
    An advertisement can be displayed in accordance with such deemed consent without application to the planning authority (subs. (b)). It should be noted that such a consent enures to the benefit of the site and all persons having an interest in it, unless revoked in terms of the Regulations [Reg. 5(2) of the 1984 Regulations].
    Advertisements not so covered, require to go through a process of obtaining an "express consent", which is akin to seeking planning consent, from the planning authority (Pt. V of the 1984 Regulations). Such "express consents" are limited to five years' duration at a time, except where the planning authority otherwise direct [Reg.18(1) of the 1984 Regulations].

Repayment of expense of removing prohibited advertisements

Repayment of expense of removing prohibited advertisements

185.—(1) Where, for the purpose of complying with any regulations made under section 182, works are carried out by any person—

(a) for removing an advertisement which was being displayed on 16th August 1948, or

(b) for discontinuing the use for the display of advertisements of a site used for that purpose on that date,

that person shall, on a claim made to the planning authority within such time and in such manner as may be prescribed, be entitled to recover from that authority compensation in respect of any expenses reasonably incurred by him in carrying out those works.

(2) Except in so far as may be otherwise provided by any regulations made under this Act, any question of disputed compensation under this section shall be referred to and determined by the Lands Tribunal.

(3) In relation to the determination of any such question, the provisions of sections 9 and 11 of the Land Compensation (Scotland) Act 1963 shall apply subject to any necessary modifications and to the provisions of any regulations made under this Act.

DEFINITIONS
    "advertisement": s.277(1).
    "Lands Tribunal": s.277(1).
    "planning authority": s.277(1).

GENERAL NOTE
    This section deals with the (presumably rare) situation of advertisement hoardings *in situ* on the taking effect of controls on the location of advertisements on August 16, 1948. Such advertisements (subject to not undergoing any substantial enlargement) are also held to enjoy a deemed consent for use. [Reg. 13(1) of the 1984 Regulations]
    Such use can only be prevented by service by the planning authority of a "discontinuance notice" on the operator of the advertisement, and the "owner, lessee or occupier" of the land affected. This power must be exercised in order to prevent "substantial injury to amenity . . . or danger" [Reg. 14(1)].
    The section deals with the obligation of the planning authority to pay compensation to any person carrying out works in compliance with the "discontinuance notice" (subs. (2)). Compensation will, in the event of dispute, be determined by the Lands Tribunal in a similar fashion to that provided under s.165 (subs. (3)).
    Whilst it is true to regard such situations as rare in the modern age, the recent decision of the Second Division in *Parker v. Secretary of State for Scotland* (1997) G.W.D. 14–628, where a deemed consent under the 1984 Regulations was held not to have been superseded by virtue of

an Application for Express Consent (see above), show that the exercise of s.185 rights is not impossible.

Enforcement of control over advertisements

Enforcement of control as to advertisements

186.—(1) Regulations under section 182 may make provision for enabling the planning authority to require—
  (a) the removal of any advertisement which is displayed in contravention of the regulations, or
  (b) the discontinuance of the use for the display of advertisements of any site which is being so used in contravention of the regulations.

(2) For that purpose the regulations may apply any of the provisions of Part VI with respect to enforcement notices or the provisions of section 143 (1) to (5), subject to such adaptations and modifications as may be specified in the regulations.

(3) Without prejudice to any provisions included in such regulations by virtue of subsection (1) or (2), if any person displays an advertisement in contravention of the regulations he shall be guilty of an offence and liable on summary conviction to a fine of such amount as may be prescribed, not exceeding level 3 on the standard scale and, in the case of a continuing offence, one-tenth of level 3 on the standard scale for each day during which the offence continues after conviction.

(4) Without prejudice to the generality of subsection (3), a person shall be deemed to display an advertisement for the purposes of that subsection if—
  (a) he is the owner or occupier of the land on which the advertisement is displayed, or
  (b) the advertisement gives publicity to his goods, trade, business or other concerns.

(5) A person shall not be guilty of an offence under subsection (3) by reason only—
  (a) of his being the owner or occupier of the land on which an advertisement is displayed, or
  (b) of his goods, trade, business or other concerns being given publicity by the advertisement,
if he proves that it was displayed without his knowledge or consent.

DEFINITIONS
  "advertisement": s.277(1).
  "enforcement notice": ss.127, 277(1).
  "planning authority": s.1(1).

GENERAL NOTE
  Since the provisions relating to advertisements stand as a form of special control, some particular means of enforcing the planning regime requires to be established. This is achieved by grafting parts of the enforcement notice procedure onto the specific provisions relating to control of advertisements via the 1984 Regulations (subs. (2)).
  Thus, the planning authority is entitled to treat the display of an advertisement not enjoying a deemed or express consent, or else in breach of a condition thereof, as constituting a breach of planning control, and may serve an enforcement notice [Reg. 24(1) of the 1984 Regulations]. Such a notice may specify steps (including the demolition of any "buildings or works" or the discontinuance of the use of any land) necessary to remedy the breach, but may also specify the steps required to bring the advertisement to an acceptable standard. [Reg. 24(3) of the 1984 Regulations. See also s.186(1)].
  The regime for carrying out enforcement notices generally is applied to advertisements by virtue of subs. (2), subject to exceptions in relation to appeals and carrying out of works by the planning authority set out in Regs. 25 and 26 of the 1984 Regulations.
  A criminal offence of displaying an advertisement in contravention of the Regulations (*i.e.* after the taking effect of a discontinuance or enforcement notice) is created against the owner or occupier of the land concerned, or else, the person whose business benefits from the continued

display of the advertisement [subss. (3) and (4)]

A defence of the offence having been committed without the knowledge or consent of the person charged with the offence is also established (sub. (5)). (Given that much advertising is carried out via agencies, it may be wondered whether there is scope for them to be prosecuted under the section, given that they may be the persons with most to gain from a breach). The maximum fine which can be imposed on summary conviction is [£1,000] (Level 3), but the fine can be increased by up to £1,000 for each day on which the offence continues to be committed. [subs. (3)]

Power to remove or obliterate placards and posters

187.—(1) Subject to the provisions of this section, a planning authority may remove or obliterate any placard or poster—

(a) which is displayed in their area, and

(b) which in their opinion is so displayed in contravention of regulations made under section 182.

(2) Subsection (1) does not authorise the removal or obliteration of a placard or poster displayed within a building to which there is no public right of access.

(3) Subject to subsection (4), where a placard or poster identifies the person who displayed it or caused it to be displayed, the planning authority shall not exercise any power conferred by subsection (1) unless they have first given him notice in writing—

(a) that in their opinion it is displayed in contravention of regulations made under section 182, and

(b) that they intend to remove or obliterate it on the expiry of a period specified in the notice.

(4) Subsection (3) does not apply if—

(a) the placard or poster does not give his address, and

(b) the authority do not know it and are unable to ascertain it after reasonable inquiry.

(5) The period specified in a notice under subsection (3) must be not less than 2 days from the date of service of the notice.

(6) Any person duly authorised in writing by the planning authority may at any reasonable time enter any land for the purpose of exercising a power conferred by this section if—

(a) the land is unoccupied, and

(b) it would be impossible to exercise the power without entering the land.

DEFINITIONS

"land": s.277(1).

"planning authority": s.1(1).

GENERAL NOTE

These provisions were added to the 1972 Act by s.56 of the Planning and Compensation Act 1991 (c.34), and are intended to address the problems posed by fly-posting. Conventional methods of enforcing planning control of advertisements (see comments on s.186) are clearly inadequate where posters can simply be put up in a matter of seconds (often on the front of vacant buildings) and rarely disclose their author.

Accordingly, following the publication of the Scottish Development Department (SDD) Consultation Paper *Efficient Planning*, (1989) new measures were put in place. These allow planning authorities the power to remove "posters or placards" (an undefined term), or else require the author to effect removal, where these breach the 1984 Regulations.

In subs. (1), a power is given expressly to permit removal by the planning authority in such circumstances. However, whilst exercise of this power may aid civic amenity, it may also result in considerable cost to the authority.

Thus, where the author (the person who displayed or caused to be displayed (subs. (3)) of the placard or poster can be identified via their terms, the planning authority must first notify that person of the breach of the 1984 Regulations, and intimate their intention to remove the offending items, before they can do it themselves [subs. (3)]. The power cannot be exercised until at least two days have elapsed from service of the notice. [subs. (5)]

In many cases, the poster will have been posted anonymously, or else put up at a time when it is impossible to trace the person responsible. In such a case, the planning authority do not require to go through the notification procedure [subs. (4)]. Removal or obliteration work can be carried out by any "person authorised" by the planning authority on any land, subject to the requirements of subs. (6) that:

(i) the land is then unoccupied,
(ii) entry is taken at a "reasonable time" (see note to s.176 above),
(iii) it is impossible to exercise the power without entering the land.

It should be noted that the power conferred under this section cannot be exercised in respect of placards or posters displayed from the inside of a building to which there is no public access. The reasoning presumably is that the owner or occupier of the building has either consented to the posting, or else has failed in his responsibility with regard to the security of the building. Attention should, however, be paid to the extent of the definition of "building" given in s.277, which does not prevent exercise of the power within the surrounding land or open areas. (See also SDD Circular 16/1992.)

PART VIII

ACQUISITION AND APPROPRIATION OF LAND FOR PLANNING PURPOSES ETC.

Acquisition for planning and public purposes

GENERAL NOTE

The importance of giving a remit to a planning authority to facilitate "development" by that authority being vest with sweeping powers of compulsory acquisition has been a recognised part of Town and Country Planning Legislation for many years. It attained something like its current significance as part of the 1947 Act, although similar powers could be found in the predecessor legislation. Of course, the power to progress major developments by means of compulsory acquisition had existed from the time of the early Acts authorising the construction of canals and railways, and became well-known following the passing of the (sometimes controversial to Scottish Lawyers) Lands Clauses Consolidation (Scotland) Act 1845 (c.19) and Railways Clauses Consolidation (Scotland) Act 1845 (c.33), which are still partly incorporated by reference into the current legislation.

The extent of powers provided by the 1947 Act were intentionally made as wide as possible – such was the extent of the task of repairing the very major damage suffered during World War II in many towns and cities. The powers were used in conjunction with many of the town centre re-developments of the 1960s and 1970s. Not all of these have proved to be popular, and the reduction of resources available for large-scale property acquisitions has diminished use of the powers for this purpose, in favour of acquisitions of a strategic nature for the furthering of economic development. (see below).

Nevertheless, no major inroads on the overall extent of powers available to planning authorities (*cf.* s.188(3)) under the 1947 or 1972 Acts have been made, even though innovations such as the Community Land Act 1975 (c.77) have not survived the test of time. It is submitted this has been the case because of the overall public interest, *inter alia*, in preventing one or a handful of landowners from frustrating a development which enjoys a planning consent, in circumstances where a private developer could not proceed.

The powers also allow the taking of title to areas where the ownership is doubtful or unknown, thereby offering up a single and "clean" title to pass from the planning authority to the ultimate developer of a site. Progress is further aided by the availability of the General Vesting Declaration (GVD) Procedure (see below).

On the other hand, it might be argued that almost all of the cards in furthering a development sit with the planning authority. They ultimately (unless acting contrary to an approved development plan) are the body which determine what receives a planning consent, and decide to exercise compulsory powers in furtherance of a consent.

Whilst any aggrieved landowner or tenant can take matters arising from a compulsory purchase order to a public local inquiry, it will not normally be open for the objector to question the merits of the grant of planning consent, but merely the need for compulsory acquisition powers to be exercised in respect of the property in question. This is not always a distinction understood by objectors.

Further, it has long been established that:

"The onus lies squarely on the local authority to show by clear and unambiguous evidence that the order should be granted" (*Per* Sachs J. in *Coleen Properties v. Minister of Housing and Local Government* [1971] 1 W.L.R. 433 at pp.439–440) but the difficulties facing a lay person in opposing a proposed compulsory purchase should not be underestimated. That lay objectors sometimes succeed is testimony to their determination in pursuing their interests.

Matters are not assisted by the frequently lengthy statutory notices served on objectors by virtue of the relevant Regulations. These are very often couched in the highly technical and precise language of post-war bureaucracy (see for example, the part of Sched. 15, which requires to accompany notices sent to "owners, occupiers and lessees" relating to GVDs). As a result, the rights of objectors are often difficult to ascertain and explain, even for professionals, and arguably are incomprehensible to those who do not have access to skilled advice. Thus far, this area does not appear to have been the subject of pressure to adopt "Plain English".

One clear benefit of the re-organisation of Local Government in 1996 was the removal of scope for dispute between District and Strategic planning authorities over who was entitled to exercise compulsory powers with respect to certain areas. This was particularly highlighted where structure and local plans did not agree as to the designation of a site. In this respect, exercise of compulsory acquisition powers has become more straightforward.

Acquisition of land by agreement

188.—(1) A planning authority may acquire by agreement any land which they require for any purpose for which a planning authority may be authorised to acquire land under section 189.

(2) The Lands Clauses Acts (except the provisions relating to the purchase of land otherwise than by agreement and the provisions relating to access to the special Act, and except sections 120 to 125 of the Lands Clauses Consolidation (Scotland) Act 1845) and sections 6 and 70 of the Railways Clauses Consolidation (Scotland) Act 1845, and sections 71 to 78 of that Act, as originally enacted and not as amended for certain purposes by section 15 of the Mines (Working Facilities and Support) Act 1923, shall be incorporated with this section, and in construing those Acts as so incorporated this section shall be deemed to be the special Act and references to the promoters of the undertaking or to the company shall be construed as references to the authority authorised to acquire the land under this section.

(3) The exercise by a planning authority of any power which they have under this section is subject to the provisions of sections 171A and 171B (promotion of economic development) of the Local Government (Scotland) Act 1973.

DEFINITIONS
  "land": s.277(1).
  "planning authority": s.1(1).

GENERAL NOTE
  This section empowers planning authorities to acquire voluntarily any land which they would be entitled to acquire under the compulsory powers in this Part (see s.189). Despite the incorporation of parts of the Lands Clauses Acts to this provision, it seems clear that a planning authority could equally take a disposition in common form under colour of its s.188 power (see *Compulsory Purchase in Scotland* (1983) Law Society of Scotland, para. 6.9).

  In practice, title is often taken by means of a statutory or schedule conveyance in reflection of the perceived benefits of this method as regards removing existing feuing conditions or real burdens over the land being acquired. On one view at least, the previous relationship of superior and vassal is extinguished by virtue on title being taken by conveyance, leaving the subjects free of any feudal controls.

  Opinion is not unanimous over the effect of such conveyances in the event of a further disposal onwards by the planning authority (see *Stair Memorial Encyclopedia Vol. 5, para. 87*). The effects of a departure from the style set out in Sched. A to the 1845 Act – particularly where a feudal relationship can be inferred – in making such a voluntary acquisition are also a matter of academic debate. (*ibid.* para. 84. See also the articles referred to in "*Compulsory Purchase and Compensation*", Jeremy Rowan-Robinson (W. Green) at pp. 70–1).

  Part of the uncertainty stems from an absence of clear judicial authority on this matter. A number of possible interpretations of s.80 of the Lands Clauses (Consolidation) (Scotland) Act 1845 given previously are canvassed by L.P. Clyde in *Duke of Argyll v. LMSR Co.*, 1931 S.C. 309, pp. 319–320, without the effect being determined conclusively. Part of the problem seems to stem from the apparent retention of feudal rights countenanced in s.126 of the 1845 Act. (Rowan-Robinson, *Op. Cit.*, p. 70).

  A full discussion of the extent whereby departure can be undertaken from the style prescribed in Sched. A of the 1845 Act is to be found in para. 84 of Vol. 5 of the *Stair Memorial Encyclo-*

pedia. It will be evident, however, that planning authorities may tend to shy away from voluntary acquisition by schedule conveyance where the circumstances of a proposed acquisition may denote the need to include terms in the schedule conveyance which are of questionable validity.

It should be noted that reference to the Lands Clauses Acts in this subsection also permits planning authorities to take title by means of notarial instrument (ss.74–76 of the 1845 Act). This is a procedure available to an authority which has deposited compensation in a bank to the account of a seller in circumstances where the seller is unwilling or unable to furnish a good title, or (more commonly) cannot be traced (s.76, 1845 Act).

Once expeded under the hand of a notary public and stamped, the notarial instrument has the effect of vesting the seller's estate and interest in the acquiring authority (*ibid.*). Recording has the same effect as for schedule conveyances (s.80 of the 1845 Act). It would appear that the same considerations regarding the effect of a schedule conveyance on the feudal relationship apply here, since the "manner prescribed" is that contained in s.80 of the 1845 Act (ss.74 and 76 of the 1845 Act) (see also Rowan-Robinson, *Op.Cit.*, p. 71).

Subs. (3)

This is a qualification to the exercise of the s.188 power which was introduced on foot of the re-definition of the powers of local authorities in relation to "promoting economic development" made by s.171 of the Local Government etc. (Scotland) Act 1994 (c.34). The power conferred by the 1994 Act is fairly broad in nature (see s.171A of the Local Government (Scotland) Act 1973 (c.65), as amended) but must be read as being subject to any restrictions imposed by the Secretary of State in exercising his powers to make Regulations under s.171B of the 1973 Act. Thus far, no Regulations have been made.

It is not entirely clear the extent to which, if any, the actings of a planning authority proposing to exercise s.188(1) powers will be restricted by this subsection. It may be that within "any purpose" falling within s.189 – where compulsory purchase powers can be exercised – lies an act which advances "development" but not "economic development", but these are not easy to envisage in practice.

Compulsory acquisition of land in connection with development and for other planning purposes

189.—(1) A local authority shall, on being authorised to do so by the Secretary of State, have power to acquire compulsorily any land in their area which—

(a) is suitable for and is required in order to secure the carrying out of development, redevelopment or improvement;

(b) is required for a purpose which it is necessary to achieve in the interests of the proper planning of an area in which the land is situated.

(2) A local authority and the Secretary of State in considering for the purposes of subsection (1)(a) whether land is suitable for development, redevelopment or improvement shall have regard to—

(a) the provisions of the development plan, so far as material,

(b) whether planning permission for any development on the land is in force, and

(c) any other considerations which would be material for the purpose of determining an application for planning permission for development on the land.

(3) Where a local authority exercise their powers under subsection (1) in relation to any land, they shall, on being authorised to do so by the Secretary of State, have power to acquire compulsorily—

(a) any land adjoining that land which is required for the purposes of executing works for facilitating its development or use, or

(b) where the land forms part of a common or open space, any land which is required for the purpose of being given in exchange for the land which is being acquired.

(4) It is immaterial by whom the local authority propose any activity or purpose mentioned in subsection (1) or (3)(a) is to be undertaken or achieved and in particular the local authority need not propose to undertake that activity or achieve that purpose themselves.

(5) The Secretary of State may authorise a local authority to acquire compulsorily under subsection (1) land which is not in their area.

(6) Before giving an authorisation under subsection (5), the Secretary of State shall consult the local authority within whose area the land is situated.

(7) The Acquisition of Land (Authorisation Procedure) (Scotland) Act 1947 shall apply to the compulsory acquisition of land under this section and accordingly shall have effect as if this section had been in force immediately before the commencement of that Act.

(8) The exercise by a local authority of any power which they have under this section, is subject to the provisions of sections 171A and 171B (promotion of economic development) of the Local Government (Scotland) Act 1973.

DEFINITIONS
"common": s.277(1).
"compulsory acquisition": s.277(1).
"development": s.26(1).
"development plan": s.24.
"economic development": s.171A, Local Government (Scotland) Act 1973 (c.65).
"improvement": in relation to roads, s.151(1), Roads (Scotland) Act 1984 (c.54).
"land": s.277(1).
"local authority": s.277(1), s.2, Local Government etc. (Scotland) Act 1994 (c.39).
"open space": s.277(1).
"planning permission": ss.29, 2.77(1), and Pt. III.
"use": s.277(1).

GENERAL NOTE
This section circumscribes the extent and manner in which compulsory purchase powers can be exercised by a "local authority" (an irrelevant distinction from a "planning authority" subsequent to 1996). Essentially, all of the powers available to the Secretary of State by virtue of the Acquisition of Land (Authorisation Procedure) (Scotland) Act 1947 (c.42) are applied to "local authorities" where exercising powers for the purposes specified in s.189(1), subject always to the oversight of the Secretary of State.

Subs. (1)
The subsection gives a wide power to the acquiring authority to acquire compulsorily any land in their area, provided that they are authorised to do so by the Secretary of State.

The definitions of "development, redevelopment and improvement" seem to fall to be read as subject to s.26, and matters excluded from the definition would appear to be unable to found the exercise of compulsory acquisition powers under this section. How land is established as being deemed to be "suitable for . . . development, redevelopment, or improvement" is considered in relation to subs. (2).

The subsection is equally broad in granting powers where the acquisition of land is "necessary in the interests of proper planning" of the area where the land is situated. It will be noted that the power relates to the locality of the land and not to the overall area of the acquiring authority, which may be important where sites of strategic significance are concerned. In *McMonagle v. Secretary of State for Scotland*, 1993 S.L.T. 807, it was held that "necessary" does not mean that there is no possible alternative development to that proposed, but can mean necessary in furtherance of the only proposal acceptable to the planning authority.

Subs. (2)
This sets out criteria to be considered both by the acquiring authority when deciding to exercise compulsory powers, and by the Secretary of State at the point of deciding to confirm their use, as regards the "suitable for . . . development, redevelopment or improvement" test of subs. (1). This provision was added to the 1972 Act by s.92(4) of the Local Government, Planning and Land Act 1980 (c.65).

The subsection does not make clear whether the list is exhaustive nor the weight to be given to each of the factors listed in reaching either decision. However, consideration of exercise or confirmation of compulsory powers must have regard to:
(a) the provisions of the development plan (see s.24) then in force, so far as material.
(b) whether planning permission for any development of the land is extant.
(c) any other "material considerations" which would have been taken into consideration in determining an Application for Planning Permission for development of the land.

This appears to leave either body with considerable scope for discretion in authorising the use of compulsory acquisition powers. (see also notes above to s.37(2)).

Subs. (3)

It will be recognised that the straightforward identification of land "suitable for development" and its subsequent acquisition under compulsory powers will not beget development where, for example, the site is inaccessible by road or cannot be drained properly.

In common with other compulsory acquisition provisions (see, for example, s.27 of the Railways Clauses Act 1845), an acquiring authority can be empowered to acquire adjacent land to allow works to be carried out which will make the primary area of land developable (subs. (3)(a)). Where the acquisition of the primary land involves a "common" (see s.277(1)), the acquiring authority can be authorised to purchase "any land" (not necessarily "adjoining land") intended to be given in exchange for the land acquired.

Subs. (4)

This subsection makes clear that an acquiring authority can exercise powers of compulsory acquisition as a means of assembling or servicing a site for development by another person. This applies even where the acquiring authority have originally intended to carry out development servicing themselves.

Subss. (5), (6)

These subsections recognise the possibility that land outwith the area of the acquiring authority (most likely close to the boundary of the authority's area) may require to be acquired compulsorily to permit a wider development to take place within the authority's area.

Subsection (6) requires the Secretary of State to authorise such an acquisition only after he has consulted with the local authority in whose area the acquisition will take place. The reference in subs. (5) to acquisition under subs. (1) powers may raise a question of whether this power could be exercised purely for the incidental purpose of servicing a site otherwise within the area of the acquiring authority.

Subs. (7)

As mentioned, compulsory acquisitions by "local authorities" under s.189 are deemed to be carried out as if by the Secretary of State acting under the 1947 Act. This means title may be taken by schedule conveyance and notarial instrument as well as GVD.

Subs. (8)

See note to subs. (3). The express tests governing use of the s.189 power appear to make situations in which the provisions of s.171A–B of the 1973 Act will have independent effect less likely. This will not be the case, of course, where the acquisition purports to be made in furtherance of some act of "promotion of economic development" forbidden by the Secretary of State.

Compulsory acquisition of land by Secretary of State for the Environment

190.—(1) The Secretary of State for the Environment may acquire compulsorily—

(a) any land necessary for the public service, and

(b) any land which it is proposed to use not only for the public service but also—

　　(i) to meet the interests of proper planning of the area, or

　　(ii) to secure the best, or most economic development or use of the land,

otherwise than for the public service.

(2) Where the Secretary of State for the Environment has acquired or proposes to acquire any land under subsection (1) ("the primary land") and in his opinion other land ought to be acquired together with the primary land—

(a) in the interests of the proper planning of the area concerned,

(b) for the purpose of ensuring that the primary land can be used, or developed and used, (together with that other land) in what appears to him to be the best or most economic way, or

(c) where the primary land or any land acquired, or which he proposes to acquire, by virtue of paragraph (a) or (b) of this subsection or of section 122(1)(a) or (b) of the Local Government, Planning and Land Act 1980, forms part of a common or open space, for the purpose of being given in exchange for that land,

he may compulsorily acquire that land.

(3) Subject to subsection (4), the power of acquiring land compulsorily under this section shall include power to acquire a servitude or other right over land by the grant of a new right.

(4) Subsection (3) shall not apply to a servitude or other right over any land which would for the purposes of the Acquisition of Land (Authorisation Procedure) (Scotland) Act 1947 form part of a common or open space.

(5) That Act shall apply to any compulsory acquisition by the Secretary of State for the Environment under this section as it applies to a compulsory acquisition by another Minister in a case falling within section 1(1) of that Act.

(6) In this section,"the public service" includes the service in the United Kingdom—

(a) of any international organisation or institution whether or not the United Kingdom or Her Majesty's Government in the United Kingdom is or is to become a member;

(b) of any office or agency established by such an organisation or institution or for its purposes, or established in pursuance of a treaty (whether or not the United Kingdom is or is to become a party to the treaty);

(c) of a foreign Sovereign Power or the Government of such a Power.

(7) For the purpose of subsection (6)(b), "treaty" includes any international agreement, and any protocol or annex to a treaty or international agreement.

DEFINITIONS

"common": s.277(1).
"compulsory acquisition": s.277(1).
"land": s.277(1).
"open space" s.277(1).
"public service": s.190(6).
"treaty": s.190(6).

GENERAL NOTE

This section combines provisions relative to the exercise of functions by the Secretary of State for the Environment in relation to compulsory acquisition found both in the Town and Country Planning (Scotland) Act 1972, and also s.122 of the Local Government, Land and Planning Act 1980. The Secretary of State for the Environment has certain property management and provision duties in relation to governmental buildings generally. His remit also comprises discharge of any obligations in this regard arising from treaties or international agreements entered into by the U.K.

As a result, the Secretary of State for the Environment has broadly similar compulsory acquisition powers to "local authorities" where land ("primary land") is required for the "public service" (including the discharge of treaty obligations) (subss. (1)(a),(6) and (7)). It is also possible for the Secretary of State for the Environment to acquire compulsorily land not required for "public service" (*i.e.* non-"primary land") where that other land will receive a benefit in planning terms from such acquisition, or else in order to replace "common or open land" compulsorily acquired (subss. (1)(b), (2)).

In view of the extent of the definition of "land" in s.277(1), it is necessary to grant the Secretary of State for the Environment the power to acquire a servitude by new grant, since it seems only existing servitudes fall within the definition (subs. (3)) (see also in this regard, Rowan-Robinson, *Op.Cit*, p. 58). This power cannot be exercised over "common or open land" (subs. (4)).

Otherwise, the Secretary of State for the Environment in exercising his powers under this section has the provisions of the 1947 Act applied to acquisitions by him, as they are applied to "local authorities" acting under s.189.

Powers relating to land held for planning purposes

Disposal of land held for planning purposes

191.—(1) Where a planning authority—
(a) has acquired or appropriated any land for planning purposes, and
(b) holds that land for the purposes for which it was so acquired or appropriated,
the authority may dispose of the land to such person, in such manner and subject to such conditions as may appear to them to be expedient for the purposes mentioned in subsection (2).

(2) Those purposes are to secure—
(a) the best use of that or other land and any buildings or works which have been, or are to be, erected, constructed or carried out on it, whether by themselves or by any other person, or
(b) the erection, construction or carrying out on it of any buildings or works appearing to them to be needed for the proper planning of their area.

(3) Subject to the provisions of subsection (7), any land disposed of under this section shall not be disposed of otherwise than at the best price or on the best terms that can reasonably be obtained.

(4) Where representations are made to the Secretary of State—
(a) that a planning authority have refused to dispose of any land under this section to any person or to agree with him as to the manner in which, or the terms or conditions on or subject to which, it is to be disposed of to him, and
(b) that the refusal constitutes unfair discrimination against that person or is otherwise oppressive,
the Secretary of State may cause the representations to be intimated to the authority.

(5) After considering any statement in writing made to him by the authority, the Secretary of State may, if he thinks fit, cause a public local inquiry to be held.

(6) After considering the report of the person appointed to hold the inquiry (if any), the Secretary of State may, if it appears to him that the representations are well founded and that it is expedient as mentioned in subsection (1) that the authority should dispose of the land under this section to that person, require the authority to offer to dispose of it to him, and give directions as to the manner of the disposal and as to all or any of the terms or conditions on or subject to which it is to be offered to him.

(7) In relation to land acquired or appropriated for planning purposes for a reason mentioned in section 189(1)(a) or (3), the powers conferred by this section on a planning authority shall be so exercised as to secure, so far as may be practicable, to persons who—
(a) were living or carrying on business or other activities on any such land,
(b) desire to obtain accommodation on such land, and
(c) are willing to comply with any requirements of the authority as to the development and use of such land,
an opportunity to obtain accommodation on it suitable to their reasonable requirements on terms settled with due regard to the price at which any such land has been acquired from them.

(8) In subsection (7),"development" includes redevelopment.

(9) Where land is disposed of under this section by a planning authority to any person for the erection of a church or other building for religious worship or buildings ancillary thereto, then, unless the parties otherwise agree, such disposal shall be by way of feu.

(10) In relation to any such land as is mentioned in subsection (1), this section shall have effect to the exclusion of the provisions of any enactment,

other than this Act, by virtue of or under which the planning authority are or may be authorised to dispose of land held by them.

DEFINITIONS
   "building": s.277(1).
   "development": ss.26(1), 191(8).
   "disposal": s.277(1) (except in relation to "disposals carried out under s.197(9)).
   "land": s.277(1).
   "planning authority": s.277(1).
   "planning purposes": s.201(1).

GENERAL NOTE
   It is implicit in the terms of ss.188 and 189 that an acquisition made by a "planning authority" or "local authority" under these powers will have been carried out with a view to achieving a planning purpose. The sections are not worded in such a way as to require a definite proposal for development to be in prospect, and there is always the possibility that hoped-for projects do not materialise.
   Equally, it is possible that a development will not emerge on the scale originally envisaged, or else does not require all of the land originally subject to acquisition under the two sections. It may also be the case that the authority has identified a developer for the site. In all of these circumstances, disposal of all or some of the land originally required will be necessary. It is also possible that something which the local authority has acquired compulsorily under other statutory powers may be transferred internally ("appropriated") for a development purpose.
   Against this stands the need to respect the legitimate interests of the landowner who suffered the loss (whether voluntarily or compulsorily) of his land, only to find that the handing over of title was not required for the purpose originally intended. This was, of course, the situation in which the scandal over Crichel Down emerged in the early 1950s, when a requisitioned wartime bombing range was sold by the Ministry of Agriculture without reference to the original landowner. Thus, this section contains a statutory adaptation of the "Crichel Down Rules" to address this specific situation (see also SDD Circular 38/1992).
   The basis for the sale by local authorities of any land held by them is a matter of broad regulation (see s.74, Local Government (Scotland) Act 1973 (c.65)). However, the specific provisions of s.191 operate to the exclusion of the 1973 Act where powers under ss.189 or 190 have been exercised (subs. (10)).

Subs. (1)
   Essentially, "planning authorities" enjoy a general power to dispose of any land acquired or appropriated by them for "planning purposes" (see s.201(1)), provided that they continue to hold the land for those purposes at the time of the disposal.
   It is important to appreciate that the local authority, in its wider role, may re-assign land so acquired for a different purpose (*e.g.* as part of a School or Housing development), in which case the provisions of the 1973 Act are applicable to any future disposal. Any exercise of the general power of disposal under this subsection, however, will be subject to the remaining provisions of s.191.

Subs. (2)
   The purposes for which a disposal under s.191(1) can be undertaken are fairly broadly stated. A disposal of land can take place where development, in the colloquial sense, has taken place, or else is to take place irrespective of whether the "planning authority" itself has or will carry out the works. The disposal may also be for the benefit of "other land" (subs. (2)(a)).
   Alternatively, a disposal can take place in order to facilitate the carrying out of specific works or the erection of buildings considered by the "planning authority" to be "necessary for the proper planning" of their area. In *McMonagle v. Secretary of State for Scotland*, 1993 S.L.T. 807, it was held that "necessary" does not mean that there is no possible alternative development to that proposed, but can mean necessary in furtherance of the only proposal acceptable to the planning authority.

Subs. (3)
   As with disposals carried out by a local authority under the 1973 Act, unless the provisions of subs. (7) apply, the obligation on a "planning authority" acting under this subsection is to obtain "the best price or . . . the best terms" that can reasonably be obtained. It should be noted that

there is no equivalent provision to s.74(2) of the 1973 Act, entitling the "planning authority to seek the Secretary of State's consent to a disposal at an undervalue.

Subss. (4)–(6)

These provisions are intended to prevent a "planning authority" from holding on to land which they have acquired under ss.189 and 190, where they have no immediate plans for use, but such retention goes in the face of a development proposal which could make use of the land. Such a refusal must be shown to constitute discriminatory or oppressive conduct on the part of the authority, which is a high standard of proof to achieve.

Subsection (4) is widely drawn as to circumstances in which a complaint can be made to the Secretary of State. Failure to agree terms and conditions or the manner of disposal of the land to the complainer is as important in this regard as a bald refusal to sell.

Where such a complaint is received, the Secretary of State may, presumably if the complaint appears well-founded on the face of it, forward it to the "planning authority". Under subs. (5), the "planning authority" is entitled to make a written submission to the Secretary of State on the complaint. (There is no time limit for response by the "planning authority", but the Secretary of State is obliged only to consider a submission "made" to him).

Again, the Secretary of State has a discretion over putting the matter to a Public Local Inquiry but it seems he can proceed to determine the complaint on the basis of the written material before him (subss. (5) and (6)). Where he does not so determine, the Secretary of State cannot exercise further powers without a Public Local Inquiry being held, and the report issued considered (*ibid.*). In either event, unless he determines to dismiss the complaint, the Secretary of State is empowered to order a disposal to take place to the complainer, and also to specify the manner of disposal or the terms and conditions thereof (subs. (6)).

Subss. (7), (8)

These subsections go some way towards applying part of the "Crichel Down Rules" (see above) to disposals made by a "planning authority" under s.191. In essence, the subsections require consideration to be given in any disposal to giving the opportunity to obtain "accommodation" (an undefined term, but perhaps intended to mean occupancy for business purposes) to persons who carried out "business or other activities" at the time of the original acquisition.

This provision applies only where the subjects were acquired compulsorily under s.189(1)(a) or (3). (Reference to s.189(3) is included at the recommendation of the Scottish Law Commission, who detected an apparent drafting error created by the 1980 Act which excluded this reference from the amended 1972 Act. See *Scottish Law Commission Report No. 157, (1996)* Recommendation 11)

To satisfy any test in this regard, such persons must be wishing to return to the land and prepared to comply with any requirements of the "planning authority" as regards the development or re-development of the land. A balance seems to require to be made, in balancing the terms of future grants of "accommodation" to compensation already paid.

There are several matters obscure in this provision. Does occupation of a dwellinghouse constitute an "other activity" in the sense of subs. (7)(a)? How are the terms agreed with the "planning authority" regarding "accommodation" to be incorporated into the bargain with the person to whom the land is being disponed? How great is the obligation to attempt to trace the original landowner where he has disappeared?

Subs. (9)

This provision aims to ensure that disposal of land under s.191 as a church enjoys the benefit of enforcement through the existence of feuing conditions to that effect. In this regard only, is the definition of "disposal" in s.277(1) qualified.

Subs. (10)

It is made clear that disposals of land acquired under planning powers are to be carried out subject to s.191, and not any other legislation under which the planning authority are entitled to act (see notes above).

Disposal by Secretary of State of land acquired under section 190

192.—(1) The Secretary of State may dispose of land held by him and acquired by him or any other Minister under section 190 to such person, in such manner and subject to such conditions as appear to him expedient.

(2) In particular, the Secretary of State may under subsection (1) dispose of land held by him for any purpose in order to secure its use for that purpose.

DEFINITIONS
  "land": s.277(1).
  "Minister": s.277(1).

GENERAL NOTE
  This provision is intended to act as a corollary to the acquisition powers enjoyed by the Secretary of State for the Environment under s.190. Essentially, the Secretary of State is free to dispose of land so acquired as he considers fit. Any disposals so effected will, as mentioned above, be subject to the "Crichel Down Rules" (see above), and will also be subject to the scrutiny of the Comptroller and Auditor-General and the Public Accounts Committee.
  It is no obstruction to a disposal made under s.191(1) that the disposal is made in order to effect a purpose which is not, itself, being carried out by the Secretary of State (s.192(2)). There is no explicit linkage made between the purpose of the original acquisition and that of its subsequent disposal.

Development of land held for planning purposes

193.—(1) This section applies to any land acquired or appropriated by a planning authority for planning purposes and held by them for those purposes.

(2) Subject to subsection (3), the functions of a planning authority shall include power for the authority, notwithstanding any limitation imposed by law on the capacity of the authority by virtue of its constitution, to erect, construct or carry out any building or work on any land to which this section applies.

(3) Subsection (2) confers such power only if such power is not and could not be conferred on the authority or any other person by or under any enactment, other than an enactment in this Part.

(4) The functions of a planning authority shall include power for the authority, notwithstanding any such limitation as is mentioned in subsection (2), to repair, maintain and insure any buildings or works on land to which this section applies, and generally to deal therewith in a proper course of management.

(5) Nothing in this section shall be construed as authorising any act or omission on the part of a planning authority which is actionable at the instance of any person on any ground other than such a limitation as is mentioned in subsection (2).

DEFINITIONS
  "building": s.277(1).
  "land": s.277(1).
  "planning authority": s.1(1).

GENERAL NOTE
  Section 193 is intended to clothe planning authorities with broad powers to carry out the development of any "land" (which can, in terms of s.277(1) include a "building") which they acquire under ss.188 and 189. It is important to appreciate that a number of the statutes under which local authorities discharge their statutory functions contain powers of compulsory acquisition (e.g. s.103 of the Roads (Scotland) Act 1980). However, unless what the local authority are entitled to do subsequent to such an acquisition is circumscribed, such land may be "appropriated" for "planning purposes" (see s.201(1)).
  In terms of land acquired for "planning purposes", the latitude given is fairly wide, and was used extensively in re-development schemes such as the replacement or renewal of town centre housing or retail schemes. Current restrictions on capital expenditure make direct funding of such schemes by a planning authority less likely, but this does not close the door on developments funded by loan or carried out under the Private Finance Initiative (PFI).
  Therefore, provided that the carrying out of the work to land falling within s.193 is not authorised (and, therefore, potentially restricted in its scope) by virtue of the legislation or else another Part of the Act (subs. (3)), the planning authority can carry out construction or other work on

any land which it has acquired for "planning purposes". This power exists irrespective of any other restriction on the vires of the local authority to carry out such work (subs. (2)).

Subsection (4) makes clear that the power extends beyond mere execution of any construction or building works, and in its terms establishes that the planning authority may carry out normal acts of long-term management of properties so constructed, such as maintenance, repair and insurance. (For a possible instance of the extent of "works of maintenance", see *R. v. Hackney L.B.C. ex p. Secretary of State for the Environment* (1989) 88 L.G.R. 96). Subsection (5) offers a limited defence to any action raised against the planning authority in relation to any act or omission arising from the exercise of a s.193 power insofar as a question of vires would have arisen, if not authorised under subs. (2).

Extinguishment of certain rights affecting acquired or appropriated land

Extinguishment of rights over land compulsorily acquired

194.—(1) Subject to the provisions of this section, upon the completion by the acquiring authority of a compulsory acquisition of land under this Part—
  (a) all private rights of way and rights of laying down, erecting, continuing or maintaining any apparatus on, under or over the land and all other rights or servitudes in or relating to that land shall be extinguished, and
  (b) any such apparatus shall vest in the acquiring authority.
(2) Subsection (1) shall not apply—
  (a) to any right vested in, or apparatus belonging to, statutory undertakers for the purpose of the carrying on of their undertaking,
  (b) to any right conferred by or in accordance with the telecommunications code on the operator of a telecommunications code system, or
  (c) to any telecommunication apparatus kept installed for the purposes of any such system.
(3) In respect of any right or apparatus not falling within subsection (2), subsection (1) shall have effect subject—
  (a) to any direction given by the acquiring authority before the completion of the acquisition that subsection (1) shall not apply to any right or apparatus specified in the direction, and
  (b) to any agreement which may be made (whether before or after the completion of the acquisition) between the acquiring authority and the person in or to whom the right or apparatus in question is vested or belongs.
(4) Any person who suffers loss by the extinguishment of a right or servitude or the vesting of any apparatus under this section shall be entitled to compensation from the acquiring authority.
(5) Any compensation payable under this section shall be determined in accordance with the Land Compensation (Scotland) Act 1963.

DEFINITIONS
  "acquiring authority": s.277(1).
  "apparatus": s.164(1) of the New Roads and Street Works Act 1991 (c.22).
  "building": s.277(1).
  "compulsory acquisition": s.277(1).
  "erecting": see definition of "erection" s.277(1).
  "land": s.277(1).
  "statutory undertakers": ss.214, 277(1).
  "telecommunication apparatus": para.1, Sched. 1 to the Telecommunications Act 1984 (c.12).
  "telecommunications code": s.10, Sched. 2 to the Telecommunications Act 1984 (c.12).
  "telecommunications code system": s.106(1) of the Telecommunications Act 1984 (c.12).

GENERAL NOTE
  It will be apparent that the compulsory acquisition of land for the undertaking of a planning or development purpose may be rendered pointless if possible uses are sterilised or rendered difficult by the existence of private rights of way or servitudes. On the other hand, persons having the benefit of such rights cannot be expected merely to yield these to the wider good without compensation. The position of persons generally or specifically empowered by statute ("statutory

undertakers"; see s.214) to exercise rights over land, or else to construct "apparatus" there in furtherance of their statutory authority must also be taken into account.

Subs. (1)
This subsection sets out the general principle that where land is acquired by an "acquiring authority" (defined in s.277(1) more widely than a "planning authority" in order to take account of other bodies empowered under the Act to exercise powers of compulsory acquisition) on a compulsory basis – that is under s.189 – all "private rights of way . . . and all other rights and servitudes" are extinguished on completion of the acquisition. In terms of Sched. 15, para. 7, this will mean the end of the period specified in a General Vesting Declaration.
The further principle is enunciated that where a private right of laying down, erecting, continuing any "apparatus" within the land acquired is in effect at the time of completion of the acquisition, that right is also extinguished, and the "apparatus" vests in the "acquiring authority". Presumably, vesting coincides with "completion" of the compulsory acquisition (see above). The provisions for payment of compensation where such rights are extinguished or apparatus vested are discussed below, as are the means whereby the general principle can be modified in relation to rights and/or "apparatus" which would otherwise be vested.

Subs. (2)
As mentioned previously, the general principle contained in subs. (1) does not apply where rights vested in, or apparatus belonging to "statutory undertakers" lie within land subject to a completed compulsory acquisition. Further provision is made for the protection of rights of persons operating, or operating a system under the "telecommunications code" contained in Sched. 2 to the Telecommunications Act 1984 (c.12), where such rights exist under the Code. "Apparatus" forming part of a system installed conform to the provisions of the Code is similarly protected. (Extinguishment of such rights is dealt with by the procedure set out in ss.224–227 below).

Subs. (3)
This provision modifies the general principle of subs. (1) permitting the "acquiring authority" to direct that a right mentioned in the subsection will not be extinguished, or else that "apparatus" will not vest. This power must be exercised prior to "completion" (see above) of the compulsory acquisition of the land concerned (subs. (3)(a)).
Alternatively, the effect of subs. (1) can be disapplied (or arguably in view of the terms in which it is couched, modified) in relation to any right or "apparatus" which would otherwise be affected, by agreement between the "acquiring authority" and the person to whom such right or apparatus belongs. Such an agreement can be entered before or after "completion" of the compulsory acquisition (subs. (3)(b)).
Two points can be made in relation to the latter provision: the first is that it can clearly be of no use where the ownership of the right or apparatus is unknown. If this remains the case up to "completion" of the compulsory acquisition, the "acquiring authority" will be obliged to decide whether to make a subs. (1)(a) declaration prior to "completion". The second point is that it is unclear how an agreement made under this subsection can enter the Register of Sasines or Land Register, which may be problematic for a prospective purchaser relying on the terms of subs. (1) alone.

Subss. (4), (5)
As stated above, any person suffering the loss of a right or servitude or relinquishing "apparatus" consequent upon the application of subs. (1) is entitled to compensation in terms of the Land Compensation (Scotland) Act 1963 (c.51). This falls to be determined by the Lands Tribunal in terms of the relevant principles.

General vesting declarations

195.—(1) Schedule 15 shall have effect for the purpose of enabling any authority to whom this section applies to vest in themselves by a declaration land which they are authorised by a compulsory purchase order to acquire and with respect to the effect of such a declaration, the payment and recovery of sums in respect of compensation for the acquisition of land so vested and other matters connected with it.

(2) This section applies to any Minister or local or other public authority authorised to acquire land by means of a compulsory purchase order, and any such authority is in Schedule 15 referred to as an acquiring authority.

(3) This section shall not apply to the compulsory acquisition of land with respect to which a compulsory purchase order was in force before 8th December 1969.

DEFINITIONS

"authority": see definition of "acquiring authority" (s.277(1)).
"compulsory purchase order": s.1 of the Acquisition of Land (Authorisation Procedure) (Scotland) Act 1947 (c.42).
"land": s.277(1).
"Minister": s.277(1).

GENERAL NOTE

As indicated above, s.189(7) applies the provisions of the Acquisition of Land (Authorisation Procedure) (Scotland) Act 1947 (c.42) to compulsory acquisitions made under that section. This means that the procedure for making and confirming compulsory purchase orders ("CPOs") contained in the 1947 Act is applied to such acquisitions. As indicated above in relation to s.189, once a CPO has been confirmed, title may be taken by two of the procedures (Schedule Conveyance and Notarial Instrument) provided for in the 1845 Act.

The 1947 Act innovated on this procedure by introducing the General Vesting Declaration (GVD) as a means of permitting an "acquiring authority" to complete title to all or some of the land comprised in the confirmed CPO. It seems that it is not essential for all of the land comprised in a CPO to be taken by a single GVD, which might otherwise oblige advance payments of compensation to be made early (see *Stair Memorial Encyclopedia, Vol. 5, para. 90*).

This last point is important, since a GVD regulates not only the taking of title by the "acquiring authority", but also the means by which compensation payable is to be determined. A GVD has, however, no real resemblance to any other conveyancing writ, and can simply vest a delineated area of land in the authority, leaving it with the process of payment of compensation to be resolved following vesting. (For further comments on GVDs, see the General Note to Sched. 15).

Power to override servitudes and other rights

196.—(1) The interests and rights to which this section applies are any to override servitude, liberty, privilege, right or advantage annexed to land and adversely affecting other land, including any natural right to support.

(2) Subject to subsection (3) the erection, construction or carrying out, or maintenance, of any building or work on land which has been acquired or appropriated by a planning authority for planning purposes, whether done by the planning authority or by a person deriving title from them, is authorised by virtue of this section if it is done in accordance with planning permission, notwithstanding that it involves—

   (a) interference with an interest or right to which this section applies, or

   (b) a breach of a restriction as to the use of land arising by virtue of any deed or contract.

(3) Nothing in subsection (2) authorises interference with any right of way or right of laying down, erecting, continuing or maintaining apparatus on, under or over land which is—

   (a) a right vested in or belonging to statutory undertakers for the purpose of the carrying on of their undertaking, or

   (b) a right conferred by or in accordance with the telecommunications code on the operator of a telecommunications code system.

(4) In respect of any interference or breach in pursuance of subsection (2), compensation—

   (a) shall be payable under section 61 of the Lands Clauses Consolidation (Scotland) Act 1845 or under section 6 of the Railways Clauses Consolidation (Scotland) Act 1845, and

   (b) shall be assessed in the same manner and subject to the same rules as in the case of other compensation under those sections in respect of injurious affection where—

      (i) the compensation is to be estimated in connection with a purchase under those Acts, or

(ii) the injury arises from the execution of works on land acquired under those Acts.

(5) Where a person deriving title from the planning authority by whom the land in question was acquired or appropriated—
  (a) is liable to pay compensation by virtue of subsection (4), and (b) fails to discharge that liability,
the liability shall, subject to subsection (6), be enforceable against the planning authority.

(6) Nothing in subsection (5) affects any agreement between the planning authority and any other person for indemnifying the planning authority against any liability under that subsection.

(7) Nothing in this section shall be construed as authorising any act or omission on the part of any person which is actionable at the instance of any person on any ground other than such an interference or breach as is mentioned in subsection (2).

DEFINITIONS
  "acquiring authority": s.277(1).
  "building": s.277(1).
  "compulsory acquisition": s.277(1).
  "injurious affection": s.6 of the Railways Clauses (Consolidation) (Scotland) Act 1845, as amended by the Lands Compensation (Scotland) Act 1963.
  "land": s.277(1).
  "planning authority": s.1(1).
  "planning purposes": s.201(1).
  "planning permission": see Pt. III.
  "statutory undertaker": s.214.
  "telecommunications code": s.10, Sched. 2 of the Telecommunications Act 1984.
  "telecommunications code system": s.106(1) of the Telecommunications Act 1984.

GENERAL NOTE
  This section represents a significant adjunct to the powers of compulsory acquisition and development of land acquired under compulsory powers contained in ss.189, 193 and 194 (See notes above). Where a compulsory acquisition has taken place, and development of the land (or impliedly a part of it or else a wider area involving use of the whole or part of such land) is being undertaken on foot of a planning consent for such development, existing rights of servitude and related rights referable to other land can be made to yield to the development enjoying the planning consent.
  As stated above, this power can leave a powerful weapon in the hands of the acquiring authority, who are also the arbiters – in the majority of cases – of whether an application receives planning consent. Clearly, potential financial benefit to the authority is an issue which falls to be disregarded in exercising its planning powers, but in many cases, this is difficult to eliminate from the overall background.

Subs. (1)
  This subsection lists the rights which can be obliged to yield in furtherance of a planning consent involving whole or part of the land previously compulsorily acquired by a "planning authority" (which excludes from its ambit some of the other "acquiring" authorities for present purposes). At the heart of the definition is any servitude, whether positive or negative, and express or implied. (This accounts for the inclusion of the urban servitude of support in this subsection, although it seems any other of the recognised urban or rural servitudes would satisfy this test). However, the further language referring to "any right or advantage", when read in conjunction with subs. (2)(b), arguably appears to extend the statutory extinction of rights which can occur under this section, to embrace real burdens and conditions.

Subs. (2)
  Except where the rights and apparatus of "statutory undertakers" are involved, land or buildings compulsorily acquired by a planning authority under s.189 can be developed by the authority or a "person deriving title from them" (not necessarily the immediate successor in title), if performed in accordance with a planning permission. In such circumstances, the works in question can be carried out, notwithstanding:
  (a) interference with any of the rights or interests specified in subs. (1),
  (b) any breach of a restriction on use of the land specified in "any deed or contract".

As regards (b), no definition is given in the Act of a "deed or contract", but it appears to be presumed that this term is sufficiently wide to include real burdens or conditions contained in a feu contract or disposition.

The implications for conveyancing theory are somewhat startling. What happens to any "right or interest" or a "restriction on use" swept aside by virtue of this subsection? Do the burdens or restrictions simply fly off? What is the position where the works purportedly following upon a planning permission are the subject of enforcement notice proceedings? What is the position during and subsequent to an enforcement notice appeal? It seems that the provisions of the 1947 Act, from which these provisions stem, were drafted with little concern for the position in Scots law. However, they have spawned little in the way of reported decisions, despite the apparent scope for creating uncertainty contained therein.

Subs. (3)

This is a similar provision to s.194(2) in relation to disapplication of the rights conferred by subs. (1) as regards rights of the nature therein specified, where these are vested in "statutory undertakers", or else relate to the construction or maintenance of their "apparatus". Section 194 does not, however, authorise any interference with or vesting of the "apparatus" itself.

Subs. (4)

Since subs. (1) concerns itself with interference with rights rather than the vesting of property as is the case in s.194, the basis of payment of compensation set out is somewhat different, being referable to the Lands Clauses Acts rather than the Lands Compensation Legislation. Accordingly, the assumptions made in assessing compensation will be somewhat different.

Subss. (5), (6)

It follows from the logic of permitting a "person deriving title" from the planning authority to have the benefit of s.196(1) that liability for payment of compensation, as assessed under subs. (4), should lie with the person who actually exercises that right. Since a person purchasing from the "acquiring authority" may be presumed to have taken the land in the knowledge of the existence of subs. (2), it could be argued that this is reflected in the price actually paid. Hence, it might be reasonable to look to the planning authority who made the original acquisition under compulsory powers for recovery in the event of the person liable (by implication) under the section failing to discharge that liability.

Again, there are a number of questions begged by this provision. At what point does a failure of payment by the liable person crystallise the right to go against the acquiring authority? What are the liabilities of predecessor landowners if, say, the third in line from the planning authority defaults in the obligation under subs. (5)?

It is possible for the planning authority to enter into agreement indemnifying the planning authority against action in terms of subs. (5) (subs. (6)), but can such an agreement transmit against singular successors? Does the planning authority have any protection where the Grantor of the Indemnity dies or becomes bankrupt? Again, little litigation appears to have been generated by this provision.

Subs. (7)

This is a provision similar to s.193(5), establishing that the limits of a defence to any action raised by a landowner aggrieved by works carried out in furtherance of the s.196(2) power by "any other person" is limited to interference with or breach of rights falling within that subsection.

Provisions as to churches and burial grounds

197.—(1) Any land consisting of a church or other building used or formerly used for religious worship, or the site of such a building, or a burial ground, which has been acquired by a Minister, a planning authority or statutory undertakers under this Part or under Chapter V of Part I of the Planning (Listed Buildings and Conservation Areas) (Scotland) Act 1997 or compulsorily under any other enactment, or which has been appropriated by a planning authority for planning purposes, may, subject to the following provisions of this section—

   (a) in the case of land acquired by a Minister, be used in any manner by him or on his behalf for any purpose for which he acquired the land, and

   (b) in any other case, be used by any person in any manner in accordance with planning permission, notwithstanding anything in any enactment relating to churches or such other buildings or to burial grounds or any obligation or restriction imposed under any deed or agreement or otherwise as respects that church or other building or burial ground.

(2) In the case of land which—

(a) has been acquired by the Secretary of State under section 79(1) of the National Health Service (Scotland) Act 1978, and

(b) is held, used or occupied by a health service body, as defined in section 60(7) of the National Health Service and Community Care Act 1990,

subsection (1) shall apply with the omission of paragraph (a) and, in paragraph (b), of the words "in any other case".

(3) No authority shall be required for the removal and reinterment of any human remains, or for the removal or disposal of any monuments.

(4) Nothing in this section shall be construed as authorising any act or omission on the part of any person which is actionable at the instance of any person on any ground other than contravention of any such enactment, obligation or restriction as is mentioned in subsection (1).

(5) In this section—

"burial ground" includes any churchyard, cemetery or other ground, whether consecrated or not, which has at any time been set apart for the purposes of interment, and includes part of a burial ground; and

"monument" includes a tombstone or other memorial and any fixtures or furnishings.

DEFINITIONS

"building": s.277(1).
"burial ground": s.197(5).
"health service body": s.60(7) of the National Health Service and Community Care Act 1990 (c.19).
"land": s.277(1).
"Minister": s.277(1).
"monument": s.201(5).
"planning authority": s.1(1).
"planning purposes": s.201(1).
"planning permission": Pt. III.
"statutory undertakers": ss.214(1), 277(1).

GENERAL NOTE

The overall effect of this section is to disapply the terms of any enactment or any real burden or restriction arising *ex contractu* relating to the carrying on of a church or burial ground on any land acquired compulsorily or "appropriated" by a "planning authority". Where the land has been acquired under ss.188 or 189, or in terms of the Planning (Listed Buildings and Conservation Areas) (Scotland) Act 1997 (c.9), or else "compulsorily under any enactment", the provisions of this section apply (subs. (1)).

In such cases, where the land (which can include disused churches or the site of former churches) was initially acquired by a "planning authority" other than a Minister, it can be developed in accordance with a planning permission, notwithstanding the existence of any of the aforementioned restrictions. Where acquired by a Minister, development can proceed as wished by him or by a person acting on his behalf, provided that such use falls within the original purpose behind the acquisition (subs. (1)). The former provision applies where an acquisition was made by the Secretary of State for Health and the land forms part of the assets of any "health service body", as defined in s.60(7) of the National Health Service and Community Care Act 1990 (c.19) (subs. (2)). Reference should also be made to the comments regarding the terms of s.196(2).

Perhaps surprisingly, no permission beyond that arising from s.197 and the relevant planning permission (in the case of developments other than by Ministers) is required for removal of human remains, tombstones and monuments from burial grounds in furtherance of the developments so authorised (subs. (3)). Here, it seems that reliance is being placed on the responsiveness of planning authorities or Ministers to genuine public concern regarding the removal of remains of relatives in order to prevent the powers granted under this section being used insensitively. It may be worth noting however, that no requirements regarding re-internment of remains thus removed appears in this section.

A similar defence to actions raised is provided in relation to any act or omission arising from the exercise of the subs. (1) power as for ss.193(5) and 196(7) (s.197(4)).

Use and development of land for open spaces

198.—(1) Any land being, or forming part of, a common or open space, which has been acquired by a Minister, a local authority or statutory undertakers under this Part or under Chapter V of Part I of the Planning (Listed Buildings and Conservation Areas) (Scotland) Act 1997 or compulsorily under any other enactment, or which has been appropriated by a planning authority for planning purposes, may—

    (a) in the case of land acquired by a Minister, be used in any manner by him or on his behalf for any purpose for which he acquired the land, and

    (b) in any other case, be used by any person in any manner in accordance with planning permission,

notwithstanding anything in any enactment relating to land of that kind, or in any enactment by which the land is specially regulated.

(2) Nothing in this section shall be construed as authorising any act or omission on the part of any person which is actionable at the instance of any person on any ground other than contravention of any such enactment as is mentioned in subsection (1).

DEFINITIONS
    "common" : s.277(1).
    "land": s.277(1).
    "local authority": s.2 of the Local Government etc. (Scotland) Act 1994 (c.39).
    "Minister": s.277(1).
    "open space": s.277(1).
    "planning authority": s.1(1).
    "planning purposes": s.201(1).
    "planning permission": Pt. III.
    "statutory undertaker": ss.214(1), 277(1).

GENERAL NOTE
This section makes similar provisions disapplying any general or special Act governing the operation of a "common or open space", where the land in question has been acquired in circumstances similar to those described in s.197. Where this is the case, the same test for achieving disapplication of the legislation (but not here any title or other restriction) applies, except that no provision is made in relation to "health service [bodies]" (*cf.* s.197(2)).

There are two slightly curious aspects to subs. (1); the first is that the test here refers to acquisition by a "local authority" and not a "planning authority" – as in s.197(1) – in relation to the powers enabling compulsory acquisition, although since both subsections also refer to appropriation by a "planning authority for planning purposes", this may not add up to a significant difference. Rather more difficult to construe is the reference in the definition of "open space" to a "disused burial ground", which does not sit easily with the definition of "burial ground" given in s.197(5). It seems unlikely that this represents more than slight carelessness in the drafting of the definition, and prospective developers of "burial grounds" would seem to place themselves on a stronger footing by resorting to s.197.

Again there is a defence to any action raised in relation to acts or omissions carried out in exercise of the powers granted under this section (s.198(2)).

Displacement of persons from land acquired or appropriated

199.—(1) Where—

    (a) any land has been acquired or appropriated for planning purposes,

    (b) the land is for the time being held by a planning authority for the purposes for which it was acquired or appropriated, and

    (c) the carrying out of redevelopment on the land will involve the displacement of persons residing in premises on it,

it shall be the duty of the authority, in so far as there is no other residential accommodation suitable to the reasonable requirements of those persons

available on reasonable terms, to secure the provision of such accommodation in advance of the displacements from time to time becoming necessary as the redevelopment proceeds.

(2) If the Secretary of State certifies that possession of a house which—

(a) has been acquired or appropriated by a planning authority for planning purposes, and

(b) is for the time being held by the authority for the purposes for which it
was acquired or appropriated,

is immediately required for those purposes, nothing in the Rent (Scotland)
Act 1984 shall prevent the acquiring or appropriating authority from obtaining possession of the house.

(3) Where—

(a) any land has been acquired by a Minister or a planning authority under
this Part or under Chapter V of Part I of the Planning (Listed Buildings and Conservation Areas) (Scotland) Act 1997, or has been appropriated by a planning authority for planning purposes, and

(b) possession of any building on the land is required by that Minister or
the planning authority in question, as the case may be, for the purposes
for which the land was acquired or appropriated,

then, at any time after the tenancy of the occupier has expired or has been
determined, the Minister or planning authority in question may serve a
notice on the occupier of the building requiring him to remove from it within
a period of 21 days.

(4) On the expiry of that period a certified copy of the notice to remove
shall be sufficient warrant for ejection against the occupier or any party in his
right in the event of non-compliance with the notice.

DEFINITIONS
"land": s.277(1).
"planning purposes": s.201(1).
"planning authority": s.1(1).

GENERAL NOTE
Subs. (1)
This subsection imposes a duty on planning authorities who have acquired land for "planning
purposes" (*i.e.* under ss.188 or 189 or s.47 of the Planning (Listed Buildings and Conservation
Areas) (Scotland) Act 1997 (c.9)), or else have "appropriated" such land, and who continue to
hold such land for that purpose, where a re-development (an undefined term) is about to commence, in relation to any persons who are then resident on such land.

Where such persons will require to be displaced by the re-development and are unable to find
alternative residences suitable to their needs on "reasonable terms", it is the duty of the planning
authority to "secure provision" of appropriate accommodation prior to the need actually arising. In days when the housing stock available to planning authorities from within their own
resources is limited, it is a little unclear how far this obligation actually extends.

Subs. (2)
This subsection merely provides that where the circumstances narrated in relation to subs. (1)
apply in relation to houses situated on land acquired or appropriated by a planning authority,
the protections a tenant would otherwise enjoy under the Rent (Scotland) Act 1984 (c.58)
against recovery of possession can be disapplied. This occurs where the Secretary of State certifies the house to be "immediately required" for the purposes of carrying out the
re-development.

Subss. (3), (4)
These subsections narrate the procedure whereby possession of any "building" is "required"
(in this instance, not as a matter of urgency) for the purposes of the original acquisition. A
slightly different pre-requisite to exercise of the power is provided in subs. (3)(a). Here, it may
only be exercised where land has been acquired compulsorily by the Secretary of State, or voluntarily or compulsorily by a planning authority under ss.188 or 189, or else under Pt. I (Listed
Buildings) of the Planning (Listed Buildings and Conservation Areas) (Scotland) Act 1997 (c.9),
or else has been "appropriated" by the planning authority.

If one of these tests is satisfied, and the tenancy of the "building" has expired, removal of the occupier can be required on the service of 21 days notice to remove on him. In the event of failure so to remove, certification of a copy of the notice to remove on behalf of the relevant authority grants warrant for enforcement of ejection, without resort to further process.

Modification of incorporated enactments for purposes of this Part

200.—(1) Where it is proposed that land should be acquired compulsorily under section 189 or 190 and a compulsory purchase order relating to that land is submitted to the confirming authority in accordance with Part I of Schedule 1 to the Acquisition of Land (Authorisation Procedure) (Scotland) Act 1947 or, as the case may be, is made in draft by the Secretary of State for the Environment in accordance with Part II of that Schedule, the confirming authority or the Secretary of State, as the case may be, may disregard for the purposes of that Schedule any objection to the order or draft which, in the opinion of that authority or Secretary of State, amounts in substance to an objection to the provisions of the development plan defining the proposed use of that or any other land.

(2) Where a compulsory purchase order authorising the acquisition of any land under section 189 is submitted to the Secretary of State in accordance with Part I of Schedule 1 to the said Act of 1947, then if the Secretary of State—

   (a) is satisfied that the order ought to be confirmed so far as it relates to part of the land comprised therein, but

   (b) has not for the time being determined whether it ought to be confirmed so far as it relates to any other such land,

he may confirm the order so far as it relates to the land mentioned in paragraph (a), and give directions postponing consideration of the order, so far as it relates to any other land specified in the directions, until such time as may be so specified.

(3) Where the Secretary of State gives directions under subsection (2), the notices required by paragraph 6 of Schedule 1 to the said Act of 1947 to be published and served shall include a statement of the effect of the directions.

(4) In construing the Lands Clauses Acts and section 6 of the Railways Clauses Consolidation (Scotland) Act 1845, as incorporated by virtue of paragraph 1 of Schedule 2 to the Acquisition of Land (Authorisation Procedure) (Scotland) Act 1947, in relation to any of the provisions of this Part—

   (a) references to the execution of the works or to the construction of the railway shall be construed as including references to any erection, construction or carrying out of buildings or works authorised by section 196,

   (b) in relation to the erection, construction or carrying out of any buildings or works so authorised, references in section 6 of the said Act of 1845 to the company shall be construed as references to the person by whom the buildings or works in question are erected, constructed or carried out, and

   (c) references to the execution of the works shall be construed as including also references to any erection, construction or carrying out of buildings or works on behalf of a Minister or statutory undertakers on land acquired by that Minister or those undertakers, where the buildings or works are erected, constructed or carried out for the purposes for which the land was acquired.

DEFINITIONS
"buildings": s.277(1).
"compulsory purchase order": s.1(1) of the Acquisition of Land (Authorisation Procedure) (Scotland) Act 1947 (c.42).
"confirming authority": s.2(1) of the Acquisition of Land (Authorisation Procedure) Act 1947 (c.42).
"development plan": s.24.
"land": s.277(1).

"Minister": s.277(1).
"statutory undertakers": ss.214(1), 271(1).

Subs. (1)

This subsection is designed to modify the effect of otherwise applicable parts of the 1947 Act so as to permit the "confirming authority" (usually the Secretary of State) to disregard one species of possible objection which might arise, where a CPO of land is being sought under s.189.

Reference has been made in earlier parts of the legislation to the process for objection to the adoption of structure and local plans. In view of the ability of the public to participate in the process of determining these aspects of the development plan, the Secretary of State is entitled to disregard objections to a CPO made by virtue of s.189, where that objection is substantially an objection to what the development plan proposes as a use for the land affected, or any other land.

Subss. (2), (3)

If para. 4(2), Sched. 1 to the Acquisition of Land (Authorisation Procedure) (Scotland) Act 1947 (c.42) were to be applied to s.189 CPOs unmodified, this would seem to place the Secretary of State in the position of taking an "all or nothing" approach to the matter of confirming the CPO. In a number of cases, this could lead to the rejection or delay of a CPO in circumstances where the reasons for acquisition of the bulk of the land affected were substantially upheld, but were not for a minor portion thereof.

The Secretary of State is thus empowered (subs. (2)) to confirm the CPO over a part only of the land affected and to postpone a determination on the remaining portion, until a time specified in the relevant decision letter. It is not clear whether scope is open for the Secretary of State to entertain further submissions where determination on the remaining portion is outstanding. Notice of a subs. (2) determination must be included in any notices served or advertisement made of confirmation of part of the CPO (subs. (3)).

Subs. (4)

This subsection modifies the terms of the Lands Clauses and Railways Clauses Acts to take account of the "development" purposes authorised by this part of the Act in relation to land acquired under its terms.

Interpretation of this Part

201.—(1) In this Part—

(a) any reference to the acquisition of land for planning purposes is a reference to the acquisition thereof under section 188 or 189 of this Act or section 47 of the Planning (Listed Buildings and Conservation Areas) (Scotland) Act 1997 (or, as the case may be, under section 102 or 109 of the 1972 Act), and

(b) any reference to the appropriation of land for planning purposes is a reference to the appropriation thereof for purposes for which land can be or could have been acquired under those sections.

(2) In relation to a planning authority or body corporate, nothing in sections 196 to 198 shall be construed as authorising any act or omission on their part in contravention of any limitation imposed by law on their capacity by virtue of the constitution of the authority or body.

(3) Any power conferred by section 197 or 198 to use land in a manner therein mentioned shall be construed as a power so to use the land, whether it involves the erection, construction or carrying out of any building or work, or the maintenance of any building or work or not.

"building": s.277(1).
"land": s.277(1).
"planning authority": s.1(1).
"planning purposes": subs. (1).

The expression "planning purposes" is explained in order to allow references in preceding sections to land being acquired or appropriated by the bodies variously mentioned "for planning purposes" to be construed. The reference is directed to the powers of voluntary or compulsory acquisition of land given to planning authorities and to the Secretary of State for the Environment in ss.189 or 190 respectively. The expression is also applied to "appropriations" by planning authorities (subs. (1)).

A limitation to the powers conferred on local or planning authorities by virtue of ss.196–198 is imposed by making clear that these sections do not, in themselves, authorise anything which otherwise would be *ultra vires* of that body (subs. (2)). The extent to which any power conferred in ss.197–198 can be exercised, subject to the foregoing, is specified in subs. (3).

PART IX

ROADS, FOOTPATHS AND RIGHTS OF WAY

Stopping up and diversion of roads by Secretary of State

Roads affected by development: orders by Secretary of State

202.—(1) The Secretary of State may by order authorise the stopping up or diversion of any road if he is satisfied that it is necessary to do so in order to enable development to be carried out—
 (a) in accordance with planning permission granted under Part III, or
 (b) by a government department.
 (2) Such an order may make such provision as appears to the Secretary of State to be necessary or expedient for the construction or improvement of any other road.
 (3) Such an order may direct that the other road so constructed or improved—
 (a) shall be entered by the local roads authority in the list of public roads kept by them under section 1 of the Roads (Scotland) Act 1984, or
 (b) shall be deemed for the purposes of that Act to have been constructed by the Secretary of State under section 19 of that Act and shall, on such date as may be specified in the order, become a trunk road within the meaning of that Act.
 (4) Any order made under this section may contain such incidental and consequential provisions as appear to the Secretary of State to be necessary or expedient, including in particular—
 (a) provision for authorising the Secretary of State, or requiring any other authority or person specified in the order to pay, or to make contributions in respect of, the cost of doing any work provided for by the order or any increased expenditure to be incurred which is attributable to the doing of any such work;
 (b) provision for the preservation of any rights of statutory undertakers in respect of any apparatus of theirs which immediately before the date of the order is under, in, on, over, along or across the road to which the order relates.
 (5) An order may be made under this section authorising the stopping up or diversion of any road which is temporarily stopped up or diverted under any other enactment.
 (6) This section is without prejudice to—
 (a) any power conferred on the Secretary of State by any other enactment to authorise the stopping up or diversion of a road,
 (b) section 3 of the Acquisition of Land (Authorisation Procedure) (Scotland) Act 1947, or
 (c) section 206(1)(a).

DEFINITIONS
 "apparatus": s.164(1) of the New Roads and Street Works Act 1991 (c.22).
 "government department": s.277(1).
 "local roads authority": s.277(1).
 "planning permission": Pt. III.
 "road": s.151(1) of the Roads (Scotland) Act 1984 (c.54).

"statutory undertakers": s.214(1).
"trunk road": s.151(1) of the Roads (Scotland) Act 1984 (c.54).

GENERAL NOTE
It will be apparent that one adjunct to the granting of a planning permission may be an effect on roadways which wholly or partly cross the land receiving the benefit of the planning permission. For example, the re-development of many town centres for retail purposes has involved the site being developed in such a way so as to physically block existing roadways.

Two consequences flow from such developments; the first is that the traffic using these roadways must be re-directed, particularly where the former roadways formed part of a through route. Secondly, where a roadway is adopted on to the list of public highways kept by the roads authority for the area, a public right of passage over the *solum* of the roadway is created (Roads (Scotland) Act 1984, s.1(1)), and this will conflict with the intended development, and very likely create a problem with intending developers, unless extinguished.

Prior to April 1, 1996, local planning authorities were district councils, and roads authorities were regional councils in most areas. Notwithstanding the merging of functions into single unitary authorities, the responsible local authority must have regard to its separate powers and duties in exercising of the relevant legislation. There is no guarantee that the roads authority will exercise its powers in a way which will take account of facilitating a development which obtains planning permission by, for example, agreeing to stop-up roads affected by the grant.

Subs. (1)
Application can be made to the Secretary of State for the stopping-up or diversion of any "road" (interpreted by s.151(1) of the1984 Act as being "any road (including the verge) over which there is a public right of passage"), were this necessary to permit development to be carried out in accordance with a planning permission, or else to allow a "Government Department" (which may enjoy certain forms of deemed consent under the GDO) to carry out such a development.

Where a road is stopped-up, the effect is two-fold; first, the public right of passage over the section of roadway affected may cease as from the time of the stopping-up (*cf.* s.68(4) of the 1984 Act). Secondly, the *solum* of the roadway vests in each of the adjacent proprietors fronting the topped-up section (*ibid.*, s.68(5)). This second provision is also helpful on occasions in the process of assembling land for developments, since the effect is the same whether or not the order is made under the 1984 Act or any other enactment (*ibid.*, s.68(5)) (For the powers of planning authorities in this regard, see the Note to s.207 below).

Subss. (2), (3)
Part of the process of stopping-up a roadway under this section may include the provision of an alternative route for the displaced traffic, or else the improvement of an existing roadway in order to improve its capacity. Subsection (2) establishes that requirements to this effect may form part of a s.202 stopping-up order. Provision for any roadway subject to this order being adopted for maintenance can also be made in the order.

This can occur either by adding any roadway so constructed or improved to the list of highways of the local roads authority, who will thereafter have the responsibility for future maintenance, or else become a trunk road, in which case, the responsibility rests with the Secretary of State (Roads (Scotland) Act 1984, s.2).

Subss. (4), (5)
These two subsections set out further incidental provisions to a s.202 stopping-up order. The more important provision appears in subs. (4), where the Secretary of State is granted the power to require the payment of the cost of any works arising from the making of the stopping-up order, or else the making of a contribution thereto. This power can be exercised against the relevant local authority, private persons, or else the Secretary of State himself (subs. (4)(a)). This power is exerciseable whether or not provision of an alternative roadway or improvement of an existing roadway is required as part of the stopping-up order.

Provision is also made for protecting the position of "statutory undertakers" in relation to any apparatus located within or adjacent to the stopped-up section of roadway (subs. (4)(b)). A stopping-up order is not prevented from being made where temporary stopping-up or diversion orders made under the 1984 Act are already in force over the relevant section of roadway (subs. (5)).

Subs. (6)
This subsection preserves other rights of the Secretary of State to exercise powers to stop-up roadways or to extinguish public rights of way under other legislation.

Powers of local authorities to extinguish certain rights

Order extinguishing right to use vehicles on road

203.—(1) This section applies where—

(a) a competent authority by resolution adopt a proposal for improving the amenity of part of their area, and

(b) the proposal involves a road in that area (being a road over which the public have a right of way with vehicles, but not a trunk road or a road classified as a principal road for the purposes of advances under section 3 of the Roads (Scotland) Act 1984) being changed to a footpath or bridleway.

(2) Subject to paragraph 5 of Schedule 16 and to subsection (9), the competent authority may by order provide for the extinguishment of any right which persons may have to use vehicles on that road.

(3) An order made under subsection (2) may include such provision as the competent authority (after consultation with the planning authority and the roads authority, if different from the competent authority) think fit for permitting the use on the road of vehicles (whether mechanically propelled or not) in such cases as may be specified in the order, notwithstanding the extinguishment of any such right as is mentioned in that subsection.

(4) Such provision as is mentioned in subsection (3) may be framed by reference to—

(a) particular descriptions of vehicles,

(b) particular persons by whom, or on whose authority, vehicles may be used, or

(c) the circumstances in which, or the times at which, vehicles may be used for particular purposes.

(5) No provision contained in, or having effect under, any enactment, being a provision prohibiting or restricting the use of footpaths or bridleways, shall affect any use of a vehicle on a road in relation to which an order made under subsection (2) has effect, where the use is permitted in accordance with provisions of the order included by virtue of subsections (3) and (4).

(6) Without prejudice to section 275(7), the competent authority may, subject to paragraph 5 of Schedule 16 and to subsection (9), by order revoke an order made by them in relation to a road under subsection (2); and if they do so, any right to use vehicles on the road in relation to which the order was made which was extinguished by virtue of the order under subsection (2) shall be reinstated.

(7) An order under this section—

(a) may make such provision as appears to the competent authority to be necessary or expedient for the construction or improvement of any other road (not being a trunk road such as is mentioned in paragraph (a), or a special road such as is mentioned in paragraph (b), of section 207(1)) and may direct that the other road so constructed or improved shall be entered by the local roads authority in the list of public roads kept by the local roads authority under section 1 of the Roads (Scotland) Act 1984, and

(b) may contain such incidental and consequential provisions as appear to the competent authority to be necessary or expedient, including in particular—

(i) provision for authorising the competent authority, or requiring any other authority or person specified in the order, to make such payments, repayments or contributions as are mentioned in section 202(4)(a), and

(ii) such provision as is mentioned in section 202(4)(b).

(8) This section is without prejudice to—

(a) any power conferred on the competent authority by any other enactment to authorise the stopping up or diversion of a road, or

(b) section 206(1)(b).

(9) The competent authorities for the purposes of this section and section 204 are local authorities, and a competent authority shall not make an order under subsection (2) or (6), if they are not the roads authority, without obtaining the consent of that authority.

DEFINITIONS

"bridleway": s.277(1).
"competent authorities": s.203(9).
"footpath: s.277(1).
"road": s.151(1) of the Roads (Scotland) Act 1984 (c.54).
"special road": s.151(1) of the Roads (Scotland) Act 1984 (c.54).
"trunk road": ss.7, 151(1) of the Roads (Scotland) Act 1984 (c.54).

GENERAL NOTE

Given that powers are given to planning authorities which are similar to those granted the Secretary of State under s.202 (See subs. (8) and Note to s.207 below), it is a little puzzling to see a different range of powers appearing in the following section. The powers granted by s.203 are exerciseable by "competent authorities" (local authorities by virtue of subs. (9)) in the interests of "improving the amenity of part of their area", rather than on foot of a specific planning permission.

The intention is to grant powers akin to that involving making stopping-up orders, where such a proposal entails changes to the relevant roads network which terminate or amend rights of vehicular passage and replace it with a footpath or bridleway. This power cannot be used in relation to roads (trunk and special roads) which fall under the control of the Secretary of State (subs. (1)).

The power can be used to effect a total or partial removal of vehicles from the sections of road affected by the order. The order can allow specified classes of vehicle, vehicles used by designated operators (*e.g.* fire and ambulance vehicles), or vehicles at certain times or in given circumstances to use the road lawfully after the order is in effect (subss. (2)–(5)).

The Order is capable of being revoked by a "competent authority", thereby re-instating the general right of vehicular passage (subs. (6)). Powers similar to s.202(4) are also granted, allowing the Order to deal with the construction of new roads or the improvement of existing roads, and for an obligation to make contributions to the costs thereof to be imposed. Orders under subss. (2) or (6) cannot be made unless the roads authority is consulted, where this is different from the "competent authority" (s.203(9)).

The procedure for making a s.203 Order is set out more fully in Sched. 16 (see Note below). Where a proposed s.203 Order is the subject of objection, confirmation must be undertaken by the Secretary of State. (Sched. 16, para. 5(1)).

Compensation for orders under section 203

204.—(1) Any person who, at the time of an order under section 203(2) coming into force, has an interest in land having lawful access to a road to which the order relates shall be entitled to be compensated by the competent authority in respect of—

(a) any depreciation in the value of his interest which is directly attributable to the order, and

(b) any other loss or damage which is so attributable.

(2) A claim for compensation under subsection (1) shall be made to the competent authority within the prescribed time and in the prescribed manner.

(3) For the purpose of assessing any such compensation the rules set out in section 12 of the Land Compensation (Scotland) Act 1963 shall, so far as applicable and subject to any necessary modifications, have effect as they have effect for the purpose of assessing compensation for the compulsory acquisition of an interest in land.

(4) Where an interest in land is subject to a heritable security—

(a) any compensation to which this section applies, which is payable in respect of depreciation of the value of that interest, shall be assessed as if the interest were not subject to the security,

(b) a claim for any such compensation may be made by any creditor in a heritable security over the interest, but without prejudice to the making of a claim by the person entitled to the interest,

(c) no compensation to which this section applies shall be payable in respect of the interest of the creditor in the heritable security (as distinct from the interest which is subject to the security), and

(d) any compensation to which this section applies which is payable in respect of the interest which is subject to the heritable security shall be paid to the creditor in the security, or if there is more than one such creditor, to the creditor whose security ranks first, and shall in either case be applied by him as if it were proceeds of sale by him under the powers competent to creditors in heritable securities.

(5) Except in so far as may be provided by any regulations made under this Act, any question of disputed compensation under this section shall be referred to and determined by the Lands Tribunal.

(6) In relation to the determination of any such question, the provisions of sections 9 and 11 of the Land Compensation (Scotland) Act 1963 shall apply subject to any necessary modifications and to the provisions of any regulations made under this Act.

DEFINITIONS
"competent authority": s.203(9).
"compulsory acquisition": s.277(1).
"heritable security": s.277(1).
"land": s.277(1).
"Lands Tribunal": s.277(1).
"road": s.151(1) of the Roads (Scotland) Act 1984 (c.54).

GENERAL NOTE
The making of an order under s.203(2) can potentially have the effect of making access to land impossible or more difficult once the general right of vehicular access over an existing road is extinguished. (Presumably, in the case of, say, the sole access to a field, judicious use of the s.203(4) power might be helpful).

Where this occurs, any person having an interest in land thereby affected is entitled to make a claim for compensation against the "competent authority" on the bases specified in subss. (1) and (4), again applying the principles of the Land Compensation (Scotland) Act 1963 (c.51) (subss. (3), (6)). Scope exists for reference to the lands tribunal in the event of dispute over the level of compensation (subs. (5)).

Provision of amenity for road reserved to pedestrians

205.—(1) Where an order has been made under section 203(2) in relation to a road, a competent authority may carry out and maintain any such works on or in the road, or place on or in it any such objects or structures, as appear to them—

(a) to be expedient for the purposes of—
   (i) giving effect to the order, or
   (ii) enhancing the amenity of the road and its immediate surroundings, or

(b) to be otherwise desirable for a purpose beneficial to the public.

(2) The powers exercisable by a competent authority under this section include—

(a) laying out any part of the road with lawns, trees, shrubs and flowerbeds, and

(b) providing facilities for recreation or refreshment.

(3) A competent authority may so exercise their powers under this section as to restrict the access of the public to any part of the road, but shall not so exercise them as—

(a) to prevent persons from entering the road at any place where they could enter it before the order under section 203 was made,

(b) to prevent the passage of the public along the road,

(c) to prevent normal access by pedestrians to premises adjoining the road,

(d) to prevent any use of vehicles which is permitted by an order made under section 203 and applying to the road,

(e) to prevent statutory undertakers from having access to any works of theirs under, in, on, over, along or across the road, or

(f) to prevent the operator of any telecommunications code system from having access to any works of his under, in, on, over, along or across the road.

(4) An order under section 203(6) may make provision requiring the removal of any obstruction of the road resulting from the exercise by a competent authority of their powers under this section.

(5) The competent authorities for the purposes of this section are local authorities, and a competent authority shall not exercise any powers conferred by this section, if they are not the roads authority, without obtaining the consent of that authority.

DEFINITIONS
"competent authority": s.205(5).
"road": s.151(1) if the Roads (Scotland) Act 1984 (c.54).
"statutory undertakers": s.214(1).

GENERAL NOTE
This section sets out a range of subsidiary provisions to the powers conferred on "competent authorities" by virtue of the greater power of s.203 to stop-up roads on amenity grounds.

Thus, parts of the stopped-up road (which can include all or part of the associated verge (s.151(1) of the Roads (Scotland) Act 1984), can become subject to construction of "any works" which are consequent upon the making of the s.203 Order, or which will enhance amenity or public benefit. This can include acts such as laying out park areas or providing "recreation or refreshment facilities" (subs. (2)). It is submitted that the non-exhaustive nature of the powers exerciseable in this regard provided by subs. (2), does not prevent other acts which are justifiable on amenity grounds from being carried out.

Other parts of the section restrict the use of s.205 powers in the five circumstances set out in subs. (3), which are designed primarily to avoid conflict with the provisions of s.203. Provision is made in subs. (4) for the effects of revocation of a s.203 Order, although retention of any obstructions on a re-instated road would seem to conflict with ss.83 and 87 of the Roads (Scotland) Act 1984. Again, provision is made for consultation with the roads authority where that is not the same as the "competent authority" in the exercise of s.205 powers (subs. (6)).

Extinguishment of public rights of way over land held for planning purposes

206.—(1) Where any land has been acquired or appropriated for planning purposes and is for the time being held by a local authority for the purposes for which it was acquired or appropriated—

(a) the Secretary of State may by order extinguish any public right of way over the land if he is satisfied that an alternative right of way has been or will be provided or that the provision of an alternative right of way is not required;

(b) subject to paragraph 5 of Schedule 16, the local authority may by order extinguish any such right over the land if they are so satisfied.

(2) In this section any reference to the acquisition or appropriation of land for planning purposes shall be construed in accordance with section 201 as if this section were in Part VIII.

DEFINITIONS
"land": s.271(1).
"planning purposes": s.201(1).

GENERAL NOTE
This section makes further provision relative to the consequences of any acquisition or appropriation of land "for planning purposes" see s.201(1)).

As was indicated in the Note to s.194, the continued existence of private rights of way subsequent to such an acquisition or appropriation could render the land hard to develop. The same is obviously true of existing public rights of way.

Accordingly, provided that it continues to hold the land "for planning purposes", a "local authority" can apply to the Secretary of State for the extinguishment of such rights, or else, may make such an order itself. It cannot, however, do so where objections to the proposed order are received (Sched. 16, para. 5(1)), and must leave confirmation to the Secretary of State. In either instance, confirmation is dependent upon the confirming body being satisfied that an alternative "right of way" (the section does not say this must be a public right of way) will be provided, or else that an alternative is not required (subs. (1)).

Powers of planning authorities to stop up roads, etc.

Roads affected by development: orders by planning authorities

207.—(1) Subject to paragraph 5 of Schedule 16 and to subsection (5), a planning authority may by order authorise the stopping up or diversion of any road which is not—

(a) a trunk road within the meaning of the Roads (Scotland) Act 1984, or

(b) a special road provided by the Secretary of State in pursuance of a scheme under that Act,

if they are satisfied that it is necessary to do so in order to enable the development to be carried out in accordance with planning permission granted under Part III, or by a government department.

(2) An order under this section—

(a) may make such provision as appears to the planning authority to be necessary or expedient for the construction or improvement of any other road (not being a trunk road such as is mentioned in paragraph (a), or a special road such as is mentioned in paragraph (b), of subsection (1)) and may direct that the other road so constructed or improved shall be entered by the local roads authority in the list of public roads kept by the local roads authority under section 1 of the Roads (Scotland) Act 1984, and

(b) may contain such incidental and consequential provisions as appear to the planning authority to be necessary or expedient, including in particular—

(i) provision for authorising the planning authority, or requiring any other authority or person specified in the order, to make such payments, repayments or contributions as are mentioned in section 202(4)(a), and

(ii) such provision as is mentioned in section 202(4)(b).

(3) An order may be made under this section authorising the stopping up or diversion of any road (not being a trunk road such as is mentioned in paragraph (a), or a special road such as is mentioned in paragraph (b), of subsection (1)) which is temporarily stopped up or diverted under any other enactment.

(4) This section is without prejudice to any power conferred on the planning authority by any other enactment to authorise the stopping up or diversion of a road.

(5) The planning authority shall not make an order under this section without consulting the roads authority (in a case where they are themselves not that authority).

DEFINITIONS
"planning authority": s.1(1).
"planning permission": Pt. III.
"special road": ss.7, 151(1) of the Roads (Scotland) Act 1984 (c.54).
"trunk road": s.151(1) of the Roads (Scotland) Act 1984 (c.54).

GENERAL NOTE
As will have been apparent from consideration of s.202, the Secretary of State has long been able to authorise the stopping-up of roads as a necessary consequence of the granting of a planning permission, or any development by a government department which does not require planning permission. No such power beyond promotion of orders rested with the then local authorities, and it was cumbersome to have all such orders adjudicated upon by the Scottish Office. The Local Government, Planning and Land Act 1980 (c.65) added s.198A to the 1972 Act in order to devolve parts of this function to local and general planning authorities.

Accordingly, planning authorities enjoy – subject to exceptions aftermentioned – the same power as the Secretary of State has under s.202 to make stopping-up orders as an adjunct to planning permissions. The exceptions are that s.207 Orders cannot affect trunk or special roads (subs. (1)), and must be put to the Secretary of State for confirmation where they are subject to objection (Sched. 16, para. 5(1)). Again, consultation is required with the relevant roads authority, where different to the planning authority (subs. (5)), although this is less likely to be required given the inability of such orders to affect trunk or special roads.

Similar powers to those conferred on the Secretary of State by virtue of s.202(4), in relation to requirements for construction of a replacement road or improvement of an existing road, and for expenditure, or for the requirement of contributions from private persons, are repeated in relation to planning authorities in subs. (2). There is no restriction on the exercise of the power in a local authority to make a s.207 Order, where a temporary stopping-up or diversion order is in effect (most likely under the Roads (Scotland) Act 1984 (c.54)) (subs. (3)). Exercise of the power is without prejudice to any powers of the planning authority under any other enactment to impose a stopping-up order (subs. (4)).

Footpaths and bridleways affected by development: orders by planning authorities

208.—(1) Subject to paragraph 5 of Schedule 16, a planning authority may by order authorise the stopping up or diversion of any footpath or bridleway if they are satisfied that it is necessary to do so in order to enable the development to be carried out—

    (a) in accordance with planning permission granted under Part III, or

    (b) by a government department.

(2) An order under this section may, if the planning authority are satisfied that it should do so, provide—

    (a) for the creation of an alternative footpath or bridleway for use as a replacement for the one authorised by the order to be stopped up or diverted, or for the improvement of an existing path or way for such use;

    (b) for authorising or requiring works to be carried out in relation to any footpath or bridleway for whose stopping up or diversion, creation or improvement, provision is made by the order;

    (c) for the preservation of any rights of statutory undertakers in respect of apparatus of theirs which immediately before the date of the order is under, in, on, over, along or across any such footpath or bridleway;

    (d) for requiring any person named in the order to pay, or make contributions in respect of, the cost of carrying out any such works.

(3) An order may be made under this section authorising the stopping up or diversion of a footpath or bridleway which is temporarily stopped up or diverted under any other enactment.

DEFINITIONS
"bridleway": s.47 of the Countryside (Scotland) Act 1967 (c.86).
"footpath": s.47 of the Countryside (Scotland) Act 1967 (c.86).
"planning authority": s.1(1).
"planning permission": Pt. III.

GENERAL NOTE
As with the extinguishment of public rights of way and the stopping-up of roads in furtherance of a planning permission or development by a government department mentioned above, similar provisions are made in s.208 to enable planning authorities to stop-up or divert footpaths or bridleways established under the Countryside (Scotland) Act 1967 (c.86). In essence these are

paths over which a public right of access, falling short of a public right of way, exists necessitating different provision for their stopping-up. In this instance, however, a specific provision is made for protection of the rights of statutory undertakers (subs. (2)(c)).

It seems that there is no obligation for the planning authority to require the provision of an alternative or diverted footpath or bridleway, in view of the permissive language of subs. (2). Again, Sched. 16, para. 5 applies in relation to orders under s.208 to which objection is made.

Procedure

Procedure for making and confirming orders by Secretary of State and planning authorities

209. Schedule 16 shall have effect in relation to the procedure for the making and confirming of orders under this Part by the Secretary of State and planning authorities.

GENERAL NOTE

This section applies the provisions of Sched. 16 to the procedure for making of any of the orders referred to in Pt. IX.

Recovery of costs of making orders

210.—(1) Where a person requests a local authority to make an order to which this subsection applies, the local authority may require him, as a condition of their compliance with the request, to make such provision as they consider reasonable as regards any costs to be incurred by them in so complying.

(2) The orders to which subsection (1) applies are orders under any of the following enactments—

(a) section 203 (orders extinguishing the right to use vehicles on a road);

(b) section 207 (orders authorising the stopping up or diversion of certain roads);

(c) section 208 (orders authorising the stopping up or diversion of footpaths or bridleways);

(d) section 34 of the Countryside (Scotland) Act 1967 (orders as regards the closure of public paths); and

(e) section 35 of that Act (orders as regards the diversion of public paths).

DEFINITIONS

"local authority": s.277(1).

GENERAL NOTE

Section 45 of the Local Government and Planning Act 1982 (c.43), broadened the power of a local authority in relation to the making of some of the orders which it was empowered to make under the 1972 Act and the Countryside (Scotland) Act 1967 (subs. (2)). It is certainly conceivable that the effect on the owner of a property subject to a planning permission where such an order is made, might be greater on the individual than to the locality overall. However, in the absence of any express power, it was doubtful whether a local authority could make such orders at the request of private persons, where it would not have done so of its own volition.

Section 210A of the 1972 Act (now s.210) makes clear, first, that making such a localised order is possible, and secondly, that the local authority can seek to recover the costs in making such an order from the person who made the request (subs. (1)).

Supplementary provisions

Concurrent proceedings in connection with roads

211.—(1) In relation to orders under sections 202, 203 and 207, regulations made under this Act may make provision for securing that any proceedings required to be taken for the purposes of the acquisition of land under section 104(1)(b)(i) of the Roads (Scotland) Act 1984 may be taken concurrently with any proceedings required to be taken for the purposes of the order.

(2) In relation to orders under section 206(1)(a) or (b), regulations may make provision for securing—

(a) that any proceedings required to be taken for the purposes of such an order may be taken concurrently with any proceedings required to be taken for the purposes of the acquisition of the land over which the right of way is to be extinguished, or

(b) that any proceedings required to be taken for the purposes of the acquisition of any other land under section 104(1)(b)(ii) of the Roads (Scotland) 1984 Act may be taken concurrently with either or both of the proceedings referred to in the preceding paragraph.

DEFINITIONS
  "land": s.277(1).

GENERAL NOTE
  This section ensures that the making of orders under various sections contained in Pt. IX, does not prejudice the exercise of other powers vested in the Secretary of State under s.104 of the Roads (Scotland) Act 1984 to make orders and schemes, or for acquisition of land over which a public right of way is to be extinguished prospectively by virtue of s.206.

Telecommunication apparatus

212.—(1) Where in pursuance of an order under section 202, 203 or 207 a road is stopped up, diverted or changed and immediately before the date on which the order became operative there was under, in, on, over, along or across the road any telecommunication apparatus kept installed for the purposes of a telecommunications code system, the operator of that system shall have the same powers in respect of the telecommunication apparatus as if the order had not come into force.

(2) Notwithstanding subsection (1), any person entitled to land over which the road subsisted shall be entitled to require the alteration of the apparatus.

(3) Where—

(a) any such order provides for the improvement of a road for which the Secretary of State is not the roads authority, and

(b) immediately before the date on which the order came into force, there was under, in, on, over, along or across the road any telecommunication apparatus kept installed for the purposes of a telecommunications code system,

the local roads authority shall be entitled to require the alteration of the apparatus.

(4) Subsection (3) does not have effect so far as it relates to the alteration of any telecommunication apparatus for the purpose of authority's works within the meaning of Part IV of the New Roads and Street Works Act 1991.

(5) Where an order under section 206(1)(b) extinguishing a public right of way or an order under section 208 authorising the stopping up or diversion of any footpath or bridleway is made by a planning authority and, at the time of the publication of the notice required by paragraph 6 of Schedule 16, any telecommunication apparatus was kept installed for the purposes of a telecommunications code system under, in, on, over, along or across the land over which the right of way subsisted—

(a) the power of the operator of the system to remove the apparatus shall, notwithstanding the making of the order, be exercisable at any time not later than the end of the period of 3 months from the date on which the right of way is extinguished or, as the case may be, the footpath or bridleway is stopped up or diverted and shall be exercisable in respect of the whole or any part of the apparatus after the end of that period if before the end of that period the operator of the system has given notice to the authority which made the order of his intention to remove the apparatus or that part of it, as the case may be;

   (b) the operator of the system may by notice given to the authority which made the order not later than the end of the said period of 3 months abandon the telecommunication apparatus or any part of it;

   (c) subject to paragraph (b), the operator of the system shall be deemed at the end of that period to have abandoned any part of the apparatus which the operator has then neither removed nor given notice of his intention to remove;

   (d) the operator of the system shall be entitled to recover from the authority which made the order the expense of providing, in substitution for the apparatus and any other telecommunication apparatus connected with it which is rendered useless in consequence of the removal or abandonment of the first-mentioned apparatus, any telecommunication apparatus in such other place as the operator may require; and

   (e) where under the preceding provisions of this subsection the operator of the system has abandoned the whole or any part of any telecommunication apparatus that apparatus or that part of it shall vest in the authority which made the order and shall be deemed, with its abandonment, to cease to be kept installed for the purposes of a telecommunications code system.

   (6) As soon as reasonably practicable after the making of any such order as is mentioned in subsection (5) in circumstances in which that subsection applies in relation to the operator of any telecommunications code system, the authority which made the order shall give notice to the operator of the making of the order.

   (7) Paragraph 1(2) of the telecommunications code (alteration of apparatus to include moving, removal or replacement of apparatus) shall apply for the purposes of the preceding provisions of this section as it applies for the purposes of that code.

   (8) Paragraph 21 of the telecommunications code (restriction on removal of telecommunication apparatus) shall apply in relation to any entitlement conferred by this section to require the alteration, moving or replacement of any telecommunication apparatus as it applies in relation to an entitlement to require the removal of any such apparatus.

DEFINITIONS
   "bridleway": s.47 of the Countryside (Scotland) Act 1967 (c.86).
   "footpath": s.47 of the Countryside (Scotland) Act 1967 (c.86).
   "land": s.277(1).
   "roads": s.151(1) of the Roads (Scotland) Act 1984 (c.54).
   "telecommunications apparatus": para. 1, Sched. 1 to the Telecommunications Act 1984 (c.12).
   "telecommunications code system": s.106(1) of the Telecommunications Act 1984 (c.12).

GENERAL NOTE
   This section provides protection to the operators of "Telecommunications apparatus" or systems located in, on, over, roads which are stopped-up, diverted or changed by virtue of orders made under Pt. IX (subs. (1)). Whilst the right to operate the "apparatus" is preserved, alteration thereof can be required in the circumstances narrated in subss. (2) and (3). Slightly fuller provisions are made for circumstances where a public right of way, footpath or bridleway are stopped-up or altered or diverted (subs. (5)).

Temporary road orders: mineral workings

Temporary stopping up of roads, footpaths and bridleways for mineral workings

   213.—(1) Where the Secretary of State is satisfied—

   (a) that an order under section 202 for the stopping up or diversion of a public road is required for the purpose of enabling minerals to be worked by surface working, and

(b) that the road can be restored, after the minerals have been worked, to a condition not substantially less convenient to the public,
the order may provide for the stopping up or diversion of the road during such period as may be prescribed by or under the order and for its restoration at the expiration of that period.

(2) Where a planning authority are so satisfied in respect of an order under section 207, the order may so provide.

(3) Where a planning authority are satisfied—

(a) that an order under section 208 for the stopping up or diversion of a footpath or bridleway is required for the purpose of enabling minerals to be worked by surface working, and

(b) that the footpath or bridleway can be restored, after the minerals have been worked, to a condition not substantially less convenient to the public,
the order may provide for the stopping up or diversion of the footpath or bridleway during such period as may be prescribed by or under the order and for its restoration at the expiration of that period.

(4) Without prejudice to the provisions of section 202, 207 or 208, where provision is made in any order by virtue of subsection (1), (2) or (3) that order may also contain such provisions as appear to the Secretary of State or, as the case may be, the planning authority to be expedient—

(a) for imposing upon persons who, apart from the order, would be subject to any liability with respect to the repair of the original road, footpath or bridleway during the period prescribed by or under the order a corresponding liability in respect of any road, footpath or bridleway provided in pursuance of the order;

(b) for the stopping up at the expiry of that period of any road, footpath or bridleway so provided and for the reconstruction and maintenance of the original road, footpath or bridleway;
and any provision included in the order in accordance with section 202(4), section 207(2) or section 208(2) requiring payment to be made in respect of any cost or expenditure under the order may provide for the payment of a capital sum in respect of the estimated amount of that cost or expenditure.

(5) In relation to any road which is stopped up or diverted by virtue of an order under section 202 or 207, sections 224 and 225 shall have effect as if—

(a) for references to land which has been acquired as there mentioned and to the purchasing authority there were substituted respectively references to land over which the road subsisted and to the person entitled to possession of that land, and

(b) references in subsection (6) of each of those sections to a planning authority or statutory undertaker included references to any person (other than the Secretary of State) who is entitled to possession of that land,
and sections 228 to 231 shall have effect accordingly.

DEFINITIONS
"bridleway": s.47 of the Countryside (Scotland) Act 1967 (c.86).
"footpath": s.47 of the Countryside (Scotland) Act 1967 (c.86).
"minerals": s.277(1).
"planning authority": s.1(1).
"road": s.151(1) of the Roads (Scotland) Act 1984 (c.54).

GENERAL NOTE
This section imports provisions from the Mineral Working Act 1951 (c.60) to circumstances where the working of minerals from the surface involves the stopping-up or diversion of public roads, footpaths or bridleways, during the period of extraction of the minerals. In such circumstances, the Secretary of State (in relation to public roads (subs. (1)), and a planning authority in relation to all three (subs. (2) and (3))) can provide in making orders under the relevant sections of Pt. IX that such orders shall subsist only for the period of extraction. This power can be

exercised where restoration of the stopped-up sections can be undertaken to a "condition not substantially less convenient to the public".

Such an order can impose liability for payment for repair of temporary replacement roads, footpaths and bridleways, and for the stopping-up of these upon expiry of the order. This can be undertaken in the form of a commuted capital payment to the Secretary of State or the planning authority (subs. (4)). Provision is again made in relation to the position of statutory undertakers whose rights are affected by an order, modified by virtue of s.213, effecting the stopping-up of a road (subs. (5)). (See also ss.224 and 225).

The section has been modified slightly at the recommendation of the Scottish Law Commission in order to apply the charging regime to those matters covered under s.198A(2) of the 1972 Act. (See *Scottish Law Commission Report No. 157*, (1996), Recommendation 12.)

Part X

Statutory Undertakers

Preliminary

Meaning of "statutory undertakers"

214.—(1) Subject to the following provisions of this section, in this Act "statutory undertakers" means persons authorised by any enactment to carry on any railway, light railway, tramway, road transport, water transport, canal, inland navigation, dock, harbour, pier or lighthouse undertaking or any undertaking for the supply of hydraulic power or water and a relevant airport operator (within the meaning of Part V of the Airports Act 1986).

(2) Subject to the following provisions of this section, in this Act "statutory undertaking" shall be construed in accordance with subsection (1) and, in relation to a relevant airport operator (within the meaning of Part V of the Airports Act 1986), means an airport to which that Part of that Act applies.

(3) Subject to subsection (5), for the purposes of the provisions mentioned in subsection (4) any public gas transporter, the Post Office and the Civil Aviation Authority shall be deemed to be statutory undertakers and their undertakings statutory undertakings.

(4) The provisions referred to in subsection (3) are sections 26, 57, 69, 70, 77(3), 90 to 92, 94, 99, 121(11)(b), 194(2)(a), 196 to 198, 200, 202(4)(b), 205(3)(e), 208(2), 215(1) and (2), 216, 218, 219, 221 to 236, 239(10)(a), 255, 270(9), 277(2) and (3), and Schedules 6, 7, 14 and 16.

(5) Subsection (4) shall apply—

(a) as respects the Post Office, as if the reference to sections 26, 194(2)(a), 196, 200, 202(4)(b), 205(3)(e), 208(2), 215(1) and (2) and 277(2) and (3) were omitted;

(b) as respects the Civil Aviation Authority, as if the references to sections 200, 215(1) and (2) and 277(2) and (3) were omitted and the reference to Schedule 16 included the words "except paragraph 3"; and

(c) as respects any public gas transporter, as if the reference to Schedule 7 were omitted and the reference to Schedule 16 included the words "except paragraphs 1 and 3".

(6) Any holder of a licence under section 6 of the Electricity Act 1989 shall be deemed to be a statutory undertaker and his undertaking a statutory undertaking—

(a) for the purposes of the provisions mentioned in subsection (7)(a), if he holds a licence under subsection (1) of that section;

(b) for the purposes of the provisions mentioned in subsection (7)(b), if he is entitled to exercise any power conferred by Schedule 3 to that Act; and

(c) for the purposes of the provisions mentioned in subsection (7)(c), if he is entitled to exercise any power conferred by paragraph 2 of Schedule 4 to that Act.

(7) The provisions referred to in subsection (6) are—

    (a) sections 26, 77(3), 90 to 92, 94, 99, 194(2)(a), 196, 200, 205(3)(e), 215(1)
         and (2), 216, 218, 219, 221 to 236, 239(10)(a), 255, 270(9), 277(2) and
         (3), Schedule 14 and paragraphs 2(2)(a) and (3)(a) of Schedule 16;
    (b) sections 121(11)(b), 197 and 198; and
    (c) sections 202(4)(b) and 208(2) and paragraphs 1, 6(2)(b)(iii) and (3),
         8(5) and (7) and 9(1), (3) and (4) of Schedule 16.

DEFINITIONS
    "enactment": s.277(1).
    "land": s.277(1).
    "public gas transporter": Pt. I of the Gas Act 1986 (c.44).

GENERAL NOTE
    Statutory undertakers are bodies authorised by any public general, private or local enactment
to carry on any of the undertakings specified in subs. (1). Many of the privatised industries have
lost their automatic status as statutory undertakers, although under subs. (3) any public gas
transporter is deemed to be a statutory undertaker. Similarly, subs. (6) provides for the holder of
a licence under the Electricity Act 1989 (c.29) to be deemed a statutory undertaker for the
purposes of certain provisions of this Act. Whereas in England and Wales, the Environment
Agency is deemed to be a statutory undertaker under the Town and Country Planning Act 1990
(c.8), similar provisions have not been introduced in Scotland through this Act in respect of the
Scottish Environment Protection Agency. Telecommunication operators are deemed to be
statutory undertakers for some of the provisions of this Act. This is noted under the relevant
sections.

Principle modifications of planning control in the case of statutory undertakers
    (1) Applications for planning permission under Pt. III follow normal procedure. However
s.218 requires applications for planning permission called-in by the Secretary of State, appeals to
the Secretary of State and appeals against enforcement notices to be determined jointly by the
Secretary of State and the "appropriate Minister" as defined by s.217. Similarly, s.221 and s.222
respectively apply the same arrangements in respect of revocation, modification and discontinuance orders made under Pt. III.
    (2) Where a purchase notice under s.88 has been served on a planning authority, the Secretary
of State may require that the relevant statutory undertaker acquire the land instead (s.92(4)).
Statutory undertakers may also constitute the "appropriate authority" on whom a blight notice
may be served under s.120 and Sched. 14.
    (3) The rights of statutory undertakers are not automatically extinguished upon compulsory
acquisition of their land under Pt. VIII. Section 224 (statutory undertakers) and s.225 (telecommunications code system operators) contain a detailed notification procedure. Paragraph 10 of
Sched. 1 to the Acquisition of Land (Authorisation Procedure) (Scotland) Act 1947 (c.42) confers a degree of protection upon land acquired by statutory undertakers for the purposes of their
undertaking. However, s.223 of the 1997 Act disapplies para. 10 of Sched. 1 of the 1947 Act
where an order has been made or confirmed by the appropriate Minister acting jointly with the
relevant Minister or Ministers.
    (4) Planning permission is not required for the purpose of inspecting, repairing or removing
any sewers, mains, pipes, cables or other apparatus, including the breaking open of any road or
other land for that purpose (s.26(a)(c)).
    (5) Planning conditions requiring the removal of any building or works or the discontinuance
of any permitted use cannot be granted without the consent of the statutory undertakers
concerned.
    (6) The Town and Country Planning (General Permitted Development) (Scotland) Order
1992 permits development by statutory undertakers for a wide range of activities most of which
are confined to operational land (see Sched. 1, Pt. 13). The Order also contains special provisions
in relation to development by telecommunications code system operators and aviation related
development.

Operational land
    The Act seeks to draw a distinction between land held by an undertaking for general purposes
and operational land as defined by s.215: see further notes to s.215.

Water authorities
    The Local Government etc. (Scotland) Act 1994 (c.39) established three new water author-
ities for Scotland with responsibility for water and sewerage in their areas. They are known as
the East of Scotland Water Authority; West of Scotland Water Authority and the North of

Scotland Water Authority. They are statutory undertakers under s.214(1) for the purposes of this Act and for the purposes of the Town and Country Planning (General Permitted Development) (Scotland) Order 1992 (S.I. 1992 No.223 (as amended)).

Civil Aviation Authority
    The Civil Aviation Authority ("CAA") provide air traffic control services to most Scottish aerodromes. The Civil Aviation Act 1982 (c.16) has provided the CAA with power to acquire land and rights over land and to impose restrictions on the use of land in the vicinity of aerodromes. The Authority is deemed to be a statutory undertaker for certain provisions of this Act (s.214(3)). In addition the Town and Country Planning (General Permitted Development) (Scotland) Order 1992, Sched. 1, Pt. 14 contains special provision for development by the CAA.

Relevant Airport Operators
    A "relevant airport operator" is defined in s.57(4) of the Airports Act 1986 (c.31). Part V of the Airports Act 1986 applies to all airports permitted to levy airport charges under Pt. IV and any airport owned or managed by any subsidiary of the CAA. It does not however apply to any airport owned by BAA. Under the GPDO the relevant airport operator enjoys extensive permitted development rights.

Transport Operators
    This category includes operators such as Railtrack, the newly privatised railway companies and other public transport operators.

The Post Office
    The Post Office is not a statutory undertaker but is deemed by subss. (3) to (5) to be so for certain purposes of the 1997 Act and for the purposes of the General Permitted Development Order 1992. Its operational land is defined by the Post Office Operational Land Regulations 1973 (S.I. 1973 No.310).

Public Gas Transporters
    Public gas transporters are bodies authorised by the Gas Act 1995 (c.45), s.5 to convey gas through pipes to any premises in their authorised area. They are not statutory undertakers, but are deemed to be so under subss. (3) to (5) for certain provisions of this Act and for the purposes of the General Permitted Development Order 1992.

Electricity Licence Holders
    Electricity licence holders are deemed to be statutory undertakers for various provisions of this 1997 Act, depending on the type of licence held under the Electricity Act 1989 (c.29). For the purposes of s.121 ("appropriate enactment" for blight purposes) and s.197 (provisions as to churches and burial grounds) statutory undertaker status is not conferred unless the licence includes the right to exercise any power conferred by Sched. 3 to the Electricity Act 1989 (power of compulsory acquisition of land).

Meaning of "operational land"

    215.—(1) Subject to the following provisions of this section and to section 216, in this Act "operational land" means, in relation to statutory undertakers—
        (a) land which is used for the purpose of carrying on their undertaking, and
        (b) land in which an interest is held for that purpose.
    (2) Paragraphs (a) and (b) of subsection (1) do not include land which, in respect of its nature and situation, is comparable rather with land in general than with land which is used, or in which interests are held, for the purpose of the carrying on of statutory undertakings.
    (3) In sections 77(3), 218 to 236 and paragraph 6 of Schedule 6 "operational land", in relation to the Post Office and the Civil Aviation Authority, means land of the Post Office's or, as the case may be, of the Authority's of any such class as may be prescribed by regulations.

(4) Such regulations—
(a) may define a class of land by reference to any circumstances whatsoever, and
(b) in the case of the Civil Aviation Authority, may make provision for different circumstances, including prescribing different classes of land for the purposes of different provisions.

(5) In the case of the Post Office or the Civil Aviation Authority, if any question arises as to whether land belonging to either of them falls within a class defined by such regulations, it shall be determined by the Secretary of State.

DEFINITIONS
"appropriate Minister": ss.217, 277(1).
"land": s.277(1).
"Minister": s.277(1).
"prescribed": s.277(1).
"statutory undertakings": ss.214, 277(1).

GENERAL NOTE
Many of the statutory provisions applicable to statutory undertakers extend only to their operational land. Operational land must be distinguished from land held for general purposes. For most statutory undertakings, the relevant rules are provided by this section. However for some (the Civil Aviation Authority and the Post Office) the definition is provided separately by regulations: see further below. Section 215 only applies to land purchased after December 8, 1969 unless s.216(3) or (4) applies: see commentary to s.216 below.

Subs. (1)
Subsection (1) defines two categories of operational land: (a) land which is used for the purposes of the undertaking concerned; (b) land in which an interest is held for that purpose. Thus, this provision covers land held for present or future operational use.

Subs. (2)
Subsection (2) draws a distinction between operational land as defined in subs. (1) and land which "is comparable rather with land in general". The distinction is of significance given that certain statutory provisions only apply to development of operational land. Whether land is comparable with land in general rather than land used for the purposes of the statutory undertaking is a question of fact depending upon all the circumstances of the case (*R. v. Minister of Fuel and Power, ex p. Warwickshire County Council* [1957] 1 WLR 861). Land held purely for investment is not operational land and is covered under subs. (2).

Subs. (3)
The operational land of the Post Office and the Civil Aviation Authority are defined in the following regulations:
(a) Post Office: the Post Office Operational Land Regulations 1973 (S.I. 1973 No.310), reg. 2 deems land owned by the Post Office to be operational land if it is used by it or in which an interest is held by it for any of the following purposes:
  (i) a postal office;
  (ii) a postmen's delivery office;
  (iii) the housing or supporting of apparatus used for the operation of the Post Office telecommunications services excluding therefrom the storage of such apparatus where such storage is the only purpose.
(b) Civil Aviation Authority: the Civil Aviation Authority (Operational Land Regulations 1985 (S.I. 1985 No.575), reg. 2 prescribes the following classes of land as the Authority's operational land if it is land which is used, or in which an interest is held by the CAA for:
  (i) the operation of an aerodrome or for any purpose ancillary to such use;
  (ii) the provision of facilities for the control of air traffic or for assisting the navigation of aircraft.

Subs. (5)
Any questions arising as to whether the land of the Post Office or the Civil Aviation Authority is operational land is to be determined by the Secretary of State.

Statutory undertakers. In addition to the undertakers within the definition of statutory undertakers in s.214(1), the following are deemed by virtue of s.214(3)–(7) to be statutory undertakers for the purposes of this section: any public gas transporter, the Post Office, the Civil Aviation Authority and electricity undertakers holding a licence under the s.6 of the Electricity Act 1989.

Cases in which land is to be treated as not being operational land

216.—(1) This section applies where an interest in land is held by statutory undertakers for the purpose of carrying on their undertaking and—

(a) the interest was acquired by them on or after 8th December 1969, or

(b) it was held by them immediately before that date but the circumstances were then such that the land did not fall to be treated as operational land for the purposes of the 1947 Act.

(2) Where this section applies in respect of any land then, notwithstanding the provisions of section 215, the land shall not be treated as operational land for the purposes of this Act unless it falls within subsection (3) or (4).

(3) Land falls within this subsection if—

(a) there is, or at some time has been, in force with respect to it a specific planning permission for its development, and

(b) that development, if carried out, would involve or have involved its use for the purpose of the carrying on of the statutory undertakers' undertaking.

(4) Land falls within this subsection if—

(a) the statutory undertakers' interest in the land was acquired by them as the result of a transfer under the provisions of the Transport Act 1968, the Gas Act 1986 or the Airports Act 1986 from other statutory undertakers, and

(b) immediately before transfer the land was operational land of those other undertakers.

(5) A specific planning permission for the purpose of subsection (3)(a) is a planning permission—

(a) granted on an application in that behalf made under Part III,

(b) granted by provisions of a development order granting planning permission generally for development which has received specific parliamentary approval,

(c) granted by a special development order in respect of development specifically described in the order,

(d) deemed to be granted by virtue of a direction of a government department under section 57(1), or

(e) deemed to be granted by virtue of paragraph 27 of Schedule 9 to the Post Office Act 1969.

(6) In subsection (5)—

(a) the reference in paragraph (a) to Part III includes a reference to Part III of the 1972 Act and the enactments in force before the commencement of that Act and replaced by Part III of it,

(b) the reference in paragraph (b) to development which has received specific parliamentary approval is a reference to development authorised—

(i) by a local or private Act of Parliament,

(ii) by an order approved by both Houses of Parliament, or

(iii) by an order which has been brought into operation in accordance with the provisions of the Statutory Orders (Special Procedure) Act 1945,

being an Act or order which designates specifically both the nature of the development authorised by it and the land upon which it may be carried out, and

(c) the reference in paragraph (d) to section 57(1) includes a reference to section 37 of the 1972 Act and section 32 of the 1947 Act.

(7) This section shall not apply to land in the case of which an interest of the Postmaster General's vested in the Post Office by virtue of section 16 of the Post Office Act 1969.

(8) Where an interest in land is held by the Civil Aviation Authority this section shall not apply for the purpose of determining whether the land is operational land in relation to the Authority for the purposes of this Act.

DEFINITIONS

"the 1947 Act": s.277(1).
"the 1972 Act": s.277(1).
"development": ss.26, 277(1).
"development order": ss.30, 277(1).
"enactment": s.277(1).
"government department": s.277(1).
"operational land": ss.215, 277(1).
"planning permission": s.277(1).
"statutory undertakers": ss.214, 277(1).

GENERAL NOTE

This section narrows the categories of operational land defined by s.215, by excluding land acquired by a statutory undertaker on or after December 8, 1969 and land which did not fall to be treated as operational land immediately prior to that date under the Town and Country Planning (Scotland) Act 1947 (c.53).

Acquisition of land post December 1969

Under subs. (3), land can only be treated as operational land if there is or has been a specific planning permission in force for its development for the purpose of the carrying on of the statutory undertakers' undertaking. A specific planning permission is defined in subs. (5) as planning permission:

(a) granted on an application under Pt. III;
(b) granted under the Town and Country Planning (General Permitted Development) (Scotland) Order 1992, Sched. 1, Pt. 11 (permission for development under local or private Acts or parliamentary order) or an order granted under the Statutory Orders (Special Procedures) Act 1945 (c.18);
(c) specific permission granted by a special development order;
(d) deemed to have been granted by virtue of a direction of a government department under s.57(1) (development with government authorisation);
(e) deemed to be granted under para. 27 of Sched. 9 to the Post Office Act 1969 (c.48).

Land may also be regarded as operational land if:

(a) the land was transferred from other statutory undertakers under any reorganisation or privatisation legislation specified in subs. (4)(a) and was operational land of the previous statutory undertaker immediately before the transfer.

Dispute as to operational land. Any question arising as to whether the land of statutory undertakers other than land belonging to the Post Office or Civil Aviation Authority, is operational land, is to be determined by the appropriate minister in relation to that statutory undertaker.

Statutory undertakers. In addition to the undertakers within the definition of statutory undertakers in s.214(1), the following are deemed by virtue of s.214(3)–(7) to be statutory undertakers for the purposes of this section: any public gas transporter, the Post Office, the Civil Aviation Authority and electricity undertakers holding a licence under s.6 of the Electricity Act 1989.

Meaning of "the appropriate Minister"

217.—(1) Subject to the following provisions of this section, in this Act "the appropriate Minister" means—

(a) in relation to statutory undertakers carrying on any railway, light railway, tramway, road transport, dock, harbour, pier or lighthouse undertaking, the Civil Aviation Authority or a relevant airport operator (within the meaning of Part V of the Airports Act 1986), the Secretary of State for Transport;
(b) in relation to statutory undertakers carrying on an undertaking for the supply of hydraulic power and the Post Office, the Secretary of State for Trade and Industry;
(c) in relation to statutory undertakers carrying on an undertaking for the supply of water, the Secretary of State for Scotland; and

(d) in relation to any other statutory undertakers, the Secretary of State
for the Environment.

(2) For the purposes of sections 121(11), 218 to 233, 270(9) and 277(2) and
(3) and paragraph 6 of Schedule 6, "the appropriate Minister"—

(a) in relation to a public gas transporter, means the Secretary of State for
Trade and Industry; and

(b) in relation to a holder of a licence under section 6 of the Electricity Act
1989, means the Secretary of State.

(3) References in this Act to the Secretary of State and the appropriate
Minister—

(a) if the appropriate Minister is not the one concerned as the Secretary of
State, shall be construed as references to the Secretary of State and the
appropriate Minister; and

(b) if the one concerned as the Secretary of State is also the appropriate
Minister, shall be construed as references to the Secretary of State
alone,

and similarly with references to a Minister and the appropriate Minister and
with any provision requiring the Secretary of State to act jointly with the
appropriate Minister.

DEFINITIONS
"Minister": s.277(1).
"statutory undertaking": ss.214, 277(1).

GENERAL NOTE
The "appropriate minister" is the minister with supervisory responsibility for the activities
carried on by the particular statutory undertaking. The purpose of designating the appropriate
minister under this Act is to ensure that planning and other related decisions are taken only after
the operational aspects of any proposed development have been taken into account. The appropriate minister therefore shares with the Secretary of State the functions under Pt. III of the 1997
Act of determining called-in planning and other related applications. If any question arises as to
which minister is the appropriate minister in relation to any of the statutory undertakers, that
question is to be determined by the Treasury (s.277(2)).

Application of Part III to statutory undertakers

Applications for planning permission by statutory undertakers

218.—(1) Where—

(a) an application for planning permission to develop land to which this
subsection applies is made by statutory undertakers and is referred to
the Secretary of State under Part III,

(b) an appeal is made to the Secretary of State under that Part from the
decision on such an application, or

(c) such an application is deemed to be made under subsection (7) of section 133 on an appeal under section 130 by statutory undertakers,

the application or appeal shall be dealt with by the Secretary of State and the
appropriate Minister.

(2) Subsection (1) applies to—

(a) operational land, and

(b) land in which the statutory undertakers hold or propose to acquire an
interest with a view to its being used for the purpose of carrying on
their undertaking, where the planning permission, if granted on the
application or appeal, would be for development involving the use of
the land for that purpose.

(3) Subject to the provisions of this Part as to compensation, this Act shall
apply to an application which is dealt with under this section by the Secretary
of State and the appropriate Minister as if it had been dealt with by the
Secretary of State.

(4) Subsection (2)(b) shall have effect in relation to the Civil Aviation Authority as if for the reference to development involving the use of land for the purpose of carrying on the Civil Aviation Authority's undertaking there were substituted a reference to development involving the use of land for such of the purposes of carrying on that undertaking as may be prescribed.

DEFINITIONS
"appropriate Minister": ss.217, 277(1).
"development": ss.26, 277(1).
"land": s.277(1).
"Minister": s.277(1).
"operational land": ss.215, 277(1).
"planning permission": s.277(1).
"prescribed": s.277(1).
"statutory undertakers": ss.214, 277(1).
"use": s.277(1).

GENERAL NOTE
If an application for planning permission is called-in or appealed, it is determined by the Secretary of State acting jointly with the appropriate Minister. The same rules extend to deemed planning applications under s.133 and appeals against enforcement notices under s.130. Outside this section, planning applications by statutory undertakers are dealt with in the normal way by planning authorities under Pt. III.

Display of advertisements. This section does not apply to the display of advertisements on operational land by virtue of s.236.

Statutory undertakers. In addition to the undertakers within the definition of statutory undertakers in s.214(1), the following are deemed by virtue of s.214(3)–(7) to be statutory undertakers for the purposes of this section: any public gas transporter, the Post Office, the Civil Aviation Authority and electricity undertakers holding a licence under s.6 of the Electricity Act 1989.

Conditional grants of planning permission

219. Notwithstanding anything in Part III, planning permission to develop operational land of statutory undertakers shall not, except with their consent, be granted subject to conditions requiring—
(a) that any buildings or works authorised by the permission shall be removed, or
(b) that any use of the land so authorised shall be discontinued,
at the end of a specified period.

DEFINITIONS
"building": s.277(1).
"building or works": s.277(1).
"land": s.277(1).
"operational land": ss.215, 277(1).
"planning permission": s.277(1).
"statutory undertakers": ss.214, 277(1).
"use": s.277(1).

GENERAL NOTE
This section operates so as to prevent the grant of temporary planning permission to a statutory undertaker by a planning authority.

Display of Advertisements. This section does not apply to the display of advertisements on operational land by virtue of s.236.

Statutory undertakers. In addition to the undertakers within the definition of s.214(1), the following are deemed by virtue of s.214(3)–(7) to be statutory undertakers for the purposes of this section: any public gas transporter, the Post Office, the Civil Aviation Authority and electricity undertakers holding a licence under s.6 of the Electricity Act 1989.

Development requiring authorisation of government department

220.—(1) The Secretary of State and the appropriate Minister shall not be required under section 218(1) to deal with an application for planning permission for the development of operational land if the authorisation of a government department is required in respect of that development.

(2) Subsection (1) does not apply where the relevant authorisation has been granted without any direction as to the grant of planning permission.

(3) For the purposes of this section development shall be taken to be authorised by a government department if—

(a) any consent, authority or approval to or for the development is granted by the department in pursuance of an enactment,

(b) a compulsory purchase order is confirmed by the department authorising the purchase of land for the purpose of the development,

(c) consent is granted by the department to the appropriation of land for the purpose of the development or the acquisition of land by agreement for that purpose,

(d) authority is given by the department—

(i) for the borrowing of money for the purpose of the development, or

(ii) for the application for that purpose of any money not otherwise so applicable, or

(e) any undertaking is given by the department to pay a grant in respect of the development in accordance with an enactment authorising the payment of such grants,

and references in this section to the authorisation of a government department shall be construed accordingly.

DEFINITIONS
"appropriate Minister": ss.217, 277(1).
"development": ss.26, 277(1).
"enactment": s.277(1).
"government department": s.277(1).
"land": s.277(1).
"Minister": s.277(1).
"operational land": ss.215, 277(1).
"planning permission": s.277(1).

GENERAL NOTE
This section allows the Secretary of State and the appropriate Minister to decline to determine a planning application where the authorisation of a government department is required in respect of that development. Further, in each of the cases specified in subs. (3), the government department has the power to direct that planning permission should be deemed to be granted (see s.57).

Display of Advertisements. This section does not apply to advertisements displayed on operational land by virtue of s.236.

Revocation or modification of permission to develop operational land

221. In relation to any planning permission granted on the application of statutory undertakers for the development of operational land, the provisions of Part III with respect to the revocation and modification of planning permission shall have effect as if for any reference in them to the Secretary of State there were substituted a reference to the Secretary of State and the appropriate Minister.

DEFINITIONS
"appropriate Minister": ss.217, 277(1).
"development": s.277(1).
"Minister": s.277(1).
"operational land": ss.215, 277(1).
"planning permission": s.277(1).
"statutory undertaker": ss.214, 277(1).

GENERAL NOTE
Where an unopposed order is made under Pt. III of the Act for the revocation or modification of planning permission relating to operational land, that order must be confirmed by the Secretary of State acting jointly with the appropriate Minister.

Display of Advertisements. This section does not apply to the display of advertisements by virtue of s.236.

Statutory undertakers. In addition to the undertakers within the definition of statutory undertakers in s.214(1), the following are deemed by virtue of s.214(3)–(7) to be statutory undertakers for the purposes of this section: any public gas transporter, the Post Office, the Civil Aviation Authority, and electricity undertakers holding a licence under s.6 of the Electricity Act 1989.

Order requiring discontinuance of use etc. of operational land

222. The provisions of Part III with respect to the making of orders—
(a) requiring the discontinuance of any use of land,
(b) imposing conditions on the continuance of it, or
(c) requiring buildings or works on land to be altered or removed,
and the provisions of Schedule 8 with respect to the making of orders under that Schedule shall have effect in relation to operational land of statutory undertakers as if for any reference in them to the Secretary of State there were substituted a reference to the Secretary of State and the appropriate Minister.

DEFINITIONS
"appropriate Minister": ss.217, 277(1).
"land": s.277(1).
"Minister": s.277(1).
"operational land": ss.215, 277(1).
"statutory undertakers": ss.214, 277(1).
"use": s.277(1).

GENERAL NOTE
Under s.222, in relation to operational land, the following require to be confirmed by the Secretary of State acting jointly with the appropriate Minister: orders relating to the discontinuance of any use of land, or imposing conditions, orders requiring buildings or works to be discontinued and orders relating to old mineral workings and permissions under Sched. 8.

Display of Advertisements. This section does not apply to the display of advertisements by virtue of s.236.

Statutory undertakers. In addition to the undertakers within the definition of statutory undertakers in s.214(1), the following are deemed by virtue of s.214(3)–(7) to be statutory undertakers for the purposes of this section: any public gas transporter, the Post Office, the Civil Aviation Authority and electricity undertakers holding a licence under s.6 of the Electricity Act 1989.

Acquisition of land of statutory undertakers

223.—(1) This section applies to any compulsory purchase order under this Act authorising the acquisition of land which has been acquired by statutory undertakers for the purposes of their undertaking.

(2) Paragraph 10 (protection of land of statutory undertakers) of Schedule 1 to the Acquisition of Land (Authorisation Procedure) (Scotland) Act 1947 shall not apply to such an order confirmed or made by the appropriate Minister jointly with the Minister or Ministers who would (apart from this subsection) have power to make or confirm it.

DEFINITIONS
"appropriate Minister": ss.217, 277(1).
"land": s.277(1).
"statutory undertakers": ss.214, 277(1).

GENERAL NOTE
Under para. 10 of Sched. 1 to the Acquisition of Land (Authorisation Procedure) (Scotland) Act 1947, where a compulsory purchase order includes land which has been acquired by statutory undertakers for the purposes of their undertaking and objections are made to that order within the period allowed for objection to the appropriate Minister, that Minister may block the acquisition of that land. However, s.223 of the 1997 Act disapplies para. 10 of Sched. 1 to the 1947 Act where an order has been made or confirmed by the appropriate Minister acting jointly with the relevant Minister or Ministers.

Statutory undertakers. In addition to the undertakers within the definition of statutory undertakers in s.214(1), the following are deemed by virtue of s.214(3)–(7) to be statutory undertakers for the purposes of this section: any public gas transporter, the Post Office, the Civil Aviation Authority and electricity undertakers holding a licence under s.6 of the Electricity Act 1989, whose licence includes the right to exercise any power conferred by Sched. 3 to the Electricity Act 1989 (power of compulsory acquisition of land).

Extinguishment of rights of statutory undertakers, etc.

Extinguishment of rights of statutory undertakers: preliminary notices

224.—(1) This section applies where any land has been acquired by a Minister, a planning authority or statutory undertakers under Part VIII of this Act or Chapter V of Part I of the Planning (Listed Buildings and Conservation Areas) (Scotland) Act 1997 or compulsorily under any other enactment or has been appropriated by a planning authority for planning purposes, and—
  (a) there subsists over that land a right vested in or belonging to statutory undertakers for the purpose of the carrying on of their undertaking, being a right of way or a right of laying down, erecting, continuing or maintaining apparatus on, under or over the land, or
  (b) there is on, under or over the land apparatus vested in or belonging to statutory undertakers for the purpose of the carrying on of their undertaking.
(2) For the purposes of this section the relevant period, in relation to a notice served in respect of any right or apparatus, is the period of 28 days from the date of service of the notice or such longer period as may be specified in it in relation to that right or apparatus.
(3) If the acquiring or appropriating authority is satisfied that the extinguishment of the right or, as the case may be, the removal of the apparatus is necessary for the purpose of carrying out any development with a view to which the land was acquired or appropriated, they may serve on the statutory undertakers a notice—
  (a) stating that at the end of the relevant period the right will be extinguished, or
  (b) requiring that before the end of that period the apparatus shall be removed.
(4) The statutory undertakers on whom a notice is served under subsection (3) may, before the end of the period of 28 days from the date of service of the notice, serve a counter-notice on the acquiring or appropriating authority—
  (a) stating that they object to all or any of the provisions of the notice, and
  (b) specifying the grounds of their objection.
(5) If no counter-notice is served under subsection (4)—
  (a) any right to which the notice relates shall be extinguished at the end of the relevant period, and
  (b) if at the end of that period any requirement of the notice as to the removal of any apparatus has not been complied with, the acquiring or

appropriating authority may remove the apparatus and dispose of it in any way the authority may think fit.

(6) If a counter-notice is served under subsection (4) on a planning authority or on statutory undertakers, the authority or undertakers may either—

(a) withdraw the notice (without prejudice to the service of a further notice), or

(b) apply to the Secretary of State and the appropriate Minister for an order under this section embodying the provisions of the notice, with or without modification.

(7) If a counter-notice is served under subsection (4) on a Minister—

(a) he may withdraw the notice (without prejudice to the service of a further notice), or

(b) he and the appropriate Minister may make an order under this section embodying the provisions of the notice, with or without modification.

(8) In this section any reference to the appropriation of land for planning purposes shall be construed in accordance with section 201(1) as if this section were in Part VIII.

DEFINITIONS
    "acquiring authority": s.277(1).
    "appropriate Minister": ss.217, 277(1).
    "building": s.277(1).
    "development": ss.26, 277(1).
    "enactment": ss.277(1).
    "land": s.277(1).
    "Minister": s.277(1).
    "planning authority": ss.1, 277(1).
    "statutory undertakers": ss.214, 277(1).

GENERAL NOTE
    The rights of statutory undertakers for the purposes of their undertaking, being either a right of way, the right of laying down, erecting, continuing or maintaining apparatus or where there is apparatus belonging to or vesting in the statutory undertaker on, over or under land, are not automatically overridden upon the acquisition or compulsory acquisition of land under Pt. VIII of this Act or Chap. V of Pt. I of the Planning (Listed Buildings and Conservation Areas) (Scotland) Act 1997 (c.9). This section provides a detailed notification procedure whereby the acquiring authority must serve written notice upon the statutory undertaker whose interests may be affected by any such acquisition. The statutory undertaker may object to the proposed acquisition by service of a counter-notice. If the acquiring authority chooses not to withdraw its notice, the matter is referred to the Secretary of State and the appropriate Minister for an order.

Statutory undertakers. In addition to the undertakers within the definition of statutory undertakings in s.214(1), the following are deemed by virtue of s.214(3)–(7) to be statutory undertakers for the purposes of this section: any public gas transporter, the Post Office, the Civil Aviation Authority and electricity undertakings holding a licence under s.6 of the Electricity Act 1989.

Telecommunications code system operators. Telecommunications code system operators are not statutory undertakers for the purposes of this section, but are given separate protection under s.225: see further note to s.225 below.

Extension to road orders. This section and s.225 to s.227, applies to land which is acquired or appropriated for road purposes: (Roads (Scotland) Act 1984 (c.54), s.134, as amended by the New Roads and Street Works Act 1991 (c.22).

The Notice. The acquiring authority may serve a notice on the relevant statutory undertakers stating either:
        (i) that at the end of the period specified in the notice the rights of that statutory undertaker in connection with the land in issue will be extinguished; or
        (ii) require the relevant statutory undertaker upon whom the notice is served to remove any apparatus belonging to it before the expiry of the period specified in the notice.
    The acquiring authority must be satisfied that the extinguishment of the statutory undertaker's right or the removal of its apparatus is necessary for the purpose of carrying out the

development for which the land is to be acquired. The period of time specified in the notice must not be less than 28 days from the date of service. The acquiring authority has a discretion to specify a greater period where it considers it appropriate.

The Counter-notice. The statutory undertaker upon whom a notice under subs. (3) has been served may object to all or any of the provisions contained in the notice by service of a counter-notice under subs. (4) upon the acquiring authority. This counter-notice must be served within 28 days of service of a notice under subs. (3). If a counter-notice is not served within the specified period in the notice, any right to which the notice relates becomes automatically extinguished upon the expiry of that period. Further, any apparatus remaining at the end of the specified period which was required to be removed by the notice may be disposed of by the acquiring authority in any way it may think fit. The Courts have no power to extend the period of time for service of a counter-notice.

Where the statutory undertaker does serve a counter-notice upon a planning authority or statutory undertakers who are the acquiring authority, the authority or undertakers may elect to either:

> (i) withdraw the notice served by them without prejudice to the service of a further notice at a later stage; or
> (ii) apply to the Secretary of State and the appropriate Minister for an order embodying the provisions of the notice with or without modification.

The Order. Where it is considered necessary to make an order under s.224, or under s.225 (telecommunications code systems operators), the order must first be prepared in draft and an opportunity given to the undertaker or operator to object and be heard in respect of that objection (s.227).

Compensation. A statutory undertaker is entitled to compensation under s.232(2) for the extinguishment of any of its rights or the imposition of any requirement upon it. The measure of compensation is to be calculated in accordance with s.233. A statutory undertaker may elect however for compensation to be assessed on the basis of diminution in the value of the interest in the land under s.234.

Extinguishment of rights of telecommunications code system operators: preliminary notices

225.—(1) This section applies where any land has been acquired by a Minister, a planning authority or statutory undertakers under Part VIII or under Chapter V of Part I of the Planning (Listed Buildings and Conservation Areas) (Scotland) Act 1997 or compulsorily under any other enactment or has been appropriated by a planning authority for planning purposes, and—

> (a) there subsists over that land a right conferred by or in accordance with the telecommunications code on the operator of a telecommunications code system, being a right of way or a right of laying down, erecting, continuing or maintaining apparatus on, under or over the land, or
> (b) there is on, under or over the land telecommunication apparatus kept installed for the purposes of any such system.

(2) For the purposes of this section the relevant period, in relation to a notice served in respect of any right or apparatus, is the period of 28 days from the date of service of the notice or such longer period as may be specified in it in relation to that right or apparatus.

(3) If the acquiring or appropriating authority is satisfied that the extinguishment of the right or, as the case may be, the removal of the apparatus is necessary for the purpose of carrying out any development with a view to which the land was acquired or appropriated, they may serve on the operator of the telecommunications code system a notice—

> (a) stating that at the end of the relevant period the right will be extinguished, or
> (b) requiring that before the end of that period the apparatus shall be removed.

(4) The operator of the telecommunications code system on whom a notice is served under subsection (2) may, before the end of the period of 28 days

from the date of service of the notice, serve a counter-notice on the acquiring or appropriating authority—

(a) stating that he objects to all or any of the provisions of the notice, and

(b) specifying the grounds of his objection.

(5) If no counter-notice is served under subsection (4)—

(a) any right to which the notice relates shall be extinguished at the end of the relevant period, and

(b) if at the end of that period any requirement of the notice as to the removal of any apparatus has not been complied with, the acquiring or appropriating authority may remove the apparatus and dispose of it in any way the authority may think fit.

(6) If a counter-notice is served under subsection (4) on a planning authority or on statutory undertakers, the authority or undertakers may either—

(a) withdraw the notice (without prejudice to the service of a further notice), or

(b) apply to the Secretary of State and the Secretary of State for Trade and Industry for an order under this section embodying the provisions of the notice, with or without modification.

(7) If a counter-notice is served under subsection (4) on a Minister—

(a) he may withdraw the notice (without prejudice to the service of a further notice), or

(b) he and the Secretary of State for Trade and Industry may make an order under this section embodying the provisions of the notice, with or without modification.

(8) In this section any reference to the appropriation of land for planning purposes shall be construed in accordance with section 201(1) as if this section were in Part VIII.

DEFINITIONS

"acquiring authority": s.277(1).
"building": s.277(1).
"development": ss.26, 277(1).
"enactment": s.277(1).
"land": s.277(1).
"planning authority": ss.1, 277(1).
"Minister": s.277(1).
"statutory undertakers": ss.214, 277(1).

GENERAL NOTE

This section provides a detailed notification procedure where the interests in land or apparatus on, over or under land belonging to telecommunications code systems operators are likely to be affected by the acquisition or compulsory acquisition of land. It is identical in terms to that prescribed by s.224 in the case of statutory undertakers (see note to s.224 above). The procedure for making orders is prescribed by s.227. Compensation entitlement is prescribed by s.232(3).

Statutory undertakers. In addition to the undertakers within the definition of statutory undertakings in s.214(1), the following are deemed by virtue of s.214(3)–(7) to be statutory undertakers for the purposes of this section: the Post Office, the Civil Aviation Authority and electricity undertakers holding a licence under s.6 of the Electricity Act 1989, whose licence includes the right to exercise any power conferred by Sched. 3 to the Electricity Act 1989 (power of compulsory acquisition of land).

Notice for same purposes as sections 224 and 225 but given by undertakers to developing authority

226.—(1) Subject to the provisions of this section, where land has been acquired or appropriated as mentioned in section 224(1) or 225(1) and—

(a) there is on, under or over the land any apparatus vested in or belonging to statutory undertakers, and

(b) the undertakers claim that development to be carried out on the land is such as to require, on technical or other grounds connected with the carrying on of their undertaking, the removal or re-siting of the apparatus affected by the development,

the undertakers may serve on the acquiring or appropriating authority a notice claiming the right to enter on the land and carry out such works for the removal or re-siting of the apparatus or any part of it as may be specified in the notice.

(2) No notice under this section shall be served later than 21 days after the beginning of the development of land which has been acquired or appropriated as mentioned in section 224(1) or, as the case may be, 225(1).

(3) Where a notice is served under this section, the authority on whom it is served may, before the end of the period of 28 days from the date of service, serve on the statutory undertakers a counter-notice—

(a) stating that they object to all or any of the provisions of the notice, and
(b) specifying the grounds of their objection.

(4) If no counter-notice is served under subsection (3), the statutory undertakers shall, after the end of that period, have the rights claimed in their notice.

(5) If a counter-notice is served under subsection (3), the statutory undertakers who served the notice under this section may either withdraw it or may apply to the Secretary of State and the appropriate Minister for an order under this section conferring on the undertakers the rights claimed in the notice or such modified rights as the Secretary of State and the appropriate Minister think it expedient to confer on them.

(6) Where, by virtue of this section or of an order of Ministers under it, statutory undertakers have the right to execute works for the removal or re-siting of apparatus, they may arrange with the acquiring or appropriating authority for the works to be carried out by that authority, under the superintendence of the undertakers, instead of by the undertakers themselves.

(7) In subsection (1)(a), the reference to apparatus vested in or belonging to statutory undertakers shall include a reference to telecommunication apparatus kept installed for the purposes of a telecommunications code system.

(8) For the purposes of subsection (7), in this section—

(a) references (except in subsection (1)(a)) to statutory undertakers shall have effect as references to the operator of any such system, and
(b) references to the appropriate Minister shall have effect as references to the Secretary of State for Trade and Industry.

DEFINITIONS
"acquiring authority": s.277(1).
"appropriate Minister": ss.217, 277(1).
"development": ss.26, 277(1).
"land": s.277(1).
"Minister": s.277(1).
"statutory undertakers": ss.214, 277(1).

GENERAL NOTE
This section allows a statutory undertaker or a telecommunications code system operator (subs. (7)) to initiate a procedure, by notice, for the removal of apparatus on land that has been acquired or appropriated for planning purposes or acquired compulsorily. This procedure may only be initiated in circumstances where the statutory undertaker can establish on technical or other grounds connected with their undertaking, that the development is such as to require the removal or re-siting of the apparatus.

Notice. The statutory undertaker may serve a notice upon the acquiring or appropriating authority. The notice must specify what works it intends to carry out to facilitate the removal or re-siting of its apparatus. The notice must not be served later than 21 days after the commencement of the development of the land which has been acquired or appropriated (subs. (2)).

Counter-notice. Where a notice has been served on the acquiring or appropriating authority, that authority may serve a counter-notice objecting to all or any of the provisions of the notice.

The grounds of the objection must be specified (subs. (3)). The counter-notice must be served before the expiry of the period of 28 days from the date of service of the notice. If no counter-notice is served within the specified period, the statutory undertakers are entitled to exercise the right to carry out the works specified in the notice. The Courts have no power to extend the time for service of a counter-notice.

Where a counter notice is served by the acquiring or appropriating authority, the statutory undertaker may elect to either:

(i) withdraw the notice served by them; or

(ii) apply to the Secretary of State and the appropriate Minister for an order embodying the provisions of the notice with or without modification.

Compensation. Where an undertaker has the right to remove or re-site apparatus by virtue of s.226 or an order of Ministers under s.226, the undertaker is entitled to compensation from the acquiring or appropriating authority (s.232(4)).

Statutory undertakers. In addition to the undertakers within the definition of statutory undertakings in s.214(1), the following are deemed by virtue of s.214(3)–(7) to be statutory undertakers for the purposes of this section: public gas transporters, the Post Office, the Civil Aviation Authority and electricity undertakers holding a licence under s.6 of the Electricity Act 1989.

Orders under sections 224 and 225

227.—(1) Where a Minister and the appropriate Minister propose to make an order under section 224(7) or 225(7), they shall prepare a draft of the order.

(2) Before making an order under subsection (6) or (7) of section 224, or under subsection (6) or (7) of section 225, the Ministers proposing to make the order shall give the statutory undertakers or, as the case may be, the operator of the telecommunications code system on whom notice was served under subsection (3) of section 224 or, as the case may be, under subsection (3) of section 225 an opportunity of objecting to the application for, or proposal to make, the order.

(3) If any such objection is made, before making the order the Ministers shall cause an inquiry to be held and shall give those statutory undertakers or, as the case may be, that operator (and, in a case falling within subsection (6) of either of those sections, the planning authority or statutory undertakers on whom the counter-notice was served) an opportunity of appearing before, and being heard by, a person appointed for the purpose by the Secretary of State and the appropriate Minister.

(4) After complying with subsections (2) and (3) the Ministers may, if they think fit, make the order in accordance with the application or, as the case may be, in accordance with the draft order, either with or without modification.

(5) Where an order is made under section 224 or 225—

(a) any right to which the order relates shall be extinguished at the end of the period specified in that behalf in the order, and

(b) if, at the end of the period so specified in relation to any apparatus, any requirement of the order as to the removal of the apparatus has not been complied with, the acquiring or appropriating authority may remove the apparatus and dispose of it in any way the authority may think fit.

(6) In this section references to the appropriate Minister shall in the case of an order under section 225 be taken as references to the Secretary of State for Trade and Industry.

DEFINITIONS
  "appropriate Minister": ss.217, 277(1).
  "planning authority": ss.1, 277(1).
  "Minister": s.277(1).
  "statutory undertaker": ss.214, 277(1).

GENERAL NOTE

This section sets out the procedure for making orders under ss.224 and 225. Before an order is made, the Ministers must prepare a draft order and give the statutory undertakers or telecommunications code system operators upon whom a notice was served, an opportunity of objecting to the application for, or proposal to make the order. Where an objection is made to the making of the order, an inquiry must be held in order for the affected parties to make representations (subs. (3)). A person is appointed for this purpose by the Secretary of State and the appropriate Minister. After hearing representations, the person appointed to hear the representations must make a formal report to the Ministers.

The Order. The Secretary of State and the appropriate Minister may make an order in accordance with the application or with modifications as they think fit. Where an order is made under ss.224 or 225, any pre-existing right to which the order relates thereafter becomes extinguished.

Statutory undertakers. In addition to the undertakers within the definition of statutory undertakers in s.214(1), the following are deemed by virtue of s.214(3)–(7) to be statutory undertakers for the purposes of this section: any public gas transporter, the Post Office, the Civil Aviation Authority and electricity undertakers holding a licence under s.6 of the Electricity Act 1989.

Extension or modification of statutory undertakers' functions

Extension or modification of functions of statutory undertakers

228.—(1) The powers conferred by this section shall be exercisable where, on a representation made by statutory undertakers, it appears to the Secretary of State and the appropriate Minister to be expedient that the powers and duties of those undertakers should be extended or modified, in order—

   (a) to secure the provision of services which would not otherwise be provided, or satisfactorily provided, for any purpose in connection with which a planning authority or Minister may be authorised under Part VIII or under Chapter V of Part I of the Planning (Listed Buildings and Conservation Areas) (Scotland) Act 1997 to acquire land or in connection with which any such person may compulsorily acquire land under any other enactment, or

   (b) to facilitate an adjustment of the carrying on of the undertaking necessitated by any of the acts and events mentioned in subsection (2).

   (2) Those acts and events are—

   (a) the acquisition under Part VIII or that Chapter or compulsorily under any other enactment of any land in which an interest was held, or which was used, for the purpose of the carrying on of the undertaking of the statutory undertakers in question;

   (b) the extinguishment of a right or the imposition of any requirement by virtue of section 224 or 225;

   (c) a decision on an application made by the statutory undertakers for planning permission to develop any such land as is mentioned in paragraph (a);

   (d) the revocation or modification of planning permission granted on any such application;

   (e) the making of an order under section 71 or paragraph 1 of Schedule 8 in relation to any such land.

   (3) The powers conferred by this section shall also be exercisable where, on a representation made by a planning authority or Minister, it appears to the Secretary of State and the appropriate Minister to be expedient that the powers and duties of statutory undertakers should be extended or modified in order to secure the provision of new services, or the extension of existing services, for any purpose in connection with which the planning authority or

Minister making the representation may be authorised under Part VIII or under Chapter V of Part I of the Planning (Listed Buildings and Conservation Areas) (Scotland) Act 1997 to acquire land or in connection with which the local authority or Minister may compulsorily acquire land under any other enactment.

(4) Where the powers conferred by this section are exercisable, the Secretary of State and the appropriate Minister may, if they think fit, by order provide for such extension or modification of the powers and duties of the statutory undertakers as appears to them to be requisite in order—

  (a) to secure the services in question, as mentioned in subsection (1)(a) or (3), or
  (b) to secure the adjustment in question, as mentioned in subsection (1)(b),

as the case may be.

(5) Without prejudice to the generality of subsection (4), an order under this section may make provision—

  (a) for empowering the statutory undertakers—
    (i) to acquire (whether compulsorily or by agreement) any land specified in the order, and
    (ii) to erect or construct any buildings or works so specified;
  (b) for applying in relation to the acquisition of any such land or the construction of any such works enactments relating to the acquisition of land and the construction of works;
  (c) where it has been represented that the making of the order is expedient for the purposes mentioned in subsection (1)(a) or (3), for giving effect to such financial arrangements between the planning authority or Minister and the statutory undertakers as they may agree, or as, in default of agreement, may be determined to be equitable in such manner and by such tribunal as may be specified in the order;
  (d) for such incidental and supplemental matters as appear to the Secretary of State and the appropriate Minister to be expedient for the purposes of the order.

(6) Orders under this section shall be subject to special parliamentary procedure.

DEFINITIONS
  "appropriate Minister": ss.217, 277(1).
  "building": s.277(1).
  "building or works": s.277(1).
  "conservation area": s.277(1), s.61 of the Planning (Listed Buildings and Conservation Areas) (Scotland) Act 1997 (c.9).
  "enactment": s.277(1).
  "functions": s.277(1).
  "land": s.277(1).
  "planning authority": ss.1, 277(1).
  "Minister": s.277(1).
  "planning permission": s.277(1).
  "statutory undertakers": s.214, s.277(1).

GENERAL NOTE
  In order for the statutory undertakers to exercise some of the powers under this Act, some extension or modification of their existing powers and duties may be necessary. This section provides a scheme whereby such extension or modification may be secured. A statutory undertaking may seek an order extending or modifying its functions in response to the following:
    (i) the acquisition or compulsory acquisition of land by a planning authority or a Minister;
    (ii) the compulsory acquisition of land for the purpose of carrying on the undertaking;
    (iii) the extinguishment of rights under ss.224 or 225;
    (iv) the revocation or modification of planning permission;
    (v) the making of a discontinuance order.

The statutory undertaker also has the option of seeking an order under s.230 relieving it of its obligations to provide any service.

Procedure. The power to extend or modify the functions or duties of statutory undertakers are exercisable either following a representation by the statutory undertaker concerned (subs. (1)), or by a planning authority or Minister to the Secretary of State and the appropriate Minister (subs. (3)). Where a representation is made by either the statutory undertaker or the planning authority or Minister, notice of this representation must be published (s.229).

The Order. Subsection (4) confers a wide-ranging power upon the Secretary of State and the appropriate Minister to, by order, allow for such extension or modification of the powers and duties of statutory undertakers as they think fit.

Statutory undertakers. In addition to the undertakers within the definition of statutory undertakers in s.214(1), the following are deemed by virtue of s.214(3)–(7) to be statutory undertakers for the purposes of this section: any public gas transporter, the Post Office, the Civil Aviation Authority and electricity undertakers holding a licence under s.6 of the Electricity Act 1989, whose licence includes the right to exercise any power conferred by Sched. 3 to the Electricity Act 1989 (power of compulsory acquisition).

Procedure in relation to orders under section 228

229.—(1) As soon as possible after making such a representation as is mentioned in section 228(1) or (3) the statutory undertakers, the planning authority or Minister making the representation shall publish notice of the representation.

(2) A notice under subsection (1)—

   (a) shall be published in such form and manner as the Secretary of State and the appropriate Minister may direct,

   (b) shall give such particulars as they may direct of the matters to which the representation relates, and

   (c) shall specify the time within which (being not less than 28 days), and the manner in which, objections to the making of an order on the representation may be made.

(3) A similar notice shall be served—

   (a) on any persons appearing from the valuation roll to have an interest in any land to which the representation relates, and

   (b) if directed by the Secretary of State and the appropriate Minister, on such persons, or persons of such classes, as may be so directed.

DEFINITIONS
   "appropriate Minister": ss.217, 277(1).
   "planning authority": ss.1, 277(1).
   "Minister": s.277(1).
   "statutory undertaker": ss.214, 277(1).

GENERAL NOTE
   Orders under s.228 are initiated following a representation from either the statutory undertaker, planning authority or Minister. A notice of the representation must be published in the form and manner directed by the Secretary of State, must contain such particulars as they may direct and must specify a time within which objections to the representations must be made. Subsection (3) makes special provision for service of the notice on any persons appearing on the valuation roll who may have an interest in the land to which the representation relates. The Secretary of State and the appropriate Minister also retain a discretion to direct service of the notice upon persons or particular classes of persons.

Statutory undertakers. In addition to the undertakers within the definition of statutory undertakers in s.214(1), the following are deemed by virtue of s.214(3)–(7) to be statutory undertakers for the purposes of this section: any public gas transporter, the Post Office, the Civil Aviation Authority and electricity undertakers holding a licence under the Electricity Act 1989, whose licence includes the right to exercise any power conferred by Sched. 3 to the Electricity Act 1989 (power of compulsory purchase).

Relief of statutory undertakers from obligations rendered impracticable

230.—(1) Where, on a representation made by statutory undertakers the appropriate Minister is satisfied that the fulfilment of any obligation incurred by those undertakers in connection with the carrying on of their undertaking has been rendered impracticable by an act or event to which this subsection applies, the appropriate Minister may, if he thinks fit, by order direct that the statutory undertakers shall be relieved of the fulfilment of that obligation, either absolutely or to such extent as may be specified in the order.

(2) Subsection (1) applies to the following acts and events—

(a) the compulsory acquisition under Part VIII or under Chapter V of Part I of the Planning (Listed Buildings and Conservation Areas) (Scotland) Act 1997 or under any other enactment of any land in which an interest was held, or which was used, for the purpose of the carrying on of the undertaking of the statutory undertakers, and

(b) the acts and events specified in section 228(2)(b) to (e).

(3) The appropriate Minister may direct statutory undertakers who have made a representation to him under subsection (1) to publicise it in either or both of the following ways—

(a) by publishing in such form and manner as he may direct a notice, giving such particulars as he may direct of the matters to which the representation relates and specifying the time within which (being not less than 28 days), and the manner in which, objections to the making of an order on the representation may be made;

(b) by serving such a notice on such persons, or persons of such classes, as he may direct.

(4) The statutory undertakers shall comply with any direction given to them under subsection (3) as soon as practicable after the making of the representation under subsection (1).

(5) If any objection to the making of an order under this section is duly made and is not withdrawn before the order is made, the order shall be subject to special parliamentary procedure.

(6) Immediately after an order is made under this section by the appropriate Minister, he shall—

(a) publish a notice stating that the order has been made and naming a place where a copy of it may be seen at all reasonable hours, and

(b) serve a similar notice—

(i) on any person who duly made an objection to the order and has sent to the appropriate Minister a request in writing to serve him with the notice required by this subsection, specifying an address for service, and

(ii) on such other persons (if any) as the appropriate Minister thinks fit.

(7) Subject to subsection (8), and to the provisions of Part XI, an order under this section shall become operative on the date on which the notice required by subsection (6) is first published.

(8) Where in accordance with subsection (5) the order is subject to special parliamentary procedure, subsection (7) shall not apply.

Definitions
"appropriate Minister": ss.217, 277(1).
"building": s.277(1).
"compulsory acquisition": s.277(1).
"conservation area": s.277(1), s.61 of the Planning (Listed Buildings and Conservation Areas) (Scotland) Act 1997 (c.9).

"enactment": s.277(1).
"land": s.277(1).
"Minister": s.277(1).
"statutory undertakers": ss.214, 277(1).
"use": s.277(1).

GENERAL NOTE
   This section provides for obligations binding upon statutory undertakers in connection with the carrying on of their undertaking to be discharged following a representation to the appropriate Minister. This Minister must be satisfied that the fulfilment of that obligation has been rendered impracticable by the compulsory acquisition of the land or the acts or events specified in s.228(2)(b)–(e) (see commentary to s.228 above).

   The Order. The appropriate Minister may grant an order relieving the statutory undertaking of its obligations. Where objections are made however to a representation by the statutory undertaking, an order may only be made by special parliamentary procedure. When an order is made under this section, the appropriate Minister must publish a notice to this effect (subs. (6)).

   Statutory undertakers. In addition to the undertakers within the definition of undertakers in s.214(1), the following are deemed by virtue of s.214(3)–(7) to be statutory undertakers for the purposes of this section: any public gas transporter, the Post Office, the Civil Aviation Authority and electricity undertakers holding a licence under s.6 of the Electricity Act 1989.

Objections to orders under sections 228 and 230

   231.—(1) For the purposes of sections 228 and 230, an objection to the making of an order shall not be treated as duly made unless—
   (a) the objection is made within the time and in the manner specified in the notice required by section 229 or, as the case may be, section 230, and
   (b) a statement in writing of the grounds of the objection is comprised in or submitted with the objection.
   (2) Where an objection to the making of such an order is duly made in accordance with subsection (1) and is not withdrawn, the following provisions of this section shall have effect in relation to it.
   (3) Unless the appropriate Minister decides without regard to the objection not to make the order, or decides to make a modification which is agreed to by the objector as meeting the objection, before he makes a final decision he—
   (a) shall consider the grounds of the objection as set out in the statement, and
   (b) may, if he thinks fit, require the objector to submit within a specified period a further statement in writing as to any of the matters to which the objection relates.
   (4) In so far as the appropriate Minister, after considering the grounds of the objection as set out in the original statement and in any such further statement, is satisfied that the objection relates to a matter which can be dealt with in the assessment of compensation, the appropriate Minister may treat the objection as irrelevant for the purpose of making a final decision.
   (5) If—
   (a) after considering the grounds of the objection as so set out, the appropriate Minister is satisfied that, for the purpose of making a final decision, he is sufficiently informed as to the matters to which the objection relates, or
   (b) in a case where a further statement has been required, it is not submitted within the specified period,
   the appropriate Minister may make a final decision without further investigation as to those matters.
   (6) Subject to subsections (4) and (5), before making a final decision the appropriate Minister shall give the objector an opportunity of appearing

before, and being heard by, a person appointed for the purpose by the appropriate Minister.

(7) If the objector takes that opportunity, the appropriate Minister shall give an opportunity of appearing and being heard on the same occasion to the statutory undertakers, planning authority or Minister on whose representation the order is proposed to be made, and to any other persons to whom it appears to him to be expedient to give such an opportunity.

(8) Notwithstanding anything in the previous provisions of this section, if it appears to the appropriate Minister that the matters to which the objection relates are such as to require investigation by public local inquiry before he makes a final decision, he shall cause such an inquiry to be held.

(9) Where the appropriate Minister determines to cause such an inquiry to be held, any of the requirements of subsections (3) to (7) to which effect has not been given at the time of that determination shall be dispensed with.

(10) In this section any reference to making a final decision in relation to an order is a reference to deciding whether to make the order or what modification (if any) ought to be made.

(11) In the application of this section to an order under section 228, any reference to the appropriate Minister shall be construed as a reference to the Secretary of State and the appropriate Minister.

DEFINITIONS
  "appropriate Minister": ss.217, 277(1).
  "planning authority": ss.1, 277(1).
  "Minister": s.277(1).
  "statutory undertakers": ss.214, 277(1).

GENERAL NOTE
  This section prescribes the procedure to be followed for objections to the making of an order under s.228 (extension or modification of functions of statutory undertakers) and s.230 (relief of statutory undertakers from obligations rendered impracticable).

Subs. (1)
  An objection is invalid unless it is made within the time and the manner prescribed by the notice which statutory undertakers must publish (and in some cases serve) under ss.229 or 230. The objection must be accompanied by a written statement containing the grounds of the objection. The appropriate Minister is empowered to require the objector to submit a further written statement in relation to the matters to which the objection relates. A time period for the submission of this further written statement may also be imposed under subs. (3).

Subs. (3)
  The purpose of subs. (3) is to ensure that any objections to a proposed order are fully taken into account as a "relevant consideration" before the appropriate Minister makes his decision. The amount of weight to be given to that objection however is a matter for that Minister.

Subs. (4)
  If the appropriate Minister is satisfied that the objection may be appropriately addressed when assessing compensation, he is entitled to disregard the objection on the ground that it is irrelevant.

Subs. (5)
  The appropriate Minister may make a final decision where he is satisfied that he is sufficiently informed on the nature of the objection, or where a further statement that has been required has not been submitted within the specified time period.

Subs. (7)
  Under subs. (6), the appropriate Minister must give an objector an opportunity of making oral representations before a person appointed for that purpose by that Minister (subject to subss. (4) and (5)). In these circumstances, subs. (7) allows for the relevant statutory undertaker, the planning authority or the Minister who made the representation, to be given the opportunity of responding to the objector's representations. If necessary, the appropriate Minister may cause a public local inquiry to be held into the matters to which the objection relates (subs. (8)).

Statutory undertakers. In addition to the undertakers within the definition of statutory undertakers in s.214(1), the following are deemed by virtue of s.214(3)–(7) to be statutory undertakers for the purposes of this section: any public gas transporter, the Post Office, the Civil Aviation Authority and electricity undertakers holding a licence under s.6 of the Electricity Act 1989.

Compensation

Right to compensation in respect of certain decisions and orders

232.—(1) Statutory undertakers shall, subject to the following provisions of this Part, be entitled to compensation from the planning authority—

   (a) in respect of any decision made in accordance with section 218 by which planning permission to develop operational land of those undertakers is refused or is granted subject to conditions where—

      (i) planning permission for that development would have been granted by a development order but for a direction given under such an order that planning permission so granted should not apply to the development, and

      (ii) it is not development which has received specific parliamentary approval (within the meaning of section 216(6)(b));

   (b) in respect of any order under section 65, as modified by section 221, by which planning permission which was granted on the application of those undertakers for the development of any such land is revoked or modified.

(2) Where by virtue of section 224—

   (a) any right vested in or belonging to statutory undertakers is extinguished, or

   (b) any requirement is imposed on statutory undertakers,

those undertakers shall be entitled to compensation from the acquiring or appropriating authority at whose instance the right was extinguished or the requirement imposed.

(3) Where by virtue of section 225—

   (a) any right vested in or belonging to an operator of a telecommunications code system is extinguished, or

   (b) any requirement is imposed on such an operator,

the operator shall be entitled to compensation from the acquiring or appropriating authority at whose instance the right was extinguished or the requirement imposed.

(4) Where—

   (a) works are carried out for the removal or resiting of statutory undertakers' apparatus, and

   (b) the undertakers have the right to carry out those works by virtue of section 226 or an order of Ministers under that section,

the undertakers shall be entitled to compensation from the acquiring or appropriating authority.

(5) Subsection (1) shall not apply in respect of a decision or order if—

   (a) it relates to land acquired by the statutory undertakers after 7th January 1947, and

   (b) the Secretary of State and the appropriate Minister include in the decision or order a direction that subsection (1) shall not apply to it.

(6) The Secretary of State and the appropriate Minister may give a direction under subsection (5) only if they are satisfied, having regard to the nature, situation and existing development of the land and of any neighbouring land, and to any other material considerations, that it is unreasonable that compensation should be recovered in respect of the decision or order in question.

(7) For the purposes of this section the conditions referred to in sections 58 and 59 shall be disregarded.

"appropriate Minister": ss.217, 277(1).
"acquiring authority": s.277(1).
"development": s.277(1).
"development order": s.277.
"land": s.277(1).
"Minister": s.277(1).
"operational land": ss.215, 277(1).
"planning authority": s.1, s.277(1).
"planning permission": s.277(1).
"statutory undertakers": ss.214, 277(1).
"use": s.277(1).

GENERAL NOTE
This section establishes a statutory scheme for entitlement to compensation for statutory undertakers and telecommunications code system operators. The measure of compensation is to be calculated in accordance with s.233. However, s.234 allows statutory undertakers to waive that entitlement in respect of compulsorily purchased land, in favour of the normal rules applicable to land compensation on compulsory acquisition. Section 235 prescribes the procedure for assessing compensation under s.233. In the event of any dispute, compensation is to be assessed by a tribunal (s.235(1)).

Compensation. Entitlement to compensation from a planning authority or the acquiring or appropriating authority as the case may be arises in the following circumstances:
  (i) where planning permission to develop operational land under s.218 is refused or granted subject to conditions (subs. (1));
 (ii) where planning permission has been modified or revoked pursuant to an order under s.221 (subs. (1)(b));
(iii) where any right vested in or belonging to a statutory undertaker is extinguished under s.224 (subs. (2)(a))
 (iv) where any requirement is imposed upon a statutory undertaker under s.224 (subs. (2)(b));
  (v) where any right vested in or belonging to a telecommunications code system operator is extinguished under s.225 (subs. (3)(a));
 (vi) where any requirement is imposed upon a telecommunications code system operator under s.225 (subs. (3)(b));
(vii) where undertakers works are carried out for the removal or re-siting of apparatus by virtue of s.226 or an order thereunder (subs. (4));
Secretary of State and the appropriate Minister may direct that no compensation in respect of a refusal of planning permission or grant of such permission with conditions under s.218, where it relates to land acquired after January 7, 1947, is recoverable (subs. (5)). However, a direction under s.232(5) may only be given where the Secretary of State and the appropriate Minister are satisfied that it is unreasonable that compensation should be recovered. In reaching this decision, the Secretary of State and the appropriate Minister must have regard to the nature, situation and existing development of the land, of the neighbouring land and to any other "material considerations". The amount of weight to be given to these considerations is a matter for the ministers alone.

Statutory undertakers. In addition to the undertakers within the definition of statutory undertakers in s.214(1), the following are deemed by virtue of s.214(3)–(7) to be statutory undertakers for the purposes of this section: any public gas transporter, the Post Office, the Civil Aviation Authority and electricity undertakers holding a licence under s.6 of the Electricity Act 1989.

Advertisements. Subsections (1), (5) and (6) do not apply to the display of advertisements on operational land by virtue of s.236.

Measure of compensation to statutory undertakers etc.

233.—(1) Where—
(a) statutory undertakers are entitled to compensation—
       (i) as mentioned in subsection (1), (2) or (4) of section 232,
      (ii) under the provisions of section 83 in respect of an order made under section 71 or paragraph 1, 3, 5 or 6 of Schedule 8 as modified by section 222, or

(iii) in respect of a compulsory acquisition of land which has been acquired by those undertakers for the purposes of their undertaking, where the first-mentioned acquisition is effected under a compulsory purchase order confirmed or made without the appropriate Minister's certificate, or

(b) the operator of a telecommunications code system is entitled to compensation as mentioned in section 232(3),

the amount of the compensation shall (subject to section 234) be an amount calculated in accordance with this section.

(2) Subject to subsections (4) to (6), that amount shall be the aggregate of—

(a) the amount of any expenditure reasonably incurred in acquiring land, providing apparatus, erecting buildings or doing work for the purpose of any adjustment of the carrying on of the undertaking or, as the case may be, the running of the telecommunications code system rendered necessary by the proceeding giving rise to compensation (a "business adjustment"),

(b) the appropriate amount for loss of profits, and

(c) where the compensation is under section 232(2) or (3) and is in respect of the imposition of a requirement to remove apparatus, the amount of any expenditure reasonably incurred by the statutory undertakers or, as the case may be, the operator in complying with the requirement, reduced by the value after removal of the apparatus removed.

(3) In subsection (2) "the appropriate amount for loss of profits" means—

(a) where a business adjustment is made, the aggregate of—

(i) the estimated amount of any decrease in net receipts from the carrying on of the undertaking or, as the case may be, the running of the telecommunications code system pending the adjustment, in so far as the decrease is directly attributable to the proceeding giving rise to compensation, and

(ii) such amount as appears reasonable compensation for any estimated decrease in net receipts from the carrying on of the undertaking or, as the case may be, the running of the telecommunications code system in the period after the adjustment has been completed, in so far as the decrease is directly attributable to the adjustment;

(b) where no business adjustment is made, such amount as appears reasonable compensation for any estimated decrease in net receipts from the carrying on of the undertaking or, as the case may be, the running of the telecommunications code system which is directly attributable to the proceeding giving rise to compensation.

(4) Where a business adjustment is made, the aggregate amount mentioned in subsection (2) shall be reduced by such amount (if any) as appears to the tribunal referred to in section 235(2) to be appropriate to offset—

(a) the estimated value of any property (whether moveable or heritable) belonging to the statutory undertakers or the operator and used for the carrying on of their undertaking or, as the case may be, the running of the telecommunications code system which in consequence of the adjustment ceases to be so used, in so far as the value of the property has not been taken into account under paragraph (c) of that subsection, and

(b) the estimated amount of any increase in net receipts from the carrying on of the undertaking or the running of the telecommunications code system in the period after the adjustment has been completed, in so far as that amount has not been taken into account in determining the amount mentioned in paragraph (b) of that subsection and is directly attributable to the adjustment.

(5) Where a business adjustment is made the aggregate amount mentioned in subsection (2) shall be further reduced by any amount which appears to that tribunal to be appropriate, having regard to any increase in the capital value of heritable property belonging to the statutory undertakers or the operator which is directly attributable to the adjustment, allowance being made for any reduction made under subsection (4)(b).

(6) Where—

(a) the compensation is under section 232(4), and

(b) the acquiring or appropriating authority carry out the works,

then, in addition to any reduction falling to be made under subsection (4) or (5), the aggregate amount mentioned in subsection (2) shall be reduced by the actual cost to the authority of carrying out the works.

(7) References in this section to a decrease in net receipts shall be construed as references—

(a) to the amount by which a balance of receipts over expenditure is decreased,

(b) to the amount by which a balance of expenditure over receipts is increased, or

(c) where a balance of receipts over expenditure is converted into a balance of expenditure over receipts, to the aggregate of the two balances,

and references to an increase in net receipts shall be construed accordingly.

(8) In this section—

"proceeding giving rise to compensation" means—

(a) except in relation to compensation under section 232(4), the particular action (that is to say, the decision, order, extinguishment of a right, imposition of a requirement or acquisition) in respect of which compensation falls to be assessed, as distinct from any development or project in connection with which that action may have been taken, and

(b) in relation to compensation under section 232(4), the circumstances making it necessary for the apparatus in question to be removed or resited; and

"the appropriate Minister's certificate" means such a certificate as is mentioned in paragraph 10 of Schedule 1 to the Acquisition of Land (Authorisation Procedure) (Scotland) Act 1947.

Definitions

"appropriate amount of loss of profit": subs. (3).
"appropriate Minister": ss.217, 277(1).
"appropriate Minister's certificate": subs. (8).
"acquiring authority": s.277(1).
"building": s.277(1).
"business adjustment": subs. (2)(a).
"compulsory acquisition": s.277(1).
"development": s.277(1).
"land": s.277(1).
"Minister": s.277(1).
"proceeding giving rise to compensation": subs. (8).
"statutory undertaker": ss.214, 277(1).

General Note

This section prescribes the measure of compensation to be paid to statutory undertakers and telecommunications code system operators who are entitled to such compensation under s.232. In the case of compulsory acquisition, statutory undertakers may elect by notice served under s.234 for compensation to be calculated on the basis of ordinary rules.

Method of assessment. The general principle is that the statutory undertaker or, as the case may be, the telecommunications code system operator is entitled to compensation for expenditure reasonably incurred, including loss of profits, under the provisions in s.232 giving rise to entitlement of compensation.

Statutory undertakers. In addition to the undertakers within the definition of statutory undertakers in s.214(1) the following are deemed by virtue of s.214(3)–(7) to be statutory undertakers for the purposes of this section: any public gas transporter, the Post Office, the Civil Aviation Authority and electricity undertakers holding a licence under s.6 of the Electricity Act 1989.

Exclusion of section 233 at option of statutory undertakers

234.—(1) Where statutory undertakers are entitled to compensation in respect of such a compulsory acquisition as is mentioned in section 233(1)(c), the statutory undertakers may by notice in writing under this section elect that the compensation shall be ascertained in accordance with the enactments (other than rule (5) of the rules set out in section 12 of the Land Compensation (Scotland) Act 1963) which would be applicable apart from section 233.

(2) If the statutory undertakers so elect the compensation shall be ascertained accordingly.

(3) An election under this section may be made either in respect of the whole of the land comprised in the compulsory acquisition in question or in respect of part of that land.

(4) Any notice under this section shall be given to the acquiring authority before the end of the period of 2 months from the date of service of notice to treat in respect of the interest of the statutory undertakers.

DEFINITIONS
  "acquiring authority": s.277(1).
  "compulsory acquisition": s.277(1).
  "enactment": s.277(1).
  "land": s.277(1).
  "statutory undertakers": ss.214, 277(1).

GENERAL NOTE
  A statutory undertaker may elect to have compensation assessed on the normal basis for compulsory purchase under the Land Compensation (Scotland) Act 1963 (c.51). However, the right of election only applies to land which the statutory undertakers had compulsorily acquired themselves for the purposes of their undertaking without the appropriate Minister's certificate (a certificate under the Acquisition of Land (Authorisation Procedure) (Scotland) Act 1947 (c.42)).

Statutory undertakers. In addition to the undertakers within the definition of statutory undertakers in s.214(1), the following are deemed by virtue of s.214(3)–(7) to be statutory undertakers for the purposes of this section: any public gas transporter, the Post Office, the Civil Aviation Authority and electricity undertakers holding a licence under s.6 of the Electricity Act 1989 whose licence includes the right to exercise any of the powers conferred by Sched. 3 to the Electricity Act 1989 (c.29) (power of compulsory acquisition).

Procedure for assessing compensation

235.—(1) Where the amount of any such compensation as is mentioned in subsection (1) of section 233 falls to be ascertained in accordance with the provisions of that section, the compensation shall, in default of agreement, be assessed by the tribunal mentioned in subsection (2) below, if apart from this section it would not fall to be so assessed.

(2) The tribunal referred to in subsection (1) above shall consist of 4 persons, namely—
  (a) an advocate or solicitor of not less than 7 years' standing, appointed by the Lord President of the Court of Session to act as chairman,
  (b) two persons appointed by the Secretary of State as persons having special knowledge and experience of the valuation of land and of civil engineering respectively, and

(c) for each claim coming before the tribunal, a person selected by the appropriate Minister, as a person having special knowledge and experience of statutory undertakings of the kind carried on by the claimant, from the members of a panel appointed by appropriate Ministers of persons appearing to them to have such knowledge and experience of statutory undertakings.

(3) The Treasury may pay out of money provided by Parliament to the members of the tribunal such remuneration (whether by way of salaries or by way of fees), and such allowances, as the Treasury may determine.

(4) For the purposes of any proceedings arising before the tribunal in respect of compensation falling to be ascertained as mentioned in subsection (1), sections 9 and 11 of the Land Compensation (Scotland) Act 1963 shall apply as they apply to proceedings on a question referred to the Lands Tribunal under section 8 of that Act, but with the substitution, in section 11, for references to the acquiring authority, of references to the person from whom the compensation is claimed.

DEFINITIONS
"acquiring authority": s.277(1).
"appropriate Minister": ss.217, 277(1).
"Lands Tribunal": s.277(1).
"Statutory undertakers": ss.214, 277(1).

GENERAL NOTE
This section establishes a special tribunal to adjudicate on the measure of compensation payable under s.233 in default of agreement between the parties.

Statutory undertakers. In addition to the undertakers within the definition of statutory undertakings in s.214(1), the following are deemed by virtue of s.214(3)–(7) to be statutory undertakers for the purposes of this section: any public gas transporter, the Post Office, the Civil Aviation Authority and electricity undertakers holding a licence under s.6 of the Electricity Act 1989.

Advertisements

Special provisions as to display of advertisements on operational land

236. Sections 218 to 222 and 232(1), (5) and (6) do not apply in relation to the display of advertisements on operational land of statutory undertakers.

DEFINITIONS
"advertisements": s.277(1).
"operational land": ss.215, 277(1).
"statutory undertakers": ss.214, 277(1).

PART XI

VALIDITY

Validity of development plans and certain orders, decisions and directions

237.—(1) Except as provided by this Part, the validity of—
(a) a structure plan, a local plan or any alteration, repeal or replacement of any such plan, whether before or after the plan, alteration, repeal or replacement has been approved or adopted,
(b) a simplified planning zone scheme or any alteration of any such scheme, whether before or after the adoption or approval of the scheme or alteration,
(c) an order under any provision of Part IX, whether before or after the order has been made,
(d) an order under section 230, whether before or after the order has been made,

(e) any such order as is mentioned in subsection (2), whether before or after it has been confirmed, or

(f) any such action on the part of the Secretary of State as is mentioned in subsection (3),

shall not be questioned in any legal proceedings whatsoever.

(2) The orders referred to in subsection (1)(e) are—

(a) any order under section 65 or under the provisions of that section as applied by or under any other provision of this Act;

(b) any order under section 71 or under the provisions of that section as applied by or under any other provisions of this Act;

(c) any tree preservation order;

(d) any order made in pursuance of section 183(4);

(e) any order under paragraph 1, 3, 5 or 6 of Schedule 8.

(3) The action referred to in subsection (1)(f) is action on the part of the Secretary of State of any of the following descriptions—

(a) any decision on an application referred to him under section 46;

(b) any decision on an appeal under section 47;

(c) any decision to confirm a completion notice under section 62;

(d) any decision on an appeal under section 130;

(e) any decision to confirm or not to confirm a purchase notice including—

(i) any decision not to confirm such a notice in respect of part of the land to which it relates, or

(ii) any decision to grant any permission, or give any direction, instead of confirming such a notice, either wholly or in part;

(f) any decision on an appeal under section 154 against the refusal or partial refusal of an application for a certificate under section 150 or 151;

(g) any decision on an appeal under section 180 against a notice under section 179;

(h) any decision relating—

(i) to an application for consent under a tree preservation order,

(ii) to an application for consent under any regulations made under section 182 or 183, or

(iii) to any certificate or direction under any such order or regulations, whether it is a decision on appeal or a decision on an application referred to the Secretary of State for determination in the first instance.

(4) Nothing in this section shall affect the exercise of any jurisdiction of any court in respect of any refusal or failure on the part of the Secretary of State to take any such action as is mentioned in subsection (3).

DEFINITIONS

"land": s.277(1).

"purchase notice": ss.88, 277(1).

"simplified planning zone": ss.49, 277(1).

"tree preservation order": ss.160, 277(1).

GENERAL NOTE

The nature of plan-led development and the public desire for a degree of certainty in land usage has resulted in limitations being placed upon an individual's right to challenge the validity of plans and certain types of orders and decisions. Section 237 precludes any legal challenge to the validity of the statutory plans, orders or decisions specified in s.237 except by way of application to the Court of Session under s.238. It should be noted that it is only the "validity" of planning decisions which may be subject to scrutiny by the courts and not their technical or planning merits. It is not for the court to substitute its own decision for that of the planning authority or Secretary of State. The question for the courts is simply one of vires. Any application must be made within six weeks from the published date of the adoption or approval of the plan, or the date the order, decision, direction is made. If no challenge is made within this period, this section takes effect, even where the decision being challenged is fundamentally flawed:

Smith v. East Elloe Rural District Council [1956] A.C. 736; *Hamilton v. Secretary of State for Scotland*, 1972 S.L.T. 233.

Scope of s.237. Section 237 applies to the following plans, orders, decisions and directions:
   (i)   a structure plan and a local plan, or any alteration, repeal or replacement of such plan, whether before or after it has been approved or adopted (subs. (1)(a));
   (ii)   a simplified planning zone scheme or any alteration to it whether before or after its adoption or approval (subs. (1)(b));
   (iii)   any order under Pt. IX (Roads, Footpaths and Rights of Way) whether before or after the order has been made (subs. (1)(c));
   (iv)   an order under s.230 relieving statutory undertakers from obligations rendered impracticable, whether before or after the order has been made;
   (v)   any order under s.65 modifying or revoking planning permission, or other order under that section as applied by or under the provisions of this Act, whether before or after it has been confirmed (subs. (2)(a));
   (vi)   any order under s.71 discontinuing use of or alteration to removal of buildings or works, or under the provisions of that section as applied by or under the provisions of this Act, whether before or after it has been confirmed (subs. (2)(b));
   (vii)   any tree preservation order whether before or after it has been confirmed (subs. (2)(c));
   (viii)   any order made under s.183(4) (powers to make different advertisement regulations) whether before or after it has been confirmed (subs. (2)(d));
   (ix)   any order made under paras. 1, 3, 5, 6 of Sched. 8 (old mineral workings and permissions) whether before or after it has been confirmed (subs. (2)(e));
   (x)   any decision by the Secretary of State on a called-in application (subs. (3)(a));
   (xi)   any decision on an appeal against a planning decision or failure to make a decision (subs. (3)(b));
   (xii)   any decision to confirm a completion notice under s.62 (subs. (3)(c));
   (xiii)   any decision on an appeal against an enforcement notice under s.130 (subs. (3)(d));
   (xiv)   any decision to confirm or not to confirm a purchase notice under Pt. V (subs. (3)(e));
   (xv)   any decision on an appeal under s.154 against a refusal to grant a certificate of lawfulness of existing use or development (subs. (3)(f));
   (xvi)   any decision on appeal under s.180 against a notice requiring proper maintenance served under s.179 (subs. (3)(g));
   (xvii)   any decision relating to an application for consent under a tree preservation order (subs. (3)(h)(i));
   (xviii)   any decision relating to an application for consent under any regulations made under s.182 (regulations controlling advertisement displays) or s.183 (regulations controlling different advertisements in different areas) (subs. (3)(h)(ii));
   (xix)   any decision relating to any certificate or direction under any such order or regulations, whether on appeal or application which has been referred to the Secretary of State for determination in the first instance.

Other preclusive provisions. The provisions of s.237 are not exhaustive. Where these provisions do not apply, a challenge to any decision may be made by way of judicial review. In particular, subs. (4) specifically preserves the courts' jurisdiction in respect of any refusal or failure by the Secretary of State to take any action mentioned in subs. (3). There are a number of other provisions in this and other related enactments which impose restrictions upon an individual's right to challenge a planning related decision or order. Examples include s.134 which provides that the validity of an enforcement notice shall not be questioned in any proceedings whatsoever on any of the grounds specified in s.139(1)(b)–(e) except by appeal under that section; and various orders of the Secretary of State under the Planning (Listed Buildings and Conservation Areas) (Scotland) Act 1997 (c.9). The provision itself will almost always state whether it precludes legal challenge.

Exceptions to the preclusive provisions. It is not possible to give an exhaustive list of all the provisions to which the preclusive provisions do not apply. However, examples include interlocutory decisions in the course of certain types of appeal (*Co-operative Retail Services v. Secretary of State for the Environment* [1980] 1 W.L.R. 271); decisions relating to the award of expenses in connection with appeals (*R. v. Secretary of State for the Environment, ex p. Reinisch* (1971) 22 P. & C.R. 1022, see also *R. v. Secretary of State for the Environment, ex p. Three Rivers District Council* [1983] J.P.L. 730).
   Even where there is no statutory restriction on the courts' jurisdiction to entertain a challenge to the validity of a plan, decision or order, the courts may nonetheless be reluctant to hear a

challenge. One of the major reasons for this reticence is the well established principle that any statutory remedy must normally have been exhausted before the courts' supervisory jurisdiction may be invoked. This principle is clearly illustrated by the recent decision of the first division in *Philip Lardner v. Renfrew District Council*, 1997 G.W.D. 9-393. In this case, the Lord President dismissed an appeal under s.232 of the Town and Country Planning (Scotland) Act 1972 (c.52) against the adoption of a local plan by Renfrew District Council, the statutory predecessors of the respondents, in circumstances where the appellant had not, as he was entitled, made a timeous objection to the adoption of the plan or made representations at the subsequent local inquiry. Thus, the appellant was held not to be an "aggrieved person" within the scope of s.232 (see note to s.239). Neither, will the courts normally entertain an action seeking reduction of a decision of a planning authority where there exists a right of appeal to the Secretary of State (*Bellway v. Strathclyde Regional Council*, 1980 S.L.T. 66).

Proceedings for questioning validity of development plans and certain schemes and orders

238.—(1) If any person aggrieved by a structure plan or a local plan or by any alteration, repeal or replacement of any such plan desires to question the validity of the plan or, as the case may be, the alteration, repeal or replacement on the ground—
    (a) that it is not within the powers conferred by Part II, or
    (b) that any requirement of that Part or of any regulations made under it has not been complied with in relation to the approval or adoption of the plan or, as the case may be, its alteration, repeal or replacement,
he may make an application to the Court of Session under this section.
    (2) On any application under this section the Court of Session—
    (a) may by interim order wholly or in part suspend the operation of the plan or, as the case may be, the alteration, repeal or replacement, either generally or in so far as it affects any property of the applicant, until the final determination of the proceedings;
    (b) if satisfied that the plan or, as the case may be, the alteration, repeal or replacement is wholly or to any extent outside the powers conferred by Part II, or that the interests of the applicant have been substantially prejudiced by the failure to comply with any requirement of that Part or of any regulations made under it, may wholly or in part quash the plan or, as the case may be, the alteration, repeal or replacement either generally or in so far as it affects any property of the applicant.
    (3) Subsections (1) and (2) shall apply, subject to any necessary modifications, to a simplified planning zone scheme or an alteration of such a scheme or to an order under section 202, 203, 206, 207, 208 or 230 as they apply to any plan or an alteration, repeal or replacement there mentioned.
    (4) An application under this section must be made within 6 weeks from the relevant date.
    (5) For the purposes of subsection (4) the relevant date is—
    (a) in the case of an application in respect of such a plan as is mentioned in subsection (1), the date of the publication of the first notice of the approval or adoption of the plan, alteration, repeal or replacement required by regulations under section 21;
    (b) in the case of an application by virtue of subsection (3) in respect of a simplified planning zone scheme or an alteration of such a scheme, the date of the publication of the first notice of the approval or adoption of the scheme or alteration required by regulations under paragraph 12 of Schedule 5;
    (c) in the case of an application by virtue of subsection (3) in respect of an order under section 202 or 206(1)(a), the date on which the notice required by paragraph 1(7) of Schedule 16 is first published;
    (d) in the case of an application by virtue of subsection (3) in respect of an order under section 203, 206(1)(b), 207 or 208, the date on which the notice required by paragraph 11 of Schedule 16 is first published in accordance with that paragraph; and

(e) in the case of an application by virtue of subsection (3) in respect of an order under section 230, the date on which the notice required by subsection (6) of that section is first published;

but subject, in the case of those orders made under sections 202, 203 and 230, to section 241.

(6) In their application to simplified planning zone schemes and their alteration, subsections (1) and (2) shall have effect as if they referred to Part III instead of Part II.

DEFINITIONS
　　"development": ss.26, 277(1).
　　"development plan": ss.24, 277(1).
　　"simplified planning zone": ss.49, 277(1).

GENERAL NOTE
　　Section 238 provides a detailed procedure for challenging the validity of a structure plan, local plan, simplified planning zone or any of the orders and schemes referred to in subs. (3).

Scope of s.238. Under subs. (1), any person aggrieved by a structure plan or local plan, or by its alteration, repeal or replacement may question its validity or its alteration, repeal or replacement in the Court of Session. The validity, alteration, repeal or replacement of a simplified planning zone scheme or any order specified in subs. (3) as they apply to any plan or such alteration, repeal or replacement of the order may also be challenged in the courts.

Limitations. The right to challenge is subject to two important statutory limitations:
　　(i) any application to the Court of Session must be made within six weeks from the relevant date (subs. (4)). The relevant date for these purposes is defined in subs. (5). The Court of Session has no power to extend this statutory time-limit for lodging an application. This rule may operate harshly in some circumstances: see *R. v. Secretary of State for the Environment, ex p. Kent* [1990] 1 P.L.R 128. In this case, the Court of Appeal upheld a ruling by the divisional court that the applicant could not appeal against a planning permission granted for development near to his home, in circumstances where the applicant did not know that a planning application had even been made and had subsequently been appealed to the Secretary of State. This six week period has been subject to some criticism by the courts. In the case of *Smith v. East Elloe Rural District Council,* [1956] A.C. 736, Lord Radcliffe described the six week period as "pitifully inadequate". The House of Lords by majority held that an ouster clause similar in terms to s.238, deprived them of jurisdiction once the time period had expired, notwithstanding circumstances in which bad faith was alleged. However, in the later House of Lords decision in *Anisminic v. Foreign Compensation Commission* [1969] 2 A.C. 147, the House considered *Smith v. East Elloe Rural District Council.* According to Lord Reid, where a decision or determination is being challenged as a nullity, a person is not challenging the purported decision or determination, but is maintaining that it does not exist. In those circumstances, the ouster provision is not to be interpreted as excluding the courts' jurisdiction where nullity was in question. The House of Lords proceeded to distinguish the case of *Smith v. East Elloe Rural District Council* as unsatisfactory on the basis that there was no citation of other cases given to the House in that case, on the question whether a clause ousting the jurisdiction of the court applied when a nullity was in issue. In *Hamilton v. Secretary of State for Scotland,* 1972 S.L.T. 233, *Smith* was regarded as good law and the Court of Session regarded its jurisdiction as having been totally ousted. Lord Kissen proceeded to distinguish *Anisminic* on its facts and dismissed the action as incompetent (see also *Jeary v. Chailey R.D.C.* (1973) 26 P. & C.R. 280; *Lithgow v. Secretary of State for Scotland,* 1973 S.C. 1). The Court of Appeal had an opportunity to examine the operation of an ouster clause in *R. v. Secretary of State for the Environment, ex p. Ostler* [1977] Q.D. 122. In that case, which involved the validity of a compulsory purchase order, *Anisminic* was again distinguished on its facts. The court drew a distinction between decisions which are essentially judicial and other administrative decisions. Lord Denning found the *Anisminic* decision to be more of a judicial decision compared to the administrative nature of the decision in *Ostler.* The Court of Appeal went on to hold that Mr Ostler's appeal had become statute barred after the expiry of the six week time limit (for a full discussion of these and other cases see *Harlow* [1976] P.L. 304; *Alder* [1976] J.P.L. 270; *Wade* (1977) 93 L.Q.R.; *Whomersley* [1977] C.L.J. 4; *Gravells* (1978) 41 M.L.R. 383; *Alder* (1980) 43 M.L.R. 670; *Gravells* (43) M.L.R. 173; *Leigh* [1980] P.L. 34; *Reid,* 1984 S.P.L.P. 74 and 1984 S.L.T. (News) 297). However, in the case of *McDaid v. Clydebank District Council,* 1984 S.L.T. 162, the First Division following *Anisminic,* held that an absolute ouster clause in relation to an enforcement notice did not exclude the court's jurisdiction where the notice involved a nullity. No reference was made by the court to the English decisions of *Smith,*

Hamilton and Ostler, although it is difficult to believe that the Division was unaware of them. It is not clear whether the Division regarded the *McDaid* case as distinguishable on its facts on the basis that the clause in that case sought to oust the court's jurisdiction completely and it was therefore reconcilable with the *Smith cases*, or whether it formed the view that a preclusive clause could not protect a nullity as opined by Lord Reid. Given this uncertainty, it would be advisable to treat the *McDaid* decision with some caution.

(ii) the right to challenge is exercisable only by an "aggrieved person" (see note at s.239);

Statutory grounds of appeal. Subsection (1) contains the two statutory grounds of challenge under s.238. They are:

that the plan or order is not within the scope of Pt. II of this Act (or Pt. III in relation to simplified planning zone schemes) (subs. (1)(a)); or that there had been a failure to comply with a statutory requirement under that Part or any regulations made under it (subs. (1)(b)). Where a challenge is made on the grounds that a statutory requirement has not been followed, the person aggrieved must, if he is seeking a reduction of that decision or order being challenged, show some prejudice by reason of the failure to follow that requirement. Subsection (1)(a) and (b) may be regarded as the substantive *ultra vires* and procedural *ultra vires* grounds respectively. However, this distinction in practice tends largely to be academic as a procedural irregularity such as a breach of the inquiry rules may quite properly be regarded as falling outside the scope of the Act as well as being a failure to comply with any procedural requirements (see note to s.239).

Powers and procedure. An application under this section is made directly to the Inner House in Form 41.19 and must state the grounds of the appeal: Rules of the Court of Session 1994 (S.I. 1994 No.1443), R.C.S. 41.19. It must be served upon the Secretary of State any other person as the court thinks fit, such as the planning authority (R.C.S. 41.21(1)). It is not clear why an appeal is to be made direct to the Inner House. The 1997 Act simply provides for appeal to the Court of Session, however the annotations to r.41 of the R.C.S. state that, "by long tradition" such appeals are dealt with by the Inner House. This contrasts with the position in England and Wales where appeals are to the Queen's Bench Division of the High Court. The appellant thereafter may appeal to the Court of Appeal and from there to the House of Lords on a point of law. The appellant in Scotland may find it an advantage for his appeal to be heard by three judges, however for the courts, this is a costly and time-consuming exercise which requires more justification than "long tradition". This difficulty for the courts is highlighted by the fact that where there is a conflict of evidence, it is not unusual for the Inner House to direct that such evidence be heard by a single judge. Furthermore, as appeal from the Inner House lies only to the House of Lords, the Scottish appellant is denied an intermediate tier of appeal enjoyed by his English and Welsh counterparts. There may be some scope for the rules committee of the Court of Session to investigate whether it is necessary for planning appeals, or any other statutory appeals to continue to be directed straight to the Inner rather than Outer House.

On an application under s.238(2), the Court of Session is empowered to make an interim order suspending the operation of the plan or its alteration, repeal or replacement. This interim suspension may either be in general or only insofar as it affects the applicant or his property (s.238 (2)(a)). Where the court is satisfied that the statutory grounds of challenge have been established, it has a discretion to order that the plan, or as the case may be, its alteration, repeal or replacement be quashed in whole or in part: *Peak Park Joint Planning Board v. Secretary of State for the Environment* (1979) 39 P. & C.R. 361; see also *London Borough of Richmond upon Thames v. Secretary of State for the Environment* [1984] J.P.L. 24. Where the error is not significant, the court may be prepared to exercise its discretion not to quash the decision: *Property Investment Holdings v. Secretary of State for the Environment* [1984] J.P.L. 587; *London and Clydeside Properties v. Aberdeen District Council*, 1984 S.L.T 50. In *Glasgow District Council, City of v. Secretary of State for Scotland*, 1989 S.C. 150, the court held that although the reasoning of the Secretary of State was flawed, the decision itself was untainted and correct.

Effect of quashing. When deciding whether to quash a plan, decision or order, the court may either quash the plan or leave it *in situ*. According to Lord Cameron in *British Airports Authority v. Secretary of State for Scotland,* 1979 S.C. 200, the court has "no power to vary or alter or remodel" an order or decision under review. However, the precise wording of s.238(2)(b) allows the court to quash the plan "wholly or in part". The question therefore arises whether the invalid part of the plan or order under review can be severed from the valid part so that the plan or order survives. Some guidance may be derived from the court's approach to invalid conditions. In *Hall v. Shoreham-by-Sea Urban District Council* [1964] 1 W.L.R. 240, a planning condition which required the company in effect to dedicate a road to the public at the company's expense was held to be invalid. The local planning authority argued that if the condition was *ultra vires*, then the whole planning permission should fall as a nullity as the condition was an integral part of that permission. The Court of Appeal was persuaded that the invalid condition was fundamental to the whole planning permission and proceeded to quash that permission. The suggestion in that case was that if an *ultra vires* condition is not fundamental to the whole permission the courts may be prepared to sever it from the rest of the permission. This suggestion received some support from the House of Lords in the case of *Kent County Council v. Kingsway Investments (Kent)* [1971] A.C. 72. According to their lordships (*obiter*), if the invalid conditions were unimportant or merely incidental to the permission, severance is a possibility. If the invalid conditions are part of the structure of the permission, then the permission falls with it (see also *R. v. St Edmundsbury Borough Council ex p. Investors in Industry Commercial Properties* [1985] 1 W.L.R. 1157 at 1168). In *British Airports Authority v. Secretary of State for Scotland*, 1979 S.C. 200, the First Division held that certain conditions attached to the grant of planning permission were *ultra vires,* however the court could not simply excise the invalid conditions; the courts only power was to quash the planning permission. There may be some scope for this case to be reconsidered where the conditions in issue are merely incidental to the permission as opposed to an integral part of the whole. The same considerations may apply to the exercise of the court's power under s.238(2)(b). However, it will always be a question of fact and degree depending upon all the circumstances of the case whether, first, part of the plan or order is invalid, secondly whether the invalid part is an integral part of the whole plan or order or merely incidental, thirdly whether the interests of the applicant have been substantially prejudiced by the invalid part such as to justify the court either severing the invalid part or quashing the whole plan or order.

Proceedings for questioning the validity of other orders, decisions and directions

239.—(1) If any person—

(a) is aggrieved by any order to which this section applies and wishes to question the validity of that order on the grounds—

   (i) that the order is not within the powers of this Act, or

   (ii) that any of the relevant requirements have not been complied with in relation to that order, or

(b) is aggrieved by any action on the part of the Secretary of State to which this section applies and wishes to question the validity of that action on the grounds—

   (i) that the action is not within the powers of this Act, or

   (ii) that any of the relevant requirements have not been complied with in relation to that action,

he may make an application to the Court of Session under this section.

(2) Without prejudice to subsection (1), if the authority directly concerned with any order to which this section applies, or with any action on the part of the Secretary of State to which this section applies, wish to question the validity of that order or action on any of the grounds mentioned in subsection (1), the authority may make an application to the Court of Session under this section.

(3) An application under this section must be made within 6 weeks from the date on which the order is confirmed (or, in the case of an order under section 65 which takes effect under section 67 without confirmation, the date on which it takes effect) or, as the case may be, the date on which the action is taken.

(4) This section applies to any such order as is mentioned in subsection (2) of section 237 and to any such action on the part of the Secretary of State as is mentioned in subsection (3) of that section.

(5) On any application under this section the Court of Session—

(a) may, subject to subsection (6), by interim order suspend the operation of the order or action in question until the final determination of the proceedings;

(b) if satisfied that the order or action in question is not within the powers of this Act, or that the interests of the applicant have been substantially prejudiced by failure to comply with any of the relevant requirements in relation to it, may quash that order or action.

(6) Paragraph (a) of subsection (5) shall not apply to applications questioning the validity of tree preservation orders.

(7) In relation to a tree preservation order, or to an order made in pursuance of section 183(4), the powers conferred on the Court of Session by subsection (5) shall be exercisable by way of quashing or (where applicable) suspending the operation of the order either in whole or in part, as the court may determine.

(8) References in this section to the confirmation of an order include the confirmation of an order subject to modifications as well as the confirmation of an order in the form in which it was made.

(9) In this section "the relevant requirements", in relation to any order or action to which this section applies, means any requirements of this Act or of the Tribunals and Inquiries Act 1992, or of any order, regulations or rules made under this Act or under that Act which are applicable to that order or action.

(10) Any reference in this section to the authority directly concerned with any order or action to which this section applies—

(a) in relation to any such decision as is mentioned in section 237(3)(e), where the Secretary of State confirms the notice in question, wholly or in part, with the substitution of another local authority or statutory undertakers for the planning authority, includes a reference to that local authority or those statutory undertakers;

(b) in any other case, is a reference to the planning authority.

DEFINITIONS
"planning authority": ss.1, 277(1).
"statutory undertaker": ss.214, 277(1).
"tree preservation order": ss.160, 277(1).

GENERAL NOTE
This section prescribes the only means whereby the validity of the orders mentioned in s.237(2) and any action on the part of the Secretary of State mentioned in s.237(3) may be challenged. Their validity may not otherwise be challenged in any other proceedings (s.237(1)).

Persons aggrieved. There is no statutory definition of the expression "person aggrieved". In the past, the expression was interpreted strictly by the courts. According to Salmon J. in *Buxton v. Minister of Housing and Local Government* [1961] 1 Q.B. 278, only persons whose legal rights were infringed were entitled to bring proceedings where this expression was contained in an enactment (see also *Simpson v. Edinburgh Corporation*, 1960 S.C. 313 and *Gregory v. Camden London Borough Council* [1966] 1 W.L.R. 899). This narrow interpretation was expressly disapproved of (although not overruled) by Lord Denning in *Attorney-General (Gambia) v. N'Jie* [1961] A.C. 617 who stated the expression "a person aggrieved" is "of wide import and should not be subjected to a restrictive interpretation. They do not include, of course, a mere busybody who is interfering in things which do not concern him; but they do include a person who has a genuine grievance because an order has been made which prejudicially affects his interests". These dicta were approved in a slightly different context in the later case of *Maurice v. London County Council* [1964] 2 Q.B. 362. Here the Court of Appeal held that a householder whose property would have been injuriously affected by the construction of a tall building close by, was a "person aggrieved" for the purposes of the London Building Act 1939. The *Buxton* case was again distinguished by Ackner J. in *Turner v. Secretary of State for the Environment* (1973) 28 P. & C.R. 123 and Glidewell J. in *Hollis v. Secretary of State for the Environment* [1983] J.P.L. 164 on the basis that the applicable Town and Country Planning (Inquiries Procedure) Rules 1962 specifically provided for third-party participation in planning inquiries and therefore impliedly gave them the right to insist that procedural rules should be followed, notwithstanding that they may have no direct legal interest in the site itself. The *Turner* decision however, has been criticised by Hough, "Standing in Planning Appeals" [1992] J.P.L. 319 for failing to clarify the position of third parties who do not, for whatever reason, appear at an inquiry and those who had participated in an inquiry by way of written representations (see however comments of Lord Bridge in *Bizony v. Secretary of State for the Environment* [1976] J.P.L. 306). In *Wilson v. Secretary of State for the Environment* [1988] J.P.L. 540, no issue was taken on the right of an objector to challenge a decision in circumstances where he had not taken part in the appeal process which was dealt with by way of written representations. The respondents in the cases of *Easter*

Ross Land Use Committee v. Secretary of State for Scotland, 1970 S.L.T. 317 and *Bearsden Town Council v. Glasgow Corporation,* 1971 S.C. 274, denied that the appellants were "persons aggrieved", however, this issue was not actively pursued on appeal. According to the Court of Appeal in *Times Investment v. Secretary of State for the Environment* [1990] 3 P.L.R. 111, the expression "persons aggrieved" should be taken as extending to "any person who, in the ordinary sense of the word, is aggrieved by the decision". In that case, the court held that the appellants who had purchased property which was the subject of the grant of planning permission following an appeal, could be within the scope of the expression a "person aggrieved" notwithstanding that they had no interest in the land at the time of the appeal. The point here was that the permission and its conditions runs with the land and hence binds any subsequent purchaser.

The decision of *Bizony v. Secretary of State for the Environment* [1976] J.P.L. 306 established that the expression "person aggrieved" includes those who had received notification of the inquiry and who had submitted observations and would have been entitled to appear (see p. 152D-E). Similarly, the First Division in *North East Fife District Council v. Secretary of State for Scotland,* 1992 S.L.T. 373 held that several appellants who were present at a public inquiry and had made representations were within the scope of the expression "persons aggrieved". These decisions establish that the courts are prepared to regard those persons whose legal rights are affected by decisions falling within the scope of s.238 as "persons aggrieved" or s.239, or those individuals who made written or oral representations at a public inquiry.

The important decision of the Extra Division in *Cumming v. Secretary of State for Scotland,* 1993 S.L.T. 228 confirmed the flexible approach taken by both the English and Scottish courts in recent years to the scope of the expression "person aggrieved". In that case, the appellant challenged the grant of outline planning permission for the development of a roadside service area together with a 40 bedroomed lodgehouse, restaurant and parking for up to 120 cars. The application had simply been advertised as a roadside petrol station and service area. The appellant argued that he did not make any objection to the original application as he had been misled by the advertisement as to the scale of the proposed development. In considering whether the appellant was a "person aggrieved" the court considered that the central issue was "whether the appellant was genuinely deprived by the procedure in the present planning application of an opportunity to make representations which might (at least in his view) have affected the result". The court decided to adopt a broad brush approach to this case and formed the view that "in the peculiar circumstances of the present case, there is the feature that the description of the development in the planning application form was so inadequate as to mislead or put a member of the public off his guard about what its real purpose was". The court therefore held that the appellant was a "person aggrieved". While this case is to be welcomed as suggesting that the categories of persons with the scope of the expression "person aggrieved" are not finite, the court did make clear that this was a case which was decided upon its own facts and did not seek to lay down any guidelines or principles as to when other individuals may or may not fall within the scope of the expression "person aggrieved".

The Lardner decision. The suggestion that the categories of individuals within the scope of the expression "person aggrieved" were not closed was endorsed by the First Division in the recent decision of *Philip Lardner v. Renfrewshire Council,* 1997 G.W.D. 9-395. In this case, the appellant did not object in writing or at an inquiry into proposed changes to a local plan which would have affected an area of land in the neighbourhood of his property. The appellant had suggested in his pleadings that if the plan or map of the proposals had been advertised in the Inchinnan Community Centre, it was likely that the he would have learned of the proposals within the consultation period. The proposals were advertised widely in a number of other places, including Bridgewater Place public library, Erskine which was the closest public library to the appellant's home. In those circumstances, it was difficult for the appellant to argue that the statutory consultation process had not been followed. This is apparent from the speech of the Lord President who, in the absence of any argument on a breach of statutory duty on the part of the local authority in respect of the consultation procedures, proceeded on the basis that "since no criticism was made of the procedures adopted, we are dealing with a case where the council advertised the proposal properly, made adequate arrangements for members of the public to inspect the draft plan, gave adequate time for representations to be made, considered the objections, gave notice of a public inquiry and held a public inquiry at which objectors were heard". In those circumstances, the Lord President stated that "there is a difference between *feeling* aggrieved and *being* aggrieved: for the latter expression to be appropriate, some external basis for feeling "upset" is required – some denial of affront to his expectations or rights". This approach surprisingly seems to have fallen back upon the old restrictive interpretation of the expression "person aggrieved" in the *Buxton* case which has previously been rejected by the Scottish and English courts in recent years. Furthermore, such a distinction seeks to introduce a rather technical approach into what is already a complex issue. The Division was not satisfied that the appellant's private rights were in some way affected by the adoption of the local plan on the *Buxton* approach. Neither were they satisfied that the appellant fell within the scope of the expression "person aggrieved" following the *Turner* line of cases, by reason of his failure to object at the inquiry. While the Division were reluctant to "suggest that someone who has not objected to a draft plan or taken part in an inquiry can never be "a person aggrieved", they were not prepared to extend the *Cummings* decision to an individual who did not take part in the inquiry process in the absence of any suggestion of bad faith or breach of consultation procedures.

Planning authority as a person aggrieved. The decision of the divisional court in *Ealing Corporation v. Jones* [1959] 1 Q.B. 384 is authority for the proposition that a planning authority is not a person aggrieved. In that case, Lord Parker C.J. held that if Parliament had intended a planning authority to be able to appeal to the courts (under s.238 of this Act), then it would have expressly provided for this in the legislation. However, this approach was expressly disapproved of, although not overruled, by the Court of Appeal in the case of *Cook v. Southend Borough Council* [1990] 1 All E.R. 243. The court held that the expression "person aggrieved" was to be given its ordinary natural meaning rather than the narrow interpretation adopted in previous cases. Further, a planning authority would not have to show that the decision being challenged imposed any special legal burden upon it in order to come within the scope of the expression. Interestingly, Lord Woolf drew an analogy between *locus standi* in judicial review and the expression "person aggrieved" and suggested that the approach of the courts on appeal are the same (p. 255 a–b). This view seems sensible in that it would avoid the anomaly between a public body having the necessary title and interest for a challenge in judicial review but lacking standing in parallel statutory review proceedings (note however the preclusive nature of ss.238 and 239 which excludes legal proceedings except in accordance with those sections). In contrast to the Cook decision, the case of *Strathclyde Regional Council v. Secretary of State for Scotland*, 1989 S.L.T. 821, the Second Division held that a regional council was not a "person aggrieved" for the purposes of a challenge under s.232 of the 1972 Act (now s.238). In this case, the council were dissatisfied with modifications made to its structure plans by the Secretary of State and sought to challenge their validity. The Second Division fully endorsed the *Ealing* decision. The Lord Justice Clerk pointed out that Parliament had had an opportunity in the 1972 Act to make express provision for an authority to appeal against the validity of alterations to development plans, similar to the provision in s.233 (now s.239) and had not done so. However, in the subsequent case of *Strathclyde Regional Council v. Secretary of State for Scotland (No. 2)*, 1990 S.L.T. 149 the Court of Session ruled that the planning authority was a "person aggrieved" under s.233 (now s.239). The 1989 decision in *Strathclyde Regional Council v. Secretary of State* was unconvincingly distinguished by the Lord Justice Clerk who stated that "I remain of the opinion expressed in *Strathclyde Regional Council v. Secretary of State for Scotland* 1989 that the regional planning authority were not persons aggrieved within the meaning of s.232(1). Apart from anything else, as the structure plan contained a statement of the regional planning authority's policy and general proposals, I am satisfied that the regional planning authority could never qualify to be a person aggrieved by its *own* (emphasis added) statement of policy and general proposals. That consideration, however, does not apply to s.233". This comment by the Lord Justice Clerk leaves open the question whether a planning authority can be a "person aggrieved" under s.238 in situations where the planning authority is not seeking to challenge its own policies, but amendments, alterations and repeals to those policies made by the Secretary of State.

Grounds of Challenge. Subsection (1) contains the two statutory grounds of appeal first, that the action or order is not within the powers of this Act and secondly, that any of the relevant requirements have not been complied with.

(a) *Ground 1.* "Relevant requirements" are defined further in subs. (9) as any requirements of this Act or of the Tribunals and Inquiries Act 1992 (c.53), or of any order, regulations or rules made under this Act or the Act which is applicable to the particular order or decision. The House of Lords in *Smith v. East Elloe Rural District Council* [1956] A.C. 736 adopted differing narrow interpretations of the first ground of appeal (see also *Hamilton v. Secretary of State for Scotland*, 1972 S.C. 72; *Lithgow v. Secretary of State for Scotland* 1973 S.C. 1). However, in the leading case of *Ashbridge Investments v. Minister of Housing and Local Government* [1965] 1 W.L.R. 1320, the Court of Appeal rejected this approach.

According to Denning L.J.:

> "Under this section it seems to me that the court can interfere with the Minister's decision if he has acted on no evidence; or if he has come to a conclusion to which on the evidence he could not reasonably have come; or if he has given a wrong interpretation to the words of

the statute; or if he has taken into consideration matters which he ought not to have taken into account, or *vice versa*. It is identical with the position when the Court has power to interfere with the decision of a lower tribunal which has erred in point of law" (at p. 1326).

The Ashbridge "formulae" has been impliedly accepted by the Scottish courts. According to Emslie L.J. in *Wordie Property Co. v. Secretary of State for Scotland*, 1984 S.L.T. 345, "little doubt" remains as to the scope of the statutory grounds of challenge. Lord Denning's test has since been adopted in a number of subsequent cases: see *Howard v. Minister of Housing and Local Government* (1967) 65 L.G.R. 257; *British Dredging (Services) v. Secretary of State for Wales and Monmouthshire* [1975] 1 W.L.R. 687; *Seddon Properties v. Secretary of State for the Environment* [1978] J.P.L. 835; *Eckersley v. Secretary of State for the Environment* (1977) 34 P. & C.R. 124. Further, in the case of *Bradley (Edwin H.) & Sons v. Secretary of State for the Environment* (1982) 47 P. & C.R 374, Glidewell J. (as he then was), made the point that Denning L.J. was doing no more than enunciating the same principles as those formulated by Greene L.J. in *Associated Provincial Picture Houses v. Wednesbury Corporation* [1948] 1 K.B. 233.

(b) *Ground 2.* The second ground of challenge relating to relevant requirements is qualified by the need for the appellant to show substantial prejudice by reason of the failure to comply with the relevant requirements (subs. (4)(b); see *McMillan v. Inverness-shire County Council*, 1949 S.C. 77). The court is entitled not to exercise its general discretion to quash in the absence of any substantial prejudice to the appellant: *Steele v. Minister of Housing and Local Government* (1956) 6 P. & C.R. 386; *Camden London Borough Council v. Secretary of State for the Environment* (1975) 235 E.G. 375; *Kent County Council v. Secretary of State for the Environment* (1976) 33 P. & C.R. 70; *London Borough of Greenwich v. Secretary of State for the Environment* [1981] J.P.L. 809; *Schleider v. Secretary of State for the Environment* [1983] J.P.L. 383. This ground generally raises the question of whether a procedural requirement has been fulfilled such as a breach of a mandatory or directory requirement (*James v. Secretary of State for Wales* [1966] 1 W.L.R 135; *London and Clydeside Estates v. Aberdeen District Council*, 1980 S.C. 1 (H.L.). If the breach complained of is more than a mere technicality, the courts will intervene (see for example: *McCowan v. Secretary of State for Scotland*, 1972 S.C. 93; *Peak Park Joint Planning Board v. Secretary of State for the Environment* (1979) 39 P. & C.R. 361. The circumstances of individual cases may produce an overlap between the two grounds of challenge under s.239. In those circumstances, the general rule is that the decision should be quashed unless the breach is purely technical: *London Borough of Richmond upon Thames v. Secretary of State for the Environment* [1984] J.P.L. 24 which may contrast with *Westminster City Council v. Secretary of State for the Environment* [1984] J.P.L. 27. Failure by the appellant to take an early objection to an irregularity may be taken as indicative of a lack of substantial prejudice: *Davies v. Secretary of State for Wales* [1977] J.P.L. 102; *George v. Secretary of State for the Environment* (1979) 38 P. & C.R. 609; *Midlothian District Council v. Secretary of State for Scotland*, 1980 S.C. 210; see also comments in 1981 S.P.L.P. 17).

The Seddon Properties Tests. The circumstances in which the courts will be prepared to quash a decision under the statutory grounds were summarised by Forbes J. in *Seddon Properties v. Secretary of State for the Environment* (1981) 42 P. & C.R. 26. The importance of these dicta is such that it deserves to be set out in full:

"(1) The Secretary of State must not act perversely. That is, if the court considers that no reasonable person in the position of the Secretary of State, properly directing himself on the relevant material, could have reached the conclusion which he did reach, the decision may be overturned. See *e.g.*, *Ashbridge Investments v. Minister of Housing and Local Government* [1965] 1 W.L.R. 1320, *per* Lord Denning M.R. at 1326F and Harman L.J. at 1328H. This is really no more than another example of the principle enshrined in a sentence from the judgment of Lord Greene M.R. in *Associated Provincial Picture Houses v. Wednesbury Corporation* [1948] 1 K.B. 223 at 230:

"It is true to say that, if a decision on a competent matter is so unreasonable that no reasonable authority could ever have come to it, then the courts can interfere."

(2) In reaching his conclusion the Secretary of State must not take into account irrelevant material or fail to take into account that which is relevant: see, *e.g.*, again the *Ashbridge Investments* case *per* Lord Denning M.R. *loc. cit.*

(3) The Secretary of State must abide by the statutory procedures, in particular by the Town and Country Planning (Inquiries Procedure) Rules 1974. These Rules require him to give reasons for his decision after a planning inquiry (r.13) and those reasons must be proper and adequate reasons which are clear and intelligible, and deal with the substantial points which have been raised: *Poyser and Mills Arbitration, Re* [1964] 2 Q.B. 467.

(4) The Secretary of State, in exercising his powers, which include reaching a decision such as that in this case, must not depart from the principles of natural justice: *per* Lord Russell of Killowen in *Fairmount Investments v. Secretary of State for the Environment* [1976] 1 W.L.R. 1255 at 1263D.

(5) If the Secretary of State differs from his inspector on a finding of fact or takes into account any new evidence or matter of fact not canvassed at the inquiry, he must, if this involves disagreeing with the inspector's recommendations, notify the parties and give them at least an opportunity of making further representations: (r.12 of the Scottish Inquiries Procedure Rules 1980).

There are other peripheral principles. If he differs from the inspector on an inference of fact he must have sufficient material to enable him to do so: *per* Lord Denning M.R. in *Coleen Properties v. Minister of Housing and Local Government* [1971] 1 All E.R. 1049 at 1053C. Otherwise the courts can interfere in accordance with the first principle stated above. If it is a matter of planning policy he is free to disagree with the inspector's conclusions or recommendations without bringing into operation r.12: *Pavenham (Lord Luke of) v. Minister of Housing and Local Government* [1968] 1 Q.B. 172; but of course, he must make clear what the policy is and its relevance to the issues raised at the inquiry in accordance with the third principle above. If there has been conflicting evidence at the inquiry it seems to me that he may, if he wishes, prefer one piece of evidence to another, though the material must be there to enable him to do so, he must give reasons for doing so, and if he is disagreeing with a finding of fact by the inspector he must apply the procedure of (r.12). Since the courts will interfere only if he acts beyond his powers (which is the foundation of all the above principles) it is clear that his powers include the determination of the weight to be given to any particular contention; he is entitled to attach what weight he pleases to the various arguments and contentions of the parties; the courts will not entertain a submission that he gave undue weight to one argument or failed to give any weight at all to another. Again in doing so he must, at any rate if substantial issues are involved, give clear reasons for his decision. In considering whether or not the Secretary of State has acted contrary to any of these principles the materials upon which the court may come to a conclusion are, in general, the inspector's report and the letter of the Secretary of State setting out his decision. In approaching this task it is no part of the court's duty to subject the decision letter to the kind of scrutiny appropriate to the determination of the meaning of a contract or a statute. Because the letter is addressed to the parties who are well aware of all the issues involved and of the arguments deployed at the inquiry, it is not necessary to rehearse every argument relating to each matter in ever paragraph."

The *Seddon* case should now be compared with the recent decision of *London and Midland Developments v. Secretary of State for Scotland and Dawn Construction* (1996) 55 SPEL 52.

The role of the courts when reviewing planning decisions was confirmed by Hoffman L.J in the court of appeal decision of *Somerset District Council v. Secretary of State for the Environment* [1993] 1 P.L.R. 80. In essence, the court is not entitled to substitute its own views on planning merits for that of the reporter's. This is of paramount importance in the context of the exercise of the court's supervisory jurisdiction as Hoffman L.J. makes clear:

> "The inspector is not writing an examination paper on current and draft development plans. The letter must read in good faith and references to policies must be taken in the context of the general thrust of the inspector's reasoning. A reference to a policy does not necessarily mean that it played a significant part in the reasoning: it may have been mentioned only because it was urged on the inspector by one of the representatives of the parties and he wanted to make it clear that he had not overlooked it. Sometimes his statement of policy may be elliptical but this does not necessarily show misunderstanding. One must look at what the inspector thought the important planning issues were and decide whether it appears from the way he dealt with them that he must have misunderstood a relevant policy or proposed alteration to policy."

The exercise of the court's discretion to quash. The Court of Appeal decision in *Bolton Metropolitan Borough Council v. Secretary of State for the Environment* (1990) 61 P. & C.R. 343 provides further guidance on the exercise of the court's discretion to quash a decision in circumstances where the Secretary of State has failed to take into account a material consideration. The following propositions were suggested by Glidewell L.J.:

> "(1) The expressions used in the authorities that the decision maker has failed to take into account a matter which is relevant, which is the formulation for instance in Forbes J.'s judgment in *Seddon Properties* (1981) 42 P. & C.R. 26, or that he failed to take into consideration matters which he ought to take into account, which was the way that Lord Greene put it in *Wednesbury* and Lord Denning in *Ashbridge Investments*, have the same meaning.

(2) The decision maker ought to take into account a matter which might cause him to reach a different conclusion to that which he would reach if he did not take it into account. Such a matter is relevant to his decision making process. By the verb "might", I mean where there is a real possibility that he would reach a different conclusion if he did take that consideration into account.

(3) If the matter is trivial or of small importance in relation to the particular decision, then it follows that if it were taken into account there would be a real possibility that it would make no difference to the decision and thus it is not a matter which the decision maker ought to take into account.

(4) As Hodgson J. said [at first instance], there is clearly a distinction between matters which a decision maker is obliged by statute to take into account and those where the obligation to take into account is to be implied from the nature of the decision and of the matter in question (*Creed (N.Z.) Incorporated v. Governor-General* [1981] 1 N.Z.L.R. 172).

(5) If the validity of the decision is challenged on the ground that the decision maker failed to take into account a matter in the second category, it is for the judge to decide whether it was a matter which the decision maker should have taken into account.

(6) If the judge concludes that the matter was "fundamental to the decision", or that it is clear that there is a real possibility that the consideration of the matter would have made a difference to the decision, he is thus enabled to hold that the decision was not validly made. But if the judge is uncertain whether the matter would have had this effect or was of such importance in the decision-making process, then he does not have before him the material necessary to conclude that the decision was invalid.

(7) (Though it does not arise in the circumstances of this case). Even if the judge has concluded that he could not hold that the decision is invalid, in exceptional circumstances he is entitled nevertheless, in the exercise of his discretion, not to grant any relief".

Challenges by way of judicial review. The preclusive provisions of this Part of this Act only extend to the decisions, orders or schemes mentioned in s.237. Outside these preclusive provisions, the remedy of judicial review is available. However, the courts may nonetheless still refuse to entertain a petition for judicial review on the principle that any statutory remedy must be exhausted before the court's supervisory jurisdiction may be invoked (for a detailed discussion of this principle see Reid , *"Failure to Exhaust Statutory Remedies"* 1984 J.R. 185; also see *British Railways Board v. Glasgow Corporation,* 1976 S.C. 224 *and Bellway Homes v. Strathclyde Regional Council,* 1980 S.L.T. 66).

Title and Interest. Title and interest or *"locus standi"* in judicial review proceedings is a prerequisite before the court will entertain a petition to exercise its supervisory jurisdiction. The case of *Nichol (D. & J.) v. Dundee Harbour Trs*, 1915 S.C. (H.L.) 7 held that "for a person to have such title he must be a party to some legal relation which gives him some right which the person against whom he raises the action either infringes or denies". Similarly, in the case of *Simpson v. Edinburgh Corporation*, 1960 S.C. 313, the court refused to entertain a challenge to the grant of planning permission for development of certain land from a neighbouring proprietor, on the basis that the appellant was not privy to the relationship between the planning authority and the developer. This decision can no longer be regarded as good law, given the current neighbour notification rights in existing planning rules. The liberal approach taken by the Lord Ordinary in *Wilson v. IBA*, 1979 S.L.T. 279 suggested that any member of the public would have title to enforce a public duty provided that they could demonstrate that the title was coupled with a sufficient interest in the subject matter of the petition. The nature of that interest was not defined by the court. The decision of Lord Clyde in *Scottish Old People's Welfare Council, Petrs*, 1987 S.L.T. 179 adopted a narrow interpretation of "interest". In that case, the petitioners were a pressure group who campaigned on behalf of the elderly to challenge the legality of government instructions on cold weather payments to the elderly. Although Lord Clyde held that the petitioners had sufficient title to sue, he held that their interest was too remote to give them a right to sue. This was on the basis that the petitioners were "not suing as a body of potential claimants but as a body working to protect and advance the interests of the aged". This was held to be insufficient. This approach adopts a very careful distinction between title and interest and concludes that one does not necessarily follow the other. The approach adopted by the English courts on the issue of standing has refused to follow the Scottish cases and is markedly more liberal. In recent years, the English courts have not suffered great difficulty in granting standing to the Child Poverty Action Group (*R v. Secretary of State for Social Services, ex p. Child Poverty Action Group* [1990] 2 Q.B. 540; the Equal Opportunities Commission (*R. v. Secretary of State for Employment, ex p. Equal Opportunities Commission* [1993] 1 All E.R. 1022; Greenpeace (*R. v. H.M. Inspectorate of Pollution, ex p. Greenpeace (No.2)* [1994] 4 All E.R. 329; Friends of the Earth (*R. v. Secretary of State for the Environment, ex p. Friends of the Earth* [1995] Env.L.R. 11,

Q.B.D.; the World Development Movement who challenged the grant of aid for the Pergau dam (*R. v. Secretary of State for Foreign and Commonwealth Affairs, ex p. World Development Movement* [1995] 1 All E.R. 611. The current narrow position of the Scottish law on title and interest was reaffirmed recently by the action of Greenpeace in seeking judicial review proceedings in England in relation to the ministerial approval for the disposal of the Brent Spar platform in waters of Scotland, rather than challenging this approval in the Scottish courts (*R. v. Secretary of State for Scotland, ex p. Greenpeace,* 1995 (unreported)). Although Popplewell J. declined to accept jurisdiction in that case, he accepted on the basis of opinions provided by leading Scottish counsel that Greenpeace would be likely to have difficulty in establishing sufficient title and interest in Scottish judicial review proceedings. The action taken by Greenpeace can be regarded as a lack of faith in the Scottish legal system, but also as a missed opportunity for the Scottish courts to either confirm the approach of the courts in *Scottish Old People's Welfare Council, Ptrs* or to reject it as no longer good law (for a detailed analysis of title and interest, see Munro, Standing in Judicial Review, 1995 S.L.T. 279).

Scope of the Supervisory Jurisdiction of the Court of Session. The decision of the Inner House in the case of *West v. Secretary of State for Scotland*, 1992 S.L.T. 636 made a number of important propositions (at pp. 650–1) on the scope of the supervisory jurisdiction of the Court of Session. Those propositions are set out here in full:

"(1) The Court of Session has power, in the exercise of its supervisory jurisdiction, to regulate the process by which decisions are taken by any person or body to whom a jurisdiction, power or authority has been delegated or entrusted by statute, agreement or any other instrument.

(2) The sole purpose for which the supervisory jurisdiction may be exercised is to ensure that the person or body does not exceed or abuse that jurisdiction, power or authority or fail to do what the jurisdiction, power or authority requires.

(3) The competency of the application does not depend upon any distinction between public law and private law, nor is it confined to those cases which English law has accepted as amenable to judicial review, nor is it correct in regard to issues about competency to describe judicial review under Rule of Court 260B as a public law remedy.

By way of explanation we would emphasis these important points:

(a) Judicial review is available, not to provide machinery for an appeal, but to ensure that the decision maker does not exceed or abuse his powers or fail to perform the duty entrusted to him. It is not competent for the court to review the act or decision on its merits, nor may it substitute its own opinion for that of the person or body to whom the matter had been delegated or entrusted.

(b) The word "jurisdiction" best describes the nature of the power, duty or authority committed to the person or body which is amenable to the supervisory jurisdiction of the court. It is used here as meaning simply "power to decide", and it can be applied to acts or decisions of any administrative bodies and persons with similar functions as well as those of inferior tribunals. An excess or abuse of jurisdiction may involve stepping outside it, or failing to observe its limits, or departing from the rules of natural justice, or a failure to understand the law, or the taking into account of matters which ought not to have been taken into account. The categories of what may amount to an excess or abuse of jurisdiction are not closed, and they are capable of being adapted in accordance with the development of administrative law.

(c) There is no substantial difference between English law and Scots law as to the grounds on which the process of decision making may be open to review. So reference may be made to English cases in order to determine whether there has been an excess or abuse of the jurisdiction, power or authority or a failure to do what it requires.

(d) Contractual rights and obligations, such as those between employer and employee, are not as such amenable to judicial review. The cases in which the supervisory jurisdiction is appropriate involve a tripartite relationship, between the person or body to whom the jurisdiction, power or authority has been delegated or entrusted, the person or body by whom it has been delegated or entrusted and the person or persons in respect of or for whose benefit that jurisdiction, power or authority is to be exercised."

Special provisions as to decisions relating to statutory undertakers

240. In relation to any action which—

(a) apart from the provisions of Part X, would fall to be taken by the Secretary of State and, if so taken, would be action falling within section 237(3), but

(b) by virtue of that Part, is required to be taken by the Secretary of State and the appropriate Minister,

the provisions of sections 237 and 239 shall have effect (subject to section 241) as if any reference in those provisions to the Secretary of State were a reference to the Secretary of State and the appropriate Minister.

DEFINITIONS
"appropriate Minister": ss.217, 277(1).
"Minister": s.277(1).
"statutory undertakers": ss.214, 277(1).

GENERAL NOTE
This section provides that references to action by the Secretary of State in ss.237 and 239 and action by virtue of Pt. X which is required to be taken by the Secretary of State and the appropriate Minister shall have effect as if any such reference were a reference to the Secretary of State and the appropriate Minister.

Statutory undertakers. In addition to the undertakers within the definition of s.214(1), the following are deemed by virtue of s.214(3) to (7) to be statutory undertakers for the purposes of this section: any public gas transporter, the Post Office, the Civil Aviation Authority and electricity undertakings holding a licence under s.6 of the Electricity Act 1989.

Special provisions as to orders subject to special parliamentary procedure

241.—(1) Where an order under section 202, 203 or 230 is subject to special parliamentary procedure, then—

(a) if the order is confirmed by Act of Parliament under section 2(4), as read with section 10, of the Statutory Orders (Special Procedure) Act 1945, or under section 6 of that Act, sections 237 and 238 shall not apply to the order,

(b) in any other case, section 238 shall have effect in relation to the order as if, in subsection (4) of that section, for the reference to the date there mentioned there were substituted a reference to the date on which the order becomes operative under that Act ("the operative date").

(2) Where by virtue of Part X any such action as is mentioned in section 240 is required to be embodied in an order, and that order is subject to special parliamentary procedure, then—

(a) if the order in which the action is embodied is confirmed by Act of Parliament under that Act of 1945, sections 237 and 239 shall not apply, and

(b) in any other case, the provisions of section 239 shall apply with the substitution, for any reference to the date on which the action is taken, of a reference to the operative date.

GENERAL NOTE
This section prevents a challenge to the validity of orders made under ss.202, 203 or 230 where the order is subject to special parliamentary procedure and has been confirmed by Act of Parliament (subs. (1)(a) and subs. (2)(a)). Where the order is not confirmed by an Act, then a challenge to its validity under ss.237 to 239 is competent but with substituted provisions as to the operative date of the order.

PART XII

CROWN LAND

Preliminary

Preliminary definitions

242.—(1) In this Part—
"Crown land" means land in which there is a Crown interest;
"Crown interest" means an interest belonging to Her Majesty in right of
    the Crown or belonging to a government department or held in
    trust for Her Majesty for the purposes of a government depart-
    ment; and
"private interest" means interest which is not a Crown interest.
(2) For the purposes of this Part "the appropriate authority", in relation to
any land—
(a) in the case of land belonging to Her Majesty in right of the Crown and
     forming part of the Crown Estate, means the Crown Estate
     Commissioners;
(b) in relation to any other land belonging to Her Majesty in right of the
     Crown, means the government department having the management
     of that land; and
(c) in the case of land belonging to a government department or held in
     trust for Her Majesty for the purposes of a government department,
     means that department.
(3) If any question arises as to what authority is the appropriate authority
in relation to any land, that question shall be referred to the Treasury, whose
decision shall be final.
(4) A person who is entitled to occupy Crown land by virtue of a contract in
writing shall be treated for the purposes of section 245(1)(c), so far as applicable to Parts III, VI and VII, and sections 243(2) to (7), 244, 248 and 249 as
having an interest in land and references in section 248 to the disposal of an
interest in Crown land, and in that section and sections 243(2) and 249 to a
private interest in such land, shall be construed accordingly.

DEFINITIONS
   "appropriate authority": subs. (2).
   "Crown interest": subs. (1).
   "Crown land": subs. (1).
   "disposal": s.277(1).
   "government department": s.277(1).
   "land": s.277(1).
   "private interest": subs. (1).

GENERAL NOTE
   The House of Lords, in the case of the *Lord Advocate v. Dumbarton District Council* [1990] 1
All E.R. 1, made clear that the Crown was not bound by any statutory provisions except by
express words or by necessary implication. This creates an obvious lacuna in relation to the
application of the planning legislation and its inherent controls to Crown land (see *42 H.C.
Official Report (6th Series) Written Answers col. 459 (May 12, 1983)*). The Town and Country
Planning Act 1984 (c.10) was passed in an attempt to remedy several difficulties arising out of the
status of Crown land such as the inability of the Crown to obtain planning permission for development prior to the disposal of land (see *R. v. Worthing Borough Council and Secretary of State
for the Environment, ex p. Burch (G.H.)* [1984] J.P.L. 261). Thus, the 1984 Act as amended,
allowed the appropriate authority in respect of Crown land to apply, for example, for planning
permission and listed building consent, hazardous substances consent, conservation area consent or a determination of whether planning permission is required. Part XII of the Town and

Country Planning Act 1997 consolidates previous legislation on the special status of the Crown in relation to planning matters.

Scope of the existing planning regime in respect of Crown land. Crown land is subject to a degree of planning control to the extent of:

(1) development by or on behalf of the Crown on Crown land. Although there is a general system of immunity from most planning controls, an informal system of consultation exists in terms of a Scottish Development Department Circular, *Crown Land and Crown Development SDD Circular 21/1984*;

(2) development of a privately-held interest in Crown land is subject to planning control in the normal way, although enforcement action requires the consent of the appropriate authority (s.245(2));

(3) where development has taken place by neither the Crown or a privately-owned interest, the planning authority may serve a special enforcement notice under s.243(3);

(4) the Crown or a third-party may seek planning permission in anticipation of a disposal of Crown land under s.248. The normal procedures for the grant or refusal of planning permission apply.

Development by the Crown. The informal system of consultation established by *SDD Circular 21/84 Crown Land and Crown Development*, requires that instead of an application for planning permission submitted by the Crown under the normal procedures, the appropriate authority will submit a proposed notice of development to the planning authority. The planning authority may agree thereafter, within two months, to inform the appropriate authority whether it finds the proposals acceptable with or without conditions. In the absence of agreement between the parties, the proposals may be submitted to the Secretary of State for a resolution. The Secretary of State's decision may be challenged by way of judicial review: *R. v. Secretary of State for the Environment, ex p. Gosport Borough Council* [1992] J.P.L. 476.

Application of Act as respects Crown land

Control of development on Crown land: special enforcement notices

243.—(1) No enforcement notice shall be served under section 127 in respect of development carried out by or on behalf of the Crown after 1st July 1948 on land which was Crown land at the time when the development was carried out.

(2) The following provisions of this section apply to development of Crown land carried out otherwise than by or on behalf of the Crown at a time when no person is entitled to occupy it by virtue of a private interest.

(3) Where—

(a) it appears to a planning authority that development to which this section applies has taken place in their district, and

(b) they consider it expedient to do so having regard to the provisions of the development plan and to any other material considerations,

they may issue a notice under this section (a "special enforcement notice").

(4) No special enforcement notice shall be issued except with the consent of the appropriate authority.

(5) A special enforcement notice shall specify—

(a) the matters alleged to constitute development to which this section applies, and

(b) the steps which the authority issuing the notice require to be taken for restoring the land to its condition before the development took place or for discontinuing any use of the land which has been instituted by the development.

(6) A special enforcement notice shall also specify—

(a) the date on which it is to take effect ("the specified date"), and

(b) the period within which any such steps as are mentioned in subsection (5)(b) are to be taken.

(7) A special enforcement notice may specify different periods for the taking of different steps.

DEFINITIONS
    "appropriate authority": s.242(2).
    "Crown land": s.242(1).
    "development": ss.26, 277(1).
    "development plan": s.277(1).
    "enforcement notice": ss.127, 277(1).
    "land": s.277(1).
    "planning authority": ss.1, 277(1).
    "private interest": s.242(1).
    "special enforcement notice": subs. (3).
    "specified date": subs. (6).
    "use": s.277(1).

GENERAL NOTE
    This provision only applies to development or a material change of use of Crown land otherwise than by or on behalf of the Crown or by the holder of a private interest in the Crown land.

Subs. (1)
    Subsection (1) confers immunity from enforcement in respect of development, or a material change of use by the Crown on Crown land after July 1, 1948. This immunity continues after the land ceases to be Crown land: *Newbury District Council v. Secretary of State for the Environment* [1977] J.P.L. 373. Under s.250 however, the Crown may agree that the material change of use will not continue after disposal of the land without further planning permission.

Subs. (3)
    Under subs. (3), where unauthorised development has taken place on Crown land by an individual or individuals other than or on behalf of the Crown or a person with a private interest, the planning authority is empowered to issue a special enforcement notice. The planning authority must obtain the consent of the appropriate authority (see definition in s.242(2)) in order for the special enforcement notice to be valid.

Subs. (5)
    The enforcement notice is closely modelled on the enforcement notices issued under Pt. VI of this Act. The notice must specify:
    (1) the matters which it is alleged constitute development to which this section applies;
    (2) the steps the authority require to be taken for restoring the land to its previous condition or for discontinuing any use which has been instituted by the development.

Subs. (6)
    The notice must specify the date on which it is to take effect and the period within which the planning authority require the notice to be complied with.

Supplementary provisions as to special enforcement notices

244.—(1) Not later than 28 days after the date of the issue of a special enforcement notice and not later than 28 days before the specified date, the planning authority who issued it shall serve a copy of it—
    (a) on the person who carried out the development alleged in the notice,
    (b) on any person who is occupying the land when the notice is issued, and
    (c) on the appropriate authority.
    (2) The planning authority need not serve a copy of the notice on the person mentioned in subsection (1)(a) if they are unable after reasonable enquiry to identify or trace him.
    (3) Any such person as mentioned in subsection (1)(a) or (b) may, at any time before the date specified in the notice as the date on which it is to take effect, appeal against the notice to the Secretary of State on the ground that the matters alleged in the notice—
    (a) have not taken place, or
    (b) do not constitute development to which section 243 applies.
    (4) A person may appeal against a special enforcement notice under subsection (3) whether or not he was served with a copy of it.
    (5) The provisions contained in or having effect under sections 130(2) and (3), 131(1) to (3), 132 and 133(1) shall apply to special enforcement notices

issued by planning authorities and to appeals against them under subsection (3) as they apply to enforcement notices and to appeals under section 130.

(6) The Secretary of State may by regulations apply to special enforcement notices and to appeals under subsection (3) such other provisions of this Act (with such modifications as he thinks fit) as he thinks necessary or expedient.

DEFINITIONS

"appropriate authority": s.242(2).
"development": ss.26, 277(1).
"enforcement notice": ss.127, 277(1).
"land": s.277(1).
"planning authority": ss.1, 277(1).

GENERAL NOTE

This section prescribes further requirements to be followed in respect of the service of a special enforcement notice. The person upon whom such a notice is served is entitled to appeal to the Secretary of State against the service of such a notice on the grounds that:
(1) the matters alleged in the notice have not taken place, or
(2) the matters do not constitute development to which s.243 applies.

Exercise of powers in relation to Crown land

245.—(1) Notwithstanding any interest of the Crown in Crown land, but subject to the following provisions of this section—
  (a) a plan approved, adopted or made under Part II may include proposals relating to the use of Crown land;
  (b) any power to acquire land compulsorily under Part VIII may be exercised in relation to any interest in Crown land which is for the time being held otherwise than by or on behalf of the Crown;
  (c) any restrictions or powers imposed or conferred by Part III, VI or VII, by the provisions of Chapter I of Part V relating to purchase notices, or by any of the provisions of sections 218 to 222, shall apply and be exercisable in relation to Crown land, to the extent of any interest in it for the time being held otherwise than by or on behalf of the Crown.
(2) Except with the consent of the appropriate authority—
  (a) no order or notice shall be made, issued or served under any of the provisions of section 71, 72, 125, 127, 129, 140, 145, 160 or 179 or paragraphs 1, 3, 5 and 6 of Schedule 8 or under any of those provisions as applied by any order or regulations made under Part VII, in relation to land which for the time being is Crown land;
  (b) no interest in land which for the time being is Crown land shall be acquired compulsorily under Part VIII.
(3) No purchase notice shall be served in relation to any interest in Crown land unless—
  (a) an offer has been previously made by the owner of that interest to dispose of it to the appropriate authority on equivalent terms, and
  (b) that offer has been refused by the appropriate authority.
(4) In subsection (3) "equivalent terms" means that the price payable for the interest shall be equal to (and shall, in default of agreement, be determined in the same manner as) the compensation which would be payable in respect of it if it were acquired in pursuance of a purchase notice.
(5) The rights conferred by the provisions of Chapter II of Part V shall be exercisable by a person who (within the meaning of those provisions) is an owner-occupier of a hereditament or agricultural unit which is Crown land, or is a resident owner-occupier of a hereditament which is Crown land, in the same way as they are exercisable in respect of a hereditament or agricultural unit which is not Crown land, and those provisions shall apply accordingly.

DEFINITIONS

"agricultural": s.277(1).
"appropriate authority": s.242(2).

"Crown land": s.242(1).
"development plan": ss.24, 277(1).
"equivalent terms": subs. (4).
"land": s.277(1).
"owner": s.277(1).
"purchase notice": ss.88, 277(1).
"use": s.277(1).

GENERAL NOTE
This section prescribes the general powers which are exercisable in respect of Crown land, without prejudice to the Crown's immunity from planning controls. Under subs. (1)(a), development plans may include proposals relating to the use and development of Crown land. Subsection (1)(b) contains the power of compulsory purchase in respect of any interest in Crown land which is not held by or on behalf or the Crown. Similarly, subs. (1)(c) applies the provisions relating to purchase notices to any interest in Crown land which is not held by or on behalf of the Crown. However, these powers are not exercisable without the consent of the appropriate authority. On the grant of consent by an appropriate authority, see *Molton Builders v. City of Westminster Borough Council* (1975) 30 P. & C.R. 182.

Agreements relating to Crown land

246.—(1) The appropriate authority and the planning authority for the district in which any Crown land is situated may make agreements—
  (a) for securing the use of the land, so far as may be prescribed by any such agreement, in conformity with the provisions of the development plan applicable to it, and
  (b) for the purpose of restricting or regulating the development or use of the land,
either permanently or during such period as may be prescribed by the agreement.

(2) Any such agreement may contain such consequential provisions, including provisions of a financial character, as may appear to be necessary or expedient having regard to the purposes of the agreement.

(3) Subject to subsection (4), an agreement made under subsection (1)(b) may, if it has been recorded in the appropriate Register of Sasines or, as the case may be, registered in the Land Register of Scotland, be enforceable at the instance of the planning authority against persons deriving title to the land from the appropriate authority.

(4) An agreement made under subsection (1)(b) shall not be enforceable against a third party who has in good faith and for value acquired right (whether completed by infeftment or not) to the land prior to the agreement being so recorded or, as the case may be, registered or against any person deriving title from such a third party.

(5) An agreement made under this section by a government department shall not have effect unless it is approved by the Treasury.

(6) In considering whether to make or approve an agreement under this section relating—
  (a) to land belonging to a government department, or
  (b) to land held in trust for Her Majesty for the purposes of a government department,
the department and the Treasury shall have regard to the purposes for which the land is held by or for the department.

DEFINITIONS
"appropriate authority": s.242(2).
"Crown land": s.242(1).
"development": s.277(1).
"development plan": ss.24, 277(1).
"government department": s.277(1).
"land": s.277(1).
"planning authority": ss.1, 277(1).

"prescribed": s.277(1).
"use": s.277(1).

GENERAL NOTE
    Under this section, the appropriate authority for Crown land and the planning authority may enter into agreement to secure that either development of Crown land is in accordance with the development plan, or to restrict the use of the land for development purposes. The agreement may be enforceable against subsequent purchase of the land by the planning authority, providing it is registered within the Land Register of Scotland or the appropriate Register of Sasines (subs. (3)). However, the agreement is not enforceable against a third party who has purchased the land bona fides and for value, irrespective of whether the third party is infeft (subs. (4)).
    If a government department enters into an agreement with the appropriate authority, Treasury approval is required (subs. (5)).

Supplementary provisions as to Crown interest

    247. Where there is a Crown interest in any land, sections 78 to 82 of this Act, and Schedule 3 to the Planning (Consequential Provisions) (Scotland) Act 1997 in so far as it relates to those sections or sections 155 to 157 of the 1972 Act, shall have effect in relation to any private interest as if the Crown interest were a private interest.

DEFINITIONS
    "Crown interest": s.242(1).
    "land": s.277(1).
    "planning authority": ss.1, 277(1).
    "planning permission": s.277(1).
    "private interest": s.242(1).

GENERAL NOTE
    The purpose of this section is to allow for compensation for planning decisions which restrict development to be claimed.

Provisions relating to anticipated disposal of Crown land

Application for planning permission etc. in anticipation of disposal of Crown land

    248.—(1) This section has effect for the purpose of enabling Crown land, or an interest in Crown land, to be disposed of with the benefit of planning permission or a certificate under section 151.
    (2) Notwithstanding the interest of the Crown in the land in question, an application for any such permission or certificate may be made by—
    (a) the appropriate authority, or
    (b) any person authorised by that authority in writing,
and, subject to subsections (3) to (5), all the statutory provisions relating to the making and determination of any such application shall accordingly apply as if the land were not Crown land.
    (3) Any planning permission granted by virtue of this section shall apply only—
    (a) to development carried out after the land in question has ceased to be Crown land, and
    (b) so long as that land continues to be Crown land, to development carried out by virtue of a private interest in the land.
    (4) Any application made by virtue of this section for a certificate under section 151 shall be determined as if the land were not Crown land.
    (5) The Secretary of State may by regulations—
    (a) modify or exclude any of the statutory provisions referred to in subsection (2) in their application by virtue of that subsection and any other

statutory provisions in their application to permissions or certificates granted or made by virtue of this section,

(b) make provision for requiring a planning authority to be notified of any disposal of, or of an interest in, any Crown land in respect of which an application has been made by virtue of this section, and

(c) make such other provision in relation to the making and determination of applications by virtue of this section as he thinks necessary or expedient.

(6) This section shall not be construed as affecting any right to apply for any such permission or certificate as is mentioned in subsection (1) in respect of Crown land in a case in which such an application can be made by virtue of a private interest in the land.

(7) In this section "statutory provisions" means provisions contained in or having effect under any enactment and references to the disposal of an interest in Crown land include references to the grant of an interest in such land.

DEFINITIONS
"appropriate authority": s.242(2).
"Crown Land": s.242(1).
"disposal": s.277(1).
"enactment": s.277(1).
"land": s.277(1).
"planning authority": ss.1, 277(1).
"private interest": s.242(1).
"statutory provision": subs. (7).
"use": s.277(1).

GENERAL NOTE
Prior to the introduction of this section in Scottish planning legislation, the traditional view was that " it was open neither to the Crown nor to any third party to apply for permission where there was no interest held otherwise than by or on behalf of the Crown" (*Hansard,* H.C. Vol. 42, col. 463, May 12, 1983). This section allows for an application for planning permission to be made to the planning authority in the usual way, or by a certificate of lawful use under s.151.

Subs. (3)
Planning permission granted under this provision only applies to development which is carried out after the land ceases to be Crown land, or to development carried out by virtue of a private interest in land which continues to be Crown land.

Subs. (5)
The relevant regulations are the Town and Country Planning (Crown Land Applications) (Scotland) Regulations (S.I. 1984 No. 996).

Subs. (6)
Subsection (6) preserves the right of an owner of a private interest in Crown land to apply for planning permission or any other consent under the other relevant provisions of this Act.

Tree preservation orders in anticipation of disposal of Crown land

249.—(1) A planning authority may make a tree preservation order in respect of Crown land in which no interest is for the time being held otherwise than by or on behalf of the Crown, if they consider it expedient to do so for the purpose of preserving trees or woodlands on the land in the event of its ceasing to be Crown land or becoming subject to a private interest.

(2) No tree preservation order shall be made by virtue of this section except with the consent of the appropriate authority.

(3) A tree preservation order made by virtue of this section shall not take effect until the first occurrence of a relevant event.

(4) For the purposes of subsection (3), a relevant event occurs in relation to any land if it ceases to be Crown land or becomes subject to a private interest.

(5) A tree preservation order made by virtue of this section—

(a) shall not require confirmation under section 161 until after the occurrence of the event by virtue of which it takes effect, and

(b) shall by virtue of this subsection continue in force until—

(i) the expiration of the period of 6 months beginning with the occurrence of that event, or

(ii) the date on which the order is confirmed,

whichever occurs first.

(6) Where a tree preservation order takes effect in accordance with subsection (3), the appropriate authority shall as soon as practicable give to the authority who made the order a notice in writing of the name and address of the person who has become entitled to the land in question or to a private interest in it.

(7) The procedure prescribed under section 161 in connection with the confirmation of a tree preservation order shall apply in relation to an order made by virtue of this section as if the order were made on the date on which the notice under subsection (6) is received by the authority who made it.

DEFINITIONS

"appropriate authority": s.242(2).
"Crown land": s.242(1).
"disposal": s.277(1).
"planning authority": ss.1, 277(1).
"prescribed": s.277(1).
"private interest": s.242(1).
"relevant event": subs. (4).
"tree preservation order": ss.160, 277(1).

GENERAL NOTE

This section allows the planning authority to make a tree preservation order in respect of Crown land where no interest is held by or on behalf of the Crown. The order takes effect in the event of the land ceasing to be Crown land or becoming subject to a private interest. The consent of the appropriate authority is required before an order can be made.

A tree preservation order under this section does not require to be confirmed under the procedures in s.161 until the land ceases to be Crown land or becomes subject to a private interest. The appropriate authority are obliged to provide notice in writing to the planning authority, as soon as it is practicable, of the name and address of the person to whom the land has been disposed or granted a private interest. The confirming procedures under s.161 may then be commenced.

Requirement of planning permission for continuance of use instituted by the Crown

250.—(1) A planning authority in whose area any Crown land is situated may agree with the appropriate authority that subsection (2) shall apply to such use of land by the Crown as is specified in the agreement, being a use resulting from a material change made or proposed to be made by the Crown in the use of the land.

(2) Where an agreement is made under subsection (1) in respect of any Crown land, then, if at any time the land ceases to be used by the Crown for the purpose specified in the agreement, this Act shall have effect in relation to any subsequent private use of the land as if—

(a) the specified use by the Crown had required planning permission, and

(b) that use had been authorised by planning permission granted subject to a condition requiring its discontinuance at that time.

(3) The condition referred to in subsection (2) shall not be enforceable against any person who had a private interest in the land at the time when the

agreement was made unless the planning authority by whom the agreement was made have notified him of the making of the agreement and of the effect of that subsection.

(4) An agreement made under subsection (1) shall be recorded in the appropriate Register of Sasines or, as the case may be, registered in the Land Register of Scotland, and the condition referred to in subsection (2) shall not be enforceable against any person acquiring title to the land after the agreement is made unless the agreement has been so recorded or registered before he acquired title.

(5) References in this section to the use of land by the Crown include references to its use on behalf of the Crown, and "private use" means use otherwise than by or on behalf of the Crown.

DEFINITIONS
"appropriate authority": s.242(2).
"Crown land": s.242(1).
"land": s.277(1).
"planning authority": ss.1, 277(1).
"private interest": s.242(1).
"private use": subs. (5).
"use": s.277(1).

GENERAL NOTE
This section allows the planning authority and the Crown to enter into an agreement in respect of development involving a material change of use prior to Crown land being disposed of. The effect of an agreement under subs. (1) is that under subs. (2), the use rights will cease on the disposal of the Crown land and planning permission will be required for their continued use. In these circumstances, planning permission may then be sought prior to the disposal of the Crown land pursuant to s.248. In the event of the agreement being discharged prior to the land's disposal or the refusal of planning permission, it would appear that the planning authority is placed in a position to exercise its powers under Pt. IV in the event of the land ceasing to be Crown land, although the position is unclear.

Enforcement in respect of war-time breaches of planning control by the Crown

Enforcement in respect of wartime breaches of planning control by the Crown

251.—(1) This section applies where during the war period—
(a) works not complying with planning control were carried out on land, or
(b) a use of land not complying with planning control was begun by or on behalf of the Crown.

(2) Subject to subsection (4), if at any time after the end of the war period there subsists in the land a permanent or long-term interest which is neither held by or on behalf of the Crown nor subject to any interest or right to possession so held, the planning control shall, so long as such an interest subsists in the land, be enforceable in respect of those works or that use notwithstanding—
(a) that the works were carried out or the land used by or on behalf of the Crown, or
(b) the subsistence in the land of any interest of the landlord in a lease held by or on behalf of the Crown.

(3) A person entitled to make an application under this subsection with respect to any land may apply at any time before the relevant date to an authority responsible for enforcing any planning control for a determination—
(a) whether works on the land carried out, or a use of the land begun, during the war period fail to comply with any planning control which the authority are responsible for enforcing, and

(b) if so, whether the works or use should be deemed to comply with that control.

(4) Where any works on land carried out, or use of land begun, during the war period remain or continues after the relevant date and no such determination has been given, the works or use shall by virtue of this subsection be treated for all purposes as complying with that control unless steps for enforcing the control have been begun before that date.

(5) Schedule 17 shall have effect for the purpose of making supplementary provision concerning the enforcement of breaches of planning control to which this section applies and the making and determination of applications under subsection (3).

(6) In this section and that Schedule—

"authority responsible for enforcing planning control" means, in relation to any works on land or use of land, the authority empowered by virtue of section 72 of the 1947 Act or of paragraph 28 of Schedule 22 to the 1972 Act (including that paragraph as it continues in effect by virtue of paragraph 3 of Schedule 3 to the Planning (Consequential Provisions) (Scotland) Act 1997) to serve an enforcement notice in respect of it or the authority who would be so empowered if the works had been carried out, or the use begun, otherwise than in compliance with planning control;

"the relevant date", in relation to any land, means the date with which the period of 5 years from the end of the war period ends, but for the purposes of this definition any time during which, notwithstanding subsection (2), planning control is unenforceable by reason of the subsistence in or over the land of any interest or right to possession held by or on behalf of the Crown shall be disregarded;

"owner" includes in relation to any land any person who under the Lands Clauses Acts would be enabled to sell and convey the land to the promoters of an undertaking and "owned" shall be construed accordingly;

"permanent or long-term interest", in relation to any land, means the interest of the proprietor of the dominium utile or, in the case of land other than feudal land, of the owner, a tenancy of the land granted for a term of more than 10 years and not subject to a subsisting right of the landlord to determine the tenancy at or before the expiration of 10 years from the beginning of the term, or a tenancy granted for a term of 10 years or less with a right of renewal which would enable the tenant to prolong the term of the tenancy beyond 10 years;

"tenancy" includes a tenancy under a sub-lease and a tenancy under an agreement for a lease or sub-lease, but does not include an option to take a tenancy and does not include a mortgage;

"war period" means the period extending from 3rd September 1939 to 26th March 1946; and

"works" includes any building, structure, excavation or other work on land.

(7) References in this section and that Schedule to non-compliance with planning control mean—

(a) in relation to works on land carried out, or a use of land begun, at a time when the land was subject to a resolution to prepare a scheme under the Town and Country Planning (Scotland) Act 1932, that the works were carried out or the use begun otherwise than in accordance with the terms of an interim development order or of permission granted under such an order, and

(b) in relation to works on land carried out, or a use of land begun, at a time when the land was subject to such a scheme, that the works were

carried out or the use begun otherwise than in conformity with the
provisions of the scheme,
and references in this Act to compliance with planning control shall be construed accordingly.

(8) References in this section and that Schedule to the enforcement
of planning control shall be construed as references to the exercise of the
powers conferred by section 72 of the 1947 Act or by paragraph 28 of Schedule 22 to the 1972 Act (including that paragraph as it continues in effect by
virtue of Schedule 3 to the Planning (Consequential Provisions) (Scotland)
Act 1997).

DEFINITIONS
   "1947 Act; the": s.277(1).
   "1972 Act; the": s.277(1).
   "authority responsible for planning control": subs. (6).
   "building": s.277(1).
   "development": ss.26, 277(1).
   "development order": ss.30, 277(1).
   "enforcement notice": ss.127, 277(1).
   "land": s.277(1).
   "ease": s.277(1).
   "owner": subs. (6).
   "permanent or long term interest": subs. (6).
   "relevant date": subs. (6).
   "tenancy": subs. (6).
   "use": s.277(1).
   "war period": subs. (6).
   "works": subs. (6).

GENERAL NOTE
   This section allows a planning authority to take enforcement action against a war-time breach
of planning control by the Crown, up to five years after the disposal of the land by the Crown. See
further *R. v. Secretary of State for the Environment, ex p. Bulk Storage* [1985] J.P.L. 35.

PART XIII

FINANCIAL PROVISIONS

Fees for planning applications etc.

252.—(1) The Secretary of State may by regulations make such provision
as he thinks fit for the payment of a fee of the prescribed amount to a planning authority in respect of an application made to them under the planning
Acts or any order or regulations made under them for any permission, consent, approval, determination or certificate.

(2) The Secretary of State may by regulations make such provision as he
thinks fit for the payment—
   (a) of fees of prescribed amounts to him and to the planning authority in
       respect of any application for planning permission deemed to be made
       under section 133(7), and
   (b) of a fee of the prescribed amount to him in respect of any other appli-
       cation for planning permission which is deemed to be made to him
       under this Act or any order or regulations made under it.

(3) Regulations under subsection (1) or (2) may provide for the remission
or refunding of a prescribed fee (in whole or in part) in prescribed
circumstances.

(4) No such regulations shall be made unless a draft of the regulations has
been laid before and approved by a resolution of each House of Parliament.

(5) The reference to the planning Acts in subsection (1) does not include a reference to section 251 of this Act.

DEFINITIONS
    "planning authority": ss.1, 277(1).
    "planning permission": s.277(1).
    "prescribed": s.277(1).

GENERAL NOTE
    The current regulations in force under this section are the Town and Country Planning (Fees for Applications and Deemed Applications) (Scotland) Regulations (S.I. 1990 No.147).

Grants for research and education

253. The Secretary of State may, with the consent of the Treasury, make grants for assisting establishments engaged in promoting or assisting research relating to, and education with respect to, the planning and design of the physical environment.

GENERAL NOTE
    The power under this section to make grants for research and education purposes in respect of the physical environment is supplemented by a similar power under s.153 of the Environmental Protection Act 1990 (c.43), for the Secretary of State to provide financial assistance to specified environmental bodies, schemes and programmes.

Contributions by Ministers towards compensation paid by planning authorities

254.—(1) Where—
  (a) compensation is payable by a planning authority under this Act in consequence of any decision or order to which this section applies, and
  (b) that decision or order was given or made wholly or partly in the interest of a service which is provided by a government department and the cost of which is defrayed out of money provided by Parliament,
the Minister responsible for the administration of that service may pay to that authority a contribution of such amount as he may with the consent of the Treasury determine.

    (2) This section applies to any decision or order given or made under Part III, the provisions of Part V relating to purchase notices, Part VI, Part VII or Schedule 3 or 4 or Part I of Schedule 8.

DEFINITIONS
    "government department": s.277(1).
    "Minister": s.277(1).
    "planning authority": ss.1, 277(1).
    "purchase notice": ss.88, 277(1).

GENERAL NOTE
    This section allows Ministers to pay a contribution towards the liability of planning authorities to pay compensation for decisions taken in the performance of their planning functions. Such decisions include adverse planning decisions under Pt. III, purchase notices under Pt. V, enforcement and stop notices and orders under Pt. VI.

Contributions by local authorities and statutory undertakers

255.—(1) Without prejudice to section 5(9) of the Roads (Scotland) Act 1984 (power of local roads authority to contribute towards costs incurred by Secretary of State in construction or improvement of trunk road) any local authority may contribute towards any expenses incurred by a local roads authority or the Secretary of State—
  (a) in the acquisition of land under Part VIII of this Act or Chapter V of Part I of the Planning (Listed Buildings and Conservation Areas) (Scotland) Act 1997,

  (b) in the construction or improvement of roads on land so acquired, or
  (c) in connection with any development required in the interests of the
      proper planning of the area of the local authority.
  (2) Any local authority and any statutory undertakers may contribute
towards any expenses incurred by a planning authority in or in connection
with—
  (a) the carrying out of a survey or the preparation of a structure plan or a
      local plan or the alteration, repeal or replacement of such a plan under
      Part II;
  (b) the performance of any of their functions under Part III, the pro-
      visions of Part V relating to purchase notices, Part VI (except sections
      156 and 157), Part VII (except section 168), Part VIII or Schedule 3 or
      8.
  (3) In the application of subsection (2) to a local authority, "planning authority" means a planning authority other than that local authority.

DEFINITIONS
  "building": s.277(1).
  "development": ss.26, 277(1).
  "development plan": ss.24, 277(1).
  "functions": s.277(1).
  "highway": s.277(1).
  "improvement": s.277(1).
  "land": s.277(1).
  "local authority": s.2 of the Local Government etc. (Scotland) Act 1994 (c.39).
  "local roads authority": Roads (Scotland) Act 1984 (c.54).
  "planning authority": ss.1, 277(1).
  "purchase notice": ss.88, 277(1).
  "road": Roads (Scotland) Act 1984 (c.54).
  "statutory undertakers": ss.214, 277(1).

GENERAL NOTE
  This section confers a power upon local authorities to contribute towards the costs incurred by
a local roads authority in connection with land acquisition, the construction or improvement of
roads, or development generally within the area of that local authority (subs. (1)). Subsection (2)
permits a local authority and statutory undertaker to contribute towards any expenses incurred
by a planning authority in connection with the preparation, alteration, replacement or repeal of
development plans and the performance of the planning authorities functions under the Parts of
this Act specified in subs. (2)(b).

Assistance for acquisition of property where objection made to blight notice in certain cases

  256.—(1) A local authority may, subject to such conditions as may be
approved by the Secretary of State, advance money to any person for the
purpose of enabling him to acquire a hereditament or agricultural unit in
respect of which a counter-notice has been served under section 102 specifying the grounds mentioned in subsection (4)(d) of that section as, or as one
of, the grounds of objection.
  (2) No advance may be made under subsection (1) in the case of a hereditament if its annual value exceeds such amount as may be prescribed for the
purposes of section 100(3)(a).

DEFINITIONS
  "agricultural": s.277(1).
  "local authority": s.2 of the Local Government etc. (Scotland) Act 1994 (c.39).
  "prescribed": s.277(1).

Recovery from acquiring authorities of sums paid by way of compensation

  257.—(1) This section applies where—

(a) an interest in land is compulsorily acquired or is sold to an authority possessing compulsory purchase powers, and

(b) a notice is recorded or registered under section 79(1) in respect of any of the land acquired or sold (whether before or after the completion of the acquisition or sale) in consequence of a planning decision or order made before the service of the notice to treat, or the making of the contract, in pursuance of which the acquisition or sale is effected.

(2) Where this section applies the Secretary of State shall, subject to the following provisions of this section, be entitled to recover from the acquiring authority a sum equal to so much of the amount of the compensation specified in the notice as (in accordance with section 79(2)) is to be treated as attributable to that land.

(3) If, immediately after the completion of the acquisition or sale, there is outstanding some interest in the land acquired or sold to which a person other than the acquiring authority is entitled, the sum referred to in subsection (2) shall not accrue due until that interest either ceases to exist or becomes vested in the acquiring authority.

(4) No sum shall be recoverable under this section in the case of a compulsory acquisition or sale where the Secretary of State is satisfied that the interest in question is being acquired for the purposes of the use of the land as a public open space.

(5) In this section "authority possessing compulsory purchase powers", in relation to the compulsory acquisition of an interest in land, means the person or body of persons effecting the acquisition and, in relation to any other transaction relating to an interest in land, means any person or body of persons who could be or have been authorised to acquire that interest compulsorily for the purposes for which the transaction is or was effected.

DEFINITIONS
   "acquiring authority": s.277(1).
   "authority possessing compulsory purchase powers": subs. (5).
   "compulsory acquisition": s.277(1).
   "land": s.277(1).
   "open space": s.277(1).
   "planning decision": s.277(1).
   "use": s.277(1).

GENERAL NOTE
   Where compensation is paid in respect of the compulsory acquisition of land and a s.79(1) notice is recorded or registered, the Secretary of State shall be entitled to recover from the acquiring authority a sum equal to the amount of compensation specified in the notice in the prescribed circumstances.

Sums recoverable from acquiring authorities reckonable for purposes of grant

258. Where—

(a) a sum is recoverable from any authority under section 257 by reference to an acquisition or purchase of an interest in land,

(b) a grant became or becomes payable to that or some other authority under an enactment in respect of that acquisition or purchase or of a subsequent appropriation of the land,

the power conferred by that enactment to pay the grant shall include, and shall be deemed always to have included, power to pay a grant in respect of that sum as if it had been expenditure incurred by the acquiring authority in connection with the acquisition or purchase.

DEFINITIONS
"acquiring authority": s.277(1).
"enactment": s.277(1).
"land": s.277(1).

Financial provision

259.—(1) There shall be paid out of money provided by Parliament—

(a) any expenses incurred by the Secretary of State in the payment of expenses of any committee established under section 182(2)(d),

(b) any sums necessary to enable the Secretary of State to make any payments becoming payable by him under Part IV or sections 143, 165, 166 or 185,

(c) any expenses incurred by the Secretary of State under Part IX,

(d) any expenses incurred by the Secretary of State in the making of grants under section 253, and

(e) any administrative expenses incurred by the Secretary of State for the purposes of this Act.

(2) There shall be paid out of money provided by Parliament any expenses incurred by any government department (including the Secretary of State)—

(a) in the acquisition of land under Part VIII,

(b) in the payment of compensation under section 194(4), 232(2) or 270, or

(c) under section 254.

DEFINITIONS
"government department": s.277(1).

General provision as to receipts of Secretary of State

260. Subject to section 82, any sums received by the Secretary of State under any provision of this Act shall be paid into the Consolidated Fund.

Expenses of local authorities

Expenses of, and borrowing by, local authorities

261.—(1) Any expenses incurred by a local roads authority under the provisions of this Act specified in Part I of Schedule 18 shall be defrayed in the same manner as expenses incurred by the authority on roads.

(2) Any expenses incurred by a local authority under the provisions of this Act specified in Part I of Schedule 18 in pursuance of a purchase notice or in the acquisition of land under this Act for the purposes of any function of that authority, shall be defrayed in the same manner as other expenses incurred by that authority for the purposes of that function.

(3) A local authority may borrow for the purposes of this Act in accordance with the provisions of Part VII of the Local Government (Scotland) Act 1973.

(4) Nothing in this section shall authorise the exercise of the power of borrowing money thereby conferred otherwise than in compliance with the provisions of the Local Authorities Loans Act 1945.

DEFINITIONS
"land": s.277(1).
"local authority": s.2 of the Local Government etc. (Scotland) Act 1994 (c.39).
"local roads authority": Roads (Scotland) Act 1984 (c.54).
"purchase notice": ss.88, 277(1).
"road": Roads (Scotland) Act 1984 (c.54).

PART XIV

MISCELLANEOUS AND GENERAL PROVISIONS

Application of Act in special cases

Power to modify Act in relation to minerals

262.—(1) In relation to development consisting of the winning and working of minerals or involving the depositing of mineral waste, the provisions specified in Part I of Schedule 18 shall have effect subject to such adaptations and modifications as may be prescribed by regulations.

(2) Such regulations may be made only with the consent of the Treasury and shall be of no effect unless they are approved by resolution of each House of Parliament.

(3) Any such regulations shall not apply—

(a) to the winning and working, on land held or occupied with land used for the purposes of agriculture, of any minerals reasonably required for the purposes of that use, including the fertilisation of the land so used and the maintenance, improvement or alteration of buildings or works on it which are occupied or used for those purposes, or

(b) to the winning and working of peat by any person for the domestic requirements of that person.

(4) Nothing in subsection (1) or (3) shall be construed as affecting the prerogative right of Her Majesty to any gold or silver mine.

DEFINITIONS
  "agriculture": s.277(1).
  "buildings": s.277(1).
  "buildings or works": s.277(1).
  "development": s.26, s.277(1).
  "improvement": s.277(1).
  "land": s.277(1).
  "minerals": s.277(1).
  "prescribed": s.277(1).
  "use": s.277(1).

GENERAL NOTE
  This section confers a power on the Secretary of State to adapt or modify the provisions specified in Pt. I of Sched. 18, by regulations in respect of the winning and working of minerals or the depositing of mineral waste. Schedules 3, 8, 9 and 10 of this Act contain extensive provisions relating to the mineral workings. In addition, Sched. 13 contains a power to make Regulations as to compensation in respect of orders relating to mineral workings. The current regulations are the Town and Country Planning (Compensation for Restriction on Mineral Workings) (Scotland) Regulations (S.I. 1987 No. 1529).

Exceptions. Under subs. (3), the power to modify by regulations the provisions referred to in Pt. I of Sched. 18, do not apply:
  (1) to minerals obtained on land used for agricultural purposes and required for that use, such as fertiliser;
  (2) to the winning and working of peat by any person for the domestic requirements of that person.

Exercise of Power under s.262. The current Regulations are the Town and Country Planning (Minerals) (Scotland) Regulations (S.I. 1982 No. 973). Regulations may only be made with the consent of the Treasury and are subject to positive resolution by both Houses of Parliament.

Application of certain provisions to planning authorities

263.—(1) In relation to land of planning authorities and to the development by local authorities of land in respect of which they are the planning authorities, the provisions specified in Part II of Schedule 18 shall have effect subject to such exceptions and modifications as may be prescribed by regulations.

(2) Subject to section 57, such regulations may in particular provide for securing—

    (a) that any application by such an authority for planning permission to develop such land, or for any other consent required in relation to such land under those provisions, shall be made to the Secretary of State and not to the planning authority, and

    (b) that any order or notice authorised to be made or served under those provisions in relation to such land shall be made or served by the Secretary of State and not by the planning authority.

(3) Sections 34 and 35 and 38(1) and (2) shall apply, with the necessary modifications, in relation to applications made to the Secretary of State in pursuance of such regulations as they apply in relation to applications for planning permission which fall to be determined by the planning authority.

(4) In relation to statutory undertakers who are planning authorities, section 236 and the provisions specified in that section shall have effect subject to such exceptions and modifications as may be prescribed.

(5) In relation to an urban development corporation which is the planning authority by virtue of an order under section 149(6) of the Local Government, Planning and Land Act 1980, subsections (1) to (3) shall have effect for the purposes of Part III of this Act prescribed in the order, and in relation to the kinds of development so prescribed as if—

    (a) in subsection (1) the reference to development by local authorities of land in respect of which they are the planning authorities included a reference to development by the corporation of land in respect of which it is the planning authority, and

    (b) in subsection (2)—

        (i) in paragraph (a) the words "the corporation" were substituted for the words "such an authority", and the word "corporation" were substituted for the words "planning authority", and

        (ii) in paragraph (b) the word "corporation" were substituted for the words "planning authority".

Definitions

    "development": ss.26, 277(1).

    "land": s.277(1).

    "planning authority": ss.1, 277(1).

    "planning permission": s.277(1).

    "prescribed": s.277(1).

    "statutory undertakers": ss.214, 277(1).

    "urban development corporation": s.171 of the Local Government, Planning and Land Act 1980 (c.65).

General Note

    The purpose of this section is to allow the Secretary of State to make regulations controlling the development of planning and local authority land, by planning and local authorities themselves. The current Regulations are the Town and Country Planning (Development by Planning Authorities) (Scotland) Regulations 1981 (S.I. 1981 No.829).

Subs. (1)

    Subsection (1) may cause difficulties in that it is arguably open to two conflicting interpretations. Subsection (1) provides that the provisions of Pt. II of Sched. 18 "shall have effect subject to such exceptions and modifications as may be prescribed". This may be interpreted in two ways:

    (1) that planning authorities are generally subject to this Act in respect of their own development within their area, but the Secretary of State retains power to modify and make exceptions to the specified provisions in Pt. II of Sched. 18 as they affect planning authorities; or

    (2) that the planning authorities are *only* subject to the specified provisions in Sched. 18 in relation to development of their land and to such alterations or modifications as the Secretary of State may make.

The former interpretation seems sensible as there can be no logical explanation for excluding planning authorities from general planning control. However, in the English decision of *Steeples v. Derbyshire County Council* [1981] J.P.L. 581, the second approach was adopted in relation to an equivalent provision in the Town and Country Planning Act 1971 (c.78). In that case, Webster J. held that only the provisions specified in Pt. V of Sched. 21, and regulations made thereunder applied to development by local authorities. That practice was not questioned in the cases of *R. v. Edmundsbury Borough Council, ex p. Investors in Industry Commercial Properties* [1985] 1 W.L.R. 1168. The leading Scottish text on town and country planning by Young and Rowan-Robinson does not take issue with this approach either (Scottish Planning Practice and Procedure, p. 273).

Compliance with Procedures. In *R. v. Lambeth London Borough Council, ex p. Sharp, The Times*, December 28, 1984, the court held that the English equivalent of the 1981 Regulations were mandatory. The effect of a failure to follow its requirements was to invalidate the act carried out in pursuance of the invalidity. Similarly, in *R. v. Doncaster Metropolitan Borough Council, ex p. British Railways Board* [1987] J.P.L. 444, the court proceeded to strike down a deemed grant of planning permission where there were found to be several breaches of the regulations.

Natural Heritage Areas

Natural Heritage Areas

264.—(1) Every planning authority shall compile and make available for inspection free of charge at reasonable hours and at a convenient place a list containing such particulars as the Secretary of State may determine of any area in their district which has been designated as a Natural Heritage Area under section 6 of the Natural Heritage (Scotland) Act 1991.

(2) Where any area is for the time being designated as a Natural Heritage Area, special attention shall be paid to the desirability of preserving or enhancing its character or appearance in the exercise, with respect to any land in that area, of any powers under the planning Acts.

DEFINITIONS
"Natural Heritage Area": s.6 of the Natural Heritage (Scotland) Act 1991 (c.28).
"planning authority": ss.1, 277(1).
"planning acts": s.277(1).

GENERAL NOTE
Natural Heritage Areas are designated by the Secretary of State on the advice of Scottish Natural Heritage. Such areas were previously known as "National Scenic Area Designations" (N.S.A.D.). However, since the coming into force of the 1991 Act, no new NSADs will be created and some of the existing ones may be transformed into national heritage areas. Existing controls however, remain in force for NSADs. Such areas are given special protection because of their outstanding value to the heritage of Scotland. Consideration is given to its flora and fauna, geographical location and features and its natural beauty. The natural heritage area may be regarded as the equivalent to the English designation of areas of outstanding natural beauty.

Subs. (1)
Subsection (1) requires every planning authority to compile and make available a list, of all designated Natural Heritage Areas within their district. This list must be available for inspection free of charge at a reasonable time and place.

Subs. (2)
Subsection (2) requires that "special attention" must be had to the desirability of preserving or enhancing the character or appearance of a natural heritage area in the exercise of any powers under the Planning Acts. This is a slight variation on the wording of the previous provision under the 1972 Act, which required a "special regard". It is a moot point whether the new wording strengthens, weakens or merely preserves the status quo of the status of natural heritage areas in planning decisions.

Permitted development rights in natural heritage areas are restricted by the Town and Country Planning (Restriction of Permitted Development) (Natural Scenic Areas) (Scotland) Direction 1987. This is appended to Circular 10/1984 (see also PAN 9 Nature Conservation Advice Notes).

Where the planning authority are minded to grant planning permission for specified forms of development, Scottish Natural Heritage must be consulted: see Town and Country Planning (Notification of Applications) (National Scenic Areas) (Scotland) Direction 1987, appended to Circular 9/1987.

Local inquiries and other hearings

Local inquiries

265.—(1) Subject to the provisions of this section, the Minister may cause a local inquiry to be held for the purposes of the exercise of any of his functions under this Act.

(2) The Minister shall appoint a person to hold the inquiry and to report on it to him.

(3) Notification of the time when and the place where the inquiry is to be held shall be sent to any person who has lodged and has not withdrawn objections in relation to any matter in question at the inquiry, and shall be published in such newspaper or newspapers as the Minister may direct.

(4) Subject to subsections (5) and (6), the person appointed to hold the inquiry may, on the motion of any party to it or of his own motion, serve a notice in writing on any person requiring him to attend at the time and place set forth in the notice to give evidence or to produce any books or documents in his custody or under his control which relate to any matter in question at the inquiry.

(5) No person shall be required in obedience to such a notice to attend at any place which is more than 10 miles from the place where he resides unless the necessary expenses are paid or tendered to him.

(6) Nothing in subsection (4) shall empower the person appointed to hold the inquiry to require any person to produce any book or document or to answer any question which he would be entitled, on the ground of privilege or confidentiality, to refuse to produce or to answer if the inquiry were a proceeding in a court of law.

(7) The person appointed to hold the inquiry may administer oaths and examine witnesses on oath and may accept, in place of evidence on oath by any person, a statement in writing by that person.

(8) Any person who—

(a) refuses or wilfully neglects to attend in obedience to a notice under subsection (4) or to give evidence, or

(b) wilfully alters, suppresses, conceals, destroys or refuses to produce any book or document which he may be required to produce by any such notice,

shall be guilty of an offence and liable on summary conviction to a fine not exceeding level 1 on the standard scale or to imprisonment for a period not exceeding 3 months.

(9) The Minister may make orders as to the expenses incurred—

(a) by the Minister in relation to—

(i) the inquiry, and

(ii) arrangements made for an inquiry which does not take place, and

(b) by the parties to the inquiry,

and as to the parties by whom any of the expenses mentioned in paragraphs (a) and (b) shall be paid.

(10) What may be recovered by the Minister is the entire administrative expense of the inquiry, so that, in particular—

(a) there shall be treated as expenses incurred in relation to the inquiry such reasonable sum as the Minister may determine in respect of the general staff expenses and overheads of his department, and

(b) there shall be treated as expenses incurred by the Minister holding the inquiry any expenses incurred in relation to the inquiry by any other

Minister or Government department and, where appropriate, such reasonable sum as that Minister or department may determine in respect of general staff expenses and overheads.

(11) The Minister may by regulations prescribe for any description of inquiry a standard daily amount and where an inquiry of that description does take place what may be recovered is—

(a) the prescribed standard amount in respect of each day (or an appropriate proportion of that amount in respect of a part of a day) on which the inquiry sits or the person appointed to hold the inquiry is otherwise engaged on work connected with the inquiry,

(b) expenses actually incurred in connection with the inquiry on travelling or subsistence allowances or the provision of accommodation or other facilities for the inquiry,

(c) any expenses attributable to the appointment of an assessor to assist the person appointed to hold the inquiry, and

(d) any legal expenses or disbursements incurred or made by or on behalf of the Minister in connection with the inquiry.

(12) Any order of the Minister under subsection (9) requiring any party to pay expenses may be enforced in like manner as an extract registered decree arbitral bearing a warrant for execution issued by the sheriff court of any sheriffdom in Scotland.

(13) In this section, except where the context otherwise requires, "Minister" means the Secretary of State, or any other Minister authorised under this Act to hold a local inquiry.

DEFINITIONS
  "functions": s.277(1).
  "government department": s.277(1).
  "Minister": subs. (13).

GENERAL NOTE
  This section gives the Secretary of State a wide power to cause a local inquiry to be held in the exercise of any of his functions under this Act. The inquiry must be held in public and the Secretary of State may appoint any person to chair the inquiry and report back to him.

Subs. (11)
  The current regulations which prescribe the standard daily amount are the Town and Country Planning (Cost of Inquiries, etc.) (Standard Daily Amount) (Scotland) Regulations 1995 (S.I. 1995 No.493).

Orders as to expenses of parties where no local inquiry held

266.—(1) This section applies to proceedings under this Act where the Secretary of State is required, before reaching a decision, to afford any person an opportunity of appearing before and being heard by a person appointed by him.

(2) The Secretary of State has the same power to make orders under section 265(9) in relation to proceedings to which this section applies which do not give rise to a local inquiry as he has in relation to a local inquiry.

GENERAL NOTE
  The Secretary of State is empowered under subs. (2) to make an order for expenses notwithstanding that no local inquiry is held, where expenses are incurred by the Minister and the parties in relation to the inquiry generally, and arrangements are made for an inquiry which does not subsequently take place.

Procedure on certain appeals and applications

267.—(1) The Secretary of State may by regulations prescribe the procedure to be followed in connection with proceedings under this Act where he is required, before reaching a decision, to afford any person an opportunity of appearing before and being heard by a person appointed by him and which are to be disposed of without an inquiry or hearing to which rules under section 9 of the Tribunals and Inquiries Act 1992 apply.

(2) The regulations may in particular make provision as to the procedure to be followed—
  (a) where steps have been taken with a view to the holding of such an inquiry or hearing which does not take place, or
  (b) where steps have been taken with a view to the determination of any matter by a person appointed by the Secretary of State and the proceedings are the subject of a direction that the matter shall instead be determined by the Secretary of State, or
  (c) where steps have been taken in pursuance of such a direction and a further direction is made revoking that direction,
and may provide that such steps shall be treated as compliance, in whole or in part, with the requirements of the regulations.

(3) The regulations may also—
  (a) provide for a time limit within which any party to the proceedings must lodge written submissions and any supporting documents,
  (b) prescribe the time limit (which may be different for different classes of proceedings) or enable the Secretary of State to give directions setting the time limit in a particular case or class of case,
  (c) empower the Secretary of State to proceed to a decision taking into account only such written submissions and supporting documents as were lodged within the time limit, and
  (d) empower the Secretary of State, after giving the parties written notice of his intention to do so, to proceed to a decision notwithstanding that no written submissions were lodged within the time limit, if it appears to him that he has sufficient material before him to enable him to reach a decision on the merits of the case.

GENERAL NOTE
  The current Regulations are the Town and Country Planning (Inquiries Procedure) (Scotland) Rules 1980 (S.I. 1980 No.329) and the Town and Country Planning (Appeals) (Written Submissions Procedure) (Scotland) Regulations 1990 (S.I. 1990 No.507).

Inquiries under Private Legislation Procedure (Scotland) Act 1936

268.—(1) Where the Ministers concerned so direct—
  (a) any inquiry in relation to an order under this Act which in certain events becomes subject to special parliamentary procedure, and
  (b) any hearing in connection with—
    (i) an appeal against the refusal, or the grant, subject to conditions, of an application by statutory undertakers for planning permission to develop operational land,
    (ii) such an application made by statutory undertakers and referred to the Secretary of State, or
    (iii) the revocation or modification of planning permission to develop operational land granted to statutory undertakers,
shall be held by Commissioners under the Private Legislation Procedure (Scotland) Act 1936.

(2) Any such direction shall be deemed to have been given under section 2, as read with section 10, of the Statutory Orders (Special Procedure) Act 1945.

(3) Subsections (5), (6) and (7) of section 231 shall not apply to an order mentioned in subsection (1)(a).

(4) Nothing in subsections (2) to (13) of section 265 shall apply to any inquiry to which subsection (1)(a) applies.

(5) The provisions of the Statutory Orders (Special Procedure) Act 1945 in relation to the publication of notices in the Edinburgh Gazette and in a news-

paper shall, notwithstanding anything contained in that Act, not apply to any order under this Act which is subject to special parliamentary procedure.

DEFINITIONS
  "develop": ss.26, 277(1).
  "operational land": ss.215, 277(1).
  "planning permission": s.277(1).
  "statutory undertaker": ss.214, 277(1).

Rights of entry

Rights of entry

269.—(1) Any person duly authorised in writing by the Secretary of State or by a planning authority may at any reasonable time enter upon any land for the purpose of surveying it in connection with—

  (a) the preparation, approval, adoption, making or amendment of a structure plan or local plan relating to the land under Part II, including the carrying out of any survey under that Part,

  (b) any application under Part III or sections 182 or 183, or under any order or regulations made under any of those provisions, for any permission, consent or determination to be given or made in connection with that land or any other land under that Part or those sections or under any such order or regulations, or

  (c) any proposal by the planning authority or by the Secretary of State to make or serve any order or notice under Part III (other than section 61), Part VII (other than sections 160 to 163, 167 and 172 to 175) or under any order or regulations made under any of those provisions.

(2) Any person duly authorised in writing by the Secretary of State or the planning authority may at any reasonable time enter upon any land for the purpose of ascertaining whether a stop notice or an enforcement notice is being complied with.

(3) Any person who is an officer of the Valuation Office or is duly authorised in writing by the Secretary of State may at any reasonable time enter upon any land for the purpose of surveying it, or estimating its value, in connection with a claim for compensation under this Act in respect of that land or any other land.

(4) Any person who is an officer of the Valuation Office or is duly authorised in writing by a planning authority may at any reasonable time enter upon any land for the purpose of surveying it, or estimating its value, in connection with a claim for compensation in respect of that land or any other land which is payable by the planning authority under Part IV, section 204(1) or Part X (other than section 232(2) or (3) or 233(1)(a)(iii)).

(5) Any person who is an officer of the Valuation Office or is duly authorised in writing by a local authority or Minister authorised to acquire land under section 189 or 190, or by a local authority who have power to acquire land under Part VIII, may at any reasonable time enter upon any land for the purpose of surveying it, or estimating its value, in connection with any proposal to acquire that land or any other land, or in connection with any claim for compensation in respect of any such acquisition.

(6) Subject to section 270, any power conferred by this section to survey land shall be construed as including power to search and bore for the purpose of ascertaining the nature of the subsoil or the presence of minerals in it.

DEFINITIONS
  "building": s.277(1).
  "development": ss.26, 277(1).
  "development plan": s.24.
  "functions": s.277(1).
  "land": s.277(1).

"local authority": s.2 of the Local Government etc. (Scotland) Act 1994 (c.39).
"planning authority": ss.1, 277(1).
"minerals": s.277(1).
"Minister": s.277(1).
"Valuation office": s.277(1).

GENERAL NOTE

This section confers rights of entry upon land by any person who is an officer of the Valuation Office or any person authorised in writing by the Secretary of State or by the Planning authority, for surveying purposes in connection with:

(1) the preparation of statutory plans (subs. (1)(a));

(2) applications for planning permission, applications in connection with advertisements;

(3) any proposals by the planning authority or the Secretary of State to make an order under the provisions contained within Pt. III or Pt. VII, other than the specified provisions.

Supplementary provisions as to rights of entry

270.—(1) A person authorised under section 269 to enter upon any land—

(a) shall, if so required, produce evidence of his authority and state the purpose of his entry before so entering, and

(b) shall not demand admission as of right to any land which is occupied unless 24 hours' notice of the intended entry has been given to the occupier.

(2) Any person who wilfully obstructs a person acting in the exercise of his powers under section 269 shall be guilty of an offence and liable on summary conviction to a fine not exceeding level 3 on the standard scale.

(3) If any person who, in compliance with the provisions of section 269, is admitted into a factory, workshop or workplace discloses to any person any information obtained by him therein as to any manufacturing process or trade secret, he shall be guilty of an offence.

(4) Subsection (3) does not apply if the disclosure is made in the course of performing his duty in connection with the purpose for which he was authorised to enter the land.

(5) A person who is guilty of an offence under subsection (3) shall be liable—

(a) on summary conviction to a fine not exceeding the statutory maximum, and

(b) on conviction on indictment to imprisonment for a term not exceeding 2 years or a fine or both.

(6) Where any damage is caused to land or moveable property—

(a) in the exercise of a right of entry conferred under section 269, or

(b) in the making of any survey for the purpose of which any such right of entry has been so conferred,

compensation may be recovered by any person suffering the damage from the Secretary of State or authority on whose behalf the entry was effected.

(7) Section 86 shall apply in relation to compensation under subsection (6) as it applies in relation to compensation under Part IV.

(8) No person shall carry out under section 269 any works authorised by virtue of subsection (6) of that section unless notice of his intention to do so was included in the notice required by subsection (1).

(9) The authority of the appropriate Minister shall be required for the carrying out under section 269(6) of works so authorised if the land in question is held by statutory undertakers, and they object to the proposed works on the ground that the carrying out of the work would be seriously detrimental to the carrying on of their undertaking.

DEFINITIONS

"appropriate Minister": ss.217, 277(1).
"Statutory undertaker": ss.214, 277(1).

GENERAL NOTE

This section provides that any person authorised to enter upon land for the purposes specified in s.269, must produce evidence of his authority to enter the land and give 24 hours notice of the intended entry. It is an offence to wilfully obstruct any person exercising his powers under s.269.

Subs. (6)

Compensation is payable under subs. (6) where damage is caused to the land or moveable property situated upon it, in the exercise of the purposes for which the right of entry was obtained. Any dispute as to the amount of compensation is to be determined by the Lands Tribunal.

Miscellaneous and general provisions

Service of notices

271.—(1) Subject to the provisions of this section, any notice or other document required or authorised to be served or given under this Act may be served or given—

(a) by delivering it to the person on whom it is to be served or to whom it is to be given,

(b) by leaving it at the usual or last known place of abode of that person or, in a case where an address for service has been given by that person, at that address,

(c) by sending it in a prepaid registered letter, or by the recorded delivery service, addressed to that person at his usual or last known place of abode, or, in a case where an address for service has been given by that person, at that address,

(d) in the case of a person on whom the notice is required to be served as being a person appearing from the valuation roll to have an interest in land, by sending it in a prepaid registered letter, or by the recorded delivery service, addressed to that person at his address as entered in the valuation roll, or

(e) in the case of an incorporated company or body by delivering it to the secretary or clerk of the company or body at their registered or principal office, or sending it in a prepaid registered letter, or by the recorded delivery service, addressed to the secretary or clerk of the company or body at that office.

(2) Where the notice or document is required or authorised to be served on any person as having an interest in premises, and the name of that person cannot be ascertained after reasonable inquiry, or where the notice or document is required or authorised to be served on any person as an occupier of premises, the notice or document shall be taken to be duly served if—

(a) being addressed to him either by name or by the description of "the owner", "the lessee" or "the occupier", as the case may be, of the premises (describing them) it is delivered or sent in the manner specified in subsection (1)(a), (b) or (c), or

(b) it is so addressed and is marked in such manner as may be prescribed for securing that it shall be plainly identifiable as a communication of importance, and—

    (i) it is sent to the premises in a prepaid registered letter or by the recorded delivery service and is not returned to the authority sending it, or

    (ii) is delivered to some person on those premises, or is affixed conspicuously to some object on those premises.

(3) Where—

(a) the notice or other document is required to be served on or given to all persons who have interests in or are occupiers of premises comprised in any land, and

(b) it appears to the authority required or authorised to serve or give the notice or other document that any part of that land is unoccupied, the notice or document shall be taken to be duly served on all persons having interests in, and on any occupiers of, premises comprised in that part of the land (other than a person who has given to that authority an address for the service of the notice or document on him) if it is addressed to "the owners and any lessees and occupiers" of that part of the land (describing it) and is affixed conspicuously to some object on the land.

DEFINITIONS
  "land": s.277(1).
  "owner": s.277(1).
  "prescribed": s.277(1).

Power to require information as to interests in land

272.—(1) For the purpose of enabling any order to be made or any notice or other document to be served by him or them under this Act, the Secretary of State or a local authority may in writing require the occupier of any land and any person who, either directly or indirectly, receives rent in respect of any land to supply in writing such information as to the matters mentioned in subsection (2) as may be so specified.

(2) Those matters are—
  (a) the nature of his interest in the land,
  (b) the name and address of any other person known to him as having an interest in the land, whether as superior, owner, heritable creditor, lessee or otherwise,
  (c) the purpose for which the land is currently being used,
  (d) the time when that use began,
  (e) the name and address of any person known to the person on whom the notice is served as having used the premises for that purpose, and
  (f) the time when any activities being carried out on the premises began.

(3) A notice under subsection (1) may require information to be given within a specified period which is not less than 21 days from the date of service on him.

(4) Any person who has been required under subsection (1) to give any information and fails to give it shall be guilty of an offence and liable on summary conviction to a fine not exceeding level 3 on the standard scale.

(5) Any person who has been so required to give any information and knowingly makes any misstatement in respect of it shall be guilty of an offence and liable—
  (a) on summary conviction to a fine not exceeding the statutory maximum, and
  (b) on conviction on indictment to imprisonment for a term not exceeding 2 years or to a fine or both.

(6) It shall be a defence in any proceedings under subsection (4) that the accused did not know and had no reasonable cause to know the information required of him.

DEFINITIONS
  "land": s.277(1).
  "planning authority": ss.1, 277(1).
  "local authority": s.2 of the Local Government etc. (Scotland) Act 1994 (c.39).
  "use": s.277(1).

GENERAL NOTE
  This section allows the Secretary of State or a local authority to require information from the occupier of land, or any person who receives rent in respect of any land in relation to the matters specified in subs. (2). It is an offence to fail to give the information required or to knowingly make a misstatement in respect of that information (subs. (5)). However, it is a defence in any

subsequent criminal proceedings if the accused did not know what information was required of him.

Offences by corporations

273.—(1) Where an offence under this Act which has been committed by a body corporate is proved to have been committed with the consent or connivance of, or to be attributable to any neglect on the part of—

(a) a director, manager, secretary or other similar officer of the body corporate, or

(b) any person who was purporting to act in any such capacity,

he, as well as the body corporate, shall be guilty of that offence and be liable to be proceeded against accordingly.

(2) In subsection (1) "director", in relation to any body corporate—

(a) which was established by or under an enactment for the purpose of carrying on under national ownership an industry or part of an industry or undertaking, and

(b) whose affairs are managed by its members,

means a member of that body corporate.

DEFINITIONS
"director": subs. (2).

Combined applications

274.—(1) Regulations may provide for the combination in a single document, made in such form and transmitted to such authority as may be prescribed, of—

(a) an application for planning permission in respect of any development and

(b) an application required, under any enactment specified in the regulations, to be made to a local authority in respect of that development.

(2) Before making such regulations, the Secretary of State shall consult such local authorities or associations of local authorities as appear to him to be concerned.

(3) Different provision may be made by any such regulations in relation to areas in which different enactments are in force.

(4) If an application required to be made to a local authority under an enactment specified in any such regulations is made in accordance with the provisions of the regulations, it shall be valid notwithstanding anything in that enactment prescribing, or enabling any authority to prescribe, the form in which, or the manner in which, such an application is to be made.

(5) Subsection (4) is without prejudice to—

(a) the validity of any application made in accordance with the enactment in question, or

(b) any provision of that enactment enabling a local authority to require further particulars of the matters to which the application relates.

(6) In this section "application" includes a submission.

(7) Subsection (1) shall apply in relation to applications for an approval required by a development order as it applies in relation to applications for planning permission.

DEFINITIONS
"application": subs. (6).
"development": ss.26, 277(1).
"development order": ss.30, 277(1).
"enactment": s.277(1).
"local authority": s.4 of the Local Government, etc. (Scotland) Act 1994 (c.39).

"planning permission": s.277(1).
"prescribed": s.277(1).

Regulations and orders

275.—(1) The Secretary of State may make regulations—

(a) for prescribing the form of any notice, order or other document authorised or required by this Act to be served, made or issued by any
planning authority which is a local authority,

(b) for any purpose for which regulations are authorised or required to be
made under this Act, other than a purpose for which regulations are
authorised or required to be made by another Minister, and

(c) for any of the purposes mentioned in section 28 of the Land Compensation (Scotland) Act 1963 (power to prescribe matters relevant to
Part IV).

(2) Any power conferred by this Act to make regulations shall be exercisable by statutory instrument.

(3) Any statutory instrument containing regulations made under this Act
(except regulations which, by virtue of any provision of this Act, are of no
effect unless approved by a resolution of each House of Parliament) shall be
subject to annulment in pursuance of a resolution of either House of
Parliament.

(4) The power to make development orders under section 30 and to make
orders under sections 5, 26(2)(f), 54 and 100(3)(a) or paragraph 7 or 8 of
Schedule 1 shall be exercisable by statutory instrument.

(5) Any statutory instrument which contains a development order or an
order under section 5, 54 or 100(3)(a) or paragraph 4(5) or 5(5) of Schedule 9
shall be subject to annulment in pursuance of a resolution of either House of
Parliament.

(6) Without prejudice to subsection (5), where a development order
makes provision for excluding or modifying any enactment contained in a
public general Act (other than an enactment specified in subsection (7)) the
order shall not have effect until that provision is approved by a resolution of
each House of Parliament.

(7) The enactments referred to in subsection (6) are—

(a) section 32(1) of the Public Health (Scotland) Act 1897,

(b) any enactment making such provision as might by virtue of any Act of
Parliament have been made in relation to the area to which the development order applies by means of a byelaw, order or regulation not
requiring confirmation by Parliament, and

(c) any enactment which has been previously excluded or modified by a
development order, and any enactment having substantially the same
effect as any such enactment.

(8) Without prejudice to section 14 of the Interpretation Act 1978, any
power conferred by this Act to make an order shall include power to vary or
revoke any such order by a subsequent order.

DEFINITIONS
"development order": ss.30, 277(1).
"enactment": s.277(1).
"local authority": s.4 of the Local Government, etc. (Scotland) Act 1994 (c.39).
"Minister": s.277(1).
"planning authority": ss.1, 277(1).

Act not excluded by special enactments

276. For the avoidance of doubt it is hereby declared that the provisions of
this Act, and any restrictions or powers thereby imposed or conferred in
relation to land, apply and may be exercised in relation to any land notwithstanding that provision is made by any enactment in force at the passing of

the 1947 Act, or by any local Act passed at any time during the Session of Parliament held during the regnal years 10 & 11 Geo. 6, for authorising or regulating any development of the land.

Interpretation

277.—(1) In this Act, except in so far as the context otherwise requires and subject to the following provisions of this section and to any transitional provision made by the Planning (Consequential Provisions) (Scotland) Act 1997—

"acquiring authority", in relation to the acquisition of an interest in land (whether compulsorily or by agreement) or to a proposal so to acquire such an interest, means the government department, local authority or other body by whom the interest is, or is proposed to be, acquired;

"the 1947 Act" means the Town and Country Planning (Scotland) Act 1947;

"the 1972 Act" means the Town and Country Planning (Scotland) Act 1972;

"advertisement" means any word, letter, model, sign, placard, board, notice, awning, blind, device or representation, whether illuminated or not, in the nature of, and employed wholly or partly for the purposes of, advertisement, announcement or direction, and (without prejudice to the foregoing provisions of this definition), includes any hoarding or similar structure used or designed, or adapted for use and anything else used, or designed or adapted principally for use, for the display of advertisements, and references to the display of advertisements shall be construed accordingly;

"aftercare condition" has the meaning given by paragraph 2(2) of Schedule 3;

"agriculture" includes horticulture, fruit growing, seed growing, dairy farming, the breeding and keeping of livestock (including any creature kept for the production of food, wool, skins or fur, or for the purpose of its use in the farming of land), the use of land as grazing land, meadow land, osier land, market gardens and nursery grounds, and the use of land for woodlands where that use is ancillary to the farming of land for other agricultural purposes, and "agricultural" shall be construed accordingly;

"the appropriate Minister" has the meaning given by section 217;

"breach of condition notice" has the meaning given by section 145;

"breach of planning control" has the meaning given by section 123;

"bridleway" has the same meaning as in section 47 of the Countryside (Scotland) Act 1967;

"building" includes any structure or erection, and any part of a building, as so defined, but does not include plant or machinery comprised in a building;

"building or works" includes waste materials, refuse and other matters deposited on land, and references to the erection or construction of buildings or works shall be construed accordingly and references to the removal of buildings or works include demolition of buildings and filling in of trenches;

"building operations" has the meaning given by section 26;

"caravan site" has the meaning given by section 1(4) of the Caravan Sites and Control of Development Act 1960;

"common" includes any town or village green;

"compliance period", in relation to an enforcement notice, shall be construed in accordance with section 135(11);

"compulsory acquisition" does not include the vesting in a person by an Act of Parliament of property previously vested in some other person;

"conservation area" means an area designated under section 61 of the Planning (Listed Buildings and Conservation Areas) (Scotland) Act 1997;

"depositing of mineral waste" means any process whereby a mineral-working deposit is created or enlarged and "depositing of refuse or waste materials" includes the depositing of mineral waste;

"development" has the meaning given by section 26, and "develop" shall be construed accordingly;

"development order" has the meaning given by section 30;

"development plan" shall be construed in accordance with section 24;

"disposal", except in section 191(9), means disposal by way of sale, excambion or lease, or by way of the creation of any servitude, right or privilege, or in any other manner, except by way of appropriation, gift or the creation of a heritable security, and "dispose of" shall be construed accordingly;

"enactment" includes an enactment in any local or private Act of Parliament, and an order, rule, regulation, byelaw or scheme made under an Act of Parliament, including an order or scheme confirmed by Parliament;

"enforcement notice" means a notice under section 127;

"engineering operations" includes the formation or laying out of means of access to roads;

"enterprise zone scheme" means a scheme or modified scheme having effect to grant planning permission in accordance with section 55;

"erection", in relation to buildings as defined in this subsection, includes, extension, alteration and re-erection;

"footpath" has the same meaning as in section 47 of the Countryside (Scotland) Act 1967;

"functions" includes powers and duties;

"government department" includes any Minister of the Crown;

"heritable security" means—

(a) a heritable security within the meaning of the Conveyancing (Scotland) Act 1924, but excluding a security by way of ground annual and a real burden ad factum praestandum and including a security constituted by way of ex facie absolute disposition, or

(b) an assignation in security of a lease recorded under the Registration of Leases (Scotland) Act 1857,

and "heritable creditor" shall be construed accordingly;

"improvement", in relation to a road, has the same meaning as in the Roads (Scotland) Act 1984;

"land" includes land covered with water and any building as defined by this section and, in relation to the acquisition of land under Part VIII, includes any interest in land and any servitude or right in or over land;

"Lands Tribunal" means the Lands Tribunal for Scotland;

"lease" includes a sub-lease, but does not include an option to take a lease;

"local authority" means a council constituted under section 2 of the Local Government etc. (Scotland) Act 1994;

"local roads authority" has the same meaning as in the Roads (Scotland) Act 1984;

"mineral-working deposit" means any deposit of material remaining after minerals have been extracted from land or otherwise deriving

from the carrying out of operations for the winning and working of
minerals in, on or under land;

"minerals" includes all substances of a kind ordinarily worked for
removal by underground or surface working;

"mining operations" has the meaning given by section 26;

"Minister" means any Minister of the Crown or other government
department;

"open space" means any land laid out as a public garden, or used for the
purposes of public recreation, or land which is a disused burial
ground;

"operational land" has the meaning given by section 215;

"owner", in relation to any land, includes (except in section 35) any person who under the Lands Clauses Acts would be enabled to sell and
convey the land to the promoters of an undertaking, and includes
also a lessee under a lease of agreement, the unexpired period of
which exceeds 3 years;

"the planning Acts" means this Act, the Planning (Listed Buildings and
Conservation Areas) (Scotland) Act 1997, the Planning (Hazardous Substances) (Scotland) Act 1997 and the Planning (Consequential Provisions) (Scotland) Act 1997;

"planning authority" has the meaning given by section 1;

"planning contravention notice" has the meaning given by section 125;

"planning decision" means a decision made on an application under
Part III;

"planning permission" means permission under Part III;

"planning permission granted for a limited period" has the meaning
given by section 41(3);

"prescribed" (except in relation to matters expressly required or authorised by this Act to be prescribed in some other way) means prescribed by regulations under this Act;

"public gas transporter" has the same meaning as in Part I of the Gas Act
1986;

"purchase notice" has the meaning given by section 88;

"restoration condition" has the meaning given by paragraph 2(2) of
Schedule 3;

"road" has the same meaning as in the Roads (Scotland) Act 1984;

"simplified planning zone" and "simplified planning zone scheme" shall
be construed in accordance with section 49;

"statutory undertakers" and "statutory undertaking" have the meanings given by section 214;

"steps for the protection of the environment" has the meaning given by
paragraph 5(3) of Schedule 8;

"stop notice" has the meaning given by section 140;

"suspension order" and "supplementary suspension order" have the
meanings given by paragraphs 5 and 6 respectively of Schedule 8;

"tree preservation order" has the meaning given by section 160;

"urban development area" and "urban development corporation" have
the same meaning as in section 171 of the Local Government, Planning and Land Act 1980;

"use", in relation to land, does not include the use of land for the carrying out of any building or other operations on it;

"Valuation Office" means the Valuation Office of the Inland Revenue
Department; and

"the winning and working of minerals" includes the extraction of minerals from a mineral working deposit.

(2) If, in relation to anything required or authorised to be done under this
Act, any question arises as to which Minister is or was the appropriate Minis-

ter in relation to any statutory undertakers, that question shall be determined by the Treasury.

(3) If any question so arises whether land of statutory undertakers is operational land, that question shall be determined by the Minister who is the appropriate Minister in relation to those undertakers.

(4) Words in this Act importing a reference to service of a notice to treat shall be construed as including a reference to the constructive service of such a notice which, by virtue of any enactment, is to be deemed to be served.

(5) With respect to references in this Act to planning decisions—

(a) in relation to a decision altered on appeal by the reversal or variation of the whole or part of it, such references shall be construed as references to the decision as so altered;

(b) in relation to a decision upheld on appeal, such references shall be construed as references to the decision of the planning authority and not to the decision of the Secretary of State on the appeal;

(c) in relation to a decision given on an appeal in the circumstances mentioned in section 47(2), such references shall be construed as references to the decision so given;

(d) the time of a planning decision, in a case where there is or was an appeal, shall be taken to be or have been the time of the decision as made by the planning authority (whether or not that decision is or was altered on that appeal) or, in the case of a decision given on an appeal in the circumstances mentioned in section 47(2), the time when in accordance with that section notification of a decision of the planning authority is deemed to have been received.

(6) Section 27 shall apply for determining for the purposes of this Act when development of land shall be taken to be initiated.

(7) In this Act any reference to a sale or purchase includes a reference to a sale or purchase by way of feu, and any reference to the price in relation to a sale or purchase includes a reference to grassum, feuduty and ground annual.

(8) Any reference in this Act to the dominium utile in relation to land which is not held on feudal tenure shall be construed as a reference to the interest in the land of the owner of it.

(9) References in the Planning Acts to any of the provisions in Part II of Schedule 18 include, except where the context otherwise requires, references to those provisions as modified under section 263(1) to (4).

(10) Without prejudice to section 20(2) of the Interpretation Act 1978, references in this Act to any enactment shall, except where the context otherwise requires, be construed as references to that enactment as amended by or under any other enactment.

Citation, commencement and extent

278.—(1) This Act may be cited as the Town and Country Planning (Scotland) Act 1997.

(2) Except as provided in Schedule 3 to the Planning (Consequential Provisions) (Scotland) Act 1997, this Act shall come into force at the end of the period of 3 months beginning with the day on which it is passed.

(3) Subject to subsection (4), this Act extends to Scotland only.

(4) Section 70 and Schedule 7 extend also to England and Wales.

SCHEDULES

Section 24(4)   SCHEDULE 1

OLD DEVELOPMENT PLANS

Preliminary

1. In this Schedule "old development plan" means a development plan to which paragraph 2 of Schedule 5 to the 1972 Act (continuation in force of development plans prepared before structure plans became operative) applied immediately before the commencement of this Act.

Continuation in force of old development plans

2. Any old development plan which immediately before the commencement of this Act was in force as respects any area shall, subject to the provisions of this Schedule, continue in force as respects that area and be treated for the purposes of this Act, any other enactment relating to town and country planning and the Land Compensation (Scotland) Act 1963 as being comprised in the development plan for that area.

Structure plans to prevail over old development plans

3. Subject to the following provisions of this Schedule, where by virtue of paragraph 2 the old development plan for any area is treated as being comprised in a development plan for that area and there is a conflict between any of its provisions and those of the structure plan for that area, the provisions of the structure plan shall be taken to prevail for the purposes of Parts III and V to VIII and section 85 of this Act, the Planning (Listed Buildings and Conservation Areas) (Scotland) Act 1997 and the Planning (Hazardous Substances) (Scotland) Act 1997.

Street authorisation maps

4. Where immediately before the commencement of this Act a street authorisation map prepared in pursuance of the Town and Country Planning (Development Plans) (Scotland) Regulations 1966 was treated for the purposes of the 1972 Act as having been adopted as a local plan for an area by a planning authority, it shall continue to be so treated.

Development plans for compensation purposes

5. Where there is no local plan in force in an area to which a structure plan applies, then, for any of the purposes of the Land Compensation (Scotland) Act 1963—
  (a) the development plan or current development plan shall as respects that area be taken as being—
        (i) the structure plan so far as applicable to the area, and any alterations to it, together with the Secretary of State's notice of approval of the plan and alterations, or
        (ii) the old development plan,
      whichever gives rise to those assumptions as to the grant of planning permission which are more favourable to the owner of the land acquired, for that purpose, and
  (b) land situated in an area defined in the current development plan as an area of comprehensive development shall be taken to be situated in—
        (i) any area wholly or partly within that area selected by the structure plan as an action area, or
        (ii) the area so defined in the old development plan,
      whichever leads to such assumptions as are mentioned in paragraph (a).

Discontinuance of old development plan on adoption of local plan

6. Subject to paragraph 7, on the adoption or approval of a local plan under section 17 or 19 so much of any old development plan as relates to the area to which the local plan relates shall cease to have effect.

7. The Secretary of State may by order direct that any of the provisions of the old development plan shall continue in force in relation to the area to which the local plan relates and, if he does so, the provisions of the old development plan specified in the order shall continue in force to the extent so specified.

8. The Secretary of State may by order wholly or partly revoke a development plan continued in force under this Schedule whether in its application to the whole of the district of a planning authority or in its application to part of that district and make such consequential amendments to the plan as appear to him to be necessary or expedient.

9. Before making an order with respect to a development plan under paragraph 7 or 8, the Secretary of State shall consult the planning authority for the district to which the plan relates.

Section 28(7)   SCHEDULE 2

1. Where on 1st July 1948 land was being temporarily used for a purpose other than the purpose for which it was normally used, planning permission is not required for the resumption of the use of the land for the latter purpose before 8th December 1969.

2. Where on 1st July 1948 land was normally used for one purpose and was also used on occasions, whether at regular intervals or not, for another purpose, planning permission is not required in respect of the use of the land for that other purpose on similar occasions on or after 8th December 1969 if the land has been used for that other purpose on at least one similar occasion since 1st July 1948 and before the beginning of 1969.

3. Where land was unoccupied on 1st July 1948, but had before that date been occupied at some time on or after 7th January 1937, planning permission is not required in respect of any use of the land begun before 8th December 1969 for the purpose for which the land was last used before 1st July 1948.

4. Notwithstanding anything in paragraphs 1 to 3, the use of land as a caravan site shall not, by virtue of any of those paragraphs, be treated as a use for which planning permission is not required, unless the land was so used on one occasion at least during the period of 2 years ending with 9th March 1960.

Sections 41(6) and 65(5)   SCHEDULE 3

CONDITIONS RELATING TO MINERAL WORKING

PART I

CONDITIONS IMPOSED ON GRANT OF PERMISSION

Duration of development

1.—(1) Every planning permission for development—
(a) consisting of the winning and working of minerals, or
(b) involving the depositing of mineral waste,
shall be subject to a condition as to the duration of the development.

(2) Except where a condition is specified under sub-paragraph (3), the condition in the case of planning permission granted or deemed to be granted after 22nd February 1982 is that the winning and working of minerals or the depositing of mineral waste must cease not later than the expiration of the period of 60 years beginning with the date of the permission.

(3) An authority granting planning permission after that date or directing after that date that planning permission shall be deemed to be granted may specify a longer or shorter period than 60 years, and if they do so, the condition is that the winning and working of minerals or the depositing of mineral waste must cease not later than the expiration of a period of the specified length beginning with the date of the permission.

(4) A longer or shorter period than 60 years may be prescribed for the purposes of sub-paragraphs (2) and (3).

(5) The condition in the case of planning permission granted or deemed to have been granted before 22nd February 1982 is that the winning and working of minerals or the depositing of mineral waste must cease not later than the expiration of the period of 60 years beginning with that date.

(6) A condition to which planning permission for development is subject by virtue of this paragraph—
(a) is not to be regarded for the purposes of the planning Acts as a condition such as is mentioned in section 41(1)(b), but
(b) is to be regarded for the purposes of sections 47 and 48 as a condition imposed by a decision of the planning authority, and may accordingly be the subject of an appeal under section 47.

Power to impose aftercare conditions

2.—(1) Where—
(a) planning permission for development consisting of the winning and working of minerals or involving the depositing of refuse or waste materials is granted, and

(b) the permission is granted subject to a restoration condition,

it may be granted subject also to any such aftercare condition as the planning authority think fit.

(2) In this Act—

"restoration condition" means a condition requiring that after the winning and working is completed or the depositing has ceased, the site shall be restored by the use of any or all of the following, namely, subsoil, topsoil and soil-making material; and

"aftercare condition" means a condition requiring that such steps shall be taken as may be necessary to bring land to the required standard for whichever of the following uses is specified in the condition, namely—

(a) use for agriculture,

(b) use for forestry, or

(c) use for amenity.

(3) An aftercare condition may either—

(a) specify the steps to be taken, or

(b) require that the steps be taken in accordance with a scheme (in this Schedule referred to as an "aftercare scheme") approved by the planning authority.

(4) A planning authority may approve an aftercare scheme in the form in which it is submitted to them or may modify it and approve it as modified.

(5) The steps that may be specified in an aftercare condition or an aftercare scheme may consist of planting, cultivating, fertilising, watering, draining or otherwise treating the land.

(6) Where a step is specified in a condition or a scheme, the period during which it is to be taken may also be specified, but no step may be required to be taken after the expiry of the aftercare period.

(7) In sub-paragraph (6) "the aftercare period" means a period of 5 years from compliance with the restoration condition or such other maximum period after compliance with that condition as may be prescribed; and in respect of any part of a site, the aftercare period shall commence on compliance with the restoration condition in respect of that part.

(8) The power to prescribe maximum periods conferred by sub-paragraph (7) includes power to prescribe maximum periods differing according to the use specified.

(9) In this paragraph "forestry" means the growing of a utilisable crop of timber.

Meaning of "required standard"

3.—(1) In a case where—

(a) the use specified in an aftercare condition is a use for agriculture,

(b) the land was in use for agriculture at the time of the grant of the planning permission or had previously been used for that purpose and had not at the time of the grant been used for any authorised purpose since its use for agriculture ceased, and

(c) the planning authority is aware of, or can readily ascertain, the physical characteristics of the land when it was last used for agriculture,

the land is brought to the required standard when its physical characteristics are restored, so far as it is practicable to do so, to what they were when it was last used for agriculture.

(2) In any other case where the use specified in an aftercare condition is a use for agriculture, the land is brought to the required standard when it is reasonably fit for that use.

(3) Where the use specified in an aftercare condition is a use for forestry, the land is brought to the required standard when it is reasonably fit for that use.

(4) Where the use specified in an aftercare condition is a use for amenity, the land is brought to the required standard when it is suitable for sustaining trees, shrubs or other plants.

(5) In this paragraph—

"authorised " means authorised by planning permission; and

"forestry" has the same meaning as in paragraph 2.

Consultations

4.—(1) Before imposing an aftercare condition specifying a use for forestry, the planning authority shall consult the Forestry Commission as to whether it is appropriate to specify that use.

(2) Where after consultations required by sub-paragraph (1) the planning authority are satisfied that the use that they ought to specify is a use for forestry, they shall consult the Forestry Commission with regard to whether the steps to be taken should be specified in the aftercare condition or in an aftercare scheme.

(3) The planning authority shall also consult the Forestry Commission—

(a) as to the steps to be specified in an aftercare condition which specifies a use for agriculture or for forestry, and

(b) before approving an aftercare scheme submitted in accordance with an aftercare condition which specifies such a use.

(4) The planning authority shall also, from time to time as they consider expedient, consult the Forestry Commission as to whether the steps specified in an aftercare condition or an aftercare scheme are being taken.

(5) In this paragraph "forestry" has the same meaning as in paragraph 2.

Certificate of compliance

5. If, on the application of any person with an interest in land in respect of which an aftercare condition has been imposed, the planning authority are satisfied that the condition has been complied with they shall issue a certificate to that effect.

Recovery of expenses of compliance

6. A person who has complied with an aftercare condition but who has not himself won and worked minerals or deposited refuse or waste materials shall be entitled, subject to any condition to the contrary contained in a contract which is enforceable against him by the person who last carried out such operations, to recover from that person any expenses reasonably incurred in complying with the aftercare condition.

PART II

CONDITIONS IMPOSED ON REVOCATION OR MODIFICATION OF PERMISSION

7. An order under section 65 may, in relation to planning permission for development consisting of the winning and working of minerals or involving the depositing of refuse or waste materials, include such aftercare condition as the planning authority think fit if—
   (a) it also includes a restoration condition, or
   (b) a restoration condition has previously been imposed in relation to the land by virtue of any provision of this Act.

8. Paragraphs 2(3) to (9) and 3 to 6 shall apply in relation to an aftercare condition so imposed as they apply in relation to such a condition imposed under paragraph 2.

Sections 48, 131, 154, 169 and 180   SCHEDULE 4

DETERMINATION OF CERTAIN APPEALS BY PERSON APPOINTED BY SECRETARY OF STATE

Determination of appeals by appointed person

1.—(1) The Secretary of State may by regulations prescribe classes of appeals under sections 47, 130, 154, 169 and 180 which are to be determined by a person appointed by the Secretary of State for the purpose instead of by the Secretary of State.

(2) Those classes of appeals shall be so determined except in such classes of case—
   (a) as may for the time being be prescribed, or
   (b) as may be specified in directions given by the Secretary of State.

(3) Such regulations may provide for the giving of publicity to any directions given by the Secretary of State under this paragraph.

(4) This paragraph shall not affect any provision in this Act or any instrument made under it that an appeal shall lie to, or a notice of appeal shall be served on, the Secretary of State.

(5) A person appointed under this paragraph is referred to in this Schedule as an "appointed person".

Powers and duties of appointed persons

2.—(1) An appointed person shall have the same powers and duties—
   (a) in relation to an appeal under section 47, as the Secretary of State has under section 48(1), (3), (5) and (8);
   (b) in relation to an appeal under section 130, as he has under sections 132(1), (2) and (4) and 133(1) to (4);
   (c) in relation to an appeal under section 154, as he has under subsection (2) and (3) of that section;
   (d) in relation to an appeal under section 169, as he has under subsections (5), (6), (8) and (9) of that section;
   (e) in relation to an appeal under section 180, as he has under subsections (4) and (6) of that section; and

(f) in relation to an appeal under paragraph 6(11) or (12) or 11(1) of Schedule 9 or paragraph 9(1) of Schedule 10, as he has under paragraph 18 of Schedule 8.

(2) Sections 48(2), 131(2) and 155(1) shall not apply to an appeal which falls to be determined by an appointed person, but before it is determined the Secretary of State shall ask the appellant and the planning authority whether they wish to appear before and be heard by the appointed person.

(3) If both the parties express a wish not to appear and be heard, the appeal may be determined without their being heard.

(4) If either of the parties expresses a wish to appear and be heard, the appointed person shall give them both an opportunity of doing so.

(5) Sub-paragraph (2) does not apply in the case of an appeal under section 47 if the appeal is referred to a Planning Inquiry Commission under section 69.

(6) Where an appeal has been determined by an appointed person, his decision shall be treated as that of the Secretary of State.

(7) Except as provided by section 239, the decision of an appointed person on an appeal shall be final.

Determination of appeals by Secretary of State

3.—(1) The Secretary of State may, if he thinks fit, direct that an appeal which would otherwise fall to be determined by an appointed person shall instead be determined by the Secretary of State.

(2) Such a direction shall state the reasons for which it is given and shall be served on the appellant, the planning authority and any person who has made representations relating to the subject matter of the appeal which the authority are required to take into account under section 38(2) and, if any person has been appointed under paragraph 1, on him.

(3) Where in consequence of such a direction an appeal falls to be determined by the Secretary of State himself, the provisions of this Act which are relevant to the appeal shall, subject to the following provisions of this paragraph, apply to the appeal as if this Schedule had never applied to it.

(4) The Secretary of State shall give the appellant, the planning authority and any person who has made any such representations as mentioned in sub-paragraph (2) an opportunity of appearing before and being heard by a person appointed by the Secretary of State for that purpose if—

(a) the reasons for the direction raise matters with respect to which any of those persons have not made representations, or

(b) in the case of the appellant or the planning authority, either of them was not asked in pursuance of paragraph 2(2) whether they wish to appear before and be heard by the appointed person, or expressed no wish in answer to that question, or expressed a wish to appear and be heard, but was not given an opportunity of doing so.

(5) Sub-paragraph (4) does not apply in the case of an appeal under section 47 if the appeal is referred to a Planning Inquiry Commission under section 69.

(6) Except as provided by sub-paragraph (4), the Secretary of State need not give any person an opportunity of appearing before and being heard by a person appointed for the purpose, or of making fresh representations or making or withdrawing any representations already made.

(7) In determining the appeal the Secretary of State may take into account any report made to him by any person previously appointed to determine it.

4.—(1) The Secretary of State may by a further direction revoke a direction under paragraph 3 at any time before the determination of the appeal.

(2) Such a further direction shall state the reasons for which it is given and shall be served on the person, if any, previously appointed to determine the appeal, the appellant, the planning authority and any person who has made representations relating to the subject matter of the appeal which the authority are required to take into account under section 38(2).

(3) Where such a further direction has been given, the provisions of this Schedule relevant to the appeal shall apply, subject to sub-paragraph (4), as if no direction under paragraph 3 had been given.

(4) Anything done by or on behalf of the Secretary of State in connection with the appeal which might have been done by the appointed person (including any arrangements made for the holding of a hearing or local inquiry) shall, unless that person directs otherwise, be treated as having been done by him.

Appointment of another person to determine appeal

5.—(1) At any time before the appointed person has determined the appeal the Secretary of State may—

(a) revoke his appointment, and

(b) appoint another person under paragraph 1 to determine the appeal instead.

(2) Where such a new appointment is made the consideration of the appeal or any inquiry or other hearing in connection with it shall be begun afresh.

(3) Nothing in sub-paragraph (2) shall require—

(a) the question referred to in paragraph 2(2) to be asked again with reference to the new appointed person if before his appointment it was asked with reference to the previous appointed person (any answers being treated as given with reference to the new appointed person), or

(b) any person to be given an opportunity of making fresh representations or modifying or withdrawing any representations already made.

Local inquiries and hearings

6.—(1) Whether or not the parties to an appeal have asked for an opportunity to appear and be heard, an appointed person—

(a) may hold a local inquiry in connection with the appeal, and

(b) shall do so if the Secretary of State so directs.

(2) Where an appointed person—

(a) holds a hearing by virtue of paragraph 2(4), or

(b) holds an inquiry by virtue of this paragraph,

an assessor may be appointed by the Secretary of State to sit with the appointed person at the hearing or inquiry to advise him on any matters arising, notwithstanding that the appointed person is to determine the appeal.

(3) Subject to sub-paragraph (4), the expenses of any such hearing or inquiry shall be paid by the Secretary of State.

(4) Subsections (4) to (13) of section 265 apply to an inquiry held under this paragraph as they apply to an inquiry held under that section.

(5) The appointed person has the same power to make orders under subsection (9) of that section in relation to proceedings under this Schedule which do not give rise to an inquiry as he has in relation to such an inquiry.

(6) For the purposes of this paragraph, references to the Minister in subsections (9) and (12) of that section shall be treated as references to the appointed person.

Supplementary provisions

7. If, before or during the determination of an appeal under section 47 which is to be or is being determined in accordance with paragraph 1, the Secretary of State forms the opinion mentioned in section 48(7), he may direct that the determination shall not be begun or proceeded with.

8.—(1) The Tribunals and Inquiries Act 1992 shall apply to a local inquiry or other hearing held in pursuance of this Schedule as it applies to a statutory inquiry held by the Secretary of State, but as if in section 10(1) of that Act (statement of reasons for decisions) the reference to any decision taken by the Secretary of State were a reference to a decision taken by an appointed person.

(2) The functions of determining an appeal and doing anything in connection with it conferred by this Schedule on an appointed person who is an officer of the Scottish Office shall be treated for the purposes of the Parliamentary Commissioner Act 1967 as functions of that Office.

Section 50(3)   SCHEDULE 5

SIMPLIFIED PLANNING ZONES

General

1.—(1) A simplified planning zone scheme shall consist of a map and a written statement, and such diagrams, illustrations and descriptive matter as the planning authority think appropriate for explaining or illustrating the provisions of the scheme.

(2) A simplified planning zone scheme shall specify—

(a) the development or classes of development permitted by the scheme,

(b) the land in relation to which permission is granted, and

(c) any conditions, limitations or exceptions subject to which it is granted,

and shall contain such other matters as may be prescribed.

Notification of proposals to make or alter scheme

2. An authority who decide under section 50(2) to make or alter a simplified planning zone scheme shall—

(a) notify the Secretary of State of their decision as soon as practicable, and
(b) determine the date on which they will begin to prepare the scheme or the alterations.

Power of Secretary of State to direct making or alteration of scheme

3.—(1) If a person requests a planning authority to make or alter a simplified planning zone scheme but the authority—

(a) refuse to do so, or
(b) do not within the period of 3 months from the date of the request decide to do so,

he may, subject to sub-paragraph (2), require them to refer the matter to the Secretary of State.

(2) A person may not require the reference of the matter to the Secretary of State if—

(a) in the case of a request to make a scheme, a simplified planning zone scheme relating to the whole or part of the land specified in the request has been adopted or approved within the 12 months preceding his request, or
(b) in the case of a request to alter the scheme, the scheme to which the request relates was adopted or approved, or any alteration to it has been adopted or approved, within that period.

(3) The Secretary of State shall, as soon as practicable after a matter is referred to him—

(a) send the authority a copy of any representations made to him by the applicant which have not been made to the authority, and
(b) notify the authority that if they wish to make any representations in the matter they should do so, in writing, within 28 days.

(4) After the Secretary of State has—

(a) considered the matter and any written representations made by the applicant or the authority, and
(b) carried out such consultations with such persons as he thinks fit,

he may give the authority a simplified planning zone direction.

(5) The Secretary of State shall notify the applicant and the authority of his decision and of his reasons for it.

4.—(1) A simplified planning zone direction is—

(a) if the request was for the making of a scheme, a direction to make a scheme which the Secretary of State considers appropriate, and
(b) if the request was for the alteration of a scheme, a direction to alter it in such manner as he considers appropriate,

and, in either case, requires the planning authority to take all the steps required by this Schedule for the adoption of proposals for the making or, as the case may be, alteration of a scheme.

(2) A direction under sub-paragraph (1)(a) or (b) may extend—

(a) to the land specified in the request to the authority,
(b) to any part of the land so specified, or
(c) to land which includes the whole or part of the land so specified,

and accordingly may direct that land shall be added to or excluded from an existing simplified planning zone.

Steps to be taken before depositing proposals

5.—(1) A planning authority proposing to make or alter a simplified planning zone scheme shall, before determining the content of their proposals, comply with this paragraph.

(2) They shall—

(a) consult—
    (i) the Secretary of State, and
    (ii) any local roads authority in whose area the proposed zone or any part of it lies,
as to the effect any proposals they may make might have on existing or future roads, and
(b) consult or notify such persons as regulations may require them to consult or, as the case may be, notify.

(3) They shall take such steps as may be prescribed, or as the Secretary of State may in a particular case direct, to publicise—

(a) the fact that they propose to make or alter a simplified planning zone scheme, and
(b) the matters which they are considering including in the proposals.

(4) They shall consider any representations that are made in accordance with regulations.

Procedure after deposit of proposals

6. Where a planning authority have prepared a proposed simplified planning zone scheme, or proposed alterations to a simplified planning zone scheme, they shall—

(a) make copies of the proposed scheme or alterations available for inspection at such places as may be prescribed,

   (b) take such steps as may be prescribed for the purpose of advertising the fact that the pro-
      posed scheme or alterations are so available and the places at which, and times during
      which, they may be inspected,
   (c) take such steps as may be prescribed for inviting representations or objections to be made
      within such period as may be prescribed, and
   (d) send a copy of the proposed scheme or alterations to the Secretary of State and to any
      local roads authority whom they have consulted under paragraph 5(2)(a).

Procedure for dealing with objections

7.—(1) Where objections to the proposed scheme or alterations are made, the planning authority may—
   (a) for the purpose of considering the objections, cause a local inquiry or other hearing to be
      held by a person appointed by the Secretary of State or, in such cases as may be pre-
      scribed, appointed by the authority, or
   (b) require the objections to be considered by a person appointed by the Secretary of State.
   (2) A planning authority shall exercise the power under sub-paragraph (1), or paragraph (a)
or (b) of that sub-paragraph, if directed to do so by the Secretary of State.
   (3) Regulations may—
   (a) make provision with respect to the appointment, and qualifications for appointment, of
      persons for the purposes of this paragraph;
   (b) include provision enabling the Secretary of State to direct a planning authority to appoint
      a particular person, or one of a specified list or class of persons;
   (c) make provision with respect to the remuneration and allowances of the person appointed.
   (4) The Tribunals and Inquiries Act 1992 applies to a local inquiry or other hearing held under
this paragraph as it applies to a statutory inquiry held by the Secretary of State, with the substitution in section 10(1) (statement of reasons for decision) for the references to a decision taken
by the Secretary of State of references to a decision taken by a planning authority.
   (5) The planning authority shall—
   (a) where a person appointed under or by virtue of this paragraph is in the public service of
      the Crown, pay the Secretary of State, and
   (b) in any other case, pay the person so appointed,
a sum, determined in accordance with regulations under sub-paragraph (6), in respect of the
performance by the person so appointed of his functions in relation to the inquiry or hearing
(whether or not it takes place).
   (6) Regulations made by the Secretary of State may make provision with respect to the determination of the sum referred to in sub-paragraph (5) and may in particular prescribe, in relation
to any class of person appointed under or by virtue of this paragraph, a standard daily amount
applicable in respect of each day on which a person of that class is engaged in holding, or in work
connected with, the inquiry or hearing.
   (7) Without prejudice to the generality of sub-paragraph (6), the Secretary of State may, in
prescribing by virtue of that sub-paragraph a standard daily amount for any class of person—
   (a) where the persons of that class are in the public service of the Crown, have regard to the
      general staff costs and overheads of his department, and
   (b) in any other case, have regard to the general administrative costs incurred by persons of
      that class in connection with the performance by them of their functions in relation to such
      inquiries and hearings.

Adoption of proposals by planning authority

8.—(1) After the expiry of the period for making objections or, if objections have been made
in accordance with the regulations, after considering those objections and the views of any person holding an inquiry or hearing or considering the objections under paragraph 7, the planning
authority may by resolution adopt the proposals (subject to the following provisions of this
paragraph and of paragraph 9).
   (2) They may adopt the proposals as originally prepared or as modified so as to take account
of—
   (a) any such objections as are mentioned in sub-paragraph (1) or any other objections to the
      proposals, or
   (b) any other considerations which appear to the authority to be material.
   (3) After copies of the proposals have been sent to the Secretary of State and before they have
been adopted by the planning authority, the Secretary of State may, if it appears to him that the
proposals are unsatisfactory, direct the authority to consider modifying the proposals in such
respects as are indicated in the direction.

(4) An authority to whom a direction is given shall not adopt the proposals unless they satisfy the Secretary of State that they have made the modification necessary to conform with the direction or the direction is withdrawn.

Calling in of proposals for approval by Secretary of State

9.—(1) After copies of proposals have been sent to the Secretary of State and before they have been adopted by the planning authority, the Secretary of State may direct that the proposals shall be submitted to him for his approval.

(2) In that event—

(a) the authority shall not take any further steps for the adoption of the proposals, and in particular shall not hold or proceed with a local inquiry or other hearing or any consideration of objections in respect of the proposals under paragraph 7, and

(b) the proposals shall not have effect unless approved by the Secretary of State and shall not require adoption by the authority.

Approval of proposals by Secretary of State

10.—(1) The Secretary of State may after considering proposals submitted to him under paragraph 9 either approve them, in whole or in part and with or without modifications, or reject them.

(2) In considering the proposals he may take into account any matters he thinks are relevant, whether or not they were taken into account in the proposals as submitted to him.

(3) Where on taking the proposals into consideration the Secretary of State does not determine then to reject them he shall, before determining whether or not to approve them, consider any objections made in accordance with regulations (and not withdrawn) except objections which—

(a) have already been considered by the planning authority or by a person appointed by the Secretary of State, or

(b) have already been considered at a local inquiry or other hearing.

(4) The Secretary of State may—

(a) for the purpose of considering any objections and the views of the planning authority and of such other persons as he thinks fit, cause a local inquiry or other hearing to be held by a person appointed by him, or

(b) require such objections and views to be considered by a person appointed by him.

(5) In considering the proposals the Secretary of State may consult, or consider the views of, any planning authority or any other person; but he need not do so, or give an opportunity for the making or consideration of representations or objections, except so far as he is required to do so by sub-paragraph (3) of this paragraph.

Default powers

11.—(1) Where—

(a) a planning authority are directed under paragraph 3 to make a simplified planning zone scheme which the Secretary of State considers appropriate or to alter such a scheme in such manner as he considers appropriate, and

(b) the Secretary of State is satisfied, after holding a local inquiry or other hearing, that the authority are not taking within a reasonable period the steps required by this Schedule for the adoption of proposals for the making or, as the case may be, alteration of a scheme,

he may himself make a scheme or, as the case may be, the alterations.

(2) Where under this paragraph anything which ought to have been done by a planning authority is done by the Secretary of State, the preceding provisions of this Schedule apply, so far as practicable, with any necessary modifications in relation to the doing of that thing by the Secretary of State and the thing so done.

(3) Where the Secretary of State incurs expenses under this paragraph in connection with the doing of anything which should have been done by a planning authority, so much of those expenses as may be certified by the Secretary of State to have been incurred in the performance of functions of that authority shall on demand be repaid by the authority to the Secretary of State.

Regulations and directions

12.—(1) Without prejudice to the preceding provisions of this Schedule, the Secretary of State may make regulations with respect to the form and content of simplified planning zone schemes and with respect to the procedure to be followed in connection with their preparation, withdrawal, adoption, submission, approval, making or alteration.

(2) Any such regulations may in particular—

(a) provide for the notice to be given of, or the publicity to be given to, matters included or proposed to be included in a simplified planning zone scheme and the adoption or approval of such a scheme, or of any alteration of it, or any other prescribed procedural step, and for publicity to be given to the procedure to be followed in these respects;

(b) make provision with respect to the making and consideration of representations as to matters to be included in, or objections to, any such scheme or proposals for its alteration;

(c) make provision with respect to the circumstances in which representations with respect to the matters to be included in such a scheme or proposals for its alteration are to be treated, for the purposes of this Schedule, as being objections made in accordance with regulations;

(d) without prejudice to paragraph (a), provide for notice to be given to particular persons of the adoption or approval of a simplified planning zone scheme, or an alteration to such a scheme, if they have objected to the proposals and have notified the planning authority of their wish to receive notice, subject (if the regulations so provide) to the payment of a reasonable charge;

(e) require or authorise a planning authority to consult with, or consider the views of, other persons before taking any prescribed procedural step;

(f) require a planning authority, in such cases as may be prescribed or in such particular cases as the Secretary of State may direct, to provide persons making a request in that behalf with copies of any document which has been made public, subject (if the regulations so provide) to the payment of a reasonable charge;

(g) provide for the publication and inspection of a simplified planning zone scheme which has been adopted or approved, or any document adopted or approved altering such a scheme, and for copies of any such scheme or document to be made available on sale.

(3) Regulations under this paragraph may extend throughout Scotland or to specified areas only and may make different provision for different cases.

(4) Subject to the preceding provisions of this Schedule and to any regulations under this paragraph, the Secretary of State may give directions to any planning authority or to planning authorities generally—

(a) for formulating the procedure for the carrying out of their functions under this Schedule;

(b) for requiring them to give him such information as he may require for carrying out any of his functions under this Schedule.

Section 69(4)   SCHEDULE 6

PLANNING INQUIRY COMMISSIONS

Constitution

1.—(1) A Planning Inquiry Commission ("a commission") shall consist of a chairman and not less than 2 nor more than 4 other members appointed by the Secretary of State.

(2) The Secretary of State may—

(a) pay to the members of a commission such remuneration and allowances as he may with the consent of the Treasury determine, and

(b) provide for a commission such officers or servants, and such accommodation, as appears to him expedient to provide for the purpose of assisting the commission in the discharge of their functions.

(3) The validity of any proceedings of a commission shall not be affected by any vacancy among the members of the commission or by any defect in the appointment of any member.

References

2.—(1) Two or more of the matters mentioned in section 69(2) may be referred to the same commission if it appears to the responsible Minister or Ministers that they relate to proposals to carry out development for similar purposes on different sites.

(2) Where a matter referred to a commission under section 69(2) relates to a proposal to carry out development for any purpose at a particular site, the responsible Minister or Ministers may also refer to the commission the question whether development for that purpose should instead be carried out at an alternative site.

(3) On referring a matter to a commission under section 69(2), the responsible Minister or Ministers—

(a) shall state in the reference the reasons for the reference, and

(b) may draw the attention of the commission to any points which seem to him or them to be relevant to their inquiry.

Procedure on reference

3.—(1) A reference to a commission of a proposal that development should be carried out by or on behalf of a government department may be made at any time.

(2) A reference of any other matter mentioned in section 69(2) may be made at any time before, but not after, the determination of the relevant application referred under section 46 or the relevant appeal under section 47 or, as the case may be, the giving of the relevant direction under section 57.

(3) The fact that an inquiry or other hearing has been held into a proposal by a person appointed by any Minister for the purpose shall not prevent a reference of the proposal to a commission.

(4) Notice of the making of a reference to a commission shall be published in the prescribed manner.

(5) A copy of the notice shall be served on the planning authority for the area in which it is proposed that the relevant development shall be carried out, and—
- (a) in the case of an application for planning permission referred under section 46 or an appeal under section 47, on the applicant and any person who has made representations relating to the subject matter of the application or appeal which the authority are required to take into account under section 38(1) or (2);
- (b) in the case of a proposal that a direction should be given under section 57 with respect to any development, on the local authority or statutory undertakers applying for authorisation to carry out that development.

(6) Subject to the provisions of this Schedule and to any directions given to them by the responsible Minister or Ministers, a commission shall have power to regulate their own procedure.

Functions on reference

4.—(1) A commission inquiring into a matter referred to them under section 69(2) shall—
- (a) identify and investigate the considerations relevant to, or the technical or scientific aspects of, that matter which in their opinion are relevant to the question whether the proposed development should be permitted to be carried out, and
- (b) assess the importance to be attached to those considerations or aspects.

(2) If—
- (a) in the case of a matter mentioned in section 69(2)(a), (b) or (c), the applicant, or
- (b) in any case, the planning authority,

so wish, the commission shall give to each of them, and, in the case of an application or appeal mentioned in section 69(2)(a) or (b), also to any person who has made representations relating to the subject matter of the application or appeal which the authority are required to take into account under section 38(1) or (2), an opportunity of appearing before and being heard by one or more members of the commission.

(3) The commission shall then report to the responsible Minister or Ministers on the matter referred to them.

(4) A commission may, with the approval of the Secretary of State and at his expense, arrange for the carrying out (whether by the commission themselves or by others) of research of any kind appearing to them to be relevant to a matter referred to them for inquiry and report.

Local inquiries held by commission

5.—(1) A commission shall, for the purpose of complying with paragraph 4(2), hold a local inquiry.

(2) They may hold such an inquiry, if they think it necessary for the proper discharge of their functions, although neither the applicant nor the planning authority wish an opportunity to appear and be heard.

(3) Where a commission are to hold a local inquiry under this paragraph in connection with a matter referred to them, and it appears to the responsible Minister or Ministers, in the case of some other matter falling to be determined by a Minister of the Crown and required or authorised by an enactment other than paragraph 4 and this paragraph to be the subject of a local inquiry, that the two matters are so far cognate that they should be considered together, he or, as the case may be, they may direct that the two inquiries be held concurrently or combined as one inquiry.

(4) An inquiry held by a commission under this paragraph shall be treated for the purposes of the Tribunals and Inquiries Act 1992 as one held by a Minister in pursuance of a duty imposed by a statutory provision.

(5) Subsections (4) to (13) of section 265 (power to summon and examine witnesses, and expenses at inquiries) shall apply to an inquiry held under this paragraph as they apply to an inquiry held under that section.

"The responsible Minister or Ministers"

6.—(1) In section 69 and this Schedule "the responsible Minister or Ministers" means, in relation to a matter specified in column 1 of the following Table (matters which may be referred to a Planning Inquiry Commission under section 69(2)), the Minister or Ministers specified opposite in column 2.

(2) Where an entry in column 2 of the Table specifies two or more Ministers, that entry shall be construed as referring to those Ministers acting jointly.

TABLE

Referred Matter	Responsible Minister or Ministers
1. Application for planning permission or appeal under section 47— (a) relating to land to which section 218(1) applies; (b) relating to other land.	(a) the Secretary of State and the appropriate Minister (if different); (b) the Secretary of State.
2. Proposal that a government department should give a direction under section 57(1) or that development should be carried out by or on behalf of a government department.	The Secretary of State and the Minister (if different) in charge of the government department concerned.

Section 70(4)   SCHEDULE 7

JOINT PLANNING INQUIRY COMMISSIONS

Constitution

1.—(1) A Joint Planning Inquiry Commission (a "joint commission") shall consist of a chairman and not less than 2 nor more than 4 other members appointed by the Ministers.

(2) The Ministers may—

(a) pay to the members of a joint commission such remuneration and allowances as they may with the consent of the Treasury determine, and

(b) provide for a joint commission such officers or servants, and such accommodation, as appears to them expedient to provide for the purpose of assisting the commission in the discharge of their functions.

(3) The validity of any proceedings of a joint commission shall not be affected by any vacancy among the members of the commission or by any defect in the appointment of any member.

References

2.—(1) Two or more of the matters mentioned in section 70(2) ("referred matters") may be referred to the same joint commission if it appears to the responsible Ministers that they relate to proposals to carry out development for similar purposes on different sites.

(2) Where a referred matter relates to a proposal to carry out development for any purpose at a particular site, the responsible Ministers may also refer to the commission the question whether development for that purpose should be instead carried out at an alternative site, whether in Scotland or in England, or partly in one and partly in the other.

(3) On referring a matter to a joint commission, the responsible Ministers—

(a) shall state in the reference the reasons for it, and

(b) may draw the attention of the commission to any points which seem to them to be relevant to their inquiry.

Procedure on reference

3.—(1) A reference to a joint commission of a proposal that development should be carried out by or on behalf of a government department may be made at any time.

(2) A reference of any other matter mentioned in section 70(2) may be made at any time before, but not after, the determination of the relevant referred application or the relevant

appeal or, as the case may be, the giving of the relevant direction, notwithstanding that an inquiry or other hearing has been held into the proposal by a person appointed by any Minister for the purpose.

(3) Notice of the making of a reference to a joint commission shall be published in the prescribed manner.

(4) A copy of the notice shall be served on the planning authority for the district, or as the case may be the local planning authority for the area, in which it is proposed that the relevant development shall be carried out.

(5) In the case of an application for planning permission referred under section 46 of this Act or section 77 of the 1990 Act or an appeal under section 47 of this Act or section 78 of the 1990 Act, notice shall also be served—

(a) on the applicant or appellant, and

(b) on any person who has made representations, relating to the subject matter of the application or appeal, which the planning authority are required to take into account under section 38(1) or (2) of this Act or, as the case may be, the local planning authority are required to take into account under section 71(1) or (2) of the 1990 Act.

(6) In the case of a proposal that a direction should be given by a government department under section 57(1) of this Act or section 90(1) of the 1990 Act with respect to any development, notice shall also be served on the local authority or statutory undertakers applying for authorisation to carry out that development.

(7) Subject to the provisions of this Schedule, and to any directions given to them by the responsible Ministers, a joint commission shall have power to regulate their own procedure.

(8) In this paragraph "prescribed" means prescribed by regulations made by the Secretary of State and the Secretary of State for the Environment jointly in the exercise of their respective powers under this Act and the 1990 Act.

Functions on reference

4. A joint commission inquiring into a referred matter shall—

(a) identify and investigate the considerations relevant to, or the technical or scientific aspects of, that matter which in their opinion are relevant to the question whether the proposed development should be permitted to be carried out,

(b) assess the importance to be attached to those considerations or aspects,

(c) give to persons an opportunity of appearing before, and being heard by, one or more members of the commission in accordance with paragraph 5, and

(d) report to the responsible Ministers on the matter.

5. A joint commission shall give an opportunity of appearing and being heard by one or more of its members to—

(a) in any case, the planning authority or, as the case may be, the local planning authority, if the authority so wish,

(b) in the case of a matter mentioned in section 69(2)(a), (b) or (c) of this Act or section 101(2)(a), (b) or (c) of the 1990 Act, the applicant, if he so wishes, and

(c) in the case of an application or appeal mentioned in section 69(2)(a) or (b) of this Act or section 101(2)(a) or (b) of the 1990 Act, any person who has made representations relating to the subject matter of the application or appeal which the planning authority are required to take into account under section 38(1) or (2) of this Act or, as the case may be, the local planning authority are required to take into account under section 71(1) or (2) of the 1990 Act.

6. A joint commission may, with the approval of the Ministers and at their expense, arrange for the carrying out, by themselves or others, of research of any kind appearing to them to be relevant to a referred matter.

7. The provisions of sections 46(5) and 48(2) of this Act and sections 77(5) and 79(2) of the 1990 Act and the provisions of Schedule 4 to this Act and Schedule 6 to the 1990 Act, relating to the giving of an opportunity of appearing before, and being heard by, a person appointed by the Secretary of State, shall not apply to an application for planning permission, or an appeal, referred to a joint commission.

Local inquiries

8.—(1) A joint commission shall, for the purpose of complying with paragraph 5, hold a local inquiry.

(2) A joint commission may hold such an inquiry if they think it necessary for the proper discharge of their functions, although neither the applicant nor the planning authority or, as the case may be, the local planning authority wish an opportunity to appear and be heard.

(3) Where a joint commission are to hold a local inquiry in connection with a referred matter and it appears to the responsible Ministers, in the case of some other matter falling to be determined by a Minister of the Crown and required or authorised by an enactment other than this Schedule to be the subject of a local inquiry, that the two matters are so far cognate that they should be considered together, the responsible Minister may direct that the two inquiries be held concurrently or combined as one inquiry.

(4) For the purposes of the Tribunals and Inquiries Act 1992 a local inquiry held by a joint commission—

    (a) if held in Scotland, shall be treated as one held by the Secretary of State in pursuance of a duty imposed by a statutory provision, and

    (b) if held in England, shall be treated as one held by the Secretary of State for the Environment in pursuance of a duty so imposed.

(5) Subsections (4) to (13) of section 265 shall apply to a local inquiry held by a joint commission in Scotland as they apply to an inquiry held under that section.

(6) Subsections (2) to (5) of section 250 of the Local Government Act 1972 (evidence and costs at local inquiries) shall apply in relation to a local inquiry held by a joint commission in England as they apply in relation to an inquiry caused to be held by a Minister under subsection (1) of that section, with the substitution for references to a Minister causing the inquiry to be held (other than the first reference in subsection (4)) of references to the responsible Ministers.

Interpretation

9. In this Schedule—

    "the 1990 Act" means the Town and Country Planning Act 1990;

    "the Ministers" has the meaning given in section 70(3), except that their functions under paragraphs 1(2) and 6 may, by arrangements between them, be exercised by either acting on behalf of both; and

    "the responsible Ministers" means, in relation to a matter specified in column 1 of the following Table (matters which may be referred to a Joint Planning Inquiry Commission under section 70(2)), those specified opposite in column 2, acting jointly.

TABLE

Referred Matter	Responsible Ministers
1. Application for planning permission or appeal under section 47 of this Act— (a) relating to land to which section 218(1) of this Act or section 266(1) of the 1990 Act applies;	(a) the Secretaries of State for the time being having general responsibility in planning matters in relation to Scotland and in relation to England and the appropriate Minister (if different).

Referred Matter	Responsible Ministers
(b) relating to other land.	(b) the Secretaries of State for the time being having general responsibility in planning matters in relation to Scotland and in relation to England.
2. Proposal that a government department should give a direction under section 57(1) of this Act or section 90(1) of the 1990 Act, or that development should be carried out by or on behalf of a government department.	The Secretaries of State for the time being having general responsibility in planning matters in relation to Scotland and in relation to England and the Minister (if different) in charge of the government department concerned.

Section 71(8)   SCHEDULE 8

OLD MINERAL WORKINGS AND PERMISSIONS

PART I

REQUIREMENTS RELATING TO DISCONTINUANCE OF MINERAL WORKING

Orders requiring discontinuance of mineral working

1.—(1) If, having regard to the development plan and to any other material considerations, it appears to a planning authority that it is expedient in the interests of the proper planning of their district (including the interests of amenity)—

   (a) that any use of land for development consisting of the winning and working of minerals or involving the deposit of refuse or waste materials in, on or under the land should be discontinued, or that any conditions should be imposed on the continuance of that use of land,

   (b) that any buildings or works on land so used should be altered or removed, or

   (c) that any plant or machinery used for the winning and working of or depositing of minerals should be altered or removed,

the planning authority may by order require the discontinuance of that use, or impose such conditions as may be specified in the order on the continuance of it or, as the case may be, require such steps as may be so specified to be taken for the alteration or removal of the buildings or works or plant or machinery.

   (2) Subsections (2) to (5) and (7) of section 71 and section 72 apply to orders under this paragraph as they apply to orders under section 71.

2.—(1) Where development consisting of the winning and working of minerals or involving the deposit of refuse or waste materials is being carried out in, on or under any land, the conditions which an order under paragraph 1 may impose include a restoration condition.

   (2) If—

   (a) such an order includes a restoration condition, or

   (b) a restoration condition has previously been imposed in relation to the land by virtue of any provision of this Act,

the order may also include any such aftercare condition as the planning authority think fit.

   (3) An order under paragraph 1 may grant planning permission for any development of the land to which the order relates, subject to such conditions as may be—

   (a) required by paragraph 1 of Schedule 3, or

   (b) specified in the order.

   (4) In a case where—

   (a) the use specified in an aftercare condition is a use for agriculture,

   (b) the land was in use for agriculture immediately before the development began or had previously been used for agriculture and had not been used for any authorised purpose since its use for agriculture ceased, and

   (c) the planning authority is aware of or can readily ascertain the physical characteristics of the land when it was last used for agriculture,

the land is brought to the required standard when its physical characteristics are restored, so far as it is practicable to do so, to what they were when it was last used for agriculture.

   (5) In any other case where the use specified in an aftercare condition is a use for agriculture, the land is brought to the required standard when it is reasonably fit for that use.

Prohibition of resumption of mineral working

3.—(1) Where it appears to the planning authority that development of land consisting of the winning and working of minerals or involving the depositing of mineral waste has occurred, but the winning and working or depositing has permanently ceased, the planning authority may by order—

   (a) prohibit the resumption of the winning and working or the depositing, and

   (b) impose, in relation to the site, any such requirement as is specified in sub-paragraph (3).

   (2) The planning authority may assume that the winning and working or the depositing has permanently ceased only when—

   (a) no winning and working or depositing has occurred, to any substantial extent, at the site for a period of at least 2 years, and

   (b) it appears to the planning authority, on the evidence available to them at the time when they make the order, that resumption of the winning and working or the depositing to any substantial extent at the site is unlikely.

(3) The requirements mentioned in sub-paragraph (1) are—

(a) a requirement to alter or remove plant or machinery which was used for the purpose of the winning and working or the depositing or for any purpose ancillary to that purpose,

(b) a requirement to take such steps as may be specified in the order, within such period as may be so specified, for the purpose of removing or alleviating any injury to amenity which has been caused by the winning and working or depositing, other than injury due to subsidence caused by underground mining operations,

(c) a requirement that any condition subject to which planning permission for the development was granted or which has been imposed by virtue of any provision of this Act shall be complied with, and

(d) a restoration condition.

(4) If—

(a) an order under this paragraph includes a restoration condition, or

(b) a restoration condition has previously been imposed in relation to the site by virtue of any provision of this Act,

the order may include any such aftercare condition as the planning authority think fit.

(5) Paragraphs 2(3) to (9), 3(3) and (4) and 4 to 6 of Schedule 3 apply in relation to an aftercare condition imposed under this paragraph as they apply to such a condition imposed under paragraph 2 of that Schedule.

(6) In a case where—

(a) the use specified in an aftercare condition is a use for agriculture,

(b) the land was in use for agriculture immediately before development consisting of the winning and working of minerals began to be carried out in, on, or under it or had previously been used for any authorised purpose since its use for agriculture ceased, and

(c) the planning authority is aware of or can readily ascertain the physical characteristics of the land when it was last used for agriculture,

the land is brought to the required standard when its physical characteristics are restored, so far as it is practicable to do so, to what they were when it was last used for agriculture.

(7) In any other case where the use specified is a use for agriculture the land is brought to the required standard when it is reasonably fit for that use.

4.—(1) An order under paragraph 3 shall not take effect unless it is confirmed by the Secretary of State, either without modification or subject to such modifications as he considers expedient.

(2) Where a planning authority submit such an order to the Secretary of State for his confirmation under this paragraph, the authority shall serve notice of the order—

(a) on any person who is an owner or occupier of any of the land to which the order relates, and

(b) on any other person who in their opinion will be affected by it.

(3) The notice shall specify the period within which any person on whom the notice is served may require the Secretary of State to give him an opportunity of appearing before, and being heard by, a person appointed by the Secretary of State for that purpose.

(4) If within that period such a person so requires, the Secretary of State shall, before confirming the order, give such an opportunity both to that person and to the planning authority.

(5) The period referred to in sub-paragraph (3) must not be less than 28 days from the service of the notice.

(6) Where an order under paragraph 3 has been confirmed by the Secretary of State, the planning authority shall serve a copy of the order on every person who was entitled to be served with notice under sub-paragraph (2).

(7) When an order under paragraph 3 takes effect any planning permission for the development to which the order relates shall cease to have effect.

(8) Sub-paragraph (7) is without prejudice to the power of the planning authority, on revoking the order, to make a further grant of planning permission for development consisting of the winning and working of minerals or involving the depositing of mineral waste.

Orders after suspension of winning and working of minerals

5.—(1) Where it appears to the planning authority—

(a) that development of land—

(i) consisting of the winning and working of minerals, or

(ii) involving the depositing of mineral waste,

has occurred, but

(b) the winning and working or depositing has been temporarily suspended,

the planning authority may by order (in this Act referred to as a "suspension order") require that steps be taken for the protection of the environment.

(2) The planning authority may assume that the winning and working or the depositing has been temporarily suspended only when—

(a) no such winning and working or depositing has occurred, to any substantial extent, at the site for a period of at least 12 months, but

(b) it appears to the planning authority, on the evidence available to them at the time when they make the order, that a resumption of such winning and working or depositing to a substantial extent is likely.

(3) In this Act "steps for the protection of the environment" means steps for the purpose of—

(a) preserving the amenities of the area in which the land in, on or under which the development was carried out is situated during the period while the winning and working or the depositing is suspended,

(b) protecting that area from damage during that period, or

(c) preventing any deterioration in the condition of the land during that period.

(4) A suspension order shall specify a period, commencing with the date on which it is to take effect, within which any required step for the protection of the environment is to be taken and may specify different periods for the taking of different steps.

Supplementary suspension orders

6.—(1) At any time when a suspension order is in operation the planning authority may by order direct—

(a) that steps for the protection of the environment shall be taken in addition to or in substitution for any of the steps which the suspension order or a previous order under this sub-paragraph specified as required to be taken, or

(b) that the suspension order or any order under this sub-paragraph shall cease to have effect.

(2) An order under sub-paragraph (1) is in this Act referred to as a "supplementary suspension order".

Confirmation and coming into operation of suspension orders

7.—(1) Subject to sub-paragraph (2) and without prejudice to paragraph 8, a suspension order or a supplementary suspension order shall not take effect unless it is confirmed by the Secretary of State, either without modification or subject to such modifications as he considers expedient.

(2) A supplementary suspension order revoking a suspension order or a previous supplementary suspension order and not requiring that any fresh step shall be taken for the protection of the environment shall take effect without confirmation.

(3) Sub-paragraphs (2) to (5) of paragraph 4 shall have effect in relation to a suspension order or supplementary suspension order submitted to the Secretary of State for his confirmation as they have effect in relation to an order submitted to him for his confirmation under that paragraph.

(4) Where a suspension order or supplementary suspension order has been confirmed by the Secretary of State, the planning authority shall serve a copy of the order on every person who was entitled to be served with notice of the order by virtue of sub-paragraph (3).

Registration of suspension orders

8. An order made under paragraph 3, 5 or 6 shall not take effect until it is registered either—

(a) in a case where the land affected by the order is registered in that Register, in the Land Register for Scotland, or

(b) in any other case, in the appropriate division of the General Register of Sasines.

Review of suspension orders

9.—(1) It shall be the duty of a planning authority—

(a) to undertake in accordance with the following provisions of this paragraph reviews of suspension orders and supplementary suspension orders which are in operation in their district, and

(b) to determine whether they should make in relation to any land to which a suspension order or supplementary suspension order applies—

(i) an order under paragraph 3, or

(ii) a supplementary suspension order.

(2) The first review of a suspension order shall be undertaken not more than 5 years from the date on which the order takes effect.

(3) Each subsequent review shall be undertaken not more than 5 years after the previous review.

(4) If a supplementary suspension order is in operation for any part of the area for which a suspension order is in operation, they shall be reviewed together.

(5) If a planning authority have made a supplementary suspension order which requires the taking of steps for the protection of the environment in substitution for all the steps required to

be taken by a previous suspension order or supplementary suspension order, the authority shall undertake reviews of the supplementary suspension order in accordance with sub-paragraphs (6) and (7).

(6) The first review shall be undertaken not more than 5 years from the date on which the order takes effect.

(7) Each subsequent review shall be undertaken not more than 5 years after the previous review.

Old mining permissions

10.—(1) In this paragraph and Part II of this Schedule, "old mining permission" means any planning permission for development—

(a) consisting of the winning and working of minerals, or

(b) involving the depositing of mineral waste,

which is deemed to have been granted by virtue of paragraph 77 of Schedule 22 to the 1972 Act (development authorised under interim development orders after 10th November 1943).

(2) An old mining permission shall, if an application under Part II of this Schedule to determine the conditions to which the permission is to be subject is finally determined, have effect as from the final determination as if granted on the terms required to be registered.

(3) If no such development has, at any time in the period of 2 years ending with 16th May 1991, been carried out to any substantial extent anywhere in, on or under the land to which an old mining permission relates, that permission shall not authorise any such development to be carried out after 24 January 1992 unless—

(a) the permission has effect in accordance with sub-paragraph (2), and

(b) the development is carried out after such an application is finally determined.

(4) An old mining permission shall—

(a) if no application for the registration of the permission is made under Part II of this Schedule, cease to have effect on the day following the last date on which such an application may be made, and

(b) if such an application is refused, cease to have effect on the day following the date on which the application is finally determined.

(5) An old mining permission shall, if—

(a) such an application is granted, but

(b) an application under Part II of this Schedule to determine the conditions to which the permission is to be subject is required to be served before the end of any period and is not so served,

cease to have effect on the day following the last date on which the application to determine those conditions may be served.

(6) Subject to sub-paragraph (3), this paragraph—

(a) shall not affect any development carried out under an old mining permission before an application under Part II of this Schedule to determine the conditions to which the permission is to be subject is finally determined or, as the case may be, the date on which the permission ceases to have effect, and

(b) shall not affect any order made or having effect as if made under paragraphs 1 to 9 and 11.

Resumption of mineral working after suspension order

11.—(1) Subject to sub-paragraph (2), nothing in a suspension order or a supplementary suspension order shall prevent the recommencement of development consisting of the winning and working of minerals or involving the depositing of mineral waste at the site in relation to which the order has effect.

(2) No person shall recommence such development without first giving the planning authority notice of his intention to do so.

(3) A notice under sub-paragraph (2) shall specify the date on which the person giving the notice intends to recommence the development.

(4) The planning authority shall revoke the order if the winning and working of minerals or the depositing of mineral waste has recommenced to a substantial extent at the site in relation to which the order has effect.

(5) If the authority do not revoke the order before the end of the period of 2 months from the date specified in the notice under sub-paragraph (2), the person who gave that notice may apply to the Secretary of State for the revocation of the order.

(6) Notice of an application under sub-paragraph (5) shall be given by the applicant to the planning authority.

(7) If he is required to do so by the person who gave the notice or by the planning authority, the Secretary of State shall, before deciding whether to revoke the order, give him and the planning

authority an opportunity of appearing before, and being heard by, a person appointed by the Secretary of State for the purpose.

(8) If the Secretary of State is satisfied that the winning and working of minerals or the depositing of mineral waste has recommenced to a substantial extent at the site in relation to which the order has effect, he shall revoke the order.

(9) If the Secretary of State revokes an order by virtue of sub-paragraph (8), he shall give notice of its revocation—

(a) to the person who applied to him for the revocation, and

(b) to the planning authority.

Default powers of Secretary of State

12.—(1) If it appears to the Secretary of State that it is expedient that any order should be made under paragraph 1, 3, 5 or 6, he may himself make such an order.

(2) Such an order made by the Secretary of State shall have the same effect as if it had been made by the planning authority and confirmed by the Secretary of State.

(3) The Secretary of State shall not make such an order without consulting the planning authority.

(4) Where the Secretary of State proposes to make an order under paragraph 1 he shall serve a notice of the proposal on the planning authority.

(5) The notice shall specify the period (which must not be less than 28 days from the date of its service) within which the authority may require an opportunity of appearing before and being heard by a person appointed by the Secretary of State for the purpose.

(6) If within that period the authority so require, the Secretary of State shall, before making the order, give the authority such an opportunity.

(7) The provisions of this Schedule and of any regulations made under this Act with respect to the procedure to be followed in connection with the submission by the planning authority of any order under paragraph 1, 3, 5 or 6, as the case may be, its confirmation by the Secretary of State and the service of copies of it as confirmed shall have effect, subject to any necessary modifications, in relation to any proposal by the Secretary of State to make such an order by virtue of sub-paragraph (1), its making by him and the service of copies of it.

PART II

REGISTRATION OF OLD MINING PERMISSIONS

Application for registration

13.—(1) Any person who is an owner of any land to which an old mining permission relates, or is entitled to an interest in a mineral to which such a permission relates, may apply to the planning authority for the permission to be registered.

(2) The application must specify the development which the applicant claims is authorised by the permission, including the land to which the permission relates, and the conditions (if any) to which the permission is subject.

(3) The application must be served on the planning authority before the end of the period of 6 months beginning on 24 January 1992.

(4) On an application under this paragraph, the planning authority must—

(a) if they are satisfied that (apart from paragraph 10(3)) the permission authorises development consisting of the winning and working of minerals or involving the depositing of mineral waste, ascertain—

(i) the area of land to which the permission relates, and

(ii) the conditions (if any) to which the permission is subject,

and grant the application, and

(b) in any other case, refuse the application.

(5) Where—

(a) application has been made under this paragraph, but

(b) the planning authority have not given the applicant notice of their determination within the period of 3 months beginning with the service of notice of the application (or within such extended period as may at any time be agreed upon in writing between the applicant and the authority),

the application is to be treated for the purposes of paragraph 10 and this Part of this Schedule as having been refused by the authority.

Determination of conditions

14.—(1) The conditions to which an old mining permission is to be subject—

(a) may include any conditions which may be imposed on a grant of planning permission for development consisting of the winning and working of minerals or involving the depositing of mineral waste,

(b) may be imposed in addition to, or in substitution for, any conditions ascertained under paragraph 13(4)(a), and

(c) must include a condition that the winning and working of minerals or depositing of mineral waste must cease not later than 21st February 2042.

(2) Where an application for the registration of an old mining permission has been granted, any person who is an owner of any land to which the permission relates, or is entitled to an interest in a mineral to which the permission relates, may apply to the planning authority to determine the conditions to which the permission is to be subject.

(3) The application must set out proposed conditions.

(4) The application must be served on the planning authority—

(a) after the date mentioned in sub-paragraph (5), and

(b) except where paragraph 10(3) applies, before the end of the period of 12 months beginning with that date or such extended period as may at any time be agreed upon in writing between the applicant and the authority.

(5) The date referred to in sub-paragraph (4) is—

(a) the date on which the application for registration is granted by the planning authority, if no appeal is made to the Secretary of State under paragraph 17, and

(b) in any other case, the date on which the application for registration is finally determined.

(6) On an application under this paragraph—

(a) the planning authority must determine the conditions to which the permission is to be subject, and

(b) if, within the period of 3 months beginning with the service of notice of the application (or within such extended period as may at any time be agreed upon in writing between the applicant and the authority) the authority have not given the applicant notice of their determination, the authority shall be treated for the purposes of paragraph 10 and this Part of this Schedule as having determined that the permission is to be subject to the conditions set out in the application.

(7) The condition to which an old mining permission is to be subject by reason of sub-paragraph (1)(c) is not to be regarded for the purposes of the planning Acts as a condition such as is mentioned in section 41(1)(b) (planning permission granted for a limited period).

(8) This paragraph does not apply to an old mining permission which has ceased to have effect since the application under paragraph 13 was granted.

Registration

15.—(1) Where an application for the registration of an old mining permission is granted, the permission must be entered in the appropriate part of the register kept under section 36 and the entry must specify the area of land ascertained under paragraph 13(4)(a).

(2) Where an application to determine the conditions to which an old mining permission is to be subject is finally determined, the conditions must be entered in the appropriate part of that register.

(3) The matters required to be entered in the register under this paragraph must be entered as soon as reasonably practicable.

General provisions about applications

16.—(1) An application under paragraph 13 or 14 is an application which is—

(a) made on an official form, and

(b) accompanied by an appropriate certificate.

(2) The applicant must, so far as reasonably practicable, give the information required by the form.

(3) Where the planning authority receive an application under paragraph 13 or 14, they must as soon as reasonably practicable give to the applicant a written acknowledgement of the application.

(4) Where the planning authority determine an application under either of those paragraphs, they must as soon as reasonably practicable give written notice of their determination to the applicant.

(5) An appropriate certificate is such a certificate—

(a) as would be required under sections 34 or 35 to accompany the application if it were an application for planning permission for development consisting of the winning and working of minerals or involving the depositing of mineral waste, but

(b) with such modifications as are required for the purposes of this Part of this Schedule.

(6) Sections 34(3) and (4) and 35(5) (offences) shall also have effect in relation to any certificate purporting to be an appropriate certificate.

Right of appeal

17.—(1) Where the planning authority—

(a) refuse an application under paragraph 13, or

(b) in granting such an application, ascertain an area of land, or conditions, which differ from those specified in the application,

the applicant may appeal to the Secretary of State.

(2) Where, on an application under paragraph 14, the planning authority determine conditions that differ in any respect from the conditions set out in the application, the applicant may appeal to the Secretary of State.

(3) An appeal under this paragraph must be made by giving notice of appeal to the Secretary of State.

(4) In the case of an appeal under sub-paragraph (1), the notice must be given to the Secretary of State before the end of the period of 3 months beginning with the determination or, in the case of an application treated as refused by virtue of paragraph 13(5), beginning at the end of the period or extended period referred to in paragraph 13(5)(b).

(5) In the case of an appeal under sub-paragraph (2), the notice must be given to the Secretary of State before the end of the period of 6 months beginning with the determination.

(6) A notice of appeal under this paragraph is a notice which—

(a) is made on an official form, and

(b) is accompanied by an appropriate certificate.

(7) The appellant must, so far as reasonably practicable, give the information required by the form.

(8) Paragraph 16(5) and (6) shall apply for the purposes of sub-paragraph (7) as it applies for the purposes of paragraph 16(1).

Determination of appeal

18.—(1) On an appeal under paragraph 17 the Secretary of State may—

(a) allow or dismiss the appeal, or

(b) reverse or vary any part of the decision of the planning authority (whether the appeal relates to that part of it or not),

and may deal with the application as if it had been made to him in the first instance.

(2) Before determining such an appeal the Secretary of State must, if either the appellant or the planning authority so wish, give each of them an opportunity of appearing before and being heard by a person appointed by the Secretary of State for the purpose.

(3) If at any time before or during the determination of such an appeal it appears to the Secretary of State that the appellant is responsible for undue delay in the progress of the appeal, he may—

(a) give the appellant notice that the appeal will be dismissed unless the appellant takes, within the period specified in the notice, such steps as are specified in the notice for the expedition of the appeal, and

(b) if the appellant fails to take those steps within that period, dismiss the appeal accordingly.

(4) The decision of the Secretary of State on such an appeal shall be final.

Reference of applications to Secretary of State

19.—(1) The Secretary of State may give directions requiring applications under this Part of this Schedule to any planning authority to be referred to him for determination instead of being dealt with by the authority.

(2) The direction may relate either to a particular application or to applications of a class specified in the direction.

(3) Where an application is referred to him under this paragraph—

(a) subject to paragraph (b) and sub-paragraph (4), the following provisions of this Schedule—

(i) paragraph 13(1) to (4),

(ii) paragraph 14(1) to (6)(a), (7) and (8),

(iii) paragraphs 15 and 16, and

(iv) paragraphs 20 to 22,

shall apply, with any necessary modifications, as they apply to applications which fall to be determined by the planning authority,

(b) before determining the application the Secretary of State must, if either the applicant or the planning authority so wish, give each of them an opportunity of appearing before and being heard by a person appointed by the Secretary of State for the purpose, and

(c) the decision of the Secretary of State on the application shall be final.

(4) Where an application under paragraph 13 is so referred to him, paragraph 14(5) shall apply as if for paragraphs (a) and (b) there were substituted "the date on which the application for registration is finally determined".

Two or more applicants

20.—(1) Where a person has served an application under paragraph 13 or 14 in respect of an old mining permission—

(a) he may not serve any further application under the paragraph in question in respect of the same permission, and

(b) if the application has been determined, whether or not it has been finally determined, no other person may serve an application under the paragraph in question in respect of the same permission.

(2) Where—

(a) a person has served an application under paragraph 13 or 14 in respect of an old mining permission, and

(b) another person duly serves an application under the paragraph in question in respect of the same permission,

then for the purpose of the determination of the applications and any appeal against such a determination, this Part of this Schedule shall have effect as if the applications were a single application served on the date on which the later application was served and references to the applicant shall be read as references to either or any of the applicants.

Application of provisions relating to planning permission

21.—(1) Subject to paragraph 15, section 36 and any provision of regulations or a development order made by virtue of that section shall have effect with any necessary modifications as if references to applications for planning permission included applications under paragraph 13 or 14.

(2) Where the planning authority are not the authority required to keep the register under that section, the planning authority must provide the authority required to keep the register with such information and documents as that authority requires to comply with paragraph 15 and with that section as applied by this paragraph.

(3) Sections 237 and 239 (validity of certain decisions and proceedings for questioning their validity) shall have effect as if the action mentioned in section 237(3) included any decision of the Secretary of State on an appeal under paragraph 17 or on an application referred to him under paragraph 19.

Interpretation

22.—(1) In this Part of this Schedule—

"official form" means, in relation to an application or appeal, a document supplied by or on behalf of the Secretary of State for use for the purpose in question, and

"owner" in relation to any land means any person who under the Lands Clauses Acts would be enabled to sell and convey the land to the promoters of an undertaking and includes any person entitled to possession of the land as lessee under a lease the unexpired portion of which is not less than 7 years.

(2) For the purposes of paragraph 10 and this Part of this Schedule, an application under paragraph 13 or 14 is finally determined when the following conditions are met—

(a) the proceedings on the application, including any proceedings on or in consequence of an application under section 239, have been determined, and

(b) any time for appealing under paragraph 17, or applying or further applying under that section (where there is a right to do so), has expired.

Section 74   SCHEDULE 9

<small>REVIEW OF OLD MINERAL PLANNING PERMISSIONS</small>

Interpretation

1.—(1) In this Schedule—

"dormant site" means a Phase I or Phase II site in, on or under which no minerals development has been carried out to any substantial extent at any time in the period beginning on 22nd February 1982 and ending with 6th June 1995 otherwise than by virtue of a planning permission which is not a relevant planning permission relating to the site;

"first list", in relation to a planning authority, means the list prepared by them pursuant to paragraph 3;

"mineral site" has the meaning given by sub-paragraph (2);

"old mining permission" has the meaning given by paragraph 10(1) of Schedule 8;

"owner", in relation to any land, has the meaning given by paragraph 22(1) of Schedule 8;

"Phase I site" and "Phase II site" have the meaning given by paragraph 2;

"relevant planning permission" means any planning permission, other than an old mining permission or a planning permission granted by a development order, granted after 30th June 1948 for minerals development; and

"second list", in relation to a planning authority, means the list prepared by them pursuant to paragraph 4.

(2) For the purposes of this Schedule, but subject to sub-paragraph (3), "mineral site" means—

(a) in a case where it appears to the planning authority to be expedient to treat as a single site the aggregate of the land to which any two or more relevant planning permissions relate, the aggregate of the land to which those permissions relate, and

(b) in any other case, the land to which a relevant planning permission relates.

(3) In determining whether it appears to them to be expedient to treat as a single site the aggregate of the land to which two or more relevant planning permissions relate a planning authority shall have regard to any guidance issued for the purpose by the Secretary of State.

(4) Any reference (however expressed) in this Schedule to an old mining permission or a relevant planning permission relating to a mineral site is a reference to the mineral site, or some part of it, being the land to which the permission relates; and where any such permission authorises the carrying out of development consisting of the winning and working of minerals but only in respect of any particular mineral or minerals, that permission shall not be taken, for the purposes of this Schedule, as relating to any other mineral in, on or under the land to which the permission relates.

(5) For the purposes of this Schedule, a mineral site which is a Phase I site or a Phase II site is active if it is not a dormant site.

(6) For the purposes of this Schedule, working rights are restricted in respect of a mineral site if any of—

(a) the size of the area which may be used for the winning and working of minerals or the depositing of mineral waste,

(b) the depth to which operations for the winning and working of minerals may extend,

(c) the height of any deposit of mineral waste,

(d) the rate at which any particular mineral may be extracted,

(e) the rate at which any particular mineral waste may be deposited,

(f) the period at the expiry of which any winning or working of minerals or depositing of mineral waste is to cease, or

(g) the total quantity of minerals which may be extracted from, or of mineral waste which may be deposited on, the site,

is restricted or reduced in respect of the mineral site in question.

(7) For the purposes of this Schedule, where an application is made under paragraph 9 for the determination of the conditions to which the relevant planning permissions relating to the mineral site to which the application relates are to be subject, those conditions are finally determined when—

(a) the proceedings on the application, including any proceedings on or in consequence of an application under section 239, have been determined, and

(b) any time for appealing under paragraph 11(1), or applying or further applying under paragraph 9, (where there is a right to do so) has expired.

Phase I and II sites

2.—(1) This paragraph has effect for the purposes of determining which mineral sites are Phase I sites, which are Phase II sites, and which are neither Phase I nor Phase II sites.

(2) A mineral site is neither a Phase I site nor a Phase II site where—

(a) all the relevant planning permissions which relate to the site have been granted after 21st February 1982, or

(b) some only of the relevant planning permissions which relate to the site have been granted after 21st February 1982, and the parts of the site to which those permissions relate constitute the greater part of that site.

(3) With the exception of those mineral sites which, by virtue of sub-paragraph (2), are neither Phase I nor Phase II sites, every mineral site is either a Phase I site or a Phase II site.

(4) Subject to sub-paragraph (2), where any part of a mineral site is situated within—

(a) a site in respect of which a notification under section 28 of the Wildlife and Countryside Act 1981 (sites of special scientific interest) is in force,

(b) an area designated as a National Scenic Area under section 262C of the 1972 Act, or

(c) an area designated as a Natural Heritage Area under section 6 of the Natural Heritage (Scotland) Act 1991,

that site is a Phase I site.

(5) Subject to sub-paragraphs (2) and (4), where—

(a) all the relevant planning permissions which relate to a mineral site, and which were not granted after 21st February 1982, were granted after 7th December 1969, or

(b) the parts of a mineral site to which relate such of the relevant planning permissions relating to the site as were granted after 7th December 1969 but before 22nd February 1982 constitute a greater part of the site than is constituted by those parts of the site to which no such relevant planning permission relates but to which a relevant planning permission granted on or before 7th December 1969 does relate,

the mineral site is a Phase II site.

(6) Every other mineral site, that is to say any mineral site other than one—

(a) which is, by virtue of sub-paragraph (2), neither a Phase I nor a Phase II site,

(b) which is a Phase I site by virtue of sub-paragraph (4), or

(c) which is a Phase II site by virtue of sub-paragraph (5),

is a Phase I site.

(7) In ascertaining, for the purposes of sub-paragraph (2) or (5), whether any parts of a mineral site constitute the greater part of that site, or whether a part of a mineral site is greater than any other part, that mineral site shall be treated as not including any part of the site—

(a) to which an old mining permission relates, or

(b) which is a part where minerals development has been (but is no longer being) carried out and which has, in the opinion of the planning authority, been satisfactorily restored;

but no part of a site shall be treated, by virtue of paragraph (b), as being not included in the site unless the planning authority are satisfied that any aftercare conditions which relate to that part have, so far as relating to that part, been complied with.

The "first list"

3.—(1) A planning authority shall, in accordance with the following provisions of this paragraph, prepare a list of mineral sites in their area (the "first list").

(2) A site shall, but shall only, be included in the first list if it is a mineral site in the area of the planning authority and is either—

(a) an active Phase I site,

(b) an active Phase II site, or

(c) a dormant site.

(3) In respect of each site included in the first list, the list shall indicate whether the site is an active Phase I site, an active Phase II site or a dormant site.

(4) In respect of each active Phase I site included in the first list, that list shall specify the date by which an application is to be made to the planning authority under paragraph 9.

(5) Any date specified pursuant to sub-paragraph (4) shall be a date—

(a) not earlier than the date upon which expires the period of 12 months from the date on which the first list is first advertised in accordance with paragraph 5, and

(b) not later than the date upon which expires the period of three years from the date upon which the provisions of this Schedule come into force.

(6) The preparation of the first list shall be completed before the day upon which it is first advertised in accordance with paragraph 5.

The "second list"

4.—(1) A planning authority shall, in accordance with the following provisions of this paragraph, prepare a list of the active Phase II sites in their area (the "second list").

(2) The second list shall include each mineral site in the planning authority's area which is an active Phase II site.

(3) In respect of each site included in the second list, that list shall indicate the date by which an application is to be made to the planning authority under paragraph 9.

(4) Subject to sub-paragraph (5), any date specified pursuant to sub-paragraph (3) shall be a date—

(a) not earlier than the date upon which expires the period of 12 months from the date on which the second list is first advertised in accordance with paragraph 5, and

(b) not later than the date upon which expires the period of six years from the date upon which the provisions of this Schedule come into force.

(5) The Secretary of State may by order provide that sub-paragraph (4)(b) shall have effect as if for the period of six years referred to in that paragraph there were substituted such longer period specified in the order.

(6) The preparation of the second list shall be completed before the day upon which it is first advertised in accordance with paragraph 5.

Advertisement of the first and second lists

5.—(1) This paragraph makes provision for the advertisement of the first and second lists prepared by a planning authority.

(2) The planning authority shall advertise each of the first and second lists by causing to be published, in each of two successive weeks, in one or more newspapers circulating in its area, notice of the list having been prepared.

(3) In respect of each of those lists, such notice shall—

(a) state that the list has been prepared by the authority, and

(b) specify one or more places within the area of the authority at which the list may be inspected, and in respect of each such place specify the times (which shall be reasonable times) during which facilities for inspection of the list will be afforded.

(4) In respect of the first list, such notice shall—

(a) be first published no later than the day upon which expires the period of three months from the date upon which the provisions of this Schedule come into force,

(b) explain the general effect of a mineral site being classified as a dormant site or, as the case may be, as an active Phase I site or an active Phase II site,

(c) explain the consequences which will occur if no application is made under paragraph 9 in respect of an active Phase I site included in the list by the date specified in the list for that site,

(d) explain the effects for any dormant or active Phase I or II site not included in the list of its not being included in the list and—

(i) set out the right to make an application to the authority for that site to be included in the list,

(ii) set out the date by which such an application must be made, and

(iii) state that the owner of such a site has a right of appeal against any decision of the authority upon such an application, and

(e) explain that the owner of an active Phase I site has a right to apply for postponement of the date specified in the list for the making of an application under paragraph 9, and set out the date by which an application for such postponement must be made.

(5) In respect of the second list, such notice shall—

(a) be first published no later than the day upon which expires the period of three years, or such longer period as the Secretary of State may by order specify, from the date upon which the provisions of this Schedule come into force, and

(b) explain the consequences which will occur if no application is made under paragraph 9 in respect of an active Phase II site included in the list by the date specified in the list for that site.

Applications for inclusion in the first list of sites not included in that list as originally prepared and appeals from decisions upon such applications

6.—(1) Any person who is the owner of any land, or is entitled to an interest in a mineral, may, if that land or interest is not a mineral site included in the first list and does not form part of any mineral site included in that list, apply to the planning authority for that land or interest to be included in that list.

(2) An application under sub-paragraph (1) shall be made no later than the day upon which expires the period of three months from the day when the first list was first advertised in accordance with paragraph 5.

(3) Where the planning authority consider that—

(a) the land or interest is, or forms part of, any dormant or active Phase I or II site, they shall accede to the application, or

(b) part only of the land or interest is, or forms part of, any dormant or active Phase I or II site, they shall accede to the application so far as it relates to that part of the land or interest,

but shall otherwise refuse the application.

(4) On acceding, whether in whole or in part, to an application made under sub-paragraph (1), the planning authority shall amend the first list as follows—

(a) where they consider that the land or interest, or any part of the land or interest, is a dormant site or an active Phase I or II site, they shall add the mineral site consisting of the land or interest or, as the case may be, that part, to the first list and shall cause the list to indicate whether the site is an active Phase I site, an active Phase II site or a dormant site;

(b) where they consider that the land or interest, or any part of the land or interest, forms part of any mineral site included in the first list, they shall amend the entry in the first list for that site accordingly.

(5) Where the planning authority amend the first list in accordance with sub-paragraph (4), they shall also—

(a) in a case where an active Phase I site is added to the first list pursuant to sub-paragraph (4)(a), cause that list to specify, in respect of that site, the date by which an application is to be made to the planning authority under paragraph 9;

(b) in a case where—

(i) the entry for an active Phase I site included in the first list is amended pursuant to sub-paragraph (4)(b), and

(ii) the date specified in that list in respect of that site as the date by which an application is to be made to the planning authority under paragraph 9 is a date falling less than 12 months after the date upon which the authority make their decision upon the application in question,

cause that date to be amended so as to specify instead the date upon which expires the period of 12 months from the date on which the applicant is notified under sub-paragraph (10) of the authority's decision upon his application.

(6) Any date specified pursuant to sub-paragraph (5)(a) shall be a date—

(a) not earlier than the date upon which expires the period of 12 months from the date on which the applicant is notified under sub-paragraph (10) of the planning authority's decision upon his application, and

(b) not later than the later of—

(i) the date upon which expires the period of three years from the date upon which the provisions of this Schedule come into force; and

(ii) the date mentioned in paragraph (a).

(7) On acceding, whether in whole or in part, to an application made under sub-paragraph (1), the planning authority shall, if the second list has been first advertised in accordance with paragraph 5 prior to the time at which they make their decision on the application, amend the second list as follows—

(a) where they consider that the land or interest, or any part of the land or interest, is an active Phase II site, they shall add the mineral site consisting of the land or interest or, as the case may be, that part, to the second list;

(b) where they consider that the land or interest, or any part of the land or interest, forms part of any active Phase II site included in the second list, they shall amend the entry in that list for that site accordingly.

(8) Where the planning authority amend the second list in accordance with sub-paragraph (7), they shall also—

(a) in a case where an active Phase II site is added to the second list pursuant to sub-paragraph (7)(a), cause that list to specify, in respect of that site, the date by which an application is to be made to the authority under paragraph 9;

(b) in a case where—

(i) the entry for an active Phase II site included in the second list is amended pursuant to sub-paragraph (7)(b), and

(ii) the date specified in that list in respect of that site as the date by which an application is to be made to the authority under paragraph 9 is a date falling less than 12 months after the date upon which the authority make their decision upon the application in question,

cause that date to be amended so as to specify instead the date upon which expires the period of 12 months from the date on which the applicant is notified under sub-paragraph (10) of the authority's decision upon his application.

(9) Any date specified pursuant to sub-paragraph (8)(a) shall be a date—

(a) not earlier than the date upon which expires the period of 12 months from the date on which the applicant is notified under sub-paragraph (10) of the planning authority's decision upon his application, and

(b) not later than the later of—

(i) the date upon which expires the period of six years from the date upon which the provisions of this Schedule come into force, and

(ii) the date mentioned in paragraph (a).

(10) When a planning authority determine an application made under sub-paragraph (1), they shall notify the applicant in writing of their decision and, in a case where they have acceded to the application, whether in whole or in part, shall supply the applicant with details of any amendment to be made to the first or second list in accordance with sub-paragraph (4) or (8).

(11) Where a planning authority—

(a) refuse an application made under sub-paragraph (1), or

(b) accede to such an application only so far as it relates to part of the land or interest in respect of which it was made,

the applicant may by notice appeal to the Secretary of State.

(12) A person who has made such an application may also appeal to the Secretary of State if the planning authority have not given notice to the applicant of their decision on the application within eight weeks of their having received the application or within such extended period as may at any time be agreed upon in writing between the applicant and the authority.

(13) An appeal under sub-paragraph (11) or (12) must be made by giving notice of appeal to the Secretary of State before the end of the period of six months beginning with—

(a) in the case of an appeal under sub-paragraph (11), the determination, or

(b) in the case of an appeal under sub-paragraph (12), the end of the period of eight weeks mentioned in that sub-paragraph or, as the case may be, the end of the extended period mentioned in that sub-paragraph.

Postponement of the date specified in the first or second list for review of the permissions relating to a Phase I or II site in cases where the existing conditions are satisfactory

7.—(1) Any person who is the owner of any land, or of any interest in any mineral, comprised in—

(a) an active Phase I site included in the first list, or

(b) an active Phase II site included in the second list,

may apply to the planning authority for the postponement of the date specified in that list in respect of that site as the date by which an application is to be made to the authority under paragraph 9 (in this paragraph referred to as "the specified date").

(2) Subject to sub-paragraph (3), an application under sub-paragraph (1) shall be made no later than the day upon which expires the period of three months from the day when—

(a) in the case of an active Phase I site, the first list, or

(b) in the case of an active Phase II site, the second list,

was first advertised in accordance with paragraph 5.

(3) In the case of—

(a) an active Phase I site—

(i) added to the first list in accordance with paragraph 6(4)(a); or

(ii) in respect of which the entry in the first list was amended in accordance with paragraph 6(4)(b);

or

(b) an active Phase II site—

(i) added to the second list in accordance with paragraph 6(7)(a); or

(ii) in respect of which the entry in the second list was amended in accordance with paragraph 6(7)(b),

an application under sub-paragraph (1) shall be made no later than the day upon which expires the period of three months from the day on which notice was given under paragraph 6(10) of the planning authority's decision to add the site to or, as the case may be, so to amend the list in question.

(4) An application under sub-paragraph (1) shall be in writing and shall—

(a) set out the conditions to which each relevant planning permission relating to the site is subject,

(b) set out the applicant's reasons for considering those conditions to be satisfactory,

(c) set out the date which the applicant wishes to be substituted for the specified date, and

(d) be accompanied by the appropriate certificate.

(5) For the purposes of sub-paragraph (4)(d), the appropriate certificate is each of the certificates which would be required, under or by virtue of sections 34 and 35, to accompany the application if it were an application for planning permission for minerals development, but with such modifications as are required for the purposes of this paragraph; and sections 34(3) and (4) and 35(5) shall have effect in relation to any certificate purporting to be the appropriate certificate.

(6) Where the planning authority receive an application made under sub-paragraph (1)—

(a) if they consider the conditions referred to in sub-paragraph (4)(a) to be satisfactory they shall agree to the specified date being postponed in which event they shall determine the date to be substituted for that date,

(b) in any other case they shall refuse the application.

(7) Where the planning authority agree to the specified date being postponed they shall cause the first or, as the case may be, the second list to be amended accordingly.

(8) When a planning authority determine an application made under sub-paragraph (1), they shall notify the applicant in writing of their decision and, in a case where they have agreed to the postponement of the specified date, shall notify the applicant of the date which they have determined should be substituted for the specified date.

(9) Where, within three months of the planning authority having received an application under sub-paragraph (1), or within such extended period as may at any time be agreed upon in writing between the applicant and the authority, the authority have not given notice, under sub-paragraph (8), to the applicant of their decision upon the application, the authority shall be treated as—

(a) having agreed to the specified date being postponed, and

(b) having determined that the date referred to in sub-paragraph (4)(c) be substituted for the specified date,

and sub-paragraph (7) shall apply accordingly.

Service on owners etc. of notice of preparation of the first and second lists

8.—(1) The planning authority shall, no later than the date upon which the first list is first advertised in accordance with paragraph 5, serve notice in writing of the first list having been prepared on each person appearing to them to be the owner of any land, or entitled to an interest in any mineral, included within a mineral site included in the first list, but this sub-paragraph is subject to sub-paragraph (7).

(2) A notice required to be served by sub-paragraph (1) shall—

(a) indicate whether the mineral site in question is a dormant site or an active Phase I or II site, and

(b) where that site is an active Phase I site—

    (i) indicate the date specified in the first list in relation to that site as the date by which an application is to be made to the planning authority under paragraph 9,

    (ii) explain the consequences which will occur if such an application is not made by the date so specified, and

    (iii) explain the right to apply to have that date postponed, and indicate the date by which such an application must be made.

(3) Where, in relation to any land or mineral included in an active Phase I site, the planning authority—

(a) have served notice on any person under sub-paragraph (1), and

(b) have received no application under paragraph 9 from that person by the date falling eight weeks before the date specified in the first list as the date by which such applications should be made in respect of the site in question,

the authority shall serve a written reminder on that person, and such a reminder shall—

    (i) indicate that the land or mineral in question is included in an active Phase I site,

    (ii) comply with the requirements of sub-paragraph (2)(b)(i) and (ii), and

    (iii) be served on that person on or before the date falling four weeks before the date specified in the first list in respect of that site as the date by which an application is to be made to the authority under paragraph 9.

(4) The planning authority shall, no later than the date upon which the second list is first advertised in accordance with paragraph 5, serve notice in writing of the second list having been prepared on each person appearing to them to be the owner of any land, or entitled to an interest in any mineral, included within an active Phase II site included in the second list, but this sub-paragraph is subject to sub-paragraph (7).

(5) A notice required to be served by sub-paragraph (4) shall—

(a) indicate that the mineral site in question is an active Phase II site,

(b) indicate the date specified in the second list in relation to that site as the date by which an application is to be made to the planning authority under paragraph 9,

(c) explain the consequences which will occur if such an application is not made by the date so specified, and

(d) explain the right to apply to have that date postponed, and indicate the date by which such an application must be made.

(6) Where, in relation to any land or mineral included in an active Phase II site, the planning authority—

(a) have served notice on any person under sub-paragraph (4), and

(b) have received no application under paragraph 9 from that person by the date falling eight weeks before the date specified in the second list as the date by which such applications should be made in respect of the site in question, the authority shall serve a written reminder on that person, and such a reminder shall—

    (i) comply with the requirements of sub-paragraph (5)(a) to (c), and

    (ii) be served on that person on or before the date falling four weeks before the date specified in the second list in respect of that site as the date by which an application is to be made to the authority under paragraph 9.

(7) Sub-paragraph (1) or (4) shall not require the planning authority to serve notice under that sub-paragraph upon any person whose identity or address for service is not known to and cannot practicably, after reasonable inquiry, be ascertained by them, but in any such case the authority shall cause to be firmly affixed, to each of one or more conspicuous objects on the land or, as the case may be, on the surface of the land above the interest in question, a copy of the notice which they would (apart from the provisions of this sub-paragraph) have had to serve under that sub-paragraph on the owner of that land or interest.

(8) If, in a case where sub-paragraph (7) applies, no person makes an application to the authority under paragraph 9 in respect of the active Phase I or II site which includes the land or interest in question by the date falling eight weeks before the date specified in the first or, as the case may be, the second list as the date by which such applications should be made in respect of that site, the authority shall cause to be firmly affixed, to each of one or more conspicuous objects on the land or, as the case may be, on the surface of the land above the interest in question, a copy of the written reminder that would, in a case not falling within sub-paragraph (7), have been served under sub-paragraph (3) or (6).

(9) Where by sub-paragraph (7) or (8) a copy of any notice is required to be affixed to an object on any land that copy shall—

  (a) be displayed in such a way as to be easily visible and legible,

  (b) be first displayed—

    (i) in a case where the requirement arises under sub-paragraph (7), no later than the date upon which the first or, as the case may be, the second list is first advertised in accordance with paragraph 5, or

    (ii) in a case where the requirement arises under sub-paragraph (8), no later than the date falling four weeks before the date specified in the first or, as the case may be, the second list in respect of the site in question as the date by which an application is to be made to the authority under paragraph 9, and

  (c) be left in position for at least the period of 21 days from the date when it is first displayed, but where the notice is, without fault or intention of the authority, removed, obscured or defaced before that period has elapsed, that requirement shall be treated as having been complied with if the authority have taken reasonable steps for protection of the notice and, if need be, its replacement.

(10) In sub-paragraphs (7) and (8), any reference to a conspicuous object on any land includes, in a case where the person serving a notice considers that there are no or insufficient such objects on the land, a reference to a post driven into or erected upon the land by the person serving the notice for the purpose of having affixed to it the notice in question.

(11) Where the planning authority, being required—

  (a) by sub-paragraph (3) or (6) to serve a written reminder on any person, or

  (b) by sub-paragraph (8) to cause a copy of such a reminder to be displayed in the manner set out in that sub-paragraph,

fail to comply with that requirement by the date specified for the purpose, they may at any later time serve or, as the case may be, cause to be displayed, such a written reminder and, in any such case, the date by which an application in relation to the mineral site in question is to be made under paragraph 9 is the date upon which expires the period of three months from the date when the reminder was served or posted in accordance with the provisions of this sub-paragraph.

Applications for approval of conditions and appeals in cases where the conditions approved are not those proposed

9.—(1) Any person who is the owner of any land, or who is entitled to an interest in a mineral, may, if that land or mineral is or forms part of a dormant site or an active Phase I or II site, apply to the planning authority to determine the conditions to which the relevant planning permissions relating to that site are to be subject.

(2) An application under this paragraph shall be in writing and shall—

  (a) identify the mineral site to which the application relates,

  (b) specify the land or minerals comprised in the site of which the applicant is the owner or, as the case may be, in which the applicant is entitled to an interest,

  (c) identify any relevant planning permissions relating to the site,

  (d) identify, and give an address for, each other person that the applicant knows or, after reasonable inquiry, has cause to believe to be an owner of any land, or entitled to any interest in any mineral, comprised in the site,

(e) set out the conditions to which the applicant proposes the permissions referred to in paragraph (c) should be subject, and

(f) be accompanied by the appropriate certificate.

(3) For the purposes of sub-paragraph (2), the appropriate certificate is each of the certificates which would be required, under or by virtue of sections 34 and 35, to accompany the application if it were an application for planning permission for minerals development, but with such modifications as are required for the purposes of this paragraph; and sections 34(3) and (4) and 35(5) shall have effect in relation to any certificate purporting to be the appropriate certificate.

(4) Section 35 shall have effect, with any necessary modifications, as if subsection (1) also authorised a development order to provide for publicising applications under this paragraph.

(5) Where the planning authority receive an application under this paragraph in relation to a dormant site or an active Phase I or II site they shall determine the conditions to which each relevant planning permission relating to the site is to be subject; and any such permission shall, from the date when the conditions to which it is to be subject are finally determined, have effect subject to the conditions which are determined under this Schedule as being the conditions to which it is to be subject.

(6) The conditions imposed by virtue of a determination under sub-paragraph (5)—

(a) may include any conditions which may be imposed on a grant of planning permission for minerals development;

(b) may be in addition to, or in substitution for, any existing conditions to which the permission in question is subject.

(7) In determining that a relevant planning permission is to be subject to any condition relating to development for which planning permission is granted by a development order, the planning authority shall have regard to any guidance issued for the purpose by the Secretary of State.

(8) Subject to sub-paragraph (9), where, within the period of three months from the planning authority having received an application under this paragraph, or within such extended period as may at any time be agreed upon in writing between the applicant and the authority, the authority have not given notice to the applicant of their decision upon the application, the authority shall be treated as having at the end of that period or, as the case may be, that extended period, determined that the conditions to which any relevant planning permission to which the application relates is to be subject are those specified in the application as being proposed in relation to that permission; and any such permission shall, from that time, have effect subject to those conditions.

(9) Where a planning authority, having received an application under this paragraph, are of the opinion that they are unable to determine the application unless further details are supplied to them, they shall within the period of one month from having received the application give notice to the applicant—

(a) stating that they are of such opinion, and

(b) specifying the further details which they require,

and where the authority so serve such a notice the period of three months referred to in sub-paragraph (8) shall run not from the authority having received the application but from the time when the authority have received all the further details specified in the notice.

(10) Without prejudice to the generality of sub-paragraph (9), the further details which may be specified in a notice under that sub-paragraph include any—

(a) information, plans or drawings, or

(b) evidence verifying any particulars of details supplied to the authority in respect of the application in question,

which it is reasonable for the authority to request for the purpose of enabling them to determine the application.

Notice of determination of conditions to be accompanied by additional information in certain cases

10.—(1) This paragraph applies in a case where—

(a) on an application made to the planning authority under paragraph 9 in respect of an active Phase I or II site the authority determine under that paragraph the conditions to which the relevant planning permissions relating to the site are to be subject,

(b) those conditions differ in any respect from the proposed conditions set out in the application, and

(c) the effect of the conditions, other than any restoration or aftercare conditions, so determined by the authority, as compared with the effect of the conditions, other than any restoration or aftercare conditions, to which the relevant planning permissions in question were subject immediately prior to the authority making the determination, is to restrict working rights in respect of the site.

(2) In a case where this paragraph applies, the planning authority shall, upon giving to the applicant notice of the conditions determined by the authority under paragraph 9, also give to the applicant notice—

(a) stating that the conditions determined by the authority differ in some respect from the proposed conditions set out in the application,

(b) stating that the effect of the conditions, other than any restoration or aftercare conditions, determined by the authority, as compared with the effect of the conditions, other than any restoration or aftercare conditions, to which the relevant planning permissions relating to the site in question were subject immediately prior to the making of the authority's determination, is to restrict working rights in respect of the site,

(c) identifying the working rights so restricted, and

(d) stating whether, in the opinion of the authority, the effect of that restriction of working rights would be such as to prejudice adversely to an unreasonable degree—

(i) the economic viability of operating the site, or

(ii) the asset value of the site.

(3) In determining whether, in their opinion, the effect of that restriction of working rights would be such as is mentioned in sub-paragraph (2)(d), a planning authority shall have regard to any guidance issued for the purpose by the Secretary of State.

(4) In this paragraph, "the applicant" means the person who made the application in question under paragraph 9.

Right to appeal against planning authority's determination of conditions etc.

11.—(1) Where the planning authority—

(a) on an application under paragraph 9 determine under that paragraph conditions that differ in any respect from the proposed conditions set out in the application, or

(b) give notice, under paragraph 10(2)(d), stating that, in their opinion, the restriction of working rights in question would not be such as to prejudice adversely to an unreasonable degree either of the matters referred to in paragraph 10(2)(d)(i) and (ii),

the person who made the application may appeal to the Secretary of State.

(2) An appeal under sub-paragraph (1) must be made by giving notice of appeal to the Secretary of State before the end of the period of six months beginning with the date on which the authority give notice to the applicant of their determination or, as the case may be, stating their opinion.

Permissions ceasing to have effect

12.—(1) Subject to paragraph 8(11), where no application under paragraph 9 in respect of an active Phase I or II site has been served on the planning authority by the date specified in the first or, as the case may be, the second list as the date by which applications under that paragraph in respect of that site are to be made, or by such later date as may at any time be agreed upon in writing between the applicant and the authority, each relevant planning permission relating to the site shall cease to have effect, except in so far as it imposes any restoration or aftercare condition, on the day following the last date on which such an application may be made.

(2) The reference in sub-paragraph (1) to the date specified in the first or, as the case may be, the second list as the date by which applications under paragraph 9 are to be made in respect of any Phase I or II site is a reference to the date specified for that purpose in respect of that site in that list as prepared by the planning authority or, where that date has been varied by virtue of any provision of this Schedule, to that date as so varied.

(3) Subject to sub-paragraph (4), no relevant planning permission which relates to a dormant site shall have effect to authorise the carrying out of minerals development unless—

(a) an application has been made under paragraph 9 in respect of that site, and

(b) that permission has effect in accordance with paragraph 9(5).

(4) A relevant planning permission which relates to a Phase I or II site not included in the first list shall cease to have effect, except in so far as it imposes any restoration or aftercare condition, on the day following the last date on which an application under sub-paragraph (1) of paragraph 6 may be made in respect of that site unless an application has been made under that sub-paragraph by that date in which event, unless the site is added to that list, such a permission shall cease to have effect when the following conditions are met—

(a) the proceedings on that application, including any proceedings on or in consequence of the application under section 239, have been determined, and

(b) any time for appealing under paragraph 6(11) or (12), or applying or further applying under paragraph 6(1), (where there is a right to do so) has expired.

Reference of applications to the Secretary of State

13.—(1) The Secretary of State may give directions requiring applications under paragraph 9 to any planning authority to be referred to him for determination instead of being dealt with by the authority.

(2) Any such direction may relate either to a particular application or to applications of a class specified in the direction.

(3) Where an application is referred to the Secretary of State in accordance with such a direction—
  (a) subject to paragraph (b), the following provisions of this Schedule—
      (i) paragraph 9(5) and (6),
      (ii) paragraph 10, and
      (iii) paragraph 14 so far as relating to applications under paragraph 9,
    shall apply, with any necessary modifications, as they apply to applications which fall to be determined by the planning authority,
  (b) before determining the application the Secretary of State must, if either the applicant or the planning authority so wish, give each of them an opportunity of appearing before and being heard by a person appointed by the Secretary of State for the purpose, and
  (c) the decision of the Secretary of State on the application shall be final.

Two or more applicants

14.—(1) Where a planning authority have received from any person a duly made application under paragraph 7(1) or 9—
  (a) that person may not make any further application under the paragraph in question in respect of the same site, and
  (b) if the application has been determined, whether or not in the case of an application under paragraph 9 it has been finally determined, no other person may make an application under the paragraph in question in respect of the same site.

(2) Where—
  (a) a planning authority have received from any person in respect of a mineral site a duly made application under paragraph 7(1) or 9, and
  (b) the authority receive from another person a duly made application under the paragraph in question in respect of the same site,
then for the purpose of the determination of the applications and any appeal against such a determination, this Schedule shall have effect as if the applications were a single application received by the authority on the date on which the later application was received by the authority and references to the applicant shall be read as references to either or any of the applicants.

Compensation

15.—(1) This paragraph applies in a case where—
  (a) an application made under paragraph 9 in respect of an active Phase I or II site is finally determined, and
  (b) the requirements of either sub-paragraph (2) or (3) are satisfied.

(2) The requirements of this sub-paragraph are—
  (a) that the conditions to which the relevant planning permissions relating to the site are to be subject were determined by the planning authority,
  (b) no appeal was made under paragraph 11(1)(a) in respect of that determination or any such appeal was withdrawn or dismissed, and
  (c) the authority gave notice under paragraph 10(2)(d) and either—
      (i) that notice stated that, in the authority's opinion, the restriction of working rights in question would be such as to prejudice adversely to an unreasonable degree either of the matters referred to in paragraph 10(2)(d)(i) and (ii), or
      (ii) that notice stated that, in the authority's opinion, the restriction in question would not be such as would so prejudice either of those matters but an appeal under paragraph 11(1) in respect of the giving of the notice has been allowed.

(3) The requirements of this sub-paragraph are that the conditions to which the relevant planning permissions are to be subject were determined by the Secretary of State (whether upon an appeal under paragraph 11(1)(a) or upon a reference under paragraph 13) and—

(a) in a case where those conditions were determined upon an appeal under paragraph 11(1)(a) either—

(i) the planning authority gave notice under paragraph 10(2)(d) stating that, in their opinion, the restriction of working rights in question would be such as to prejudice adversely to an unreasonable degree either of the matters referred to in paragraph 10(2)(d)(i) and (ii), or

(ii) the authority gave a notice under paragraph 10(2)(d) stating that, in their opinion, the restriction in question would not be such as would so prejudice either of those matters but an appeal under paragraph 11(1)(b) in respect of the giving of that notice has been allowed,

or

(b) in a case where those conditions were determined upon a reference under paragraph 13, the Secretary of State gave notice under paragraph 10(2)(d) stating that, in his opinion, the restriction of working rights in question would be such as to prejudice adversely to an unreasonable degree either of the matters referred to in paragraph 10(2)(d)(i) and (ii).

(4) In a case to which this paragraph applies Parts IV and X of this Act shall have effect as if an order made under section 65 had been confirmed by the Secretary of State under section 66 at the time when the application in question was finally determined and, as so confirmed, had effect to modify those permissions to the extent specified in sub-paragraph (5).

(5) For the purposes of sub-paragraph (4), the order which is treated by virtue of that sub-paragraph as having been made under section 65 is one whose only effect adverse to the interests of any person having an interest in the land or minerals comprised in the mineral site is to restrict working rights in respect of the site to the same extent as the relevant restriction.

(6) For the purposes of Schedule 13 and of any regulations made under that Schedule, the permissions treated as being modified by the order mentioned in sub-paragraph (4) shall be treated as if they were planning permissions for development which neither consists of nor includes any minerals development.

Appeals: general procedural provisions

16.—(1) This paragraph applies to appeals under paragraph 6(11) or (12) or 11(1).

(2) Notice of appeal in respect of an appeal to which this paragraph applies shall be given on a form supplied by or on behalf of the Secretary of State for use for that purpose, and giving, so far as reasonably practicable, the information required by that form.

(3) Paragraph 18 of Schedule 8 shall apply to an appeal to which this paragraph applies as it applies to appeals under paragraph 17 of that Schedule.

(4) Sections 237 to 239 shall have effect as if the action mentioned in section 237(3) included any decision of the Secretary of State—

(a) on an appeal to which this paragraph applies, or

(b) on an application under paragraph 9 referred to him under paragraph 13.

(5) Schedule 4 shall apply to appeals to which this paragraph applies.

Section 74   SCHEDULE 10

PERIODIC REVIEW OF MINERAL PLANNING PERMISSIONS

Duty to carry out periodic reviews

1. The planning authority shall, in accordance with the provisions of this Schedule, cause periodic reviews to be carried out of the mineral permissions relating to a mining site.

Interpretation

2.—(1) For the purposes of this Schedule—

"first review date", in relation to a mining site, shall, subject to paragraph 5, be ascertained in accordance with paragraph 3;

"mineral permission" means any planning permission, other than a planning permission granted by a development order, for minerals development;

"mining site" means—

(a) in a case where it appears to the planning authority to be expedient to treat as a single site the aggregate of the land to which any two or more mineral permissions relate, the aggregate of the land to which those permissions relate; and

(b) in any other case, the land to which a mineral permission relates;
"old mining permission" has the meaning given by paragraph 10(1) of Schedule 8; and
"owner", in relation to any land, has the meaning given by paragraph 22(1) of Schedule 8.

(2) In determining whether it appears to them to be expedient to treat as a single site the aggregate of the land to which two or more mineral permissions relate a planning authority shall have regard to any guidance issued for the purpose by the Secretary of State.

(3) Any reference (however expressed) in this Schedule to a mining site being a site to which relates—

(a) an old mining permission, or

(b) a mineral permission,

is a reference to the mining site, or some part of it, being the land to which the permission relates.

(4) For the purposes of this Schedule, an application made under paragraph 6 is finally determined when—

(a) the proceedings on the application, including any proceedings on or in consequence of an application under section 239, have been determined, and

(b) any time for appealing under paragraph 9(1), or applying or further applying under paragraph 6, (where there is a right to do so) has expired.

The first review date

3.—(1) Subject to sub-paragraph (7), in a case where the mineral permissions relating to a mining site include an old mining permission, the first review date means—

(a) the date falling fifteen years after the date upon which, pursuant to an application made under paragraph 14 of Schedule 8, the conditions to which that old mining permission is to be subject are finally determined under that Schedule, or

(b) where there are two or more old mining permissions relating to that site, and the date upon which those conditions are finally determined is not the same date for each of those permissions, the date falling fifteen years after the date upon which was made the last such final determination to be so made in respect of any of those permissions,

and paragraph 22(2) of that Schedule shall apply for the purposes of this sub-paragraph as it applies for the purposes of paragraph 10 and Part II of that Schedule.

(2) Subject to sub-paragraph (7), in the case of a mining site which is a Phase I or II site within the meaning of Schedule 9, the first review date means the date falling fifteen years after the date upon which, pursuant to an application made under paragraph 9 of that Schedule, there is determined under that paragraph the conditions to which the relevant planning permissions (within the meaning of that Schedule) relating to the site are to be subject.

(3) Subject to sub-paragraphs (4) and (7), in the case of a mining site—

(a) which is not a Phase I or II site within the meaning of Schedule 9, and

(b) to which no old mining permission relates,

the first review date is the date falling fifteen years after the date upon which was granted the most recent mineral permission which relates to the site.

(4) Where, in the case of a mining site falling within sub-paragraph (3), the most recent mineral permission relating to that site relates, or the most recent such permissions (whether or not granted on the same date) between them relate, to part only of the site, and in the opinion of the planning authority it is expedient, for the purpose of ascertaining, under that sub-paragraph, the first review date in respect of that site, to treat that permission or those permissions as having been granted at the same time as the last of the other mineral permissions relating to the site, the first review date for that site shall be ascertained under that sub-paragraph accordingly.

(5) A planning authority shall, in deciding whether they are of such an opinion as is mentioned in sub-paragraph (4), have regard to any guidance issued by the Secretary of State for the purpose.

(6) Subject to sub-paragraph (7), in the case of a mining site—

(a) to which relates a mineral permission in respect of which an order has been made under section 65, or

(b) in respect of which, or any part of which, an order has been made under paragraph 1 of Schedule 8,

the first review date shall be the date falling fifteen years after the date upon which the order took effect or, in a case where there is more than one such order, upon which the last of those orders to take effect took effect.

(7) In the case of a mining site for which the preceding provisions of this paragraph have effect to specify two or more different dates as the first review date, the first review date shall be the latest of those dates.

Service of notice of first periodic review

4.—(1) The planning authority shall, in connection with the first periodic review of the mineral permissions relating to a mining site, no later than 12 months before the first review date, serve notice upon each person appearing to them to be the owner of any land, or entitled to an interest in any mineral, included in that site.

(2) A notice required to be served under sub-paragraph (1) shall—

(a) specify the mining site to which it relates,

(b) identify the mineral permissions relating to that site,

(c) state the first review date,

(d) state that the first review date is the date by which an application must be made for approval of the conditions to which the mineral permissions relating to the site are to be subject and explain the consequences which will occur if no such application is made by that date, and

(e) explain the right to apply for postponement of the first review date and give the date by which such an application has to be made.

(3) Where, in relation to any land or mineral included in a mining site, the planning authority—

(a) have served notice on any person under sub-paragraph (1), and

(b) have received no application under paragraph 6 from that person by the date falling eight weeks before the first review date,

the authority shall serve a written reminder on that person.

(4) A reminder required to be served under sub-paragraph (3) shall—

(a) indicate that the land or mineral in question is included in a mining site,

(b) comply with the requirements of sub-paragraph (2)(a) to (d), and

(c) be served on the person in question on or before the date falling four weeks before the first review date.

(5) Sub-paragraph (1) shall not require the planning authority to serve notice under that sub-paragraph upon any person whose identity or address for service is not known to and cannot practicably, after reasonable inquiry, be ascertained by them, but in any such case the authority shall cause to be firmly affixed, to each of one or more conspicuous objects on the land or, as the case may be, on the surface of the land above the interest in question, a copy of the notice which they would (apart from the provisions of this sub-paragraph) have had to serve under that sub-paragraph on the owner of that land or interest.

(6) If, in a case where sub-paragraph (5) applies, no person makes an application to the authority under paragraph 6 in respect of the mining site which includes the land or interest in question by the date falling eight weeks before the first review date, the authority shall cause to be firmly affixed, to each of one or more conspicuous objects on the land or, as the case may be, on the surface of the land above the interest in question, a copy of the written reminder that would, in a case not falling within sub-paragraph (5), have been served under sub-paragraph (3).

(7) Where by sub-paragraph (5) or (6) a copy of any notice is required to be affixed to an object on any land that copy shall—

(a) be displayed in such a way as to be easily visible and legible,

(b) be first displayed—

(i) in a case where the requirement arises under sub-paragraph (5), no later than 12 months before the first review date, or

(ii) in a case where the requirement arises under sub-paragraph (6), no later than the date falling four weeks before the first review date,

and

(c) be left in position for at least the period of 21 days from the date when it is first displayed, but where the notice is, without fault or intention of the authority, removed, obscured or defaced before that period has elapsed, that requirement shall be treated as having been complied with if the authority have taken reasonable steps for protection of the notice and, if need be, its replacement.

(8) In sub-paragraphs (5) and (6), any reference to a conspicuous object on any land includes, in a case where the person serving a notice considers that there are no or insufficient such objects on the land, a reference to a post driven into or erected upon the land by the person serving the notice for the purpose of having affixed to it a copy of the notice in question.

Application for postponement of the first review date

5.—(1) Any person who is the owner of any land, or of any interest in any mineral, comprised in a mining site may, no later than the day upon which expires the period of three months from the day upon which notice was served upon him under paragraph 4, apply under this paragraph to the planning authority for the postponement of the first review date.

(2) An application under this paragraph shall be in writing and shall set out—

(a) the conditions to which each mineral permission relating to the site is subject,

(b) the applicant's reasons for considering those conditions to be satisfactory, and

(c) the date which the applicant wishes to have substituted for the first review date.

(3) Where the planning authority receive an application made under this paragraph—

(a) if they consider the conditions referred to in sub-paragraph (2)(a) to be satisfactory they shall agree to the first review date being postponed in which event they shall determine the date to be substituted for that date;

(b) in any other case they shall refuse the application.

(4) When a planning authority determine an application made under this paragraph, they shall notify the applicant in writing of their decision and, in a case where they have agreed to the postponement of the first review date, shall notify the applicant of the date which they have determined should be substituted for the first review date.

(5) Where, within the period of three months of the planning authority having received an application under this paragraph, or within such extended period as may at any time be agreed upon in writing between the applicant and the authority, the authority have not given notice, under sub-paragraph (4), to the applicant of their decision upon the application, the authority shall be treated as having, at the end of that period or, as the case may be, that extended period—

(a) agreed to the first review date being postponed, and

(b) determined that the date referred to in sub-paragraph (2)(c) be substituted for the first review date.

Application to determine the conditions to which the mineral permissions relating to a mining site are to be subject

6.—(1) Any person who is the owner of any land, or who is entitled to an interest in a mineral, may, if that land or mineral is or forms part of a mining site, apply to the planning authority to determine the conditions to which the mineral permissions relating to that site are to be subject.

(2) An application under this paragraph shall be in writing and shall—

(a) identify the mining site in respect of which the application is made and state that the application is made in connection with the first periodic review of the mineral permissions relating to that site,

(b) specify the land or minerals comprised in the site of which the applicant is the owner or, as the case may be, in which the applicant is entitled to an interest,

(c) identify the mineral permissions relating to the site,

(d) identify, and give an address for, each other person that the applicant knows or, after reasonable inquiry, has cause to believe to be an owner of any land, or entitled to any interest in any mineral, comprised in the site,

(e) set out the conditions to which the applicant proposes the permissions referred to in paragraph (c) should be subject, and

(f) be accompanied by the appropriate certificate.

(3) For the purposes of sub-paragraph (2), the appropriate certificate is each of the certificates which would be required, under or by virtue of sections 34 and 35, to accompany the application if it were an application for planning permission for minerals development, but with such modifications as are required for the purposes of this paragraph; and sections 34(3) and(4) and 35(5) shall have effect in relation to any certificate purporting to be the appropriate certificate.

(4) Where the planning authority receive an application under this paragraph in relation to a mining site they shall determine the conditions to which each mineral permission relating to the site is to be subject.

(5) The conditions imposed by virtue of a determination under sub-paragraph (4)—

(a) may include any conditions which may be imposed on a grant of planning permission for minerals development;

(b) may be in addition to, or in substitution for, any existing conditions to which the permission in question is subject.

(6) In determining that a mineral permission is to be subject to any condition relating to development for which planning permission is granted by a development order, the planning authority shall have regard to any guidance issued for the purpose by the Secretary of State.

(7) Subject to sub-paragraph (8), where, within the period of three months of the planning authority having received an application under this paragraph, or within such extended period as may at any time be agreed upon in writing between the applicant and the authority, the authority have not given notice to the applicant of their decision upon the application, the authority shall be treated as having at the end of that period or, as the case may be, that extended period, determined that the conditions to which any mineral permission to which the application relates

is to be subject are those specified in the application as being proposed in relation to that permission; and any such permission shall, from that time, have effect subject to those conditions.

(8) Where a planning authority, having received an application under this paragraph, are of the opinion that they are unable to determine the application unless further details are supplied to them, they shall within the period of one month from having received the application give notice to the applicant—

(a) stating that they are of such opinion, and

(b) specifying the further details which they require,

and where the authority so serve such a notice the period of three months referred to in sub-paragraph (7) shall run not from the authority having received the application but from the time when the authority have received all the further details specified in the notice.

(9) Without prejudice to the generality of sub-paragraph (8), the further details which may be specified in a notice under that sub-paragraph include any—

(a) information, plans or drawings, or

(b) evidence verifying any particulars of details supplied to the authority in respect of the application in question,

which it is reasonable for the authority to request for the purpose of enabling them to determine the application.

Permissions ceasing to have effect

7. Where no application under paragraph 6 in respect of a mining site has been served on the planning authority by the first review date, or by such later date as may at any time be agreed upon in writing between the applicant and the authority, each mineral permission—

(a) relating to the site, and

(b) identified in the notice served in relation to the site under paragraph 4,

shall cease to have effect, except in so far as it imposes any restoration or aftercare condition, on the day following the first review date or, as the case may be, such later agreed date.

Reference of applications to the Secretary of State

8.—(1) The Secretary of State may give directions requiring applications made under paragraph 6 to any planning authority to be referred to him for determination instead of being dealt with by the authority.

(2) A direction under sub-paragraph (1) may relate either to a particular application or to applications of a class specified in the direction.

(3) Where an application is referred to the Secretary of State in accordance with a direction under sub-paragraph (1)—

(a) subject to paragraph (b), paragraph 6(4) and (5), and paragraph 11 so far as relating to applications under paragraph 6, shall apply, with any necessary modifications, to his determination of the application as they apply to the determination of applications by the planning authority,

(b) before determining the application the Secretary of State must, if either the applicant or the planning authority so wish, give each of them an opportunity of appearing before and being heard by a person appointed by the Secretary of State for the purpose, and

(c) the decision of the Secretary of State on the application shall be final.

Appeals

9.—(1) Where on an application under paragraph 6 the planning authority determine conditions that differ in any respect from the proposed conditions set out in the application, the applicant may appeal to the Secretary of State.

(2) An appeal under sub-paragraph (1) must be made by giving notice of appeal to the Secretary of State, before the end of the period of six months beginning with the determination, on a form supplied by or on behalf of the Secretary of State for use for that purpose, and giving, so far as reasonably practicable, the information required by that form.

(3) Paragraph 18 of Schedule 8 shall apply to appeals under sub-paragraph (1) as it applies to appeals under paragraph 17 of that Schedule.

(4) Sections 237 to 239 shall have effect as if the action mentioned in section 237(3) included any decision of the Secretary of State—

(a) on an appeal under sub-paragraph (1), or

(b) on an application under paragraph 6 referred to him under paragraph 8.

(5) Schedule 4 shall apply to appeals under sub-paragraph (1).

Time from which conditions determined under this Schedule are to take effect

10.—(1) Where an application has been made under paragraph 6 in respect of a mining site, each of the mineral permissions relating to the site shall, from the time when the application is finally determined, have effect subject to the conditions to which it is determined under this Schedule that that permission is to be subject.

(2) Sub-paragraph (1) is without prejudice to paragraph 6(7).

Two or more applicants

11.—(1) Where a planning authority have received from any person a duly made application under paragraph 5 or 6—

(a) that person may not make any further application under the paragraph in question in respect of the same site, and

(b) if the application has been determined, whether or not in the case of an application under paragraph 6 it has been finally determined, no other person may make an application under the paragraph in question in respect of the same site.

(2) Where—

(a) a planning authority have received from any person in respect of a mineral site a duly made application under paragraph 5 or 6; and

(b) the authority receive from another person a duly made application under the paragraph in question in respect of the same site,

then for the purpose of the determination of the applications and any appeal against such a determination, this Schedule shall have effect as if the applications were a single application received by the authority on the date on which the later application was received by the authority and references to the applicant shall be read as references to either or any of the applicants.

Second and subsequent periodic reviews

12.—(1) In this paragraph, in relation to a mining site, but subject to paragraph 5 as applied by sub-paragraph (2), "review date" means—

(a) in the case of the second periodic review, the date falling fifteen years after the date upon which was finally determined an application made under paragraph 6 in respect of the site, and

(b) in the case of subsequent periodic reviews, the date falling fifteen years after the date upon which there was last finally determined under this Schedule an application made in respect of that site under paragraph 6 as applied by sub-paragraph (2).

(2) Paragraphs 4 to 11 shall apply in respect of the second or any subsequent periodic review of the mineral permissions relating to a mining site as they apply to the first such periodic review, but as if—

(a) any reference in those paragraphs to the "first review date" were a reference to the review date, and

(b) the references in paragraphs 4(1) and 6(2)(a) to the first periodic review were references to the periodic review in question.

Compensation

13.—(1) This paragraph applies where—

(a) an application made under paragraph 6 in respect of a mining site is finally determined,

(b) the conditions to which the mineral permissions relating to the site are to be subject, as determined under this Schedule, differ in any respect from the proposed conditions set out in the application, and

(c) the effect of the new conditions, except in so far as they are restoration or aftercare conditions, as compared with the effect of the existing conditions, except in so far as they were restoration or aftercare conditions, is to restrict working rights in respect of the site.

(2) For the purposes of this paragraph—

"the new conditions", in relation to a mining site, means the conditions, determined under this Schedule, to which the mineral permissions relating to the site are to be subject; and

"the existing conditions", in relation to a mining site, means the conditions to which the mineral permissions relating to the site were subject immediately prior to the final determination of the application made under paragraph 6 in respect of that site.

(3) For the purposes of this paragraph, working rights are restricted in respect of a mining site if any of—

(a) the size of the area which may be used for the winning and working of minerals or the depositing of mineral waste,

(b) the depth to which operations for the winning and working of minerals may extend,

(c) the height of any deposit of mineral waste,

(d) the rate at which any particular mineral may be extracted,

(e) the rate at which any particular mineral waste may be deposited,

(f) the period at the expiry of which any winning or working of minerals or depositing of mineral waste is to cease, or

(g) the total quantity of minerals which may be extracted from, or of mineral waste which may be deposited on, the site,

is restricted or reduced in respect of the mining site in question.

(4) In a case to which this paragraph applies, but subject to sub-paragraph (6), Parts IV and X of this Act shall have effect as if an order made under section 65—

(a) had been confirmed by the Secretary of State under section 66 at the time when the application in question was finally determined, and

(b) as so confirmed, had effect to modify those permissions to the extent specified in sub-paragraph (6).

(5) For the purposes of this paragraph, the order referred to in sub-paragraph (4) is one whose only effect adverse to the interests of any person having an interest in the land or minerals comprised in the mineral site is to restrict working rights in respect of the site to the same extent as the relevant restriction.

(6) For the purposes of Schedule 13 and of any regulations made under that Schedule, the permissions treated as being modified by the order mentioned in sub-paragraph (4) shall be treated as if they were planning permissions for development which neither consists of nor includes any minerals development.

Sections 76 and 89   SCHEDULE 11

DEVELOPMENT NOT CONSTITUTING NEW DEVELOPMENT

1.—(1) The carrying out of—

(a) the rebuilding, as often as occasion may require, of any building which was in existence on 1st July 1948, or of any building which was in existence before that date but was destroyed or demolished after 7th January 1937, including the making good of war damage sustained by any such building;

(b) the rebuilding, as often as occasion may require, of any building erected after 1st July 1948 which was in existence at a material date;

(c) works for the maintenance, improvement or other alteration of any building, being works which—

(i) affect only the interior of the building, or do not materially affect the external appearance of the building, and

(ii) are works for making good war damage,

so long as the cubic content of the original building, as ascertained by external measurement, is not substantially exceeded.

(2) In sub-paragraph (1) "war damage" has the same meaning as in the War Damage Act 1943.

2. The use as two or more separate dwellinghouses of any building which at a material date was used as a single dwellinghouse.

3. Where after 1st July 1948—

(a) any buildings or works have been erected or constructed, or any use of land has been instituted, and

(b) any condition imposed under Part III of this Act, limiting the period for which those buildings or works may be retained, or that use may be continued, has effect in relation to those buildings or works or that use,

this Schedule shall not operate except as respects the period specified in that condition.

4. For the purposes of paragraph 1 the cubic content of a building is substantially exceeded—

(a) in the case of a dwellinghouse, if it is exceeded by more than one-tenth or 1,750 cubic feet, whichever is the greater, and

(b) in any other case, if it is exceeded by more than one-tenth.

5.—(1) In this Schedule "at a material date" means at either—

(a) 1st July 1948, or

(b) the date by reference to which this Schedule falls to be applied in the particular case in question.

(2) Sub-paragraph (1)(b) shall not apply in relation to any buildings, works or use of land in respect of which, whether before or after the date mentioned in that sub-paragraph, an enforcement notice served before that date has become or becomes effective.

6.—(1) In relation to a building erected after 1st July 1948 which results from the carrying out of any such works as are described in paragraph 1, any reference in this Schedule to the original building is a reference to the building in relation to which those works were carried out and not to the building resulting from the carrying out of those works.

(2) This paragraph does not apply for the purposes of sections 82 or 88.

Section 80(5)   SCHEDULE 12

CONDITION TREATED AS APPLICABLE TO REBUILDING AND ALTERATIONS

1. Where the building to be rebuilt or altered is the original building, the amount of gross floor space in the building as rebuilt or altered which may be used for any purpose shall not exceed by more than 10 per cent. the amount of gross floor space which was last used for that purpose in the original building.

2. Where the building to be rebuilt or altered is not the original building, the amount of gross floor space in the building as rebuilt or altered which may be used for any purpose shall not exceed the amount of gross floor space which was last used for that purpose in the building before the rebuilding or alteration.

3. In determining under this Schedule the purpose for which floor space was last used in any building, no account shall be taken of any use in respect of which an effective enforcement notice has been or could be served or, in the case of a use which has been discontinued, could have been served immediately before the discontinuance.

4.—(1) For the purposes of this Schedule gross floor space shall be ascertained by external measurement.

(2) Where different parts of a building are used for different purposes, floor space common to those purposes shall be apportioned rateably.

5. In relation to a building erected after 1st July 1948 which is a building resulting from the carrying out of any such works as are described in paragraph 1 of Schedule 11, any reference in this Schedule to the original building is a reference to the building in relation to which those works were carried out and not to the building resulting from the carrying out of those works.

Section 84   SCHEDULE 13

REGULATIONS AS TO COMPENSATION IN RESPECT OF ORDERS RELATING TO MINERAL WORKING

Power to modify compensation provisions

1.—(1) The Secretary of State may by regulations made with the consent of the Treasury provide, in relation to orders made under—

(a) section 65 modifying planning permission for development consisting of the winning or working of minerals or involving the depositing of mineral waste, or

(b) section 71, and paragraph 1, 3, 5 or 6 of Schedule 8 with respect to such winning and working or depositing,

that sections 76, 83, 87, 232 and 233 shall have effect subject, in such cases as may be prescribed, to such modifications as may be prescribed.

(2) Without prejudice to the generality of sub-paragraph (1), such regulations may make provision—

(a) as to circumstances in which compensation is not to be payable;

(b) for the modification of the basis on which any amount to be paid by way of compensation is to be assessed;

(c) for the assessment of any such amount on a basis different from that on which it would otherwise have been assessed,

and may also make different provision for different cases, and incidental or supplementary provision.

(3) Such regulations shall be of no effect unless approved by a resolution of each House of Parliament.

(4) Before making any such regulations, the Secretary of State shall consult such persons as appear to him to be representative of—

(a) persons carrying out mining operations;

(b) owners of interests in land containing minerals;

(c) planning authorities.

Determination of claims

2. The references in section 86 to questions of disputed compensation under Part IV include references to questions of disputed compensation under sections 76, 83, 87, 232 and 233 as modified by regulations under paragraph 1.

     SCHEDULE 14

BLIGHTED LAND

Land allocated for public authority functions in development plans etc.

1.—(1) This paragraph applies to land indicated in a structure plan in force for the area in which it is situated either—

  (a) as land which may be required for the purposes—

      (i) of the functions of a government department, local authority or statutory undertakers, or

      (ii) of the establishment or running by a public telecommunications operator of a telecommunication system, or

  (b) as land which may be included in an action area.

(2) This paragraph does not apply to land situated in an area for which a local plan is in force, where that plan—

  (a) allocates any land in the area for the purposes of such functions as are mentioned in this paragraph, or

  (b) defines any land in the area as the site of proposed development for the purposes of any such functions.

(3) This paragraph does not apply to land to which paragraph 3 or 4 applies.

(4) In sub-paragraph (1) the reference to a structure plan in force includes a reference to—

  (a) a structure plan which has been submitted to the Secretary of State under section 6,

  (b) proposals for the alteration or repeal and replacement of a structure plan which have been submitted to the Secretary of State under section 9, and

  (c) modifications proposed to be made by the Secretary of State in any such plan or proposals, being modifications of which he has given notice in accordance with regulations under Part II.

(5) Sub-paragraph (4) shall cease to apply—

  (a) if the copies of the proposals made available for inspection are withdrawn under section 8(10),

  (b) when the relevant proposals come into force (whether in their original form or with modifications), or

  (c) when the Secretary of State decides to reject the proposals in accordance with section 10 and notice of the decision has been given by advertisement.

(6) In sub-paragraph (4) references to anything done under any provision include reference to anything done under that provision as it applies by virtue of section 22.

2.—(1) This paragraph applies to land which—

  (a) is allocated for the purposes of any such functions as are mentioned in paragraph 1(1)(a)(i) or (ii) by a local plan in force, or

  (b) is land defined in such a plan as the site of proposed development for the purposes of any such functions.

(2) In sub-paragraph (1) the reference to a local plan in force includes a reference to—

  (a) a local plan of which copies have been made available for inspection under section 12(3),

  (b) proposals for the alteration or repeal and replacement of a local plan of which copies have been made available for inspection under section 12(3), and

  (c) modifications proposed to be made by the planning authority or the Secretary of State in any such plan or proposals as are mentioned in paragraph (a) or (b), being modifications of which notice has been given by the authority or the Secretary of State in accordance with regulations under Part II.

(3) Sub-paragraph (2) shall cease to apply—

  (a) if the copies of the plan or proposals made available for inspection are withdrawn under section 8(10),

  (b) when the relevant plan or proposals come into force (whether in their original form or with modifications), or

  (c) when the Secretary of State decides to reject, or the planning authority decide to abandon, the plan or proposals and notice of the decision has been given by advertisement.

(4) In sub-paragraph (2) references to anything done under any provision include references to anything done under that provision as it applies by virtue of section 22.

3. This paragraph applies to land indicated in a plan (other than a development plan) approved by a resolution passed by a planning authority for the purpose of the exercise of their powers under Part III as land which may be required for the purposes of any functions of a government department, local authority or statutory undertakers.

4. This paragraph applies to land in respect of which a planning authority—

(a) have resolved to take action to safeguard it for development for the purposes of any such functions as are mentioned in paragraph 3, or

(b) have been directed by the Secretary of State to restrict the grant of planning permission in order to safeguard it for such development.

New towns and urban development areas

5.—(1) This paragraph applies to land within an area described as the site of a proposed new town in the draft of an order in respect of which a notice has been published under paragraph 2 of Schedule 1 to the New Towns (Scotland) Act 1968.

(2) Land shall cease to be within this paragraph when—

(a) the order comes into force (whether in the form of the draft or with modifications), or

(b) the Secretary of State decides not to make the order.

6. This paragraph applies to land within an area designated as the site of a proposed new town by an order which has come into operation under section 1 of the New Towns (Scotland) Act 1968.

7.—(1) This paragraph applies to land which is—

(a) within an area intended to be designated as an urban development area by an order which has been made under section 134 of the Local Government, Planning and Land Act 1980 but has not come into effect, or

(b) within an area which has been so designated by an order under that section which has come into effect.

(2) Land shall cease to be within this paragraph when the order comes into force.

Housing action areas

8. This paragraph applies to land within an area declared to be a housing action area by a resolution under section 89, 90 or 91 of the Housing (Scotland) Act 1987 in relation to houses or parts of buildings which have been identified in accordance with section 92(4)(c) of that Act.

9. This paragraph applies to land which is surrounded by or adjoining an area declared to be a housing action area by a resolution under section 89, 90 or 91 of the Housing (Scotland) Act 1987 whether or not the resolution identifies any of the buildings in accordance with section 92(4)(a) of that Act.

Roads

10. This paragraph applies to land indicated in a development plan (otherwise than by being dealt with in a manner mentioned in paragraphs 1, 2, 3 and 4) as—

(a) land on which a road is proposed to be constructed, or

(b) land to be included in a road as proposed to be improved or altered.

11.—(1) This paragraph applies to land on or adjacent to the line of a road proposed to be constructed, improved or altered, as indicated in an order or scheme—

(a) which has come into operation under, or

(b) which is proposed to be made or conferred under, and in respect of which a notice has been published under Schedule 1 to,

the Roads (Scotland) Act 1984, being land in relation to which a power of compulsory acquisition conferred by that Act may become exercisable, as being land required for purposes of construction, improvement or alteration as indicated in the order or scheme.

(2) Land shall cease to be within sub-paragraph (1)(b) when—

(a) the relevant order or scheme comes into operation (whether in its original form or with modifications), or

(b) the Secretary of State decides not to confirm or make the order or scheme.

12. This paragraph applies to land shown on plans approved by a resolution of a roads authority as land comprised in the site of a road as proposed to be constructed, improved or altered by that authority.

13. This paragraph applies to land comprised in the site of a road as proposed to be constructed, improved or altered by the Secretary of State if the Secretary of State has given written notice of the proposal, together with maps or plans sufficient to identify the land in question, to the planning authority.

Compulsory purchase

14. This paragraph applies to land authorised by a special enactment to be compulsorily acquired, or land falling within the limits of deviation within which powers of compulsory acquisition conferred by a special enactment are exercisable.

15.—(1) This paragraph applies to land in respect of which—

(a) a compulsory purchase order is in force, or

(b) there is in force a compulsory purchase order providing for the acquisition of a right in or over that land,

and the appropriate authority have power to serve, but have not served, notice to treat in respect of the land or, as the case may be, the right or rights.

(2) This paragraph applies also to land in respect of which—

(a) a compulsory purchase order has been submitted for confirmation to, or been prepared in draft by, a Minister, and

(b) a notice has been published under paragraph 3(1)(a) of Schedule 1 to the Acquisition of Land (Authorisation Procedure) (Scotland) Act 1947 or under any corresponding enactment applicable to it.

(3) Sub-paragraph (2) shall cease to apply when—

(a) the relevant compulsory purchase order comes into force (whether in its original form or with modifications), or

(b) the Minister concerned decides not to confirm or make the order.

Section 195   SCHEDULE 15

GENERAL VESTING DECLARATIONS

PART I

GENERAL PROVISIONS

Execution of general vesting declarations

1.—(1) Where a compulsory purchase order authorising an acquiring authority to acquire any land has come into operation, the authority may execute in respect of any of the land which they are authorised to acquire by the compulsory purchase order a declaration in the prescribed form (in this Schedule referred to as a "general vesting declaration") vesting the land in themselves as from the end of such period as may be specified in the declaration (not being less than 28 days) from the date on which the service of notices required by paragraph 4 is completed.

(2) A general vesting declaration shall contain a particular description of the lands affected or a description by reference of those lands in the manner provided by section 61 of the Conveyancing (Scotland) Act 1874.

2.—(1) Before making a general vesting declaration with respect to any land which is subject to a compulsory purchase order, the acquiring authority shall include in the notice of the making or confirmation of the order which is required to be published or served by paragraph 6 of Schedule 1 to the Acquisition Act 1947 or any other provision of the relevant enactments corresponding to that paragraph, or in a notice given subsequently and before the service of the notice to treat in respect of that land—

(a) such a statement of the effect of paragraphs 1 to 8 as may be prescribed, and

(b) a notification to the effect that every person who, if a general vesting declaration were made in respect of all the land comprised in the order in respect of which notice to treat has not been given, would be entitled to claim compensation in respect of any such land is invited to give information to the authority making the declaration in the prescribed form with respect to his name and address and the land in question.

(2) The requirements of the relevant enactments with respect to the publication and service of a notice of the making or confirmation of a compulsory purchase order shall apply to a notice under this paragraph given subsequently to the first-mentioned notice.

3.—(1) Subject to sub-paragraph (2), a general vesting declaration shall not be executed before the end of the period of 2 months beginning with the date of the first publication of the notice complying with paragraph 2(1), or such longer period, if any, as may be specified in the notice.

(2) The acquiring authority may, with the consent in writing of every occupier of any of the land specified in the declaration, execute a general vesting declaration before the end of that period of 2 months, or of the longer period so specified, as the case may be.

4. As soon as may be after executing a general vesting declaration, the acquiring authority shall serve—

(a) on every occupier of any of the land specified in the declaration (other than land in which there subsists a short tenancy or a long tenancy which is about to expire), and

(b) on every other person who has given information to the authority with respect to any of that land in pursuance of the invitation published and served under paragraph 2(1), a notice in the prescribed form specifying the land and stating the effect of the declaration.

5. For the purposes of this Schedule, a certificate by the acquiring authority that the service of notices required by paragraph 4 was completed on a date specified in the certificate shall be conclusive evidence of the fact so stated.

Effect of general vesting declaration

6. At the end of the period specified in a general vesting declaration, the provisions of the Lands Clauses Acts and of section 6 of the Railways Clauses Consolidation (Scotland) Act 1845 (both as incorporated by Schedule 2 to the Acquisition Act 1947) and of the Land Compensation (Scotland) Act 1963 shall apply as if, on the date on which the declaration was made, a notice to treat had been served on every person on whom, under section 17 of the Lands Clauses Consolidation (Scotland) Act 1845 (on the assumption that they required to take the whole of the land specified in the declaration and had knowledge of all the parties referred to in that section) the acquiring authority could have served such a notice, other than—

(a) any person entitled to an interest in the land in respect of which such a notice had actually been served before the end of that period, and

(b) any person entitled to a short tenancy or a long tenancy which is about to expire.

7. At the end of the period specified in a general vesting declaration, the land specified in the declaration, together with the right to enter upon and take possession of it, shall vest in the acquiring authority as if the circumstances in which under the said Act of 1845 an authority authorised to purchase land compulsorily have any power to expede a notarial instrument (whether for vesting land or any interest in land in themselves or for extinguishing the whole or part of any feuduty, ground annual or rent, or other payment or incumbrance) had arisen in respect of all the land and all interests in it, and the acquiring authority had duly exercised that power accordingly at the end of that period.

8. Where any land specified in a general vesting declaration is land in which there subsists a short tenancy or a long tenancy which is about to expire—

(a) the right of entry conferred by paragraph 7 shall not be exercisable in respect of that land unless, after serving a notice to treat in respect of that tenancy, the acquiring authority have served upon every occupier of any of the land in which the tenancy subsists a notice stating that, at the end of such period as is specified in the notice (not being less than 14 days) from the date on which the notice is served, they intend to enter upon and take possession of such land as is specified in the notice, and that period has expired, and

(b) the vesting of the land in the acquiring authority shall be subject to the tenancy until that period expires, or the tenancy comes to an end, whichever first occurs.

Recovery of compensation overpaid

9. Paragraphs 10 to 14 shall have effect where, after the acquiring authority have made a general vesting declaration in respect of any land, a person claims compensation in respect of the acquisition by the authority of an interest in any land by virtue of the declaration, and the authority pay compensation in respect of that interest.

10. If, in a case falling within paragraph 9, it is subsequently shown—

(a) that the land, or the claimant's interest in it, was subject to an incumbrance which was not disclosed in the particulars of his claim, and

(b) that by reason of that incumbrance the compensation paid exceeded the compensation to which the claimant was entitled in respect of that interest,

the acquiring authority may recover the amount of the excess from the claimant.

11. If in a case falling within paragraph 9, it is subsequently shown that the claimant was not entitled to the interest in question, either in the whole or in part of the land to which the claim related, the acquiring authority may recover from him an amount equal to the compensation paid, or to so much of that compensation as, on a proper apportionment of it, is attributable to that part of the land, as the case may be.

12. Any question arising under paragraph 10 or 11—

(a) as to the amount of the compensation to which the claimant was entitled in respect of an interest in land, or

(b) as to the apportionment of any compensation paid,

shall be referred to and determined by the Lands Tribunal; and in relation to the determination of any such question, the provisions of section 9 of the Land Compensation (Scotland) Act 1963 shall apply, subject to any necessary modifications.

13. Subject to paragraph 12, any amount recoverable by the acquiring authority under paragraph 10 or 11 shall be recoverable in any court of competent jurisdiction.

14. Any sum recovered under paragraph 10 or 11 in respect of land by an acquiring authority who are a local authority shall be applied towards the repayment of any debt incurred in acquir-

ing or redeveloping that land or if no debt was so incurred shall be paid into the account out of which the compensation in respect of the acquisition of that land was paid.

Penalty for false information in claiming compensation

15.—(1) If any person for the purpose of obtaining for himself or for any other person any compensation in respect of the acquisition by the acquiring authority of an interest in land by virtue of a general vesting declaration—

(a) knowingly or recklessly makes a statement which is false in a material particular,

(b) with intent to deceive produces, furnishes, sends or otherwise makes use of any book, account, or other document which is false in a material particular, or

(c) with intent to deceive withholds any material information,

he shall be guilty of an offence.

(2) Any person guilty of an offence under this paragraph shall (without prejudice to the recovery of any sum under paragraph 10 or 11) be liable—

(a) on summary conviction, to a fine not exceeding the statutory maximum, and

(b) on conviction on indictment, to imprisonment for a term not exceeding 2 years or a fine, or both.

PART II

SUPPLEMENTARY PROVISIONS

16. This Part shall have effect for the purposes of paragraphs 6 to 8.

Exclusion of power of entry under the Acquisition Act 1947

17. Paragraph 3 of Schedule 2 to the Acquisition Act 1947 (power to enter upon land after service of notice to treat) shall not apply to land specified in a general vesting declaration under this Act.

Restriction on withdrawal of constructive notice to treat

18. The power conferred by section 39 of the Land Compensation (Scotland) Act 1963 to withdraw notice to treat shall not be exercisable, in respect of a notice to treat which is deemed to be served under paragraphs 6 to 8, at any time after the interest in respect of which the notice is deemed to be served has vested in an acquiring authority by virtue of paragraph 7.

Objection to severance

19. Paragraph 4 of Schedule 2 to the Acquisition Act 1947 shall not apply to land in respect of which a general vesting declaration is made under this Act.

20.—(1) If a general vesting declaration under this Act comprises part only of a house, building or factory, or of a park or garden belonging to a house, any person who is able to sell the whole of the house, building, factory, park or garden may by notice served on the acquiring authority (in this Part referred to as a "notice of objection to severance") require them to purchase his interest in the whole.

(2) Except as provided by paragraph 29, a notice of objection to severance served by any person shall not have effect if it is served more than 28 days after the date on which the notice required by paragraph 4 above is served on him.

21. Where a notice of objection to severance is served in respect of a person's interest in any land (in this Part referred to as "the land proposed to be severed"), and is so served within the time allowed in accordance with paragraph 20(2), then, notwithstanding anything in paragraph 7—

(a) that interest shall not vest in the acquiring authority, and

(b) if he is entitled to possession of that land, the acquiring authority shall not be entitled to enter upon or take possession of it,

until the notice has been disposed of in accordance with the following provisions of this Schedule.

22. Within 3 months after a person has served on an acquiring authority a notice of objection to severance, the acquiring authority shall either—

(a) serve notice on him withdrawing the notice to treat deemed to have been served on him in respect of his interest in the land proposed to be severed,

(b) serve notice on him that the general vesting declaration shall have effect, in relation to his interest in the land proposed to be severed, as if the whole of that land had been comprised in the declaration (and in the compulsory purchase order, if part only of that land was comprised in that order), or

(c) refer the notice of objection to severance to the Lands Tribunal and notify him that it has been so referred.

23. If the acquiring authority do not take action in accordance with paragraph 22 within the period allowed by that paragraph, then at the end of that period they shall be deemed to have acted in accordance with sub-paragraph (a) of that paragraph.

24. Where in accordance with paragraph 22 or 23 the notice to treat deemed to have been served in respect of a person's interest in the land proposed to be severed is withdrawn, or is deemed to have been withdrawn—

(a) that interest shall not vest in the acquiring authority by virtue of the general vesting declaration, and

(b) if he is entitled to possession of that land, the acquiring authority shall not be entitled by virtue of that declaration to enter upon or take possession of it.

25. Where an acquiring authority take action in accordance with paragraph 22(b), the general vesting declaration (and, where applicable, the compulsory purchase order) shall have effect as mentioned in that paragraph, whether apart from this Schedule the acquiring authority could have been authorised to acquire the interest in question in the whole of the land proposed to be severed or not.

26. Where in accordance with paragraph 22(c) an acquiring authority refer a notice of objection to severance to the Lands Tribunal, and on that reference the Tribunal determines that the part of the land proposed to be severed which is comprised in the general vesting declaration can be taken—

(a) in the case of a house, building or factory, without material detriment, or

(b) in the case of a park or garden, without seriously affecting the amenity or convenience of the house,

paragraph 21 shall thereupon cease to have effect in relation to that notice.

27.—(1) If on such a reference the Lands Tribunal does not make a determination in accordance with paragraph 26, the Tribunal shall determine the area of that land (being the whole of it or a part of it which includes the part comprised in the general vesting declaration) which the acquiring authority ought to be required to take; and the general vesting declaration shall have effect, in relation to the interest in that area of the person who served the notice of objection to severance, as if the whole of that area had been comprised in the general vesting declaration, whether apart from this Schedule the acquiring authority could have been authorised to acquire that interest in the whole of that area or not.

(2) Where sub-paragraph (1) applies, and part of the area determined by the Lands Tribunal was not comprised in the compulsory purchase order, the general vesting declaration shall have effect as mentioned in that sub-paragraph as if the whole of that area had been comprised in the compulsory purchase order as well as in the declaration.

28. Where by virtue of paragraph 22(a), 23, 25 or 27 a general vesting declaration is to have effect in relation to a different area of land from that originally comprised in the declaration, the acquiring authority shall alter accordingly the description of the land affected by the declaration.

29.—(1) Where in accordance with paragraph 20(1) a person is entitled to serve a notice of objection to severance, and it is proved—

(a) that he did not receive the notice required by paragraph 4 to be served on him, or received that notice less than 28 days before, or on or after, the date on which the period specified in the general vesting declaration expired, and

(b) that a notice of objection to severance served by him was served not more than 28 days after the date on which he first had knowledge of the execution of the general vesting declaration,

that notice shall have effect notwithstanding that it is served after the time allowed in accordance with paragraph 20(2) has expired.

(2) Where, in the circumstances specified in sub-paragraph (1), a person serves a notice of objection to severance after the end of the period specified in the general vesting declaration,—

(a) paragraphs 21 and 24 shall not have effect in relation to that notice,

(b) paragraph 22 shall have effect in relation to that notice as if sub-paragraph (a) of that paragraph were omitted,

(c) paragraph 23 shall have effect in relation to that notice with the substitution, for the words "sub-paragraph (a)", of the words "sub-paragraph (b)", and

(d) paragraph 26 shall not have effect in relation to that notice, but without prejudice to the making by the Tribunal of any such determination as is mentioned in that paragraph.

Compensation

30. Where any of the land specified in a general vesting declaration under this Act has become vested in an acquiring authority by virtue of paragraphs 6 to 8, the acquiring authority shall be liable to pay the like compensation, and the like interest on the compensation agreed or

awarded, as they would have been required to pay if they had taken possession of the land under paragraph 3 of Schedule 2 to the Acquisition Act 1947.

31. Sections 56 to 60 and sections 63 to 66 of the Lands Clauses Consolidation (Scotland) Act 1845 (absent and untraced owners) and sections 117 to 119 of that Act (interests omitted from purchase) shall not apply to the compensation to be paid for any interest in land in respect of which a notice to treat is deemed to have been served by virtue of paragraphs 6 to 8.

Charges and tenancies

32.—(1) Where land specified in a general vesting declaration under this Act is, together with other land not so specified, charged with a charge, such proportion of the charge as may be apportioned under section 109 of the Lands Clauses Consolidation (Scotland) Act 1845 to the first mentioned land shall, subject to sub-paragraph (3), be treated as having been extinguished by virtue of paragraphs 6 to 8 on the vesting of that land in the acquiring authority under those paragraphs.

(2) Where by virtue of sub-paragraph (1) a portion of a charge is treated as having been extinguished, sections 108 to 111 of the Act of 1845 shall have effect as if the extinguishment had taken place under section 110 of that Act.

(3) If, in the circumstances described in sub-paragraph (1), the person entitled to the charge and the owner of the land subject to it enter into an agreement to that effect, sections 108 to 111 of the Act of 1845 shall have effect as if, at the time of the vesting of the land in the acquiring authority under paragraphs 6 to 8, the person entitled to the charge had released that land from the charge on the condition mentioned in section 109 of that Act; and in that case no part of the charge shall be treated as having been extinguished as regards the remaining part of the land charged with it.

(4) In this paragraph "charge" means any such feuduty, ground annual or rent or other payment or incumbrance as is mentioned in the introductory words to sections 107 to 111 of the Act of 1845.

33. Where land specified in a general vesting declaration under this Act is, together with other land not so specified, comprised in a tenancy for a term of years unexpired, section 112 of the Lands Clauses Consolidation (Scotland) Act 1845 shall have effect in relation to it as if for references to the time of the apportionment of rent mentioned in it there were substituted references to the time of the vesting of the tenancy in the acquiring authority.

34. Where any of the land specified in a general vesting declaration under this Act has become vested in an acquiring authority under paragraphs 6 to 8, any person who, in consequence of it, is relieved from any liability (whether in respect of a feuduty, ground annual, rent, interest on a heritable security or any other payment) and makes any payment as in satisfaction or part satisfaction of that liability shall, if he shows that when he made the payment he did not know of the facts which constituted the cause of his being so relieved, or of one or more of those facts, be entitled to recover the sum paid from the person to whom it was paid.

Miscellaneous

35. Where, after land has become vested in an acquiring authority under paragraphs 6 to 8, a person retains possession of any document relating to the title to the land, he shall be deemed to have given to the acquiring authority an acknowledgement in writing of the right of the acquiring authority to production of that document and to delivery of copies of it and (except where he retains possession of the document as heritable creditor or as trustee or otherwise in a fiduciary capacity) an undertaking for safe custody of it.

36.—(1) The time within which a question of disputed compensation, arising out of an acquisition of an interest in land in respect of which a notice to treat is deemed to have been served by virtue of paragraphs 6 to 8, may be referred to the Lands Tribunal shall be 6 years from the date at which the person claiming compensation, or a person from whom he derives title, first knew, or could reasonably be expected to have known, of the vesting of the interest by virtue of those paragraphs.

(2) In reckoning the period of 6 years referred to in sub-paragraph (1), no account shall be taken of any period during which the person claiming compensation or the person from whom he derives title was under legal disability by reason of nonage or otherwise.

37. At the end of the period specified in a general vesting declaration or, if a notice of objection to severance is served under this Schedule, when that notice has been disposed of in accordance with the provisions of this Schedule, that declaration, if still being proceeded with or, as the case may be, that declaration as altered under paragraph 28, shall be recorded in the General Register of Sasines or, as the case may be, registered in the Land Register of Scotland, and on being so recorded or registered shall have the same effect as a conveyance registered in accordance with section 80 of the Lands Clauses Consolidation (Scotland) Act 1845.

PART III

INTERPRETATION

38.—(1) In this Schedule—
"short tenancy" means a tenancy for a year or from year to year or any lesser interest, and
"long tenancy which is about to expire", in relation to a general vesting declaration, means a
    tenancy granted for an interest greater than a short tenancy, but having at the date of
    the declaration a period still to run which is not more than the specified period (that is
    to say, such period, longer than one year, as may for the purposes of this paragraph be
    specified in the declaration in relation to the land in which the tenancy subsists).
(2) In determining for the purposes of this paragraph what period a tenancy still has to run at
the date of a general vesting declaration it shall be assumed—
  (a) that the tenant will exercise any option to renew the tenancy, and will not exercise any
      option to terminate the tenancy, then or later available to him, and
  (b) that the landlord will exercise any option to terminate the tenancy then or later available
      to him.
39. In this Schedule—
"Acquisition Act 1947" means the Acquisition of Land (Authorisation Procedure) (Scot-
    land) Act 1947;
"relevant enactments", in relation to an acquiring authority, means the enactments under
    which that authority may acquire or be authorised to acquire land compulsorily and
    which prescribe a procedure for effecting the compulsory acquisition of land by them
    by means of a compulsory purchase order; and
"land", in relation to compulsory acquisition by an acquiring authority, has the same mean-
    ing as in the relevant enactments.

GENERAL NOTE
    This Schedule sets out fully the procedure for the making of a General Vesting Declaration
(GVD).
    Any GVD must be preceded by the relative Compulsory Purchase Order (CPO) "coming into
operation" (para. 1(1)), that is being confirmed by the Secretary of State, and the date specified
in the notice of confirmation having passed without judicial challenge arising. At this point, the
acquiring authority will intimate whether it intends to proceed to complete title by means of a
GVD (see Reg.3(e), Compulsory Purchase of Land (Scotland) Regulations 1976 (S.I. 1976
No.820). In practice, the authority will almost certainly wish to leave this option open where it
has not reached the stage of concluded missives with all the affected proprietors. Even then, a
GVD may offer a simpler means of taking title given the broad terms in which para. 1(2) is
couched.
    The process means that the intention to make a GVD will be advertised at the time of confir-
mation (para. 2(1)), but also that the GVD cannot be made for a further two months from the
date of first publication of the confirmation notice (para. 3(1)), unless all the affected proprietors
consent in writing to an earlier date (para. 3(1)). Provision is thereafter made for service of
notice of execution of the GVD on persons affected, and for certification of the same (paras. 4
and 5).
    The effect of a GVD is equated in the Schedule to an expeded notarial instrument made in
terms of s.76 of the Lands Clauses Consolidation (Scotland) Act 1845 (c.19) (para. 7, see also
Note to s.189). The effect is to vest and to grant entry to the land comprised within the GVD in
the acquiring authority, subject to the rights of persons who are in occupation under a "short
tenancy" or "long tenancy which is about to expire" (see para. 38(1)) enjoying protection as
specified in para. 8. Otherwise, the authority is free to intromit with the land acquired, subject to
the provisions of Pt. VII.
    Provision is made in relation to payments of compensation which have been over-paid or
obtained by giving false information (paras. 9–15). Adaptations to the regime relative to severance of land set out in Sched. 2 to the 1947 Act are applied to vesting undertaken on foot of a
GVD (paras. 16–29). Other provisions relate to how compensation is to be assessed (paras.
30–31), as well as land charges (feu duties, ground annuals, etc.) and tenancies subsisting over
land vested by means of a GVD in addition to other land (paras. 32–34).
    The form of a GVD is set out in Form 7 of the 1976 Regulations, and Forms to be used in the
process are set out in Forms 8–11. For a fuller exposition of the process behind executing and
recording a GVD, see "*Compulsory Purchase in Scotland*" (1983) (Law Society of Scotland),
pp.65–69.

SCHEDULE 16

PROCEDURE FOR MAKING AND CONFIRMING ORDERS RELATING TO ROADS AND RIGHTS OF WAY

PART I

MAKING ORDERS

Procedure for making of orders by Secretary of State

1.—(1) Before making an order under section 202 or 206(1)(a) the Secretary of State shall publish in at least one local newspaper circulating in the relevant area, and in the Edinburgh Gazette, a notice—

(a) stating the general effect of the order,

(b) specifying a place in the relevant area where a copy of the draft order and of any relevant map or plan may be inspected by any person free of charge at all reasonable hours during a period of 28 days from the last day on which publication of the notice has taken place, and

(c) stating that, within the period, any person may by notice to the Secretary of State object to the making of the order.

(2) Not later than the last day on which publication has taken place in accordance with sub-paragraph (1), the Secretary of State—

(a) shall serve a copy of the notice, together with a copy of the draft order and of any relevant map or plan, on every local authority in whose area any road or, as the case may be, any land to which the order relates is situated, and on any water, hydraulic power or electricity undertakers or public gas transporter having any cables, mains, pipes or wires laid along, across, under or over any road to be stopped up or diverted or, as the case may be, any land over which a right of way is to be extinguished, under the order, and

(b) shall cause a copy of the notice to be displayed in a prominent position at the ends of so much of any road as is proposed to be stopped up or diverted or, as the case may be, of the right of way proposed to be extinguished under the order.

(3) Subject to sub-paragraph (4), if before the end of the said period of 28 days an objection is received by the Secretary of State from any local authority, undertakers or transporter on whom a notice is required to be served under sub-paragraph (2), or from any other person appearing to him to be affected by the order, and the objection is not withdrawn, the Secretary of State shall cause a local inquiry to be held.

(4) If the objection is made by a person other than such a local authority, undertakers or transporter, the Secretary of State may dispense with such an inquiry if he is satisfied that in the special circumstances of the case the holding of such an inquiry is unnecessary.

(5) After considering any objections to the order which are not withdrawn and, where a local inquiry is held, the report of the person who held the inquiry, the Secretary of State (subject to sub-paragraph (6)) may make the order either without modification or subject to such modifications as he thinks fit.

(6) Where the order contains a provision requiring any such payment, repayment or contribution as is mentioned in section 202(4)(a), and objection to that provision is duly made, in accordance with sub-paragraph (3), by an authority or person who would be required by it to make such a payment, repayment or contribution, and the objection is not withdrawn, the order shall be subject to special parliamentary procedure.

(7) Immediately after the order has been made, the Secretary of State shall publish, in the manner specified in sub-paragraph (1), a notice stating that the order has been made, and naming a place where a copy of the order may be seen at all reasonable hours; and sub-paragraph (2) shall have effect in relation to any such notice as it has effect in relation to a notice under sub-paragraph (1).

(8) In this paragraph "the relevant area", in relation to an order, means the area in which any road or land to which the order relates is situated.

Procedure in anticipation of planning permission, etc.

2.—(1) Where the Secretary of State would, if planning permission for any development had been granted under Part III, have power to make an order under section 202 authorising the stopping-up or diversion of a road in order to enable that development to be carried out, then, notwithstanding that such permission has not been granted, the Secretary of State may, in the circumstances specified in sub-paragraphs (2) to (4), publish notice of the draft of such an order in accordance with paragraph 1.

(2) The Secretary of State may publish such a notice where the relevant development is the subject of an application for planning permission and either—

(a) that application is made by a local authority or statutory undertakers,

(b) that application stands referred to the Secretary of State in pursuance of a direction under section 46, or

(c) the applicant has appealed to the Secretary of State under section 47 against a refusal of planning permission or of approval required under a development order, or against a condition of any such permission or approval.

(3) The Secretary of State may publish such a notice where—

(a) the relevant development is to be carried out by a local authority or statutory undertakers and requires, by virtue of an enactment, the authorisation of a government department, and

(b) the developers have made application to the department for that authorisation and also requested a direction under section 57 that planning permission be deemed to be granted for that development.

(4) The Secretary of State may publish such a notice where the planning authority certify that they have begun to take such steps, in accordance with regulations made by virtue of section 263, as are requisite in order to enable them to obtain planning permission for the relevant development.

(5) Paragraph 1(5) shall not be construed as authorising the Secretary of State to make an order under section 202 of which notice has been published by virtue of sub-paragraph (1) until planning permission is granted for the development which occasions the making of the order.

Further procedure in anticipation of planning permission, etc.

3.—(1) Where a planning authority would, if planning permission for any development had been granted under Part III, have power to make an order under section 207 authorising the stopping-up or diversion of a road in order to enable that development to be carried out, then, notwithstanding that such permission has not been granted, the authority may, in the circumstances specified in sub-paragraphs (3) to (5), publish notice of the draft of such an order in accordance with the following provisions of this Schedule.

(2) Nothing in those provisions shall be construed as authorising the authority to make the order in anticipation of such permission.

(3) The authority may publish such a notice where the development is the subject of an application for planning permission.

(4) The authority may publish such a notice where—

(a) the development is to be carried out by a local authority or statutory undertakers and requires, by virtue of an enactment, the authorisation of a government department, and

(b) the developers have made an application to the department for that authorisation and also requested a direction under section 57 that planning permission be deemed to be granted for that development.

(5) The planning authority may publish such a notice where they have begun to take such steps, in accordance with regulations made by virtue of section 263, as are requisite in order to enable them to obtain planning permission for the development.

PART II

CONFIRMATION OF ORDERS

Application

4.—(1) This Part shall have effect with respect to the confirmation of orders under section 203, 206(1)(b), 207 and 208 and the publicity for such orders after they are confirmed.

(2) This Part has no application as regards orders made by the Secretary of State.

Confirmation of orders made by other authorities

5.—(1) An order made under section 203 by a competent authority, section 206(1)(b) by a local authority or section 207 or 208 by a planning authority shall not take effect unless confirmed—

(a) by the Secretary of State in a case where the order is opposed, and

(b) in any other case by the authority making the order.

(2) The Secretary of State shall not confirm any such order unless satisfied as to every matter of which the authority making the order are required under section 206(1)(b), 207 or 208 (as the case may be) to be satisfied.

(3) The time specified—

(a) in an order under section 203 as the time from which a right is to be extinguished,

(b) in an order under section 206(1)(b) as the time from which a right of way is to be extinguished,

(c) in an order under section 207 as the time from which a road is to be stopped up or diverted, or

(d) in an order under section 208 as the time from which a footpath or bridleway is to be stopped up or diverted,

shall not be earlier than confirmation of the order.

6.—(1) Before an order under section 203, 206(1)(b), 207 or 208 is submitted to the Secretary of State for confirmation or confirmed as an unopposed order, the authority by whom the order was made shall give notice in the prescribed form—

(a) stating the general effect of the order and that it has been made and is about to be submitted for confirmation or to be confirmed as an unopposed order,

(b) naming a place in the area in which the land to which the order relates is situated where a copy of the order may be inspected free of charge at all reasonable hours, and

(c) specifying the time (not being less than 28 days from the date of the first publication of the notice) within which, and the manner in which, representations or objections with respect to the order may be made.

(2) Subject to sub-paragraph (3), the notice to be given under sub-paragraph (1) shall be given—

(a) by publication in the Edinburgh Gazette and in at least one local newspaper circulating in the area in which the land to which the order relates is situated, and

(b) by serving a similar notice on—

(i) every owner, occupier and lessee (except tenants for a month or a period less than a month and statutory tenants within the meaning of the Rent (Scotland) Act 1984) of any of that land,

(ii) every local authority whose area includes any of that land,

(iii) any statutory undertakers to whom there belongs, or by whom there is used, for the purposes of their undertaking, any apparatus under, in, on, over, along or across that land, and

(iv) any person named in the order by virtue of section 208(2)(d), and

(c) by causing a copy of the notice to be displayed in a prominent position at the ends of so much of any footpath or bridleway as is to be stopped up, diverted or extinguished by virtue of the order.

(3) Except in the case of an owner, occupier or lessee being a local authority or statutory undertakers, the Secretary of State may in any particular case direct that it shall not be necessary to comply with sub-paragraph (2)(b)(i).

(4) If he so directs in the case of any land, then in addition to publication—

(a) the notice shall be addressed to "the owners and any occupiers" of the land (describing it), and

(b) a copy or copies of the notice shall be affixed to some conspicuous object or objects on the land.

7. If no representations or objections are duly made, or if any so made are withdrawn, the authority by whom the order was made may, instead of submitting the order to the Secretary of State themselves confirm the order (but without any modification).

8.—(1) This paragraph applies where any representation or objection duly made is not withdrawn.

(2) If the objection is made by a local authority, the Secretary of State shall, before confirming the order, cause a local inquiry to be held.

(3) If the representation or objection is made by a person other than a local authority, the Secretary of State shall, before confirming the order, either—

(a) cause a local inquiry to be held, or

(b) give any person by whom any representation or objection has been duly made and not withdrawn an opportunity of being heard by a person appointed by the Secretary of State for the purpose.

(4) After considering the report of the person appointed under sub-paragraph (2) or (3) to hold the inquiry or hear representations or objections, the Secretary of State may confirm the order, with or without modifications.

(5) In the case of an order under section 207 or 208, if objection is made by statutory undertakers on the ground that the order provides for the creation of a public right of way over land covered by works used for the purpose of their undertaking, or over the curtilage of such land, and the objection is not withdrawn, the order shall be subject to special parliamentary procedure.

(6) Notwithstanding anything in the previous provisions of this paragraph, the Secretary of State shall not confirm an order so as to affect land not affected by the order as submitted to him, except after—

   (a) giving such notice as appears to him requisite of his proposal so to modify the order, specifying the time (which must not be less than 28 days from the date of the first publication of the notice) within which, and the manner in which, representations or objections with respect to the proposal may be made,

   (b) holding a local inquiry or affording to any person by whom any representation or objection has been duly made and not withdrawn an opportunity of being heard by a person appointed by the Secretary of State for the purpose, and

   (c) considering the report of the person appointed to hold the inquiry or, as the case may be, to hear representations or objections.

   (7) In the case of an order under section 207 or 208, if objection is made by statutory undertakers on the ground that the order as modified would provide for the creation of a public right of way over land covered by works used for the purposes of their undertaking, or over the curtilage of such land, and the objection is not withdrawn, the order shall be subject to special parliamentary procedure.

   9.—(1) The Secretary of State shall not confirm an order under section 203, 207 or 208 which extinguishes a right of way over land under, in, on, over, along or across which there is any apparatus belonging to or used by statutory undertakers for the purposes of their undertaking, unless the undertakers have consented to the confirmation of the order.

   (2) Any such consent may be given subject to the condition that there are included in the order such provisions for the protection of the undertakers as they may reasonably require.

   (3) The consent of statutory undertakers to any such order shall not be unreasonably withheld.

   (4) Any question arising under this paragraph whether the withholding of consent is unreasonable, or whether any requirement is reasonable, shall be determined by whichever Minister is the appropriate Minister in relation to the statutory undertakers concerned.

   10. Regulations may, subject to this Part, make such provision as the Secretary of State thinks expedient as to the procedure on the making, submission and confirmation of orders under sections 203, 206(1)(b), 207 and 208.

PART III

PUBLICITY FOR ORDERS AFTER CONFIRMATION

   11.—(1) As soon as may be after an order under sections 203, 206(1)(b), 207 and 208 has been confirmed by the Secretary of State or confirmed as an unopposed order, the authority by whom the order was made shall—

   (a) publish, in the manner required by paragraph 6(2), a notice in the prescribed form—

      (i) describing the general effect of the order,

      (ii) stating that it has been confirmed, and

      (iii) naming a place in the area in which the land to which the order relates is situated where a copy of the order as confirmed may be inspected free of charge at all reasonable hours,

   (b) serve a similar notice and a copy of the order as confirmed on any persons on whom notices were required to be served under paragraph 6(2), and

   (c) cause a similar notice to be displayed in the similar manner as the notice required to be displayed under paragraph 6(2).

   (2) No such notice or copy need be served on a person unless he has sent to the authority a request in that behalf, specifying an address for service.

GENERAL NOTE

   This Schedule establishes two separate regimes in relation to the confirmation of orders made under Pt. IX either by the Secretary of State (in relation to orders made under ss.202 and 206(1)) (para. 1(1)) or else by the "competent authority" (s.203), the "local authority" (s.206(1)(b)), or the "planning authority" (ss.207, 208) (para. 5(1)).

   As regards the orders which fall to be made other than by the Secretary of State, it should be borne in mind that the "competent authority" or "planning authority" will be the local authority for the area concerned unless the roads authority bears a different identity. Subsequent to 1996, this difference does not seem to matter, as all 27 mainland authorities and three Islands authorities are also the roads authorities for their area. Moreover, such authorities are empowered to confirm orders delegated to them where no objections are received thereto (para. 5(1)(b)).

   Both regimes have provision for the publication and advertisement of proposed orders, for the submission of objections and the holding, if necessary, of Public Local Inquiries, as well as for publication of confirmation of an order. It may be worth noting that both the Secretary of State, in relation to s.202 Orders, and the "planning authority", in relation to s.207 Orders, enjoy limited powers to promote draft orders in anticipation of a grant of planning permission (paras. 2(1) and 3(1)).

Section 251(5) SCHEDULE 17

ENFORCEMENT AS RESPECTS WAR-TIME BREACHES BY THE CROWN OF PLANNING CONTROL

Preliminary

1. In this Schedule—
  "authority" means an authority responsible for enforcing planning control,
  "compliance determination application" means an application under section 251(3), and
  "compliance determination" means a determination given on such an application.

Making of compliance determination applications

2.—(1) A compliance determination application may be made with respect to any land—
(a) by the owner or occupier of the land, or
(b) by any person who proves that he has or intends to acquire an interest in the land which will be affected by a compliance determination or that he has borne any of the cost of carrying out works on the land during the war period.

(2) In the case of land owned or occupied by or on behalf of the Crown, or leased to, or to a person acting on behalf of, the Crown, or land with respect to which it is proved that there is held, or intended to be acquired, by or on behalf of the Crown an interest in the land which will be affected as mentioned in sub-paragraph (1) or that any of the cost there mentioned has been borne by the Crown, a compliance determination application may be made by any person acting on behalf of the Crown.

3. A compliance determination application shall be accompanied by such plans and other information as are necessary to enable the application to be determined.

4.—(1) The authority to whom a compliance determination application is made shall within 14 days from the receipt of the application publish notice of it in one or more local newspapers circulating in the area in which the land is situated and serve notice of it on any person appearing to the authority to be specially affected by the application.

(2) The authority shall take into consideration any representations made to them in connection with the application within 14 days from the publication of the notice.

Determination of applications

5.—(1) Where a compliance determination application is made to an authority the authority shall determine whether the works or use in question fail to comply with any planning control which the authority are responsible for enforcing and, if so, shall specify the control in question.

(2) Where the authority determine that works or a use fail so to comply they shall further determine whether having regard to all relevant circumstances the works or use shall, notwithstanding the failure, be deemed so to comply, either unconditionally or subject to such conditions as to the time for which the works or use may be continued, the carrying out of alterations, or other matters, as the authority think expedient.

Appeals against compliance determinations or failure to make such determinations

6.—(1) Where the applicant is aggrieved by a compliance determination, or where a person by whom representations have been made as mentioned in paragraph 4 is aggrieved by such a determination, he may appeal to the Secretary of State.

(2) The applicant may also appeal if he is aggrieved by the failure of the authority to determine the application within 2 months from the last day on which representations under paragraph 4 may be made and has served notice on the authority that he appeals to the Secretary of State.

(3) An appeal under this paragraph must be made within the period of 28 days after the applicant has notice of the determination or, in the case of an appeal under sub-paragraph (2), after the applicant has served notice on the authority of the appeal, or within such extended period as the Secretary of State may allow.

7.—(1) On such an appeal the Secretary of State may give, in substitution for the determination, if any, given by the authority, such determination as appears to him to be proper having regard to all relevant circumstances, or, if he is satisfied that the applicant was not a person entitled to make the application, may decide that the application is not to be entertained.

(2) At any stage of the proceedings on such an appeal to him the Secretary of State may, and shall if so directed by the Court of Session, state in the form of a special case for the opinion of the Court of Session any question of law arising in connection with the appeal.

8. Subject to paragraph 9 and to any determination or decision of the Secretary of State on an appeal under paragraph 7, any compliance determination shall be final and any such failure to give a determination as mentioned in paragraph 6(2) shall be taken on the service of the notice there mentioned as a final refusal by the authority to entertain the application, and any determination or decision of the Secretary of State on an appeal under paragraph 7 shall be final.

Fresh applications where alteration in circumstances

9. Where a compliance determination has been given that works on land or a use of land shall not be deemed to comply with planning control or shall be deemed to comply with it subject to conditions, then if a person entitled to make a compliance determination application with respect to the land satisfies the authority or on appeal the Secretary of State that there has been a material change of circumstances since the previous application was determined, he may make a subsequent application and on such an application the authority or on appeal the Secretary of State may substitute for the compliance determination such determination as appears proper having regard to all relevant circumstances.

References of application to Secretary of State

10.—(1) If it appears to the Secretary of State that it is expedient, having regard to considerations affecting the public interest (whether generally or in the locality concerned), that any compliance determination application to an authority, or any class or description of such applications, should instead of being determined by the authority be referred to him for decision, he may give directions to the authority requiring that application, or applications of that class or description, to be so referred.

(2) This Schedule shall apply to any such reference as if it were an appeal under paragraph 6(2) following the failure of the authority to determine the application.

Information

11. The Secretary of State may give directions to any authority requiring them to furnish him with such information with respect to compliance determination applications received by them as he considers necessary or expedient in connection with the exercise of his functions under this Schedule.

Opportunity for hearing

12.—(1) On a compliance determination application the applicant may require the authority to give him an opportunity before the application is determined of appearing before and being heard by a person appointed by the authority for the purpose.

(2) In the case of—
(a) a compliance determination application referred to the Secretary of State for decision, or
(b) an appeal under this Schedule,
the applicant or the authority may require the Secretary of State to give him or them an opportunity before the application or appeal is determined of appearing before and being heard by a person appointed by the Secretary of State for the purpose.

Notice of proposed enforcement

13.—(1) This paragraph applies where before the relevant date any person proposes to take steps for enforcing a planning control in the case of such works or such a use as is mentioned in section 251(1).

(2) Subject to sub-paragraph (4), unless a compliance determination application has been made in relation to the land which has not been finally determined, that person shall serve on every owner and occupier of the land not less than 28 days' notice of the proposal, and if within that period any person makes such an application in relation to the land and within 7 days of making it serves on the person proposing to take steps as aforesaid notice that the application

has been made, no steps for enforcing the control shall be taken until the final determination of the application.

(3) If such an application has been made which has not been finally determined, no such steps shall be taken until the final determination of it.

(4) No notice shall be required under sub-paragraph (2) if steps for enforcing a planning control in the case of any works on land are begun within 28 days of the final determination of a compliance determination application in relation to the land.

(5) For the purpose of this paragraph a compliance determination application shall be treated as having been finally determined notwithstanding that a subsequent application may be made under paragraph 9.

Power of entry

14.—(1) At any time before the relevant date any officer of an authority shall, on producing, if so required, some duly authenticated document showing his authority to act for the purposes of this paragraph, have a right, subject to the provisions of this paragraph, to enter any premises at all reasonable hours—

(a) for the purpose of ascertaining whether there are on the premises any works carried out during the war period which do not comply with planning control, or whether a use of the premises continues which was begun during that period and does not comply with it;

(b) where a compliance determination application has been made to the authority, for the purpose of obtaining any information required by the authority for the exercise of their functions under section 251 and this Schedule in relation to the application.

(2) Admission to any premises which are occupied shall not be demanded as of right unless 24 hours' notice of the intended entry has been served on the occupier.

(3) Any person who wilfully obstructs any officer of an authority acting in the exercise of his powers under this section shall be guilty of an offence and liable on summary conviction to a fine not exceeding level 1 on the standard scale.

(4) If any person who in compliance with this paragraph is admitted into a factory, workshop or workplace discloses to any person any information obtained by him in it with regard to any manufacturing process or trade secret, he shall, unless such disclosure was made in the performance of his duty, be guilty of an offence and liable on summary conviction to a fine not exceeding level 3 on the standard scale or to imprisonment for a term not exceeding 3 months.

Service of notices

15.—(1) Any notice or other document required or authorised to be served under this Schedule may be served on any person either by delivering it to him, or by leaving it at his proper address, or by post.

(2) Any such document required or authorised to be served upon an incorporated company or body shall be duly served if it is served upon the secretary or clerk of the company or body.

(3) For the purposes of this paragraph and of section 7 of the Interpretation Act 1978, the proper address of any person upon whom any such document is to be served is—

(a) in the case of the secretary or clerk of any incorporated company or body, that of the registered or principal office of the company or body, and

(b) in any other case, the last known address of the person to be served.

(4) If it is not practicable after reasonable enquiry to ascertain the name or address of an owner or occupier of land on whom any such document is to be served, the document may be served by addressing it to him by the description of "owner" or "occupier" of the premises (describing them) to which it relates, and by delivering it to some person on the premises or, if there is no person on the premises to whom it can be delivered, by affixing it, or a copy of it, to some conspicuous part of the premises.

Supplementary provisions

16. Parts XIII and XIV do not apply to section 251 and this Schedule.

SCHEDULE 18

PROVISIONS OF THIS ACT REFERRED TO IN SECTIONS 261 TO 263

PART I

PROVISIONS REFERRED TO IN SECTIONS 261(1) AND (2) AND 262(1)

Sections 4 to 22.
Section 24.
Section 26.
Section 27(2) to (6) so far as applying for the purposes of sections 58, 59 and 61.
Section 28.
Section 30.
Section 31 except subsection (4).
Sections 32 to 34.
Section 36.
Section 37(1) to (3).
Section 39.
Section 41(1) to (5).
Sections 43 and 44.
Sections 46 to 48.
Section 57(1), (3) and (4).
Sections 58 to 63.
Sections 65 to 73.
Sections 75 to 77.
Section 83.
Sections 86 to 89.
Section 90(1) to (5).
Sections 91 and 92.
Section 93.
Section 94(1) to (7).
Section 95.
In section 99(1), the definition of "the relevant provisions".
Section 108(1) and (2).
Sections 113 and 114.
Section 117.
Sections 123 to 126.
Sections 130 to 136.
Sections 138 to 145.
Sections 148 to 158.
Sections 160 to 162.
Sections 164 and 165.
Section 169(10).
Sections 170 and 171.
Section 172(4).
Sections 176 to 180.
Sections 182 to 186.
Section 188.
Section 189(1) to (7).
Sections 190 to 194.
Sections 196 to 206.
Section 208.
Sections 211 and 212.
Section 215(1) and (2).
Section 216(1) to (6).
Section 217(1) and (3).
Section 218(1) to (3).
Sections 219 to 236.
Section 237(1) except paragraphs (e) and (f).
Section 238.
Section 241, with the omission in subsection (2) of the references to section 239.
Section 242(1), with the omission of the definition of "private interest", (2) and (3).
Section 243(1).
Section 245(1) to (4) (the reference, in subsection (1)(c), to Part III being construed as not referring to sections 34 and 35).

Section 246.
Sections 253 to 256.
Sections 261 and 262.
Section 263(1) to (4).
Section 269 except subsection (3).
Section 270.
Sections 272 and 273.
In section 275, subsections (4) and (5) so far as relating to section 5, and subsection (7).
In section 277(1), the definition of "mineral working deposit".
Schedule 1.
Schedule 2 paragraphs 1 to 3.
Schedule 3 paragraphs 7 and 8.
Schedule 4.
Schedule 5 paragraph 7(5).
Schedules 6 and 7.
Schedule 8 paragraphs 1 to 12.
Schedule 11.
Schedule 13 paragraph 2.
Schedule 16 paragraphs 1, 2 and 4 to 11.
Any other provisions of the planning Acts in so far as they apply, or have effect for the purposes of, any of the provisions specified above.

Part II

Provisions referred to in section 263(1)

Section 26.
Section 27(2) to (6) so far as applying for the purposes of sections 52(2), 53(6) and 54(4).
Section 28.
Sections 30 to 33.
Section 36(1) and (4).
Section 37(1) to (3).
Section 38(4) and (5).
Section 41.
Section 43(1).
Section 44.
Sections 46 to 54.
Section 57(1), (3) and (4).
Sections 65 and 66.
Sections 71 and 72.
Section 75.
Sections 123 to 138.
Sections 140 and 141.
Section 143(1) to (5).
Sections 144 and 145.
Sections 147 to 155.
Sections 160 to 162.
Section 169(2) to (9).
Section 171.
Section 172(4).
Sections 179 to 184.
Section 186.
Schedule 2.
Schedule 3 paragraphs 7 and 8.
Schedule 8 paragraphs 1 to 11.

TABLE OF DERIVATIONS

Notes:

1. This Table shows the derivation of the provisions of the Bill.
2. The following abbreviations are used in the Table—

Acts of Parliament

1972	=	The Town and Country Planning (Scotland) Act 1972 (c. 52)
1973C	=	The Land Compensation (Scotland) Act 1973 (c. 56)
1973	=	The Local Government (Scotland) Act 1973 (c. 65)
1977	=	The Town and Country Planning (Scotland) Act 1977 (c. 10)
1980	=	The Local Government, Planning and Land Act 1980 (c. 65)

1981MP	= The Local Government (Miscellaneous Provisions) (Scotland) Act 1981 (c. 23)
1981	= The Town and Country Planning (Minerals) Act 1981 (c. 36)
1982	= The Local Government and Planning (Scotland) Act 1982 (c. 43)
1984P	= The Town and Country Planning Act 1984 (c. 10)
1984T	= The Telecommunications Act 1984 (c. 12)
1984	= The Roads (Scotland) Act 1984 (c. 54)
1986	= The Housing and Planning Act 1986 (c. 63)
1991	= The Planning and Compensation Act 1991 (c. 34)
1994	= The Local Government etc. (Scotland) Act 1994 (c. 39)

3. The Table does not show the effect of Transfer of Functions orders.

4. The Table does not give details of the effect of section 172(2) of the Local Government (Scotland) Act 1973 (c. 65), which omitted the word "local" in the expression "local planning authority" where it occurs in any enactment or instrument.

5. "Sc Law Com Rec No." followed by a number indicates that the provision gives effect to the Recommendation bearing that number in Appendix 1 to the Scottish Law Commission's Report on the Consolidation of Certain Enactments relating to Town and Country Planning in Scotland (Cmnd. 3644).

Provision	Derivation
1(1)	1973 s.172(1); 1994 Sch. 13 para. 92(57).
(2)	1973 s.172(3); 1994 Sch. 13 para. 92(57).
2(1)	1980 Sch. 32 para. 5(8).
(2)	1980 Sch. 32 para. 15(2)(b)(ii).
(3)	1980 Sch. 32 para. 20(2).
(4)	1980 Sch. 32 para. 25(1)(c).
(5)	1980 Sch. 32 para. 25(2).
3(1)	1980 s.149(6).
(2)	1980 s.149(8)(a).
4(1)	1972 s.4(1); 1994 Sch. 4 para. 2(a).
(2)	1972 s.4(2); 1994 Sch. 4 para. 2(b).
(3)	1972 s.4(3).
(4)	1972 s.4(4).
5(1)	1972 s.4A(1); 1994 s.33(1).
(2)	1972 s.4A(2); 1994 s.33(1).
(3)	1972 s.4A(3); 1994 s.33(1).
(4)	1972 s.4A(4); 1994 s.33(1).
6(1)	Drafting.
(2)	1972 s.5(1); 1994 Sch. 4 para. 3.
(3)	1972 s.5(1A); 1994 Sch. 4 para. 3.
(4)	1972 s.5(1B); 1994 Sch. 4 para. 3.
(5)	1972 s.5(1C); 1994 Sch. 4 para. 3.
(6)	1972 s.5(1D); 1994 Sch. 4 para. 3.
(7)	1972 s.5(2); 1981MP Sch. 2 para. 17(a)
(8)	1972 s.6A; 1994 Sch. 4 para. 5.
7(1)	1972 s.5(3); 1991 Sch. 13 para. 3.
(2)	1972 s.5(4).
(3)	1972 s.5(6).
8(1), (2)	1972 s.6(1).
(3)	1972 s.6(1A); 1994 Sch. 4 para. 4.
(4), (5)	1972 s.6(2).
(6)	1972 s.6(3).
(7), (8)	1972 s.6(4).
(9)	1972 s.6(5).
(10)	1972 s.6(6).
(11)	1972 s.6(7).
9(1)	1972 s.8(1); 1982 s.37(a).
(2)	1972 s.8(1).
(3)	1972 s.8(2); 1982 s.37(b).
(4)	1972 ss.6A, 8(3); 1982 s.37(c); 1994 Sch. 4 para. 5.
(5)	1972 s.8(4); 1982 s.37(c).
(6)	1972 s.8(5); 1982 s.37(c).
(7)	1972 s.8(6); 1982 s.37(c).

Provision	Derivation
9(8)	1972 s.8(7); 1982 s.37(c).
(9)	1972 s.8(8); 1982 s.37(c).
10(1), (2)	1972 ss.7(1), 8(2); 1994 Sch. 4 para. 6.
(3)	1972 ss.7(2), 8(2).
(4)	1972 ss.7(3), 8(2); 1973 s.175(1); 1982 s.36.
(5)	1972 ss.7(4), 8(2); 1973 s.175(1).
(6)	1972 ss.7(5), 8(2); 1973 s.175(1).
(7)	1972 ss.7(5) proviso, 8(2); 1973 s.175(1).
(8)	1972 ss.7(6), 8(2); 1973 s.175(1); Tribunals and Inquiries Act 1992 (c. 53) Sch. 3 para. 3
(9)	1972 ss.7(7), 8(2); 1973 s.175(1).
(10)	1972 ss.7(8), 8(2); 1973 s.175(1).
11(1)	1972 s.9(1A); 1994 Sch. 4 para. 7.
(2)	1972 s.9(4A); 1977 s.2(1)(a).
(3)	1972 s.9(3), (5); 1991 Sch. 13 para. 4.
(4)	1972 s.9(4).
(5)	1972 s.9(9); 1977 s.2(1)(b).
(6)	1972 s.9(6).
12(1)	1972 ss.10(1), 13(3); 1977 s.2(2).
(2)	1972 ss.10(1), 13(3).
(3)	1972 ss.10(2), 13(3); 1981MP Sch. 2 para. 19(a).
(4)	1972 ss.10(2), 13(3).
(5)	1972 ss.10(3), 13(3); 1981MP Sch. 3 para. 15.
(6)	1972 s.13(4); 1982 s.40(c).
13(1)	1972 s.13(1); 1982 s.40(a).
(2)	1972 s.13(3); 1982 s.40(c).
(3), (4)	1972 s.13(1); 1982 s.40(a).
14(1)	1972 ss.9(7), 13(2); 1981MP Sch. 2 para. 20.
(2)	1972 ss.9(8), 13(2); 1981MP Sch. 2 paras. 18(c)(i), 20.
(3)	1972 ss.9(7), 13(2); 1981MP Sch. 2 para. 20.
(4)	1972 ss.9(10), 13(3).
(5)	1972 ss.9(7), (11), 13(2), (3).
15(1) to (3)	1972 ss.11(1), 13(3); 1982 s.38(a), (b).
(4)	1972 ss.11(2), 13(3).
(5)	1972 ss.11(1)(a), 13(3).
(6)	1972 ss.11(1)(b), 13(3); Tribunals and Inquiries Act 1992 (c. 53) Sch. 3 para. 4.
16(1)	1972 s.11(1A); Town and Country Planning (Costs of Inquiries etc.) Act 1995 (c. 49) s.3(2)(a).
(2)	1972 s.11(1B); Town and Country Planning (Costs of Inquiries etc.) Act 1995 (c. 49) s.3(2)(a).
(3)	1972 s.11(1C); Town and Country Planning (Costs of Inquiries etc.) Act 1995 (c. 49) s.3(2)(a).
17(1)	1972 ss.12(1), 13(3); 1986 Sch. 11 para. 28(2).
(2)	1972 ss.12(1), 13(3); 1982 s.39.
(3)	1972 ss.12(2), 13(3); 1977 s.2(3).
(4)	1972 ss.12(2A), 13(3); 1986 Sch. 11 para. 28(1).
(5)	1972 ss.12(2B), 13(3); 1986 Sch. 11 para. 28(1).
18(1)	1972 ss.12(3), 13(3).
(2)	1972 ss.12(3), (4), 13(3); 1973 s.175(2).
19(1) to (4)	1972 ss.12(4), 13(3); 1973 s.175(2).
20	1972 s.14; 1984 Sch. 9 para. 70(2).
21(1), (2)	1972 s.16(1); 1982 Sch. 2 para. 1.
(3)	1972 s.16(2).
(4)	1972 s.16(3).
(5)	1972 s.16(4).
22(1)	1972 s.15(1); 1973 Sch. 23 para. 17(b); 1994 Sch. 4 para. 8(a)(ii), Sch. 14.
(2)	1972 s.15(2).
(3)	1972 s.15(2A); 1994 Sch. 4 para. 8(b).

Provision	Derivation
22(4)	1972 s.15(3).
(5)	1972 s.15(4), (5).
23(1)	1980 Sch. 32 para. 24(1); drafting.
(2)	1980 Sch. 32 para. 24(2), (3); drafting.
24(1)	1972 s.17(1).
(2)	1972 s.17(2).
(3)	1972 s.17(3).
(4)	1972 s.17(4).
(5)	1972 s.17(5); 1994 Sch. 4 para. 9.
(6)	1972 Sch. 21 Pt. I; 1977 s.5(7).
25	1972 s.18A; 1991 s.58.
26(1)	1972 s.19(1).
(2)	1972 s.19(2); 1984 Sch. 9 para. 70(3); 1986 Sch. 11 para. 29; 1991 s.44(2).
(3)	1972 s.19(3).
(4)	1972 s.19(1A); 1991 s.44(1).
(5)	1972 s.19(3A); 1981 s.19(1).
(6)	1972 s.19(3B); 1991 s.45.
(7)	1972 s.19(4).
27(1)	1972 s.275(5).
(2), (3)	1972 ss.21C(4), 21D(6), 21E(4), 40(1), 41(1); 1980 Sch. 32 para. 26(1A); Housing and Planning Act 1986 (c. 63) ss.26(1), 54(2).
(4)	1972 s.40(2); 1991 Sch. 13 para. 15.
(5)	1972 s.40(3); 1991 Sch. 12 para. 10.
(6)	1972 s.40(3).
28(1)	1972 s.20(1).
(2)	1972 s.20(5).
(3)	1972 s.20(8).
(4)	1972 s.20(9).
(5)	1972 s.20(6), (8).
(6)	1972, s.20(10); drafting.
(7)	Drafting.
29(1) to (3)	Drafting.
30(1)	1972 s.21(1); 1991 Sch. 13 para. 5.
(2)	1972 s.21(2); 1991 Sch. 13 para. 5.
(3)	1972 s.21(3); 1991 Sch. 13 para. 5.
31(1)	1972 s.21(4).
(2), (3)	1972 s.21(5).
(4)	1972 s.21(6).
(5)	1972 s.21(7).
32	1972 s.22(1); 1982 Sch. 2 para. 2.
33(1)	1972 s.29(1); 1991 Sch. 13 para. 8.
(2)	1972 s.29(2); 1991 Sch. 13 para. 8.
(3)	1972 s.29(3); 1991 Sch. 13 para. 8.
34(1)	1972 s.23(1); 1982 s.41; 1991 Sch. 13 para. 6.
(2)	1972 s.23(2); 1982 s.41.
(3)	1972 s.23(3); 1982 s.41.
(4)	1972 s.23(3); 1982 s.41; Criminal Procedure (Consequential Provisions) (Scotland) Act 1995 (c. 40) Sch. 1 paras. 5, 6; Criminal Procedure (Scotland) Act 1995 (c. 46) s.225.
(5)	1972 s.23(4); 1991 Sch. 13 para. 6.
(6)	1972 s.23(5); 1991 Sch. 13 para. 6.
35(1) to (8)	1972 s.24; 1991 s.46(1).
36(1)	1972 s.31(2), (5); 1982 Sch. 2 para. 9; 1986 Sch. 6 Pt. IV para. 1; 1991 Sch. 13 para. 9.
(2)	1972 s.31(3), (5); 1991 Sch. 13 para. 9.
(3)	1972 s.31(3), (5); 1991 Sch. 13 para. 9.
(4)	1972 s.31(4), (5).
37(1)	1972 s.26(1); 1986 Sch. 11 para. 54.

Provision	Derivation
37(2)	1972 s.26(1).
(3)	1972 s.26(1); drafting.
(4)	1972 s.30A; 1982 Sch. 2 para. 8.
38(1)	1972 s.26(2); 1982 Sch. 2 para. 5.
(2)	1972 s.26(3); 1991 s.46(2).
(3)	1972 s.26(3A); 1991 s.46(2).
(4)	1972 s.26(5).
(5)	1972 s.26(6).
39(1) to (3)	1972 s.26A; 1991 s.47(1).
40(1) to (3)	1972 s.26B; 1991 s.48.
41(1)	1972 s.27(1).
(2)	1972 s.27(1) proviso.
(3)	1972 s.27(2); 1981 Sch. 2 para. 1.
(4)	1972 s.27(3).
(5)	1972 s.27(3).
(6)	Drafting.
42(1)	1972 s.28A(1); 1986 Sch. 11 para. 31.
(2)	1972 s.28A(3); 1986 Sch. 11 para. 31.
(3)	1972 s.28A(2); 1986 Sch. 11 para. 31.
(4)	1972 s.28A(4); 1986 Sch. 11 para. 31.
43(1)	1972 s.28(1); 1982 Sch. 2 para. 6(a); 1991 Sch. 13 para. 7.
(2)	1972 s.28(2); 1982 Sch. 2 para. 6(b); 1991 Sch. 13 para. 7(b).
44(1)	1972 s.30(1).
(2), (3)	1972 s.30(2).
45(1)	1972 s.26(4A); 1981MP s.36.
(2)	1972 s.26(4A); 1981MP s.36.
46(1)	1972 s.32(1); 1982 Sch. 2 para. 10(a).
(2)	1972 s.32(2).
(3)	1972 s.32(3).
(4)	1972 s.32(4); 1982 Sch. 2 para. 10(b)(ii), (iii); 1981 Sch. 2 para. 2; 1986 Sch. 11 para. 55; 1991 Sch. 13 para. 10.
(5), (6)	1972 s.32(5).
(7)	1972 s.32(6).
47(1)	1972 s.33(1); 1982 Sch. 2 para. 11(a).
(2)	1972 s.34; 1982 Sch. 2 para. 12; 1991 s.47(2); Sch. 13 para. 12.
(3)	1972 s.33(2); 1991 Sch. 13 para. 11(a).
(4)	1972 ss.33(2), 34.
(5)	1972 s.34; Sc Law Com Rec No. 1.
48(1)	1972 s.33(3).
(2)	1972 s.33(4).
(3)	1972 s.33(3) proviso.
(4)	1972 s.33(4).
(5)	1972 s.33(5); 1981 Sch. 2 para. 3; 1982 Sch. 2 para. 11(b); 1986 Sch. 11 para. 55; 1991 Sch. 13 para. 11(b).
(6)	1972 s.33(6).
(7)	1972 s.33(7); 1986 Sch. 11 para. 56; 1991 Sch. 13 para. 11(c).
(8)	1972 s.33(7A); 1991 s.50(1).
(9)	1972 s.33(8).
49(1) to (3)	1972 s.21A(1) to (3); 1986 s.26(1).
50(1)	1972 s.21A(4)(a); 1986 s.26(1).
(2)	1972 s.21A(4)(b), (5); Sch. 6A para. 2(1); 1986 s.26(1).
(3)	1972 s.21A(5); 1986 s.26(1).
51(1), (2)	1972 s.21B(1); 1986 s.26(1).
(3), (4)	1972 s.21B(2); 1986 s.26(1).
52(1), (2)	1972 s.21C; 1986 s.26(1), (2)
53(1) to (5)	1972 s.21D(1) to (5); 1986 s.26(1).
(6)	1972 ss.21D(6), 27(2), (3); 1986 s.26(1).

Provision	Derivation
54(1) to (3)	1972 s.21E(1) to (3); 1986 s.26(1).
(4)	1972 ss.21E(4), 27(2), (3); 1986 s.26(1).
55(1)	1980 Sch. 32 paras. 5(4)(a), 17(1).
(2)	1980 Sch. 32 paras. 11(3), 17(2).
(3)	1980 Sch. 32 para. 17(3).
(4)	1980 Sch. 32 para. 17(4).
(5)	1980 Sch. 32 para. 17(5).
(6)	1980 Sch. 32 para. 17(6).
(7)	1980 Sch. 32 para. 25(1)(a), (b).
(8)	1980 Sch. 32 para. 25(2).
(9)	1980 Sch. 32 para. 17(7).
(10)	1980 Sch. 32 para. 17(8).
56(1)	1980 Sch. 32 para. 21; 1986 s.54(1).
(2)	1980 Sch. 32 para. 22(1); 1986 s.54(1).
57(1)	1972 s.37(1).
(2)	Electricity Act 1989 (c. 29) Sch. 8 para. 7(1).
(3)	1972 s.37(2); Electricity Act 1989 (c. 29) Sch. 8 para. 7(3); 1991 Sch. 12 para. 9.
(4)	1972 s.37(3).
(5)	Electricity Act 1989 (c. 29) Sch. 8 para. 7(4).
58(1), (2)	1972 s.38(1).
(3)	1972 s.38(2).
(4)	1972 s.38(3); 1980 Sch. 32 para. 19(2); 1981 s.23; 1986 Sch. 6 Pt. IV para. 2; 1991 Sch. 8 para. 3; Sch. 13 para. 13.
59(1)	1972 s.39(1); 1991 Sch. 13 para. 14.
(2), (3)	1972 s.39(2); 1982 Sch. 2 para. 13.
(4)	1972 s.39(3).
(5)	1972 s.39(4).
(6)	1972 s.39(5).
(7)	1972 s.39(6).
60(1)	1972 s.40(4); Electricity Act 1989 (c. 29) Sch. 8 para. 7(3).
(2)	1972 s.40(5).
(3)	1972 s.40(6).
(4)	1972 s.40(7).
61(1)	1972 ss.21C(3), 41(1); 1980 Sch. 32 para. 22(2)(b); 1986 ss.26(1), 54.
(2), (3)	1972 s.41(2).
(4)	1972 s.41(3)(a).
(5), (6)	1972 s.41(6).
62(1), (2)	1972 s.41(3)(b).
(3)	1972 s.41(4).
(4), (5)	1972 s.41(5).
63(1) to (3)	1972 s.260(5).
(4)	Sc Law Com Rec No. 2.
64	1972 s.31A; 1982 s.46.
65(1), (2)	1972 s.42(1).
(3)	1972 s.42(4).
(4)	1972 s.42(4) proviso.
(5)	1972 s.42(5); 1981 s.25.
66(1)	1972 s.42(2).
(2) to (5)	1972 s.42(3).
(6)	1972 s.42(2).
67(1)	1972 s.43(1).
(2)	1972 s.43(1), (2).
(3)	1972 s.43(3).
(4)	1972 s.43(2)(a).
(5)	1972 s.43(2)(b).
(6)	1972 s.43(4).
(7)	1972 s.43(5).
(8)	1972 s.43(6).
68(1)	1972 s.260(1), (2).

Provision	Derivation
68(2), (3)	1972 s.260(1).
(4) to (6)	1972 s.260(4).
(7)	1972 s.260(3).
(8)	1972 s.42(5); 1981 s.25.
69(1)	1972 s.44(1).
(2)	1972 s.45(1).
(3)	1972 s.45(2).
(4)	1972 s.45(8); drafting.
70(1)	1972 s.47(1).
(2)	1972 s.47(1); Planning (Consequential Provisions) Act 1990 (c. 11) Sch. 2 para. 27(1).
(3)	1972 s.47(6).
(4)	1972 s.47(7); drafting.
71(1)	1972 s.49(1).
(2), (3)	1972 s.49(2).
(4)	1972 s.49(3); 1991 Sch. 13 para. 16.
(5)	1972 s.49(3A); 1991 Sch. 13 para. 16.
(6)	1972 s.49(7); 1991 Sch. 8 para. 5(7).
(7)	1972 s.49(8).
(8)	1972 s.49(1A); 1981 s.26; 1991 Sch. 8 para. 5.
72(1)	1972 s.49(4).
(2) to (4)	1972 s.49(5).
(5)	1972 s.49(6).
73(1)	1972 s.260(1), (2).
(2), (3)	1972 s.260(1).
(4) to (6)	1972 s.260(4).
(7)	1972 s.260(3).
74(1)	Environment Act 1995 (c. 25) s.96(1), (3).
(2)	Environment Act 1995 (c. 25) s.96(5).
(3)	Environment Act 1995 (c. 25) s.96(6).
75(1), (2)	1972 s.50(1).
(3)	1972 s.50(2); 1991 s.49(1).
(4)	1972 s.50(2) proviso.
(5)	1972 s.50(3).
76(1)	1972 s.153(1); 1981 Sch. 2 para. 4.
(2)	1972 s.153(2).
(3)	1972 s.153(3).
(4)	1972 s.153(4); 1991 Sch. 12 para. 14.
(5)	1972 s.153(5).
77(1)	1972 s.154(1), (2).
(2)	1972 s.154(1A); Town and Country Planning (Compensation) Act 1985 (c. 19) s.2(1).
(3)	1972 s.154(3).
(4)	1972 s.154(3A); 1991 s.44(3).
78(1)	1972 s.155(1).
(2)	1972 ss.154(2), 155(2).
(3)	1972 s.155(3); 1991 Sch. 12 para. 15(a).
(4)	1972 s.155(4).
(5)	1972 ss.154(2), 155(6); 1991 Sch. 19 Pt. IV.
79(1)	1972 s.155(5); Land Registration (Scotland) Act 1979 (c. 33) s.29(2).
(2)	1972 s.155(5A); 1991 Sch. 12 para. 15(c).
80(1) to (6)	1972 s.156A; 1991 Sch. 12 para. 17.
81(1) to (7)	1972 s.156B; 1991 Sch. 12 para. 17.
82(1)	1972 s.157(2); 1991 Sch. 12 para. 18(b).
(2)	1972 s.157(3).
(3)	1972 s.157(3) proviso.
83(1)	1972 s.159(1); Sc Law Com Rec No. 3.
(2)	1972 s.159(2).
(3)	1972 s.159(3).
(4)	1972 s.159(4).

Provision	Derivation
84	Drafting.
85(1)	1972 s.145(1); 1991 Sch. 13 para. 28.
(2)	1972 s.145(2).
(3)	1972 s.145(3).
86(1)	1972 s.168(1); 1981 ss.32, 35.
(2)	1972 s.168(2).
87(1)	1972 s.167(1).
(2)	1972 s.167(2); 1981 Sch. 2 para. 6.
(3)	1972 s.167(3).
(4)	1972 s.167(4).
88(1)	1972 ss.169(1), 177(1), 178(1).
(2)	1972 ss.169(1), (7), 177(1), (2), 178(1), (2).
(3)	1972 ss.169(1), 177(1).
(4)	1972 s.178(1).
(5)	1972 s.169(4).
(6)	1972 s.169(5).
(7)	1972 s.169(6).
(8)	1972 s.178(5).
89	1972 ss.169(2), 177(2), 178(2); 1991 Sch. 12 para. 19.
90(1)	1972 ss.170(1), 177(2), 178(2); 1986 Sch. 11 para. 35(1)(a).
(2)	1972 ss.170(1), 177(2), 178(2).
(3)	1972 ss.170(2), 177(2), 178(2).
(4)	1972 ss.170(3), 177(2), 178(2); 1986 Sch. 11 para. 35(1)(b).
(5)	1972 ss.170(4), 177(2), 178(2).
(6)	1972 s.197.
91(1)	1972 ss.171(1), 177(2), 178(2).
(2)	1972 ss.171(2), 177(2), 178(2).
(3), (4)	1972 ss.171(3), 177(2), 178(2).
(5)	1972 ss.171(4), 177(2), 178(2).
92(1)	1972 ss.172(1), 177(2), 178(2); Sc Law Com Rec No. 4.
(2)	1972 ss.172(2), 177(2), (3), 178(2), (3).
(3)	1972 ss.172(3), 177(2), 178(2).
(4)	1972 ss.172(4), 177(2), 178(2).
(5)	1972 s.172(5).
93(1)	1972 ss.173(1), 177(2), 178(2); 1986 Sch. 11 para. 36; Sc Law Com Recs Nos. 4, 5.
(2)	1972 s.173(2), 177(2), 178(2).
(3)	1972 s.173(3), 177(2), 178(2); 1986 Sch. 11 para. 36.
94(1)	1972 ss.175(1), 177(2), 178(2).
(2)	1972 s.175(2), 177(2), 178(2).
(3)	1972 ss.175(3), 177(2), 178(2); 1986 Sch. 11 para. 37(1).
(4)	1972 ss.175(3A), 177(2), 178(2); 1986 Sch. 11 para. 37(1).
(5), (6)	1972 ss.175(4), 177(2), 178(2).
(7)	1972 ss.175(5), 177(2), 178(2).
(8)	1972 s.197.
95(1)	1972 ss.176(1), 177(2), 178(2).
(2)	1972 ss.176(2), 177(2), 178(2); 1991 Sch. 12 para. 20(a).
(3), (4)	1972 ss.176(3), 177(2), 178(2).
(5)	1972 ss.176(4), 177(2), 178(2).
(6)	1972 ss.176(5), 177(2), 178(2); 1991 Sch. 12 para. 20(b).
(7)	1972 s.178(4).
96(1), (2)	1973C s.49(1), (5).
(3)	1973C s.49(3), (5).
(4)	1973C s.49(4), (5).
(5)	1973C s.49(2), (5).
(6)	1973C s.49(1), (2), (5).
(7)	1973C s.49(5), (6).
97(1), (2)	1973C ss.49(5), 50(1).
(3)	1973C ss.49(5), 50(2).
(4), (5)	1973C ss.49(5), 50(3).

Provision	Derivation
97(6)	1973C ss.49(5), 50(4).
(7)	1973C ss.49(5), 50(5).
(8), (9)	1973C ss.49(5), 50(6).
(10)	1973C ss.49(5), 50(7).
(11)	1973C ss.49(5), 50(8).
98(1)	1973C ss.49(5), 78(2).
(2)	1973C ss.49(5), 80(1).
99(1)	1972 ss.170(5), 175(6), 180A; 1984T Sch. 4 para. 54(5).
(2)	Sc Law Com Rec No. 4.
100(1)	1972 s.181(1); drafting.
(2)	1972 s.181(3), (4), (5).
(3)	1972 s.181(4).
(4)	1972 s.181(4A); Local Government Finance Act 1988 (c. 41) Sch. 12 para. 9.
(5)	1972 s.181(4), (5).
(6)	1972 s.181(6); 1973C s.71(2)(b), 77(2).
101(1)	1972 s.182(1); 1973C s.72(1) Sch. 3; 1991 Sch. 17 para. 11.
(2)	1972 s.182(2).
(3)	1972 s.182(2) proviso.
(4)	1972 s.182(4).
(5)	1972 s.182(5); Crofting Reform (Scotland) Act 1976 (c. 21) Sch. 1 para. 1; Sc Law Com Rec No. 6.
102(1), (2)	1972 s.183(1).
(3)	1972 s.183(4); 1973C s.77(3).
(4)	1972 s.183(2); 1980 s.92(7).
(5)	1972 s.183(3A); 1973C s.71(3)(a).
(6)	1972 s.183(3).
(7)	1973C s.69(2).
(8)	1972 s.183(5); 1973C s.71(3)(b).
103(1)	1973C ss.64(6), 65(3); 1984 Sch. 9 para. 72(7)(b).
(2)	1973C s.64(6), 65(3); 1984 Sch. 9 para. 72(7)(b).
104(1), (2)	1972 s.184(1).
(3)	1972 s.184(2).
(4)	1972 s.184(3).
(5)	1972 s.184(4).
(6)	1972 s.184(5).
(7)	1972 s.184(6); Crofting Reform (Scotland) Act 1976 (c. 21) Sch. 1 para. 2; Sc Law Com Rec No. 6.
(8)	1973C s.64(6).
105(1), (2)	1972 s.185(1).
(3)	1972 s.185(2).
(4), (5)	1972 s.185(3).
(6)	1972 s.185(4).
(7)	1972 s.185(5); Crofting Reform (Scotland) Act 1976 (c. 21) Sch. 1 para. 3; Sc Law Com Rec No. 6.
106(1)	1972 s.188(1).
(2)	1972 s.188(2).
(3)	1972 s.188(3).
(4)	1972 s.188(4).
(5)	1972 s.188(5); Crofting Reform (Scotland) Act 1976 (c. 21) Sch. 1 para. 4; Sc Law Com Rec No. 6.
107(1), (2)	1972 s.187(1).
(3)	1972 s.187(2).
(4)	1972 s.187(3).
108(1)	1972 s.186.
(2)	1972 s.186; Housing (Scotland) Act 1974 (c. 45) Sch. 3 para. 47; Housing (Scotland) Act 1987 (c. 26) Sch. 23 para. 18.
(3)	1973C s.76(6).
(4)	1973C s.76(7).
109(1), (2)	1973C s.74(1).

Provision	Derivation
109(3)	1973C s.74(2).
(4)	1973C s.74(3); Crofting Reform (Scotland) Act 1976 (c. 21) Sch. 1 para. 8; Sc Law Com Rec No. 6.
110(1)	1973C s.75(1).
(2), (3)	1973C s.75(2).
(4)	1973C s.75(3).
(5)	1973C s.75(4).
(6)	1973C s.75(5).
(7)	1973C s.75(6).
(8)	1973C s.75(7).
111(1)	1973C s.76(1).
(2)	1973C s.76(2).
(3)	1973C s.76(3).
(4)	1973C s.76(4).
(5)	1973C s.76(5).
(6)	1973C s.76(7).
(7)	1973C s.76(9); Crofting Reform (Scotland) Act 1976 (c. 21) Sch. 1 para. 9; Sc Law Com Rec No. 6.
112(1)	1972, s.189; 1973C s.76(8); Sc Law Com Rec No. 7.
(2)	1973C s.73(1).
(3)	1973C s.73(2).
(4)	1973C s.73(2) proviso.
(5)	1973C s.73(3); Sc Law Com Rec No. 8.
113(1)	1972 s.190(1); 1973C s.72(1); 1991 Sch. 17 para. 11.
(2)	1972 s.190(2).
(3)	1972 s.190(2) proviso.
(4)	1972 s.190(3).
(5)	1972 s.190(6); Sc Law Com Rec No. 8.
114(1)	1972 s.190(4); 1973C s.73(4).
(2)	1972 s.190(5); 1973C s.73(4).
115(1)	1972 s.193(1).
(2)	1972 s.193(2).
(3)	1972 s.193(3).
(4)	1972 s.193(4); Interpretation Act 1978 (c. 30) s.25(2), Sch. 1.
(5)	1972 s.193(5).
116(1), (2)	1973C s.68(4); 1980 s.147(4).
(3)	1973C s.68(5); 1980 s.147(5).
(4)	1973C s.68(6); Crofting Reform (Scotland) Act 1976 (c. 21) Sch. 1 para. 7; Sc Law Com Rec No. 6.
117(1)	1972 s.191(1), (2).
(2)	1972 s.191(2).
118	1972 s.197.
119(1)	1972 s.192(1).
(2)	1972 s.192(2).
(3)	1972 s.192(3).
(4)	1972 s.192(4); Crofting Reform (Scotland) Act 1976 (c. 21) s.11, Sch. 1 para. 5; Sc Law Com Rec No. 6.
120(1)	1972 s.194(1); 1984T Sch. 4 para. 54(6).
(2)	1972 s.194(2); 1984 Sch. 9 para. 70(6).
(3)	1972 s.194(3).
(4)	1973C s.68(3); 1980 s.147(3).
121(1)	1972 s.195(1); 1973C s.71(4).
(2)	1972 s.195(2).
(3)	1973C s.64(9).
(4)	1973C s.67(3).
(5)	1973C s.68(3); 1980 s.147(3).
(6)	1973C s.69(3); Housing (Scotland) Act 1974 (c. 45) Sch. 3 para. 51(d); Housing (Scotland) Act 1987 (c. 26) Sch. 23 para. 19(10).
(7)	1973C s.66(3).
(8)	1972 s.195(3); 1984 Sch. 9 para. 70(7)(a).

Provision	Derivation
121(9)	1972 s.195(4)(aa), (c); 1984 Sch. 9 para. 70(7)(b).
(10)	1972 s.195(5).
(11)	1972 s.195(6).
122(1)	1972 s.196(1); Crofting Reform (Scotland) Act 1976 (c. 21) Sch. 1 para. 6; Crofters (Scotland) Act 1993 (c. 44) Sch. 6 para. 3; Sc Law Com Rec No. 6.
(2)	1972 s.196(2).
(3)	1972 s.196(3).
(4)	1972 s.196(4).
(5)	1972 s.196(5).
123(1) to (3)	1972 s.83A; 1991 s.36(1).
124(1) to (4)	1972 s.83B; 1991 s.36(1).
125(1) to (8)	1972 s.83C; 1991 s.33.
126(1) to (6)	1972 s.83D; 1991 s.33.
127(1) to (3)	1972 s.84; 1991 s.37.
128(1) to (14)	1972 s.84AA; 1991 s.37.
129(1) to (4)	1972 s.84AB; 1991 s.37.
130(1)	1972 s.85(1); 1991 s.38(1).
(2)	1972 s.85(2); 1991 s.38(1).
(3)	1972 s.85(2A); 1982 Sch. 2 para. 20(b).
131(1)	1972 s.85(2B); 1982 Sch. 2 para. 20(b); 1991 Sch. 13 para. 20(a).
(2)	1972 s.85(2D); 1982 Sch. 2 para. 20(b).
(3)	1972 s.85(3).
(4)	1972 s.85(9).
132(1)	1972 s.85(5).
(2)	1972 s.85(4)(a); 1991 Sch. 13 para. 20(b)(i).
(3)	1972 s.85(2C); 1982 Sch. 2 para. 20(b).
(4)	1972 s.85(4)(b); 1991 Sch. 13 para. 20(b)(ii).
133(1)	1972 s.85(5); 1982 Sch. 2 para. 20(c); 1991 Sch. 13 para. 20(c).
(2)	1972 s.85(5A); 1991 Sch. 13 para. 20(d).
(3)	1972 s.85(5B); 1991 Sch. 13 para. 20(d).
(4)	1972 s.85(6).
(5)	1972 s.85(6A); 1991 Sch. 13 para. 20(e).
(6)	1972 s.85(6B); 1991 Sch. 13 para.. 20(e).
(7)	1972 s.85(7); 1991 Sch. 13 para. 20(f).
(8)	1972 s.85(7A); 1991 s.38(2).
(9)	1972 s.85(7)(a).
(10)	1972 s.85(7)(b).
(11)	1972 s.85(7)(c).
134	1972 s.85(10).
135(1)	1972 s.88(1); 1991 Sch. 19 Pt. IV.
(2)	1972 s.88(1).
(3)	1972 s.88(1A); 1982 Sch. 2 para. 23(a).
(4)	1972 s.88(2).
(5)	1972 s.88(3); 1982 Sch. 2 para. 23(b).
(6), (7)	1972 s.88(4); 1982 Sch. 2 para. 23(b).
(8), (9)	1972 s.88(5); 1982 Sch. 2 para. 23(b).
(10)	1972 s.88(6); 1991 s.39.
(11)	1972 s.88(1); Sc Law Com Rec No. 9.
136(1) to (9)	1972 s.86; 1991 s.40.
137(1) to (3)	1972 s.89A; 1982 Sch. 2 para. 25; 1991 Sch. 13 para. 25.
138(1)	1972 s.89(1); 1991 Sch. 13 para. 24(a).
(2)	1972 s.89(2).
(3)	1972 s.89(3); 1991 Sch. 13 para. 24(b).
(4)	1972 s.89(4); 1982 Sch. 2 para. 24; 1991 Sch. 13 para. 24; Criminal Procedure (Consequential Provisions) (Scotland) Act 1995 (c. 40) Sch. 1 paras. 5, 6; Criminal Procedure (Scotland) Act 1995 (c. 46) s.225.
139(1) to (3)	1972 s.260(5).
(4)	1972 s.260(5) proviso; Sc Law Com Rec No. 2.

Provision	Derivation
140(1)	1972 s.87(1); 1977 s.4; 1991 s.41(1).
(2)	1972 s.87(2); 1977 s.4; 1991 s.41(1).
(3)	1972 s.87(2A); 1991 s.41(1).
(4)	1972 s.87(2B); 1991 s.41(1).
(5)	1972 s.87(2C); 1991 s.41(1).
(6)	1972 s.87(2D); 1991 s.41(1).
(7)	1972 s.87(3); 1977 s.4; 1991 s.41(1).
(8)	1972 s.87(6); 1977 s.4; 1991 Sch. 13 para. 21(c).
(9)	1972 s.87(10); 1977 s.4.
141(1)	1972 s.87(4); 1977 s.4; 1991 Sch. 13 para. 21(a).
(2)	1972 s.87(5); 1977 s.4; 1991 Sch. 13 para. 21(b).
(3)	1972 s.87(7); 1977 s.4(7).
(4)	1972 s.87(9); 1977 s.4; 1991 Sch. 13 para. 21(d).
142(1) to (3)	1972 s.260(5).
(4)	1972 s.260(5) proviso; Sc Law Com Rec No. 2.
143(1)	1972 s.166(1); 1977 s.5(2)(a); 1991 Sch. 13 para. 29.
(2)	1972 s.166(2); 1991 Sch. 13 para. 30.
(3)	1972 s.166(4).
(4)	1972 s.166(5).
(5)	1972 s.166(6); 1977 s.5(2)(d); 1991 s.41(3).
(6)	1972 s.168(1).
(7)	1972 s.168(2).
144(1)	1972 s.87(8); 1991 s.41(2).
(2)	1972 s.87(8A); 1991 s.41(2).
(3)	1972 s.87(8B); 1991 s.41(2).
(4)	1972 s.87(8C); 1991 s.41(2).
(5)	1972 s.87(8D); 1991 s.41(2).
(6)	1972 s.87(8E); 1991 s.41(2).
145(1) to (13)	1972 s.87AA; 1991 s.34.
146(1) to (3)	1972 s.260A; 1991 s.35.
147(1), (2)	1972 s.87A(1), (2); 1982 s.44; 1991 Sch. 13 para. 22.
148(1)	1972 s.100(1); 1981 s.28; 1991 Sch. 8 para. 9.
(2)	1972 s.100(2); 1981 s.28.
(3)	1972 s.100(3); 1981 s.28.
(4)	1972 s.100(6); 1981 s.28.
(5)	1972 s.100(7); 1981 s.28.
149(1), (2)	1972 s.100(4); 1981 s.28.
(3), (4)	1972 s.100(5); 1981 s.28.
150(1) to (7)	1972 s.90; 1991 s.42(1).
151(1) to (4)	1972 s.90A; 1991 s.42(1).
152(1) to (8)	1972 s.90B; 1991 s.42(1).
153(1), (2)	1972 s.90C; 1991 s.42(1).
154(1)	1972 s.91(2); 1991 Sch. 13 para. 26(a); Sc Law Com Rec No. 10.
(2)	Sc Law Com Rec No. 10.
(3)	1972 s.91(2); 1991 Sch. 13 para. 26(a); Sc Law Com Rec No. 10.
(4)	1972 s.91(2).
(5)	1972 s.91(6).
155(1)	1972 s.91(4); 1981MP Sch. 2 para. 24(c).
(2)	1972 s.91(7); 1991 Sch. 13 para. 26(c).
156(1) to (4)	1972 s.91A; 1991 s.43(1).
157(1) to (3)	1972 s.91B; 1991 s.43(1).
158(1) to (7)	1972 s.91C; 1991 s.43(1).
159	1972 s.57.
160(1), (2)	1972 s.58(1).
(3)	1972 s.58(1); Town and Country Amenities Act 1974 (c. 32) s.11(1).
(4)	1972 s.58(2); 1991 Sch. 12 para. 12.
(5)	1972 s.58(3).
(6)	1972 s.58(6); Town and Country Amenities Act 1974 (c. 32) s.11(2)(a).
(7)	1972 s.58(10); 1986 Sch. 12 Pt. II.

Provision	Derivation
161(1)	1972 s.58(4); 1981MP Sch. 2 para. 22(1)(a); 1984P s.2(6).
(2)	1972 s.58(4); Land Registration (Scotland) Act 1979 (c. 33) s.29(2).
(3)	1972 s.58(5).
(4)	1972 s.58(5); 1981MP Sch. 2 para. 22(1)(b).
162(1)	1972 s.58(7).
(2)	1972 s.58(7); Interpretation Act 1978 (c. 30) s.17(2)(a).
(3)	1972 s.58(8); Interpretation Act 1978 (c. 30) s.17(2)(a).
(4)	1972 s.58(7), (9); Interpretation Act 1978 (c. 30) s.17(2)(a).
163(1)	1972 s.59(1).
(2)	1972 s.59(2).
(3)	1972 s.59(3).
164(1)	1972 s.260(1), (2)(c).
(2)	1972 s.260(1), (2)(c); 1986 Sch. 11 para. 51.
(3)	1972 s.260(1).
(4)	1972 s.260(3).
165(1)	1972 s.163.
(2), (3)	1972 s.168.
166(1)	1972 s.164(1), (2).
(2)	1972 s.164(2).
(3)	1972 s.164(3).
(4)	1972 s.164(4).
(5)	1972 s.164(5).
167(1)	1972 s.60(1); Town and Country Amenities Act 1974 (c. 32) s.11(2)(b); Town and Country Planning (Amendment) Act 1985 (c. 52) s.2(2).
(2)	1972 s.60(1).
(3)	1972 s.60(1A); Town and Country Planning (Amendment) Act 1985 (c. 52) s.2(3).
(4)	1972 s.60(2).
(5)	1972 s.60(3).
168(1), (2)	1972 s.99(1).
(3)	1972 s.99(2); 1991 s.54(2).
(4)	1972 s.60(3).
169(1)	1972 s.99(3); 1986 Sch. 11 Pt. II para. 46; 1991 s.54(2)(b)(ii).
(2)	1972 ss.85(2), 99(3); 1991 s.54(2)(b)(i).
(3)	1972 ss.85(2A), 99(3); 1986 Sch. 11 para. 46.
(4)	1972 ss.85(2B), 99(3); 1986 Sch. 11 para. 46; 1991 Sch. 13 para. 20.
(5)	1972 ss.85(2C), 99(3); 1986 Sch. 11 para. 46.
(6)	1972 ss.85(2D), 99(3); 1986 Sch. 11 para. 46.
(7)	1972 ss.85(3), 99(3).
(8)	1972 ss.85(4)(a), 99(3); 1991 Sch. 13 para. 20.
(9)	1972 s.85(5), 99(3).
(10)	1972 s.99(4).
170(1), (2)	1972 ss.88(1), 99(5).
(3)	1972 ss.88(1A), 99(5); 1982 Sch. 2 para. 23(a).
(4)	1972 ss.88(2), 99(5).
(5)	1972 ss.88(3), 99(5); 1982 Sch. 2 para. 23(b).
(6), (7)	1972 ss.88(4), 99(5); 1982 Sch. 2 para. 23(b).
(8), (9)	1972 ss.88(5), 99(5); 1982 Sch. 2 para. 23(b).
(10)	1972 s.99(6); 1991 s.54(2)(c).
171(1)	1972 s.98(1); Town and Country Amenities Act 1974 (c. 32) s.11(3).
(2)	1972 s.98(1); Town and Country Amenities Act 1974 (c. 32) s.11(3); 1991 s.54(1)(a).
(3)	1972 s.98(1); Town and Country Amenities Act 1974 (c. 32) s.11(3).
(4)	1972 s.98(2); Town and Country Amenities Act 1974 (c. 32) s.11(4); Criminal Procedure (Consequential Provisions) (Scotland) Act 1995 (c. 40) Sch. 1 paras. 5, 6; Criminal Procedure (Scotland) Act 1995 (c. 46) s.225.
172(1)	1972 s.59A(1); Town and Country Amenities Act 1974 (c. 32) s.9.
(2)	1972 s.59A(2); Town and Country Amenities Act 1974 (c. 32) s.9.
(3)	1972 s.59A(3); Town and Country Amenities Act 1974 (c. 32) s.9.

Provision	Derivation
172(4)	1972 s.98(4); Town and Country Amenities Act 1974 (c. 32) s.11(6).
173(1)	1972 s.59A(4); Town and Country Amenities Act 1974 (c. 32) s.9.
(2)	1972 s.59A(5); Town and Country Amenities Act 1974 (c. 32) s.9.
(3)	1972 s.59A(5); Town and Country Amenities Act 1974 (c. 32) s.9.
(4)	1972 s.59A(6); Town and Country Amenities Act 1974 (c. 32) s.9.
174(1), (2)	1972 s.59A(8); Town and Country Amenities Act 1974 (c. 32) s.9.
(3)	1972 s.59A(9); Town and Country Amenities Act 1974 (c. 32) s.9.
175	1972 s.59A(7); Town and Country Amenities Act 1974 (c. 32) s.9.
176(1) to (8)	1972 s.99A; 1991 s.54(3).
177(1) to (3)	1972 s.99B; 1991 s.54(3).
178(1) to (4)	1972 s.99C; 1991 s.54(3).
179(1)	1972 s.63(1); 1982 Sch. 2 para 17(a); 1986 Sch. 11 para. 32(1).
(2)	1972 s.63(1A); 1982 Sch. 2 para. 17(a).
(3)	1972 s.63(1B); 1982 Sch. 2 para. 17(a); 1986 Sch. 11 para. 32(2).
(4)	1972 s.63(1C); 1982 Sch. 2 para. 17(a); 1986 Sch. 11 para. 32(2).
(5)	1972 s.63(2).
(6)	1972 s.63(3).
180(1)	1972 s.63A(1); 1982 Sch. 2 para. 18; 1986 Sch. 11 para. 33(1).
(2)	1972 s.63A(2); 1982 Sch. 2 para. 18.
(3)	1972 s.63A(3); 1982 Sch. 2 para. 18.
(4)	1972 s.63A(4); 1982 Sch. 2 para. 18.
(5)	1972 s.63A(5); 1982 Sch. 2 para. 18; 1986 Sch. 11 para. 33(1).
(6)	1972 s.63A(6); 1982 Sch. 2 para. 18.
(7)	1972 s.63A(7); 1986 Sch. 11 para. 34(1).
181(1), (2)	1972 s.87A(1), (2); 1982 s.44; 1991 Sch. 13 para. 22.
182(1)	1972 s.61(1).
(2)	1972 s.61(2).
(3)	1972 ss.61(2)(c), 180(1).
183(1) to (3)	1972 s.61(3); Town and Country Amenities Act 1974 (c. 32) s.3(2).
(4)	1972 s.61(4).
(5)	1972 s.61(5).
(6)	1972 s.61(8).
184	1972 s.62.
185(1)	1972 s.165.
(2)	1972 s.168(1); 1981 s.32.
(3)	1972 s.168(2).
186(1), (2)	1972 s.101(1).
(3)	1972 s.101(2); 1986 Sch. 11 para. 44; 1991 Sch. 13 para. 27.
(4)	1972 s.101(3).
(5)	1972 s.101(3) proviso.
187(1) to (6)	1972 s.101A; 1991 s.56.
188(1)	1972 s.109(1); 1973 Sch. 23 para. 23.
(2)	1972 s.109(2).
(3)	1973 s.171C; 1994 s.171.
189(1)	1972 s.102(1); 1980 s.92(4).
(2)	1972 s.102(1A); 1980 s.92(4).
(3)	1972 s.102(1B); 1980 s.92(4).
(4)	1972 s.102(1C); 1980 s.92(4).
(5)	1972 s.102(2).
(6)	1972 s.102(3); 1973 Sch. 23 para. 21(a); 1994 Sch. 4 para. 10.
(7)	1972 s.102(4).
(8)	1973 s.171C; 1994 s.171.
190(1)	1972 s.103(1); 1980 s.122(2).
(2)	1980 s.122(1).
(3)	1972 s.103(2).
(4)	1972 s.103(2) proviso.
(5)	1972 s.103(3).
(6), (7)	1980 s.122(3).
191(1), (2)	1972 s.113(1).

Provision	Derivation
191(3)	1972 s.113(3).
(4) to (6)	1972 s.113(5).
(7)	1972 s.113(6); Sc Law Com Rec No. 11.
(8)	1972 s.113(6).
(9)	1972 s.113(7).
(10)	1972 s.113(8).
192(1), (2)	1980 s.122(6).
193(1)	1972 s.114(2).
(2)	1972 s.114(1).
(3)	1972 s.114(1), (7).
(4)	1972 s.114(5).
(5)	1972 s.114(6).
194(1)	1972 s.108(1).
(2)	1972 s.108(2); 1984T Sch. 4 para. 54(3).
(3)	1972 s.108(3).
(4)	1972 s.108(4).
(5)	1972 s.108(5).
195(1) to (3)	1972 s.278.
196(1)	1972 s.117(2).
(2)	1972 s.117(1).
(3)	1972 s.117(1) proviso; 1984T Sch. 4 para. 54(4).
(4)	1972 s. 117(3).
(5)	1972 s.117(4).
(6)	1972 s.117(4) proviso.
(7)	1972 s.117(5).
197(1)	1972 s.118(1).
(2)	1972 s.118(1A); National Health Service and Community Care Act 1990 (c. 19) Sch. 8 para. 7.
(3)	1972 s.118(3).
(4)	1972 s.118(4).
(5)	1972 s.118(5).
198(1)	1972 s.119(1).
(2)	1972 s.119(2).
199(1)	1972 s.120(1).
(2)	1972 s.120(3).
(3), (4)	1972 s.120(4).
200(1)	1972 s.121(1).
(2)	1972 s.121(2).
(3)	1972 s.121(3).
(4)	1972 s.121(4).
201(1)	1972 s.122(1).
(2)	1972 s.122(2).
(3)	1972 s.122(3).
202(1)	1972 s.198(1); 1980 Sch. 32 para. 19(4); 1984 Sch. 9 para. 70(8)(a).
(2), (3)	1972 s.198(2); 1984 Sch. 9 para. 70(8)(b).
(4)	1972 s.198(3); 1984 Sch. 9 para. 70(8)(c).
(5)	1972 s.198(4); 1984 Sch. 9 para. 70(8)(d).
(6)	1972 s.198(5); 1984 Sch. 9 para. 70(8)(d).
203(1)	1972 s.201(1); 1984 Sch. 9 para. 70(10)(a).
(2)	1972 s.201(2); 1981MP Sch. 2 para. 27(1)(a); 1984 Sch. 9 para. 70(10)(b).
(3)	1972 s.201(3); 198MP Sch. 2 para. 27(1)(b); 1984 Sch. 9 para. 70(10)(b), (c).
(4)	1972 s.201(3).
(5)	1972 s.201(4); 1984 Sch. 9 para. 70(10)(d).
(6)	1972 s.201(8); 1981MP Sch. 2 para. 27(1)(c); 1984 Sch. 9 para. 70(10)(d).
(7)	1972 s.201(10); 1981MP Sch. 2 para. 27(1)(e); 1984 Sch. 9 para. 70(10)(f).
(8)	1972 s.201(11); 1981MP Sch. 2 para. 27(1)(e); 1984 Sch. 9 para. 70(10)(g).
(9)	1972 s.201(9); 1973 Sch. 23 para. 27; 1981MP Sch. 2 para. 27(1)(d), (2); 1984 Sch. 9 para. 70(10)(e); 1994 Sch. 4 para. 11.
204(1)	1972 s.201(5); 1984 Sch. 9 para. 70(10)(d).
(2)	1972 s.201(6).

Provision	Derivation
204(3)	1972 ss.167(1), 201(7).
(4)	1972 ss.167(4), 201(7).
(5)	1972 ss.168(1), 201(7).
(6)	1972 ss.168(2), 201(7).
205(1)	1972 s.202(1); 1984 Sch. 9 para. 70(11).
(2)	1972 s.202(2); 1984 Sch. 9 para. 70(11).
(3)	1972 s.202(3); 1984T Sch. 4 para. 54(7); 1984 Sch. 9 para. 70(11).
(4)	1972 s.202(4); 1984 Sch. 9 para. 70(11).
(5)	1972 s.202(5); 1994 Sch. 4 para. 12.
206(1)	1972 s.203(1).
(2)	1972 s.203(2).
207(1)	1972 s.198A(1); 1981MP Sch. 2 para. 25; 1984 Sch. 9 para. 70(9)(a).
(2)	1972 s.198A(2); 1981MP Sch. 2 para. 25; 1984 Sch. 9 para. 70(9)(b).
(3)	1972 s.198A(3); 1981MP Sch. 2 para. 25; 1984 Sch. 9 para. 70(9)(c).
(4)	1972 s.198A(4); 1981MP Sch. 2 para. 25; 1984 Sch. 9 para. 70(9)(c).
(5)	1972 s.198A(5); 1981MP Sch. 2 para. 25; 1984 Sch. 9 para. 70(9)(d).
208(1)	1972 s.199(1).
(2)	1972 s.199(2).
(3)	1972 s.199(3).
209	Drafting.
210(1)	1972 s.210A(1); 1982 s.45(1); 1984 Sch. 9 para. 70(18)(a).
(2)	1972 s.210A(2); 1982 s.45(2); 1984 Sch. 9 para. 70(18)(b).
211(1)	1972 s.208(1); 1981MP Sch. 3 para. 19(a); 1984 Sch. 9 para. 70(16)(a).
(2)	1972 s.208(2); 1981MP Sch. 3 para. 19(b); 1984 Sch. 9 para. 16(b).
212(1)	1972 s.209(1); 1984T Sch. 4 para. 54(8); 1984 Sch. 9 para. 70(17)(a).
(2)	1972 s.209(1); 1984T Sch. 4 para. 54(8).
(3)	1972 s.209(2); 1984T Sch. 4 para. 54(8); 1984 Sch. 9 para. 70(17)(b); New Roads and Street Works Act 1991 (c. 22) Sch. 8 para. 104(a).
(4)	1972 s.209(2); 1984T Sch. 4 para. 54(8); New Roads and Street Works Act 1991 (c. 22) Sch. 8 para. 104(b).
(5)	1972 s.209(3); 1984T Sch. 4 para. 54(8).
(6)	1972 s.209(4); 1984T Sch. 4 para. 54(8).
(7)	1972 s.209(5); 1984T Sch. 4 para. 54(8).
(8)	1972 s.209(6); 1984T Sch. 4 para. 54(8).
213(1) to (3)	Mineral Workings Act 1951 (c. 60) s.32(1); 1984 Sch. 9 para. 41.
(4)	Mineral Workings Act 1951 (c. 60) s.32(2); 1984 Sch. 9 para. 41; Sc Law Com Rec No. 12.
(5)	Mineral Workings Act 1951 (c. 60) s.32(3); 1984 Sch. 9 para. 41.
214(1)	1972 s.275(1); Airports Act 1986 (c. 31) Sch. 2 para. 1(1); Electricity Act 1989 (c. 29) Sch. 18.
(2)	1972 s.275(1); Airports Act 1986 (c. 31) Sch. 2 para. 1(1).
(3) to (5)	Post Office Act 1969 (c. 48) Sch. 4 para. 93(1)(xxxiv); 1972 Sch. 21 Pt. II; 1981MP Sch. 3 para. 13; British Telecommunications Act 1981 (c. 38) Sch. 3 para. 10(2)(d); Civil Aviation Act 1982 (c. 16) Sch. 2 para. 4; 1986 Sch. 7 Pt. II para. 8; Gas Act 1995 (c. 45) Sch. 4 para. 2(1)(xix).
(6), (7)	Electricity Act 1989 (c. 29) Sch. 16 paras. 1(1)(xxiii), (xxvi), 2(2)(d), (7).
215(1), (2)	1972 s.211.
(3)	Post Office Act 1969 (c. 48) Sch. 4 para. 93(4); 1972 Sch. 21 Pt. II; Civil Aviation Act 1982 (c. 16) Sch. 2 para. 5.
(4)	Post Office Act 1969 (c. 48) Sch. 4 para. 93(4); Civil Aviation Act 1982 (c. 16) Sch. 2 para. 5, Sch. 13 Pt. III para. 1.
(5)	Post Office Act 1969 (c. 48) Sch. 4 para. 93(4); Civil Aviation Act 1982 (c. 16) Sch. 2 para. 5.
216(1)	1972 s.212(1).
(2)	1972 s.212(1), (2).
(3)	1972 s.212(2)(a).
(4)	1972 s.212(2)(b); Gas Act 1986 (c. 44) Sch. 7 para. 13; Airports Act 1986 (c. 31) Sch. 4 para. 2.
(5)	1972 s.212(3).
(6)	Post Office Act 1969 (c. 48) Sch. 9 para. 27(11); 1972 s.212(3).

Provision	Derivation
216(7)	Post Office Act 1969 (c. 48) Sch. 4 para. 92(2).
(8)	Civil Aviation Act 1982 (c. 16) Sch. 2 para. 7(1).
217(1)	1972 s.213(1); Airports Act 1986 (c. 31) Sch. 2 para. 1(2), Sch. 6.
(2)	Electricity Act 1989 (c. 29) Sch. 16 para. 3(2)(e); Gas Act 1995 (c. 45) Sch. 4 para. 2(10).
(3)	1972 s.213(2).
218(1)	1972 s.214(1).
(2)	1972 s.214(2).
(3)	1972 s.214(5).
(4)	Civil Aviation Act 1982 (c. 16) Sch. 2 para. 7(2).
219	1972 s.214(4).
220(1), (2)	1972 s.215(1).
(3)	1972 ss.37(3); 215(2).
221	1972 s.216; Sc Law Com Rec No. 13.
222	1972 s.217; Sc Law Com Recs Nos. 13, 14.
223(1), (2)	1972 s.218; 1991 Sch. 17 para. 12.
224(1) to (3)	1972 s.219(1).
(4)	1972 s.219(2).
(5)	1972 s.219(3).
(6)	1972 s.219(4).
(7)	1972 s.219(5).
(8)	1972 s.219(6).
225(1) to (3)	1972 s.219(1), (7); 1984T Sch. 4 para. 54(10).
(4)	1972 s.219(2), (7); 1984T Sch. 4 para. 54(10).
(5)	1972 s.219(3), (7); 1984T Sch. 4 para. 54(10).
(6)	1972 s.219(4), (7); 1984T Sch. 4 para. 54(10).
(7)	1972 s.219(5), (7); 1984T Sch. 4 para. 54(10).
(8)	1972 s.219(6), (7); 1984T Sch. 4 para. 54(10).
226(1)	1972 s.221(1).
(2)	1972 s.221(2).
(3)	1972 s.221(3).
(4)	1972 s.221(4).
(5)	1972 s.221(5).
(6)	1972 s.221(6).
(7), (8)	1972 s.221(7); 1984T Sch. 4 para. 54(11).
227(1)	1972 s.220(1).
(2)	1972 s.220(2).
(3)	1972 s.220(2); Sc Law Com Rec No. 15.
(4)	1972 s.220(2).
(5)	1972 s.220(3).
(6)	1972 s.219(7); 1984T Sch. 4 para. 54(10).
228(1)	1972 s.222.
(2) to (6)	1972 s.223(2).
229(1) to (3)	1972 s.223(1).
230(1)	1972 s.224(1).
(2)	1972 s.224(2).
(3), (4)	1972 s.224(3).
(5)	1972 s.224(4).
(6)	1972 s.224(5).
(7)	1972 s.224(6).
(8)	1972 s.224(7).
231(1)	1972 s.225(1).
(2)	1972 s.225(2).
(3)	1972 s.225(3).
(4)	1972 s.225(4).
(5)	1972 s.225(5).
(6), (7)	1972 s.225(6).
(8), (9)	1972 s.225(7).
(10)	1972 s.225(8).
(11)	1972 s.225(2) proviso.

Provision	Derivation
232(1)	1972 s.226(1).
(2)	1972 s.226(2).
(3)	1972 ss.219(7), 226(2); 1984T Sch. 4 para. 54(10).
(4)	1972 s.226(3).
(5), (6)	1972 s.226(4).
(7)	1972 s.226(5).
233(1)	1972 s.227(1); 1981 Sch. 2 para. 7; 1984T Sch. 4 para. 54(10).
(2), (3)	1972 s.227(2); 1984T Sch. 4 para. 54(10).
(4), (5)	1972 s.227(3); 1984T Sch. 4 para. 54(10).
(6)	1972 s.227(4).
(7)	1972 s.227(5).
(8)	1972 s.227(6).
234(1), (2)	1972 s.228(1).
(3)	1972 s.228(2).
(4)	1972 s.228(3).
235(1) to (4)	1972 s.229.
236	1972 s.230.
237(1)	1972 s.231(1); 1986 Sch. 6 Pt. IV para. 4.
(2)	1972 s.231(2); 1981 Sch. 2 para. 8; 1986 Sch. 11 para. 50(b).
(3)	1972 s.231(3); 1982 s.47(a), (c), Sch. 2 para. 35(a), (b); 1986 Sch. 7 para. 2; 1991 Sch. 13 para. 33.
(4)	1972 s.231(4).
238(1)	1972 s.232(1).
(2)	1972 s.232(2).
(3)	1972 s.232(3), (4); 1982 Sch. 2 para. 36; 1986 Sch. 6 Pt. IV para. 5.
(4)	1972 s.232(1).
(5)	1972 s.232(1), (3); 1982 Sch. 2 para. 36; 1986 Sch. 6 Pt. IV para. 5.
(6)	1972 s.232(4); 1986 Sch. 6 Pt. IV para. 5.
239(1)	1972 s.233(1).
(2)	1972 s.233(2).
(3)	1972 s.233(1), (2); Sc Law Com Rec No. 16.
(4)	1972 s.233(3).
(5)	1972 s.233(4).
(6)	1972 s.233(4) proviso.
(7)	1972 s.233(5).
(8)	1972 s.233(6).
(9), (10)	1972 s.233(7).
240	1972 s.235.
241(1)	1972 s.236(1).
(2)	1972 s.236(2).
242(1)	1972 ss.253(7), 255; 1984P s.6(1).
(2), (3)	1972 s.253(7).
(4)	1984P s.4(1).
243(1)	1972 s.253(3).
(2)	1984P s.3(1).
(3)	1984P s.3(2).
(4)	1984P s.3(3).
(5)	1984P s.3(4).
(6),(7)	1984P s.3(5).
244(1), (2)	1984P s.3(6).
(3), (4)	1984P s.3(7).
(5), (6)	1984P s.3(9).
245(1)	1972 s.253(1).
(2)	1972 s.253(2); 1981 Sch. 2 para. 9; 1986 Sch. 7 Pt. 2 para. 3; 1991 Sch. 13 para. 37.
(3), (4)	1972 s.253(5).
(5)	1972 s.253(6).
246(1)	1972 s.254(1); 1991 s.49(2).
(2)	1972 s.254(1).
(3)	1972 s.254(1A); 1991 s.49(3).

Provision	Derivation
246(4)	1972 s.254(1B); 1991 s.49(3).
(5)	1972 s.254(2).
(6)	1972 s.254(3).
247	1972 s.255(1); 1991 Sch. 12 para. 29.
248(1)	1984P s.1(1); 1991 Sch. 13 para. 47(2).
(2)	1984P s.1(2); 1991 sch. 13 para. 47(3).
(3)	1984P s.1(3).
(4)	1984P s.1(4); 1991 Sch. 13 para. 47(4).
(5)	1984P s.1(5); 1991 Sch. 13 para. 47(5).
(6)	1984P s.1(7); 1991 Sch. 13 para. 47(6).
(7)	1984P s.1(6).
249(1)	1984P s.2(1).
(2)	1984P s.2(2).
(3), (4)	1984P s.2(3).
(5)	1984P s.2(4).
(6)	1984P s.2(5).
(7)	1984P s.2(5), (6).
250(1)	1984P s.5(1).
(2)	1984P s.5(2).
(3)	1984P s.5(3).
(4)	1984P s.5(5).
(6)	1984P s.5(6).
251(1)	Building Restrictions (War-Time Contraventions) Act 1946 (c. 35) ss.1(2), 7(6).
(2)	Building Restrictions (War-Time Contraventions) Act 1946 (c. 35) ss.1(2), 7(6), 8(3).
(3)	Building Restrictions (War-Time Contraventions) Act 1946 (c. 35) ss.2(1) to (3).
(4)	Building Restrictions (War-Time Contraventions) Act 1946 (c. 35) s.4(1).
(5)	Drafting.
(6)	Building Restrictions (War-Time Contraventions) Act 1946 (c. 35) ss.1(2), (3), (5), 2(1), 4(1), 7(1), (6), 8(3), (5); Statute Law (Repeals) Act 1989 (c. 43) Sch. 2 para. 11.
(7)	Building Restrictions (War-Time Contraventions) Act 1946 (c. 35) s.7(3); Sc Law Com Rec No. 17
(8)	Building Restrictions (War-Time Contraventions) Act 1946 (c. 35) ss.7(5), 8(5).
252(1)	1980 s.87(1).
(2)	1980 s.87(3); 1991 Sch. 13 para. 45.
(3)	1980 s.87(4).
(4), (5)	1980 s.87(6).
253	1972 s.240.
254(1), (2)	1972 s.241.
255(1)	1972 s.242(1); 1973 Sch. 14 para. 89; 1984 Sch. 9 para. 70(19); 1994 Sch. 4 para. 13.
(2)	1972 s.242(2); 1973 s.172(2); 1991 Sch. 13 para. 35; Sc Law Com Rec No. 18.
(3)	Drafting.
256(1), (2)	1972 s.243; 1973 Sch. 23 para. 29; 1994 Sch. 4 para. 14.
257(1)	1972 s.244(1), (2).
(2)	1972 s.244(1); 1991 Sch. 12 para. 23(a).
(3)	1972 s.244(3).
(4)	1972 s.244(4).
(5)	1972 s.275(1).
258	1972 s.246.
259(1)	Mineral Workings Act 1951 (c. 60) s.40(6); 1972 s.247(1); 1991 Sch. 12 para. 26, Sch. 13 para. 36.
(2)	1972 s.247(2).
260	1972 s.249; 1980 s.87(7).
261(1)	1972 s.250(1); 1984 Sch. 9 para. 70(20).
(2)	1972 s.250(2).

Provision	Derivation
261(3)	1972 s.250(3); 1973 Sch. 23 para. 30.
(4)	1972 s.250(4).
262(1)	1972 s.251(1); 1991 Sch. 8 para. 9.
(2)	1972 s.251(1), (2).
(3), (4)	1972 s.251(3).
263(1)	1972 s.256(1).
(2)	1972 s.256(2).
(3)	1972 s.256(3).
(4)	1972 s.258.
(5)	1980 s.149(10).
264(1), (2)	1972 s.262C(3), (4); 1986 Sch. 11 para. 38; Natural Heritage (Scotland) Act 1991 (c. 28) s.6(8).
265(1)	1972 s.267(1).
(2)	1972 s.267(2).
(3)	1972 s.267(3).
(4)	1972 s.267(4).
(5)	1972 s.267(4) proviso (i).
(6)	1972 s.267(4) proviso (ii).
(7)	1972 s.267(5).
265(8)	1972 s.267(6); Criminal Procedure (Consequential Provisions) (Scotland) Act 1995 (c. 40) Sch. 1 paras. 5, 6; Criminal Procedure (Scotland) Act 1995 (c. 46) s.225.
(9)	1972 s.267(7); 1986 Sch. 11 para. 39.
(10)	1972 s.267(7A); 1986 Sch. 11 para. 39.
(11)	1972 s.267(7B); 1986 Sch. 11 para. 39.
(12)	1972 s.267(8); Debtors (Scotland) Act 1987 (c. 18) Sch. 6 para. 15.
(13)	1972 s.267(9); 1986 Sch. 11 para. 58.
266(1), (2)	1972 s.267A; 1986 Sch. 11 para. 40(1).
267(1) to (3)	1972 s.267B; 1986 Sch. 11 para. 41.
268(1)	1972 s.268.
269(1)	1972 s.265(1); 1982 Sch. 2 para. 40; 1991 Sch. 13 para. 38.
(2)	1972 s.265(2A); 1977 s.5(3).
(3)	1972 s.265(5).
(4)	1972 s.265(6); 1991 Sch. 13 para. 38(f).
(5)	1972 s.265(7).
(6)	1972 s.265(8).
270(1)	1972 s.266(1); 1991 Sch. 13 para. 39.
(2)	1972 s.266(2); 1982 Sch. 2 para. 41; Criminal Procedure (Consequential Provisions) (Scotland) Act 1995 (c. 40) Sch. 1 paras. 5, 6; Criminal Procedure (Scotland) Act 1995 (c. 46) s.225.
(3)	1972 s.266(3).
(4)	1972 s.266(3); 1991 Sch. 13 para. 39.
(5)	1972 s.266(3); Criminal Procedure (Consequential Provisions) (Scotland) Act 1995 (c. 40) Sch. 1 para. 2.
(6)	1972 s.266(4); 1991 s.43(2).
(7)	1972 s.266(5).
(8), (9)	1972 s.266(6).
271(1)	1972 s.269(1).
(2)	1972 s.269(2).
(3)	1972 s.269(3).
272(1)	1972 s.270(1); 1977 s.5(4)(a).
(2)	1972 s.270(1); 1977 s.5(4)(a); 1986 Sch. 11 para. 52.
(3)	1972 s.270(1); 1977 s.5(4)(a).
(4)	1972 s.270(2); Criminal Procedure (Consequential Provisions) (Scotland) Act 1995 (c. 40) Sch. 1 paras. 5, 6; Criminal Procedure (Scotland) Act 1995 (c. 46) s.225.
(5)	1972 s.270(3); Criminal Procedure (Consequential Provisions) (Scotland) Act 1995 (c. 40) Sch. 1 para. 2.
(6)	1972 s.270(4); 1977 s.5(4)(b).
273(1), (2)	1972 s.271.
274(1)	1972 s.272(1).
(2)	1972 s.272(2).

Provision	Derivation
274(3)	1972 s.272(3).
(4)	1972 s.272(4).
(5)	1972 s.272(5).
(6)	1972 s.272(6).
(7)	1972 s.272(7); 1982 Sch. 2 para. 42.
275(1)	1972 s.273(1); 1991 Sch. 17 para. 18.
(2), (3)	1972 s.273(2); 1980 s.87(5).
(4)	1972 ss.4A(5); 273(4); 1986 Sch. 6 Pt. IV para. 6(a), Sch. 9 Pt. II para. 18(2); 1994 s.33(1).
(5)	1972 ss.4A(5), 273(5); 1981MP Sch. 3 para. 22; 1986 Sch. 6 Pt. IV para. 6(b); 1994 s.33(1).
(6)	1972 s.273(6).
(7)	1972 Sch. 20.
(8)	1972 s.273(3).
276	1972 s.274.
277(1)	1972 ss.251(1A), 275(1); 1973 Sch. 23 para. 32(a); 1980 Sch. 32 para. 19(5); 1981 Sch. 2 para. 11; 1984 Sch. 9 para. 70(21); 1986 Sch. 7 Pt. II para. 6(c);1991 s.55, Schs. 8, 12, 13; 1994 Sch. 4 para. 15; Gas Act 1995 (c. 45) Sch. 4 para. 1; Sc Law Com Rec No. 19.
(2), (3)	1972 s.275(2).
(4) to(6)	1972 s.275(3) to (5).
(7) to (10)	1972 s.275(7) to (10).
278(1), (2)	Drafting.
(3), (4)	1972 s.281(3).
Sch. 1	
paras. 1, 2	1972 Sch. 5 para. 2.
para. 3	1972 Sch. 5 para. 3.
para. 4	1972 Sch. 5 para. 4.
para. 5	1972 Sch. 5 para. 5.
paras. 6, 7	1972 Sch. 5, para. 5A; 1977 s.5(5).
para. 8	1972 Sch. 5 para. 6.
para. 9	1972 Sch. 5 para. 7.
Sch. 2	
para. 1	1972 s.20(2).
para. 2	1972 s.20(3).
para. 3	1972 s.20(4).
para. 4	1972 s.20(7).
Sch. 3	
para. 1	1972 s.41A; 1981 s.24; 1991 Sch. 8 para. 4.
para. 2	1972 s.27A(1) to (8), (9), (19); 1981 s.22; 1991 Sch. 8 para. 2(a),(b).
para. 3	1972 s.27A(9) to (12), (19); 1981 s.22.
para. 4	1972 s.27A(13) to (16), (19); 1981 s.22.
para. 5	1972 s.27A(17); 1981 s.22.
para. 6	1972 s.27A(18); 1981 s.22; 1991 Sch. 8 para. 2(c).
para. 7	1972 s.42(5); 1981 s.25.
para. 8	1972 s.42(6); 1981 s.25.
Sch. 4	
para. 1	1972 Sch. 7 para. 1; drafting.
para. 2	1972 Sch. 7 para. 2; 1986 Sch. 11 para. 34(2); 1991 s.50(2), Sch. 13 para. 41(1), Sch. 19 Pt. IV; Environment Act 1995 (c. 25) Sch. 22 para. 16; Sc Law Com Rec No. 20.
para. 3	1972 Sch. 7 para. 3; 1991 Sch. 13 para. 41(3).
para. 4	1972 Sch. 7 para. 3A; 1986 Sch. 11 para. 42; 1991 Sch. 13 para. 41(3).
para. 5	1972 Sch. 7 para. 4.
para. 6	1972 Sch. 7 para. 5; 1986 Sch. 11 paras. 40(2), 43.
para. 7	1972 Sch. 7 para. 6.
para. 8	1972 Sch. 7 para. 7; Tribunals and Inquiries Act 1992 (c. 53) Sch. 3 para. 7(b).
Sch. 5	
para. 1	1972 Sch. 6A para. 1; 1986 Sch. 6 Pt. III.
para. 2	1972 Sch. 6A para. 2(2); 1986 Sch. 6 Pt. III.
para. 3	1972 Sch. 6A para. 3; 1986 Sch. 6 Pt. III.
para. 4	1972 Sch. 6A para. 4; 1986 Sch. 6 Pt. III; 1991 Sch. 11 para. 4.

Provision	Derivation
Sch. 5	
para. 5	1972 Sch. 6A para. 5; 1986 Sch. 6 pt. III; 1991 Sch. 11 para. 1.
para. 6	1972 Sch. 6A para. 6; 1986 Sch. 6 Pt. III; 1991 Sch. 11 para. 1.
para. 7	1972 Sch. 6 para. 7(4), Sch. 6A para. 7, Sch. 7 para. 7(5); 1986 Sch. 6 Pt. III; 1991 Sch. 11 paras. 2, 5; Tribunals and Inquiries Act 1992 (c. 53) Sch. 3 para. 6; Town and Country Planning (Costs of Inquiries etc.) Act 1995 (c. 49) s.3(3)(a).
para. 8	1972 Sch. 6A para. 8(1); 1986 Sch. 6 Pt. III; 1991 Sch. 11 para. 6.
para. 9	1972 Sch. 6A para. 9; 1986 Sch. 6 Pt. III; 1991 Sch. 11 para. 7.
para. 10	1972 Sch. 6A para. 10; 1986 Sch. 6 Pt. III; 1991 Sch. 11 para. 2(2).
para. 11	1972 Sch. 6A para. 11; 1986 Sch. 6 Pt. III; 1991 Sch. 11 para. 8.
para. 12	1972 Sch. 6A para. 12; 1986 Sch. 6 Pt. III; 1991 Sch. 11 para. 9.
Sch. 6	
para. 1	1972 s.44(2) to (4).
para. 2	1972 s.45(3) to (5).
para. 3	1972 s.46(1), (2), (7).
para. 4	1972 s.45(6), (7).
para. 5	1972 s.46(3) to (6); Tribunals and Inquiries Act 1992 (c. 53) Sch. 3 para. 5.
para. 6	1972 s.45(8), Sch. 8 paras. 1, 2; drafting.
Sch. 7	
para. 1	1972 s.47(2) to (4).
para. 2	1972 Sch. 9 paras. 3 to 5.
para. 3	1972 Sch. 9 paras. 6, 7, 16; Planning (Consequential Provisions) Act 1990 (c. 11) Sch. 2 para. 27(2)(c).
para. 4	1972 Sch. 9 para. 8.
para. 5	1972 Sch. 9 para. 9; Planning (Consequential Provisions) Act 1990 (c. 11) Sch. 2 para. 27(2)(d), (e).
para. 6	1972 Sch. 9 para. 15(1).
para. 7	1972 Sch. 9 para. 10; Planning (Consequential Provisions) Act 1990 (c. 11) Sch. 2 para. 27(2)(f).
para. 8	1972 Sch. 9 paras. 11 to 14; Local Government Act 1972 (c. 70) s.272(2); Tribunals and Inquiries Act 1992 (c. 53) Sch.3 para. 8.
para. 9	1972 s.47(6), Sch. 9 paras. 1, 2, 15(2); Planning (Consequential Provisions) Act 1990 (c. 11) Sch. 2 para. 27(2)(a).
Sch. 8	
para. 1	1972 s.49(1) to (1B), (2) to (8); 1981 s.26; 1991 Sch. 8 para. 5(2), (3); drafting.
para. 2	1972 ss.49(1C) to (1G); 1981 s.26; 1991 Sch. 8 para. 5(4) to (6).
para. 3	1972 s.49A(1) to (7); 1981 s.27; 1991 Sch. 8 para. 6.
para. 4	1972 s.49A(8) to (11); 1981 s.27; 1991 Sch. 8 para. 6(2).
para. 5	1972 s.49B(1) to (4); 1981 s.27; 1991 Sch. 8 para. 7.
para. 6	1972 s.49B(5); 1981 s.27.
para. 7	1972 s.49C; 1981 s.27.
para. 8	1972 s.49D; 1981 s.27.
para. 9	1972 s.49E; 1981 s.27.
para. 10	1972 s.49H; 1991 s.52.
para. 11	1972 s.49F; 1981 s.27; 1991 Sch. 8 para. 8.
para. 12	1972 s.260(1) to (4); 1981 Sch. 2 para. 10.
para. 13.	1972 Sch. 10A para. 1; 1991 Sch. 9.
para. 14	1972 Sch. 10A para. 2; 1991 Sch. 9.
para. 15	1972 Sch. 10A para. 3; 1991 Sch. 9.
para. 16	1972 Sch. 10A para. 4; 1991 Sch. 9.
para. 17	1972 Sch. 10A para. 5; 1991 Sch. 9.
para. 18	1972 Sch. 10A para. 6; 1991 Sch. 9.
para. 19	1972 Sch. 10A para. 7; 1991 Sch. 9.
para. 20	1972 Sch. 10A para. 8; 1991 Sch. 9.
para. 21	1972 Sch. 10A para. 9; 1991 Sch. 9.
para. 22	1972 Sch. 10A para. 10; 1991 Sch. 9.
Sch. 9	Environment Act 1995 (c. 25) Sch. 13.
Sch. 10	Environment Act 1995 (c. 25) Sch. 14.

Provision	Derivation
Sch. 11	
para. 1	1972 Sch. 6 paras. 1, 10.
para. 2	1972 Sch. 6 para. 2.
para. 3	1972 Sch. 6 para. 11.
para. 4	1972 Sch. 6 para. 1.
para. 5	1972 Sch. 6 para. 13.
para. 6	1972 Sch. 6 para. 14; 1991 Sch. 12 para. 32(b).
Sch. 12	1972 Sch. 16.
Sch. 13	
para. 1	1972 s.167A; 1981 s.31; 1991 Sch. 8 para. 11.
para. 2	1972 s.168(1); 1981 s.32.
Sch. 14	
para. 1	1972 s.181(1)(a), (2); 1973C ss.64(1), (4), (5), (7), 67(2); 1984T Sch. 4 para. 54(6); Coal Industry Act 1987 (c. 3) Sch. 1 para. 20; Sc Law Com Rec No. 21.
para. 2	1972 s.181(1)(b); 1973C ss.64(2), (4), (5), (7) to (9); Sc Law Com Rec No. 21.
para. 3	1973C s.67(1)(a).
para. 4	1973C s.67(1)(b).
para. 5	1973C s.68(1)(a), (2).
para. 6	1973C s.68(1)(b).
para. 7	1980 s.147(1), (2).
para. 8	1973C s.69(1)(a); Housing (Scotland) Act 1974 (c. 45) Sch. 3 para. 51(a), (b); Housing (Scotland) Act 1987 (c. 26) Sch. 23 para. 19(9)(a).
para. 9	1973C s.69(1)(b); Housing (Scotland) Act 1974 (c. 45) Sch. 3 para. 51(a), (c); Housing (Scotland) Act 1987 (c. 26) Sch. 23 para. 19(9)(b).
para. 10	1972 s.181(1)(c).
para. 11	1972 s.181(1)(e); 1973C s.65(2); 1984 Sch. 9 paras. 70(5)(a), 72(7)(b).
para. 12	1972 s.181(1)(f); 1984 Sch. 9 para. 70(5)(b).
para. 13	1972 s.181(1); 1991 Sch. 17 para. 17.
para. 14	1972 s.181(1)(d).
para. 15	1972 s.181(1)(g)(i); 1973C ss.66(1), (2), 71(1), (2)(a).
Sch. 15	1972 Sch. 24; Criminal Procedure (Consequential Provisions) (Scotland) Act 1995 (c. 40) Sch. 1 para. 2.
Sch. 16	
para. 1	1972 s.204(1) to (7); 1984 Sch. 9 para. 70(12); Gas Act 1995 (c. 45) Sch. 4 para. 2(2)(e); Sc Law Com Rec No. 22.
para. 2	1972 s.205(1) to (5); 1984 Sch. 9 para. 70(13); 1986 Sch. 11 paras. 48, 49.
para. 3	1972 s.205A(1) to (4); 1981MP Sch. 3 para. 16; 1984 Sch. 9 para. 70(13), (14); 1986 Sch. 11 para. 48.
para. 4	1972 s.206(4); 1981MP Sch. 3 para. 17(d).
para. 5	1972 s.206(1) to (3); 1981MP Sch. 3 para. 17(a) to (c); 1984 Sch. 9 para. 70(15).
para. 6	1972 Sch. 18 para. 1; 1973 Sch. 23 para. 34; 1981MP Sch. 3 para. 23(a).
para. 7	1972 Sch. 18 para. 2.
para. 8	1972 Sch. 18 para. 3(1), (2); 1981MP Sch. 3 para. 23(b); 1984 Sch. 9 para. 70(22)(a).
para. 9	1972 Sch. 18 para. 4; 1981MP Sch. 3 para. 23(c).
para. 10	1972 Sch. 18 para. 5; 1981MP Sch. 3 para. 23(a).
para. 11	1972 Sch. 18 para. 6; 1981MP Sch. 3 para. 23(a); Sc Law Com Rec No. 23.
Sch. 17	
para. 1	Drafting.
para. 2	Building Restrictions (War-Time Contraventions) Act 1946 (c. 35) ss.2(4), (5), (6), 8.
para. 3	Building Restrictions (War-Time Contraventions) Act 1946 (c. 35) ss.2(6), 8.
para. 4	Building Restrictions (War-Time Contraventions) Act 1946 (c. 35) ss.2(7), 8.
para. 5	Building Restrictions (War-Time Contraventions) Act 1946 (c. 35) ss.2(2), (3), 8.

Provision	Derivation
Sch. 17	
para. 6	Building Restrictions (War-Time Contraventions) Act 1946 (c. 35) ss.2(7), (8), 8.
para. 7	Building Restrictions (War-Time Contraventions) Act 1946 (c. 35) ss.2(8), 8(2), (4).
para. 8	Building Restrictions (War-Time Contraventions) Act 1946 (c. 35) ss.2(9), 8(2).
para. 9	Building Restrictions (War-Time Contraventions) Act 1946 (c. 35) ss.2(9), proviso 8(2).
para. 10	Building Restrictions (War-Time Contraventions) Act 1946 (c. 35) ss.2(10), 8(2).
para. 11	Building Restrictions (War-Time Contraventions) Act 1946 (c. 35) ss.2(11), 8(2).
para. 12	Building Restrictions (War-Time Contraventions) Act 1946 (c. 35) ss.2(12), 8(2).
para. 13	Building Restrictions (War-Time Contraventions) Act 1946 (c. 35) ss.3(1), (7), 8(1).
para. 14	Building Restrictions (War-Time Contraventions) Act 1946 (c. 35) ss.5, 8; Criminal Procedure (Consequential Provisions) (Scotland) Act 1995 (c. 40) Sch. 1 paras. 5, 6; Criminal Procedure (Scotland) Act 1995 (c. 46) s.225.
para. 15	Building Restrictions (War-Time Contraventions) Act 1946 (c. 35) ss.6, 8.
para. 16	Drafting.
Sch. 18	1972 Sch. 19.

TABLE OF DESTINATIONS

Building Restrictions (War-Time Contraventions) Act 1946
(c.35)

1946	1997
s.1(2).........	s.251(1), (2), (6)
(3), (5).....	251(6)
2(1).........	251(3), (6)
(2).........	251(3)
	Sched. 17, para. 5
(3).........	s.251(3), Sched. 17, para. 5
(4), (5).....	Sched. 17, para. 2
(6).........	Sched. 17, paras. 2, 3
(7).........	Sched. 17, paras. 4, 6
2(8).........	Sched. 17, paras. 6, 7

1946	1997
s.2(9).........	Sched. 17, para. 8
(9) proviso .	Sched. 17, para. 9
(10).........	Sched. 17, para. 10
(11).........	Sched. 17, para. 11
(12).........	Sched. 17, para. 12
3(1), (7).....	Sched. 17, para. 13
4(1).........	s.251(4), (6)
5	Sched. 17, para. 14
6	Sched. 17, para. 15

1946	1997
s.7(1).........	s.251(6)
(3).........	251(7)
(5).........	251(8)
(6).........	251(1), (2), (6)
8	Sched. 17, paras. 2, 3, 4, 5, 6, 14, 15
(1).........	Sched. 17, para. 13
(2).........	Sched. 17, paras. 7, 8, 9, 10, 11, 12
(3).........	s.251(2), (6)
(4).........	Sched. 17, para. 7
(5).........	s.251(6), (8)

Mineral Workings Act 1951
(c.60)

1951	1997
s.32(1).......	s.213(1)–(3)
32(2).......	213(4)
32(3).......	213(5)
40(6).......	259(1)

Post Office Act 1969
(c.48)

1969	1997
Sched. 4, para. 92(2) ..	s.216(7)
para. 93(1) (xxxiv)	214(3)–(5)
para. 93(4)...	215(3), (4), (5)
Sched. 9, para. 27(11) .	216(6)

The Town and Country Planning (Scotland) Act 1972
(c.52)

1972	1997
s.4(1)–(4).....	s.4(1)–(4)
4A(1).......	5(1)
(2).......	5(2)
(3).......	5(3)
(4).......	5(4)
(5)......	275(4), (5)
5(1).........	6(2)
(1A).......	6(3)
(1B).......	6(4)
(1C).......	6(5)
(1D).......	6(6)
(2).........	6(7)
(3).........	7(1)

1972	1997
s.5(4).........	s.7(2)
(6).........	7(3)
6(1).........	8(1), (2)
(1A).......	8(3)
(2).........	8(4), (5)
(3).........	8(6)
(4).........	8(7), (8)
(5).........	8(9)
(6).........	8(10)
(7).........	8(11)
6A..........	ss.6(8), 8(4)
7(1).........	s.10(1), (2)
(2).........	10(3)

1972	1997
s.7(3).........	s.10(4)
(4).........	10(5)
(5) proviso .	10(6), (7)
(6).........	10(8)
(7).........	10(9)
(8).........	10(10)
8(1).........	9(1), (2)
(2).........	ss.9(3), 10(1), (2), (3), (4), (5), (6), (7), (8), (9), (10)
(3).........	s.9(4)
(4).........	9(5)

1972	1997
s.8(5)	s.9(6)
(6)	9(7)
(7)	9(8)
(8)	9(9)
9(1A)	11(1)
(3)	11(3)
(4)	11(4)
(4A)	11(2)
(5)	11(3)
(6)	11(6)
(7)	14(1), (3), (5)
(8)	14(2)
(9)	11(5)
(10)	14(4)
(11)	14(5)
10(1)	12(1), (2)
(2)	12(3), (4)
(3)	12(5)
11(1)	15(1)–(3)
(1)(a)	15(5)
(1)(b)	15(6)
(1A)	16(1)
(1B)	16(2)
(1C)	16(3)
(2)	15(4)
12(1)	17(1), (2)
(2)	17(3)
(2A)	17(4)
(2B)	17(5)
(3)	18(1), (2)
(4)	ss.18(2), 19(1)–(4)
13(1)	s.13(1), (3), (4)
(2)	14(1), (2), (3), (5)
(3)	ss.12(1), (2), (3), (4), (5), 13(2), 14(4), (5), 15(1)–(3), (4), (5), (6), 17(1), (2), (3), (4), (5), 18(1), (2), 19(1)–(4)
(4)	s.12(6)
14	20
15(1)	22(1)
(2)	22(2)
(2A)	22(3)
(3)	22(4)
(4), (5)	22(5)
16(1)	21(1), (2)
(2)	21(3)
(3)	21(4)
(4)	21(5)
17(1)	24(1)
(2)	24(2)
(3)	24(3)
(4)	24(4)
(5)	24(5)
18A	25
19(1)	26(1)
(1A)	26(4)
(2)	26(2)
(3)	26(3)
(3A)	26(5)
(3B)	26(6)
(4)	26(7)
20(1)	28(1)
(2)	Sched. 2, para. 1

1972	1997
s.20(3)	Sched. 2, para. 2
(4)	Sched. 2, para. 3
(5)	s.28(2)
(6)	28(5)
(7)	Sched. 2, para. 4
(8)	s.28(3), (5)
(9)	28(4)
(10)	28(6)
21(1)	30(1)
(2)	30(2)
(3)	30(3)
(4)	31(1)
(5)	31(2), (3)
(6)	31(4)
(7)	31(5)
21A(1)–(3)	49(1)–(3)
(4)(a)	50(1)
(4)(b)	50(2)
(5)	50(2), (3)
21B(1)	51(1), (2)
(2)	51(3), (4)
21C	52(1), (2)
(3)	61(1)
(4)	27(2), (3)
21D(1)–(5)	53(1)–(5)
(6)	ss.27(2), (3), 53(6)
21E(1)–(3)	s.54(1)–(3)
(4)	ss.27(2), (3), 54(4)
22(1)	s.32
23(1)	34(1)
(2)	34(2)
(3)	34(3), (4)
(4)	34(5)
(5)	34(6)
24	35(1)–(8)
26(1)	37(1), (2), (3)
(2)	38(1)
(3)	38(2)
(3A)	38(3)
(5)	38(4)
(6)	38(5)
(4A)	45(1), (2)
26A	39(1)–(3)
26B	40(1)–(3)
27(1)	41(1)
(1) proviso	41(2)
(2)	ss.41(3), 53(6), 54(4)
(3)	41(4), (5), 53(6), 54(4)
27A(1)–(8)	Sched. 3, para. 2
(9)–(12)	Sched. 3, para. 3
(13)–(16)	Sched. 3, para. 4
(17)	Sched. 3, para. 5
(18)	Sched. 3, para. 6
(19)	Sched. 3, paras. 2, 3, 4
28(1)	s.43(1)
(2)	43(2)

1946	1997
s.28A(1)	s.42(1)
(2)	42(3)
(3)	42(2)
(4)	42(4)
29(1)	33(1)
(2)	33(2)
(3)	33(3)
30(1)	44(1)
(2)	44(2), (3)
30A	37(4)
31(2)	36(1)
(3)	36(2), (3)
(4)	36(4)
(5)	36(1), (2), (3), (4)
32(1)	46(1)
(2)	46(2)
(3)	46(3)
(4)	46(4)
(5)	46(5), (6)
(6)	46(7)
33(1)	47(1)
(2)	47(3), (4)
(3)	48(1)
(3) proviso	48(3)
(4)	48(2), (4)
(5)	48(5)
(6)	48(6)
(7)	48(7)
(7A)	48(8)
(8)	48(9)
34	47(2), (4), (5)
37(1)	57(1)
(2)	57(3)
(3)	ss.57(4), 220(3)
38(1)	s.58(1), (2)
(2)	58(3)
(3)	58(4)
39(1)	59(1)
(2)	59(2), (3)
(3)	59(4)
(4)	59(5)
(5)	59(6)
(6)	59(7)
40(1)	27(2), (3)
(2)	27(4)
(3)	27(5), (6)
(4)	60(1)
(5)	60(2)
(6)	60(3)
(7)	60(4)
41(1)	ss.27(2), (3), 61(1)
(2)	s.61(2), (3)
(3)(a)	61(4)
(3)(b)	62(1), (2)
(4)	62(3)
(5)	62(4), (5)
(6)	61(5), (6)
41A	Sched. 3, para. 1
42(1)	s.65(1), (2)
(2)	66(1), (3)
(3)	66(2)
(4)	65(3)
(4) proviso	65(4)
(5)	ss.65(5), 68(8), Sched. 3, para. 7

TABLE OF DESTINATIONS

1972	1997
s.177(2)	ss.88(2), 89, 90(1), (2), (3), (4), (5), 91(1), (2), (3), (4), (5), 92(1), (2), (3), (4), 93(1), (2), (3), 94(1), (2), (3), (4), (5), (6), (7), 95(1), (2), (3), (4), (5), (6)
(3)	s.92(2)
178(1)	88(1), (2), (4)
(2)	ss.88(2), 89, 90(1), (2), (3), (4), (5), 91(1), (2), (3), (4), (5), 92(1), (2), (3), (4), 93(1), (2), (3), 94(1), (2), (3), (4), (5), (6), (7), 95(1), (2), (3), (4), (5), (6)
(3)	s.92(2)
(4)	95(7)
(5)	88(8)
180(1)	182(3)
180A	99(1)
181(1)	100(1), Sched. 14, para. 13
(1)(a)	Sched. 14, para. 1
(1)(b)	Sched. 14, para. 2
(1)(c)	Sched. 14, para. 10
(1)(d)	Sched. 14, para. 14
(1)(e)	Sched. 14, para. 11
(1)(f)	Sched. 14, para. 12
(1)(g)(i)	Sched. 14, para. 15
(2)	Sched. 14, para. 1
(3)	s.100(2)
(4)	100(2), (3), (5)
(4A)	100(4)
(5)	100(2), (5)
(6)	100(6)
182(1)	101(1)
(2)	101(2)
proviso	101(3)
(4)	101(4)
(5)	101(5)
183(1)	102(1), (2)
(2)	102(4)
(3)	102(6)
(3A)	102(5)
(4)	102(3)
(5)	102(8)
184(1)	104(1), (2)
(2)	104(3)
(3)	104(4)

1972	1997
s.184(4)	s.104(5)
(5)	104(6)
(6)	104(7)
185(1)	105(1), (2)
(2)	105(3)
(3)	105(4), (5)
(4)	105(6)
(5)	105(7)
186	108(1), (2)
187(1)	107(1), (2)
187(2)	107(3)
(3)	107(4)
188(1)	106(1)
(2)	106(2)
(3)	106(3)
(4)	106(4)
(5)	106(5)
189	112(1)
190(1)	113(1)
(2)	113(2)
proviso	113(3)
(3)	113(4)
(4)	114(1)
(5)	114(2)
(6)	113(5)
191(1)	117(1)
(2)	117(1), (2)
192(1)	119(1)
(2)	119(2)
(3)	119(3)
(4)	119(4)
193(1)	115(1)
(2)	115(2)
(3)	115(3)
(4)	115(4)
(5)	115(5)
194(1)	120(1)
(2)	120(2)
(3)	120(3)
195(1)	121(1)
(2)	121(2)
(3)	121(8)
(4)(c)	121(9)
(4)(aa)	121(9)
(5)	121(10)
(6)	121(11)
196(1)	122(1)
(2)	122(2)
(3)	122(3)
(4)	122(4)
(5)	122(5)
197	ss.90(6), 98(8), 118
198(1)	s.202(1)
(2)	202(2)
(3)	202(3)
(4)	202(4)
(5)	202(5)
198A(1)	207(1)
(2)	207(2)
(3)	207(3)
(4)	207(4)
(5)	207(5)
199(1)	208(1)
(2)	208(2)
(3)	208(3)
201(1)	203(1)
(2)	203(2)

1972	1997
s.201(3)	s.203(3), (4)
(4)	203(5)
(5)	204(1)
(6)	204(2)
(7)	204(3), (4), (5), (6)
(8)	203(6)
(9)	203(9)
(10)	203(7)
(11)	203(8)
202(1)	205(1)
(2)	205(2)
(3)	205(3)
(4)	205(4)
(5)	205(5)
203(1)	206(1)
(2)	206(2)
204(1)–(7)	Sched. 16, para. 1
205(1)–(5)	Sched. 16, para. 2
205A(1)–(4)	Sched. 16, para. 3
206(1)–(3)	Sched. 16, para. 5
(4)	Sched. 16, para. 4
208(1)	s.211(1)
(2)	211(2)
209(1)	212(1), (2)
(2)	212(3), (4)
(3)	212(5)
(4)	212(6)
(5)	212(7)
(6)	212(8)
210A(1)	210(1)
(2)	210(2)
211	215(1), (2)
212(1)	216(1), (2)
(2)	216(2)
(2)(a)	216(3)
(2)(b)	216(4)
(3)	216(5), (6)
213(1)	217(1)
(2)	217(3)
214(1)	218(1)
(2)	218(2)
(4)	219
(5)	218(3)
215(1)	220(1), (2)
(2)	220(3)
216	221
217	222
218	223(1), (2)
219(1)	ss.224(1)–(3), 225(1)–(3)
(2)	224(4), 225(4)
(3)	224(5), 225(5)
(4)	224(6), 225(6)
(5)	224(7), 225(7)
(6)	224(8), 225(8)
(7)	225(1)–(3), (4), (5), (6), (7), (8), 227(6), 232(3)

8–381

LOCAL GOVERNMENT ACT 1972
(c.70)

TABLE OF DESTINATIONS

THE LAND COMPENSATION (SCOTLAND) ACT 1973
(c.56)

1973	1997
s.49(1)........	s.96(1), (2), (6)
(2)........	96(5), (6)
(3)........	96(3)
(4)........	96(4)
(5)........	ss.96(1), (2), (3), (4), (5), (6), (7), 97(1), (2), (3), (4), (5), (6), (7), (8), (9), (10), (11), 98(1), (2)
(6)........	s.96(7)
50(1)........	97(1), (2)
(2)........	97(3)
(3)........	97(4), (5)
(4)........	97(6)
(5)........	97(7)
(6)........	97(8), (9)
(7)........	97(10)
(8)........	97(11)
64(1)........	Sched. 14, para. 1
(2)........	Sched. 14, para. 2
(4)........	Sched. 14, paras. 1, 2
(5)........	Sched. 14, paras. 1, 2
(6)........	ss.103(1), (2), 104(8)
(7)........	Sched. 14, paras. 1, 2
(8)........	Sched. 14, para. 2
(9)........	s.121(3), Sched. 14, para. 2

1973	1997
s.65(2)........	Sched. 14, para. 11
(3)........	s.103(1), (2)
66(1)........	Sched. 14, para. 15
(2)........	Sched. 14, para. 15
(3)........	s.121(7)
67(1)(a)....	Sched. 14, para. 3
(1)(b)....	Sched. 14, para. 4
(2)........	Sched. 14, para. 1
(3)........	s.121(4)
68(1)(a)....	Sched. 14, para. 5
(1)(b)....	Sched. 14, para. 6
(2)........	Sched. 14, para. 5
(3)........	ss.120(4), 121(5)
(4)........	s.116(1), (2)
(5)........	116(3)
(6)........	116(4)
69(1)(a)....	Sched. 14, para. 8
(1)(b)....	Sched. 14, para. 9
(3)........	s.121(6)
71(1)........	Sched. 14, para. 15
(2)(a)....	Sched. 14, para. 15
(2)(b)....	s.100(6)

1973	1997
s.71(3)(a)....	s.102(5)
(3)(b)....	102(8)
(4)........	121(1)
72(1)........	ss.101(1), 113(1)
73(1)........	s.112(2)
(2)........	112(3)
(2) proviso	112(4)
(3)........	112(5)
(4)........	114(1), (2)
74(1)........	109(1), (2)
(2)........	109(3)
(3)........	109(4)
75(1)........	110(1)
(2)........	110(2), (3)
(3)........	110(4)
(4)........	110(5)
(5)........	110(6)
(6)........	110(7)
(7)........	110(8)
76(1)........	111(1)
(2)........	111(2)
(3)........	111(3)
(4)........	111(4)
(5)........	111(5)
(6)........	108(3)
(7)........	ss.108(4), 111(6)
(8)........	s.112(1)
(9)........	111(7)
77(2)........	100(6)
(3)........	102(3)
78(2)........	98(1)
80(1)........	98(2)
Sched. 3	101(1)

THE LOCAL GOVERNMENT (SCOTLAND) ACT 1973
(c.65)

1973	1997
s.171C........	ss.188(3), 189(8)
172(1)	s.1(1)
(2)	255(2)
(3)	1(2)
175(1)	10(4), (5), (6), (7), (8), (9), (10)
(2)	ss.18(2), 19(1)–(4)
Sched. 14, para. 89	s.255(1)
Sched. 23, para. 17(b) ..	22(1)
para. 21(a)...	189(6)
para. 23	188(1)
para. 27	203(9)
para. 29	256(1), (2)
para. 30	261(3)
para. 32(a)...	277(1)
para. 34	Sched. 16, para. 6

TABLE OF DESTINATIONS

TOWN AND COUNTRY AMENITIES ACT 1974
(C.32)

1974	1997
s.3(2).........	s.183(1)–(3)
9	ss.172(1), (2), (3), 173(1), (2), (3), (4), 174(1), (2), (3), 175
11(1)........	s.160(3)
(2)(a).....	160(6)
(2)(b).....	167(1)
(3)........	171(1), (2), (3)
(4)........	171(4)
(6)........	172(4)

HOUSING (SCOTLAND) ACT 1974
(C.45)

1974	1997
Sched. 3,	
para. 47	s.108(2)
para. 51(a)...	Sched. 14, paras. 8, 9
para. 51(b) ..	Sched. 14, para. 8
para. 51(c)...	Sched. 14, para. 9
para. 51(d) ..	s.121(6)

CROFTING REFORM (SCOTLAND) ACT 1976
(C.21)

1976	1997
s.11	s.119(4)
Sched. 1,	
para. 1	101(5)
para. 2	104(7)
para. 3	105(7)
para. 4	106(5)
para. 5	119(4)
para. 6	122(1)
para. 7	116(4)
para. 8	109(4)
para. 9	111(7)

TOWN AND COUNTRY PLANNING (SCOTLAND) ACT 1977
(C.10)

1977	1997
s.2(1)(a)......	s.11(2)
(1)(b)......	11(5)
(2)........	12(1)
(3)........	17(3)
4	ss.140(1), (2), (7), (8), (9), 141(1), (2), (4)
(7)........	s.141(3)
5(2)(a).....	143(1)
(2)(d).....	143(5)
(3)........	269(2)
(4)(a).....	272(1), (2), (3)
(4)(b).....	272(6)
(5)........	Sched. 1, paras. 6, 7
(7)........	s.24(6)

TABLE OF DESTINATIONS

INTERPRETATION ACT 1978
(c.30)

1978	1997
s.17(2)(a)	s.162(2), (3), (4)
25(2)	115(4)
Sched. 1	115(4)

LAND REGISTRATION (SCOTLAND) ACT 1979
(c.33)

1979	1997
s.29(2)	ss.79(1), 161(2)

LOCAL GOVERNMENT, PLANNING AND LAND ACT 1980
(c.65)

1980	1997	1981	1997	1981	1997
s.87(1)	s.252(1)	s.149(6)	s.3(1)	para. 17(8)	s.55(10)
(3)	252(2)	(8)(a)	3(2)	para. 19(2)	58(4)
(4)	252(3)	(10)	263(5)	para. 19(4)	202(1)
(5)	275(2), (3)	Sched. 32,		para. 19(5)	277(1)
(6)	252(4), (5)	para. 5(4)(a)	55(1)	para. 20(2)	2(3)
(7)	260	para. 5(8)	2(1)	para. 21	56(1)
92(4)	189(1), (2), (3), (4)	para. 11(3)	55(2)	para. 22(1)	56(2)
		para. 15(2)(b)		para. 22(2)(b)	61(1)
(7)	102(4)	(ii)	2(2)	para. 24(1)	23(1)
122(1)	190(2)	para. 17(1)	55(1)	para. 24(2)	23(2)
(2)	190(1)	para. 17(2)	55(2)	para. 24(3)	23(2)
(3)	190(6), (7)	para. 17(3)	55(3)	para. 25(1)(a)	55(7)
(6)	192(1), (2)	para. 17(4)	55(4)	para. 25(1)(b)	55(7)
147(3)	ss.120(4), 121(5)	para. 17(5)	55(5)	para. 25(1)(c)	2(4)
(4)	s.116(1), (2)	para. 17(6)	55(6)	para. 25(2)	ss.2(5), 55(8)
(5)	116(3)	para. 17(7)	55(9)	para. 26(1A)	s.27(2), (3)

LOCAL GOVERNMENT (MISCELLANEOUS PROVISIONS) (SCOTLAND) ACT 1981
(c.23)

1981	1997	1981	1997	1981	1997
s.36	s.45(1), (2)	Sched. 2—cont.		Sched. 3—cont.	
Sched. 2,		para. 27(1)(c)	s.203(6)	para. 17(d)	Sched. 16, para. 4
para. 17(a)	6(7)	para. 27(1)(d)	203(9)		
para. 18(c)(i)	14(2)	para. 27(1)(e)	203(7), (8)	para. 19(a)	s.211(1)
para. 19(a)	12(3)	para. 27(2)	203(9)	para. 19(b)	211(2)
para. 20	14(1), (2), (3)	Sched. 3,		para. 22	275(5)
para. 22(1)(a)	161(1)	para. 13	214(3)–(5)	para. 23(a)	Sched. 16, paras. 6, 10, 11
para. 22(1)(b)	161(4)	para. 15	12(5)		
para. 24(c)	155(1)	para. 16	Sched. 16, para. 3		
para. 25	207(1), (2), (3), (4), (5)	para. 17(a)–		para. 23(b)	Sched. 16, para. 8
		(c)	Sched. 16, para. 5	para. 23(c)	Sched. 16, para. 9
para. 27(1)(a)	203(2)				
para. 27(1)(b)	203(3)				

TOWN AND COUNTRY PLANNING (MINERALS) ACT 1981
(c.36)

BRITISH TELECOMMUNICATIONS ACT 1981
(c.38)

CIVIL AVIATION ACT 1982
(c.16)

LOCAL GOVERNMENT AND PLANNING (SCOTLAND) ACT 1982
(c.43)

TABLE OF DESTINATIONS

TOWN AND COUNTRY PLANNING ACT 1984
(C.10)

1984	1997	1984	1997	1984	1997
s.1(1)........	s.248(1)	s.2(4)........	s.249(5)	s.3(7)........	s.244(3), (4)
(2)........	248(2)	(5)........	249(6),(7)	(9)........	244(5), (6)
(3)........	248(3)	(6)........	ss.161(1),	4(1)........	242(4)
(4)........	248(4)		249(7)	5(1)........	250(1)
(5)........	248(5)	3(1)........	s.243(2)	(2)........	250(2)
(6)........	248(7)	(2)........	243(3)	(3)........	250(3)
(7)........	248(6)	(3)........	243(4)	(5)........	250(4)
2(1)........	249(1)	(4)........	243(5)	(6)........	250(5)
(2)........	249(2)	(5)........	243(6), (7)	6(1)........	242(1)
(3)........	249(3), (4)	(6)........	244(1), (2)		

TELECOMMUNICATIONS ACT 1984
(C.12)

1984	1997
Sched. 4, para.	
54(3)........	s.194(2)
para. 54(4)...	196(3)
para. 54(5)...	99(1)
para. 54(6)...	120(1), Sched. 14, para. 1
para. 54(7)...	205(3)
para. 54(8)...	212(1), (2), (3), (4), (5), (6), (7), (8)
para. 54(10) .	ss.225(1)–(3), (4), (5), (6), (7), (8), 227(6), 232(3), 233(1), (2), (3), (4), (5)
para. 54(11) .	s.226(7), (8)

ROADS (SCOTLAND) ACT 1984
(C.54)

1984	1997	1984	1997	1984	1997
Sched. 9, para.		Sched. 9—cont.		Sched. 9—cont.	
41	s.213(1)–(3), (4), (5)	para. 70(10)(b)....	s.203(2), (3)	para. 70(15) .	Sched. 16, para. 5
para. 70(2)...	20	para. 70(10)(c)....	203(3)	para. 70(16)(a)....	s.211(1)
para. 70(3)...	26(2)	para. 70(10)(d)....	ss.203(5), (6), 204(1)	para. 70(16)(b)....	211(2)
para. 70(5)(a)	Sched. 14, para. 11	para. 70(10)(e)....	s.203(9)	para. 70(17)(a)....	212(1)
para. 70(5)(b)	Sched. 14, para. 12	para. 70(10)(f)	203(7)	para. 70(17)(b)....	212(3)
para. 70(6)...	s.120(2)	para. 70(10)(g)....	203(8)	para. 70(18)(a)....	210(1)
para. 70(7)(a)	121(8)	para. 70(11) .	205(1), (2), (3), (4)	para. 70(18)(b)....	210(2)
para. 70(7)(b)	121(9)	para. 70(12) .	Sched. 16, para. 1	para. 70(19) .	255(1)
para. 70(8)(a)	202(1)	para. 70(13) .	Sched. 16, paras. 2, 3	para. 70(20) .	261(1)
para. 70(8)(b)	202(2), (3)	para. 70(14) .	Sched. 16, para. 3	para. 70(21) .	277(1)
para. 70(8)(c)	202(4)			para. 70(22)(a)....	Sched. 16, para. 8
para. 70(8)(d)	202(5), (6)			para. 72(7)(b)	s.103(1), (2), Sched. 14, para. 11
para. 70(9)(a)	207(1)				
para. 70(9)(b)	207(2)				
para. 70(9)(c)	207(3), (4)				
para. 70(9)(d)	207(5)				
para. 70(10)(a)....	203(1)				

TABLE OF DESTINATIONS

TOWN AND COUNTRY PLANNING (COMPENSATION) ACT 1985
(C.19)

1985	1997
s.2(1)	s.77(2)

TOWN AND COUNTRY PLANNING (AMENDMENT) ACT 1985
(C.52)

1985	1997
s.2(2)	s.167(1)
2(3)	167(3)

NATURAL HERITAGE (SCOTLAND) ACT 1986
(C.28)

1986	1997
s.6(8)	s.264(1), (2)

AIRPORTS ACT 1986
(C.31)

1986	1997
Sched. 2,	
para. 1(1)	s.214(1), (2)
para. 1(2)	217(1)
Sched. 4,	
para. 2	216(4)
Sched. 6	217(1)

GAS ACT 1986
(C.44)

1986	1997
Sched. 7,	
para. 13	s.216(4)

THE HOUSING AND PLANNING ACT 1986
(C.63)

1986	1997
s.26(1)	ss.27(2), (3), 49(1)–(3), 50(1), (2), (3), 51(1), (2), (3), (4), 52(1), (2), 53(1)–(5), (6), 54(1)–(3), (4), 61(1)
26(2)	s.52(1), (2)
54	61(1)
54(1)	56(1), (2)
54(2)	27(2), (3)
Sched. 6,	
Pt. III	Sched. 5, paras. 1, 2, 3, 4, 5, 6, 7, 8, 9, 10, 11, 12
Pt. IV,	
para. 1	s.36(1)
para. 2	58(4)
para. 4	237(1)
para. 5	238(3), (5), (6)
para. 6(a)	275(4)
para. 6(b)	275(5)

1986	1997
Sched. 7,	
para. 2	s.237(3)
Pt. II,	
para. 3	245(2)
para. 6(c)	277(1)
para. 8	214(3)–(5)
Sched. 9,	
Pt. II,	
para. 18(2)	275(4)
Sched. 11,	
para. 28(1)	17(4), (5)
para. 28(2)	17(1)
para. 29	26(2)
para. 31	42(1), (2), (3), (4)
para. 32(1)	179(1)
para. 32(2)	179(3), (4)
para. 33(1)	180(1), (5)
para. 34(1)	180(7)
para. 34(2)	Sched. 4, para. 2
para. 35(1)(a)	s.90(1)
para. 35(1)(b)	90(4)
para. 36	93(1), (3)
para. 37(1)	94(3), (4)
para. 38	s.264(1), (2)

1986	1997
Sched. 11—cont.	
para. 39	s.265(9), (10), (11)
para. 40(1)	266(1), (2)
para. 40(2)	Sched. 4, para. 6
para. 41	s.267(1)–(3)
para. 42	Sched. 4, para. 4
para. 43	Sched. 4, para. 6
para. 44	s.186(3)
para. 46	s.169(1), (3), (4), (5), (6)
para. 48	Sched. 16, paras. 2, 3
para. 49	Sched. 16, para. 2
para. 50(b)	s.237(2)
para. 51	164(2)
para. 52	272(2)
para. 54	37(1)
para. 55	ss.46(4), 48(5)
para. 56	s.48(7)
para. 58	265(13)
Sched. 12,	
Pt. II	160(7)

TABLE OF DESTINATIONS

COAL INDUSTRY ACT 1987
(c.3)

1987	1997
Sched. 1,	
para. 20	Sched. 14, para. 1

DEBTORS (SCOTLAND) ACT 1987
(c.18)

1987	1997
Sched. 6,	
para. 15	s.265(12)

HOUSING (SCOTLAND) ACT 1987
(c.26)

1987	1997
Sched. 23	
para. 18	s.108(2)
para. 19(9)(a)	Sched. 14, para. 8
para. 19(9)(b)	Sched. 14, para. 9
para. 19(10) .	s.121(6)

LOCAL GOVERNMENT FINANCE ACT 1988
(c.41)

1988	1997
Sched. 12,	
para. 9	s.100(4)

ELECTRICITY ACT 1989
(c.29)

1989	1997
Sched. 8,	
para. 7(1) . . .	s.57(2)
para. 7(3). . . .	ss.57(3), 60(1)
para. 7(4). . . .	s.57(5)
Sched. 16,	
para. 1(1)	
(xxiii)	214(6), (7)
para. 1(1)	
(xxvi)	214(6), (7)
para. 2(2)(d).	214(6), (7)
para. 2(7). . . .	214(6), (7)
para. 3(2)(e).	217(2)
Sched. 18	214(1)

STATUTE LAW (REPEALS) ACT 1989
(c.43)

1989	1997
Sched. 2,	
para. 11	s.251(6)

TABLE OF DESTINATIONS

PLANNING (CONSEQUENTIAL PROVISIONS) ACT 1990
(C.11)

1990	1997
Sched. 2,	
para. 27(1)	s.70(2)
para. 27(2)(a)	Sched. 7, para. 9
para. 27(2)(c)	Sched. 7, para. 3
para. 27(2)(d)	Sched. 7, para. 5
para. 27(2)(e)	Sched. 7, para. 5
para. 27(2)(f)	Sched. 7, para. 7

NATIONAL HEALTH SERVICE AND COMMUNITY CARE ACT 1990
(C.19)

1990	1997
Sched. 8,	
para. 7	s.197(2)

NEW ROADS AND STREET WORKS ACT 1991
(C.22)

1991	1997
Sched. 8,	
para. 104(a)	s.212(3)
para. 104(b)	212(4)

PLANNING COMPENSATION ACT 1991
(C.34)

1991	1997
s.33	ss.125(1)–(8), 126(1)–(6)
34	s.145(1)–(13)
35	146(1)–(3)
36(1)	ss.123(1)–(3), 124(1)–(4)
37	127(1)–(3), 128(1)–(14), 129(1)–(4)
38(1)	s.130(1), (2)
(2)	133(8)
39	135(10)
40	136(1)–(9)
41(1)	140(1), (2), (3), (4), (5), (6), (7)
(2)	144(1), (2), (3), (4), (5), (6)
(3)	143(5)
42(1)	ss.150(1)–(7), 151(1)–(4), 152(1)–(8), 153(1), (2)
43(1)	156(1)–(4), 157(1)–(3), 158(1)–(7)
43(2)	s.270(6)
44(1)	26(4)
(3)	77(4)
45	26(6)

1991	1997
s.46(1)	s.35(1)–(8)
(2)	38(2), (3)
47(1)	39(1)–(3)
(2)	47(2)
48	40(1)–(3)
49(1)	75(3)
(2)	246(1)
(3)	246(3), (4)
50(1)	48(8)
50(2)	Sched. 4, para. 2
54(1)(a)	s.171(2)
54(2)	168(3)
(2)(b)(i)	169(2)
(2)(b)(ii)	169(1)
(2)(c)	170(10)
(3)	ss.176(1)–(8), 177(1)–(3), 178(1)–(4)
55	s.277(1)
56	187(1)–(6)
58	5
Sched. 8,	277(1)
paras. 2(a), (b)	Sched. 3, para. 2
para. 2(c)	Sched. 3, para. 6
para. 3	s.58(4)
para. 4	Sched. 3, para. 1

1991	1997
Sched. 8—cont.	
para. 5	s.71(8)
para. 5(2), (3)	Sched. 8, para. 1
para. 5(4)–(6)	Sched. 8, para. 2
para. 5(7)	s.71(6)
para. 6	Sched. 8, para. 3
para. 6(2)	Sched. 8, para. 4
para. 7	Sched. 8, para. 5
para. 8	Sched. 8, para. 11
para. 9	ss.148(1), 262(1)
para. 11	Sched. 13, para. 1
Sched. 9	Sched. 8, paras. 13, 14, 15, 16, 17, 18, 19, 20, 21, 22
Sched. 11,	
para. 1	Sched. 5, paras. 5, 6
para. 2	Sched. 5, para. 7
para. 2(2)	Sched. 5, para. 10
para. 4	Sched. 5, para. 3

TRIBUNALS AND INQUIRIES ACT 1992
(C.53)

CROFTERS (SCOTLAND) ACT 1993
(C.44)

TABLE OF DESTINATIONS

LOCAL GOVERNMENT ETC. (SCOTLAND) ACT 1994
(C.39)

1994	1997
s.33(1)........	ss.5(1), (2), (3), (4), 275(4), (5)
171	188(3), 189(8)
Sched. 4,	
para. 2(a) ...	s.4(1)
para. 2(b)....	4(2)
para. 3	6(2), (3), (4), (5), (6), (8)
para. 4	8(3)
para. 5	9(4)
para. 6	10(1), (2)
para. 7	11(1)
para. 8(a)(ii).	22(1)
para. 8(b)....	22(3)
para. 9	24(5)
para. 10	189(6)
para. 11	203(9)
para. 12	205(5)
para. 13	255(1)
para. 14	256(1), (2)
para. 15	277(1)
Sched. 13,	
para. 92(57) .	1(1), (2)
Sched. 14	22(1)

ENVIRONMENT ACT 1995
(C.25)

1995	1997
s.96(1), (3)....	s.74(1)
96(5)........	74(2)
96(6)........	74(3)
Sched. 13	Sched. 9
Sched. 14	Sched. 10
Sched. 22,	
para. 16	Sched. 4, para. 2

CRIMINAL PROCEDURE (CONSEQUENTIAL PROVISIONS) (SCOTLAND) ACT 1995
(C.40)

1995	1997
Sched. 1,	
para. 2	ss.270(5), 272(5), Sched. 15
para. 5	34(4), 138(4), 171(4), 265(8), 270(2), 272(4), Sched. 17, para. 14
para. 6	34(4), 138(4), 171(4), 265(8), 270(2), 272(4), Sched. 17, para. 14

GAS ACT 1995
(C.45)

1995	1997
Sched. 4,	
para. 1	s.277(1)
para. 2(1)	
(xix)	214(3)–(5)
para. 2(2)(e) .	Sched. 16,
	para. 1
para. 2(10)...	217(2)

CRIMINAL PROCEDURE (SCOTLAND) ACT 1995
(C.46)

1995	1997
s.225	ss.34(4), 138(4),
	171(4),
	265(8),
	270(2),
	272(4),
	Sched. 17,
	para. 14

TOWN AND COUNTRY PLANNING (COSTS OF INQUIRIES ETC.) ACT 1995
(C.49)

1995	1997
s.3(2)(a)......	s.16(1), (2), (3)
(3)(a)......	Sched. 5,
	para. 7

SCOTTISH LAW COMMISSION'S REPORT ON THE CONSOLIDATION OF CERTAIN ENACTMENTS RELATING
TO TOWN AND COUNTRY PLANNING IN SCOTLAND
(SCOT LAW COM. NO. 157) (CMND.3644)

1996	1997
App.1	
No.1	s.47(5)
No.2	ss.63(4), 139(4),
	142(4)
No.3	s.83(1)
No.4	ss.92(1), 93(1),
	99(2)
No.5	s.93(1)
No.6	ss.101(5),
	104(7), 105(7),
	106(5), 109(4),
	111(7), 116(4),
	119(4), 122(1)
No.7	s.112(1)
No.8	ss.112(5),
	113(5)
No.9	s.135(11)
No.10	154(1), (2),
	(3)
No.11	191(7)
No.12	213(4)
No.13	ss.221, 222
No.14	s.222
No.15	227(3)
No.16	239(3)
No.18	255(2)
No.19	277(1)
No.20	Sched. 4,
	para. 2
No.21	Sched. 14,
	paras. 1, 2
No.22	Sched. 16,
	para. 1
No.23	Sched. 16,
	para. 11

INDEX

References are to sections and Schedules

8–395

PLANNING (LISTED BUILDINGS AND CONSERVATION AREAS) (SCOTLAND) ACT 1997*

(1997 c. 9)

[A Table showing the destination of provisions of various Acts to this consolidation Act will be found at the end of the Act. The Table has no official status.]

ARRANGEMENT OF SECTIONS

PART I

LISTED BUILDINGS

CHAPTER I

LISTING OF SPECIAL BUILDINGS

---

* Annotations by Jacqueline Williamson LL.B.(Hons.), LL.M., Advocate, Barrister of the Inner Temple.

Chapter III

Rights of Owners etc.

Compensation

Listed building purchase notices

Chapter IV

Enforcement

Chapter V

Prevention of Deterioration and Damage

Compulsory acquisition of listed building in need of repair

Acquisition by agreement

Management of acquired buildings

Urgent preservation

Grants for repair and maintenance

Damage to listed buildings

Chapter VI

Miscellaneous and Supplemental

Exceptions for church buildings and ancient monuments

Local authority notices and works affecting listed buildings

An Act to consolidate certain enactments relating to special controls in respect of buildings and areas of special architectural or historic interest with amendments to give effect to recommendations of the Scottish Law Commission. [27th February 1997]

PARLIAMENTARY DEBATES
Hansard, H.L. Vol. 576, cols. 122, 588, 673; Vol. 577, cols. 560, 1082. H.C. Vol. 291, col. 196.

INTRODUCTION AND GENERAL NOTE

The Planning (Listed Buildings and Conservation Areas) (Scotland) Act 1997 (c. 9) is one of a package of four Statutes to consolidate town and country planning in Scotland. The others are the Town and Country Planning (Scotland) Act 1997 (c. 8), the Planning (Hazardous Substances) (Scotland) Act 1997 (c. 10), and the Planning (Consequential Provisions) (Scotland) Act 1997 (c. 11). The Acts may be collectively known as the "Planning Acts", all four of which came into force on May 27, 1997. The Planning (Listed Buildings and Conservation Areas) (Scotland) Act 1997 now provides a self-contained scheme for the protection of Scotland's architectural and landscape heritage. While it is related to the Town and Country Planning (Scotland) Act 1997 (c. 8), its provisions operate independently of the relevant provisions of that statute. The legislation relating to scheduled monuments have not been incorporated into the Planning (Listed Buildings and Conservation Areas) (Scotland) Act 1997 and remain contained within the Ancient Monuments and Archaeological Areas Act 1979 (c. 46). Where a building is listed both under this Act and a scheduled monument under the 1979 Act, the provisions of the 1979 Act are to prevail. Given the similarity between the Scottish provisions on listed buildings and conservation areas control, and the equivalent English provisions, reference has been made, where relevant to English case law.

Part I of this Act is concerned with listed buildings and contains the relevant provisions relating to the listing of buildings, listed building consents, compensation to owners and listed building purchase notices, enforcement of listed building control and the prevention of deterioration and damage to listed buildings. It remains an offence under s.8 of Pt. I of this Act to carry out works to a listed building which affect its character as a building of special architectural or historic interest, without the benefit of listed building consent. This punitive provision is supplemented by enforcement powers to require the restoration of a building to its previous condition. Part I also confers extensive powers on planning authorities to undertake urgent works to preserve unoccupied listed buildings and to recover their expenses for such works. Where necessary, the Secretary of State may authorise a planning authority to compulsorily acquire a listed building which is in need of repair.

Part II of this Act is concerned with the designation and control of development within conservation areas. This Part imposes a duty upon planning authorities to determine which parts of their district are areas of special architectural or historic interest, the character or appearance of which it is desirable to preserve or enhance. Planning authorities are required to pay special attention to the desirability of preserving or enhancing the character or appearance of conservation area in the exercise of its planning functions. It is arguable that this creates a rebuttable presumption against development which may have an adverse impact upon the character or appearance of a conservation area.

Part III contains special provisions relating to the land and works of planning authorities and the exercise of the powers in this Act in relation to Crown land.

Part IV is concerned with supplementary provisions.

Allocation of Functions

The functions under the Act are distributed amongst:

(1) the Secretary of State who has the powers of determination of appeals, call-in, and several reserve powers. Historic Scotland is the department within the Scottish Office with responsibility for administration of the Secretary of State's powers relating to listed buildings. Executive agency status was conferred on Historic Scotland during the previous Government's "Next Steps" policy. However, the Agency remains a part of the Scottish Office.

(2) Planning authorities, who were established following local government reorganisation under the Local Government etc. (Scotland) Act 1994 (c. 39). Local government reorganisation in Scotland took effect on April 1, 1996. Twenty-nine unitary authorities replaced the previous two-tier arrangement of regional and district councils. The new unitary councils exercise all local authority functions including all planning functions for their area (s.2 of the Local Government etc. (Scotland) Act 1994).

(3) Local authorities who are defined by s.2 of the Local Government etc. (Scotland) Act 1994.

Parliamentary Proceedings

The consolidation was undertaken by the Scottish Law Commission which reported to the House in November 1996 (*Report on the Consolidation of Certain Enactments Relating to Town*

and Country Planning in Scotland—Scot Law Com No.157). The Report contained 42 recommendations in relation to consolidation of the previous legislation, 11 of which relate to this
Act. The Bill was introduced in the Lords and received its first reading on November 26, 1996 as
part of the package of four consolidating bills. Its second reading was uneventful and took place
on December 3, 1996 whereon it was subsequently referred to the Joint Committee on Consolidation Bills. The order of recommitment was discharged on January 21, 1997 in the absence of
any indication of an intention to move a manuscript amendment or a wish by any of the Lords to
speak in committee on recommitment.
The Bill received its third reading in the Lords on January 28, 1997 without much debate,
following which the Bill was referred to the Commons. It is notable that at this stage, a privileged
amendment was made to the Bill in the form of an insertion of subs. (4) to cl. 83. The amendment
prescribed the imposition or alteration of any charge on the people or public funds. This amendment was removed in the Commons during the Bill's second reading in that House on February
25, 1997 (see *Hansard,* H.C. Vol. 291, col. 196). The Bill had a formal third reading on the same
day and received Royal Assent on February 27, 1997.

Policy Guidance
Scotland does not have dedicated national policy guidelines on historic buildings and conservation areas (see PPG15 which applies to England only). PAN 42 is not in terms concerned with
historic buildings and conservation areas, but is limited to archaeology and scheduled monuments. This guidance note may be of some relevance however, where a listed building is also
scheduled as an ancient monument, or where a listed building or ancient monument is situated
within a conservation area. It should be noted that these controls do not operate in a vacuum—a
degree of overlap should be anticipated. The main guidance on listed buildings and conservation
areas is contained in Historic Scotland's Memorandum of Guidance on Listed Buildings and
Conservation Areas 1993 , issued with Circular No.27/1993 (revised guidance due in Autumn
1997). A booklet is also published by Historic Scotland called *Scotland's Listed Buildings—A
Guide to their Protection.*

ABBREVIATIONS
"1987 Regulations": the Town and Country Planning (Listed Buildings and Buildings in Conservation Areas) (Scotland) Regulations 1987 (S.I. 1987 No. 1529).
"the Principal Act": the Town and Country Planning (Scotland) Act 1997 (c. 8).

COMMENCEMENT
This Act came into force on May 27, 1997, three months after Royal Assent.

PART I

LISTED BUILDINGS

CHAPTER I

LISTING OF SPECIAL BUILDINGS

Listing of buildings of special architectural or historic interest

1.—(1) For the purposes of this Act and with a view to the guidance of
planning authorities in the performance of their functions under this Act in
relation to buildings of special architectural or historic interest, the Secretary
of State shall compile lists of such buildings or approve, with or without
modifications, such lists compiled by other persons or bodies of persons, and
may amend any list so compiled or approved.
(2) In considering whether to include a building in a list compiled or
approved under this section, the Secretary of State may take into account not
only the building itself but also—
(a) any respect in which its exterior contributes to the architectural or
historic interest of any group of buildings of which it forms part, and
(b) the desirability of preserving, on the ground of its architectural or historic interest, any feature of the building consisting of a man-made
object or structure fixed to the building or forming part of the land and
comprised within the curtilage of the building.

(3) Before compiling or approving, with or without modifications, any list under this section or amending any such list the Secretary of State shall consult such persons or bodies of persons as appear to him appropriate as having special knowledge of, or interest in, buildings of architectural or historic interest.

(4) In this Act "listed building" means a building which is for the time being included in a list compiled or approved by the Secretary of State under this section; and, for the purposes of this Act, the following shall be treated as part of the building—

(a) any object or structure fixed to the building, and

(b) any object or structure within the curtilage of the building which, though not fixed to the building, forms part of the land and has done so since before 1st July 1948.

(5) Schedule 1 (which makes provision as to the treatment as listed buildings of certain buildings formerly subject to building preservation orders) shall have effect.

DEFINITIONS
    "building": s.81(2).
    "functions": s.81(2).
    "land": s.81(2).
    "listed building": subs. (4).
    "planning authority": s.81(2).
    "principle Act": s.81(1).

GENERAL NOTE

Purpose of the Section
    This provision introduces the statutory scheme for the identification and protection of buildings of special architectural or historical interest. It is a discriminating system: only buildings which are individually identified as being of special interest are listed. The lists of buildings are essentially an archive. They are subject to constant change, whether as a result of new additions or through deletions. One of the main consequences of listing a building, is that it becomes a criminal offence to carry out any works which demolish, alter, extend or in any way affect its special character, without consent. In addition, the protection afforded by this Act may be temporarily conferred upon a building by service of a building preservation notice, under ss.3 or 4. It should be noted that a building may also be indirectly protected under Pt. II of this Act insofar as it may be situated within a designated conservation area. This is the case notwithstanding that the building itself may not be listed.

Development of Listing
    There are currently 42,000 buildings listed in Scotland. Following upon the losses sustained in England, Wales and Scotland during the second world war, planning authorities were empowered under the original protective legislation, the Town and Country Planning (Scotland) Act 1947 (c. 53), to make building preservation orders in respect of buildings of historic interest. The Secretary of State could compile lists of buildings which were the subject of these preservation orders, however the consequences following upon listing was not as significant then as it is under the present law. The Secretary of State is now subject to a statutory duty to compile and keep a list of buildings identified as being of special architectural or historic interest. A full list must be made available for public inspection.
    While it is undoubtedly desirable that buildings of architectural and historic interest should be preserved, the restrictions imposed upon the demolition or alteration of a building following listing, may decrease the value of that building. This was illustrated by the English Court of Appeal decision of *Amalgamated Investment & Property Co. v. Walker (John) & Sons* [1977] 1 WLR 164. In this case, the Court of Appeal rejected an action for recission of a contract for the purchase of a warehouse for redevelopment, where the building became listed two days after the contract was signed. The Court held that listing after the exchange of contracts, was not an unforeseeable risk but an inherent one which is accepted by the purchaser.

The Listing Procedure
    The identification of buildings for listing purposes is currently being carried out as part of a comprehensive re-survey of the country by Historic Scotland, which began in 1979 and is due to be completed by the year 2005. This re-survey aims to re-assess all buildings eligible for listing on

an area by area basis. However, the re-survey is not intended to preclude members of the public or organisations from suggesting further buildings for listing. Individuals may suggest buildings to be considered for listing to Historic Scotland on behalf of the Secretary of State.

Definition of Building

Section 81(2) of this Act defines a building by reference to s.277(1) of the Principal Act to include "any structure or erection, and any part of a building as so defined but does not include plant or machinery comprised in a building". However, when considering whether to list a building, s.1(2) of this Act empowers the Secretary of State to take into account not just the building itself, but any respect in which its exterior contributes to the architectural or historic interest of any group of buildings of which it forms part, or any feature of the building consisting of a man-made object or structure fixed to the building or forming part of the land and comprised within the curtilage of the building. This does not entitle the feature or fixture to be listed in its own right, the Secretary of State is merely required to take into account the desirability of preserving the feature or fixture when considering whether to list the building.

Objects and Structures fixed to the building

In *Corthorn Land and Timber Co. v. Minister of Housing and Local Government* (1965) 17 P. & C.R. 210, the Court upheld the validity of a building preservation order which provided that not only should a building which consisted of a mansion, not be demolished, altered or extended without consent, but that a number of items comprising of portraits, oak panelling, a large wood carving in the Great Hall and a medieval wooden equestrian figure, were fixtures and should not be removed. The Court in essence applied the English common law of fixtures and fittings to references to the term "fixed" where it appeared within the relevant legislation relating to listed buildings (see also comments by Lord Mackay of Clashfern in *Debenhams v. Westminster City Council* [1987] A.C. 396.

In the case of *R. v. Secretary of State for Wales, ex p. Kennedy* [1996] JPL 645, the High Court applied the definition of fixture for the purposes of the term "fixed" where it appeared in the listed building legislation and upheld enforcement notices which required the return and restoration of property which had been removed from Leighton Hall, a Grade II mansion in Welshpool.

Objects or Structures within the Curtilage

Section 1(4)(b) provides that any object or structure within the curtilage of the building which forms part of the land and has done so since before July 1, 1948 shall be protected by the listing of the building. It is not necessary for the object or structure to be fixed to the building. There is no statutory definition of the term 'curtilage', however the Court of Appeal in *Att.-Gen., ex rel. Sutcliffe, Rouse and Hughes v. Calderdale Borough Council* [1983] JPL 310 set out three factors to be taken into account in deciding whether a structure or object was within the curtilage of a listed building:

(i)   the physical layout of the building and the structure;
(ii) their ownership, past and present; and
(iii) their use or function, past and present.

Applying these criteria, the Court held that a row of mill-workers cottages adjacent to and linked only by a bridge to the mill, which was a listed building, was within the curtilage of the mill and therefore included in the listing. However, this case was distinguished by the House of Lords in *Debenhams v. Westminster City Council* [1987] A.C. 396 (Lord Ackner dissenting). According to Lord Keith of Kinkel, the phrase "structure fixed to a building" within the meaning of the English provisions relating to listed buildings:

> "is intended to convey a limitation to such structures as are ancillary to the listed building itself, for example the stable block of a mansion house, or the steading of a farmhouse, either fixed to the main building or within its curtilage. In my opinion, the concept envisaged is that of principal and accessory. It does not follow that I would overrule the decision in the *Calderdale* case, though I would not accept the width of the reasoning of Stephenson L.J. There was, in my opinion, room for the view that the terrace of cottages was ancillary to the mill."

This view was reinforced in the case of *Watts v. Secretary of State for the Environment* [1991] 1 PLR 61 where the Divisional Court allowed an appeal against an enforcement notice which required the reinstatement of a demolished wall. The wall had been in a different curtilage and separate ownership at the time and therefore was not a fixture in relation to the separately owned listed building. Similarly, in *R. v. Camden London Borough Council, ex. p. Bellamy* [1992] JPL 255, the High Court held that it was necessary to decide whether the adjacent building was a structure ancillary or subordinate to the listed building, whether it served to secure the curtilage and whether the two buildings had been in common ownership since the time of listing. Paragraph 6 to App. 1 of the *Memorandum of Guidance on Listed Buildings and Conservation Areas 1993*, contains detailed guidance from Historic Scotland on the issue of curtilage. In particular, para. 6.4.0 provides general guidelines on new development within the curtilage of listed buildings.

Criteria for Listing
Three classifications are used by Historic Scotland for listing buildings. These are A, B and C(S). Pending the completion of the re-survey, some buildings are currently classified as 'B for group'. However, it is anticipated that by the end of the survey, those buildings falling within this category will be assigned to one of the three main categories will henceforth no longer exist. The categories used by Historic Scotland are defined in the *1993 Memorandum of Guidance* as follows:

Category A: buildings of national or international importance, either architectural or historic, or fine little-altered examples of some particular period, style or period building type;
Category B: buildings of regional or more than local importance, or major examples of some period, style or building type which may have been somewhat altered.
Category C: buildings of local importance; lesser examples of any period, style or building type whether as originally constructed or as the result of subsequent alteration; simple, well-proportioned traditional buildings, often forming part of a planned group, *e.g.* an estate or an industrial complex, or grouping well in association with buildings in a higher category.

Principles for selection
The principles of selection for listing are set out in the *1993 Memorandum of Guidance* as:
"—all buildings erected prior to 1840 which are of any quality, even if plain, and survive in anything like their original form are listed;
—all buildings erected between 1840 and 1914 which are of definite quality and character either individually or as part of a group are listed;
—buildings erected between 1914 and 1945 are listed if they are good examples of the works of an important architect, or of a particular style whether it be traditional, progressive or international modern;
—after 1945 buildings of outstanding quality and some vintage may be listed; a very high degree of selection is exercised.
In choosing buildings, beside age, particular attention is paid to:
—the works of better known architects;
—the special value of particular building types either for architectural or planning reasons or as illustrating social and economic history, *e.g.* industrial buildings both urban and rural, railway and other transport buildings, schools, hospitals, theatres, civic buildings, markets, exchanges, charitable institutions, prisons, street furniture and public memorials;
—distinctive regional variations in design and use of materials;
—association with well known persons or events; and
—group value, especially examples of town planning, *e.g.* squares, terraces, model villages, townscape and landscape value."

Demolition of Listed Buildings without Consent
Demolition of a listed building without the requisite consent, cannot defeat the purposes of the legislation. It may be possible to serve a listed building enforcement notice requiring restoration of a listed building notwithstanding its demolition, provided sufficient components exist to restore it: *R. v. Leominster District Council, ex p. Antique Country Buildings* [1988] JPL 554 and *Leominster District Council v. British Historic Buildings and S.P.S. Shipping* [1987] JPL 350.

Publication of lists

2.—(1) As soon as possible after any list has been compiled or approved under section 1, or any amendments of such a list have been made, a copy of so much of the list as relates to the district of any planning authority or the area of the local authority for the purposes of the Housing (Scotland) Act 1987, or of so much of the amendments as so relates, certified by or on behalf of the Secretary of State to be a true copy, shall be deposited with the clerk of that authority.

(2) As soon as possible after the inclusion of any building in a list under section 1, whether on the compilation or approval of the list or by amend-

ment, or as soon as possible after any such list has been amended by the exclusion of any building from it—

(a) the Secretary of State shall inform the planning authority in whose district the building is situated of the inclusion or exclusion, and

(b) the planning authority shall serve a notice in the prescribed form on every owner, lessee and occupier of the building, stating that the building has been included in, or excluded from, the list.

(3) The Secretary of State shall keep available for public inspection, free of charge, at reasonable hours and at a convenient place, copies of all lists and amendments of lists compiled, approved or made by him under section 1.

(4) Every authority with whose clerk copies of any list or amendments are deposited under this section shall similarly keep available copies of so much of any such list or amendment as relates to buildings within their district or area.

DEFINITIONS
"building": s.81(2).
"land": s.81(2).
"owner": s.81(2).
"planning authority": s.81(2).
"prescribed": s.81(1).

GENERAL NOTE
This provision describes the practice to be adopted upon the inclusion of a building, or an amendment to the statutory lists of buildings. Subsection (1) requires the Secretary of State to lodge a certified copy of the list or the relevant amendments with the Clerk to the relevant authority. Furthermore, subs. (2) requires the Secretary of State to inform the planning authority in whose district or area, the building is situated, of its inclusion or exclusion in the list. Thereafter, the planning authority is obliged to inform the owner, lessee or occupier of the building of its inclusion or exclusion from the list. The need to inform the owner as soon as is reasonably practicable cannot be over-emphasised. It is obviously vital that information on a building's listed status is passed on as soon as possible, especially in situations where the property is about to change ownership. In England and Wales, a deposited list is registered as a local land charge by virtue of s.2(2) of the Planning (Listed Buildings and Conservation Areas) Act 1990 (c. 9). The importance of this is that registration gives notice of a building's listed status to prospective purchasers and all others involved with the land. No such system of registration exists in Scotland. It is no defence to a prosecution for works carried out without the requisite consent that the listing had not been registered: *Abbey National Building Society v. Cann* [1990] 1 All E.R. 1085.

Copies of the Lists
The Secretary of State is required by subs. (3) to keep a copy of the full list available for public inspection. This list is currently held at Historic Scotland's Headquarters, Longmore House, Salisbury Place, Edinburgh, EH9 1SH. Certified copies of the statutory lists relevant for a particular area, are deposited by the Secretary of State with planning authorities for inspection.

Temporary listing: building preservation notices

3.—(1) If it appears to a planning authority that a building in their district which is not a listed building—

(a) is of special architectural or historic interest, and

(b) is in danger of demolition or of alteration in such a way as to affect its character as a building of such interest,

they may serve on the owner, lessee and occupier of the building a notice (in this Act referred to as a "building preservation notice").

(2) A building preservation notice shall—

(a) state that the building appears to the planning authority to be of special architectural or historic interest and that they have requested the Secretary of State to consider including it in a list compiled or approved under section 1, and

(b) explain the effect of subsections (3) to (5) and Schedule 2.

(3) A building preservation notice—

(a) shall come into force as soon as it has been served on the owner, lessee and occupier of the building to which it relates, and

(b) subject to subsection (4), shall remain in force for 6 months from the date when it is served or, as the case may be, last served.

(4) A building preservation notice shall cease to be in force if the Secretary of State—

(a) includes the building in a list compiled or approved under section 1, or

(b) notifies the planning authority in writing that he does not intend to do so.

(5) While a building preservation notice is in force with respect to a building, the provisions of this Act (other than section 53) and the principal Act shall have effect in relation to the building as if it were a listed building.

(6) If, following the service of a building preservation notice, the Secretary of State notifies the planning authority that he does not propose to include the building in a list compiled or approved under section 1, the authority—

(a) shall immediately give notice of the Secretary of State's decision to the owner, lessee and occupier of the building, and

(b) shall not, within the period of 12 months beginning with the date of the Secretary of State's notification, serve another building preservation notice in respect of the building.

DEFINITIONS

"building": s.81(2).
"building preservation notice": s.81(1).
"functions": s.81(2).
"listed building": s.1(4).
"owner": s.81(2).
"planning authority": s.81(2).
"the Principal Act": s.81(1).

GENERAL NOTE

This provision empowers a planning authority to take interim steps, by way of a building preservation notice, to protect a building in their district which is not listed, but which appears to them to be of special architectural or historic interest. However, the power is only exercisable in relation to those buildings which appear to them to be in danger of demolition or alteration in such a way as to affect its character. Service of the notice confers the same degree of protection upon a building as inclusion in the statutory list, for a period not exceeding six months. During this period, the Secretary of State may:

(i) list the building, in which case the building preservation notice ceases to have effect: (subs. (4)(a));

(ii) serve written notice upon the planning authority that he does not intend to list the building, in which case the building preservation notice ceases to have effect: (subs. (4)(b)).

Exceptions for Church Buildings and Ancient Monuments

A building preservation order cannot be served in respect of any ecclesiastical building which is for the time being used for ecclesiastical purposes (s.54(1) of this Act). Further, s.55(1) excludes a scheduled ancient monument from the scope of s.3.

Compensation

Under subs. (6), where the Secretary of State notifies the planning authority that he does not intend to include the building in the statutory list, the planning authority must immediately give notice of this to the owner, occupier or lessee of the building. They are then precluded from serving another building preservation order in respect of the same building, within the period of 12 months from the date of the Secretary of State's notification (subs. (6)(b)). Any person who had an interest in the building at the time the building preservation notice is served, is entitled to compensation from the planning authority who served the notice, in respect of any loss or damage which is directly attributable to the effect of the notice, pursuant to s.26(2). See further, General Note to s.26.

Temporary listing in urgent cases

4.—(1) If it appears to the planning authority to be urgent that a building preservation notice should come into force, they may, instead of serving the notice on the owner, lessee and occupier of the building to which it relates, affix the notice conspicuously to some object on the building.

(2) The affixing of a notice under subsection (1) shall be treated for all the purposes of section 3, this section, sections 9 to 24 and Schedule 2 as service of the notice.

(3) A notice which is so affixed must explain that by virtue of being so affixed it is treated as being served for those purposes.

DEFINITIONS
  "building": s.81(2).
  "building preservation notice": s.3(1).
  "functions": s.81(2).
  "listed building": s.1(4).
  "owner": s.81(2).
  "planning authority": s.81(2).

GENERAL NOTE
  It will have been noted that s.3 requires service of a building preservation order, before it can take effect: see *Maltglade v. St. Albans Rural District Council* (1972) 24 P. & C.R. 32. However, this may allow the unscrupulous appellant to assert that the notice had not been served in time in accordance with the normal rules of service and in any event, before the demolition works had commenced. Section 4 therefore authorises the planning authority to affix a building preservation notice conspicuously to some object on the building, which is then to be treated as service.

Provisions applicable on lapse of building preservation notice

5. Schedule 2 (which makes provision as respects the lapse of building preservation notices) shall have effect.

DEFINITIONS
  "building": s.81(2).
  "building preservation notice": s.3(1).

GENERAL NOTE
  Section 5 applies the provisions of Sched. 2 to this Act to the lapse of building preservation notices. Paragraph 1 of Sched. 2 provides for a building preservation notice to lapse in two circumstances:
  (a) on the expiry of the six months period from the date it was granted: or
  (b) on the service of a notification by the Secretary of State under s.3(4)(b) that he does not intend to include the building which forms the subject of the building preservation notice, in the statutory list;
  The significance of this is that any proceedings on or arising out of an application for listed building consent while the building preservation notice was in force and any such consent granted will lapse (para. 3). Further, any listed building enforcement notice served by the planning authority while the building preservation notice was in force, ceases to have effect. However, the liability of a person for an offence under s.8 (unauthorised works) or s.39 (non-compliance with a listed buildings enforcement notice) is preserved by para. 2 of Sched. 3.

CHAPTER II

AUTHORISATION OF WORKS AFFECTING LISTED BUILDINGS

Control of works in respect of listed buildings

Restriction on works affecting listed buildings

6. Subject to the following provisions of this Act, no person shall execute or cause to be executed any works for the demolition of a listed building or for its alteration or extension in any manner which would affect its character as a building of special architectural or historic interest, unless the works are authorised.

DEFINITIONS
"authorised": s.8.
"building": s.81(2).
"listed building": s.1(4).

GENERAL NOTE
This provision contains a clear prohibition against any works intended to be carried out to listed buildings without the requisite consent granted under the relevant provisions of this Act. A breach of s.6 is an offence under s.8.

Extent of Prohibition
This prohibition extends to:
(a) buildings which are subject to building preservation notices pursuant to s.3:
(b) buildings in conservation areas, pursuant to s.66(3). The logic behind the extension of this provision is that the value of a conservation area does not exclusively lie in individual listed buildings, but in the contribution which all the buildings in the conservation area make as a whole. Thus, the demolition or alteration of a single building within a conservation area, may affect its overall character or appearance.

Exceptions
The exceptions to the prohibition contained in s.6 are:
(a) ecclesiastical buildings which are for the time being, used for ecclesiastical purposes (s.54), see also para. 2.6 of the *Memorandum of Guidance* 1993;
(b) buildings which are included in the Schedule of monuments maintained under the Ancient Monuments and Archaeological Areas Act 1979 (c. 46);
(c) buildings owned by the Crown, notwithstanding that they may be listed pursuant to s.1. Section 74 seeks to apply the majority of provisions of this Act to Crown land. In practice however, a non-statutory procedure exists whereby Crown developers are required to consult the appropriate planning authority about any plans to demolish, alter or extend a listed building in any way which would affect its character or appearance as a building of special architectural or historic interest. SDD Circular No.21/1984 *"Crown Land and Crown Development"* sets out the details of the procedure to be followed (see paras. 26 to 28).

Planning Control
The requirement to obtain consent before executing any works for the demolition, alteration or extension of a listed building, is without prejudice to the likelihood of the need to obtain separate planning permission for works which constitute development under Pt. III of the Town and Country Planning (Scotland) Act 1997 (c. 8). A separate application for planning permission would be required in these circumstances. See the decision of the High Court in *Windsor and Maidenhead Borough Council v. Secretary of State for the Environment* [1988] 2 PLR 17; [1988] JPL 410. In this case, Mann J. held that the repainting of a listed building, for which listed building was required, was capable of also constituting development requiring planning permission.

Extension to conservation areas
This provision is extended to buildings in conservation areas by virtue of s.66.

Authorisation of works: listed building consent

7.—(1) Works for the alteration or extension of a listed building are authorised if—
   (a) the planning authority or the Secretary of State has granted written consent for the execution of the works, and
   (b) the works are executed in accordance with the terms of the consent and of any conditions attached to it.
   (2) Works for the demolition of a listed building are authorised if—
   (a) such consent has been granted for their execution,
   (b) notice of the proposal to execute the works has been given to the Royal Commission,

(c) after such notice has been given either—
        (i) for a period of at least 3 months following the grant of listed building consent, and before the commencement of the works, reasonable access to the building has been made available to members or officers of the Commission for the purpose of recording it, or
        (ii) the Secretary of the Commission or other officer of theirs with authority to act on their behalf for the purposes of this section has stated in writing that they have completed their recording of the building or that they do not wish to record it, and
(d) the works are executed in accordance with the terms of the consent and of any conditions attached to it.
(3) Where—
(a) works for the alteration, extension or demolition of a listed building have been executed without such consent, and
(b) written consent is granted by the planning authority or the Secretary of State for the retention of the works,
the works are authorised from the grant of that consent.

(4) In this section "the Royal Commission" means the Royal Commission on the Ancient and Historical Monuments of Scotland.

(5) The Secretary of State may by order provide that subsection (2) shall have effect with the substitution for the reference to the Royal Commission of a reference to such other body as may be so specified.

(6) Such an order shall apply in the case of works executed or to be executed on or after such date as may be specified in the order.

(7) Consent under subsection (1), (2) or (3) is referred to in this Act as "listed building consent".

DEFINITIONS
    "building": s.81(2).
    "land": s.81(2).
    "listed building": s.1(4).
    "listed building consent": s.7(7).
    "planning authority": s.81(2).
    "Royal Commission": subs. (4).

GENERAL NOTE
    This section establishes the requirements which must be satisfied before works for the demolition, alteration or extension of a listed building can be authorised. Section 7 draws a distinction between works for the alteration or extension to a listed building (subs. (1) and demolition (subs. (2)).

Alteration or extension or demolition
    In *Shimizu (U.K) v. Westminster City Council* [1997] 1 WLR 168; [1997] 1 All E.R. 481, the appellants purchased a listed building with consent to demolish the entire building except for the façade, chimney breasts and chimney stacks. The appellants proceeded to carry out the demolition pursuant to the consent. Thereafter, they applied for listed building consent for the removal of the internal chimney breasts in order to provide an extra floor to their proposed new development. The application was refused by the Secretary of State. The appellants sought substantial compensation from the local planning authority under the now repealed s.27(1)(a) of the Planning (Listed Buildings and Conservation Areas) Act 1990 (c. 9), on the grounds that the removal of the chimney breasts amounted to an "alteration of ... a listed building" and did not constitute development. The Lands Tribunal held that the proposed works constituted alterations to a listed building, with the result that compensation was payable by the planning authority. This was overturned by the Court of Appeal on the grounds that the concepts of "demolition" and "alteration" were mutually exclusive and that the removal of the chimney breasts amounted to the demolition of a listed building or part of a listed building in respect of which compensation was not payable by the local planning authority under s.27(1)(a) (repealed by Pt. II of Sched. 19 to the Planning and Compensation Act 1991 (c. 34)). The appellants appealed.
    The House of Lords (Griffiths L.J. dissenting) held that "demolition" referred to pulling down a building so that it was completely destroyed and broken up. It therefore followed that works which involved the demolition of part only of a listed building falling short of the destruction of the whole building, fell within the expression "alteration" and did not constitute

demolition for the purposes of the Act unless the works to be carried out to the listed building as a whole were so substantial as to amount to a clearing of the whole site for redevelopment. Whether works were "demolition" or alteration" was ultimately a question of fact in each case and the Lands Tribunal had been entitled to hold on the facts that the proposed works were works of alteration and not works of demolition.

This is an important judgment which, in the words of the dissenting speech of Griffiths L.J., brings about "a fundamental change to the basis upon which the legislation has hitherto been administered". The conventional approach to the term "listed building", which was accepted in the Court of Appeal, was that this term included part of a listed building. Indeed, s.91 of the 1990 Act provides that the word "building" has the same meaning as in s.336 of the Town and Country Planning Act 1990 (c. 8), which provides that "building" includes "any part of a building". This English provision is replicated in s.81 of the Planning (Listed Buildings and Conservation Areas) (Scotland) Act 1997 (c. 9), which defines the term "building" by reference to s.278 of the Town and Country Planning (Scotland) Act 1997 (c. 8). The difficulty therefore which the Court of Appeal and subsequently the House of Lords had to grapple with was how to differentiate between the terms "demolition" and "alteration" when the term "building" included "part of a building". It is notable that Russell L.J. in the Court of Appeal observed that his dissatisfaction with these terms was "only slightly lessened by the reflection that Parliament has resolved the anomaly by withdrawing the right to compensation".

The lead speech of Hope L.J. is of particular interest in that he focuses upon the definition of the term "listed building" rather than "building". While he acknowledges the statutory extension to the term "building" to include "part of a building", Hope L.J. forms the view in *Shimizu (U.K)* that no such extension applies to the term "listed building":

> "Mr Barnes accepted that the difficulty which has arisen in this case is due entirely to the extended meaning which is given to the word 'building' in the Principal Act as including "any part of a building" ... If s.27(1)(a) is to be read as directing that the section is to have effect where "an application for listed building consent for the alteration or extension of a listed building or *part of a listed building*", one could without much difficulty say that the applicants" application did not meet the requirement because it was an application to demolish a part of the listed building—namely the chimney breasts—not to alter or extend that part of the listed building ... But, ... I do not think that it is self-evident that the expression "listed building" must be read in this way."

The effect of this approach is that once a building or part of a building is included in the statutory list by the Secretary of State, the term "listed building" is to be read in the context of the entire building or the part so listed. Thus, demolition must be defined by reference to the unit which is listed, and not just a part of it. Therefore, works which fall short of the destruction of the unit which is listed, falls within the term "alteration" and not "demolition". Lord Hope's speech went even further in that he points out that the advice contained in DOE Circular 8/87 and a decision of the Queen's Bench Division in *R. v. North Hertfordshire District Council, ex p. Sullivan* [1981] JPL 752 and para. 4.28 of PPG 15, was now inconsistent with his speech in *Shimizu*, and required to be reconsidered. In essence, Lord Hope has formed the view that there can no longer be any question of the word "demolition" within the meaning of the Act being applied to works of alteration which affect only part of a listed building. The implications of this view nationally for all those involved in the preservation of listed buildings must be a cause for concern. This was certainly acknowledged in the dissenting speech of Lord Griffiths at p. 484G-H, who adopted a pragmatic approach to the whole issue:

> "The appellants acquired the building (on November 2, 1989) before any demolition had commenced. They could before starting demolition have applied for the planning consent to be varied to enable them to demolish the chimney breasts. This we know would have been refused. The appellants would have been thereby deprived of additional floor space, but would not have been entitled to compensation.
>
> In fact they choose to demolish the building and then to apply to demolish the chimney breasts. And it is said that by making the application later rather than earlier they turn demolition into alteration and, hey presto, are entitled to £1.8m. My Lords, that does not seem right to me. Taking down and destroying the chimney breast was part and parcel of the demolition of the old listed building whether it took place before or during the construction of the new building and I would dismiss the appeal".

The *Shimizu* decision is unlikely to have settled the question of when works to a listed building are to be regarded as demolition or as alteration. This is especially likely to be the case where only part of a building is listed such as the façade. In this situation, the question then arises whether the building behind the façade is also listed. The answer would seem to depend on whether the *Debenhams v. Westminster City Council* [1987] 1 All E.R. 51 test can be said to apply (the ancillary/subordinate approach: see commentary to s.1). However, it is clearly intellectually dissatisfying to regard the building behind the façade as ancillary or subordinate to the façade! Equally, it is dissatisfying to regard the total removal of the building behind the façade as an alteration to a listed building rather than as a demolition as Lord Hope's interpretation appears to suggest. The decision of the House of Lords in *Shimizu* also creates difficulties where the listed unit comprises of more than one building, such as a row of terraced houses or a number of buildings within the curtilage of the principal listed building. It is now unclear in these circumstances whether the removal of one building from the terrace or curtilage would constitute demolition, or alteration. Ultimately, each case will turn upon its individual facts and circumstances.

Notification to the Royal Commission
The Royal Commission on the Ancient and Historical Monuments of Scotland was created in 1908 by the Royal Prerogative and operates under the terms of a Royal Warrant (revised in 1992). It is a non-departmental public body sponsored by Historic Scotland and funded by the Scottish Office. Subsection (2) requires the Royal Commission to be notified of the proposal to execute works for the demolition of a listed building. It appears logical that the Royal Commission must be notified as a matter of course *before* listed building consent is granted, of all proposals for demolition. This would provide the Royal Commission with an opportunity to make representations on the appropriateness or otherwise of the proposal *before* consent is granted. Thereafter, if listed building consent is granted for the demolition of the building, notification of the decision under subs. (2)(c) must be given so as to allow the Royal Commission access to the building for recording purposes.

The effect of the *Shimizu* decision on the role of the Royal Commission is unclear. It appears reasonably certain that the number of applications for demolition may fall following *Shimizu*, insofar as these applications will now become applications for alteration, rather than demolition. This will be disappointing as the loss of architectural features in some circumstances may be as significant as the loss of the building itself. The Royal Commission on the Ancient and Historical Monuments of Scotland, is based at John Sinclair House, 16 Bernard Crescent, Edinburgh, EH8 9NX.

Extension to conservation areas
This provision is extended to buildings in conservation areas by virtue of s.66.

Offences

8.—(1) If a person contravenes section 6 he shall be guilty of an offence.

(2) Without prejudice to subsection (1), if a person executing or causing to be executed any works in relation to a listed building under a listed building consent fails to comply with any condition attached to the consent, he shall be guilty of an offence.

(3) In proceedings for an offence under this section it shall be a defence to prove the following matters—

(a) that works to the building were urgently necessary in the interests of safety or health or for the preservation of the building,

(b) that it was not practicable to secure safety or health or, as the case may be, the preservation of the building by works of repair or works for affording temporary support or shelter,

(c) that the works carried out were limited to the minimum measures immediately necessary, and

(d) that notice in writing justifying in detail the carrying out of the works was given to the planning authority as soon as reasonably practicable.

(4) A person guilty of an offence under this section shall be liable—

(a) on summary conviction to imprisonment for a term not exceeding 6 months or a fine not exceeding £20,000, or both, or

(b) on conviction on indictment to imprisonment for a term not exceeding 2 years or a fine, or both.

(5) In determining the amount of any fine to be imposed on a person convicted of an offence under this section, the court shall in particular have regard to any financial benefit which has accrued or appears likely to accrue to him in consequence of the offence.

DEFINITIONS
  "building": s.81(2).
  "listed building": s.1(4).
  "listed building consent": s.7.
  "planning authority": s.81(2).

GENERAL NOTE
  This section establishes two separate offences:
  (a) it is an offence to contravene s.6 which restricts works affecting listed buildings without
     the requisite consent under s.7;
  (b) it is an offence to fail to comply with the conditions attached to any listed building consent.
  The offences created under this section are extended by s.66(3) to buildings in conservation
areas and by s.3(4) to buildings which are the subject of a building preservation notice. In Scotland, only the Procurator Fiscal is empowered to bring criminal proceedings for an offences
under this Act. This contrasts with the position in England and Wales, whereby local planning
authorities are empowered to undertake prosecutions in respect of breach of planning control.

Exceptions
  It is not an offence under s.8 to carry out unauthorised work to listed buildings in relation to
the following buildings:
  (a) ecclesiastical buildings which are for the time being, used for ecclesiastical purposes
     (s.54), see also para. 2.6 of the *1993 Memorandum of Guidance*;
  (b) buildings which are included in the Schedule of monuments maintained under the
     Ancient Monuments and Archaeological Areas Act 1979;
  (c) buildings owned by the Crown, notwithstanding that they may be listed pursuant to s.1.
     Section 74 seeks to apply the majority of provisions of this Act to Crown land. In practice
     however, a non-statutory procedure exists whereby Crown developers are required to
     consult the appropriate planning authority about any plans to demolish, alter or extend a
     listed building in any way which would affect its character or appearance as a building of
     special architectural or historic interest. SDD Circular No.21/1984 *"Crown Land and
     Crown Development"* sets out the details of the procedure to be followed (see paras. 26 to
     28).

Scope of the Offences

Subs. (1)
  It is an offence of strict liability to carry out unauthorised works for the demolition, alteration
or extension to a listed building: see decision of the Queen's Bench Division in *R. v. Wells Street
Metropolitan Stipendiary Magistrate, ex p. Westminster City Council* [1986] 3 All E.R. 4, [1986]
JPL 903, on an identical provision in the English Town and Country Planning Act 1971 (c. 78).
Liability is created by any person executing or causing to be executed any unauthorised works in
relation to a listed building. It is notable that liability only arises therefore out of a positive act.
Knowingly permitting unauthorised works to be executed does not give rise to an offence under
this section.
  Liability arises from the date the building becomes listed. This further illustrates the importance of notifying all the relevant owners or occupiers as soon as the building becomes listed.

Subs. (2)
  This provision overlaps considerably with the offence created by subs. (1), in that works are
only authorised under subs. (1) where they are executed in accordance with the terms of the
consent and any conditions attached to it (s.7(1)(b)). However, it is likely that Parliament has
seen fit to create a specific offence of contravention of a condition without prejudice to subs. (1)
for the purposes of clarity.

Damage to Listed Buildings
  Section 53 creates a specific offence of intentionally causing damage to a listed building or
permitting any act which causes or is likely to result in damage to the building. This provision
differs from the criminal liability created under s.8, in that it is intended to encompass deliberate
acts of damage to a listed building, rather than unauthorised alteration.

Defence

The burden of establishing the statutory defence lies on the accused. There are five elements to the defence, each of which must be established:
(i)   that the works were urgently necessary;
(ii)   that it was in the interests of health and safety or preservation of the building;
(iii) works of repair or temporary support or shelter was not practicable;
(iv)   works were limited to the minimum measures which must be immediately necessary;
(v)   notice in writing and in detail must be given to the planning authority as soon as reasonably practicable.

It can be seen that this is not a defence which will be easily established and is likely to require expert evidence.

Penalties

An offence under this provision may be tried either summarily or on indictment. An individual convicted under s.8 may be fined or imprisoned or both. If tried summarily, the maximum fine is £20,000 and the maximum imprisonment is six months. If tried on indictment, an individual may face an unlimited fine or imprisonment not exceeding two years. The sentencing court is required to have particular regard to any financial benefit which the individual has had or which is likely to accrue to him. This can be illustrated by the two decisions reported in [1990] JPL 397. The first case involved the imposition of a £14,000 fine by Horseferry Road Magistrates Court on a company director and Seasons Builders of Hemel Hempstead, following their guilty plea to unauthorised works to a Grade II listed building in Soho, London. They were also ordered to pay £10,000 in expenses to Westminster City Council and English Heritage, who brought the prosecution. The second case involved the imposition of a £25,000 fine for contempt of court on Kingsland Investments, a property investment company. This followed a breach of an injunction by the company obtained by Forest Heath District Council, to prevent any further unauthorised work to Palace House Mansion, a Grade II listed building in Palace Street.

Other enforcement powers

The planning authority have additional extensive powers under ss.34–41 in respect of contravention of listed building control. In particular, it is an offence to fail to comply with a listed building enforcement notice under s.39: see further commentary to s.39.

Extension to conservation areas

This provision is extended to buildings in conservation areas by virtue of s.66.

Applications for listed building consent

Making of applications for listed building consent

9.—(1) Except as provided in sections 11 to 14, an application for listed building consent shall be made to and dealt with by the planning authority.

(2) Such an application shall be made in such form as the planning authority may require and shall contain—
(a) sufficient particulars to identify the building to which it relates, including a plan,
(b) such other plans and drawings as are necessary to describe the works which are the subject of the application, and
(c) such other particulars as may be required by the planning authority.

(3) Provision may be made by regulations with respect to—
(a) the manner in which applications for listed building consent are to be made,
(b) the manner in which such applications are to be advertised, and
(c) the time within which they are to be dealt with by planning authorities or, as the case may be, by the Secretary of State.

DEFINITIONS
"building": s.81(2).
"listed building": s.1(4).
"listed building consent": s.7.
"planning authority": s.81(2).

Applications for consent
This section prescribes the form of applications for listed building consent. Its provisions extend to:
(i) buildings which are the subject of building preservation notices under s.3;
(ii) applications for conservation area consent (see s.66 and reg. 3(1) of the Town and Country Planning (Listed Buildings and Buildings in Conservation Areas) (Scotland) Regulations 1987 (S.I. 1987 No. 1529));
(iii) applications to vary or discharge conditions attached to listed building consent (s.17(2)) or to conservation area consent (see s.66 and reg. 4 of the Town and Country Planning (Listed Buildings and Buildings in Conservation Areas) (Scotland) Regulations 1987).

Form of application
The 1987 Regulations prescribe the procedures for making and determining applications for listed building and conservation area consent. The application must be made on a form prescribed by the planning authority and be lodged together with two copies of the form and such documents or certificates as may be required. Regulation 3 confers a wide discretion upon the planning authority to require the applicant to provide such further information as they may require to enable them to determine the application and to verify the information submitted to them. This is in addition to the information which an application must contain under subs. (2).
Under subs. (2), an application must contain:
(i) sufficient particulars to identify the building, including a plan;
(ii) such other plans and drawings as are necessary to describe the works which are the subject of the application; and
(iii) such other particulars as may be required by the planning authority.
The planning authority may not necessarily determine the application itself. Under reg. 3 of the 1987 Regulations, the planning authority may simply fail to determine the application within the requisite two-month time limit (which gives rise to the right of appeal to the Secretary of State) or refer the application to the Secretary of State for his determination.

Certificates to accompany applications
Regulation 6 of the 1987 Regulations provides that the application must be accompanied by a certificate signed by or on behalf of the applicant which certifies that either:
(i) the applicant was the owner of the building or any part of the building to which the application relates for a period of not less than 21 days prior to the date the application was made; or
(ii) the applicant has given the requisite notice to all persons who were the owners of the building or part of the building to which the application relates for a period of not less than 21 days prior to the date the application was made. This certificate must include the names and addresses of all persons to whom notice of the application was given and the date upon which each notice was served; or
(iii) that the applicant has issued such a notice to all owners of the building or part of the building to which the application relates, who are reasonably ascertainable; or
(iv) that no owners were reasonably ascertainable.
Part I of Sched. 2 to the 1987 Regulations prescribes the standard form which those certificates are required to follow.

Advertisements of Applications
Under Reg. 5 of the 1987 Regulations, planning authorities are required to advertise applications for listed building consent. Such advertisements must appear in both the Edinburgh Gazette and the local newspaper simultaneously and state where the application and its accompanying plans may be inspected during reasonable hours. The application and the plans must be available for inspection by the public for a period of not less than 21 days beginning with the date of publication of the notice. The notice must also state that representations may be made to the planning authority in writing within that period.
The planning authority must display a notice on or near the building to which the application relates, for not less than seven days. The planning authority have no power to determine the application until the expiry of the requisite period of notice. The *1993 Memorandum of Guidance* recommends that planning authorities keep a register of applications for listed building consent. This is a matter of good practice, rather than any statutory requirement.

Crown Land

The Crown do not require consent to carry out works to a listed building which is situated on Crown land, although s.74, seeks to apply the majority of provisions of this Act to Crown land. In practice however, a non-statutory procedure exists whereby Crown developers are required to consult the appropriate planning authority about any plans to demolish, alter or extend a listed building in any way which would affect its character or appearance as a building of special architectural or historic interest. SDD Circular No. 21/1984 *"Crown Land and Crown Development"* sets out the details of the procedure to be followed (see paras. 26 to 28). Further guidance may be obtained from paras. 2.73 to 2.79 of the *1993 Memorandum of Guidance*. See further commentary to s.74.

Where an interest, other than an interest held on behalf of the Crown, is held in a listed building which is situated on Crown land, the holder of the interest is required to make an application for listed building consent in the normal way. Certification is required under s.10 that the Crown has been notified of the application.

Applications by planning authorities

Planning authorities who wish to carry out works which require listed building consent are required to make an application for consent to the Secretary of State: see s.73 and reg. 11 of the 1987 Regulations.

Certificates as to interests in listed building etc.

10.—(1) Regulations may provide that an application for listed building consent shall not be entertained unless it is accompanied by a certificate in the prescribed form as to the interests in the building to which the application relates.

(2) Any such regulations may—

(a) include requirements corresponding to those mentioned in sections 35 and 38(2) of the principal Act,

(b) make provision as to who, in the case of any building, is to be treated as the owner for the purposes of any provision of the regulations, and

(c) make different provision for different cases or classes of case.

(3) If any person—

(a) issues a certificate which purports to comply with the requirements of regulations made by virtue of this section and which contains a statement which he knows to be false or misleading in a material particular, or

(b) recklessly issues a certificate which purports to comply with those requirements and which contains a statement which is false or misleading in a material particular,

he shall be guilty of an offence and liable on summary conviction to a fine not exceeding level 3 on the standard scale.

DEFINITIONS

"building": s.81(2).
"listed building": s.1(4).
"listed building consent": s.7(7).
"owner": s.81(2).
"planning authority": s.81(2).
"prescribed": s.81(1).

GENERAL NOTE

This provision extends to applications in relation to:

(i) buildings which are the subject of building preservation notices under s.3;

(ii) applications for conservation area consent (see s.66 and reg. 3(1) of the Town and Country Planning (Listed Buildings and Buildings in Conservation Areas) (Scotland) Regulations 1987 (S.I. 1987 No. 1529));

(iii) applications to vary or discharge conditions attached to listed building consent (s.17(2)) or to conservation area consent (see s.66 and reg. 4 of the Town and Country Planning (Listed Buildings and Buildings in Conservation Areas) (Scotland) Regulations 1987). However, such an application may only be made by an individual with an "interest" in the listed building.

Subs. (3)

It is an offence under subs. (3) to knowingly or recklessly provide false or misleading information. This offence is triable summarily only.

Reference of certain applications to Secretary of State

11.—(1) The Secretary of State may give directions requiring applications for listed building consent to be referred to him instead of being dealt with by the planning authority.

(2) A direction under this section may relate either to a particular application or to applications in respect of such buildings as may be specified in the direction.

(3) An application in respect of which a direction under this section has effect shall be referred to the Secretary of State accordingly.

(4) Before determining an application referred to him under this section, the Secretary of State shall, if either the applicant or the authority so desire, afford to each of them an opportunity of appearing before, and being heard by, a person appointed by the Secretary of State.

(5) The decision of the Secretary of State on any application referred to him under this section shall be final.

DEFINITIONS

"building": s.81(2).
"listed building": s.1(4).
"listed building consent": s.7(7).
"planning authority": s.81(2).

GENERAL NOTE

This section empowers the Secretary of State to "call-in" an application for listed building consent for his own determination in the first instance. This power is parallel to that contained in s.46 of the Principal Act and allows the Secretary of State to exercise considerable control over planning decisions.

The Secretary of State has a considerable discretion under s.11 to call-in an application: see further *R. v. Secretary of State for the Environment, ex p. Southwark London Borough Council* (1987) 54 P. & C.R. 226; [1987] JPL 587 and *R. v. Secretary of State for the Environment, ex p. Middlesbrough Borough Council* [1988] 3 PLR 52. There are no provisions within the legislation for individuals to request the Secretary of State to exercise his powers of call-in, although they may informally do so. In *R. v. Secretary of State for the Environment, ex p. Newprop* [1983] JPL 386, Forbes J. held that the Secretary of State's refusal to call-in an application could only be challenged if his decision was "wildly perverse". However, in *Rhys Williams v. Secretary of State for Wales* [1985] JPL 29, the Court of Appeal applied the normal principles of Wednesbury unreasonableness to the question of whether the Secretary of State ought to have exercised his powers to call in an application. However, in *Lakin v. Secretary of State for Scotland* [1988] SLT 780, the Court of Session quashed a decision of the Secretary of State to refuse to call-in an application, in circumstances where this refusal prejudiced the outcome of a planning application by the Petitioners and defeated their legitimate expectation of a hearing into alternative sites.

Title and Interest to challenge

While it is open to any member of the public to request the Secretary of State to exercise his powers under s.11, he is not obliged to accede to such a request or to give reasons for not doing so. Furthermore, a member of the public must establish title and interest in judicial review proceedings, before the courts will entertain a petition to exercise its supervisory jurisdiction. At present, there is a marked divergence between the Scottish approach to title and interest and the English rules pertaining to *locus standi*, the latter approach being much more liberal. In *Wilson v. I.B.A.*, 1979 SLT 279, the Lord Ordinary suggested that any member of the public would have title to enforce a public duty provided that they could demonstrate that the title was coupled with a sufficient interest in the subject matter to which the petition relates. The nature of that interest was undefined. However in *Scottish Old People's Welfare Council, Petrs.*, 1987 SLT 179, Lord Clyde adopted a narrow interpretation of "interest". In that case, the petitioners were a pressure group who campaigned on behalf of the elderly to challenge the legality of government instructions on cold weather payments to the elderly. Although Lord Clyde held that the petitioners had sufficient title to challenge, he held that their interest was too remote to give them a right to sue. This was on the basis that the petitioners were "not suing as a body of potential claimants, but as a body working to protect and advance the interests of the aged". This was held to be insufficient. This approach adopts a careful distinction between title on the one hand and interest on the other, and concludes that one does not necessarily follow the other.

Notification of call-in
The Town and Country Planning (Listed Buildings and Buildings in Conservation Areas) (Scotland) Regulations 1987 (S.I. 1987 No. 1529), requires the planning authority to notify an applicant for listed building consent, in writing where the application has been called-in.

Applications by planning authorities
The Town and Country Planning (Listed Buildings and Buildings in Conservation Areas) (Scotland) Regulations 1987 (S.I. 1987 No. 1529) require a planning authority to submit an application for listed building consent to the planning authority in the usual way. However, reg. 11(2) requires the application to be submitted to the Secretary of State. The procedure thereafter follows that which applies to the determination of appeals.

Secretary of State's decision final
Section 11(5) is subject to the provisions of s.58 which allows for a decision under s.11 to be challenged in the Court of Session: see further commentary to s.58.

Extension to conservation areas
This provision applies to buildings in conservation areas by virtue of s.66.

Duty to notify Secretary of State of applications

12.—(1) If a planning authority to whom application is made for listed building consent intend to grant such consent they shall first notify the Secretary of State of the application giving particulars of the works for which the consent is required.

(2) The Secretary of State may within the period of 28 days beginning with the date of the notification—

(a) direct the reference of the application to him under section 11, or
(b) give notice to the authority that he requires further time in which to consider whether to require such a reference.

(3) The planning authority shall not grant listed building consent until—

(a) the period mentioned in subsection (2) has expired without the Secretary of State directing the reference of the application to him or giving them notice under paragraph (b) of that subsection, or
(b) the Secretary of State has notified them that he does not intend to require the reference of the application.

DEFINITIONS
  "buildings": s.81(2).
  "listed building": s.1(4).
  "listed building consent": s.7(7).
  "planning authority": s.81(2).

GENERAL NOTE
Section 12 requires planning authorities to notify the Secretary of State of applications made for listed building consent, where they propose to grant consent. The Secretary of State thereafter has 28 days from the date of notification to direct that the application be referred to him under s.11, or give notice that he requires further time in which to consider whether to require such a reference. Applications in respect of which the planning authority does not intend to grant consent, need not be referred to the Secretary of State. The notification requirement also applies to buildings which are the subject of building preservation notices (s.3(5)).

Notification to the Secretary of State
Planning authorities have no power to grant listed building consent until the Secretary of State has been notified and until after the expiry of the 28 day notification period. In the absence of the exercise of his call-in powers by the Secretary of State under s.11, the planning authority may only then proceed to grant consent. Paragraph 2.52 of the *1993 Memorandum of Guidance* suggests that notification to the Secretary of State be accompanied by:

— a copy of the application, together with plans drawings and all of the information necessary to identify the buildings and to consider the detail of the works. Where appropriate, a structural report should also be provided;
— an indication of the reasons why the planning authority are disposed to grant consent;
— copies of representations, if any, particularly in response to the advertisement and, in the case of demolitions, the notification sent to the Royal Commission on the Ancient and Historical Monuments of Scotland.

Extension to conservation areas
This provision applies to buildings in conservation areas by virtue of s.66.

Directions concerning notification of applications etc.

13.—(1) The Secretary of State may give directions that, in the case of such descriptions of applications for listed building consent as he may specify, other than such consent for the demolition of a building, section 12 shall not apply.

(2) Where a direction is in force under subsection (1) in respect of any description of application, planning authorities may determine applications of that description in any manner they think fit, without notifying the Secretary of State.

(3) Without prejudice to sections 9 to 12, the Secretary of State may give directions to planning authorities requiring them, in such cases or classes of case as may be specified in the directions, to notify to him and to such other persons as may be so specified—

(a) any applications made to them for listed building consent, and
(b) the decisions taken by the authorities on those applications.

DEFINITIONS
"buildings": s.81(2).
"land": s.81(2).
"listed building": s.1(4).
"listed building consent": s.7(7).
"planning authority": s.81(2).

GENERAL NOTE
This provision empowers the Secretary of State to issue directions relaxing the notification requirements contained in s.12. A direction under this provision is not made by statutory instrument and is not subject to parliamentary supervision. The existing directions are contained in Annex III to Circular 17/1987 which provides:

"Under the powers contained in paragraph 6(1) of Schedule 10 to the Town and Country Planning (Scotland) Act 1972 (now superseded by s.13 of this Act), the Secretary of State hereby directs that:

(a) applications for alterations or extensions to category C(S) and B for group buildings; and
(b) applications for varying or modifying of conditions attached to earlier consents relating to the alteration or extension of buildings in these categories

which are received by planning authorities on or after January 1, 1988 shall not be required to be notified to him under paragraph 5 of Schedule 10 to the 1972 Act."

A planning authority which receives an application for listed building consent which falls within the scope of this direction is entitled to grant the application without notifying the Secretary of State.

However, it should be noted that under subs. (3), the Secretary of State may still require a planning authority to notify him of applications for listed building consent or decisions taken by planning authorities on those applications, without prejudice to the power to issue a direction under subs. (1).

Extension to conservation areas
This provision applies to buildings in conservation areas by virtue of s.66.

Decision on application

14.—(1) Subject to the previous provisions of this Part, the planning authority or, as the case may be, the Secretary of State may grant or refuse an application for listed building consent and, if granting consent, may grant it subject to conditions.

(2) In considering whether to grant listed building consent for any works, the planning authority or the Secretary of State, as the case may be, shall have special regard to the desirability of preserving the building or its setting or any features of special architectural or historic interest which it possesses.

(3) Any listed building consent shall (except in so far as it otherwise provides) enure for the benefit of the building and of all persons for the time being interested in it.

DEFINITIONS
  "building": s.81(2).
  "listed building": s.1(4).
  "listed building consent": s.7(7).
  "planning authority": s.81(2).

GENERAL NOTE
This provision establishes the power of the planning authority or the Secretary of State to grant listed building consent, subject to the previous provisions of this Act and attached conditions. In reaching a decision whether or not to grant consent, the planning authority are required to have "special regard to the desirability of preserving the building or its setting or any features of special architectural or historic interest which it possesses". In *Simpson v. Corporation of the City of Edinburgh,* 1960 S.C. 313, the Court of Session said that in dealing with applications for planning permission the local authority had to "have regard" to the material provisions of the development plan. Lord Guest said (at 318):
  "To 'have regard to' does not, in my view, mean 'slavishly to adhere to'. It requires the planning authority to consider the development plan, but does not oblige them to follow it."
Further, in *R. v. C.D.* [1976] 1 N.Z.L.R. 436 at 437, Somers J. said:
  "I do not think that [the words have regard to] are synonymous with 'shall take into account' ... I think that the legislative intent is that the court has a complete discretion but that the seven matters, or as many as are appropriate, are to be considered. In any particular case, all or any of the appropriate matters may be rejected or given such weight as the case suggests is suitable."
These dicta were approved by the Inner House of the Court of Session in *King v. East Ayrshire Council* 1997 GWD.

Policy Advice
The Secretary of State's guidance as to the factors planning authorities should take into account in reaching decisions on listed building applications, are contained in paras. 2.10 to 2.23 of the *1993 Memorandum of Guidance.*

Owners' representations
The planning authority is required to take into account any representations by the owner of a listed building and to give notice of their decision to such a person (reg. 3 of the Town and Country Planning (Listed Buildings and Buildings in Conservation Areas) (Scotland) Regulations 1987 (S.I. 1987 No. 1529).

Extension to conservation areas
This provision applies to buildings in conservation areas by virtue of s.66.

Grant of consent subject to conditions

Power to impose conditions on grant of listed building consent

15.—(1) Without prejudice to the generality of section 14(1), the conditions subject to which listed building consent may be granted may include conditions with respect to—
  (a) the preservation of particular features of the building, either as part of it or after severance from it;

(b) the making good, after the works are completed, of any damage caused to the building by the works;

(c) the reconstruction of the building or any part of it following the execution of any works, with the use of original materials so far as practicable and with such alterations of the interior of the building as may be specified in the conditions.

(2) Listed building consent may also be granted subject to a condition reserving specified details of the works (whether or not set out in the application) for subsequent approval by the planning authority or, in the case of consent granted by Secretary of State, specifying whether the reserved details are to be approved by the planning authority or by him.

(3) In granting a listed building consent a planning authority may attach to the consent a condition that no demolition of the listed building shall take place until either or both of the following requirements have been met—

(a) an agreement for the regulation of the development of the site of the listed building in accordance with a current planning permission has been made and recorded under section 75 of the principal Act;

(b) the planning authority are satisfied that contracts have been placed either—

      (i) for the redevelopment of the site, or

      (ii) for its conversion to an acceptable open space,

in accordance with a current planning permission.

DEFINITIONS
"building": s.81(2).
"development": s.81(2).
"listed building": s.1(4).
"listed building consent": s.7(7).
"planning authority": s.81(2).
"planning permission": s.81(2).

GENERAL NOTE
This provision provides for the imposition of conditions by the planning authority on the grant of listed building consent. It should be noted that this power is in addition to existing power in the Principal Act to attach conditions to the grant of any requisite planning permission.

Subs. (1)
Subsection (1) sets out the type of conditions which may be attached to the grant of listed building consent. Subsection (1) is not intended to be definitive, but merely lists the type of conditions which are commonly seen. They include:

(a) conditions requiring preservation of particular features of the building;
(b) conditions requiring restoration of any damage caused to the building during works;
(c) reconstruction of the building using the original materials as far as reasonably practicable;

Subs. (2)
While a condition may reserve matters of detail for subsequent approval, this does not derogate from the need for the condition to satisfy the requirement of certainty. This is of particular importance considering the criminal sanctions which may be imposed following a breach of condition. It should be noted that the *1993 Memorandum of Guidance* states that the grant of listed building consent subject to a condition under subs. (2), is not intended to foster the granting of outline listed building consent, leaving major details crucial to the assessment of a proposal's merit unclear (para. 2.82).

Criteria for validity
In *Newbury District Council v. Secretary of State for the Environment* [1981] A.C. 636, Viscount Dilhorne stated that:
"The conditions imposed must be for a planning purpose and not for an ulterior one, and . . . they must fairly and reasonably relate to the development permitted. Also they must not be so unreasonable that no reasonable planning authority could have imposed them".

Apart from the three well known tests laid down in the *Newbury* case, a condition may also be void for uncertainty (*Fawcett Properties v. Buckingham County Council* [1961] A.C. 636; contrast *Lowe (David) & Sons v. Burgh of Musselburgh,* 1974 SLT 5); or unenforceable insofar as it concerns matters outwith the control of the applicant (*British Airports Authority v. Secretary of State for Scotland* [1980] JPL 260); although the use of *Grampian*-type conditions may overcome this difficulty (*Grampian Regional Council v. City of Aberdeen District Council* (1984) 47 P. & C.R. 633. A condition must not be imposed for an ulterior motive : *R. v. Hillingdon London Borough Council, ex p. Royco Homes* [1974] Q.B. 720, see also *"the Hillingdon ('Royco') Case"* [1974] JPL 507.

Severance of Invalid Conditions
Prior to 1986, one of the dilemma's facing landowners seeking to challenge the validity of a condition, was whether the Courts would be prepared to sever the invalid condition from the permission, or whether the condition could not be severed so that the whole planning permission was held to be void *ab initio.* In *Hall & Co. v. Shoreham-by-Sea Urban District Council* [1964] 1 WLR 240, a condition which effectively required a company to dedicate a road to the public at the public's expense was held to be invalid. However, the Court of Appeal was persuaded that as the condition was fundamental to the whole permission, the planning permission was a nullity. This decision gave rise to the trivial/fundamental test which was supported by the House of Lords in *Kent County Council v. Kingsway Investments (Kent)* [1971] A.C. 72. Section 17 of this Act was originally introduced by the Housing and Planning Act 1986 (c. 63) and now allows an applicant to apply to a planning authority to vary or discharge conditions attached to the grant of listed building or planning consent.

Appeal against condition
Section 18 allows a landowner to appeal to the Secretary of State against the imposition of a condition attached to a listed building consent. The consequence of an appeal against a condition however, is that the Secretary of State may treat the appeal as if the application for listed building consent was made to him in the first instance. This may lead to the loss of the consent, as well as the condition, if the appeal is successful. Contrast the position of an appeal against a refusal of an application to vary or discharge a condition.

Extension to conservation area consent
This provision extends to buildings in conservation areas, by virtue of s.66.

Limit of duration of listed building consent

16.—(1) Any listed building consent shall be granted subject to a condition that works permitted by that consent shall be commenced within such period as the planning authority may specify in the consent.

(2) If no time limit is specified in any grant of listed building consent under subsection (1), the grant shall be deemed to have been made subject to a condition that works in terms of the consent shall be commenced within 5 years from the date of the grant.

(3) Nothing in this section applies to any consent to the retention of works granted under section 7(3).

(4) The date of the granting or of the refusal of an application for listed building consent shall be the date on which the notice of the planning authority's decision bears to have been signed on behalf of the authority.

DEFINITIONS
  "building": s.81(2).
  "listed building": s.1(4).
  "listed building consent": s.7(7).
  "planning authority": s.81(2).

GENERAL NOTE
  This provision requires a planning authority to impose a time limit within which works permitted by listed building consent must be commenced. A time limit of five years is deemed to apply to any listed building consent in the absence of express provision by the planning authority. A failure to carry out works the subject of a listed building consent, results in a lapse of that consent. Works carried out outwith the time limit constitutes an offence under s.8(2).

Extension to conservation area consent

This provision extends to buildings in conservation areas, by virtue of s.66.

Application for variation or discharge of conditions

17.—(1) Any person interested in a listed building with respect to which listed building consent has been granted subject to conditions may apply to the planning authority for the variation or discharge of the conditions.

(2) The application shall indicate what variation or discharge of conditions is applied for and the provisions of sections 9 to 13, 14(3) and 18 to 20 apply to such an application as they apply to an application for listed building consent.

(3) On such an application the planning authority or, as the case may be, the Secretary of State may vary or discharge the conditions attached to the consent, and may add new conditions consequential upon the variation or discharge, as they or he think fit.

DEFINITIONS

"building": s.81(2).
"listed building": s.1(4).
"listed building consent": s.7(7).
"planning authority": s.81(2).

GENERAL NOTE

Prior to 1986, a condition could only be varied or discharged by appeal or by seeking a fresh consent. The Housing and Planning Act 1986 (c. 63) introduced a new procedure whereby application may be made to the planning authority for variation and discharge of conditions attached to a consent.

"any person interested"

This phrase appears to limit the scope of individuals who are entitled to make an application under this provision to those with a property interest in the building: see *Jones v. Secretary of State for Wales* (1974) 28 P. & C.R. 280, but compare *Pennine Raceway v. Kirklees Metropolitan District Council (Ref/45/1980)* [1982] 3 All E.R. 628. This is significant as applicants for planning permission need not have a propriety interest in the land which forms the subject matter of the application. However, unlike a planning condition, given that a condition attached to listed building consent may give rise to criminal liability, it is sensible that third parties without a propriety interest may not seek to vary that condition. See Annex 1 to Circular No. 17/1987 for further guidance.

Determination of the application

On an application under s.17, subs. (3) empowers the planning authority or, as the case may be, the Secretary of State to vary or discharge the conditions attached to the consent. Application must be made to the planning authority in the first instance following normal applications procedures, including advertisement: Regs. 4 and 5 of the 1987 Regs. Appeal lies to the Secretary of State under s.19 against a refusal by the planning authority of an application submitted under s.17.

Power to impose further conditions

On an application submitted to them under s.17, the planning authority's powers are not restricted to determining the application in isolation. Subsection (3) empowers the planning authority to substitute whatever new conditions it thinks fit. However, this power can only be exercised where there is an identifiable relationship between the condition which forms the subject of the application and the new condition. This is clear from the wording of the provision which provides for the addition of "new conditions *consequential* upon the variation or discharge" (author emphasis). If the planning authority are of the view that variation or discharge should not take place except on a fundamentally different basis, then the proper course of action is for consent under s.17 to be refused and for the applicant to be advised to submit a fresh application for listed building consent under s.9.

Extension to conservation area consent
This provision extends to buildings in conservation areas, by virtue of s.66.

Appeals

Right to appeal against decision or failure to take decision

18.—(1) Where a planning authority—

(a) refuse an application for listed building consent or grant it subject to conditions,

(b) refuse an application for variation or discharge of conditions subject to which such consent has been granted or grant it and add new conditions, or

(c) refuse an application for approval required by a condition imposed on the granting of listed building consent with respect to details of works or grant it subject to conditions,

the applicant, if he is aggrieved by the decision, may appeal to the Secretary of State.

(2) A person who has made such an application may also appeal to the Secretary of State if the planning authority have neither—

(a) given notice to the applicant of their decision on the application, nor

(b) in the case of such an application as is mentioned in subsection (1)(a) or (b), given notice to the applicant that the application has been referred to the Secretary of State in accordance with directions given under section 11,

within the relevant period from the date of the receipt of the application or within such extended period as may at any time be agreed upon in writing between the applicant and the authority.

(3) In this section "the relevant period" means—

(a) in the case of such an application as is mentioned in subsection (1)(a) or (b), such period as may be prescribed, and

(b) in the case of such an application for approval as is mentioned in subsection (1)(c), the period of two months from the date of the receipt of the application.

(4) For the purposes of the application of sections 20(1) and 58(7)(a) in relation to an appeal under subsection (2), the authority shall be treated as having refused the application in question.

DEFINITIONS
"building": s.81(2).
"listed building": s.1(4).
"listed building consent": s.7(7).
"planning authority": s.81(2).
"prescribed": s.81(2).

GENERAL NOTE
This provision establishes the right to appeal to the Secretary of State against a determination or non-determination by a planning authority of an application submitted to it under this Act. An appeal may be submitted in respect of:

(1) a refusal of listed building consent (subs. (1)(a));

(2) any conditions attached to the grant of consent (subs. (1)(a));

(3) a refusal of an application under s.17 for the variation or discharge of a condition attached to a consent, or the imposition of a new condition (subs. (1)(b)): the distinction between an appeal against a condition attached to a consent on application under s.9 and an appeal against a refusal to vary or discharge a condition on application under s.17 should be noted; an appeal against the former operates so as to place the entire consent before the Secretary of State, whereas an appeal against the former is restricted to the condition itself;

(4) a refusal or conditional grant of an application for approval of reserved matters required by a condition (subs. (1)(c));

(5) a refusal or conditional grant of conservation area consent (s.66(3));

  (6) a refusal of an application under s.17 for the variation or discharge of a condition attached to a conservation area consent, or the imposition of a new condition on an application under s.17 as applied by s.66(3);

  (7) a failure by the planning authority to determine an application for listed building or conservation area consent with the period prescribed by the 1987 Regulations.

In addition to the above, an applicant may appeal under s.18 where the planning authority have failed to give notice of their decision to the applicant, or of a direction that an application has been called in (subs. (2)).

"Persons aggrieved"
  Only an applicant who is aggrieved by a decision is entitled to appeal under this provision to the Secretary of State. On the meaning of "persons aggrieved", see General Note to s. 58.

Planning Appeals
  An application for listed building consent does not derogate from the need to apply for planning permission where the proposed works constitute "development" under s.26 of the Principal Act. In cases where planning permission is refused, a separate appeal is required to be made under the Principal Act, although it is likely that the two appeals will be conjoined.

Transferred jurisdiction
  Under the Town and Country Planning (Determination of Appeals by Appointed Persons) (Prescribed Classes) (Scotland) Regulations 1987 (S.I. 1987 No. 1531), the Secretary of State is empowered to delegate decisions on listed building appeal cases to Reporters.

Extension to conservation area consent
  This provision extends to buildings in conservation areas, by virtue of s.66.

Appeals: supplementary provisions

  19.—(1) An appeal under section 18 must be made by notice served in the prescribed manner within such period as may be prescribed.

  (2) The period which may be prescribed under subsection (1) must not be less than—

    (a) in the case of an appeal under section 18(1), 28 days from the receipt by the applicant of notification of the decision, or

    (b) in the case of an appeal under section 18(2), 28 days from the end of the relevant period within the meaning of that section or, as the case may be, the extended period there mentioned.

  (3) The notice of appeal may include as the ground or one of the grounds of the appeal a claim that the building is not of special architectural or historic interest and ought to be removed from any list compiled or approved by the Secretary of State under section 1.

  (4) In the case of a building in respect of which a building preservation notice is in force, the notice may include a claim that the building should not be included in such a list.

  (5) Regulations may provide that an appeal in respect of an application for listed building consent, or for the variation or discharge of conditions subject to which such consent has been granted, shall not be entertained unless it is accompanied by a certificate in the prescribed form as to the interests in the building to which the appeal relates.

  (6) Any such regulations may include provisions corresponding to those which may be included in regulations under section 10 by virtue of section 10(2).

  (7) If any person—

    (a) issues a certificate which purports to comply with the requirements of regulations made by virtue of subsection (5) or (6) and which contains a statement which he knows to be false or misleading in a material particular, or

    (b) recklessly issues a certificate which purports to comply with those requirements and which contains a statement which is false or misleading in a material particular, he shall be guilty of an offence and liable on summary conviction to a fine not exceeding level 3 on the standard scale.

    "building": s.81(2).
    "listed building": s.1(4).
    "listed building consent": s.7(7).
    "planning authority": s.81(2).
    "prescribed": s.81(2).

GENERAL NOTE
    An applicant wishing to appeal under s.18, is required to serve notice of his appeal on the prescribed form obtainable from the Scottish office Inquiry Reporters Unit, 2 Greenside Lane, Edinburgh. The period within which an appeal may be made is six months from receipt of the decision or expiry of the time within which the planning authority may determine the application (reg. 8 of the 1987 Regulations). The Secretary of State has a discretion to extend this time period where appropriate (reg. 8(1)). However, para. 7.2 of the *1993 Memorandum of Guidance* suggests that he will be reluctant to do so unless there are special circumstances which excuse the delay in giving notice of appeal.

Documents to accompany an application
    Regulation 8 of the 1987 Regulations requires the following documents to accompany an application:
    — the application made to the planning authority;
    — all relevant plans, drawings, particulars or documents submitted with the application, including a copy of the certificate given in accordance with reg. 6 (certificates relating to ownership) or in respect of applications relating to Crown land, a copy of documents lodged in accordance with reg. 7 (certificate as to interest or authorisation);
    — the notice of the planning authority's decision—if any;
    — all other relevant correspondence with the planning authority.
    It is an offence under subs. (7) to knowingly or recklessly issue a certificate which contains a statement which is false or misleading in a material way.

Grounds of Appeal
    Subsection (3) provides that the grounds of appeal may include a claim that the building is not of special architectural or historic interest and should be removed from the list.

Extension to conservation area consent
    This provision extends to buildings in conservation areas, by virtue of s.66.

Determination of appeals

   20.—(1) The Secretary of State may allow or dismiss an appeal under section 18, or may reverse or vary any part of the decision of the authority, whether or not the appeal relates to that part, and—
    (a) may deal with the application as if it had been made to him in the first instance, and
    (b) may exercise his power under section 1 to amend any list compiled or approved under that section by removing from it the building to which the appeal relates.
   (2) Before determining the appeal the Secretary of State shall, if either the appellant or the planning authority so wish, give each of them an opportunity of appearing before, and being heard by, a person appointed by the Secretary of State for the purpose.
   (3) The decision of the Secretary of State on the appeal shall be final.
   (4) Schedule 3 (which makes provision regarding the determination of certain appeals by a person appointed by the Secretary of State) applies to appeals under section 18.

    "building": s.81(2).
    "planning authority": s.81(2).

GENERAL NOTE
Appeals to the Secretary of State broadly correspond to appeals under s.48 of the Principal Act. Before determining an appeal, the Secretary of State is obliged to allow parties an opportunity to make oral representations at a public local inquiry. However, the majority of appeals are dealt with on the basis of written representations under the Town and Country Planning (Appeals) (Written Submissions Procedure) (Scotland) Regulations 1990 (S.I. 1990 No. 507). See further Circular SDD7/1990.

Application to the Court of Session
The Secretary of State's decision is expressed to be final (subs. (3)). However, this is subject to the right of any person aggrieved to apply to the Court of Session under s.58. See further General Note to s.58.

Extension to conservation area consent
This provision extends to buildings in conservation areas, by virtue of s.66.

Revocation and modification of consent

Revocation and modification of listed building consent by planning authority

21.—(1) If it appears to the planning authority that it is expedient to revoke or modify listed building consent granted on an application made under this Act, the authority may revoke or modify the consent to such extent as they consider expedient.

(2) In performing their functions under subsection (1) the authority shall have regard to the development plan and to any other material considerations.

(3) The power conferred by this section to revoke or modify listed building consent in respect of any works may be exercised at any time before those works have been completed, but the revocation or modification shall not affect so much of those works as has been previously carried out.

DEFINITIONS
"building": s.81(2).
"development": s.81(2).
"development plan": s.81(2).
"functions": s.81(2).
"listed building": s.1(4).
"listed building consent": s.7(7).
"planning authority": s.81(2).

GENERAL NOTE
This provision establishes the general power for planning authorities to revoke or modify listed building consent as they consider expedient.

Scope of power
The power to revoke or modify consent does not apply retrospectively to work that has already been carried out (subs. (3)). However, it does apply to works which have not yet begun or works which are not yet completed.

Extension to conservation areas
This provision extends to buildings in conservation areas, by virtue of s.66.

Procedure for section 21 orders: opposed cases

22.—(1) Except as provided in section 23, an order made by a planning authority under section 21 shall not take effect unless it is confirmed by the Secretary of State.

(2) Where a planning authority submit an order to the Secretary of State for confirmation, they shall serve notice on—
(a) the owner of the building affected,
(b) the lessee of that building,

(c) the occupier of that building, and

(d) any other person who in their opinion will be affected by the order.

(3) The notice shall specify the period (which must not be less than 28 days after its service) within which any person on whom it is served may require an opportunity of appearing before and being heard by a person appointed by the Secretary of State for the purpose.

(4) If within that period a person on whom the notice is served so requires, the Secretary of State shall, before he confirms the order, give such an opportunity both to that person and to the planning authority.

(5) The Secretary of State may confirm any such order submitted to him either without modification or subject to such modifications as he considers expedient.

DEFINITIONS

"building": s.81(2).
"owner": s.81(2).
"planning authority": s.81(2).

GENERAL NOTE

An order under s.21 is of no effect until it is confirmed by the Secretary of State (subs. (1)). (See further *Caledonian Terminal Investments v. Edinburgh Corporation,* 1970 S.C. 271.) However, this power is weakened by the likely delay between the service of an order under s.21 and the date of confirmation by the Secretary of State, insofar as works may still be carried out until confirmation of the order. The individuals specified in subs. (2) must notify the planning authority in writing of any objection to such an order within 28 days of service of the s.21 notice upon them. Those who object to the order are entitled to an opportunity to be heard by the Secretary of State. The Secretary of State may confirm the order with or without modifications or reject it.

Extension to conservation areas

This provision extends to buildings in conservation areas, by virtue of s.66.

Compensation

Entitlement to compensation as a result of the revocation or modification of listed building consent arises under s.25.

Procedure for section 21 orders: unopposed cases

23.—(1) This section shall have effect where—

(a) the planning authority have made an order under section 21 revoking or modifying a listed building consent granted by them, and

(b) the owner, lessee and occupier of the land and all persons who in the authority's opinion will be affected by the order have notified the authority in writing that they do not object to the order.

(2) Where this section applies, instead of submitting the order to the Secretary of State for confirmation the authority shall—

(a) advertise in the prescribed manner the fact that the order has been made, and the advertisement shall specify—

(i) the period within which persons affected by the order may give notice to the Secretary of State that they wish an opportunity of appearing before, and being heard by, a person appointed by the Secretary of State for the purpose, and

(ii) the period at the end of which, if no such notice is given to the Secretary of State, the order may take effect by virtue of this section and without being confirmed by him,

(b) serve notice to the same effect on the persons mentioned in subsection (1)(b), and

(c) send a copy of any such advertisement to the Secretary of State not more than 3 days after its publication.

(3) A notice under subsection (2)(b) shall include a statement to the effect that no compensation is payable under section 25 in respect of an order under section 21 which takes effect by virtue of subsection (4) of this section.

(4) If—

(a) no person claiming to be affected by the order has given notice to the Secretary of State as mentioned in subsection (2)(a)(i) within the period referred to in that subsection, and

(b) the Secretary of State has not directed that the order be submitted to him for confirmation,

the order shall take effect at the end of the period referred to in subsection (2)(a)(ii) without being confirmed by the Secretary of State as required by section 22(1).

(5) The period referred to in subsection (2)(a)(i) must not be less than 28 days from the date on which the advertisement first appears.

(6) The period referred to in subsection (2)(a)(ii) must not be less than 14 days from the end of the period referred to in subsection (2)(a)(i).

DEFINITIONS
"building": s.81(2).
"land": s.81(2).
"listed building": s.1(4).
"listed building consent": s.7(7).
"owner": s.81(2).
"planning authority": s.81(2).
"prescribed": s.81(2).

GENERAL NOTE
This provision concerns the procedure where the owner, lessee and occupier of a building the subject of an order under s.21 may notify the planning authority in writing that they do not object to the order. In these circumstances, the authority need not submit the order for confirmation by the Secretary of State. Instead, the planning authority is required to advertise the making of an order and to submit a copy of the advertisement to the Secretary of State. A copy of the advertisement must also be sent to the individuals specified in subs. (1)(b). The advertisement must specify a period within which any person affected by the order may give notice to the Secretary of State, within 28 days of the advertisement first appearing, that they desire an opportunity to be heard. There is no right to compensation where an order under s.21 is unopposed.

Extension to conservation areas
This provision extends to buildings in conservation areas, by virtue of s.66.

Listed building purchase notice
It should be noted that an owner may serve a listed building purchase notice upon the planning authority pursuant to s.28, requiring a planning authority to purchase his interest in the property, following the making of an order under s.21.

Revocation and modification of listed building consent by Secretary of State

24.—(1) If it appears to the Secretary of State that it is expedient that an order should be made under section 21 revoking or modifying any listed building consent granted on an application under this Act, he may himself make such an order revoking or modifying the consent to such extent as he considers expedient.

(2) In performing his functions under subsection (1) the Secretary of State shall have regard to the development plan and to any other material considerations.

(3) The Secretary of State shall not make an order under that subsection without consulting the planning authority.

(4) Where the Secretary of State proposes to make such an order he shall serve notice on—

(a) the owner of the building affected,
(b) the lessee of that building,
(c) the occupier of that building, and
(d) any other person who in his opinion will be affected by the order.

(5) The notice shall specify the period (which must not be less than 28 days after its service) within which any person on whom it is served may require an opportunity of appearing before and being heard by a person appointed by the Secretary of State for the purpose.

(6) If within that period a person on whom the notice is served so requires, the Secretary of State shall, before he makes the order, give such an opportunity both to that person and to the planning authority.

(7) The power conferred by this section to revoke or modify listed building consent in respect of any works may be exercised at any time before those works have been completed, but the revocation or modification shall not affect so much of those works as has been previously carried out.

(8) An order under this section shall have the same effect as if it had been made by the planning authority under section 21 and confirmed by the Secretary of State under section 22.

DEFINITIONS
    "building": s.81(2).
    "development": s.81(2).
    "development plan": s.81(2).
    "functions": s.81(2).
    "listed building": s.1(4).
    "listed building consent": s.7(7).
    "owner": s.81(2).
    "planning authority": s.81(2).

GENERAL NOTE
    The Secretary of State himself is empowered under this provision to make an order under s.21 revoking or modifying listed building consent, as he deems expedient, following consultation with the planning authority. The procedure for making an order is broadly similar to that in relation to s.21 orders by planning authorities.

Extension to conservation areas
    This provision extends to buildings in conservation areas, by virtue of s.66.

Compensation
    Entitlement to compensation as a result of the revocation or modification of listed building consent arises under s.25.

CHAPTER III

RIGHTS OF OWNERS ETC.

Compensation

Compensation where listed building consent revoked or modified

25.—(1) This section shall have effect where listed building consent is revoked or modified by an order under section 21 (other than an order which takes effect by virtue of section 23).

(2) If, on a claim made to the planning authority within the prescribed time and in the prescribed manner, it is shown that a person interested in the building—

(a) has incurred expenditure in carrying out works which are rendered abortive by the revocation or modification, or
(b) has otherwise sustained loss or damage which is directly attributable to the revocation or modification,

the authority shall pay to that person compensation in respect of that expenditure, loss or damage.

(3) Subject to subsection (4), no compensation shall be paid under this section in respect of—

   (a) any works carried out before the grant of the listed building consent which is revoked or modified, or

   (b) any other loss or damage (not being loss or damage consisting of depreciation of the value of an interest in land) arising out of anything done or omitted to be done before the grant of that consent.

(4) For the purposes of this section, expenditure incurred in the preparation of plans for the purposes of any works, or upon other similar matters preparatory to any works, shall be taken to be included in the expenditure incurred in carrying out those works.

DEFINITIONS

   "building": s.81(2).
   "land": s.81(2).
   "listed building": s.1(4).
   "listed building consent": s.7(7).
   "planning authority": s.81(2).
   "prescribed": s.81(2).

GENERAL NOTE

This provision establishes entitlement to compensation for the revocation or modification of listed building consent. It does not apply in the case of orders under s.21 which are not opposed. An application for compensation must be made to the planning authority within six months from the date of confirmation or the date of the order (reg. 9 of the 1987 Regs). Those persons entitled to apply for compensation are those individuals referred to in s.22(2) or s.24(4) or others with a legal interest in the building.

Entitlement to compensation does not extend to works carried out prior to the making of the order, however it does arise under subs. (2) if the person making the claim can establish that he has incurred expenditure in carrying out works which are rendered abortive, or has sustained loss or damage directly attributable to the s.21 order.

Extension to conservation areas

This provision extends to buildings in conservation areas, by virtue of s.66.

Compensation for loss or damage caused by service of building preservation notice

26.—(1) This section applies where a building preservation notice ceases to have effect without the building having been included in a list compiled or approved by the Secretary of State under section 1.

(2) Any person who at the time when the notice was served had an interest in the building shall, on making a claim to the planning authority within the prescribed time and in the prescribed manner, be entitled to be paid compensation by the authority in respect of any loss or damage directly attributable to the effect of the notice.

(3) The loss or damage in respect of which compensation is payable under subsection (2) shall include a sum payable in respect of any breach of contract caused by the necessity of discontinuing or countermanding any works to the building on account of the building preservation notice being in force with respect to it.

DEFINITIONS

   "building": s.81(2).
   "building preservation notice": s.3(1).
   "planning authority": s.81(2).
   "prescribed": s.81(2).

GENERAL NOTE

Entitlement to compensation in respect of a building preservation notice arises where a building does not subsequently become listed within the period of six months specified in s.3(3). Compensation is payable in respect of any loss or damage directly attributable to the effect of the notice. The planning authority may be required to indemnify the applicant in respect of any liability he may have incurred for breach of contract with third parties caused by the effects of the notice.

General provisions as to compensation for depreciation under this Part

27.—(1) For the purpose of assessing any compensation to which this section applies, the rules set out in section 12 of the Land Compensation (Scotland) Act 1963 shall, so far as applicable and subject to any necessary modifications, have effect as they have effect for the purpose of assessing compensation for the compulsory acquisition of an interest in land.

(2) This section applies to any compensation which is payable under section 25 or 26 in respect of depreciation of the value of an interest in land.

(3) Where an interest in land is subject to a heritable security—

(a) any compensation to which this section applies which is payable in respect of depreciation of the value of that interest, shall be assessed as if the interest were not subject to the security.

(b) a claim for any such compensation may be made by any creditor in a heritable security over the interest, but without prejudice to the making of a claim by the person entitled to the interest,

(c) no compensation to which this section applies shall be payable in respect of the interest of the creditor in the heritable security (as distinct from the interest which is subject to the security), and

(d) any compensation to which this section applies which is payable in respect of the interest which is subject to the heritable security shall be paid to the creditor in the security or, if there is more than one such creditor, to the creditor whose security ranks first, and shall in either case be applied by him as if it were proceeds of sale by him under the powers competent to creditors in heritable securities.

(4) Except in so far as may be otherwise provided by any regulations made under this Act, any question of disputed compensation under section 25 or 26 shall be referred to and determined by the Lands Tribunal.

(5) In relation to the determination of any such question, the provisions of sections 9 and 11 of the Land Compensation (Scotland) Act 1963 shall apply, subject to any necessary modifications and to the provisions of any regulations made under this Act.

DEFINITIONS
"building": s.81(2).
"compulsory acquisition": s.81(2).
"land": s.81(2).
"listed building": s.1(4).
"listed building purchase notice": s.28(1).

GENERAL NOTE
This provision applies the ordinary rules relating to compensation for compulsory purchase under the Land Compensation (Scotland) Act 1963 (c. 51), to the assessment of compensation under the preceding sections. Disputed claims are to be referred and determined by the Lands Tribunal. Section 12 of the 1963 Act contains the rules for assessing compensation which state:
    "Compensation in respect of any compulsory purchase acquisition shall be assessed in accordance with the following rules:
        (1) No allowance shall be made on account of the acquisition being compulsory;
        (2) The value of land shall, subject as hereinafter provided, be taken to be the amount which the land if sold in the open market by a willing seller might be expected to realise;
        (3) The special suitability or adaptability of the land for any purpose shall not be taken into account if that purpose is a purpose to which it could be applied only in pursuance of statutory powers, or for which there is no market apart from the requirements of any authority possessing compulsory purchase powers;
        (4) Where the value of the land is increased by reason of the use of thereof or of any premises thereon in a manner which could be restrained by any court, or is contrary

to law, or is detrimental to the health of the occupants of the premises or to the public health, the amount of that increase shall not be taken into account;

(5) Where land is, and but for the compulsory acquisition would continue to be, devoted to a purpose of such a nature that there is no general demand or market for land for that purpose, the compensation may, if the official arbiter is satisfied that reinstatement in some other place is bona fide intended, be assessed on the basis of the reasonable cost of equivalent reinstatement;

(6) The provisions of rule (2) shall not affect the assessment of compensation for disturbance or any other matter not directly based on the value of land;

and the following provisions of this Part of this Act shall have effect with respect to the assessment."

Heritable Securities

Where the interest in land is subject to a heritable security (mortgage), this does not operate so as to affect the valuation of any compensation (subs. (3)(a)). The creditor is entitled to make the claim for compensation and any compensation in respect of the interest which forms the subject of the heritable security, is required to be paid over to the creditor (without prejudice to the rights of the debtor).

Listed building purchase notices

Purchase notice on refusal or conditional grant of listed building consent

28.—(1) Where—

(a) listed building consent in respect of a building is refused or is granted subject to conditions, or is revoked or modified by an order under section 21 or 24, and

(b) any owner or lessee of the building claims that—

(i) the conditions mentioned in subsection (2) are satisfied with respect to it and any land comprising the building, or contiguous or adjacent to it, and owned or occupied with it, and

(ii) the conditions mentioned in subsection (3) are satisfied with respect to that land,

he may, within the prescribed time and in the prescribed manner, serve on the planning authority in whose district the building and land is situated a notice (in this Act referred to as a "listed building purchase notice") requiring that authority to purchase his interest in the building and the land in accordance with sections 29 to 33.

(2) The conditions mentioned in subsection (1)(b)(i) are—

(a) that the building and land in respect of which the notice is served have become incapable of reasonably beneficial use in their existing state,

(b) in a case where listed building consent has been granted subject to conditions with respect to the execution of the works or has been modified by the imposition of such conditions, that the building and land cannot be rendered capable of such use by the carrying out of the works in accordance with those conditions, and

(c) in any case, that the building and land cannot be rendered capable of such use by the carrying out of any other works for which listed building consent has been granted or for which the planning authority or the Secretary of State has undertaken to grant such consent.

(3) The conditions mentioned in subsection (1)(b)(ii) are that the use of the land is substantially inseparable from that of the building and that it ought to be treated, together with the building, as a single holding.

(4) Where, for the purpose of determining whether the conditions mentioned in subsection (2) are satisfied in relation to any building and land, any question arises as to what is or would in any particular circumstances be a reasonably beneficial use of the building and land, no account shall be taken of any prospective use which would involve the carrying out of development (other than any development specified in paragraph 1 or 2 of Schedule 11 to

the principal Act) or of any works requiring listed building consent which might be executed to the building, other than works for which the planning authority or the Secretary of State has undertaken to grant such consent.

DEFINITIONS
"building": s.81(2).
"development": s.81(2).
"land": s.81(2).
"listed building": s.1(4).
"listed building consent": s.7(7).
"listed building purchase notice": subs. (1).
"owner": s.81(2).
"planning authority": s.81(2).
"prescribed": s.81(2).
"use": s.81(2).

GENERAL NOTE
Where listed building consent has been refused, or granted subject to conditions or revoked or modified by an order under ss.21 or 24, the owner or lessee of a building is entitled to serve a listed building purchase notice upon the planning authority requiring that authority to purchase his interest in the land. This provision is broadly similar to that contained in s.88 of the Principal Act.

Scope of Notice
It is not necessary for the notice to be confined to the building alone. Subsection (1) extends the scope of the notice to any land comprising the building or contiguous or adjacent to it, and owned and occupied with it. However, in order for the land to be included within the notice, it must be substantially inseparable from that of the building, so as to be treated together with the building as a single holding.

Beneficial Use
Paragraph 7.21 of the *1993 Memorandum of Guidance* provides that:
"The remedy by way of listed building purchase notice is not intended for the case where the owner shows merely that he is unable to realise the full development value of his land: it is intended to provide for situations in which refusal of consent has left the building incapable of any reasonably beneficial use, whether or not a concrete proposal for such use is in prospect. It should not therefore be assumed that a refusal of listed building consent will necessarily be followed by a successful listed building purchase notice".
This advice seems slightly inconsistent with case law where the courts have consistently held that it is not incumbent upon the claimant to establish that the land has become incapable of reasonably beneficial use as a direct consequence of the refusal of consent: see *Leominster Borough Council v. Minister of Housing and Local Government* (1971) 218 E.G. 1419; *West Bromwich County Borough Council v. Minister of Housing and Local Government* (1968) 206 E.G. 1085. In *R. v. Minister of Housing and Local Government, ex p. Chichester R.D.C.* [1960] 1 WLR 587, Lord Parker C.J. stated that "the test was whether it has become incapable of beneficial use in its existing state".

Time Limit
Under reg. 9 of the 1987 Regs., a purchase notice must be served on a planning authority within 12 months of the date of the decision giving rise to an entitlement under s.28. The Secretary of State has a discretion to extend this time limit in appropriate circumstances.

Policy Guidance
Policy guidance on purchase notices in general may be found in DHS Circular 14/1959.

Extension to conservation areas
This provision extends to buildings in conservation areas, by virtue of s.66.

Action by planning authority on whom listed building purchase notice served

29.—(1) The planning authority on whom a listed building purchase notice is served under section 28 shall serve on the owner or lessee by whom the notice was served a notice stating—

(a) that the authority are willing to comply with the purchase notice,

(b) that another planning authority or statutory undertakers specified in the notice under this subsection have agreed to comply with it in their place, or

(c) that for reasons specified in the notice under this subsection the authority are not willing to comply with the purchase notice and have not found any other planning authority or statutory undertakers who will agree to comply with it in their place, and that they have sent to the Secretary of State a copy of the purchase notice and of the notice under this subsection.

(2) A notice under subsection (1) must be served before the end of the period of 3 months beginning with the date of service of the listed building purchase notice.

(3) Where the planning authority on whom a listed building purchase notice is served by an owner or lessee have served on him a notice in accordance with subsection (1)(a) or (b) the authority, or the other planning authority or statutory undertakers specified in the notice, as the case may be, shall be deemed—

(a) to be authorised to acquire the interest of the owner or lessee compulsorily in accordance with the provisions of section 42, and

(b) to have served a notice to treat in respect of it on the date of service of the notice under that subsection.

(4) Where the planning authority propose to serve such a notice as is mentioned in subsection (1)(c), they shall first send to the Secretary of State a copy of—

(a) the proposed notice, and

(b) the listed building purchase notice which was served on them.

DEFINITIONS

"building": s.81(2).

"listed building": s.1(4).

"listed building purchase notice": s.28(1).

"owner": s.81(2).

"planning authority": s.81(2).

"statutory undertaker": s.81(2).

GENERAL NOTE

This provision establishes the procedures to be followed by a planning authority following the service of a listed building purchase notice on them pursuant to s.28. Subsection (1) essentially contains a notice and counter-notice procedure. If the planning authority are content to comply with the notice or another planning authority or statutory undertaker is willing to do so in their place, subs. (3) deems the planning authority or statutory undertaker as the case may be, to be authorised to compulsorily acquire the interest of the owner or lessee. The procedures for compulsory acquisition under s.42 are then triggered, together with entitlement to compensation. If the planning authority propose to serve a counter notice under subs. (1)(c), they must first send a copy of the proposed counter notice and the listed building purchase notice served upon them to the Secretary of State, whereby the matter becomes referred to him for a determination in accordance with the procedures under s.30.

Extension to conservation areas

This provision extends to buildings in conservation areas, by virtue of s.66.

Procedure on reference of listed building purchase notice to Secretary of State

30.—(1) Where a copy of a listed building purchase notice is sent to the Secretary of State under section 29(4), he shall consider whether to confirm the notice or to take other action under section 31 in respect of it.

(2) Before confirming such a notice or taking such other action, the Secretary of State shall give notice of his proposed action—

(a) to the person who served the notice,

(b) to the planning authority on whom it was served, and

(c) if the Secretary of State proposes to substitute any other planning authority or statutory undertakers for the planning authority on whom the notice was served, to them.

(3) A notice under subsection (2) shall specify the period (which must not be less than 28 days from its service) within which any of the persons, authorities or statutory undertakers on whom it is served may require the Secretary of State to give them an opportunity of appearing before, and being heard by, a person appointed by the Secretary of State for the purpose.

(4) If within that period any of those persons, authorities or statutory undertakers so requires, the Secretary of State shall, before he confirms the listed building purchase notice or takes any other action under section 31 in respect of it, give each of them such an opportunity.

(5) If, after any of those persons, authorities or statutory undertakers have appeared before and been heard by the appointed person, or the persons, authorities and statutory undertakers concerned have agreed to dispense with such a hearing, it appears to the Secretary of State to be expedient to take action under section 31 otherwise than in accordance with the notice given by him, the Secretary of State may take that action accordingly.

(6) In this section and sections 31 to 33, "land" means the building and the land in respect of which the notice under section 28(1) is served.

DEFINITIONS
"building": s.81(2).
"listed building": s.1(4).
"listed building purchase notice": s.28(1).
"owner": s.81(2).
"planning authority": s.81(2).
"statutory undertaker": s.81(2).

GENERAL NOTE
The Secretary of State is required to consider whether to confirm the listed building purchase notice and to give notice of what action he proposes to take to the respective parties. A copy of this notice must be served on all the interested parties, and give them an opportunity to make representations if they so desire.

Extension to conservation areas
This provision extends to buildings in conservation areas, by virtue of s.66.

Action by Secretary of State in relation to listed building purchase notice

31.—(1) Subject to the following provisions of this section, if the Secretary of State is satisfied that the conditions specified in section 28(2)(a) to (c) are satisfied in the case of any listed building purchase notice, he shall confirm the notice.

(2) If the Secretary of State is satisfied that those conditions are fulfilled only in respect of part of the land, he shall confirm the notice only in respect of that part and the notice shall have effect accordingly.

(3) The Secretary of State shall not confirm the notice unless he is satisfied that the land comprises such land contiguous or adjacent to the building as is in his opinion required—

(a) for preserving the building or its amenities,

(b) for affording access to it, or

(c) for its proper control or management.

(4) If it appears to the Secretary of State to be expedient to do so he may, instead of confirming the notice—

(a) in the case of a notice served on account of the refusal of listed building consent for any works, grant such consent for those works,

(b) in the case of a notice served on account of such consent being granted subject to conditions, revoke or amend those conditions so far as it appears to him to be required in order to enable the land to be rendered capable of reasonably beneficial use by the carrying out of those works,

(c) in the case of a notice served on account of such consent being revoked by an order under section 21 or 24, cancel the order revoking the consent, or

(d) in the case of a notice served on account of such consent being modified by such an order by the imposition of conditions, revoke or amend those conditions so far as appears to him to be required in order to enable the land to be rendered capable of reasonably beneficial use by the carrying out of the works in respect of which the consent was granted.

(5) If it appears to the Secretary of State that the land, or any part of it, could be rendered capable of reasonably beneficial use within a reasonable time by the carrying out—

(a) of any other works for which listed building consent ought to be granted, or

(b) of any development for which planning permission ought to be granted,

he may, instead of confirming the listed building purchase notice (or confirming it so far as it relates to that part), direct that if an application is made for such consent for those works, or as the case may be for planning permission for that development, it shall be granted.

(6) If it appears to the Secretary of State, having regard to the probable ultimate use of the building or its site, that it is expedient to do so he may, if he confirms the notice, modify it in relation to either the whole or any part of the land, by substituting another planning authority or statutory undertakers for the authority on whom the notice was served.

(7) Any reference in section 30 to the taking of action by the Secretary of State under this section includes a reference to the taking by him of a decision not to confirm the purchase notice on the grounds that any of the conditions referred to in subsection (1) of this section are not satisfied.

DEFINITIONS
"land": s.81(2).
"listed building": s.1(4).
"listed building consent": s.7(7).
"listed building purchase notice": s.28(1).
"planning authority": s.81(2).
"statutory undertaker": s.81(2).
"use": s.81(2).

GENERAL NOTE
If the Secretary of State is satisfied that the conditions specified in s.28 are satisfied, he must confirm the notice, unless he is not also satisfied that the land included in the listed building purchase notice is contiguous or adjacent to the building.

Extension to conservation areas
This provision extends to buildings in conservation areas, by virtue of s.66.

Effect of Secretary of State's action in relation to listed building purchase notice

32.—(1) Where the Secretary of State confirms a listed building purchase notice, the authority on whom the notice was served shall be deemed—

(a) to be authorised to acquire the owner's or lessee's interest in the land compulsorily in accordance with the provisions of section 42, and

(b) to have served a notice to treat in respect of it on such date as the Secretary of State may direct.

(2) If before the end of the relevant period the Secretary of State has neither—

(a) confirmed the listed building purchase notice, nor
(b) notified the owner or lessee by whom it was served that he does not propose to confirm it, nor
(c) taken any such action in respect of it as is mentioned in subsection (4) or (5) of section 31,

the notice shall be deemed to be confirmed at the end of that period and the authority on whom the notice was served shall be deemed to have been authorised as is mentioned in subsection (1)(a) and to have served a notice to treat in respect of the owner's or lessee's interest at the end of that period.

(3) Where a listed building purchase notice is confirmed in respect of only part of the land, references in this section to the owner's or lessee's interest in the land are references to the owner's or lessee's interest in that part.

(4) Where a listed building purchase notice is modified under section 31(6) by the substitution of another planning authority or statutory undertakers for the authority on whom the notice was served, the reference in subsection (1) to that authority is to that other planning authority or those statutory undertakers.

(5) In this section "the relevant period" means, subject to subsection (6)—
(a) the period of 9 months beginning with the date of the service of the listed building purchase notice, or
(b) if it ends earlier, the period of 6 months beginning with the date on which a copy of the purchase notice was sent to the Secretary of State.

(6) The relevant period does not run if the Secretary of State has before him at the same time both—
(a) a copy of the listed building purchase notice sent to him under section 29(4), and
(b) a notice of appeal under section 18 or 35 relating to any of the land to which the purchase notice relates.

(7) Where any decision by the Secretary of State to confirm or not to confirm a listed building purchase notice (including any decision to confirm the notice only in respect of part of the land, or to give any direction as to the granting of listed building consent or planning permission) is quashed under section 58, the notice shall be treated as cancelled, but the owner or lessee may serve a further notice in its place.

(8) For the purposes of determining whether such a further notice has been served within the period prescribed for the service of listed building purchase notices, the decision concerning listed building consent on account of which the notice has been served shall be treated as having been made on the date on which the decision of the Secretary of State was quashed.

DEFINITIONS
"land": s.81(2).
"listed building": s.1(4).
"listed building consent": s.7(7).
"listed building purchase notice": s.28(1).
"planning authority": s.81(2).
"statutory undertaker": s.81(2).

GENERAL NOTE
If the Secretary of State fails to take any steps in relation to a listed building purchase notice within the requisite period, he is deemed to have confirmed the notice.

Extension to conservation areas
This provision extends to buildings in conservation areas, by virtue of s.66.

Reduction of compensation on acquisition where section 25 compensation payable

33. Where compensation is payable under section 25 in respect of expenditure incurred in carrying out any works to a building, any compensation which then becomes payable in respect of the acquisition of an interest in the land in pursuance of a listed building purchase notice shall be reduced by an amount equal to the value of those works.

DEFINITIONS
  "building": s.81(2).
  "listed building purchase notice": s.81(2).

CHAPTER IV

ENFORCEMENT

Power to issue listed building enforcement notice

34.—(1) Where it appears to the planning authority—
  (a) that any works have been, or are being, executed to a listed building in their district, and
  (b) that the works are such as to involve a contravention of section 8(1) or (2),
they may, if they consider it expedient to do so having regard to the effect of the works on the character of the building as one of special architectural or historic interest, serve a notice under this section (in this Act referred to as a "listed building enforcement notice").

(2) A listed building enforcement notice shall specify the alleged contravention and require such steps as may be specified in the notice to be taken—
  (a) for restoring the building to its former state,
  (b) if the authority consider that such restoration would not be reasonably practicable or would be undesirable, for executing such further works specified in the notice as they consider are required to alleviate in a manner acceptable to them the effect of the works which were carried out without listed building consent, or
  (c) for bringing the building to the state it would have been in if the terms and conditions of any listed building consent for the works had been complied with.

(3) In considering whether such restoration is undesirable under subsection (2)(b), the authority shall have regard to the desirability of preserving—
  (a) the character of the building, or
  (b) its features of architectural or historical interest.

(4) Where such further works as are mentioned in subsection (2)(b) have been carried out on a building, listed building consent shall be deemed to have been granted in respect of the works carried out on that building.

(5) A listed building enforcement notice—
  (a) shall specify the date upon which it is to take effect and, subject to section 35(3), shall take effect on that date, and
  (b) shall specify the period (the "period for compliance") within which any steps are required to be taken and may specify different periods for different steps,
and, where different periods apply to different steps, references in this Act to the period for compliance with a listed building enforcement notice, in relation to any step, are to the period within which the step is required to be taken.

(6) A copy of a listed building enforcement notice shall be served—
  (a) on the owner, on the lessee and on the occupier of the building to which it relates, and
  (b) on any other person having an interest in the building, being an interest which in the opinion of the authority is materially affected by the notice.

(7) The planning authority may—
(a) withdraw a listed building enforcement notice (without prejudice to their power to issue another), or
(b) waive or relax any requirement of such a notice and, in particular, extend the period specified in accordance with subsection (5),
and the powers conferred by this subsection may be exercised whether or not the notice has taken effect.

(8) The planning authority shall, immediately after exercising the powers conferred by subsection (7), give notice of the exercise to every person who has been served with a copy of the listed building enforcement notice or would, if the notice were reissued, be served with a copy of it.

(9) Every planning authority shall keep available for public inspection free of charge at reasonable hours and at a convenient place a list containing particulars of any building in their district in respect of which a listed building enforcement notice has been served.

DEFINITIONS
"building": s.81(2).
"listed building": s.1(4).
"listed building consent": s.7(7).
"listed building enforcement notice": subs. (1).
"planning authority": s.81(2).
"owner": s.81(2).

GENERAL NOTE
The statutory provisions on enforcement of listed building control are similar to that contained in Pt. VI of the Principal Act in relation to breaches of planning control. However, unlike the Principal Act, criminal liability arises independently under s.8 of this Act, irrespective of any enforcement action. However, failure to comply with the terms of an enforcement notice is an offence under s.39.

Scope of Power to issue an enforcement notice
A planning authority is empowered to issue a listed building enforcement notice where it appears to it that works are or have been executed to a listed building which are such as to involve a contravention of s.8. Merely failure to keep a listed building in repair is insufficient to entitle the planning authority to issue an enforcement notice. In any event, the planning authority already possesses extensive powers in relation to disrepair under Chap. V of this Act. The planning authority is not obliged to issue an enforcement notice, it is a matter for its discretion: see *Perry v. Stanborough (Developments)* (1977) 244 E.G. 551.

Content of enforcement notice
An enforcement notice must contain specific information so as to give sufficient notice to the recipient of what the planning authority requires to be carried out in order to comply with the notice. The importance of specification is heightened by the fact that non-compliance is a criminal offence. A notice which lacks specification is a nullity. However, see the case of *Bath City Council v. Secretary of State for the Environment* [1983] JPL 737 who stated:
"... the person carrying out the works should be in the best position to know what steps were needed in order to rectify the breach of the listed buildings provisions which he had committed and if he did not know he could not complain if this meant, for example, he must retile the whole roof, although otherwise he would only be required to retile part. He could not ... refuse to comply because his own default made it more difficult for him to do so."
The validity of an enforcement notice is prohibited by s.37(6) from being questioned in any legal proceedings. However, this does not operate so as to preclude a notice from being challenged on the basis that it is a nullity. An enforcement notice must be interpreted strictly given that it carries criminal liability: *Browning v. Tameside Metropolitan Borough Council* [1997] EGCS 38.

Service of an enforcement notice
A listed building enforcement notice must be served on the owner, lessee and occupier of the building to which it relates and any other person who the planning authority thinks may be materially affected by the notice who have an interest in the building. The notice must specify the date upon which it is to take effect, what steps are required in order to comply with it and the period within which any steps are required to be taken. A copy of the enforcement notice must also be made available for inspection by the public at reasonable hours and in a convenient place.

Withdrawal of an enforcement notice

An enforcement notice may be withdrawn, or any requirement contained therein waived or relaxed at any time by the planning authority, irrespective of whether or not the notice has taken effect. This is without prejudice to the power of the authority to issue another: (subs. (7)).

Right of Appeal

Recipients of a listed building enforcement notice have a right of appeal to the Secretary of State under s.35. Such an appeal must be made before the notice takes effect. This has the effect of suspending the operation of the notice pending the outcome of the appeal. However, this does not affect any criminal liability which may have arisen under s.8.

Interdicts

If necessary, a planning authority may seek an interdict to restrain a continuing breach of an enforcement notice: see *Leominster District Council v. British Historic Buildings and S.P.S. Shipping* [1987] JPL 350.

Extension to conservation areas

This provision extends to buildings in conservation areas, by virtue of s.66.

Appeal against listed building enforcement notice

35.—(1) A person on whom a listed building enforcement notice is served or any other person having an interest in the building to which it relates may, at any time before the date specified in the notice as the date on which it is to take effect, appeal to the Secretary of State against the notice on any of the following grounds—

(a) that the building is not of special architectural or historic interest;

(b) that the matters alleged to constitute a contravention of section 8(1) or (2) have not occurred;

(c) that those matters (if they occurred) do not constitute such a contravention;

(d) that—

(i) works to the building were urgently necessary in the interests of safety or health, or for the preservation of the building,

(ii) it was not practicable to secure safety or health or, as the case may be, the preservation of the building by works of repair or works for affording temporary support or shelter, and

(iii) the works carried out were limited to the minimum measures immediately necessary;

(e) that listed building consent ought to be granted for the works, or that any relevant condition of such consent which has been granted ought to be discharged, or different conditions substituted;

(f) that copies of the notice were not served as required by section 34(6);

(g) except in relation to such a requirement as is mentioned in section 34(2)(b) or (c), that the requirements of the notice exceed what is necessary for restoring the building to its condition before the works were carried out;

(h) that the period specified in the notice as the period within which any step required by the notice is to be taken falls short of what should reasonably be allowed;

(i) that the steps required by the notice for the purpose of restoring the character of the building to its former state would not serve that purpose;

(j) that steps required to be taken by virtue of section 34(2)(b) exceed what is necessary to alleviate the effect of the works executed to the building;

(k) that steps required to be taken by virtue of section 34(2)(c) exceed what may reasonably be required to bring the building to the state in which it would have been if the terms and conditions of the listed building consent had been complied with.

(2) An appeal under this section shall be made either—

(a) by giving written notice of the appeal to the Secretary of State before the date specified in the listed building enforcement notice as the date on which it is to take effect, or

(b) by sending such notice to him in a properly addressed and prepaid letter posted to him at such time that, in the ordinary course of post, it would be delivered to him before that date.

(3) Where an appeal is brought under this section the notice shall be of no effect pending the final determination or withdrawal of the appeal.

(4) A person who gives notice of appeal under this section shall submit to the Secretary of State, either when giving the notice or within such time as may be prescribed, a statement in writing—

(a) specifying the grounds on which he is appealing against the listed building enforcement notice, and

(b) giving such further information as may be prescribed.

(5) Schedule 3 (which makes provision regarding the determination of certain appeals by a person appointed by the Secretary of State) applies in relation to appeals under this section.

DEFINITIONS
"building": s.81(2).
"listed building": s.1(4).
"listed building consent": s.7(7).
"listed building enforcement notice": s.34(1).
"planning authority": s.81(2).
"prescribed": s.81(2).

GENERAL NOTE
An appeal may be made by a person on whom an enforcement notice has been served or any other person who has an interest in the building. The Town and Country Planning (Enforcement of Control) (Scotland) Regulations 1992 (S.I. 1992 No. 477) contains the detailed procedure to be followed for submission of a notice of appeal.

The grounds of appeal
The grounds upon which an enforcement notice may be challenged under s.35 are comprehensively set out under subs. (1). A written statement containing the grounds of appeal must be submitted at the same time of the service of notice of appeal, or within 14 days of being required to do so by the Secretary of State (Town and Country Planning (Enforcement of Control) (Scotland) Regulations 1992).

Effect of an appeal
The service of a notice of appeal is effective to suspend the operation of the enforcement notice. This does not affect any criminal liability which may arise under s.8.

Transferred jurisdiction
The Secretary of State is empowered to delegate decisions on appeals under s.35 to Reporters under the Town and Country Planning (Determination of Appeals by Appointed Persons) (Prescribed Classes) (Scotland) Regulations 1987. Further guidance on the determination of appeals may be obtained from paras. 7.4 to 7.10 of the *1993 Memorandum of Guidance*.

Extension to conservation areas
This provision extends to buildings in conservation areas, by virtue of s.66.

Appeals: supplementary provisions

36.—(1) The Secretary of State may prescribe the procedure to be followed on appeals under section 35, and may in particular—

(a) require the planning authority to submit, within such time as may be prescribed, a statement indicating the submissions which they propose to put forward on the appeal,

(b) specify the matters to be included in such a statement,

(c) require the authority or the appellant to give such notice of such an appeal as may be prescribed to such persons as may be prescribed, and

(d) require the authority to send to the Secretary of State, within such period from the date of the bringing of the appeal as may be pre-scribed, a copy of the enforcement notice and a list of the persons served with copies of it.

(2) Subject to section 37(3), the Secretary of State shall, if either the plan-ning authority or the appellant so requires, give each of them an opportunity of appearing before and being heard by a person appointed by him for the purpose.

<small>DEFINITIONS</small>
> "planning authority": s.81(2).
> "prescribed": s.81(1).

Determination of appeals under section 35

37.—(1) On the determination of an appeal under section 35 the Secretary of State shall give directions for giving effect to the determination, including where appropriate directions for quashing the listed building enforcement notice.

(2) On such an appeal the Secretary of State—
(a) may—
> (i) correct any defect, error or misdescription in the listed build-ing enforcement notice, or
> (ii) vary the terms of the listed building enforcement notice,
> if he is satisfied that the correction or variation will not cause injustice to the appellant or the planning authority, and
(b) in a case where it would otherwise be a ground for determining the appeal in favour of the appellant that a person required by section 34(6) to be served with a copy of the notice was not served, may disre-gard that fact if he is satisfied that the person has not been substantially prejudiced by the failure to serve him.

(3) The Secretary of State may—
(a) dismiss such an appeal if the appellant fails to comply with section 35(4) within the prescribed time;
(b) allow such an appeal or quash the listed building enforcement notice if the planning authority fail to comply within the prescribed period with any requirement imposed by regulations made by virtue of section 36(1)(a), (b) or (d).

(4) On the determination of an appeal under section 35 the Secretary of State may—
(a) grant listed building consent for the works to which the listed building enforcement notice relates,
(b) discharge any condition subject to which such consent was granted and substitute any other condition, whether more or less onerous, or
(c) if he thinks fit, exercise his power under section 1 to amend any list compiled or approved under that section by removing from it the building to which the appeal relates.

(5) Any listed building consent granted by the Secretary of State under subsection (4) shall be treated as granted on an application for the same con-sent under section 9.

(6) The validity of a listed building enforcement notice shall not, except by way of appeal under section 35, be questioned in any proceedings whatso-ever on the grounds specified in section 35(1)(b) and (f).

<small>DEFINITIONS</small>
> "building": s.81(2).
> "listed building": s.1(4).
> "listed building consent": s.7(7).
> "listed building enforcement notice": s.34(1).
> "planning authority": s.81(2).
> "prescribed": s.81(2).

The Secretary of State has extensive powers under this provision to give directions for giving effect to the enforcement notice, or quashing it. In addition, the Secretary of State may amend the statutory list or grant listed building consent.

Extension to conservation areas
This provision extends to buildings in conservation areas, by virtue of s.66.

Execution of works required by listed building enforcement notice

38.—(1) If any of the steps specified in the listed building enforcement notice have not been taken within the period for compliance with the notice, the authority may—

(a) enter on the land and take those steps, and

(b) recover from the person who is then the owner or lessee of the land any expenses reasonably incurred by them in doing so.

(2) Where a listed building enforcement notice has been served in respect of a building—

(a) any expenses incurred by the owner, lessee or occupier of a building for the purpose of complying with it, and

(b) any sums paid by the owner or lessee of a building under subsection (1) in respect of expenses incurred by the planning authority in taking steps required by it,

shall be deemed to be incurred or paid for the use and at the request of the person who carried out the works to which the notice relates.

(3) If on a complaint by the owner of any land it appears to the sheriff that the occupier of the land is preventing the owner from carrying out work required to be carried out by a listed building enforcement notice, the sheriff may by warrant authorise the owner to go on the land and carry out that work.

(4) A planning authority taking steps under subsection (1) may sell any materials removed by them from the land unless those materials are claimed by the owner within 3 days of their removal.

(5) After any such sale the planning authority shall pay the proceeds to the owner less the expenses recoverable by them from him.

(6) Where a planning authority seek, under subsection (1), to recover any expenses from a person on the basis that he is the owner of any land, and such person proves that—

(a) he is receiving the rent in respect of that land merely as trustee, tutor, curator, factor or agent of some other person, and

(b) he has not, and since the date of the service on him of the demand for payment has not had, in his hands on behalf of that other person sufficient money to discharge the whole demand of the authority,

his liability shall be limited to the total amount of the money which he has or has had in his hands on behalf of that other person.

(7) A planning authority who by reason of subsection (6) have not recovered the whole of any such expenses from a trustee, tutor, curator, factor or agent may recover any unpaid balance from the person on whose behalf the rent is received.

(8) Any person who wilfully obstructs a person acting in the exercise of powers under subsection (1) shall be guilty of an offence and liable on summary conviction to a fine not exceeding level 3 on the standard scale.

Definitions
"building": s.81(2).
"land": s.81(2).
"listed building": s.1(4).
"listed building consent": s.7(7).
"listed building enforcement notice": s.34(1).
"owner": s.81(2).
"planning authority": s.81(2).
"use": s.81(2).

GENERAL NOTE

On judicial review of a planning authority's decision to take enforcement action under this provision see: *R. v. Greenwich London Borough Council, ex p. Patel* [1985] JPL 851. The court will interpret an enforcement notice strictly in an action to recover its expenses under this provision: *Browning v. Tameside Metropolitan Borough Council* [1997] EGCS 38.

Extension to conservation areas

This provision extends to buildings in conservation areas, by virtue of s.66.

Offence where listed building enforcement notice not complied with

39.—(1) Where, after the end of the period for compliance with the notice, any step required by a listed building enforcement notice to be taken has not been taken, the person who is for the time being owner of the land is in breach of the notice.

(2) If at any time the owner of the land is in breach of a listed building enforcement notice he shall be guilty of an offence.

(3) An offence under this section may be charged by reference to any day or longer period of time and a person may be convicted of a second or subsequent offence under this section by reference to any period of time following the preceding conviction for such an offence.

(4) In proceedings against any person for an offence under this section, it shall be a defence for him to show—

   (a) that he did everything he could be expected to do to secure that all the steps required by the notice were taken, or

   (b) that he was not served with a copy of the listed building enforcement notice and was not aware of its existence.

(5) A person guilty of an offence under this section shall be liable—

   (a) on summary conviction, to a fine not exceeding £20,000, and

   (b) on conviction on indictment, to a fine.

(6) In determining the amount of any fine to be imposed on a person convicted of an offence under this section, the court shall in particular have regard to any financial benefit which has accrued or appears likely to accrue to him in consequence of the offence.

DEFINITIONS

   "building": s.81(2).
   "listed building": s.1(4).
   "listed building enforcement notice": s.34(1).
   "owner": s.81(2).

GENERAL NOTE

This provision establishes criminal liability on the part of the owner of land the subject of a listed building enforcement notice. Subsection (4) prescribes the defences upon which an owner may rely.

Extension to conservation areas

This provision extends to buildings in conservation areas, by virtue of s.66.

Effect of listed building consent on listed building enforcement notice

40.—(1) If, after the issue of a listed building enforcement notice, consent is granted under section 7(3)—

   (a) for the retention of any work to which the listed building enforcement notice relates, or

   (b) permitting the retention of works without complying with some condition subject to which a previous listed building consent was granted,

the listed building enforcement notice shall cease to have effect in so far as it requires steps to be taken involving the works not being retained or, as the case may be, for complying with that condition.

(2) The fact that such a notice has wholly or partly ceased to have effect under subsection (1) shall not affect the liability of any person for an offence in respect of a previous failure to comply with that notice.

DEFINITIONS
  "building": s.81(2).
  "listed building": s.1(4).
  "listed building enforcement notice": s.34(1).
  "owner": s.81(2).

GENERAL NOTE
  This section provides for a listed building enforcement notice to cease to have effect where listed building consent is granted. This is without prejudice however, to any criminal liability which may have arisen while the notice was in force.

Extension to conservation areas
  This provision extends to buildings in conservation areas, by virtue of s.66.

Enforcement by Secretary of State

41.—(1) If it appears to the Secretary of State that it is expedient that a listed building enforcement notice should be served in respect of any land, he may himself serve such a notice under section 34.

(2) A listed building enforcement notice served by the Secretary of State shall have the same effect as a notice served by the planning authority.

(3) The Secretary of State shall not serve such a notice without consulting the planning authority.

(4) The provisions of this Act relating to listed building enforcement notices apply, so far as relevant, to a listed building enforcement notice served by the Secretary of State as they apply to a listed building enforcement notice served by a planning authority, but with the substitution for any reference to the planning authority of a reference to the Secretary of State, and any other necessary modifications.

DEFINITIONS
  "building": s.81(2).
  "land": s.81(2).
  "listed building": s.1(4).
  "listed building enforcement notice": s.34(1).
  "planning authority": s.81(1).

GENERAL NOTE
  This provision empowers the Secretary of State to serve an enforcement notice himself under s.34 after consultation with the planning authority.

Extension to conservation areas
  This provision extends to buildings in conservation areas, by virtue of s.66.

CHAPTER V

PREVENTION OF DETERIORATION AND DAMAGE

Compulsory acquisition of listed building in need of repair

Compulsory acquisition of listed building in need of repair

42.—(1) If it appears to the Secretary of State that reasonable steps are not being taken for properly preserving a listed building, he—
  (a) may authorise the planning authority for the district in which the building is situated to acquire compulsorily under this section the building and any relevant land, or
  (b) may himself compulsorily acquire them under this section.

(2) The Secretary of State shall not make or confirm a compulsory purchase order for the acquisition of any building by virtue of this section unless he is satisfied that it is expedient to make provision for the preservation of the building and to authorise its compulsory acquisition for that purpose.

(3) The Acquisition of Land (Authorisation Procedure) (Scotland) Act 1947 shall apply to the compulsory acquisition of land under this section and accordingly shall have effect—

  (a) as if this section had been in force immediately before the commencement of that Act, and

  (b) as if references in it to the Minister of Transport and to the enactments specified in section 1(1)(b) of that Act included respectively references to the Secretary of State and to this section.

(4) Any person having an interest in a building which it is proposed to acquire compulsorily under this section may, within 28 days after the service of the notice required to be served under paragraph 3(b) of Schedule 1 to that Act of 1947, apply to the sheriff for an order prohibiting further proceedings on the compulsory purchase order.

(5) If on an application under subsection (4) the sheriff is satisfied that reasonable steps have been taken for properly preserving the building, he shall make an order accordingly.

(6) Any person aggrieved by the decision of the sheriff on an application under subsection (4) may appeal against the decision to the Court of Session, but only on a question of law.

(7) In this section "relevant land", in relation to any building, means the land comprising or contiguous or adjacent to it which appears to the Secretary of State to be required for preserving the building or its amenities, or for affording access to it, or for its proper control or management.

DEFINITIONS
  "building": s.81(2).
  "compulsory acquisition": s.91(2).
  "land": s.81(2).
  "listed building": s.1(4).
  "relevant land": subs. (7).

GENERAL NOTE
  This provision enables the planning authority or the Secretary of State to compulsorily acquire a listed building which is in need of repair. A repairs notice must be served upon the owner of the listed building as a necessary preliminary step under s.43. This must specify what works are considered necessary for the preservation of the building. This also essentially provides the owner with an opportunity to carry out the repairs himself and thereby avoid the drastic use of compulsory acquisition powers against him. Failure to comply with a notice served under s.43 thereafter triggers the entitlement by the planning authority or the Secretary of State to exercise their powers of compulsory purchase under s.42. The exercise of powers under this provision are limited to circumstances where it is considered expedient for the preservation of the building.

Validity of repairs notice
  See the House of Lords decision in *Robbins v. Secretary of State for the Environment* [1989] 1 All E.R. 878 and *Rolf v. North Shropshire District Council* [1988] JPL 103.

Application to Sheriff Court
  An application may be made to the Sheriff prohibiting all further proceedings in relation to a proposal to compulsorily acquire a listed building. The sheriff is empowered to make an order to this effect where he is satisfied that all reasonable steps have been taken by the owner to preserve the building.

Compensation
  The provisions of the Acquisition of Land (Authorisation Procedure) (Scotland) Act 1947 (c. 42) apply to the assessment of compensation following a compulsory acquisition under this provision. Where the planning authority or the Secretary of State are satisfied that the building

was deliberately allowed to fall into disrepair, they may make a direction under s.45 for the payment of minimum compensation. See paras. 3.27 to 3.30 of the *1993 Memorandum of Guidance* for guidance as to when a direction is likely to be applied.

Repairs notice as preliminary to acquisition under section 42

43.—(1) The compulsory purchase of a building under section 42 shall not be started by the planning authority or by the Secretary of State unless at least 2 months previously the authority or, as the case may be, the Secretary of State has served on the owner of the building a notice under this section (in this section referred to as a "repairs notice")—

  (a) specifying the works which the authority or, as the case may be, the Secretary of State considers reasonably necessary for the proper preservation of the building, and

  (b) explaining the effect of sections 42 to 45,

and the repairs notice has not been withdrawn.

  (2) Where—

  (a) a building is demolished after a repairs notice has been served in respect of it by a planning authority or the Secretary of State, but

  (b) the Secretary of State is satisfied that he would have confirmed or, as the case may be, would have made a compulsory purchase order in respect of the building had it not been demolished,

the demolition of the building shall not prevent the authority or the Secretary of State from being authorised under section 42 to acquire compulsorily the site of the building.

  (3) A planning authority or the Secretary of State may at any time withdraw a repairs notice served by them or him on any person and shall, in that event, immediately give him notice of the withdrawal.

  (4) Where a repairs notice has been served on a person in respect of a building, he shall not be entitled to serve a listed building purchase notice in respect of it until the expiration of 3 months beginning with the date of the service of the repairs notice or, if during that period the compulsory acquisition of the building is begun under section 42, unless and until the compulsory acquisition is discontinued.

  (5) For the purposes of this section a compulsory acquisition—

  (a) is started when the planning authority or the Secretary of State, as the case may be, serves the notice required by paragraph 3(b) of Schedule 1 to the Acquisition of Land (Authorisation Procedure) (Scotland) Act 1947, and

  (b) is discontinued—

      (i) in the case of acquisition by the Secretary of State, when he decides not to make the compulsory purchase order, and

      (ii) in any other case, where the order is withdrawn or the Secretary of State decides not to confirm it.

DEFINITIONS
  "building": s.81(2).
  "compulsory acquisition": s.91(2).
  "land": s.81(2).
  "listed building": s.1(4).

GENERAL NOTE
  See para. 31 of the *1993 Memorandum of Guidance* for information on the content of repair notices.

Compensation on compulsory acquisition of listed building

44. Subject to section 45, for the purpose of assessing compensation in respect of any compulsory acquisition of land including a building which immediately before the date of the compulsory purchase order was listed, it shall be assumed that listed building consent would be granted—

(a) for any works for the alteration or extension of the building, or
(b) for the demolition of the building for the purpose of development of any class specified in Schedule 11 to the principal Act (development not constituting new development).

DEFINITIONS
    "building": s.81(2).
    "compulsory acquisition": s.91(2).
    "development": s.81(2).
    "land": s.81(2).
    "listed building": s.1(4).
    "new development": s.81(2).

GENERAL NOTE
    This provision provides for compensation to be assessed on the assumption that the necessary consents have been obtained. The effect of this assumption is to substantially increase the amount of compensation that becomes payable.

Minimum compensation in case of listed building deliberately left derelict

45.—(1) If a planning authority—
(a) propose to acquire a building compulsorily under section 42, and
(b) are satisfied that the building has been deliberately allowed to fall into disrepair for the purpose of justifying its demolition and the development or redevelopment of the site or any adjoining site,
they may make a direction for minimum compensation.
    (2) Subject to the provisions of this section, if the Secretary of State acquires a building compulsorily under section 42 he may, if he is satisfied as mentioned in subsection (1)(b), include a direction for minimum compensation in the compulsory purchase order.
    (3) Without prejudice to so much of paragraph 3(b) of Schedule 1 to the Acquisition of Land (Authorisation Procedure) (Scotland) Act 1947 (notices stating effect of compulsory purchase order or, as the case may be, draft order) as requires the notice to state the effect of the order, the notice required to be served in accordance with that provision shall—
(a) include a statement that the authority have made a direction for minimum compensation or, as the case may be, that the Secretary of State has included such a direction in the draft order prepared by him in accordance with paragraph 7 of that Schedule, and
(b) explain the meaning of the expression "direction for minimum compensation".
    (4) A direction for minimum compensation in relation to a building compulsorily acquired is a direction that for the purpose of assessing compensation it is to be assumed, notwithstanding anything to the contrary in the Land Compensation (Scotland) Act 1963, the principal Act or this Act—
(a) that planning permission would not be granted for any development or redevelopment of the site of the building, and
(b) that listed building consent would not be granted for any works for the demolition, alteration or extension of the building other than development or works necessary for restoring it to, and maintaining it in, a proper state of repair.
    (5) If—
(a) a planning authority have made a direction for minimum compensation and the Secretary of State confirms the compulsory purchase order relating to the acquisition of the building in question, or
(b) the Secretary of State, under subsection (2) above, includes such a direction in a compulsory purchase order made by him,
the compensation in respect of the compulsory acquisition shall be assessed in accordance with the direction.

(6) Where a planning authority make a direction for minimum compensation, or the Secretary of State includes such a direction in a draft compulsory purchase order prepared by him, any person having an interest in the building may, within 28 days after the service of the notice mentioned in subsection (3), apply to the sheriff for an order that the planning authority's direction for minimum compensation be reversed or, as the case may be, that such a direction be not included in the compulsory purchase order as made by the Secretary of State.

(7) If the sheriff is satisfied that the building has not been deliberately allowed to fall into disrepair for the purpose mentioned in subsection (1), he shall make the order applied for.

(8) A person aggrieved by the decision of the sheriff on an application under subsection (6) may appeal against the decision to the Court of Session, but only on a question of law.

(9) The rights conferred by subsections (6) and (8) shall not prejudice those conferred by section 42(4) and (6).

DEFINITIONS
  "building": s.81(2).
  "compulsory acquisition": s.91(2).
  "development": s.81(2).
  "land": s.81(2).
  "listed building": s.1(4).
  "new development": s.81(2).

GENERAL NOTE
  This provision operates so as to discourage owners of listed buildings from deliberately allowing the building to fall into disrepair as a means of compelling a planning authority to exercise its powers of compulsory purchase under s.42. In these circumstances, a planning authority may issue a direction under s.46 that only minimum compensation will be payable upon confirmation of a compulsory purchase order. Under subs. (4), minimum compensation is assessed at the value of the land without the benefit of planning permission or listed consent.
  See paras. 3.27 to 3.30 of the *1993 Memorandum of Guidance.*

Ending of rights over land compulsorily acquired

46.—(1) Subject to the provisions of this section, upon the completion by the acquiring authority of a compulsory acquisition of land under section 42—
  (a) all private rights of way and rights of laying down, erecting, continuing or maintaining any apparatus on, under or over the land and all other rights or servitudes in or relating to that land shall be extinguished, and
  (b) any such apparatus shall vest in the acquiring authority.

(2) Subsection (1) shall not apply to—
  (a) any right vested in, or apparatus belonging to, statutory undertakers for the purpose of the carrying on of their undertaking,
  (b) any right conferred by or in accordance with the telecommunications code on the operator of a telecommunications code system, or
  (c) any telecommunications apparatus kept installed for the purposes of any such system.

(3) In respect of any right or apparatus not falling within subsection (2), subsection (1) shall have effect subject to—
  (a) any direction given by the acquiring authority before the completion of the acquisition that subsection (1) shall not apply to any right or apparatus specified in the direction, and
  (b) any agreement which may be made (whether before or after the completion of the acquisition) between the acquiring authority and the person in or to whom the right or apparatus in question is vested or belongs.

(4) Any person who suffers loss by the extinguishment of a right or servitude or the vesting of any apparatus under this section shall be entitled to compensation from the acquiring authority.

(5) Any compensation payable under this section shall be determined in accordance with the Land Compensation (Scotland) Act 1963.

DEFINITIONS
   "acquiring authority": s.81(2).
   "compulsory acquisition": s.81(2).
   "land": s.81(2).
   "statutory undertaker": s.81(2).

GENERAL NOTE
   Compulsory purchase of land as a general rule is effective to extinguish all private rights in, over or under land. Further, pursuant to subs. (1)(b), any apparatus which remains on the land at the time of compulsory acquisition vests in the acquiring authority.

Exceptions
   The provisions of subs. (1) do not apply to:
   (a) any right vested in or apparatus belonging to statutory undertakers, for the purpose of carrying out their undertaking;
   (b) any right conferred by or in accordance with the telecommunications code or on the operator of a telecommunications code system;
   (c) any telecommunications apparatus installed for the purpose of any such system.
   See commentary to s.214 of the Principal Act for identification of statutory undertakers.

Acquisition by agreement

Acquisition of land by agreement

   47.—(1) A planning authority may acquire by agreement—
   (a) any building appearing to them to be of special architectural or historic interest, and
   (b) any land comprising or contiguous or adjacent to such a building which appears to them to be required—
         (i) for preserving the building or its amenities,
         (ii) for affording access to it, or
         (iii) for its proper control or management.
   (2) The enactments mentioned in subsection (3) shall apply in relation to the acquisition of land under subsection (1).
   (3) Those enactments are—
   (a) the Lands Clauses Acts (except the provisions relating to the purchase of land otherwise than by agreement and the provisions relating to access to the special Act, and except sections 120 to 125 of the Lands Clauses Consolidation (Scotland) Act 1845), and
   (b) sections 6 and 70 of the Railways Clauses Consolidation (Scotland) Act 1845, and sections 71 to 78 of that Act, as originally enacted and not as amended for certain purposes by section 15 of the Mines (Working Facilities and Support) Act 1923.
   (4) For the purposes of the application of those enactments—
   (a) this section shall be deemed to be the special Act, and
   (b) references to the promoters of the undertaking or to the company shall be construed as references to the authority authorised to acquire the land under this section.

DEFINITIONS
   "building": s.81(2).
   "land": s.81(2).
   "planning authority": s.81(2).

Management of acquired buildings

Management of listed buildings acquired under this Act

   48.—(1) Where a planning authority acquire any building or other land under section 42(1) or 47(1)(a) or (b), they may make such arrangements as to its management, use or disposal as they consider appropriate for the purpose of its preservation.

(2) Where the Secretary of State acquires any building or other land under section 42(1), he may—
   (a) make such arrangements as he thinks fit as to the management, custody or use of the building or land, and
   (b) dispose of or otherwise deal with any such building or land as he may from time to time determine.

DEFINITIONS
   "building": s.81(2).
   "disposal": s.81(2).
   "land": s.81(2).
   "listed building": s.1(4).
   "planning authority": s.81(2).

GENERAL NOTE
   This provision empowers the planning authority or, as the case may be the Secretary of State to secure the management or custody of a building compulsorily acquired as they see fit.

Urgent preservation

Urgent works to preserve unoccupied listed buildings

49.—(1) A planning authority may execute any works which appear to them to be urgently necessary for the preservation of a listed building in their district.

(2) The Secretary of State may execute any works which appear to him to be urgently necessary for the preservation of a listed building.

(3) The works which may be executed under this section may consist of or include works for affording temporary support or shelter for the building.

(4) If the building is occupied works may be carried out only to those parts which are not in use.

(5) The owner of the building shall be given not less than 7 days' notice in writing of the intention to carry out the works.

(6) The notice shall describe the works proposed to be carried out.

DEFINITIONS
   "building": s.81(2).
   "functions": s.81(2).
   "land": s.81(2).
   "listed building": s.1(4).
   "planning authority": s.81(2).

GENERAL NOTE
   This provision entitles a planning authority or, as the case may be, the Secretary of State, to carry out urgent works to secure the preservation of a listed building. Before carrying out those works, the owner of the building is entitled to no less than seven days' notice in writing of an intention to carry out those works. A notice should specify in detail what works are proposed to be carried out. See also *R. v. Camden London Borough Council, ex p. Comyn Ching & Co. (London)* (1984) 47 P. & C.R. 1417.

Recovery of expenses of works under section 49

50.—(1) This section has effect for enabling the expenses of works executed under section 49 to be recovered.

(2) The planning authority or, as the case may be, the Secretary of State may give notice to the owner of the building requiring him to pay the expenses of the works.

(3) Where the works consist of or include works for affording temporary support or shelter for the building—
   (a) the expenses which may be recovered include any continuing expenses involved in making available the apparatus or materials used, and

(b) notices under subsection (2) in respect of any such continuing expenses may be given from time to time.

(4) The owner may within 28 days of the service of the notice represent to the Secretary of State—

(a) that some or all of the works were unnecessary for the preservation of the building,

(b) in the case of works for affording temporary support or shelter, that the temporary arrangements have continued for an unreasonable length of time, or

(c) that the amount specified in the notice is unreasonable or that the recovery of it would cause him hardship.

and the Secretary of State shall determine to what extent the representations are justified.

(5) The Secretary of State shall give notice of his determination, the reasons for it and the amount recoverable—

(a) to the owner of the building, and

(b) to the planning authority, if they carried out the works.

DEFINITIONS
"building": s.81(2).
"planning authority": s.81(2).
"owner": s.81(2).

GENERAL NOTE
This provision empowers the planning authority or the Secretary of State to recover their expenses of carrying out works under s.49 from the owner.

Notice to owner
While the provision does not specify what type of notice should be given, the Court of Appeal in *Bolton Metropolitan Borough Council v. Jolley* [1989] 1 PLR 97, held that this required more than the submission of a bare account.

Grants for repair and maintenance

Power of local authority to contribute to preservation of listed buildings etc.

51.—(1) A local authority may contribute towards the expenses incurred or to be incurred in the repair or maintenance—

(a) of a listed building which is situated in or in the vicinity of their area, or

(b) of a building in their area which is not listed but appears to them to be of architectural or historic interest.

(2) At the time of making such a contribution the local authority may also contribute towards the expenses incurred, or to be incurred, in the upkeep of any garden occupied with the building and contiguous or adjacent to it.

(3) A contribution under this section may be made by grant or loan.

(4) A contribution by way of loan may be made upon such terms and conditions as the local authority may determine including (but without prejudice to the foregoing) a term that the loan shall be free of interest.

(5) A local authority—

(a) may renounce their right to repayment of such a loan or any interest for the time being outstanding, and

(b) by agreement with the borrower may otherwise vary any of the terms and conditions on which such a loan is made.

(6) A local authority may require as a condition of the making by them of a contribution under this section by way of grant towards the expenses of the repair or maintenance or upkeep of any property that the person to whom the grant is made shall enter into an agreement with them for the purpose of enabling the public to have access to the property or part of it during such period and at such times as the agreement may provide.

DEFINITIONS
  "building": s.81(2).
  "land": s.81(2).
  "listed building": s.1(4).
  "local authority": s.81(2).

GENERAL NOTE

This provision empowers a local authority to make a contribution towards the expenses incurred in the repair and maintenance of a listed building in their area, or a building which appears to them to be of architectural or historic interest. The power extends to any garden contiguous or adjacent to the building. The local authority may make its contribution by way of a loan or a grant. If a contribution is made by way of a loan, it may be upon such terms as the local authority deem fit. Furthermore, they are empowered to renounce their right to repayment of the loan or any interest.

Recovery of grants under section 51

52.—(1) If, during the period of 3 years beginning with the day on which a grant is made under section 51 towards the repair or maintenance or upkeep of any property ("the grant property"), the grantee disposes of the interest held by him in the property on that day or any part of that interest, by way of sale or excambion or lease for a term of not less than 21 years, the local authority may recover the amount of the grant, or such part of it as they think fit, from the grantee.

(2) If the grantee gives the whole of that interest to any person (whether directly or indirectly, but otherwise than by will) subsection (1) shall have effect as if the donee were the grantee.

(3) If the grantee gives part of that interest to any person (whether directly or indirectly, but otherwise than by will) subsection (1) shall have effect as if any disposal or part disposal of that interest by the donee were a disposal by the grantee.

(4) If any condition imposed on the making of a grant to which this section applies is contravened or not complied with, the local authority may recover the amount of the grant, or such part of it as they think fit, from the grantee.

(5) Nothing in this section entitles a local authority to recover amounts in the aggregate exceeding the amount of the grant (for example by virtue of a breach of more than one condition or disposals of several parts of an interest in the grant property).

DEFINITIONS
  "building": s.81(2).
  "disposal": s.81(2).
  "lease": s.81(2).
  "local authority": s.81(2).

Damage to listed buildings

Acts causing or likely to result in damage to listed buildings

53.—(1) If, with the intention of causing damage to a listed building, any relevant person does or permits the doing of any act which causes or is likely to result in damage to the building, he shall be guilty of an offence and liable on summary conviction to a fine not exceeding level 3 on the standard scale.

(2) A person is a relevant person for the purpose of subsection (1) if apart from that subsection he would be entitled to do or permit the act in question.

(3) Subsection (1) does not apply to an act for the execution of works—

  (a) authorised by planning permission granted or deemed to be granted in pursuance of an application under the principal Act, or

  (b) for which listed building consent has been given under this Act.

(4) If a person convicted of an offence under this section fails to take such reasonable steps as may be necessary to prevent any damage or further damage resulting from the offence, he shall be guilty of a further offence and

liable on summary conviction to a fine not exceeding one-tenth of level 3 on the standard scale for each day on which the failure continues.

DEFINITIONS
  "building": s.81(2).
  "listed building": s.1(4).
  "listed building consent": s.7(7).
  "planning permission": s.81(2).
  "relevant person": subs. (2).

GENERAL NOTE
  It is a criminal offence to cause or permit the doing of any act which causes or is likely to result in damage to a listed building. This provision is distinct from s.8 relating to "works", in that it encompasses any act, which may cause damage and is not restricted to circumstances where the character of the building as a building of special architectural or historic interest may be affected.

CHAPTER VI

MISCELLANEOUS AND SUPPLEMENTAL

Exceptions for church buildings and ancient monuments

Exceptions for ecclesiastical buildings

54.—(1) The provisions mentioned in subsection (2) shall not apply to any ecclesiastical building which is for the time being used for ecclesiastical purposes.

(2) Those provisions are sections 3, 4, 6 to 8, 42, 49 and 53.

(3) For the purposes of subsection (1), a building used or available for use by a minister of religion wholly or mainly as a residence from which to perform the duties of his office shall be treated as not being an ecclesiastical building.

(4) For the purposes of sections 6 to 8 a building shall be taken to be used for the time being for ecclesiastical purposes if it would be so used but for the works in question.

(5) The Secretary of State may by order provide for restricting or excluding the operation of subsections (1) to (3) in such cases as may be specified in the order.

(6) An order under subsection (5) may—

(a) make provision for buildings generally, for descriptions of building or for particular buildings;

(b) make different provision for buildings in different areas, for buildings of different religious faiths or denominations or according to the use made of the building;

(c) make such provision in relation to a part of a building (including, in particular, an object or structure falling to be treated as part of the building by virtue of section 1(4)) as may be made in relation to a building and make different provision for different parts of the same building;

(d) make different provision with respect to works of different descriptions or according to the extent of the works;

(e) make such consequential adaptations or modifications of the operation of any other provision of this Act or the principal Act, or of any instrument made under either of those Acts, as appear to the Secretary of State to be appropriate.

(7) Subsections (5) and (6) are without prejudice to the Church of Scotland Act 1921.

Exceptions for ancient monuments etc.

55.—(1) The provisions mentioned in subsection (2) shall not apply to any building for the time being included in the Schedule of monuments compiled and maintained under section 1 of the Ancient Monuments and Archaeological Areas Act 1979.

(2) Those provisions are sections 3, 4, 6 to 8, 42, 49 and 53.

GENERAL NOTE

A building may be both listed under this Act and a scheduled ancient monument under the terms of the Ancient Monuments and Archaeological Areas Act 1979 (c. 46). In these circumstances, the provisions of the 1979 Act are to prevail. Section 2 of that Act provides that it is an offence, except in accordance with a grant of scheduled monument consent to carry out:

"(a) any works resulting in the demolition or destruction or any damage to a scheduled monument;

(b) any works for the purpose of removing or repairing a scheduled monument or any part of it or of making any alterations or additions thereto; and

(c) any flooding or tipping operations on land in, or under which there is a scheduled monument."

Local authority notices and works affecting listed buildings

Intimation of local authority notices etc. affecting listed buildings

56.—(1) Where, as respects a listed building owned, leased or occupied by a local authority, the authority—

(a) have, under or by virtue of any enactment, served a notice requiring any person to show why the building should not conform to the building regulations,

(b) have, under or by virtue of any enactment, served a notice or made an order requiring the demolition of, or the carrying out of works affecting, the building, or

(c) propose (whether under or by virtue of any enactment or otherwise) to carry out emergency works or demolitions affecting the building,

they shall forthwith give written intimation of the notice, order or proposal to the Secretary of State.

(2) Where the safety of the public requires that any demolition or works be carried out without such delay as would result from compliance with subsection (1), the intimation (which may, in such a case, initially be oral) shall be given as long before the commencement of the demolition or works as is consistent with that requirement.

Validity of instruments, decisions and proceedings

Validity of certain orders and decisions

57.—(1) Except as provided by section 58, the validity of—

(a) any order under section 21, whether before or after it has been confirmed,

(b) any order under section 24, or

(c) any such decision on the part of the Secretary of State as is mentioned in subsection (2),

shall not be questioned in any legal proceedings whatsoever.

(2) Those decisions are—

(a) any decision on an application referred to the Secretary of State under section 11 or on an appeal under section 18,

(b) any decision of the Secretary of State to confirm or not to confirm a listed building purchase notice including—

(i) any decision not to confirm such a notice in respect of part of the land to which it relates, and

(ii) any decision to grant any consent, or give any direction, in lieu of confirming such a notice, either wholly or in part, and

(c) any decision of the Secretary of State on an appeal under section 35.

(3) Nothing in this section shall affect the exercise of any jurisdiction of any court in respect of any refusal or failure on the part of the Secretary of State to take any such action as is mentioned in subsection (2).

DEFINITIONS
  "building": s.81(2).
  "land": s.81(2).
  "listed building purchase notice": s.34(1).

GENERAL NOTE
  The public desire for a degree of certainty in land usage has resulted in limitations being placed upon an individual's right to challenge the validity of certain types of orders and decisions. Section 57 precludes any legal challenge to the validity of orders under ss.21 or 24 or decisions by the Secretary of State specified in subs. (2) except by way of application to the Court of Session under s.58. It should be noted that it is only the "validity" of planning decisions which may be subject to scrutiny by the courts and not their technical or planning merits. It is not for the court to substitute its own decision for that of the planning authority or Secretary of State. The question for the courts is simply one of vires. Any application must be made within six weeks from the published date of the adoption or approval of the plan, or the date the order, decision, direction is made. If no challenge is made within this period, this section takes effect, even where the decision being challenged is fundamentally flawed: *Smith v. East Elloe Rural District Council* [1956] A.C. 736; *Hamilton v. Secretary of State for Scotland,* 1972 S.L.T. 233.

Other preclusive provisions
  The provisions of s.57 are not exhaustive. Where these provisions do not apply, a challenge to any decision may be made by way of judicial review. In particular, subs. (3) specifically preserves the courts' jurisdiction in respect of any refusal or failure by the Secretary of State to take any action mentioned in subs. (2). There are a number of other provisions in this and other related enactments which impose restrictions upon an individual's right to challenge a planning related decision or order. Examples include s.34 which provides that the validity of a listed building enforcement notice shall not be questioned in any proceedings whatsoever on any of the grounds specified in s.35 except by appeal under that section. The provision itself will almost always state whether it precludes legal challenge.

Exceptions to the preclusive provisions
  It is not possible to give an exhaustive list of all the provisions to which the preclusive provisions do not apply. However, examples include interlocutory decisions in the course of certain types of appeal (*Co-operative Retail Services v. Secretary of State for the Environment* [1980] 1 W.L.R. 271); decisions relating to the award of expenses in connection with appeals (*R. v. Secretary of State for the Environment, ex p. Reinisch* (1971) 22 P. & C.R. 1022, see also *R. v. Secretary of State for the Environment, ex p. Three Rivers District Council* [1983] JPL 730).

  Even where there is no statutory restriction on the courts' jurisdiction to entertain a challenge to the validity of a plan, decision or order, the courts may nonetheless be reluctant to hear a challenge. One of the major reasons for this reticence is the well established principle that any statutory remedy must normally have been exhausted before the courts' supervisory jurisdiction may be invoked. This principle is clearly illustrated by the recent decision of the first division in *Philip Lardner v. Renfrew District Council* 1997 GWD 9-393. In this case, the Lord President dismissed an appeal under s.232 of the Town and Country Planning (Scotland) Act 1972 (c. 52) against the adoption of a local plan by Renfrew District Council, the statutory predecessors of the respondents, in circumstances where the appellant had not, as he was entitled, made a time-ous objection to the adoption of the plan or made representations at the subsequent local inquiry. Thus, the appellant was held not to be an "aggrieved person" within the scope of s.232 (see note to s.239). Neither, will the courts normally entertain an action seeking reduction of a decision of a planning authority where there exists a right of appeal to the Secretary of State (*Bellway v. Strathclyde Regional Council*, 1980 SLT 66).

Proceedings for questioning validity of other orders, decisions and directions

58.—(1) If any person is aggrieved by any such order or decision as is mentioned in section 57(1) and wishes to question its validity on the grounds—

(a) that it is not within the powers of this Act, or

(b) that any of the relevant requirements have not been complied with in relation to it,

he may make an application to the Court of Session under this section.

(2) Without prejudice to subsection (1), if the authority directly concerned with any such order or decision wish to question its validity on any of those grounds, the authority may make an application to the Court of Session under this section.

(3) An application under this section must be made within 6 weeks from the date on which the order is confirmed (or, in the case of an order under section 21 which takes effect under section 23 without confirmation, the date on which it takes effect) or, as the case may be, the date on which the decision is made.

(4) On any application under this section the Court of Session—

(a) may by interim order suspend the operation of the order or decision the validity of which is questioned by the application, until the final determination of the proceedings, and

(b) if satisfied—

(i) that the order or decision is not within the powers of this Act, or

(ii) that the interests of the applicant have been substantially prejudiced by a failure to comply with any of the relevant requirements in relation to it,

may quash that order or decision.

(5) References in this section to the confirmation of an order include the confirmation of an order subject to modifications as well as the confirmation of an order in the form in which it was made.

(6) In this section "the relevant requirements", in relation to any order or decision, means any requirements of this Act or of the Tribunals and Inquiries Act 1992, or of any order, regulations or rules made under either of those Acts, which are applicable to that order or decision.

(7) For the purposes of subsection (2) the authority directly concerned with any order or decision is—

(a) the planning authority, and

(b) in relation to any such decision as is mentioned in section 57(2)(b) where the Secretary of State has modified the notice wholly or in part by substituting another planning authority or statutory undertakers for the planning authority, also that authority or those statutory undertakers.

DEFINITIONS

"development": s.81(2).

"planning authority": s.81(2).

"relevant requirement": subs. (6).

GENERAL NOTE

Section 58 provides a detailed procedure for challenging the validity of any of the order, decisions or directions contained in s.57(1).

Limitations

The right to challenge is subject to two important statutory limitations. First, any application to the Court of Session must be made within six weeks from the date an order is confirmed or takes effect. The Court of Session has no power to extend this statutory time limit for lodging an application. This rule may operate harshly in some circumstances: see *R. v. Secretary of State for the Environment, ex p. Kent* [1990] 1 PLR 128. In this case, the Court of Appeal upheld a ruling by the divisional court that the applicant could not appeal against a planning permission granted for development near to his home, in circumstances where the applicant did not know that a planning application had even been made and had subsequently been appealed to the Secretary of State. This six week period has been subject to some criticism by the courts. In the case of *Smith v. East Elloe Rural District Council* [1956] A.C. 736, Lord Radcliffe described the six week period as "pitifully inadequate". The House of Lords by majority held that an ouster clause similar in terms to s.58 deprived them of jurisdiction once the time period had expired, notwithstanding circumstances in which bad faith was alleged. However, in the later House of Lords decision in *Anisminic v. Foreign Compensation Commission* [1969] 2 A.C. 147, the House considered *Smith v. East Elloe Rural District Council*. According to Lord Reid, where a decision or determination is being challenged as a nullity, a person is not challenging the purported decision or determination, but is maintaining that it does not exist. In those circumstances, the ouster provision is not to be interpreted as excluding the courts" jurisdiction where nullity was in question. The House of Lords proceeded to distinguish the case of *Smith v. East Elloe Rural District Council* as unsatisfactory on the basis that there was no citation of other cases given to the House in that case, on the question whether a clause ousting the jurisdiction of the court applied when a nullity was in issue. In *Hamilton v. Secretary of State for Scotland,* 1972 SLT 233, *Smith* was regarded as good law and the Court of Session regarded its jurisdiction as having been totally ousted. Lord Kissen proceeded to distinguish *Anisminic* on its facts and dismissed the action as incompetent (see also *Jeary v. Chailey Rural District Council* (1973) 26 P. & C.R. 280; *Lithgow v. Secretary of State for Scotland,* 1973 S.C. 1). The Court of Appeal had an opportunity to examine the operation of an ouster clause in *R. v. Secretary of State for the Environment, ex p. Ostler* [1976] 3 All E.R. 90. In that case, which involved the validity of a compulsory purchase order, *Anisminic* was again distinguished on its facts. The court drew a distinction between decisions which are essentially judicial and other administrative decisions. Lord Denning found the *Anisminic* decision to be more of a judicial decision compared to the administrative nature of the decision in *Ostler*. The Court of Appeal went on to hold that Mr Ostler's appeal had become statute barred after the expiry of the six week time limit (for a full discussion of these and other cases see *Harlow* [1976] P.L. 304; *Alder* [1976] JPL 270; *Wade* (1977) 93 LQR; *Whomersley* [1977] CLJ 4; *Gravells* (1978) 41 MLR 383; *Alder* (1980) 43 MLR 670; *Gravells* (1980) 43 MLR 173; *Leigh* [1980] P.L. 34; *Reid,* 1984 SPLP 74 and 1984 SLT (News) 297). However, in the case of *McDaid v. Clydebank District Council,* 1984 SLT 162, the First Division following *Anisminic,* held that an absolute ouster clause in relation to an enforcement notice did not exclude the court's jurisdiction where the notice involved a nullity. No reference was made by the court to the English decisions of *Smith, Hamilton* and *Ostler,* although it is difficult to believe that the Division were unaware of them. It is not clear whether the Division regarded the *McDaid* case as distinguishable on its facts on the basis that the clause in that case sought to oust the court's jurisdiction completely and it was therefore reconcilable with the *Smith cases,* or whether it formed the view that a preclusive clause could not protect a nullity as opined by Lord Reid. Given this uncertainty, it would be advisable to treat the *McDaid* decision with some caution.

Secondly, the right to challenge is exercisable only by an "aggrieved person"; see further commentary below.

Powers and procedure

An application under this section is made directly to the Inner House in Form 41.19 and must state the grounds of the appeal: Rules of the Court of Session 1994 (S.I. 1994 No.1443), R.C.S. 41.19. It must be served upon the Secretary of State and any other person as the court thinks fit, such as the planning authority (R.C.S. 41.21(1)). It is not clear why appeal is direct to the Inner House. The 1997 Act simply provides for appeal to the Court of Session, however the annotations to r. 41 of the R.C.S. state that, "by long tradition" such appeals are dealt with by the Inner House. This contrasts with the position in England and Wales where appeals are to the Queen's Bench Division of the High Court. The appellant in England and Wales thereafter may appeal to the Court of Appeal and from there to the House of Lords on a point of law. The appellant in Scotland may find it an advantage for his appeal under s.58 to the Court of Session to be heard by three judges, however for the courts, this is a costly and time-consuming exercise which requires more justification than "long tradition". This difficulty for the courts is highlighted by the fact that where there is a conflict of evidence, it is not unusual for the Inner House to direct that such evidence be heard by a single judge. Furthermore, as appeal from the Inner House lies only to the House of Lords, the Scottish appellant is denied an intermediate tier of appeal enjoyed by his English and Welsh counterparts. There may be some scope for the rules committee of the Court of Session to investigate whether it is necessary for planning appeals, or indeed any other statutory appeals to continue to be directed straight to the Inner rather than Outer House.

On an application under s.58(4), the Court of Session is empowered to make an interim order suspending the operation of the plan or its alteration, repeal or replacement. Where the court is satisfied that the statutory grounds of challenge have been established, it has a discretion to order that the plan, or as the case may be, its alteration, repeal or replacement be quashed in whole or in part: *Peak Park Joint Planning Board v. Secretary of State for the Environment and Imperial Chemical Industries* (1979) 39 P. & C.R. 361; see also *London Borough of Richmond upon Thames v. Secretary of State for the Environment* [1984] JPL 24. Where the error is not significant, the court may be prepared to exercise its discretion not to quash the decision: *Property Investment Holdings v. Secretary of State for the Environment and Reigate and Banstead Borough Council* [1984] JPL 587; *London and Clydeside Properties v. City of Aberdeen District Council,* 1984 SLT 50. In *Glasgow District Council v. Secretary of State for Scotland,* 1989 S.C. 150, the court held that although the reasoning of the Secretary of State was flawed, the decision itself was untainted and correct.

Persons aggrieved

There is no statutory definition of the expression "person aggrieved". In the past, the expression was interpreted strictly by the courts. According to Salmon J. in *Buxton v. Minister of Housing and Local Government* [1961] 1 Q.B. 278, only persons whose legal rights were infringed were entitled to brings proceedings where this expression was contained in an enactment (see also *Simpson v. Edinburgh Corporation,* 1960 S.C. 313 and *Gregory v. Camden London Borough Council* [1966] 1 WLR 899). This narrow interpretation was expressly disapproved of (although not overruled) by Lord Denning in *Att.-Gen. (Gambia) v. N'Jie* [1961] A.C. 617 who stated the expression "a person aggrieved" is "of wide import and should not be subjected to a restrictive interpretation. They do not include, of course, a mere busybody who is interfering in things which do not concern him; but they do include a person who has a genuine grievance because an order has been made which prejudicially affects his interests". These dicta were approved in a slightly different context in the later case of *Maurice v. London County Council* [1964] 2 Q.B. 362. Here the Court of Appeal held that a householder whose property would have been injuriously affected by the construction of a tall building close by, was a "person aggrieved" for the purposes of the London Building Act 1939. The *Buxton* case was again distinguished by Ackner J. in *Turner v. Secretary of State for the Environment* (1973) 28 P. & C.R. 123 and Glidewell J. in *Hollos v. Secretary of State for the Environment* [1983] JPL 164 on the basis that the applicable Town and Country Planning (Inquiries Procedure) Rules 1962 (S.I. (S.) 1980 No. 1676) specifically provided for third-party participation in planning inquiries and therefore impliedly gave them the right to insist that procedural rules should be followed, notwithstanding that they may have no direct legal interest in the site itself. The *Turner* decision however, has been criticised by Hough, "Standing in Planning Appeals" [1992] JPL 319 for failing to clarify the position of third parties who do not, for whatever reason, appear at an inquiry and those who had participated in an inquiry by way of written representations (see however comments of Lord Bridge in *Bizony v. Secretary of State for the Environment* [1976] JPL 306). In *Wilson v. Secretary of State for the Environment* [1988] JPL 540, no issue was taken on the right of an objector to challenge a decision in circumstances where he had not taken part in the appeal process which was dealt with by way of written representations. The respondents in the cases of *Easter Ross Land Use Committee v. Secretary of State for Scotland,* 1970 SLT 317 and *Bearsden Town Council v. Glasgow Corporation,* 1971 S.C. 274, denied that the appellants were "persons aggrieved", however, this issue was not actively pursued on appeal. According to the Court of Appeal in *Times Investment v. Secretary of State for the Environment* [1990] 3 PLR 111, the expression "persons aggrieved" should be taken as extending to "any person who, in the ordinary sense of the word, is aggrieved by the decision". In that case, the court held that the appellants who had purchased property which was the subject of the grant of planning permission following an appeal, could be within the scope of the expression a "person aggrieved" notwithstanding that they had no interest in the land at the time of the appeal. The point here was that the permission and its conditions run with the land and hence bind any subsequent purchaser.

The decision of *Bizony v. Secretary of State for the Environment* [1976] JPL 306 established that the expression "person aggrieved" includes those who had received notification of the inquiry and who had submitted observations and would have been entitled to appear (see p.152D-E). Similarly, the First Division in *North East Fife District Council v. Secretary of State for Scotland,* 1992 S.L.T. 373 held that several appellants who were present at a public inquiry and had made representations were within the scope of the expression "persons aggrieved". These decisions establish that the courts are prepared to regard those persons whose legal rights are affected by decisions falling within the scope of s.58 as "persons aggrieved".

The important decision of the Extra Division in *Cumming v. Secretary of State for Scotland,* 1993 SLT 228 confirmed the flexible approach taken by both the English and Scottish courts in recent years to the scope of the expression "person aggrieved". In that case, the appellant challenged the grant of outline planning permission for the development of a roadside service area together with a 40 bedroomed lodgehouse, restaurant and parking for up to 120 cars. The application had simply been advertised as a roadside petrol station and service area. The appellant argued that he did not make any objection to the original application as he had been misled by the advertisement as to the scale of the proposed development. In considering whether the appellant was a "person aggrieved" the court considered that the central issue was "whether the appellant was genuinely deprived by the procedure in the present planning application of an opportunity to make representations which might (at least in his view) have affected the result". The court decided to adopt a broad brush approach to this case and formed the view that "in the peculiar circumstances of the present case, there is the feature that the description of the development in the planning application form was so inadequate as to mislead or put a member of the public off his guard about what its real purpose was". The court therefore held that the appellant was a "person aggrieved". While this case is to be welcomed as suggesting that the categories of persons with the scope of the expression "person aggrieved" are not finite, the court did make clear that this was a case which was decided upon its own facts and did not seek to lay down any guidelines or principles as to when other individuals may or may not fall within the scope of the expression "person aggrieved".

The Lardner decision
The suggestion that the categories of individuals within the scope of the expression "person aggrieved" were not closed was endorsed by the First Division in the recent decision of *Philip Lardner v. Renfrewshire Council,* 1997 SLT 1027. In this case, the appellant did not object in writing or at an inquiry into proposed changes to a local plan which would have affected an area of land in the neighbourhood of his property. The appellant had suggested in his pleadings that if the plan or map of the proposals had been advertised in the Inchinnan Community Centre, it was likely that he would have learned of the proposals within the consultation period. The proposals were advertised widely in a number of other places, including Bridgewater Place public library, Erskine, which was the closest public library to the appellant's home. In those circumstances, it was difficult for the appellant to argue that the statutory consultation process had not been followed. This is apparent from the speech of the Lord President who, in the absence of any argument on a breach of statutory duty on the part of the local authority in respect of the consultation procedures, proceeded on the basis that "since no criticism was made of the procedures adopted, we are dealing with a case where the council advertised the proposal properly, made adequate arrangements for members of the public to inspect the draft plan, gave adequate time for representations to be made, considered the objections, gave notice of a public inquiry and held a public inquiry at which objectors were heard". In those circumstances, the Lord President stated that "there is a difference between *feeling* aggrieved and *being* aggrieved: for the latter expression to be appropriate, some external basis for feeling "upset" is required—some denial of affront to his expectations or rights". This approach surprisingly seems to have fallen back upon the old restrictive interpretation of the expression "person aggrieved" in the *Buxton* case which has previously been rejected by the Scottish and English courts in recent years. Furthermore, such a distinction seeks to introduce a rather technical approach into what is already a complex issue. The Division was not satisfied that the appellant's private rights were in some way affected by the adoption of the local plan. Thus they were not satisfied that the appellant fell within the scope of the expression "person aggrieved", by reason of his failure to object at the inquiry. While the Division were reluctant to suggest that someone who has not objected to a draft plan or taken part in an inquiry can never be "a person aggrieved", they were not prepared to extend the *Cumming* decision to an individual who did not take part in the inquiry process in the absence of any suggestion of bad faith or breach of consultation procedures.

Planning authority as a person aggrieved
The decision of the divisional court in *Ealing Corporation v. Jones* [1959] 1 Q.B. 384 is authority for the proposition that a planning authority is not a person aggrieved. In that case, Lord Parker C.J. held that if Parliament had intended a planning authority to be able to appeal to the courts (under s.238 of the Principal Act), then it would have expressly provided for this in the legislation. However, this approach was expressly disapproved of, although not overruled, by the Court of Appeal in the case of *Cook v. Southend Borough Council* [1990] 1 All E.R. 243. The court held that the expression "person aggrieved" was to be given its ordinary natural meaning rather than the narrow interpretation adopted in previous cases. Further, a planning authority would not have to show that the decision being challenged imposed any special legal burden

upon it in order to come within the scope of the expression. Interestingly, Lord Woolf drew an analogy between *locus standi* in judicial review and the expression "person aggrieved" and suggested that the approach of the courts on appeal are the same (p.255 a-b). This view seems sensible in that it would avoid the anomaly between a public body having the necessary title and interest for a challenge in judicial review but lacking standing in parallel statutory review proceedings. In contrast to the *Cook* decision, in the case of *Strathclyde Regional Council v. Secretary of State for Scotland*, 1989 SLT 821, the Second Division held that a regional council was not a "person aggrieved" for the purposes of a challenge under s.232 of the 1972 Act (now s.238). In this case, the council were dissatisfied with modifications made to its structure plans by the Secretary of State and sought to challenge their validity. The Second Division fully endorsed the *Ealing* decision. The Lord Justice Clerk pointed out that Parliament had had an opportunity in the 1972 Act to make express provision for an authority to appeal against the validity of alterations to development plans, similar to the provision in s.233 (now s.239) and had not done so. However, in the subsequent case of *Strathclyde Regional Council v. Secretary of State for Scotland (No. 2)*, 1990 SLT 149 the Court of Session ruled that the planning authority was a "person aggrieved" under s.233 (now s.239). The 1989 decision in *Strathclyde Regional Council v. Secretary of State* was unconvincingly distinguished by the Lord Justice Clerk who stated that "I remain of the opinion expressed in *Strathclyde Regional Council v. Secretary of State for Scotland* 1989 that the regional planning authority were not persons aggrieved within the meaning of s.232(1). Apart from anything else, as the structure plan contained a statement of the regional planning authority's policy and general proposals, I am satisfied that the regional planning authority could never qualify to be a person aggrieved by its *own* (author emphasis) statement of policy and general proposals. That consideration, however, does not apply to s.233". This comment by the Lord Justice Clerk leaves open the question whether a planning authority can be a "person aggrieved" under s.238 in situations where the planning authority is not seeking to challenge its own policies, but amendments, alterations and repeals to those policies made by the Secretary of State.

Grounds of Challenge

Section 58 contains the two statutory grounds of appeal, first, that the action or order is not within the powers of this Act and secondly, that any of the relevant requirements have not been complied with.

(a) Ground 1

"Relevant requirements" are defined further in subs. (9) as any requirements of this Act or of the Tribunals and Inquiries Act 1992 (c. 53), or of any order, regulations or rules made under this Act or the Act which is applicable to the particular order or decision. The House of Lords in *Smith v. East Elloe Rural District Council* [1956] A.C. 736 adopted differing narrow interpretations of the first ground of appeal (see also *Hamilton v. Secretary of State for Scotland*, 1972 S.C. 233; *Lithgow v. Secretary of State for Scotland*, 1973 S.C. 1). However, in the leading case of *Ashbridge Investments v. Minister of Housing and Local Government* [1965] 1 WLR 1320, the Court of Appeal rejected this approach. According to Lord Denning:

"Under this section it seems to me that the court can interfere with the Minister's decision if he has acted on no evidence; or if he has come to a conclusion to which on the evidence he could not reasonably have come; or if he has given a wrong interpretation to the words of the statute; or if he has taken into consideration matters which he ought not to have taken into account, or *vice versa*. It is identical with the position when the Court has power to interfere with the decision of a lower tribunal which has erred in point of law" (p.1326).

The Ashbridge "formulae" has been impliedly accepted by the Scottish courts. According to Lord Emslie in *Wordie Property Co. v. Secretary of State for Scotland*, 1984 SLT 345, "little doubt" remains as to the scope of the statutory grounds of challenge. Lord Denning's test has since been adopted in a number of subsequent cases: see *Howard v. Minister of Housing and Local Government* (1967) 65 LGR 257; *British Dredging (Services) v. Secretary of State for Wales and Monmouthshire* [1975] 1 WLR 687; *Seddon Properties v. Secretary of State for the Environment* [1978] JPL 835; *Eckersley v. Secretary of State for the Environment* (1977) 34 P. & C.R. 124. Further, in the case of *Bradley (Edwin H.) & Sons v. Secretary of State for the Environment* (1982) 47 P. & C.R. 374, Glidewell J. (as he then was), made the point that Lord Denning was doing no more than enunciating the same principles as those formulated by Lord Greene in *Associated Provincial Picture Houses v. Wednesbury Corporation* [1948] 1 K.B. 223.

(b) Ground 2

The second ground of challenge relating to relevant requirements is qualified by the need for the appellant to show substantial prejudice by reason of the failure to comply with the relevant requirements (subs. (4)(b)); see *M'Millan v. Inverness-shire County Council,* 1949 S.C. 77. The court is entitled not to exercise its general discretion to quash in the absence of any substantial prejudice to the appellant: *Steele v. Minister of Housing and Local Government* (1956) 6 P. & C.R. 386; *Camden London Borough Council v. Secretary of State for the Environment* (1975) 235 E.G. 375; *Kent County Council v. Secretary of State for the Environment* (1976) 33 P. & C.R. 70; *London Borough of Greenwich v. Secretary of State for the Environment* [1981] JPL 809; *Schleider v. Secretary of State for the Environment* [1983] JPL 383. This ground generally raises the question of whether a procedural requirement has been fulfilled such as a breach of a mandatory or directory requirement (*James v. Secretary of State for Wales* [1966] 1 WLR 135; *London and Clydeside Estates v. Aberdeen District Council,* 1980 S.C. (H.L.) 1. If the breach complained of is more than a mere technicality, the courts will intervene (see for example: *McCowan v. Secretary of State for Scotland,* 1972 S.C. 93; *Peak Park Joint Planning Board v. Secretary of State for the Environment* (1976) 39 P. & C.R. 361. The circumstances of individual cases may produce an overlap between the two grounds of challenge under s.239. In those circumstances, the general rule is that the decision should be quashed unless the breach is purely technical: *London Borough of Richmond upon Thames v. Secretary of State for the Environment* [1984] JPL 24 which may contrast with *Westminster City Council v. Secretary of State for the Environment* [1984] JPL 27. Failure by the appellant to take an early objection to an irregularity may be taken as indicative of a lack of substantial prejudice: *Davies v. Secretary of State for Wales* [1977] JPL 102; *George v. Secretary of State for the Environment* (1979) 38 P. & C.R. 609; *Midlothian District Council v. Secretary of State for Scotland,* 1980 S.C. 210; see also comments in 1981 SPLP 17).

The Seddon Properties Tests

The circumstances in which the courts will be prepared to quash a decision under the statutory grounds were summarised by Forbes J. in *Seddon Properties v. Secretary of State for the Environment* (1978) 42 P. & C.R. 26. The importance of these dicta is such that it deserves to be set out in full:

"(1) The Secretary of State must not act perversely. That is, if the court considers that no reasonable person in the position of the Secretary of State, properly directing himself on the relevant material, could have reached the conclusion which he did reach, the decision may be overturned. See *e.g., Ashbridge Investments v. Minister of Housing and Local Government* [1965] 1 WLR 1320, *per* Lord Denning M.R. at 1326F and Harman L.J. at 1328H. This is really no more than another example of the principle enshrined in a sentence from the judgment of Lord Greene M.R. in *Associated Provincial Picture Houses v. Wednesbury Corporation* [1948] 1 K.B. 223 at 230:

"It is true to say that, if a decision on a competent matter is so unreasonable that no reasonable authority could ever have come to it, then the courts can interfere."

(2) In reaching his conclusion the Secretary of State must not take into account irrelevant material or fail to take into account that which is relevant: see, *e.g.,* again the *Ashbridge Investments* case *per* Lord Denning M.R. *loc. cit.*

(3) The Secretary of State must abide by the statutory procedures, in particular by the Town and Country Planning (Inquiries Procedure) Rules 1974. These Rules require him to give reasons for his decision after a planning inquiry and those reasons must be proper and adequate reasons which are clear and intelligible, and deal with the substantial points which have been raised: *Re Poyser and Mills Arbitration* [1964] 2 Q.B. 467.

(4) The Secretary of State, in exercising his powers, which include reaching a decision such as that in this case, must not depart from the principles of natural justice: *per* Lord Russell of Killowen in *Fairmount Investments v. Secretary of State for the Environment* [1976] 1 WLR 1255 at 1263D.

(5) If the Secretary of State differs from his inspector on a finding of fact or takes into account any new evidence or matter of fact not canvassed at the inquiry he must, if this involves disagreeing with the inspector's recommendations, notify the parties and give them at least an opportunity of making further representations.

There are other peripheral principles. If he differs from the inspector on an inference of fact he must have sufficient material to enable him to do so: *per* Lord Denning M.R. in *Coleen Properties v. Minister of Housing and Local Government* [1971] 1 All E.R. 1049 at 1053C. Otherwise the courts can interfere in accordance with the first principle stated above. If it is a matter of planning policy he is free to disagree with the inspector's conclusions or recommendations without bringing into operation rule 12: *Pavenham (Lord Luke of) v. Minister of Housing and Local Government* [1968] 1 Q.B. 172; but of course, he must make clear what the policy is and its relevance to the issues raised at the inquiry in accordance with the third principle above. If there has been conflicting evidence at the inquiry it seems to me that he may, if he wishes, prefer one piece of evidence to another, though the material must be there to enable him to do so, he must give reasons for doing so, and if he is disagreeing with a finding of fact by the inspector he must apply the procedure. Since the courts will interfere only if he acts beyond his powers (which is the foundation of all the above principles) it is clear that his powers include the determination of the weight to be given to any particular contention; he is entitled to attach what weight he pleases to the various arguments and contentions of the parties; the courts will not entertain a submission that he gave undue weight to one argument or failed to give any weight at all to another. Again in doing so he must, at any rate if substantial issues are involved, give clear reasons for his decision. In considering whether or not the Secretary of State has acted contrary to any of these principles the materials upon which the court may come to a conclusion are, in general, the inspector's report and the letter of the Secretary of State setting out his decision. In approaching this task it is no part of the court's duty to subject the decision letter to the kind of scrutiny appropriate to the determination of the meaning of a contract or a statute. Because the letter is addressed to the parties who are well aware of all the issues involved and of the arguments deployed at the inquiry, it is not necessary to rehearse every argument relating to each matter in every paragraph."

The Seddon case should now be compared with the recent decision of *London and Midland Developments v. Secretary of State for Scotland and Dawn Construction* (1996) SS SPEL 52.

The role of the courts when reviewing planning decisions was confirmed by Hoffmann L.J. in the court of appeal decision of *Somerset District Council v. Secretary of State for the Environment* [1993] 1 PLR 80. In essence, the court is not entitled to substitute its own views on planning merits for that of the reporter's. This is of paramount importance in the context of exercise of the court's supervisory jurisdiction as Hoffmann L.J. makes clear:

"The inspector is not writing an examination paper on current and draft development plans. The letter must read in good faith and references to policies must be taken in the context of the general thrust of the inspector's reasoning. A reference to a policy does not necessarily mean that it played a significant part in the reasoning: it may have been mentioned only because it was urged on the inspector by one of the representatives of the parties and he wanted to make it clear that he had not overlooked it. Sometimes his statement of policy may be elliptical but this does not necessarily show misunderstanding. One must look at what the inspector thought the important planning issues were and decide whether it appears from the way he dealt with them that he must have misunderstood a relevant policy or proposed alteration to policy."

The exercise of the court's discretion to quash

The Court of Appeal decision in *Bolton Metropolitan Borough Council v. Secretary of State for the Environment* (1990) 61 P. & C.R. 343 provides further guidance on the exercise of the court's discretion to quash a decision in circumstances where the Secretary of State has failed to take into account a material consideration. The following propositions were suggested by Glidewell L.J.:

"(1) The expressions used in the authorities that the decision maker has failed to take into account a matter which is relevant, which is the formulation for instance in Forbes J.'s judgment in *Seddon Properties* (1981) P. & C.R. 26, or that he failed to take into consideration matters which he ought to take into account, which was the way that Lord Greene put it in *Wednesbury* and Lord Denning in *Ashbridge Investments*, have the same meaning.

(2) The decision maker ought to take into account a matter which might cause him to reach a different conclusion to that which he would reach if he did not take it into account. Such a matter is relevant to his decision making process. By the verb 'might', I mean where there is a real possibility that he would reach a different conclusion if he did take that consideration into account.

(3) If the matter is trivial or of small importance in relation to the particular decision, then it follows that if it were taken into account there would be a real possibility that it would make no difference to the decision and thus it is not a matter which the decision maker ought to take into account.

(4) As Hodgson J. said [at first instance], there is clearly a distinction between matters which a decision maker is obliged by statute to take into account and those where the obligation to take into account is to be implied from the nature of the decision and of the matter in question (*Creed (N.Z.) Incorporated v. Governor-General* [1981] 1 NZLR 172).

(5) If the validity of the decision is challenged on the ground that the decision maker failed to take into account a matter in the second category, it is for the judge to decide whether it was a matter which the decision maker should have taken into account.

(6) If the judge concludes that the matter was "fundamental to the decision", or that it is clear that there is a real possibility that the consideration of the matter would have made a difference to the decision, he is thus enabled to hold that the decision was not validly made. But if the judge is uncertain whether the matter would have had this effect or was of such importance in the decision making process, then he does not have before him the material necessary to conclude that the decision was invalid.

(7) (Though it does not arise in the circumstances of this case). Even if the judge has concluded that he could not hold that the decision is invalid, in exceptional circumstances he is entitled nevertheless, in the exercise of his discretion, not to grant any relief".

Challenges by way of judicial review

The preclusive provisions of this Part of the Act only extend to the decisions, orders or schemes mentioned in s.237. Outside these preclusive provisions, the remedy of judicial review is available. However, the courts may nonetheless still refuse to entertain a petition for judicial review on the principle that any statutory remedy must be exhausted before the court's supervisory jurisdiction may be invoked (for a detailed discussion of this principle see Reid, "Failure to Exhaust Statutory Remedies" 1984 J.R. 185; also see *British Railways Board v. Glasgow Corporation,* 1976 SC 224 *and Bellway Homes v. Strathclyde Regional Council,* 1980 SLT 66 and *Lardener v. Renfrewshire Council,* 1997 SLT 1027).

Title and Interest

Title and interest in judicial review proceedings is a prerequisite before the court will entertain a petition to exercise its supervisory jurisdiction. The case of *D. & J. Nichol v. Dundee Harbour Trs,* 1915 S.C. (H.L.) 7 held that "for a person to have such title he must be a party to some legal relation which gives him some right which the person against whom he raises the action either infringes or denies". Similarly, in the case of *Simpson v. Edinburgh Corporation,* 1960 S.C. 313, the court refused to entertain a challenge to the grant of planning permission for development of certain land from a neighbouring proprietor, on the basis that the appellant was not privy to the relationship between the planning authority and the developer. This decision can no longer be regarded as good law, given the current neighbour notification rights in existing planning rules. The liberal approach taken by the Lord Ordinary in *Wilson v. IBA,* 1979 SLT 279 suggested that any member of the public would have title to enforce a public duty provided that they could demonstrate that the title was coupled with a sufficient interest in the subject matter of the petition. The nature of that interest was not defined by the court. The decision of Lord Clyde in *Scottish Old People's Welfare Council, Petrs,* 1987 SLT 179 adopted a narrow interpretation of "interest". In that case, the petitioners were a pressure group who campaigned on behalf of the elderly to challenge the legality of government instructions on cold weather payments to the elderly. Although Lord Clyde held that the petitioners had sufficient title to sue, he held that their interest was too remote to give them a right to sue. This was on the basis that the petitioners were "not suing as a body of potential claiments but as a body working to protect and advance the interests of the aged". This was held to be insufficient. This approach adopts a very careful distinction between title and interest and concludes that one does not necessarily follow the other. The approach adopted by the English courts on the issue of standing has refused to follow the Scottish cases and is markedly more liberal. In recent years, the English courts have not suffered great difficulty in granting standing to the Child Poverty Action Group (*R. v. Secretary of State for Social Services, ex p. the Child Poverty Action Group* [1990] 2 Q.B. 540; the Equal Opportunities Commission (*R. v. Secretary of State for Employment, ex p. Equal Opportunities Commission* [1993] 1 All E.R. 1022; Greenpeace (*R. v. H.M. Inspectorate of Pollution, ex p. Greenpeace (No.2)* [1994] 4 All E.R. 329; Friends of the Earth (*R. v. Secretary of State for the Environment, ex p. Friends of the Earth* [1995] Env.L.R. 11, QBD; the World Development Movement who challenged the grant of aid for the Pergau dam (*R. v. Secretary of State for Foreign and Commonwealth Affairs, ex p. World Development Movement* [1995] 1 All E.R. 611. The current narrow position of the Scottish law on title and interest was reaffirmed recently by the action of Greenpeace in seeking judicial review proceedings in England in relation to the ministerial approval for the disposal of the Brent Spar platform in waters off Scotland, rather than challenging this approval in the Scottish courts (*R. v. Secretary of State for Scotland, ex p. Greenpeace,* 1995 (unreported)). Although Popplewell J. declined to accept jurisdiction in that case, he accepted on the basis of opinions provided by leading Scottish counsel that Greenpeace would be likely to have difficulty in establishing sufficient title and interest in Scottish judicial review proceedings. The action taken by Greenpeace can be regarded as a lack of faith in the Scottish legal system, but also as a missed opportunity for the Scottish courts to either confirm the approach of the courts in *Scottish Old People's Welfare Council, Petrs* or to reject it as no longer good law (for a detailed analysis of title and interest, see Munro, Standing in Judicial Review, 1995 SLT 279).

Scope of the Supervisory Jurisdiction of the Court of Session
The decision of the Inner House in the case of *West v. Secretary of State for Scotland,* 1992 SLT 636 made a number of important propositions (at p.650) on the scope of the supervisory jurisdiction of the Court of Session. Those propositions are set out here in full:

"(1) The Court of Session has power, in the exercise of its supervisory jurisdiction, to regulate the process by which decisions are taken by any person or body to whom a jurisdiction, power or authority has been delegated or entrusted by statute, agreement or any other instrument.
(2) The sole purpose for which the supervisory jurisdiction may be exercised is to ensure that the person or body does not exceed or abuse that jurisdiction, power or authority or fail to do what the jurisdiction, power or authority requires.
(3) The competency of the application does not depend upon any distinction between public law and private law, nor is it confined to those cases which English law has accepted as amenable to judicial review, nor is it correct in regard to issues about competency to describe judicial review under Rule of Court 260B as a public law remedy.

By way of explanation we would emphasise these important points:
(a) Judicial review is available, not to provide machinery for an appeal, but to ensure that the decision maker does not exceed or abuse his powers or fail to perform the duty entrusted to him. It is not competent for the court to review the act or decision on its merits, nor may it substitute its own opinion for that of the person or body to whom the matter had been delegated or entrusted.
(b) The word "jurisdiction" best describes the nature of the power, duty or authority committed to the person or body which is amenable to the supervisory jurisdiction of the court. It is used here as meaning simply "power to decide", and it can be applied to acts or decisions of any administrative bodies and persons with similar functions as well as those of inferior tribunals. An excess or abuse of jurisdiction may involve stepping outside it, or failing to observe its limits, or departing from the rules of natural justice, or a failure to understand the law, or the taking into account of matters which ought not to have been taken into account. The categories of what may amount to an excess or abuse of jurisdiction are not closed, and they are capable of being adapted in accordance with the development of administrative law.
(c) There is no substantial difference between English law and Scots law as to the grounds on which the process of decision making may be open to review. So reference may be made to English cases in order to determine whether there has been an excess or abuse of the jurisdiction, power or authority or a failure to do what it requires.
(d) Contractual rights and obligations, such as those between employer and employee, are not as such amenable to judicial review. The cases in which the supervisory jurisdiction is appropriate involve a tripartite relationship, between the person or body to whom the jurisdiction, power or authority has been delegated or entrusted, the person or body by whom it has been delegated or entrusted and the person or persons in respect of or for whose benefit that jurisdiction, power or authority is to be exercised."

Effect of quashing
When deciding whether to quash a plan, decision or order, the court may either quash the plan or leave it *in situ.* According to Lord Cameron in *British Airports Authority v. Secretary of State for Scotland,* 1979 S.C. 200, the court has "no power to vary or alter or remodel" an order or decision under review. However, the precise wording of s.238(2)(b) allows the court to quash the plan. No distinction is drawn on the issue of whether the Court may quash in whole or in part.

Special considerations affecting planning functions

General duty as respects listed buildings in exercise of planning functions

59.—(1) In considering whether to grant planning permission for development which affects a listed building or its setting, a planning authority or the Secretary of State, as the case may be, shall have special regard to the desirability of preserving the building or its setting or any features of special architectural or historic interest which it possesses.

(2) Without prejudice to section 64, in the exercise of the powers of disposal and development conferred by the provisions of sections 191 and 193 of the principal Act, a planning authority shall have regard to the desirability of

preserving features of special architectural or historic interest and, in particular, listed buildings.

(3) In this section, "preserving", in relation to a building, means preserving it either in its existing state or subject only to such alterations or extensions as can be carried out without serious detriment to its character, and "development" includes redevelopment.

DEFINITIONS
"buildings": s.81(2).
"development": s.81(2).
"disposal": s.81(2).
"functions": s.81(2).
"listed building": s.1(4).
"planning authority": s.81(2).
"planning permission": s.81(2).

GENERAL NOTE
This provision is designed to ensure that planning decisions are not taken in a vacuum. Regard must be had to considerations relating to listing building control.

Publicity for applications affecting setting of listed buildings

60.—(1) This section applies where an application for planning permission for any development of land is made to a planning authority and the development would, in the opinion of the authority, affect the setting of a listed building.

(2) The planning authority shall—
(a) publish in a local newspaper circulating in the locality in which the land is situated, and
(b) for not less than 7 days display on or near the land,
a notice indicating the nature of the development in question and naming a place within the locality where a copy of the application, and of all plans and other documents submitted with it, will be open to inspection by the public at all reasonable hours during the period of 21 days beginning with the date of publication of the notice under paragraph (a).

(3) The application shall not be determined by the planning authority before both the following periods have elapsed, namely—
(a) the period of 21 days referred to in subsection (2), and
(b) the period of 21 days beginning with the date on which the notice required by that subsection to be displayed was first displayed.

(4) In determining any application for planning permission to which this section applies, the planning authority shall take into account any representations relating to the application which are received by them before the periods mentioned in subsection (3) have elapsed.

(5) In this section references to planning permission do not include references to planning permission falling within section 33(1) of the principal Act.

DEFINITIONS
"building": s.81(2).
"development": s.81(2).
"land": s.81(2).
"listed building": s.1(4).
"planning authority": s.81(2).

GENERAL NOTE
This provision requires the planning authority to publicise applications for developments which would in their opinion affect the setting of a listed building. This is consistent with the need to integrate the planning functions of the planning authority with considerations relating to listed building control.

Part II

Conservation Areas

Designation

Designation of conservation areas

61.—(1) Every planning authority shall—
(a) from time to time determine which parts of their district are areas of special architectural or historic interest the character or appearance of which it is desirable to preserve or enhance, and
(b) designate such areas as conservation areas.

(2) The Secretary of State may from time to time, after consultation with a planning authority, determine that any part of the authority's district which is not for the time being designated as a conservation area is an area of special architectural or historic interest the character or appearance of which it is desirable to preserve or enhance; and, if he so determines, he may designate that part as a conservation area.

Definitions
    "conservation area": s.61.
    "functions": s.81(2).
    "land": s.81(2).
    "planning authority": s.81(2).

General Note
    This provision requires every planning authority to determine which parts of their area are to be considered areas of special architectural or historic interest, the character or appearance of which it is desirable to preserve. Those areas so identified are to be designated as conservation areas. The Secretary of State is also empowered to make such designations in relation to any part of a planning authority's district in consultation with the planning authority. The duty is a continuing one. The planning authority must periodically review those designations and, where appropriate, designate new areas.

Designation of conservation areas: supplementary provisions

62.—(1) A planning authority shall give notice to the Secretary of State of the designation of any part of their district as a conservation area under section 61(1), and of any variation or cancellation of any such designation.

(2) The Secretary of State shall give notice to a planning authority of the designation of any part of their district as a conservation area under section 61(2), and of any variation or cancellation of any such designation.

(3) A notice under subsection (1) or (2) shall contain sufficient particulars to identify the area affected.

(4) Notice of any such designation, variation or cancellation, with particulars of its effect, shall be published in the Edinburgh Gazette and in at least one newspaper circulating in the district of the planning authority by that authority or, as the case may be, the Secretary of State.

(5) Every planning authority shall compile and keep available for public inspection free of charge at reasonable hours and at a convenient place a list containing such particulars as the Secretary of State may determine of any part of their district which has been designated as a conservation area.

Definitions
    "conservation area": s.61.
    "land": s.81(2).
    "planning authority": s.81(2).

General Note
    This provision requires the planning authority to serve notice of the designation of any part of their district upon the Secretary of State, including any variation or cancellation. They are also

required to publish notice of any designation, variation or cancellation in the Edinburgh Gazette and at least one other newspaper.

General duties of planning authorities

Proposals for preservation and enhancement of conservation areas

63.—(1) It shall be the duty of a planning authority to formulate and publish, from time to time, proposals for the preservation and enhancement of any parts of their district which are conservation areas.

(2) Proposals under this section shall be submitted for consideration to a public meeting in the area to which they relate.

(3) The planning authority shall have regard to any views concerning the proposals expressed by persons attending the meeting.

DEFINITIONS
"conservation area": s.61.
"planning authority": s.81(2).

GENERAL NOTE
This provision operates so as to place the planning authority under a continuous duty to review and formulate proposals for the preservation and enhancement of conservation areas.

General duty as respects conservation areas in exercise of planning functions

64.—(1) In the exercise, with respect to any buildings or other land in a conservation area, of any powers under any of the provisions in subsection (2), special attention shall be paid to the desirability of preserving or enhancing the character or appearance of that area.

(2) Those provisions are—
(a) the planning Acts, and
(b) Part I of the Historic Buildings and Ancient Monuments Act 1953.

DEFINITIONS
"building": s.81(2).
"conservation area": s.61.
"functions": s.81(2).
"land": s.81(2).

GENERAL NOTE
In the House of Lords decision in *South Lakeland District Council v. Secretary of State for the Environment* [1992] 1 All E.R. 45, the Law Lords held that on its true construction, the word "preserving" was to be interpreted in the wider sense of keeping safe from harm and not in the narrower sense of making a positive contribution to the character or appearance of the conservation area in question. Lord Bridge (with whom the other Lords concurred) further accepted that the stricter development control was justified in conservation areas, but the objective of the legislation on conservation areas did not go so far as to inhibit all development. See also paras. 4.15 to 4.21 of the *1993 Memorandum of Guidance.*

Publicity for applications affecting conservation areas

65.—(1) This section applies where an application for planning permission for any development of land is made to a planning authority and the development would, in the opinion of the authority, affect the character or appearance of a conservation area.

(2) The planning authority shall—
(a) publish in a local newspaper circulating in the locality in which the land is situated, and
(b) for not less than 7 days display on or near the land,
a notice indicating the nature of the development in question and naming a place within the locality where a copy of the application, and of all plans and other documents submitted with it, will be open to inspection by the public at all reasonable hours during the period of 21 days beginning with the date of publication of the notice under paragraph (a).

(3) The application shall not be determined by the planning authority before both the following periods have elapsed, namely—

(a) the period of 21 days referred to in subsection (2), and

(b) the period of 21 days beginning with the date on which the notice required by that subsection to be displayed was first displayed.

(4) In determining any application for planning permission to which this section applies, the planning authority shall take into account any representations relating to the application which are received by them before the periods mentioned in subsection (3) have elapsed.

(5) In this section references to planning permission do not include references to planning permission falling within section 33(1) of the principal Act.

DEFINITIONS

"conservation area": s.61.
"functions": s.81(2).
"land": s.81(2).
"planning authority": s.81(2).
"planning permission": s.81(2).

GENERAL NOTE

This provision requires planning authorities to publicise applications for planning permission which in the opinion of the authority would affect the character or appearance of the conservation area. This publicity requirement for applications affecting conservation areas is additional to the existing requirement to publicise general planning applications.

Control of demolition

Control of demolition in conservation areas

66.—(1) A building in a conservation area shall not be demolished without the consent of the appropriate authority (in this Act referred to as "conservation area consent").

(2) The appropriate authority for the purposes of this section is—

(a) in relation to applications for consent made by planning authorities, the Secretary of State, and

(b) in relation to other applications, the planning authority or the Secretary of State.

(3) The following provisions of this Act, namely—

sections 6 to 25,
sections 28 to 41,
sections 56 to 58,
section 59(1),
section 73(2) to (4),
section 74(1)(b), (3) and (4), and
section 80(2),

shall have effect in relation to buildings in conservation areas as they have effect in relation to listed buildings subject to such exceptions and modifications as may be prescribed by regulations.

(4) Any such regulations may make different provision in relation to—

(a) applications made by planning authorities, and

(b) other applications.

DEFINITIONS

"building": s.81(2).
"conservation area": s.61.
"listed building": s.1(4)
"planning authority": s.81(2).
"prescribed": s.81(2).

GENERAL NOTE

This section provides for the application of controls in relation to listed buildings to apply in relation to buildings situated within conservation areas. The effect of this section is to extend the majority of controls which apply to listed buildings to the demolition of buildings in conservation areas. Section 67 contains the exceptions to s.66.

Cases in which section 66 does not apply

67.—(1) Section 66 does not apply to—

(a) listed buildings,

(b) ecclesiastical buildings which are for the time being used for ecclesiastical purposes,

(c) buildings for the time being included in the Schedule of Monuments compiled and maintained under section 1 of the Ancient Monuments and Archaeological Areas Act 1979, or

(d) buildings in relation to which a direction under subsection (2) is for the time being in force.

(2) The Secretary of State may direct that section 66 shall not apply to any description of buildings specified in the direction.

(3) A direction under subsection (2) may be given either to an individual planning authority or to planning authorities generally.

(4) The Secretary of State may vary or revoke a direction under subsection (2) by a further direction under that subsection.

(5) For the purposes of subsection (1)(b), a building used or available for use by a minister of religion wholly or mainly as a residence from which to perform the duties of his office shall be treated as not being an ecclesiastical building.

(6) For the purposes of sections 6 to 8 as they apply by virtue of section 66(3) a building shall be taken to be used for the time being for ecclesiastical purposes if it would be so used but for the works in question.

(7) The Secretary of State may by order provide for restricting or excluding the operation of subsection (1)(b) in such cases as may be specified in the order.

(8) An order under subsection (7) may—

(a) make provision for buildings generally, for descriptions of building or for particular buildings;

(b) make different provision for buildings in different areas, for buildings of different religious faiths or denominations or according to the use made of the building;

(c) make such provision in relation to a part of a building (including, in particular, an object or structure falling to be treated as part of the building by virtue of section 1(4)) as may be made in relation to a building and make different provision for different parts of the same building;

(d) make different provision with respect to works of different descriptions or according to the extent of the works;

(e) make such consequential adaptations or modifications of the operation of any other provision of this Act or the principal Act, or of any instrument made under either of those Acts, as appear to the Secretary of State to be appropriate.

(9) Subsections (7) and (8) are without prejudice to the Church of Scotland Act 1921.

(10) Any proceedings on or arising out of an application for conservation area consent made while section 66 applies to a building shall lapse when it ceases to apply to it, and any such consent granted with respect to the building shall also lapse.

(11) The fact that that section has ceased to apply to a building shall not affect the liability of any person to be prosecuted and punished for an offence under section 8 or 39 committed with respect to the building while that section did apply to it.

DEFINITIONS

"building": s.81(2).

"conservation area consent": s.66(1).

"conservation area": s.61.

"functions": s.81(2).

"land": s.81(2).
"listed buildings": s.1(4).
"planning authority": s.81(2).
"use": s.81(2).

GENERAL NOTE
This section prescribes the cases to which the application of controls under s.66 do not apply.

Urgent works to preserve unoccupied buildings in conservation areas

68. If it appears to the Secretary of State that the preservation of a building in a conservation area is important for maintaining the character or appearance of that area, he may direct that section 49 shall apply to it as it applies to listed buildings.

DEFINITIONS
"building": s.81(2).
"conservation area": s.61.
"listed building": s.1(4).

GENERAL NOTE
This provision extends the powers of the Secretary of State to preserve listed buildings in conservation areas. See further commentary to s.49.

Grants

Grants and loans for preservation or enhancement of conservation areas

69.—(1) If in the opinion of the Secretary of State any conservation area is an area of outstanding architectural or historic interest, he may make grants or loans for the purpose of defraying in whole or in part any expenditure incurred or to be incurred in or in connection with, or with a view to the promotion of, the preservation or enhancement of the character or appearance of the area or any part of it.

(2) A grant or loan under this section may be made subject to such conditions as the Secretary of State may think fit to impose.

(3) Any loan under this section shall be made on such terms as to repayment, payment of interest and otherwise as the Secretary of State may with the approval of the Treasury determine.

(4) Unless the making of a grant or loan under this section appears to the Secretary of State to be a matter of immediate urgency, before making the grant or loan the Secretary of State shall consult the Historic Buildings Council for Scotland as to its making and the conditions subject to which it should be made.

(5) The Secretary of State may pay such remuneration and allowances as he may with the approval of the Treasury determine to any member of the Council by whom services are rendered in connection with any question as to the exercise of his powers under this section.

(6) If any such member is also a member of the House of Commons, those payments shall extend only to allowances in respect of travelling and subsistence expenses, and any other expenses necessarily incurred by that member in connection with those services.

DEFINITIONS
"building": s.81(2).
"conservation area": s.61.
"land": s.81(2).

Recovery of grants under section 69

70.—(1) This section applies to any grant under section 69 made on terms that it shall be recoverable under this section.

(2) A grant shall be regarded as made on those terms only if before or on making the grant the Secretary of State gives to the grantee notice in writing—

(a) summarising the effect of this section, and
(b) if the grant is made for the purpose of defraying the whole or part of expenditure in relation to any particular property ("the grant property"), specifying the recovery period.

(3) In this section "the recovery period" means the period, beginning with the day on which the grant is made and ending not more than 10 years after that day, during which the grant is recoverable in accordance with subsection (4).

(4) If during the recovery period the grantee disposes of the interest which was held by him in the grant property on the day on which the grant was made or any part of that interest by way of sale or excambion or lease for a term of not less than 21 years, the Secretary of State may recover the amount of the grant, or such part of it as he thinks fit, from the grantee.

(5) If the grantee gives the whole of that interest to any person (whether directly or indirectly, but otherwise than by will) subsection (4) shall have effect as if the donee were the grantee.

(6) If the grantee gives part of that interest to any person (whether directly or indirectly but otherwise than by will) subsection (4) shall have effect as if any disposal or part disposal of that interest by the donee were a disposal by the grantee.

(7) If any condition imposed on the making of a grant to which this section applies is contravened or not complied with, the Secretary of State may recover the amount of the grant, or such part of it as he thinks fit, from the grantee.

(8) Nothing in this section entitles the Secretary of State to recover amounts in the aggregate exceeding the amount of the grant (for example by virtue of a breach of more than one condition or disposals of several parts of an interest in the grant property).

DEFINITIONS
"disposal": s.81(2).
"grant property": subs. (2)(b).
"recovery period": subs. (2).

Town schemes

Town scheme agreements

71.—(1) The Secretary of State and a local authority may enter an agreement (in this Act referred to as a "town scheme agreement") that a specified sum of money shall be set aside for a specified period of years for the purpose of making grants for the repair of the buildings which are—
(a) included in a list compiled for the purposes of such an agreement by the Secretary of State and the authority, or
(b) shown on a map prepared by them for those purposes.

(2) Before such a list is compiled or such a map is prepared the Secretary of State and the local authority concerned shall consult the Historic Buildings Council for Scotland.

DEFINITIONS
"building": s.81(2).
"land": s.81(2).
"local authority": s.81(2).
"town scheme agreement": subs. (1).

GENERAL NOTE
This provision empowers the Secretary of State and the local authority to enter into an agreement for establishing a scheme of grant-aid dedicated to the repair of listed buildings.

Grants for repairing of buildings in town schemes

72.—(1) The Secretary of State may make grants for the purpose of defraying the whole or part of any expenditure incurred or to be incurred in the repair of any building which—

(a) is the subject of a town scheme agreement, and

(b) is situated in a conservation area which appears to him to be of outstanding architectural or historic interest.

(2) A grant under this section may be made subject to conditions imposed by the Secretary of State for such purposes as he thinks fit.

(3) Unless the making of a grant under this section appears to the Secretary of State to be a matter of immediate urgency, before making the grant the Secretary of State may consult the Historic Buildings Council for Scotland as to the making of the grant and the conditions subject to which it should be made.

(4) The Secretary of State may—

(a) pay any grant under this section to any authority which is a party to a town scheme agreement, and

(b) make arrangements with any such authority for the way in which the agreement is to be carried out.

(5) Those arrangements may include such arrangements for the offer and payment of grants under this section as the parties may agree.

(6) Section 70(4) to (8) shall apply to a grant made under this section as it applies to a grant made under that section, but taking the recovery period to be 3 years beginning with the date on which the grant is made.

DEFINITIONS
"building": s.81(2).
"land": s.81(2).
"local authority": s.81(2).
"town scheme agreement": subs. (1).

PART III

GENERAL

Special cases

Application of Act to land and works of planning authorities

73.—(1) In relation to land of planning authorities, sections 1(1) and (3) and 2 shall have effect subject to such exceptions and modifications as may be prescribed by regulations.

(2) The provisions mentioned in subsection (3) shall have effect for the purpose of applications by planning authorities relating to the execution of works for the demolition, alteration or extension of listed buildings, subject to such exceptions and modifications as may be prescribed by regulations.

(3) Those provisions are—

section 1(2), (4) and (5),

sections 3 to 26,

sections 28 to 45,

sections 56 to 58,

section 59(1),

section 60(2)(b), (3) and (4),

section 65(2)(b), (3) and (4),

Schedules 1 and 2, and

sections 54(1) to (4) and 55 as they apply with respect to the foregoing provisions.

(4) The regulations may in particular provide—

(a) for the making of applications for listed building consent to the Secretary of State, and

(b) for the service by him of notices under section 2(2) and the provisions mentioned in subsection (3) of this section.

DEFINITIONS
"building": s.81(2).
"land": s.81(2).
"listed building": s.1(4).
"listed building consent": s.7(7).
"planning authority": s.81(2).
"prescribed": s.81(2).

GENERAL NOTE
This section applies the provisions of this Act to the land of planning authorities. In essence, planning authorities enjoy no immunity from the controls in this Act. However, the Secretary of State does retain power to modify the application of this Act to planning authorities.

Exercise of powers in relation to Crown land

74.—(1) Notwithstanding any interest of the Crown in Crown land, but subject to the following provisions of this section—
    (a) a building which for the time being is Crown land may be included in a list compiled or approved by the Secretary of State under section 1,
    (b) any restrictions imposed or powers conferred by any of sections 1 to 24, 28 to 41, 49, 50, 53 to 56, 59(1), 60, 65 and 68 and Schedules 1 to 3 shall apply and be exercisable in relation to Crown land, to the extent of any interest in it for the time being held otherwise than by or on behalf of the Crown, and
    (c) any power to acquire land compulsorily under section 42 may be exercised in relation to any interest in the land which is for the time being held otherwise than by or on behalf of the Crown.
    (2) Except with the consent of the appropriate authority—
    (a) no notice shall be served under section 34 in relation to land which for the time being is Crown land, and
    (b) no interest in land which for the time being is Crown land shall be acquired compulsorily under section 42.
    (3) No listed building enforcement notice shall be served in respect of works executed by or on behalf of the Crown in respect of a building which was Crown land at the time when the works were executed.
    (4) No listed building purchase notice shall be served in relation to any interest in Crown land unless—
    (a) an offer has previously been made by the owner of the interest to dispose of it to the appropriate authority on terms that the price payable for it—
        (i) shall be equal to the compensation which would be payable in respect of the interest if it were acquired in pursuance of such a notice, or
        (ii) in default of agreement shall be determined in a similar manner to that in which that compensation would be determined, and
    (b) that offer has been refused by the appropriate authority.
    (5) A person who is entitled to occupy Crown land by virtue of a contract in writing shall be treated for the purposes of subsection (1)(b) as having an interest in land.
    (6) In this section—
    "Crown land" means land in which there is a Crown interest, and
    "Crown interest" means an interest belonging to Her Majesty in right of the Crown, or belonging to a government department, or held in

trust for Her Majesty for the purposes of a government department.

(7) For the purposes of this section "the appropriate authority", in relation to any land—

(a) in the case of land belonging to Her Majesty in right of the Crown and forming part of the Crown Estate, means the Crown Estate Commissioners,

(b) in relation to any other land belonging to Her Majesty in right of the Crown, means the government department having the management of that land, and

(c) in the case of land belonging to a government department or held in trust for Her Majesty for the purposes of a government department, means that department.

(8) If any question arises as to what authority is the appropriate authority in relation to any land, that question shall be referred to the Treasury, whose decision shall be final.

DEFINITIONS
"appropriate authority": subs. (7).
"building": s.81(2).
"Crown land": subs. (6).
"Crown interest": subs. (5).
"government department": s.81(2).
"land": s.81(2).
"listed building": s.1(4).
"listed building enforcement notice": s.34(1).
"listed building purchase notice": s.28(1).
"owner": s.81(2).

GENERAL NOTE
The Crown is generally immune from listed building control; see *Lord Advocate v. Dumbarton District Council* [1990] 1 All E.R. 1. However, see further General Note to s.6.

Application for listed building or conservation area consent in anticipation of disposal of Crown land

75.—(1) This section has effect for the purpose of enabling Crown land, or an interest in Crown land, to be disposed of with the benefit of listed building consent or conservation area consent.

(2) Notwithstanding the interest of the Crown in the land in question, an application for any such consent may be made by—

(a) the appropriate authority, or

(b) any person authorised by that authority in writing,

and, subject to subsections (3) and (4), all the statutory provisions relating to the making and determination of any such application shall accordingly apply as if the land were not Crown land.

(3) Any listed building consent or conservation area consent granted by virtue of this section shall apply only—

(a) to works carried out after the land in question has ceased to be Crown land, and

(b) so long as that land continues to be Crown land, to works carried out by virtue of a private interest in the land.

(4) The Secretary of State may by regulations—

(a) modify or exclude—

(i) any of the statutory provisions referred to in subsection (2), and

(ii) any other statutory provisions,

in their application to consents granted by virtue of this section,

(b) make provision for requiring a planning authority to be notified of any disposal of, or of an interest in, any Crown land in respect of which an application has been made by virtue of this section, and

(c) make such other provision in relation to the making and determination of applications by virtue of this section as he thinks necessary or expedient.

(5) This section shall not be construed as affecting any right to apply for any listed building consent or conservation area consent in respect of Crown land in a case in which such an application can be made by virtue of a private interest in the land.

(6) A person who is entitled to occupy Crown land by virtue of a contract in writing shall be treated for the purpose of this section as having an interest in land and references to the disposal or grant of an interest in Crown land and to a private interest in such land shall be construed accordingly.

(7) In this section "statutory provisions" means provisions contained in or having effect under any enactment and references to the disposal of an interest in Crown land include references to the grant of an interest in such land.

(8) Subsections (6) to (8) of section 74 apply for the purposes of this section as they apply for the purposes of that section.

DEFINITIONS
"building": s.81(2).
"conservation area": s.61.
"conservation area consent": s.66(1).
"disposal": s.81(2).
"enactment": s.81(2).
"land": s.81(2).
"listed building": s.1(4).
"listed building consent": s.7(7).
"planning authority": s.81(2).

GENERAL NOTE
This provision is parallel to that contained in s.243 of the Principal Act and allows the Crown to choose to make use of the planning controls in anticipation of the disposal of Crown land. See further General Note to s.243 of the Principal Act.

Miscellaneous provisions

Rights of entry

76.—(1) Any person duly authorised in writing by the Secretary of State may at any reasonable time enter upon any land for the purpose of surveying any building on that or any other land in connection with a proposal to include the building in, or exclude it from, a list compiled or approved under section 1.

(2) Any person duly authorised in writing by the Secretary of State or the planning authority may at any reasonable time enter upon any land for any of the following purposes—
   (a) surveying it in connection with any proposal by the authority or the Secretary of State to make or serve any order or notice under or by virtue of any provision of this Act other than sections 25 to 33, 42, 44 to 48, 51, 52, 57, 58, 59(2) and (3), 61 to 67, 69 to 75, 79 to 83 and Schedule 3,
   (b) ascertaining whether an offence has been, or is being, committed with respect to any building on that or any other land, under section 8, 10, 39 or 53,
   (c) ascertaining whether any such building is being maintained in a proper state of repair,
   (d) ascertaining whether any of the functions conferred by section 49 should or may be exercised in connection with the land, or
   (e) exercising any of those functions in connection with the land.

(3) Any person who is an officer of the Valuation Office or a person duly authorised in writing by the Secretary of State may at any reasonable time

enter any land for the purpose of surveying it, or estimating its value, in connection with a claim for compensation payable under this Act in respect of any land.

(4) Any person who is an officer of the Valuation Office or a person duly authorised in writing by a planning authority may at any reasonable time enter any land for the purpose of surveying it, or estimating its value, in connection with a claim for compensation payable under section 25 or 26 in respect of any land.

(5) Any person who is an officer of the Valuation Office or is duly authorised in writing by a planning authority having power to acquire land under sections 42 to 47 may at any reasonable time enter any land for the purpose of surveying it, or estimating its value, in connection with any proposal to acquire that land or any other land, or in connection with any claim for compensation in respect of any such acquisition.

(6) Subject to sections 77 and 78, any power conferred by this section to survey land shall be construed as including power to search and bore for the purpose of ascertaining the nature of the subsoil or the presence of minerals in it.

DEFINITIONS
  "building": s.81(2).
  "functions": s.81(2).
  "land": s.81(2).
  "planning authority": s.81(2).
  "valuation office": s.81(2).

Power to issue warrant

77.—(1) If in relation to rights of entry exercised under section 76 the sheriff is satisfied—

(a) that there are reasonable grounds for entering any land for any of the purposes mentioned in that section, and

(b) that—

(i) admission to the land has been refused, or a refusal is reasonably apprehended, or

(ii) the case is one of urgency,

he may issue a warrant authorising any person duly authorised in writing to enter the land.

(2) For the purposes of subsection (1)(b)(i) admission to land shall be regarded as having been refused if no reply is received to a request for admission within a reasonable period.

(3) A warrant authorises entry on one occasion only and that entry must be—

(a) within one month from the date of the issue of the warrant, and

(b) at a reasonable hour, unless the case is one of urgency.

DEFINITIONS
  "land": s.81(2).

Rights of entry: supplementary provisions

78.—(1) Subject to subsection (2), a person authorised to enter any land in pursuance of a right of entry conferred under or by virtue of section 76 or 77 (referred to in this section as "a right of entry")—

(a) shall, if so required, produce evidence of his authority and state the purpose of his entry before so entering,

(b) may take with him such other persons as may be necessary, and

(c) on leaving the land shall, if the owner or occupier is not then present, leave it as effectively secured against trespassers as he found it.

(2) Admission to any land which is occupied shall not be demanded as of right by virtue of section 76 or of this section unless 24 hours' notice of the intended entry has been given to the occupier of the land.

(3) Any person who wilfully obstructs a person acting in the exercise of a right of entry shall be guilty of an offence and liable on summary conviction to a fine not exceeding level 3 on the standard scale.

(4) If any damage is caused to land or moveable property in the exercise of a right of entry, compensation may be recovered by any person suffering the damage from the authority who gave the written authority for the entry or, as the case may be, the Secretary of State; and subsections (4) and (5) of section 27 shall apply in relation to compensation under this subsection as they apply in relation to compensation under sections 25 to 27.

(5) If any person who enters any land in exercise of a right of entry discloses to any person any information obtained by him while on the land as to any manufacturing process or trade secret, he shall be guilty of an offence.

(6) Subsection (5) does not apply if the disclosure is made by a person in the course of performing his duty in connection with the purpose for which he was authorised to enter the land.

(7) A person who is guilty of an offence under subsection (5) shall be liable—

    (a) on summary conviction to a fine not exceeding the statutory maximum, or

    (b) on conviction on indictment to imprisonment for a term not exceeding 2 years or a fine or both.

(8) No person shall carry out any works in exercise of a power conferred under section 49 unless notice of his intention to do so was included in the notice required by subsection (2) of this section.

(9) The authority of the appropriate Minister shall be required for the carrying out of works in exercise of a power conferred under section 49 if—

    (a) the land in question is held by statutory undertakers, and

    (b) they object to the proposed works on the ground that the execution of the works would be seriously detrimental to the carrying on of their undertaking.

(10) Section 217(1) of the principal Act applies for the purposes of subsection (9) as it applies for the purposes of section 270(9) of the principal Act.

DEFINITIONS

    "land": s.81(2).

Application of certain general provisions of principal Act

79.—(1) Subject to subsection (2), the following provisions of the principal Act shall apply for the purposes of this Act as they apply for the purposes of that Act—

    section 85 (power to make provision for determination of claims),

    section 146 (interdicts restraining breaches of planning control),

    section 195 (general vesting declarations),

    section 263 (local inquiries),

    section 266 (orders as to expenses of parties where no local inquiry held),

    section 267 (procedure on certain appeals and applications),

    section 271 (service of notices),

    section 272 (power to require information as to interests in land),

    section 273 (offences by corporations), and

    section 276 (Act not excluded by special enactments).

(2) Section 273 of that Act shall not apply to offences under section 53 of this Act.

Financial provisions

80.—(1) Where—

    (a) compensation is payable by a planning authority under this Act in consequence of any decision or order given or made under any provision of this Act other than sections 25 to 27, 42, 43(1) to (3), 44 to 52,

57, 58, 59(2) and (3), 61 to 64, 66, 67(1) to (4), (10) and (11) and 68 to 83, and

(b) that decision or order was given or made wholly or partly in the interest of a service which is provided by a government department and the cost of which is defrayed out of money provided by Parliament,

the Minister responsible for the administration of that service may pay that authority a contribution of such amount as he may with the consent of the Treasury determine.

(2) Any local authority and any statutory undertakers may contribute towards any expenses incurred by a planning authority in or in connection with the performance of any of their functions under the provisions of sections 1 to 24, 28 to 47, 50, 53, 54, 56, 59, 77 and 78 and Schedules 1 and 2.

(3) In the application of subsection (2) to a local authority, "planning authority" means a planning authority other than that local authority.

(4) Any expenses incurred by a planning authority under sections 28 to 30 and 42 to 47 in pursuance of a listed building purchase notice or in the acquisition of land under this Act for the purposes of any function of that authority shall be defrayed in the same manner as other expenses incurred by that authority for the purposes of that function.

(5) Subsections (3) and (4) of section 261 of the principal Act (borrowing by authorities for purposes of the principal Act) shall apply for the purposes of this Act as they apply for the purposes of that Act.

(6) There shall be paid out of money provided by Parliament—

(a) any sums necessary to enable the Secretary of State to make any payments becoming payable by him under sections 25 and 26,

(b) any expenses incurred by any government department including the Secretary of State in the acquisition of land under sections 42 to 47 or in the payment of compensation under section 46(4) or 78(4) or under subsection (1),

(c) any sums necessary to enable the Secretary of State to make grants or loans under sections 69 and 72, and

(d) any administrative expenses incurred by the Secretary of State for the purposes of this Act.

(7) Any sums received by the Secretary of State under this Act shall be paid into the Consolidated Fund.

DEFINITIONS

"land": s.81(2).
"local authority": s.81(2).
"minister": s.81(2).
"planning authority": s.81(2).
"Principal Act": s.81(2).
"statutory undertaker": s.81(3).

PART IV

SUPPLEMENTAL

Interpretation

81.—(1) In this Act, except in so far as the context otherwise requires—

"building preservation notice" has the meaning given in section 3(1),

"conservation area" means an area for the time being designated under section 61,

"conservation area consent" has the meaning given in section 66(1),

"listed building" has the meaning given in section 1(4),

"listed building consent" has the meaning given in section 7(7),

"listed building enforcement notice" has the meaning given in section 34(1),

"listed building purchase notice" has the meaning given in section 28(1),

"period for compliance", in relation to a listed building enforcement notice, has the meaning given in section 34(5), "prescribed" (except in relation to matters expressly required or authorised by this Act to be prescribed in some other way) means prescribed by regulations under this Act,

"the principal Act" means the Town and Country Planning (Scotland) Act 1997, and

"town scheme agreement" has the meaning given in section 71,

(2) Subject to subsection (6), and except in so far as the context otherwise requires, the following expressions have the same meaning as in the principal Act—

"acquiring authority"
"advertisement"
"building"
"compulsory acquisition"
"development"
"development order"
"development plan"
"disposal"
"enactment"
"functions"
"government department"
"land"
"lease"
"local authority"
"minerals"
"Minister"
"owner"
"the planning Acts"
"planning authority"
"planning permission"
"public gas transporter"
"use"
"Valuation Office".

(3) In this Act "statutory undertakers" has the same meaning as in the principal Act except that—

(a) in sections 29 to 32 it shall be deemed to include references to a public telecommunications operator,

(b) in sections 29 to 32 and 80(2) it shall be deemed to include the Post Office, and

(c) in sections 29 to 32, 46(2)(a) and 80(2) it shall be deemed to include the Civil Aviation Authority, a public gas transporter and a holder of a licence under section 6 of the Electricity Act 1989.

(4) References in the planning Acts to any of the provisions mentioned in section 73 include, except where the context otherwise requires, references to those provisions as modified under that section.

(5) Words in this Act importing a reference to service of a notice to treat shall be construed as including a reference to the constructive service of such a notice which, by virtue of any enactment, is to be deemed to be served.

(6) For the purposes of subsection (1)(b) of section 51 and subsection (2) as it applies for the purposes of that subsection the definition of "building" in the principal Act shall apply with the omission of the words "but does not include plant or machinery comprised in a building".

(7) In this Act any reference to a sale or purchase includes a reference to a sale or purchase by way of feu, and any reference to the price in relation to a sale or purchase includes a reference to grassum, feuduty and ground annual.

(8) Without prejudice to section 20(2) of the Interpretation Act 1978, references in this Act to any enactment shall, except where the context otherwise requires, be construed as references to that enactment as amended by or under any other enactment.

Regulations and orders

82.—(1) The Secretary of State may make regulations—

(a) for prescribing the form of any notice, order or other document authorised or required by this Act to be served, made or issued by a planning authority which is a local authority;

(b) for any purpose for which regulations are authorised or required to be made under this Act.

(2) Any power conferred by this Act to make regulations shall be exercisable by statutory instrument.

(3) Any statutory instrument containing regulations made under this Act shall be subject to annulment in pursuance of a resolution of either House of Parliament.

(4) The power to make orders under sections 7(5), 54(5) and 67(7) shall be exercisable by statutory instrument.

(5) Any statutory instrument which contains an order under section 54(5) or 67(7) shall be subject to annulment in pursuance of a resolution of either House of Parliament.

(6) Any order under section 54(5) or 67(7) may contain such supplementary and incidental provisions as may appear to the Secretary of State appropriate.

(7) Without prejudice to section 14 of the Interpretation Act 1978, any power conferred by this Act to make an order shall include power to vary or revoke any such order by a subsequent order.

Short title, commencement and extent

83.—(1) This Act may be cited as the Planning (Listed Buildings and Conservation Areas) (Scotland) Act 1997.

(2) This Act shall come into force at the end of the period of 3 months beginning with the day on which it is passed.

(3) This Act extends to Scotland only.

SCHEDULES

Section 1(5)   SCHEDULE 1

BUILDINGS FORMERLY SUBJECT TO BUILDING PRESERVATION ORDERS

1. Subject to paragraph 2, every building which immediately before 3rd August 1970 was subject to a building preservation order under section 27 of the Town and Country Planning (Scotland) Act 1947 but was not then included in a list compiled or approved under section 28 of that Act shall be deemed to be a listed building.

2.—(1) The Secretary of State may at any time direct, in the case of any building, that paragraph 1 shall no longer apply to it.

(2) The planning authority in whose district the building in respect of which such a direction is given is situated, on being notified of the direction, shall give notice of it to the owner, lessee and occupier of the building.

(3) Before giving such a direction in relation to a building, the Secretary of State shall consult the planning authority and the owner, lessee and occupier of the building.

3. In the case of a building to which paragraph 1 applies—

(a) a notice of appeal under section 18 may include a claim that the Secretary of State should give a direction under paragraph 2 with respect to the building and on such an appeal the Secretary of State may give such a direction; and

(b) such a direction may also be given on an appeal under section 35.

Section 5   SCHEDULE 2

LAPSE OF BUILDING PRESERVATION NOTICE

1. This Schedule applies where a building preservation notice ceases to be in force by virtue of—

(a) the expiry of the 6 months period mentioned in subsection (3)(b) of section 3; or

(b) the service of a notification by the Secretary of State under subsection (4)(b) of that section.

2. The fact that the notice has ceased to be in force shall not affect the liability of any person to be prosecuted and punished for an offence under section 8 or 39 committed by him with respect to the building while it was in force.

3. Any proceedings on or arising out of an application for listed building consent with respect to the building made while the notice was in force and any such consent granted while it was in force shall lapse.

4.—(1) Any listed building enforcement notice served by the planning authority while the building preservation notice was in force shall cease to have effect.

(2) Any proceedings on it under sections 34 to 37 shall lapse.

(3) Notwithstanding sub-paragraph (1), section 38(1) and (2) shall continue to have effect as respects any expenses incurred by the planning authority, owner, lessee or occupier as mentioned in that section and with respect to any sums paid on account of such expenses.

Sections 20(4) and 35(5) SCHEDULE 3

DETERMINATION OF CERTAIN APPEALS BY PERSON APPOINTED BY SECRETARY OF STATE

Determination of appeals by appointed person

1.—(1) The Secretary of State may by regulations prescribe classes of appeals under sections 18 and 35 which are to be determined by a person appointed by the Secretary of State for the purpose instead of by the Secretary of State.

(2) Those classes of appeals shall be so determined except in such classes of case—

(a) as may for the time being be prescribed, or

(b) as may be specified in directions given by the Secretary of State.

(3) Such regulations may provide for the giving of publicity to any directions given by the Secretary of State under this paragraph.

(4) This paragraph shall not affect any provision contained in this Act or any instrument made under it that an appeal shall lie to, or a notice of appeal shall be served on, the Secretary of State.

(5) A person appointed under this paragraph is referred to in this Schedule as an "appointed person".

Powers and duties of appointed person

2.—(1) An appointed person shall have the same powers and duties—

(a) in relation to an appeal under section 18 as the Secretary of State has under subsection (1) of section 20 and paragraph 2 of Schedule 1, and

(b) in relation to an appeal under section 35, as he has under section 37(1), (2) and (4) and paragaph 2 of Schedule 1.

(2) Sections 20(2) and 36(2) shall not apply to an appeal which falls to be determined by an appointed person, but before it is determined the Secretary of State shall ask the appellant and the planning authority whether they wish to appear before and be heard by the appointed person.

(3) If both the parties express a wish not to appear and be heard, the appeal may be determined without their being heard.

(4) If either of the parties expresses a wish to appear and be heard, the appointed person shall give them both an opportunity of doing so.

(5) Where an appeal has been determined by an appointed person, his decision shall be treated as that of the Secretary of State.

(6) Except as provided by sections 57 and 58, the decision of an appointed person on any appeal shall be final.

Determination of appeals by Secretary of State

3.—(1) The Secretary of State may, if he thinks fit, direct that an appeal which would otherwise fall to be determined by an appointed person shall instead be determined by the Secretary of State.

(2) Such a direction shall state the reasons for which it is given and shall be served on the appellant, the planning authority, any person who made representations relating to the subject matter of the appeal which the authority are required to take into account by regulations made under section 10(2) and, if any person has been appointed under paragraph 1, on him.

(3) Where in consequence of such a direction an appeal under section 18 or 35 falls to be determined by the Secretary of State himself, the provisions of this Act which are relevant to the appeal shall, subject to the following provisions of this paragraph, apply to the appeal as if this Schedule had never applied to it.

(4) The Secretary of State shall give the appellant, the planning authority and any person who has made such representations as are referred to in sub-paragraph (2) an opportunity of appearing before and being heard by a person appointed by the Secretary of State for that purpose if—

(a) the reasons for the direction raise matters with respect to which any of those persons have not made representations, or

(b) in the case of the appellant or the planning authority, either of them was not asked in pursuance of paragraph 2(2) whether they wish to appear before and be heard by the appointed person or expressed no wish in answer to that question, or expressed a wish to appear and be heard, but was not given an opportunity of doing so.

(5) Except as provided by sub-paragraph (4), the Secretary of State need not give any person an opportunity of appearing before and being heard by a person appointed for the purpose, or of making fresh representations or making or withdrawing any representations already made.

(6) In determining the appeal the Secretary of State may take into account any report made to him by any person previously appointed to determine it.

4.—(1) The Secretary of State may by a further direction revoke a direction under paragraph 3 at any time before the determination of the appeal.

(2) Such a further direction shall state the reasons for which it is given and shall be served on the person, if any, previously appointed to determine the appeal, the appellant, the planning authority and any person who has made representations relating to the subject matter of the appeal which the authority are required to take into account by regulations made under section 10(2).

(3) Where such a further direction has been given, the provisions of this Schedule relevant to the appeal shall apply, subject to sub-paragraph (4), as if no direction under paragraph 3 had been given.

(4) Anything done by or on behalf of the Secretary of State in connection with the appeal which might have been done by the appointed person (including any arrangements made for the holding of a hearing or local inquiry) shall, unless that person directs otherwise, be treated as having been done by him.

Appointment of another person to determine appeal

5.—(1) At any time before the appointed person has determined the appeal the Secretary of State may—

(a) revoke his appointment, and

(b) appoint another person under paragraph 1 to determine the appeal instead.

(2) Where such a new appointment is made the consideration of the appeal or any inquiry or other hearing in connection with it shall be begun afresh.

(3) Nothing in sub-paragraph (2) shall require—

(a) the question referred to in paragraph 2(2) to be asked again with reference to the new appointed person if before his appointment it was asked with reference to the previous appointed person (any answers being treated as given with reference to the new appointed person), or

(b) any person to be given an opportunity of making fresh representations or modifying or withdrawing any representations already made.

Local inquiries and hearings

6.—(1) Whether or not the parties to an appeal have asked for an opportunity to appear and be heard, an appointed person—

(a) may hold a local inquiry in connection with the appeal, and

(b) shall do so if the Secretary of State so directs.

(2) Where an appointed person—

(a) holds a hearing by virtue of paragraph 2(4), or

(b) holds an inquiry by virtue of this paragraph,

an assessor may be appointed by the Secretary of State to sit with the appointed person at the hearing or inquiry to advise him on any matters arising, notwithstanding that the appointed person is to determine the appeal.

(3) Subject to sub-paragraph (4), the expenses of any such hearing or inquiry shall be paid by the Secretary of State.

(4) Subsections (4) to (13) of section 265 of the principal Act apply to an inquiry held under this paragraph as they apply to an inquiry held under that section.

(5) The appointed person has the same power to make orders under subsection (9) of that section in relation to proceedings under this Schedule which do not give rise to an inquiry as he has in relation to such an inquiry.

(6) For the purposes of this paragraph, references to the Minister in subsections (9) and (12) of that section shall be read as references to the appointed person.

Supplementary provisions

7.—(1) The Tribunals and Inquiries Act 1992 shall apply to a local inquiry or other hearing held in pursuance of this Schedule as it applies to a statutory inquiry held by the Secretary of

State, but as if in section 10(1) of that Act (statement of reasons for decisions) the reference to any decision taken by the Secretary of State were a reference to a decision taken by an appointed person.

(2) The functions of determining an appeal and doing anything in connection with it conferred by this Schedule on an appointed person who is an officer of the Scottish Office shall be treated for the purposes of the Parliamentary Commissioner Act 1967 as functions of that office.

TABLE OF DERIVATIONS

Notes:

1. This Table shows the derivation of the provisions of the Bill.
2. The following abbreviations are used in the Table—

1972AM	= The Town and Country Planning (Amendment) Act 1972 (c. 42)
1972	= The Town and Country Planning (Scotland) Act 1972 (c. 52)
1974	= The Town and Country Amenities Act 1974 (c. 32)
1982	= The Local Government and Planning (Scotland) Act 1982 (c. 43)
1986	= The Housing and Planning Act 1986 (c. 63)
1991	= The Planning and Compensation Act 1991 (c. 34)

3. The Table does not show the effect of Transfer of Functions orders.
4. The Table does not give details of the effect of section 172(2) of the Local Government (Scotland) Act 1973 (c. 65), which omitted the word "local" in the expression "local planning authority" where it occurs in any enactment or instrument.
5. "Sc Law Com Rec No." followed by a number indicates that the provision gives effect to the Recommendation bearing that number in Appendix 1 to the Scottish Law Commission's Report on the Consolidation of Certain Enactments relating to Town and Country Planning in Scotland (Cmnd. 3644).

Provision	Derivation
1(1) to (3)	1972 s.52(1) to (3).
(4)	1972 s.52(7); 1986 Sch. 9 para. 13(1).
(5)	Drafting.
2(1)	1972 s.52(4); Local Government (Scotland) Act 1973 (c. 65) Sch. 23, para. 19; Housing (Scotland) Act 1987 (c. 26) Sch. 22, para. 3.
(2)	1972 s.52(5).
(3), (4)	1972 s.52(6).
3(1), (2)	1972 s.56(1)
(3), (4)	1972 s.56(3).
(5)	1972 s.56(4)
(6)	1972 s.56(5).
4(1) to (3)	1972 s.56(6).
5	1972 s.56(4).
6	1972 s.53(1); 1986 Sch. 9 para. 14(1).
7(1), (2)	1972 s.53(2); Sc Law Com Rec No. 24.
(3)	1972 s.53(2A); 1986 Sch. 9 para. 14(2).
(4) to (6)	1972 s.53(3).
(7)	1972 s.53(3A); 1986 Sch. 9 para. 14(3).
8(1)	1972 s.53(1); 1986 Sch. 9 para. 14(1).
(2)	1972 s.53(4).
(3)	1972 s.53(6); 1986 Sch. 9 para. 15(1).
(4), (5)	1972 s.53(5); 1991 Sch. 10 para. 2.
9(1), (2)	1972 Sch. 10 para. 1(1); 1986 Sch. 9 para. 22.
(3)	1972 Sch. 10 para. 1(1A); 1986 Sch. 9 para. 22.
10(1)	1972 s.24(1), Sch. 10 para. 2(1); 1991 Sch. 13 para. 42(a).
(2)	1972 s.26(3A), Sch. 10 para. 2(1); 1991 Sch. 13 para. 42(b).
(3)	1972 Sch. 10 para. 2(2); Criminal Procedure (Consequential Provisions) (Scotland) Act 1995 (c. 40) Sch. 1 paras. 5, 6; Criminal Procedure (Scotland) Act 1995 (c. 46) s.225.
11(1) to (5)	1972 Sch. 10 para. 4.
12(1)	1972 Sch. 10 para. 5(1).
(2)	1972 Sch. 10 para. 5(1), (2).
(3)	1972 Sch. 10 para. 5(2); 1986 Sch. 9 para. 23.
13(1) to (3)	1972 Sch. 10 para. 6.

Provision	Derivation
14(1)	1972 s.54(4); 1982 Sch. 2 para. 15(b).
(2)	1972 s.54(3); 1982 Sch. 2 para. 15(a).
(3)	1972 Sch. 10 para. 1(2).
15(1)	1972 s.54(4); 1982 Sch. 2 para. 15(b).
(2)	1972 s.54(4A); 1986 Sch. 9 para. 16(1).
(3)	1972 s.54(5); 1982 Sch. 2 para. 15(c).
16(1), (2)	1972 s.54A(1), (2); 1982 Sch. 2 para. 16.
(3)	1972 s.54A(5); 1986 Sch. 9 para. 14(4).
(4)	1972 s.54B; 1982 Sch. 2 para. 16.
17(1) to (3)	1972 s.54D(1) to (3); 1986 Sch. 9 para. 17.
18(1)	1972 s.54D(2), Sch. 10 para. 7(1); 1986 Sch. 9 paras. 16(2), 17.
(2)	1972 s.54D(2), Sch. 10 para. 8; 1986 Sch. 9 para. 16(3).
(3)	1972 s.54D(2), Sch. 10 para. 8; 1986 Sch. 9 para. 16(3).
(4)	1972 s.54D(2), Sch. 10 para. 8; 1986 Sch. 9 para. 16(3).
19(1)	1972 Sch. 10 para. 7(1); 1986 Sch. 9 para. 16(2).
(2)	1972 Sch. 10 para. 7(1), 8; 1986 Sch. 9 para. 16(2), (3).
(3), (4)	1972 Sch. 10 para. 7(2).
(5), (6)	1972 s.54D(2), Sch. 10 para. 2(1); 1991 Sch. 13 para. 42.
(7)	1972 s.54D(2), Sch. 10 para. 2(2); Criminal Procedure (Consequential Provisions) (Scotland) Act 1995 (c. 40) Sch. 1 paras. 5, 6; Criminal Procedure (Scotland) Act 1995 (c. 46) s.225.
20(1) to (4)	1972 Sch. 10 para. 7(3) to (6).
21(1), (2)	1972 Sch. 10 para. 9(1).
(3)	1972 Sch. 10 para. 9(4).
22(1)	1972 Sch. 10 para. 9(2).
(2) to (4)	1972 Sch. 10 para. 9(3).
(5)	1972 Sch. 10 para. 9(2).
23(1)	1972 Sch. 10 para. 11(1), (6).
(2)	1972 Sch. 10 para. 11(1) to (4); drafting.
(3)	1972 Sch. 10 para. 11(3).
(4)	1972 Sch. 10 para. 11(5).
(5), (6)	1972 Sch. 10 para. 11(2).
24(1)	1972 Sch. 10 paras. 9(1), 10(1).
(2)	1972 Sch. 10 paras. 9(1), 10(2).
(3)	1972 Sch. 10 para. 10(1).
(4) to (6)	1972 Sch. 10 paras. 9(3), 10(2).
(7)	1972 Sch. 10 paras. 9(4), 10(2).
(8)	1972 Sch. 10 para. 10(1).
25(1), (2)	1972 s.161(1).
(3)	1972 s.161(3).
(4)	1972 s.161(2).
26(1)	1972 s.162(1), (3).
(2)	1972 s.162(3).
(3)	1972 s.162(4).
27(1)	1972 s.167(1).
(2)	1972 s.167(2).
(3)	1972 s.167(4).
(4)	1972 s.168(1).
(5)	1972 s.168(2).
28(1), (2)	1972 s.179(1), (5).
(3)	1972 s.179(3).
(4)	1972 s.179(2); 1991 Sch. 12 para. 21.
29(1)	1972 Sch. 17 para. 1(1); 1986 Sch. 11 para. 35(2)(a).
(2)	1972 Sch. 17 para. 1(1).
(3)	1972 Sch. 17 para. 1(2).
(4)	1972 Sch. 17 para. 1(3); 1986 Sch. 11 para. 35(2)(b).
30(1)	1972 s.171(1), Sch. 17 paras. 1(3), 2(8).
(2)	1972 s.171(2), Sch. 17 paras. 1(3), 2(8).
(3),(4)	1972 s.171(3), Sch. 17 paras. 1(3), 2(8).

Provision	Derivation
30(5)	1972 s.171(4), Sch. 17 paras. 1(3), 2(8); drafting.
(6)	1972 s.179(3).
31(1), (2)	1972 Sch. 17 para. 2(1).
(3)	1972 Sch. 17 para. 2(2).
(4)	1972 Sch. 17 para. 2(3), (4).
(5)	1972 Sch. 17 para. 2(5), (6).
(6)	1972 Sch. 17 para. 2(7).
(7)	1972 Sch. 17 para. 2(8).
32(1)	1972 Sch. 17 para. 3(1).
(2)	1972 Sch. 17 para. 3(2).
(3)	1972 Sch. 17 para. 3(3)(a).
(4)	1972 Sch. 17 para. 3(1).
(5)	1972 Sch. 17 para. 3(3)(b); 1986 Sch. 11 para. 37(2).
(6)	1972 Sch. 17 para. 3(3A); 1986 Sch. 11 para. 37(2).
(7)	1972 Sch. 17 para. 3(4); Sc Law Com Rec No. 25.
(8)	1972 Sch. 17 para. 3(5); Sc Law Com Rec No. 26.
33	1972 Sch. 17 para. 4.
34(1)	1972 s.92(1), (2).
(2)	1972 s.92(1), (1A); 1982 Sch. 2 para. 26(a), (b).
(3)	1972 s.92(1A); 1982 Sch. 2 para. 26(b).
(4)	1972 s.92(2A); 1982 Sch. 2 para. 26(c).
(5)	1972 s.92(4); 1991 Sch. 10 para. 4(b).
(6)	1972 s.92(3), (3A); 1982 Sch. 2 para. 26(d).
(7)	1972 s.92(5); 1991 Sch. 10 para. 5.
(8)	1972 s.92(5A); 1991 Sch. 10 para. 5.
(9)	1972 s.92(6).
35(1)	1972 s.93(1); 1982 Sch. 2 para. 27(a); 1986 Sch. 9 para. 15(2); 1991 Sch. 10 para. 6(2)(a); drafting.
(2)	1972 s.93(2); 1982 Sch. 2 para. 27(b); 1991 Sch. 10 para. 6(3).
(3)	1972 s.93(3).
(4)	1972 ss.85(2A), (2B)(a), 93(2A); 1982 Sch. 2 paras. 20(b), 27(b).
(5)	1972 s.93(8).
36(1)	1972 ss.85(2B), 93(2A); 1982 Sch. 2 paras. 20(b), 27(b); 1991 Sch. 13 para. 20(a).
(2)	1972 ss.85(2D), 93(2A); 1982 Sch. 2 paras. 20(b), 27(b).
37(1)	1972 s.93(5).
(2)	1972 s.93(4); 1991 Sch. 10 para. 6(4).
(3)	1972 ss.85(2C), 93(2A); 1982 Sch. 2 paras. 20(b), 27(b).
(4)	1972 s.93(5).
(5)	1972 s.93(6); 1982 Sch. 2 para. 27(c).
(6)	1972 s.93(7).
38(1), (2)	1972 s.95(1), (2).
(3)	1972 ss.88(3), 95(3); 1982 Sch. 2 para. 23(b).
(4), (5)	1972 ss.88(4), 95(3); 1982 Sch. 2 para. 23(b).
(6), (7)	1972 ss.88(5), 95(3); 1982 Sch. 2 para. 23(b); Sc Law Com Rec No. 27.
(8)	1972 s.95(4); 1991 Sch. 10 para. 8.
39(1) to (6)	1972 s.94; 1991 Sch. 10 para. 7.
40(1)	1972 s.95A(1), (2); 1986 Sch. 9 para. 19.
(2)	1972 s.95A(3); 1986 Sch. 9 para. 19.
41(1) to (3)	1972 s.260(5).
(4)	1972 s.260(5); Sc Law Com Rec No. 2.
42(1)	1972 s.104(1), (2).
(2)	1972 s.104(4).
(3)	1972 s.104(5).
(4), (5)	1972 s.104(6).
(6)	1972 s.104(7).
(7)	1972 s.104(1).
43(1) to (3)	1972 s.105(1) to (3).
(4)	1972 ss.169(5), 170(4).

Provision	Derivation
43(5)	1972 ss.105(4), 169(6).
44	1972 s.106.
45(1)	1972 s.107(1); Local Government (Scotland) Act 1973 (c. 65) Sch. 23 para. 22(a).
(2), (3)	1972 s.107(2), (3).
(4)	1972 s.107(4).
(5)	1972 s.107(4); Sc Law Com Rec No. 28.
(6)	1972 s.107(5); Local Government (Scotland) Act 1973 (c. 65) Sch. 23 para. 22(c).
(7)	1972 s.107(5).
(8)	1972 s.107(6).
(9)	1972 s.107(7).
46(1)	1972 s.108(1).
(2)	1972 s.108(2); Telecommunications Act 1984 (c. 12) Sch. 4 para. 54(3).
(3) to (5)	1972 s.108(3) to (5).
47(1)	1972 s.109(1); Local Government (Scotland) Act 1973 (c. 65) Sch. 23 para. 23.
(2) to (4)	1972 s.109(2).
48(1)	1972 s.116(1); Sc Law Com Rec No. 29.
(2)	Historic Buildings and Ancient Monuments Act 1953 (c. 49) s.5(3); 1972 s.116(2).
49(1) to (3)	1972 s.97(1); 1986 Sch. 9 para. 20.
(4)	1972 s.97(3); 1986 Sch. 9 para. 20.
(5), (6)	1972 s.97(4); 1986 Sch. 9 para. 20.
50(1) to (5)	1972 s.97A; 1986 Sch. 9 para. 20.
51(1) to (6)	Civic Amenities Act 1967 (c. 69) s.5; Planning (Listed Buildings and Conservation Areas) Act 1990 (c. 9) s.57; Planning (Consequential Provisions) Act 1990 (c. 11) Sch. 2 para. 16.
52(1) to (5)	Civic Amenities Act 1967 (c. 69) s.5; Planning (Listed Buildings and Conservation Areas) Act 1990 (c. 9) s.58; Planning (Consequential Provisions) Act 1990 (c. 11) Sch. 2 para. 16.
53(1)	1972 s.55(1); Criminal Procedure (Consequential Provisions) (Scotland) Act 1995 (c. 40) Sch. 1 paras. 5, 6; Criminal Procedure (Scotland) Act 1995 (c. 46) s.225.
(2)	1972 s.55(1).
(3)	1972 s.55(2).
(4)	1972 s.55(3); 1986 Sch. 11 para. 44(1); 1991 Sch. 13 para. 18.
54(1), (2)	1972 ss.54(1), 56(2), 97(3), 104(3); 1986 Sch. 9 para. 20.
(3), (4)	1972 s.54(1).
(5) to (7)	1972 s.56AA(1) to (3); 1986 Sch. 9 para. 18(1).
55(1), (2)	1972 ss.54(1), 56(2), 97(3), 104(3); Ancient Monuments and Archaeological Areas Act 1979 (c. 46) Sch. 4 para. 12; 1986 Sch. 9 para. 20.
56(1) to (3).	1972 s.54C; 1982 s.42.
57(1)	1972 s.231(1)(d), (e), (2)(f).
(2)	1972 s.231(3)(h) to (k); 1982 s.47(c), Sch. 2 para. 35(b).
(3)	1972 s.231(4).
58(1)	1972 s.233(1), (3).
(2)	1972 s.233(2).
(3)	1972 s.233(1), (2); Sc Law Com Rec No. 16.
(4)	1972 s.233(4).
(5)	1972 s.233(6).
(6), (7)	1972 s.233(7).
59(1)	1972 s.54(3); 1982 Sch. 2 para. 15(a).
(2)	1972 s.115(1), (4).
(3)	1972 s.115(3); Local Government (Scotland) Act 1973 (c. 65) Sch. 23, para. 25.
60(1)	1972 s.25(1); 1974 s.4(2).
(2), (3)	1972 s.25(2), (3).
(4)	1972 s.26(4).
(5)	Drafting.

Provision	Derivation
61(1)	1972 s.262(1); 1974 s.2(1).
(2)	1972 s.262(4); 1974 s.2(1).
62(1) to (3)	1972 s.262(6); 1974 s.2(1).
(4)	1972 s.262(7); 1974 s.2(1).
(5)	1972 s.262(9); 1974 s.2(1).
63(1)	1972 s.262B(1); 1974 s.2(1); 1982 Sch. 2 para. 39.
(2), (3)	1972 s.262B(2); 1974 s.2(1).
64(1), (2)	1972 s.262(8); 1974 s.2(1).
65(1)	1972 s.25(1); 1974 s.4(2).
(2), (3)	1972 s.25(2), (3).
(4)	1972 s.26(4).
(5)	Drafting.
66(1)	1972 s.262A(2); 1974 s.2(1).
(2)	1972 s.262A(7); 1974 s.2(1).
(3)	1972 s.262A(8); 1974 s.2(1); 1986 Sch. 9 para. 21.
(4)	1972 s.262A(9); 1974 s.2(1).
67(1)	1972 s.262A(1); 1974 s.2(1).
(2)	1972 s.262A(4); 1974 s.2(1).
(3)	1972 s.262A(5); 1974 s.2(1).
(4)	1972 s.262A(6); 1974 s.2(1).
(5)	1972 ss.56(2), 262A(1); 1974 s.2(1).
(6)	1972 s.54(1); 1974 s.2(1).
(7) to (9)	1972 ss.56AA(1), 262A(8); 1986 Sch. 9 para. 18(1), 21(a).
(10), (11)	1972 s.262A(10); 1974 s.2(1).
68	1972 s.97(1), (2); 1986 Sch. 9 para. 20.
69(1)	1972AM s.10(1); 1972 Sh. 21 Pt. II; 1974 s.13(2).
(2)	1972AM s.10(2).
(3)	1972AM s.10(3); National Heritage Act 1983 (c. 47) Sch. 4 para. 22(6).
(4)	1972AM s.10(4).
(5), (6)	1972AM s.10(5).
70(1)	1972AM s.10A(1); Ancient Monuments and Archaeological Areas Act 1979 (c. 46) s.48(1).
(2)	1972AM s.10A(1), (4); Ancient Monuments and Archaeological Areas Act 1979 (c. 46) s.48(1).
(4)	1972AM s.10A(4), (5); Ancient Monuments and Archaeological Areas Act 1979 (c. 46) s.48(1).
(6)	1972AM s.10A(4), (6); Ancient Monuments and Archaeological Areas Act 1979 (c. 46) s.48(1).
(7)	1972AM s.10A(3); Ancient Monuments and Archaeological Areas Act 1979 (c. 46) s.48(1).
(8)	1972AM s.10A(8); Ancient Monuments and Archaeological Areas Act 1979 (c. 46) s.48(1); Sc Law com Rec No. 30.
71(1)	1972AM s.10C(4); 1986 s.51.
(2)	1972AM s.10C(3); 1986 s.51.
72(1)	1972AM s.10C(1), (2); 1986 s.51.
(2)	1972AM s.10C(5); 1986 s.51.
(3)	1972AM s.10C(6), (7); 1986 s.51.
(4)	1972AM s.10C(8); 1986 s.51.
(5)	1972AM s.10C(9); 1986 s.51.
(6)	1972AM s.10C(10); 1986 s.51; Planning (Listed Buildings and Conservation Areas) Act 1990 (c. 9) s.58; Planning (Consequential Provisions) Act 1990 (c. 11) Sch. 2 para. 26.
73(1)	1972 s.256(1), Sch. 19 Pt. III.
(2)	1972 s.257; 1974 s.7(2).
(3)	1972 s.257, Sch. 19 Pt. IV; 1974 s.7(2); 1986 Sch. 9 para. 24; Sc Law Com Rec No 31.
(4)	1972 ss.256(2), 257; 1974 s.7(2).
74(1)	1972 s.253(1).
(2)	1972 s.253(2); 1986 Sch. 7 Pt. II para. 3.

Provision	Derivation
74(3)	1972 s.253(4).
(4)	1972 s.253(5).
(5)	Town and Country Planning Act 1984 (c. 10) s.4(1).
(6) to (8)	1972 s.253(7).
75(1) to (3)	Town and Country Planning Act 1984 (c. 10) s.1(1) to (3).
(4)	Town and Country Planning Act 1984 (c. 10) s.1(5).
(5)	Town and Country Planning Act 1984 (c. 10) s.1(7).
(6)	Town and Country Planning Act 1984 (c. 10) s.4(1).
(7)	Town and Country Planning Act 1984 (c. 10) s.1(6).
(8)	Town and Country Planning Act 1984 (c. 10) s.6(1).
76(1)	1972 s.265(2); 1991 Sch. 10 para. 12(a).
(2)	1972 s.265(1)(c), (3), (4); Town and Country Planning (Scotland) Act 1977 (c. 10) s.5(3); 1991 Sch. 10 para. 12(b), Sch. 13 para. 38(b); Sc Law Com Rec No. 32.
(3) to (6)	1972 s.265(5) to (8).
77(1) to (3)	1972 s.97AB; 1991 Sch. 10 para. 10.
78(1) to(10)	1972 s.97AC; 1991 Sch. 10 para. 10.
79(1)	1972 ss.145, 260A, 267 to 267B, 269 to 271, 274, 278; 1991 s.35.
(2)	1972 s.271(1).
80(1)	1972 s.241; Sc Law Com Rec No. 33.
(2)	1972 s.242(2).
(3)	Drafting.
(4)	1972 s.250(2), Sch. 19 Pts. I and II.
(5)	1972 s.250(3), (4); Local Government (Scotland) Act 1973 (c. 65) Sch. 23 para. 30.
(6)	1972 s.247(1)(b), (f), (2); 1972AM s.10(1), (5); 1986 s.56(1).
(7)	1972 s.249.
81(1), (2)	1972 s.275(1); drafting.
(3)	Post Office Act 1969 (c. 48) Sch. 4 para. 93(1)(xxxiv); 1972 ss.180A, 275, Sch. 21 Pt. II; Civil Aviation Act 1982 (c. 16) Sch. 2 para. 4; Telecommunications Act 1984 (c. 12) Sch. 4 para. 54(3), (5); Electricity Act 1989 (c. 29) Sch. 16 para. 1(1)(xxiii); Gas Act 1995 (c. 45) Sch. 4 para. 2(1) (xix).
(4)	1972 s.275(9).
(5)	1972 s.275(3).
(6)	Civic Amenities Act 1967 (c. 69) s.5; Planning (Listed Buildings and Conservation Areas) Act 1990 (c. 9) s.57, 91(7); Planning (Consequential Provisions) Act 1990 (c. 11) Sch. 2 para. 16.
(7)	1972 s.275(7).
(8)	1972 s.275(10).
82(1)	1972 s.273(1).
(2), (3)	1972 s.273(2).
(4)	1972 s.273(4); 1986 Sch. 9 para. 18(2)(a).
(5)	1972 s.273(5); 1986 Sch. 9 para. 18(2)(b).
(6)	1972 s.273(9); Sc Law Com Rec No. 34.
(7)	1972 s.273(3).
83(1) to (3)	Drafting.
Sch. 1	
para. 1	1972 s.52(8).
para. 2	1972 s.52(8), (9).
para. 3	1972 s.93(5)(c), Sch. 10 para. 7(2)(a), (3)(b).
Sch. 2	
para. 1	1972 Sch. 10 para. 12.
para. 2	1972 Sch. 10 para. 13.
para. 3	1972 Sch. 10 para. 14.
para. 4	1972 Sch. 10 para. 15; Local Government (Scotland) Act 1973 (c. 65) Sch. 23 para. 33.
Sch. 3	
para. 1	1972 Sch. 7 para. 1(1) to (3); drafting.

Provision	Derivation
para. 2	1972 Sch. 7 para. 2(1) to (4); 1986 Sch. 11 para. 53; 1991 Sch. 13 para. 41(2).
para. 3	1972 Sch. 7 para. 3(1) to(5); 1991 Sch. 13 para. 41(3).
para. 4	1972 Sch. 7 para. 3A(1) to (4); 1986 Sch. 11 para. 42; 1991 Sch. 13 para. 41(4).
para. 5	1972 Sch. 7 para. 4(1), (3).
para. 6	1972 Sch. 7 para. 5; 1986 Sch. 11 paras. 40(2), 43.
para. 7	1972 Sch. 7 para. 7; Tribunals and Inquiries Act 1992 (c.53) Sch. 3 para. 7.

TABLE OF DESTINATIONS

Historic Buildings and Ancient Monuments Act 1953
(c.49)

1953	1997
s.5(3)........	s.48(2)

Civic Amenities Act 1967
(c.69)

1967	1997
s.5	ss.51(1)–(6), 52(1)–(5), 81(6)

Post Office Act 1969
(c.48)

1969	1997
Sched. 4, para.93(1) (xxxiv)	s.81(3)

Town and Country Planning (Amendment) Act 1972
(c.42)

1972	1997	1972	1997	1972	1997
s.10(1).......	ss.69(1), 80(6)	s.10A(3)......	s.70(7)	s.10C(3)......	s.71(2)
(2)........	s.69(2)	(4).....	70(2), (4), (5), (6)	(4).....	71(1)
(3)........	69(3)			(5).....	72(2)
(4)........	69(4)	(5).....	70(4)	(6), (7) ..	72(3)
(5)........	ss.69(5), (6), 80(6)	(6).....	70(6)	(8).....	72(4)
10A(1)......	s.70(1), (2)	(7).....	70(5)	(9).....	72(5)
10A(2)......	70(3)	(8).....	70(8)	(10).....	72(6)
		10C(1), (2) ..	72(1)		

Town and Country Planning (Scotland) Act 1972
(c.52)

1972	1997	1972	1997	1972	1997
s.24(1).......	s.10(1)	s.54(4).......	ss.14(1), 15(1)	s.56AA(1)....	ss.54(5)–(7), 67(7)–(9)
25(1).......	ss.60(1), 65(1)	(4A)......	s.15(2)	(2), (3)	s.54(5)–(7)
(2), (3)....	60(2), (3), 65(2), (3)	(5)........	15(3)	85(2A)......	35(4)
26(3A)......	s.10(2)	54A(1), (2)..	16(1), (2)	(2B)......	36(1)
(4)........	ss.60(4), 65(4)	(5).....	16(3)	(2B)(a) ...	35(4)
52(1)–(3)....	s.1(1)–(3)	54B.........	16(4)	(2C)......	37(3)
(4)........	2(1)	54C.........	56(1)–(3)	(2D)......	36(2)
(5).......	2(2)	54D(1)......	17(1)–(3)	88(3)........	38(3)
(6).......	2(3)	(2).....	ss.17(1)–(3), 18(1), (2), (3), (4), 19(5), (6), (7)	(4)........	38(4), (5)
(7)........	1(4)			(5)........	38(6), (7)
(8)........	Sched. 1, para.1 para.2			92(1)........	34(1), (2)
(9)........	Sched. 1, para.2	(3)......	s.17(1)–(3)	(1A)......	34(2), (3)
53(1)........	ss.6, 8(1)	55(1).......	53(1), (2)	(2)........	34(1)
(2)........	s.7(1), (2)	(2)........	53(3)	(2A)......	34(4)
(2A)......	7(3)	(3).......	53(4)	(3), (3A)..	34(6)
(3)........	7(4)–(6)	56(1).......	3(1), (2)	(4)........	34(5)
(3A)......	7(7)	(2).......	ss.54(1), (2), 55(1), (2), 67(5)	(5)........	34(7)
(4)........	8(2)			(5A)......	34(8)
(5).......	8(4), (5)			(6)........	34(9)
(6).......	8(3)	(3).......	s.3(3), (4)	93(1)........	35(1)
54(1)........	ss.54(1), (2), (3), (4), 55(1), (2), 67(6)	(4)........	ss.3(5), 5	(2)........	35(2)
		(5)........	s.3(6)	(2A)......	ss.35(4), 36(1), (2), 37(3)
(3)........	14(2), 59(1)	(6)........	4(1)–(3)	(3)........	s.35(3)
				(4)........	37(2)

9–95

1972	1997
s.93(5).	s.37(1), (4)
(c).	Sched. 1,
	para. 3
(6).	s.37(5)
(7).	37(6)
(8).	35(5)
94	39(1)–(6)
95(1), (2). . .	38(1), (2)
(3).	38(3), (4), (5),
	(6), (7)
(4).	38(8)
95A(1), (2). .	40(1)
(3).	40(2)
97(1).	ss.49(1)–(3), 68
(2).	s.68
(3).	ss.49(4), 54(1),
	(2), 55(1), (2)
(4).	s.49(5), (6)
97A	50(1)–(5)
97AB	77(1)–(3)
97AC	78(1)–(10)
104(1)	42(1), (7)
(2)	42(1)
(3)	ss.54(1), (2),
	55(1), (2)
(4)	s.42(2)
(5)	42(3)
(6)	42(4), (5)
(7)	42(6)
105(1)–(3). . .	43(1)–(3)
(4)	43(5)
106	44
107(1)	45(1)
(2), (3). . .	45(2), (3)
(4)	45(4), (5)
(5)	45(6), (7)
(6)	45(8)
(7)	45(9)
108(1)	46(1)
(2)	46(2)
(3)–(5). . .	46(3)–(5)
109(1)	47(1)
(2)	47(2)
115(1)	59(2)
(3)	59(3)
(4)	59(2)
116(1)	48(1)
(2)	48(2)
145	79(1)
161(1)	25(1), (2)
(2)	25(4)
(3)	25(3)
162(1)	26(1)
(3)	26(1), (2)
(4)	26(3)
167(1)	27(1)
(2)	27(2)
(4)	27(3)
168(1)	27(4)
(2)	27(5)
169(5)	43(4)
(6)	43(5)
171(1)	30(1)
(2)	30(2)
(3)	30(3), (4)
(4)	30(5)
179(1)	28(1), (2)
(2)	28(4)
(3)	ss.28(3), 30(6)
(4)	s.43(4)
(5)	28(1), (2)

1972	1997
s.180A	s.81(3)
231(1)(d), (e)	57(1)
(2)(f)	57(1)
(3)(h)–(k)	57(2)
(4)	57(3)
233(1)	58(1), (3)
(2)	58(2), (3)
(3)	58(3)
(4)	58(4)
(6)	58(5)
(7)	58(6), (7)
241	80(1)
242(2)	80(2)
247(1)(b), (c)	80(6)
(2)	80(6)
249	80(7)
250(2)	80(4)
(3)	80(5)
(4)	80(5)
253(1)	74(1)
(2)	74(2)
(4)	74(3)
(5)	74(4)
(7)	74(6)–(8)
256(1)	73(1)
(2)	73(4)
257	73(2), (3), (4)
260(5)	41(1)–(3), (4)
260A	79(1)
262(1)	61(1)
(4)	61(2)
(6)	62(1)–(3)
(7)	62(4)
(8)	64(1), (2)
(9)	62(5)
262A(1). . . .	67(1), (5)
(2). . . .	66(1)
(4). . . .	67(2)
(5). . . .	67(3)
(6). . . .	67(4)
(7). . . .	66(2)
(8). . . .	ss.66(3),
	67(7)–(9)
(9). . . .	s.66(4)
(10). . . .	67(10), (11)
262B(1). . . .	63(1)
(2). . . .	63(2), (3)
265(1)(c). . . .	76(2)
(2)	76(1)
(3), (4). . .	76(2)
(5)–(8). . .	76(3)–(6)
267	79(1)
267A, B.	79(1)
269	79(1)
270	79(1)
271	79(1)
(1)	79(2)
273(1)	82(1)
(2)	82(2), (3)
(3)	82(7)
(4)	82(4)
(5)	82(5)
(9)	82(6)
274	79(1)
275	81(3)
(1)	81(1), (2)
(3)	81(5)
(7)	81(7)
(9)	81(4)
(10)	81(8)
278	79(1)

1972	1997
Sched. 7,	
para. 1(1). . .	Sched. 3,
	para. 1
(2). . .	Sched. 3,
	para. 1
(3). . .	Sched. 3,
	para. 1
para. 2(1). . .	Sched. 3,
	para. 2
(2). . .	Sched. 3,
	para. 2
(3). . .	Sched. 3,
	para. 2
(4). . .	Sched. 3,
	para. 2
para. 3(1). . .	Sched. 3,
	para. 3
(2). . .	Sched. 3,
	para. 3
(3). . .	Sched. 3,
	para. 3
(4). . .	Sched. 3,
	para. 3
(5). . .	Sched. 3,
	para. 3
para. 3A(1).	Sched. 3,
	para. 4
(2).	Sched. 3,
	para. 4
(3).	Sched. 3,
	para. 4
(4).	Sched. 3,
	para. 4
para. 4(1). . .	Sched. 3,
	para. 5
(3). . .	Sched. 3,
	para. 5
para. 5	Sched. 3,
	para. 6
para. 7	Sched. 3,
	para. 7
Sched. 10,	
para. 1(1). . .	s.9(1), (2)
(1A).	9(3)
(2). . .	14(3)
para. 2(1). . .	ss.10(1), (2),
	19(5), (6)
(2). . .	10(3), 19(7)
para. 4	s.11(1)–(5)
para. 5(1). . .	12(1), (2)
(2). . .	12(2), (3)
para. 6	13(1)–(3)
para. 7(1). . .	ss.18(1), 19(1),
	(2)
(2). . .	s.19(3), (4)
(a)	Sched. 1,
	para. 3
(3). . .	s.20(1)–(4)
(b)	Sched. 1,
	para. 3
(4)–(6)	s.20(1)–(4)
para. 8	ss.18(2), (3),
	(4), 19(2)
para. 9(1). . .	21(1), (2),
	24(1)
(2). . .	22(1), (5),
	24(2)
(3). . .	22(2)–(4),
	24(4)–(6)
(4). . .	21(3), 24(7)

TABLE OF DESTINATIONS

LOCAL GOVERNMENT (SCOTLAND) ACT 1973
(c.65)

TOWN AND COUNTRY AMENITIES ACT 1974
(c.32)

TOWN AND COUNTRY PLANNING (SCOTLAND) ACT 1977
(c.10)

ANCIENT MONUMENTS AND ARCHAEOLOGICAL AREAS ACT 1979
(c.46)

TABLE OF DESTINATIONS

CIVIL AVIATION ACT 1982
(c.16)

1982	1997
Sched. 2,	
para. 4	s.81(3)

LOCAL GOVERNMENT AND PLANNING (SCOTLAND) ACT 1982
(c.43)

1982	1997
s.42	s.56(1)–(3)
47(c)........	57(2)
Sched. 2,	
para. 15(a) .	ss.14(2), 59(1)
(b) .	14(1), 15(1)
(c)..	s.15(3)
para. 16	16(1), (2), (4)
para. 20(b) .	ss.35(4), 36(1), (2), 37(3)
para. 23(b) .	s.38(3), (4), (5), (6), (7)
para. 26(a) .	34(2)
(b) .	34(2), (3)
(c)..	34(4)
(d) .	34(6)
para. 27(a) .	35(1)
(b) .	ss.35(2), (4), 36(1), (2), 37(3)
(c)..	s.37(5)
para. 35(b) .	57(2)
para. 39	63(1)

NATIONAL HERITAGE ACT 1983
(c.47)

1983	1997
Sched. 4,	
para. 22(6) .	s.69(3)

TOWN AND COUNTRY PLANNING ACT 1984
(c.10)

1984	1997
s.1(1)–(3).....	s.75(1)–(3)
(5).........	75(4)
(6)........	75(7)
(7)........	75(5)
4(1)........	ss.74(5), 75(6)
6(1)........	s.75(8)

TELECOMMUNICATIONS ACT 1984
(c.12)

1984	1997
Sched. 4,	
para. 54(3) .	ss.46(2), 81(3)
(5) .	s.81(3)

TABLE OF DESTINATIONS

HOUSING AND PLANNING ACT 1986
(c.63)

HOUSING (SCOTLAND) ACT 1987
(c.26)

ELECTRICITY ACT 1989
(c.29)

PLANNING (LISTED BUILDINGS AND CONSERVATION AREAS) ACT 1990
(c.9)

PLANNING (CONSEQUENTIAL PROVISIONS) ACT 1990
(c.11)

TABLE OF DESTINATIONS

PLANNING AND COMPENSATION ACT 1991
(c.34)

1991	1997	1991	1997	1991	1997
s.35 .... s.79(1)		Sched. 10—*cont.*		Sched. 13—*cont.*	
Sched. 10,		para. 10 .... ss.77(1)–(3),		para. 41(2) . Sched. 3,	
para. 2 ..... 8(4), (5)		78(1)–(10)		para. 2	
para. 4(b) .. 34(5)		para. 12(a) . s.76(1)		(3) . Sched. 3,	
para. 5 ..... 34(7), (8)		(b) . 76(2)		para. 3	
para. 6(2)(a) 35(1)		Sched. 12,		(4) . Sched. 3,	
(3)... 35(2)		para. 21.... 28(4)		para. 4	
(4)... 37(2)		Sched. 13,		para. 42 .... s.19(5), (6)	
para. 7 ..... 39(1)–(6)		para. 18.... 53(4)		(a) . 10(1)	
para. 8 ..... 38(8)		para. 20(a) . 36(1)		(b) . 10(2)	
		para. 38(b) . 76(2)			

TRIBUNALS AND INQUIRIES ACT 1992
(c.53)

1992	1997
Sched. 3,	
para. 7..... Sched. 3,	
para. 7	

CRIMINAL PROCEDURE (CONSEQUENTIAL PROVISIONS) (SCOTLAND) ACT 1995
(c.40)

1995	1997
Sched. 1,	
para. 5..... ss.10(3), 19(7),	
53(1)	
para. 6 ..... 10(3), 19(7),	
53(1)	

GAS ACT 1995
(c.45)

1995	1997
Sched. 4,	
para. 2(1)	
(xix) .... s.81(3)	

CRIMINAL PROCEDURE (SCOTLAND) ACT 1995
(c.46)

1995	1997
s.225 .... ss.10(3), 19(7),	
53(1)	

SCOTTISH LAW COMMISSION'S REPORT ON THE CONSOLIDATION OF CERTAIN ENACTMENTS RELATING TO TOWN AND COUNTRY PLANNING IN SCOTLAND 1996
(SCOT LAW COM NO. 157) (CMND.3644)

1996	1997
App.1,	
No.2 .... s.41(4)	
No.16 ...... 58(3)	
No.24 ...... 7(1), (2)	
No.25 ...... 32(7)	
No.26 ...... 32(8)	
No.27 ...... 38(6), (7)	
No.28 ...... 45(5)	
No.29 ...... 48(1)	
No.30 ...... 70(8)	
No.31 ...... 73(3)	
No.32 ...... 76(2)	
No.33 ...... 80(1)	
No.34 ...... 82(6)	

INDEX

References are to sections and Schedules

PLANNING (HAZARDOUS SUBSTANCES) (SCOTLAND) ACT 1997*

(1997 c. 10)

ARRANGEMENT OF SECTIONS

* Annotations by Donald A. Reid, Morton Fraser Partnership, Edinburgh.

An Act to consolidate certain enactments relating to special controls in respect of hazardous substances with amendments to give effect to recommendations of the Scottish Law Commission.   [27th February 1997]

PARLIAMENTARY DEBATES
    Hansard, H.L. Vol. 576, cols. 122, 588, 672; Vol. 577, cols. 560, 1082. H.C. Vol. 291, col. 197.

INTRODUCTION AND GENERAL NOTE
    This Act represents part of the process of consolidation of Scottish Town and Country Planning and related legislation recommended by the Scottish Law Commission in its report presented to Parliament in November 1996 (SCOT LAW COM No 157).
    The Act acknowledges the separate nature of hazardous substances legislation, forming as it does a bridge between Health and Safety and Planning law, and gives effect to recommendations made by the Scottish Law Commission to remove certain anomalies in existing legislation relating to the application of hazardous substances consent.
    The new regime requiring consent to be obtained for the presence of hazardous substances came into existence on May 1, 1993 with the coming into force of the Town and Country Planning (Hazardous Substances) (Scotland) Regulations 1993 (S.I. 1993 No. 323). These marked the implementation of additional provisions inserted into the Town and Country Planning (Scotland) Act 1972 (c. 52), by ss.35 to 38 and Pt. II of Sched. 7 to the Housing and Planning Act 1986 (c. 63). The inserted provisions are ss.56A to 56O, 97B to 97C and s.257.
    Control over hazardous substances and their presence on land is shared between the Health and Safety Executive and the Planning Authorities. The Advisory Committee on Major Hazards established by the HSE in the wake of the Flixborough disaster in 1974 recommended a notification and hazard survey scheme for installations handling more than a stated quantity of prescribed substances. This initiative, coupled with the requirement to implement the EC "Seveso" Directive on the Major Accident Hazards of Certain Industrial Activities (82/501/EEC) led to the enactment of the Notification of Installations Handling Hazardous Substances Regulations (NIHHS) (S.I. 1982 No. 1357) and the Control of Industrial Major Accident Hazard Regulations (CIMAH) (S.I. 1984 No. 1902). Both these regulations made under powers contained within the Health and Safety at Work, etc. Act 1974 (c. 37). Experience with the practical application of these regulations highlighted a gap between the legislation controlling the safe use of hazardous materials (and the operation of hazardous installations) and that requiring consideration to be given to the hazardous nature of a proposed development at the time an application for planning permission is made. There were two particular anomalies. Firstly, there was no regulation of a change in the existing use of land involving the introduction of a hazardous substance or substances. Secondly, the planning system provided no control over activities involving hazardous substances which did not amount to "development" within the meaning ascribed by s.19 of the Town and Country Planning (Scotland) Act 1972 (now s.26 of the Town and Country Planning (Scotland) Act 1997 (c. 8)). To deal with the first of these, (on what turned out to be a temporary basis) amendments were made to the Town and Country Planning (Use Classes) (Scotland) Order 1989 and the Town and Country Planning (General Permitted Development) (Scotland) Order 1992. The introduction of the amendments referred to above inserted by the Housing and Planning Act 1986 finally closed other remaining gaps in the legislation and introduced the requirement for hazardous substances consent (whether there was development or not) as a parallel regime to the traditional requirement for planning permission which could still of course be additionally required for situations where there was development.
    The decision to accord the legislation on hazardous substances consent discrete consideration in a separate statute (albeit part of the more general consolidation process) both reflects its genesis and confirms the need for the hazardous substances regime to be considered concurrently with the mainstream Town and Country Planning system. In addition, other anomalies have been identified by the Scottish Law Commission in their report and are given effect to in the new legislation. Except where a particular change in the law or practice has occurred and merits specific mention, these anomalies are not listed as such in these annotations.

The Town and Country Planning (Hazardous Substances) (Scotland) Regulations 1993 (hereafter referred to as "the Regulations") which provide detailed regulations are to remain in force and the Scottish Office currently sees no immediate need to make any changes in them although it may take some suitable opportunity in the future to update them. The derivation of the sections of the Act can be found in the Table of Derivations immediately following the Schedule to the Act and these will direct the reader to the other measures that have been implemented to amend the Regulations in terms of more recent legislation.

Two Circulars have been issued by the Scottish Office to introduce and elaborate on the hazardous substances legislation. Circular 5/1993 contains detailed guidance on policy implementation and Circular 16/1993 is aimed particularly at industry.

The hazardous substances regime in outline:

Administration and control
The duty to control hazardous substances is vested in the planning authority (s.1) and that authority's consent (hazardous substance consent) is required for the presence on land of a hazardous substance (s.2). There are exemptions, for example, where the aggregate quantity of any substance is less than a prescribed amount or where a substance is only present temporarily.

Identification of substances
The Secretary of State has power to specify by regulation substances that are hazardous and the quantities of such substances as will bring them under control ("controlled quantity") (s.3).

Obtaining consent
Sections 4 to 10 deal with the application for hazardous substances consent which may be obtained in terms of the Act or deemed to have been granted, the determination of applications and the imposition of conditions to the consent.

Variation and revocation of consents
Sections 11 to 17 cover the modification, variation and continuation of consents or conditions and the availability of compensation as a result of a revocation, change in the person in control of the land to which the consent relates, etc.

Secretary of State's powers
In terms of ss.18 to 20, the Secretary of State may call in applications for hazardous substances consent and hear appeals against a refusal to grant consent. A person aggrieved by a decision of the Secretary of State can apply to the Court of Session.

Contraventions of hazardous substances control
Sections 21 to 25 provide for the service of contravention notices by the planning authority, specifying such matters (laid down by regulation) as are in contravention of the control regime (a criminal offence) and requiring the contravention to be remedied. The planning authority can also apply for an interdict to restrain or prevent any actual or potential breach.

Miscellaneous and general
Sections 26 to 40 provide for, *inter alia,* the establishment of a register of hazardous substances, applications and consents, the interaction with health and safety law, application of the Act to planning authorities and to Crown land, rights of entry, coming into force (May 27, 1997) and extent (Scotland only).

COMMENCEMENT
The changes introduced by the Act come into force on May 27, 1997.

ABBREVIATIONS
"the Act": Planning (Hazardous Substances) (Scotland) Act 1997.
"the principal Act": Town and Country Planning (Scotland) Act 1997.
"the 1972 Act": Town and Country Planning (Scotland) Act 1972.
"the Regulations": the Town and Country Planning (Hazardous Substances) (Scotland) Regulations 1993.

Administration

Planning authorities: hazardous substances

1.—(1) It shall be the duty of the planning authority to control hazardous substances in accordance with the provisions of this Act.

(2) The duty under subsection (1) applies to an urban development corporation only if they are the planning authority in relation to all kinds of development.

DEFINITIONS

"Hazardous substances": s.3. See also General Note to s.2.

"Planning authority": s.38(2) and s.1(1) of the principal Act.

"urban development corporation": s.38 and ss.3(1), 277(1) of the principal Act, the latter referring to s.171 of the Local Government, Planning and Land Act 1980 (c. 65).

GENERAL NOTE

Interestingly, the Act does not establish a "hazardous planning authority" as such, as does the Planning (Hazardous Substances) Act 1990 (c. 10) in England and Wales, a reflection of the much reduced likelihood in Scotland of overlap in planning powers between local authorities and other bodies (as with National Park Special Planning Boards in England and Wales). An urban development corporation will be hazardous substances authority only in situations where its jurisdiction is not restricted to specified kinds of development. Circular 5/1993 explains that this provision is designed to ensure that an application for hazardous substances consent will be determined by the same body that would act as planning authority in dealing with any associated application for planning permission.

Control over presence of hazardous substances

Requirement of hazardous substances consent

2.—(1) Subject to the provisions of this Act, the presence of a hazardous substance on, over or under land requires the consent of the planning authority (in this Act referred to as "hazardous substances consent").

(2) Subsection (1) does not apply if the aggregate quantity of the substance—

(a) on, over or under the land,

(b) on, over or under other land which is within 500 metres of it and controlled by the same person, or

(c) in or on a structure controlled by the same person any part of which is within 500 metres of it,

is less than the quantity prescribed as the controlled quantity for that substance.

(3) The temporary presence of a hazardous substance while it is being transported from one place to another is not to be taken into account unless it is unloaded.

(4) The Secretary of State may by regulations provide that hazardous substances consent is not required or is only required—

(a) in relation to land of prescribed descriptions;

(b) by reason of the presence of hazardous substances in prescribed circumstances.

(5) Regulations under this section may make different provision for different cases or descriptions of cases.

DEFINITIONS

"land": s.38(2) and s.277 of the principal Act.

GENERAL NOTE

This section repeats the substance of s.56C of the 1972 Act as inserted by the Housing and Planning Act 1986 (c. 63) and represents the central "core" of the hazardous substances regime, namely the requirement to have consent if the aggregate quantity of a hazardous substance on, over or under land is equal to or exceeds the controlled quantity prescribed. The hazardous substances and the controlled quantities of these substances are listed in Sched. 1 to the Regulations. Part II of the Regulations excludes from the definition of hazardous substance controlled waste as defined by s.75(4) of the Environmental Protection Act 1990 (c. 43), or radioactive waste as defined by s.2 of the Radioactive Substances Act 1993 (c. 12). The reason for these exclusions is that legislative provision sufficient to provide control over their presence on land is deemed to have been provided elsewhere. There is also an exemption from control of substances which may be hazardous in terms of the Regulations but whose presence on land is temporary while being loaded or unloaded or transported from one place to another. It will be a matter of factual judgement whether the presence is temporary or not (see paras. 14 and 15 of Scottish Office Circular 5/1993).

Subs. (2)
The reasoning behind the inclusion of other land within 500 metres is to guard against avoidance measures such as sub-division of ownership amongst different but connected persons.
"*Hazardous substances consent*": In this connection see also s.4 (consent — general), s.5 (applications), s.6 (certificates required for consent), s.7 (determination of applications), s.8 (power to impose conditions), ss.9 and 10 (deemed consent), ss.11 and 12 (variation and revocation), s.14 (compensation for revocation or modification of consent), s.18 (references to Secretary of State), s.19 (appeals procedure), s.20 (questioning validity of appeal decision), ss.21 to 25 (contravention of consent).

Power to prescribe hazardous substances

3.—(1) For the purposes of this Act the Secretary of State—
(a) shall by regulations specify—
     (i) the substances that are hazardous substances, and
     (ii) the quantity which is to be the controlled quantity of any such substance, and
(b) may by regulations provide that, except in such circumstances as may be prescribed, all hazardous substances falling within a group specified in the regulations are to be treated as a single substance.
(2) Regulations which—
(a) are made by virtue of subsection (1)(a)(i), or
(b) are made by virtue of subsection (1)(a)(ii) and reduce the controlled quantity of a substance,
may make such transitional provision as appears to the Secretary of State to be appropriate.
(3) Regulations under this section may make different provision for different cases or descriptions of cases.

General Note
This section enables the Secretary of State to specify by regulation those substances that are hazardous for the purposes of the Act and the minimum quantity of those substances required to bring them under control ("controlled quantity") (see General Note to s.2 above). Column 1 of Sched. 1 to the Regulations lists those substances which if present at or above the controlled quantities specified in col. 2 will be subject to the consent requirements. Column 1 identifies a total of 71 substances, dividing these into classifications of "toxic substances", "highly reactive substances and explosive substances" and " flammable substances".

Obtaining hazardous substances consent

Hazardous substances consent: general

4.—(1) Hazardous substances consent—
(a) may be granted on an application under this Act, or
(b) may be deemed to have been granted by virtue of section 9 or 10.
(2) Without prejudice to the provisions of this Act, any hazardous substances consent shall (except in so far as it otherwise provides) enure for the benefit of the land to which it relates and of all persons for the time being interested in the land.

General Note
Hazardous substances consent: consent is required by s.2 or may be deemed to have been granted in terms of ss.9 and 10.
Consent to enure for the benefit of the land: hazardous substances consent is not personal to the applicant. However, it differs from planning permission in that if there is a change in the

person in control of part of the land, the consent will be revoked (unless an application for continuation is granted) (see ss.15 and 16).

Applications for hazardous substances consent

5.—(1) Provision may be made by regulations with respect to—

(a) the form and manner in which applications under this Act for hazardous substances consent are to be made,

(b) the particulars which they are to contain and the evidence by which they are to be verified,

(c) the manner in which they are to be advertised, and

(d) the time within which they are to be dealt with.

(2) Regulations may—

(a) require an applicant for hazardous substances consent or the planning authority or both to give publicity to an application for hazardous substances consent in such manner as may be prescribed;

(b) require the planning authority to conduct appropriate consultations before determining applications for hazardous substances consent;

(c) provide for the manner in which such a consultation is to be carried out and the time within which—

(i) such a consultation;

(ii) any stage in such a consultation,

is to be completed;

(d) require the planning authority to determine applications for hazardous substances consent within such time as may be prescribed;

(e) require the planning authority to give prescribed persons or bodies prescribed information about applications for hazardous substances consent including information as to the manner in which such applications have been dealt with.

(3) In subsection (2) "appropriate consultations" means consultations with the Health and Safety Executive and with such persons or bodies as may be prescribed.

(4) Regulations under this section may make different provision for different cases or descriptions of cases.

GENERAL NOTE

Applications for hazardous substances consent are regulated by Pt. III of the Regulations. An application requires to be made in a prescribed manner, to include site and substance location plans (Forms 1 and 2 of Sched. 2 to the Regulations). There requires to be notification to "persons holding an interest in neighbouring land" as specified in reg. 6(2) of the Regulations and the applicant for consent must publish in a local newspaper a notice of his application in terms of Form 8. The planning authority, before determining the application, is required to consult with various consultees, such as the Health and Safety Executive, Scottish Natural Heritage, any Community Councils, the Scottish Environmental Protection Agency, public utility suppliers, etc. The planning authority is required to inform the applicant of its decision on the application within two months of the date of receipt of the application although an extended period may be agreed in writing between the applicant and the planning authority.

"*Fees*": A fee is payable with the application for hazardous substances consent or continuation of consent (see s.29 of the Act and paras. 25 and 26 of the Regulations). To reflect the increased risk and responsibility involved, the fee is much higher where any one quantity of a hazardous substance is present in more than twice the controlled quantity.

Certificates as to interests in land etc.

6.—(1) Regulations may provide that an application for hazardous substances consent, or an appeal against the refusal of such an application or against the imposition of a condition on such a consent, shall not be entertained unless it is accompanied by a certificate in the prescribed form as to the interests in the land to which the application or appeal relates.

(2) Any such regulations may—

(a) include requirements corresponding to those mentioned in sections 34(1), 35(2) and (4) and 38(2) of the principal Act,

(b) make provision as to who is to be treated as the owner of land for the purposes of any provision of the regulations, and

(c) make different provision for different cases or descriptions of case.

(3) If any person—

(a) issues a certificate which purports to comply with the requirements of regulations made by virtue of this section and which contains a statement which he knows to be false or misleading in a material particular, or

(b) recklessly issues a certificate which purports to comply with those requirements and which contains a statement which is false or misleading in a material particular,

he shall be guilty of an offence and liable on summary conviction to a fine not exceeding level 3 on the standard scale.

GENERAL NOTE

This section enables regulations to be made to require information to be provided in respect to, *inter alia*, the ownership of the land to which the application relates. The principal intention is to ensure that any owner of the land has the opportunity to make representations to the planning authority prior to its determination of the application. Paragraph 8 of the Regulations details different forms of certificate which can be provided and which cover, for example, the situation where it is not possible to identify the owner or owners.

"*Owner*": Section 6(2)(a) enables regulations to be made to provide for who shall be treated as owner. Forms 9 and 10 of Sched. 2 to the Regulations define "owner" as "a person who, in any part of the land, is the proprietor of the dominium utile or is the lessee under a lease thereof where not less than seven years remain unexpired".

Subs. (3)(a) and (b)

This subsection is designed to underline the responsibility involved in obtaining hazardous substances consent by providing penalties for the provision of false or misleading information. Successful prosecution of an offence under subs. (3)(a) would require knowledge on the part of the offender to be proved.

Determination of applications for hazardous substances consent

7.—(1) Subject to the following provisions of this Act, where an application is made to a planning authority for hazardous substances consent, that authority may—

(a) grant hazardous substances consent, either unconditionally or subject to such conditions as they think fit, or

(b) refuse hazardous substances consent.

(2) In dealing with such an application the planning authority shall have regard to any material considerations and, in particular, but without prejudice to the generality of the foregoing—

(a) to any current or contemplated use of the land to which the application relates,

(b) to the way in which land in the vicinity is being used or is likely to be used,

(c) to any planning permission that has been granted for development of land in the vicinity,

(d) to the provisions of the development plan, and

(e) to any advice which the Health and Safety Executive have given following consultations in pursuance of regulations under section 5(2).

(3) If an application relates to more than one hazardous substance, the authority may make different determinations in relation to each.

(4) It shall be the duty of a planning authority, when granting hazardous substances consent, to include in that consent—

(a) a description of the land to which the consent relates,
(b) a description of the hazardous substance or substances to which it relates, and
(c) in respect of each hazardous substance to which it relates, a statement of the maximum amount permitted by the consent to be present at any one time.

DEFINITIONS
"development plan": s.24(1) of the principal Act.

GENERAL NOTE
The planning authority must have regard to *any* material consideration. The list provided in subs. (2)(a) is therefore not exhaustive but indicates those conditions most likely to be material in the circumstances of the application to determination of consent. For conditions see the following section.

"*may grant*": for appeals procedure see s.19. Paragraph 12 of the Regulations requires the notice of a decision to be in writing and requires the planning authority to communicate the decision, as soon as is practicable, to the Health and Safety Executive, the local authority (where it is not the planning authority), every other consultee who has made representations (paras. 11(i)(a)–(n)), to every owner who has made representations and to every person holding a notifiable interest in neighbouring land who has made representations.

Power to impose conditions on grant of hazardous substances consent

8.—(1) Without prejudice to the generality of section 7(1), a planning authority may grant hazardous substances consent conditional on the commencement or partial or complete execution of development on the land which is authorised by a specified planning permission or may grant such consent subject to conditions with respect to any of the following—
(a) how and where any hazardous substance to which the consent relates is to be kept or used,
(b) times between which any such substance may be present, and
(c) the permanent removal of any such substance—
(i) on or before a date specified in the consent, or
(ii) before the end of a period specified in it and commencing on the date on which it is granted.
(2) A planning authority may only grant consent subject to conditions as to how a hazardous substance is to be kept or used if the conditions are conditions to which the Health and Safety Executive have advised the authority that any consent they might grant should be subject.
(3) It shall be the duty of a planning authority, when granting hazardous substances consent, to include in that consent, in respect of each hazardous substance to which it relates, a statement of all conditions relating to that substance subject to which the consent is granted.

GENERAL NOTE
This section is very largely self explanatory. See also Circular 5/1993, paras. 28 and 29.

Deemed hazardous substances consent: established presence

9.—(1) Hazardous substances consent deemed to be granted by a planning authority under section 38 of the Housing and Planning Act 1986 (under which hazardous substances consent is deemed to be granted in certain circumstances where a hazardous substance was present before 1st May 1993) shall continue to have effect notwithstanding the repeal of that section and shall be deemed to be granted by the authority under this section.
(2) Hazardous substances consent which is deemed to be granted under this section is subject to—

(a) the condition that the maximum aggregate quantity of the substance that may be present—
:   (i) on, over or under the land to which the claim relates,
:   (ii) on, over or under other land which is within 500 metres of it and controlled by the same person, or
:   (iii) in or on a structure controlled by the same person any part of which is within 500 metres of it,

at any one time shall not exceed the established quantity, and

(b) such other conditions (if any) as are prescribed for the purposes of this section and are applicable in the case of that consent.

(3) The provisions of this Act (except section 20) shall apply in relation to any hazardous substances consent deemed to be granted under this section as if it had been granted by the planning authority on an application to them.

(4) In this section "established quantity" means, in relation to any land—

(a) where before 1st May 1993 there was a notification in respect of a substance in accordance with any of the Notification of Installations Handling Hazardous Substances Regulations 1982—
:   (i) the quantity notified or last notified before that date, or
:   (ii) a quantity equal to twice the quantity which was so notified or last notified before the start of the period of 12 months immediately preceding that date,

whichever is the greater;

(b) where a notification was not required before that date by any of those Regulations, a quantity exceeding by 50 per cent. the maximum quantity which was present on, over or under the land at any one time within that period.

GENERAL NOTE

Section 38 of the Housing and Planning Act 1986 (c. 63) amended the principal Act to introduce a system of protection for sites where hazardous substances had been present prior to May 1, 1993. Subsection (1) continues this system of deemed consent, notwithstanding the repeal of s.38 of the Housing and Planning Act 1986 by s.3(1) of the Planning (Consequential Provisions) (Scotland) Act 1997 (c. 11). The intention according to Circular 5/1993 was to avoid undue disruption by enabling continuation of previous operations involving hazardous substances with some facility for controlled expansion. It was a requirement that an application for deemed consent had to be made no later than October 31, 1993, following which a deemed consent would automatically be held to be in place. Part IV and Sched. 3 of the Regulations dealt with the detailed procedure for claiming deemed consent. The effect of this section is to maintain in existence any deemed consents established in terms of the earlier legislation but no new deemed consents can be issued. The continuance of the consent is dependent on the same conditions as to aggregate quantities as apply to other (non-deemed) consents, except that the determinant of maximum aggregate quantity is the "established quantity" and not the "controlled quantity". For the definition of "established quantity" see s.9(4). For detailed guidance on the operation of deemed hazardous substances consent (established presence) see paras. 35 to 51 of Circular 5/1993.

Deemed hazardous substances consent: government authorisation

10.—(1) Where—

(a) the authorisation of a government department is required by virtue of an enactment in respect of development to be carried out by a local authority, or by statutory undertakers who are not a local authority, and

(b) the development would involve the presence of a hazardous substance in circumstances requiring hazardous substances consent,

the department may, on granting that authorisation, also direct that hazardous substances consent for that development shall be deemed to be granted subject to such conditions (if any) as may be specified in the directions.

(2) On granting a consent under section 36 of the Electricity Act 1989 in respect of any operation or change of use that would involve the presence of a

hazardous substance in circumstances requiring hazardous substances consent, the Secretary of State may direct that hazardous substances consent shall be deemed to be granted, subject to such conditions (if any) as may be specified in the directions.

(3) The department or, as the case may be, the Secretary of State, shall consult the Health and Safety Commission before issuing any such directions.

(4) For the purposes of this section development shall be taken to be authorised by a government department if—

(a) any consent, authority or approval to or for the development is granted by the department in pursuance of an enactment,

(b) a compulsory purchase order is confirmed by the department authorising the purchase of land for the purpose of the development,

(c) consent is granted by the department to the appropriation of land for the purpose of the development or the acquisition of land by agreement for that purpose,

(d) authority is given by the department for the borrowing of money for the purpose of the development, or for the application for that purpose of any money not otherwise so applicable, or

(e) any undertaking is given by the department to pay a grant in respect of the development in accordance with an enactment authorising the payment of such grants,

and references in this section to the authorisation of a government department shall be construed accordingly.

(5) The provisions of this Act (except section 20) shall apply in relation to any hazardous substances consent deemed to be granted by virtue of directions under this section as if it had been granted by the Secretary of State on an application referred to him under section 18.

(6) A government department or the Secretary of State shall, as respects any hazardous substances consent deemed to be granted by virtue of directions under this section, send to the planning authority concerned any such information as appears to be required by them for the purposes of a register under section 27.

DEFINITIONS
    "government department": s.277 of the principal Act.
    "development": subs. (4) and s.26 of the principal Act.
    "statutory undertaker": s.214 of the principal Act.

GENERAL NOTE
    This section deems hazardous substances consent to exist when a government department is required to grant statutory authorisation for development being carried out by a local authority or by a statutory undertaker (not being a local authority) and a consequence of that development would be the presence of a hazardous substance or substances in circumstances which would otherwise require hazardous substances consent to be granted.

Variation and revocation of consents

Applications for removal of conditions attached to hazardous substances consent

11.—(1) This section applies to an application for hazardous substances consent without a condition subject to which a previous hazardous substances consent was granted or is deemed to have been granted.

(2) On such an application the planning authority shall consider only the question of the conditions subject to which hazardous substances consent should be granted.

(3) If on such an application the planning authority determine—

(a) that hazardous substances consent should be granted subject to conditions differing from those subject to which the previous consent was granted, or

(b) that it should be granted unconditionally,

they shall grant hazardous substances consent accordingly.

(4) If on such an application the planning authority determine that hazardous substances consent should be granted subject to the same conditions as those subject to which the previous consent was granted, they shall refuse the application.

(5) Where—

(a) hazardous substances consent has been granted or is deemed to have been granted for the presence on, over or under land of more than one hazardous substance, and

(b) an application under this section does not relate to all the substances,

the planning authority shall have regard to any condition relating to a substance to which the application does not relate only to the extent that it has implications for a substance to which the application does relate.

(6) Where—

(a) more than one hazardous substances consent has been granted or is deemed to have been granted in respect of the same land, and

(b) an application under this section does not relate to all the consents,

the planning authority shall have regard to any consent to which the application does not relate only to the extent that it has implications for a consent to which the application does relate.

GENERAL NOTE

This section allows a planning authority to remove a condition attached to a previous consent but, in doing so, it cannot overturn the underlying consent. Accordingly, conditions can be varied or removed without calling into question the principle of the consent. It applies to both granted and deemed consents. For form of and procedure in applying for consent under this section, see Pt. III of the Regulations. Circular 5/1993 at para. 54 gives as an example, a condition restricting storage of a substance to a particular location. Relocation of that substance would require removal of that condition.

General power by order to revoke or modify hazardous substances consent

12.—(1) The planning authority may by order revoke a hazardous substances consent or modify it to such extent as they consider expedient if it appears to them, having regard to any material consideration, that it is expedient to revoke or modify it.

(2) The planning authority may also by order revoke a hazardous substances consent if it appears to them—

(a) that there has been a material change of use of land to which a hazardous substances consent relates,

(b) that planning permission has been granted for development the carrying out of which would involve a material change of use of such land and the development to which the permission relates has been commenced,

(c) in the case of a hazardous substances consent which relates only to one substance, that that substance has not for at least 5 years been present on, over or under the land to which the consent relates in a quantity equal to or exceeding the controlled quantity, or

(d) in the case of a hazardous substances consent which relates to a number of substances, that none of those substances has for at least 5 years been so present.

(3) An order made by virtue of subsection (2)(a) or (b) in the case of a consent relating to more than one substance may revoke it entirely or only so far as it relates to a specified substance.

(4) An order under this section shall specify the grounds on which it is made.

GENERAL NOTE
    This section embodies a general power on the part of the planning authority to revoke or modify hazardous substances consent, provided the order confirming the revocation or modification has been confirmed by the Secretary of State (see s.13), and specifies the grounds on which it is made. Subsection (1) contains a general power at the discretion of the authority to the extent deemed by it expedient and having had regard to any material condition. Subsection (2) contains particular situations where a revocation may be ordered, including a material change in the use of the land to which the consent relates.

Subs. (2)(c) and (d)
    These cover the situation where the consent has fallen into disuse as a result of there being no one substance (or none in the case of a number of substances) present on the land for over five years. Circular 5/1993 notes that the retention of a disused consent could restrict uses to which neighbouring land could be put.

Confirmation by Secretary of State of section 12 orders

13.—(1) An order under section 12 shall not take effect unless it is confirmed by the Secretary of State.

(2) The Secretary of State may confirm any such order submitted to him either without modification or subject to such modification as he considers expedient.

(3) Where a planning authority submit any such order to the Secretary of State for his confirmation under this section, the authority shall serve notice of the order—

(a) on any person who is an owner, occupier or lessee of the whole or any part of the land to which the order relates, and

(b) on any other person who in their opinion will be affected by the order.

(4) The notice shall specify the period (which must not be less than 28 days after its service) within which any person on whom it is served may require an opportunity of appearing before and being heard by a person appointed by the Secretary of State for the purpose.

(5) If within that period a person on whom the notice is served so requires, the Secretary of State shall, before he confirms the order, give such an opportunity to that person and to the planning authority.

(6) Where an order under section 12 has been confirmed by the Secretary of State, the planning authority shall serve a copy of the order on every person who was entitled to be served with notice under subsection (3).

DEFINITIONS
    "owner": s.277 of the principal Act.

GENERAL NOTE
    This section provides the detailed requirements for the obtaining of the Secretary of State's confirmation of an order made under the preceding section (a "section 12" order) and is principally concerned with ensuring that sufficient opportunity is given to those who might be affected by such an order to make representations.

Compensation in respect of orders under section 12(1)

14.—(1) This section applies where an order is made under section 12(1) revoking or modifying a hazardous substances consent.

(2) If, on a claim made to the planning authority within the prescribed time and in the prescribed manner, it is shown that any person has suffered damage in consequence of the order—

(a) by depreciation of the value of an interest in the land to which he is entitled, or

(b) by being disturbed in his enjoyment of the land,

the authority shall pay to that person compensation in respect of that damage.

(3) Without prejudice to subsection (2), any person who carries out any works in compliance with the order shall be entitled, on a claim made as mentioned in that subsection, to recover from the planning authority compensation in respect of any expenses reasonably incurred by him in that behalf.

(4) Any compensation payable to a person under this section by virtue of such an order shall be reduced by the value to him of any timber, apparatus or other materials removed for the purpose of complying with the order.

(5) Sections 85 to 87 of the principal Act (which contain general provisions as to the assessment of and the determination of claims for compensation) shall apply as if compensation under this section were compensation under section 83 of that Act.

DEFINITIONS
"prescribed time": s.85 of the principal Act.
"prescribed manner": s.85 of the principal Act.

GENERAL NOTE
Where a planning authority has made an order under s.12(1) revoking or modifying a consent and that order has caused damage to any person either by depreciating in value an interest in land or disturbing his enjoyment of the land, the authority is required to compensate that person. A claim has to be made to the planning authority (subs. (2)) and it may extend to expenses incurred in carrying out works in compliance with the order (subs. (3)), but it must be net of the value of timber, apparatus or other materials removed in compliance with the order (subs. (4)).

Guidance is given in ss.85 to 87 of the principal Act on determination of claims for compensation, referral of disputed claims to the Lands Tribunal, etc.

Revocation of hazardous substances consent on change of control of land

15.—(1) A hazardous substances consent is revoked if there is a change in the person in control of part of the land to which it relates unless an application for the continuation of the consent has previously been made to the planning authority.

(2) Regulations may make provision in relation to applications under subsection (1) corresponding to any provision that may be made by regulations under section 5 or 6 in relation to applications for hazardous substances consent.

GENERAL NOTE
This section is designed to ensure that if there should be a partial change in the person controlling the land to which a consent relates there will be an automatic revocation of the consent, unless an application for continuation is made under s.16. As has been noted (in s.4 above) hazardous substances consent runs with the land and is not personal to the applicant. Accordingly, where control of the land (most usually its ownership) is divided, some arrangement appropriate to the safe keeping of hazardous substances on one part of it only—has to be devised. See para. 57 of Circular 5/1993.

"*Regulations*": Part III of the Regulations governs the procedure for an application under this section for continuation of consent.

Determination of applications for continuation of hazardous substances consent

16.—(1) When an application is made under section 15(1) for the continuation of a hazardous substances consent, the planning authority—

(a) may modify the consent in any way they consider appropriate, or

(b) may revoke it.

(2) In dealing with such an application the authority shall have regard to any material consideration and, in particular, but without prejudice to the generality of the foregoing—

(a) to the matters to which a planning authority are required to have regard by section 7(2)(a) to (d), and

(b) to any advice which the Health and Safety Executive have given following consultations in pursuance of regulations under section 15(2).

(3) If an application relates to more than one consent, the authority may make different determinations in relation to each.

(4) If a consent relates to more than one hazardous substance, the authority may make different determinations in relation to each.

(5) It shall be the duty of a planning authority, when continuing hazardous substances consent, to attach to the consent either—

(a) a statement that is unchanged in relation to the matters included in it by virtue of sections 7(4) and 8(3), or

(b) a statement of any change in respect of those matters.

(6) The modifications which a planning authority may make by virtue of subsection (1)(a) include, without prejudice to the generality of that provision, making the consent subject to conditions with respect to any of the matters mentioned in section 8(1); and section 8(2) shall apply as respects those conditions as it applies to the grant of consent subject to conditions.

(7) Where any application under section 15(1) is made to a planning authority then, unless within such period as may be prescribed, or within such extended period as may at any time be agreed upon in writing between the applicant and the authority, the authority either—

(a) give notice to the applicant of their decision on the application, or

(b) give notice to him that the application has been referred to the Secretary of State in accordance with directions given under section 18, the application shall be deemed to have been granted.

GENERAL NOTE

This section deals with the determination by the planning authority of an application under s.15 for continuation of hazardous substances consent.

Subs. (6)

This clause gives effect to one of the recommendations of the Scottish Law Commission namely that the imposition of a restriction on the conditions that can be imposed (as dealt with by s.8(1)) should extend as well to a modification of a hazardous substances consent as to the grant of consent.

Compensation on revocation or modification of consent under section 15

17. Where on an application under section 15(1) the planning authority modify or revoke the hazardous substances consent, they shall pay to the person in control of the whole of the land before the change in control by virtue of which the application was made compensation in respect of any loss or damage sustained by him and directly attributable to the modification or revocation.

GENERAL NOTE

Under this section the person in control of the whole of the land before the change is entitled to be compensated for any loss or damage sustained as a direct consequence of the modification or revocation.

Secretary of State's powers

Reference of applications to Secretary of State

18.—(1) The Secretary of State may give directions requiring applications for hazardous substances consent or applications under section 15(1) to be referred to him instead of being dealt with by planning authorities.

(2) A direction under this section—

(a) may be given either to a particular planning authority or to planning authorities generally, and

(b) may relate either to a particular application or to applications of a class specified in the direction.

(3) Any application in respect of which a direction under this section has effect shall be referred to the Secretary of State.

(4) Before determining an application referred to him under this section, the Secretary of State shall, if either the applicant or the planning authority so wish, give to each of them an opportunity of appearing before, and being heard by, a person appointed by the Secretary of State for the purpose.

(5) The decision of the Secretary of State on any application referred to him under this section shall be final.

GENERAL NOTE

This section entitles the Secretary of State to call in an application for his determination. Circular 5/1993 envisages this as an exceptional occurrence but instances the calling in of a related planning application or matters of exceptional importance required to be considered in connection with the hazardous substances consent itself. There is a right on the part of either the applicant or the planning authority to make representations to an appointed person. The hearing will usually be at a public local enquiry. See General Note to s.19 below.

Appeals against decisions or failure to take decisions relating to hazardous substances

19.—(1) Where a planning authority—
(a) refuse an application for hazardous substances consent, an application under section 15(1) or an application for any consent, agreement or approval of the authority required by a condition imposed on the grant of such consent, or
(b) grant it subject to conditions,
the applicant may appeal to the Secretary of State.

(2) A person who has made an application for hazardous substances consent may also appeal to the Secretary of State if the planning authority have not given to the applicant—
(a) notice of their decision on the application, or
(b) notice that the application has been referred to the Secretary of State in accordance with directions given under section 18,
within such period as may be prescribed, or within such extended period as may at any time be agreed upon in writing between the applicant and the planning authority.

(3) An appeal under this section shall be made by notice served within such time and in such manner as may be prescribed.

(4) For the purposes of the application of subsection (5) in relation to an appeal under subsection (2), the authority shall be deemed to have refused the application in question.

(5) On an appeal under this section, the Secretary of State may—
(a) allow or dismiss the appeal, or
(b) reverse or vary any part of the decision of the planning authority (whether the appeal relates to that part of it or not),
and may deal with the application as if it had been made to him in the first instance.

(6) Before determining an appeal under this section the Secretary of State shall, if either the appellant or the planning authority so wish, give each of them an opportunity of appearing before and being heard by a person appointed by the Secretary of State for the purpose.

(7) If the Secretary of State proposes to reverse or vary any part of the decision of the planning authority to which the appeal does not relate, he shall give notice of his intention to the planning authority and to the appellant and shall give each of them an opportunity of making representations about his proposals.

(8) The decision of the Secretary of State on an appeal under this section shall be final.

(9) If at any time before or during the determination of an appeal under this section it appears to the Secretary of State that the appellant is responsible for undue delay in the progress of the appeal, he may—

    (a) give the appellant notice that the appeal will be dismissed unless the appellant takes, within the period specified in the notice, such steps as are specified in the notice for the expedition of the appeal, and

    (b) if the appellant fails to take those steps within that period, dismiss the appeal accordingly.

(10) The Schedule to this Act (which makes provision regarding the determination of certain appeals by a person appointed by the Secretary of State) applies to appeals under this section.

GENERAL NOTE

This section along with s.20 gives effect to another Scottish Law Commission recommendation designed to correct the anomaly of there being a right of appeal on the refusal or conditional grant of consent, agreement or approval required on the grant of planning permission but not in the case of such a refusal or conditional grant of a consent, agreement or approval required on the grant of hazardous substances consent.

The section provides for a right of appeal where the planning authority has refused an application for hazardous substances consent, an application for continuation of consent under s.15(1), an application for any consent, etc. required by a consent condition or has granted a consent subject to conditions.

As with s.18, the appellant or the planning authority shall be afforded the opportunity of appearing before a person appointed by the Secretary of State. The hearing will normally take the form of a local public inquiry. The Secretary of State may cause such an inquiry to be held even if the principal parties do not seek one, if he considers this to be the most appropriate means of disposing of the case. In the event of an inquiry neither being requested by the principal parties nor proposed by the Secretary of State, the appeal is to be determined by written representations and a site visit.

The Town and Country Planning (Inquiries Procedure) (Scotland) Rules 1997 (S.I. 1997 No. 796) which came into force on May 27, 1997 apply in the case of inquiries resulting from an application to the Secretary of State under the Act. The Town and Country Planning Appeals (Determination by Appointed Person) (Inquiries Procedure) (Scotland) Rules 1997 (S.I. 1997 No. 750) (effective from the same date) apply to any local inquiry held by a person appointed by the Secretary of State by virtue of the powers contained in the Schedule to the Act.

Regulation 14 of the Regulations specifies time limits for the making of an appeal, that the appeal is to be made by lodging a notice of appeal, the documents to accompany the notice and other administrative matters.

Validity of decisions as to applications

    20.—(1) If any person is aggrieved by any decision of the Secretary of State under section 18 or 19 and wishes to question the validity of that decision on the grounds—

    (a) that it is not within the powers of this Act, or

    (b) that any of the relevant requirements have not been complied with in relation to that decision,

he may, within 6 weeks from the date on which the decision is taken, make an application to the Court of Session under this section.

    (2) Without prejudice to subsection (1), if the planning authority who made the decision on the application to which the proceedings relate or, as the case may be, referred the application wish to question the validity of any such decision as is mentioned in that subsection on any of the grounds there mentioned, the authority may, within 6 weeks from the date on which the decision is taken, make an application to the Court of Session under this section.

    (3) On any application under this section the Court of Session—

    (a) may by interim order suspend the operation of the decision in question until the final determination of the proceedings;

(b) if satisfied that the decision in question is not within the powers of this Act, or that the interests of the applicant have been substantially prejudiced by a failure to comply with any of the relevant requirements in relation to it, may quash that decision.

(4) In this section "the relevant requirements", in relation to any decision, means any requirements of this Act or the principal Act or of the Tribunals and Inquiries Act 1992 or of any order, regulations or rules made under this Act or under either of those Acts which are applicable to that decision.

(5) Except as provided by this section, the validity of any such decision as is mentioned in subsection (1) shall not be questioned in any legal proceedings whatsoever.

(6) Nothing in subsection (5) shall affect the exercise of any jurisdiction of any court in respect of any refusal or failure on the part of the Secretary of State to take any such decision as is there mentioned.

GENERAL NOTE

This section entitles any person aggrieved by the Secretary of State's decision under either s.18 (call in by the Secretary of State) or s.19 (appeal against decisions) to challenge the validity of the decision by applying to the Court of Session, within six weeks of the date of the decision. Likewise, the planning authority which made the decision has the right to apply to the Court of Session on the same timescale. The Court may either issue an order for the interim suspension of the decision or it may quash it if the decision is not within the powers of the Act or the interests of the applicant has been substantially prejudiced by a failure to comply with relevant requirements.

Contraventions of hazardous substances control

Offences

21.—(1) Subject to the following provisions of this section, if there is a contravention of hazardous substances control, the appropriate person shall be guilty of an offence.

(2) There is a contravention of hazardous substances control if—

(a) a quantity of a hazardous substance equal to or exceeding the controlled quantity is or has been present on, over or under land and either—

    (i) there is no hazardous substances consent for the presence of the substance, or

    (ii) there is hazardous substances consent for its presence but the quantity present exceeds the maximum quantity permitted by the consent, or

(b) there is or has been a failure to comply with a condition subject to which a hazardous substances consent was granted.

(3) In subsection (1) "the appropriate person" means—

(a) in relation to a contravention falling within paragraph (a) of subsection (2)—

    (i) any person knowingly causing the substance to be present on, over or under the land;

    (ii) any person allowing it to be so present; and

(b) in relation to a contravention falling within paragraph (a) or (b) of that subsection, the occupier of the land.

(4) A person guilty of an offence under this section shall be liable—

(a) on summary conviction, to a fine not exceeding £20,000, and

(b) on conviction on indictment, to a fine.

(5) In determining the amount of any fine to be imposed on a person convicted of an offence under this section, the court shall in particular have regard to any financial benefit which has accrued or appears likely to accrue to him in consequence of the offence.

(6) In any proceedings for an offence under this section it shall be a defence for the accused to prove—

(a) that he took all reasonable precautions and exercised all due diligence to avoid commission of the offence, or

(b) that commission of the offence could be avoided only by the taking of action amounting to a breach of a statutory duty.

(7) In any proceedings for an offence consisting of a contravention falling within subsection (2)(a), it shall be a defence for the accused to prove that at the time of the alleged commission of the offence he did not know, and had no reason to believe—

(a) if the case falls within paragraph (a)(i)—
    (i) that the substance was present, or
    (ii) that it was present in a quantity equal to or exceeding the controlled quantity;

(b) if the case falls within paragraph (a)(ii), that the substance was present in a quantity exceeding the maximum quantity permitted by the consent.

(8) In any proceedings for an offence consisting of a contravention falling within subsection (2)(b), it shall be a defence for the accused to prove that he did not know, and had no reason to believe, that he was failing to comply with a condition subject to which hazardous substances consent had been granted.

GENERAL NOTE

Sections 21 to 25 deal with the enforcement of the hazardous substances consent regime. They provide a planning authority with a variety of enforcement actions to deal with a contravention of hazardous substance control, from immediate prosecution under s.21 where the unauthorised presence of a hazardous substance could have serious consequences to public health or safety, to the issue of a contravention notice under s.22 where they require steps to be taken to remedy the effects of the contravention.

Section 21 provides that if there is a contravention of a hazardous substances consent, the appropriate person is guilty of an offence. Subsection (2) establishes the circumstances which will amount to a contravention; subs. (3) the person appropriate for culpability; subs. (4) penalties; subs. (5) effect on amount of a fine of any financial benefit accruing or likely to accrue to the person convicted; subss. (6), (7) and (8) statutory defences. Note the terms of s.273 of the principal Act (as applied by s.36 of the Act) under which a director, manager, secretary or similar officer of a body corporate can be found guilty of an offence as well as the body itself.

"*appropriate person*": See subs. (3). Note that in subs. (3)(a)(i) the strict liability nature of the offence is tempered by the requirement for knowledge to be proved.

Power to issue hazardous substances contravention notice

22.—(1) Where it appears to the planning authority that there is or has been a contravention of hazardous substances control they may issue a notice—

(a) specifying the alleged contravention, and

(b) requiring such steps as may be specified in the notice to be taken to remedy wholly or partly the contravention,

if they consider it expedient to do so having regard to any material consideration.

(2) Such a notice is referred to in this Act as a "hazardous substances contravention notice".

(3) A planning authority shall not issue a hazardous substances contravention notice where it appears to them that a contravention of hazardous substances control can be avoided only by the taking of action amounting to a breach of a statutory duty.

(4) A copy of a hazardous substances contravention notice shall be served—

(a) on the owner, the lessee and the occupier of the land to which it relates, and

(b) on such other persons as may be prescribed.

(5) A hazardous substances contravention notice shall also specify—

(a) a date not less than 28 days from the date of service of copies of the notice as the date on which it is to take effect, and

(b) in respect of each of the steps required to be taken to remedy the contravention of hazardous substances control, the period from the notice taking effect within which the step is to be taken.

(6) Where a planning authority issue a hazardous substances contravention notice the steps required by the notice may, without prejudice to the generality of subsection (1)(b), if the authority think it expedient, include a requirement that the hazardous substance be removed from the land.

(7) Where a notice includes such a requirement, it may also contain a direction that at the end of such period as may be specified in the notice any hazardous substances consent for the presence of the substance shall cease to have effect or, if it relates to more than one substance, shall cease to have effect so far as it relates to the substance which is required to be removed.

(8) The planning authority may withdraw a hazardous substances contravention notice (without prejudice to their power to issue another) at any time before or after it takes effect.

(9) If they do so, they shall immediately give notice of the withdrawal to every person who was served with a copy of the notice or would, if the notice were reissued, be served with a copy of it.

GENERAL NOTE

This section, providing for the issue of a hazardous substance contravention notice, is equivalent to the similar provision in the principal Act for the issue of planning enforcement notices as are those provisions applying to appeals against contravention notices in s.23. Section 18 of Pt. V of the Regulations provides further information on the content of a notice and the persons upon whom it is to be served.

Subs. (1)
"*expedient to do so having regard to any material consideration*": For further guidance on the appropriateness of taking this enforcement action on the part of a planning authority, see Circular 5/1993, para. 81.

Subs. (3)
A contravention notice cannot be issued where the action required to remedy the contravention cannot be taken without a breach of statutory duty.

Hazardous substances contravention notices: supplementary provisions

23.—(1) The Secretary of State may by regulations—

(a) specify matters which are to be included in hazardous substances contravention notices, in addition to those which are required to be included in them by section 22;

(b) provide—

(i) for appeals to him against hazardous substances contravention notices;

(ii) for the persons by whom, grounds upon which and time within which such an appeal may be brought;

(iii) for the procedure to be followed on such appeals;

(iv) for the directions that may be given on such an appeal;

(v) for the application to such appeals, subject to such modifications as the regulations may specify, of any of the provisions of sections 130 to 134, 237(3) and 239 of the principal Act;

(c) direct that any of the provisions of sections 135 to 138, 140, 141, 143(1) to (6), 144, 145 and 147 of that Act shall have effect in relation to hazardous substances contravention notices subject to such modifications as he may specify in the regulations;

(d) make such other provision as he considers necessary or expedient in relation to hazardous substances contravention notices.

(2) If any person appeals against a hazardous substances contravention notice, the notice shall have no effect pending the final determination or the withdrawal of the appeal.

(3) Regulations under this section may make different provisions for different cases or descriptions of cases.

GENERAL NOTE

For matters to be included in a contravention notice (s.23(1)(a)) see s.18 of Pt. V of the Regulations and para. 84 of Circular 5/1993. For information and guidance on appeals against hazardous substances contravention notices (s.23(1)(b)) see ss.19 and 20 of Pt. V and Sched. 4 of the Regulations and paras. 87 and 88 of Circular 5/1993.

Variation of hazardous substances contravention notices

24.—(1) A planning authority may waive or relax any requirement of a hazardous substances contravention notice issued by them and, in particular, may extend any period specified in accordance with section 22(5)(b) in the notice.

(2) The powers conferred by subsection (1) may be exercised before or after the notice takes effect.

(3) The planning authority shall, immediately after exercising those powers, give notice of the exercise to every person who has been served with a copy of the hazardous substances contravention notice or would, if the notice were reissued, be served with a copy of it.

GENERAL NOTE

This section was added to the principal Act (s.97BA) by the Planning and Compensation Act 1991 (c. 34), Sched. 10, para. 11.

Interdicts restraining breaches of hazardous substances control

25.—(1) Whether or not they have exercised or propose to exercise any of their other powers under this Act or the principal Act, a planning authority may seek to restrain or prevent any actual or apprehended breach of any of the controls provided for by or under this Act by means of an application for interdict.

(2) On an application under subsection (1) the court may grant such interdict as it thinks appropriate for the purpose of restraining or preventing the breach.

(3) In this section "the court" means the Court of Session or the sheriff.

GENERAL NOTE

This section which is self explanatory was added (as s.260A) to the principal Act by s.35 of the Planning and Compensation Act 1991.

Miscellaneous provisions

Temporary exemption directions

26.—(1) If it appears to the Secretary of State—
(a) either—
    (i) that the community or part of it is being or is likely to be deprived of an essential service or commodity, or
    (ii) that there is or is likely to be a shortage of such a service or commodity affecting the community or part of it, and
(b) that the presence of a hazardous substance on, over or under land specified in the direction, in circumstances such that hazardous substances consent would be required, is necessary for the effective provision of that service or commodity,
he may direct that, subject to such conditions or exceptions as he thinks fit, the presence of the substance on, over or under the land is not to constitute a

contravention of hazardous substances control so long as the direction remains in force.

(2) A direction under this section—

(a) may be withdrawn at any time, and

(b) shall in any case cease to have effect at the end of the period of 3 months beginning with the day on which it was given, but without prejudice to the Secretary of State's power to give a further direction.

(3) The Secretary of State shall send a copy of any such direction to the planning authority for the land.

GENERAL NOTE

This section enables the Secretary of State to direct that, in the case of emergency, the presence of a hazardous substance (in circumstances otherwise requiring hazardous substances consent) may continue (for a maximum period of three months) without such a consent being in force and without any offence being created as a result. The Health and Safety Executive will usually be consulted before this power is exercised.

Registers etc.

27.—(1) Every planning authority shall keep, in such manner as may be prescribed, a register containing such information as may be so prescribed with respect to—

(a) applications for hazardous substances consent made to that authority,

(b) applications under section 15(1) made to that authority,

(c) hazardous substances consent having effect by virtue of section 9 or 10 with respect to land for which that authority is the planning authority,

(d) revocations or modifications of hazardous substances consent granted with respect to such land, and

(e) directions under section 26 sent to the authority by the Secretary of State,

and every such register shall also contain such information as may be prescribed as to the manner in which applications for hazardous substances consent have been dealt with.

(2) Every register kept under this section shall be available for inspection by the public at all reasonable hours.

GENERAL NOTE

This section provides for the establishment by planning authorities of registers of prescribed information with respect to hazardous substances consent. Regulation 24 of the Regulations specifies how and where registers are to be kept (at the office of every planning authority) and how entries are to be made. It also gives effect (in subs. (1)(c)) to recommendation 38 by the Scottish Law Commission that registers should include consents deemed to have been granted by virtue of a government department or the Secretary of State.

Subs. (1)

"*such information as may be prescribed*": see Pt. VI of the Regulations.

Subs. (2)

"*at all reasonable hours*": what amounts to a reasonable hour is a question of fact and will depend on the circumstances of the particular case.

Health and safety requirements

28.—(1) Nothing in—

(a) any hazardous substances consent granted or deemed to be granted or having effect by virtue of this Act, or

(b) any hazardous substances contravention notice issued under section 22,

shall require or allow anything to be done in contravention of any of the relevant statutory provisions or any prohibition notice or improvement notice served under or by virtue of any of those provisions.

(2) To the extent that such a consent or notice purports to require or allow any such thing to be done, it shall be void.

(3) Where it appears to a planning authority who have granted, or are deemed to have granted, a hazardous substances consent or who have issued a hazardous substances contravention notice that the consent or notice or part of it is rendered void by subsection (2) the authority shall, as soon as is reasonably practicable, consult the Health and Safety Executive with regard to the matter.

(4) If the Health and Safety Executive advise the authority that the consent or notice is rendered wholly void, the authority shall revoke it.

(5) If they advise that part of the consent or notice is rendered void, the authority shall so modify it as to render it wholly operative.

(6) In this section "relevant statutory provisions", "improvement notice" and "prohibition notice" have the same meanings as in Part I of the Health and Safety at Work etc. Act 1974.

DEFINITIONS

For "relevant statutory provisions", "prohibition notice" and "improvement notice" see para. 67 of Circular 5/1993 and, further, for "relevant statutory provisions" see s.53 of the Health and Safety at Work etc. Act 1974 (c. 37), (also subs. (6) below).

GENERAL NOTE

This section emphasises that health and safety aspects should prevail when the issuing of a hazardous substances consent or the existence of a deemed consent is likely to contravene any statutory provisions (or enforcement measures) relating to such aspects. The statutory provisions include not only those in Pt. I of the Health and Safety at Work, etc. Act 1974 (and those specified in Sched. 1 to it) but also the NIHHS and CIMAH Regulations (see introduction and General Note above).

Fees

29.—(1) The Secretary of State may by regulations make provision for fees of the prescribed amount in respect of applications for, or for the continuation of, hazardous substances consent—

(a) made to an urban development corporation to be paid to the corporation;

(b) referred to him under section 18 to be paid to him;

(c) deemed to have been made to him under section 133(7) of the principal Act by virtue of regulations made under section 23 to be paid to him.

(2) Regulations made under this section may provide for—

(a) the transfer to the Secretary of State of any fee received by a planning authority in respect of an application referred to in paragraph (b) or (c) of subsection (1);

(b) the remission or refunding of a prescribed fee (in whole or in part) in prescribed circumstances or in pursuance of a direction given by him;

and the regulations may make different provision for different areas or for different cases or descriptions of cases.

(3) Section 252 of the principal Act applies to an application for the continuation of hazardous substances consent.

GENERAL NOTE

This section entitles the Secretary of State to set fees to be paid for applications for hazardous substances consent and for continuation of consent. See "*Fees*" note to s.5 above.

"*may by regulations make provision*": Part VII, paras. 25 and 26 of the Regulations specify the fees payable for different applications. See also paras. 70 and 71 of Circular 5/1993.

General

Application of this Act to planning authorities

30.—(1) This Act shall have effect, subject to such exceptions and modifications as may be prescribed, in relation to granting hazardous substances consent for planning authorities.

(2) Subject to section 10, regulations made by virtue of subsection (1) may in particular provide for securing—

    (a) that any application by a planning authority for hazardous substances consent shall be made to the Secretary of State;

    (b) that any order or notice authorised to be made, issued or served under this Act by a planning authority shall instead be made, issued or served by the Secretary of State.

GENERAL NOTE

This section simply substitutes the Secretary of State (for the planning authority) as the authority competent to receive an application for hazardous substances consent where the applicant is a planning authority. Any consequential order, etc. which would otherwise have been made or served by the planning authority will instead be made or served by the Secretary of State.

Subs. (1)

"*subject to such exceptions and modifications as may be prescribed*": See s.27 of the Regulations.

Exercise of powers in relation to Crown land

31.—(1) Notwithstanding any interest of the Crown in Crown land, but subject to subsection (2), any restrictions imposed or powers conferred by any of sections 2 to 29 (except sections 20 and 25) shall apply and be exercisable in relation to Crown land, to the extent of any interest in it for the time being held otherwise than by or on behalf of the Crown.

(2) Except with the consent of the appropriate authority, no order or notice shall be made or served under any of the provisions of section 12, 13 or 22 in relation to land which for the time being is Crown land.

(3) In this section—

    "Crown land" means land in which there is a Crown interest, and

    "Crown interest" means an interest belonging to Her Majesty in right of the Crown, or belonging to a government department, or held in trust for Her Majesty for the purposes of a government department.

(4) A person who is entitled to occupy Crown land by virtue of a contract in writing shall be treated for the purposes of subsection (1) as having an interest in land.

(5) For the purposes of this section "the appropriate authority", in relation to any land—

    (a) in the case of land belonging to Her Majesty in right of the Crown and forming part of the Crown Estate, means the Crown Estate Commissioners,

    (b) in relation to any other land belonging to Her Majesty in right of the Crown, means the government department having the management of that land, and

    (c) in the case of land belonging to a government department or held in trust for Her Majesty for the purposes of a government department, means that department.

(6) If any question arises as to what authority is the appropriate authority in relation to any land, that question shall be referred to the Treasury, whose decision shall be final.

<small>DEFINITIONS</small>
"appropriate authority": subs. (5).
"Crown interest": subs. (3).
"Crown land": subs. (3).

<small>GENERAL NOTE</small>
The provisions of the Act requiring hazardous substances consent do not apply to the Crown except in so far as there may be any interest in land held by a person otherwise by or on behalf of the Crown. Where, however, a Crown body wishes, in circumstances which would have otherwise required consent, to keep or use a hazardous substance the practice is that the body will comply on a non-statutory basis with the provisions of the Act. For further information on the policy and procedure in this respect, see paras. 72 and 73 of Circular 5/1993.

Application for hazardous substances consent in anticipation of disposal of Crown land

32.—(1) This section has effect for the purpose of enabling Crown land, or an interest in Crown land, to be disposed of with the benefit of hazardous substances consent.

(2) Notwithstanding the interest of the Crown in the land in question, an application for any such consent may be made by—
  (a) the appropriate authority, or
  (b) any person authorised by that authority in writing,
and, subject to subsections (3) and (4), all the statutory provisions relating to the making and determination of any such application shall accordingly apply as if the land were not Crown land.

(3) Any hazardous substances consent granted by virtue of this section shall apply only—
  (a) to the presence of the substance to which the consent relates after the land in question has ceased to be Crown land, and
  (b) so long as that land continues to be Crown land, to the presence of the substance by virtue of a private interest in the land.

(4) The Secretary of State may by regulations—
  (a) modify or exclude—
      (i) any of the statutory provisions referred to in subsection (2), and
      (ii) any other statutory provisions,
    in their application to consents granted by virtue of this section,
  (b) make provision for requiring a planning authority to be notified of any disposal of, or of an interest in, any Crown land in respect of which an application has been made by virtue of this section, and
  (c) make such other provision in relation to the making and determination of applications by virtue of this section as he thinks necessary or expedient.

(5) This section shall not be construed as affecting any right to apply for hazardous substances consent in respect of Crown land in a case in which such an application can be made by virtue of a private interest in the land.

(6) In this section—
  "private interest" means an interest which is not a Crown interest,
  "statutory provisions" means provisions contained in or having effect under any enactment,
and references to the disposal of an interest in Crown land include references to the grant of an interest in such land.

(7) Subsections (3), (5) and (6) of section 31 apply for the purposes of this section as they apply for the purposes of that section.

(8) A person who is entitled to occupy Crown land by virtue of a contract in writing shall be treated for the purpose of this section as having an interest in land and references to the disposal or grant of an interest in Crown land and to a private interest in such land shall be construed accordingly.

GENERAL NOTE
This section establishes a procedure for the Crown Estate Commissioners or a government department, for example, to apply for hazardous substances consent in anticipation of the Crown land being disposed of. The same provisions in respect of the making and determination of consent shall apply as would if the land were not Crown land. The consent shall only apply in respect of the particular hazardous substance or substances after the land has been disposed of. This section mirrors s.248 of the principal Act, providing for the disposal of Crown land with the benefit of planning permission.

Subs. (2)(a)
For "appropriate authority" see s.31(5).

Rights of entry

33.—(1) Any person duly authorised in writing by the Secretary of State or by a planning authority may at any reasonable time enter any land for the purpose of surveying it in connection with—

(a) any application for hazardous substances consent, or

(b) any proposal to issue a hazardous substances contravention notice.

(2) Any person duly authorised in writing by the Secretary of State or by a planning authority may at any reasonable time enter any land for the purpose of ascertaining whether an offence appears to have been committed under section 21.

(3) Any person who is an officer of the Valuation Office or a person duly authorised in writing by the Secretary of State or by a planning authority may at any reasonable time enter upon any land for the purpose of surveying it, or estimating its value, in connection with a claim for compensation in respect of that land or any other land made by virtue of section 14 or 17.

(4) Any person duly authorised in writing by the Secretary of State or a planning authority may at any reasonable time enter any land in respect of which a hazardous substances contravention notice has been served for the purpose of ascertaining whether the notice has been complied with.

(5) Subject to sections 34 and 35, any power conferred by this section to survey land shall be construed as including power to search and bore for the purpose of ascertaining the nature of the subsoil or the presence of minerals in it.

GENERAL NOTE
This section provides rights of entry, subject to due authorisation by the Secretary of State or a planning authority, to persons who may require access to land for survey purposes in connection with an application for consent, for enforcement purposes (*e.g.* identification of an offence) or for valuation purposes in connection with a claim for compensation.

Subs. (3)
For "Valuation Office," see s.38 and s.277 of the principal Act.

Power to issue warrants

34.—(1) If in relation to rights of entry exercised under section 33, the sheriff is satisfied—

(a) that there are reasonable grounds for entering any land for any of the purposes mentioned in that section, and

(b) that—

(i) admission to the land has been refused, or a refusal is reasonably apprehended, or

(ii) the case is one of urgency,

he may issue a warrant authorising any person duly authorised in writing to enter the land.

(2) For the purposes of subsection (1)(b)(i) admission to land shall be regarded as having been refused if no reply is received to a request for admission within a reasonable period.

(3) A warrant authorises entry on one occasion only and that entry must be—
  (a) within one month from the date of the issue of the warrant, and
  (b) at a reasonable hour, unless the case is one of urgency.

GENERAL NOTE

In support of the rights of entry afforded by s.33, this section provides that the sheriff may issue a warrant authorising entry, provided he considers there are reasonable grounds for entering the land and that admission has been or is likely to be refused or the case is one of urgency.

Subs. (3)

For "at a reasonable hour", see general note to s.27.

Rights of entry: supplementary provisions

35.—(1) A person authorised to enter any land in pursuance of a right of entry conferred under or by virtue of section 33 or 34 (referred to in this section as "a right of entry")—
  (a) shall, if so required, produce evidence of his authority and state the purpose of his entry before so entering,
  (b) may take with him such other persons as may be necessary, and
  (c) on leaving the land shall, if the owner or occupier is not then present, leave it as effectively secured against trespassers as he found it.

(2) Any person who wilfully obstructs a person acting in the exercise of a right of entry shall be guilty of an offence and liable on summary conviction to a fine not exceeding level 3 on the standard scale.

(3) If any damage is caused to land or moveable property in the exercise of a right of entry, compensation may be recovered by any person suffering the damage from the authority who gave the written authority for the entry or, as the case may be, the Secretary of State; and section 86 of the principal Act shall apply in relation to compensation under this subsection as it applies in relation to compensation under Part IV of the principal Act.

(4) If any person who enters any land in exercise of a right of entry discloses to any person any information obtained by him while on the land as to any manufacturing process or trade secret, he shall be guilty of an offence.

(5) Subsection (4) does not apply if the disclosure is made by a person in the course of performing his duty in connection with the purpose for which he was authorised to enter the land.

(6) A person who is guilty of an offence under subsection (4) shall be liable—
  (a) on summary conviction to a fine not exceeding the statutory maximum, and
  (b) on conviction on indictment to imprisonment for a term not exceeding 2 years or a fine or both.

(7) The authority of the appropriate Minister shall be required for the carrying out of works in exercise of a power conferred under section 33(5) if—
  (a) the land in question is held by statutory undertakers, and
  (b) they object to the proposed works on the ground that the execution of the works would be seriously detrimental to the carrying on of their undertaking.

(8) Section 217(1) of the principal Act applies for the purposes of subsection (7) as it applies for the purposes of section 270(9) of that Act.

GENERAL NOTE

This section contains supplementary provisions relating to the rights of entry conferred by ss.33 and 34.

Subs. (3)

Any dispute as to compensation is to be referred to and determined by the Lands Tribunal (s.86 of the principal Act).

Application of certain general provisions of principal Act

36. The following provisions of the principal Act shall apply for the purposes of this Act as they apply for the purposes of that Act—
  section 85 (power to make provision for determination of claims),
  section 265 (local inquiries),
  section 266 (orders as to expenses of parties where no local inquiry held),
  section 267 (procedure on certain appeals and applications),
  section 271 (service of notices),
  section 272 (power to require information as to interests in land),
  section 273 (offences by corporations), and
  section 276 (Act not excluded by special enactments).

Financial provisions

37.—(1) Where—
  (a) compensation is payable by a planning authority under this Act in consequence of any decision or order given or made under sections 1 to 29 (except sections 9, 20 and 22 to 25) or the Schedule, and
  (b) that decision or order was given or made wholly or partly in the interest of a service which is provided by a government department and the cost of which is defrayed out of money provided by Parliament,
the Minister responsible for the administration of that service may pay that authority a contribution of such amount as he may with the consent of the Treasury determine.

(2) Any local authority and any statutory undertakers may contribute towards any expenses incurred by a planning authority in or in connection with the performance of any of their functions under sections 1 to 29 (except sections 9, 20 and 25), 34 and 35.

(3) In the application of subsection (2) to a local authority, "planning authority" means a planning authority other than that local authority.

(4) Subsections (3) and (4) of section 261 of the principal Act (borrowing by authorities for purposes of the principal Act) shall apply for the purposes of this Act as they apply for the purposes of that Act.

(5) There shall be paid out of money provided by Parliament any expenses of the Secretary of State or any government department under this Act.

(6) Any sums received by the Secretary of State under any provision of this Act shall be paid into the Consolidated Fund.

GENERAL NOTE
    This section provides for the contribution by the government, by a local authority or by a statutory undertaker to the expenses incurred by a planning authority under the Act.

Subs. (2)
    For "statutory undertakers" see s.38 and s.214 of the principal Act.

Supplemental

Interpretation

38.—(1) In this Act—
  "contravention of hazardous substances control" shall be construed in accordance with section 21(2),
  "hazardous substances consent" means consent required by section 2,
  "hazardous substances contravention notice" means such a notice as is mentioned in section 22(1), and

"the principal Act" means the Town and Country Planning (Scotland) Act 1997.

(2) In this Act, except in so far as the context otherwise requires and subject to the following provisions of this section, the following expressions have the same meaning as in the principal Act—

"development",
"development plan",
"enactment",
"functions",
"government department",
"land",
"local authority",
"minerals",
"Minister",
"owner",
"planning authority",
"planning permission",
"prescribed",
"public gas transporter",
"statutory undertakers",
"urban development corporation",
"use", and
"Valuation Office".

(3) For the purposes of sections 2 to 8, 10 to 19, 21 to 23 and 29(1) and (2) any two bodies corporate are to be treated as being one person if—

(a) one of them is a body corporate of which the other is a subsidiary (within the meaning of section 736 of the Companies Act 1985), or

(b) both of them are subsidiaries (within the meaning of that Act) of one and the same body corporate.

(4) For the purposes of sections 10 and 37(2) a public gas transporter shall be deemed to be a statutory undertaker.

(5) For the purposes of section 37(2) the Post Office, the Civil Aviation Authority and any holder of a licence under section 6(1) of the Electricity Act 1989 shall be deemed to be statutory undertakers.

(6) Without prejudice to section 20(2) of the Interpretation Act 1978, references in this Act to any enactment shall, except where the context otherwise requires, be construed as references to that enactment as amended by or under any other enactment.

GENERAL NOTE
Subs. (4)

This subsection gives effect to recommendation 41 of the Scottish Law Commission, curing the anomaly that the Gas Act 1995 (c. 45) failed to include on the list of provisions in respect of which a public gas transporter is deemed to be a statutory undertaker, s.56G of the 1972 Act (now s.10 of the Act)—deemed consent following statutory authorisation.

Regulations

39.—(1) The Secretary of State may make regulations—

(a) for prescribing the form of any notice, order or other document authorised or required by this Act to be served, made or issued by a planning authority which is a local authority;

(b) for any purpose for which regulations are authorised or required to be made under this Act.

(2) Any power conferred by this Act to make regulations shall be exercisable by statutory instrument.

(3) Any statutory instrument containing regulations made under this Act shall be subject to annulment in pursuance of a resolution of either House of Parliament.

GENERAL NOTE

This is a general enabling provision under which further regulations can be made by statutory instrument if required.

Short title, commencement and extent

40.—(1) This Act may be cited as the Planning (Hazardous Substances) (Scotland) Act 1997.

(2) This Act shall come into force at the end of the period of 3 months beginning with the day on which it is passed.

(3) This Act extends to Scotland only.

GENERAL NOTE

The Act came into force on May 27, 1997.

SCHEDULE

DETERMINATION OF CERTAIN APPEALS BY PERSON APPOINTED BY SECRETARY OF STATE

Determination of appeals by appointed person

1.—(1) The Secretary of State may by regulations prescribe classes of appeals under section 19 which are to be determined by a person appointed by the Secretary of State for the purpose instead of by the Secretary of State.

(2) Those classes of appeals shall be so determined except in such classes of case—

(a) as may for the time being be prescribed, or

(b) as may be specified in directions given by the Secretary of State.

(3) Such regulations may provide for the giving of publicity to any directions given by the Secretary of State under this paragraph.

(4) This paragraph shall not affect any provision in this Act or any instrument made under it that an appeal shall lie to, or a notice of appeal shall be served on, the Secretary of State.

(5) A person appointed under this paragraph is referred to in this Schedule as an "appointed person".

Powers and duties of appointed person

2.—(1) An appointed person shall have the same powers and duties as the Secretary of State has under section 19(5), (7) and (9).

(2) Subsection (6) of that section shall not apply to an appeal which falls to be determined by an appointed person, but before it is determined the Secretary of State shall ask the appellant and the planning authority whether they wish to appear before and be heard by the appointed person.

(3) If both the parties express a wish not to appear and be heard, the appeal may be determined without their being heard.

(4) If either of the parties expresses a wish to appear and be heard, the appointed person shall give them both an opportunity of doing so.

(5) Where an appeal has been determined by an appointed person, his decision shall be treated as that of the Secretary of State.

(6) Except as provided by section 20, the decision of an appointed person on an appeal shall be final.

Determination of appeals by Secretary of State

3.—(1) The Secretary of State may, if he thinks fit, direct that an appeal which would otherwise fall to be determined by an appointed person shall instead be determined by the Secretary of State.

(2) Such a direction shall state the reasons for which it is given and shall be served on the appellant, the planning authority and any person who has made representations relating to the subject matter of the appeal which the authority are required to take into account by regulations made under section 6 or, as the case may be, 15(2) and, if any person has been appointed under paragraph 1, on him.

(3) Where in consequence of such a direction an appeal under section 19 falls to be determined by the Secretary of State himself, the provisions of this Act which are relevant to the appeal shall, subject to the following provisions of this paragraph, apply to the appeal as if this Schedule had never applied to it.

(4) The Secretary of State shall give the appellant, the planning authority and any person who has made such representations as are referred to in sub-paragraph (2) an opportunity of appearing before and being heard by a person appointed by the Secretary of State for that purpose if—

    (a) the reasons for the direction raise matters with respect to which any of those persons have not made representations, or

    (b) in the case of the appellant or the planning authority, either of them was not asked in pursuance of paragraph 2(2) whether they wish to appear before and be heard by the appointed person, or expressed no wish in answer to that question, or expressed a wish to appear and be heard, but was not given an opportunity of doing so.

(5) Except as provided by sub-paragraph (4), the Secretary of State need not give any person an opportunity of appearing before and being heard by a person appointed for the purpose, or of making fresh representations or making or withdrawing any representations already made.

(6) In determining the appeal the Secretary of State may take into account any report made to him by any person previously appointed to determine it.

4.—(1) The Secretary of State may by a further direction revoke a direction under paragraph 3 at any time before the determination of the appeal.

(2) Such a further direction shall state the reasons for which it is given and shall be served on the person, if any, previously appointed to determine the appeal, the appellant, the planning authority and any person who has made representations relating to the subject matter of the appeal which the authority are required to take into account by regulations made under section 6 or, as the case may be, 15(2).

(3) Where such a further direction has been given, the provisions of this Schedule relevant to the appeal shall apply, subject to sub-paragraph (4), as if no direction under paragraph 3 had been given.

(4) Anything done by or on behalf of the Secretary of State in connection with the appeal which might have been done by the appointed person (including any arrangements made for the holding of a hearing or local inquiry) shall, unless that person directs otherwise, be treated as having been done by him.

Appointment of another person to determine appeal

5.—(1) At any time before the appointed person has determined the appeal the Secretary of State may—

    (a) revoke his appointment, and

    (b) appoint another person under paragraph 1 to determine the appeal instead.

(2) Where such a new appointment is made the consideration of the appeal or any inquiry or other hearing in connection with it shall be begun afresh.

(3) Nothing in sub-paragraph (2) shall require—

    (a) the question referred to in paragraph 2(2) to be asked again with reference to the new appointed person if before his appointment it was asked with reference to the previous appointed person (any answers being treated as given with reference to the new appointed person), or

    (b) any person to be given an opportunity of making fresh representations or modifying or withdrawing any representations already made.

Local inquiries and hearings

6.—(1) Whether or not the parties have asked for an opportunity to appear and be heard, an appointed person—

    (a) may hold a local inquiry in connection with the appeal, and

    (b) shall do so if the Secretary of State so directs.

(2) Where an appointed person—

    (a) holds a hearing by virtue of paragraph 2(4), or

    (b) holds an inquiry by virtue of this paragraph,

an assessor may be appointed by the Secretary of State to sit with the appointed person at the hearing or inquiry to advise him on any matters arising, notwithstanding that the appointed person is to determine the appeal.

(3) Subject to sub-paragraph (4), the expenses of any such hearing or inquiry shall be paid by the Secretary of State.

(4) Subsections (4) to (13) of section 265 of the principal Act apply to an inquiry held under this paragraph as they apply to an inquiry held under that section.

(5) The appointed person has the same power to make orders under subsection (9) of that section in relation to proceedings under this Schedule which do not give rise to an inquiry as he has in relation to such an inquiry.

(6) For the purposes of this paragraph, references to the Minister in subsections (9) to (12) of that section shall be read as references to the appointed person.

Supplementary provisions

7.—(1) The Tribunals and Inquiries Act 1992 shall apply to a local inquiry or other hearing held in pursuance of this Schedule as it applies to a statutory inquiry held by the Secretary of State, but as if in section 10(1) of that Act (statement of reasons for decisions) the reference to any decision taken by the Secretary of State were a reference to a decision taken by an appointed person.

(2) The functions of determining an appeal and doing anything in connection with it conferred by this Schedule on an appointed person who is an officer of the Scottish Office shall be treated for the purposes of the Parliamentary Commissioner Act 1967 as functions of that office.

TABLE OF DERIVATIONS

Notes:

1. This Table shows the derivation of the provisions of the Bill.
2. The following abbreviations are used in the Table—

    1972 = The Town and Country Planning (Scotland) Act 1972 (c. 52)
    1986 = The Housing and Planning Act 1986 (c. 63)

3. The Table does not show the effect of Transfer of Functions orders.
4. The Table does not give details of the effect of section 172(2) of the Local Government (Scotland) Act 1973 (c. 65), which omitted the word "local" in the expression "local planning authority" where it occurs in any enactment or instrument.
5. "Sc Law Com Rec No." followed by a number indicates that the provision gives effect to the Recommendation bearing that number in Appendix 1 to the Scottish Law Commission's Report on the Consolidation of Certain Enactments relating to Town and Country Planning in Scotland (Cmnd. 3644).

Provision	Derivation
1(1), (2)	1972 s.56A(1), (2); 1986 s.35.
2(1), (2)	1972 s.56C(1); 1986 s.35.
(3)	1972 s.56C(2); 1986 s.35.
(4)	1972 s.56C(3)(b); 1986 s.35.
(5)	1972 s.56C(6); 1986 s.35.
3(1)	1972 s.56C(3)(a), (c); 1986 s.35.
(2)	1972 s.56C(4); 1986 s.35.
(3)	1972 s.56C(6); 1986 s.35.
4(1)	Drafting.
(2)	1972 s.56K(1); 1986 s.35.
5(1)	1972 s.56D(1); 1986 s.35; Environmental Protection Act 1990 (c. 43) Sch. 13 para. 11(3).
(2)	1972 s.56D(4); 1986 s.35.
(3)	1972 s.56D(5); 1986 s.35; Environmental Protection Act 1990 (c. 43) Sch. 13 para. 11(4).
(4)	1972 s.56D(6); 1986 s.35.
6(1)	1972 ss.24(1), 56D(2); 1986 s.35; Planning and Compensation Act 1991 (c. 34) s.46.
(2)	1972 s.56D(2), (6); 1986 s.35.
(3)	1972 s.56D(3); 1986 s.35.
7(1)	1972 s.56E(1); 1986 s.35.
(2)	1972 s.56E(1), (2); 1986 s.35.
(3), (4)	1972 s.56E(3), (4); 1986 s.35.
8(1), (2)	1972 s.56E(5); 1986 s.35.
(3)	1972 s.56E(4)(c); 1986 s.35.
9(1)	Drafting.

Provision	Derivation
9(2)	1986 s.38(9); Environmental Protection Act 1990 (c. 43) Sch. 13 para. 12(3)(a).
(3)	Sc Law Com Rec No. 35.
(4)	1986 s.38(10).
10(1)	1972 s.56G(1); 1986 s.35.
(2)	Electricity Act 1989 (c. 29) Sch. 8 para. 7(2).
(3)	1972 s.56G(2); 1986 s.35.
(4)	1972 ss.37(3), 56G(4); 1986 s.35.
(5)	1972 s.56G(3); 1986 s.35; Electricity Act 1989 (c. 29) Sch. 8 para. 7(3), (4); Planning and Compensation Act 1991 (c. 34) Sch. 12 para. 11.
(6)	1972 s.56G(5); Environmental Protection Act 1990 (c. 43) Sch. 13 para. 11(7).
11(1)	1972 s.56H(1); 1986 s.35.
(2) to (4)	1972 s.56H(2); 1986 s.35.
(5), (6)	1972 s.56H(3), (4); 1986 s.35.
12(1)	1972 s.56J(3); 1986 s.35.
(2)	1972 s.56J(1), (2); 1986 s.35.
(3)	1972 s.56J(1); 1986 s.35.
(4)	1972 s.56J(4); 1986 s.35.
13(1), (2)	1972 s.56J(5); 1986 s.35.
(3) to (5)	1972 s.56J(6); 1986 s.35.
(6)	1972 s.56J(7); 1986 s.35.
14(1)	1972 s.56J(8); 1986 s.35.
(2)	1972 ss.56J(8), 159(2); 1986 s.35.
(3)	1972 ss.56J(8), 159(3); 1986 s.35.
(4)	1972 ss.56J(8), 159(4); 1986 s.35.
(5)	1972 s.56J(8); 1986 s.35.
15(1), (2)	1972 s.56K(2), (3); 1986 s.35.
16(1) to (5)	1972 s.56K(4) to (8); 1986 s.35.
(6)	1972 s.56K(9); 1986 s.35; Sc Law Com Rec No. 36.
(7)	1972 ss.34, 56K(10), (11)(c); 1982 Sch. 2 para. 12; 1986 s.35.
17	1972 s.56K(12); 1986 s.35.
18(1)	1972 ss.32(1), 56F, 56K(10), (11); Local Government and Planning (Scotland) Act 1982 (c. 43) Sch. 2 para. 10(a); 1986 s.35.
(2), (3)	1972 s.32(2), 56F, 56K(10), (11); 1986 s.35.
(4), (5)	1972 ss.32(5), (6), 56F, 56K(10), (11); 1986 s.35.
19(1)	1972 ss.33(1), 56F, 56K(10), (11); 1986 s.35; Sc Law Com Rec No. 37.
(2)	1972 ss.34, 56F; 1986 s.35; Sc Law Com Rec No. 37.
(3)	1972 ss.33(1), (2), 56F, 56K(10), (11); 1986 s.35.
(4)	1972 ss.34, 56F; 1986 s.35.
(5)	1972 ss.33(3), 56F, 56K(10), (11); 1986 s.35.
(6)	1972 ss.33(4), 56F, 56K(10), (11); 1986 s.35.
(7)	1972 ss.33(3), 56F, 56K(10), (11); 1986 s.35.
(8)	1972 ss.33(6), 56F, 56K(10), (11); 1986 s.35.
(9)	1972 ss.33(7A), 56F, 56K(10), (11); 1986 s.35; Planning and Compensation Act 1991 (c. 34) s.50(1).
(10)	1972 ss.33(8), 56F, 56K(10), (11); 1986 s.35.
20(1)	1972 s.233(1), (3); Sc Law Com Rec No. 37.
(2)	1972 s.233(2), (3); Sc Law Com Rec No. 37.
(3)	1972 s.233(4).
(4)	1972 s.233(7).
(5)	1972 s.231(1), (3); 1986 Sch. 7 Pt. II para. 2; Sc Law Com Rec No. 37.
(6)	1972 s.231(4).
21(1) to (3)	1972 s.56L(1) to (3); 1986 s.35.
(4)	1972 s.56L(4); 1986 s.35; Planning and Compensation Act 1991 (c. 34) Sch. 10 para. 3(a).
(5)	1972 s.56L(4A); 1986 s.35; Planning and Compensation Act 1991 (c. 34) Sch. 10 para. 3(b).
(6) to (8)	1972 s.56L(5) to (7); 1986 s.35.

Provision	Derivation
22(1)	1972 s.97B(1), (3); 1986 s.36; Planning and Compensation Act 1991 (c. 34) Sch. 10 para. 9(1)(a).
(2)	1972 s.97B(1), (3); 1986 s.36.
(3)	1972 s.97B(2); 1986 s.36.
(4) to (7)	1972 s.97B(4) to (7); 1986 s.36.
(8)	1972 s.97B(8); 1986 s.36; Planning and Compensation Act 1991 (c. 34) Sch. 10 para. 9(1)(b).
(9)	1972 s.97B(9); 1986 s.36; Planning and Compensation Act 1991 (c. 34) Sch. 10 para. 9(1)(c).
23(1)	1972 s.97B(10); 1986 s.36; Environmental Protection Act 1990 (c. 43) Sch. 13 para. 11(11).
(2), (3)	1972 s.97B(11), (12); 1986 s.36.
24(1) to (3)	1972 s.97BA; Planning and Compensation Act 1991 (c. 34) Sch. 10 para. 11.
25(1) to (3)	1972 s.260A; Planning and Compensation Act 1991 (c. 34) s.35.
26(1) to (3)	1972 s.56M(1) to (3); 1986 s.35.
27(1)	1972 s.56N(1); 1986 s.35; Environmental Protection Act 1990 (c. 43) Sch. 13 para. 11(9); Sc Law Com Rec No. 38.
(2)	1972 s.56N(3); 1986 s.35.
28(1), (2)	1972 s.56O(1); 1986 s.35.
(3)	1972 s.56O(2); 1986 s.35; Environmental Protection Act 1990 (c. 43) Sch. 13 para. 11(10).
(4)	1972 s.56O(3); 1986 s.35; Environmental Protection Act 1990 (c. 43) Sch. 13 para. 11(10).
(5), (6)	1972 s.56O(4), (5); 1986 s.35.
29(1)	1972 s.56DA(1); Environmental Protection Act 1990 (c. 43) Sch. 13 para. 11(5); Sc Law Com Rec No. 39.
(2)	1972 s.56DA(2); Environmental Protection Act 1990 (c. 43) Sch. 13 para. 11(5).
(3)	Local Government, Planning and Land Act 1980 (c. 65) s.87(9); Environmental Protection Act 1990 (c. 43) Sch. 13 para. 13.
30(1), (2)	1972 s.257A; 1986 Sch. 7 Pt. II para. 4.
31(1)	1972 s.253(1).
(2)	1972 s.253(2); 1986 Sch. 7 Pt. II para. 3.
(3)	1972 s.253(7).
(4)	Town and Country Planning Act 1984 (c. 10) s.4(1).
(5), (6)	1972 s.253(7).
32(1)	Town and Country Planning Act 1984 (c. 10) s.1(1); 1986 Sch. 7 Pt. II para. 7(a).
(2)	Town and Country Planning Act 1984 (c. 10) s.1(2).
(3)	Town and Country Planning Act 1984 (c. 10) s.1(3A); 1986 Sch. 7 Pt. II para. 7(b).
(4)	Town and Country Planning Act 1984 (c. 10) s.1(5).
(5)	Town and Country Planning Act 1984 (c. 10) s.1(7).
(6)	Town and Country Planning Act 1984 (c. 10) ss.1(6), 6(1).
(7)	Town and Country Planning Act 1984 (c. 10) s.6(1).
(8)	Town and Country Planning Act 1984 (c. 10) s.4(1).
33(1)	1972 s.265(1A); 1986 Sch. 7 Pt. II para. 5(a).
(2)	1972 s.265(4A); 1986 Sch. 7 Pt. II para. 5(b).
(3)	1972 s.265(5), (6); Sc Law Com Rec No. 40.
(4)	1972 s.265(7A); 1986 Sch. 7 Pt. II para. 5(c).
(5)	1972 s.265(8).
34(1) to (3)	1972 s.97BB; Planning and Compensation Act 1991 (c. 34) Sch. 10 para. 11.
35(1) to (8)	1972 s.97BC; Planning and Compensation Act 1991 (c. 34) Sch. 10 para. 11.
36	1972 ss.145, 267 to 267B, 269 to 271, 274; 1977 s.5(4); 1981 Sch. 2 para. 4; 1986 Sch. 11 paras. 39, 40, 41, 52, 58; Debtors (Scotland) Act 1987 (c. 18) Sch. 6 para. 15; 1991 s.60(1), Sch. 12 para. 14(1), Sch. 13 para. 28(b); Criminal Procedure (Consequential Provisions) (Scotland) Act 1995 (c. 40) Sch. 1 paras. 2, 5, 6; Criminal Procedure (Scotland) Act 1995 (c. 46) s.225.

Provision	Derivation
37(1)	1972 s.241.
(2)	1972 s.242(2).
(3)	Drafting.
(4)	1972 s.250(3), (4); Local Government (Scotland) Act 1973 (c. 65) Sch. 23 para. 30.
(5)	1972 s.247(1)(b), (f), (2)(d); 1986 s.56; 1991 Sch. 13 para. 36.
(6)	1972 s.249; 1986 s.56.
38(1)	1972 s.275(1); 1986 Sch. 7 Pt. II para. 6(a), (b).
(2)	1972 s.275(1); Gas Act 1995 (c. 45) Sch. 4 para. 2(10)(d).
(3)	1972 s.56C(7); Fair Trading Act 1973 (c. 41) s.137(5); Companies Consolidation (Consequential Provisions) Act 1985 (c. 9) Sch. 2; 1986 s.35.
(4)	Gas Act 1995 (c. 45) Sch. 4 para. 2(1)(xix); Sc Law Com Rec No. 41.
(5)	Post Office Act 1969 (c. 48) Sch. 4 para. 93(xxxiv); Civil Aviation Act 1982 (c. 16) Sch. 2 para. 4; Electricity Act 1989 (c. 29) Sch. 16 para. 1(1)(xxiii).
(6)	1972 s.275(10).
39(1)	1972 s.273(1).
(2), (3)	1972 s.273(2).
40(1) to (3)	Drafting.
Sch.	
para. 1	1972 Sch. 7 para. 1; drafting.
para. 2	1972 Sch. 7 para. 2; Planning and Compensation Act 1991 (c. 34) Sch. 13 para. 41(1); drafting.
para. 3	1972 Sch. 7 para. 3; 1991 Sch. 13 para. 41(3).
para. 4	1972 Sch. 7 para. 3A; 1986 Sch. 11 para. 42; Planning and Compensation Act 1991 (c. 34) Sch. 13 para. 41(4).
para. 5	1972 Sch. 7 para. 4.
para. 6	1972 Sch. 7 para. 5; 1986 Sch. 11 paras. 40(2), 43.
para. 7	1972 Sch. 7 para. 7; Tribunals and Inquiries Act 1992 (c. 53) Sch. 3 para. 7(b).

TABLE OF DESTINATIONS

Post Office Act 1969
(c.48)

1969	1997
Sched. 4,	
para. 93	
(xxxiv)	s.38(5)

Town and Country Planning (Scotland) Act 1972
(c.52)

1972	1997	1972	1997	1972	1997
s.24(1)........	s.6(1)	s.56J(2).......	s.12(2)	s.231(1), (3)...	s.20(5)
32(1)........	18(1)	(3)......	12(1)	(4)	20(6)
(2)........	18(2), (3)	(4)......	12(4)	233(1)	20(1)
(5), (6)....	18(4), (5)	(5)......	13(1), (2)	(2)	20(2)
33(1)........	19(1), (3)	(6)......	13(3)–(5)	(3)	20(1), (2)
(2)........	19(3)	(7)......	13(6)	(4)	20(3)
(3)........	19(5), (7)	(8)......	14(1), (2), (3),	(7)	20(4)
(4)........	19(6)		(4), (5)	241	37(1)
(6)........	19(8)	56K(1)......	4(2)	242(2)	37(2)
(7A).....	19(9)	(2), (3) ..	15(1), (2)	247(1)(b)....	37(5)
(8)........	19(10)	(4)–(8) ..	16(1)–(5)	(f)	37(5)
34	ss.16(7), 19(2),	(9)......	16(6)	(2)(d)....	37(5)
	(4)	(10)....	ss.16(7), 18(1),	249	37(6)
37(3)........	s.10(4)		(2), (3), (4),	250(3), (4)...	37(4)
56A(1), (2) ..	1(1), (2)		(5),	253(1)	31(1)
56C(1)	2(1), (2)		19(1), (3), (5),	(2)	31(2)
(2)	2(3)		(6), (7), (8),	(7)	31(3), (5), (6)
(3)(a) ...	3(1)		(9), (10)	257A	30(1), (2)
(b) ...	2(4)	(11)....	s.18(1), (2), (3),	260A	25(1)–(3)
(c) ...	3(1)		(4), (5),	265(1A).....	33(1)
(4)	3(2)		19(1), (3), (5),	(4A).....	33(2)
(6)	ss.2(5), 3(3)		(6), (7), (8),	(5), (6)...	33(3)
(7)	s.38(3)		(9), (10)	(7A).....	33(4)
56D(1).....	5(1)	(11)(c) ..	16(7)	(8)	33(5)
(2)......	6(1), (2)	(12).....	17	267	36
(3)......	6(3)	56L(1)–(3) ..	21(1)–(3)	267A, B....	36
(4)......	5(2)	(4)	21(4)	269	36
(5)......	5(3)	(4A)	21(5)	270	36
(6)	ss.5(4), 6(2)	(5)–(7) ..	21(6)–(8)	271	36
56DA(1)....	s.29(1)	56M(1)–(3)..	26(1) to (3)	273(1)	39(1)
(2)....	29(2)	56N(1).....	27(1)	(2)	39(2), (3)
56E(1)	7(1), (2)	(3).....	27(2)	274	36
(2)......	7(2)	56O(1).....	28(1), (2)	275(1)	38(1), (2)
(3), (4) ..	7(3), (4)	(2).....	28(3)	(10)	38(6)
(4)(c) ...	8(3)	(3).....	28(4)	Sched. 7,	
(5)	8(1), (2)	(4), (5)..	28(5), (6)	para. 1.....	Sched.,
56F	ss.18(1), (2),	97B(1)	22(1), (2)		para. 1
	(3), (4), (5),	(2)	22(3)	para. 2	Sched.,
	19(1), (2), (3),	(3)	22(1), (2)		para. 2
	(4), (5), (6),	(4)–(7) ..	22(4)–(7)	para. 3	Sched.,
	(7), (8), (9),	(8)	22(8)		para. 3
	(10)	(9)	22(9)	para. 3A....	Sched.,
56G(1)......	s.10(1)	(10).....	23(1)		para. 4
(2)......	10(3)	(11), (12)	23(2), (3)	para. 4	Sched.,
(3).....	10(5)	97BA	24(1)–(3)		para. 5
(4).....	10(4)	97BB	34(1)–(3)	para. 5	Sched.,
(5).....	10(6)	97BC	35(1)–(8)		para. 6
56H(1).....	11(1)	145	36	para. 7	Sched.,
(2)......	11(2)–(4)	159(2)	14(2)		para. 7
(3), (4)..	11(5), (6)	(3)	14(3)		
56J(1).......	12(2), (3)	(4)	14(4)		

TABLE OF DESTINATIONS

FAIR TRADING ACT 1973
(c.41)

1973	1997
s.137(5)	s.38(3)

LOCAL GOVERNMENT (SCOTLAND) ACT 1973
(c.65)

1973	1997
Sched. 23,	
para. 30....	s.37(4)

TOWN AND COUNTRY PLANNING (SCOTLAND) ACT 1977
(c.10)

1977	1997
s.5(4).........	s.36

LOCAL GOVERNMENT, PLANNING LAND ACT 1980
(c.65)

1980	1997
s.87(9).......	s.29(3)

TOWN AND COUNTRY PLANNING (MINERALS) ACT 1981
(c.36)

1981	1997
Sched. 2,	
para. 4.....	s.36

CIVIL AVIATION ACT 1982
(c.16)

1982	1997
Sched. 2,	
para. 4.....	s.38(5)

LOCAL GOVERNMENT AND PLANNING (SCOTLAND) ACT 1982
(c.43)

1982	1997
Sched. 2,	
para. 10(a) .	s.18(1)
12	16(7)

TOWN AND COUNTRY PLANNING ACT 1984
(c.10)

1984	1997
s.1(1).........	s.32(1)
(2).........	32(2)
(3A).......	32(3)
(5).........	32(4)
(6).........	32(6)
(7).........	32(5)
4(1).........	ss.31(4), 32(8)
6(1).........	s.32(6), (7)

TABLE OF DESTINATIONS

COMPANIES CONSOLIDATION (CONSEQUENTIAL PROVISIONS) ACT 1986
(c.9)

HOUSING AND PLANNING ACT 1986
(c.63)

DEBTORS (SCOTLAND) ACT 1987
(c.18)

ELECTRICITY ACT 1989
(c.29)

ENVIRONMENTAL PROTECTION ACT 1990
(c.43)

TABLE OF DESTINATIONS

PLANNING AND COMPENSATION ACT 1991
(C.34)

1991	1997
s.35	s.25(1)–(3)
46	6(1)
50(1).......	19(9)
60(1).......	36
Sched. 10,	
para. 3(a) ..	21(4)
(b) ..	21(5)
para. 9(1)(a)	22(1)
(b)	22(8)

1991	1997
Sched. 10—*cont.*	
para. 9(1)(c)	s.22(9)
para. 11	ss.24(1)–(3),
	34(1)–(3),
	35(1)–(8)
Sched. 12,	
para. 11	s.10(5)
para. 14(1) .	36

1991	1997
Sched. 13,	
para. 28(b) .	s.36
para. 36	37(5)
para. 41(3) .	Sched.,
	para. 3
para. 41(1) .	Sched.,
	para. 2
para. 41(4) .	Sched.,
	para. 4

TRIBUNALS AND INQUIRIES ACT 1992
(C.53)

1992	1997
Sched. 3,	
para. 7(b) ..	Sched.,
	para. 7

CRIMINAL PROCEDURE (CONSEQUENTIAL PROVISIONS) (SCOTLAND) ACT 1995
(C.40)

1995	1997
Sched. 1,	
para. 2	s.36
para. 5	36
para. 6	36

GAS ACT 1995
(C.45)

1995	1997
Sched. 4,	
para. 2(1)	
(xix)	s.38(4)
(10)(d)	38(2)

CRIMINAL PROCEDURE (SCOTLAND) ACT 1995
(C.46)

1995	1997
s.225	s.36

SCOTTISH LAW COMMISSION'S REPORT ON THE CONSOLIDATION OF CERTAIN ENACTMENTS RELATING TO TOWN AND COUNTRY PLANNING IN SCOTLAND 1996
(SCOT LAW COM NO. 157) (CMND.3644)

1996	1997
App.1,	
No.35	s.9(3)
No.36	16(6)
No.37	ss.19(1), (2),
	20(1), (2), (5)
No.38	s.27(1)
No.39	29(1)
No.41	38(4)

INDEX

References are to sections and the Schedule

PLANNING (CONSEQUENTIAL PROVISIONS) (SCOTLAND) ACT 1997

(1997 c. 11)

An Act to make provision for repeals, consequential amendments, transitional matters and savings in connection with the consolidation of enactments in the Town and Country Planning (Scotland) Act 1997, the Planning (Listed Buildings and Conservation Areas) (Scotland) Act 1997 and the Planning (Hazardous Substances) (Scotland) Act 1997 (including provisions to give effect to recommendations of the Scottish Law Commission). [27th February 1997]

PARLIAMENTARY DEBATES
Hansard, H.L. Vol. 576, cols. 122, 588, 673; Vol. 577, cols. 560, 1082. H.C. Vol. 291, col. 197.

INTRODUCTION
   This Act exists to support the Town and Country Planning (Scotland) Act 1997, the Planning (Listed Buildings and Conservation Areas) (Scotland) Act 1997 and the Planning (Hazardous Substances) (Scotland) Act 1997. It provides for repeals, consequential amendments, transitional matters and savings in connection with the consolidations contained in those three enactments.

Meaning of "the consolidating Acts", "the repealed enactments", etc.

   1.—(1) In this Act—
      "the consolidating Acts" means the principal Act, the Planning (Listed Buildings and Conservation Areas) (Scotland) Act 1997, the Planning (Hazardous Substances) (Scotland) Act 1997 and, so far as it reproduces the effect of the repealed enactments, this Act,
      "the principal Act" means the Town and Country Planning (Scotland) Act 1997, and
      "the repealed enactments" means the enactments repealed by this Act.
   (2) Expressions used in this Act and in any of the other consolidating Acts have the same meaning as in those Acts.

Continuity, and construction of references to old and new law

   2.—(1) The substitution of the consolidating Acts for the repealed enactments does not affect the continuity of the law.
   (2) Anything done or having effect as if done under or for the purposes of a provision of the repealed enactments has effect, if it could have been done

under or for the purposes of the corresponding provision of the consolidating Acts, as if done under or for the purposes of that corresponding provision.

(3) Any reference, whether express or implied, in the consolidating Acts or any other enactment, instrument or document to a provision of the consolidating Acts shall, so far as the context permits, be construed as including, in relation to the times, circumstances and purposes in relation to which the corresponding provision of the repealed enactments has effect, a reference to that corresponding provision.

(4) Any reference, whether express or implied, in any enactment, instrument or document to a provision of the repealed enactments shall be construed, so far as is required for continuing its effect, as including a reference to the corresponding provision of the consolidating Acts.

(5) In particular, where a power conferred by an Act is expressed (in whatever words) to be exercisable in relation to enactments contained in Acts passed—

(a) before or in the same Session as the Act conferring the power, or
(b) before a date determined by reference to the coming into force of particular provisions of that Act,

the power is also exercisable in relation to provisions of the consolidating Acts which reproduce such enactments.

Repeals

3.—(1) The enactments specified in Schedule 1 are repealed to the extent specified in the third column of that Schedule.

(2) Those repeals include the repeal, in accordance with Recommendations of the Scottish Law Commission, of section 18(7) and (8) of the 1972 Act as no longer of practical utility.

(3) The repeals have effect subject to any relevant savings in Schedule 3.

Consequential amendments

4. Schedule 2 (which makes consequential amendments) shall have effect, subject to any relevant transitional provisions in Schedule 3.

Transitional provisions and savings

5.—(1) Schedule 3 (which makes transitional provision and contains savings in connection with the repeals made by this Act) shall have effect.

(2) Nothing in that Schedule affects the general operation of section 16 of the Interpretation Act 1978 (general savings implied on repeal) or of the previous provisions of this Act.

Short title, commencement and extent

6.—(1) This Act may be cited as the Planning (Consequential Provisions) (Scotland) Act 1997.

(2) Subject to subsections (3) and (4), this Act shall come into force at the end of the period of 3 months beginning with the day on which it is passed.

(3) The repeal in Part I of Schedule 1 relating to section 186 of the principal Act shall come into force on such day as the Secretary of State may by order made by statutory instrument appoint, and different days may be appointed for different purposes.

(4) An order under subsection (3) may contain such supplementary, incidental, consequential and transitional provisions as the Secretary of State thinks fit.

(5) This Act does not extend to England or Wales or Northern Ireland except (subject to subsection (6)) so far as it affects other enactments so extending.

(6) The repeals in Part II of Schedule 1 extend to Scotland only and those in Part III of that Schedule to England and Wales only.

SCHEDULES

SCHEDULE 1

REPEALS

PART I

GENERAL

Chapter	Short Title	Extent of repeal
10 & 11 Geo. 6 c. 53.	The Town and Country Planning (Scotland) Act 1947.	Section 46(8). In Schedule 8, the entry relating to the Building Restrictions (War-time Contraventions) Act 1946.
14 & 15 Geo. 6 c. 60.	The Mineral Workings Act 1951.	Section 32. Section 40(6).
1967 c. 69.	The Civic Amenities Act 1967.	Section 5. In section 30(1), the definition of "the Scottish Planning Act".
1969 c. 48.	The Post Office Act 1969.	In Schedule 4, paragraph 92; and in paragraph 93, in sub-paragraph (1), paragraph (xxxiv) and the words from "Subject to" to the end, and sub-paragraph (4)(k). In Schedule 9, paragraph 27(8) and (11).
1972 c. 42.	The Town and Country Planning (Amendment) Act 1972.	The whole Act.
1972 c. 52.	The Town and Country Planning (Scotland) Act 1972.	The whole Act.
1973 c. 56.	The Land Compensation (Scotland) Act 1973.	In section 49(5) the words from "sections 169" to "or". Sections 64 to 69. Sections 71 to 77.
1973 c. 65.	The Local Government (Scotland) Act 1973.	Section 171C(b). Section 172. Section 175. In Schedule 23, paragraphs 6 and 16 to 34.
1974 c. 32.	The Town and Country Amenities Act 1974.	Section 2(1). Section 3(2). Section 4(2) and (3). Section 6. Section 7(2). Section 9. Section 11. In section 13, subsection (1)(b); and in subsection (2), the words from "and in section" to the end.
1977 c. 10.	The Town and Country Planning (Scotland) Act 1977.	The whole Act.
1979 c. 46.	The Ancient Monuments and Archaeological Areas Act 1979.	Section 48(1). In Schedule 4, paragraph 12.
1980 c. 65.	The Local Government, Planning and Land Act 1980.	Section 87. In section 92, subsections (1) to (8); and in subsection (9), the words from "section 87" to "that,".

Chapter	Short Title	Extent of repeal
		In section 122, in subsection (1) the words "or section 103 of the Town and Country Planning (Scotland) Act 1972" and "or as the case may be 103"; in subsections (2), (3), and (8) the words "and 103"; and in subsection (6) the words "or 103".
		Section 147.
		In section 149, in subsection (6), the words from "in place of" to "authority" in the third place where it occurs; in subsection (8)(a), the words from "and in place" to "them"; and subsection (10).
		In Schedule 32, paragraphs 5(8), 15(2)(b), 17, 19, 20(2), 21, 22, 24, 25 and 26(1A).
1981 c. 23.	The Local Government (Miscellaneous Provisions) (Scotland) Act 1981.	Section 36. In Schedule 2, paragraphs 16 to 25, 27 and 28. In Schedule 3, paragraphs 13, 15 to 20, 22 and 23.
1981 c. 36.	The Town and Country Planning (Minerals) Act 1981.	The whole Act.
1981 c. 38.	The British Telecommunications Act 1981.	In Schedule 3, paragraph 10(2)(d).
1982 c. 16.	The Civil Aviation Act 1982.	In Schedule 2, in paragraphs 4 and 5, the entries relating to the Town and Country Planning (Scotland) Act 1972; and paragraph 7. In Schedule 10, paragraphs 4(c) and 8(c) and, in each case, the preceding "and".
1982 c. 43.	The Local Government and Planning (Scotland) Act 1982.	Sections 36 to 48. Schedule 2.
1983 c. 47.	The National Heritage Act 1983.	In Schedule 4, paragraph 22(6).
1984 c. 10.	The Town and Country Planning Act 1984.	The whole Act.
1984 c. 12.	The Telecommunications Act 1984.	In Schedule 4, paragraph 54.
1984 c. 54.	The Roads (Scotland) Act 1984.	In Schedule 9, paragraphs 41, 70, 72(7) and (8).
1985 c. 19.	The Town and Country Planning (Compensation) Act 1985.	The whole Act.
1985 c. 52.	The Town and Country Planning (Amendment) Act 1985.	The whole Act.
1986 c. 31.	The Airports Act 1986.	In Schedule 2, in paragraph 1, in sub-paragraph (1), the entry for the Town and Country Planning (Scotland) Act 1972 and the words from "and for the purposes" to the end, and in sub-paragraph (2), the entry for the Town and Country Planning (Scotland) Act 1972. In Schedule 4, paragraph 2.
1986 c. 44.	The Gas Act 1986.	In Schedule 7, paragraph 13.
1986 c. 63.	The Housing and Planning Act 1986.	Section 26. Sections 35 to 38. Sections 50 and 51. Section 52(1)(a). Section 54(2).

Chapter	Short Title	Extent of repeal
		In section 58(2), the words from "in Part II" to "Schedule 6", the words from "in Part IV" to "Schedule 7" and the words "Part II of Schedule 9".
		In Schedule 6, Parts III and IV.
		In Schedule 7, Part II.
		In Schedule 9, paragraphs 13 to 24.
		In Schedule 11, paragraphs 28 to 60 and 62.
1987 c. 3.	The Coal Industry Act 1987.	In Schedule 1, paragraph 20.
1987 c. 18.	The Debtors (Scotland) Act 1987.	In Schedule 6, paragraph 15.
1987 c. 26.	The Housing (Scotland) Act 1987.	In Schedule 23, paragraphs 18 and 19(9) and (10).
1988 c. 41.	The Local Government Finance Act 1988.	In Schedule 12, paragraph 9.
1989 c. 29.	The Electricity Act 1989.	In Schedule 8, paragraph 7.
		In Schedule 16, in paragraph 1, in sub-paragraph (1), paragraph (xxiii) and in paragraph (xxvi) the words "and 67"; in paragraph 2, sub-paragraphs (2)(d) and (7)(a) and, in sub-paragraph (8), the words from "and section 204" to "1972"; and paragraph 3(2)(e).
1990 c. 11.	The Planning (Consequential Provisions) Act 1990.	In Schedule 2, paragraphs 3(3), 16, 24(2), 26, 27, 44(14)(c), 62, 68 and 70.
1990 c. 19.	The National Health Service and Community Care Act 1990.	In Schedule 8, paragraph 7.
1990 c. 43.	The Environmental Protection Act 1990.	In Schedule 13, paragraphs 11 to 13.
1991 c. 22.	The New Roads and Street Works Act 1991.	In Schedule 8, paragraph 104.
1991 c. 28.	The Natural Heritage (Scotland) Act 1991.	Section 6(8) and (9).
1991 c. 34.	The Planning and Compensation Act 1991.	Sections 33 to 59.
		Section 60(1) to (5), (7) and (8).
		Schedules 8 to 11.
		In Schedule 12, paragraphs 6 to 33.
		In Schedule 13, paragraphs 2 to 43 and 45 to 47.
		In Schedule 17, paragraphs 11, 12, 17 and 18.
		In Schedule 19, in Part IV, the entry relating to the Town and Country Planning (Scotland) Act 1972.
1992 c. 53.	The Tribunals and Inquiries Act 1992.	In Schedule 3, paragraphs 3 to 8.
1994 c. 21.	The Coal Industry Act 1994.	Section 68(2)(d)(v).
		In Schedule 9, paragraph 13.
		In Schedule 10, in paragraph 12, in sub-paragraph (1) the words from "and section" to "1972", and in sub-paragraph (2) the words from "or sections" to the end.
1994 c. 39.	The Local Government etc. (Scotland) Act 1994.	Section 33.
		Schedule 4.
		In Schedule 13, paragraphs 88 and 92(57).
1995 c. 25.	The Environment Act 1995.	In Schedule 22, paragraph 16.
1995 c. 45.	The Gas Act 1995.	In Schedule 4, paragraph 2(1)(xix), (2)(e) and (10)(d).
1995 c. 49.	The Town and Country Planning (Costs of Inquiries etc.) Act 1995.	Sections 3 and 4.
		In section 5, in subsection (2), the definition of "the 1972 Act"; and subsection (5).
1997 c. 8.	The Town and Country Planning (Scotland) Act 1997.	In section 186, subsections (1) and (2); and in subsection (3), the words from the beginning to "(2)".

PART II

SCOTLAND ONLY

Chapter	Short Title	Extent of repeal
9 & 10 Geo. 6 c. 35.	The Building Restrictions (War-Time Contraventions) Act 1946.	The whole Act.
1995 c. 25.	The Environment Act 1995.	Section 96. Schedules 13 and 14.

PART III

ENGLAND AND WALES ONLY

Chapter	Short Title	Extent of repeal
1995 c. 25.	The Environment Act 1995.	In section 96, in subsection (2), the words "as they apply to England and Wales" and "(as so applying)"; subsection (3); in subsection (4) the words "and section 251A of the 1972 Act"; in subsection (5) the words "or, as the case may be, section 21 of the 1972 Act"; and in subsection (6) the definition of "the 1972 Act". In Schedule 13, the words "as respects England and Wales" in each place where they occur; in paragraph 1, in sub-paragraph (1), in each of the definitions of "mineral planning authority", "old mining permission" and "owner", paragraph (b) and the preceding "and", and in sub-paragraph (7)(a) the words "or, as the case may be, section 233 of the 1972 Act"; in paragraph 2, sub-paragraph (4)(d) and (e) and, in sub-paragraph (6), paragraph (b) and the preceding "and"; in paragraph 7, in sub-paragraph (4)(d) the words "or (6)", and sub-paragraph (6); in paragraph 9, in sub-paragraph (2)(f) the words "or (4)", sub-paragraph (4) and, in sub-paragraph (5), the words "or, as respects Scotland, section 24 of the 1972 Act"; in paragraph 12(4)(a) the words "or, as the case may be, section 233 of the 1972 Act"; in paragraph 15, in sub-paragraph (4), paragraph (b) and the preceding "or" and the words "or, as the case may be, section 42 of the 1972 Act" in both places where they occur, in sub-paragraph (5) the words "or section 42 of the 1972 Act", and in sub-paragraph (6) the words "and section 167A of the 1972 Act"; and paragraph 16(5) to (7). In Schedule 14, the words "as respects England and Wales" in each place where they occur; in paragraph 2, in sub-paragraph (1), in each of the definitions of "mineral planning authority", "old mining permission" and "owner", paragraph (b) and the preceding "and", and in sub-paragraph (4) the words "or section

Chapter	Short Title	Extent of repeal
		233 of the 1972 Act"; in paragraph 3, in sub-paragraph (1) the words "or, as the case may be, paragraph 2 of Schedule 10A to 1972 Act", "or, as the case may be, paragraph 10(2) of Schedule 10A to the 1972 Act" and "or, as the case may be, section 49H of and Schedule 10A to the 1972 Act", and in sub-paragraph (6) the words "or section 42 of the 1972 Act" and "or section 49 of the 1972 Act"; in paragraph 6, in sub-paragraph (2)(f), the words "or (4)", and sub-paragraph (4); paragraph 9(5) to (7); and in paragraph 13, in sub-paragraph (4) the words "and, as respects Scotland, Parts VIII and XI of the 1972 Act" and the words "or, as the case may be, section 42 of the 1972 Act" in both places where they occur, and in sub-paragraph (6) the words "and section 167A of the 1972 Act".

Section 4

SCHEDULE 2

CONSEQUENTIAL AMENDMENTS

The Finance Act 1931 (c. 28)

1.—(1) In section 28(6) of the Finance Act 1931, for "the Town and Country Planning (Scotland) Act 1972" substitute "the Town and Country Planning (Scotland) Act 1997".

(2) In paragraph (viii) of Schedule 2 to that Act, for "section 31(2) of the Town and Country Planning (Scotland) Act 1972" substitute "section 36(1) of the Town and Country Planning (Scotland) Act 1997".

The Mineral Workings Act 1951 (c. 60)

2. In section 41(2A) of the Mineral Workings Act 1951, for "the Town and Country Planning (Scotland) Act 1972" substitute "the Town and Country Planning (Scotland) Act 1997".

The Agricultural Land (Removal of Surface Soil) Act 1953 (c. 10)

3. For section 4 of the Agricultural Land (Removal of Surface Soil) Act 1953 substitute—

"**Application to Scotland**
     4. In the application of this Act to Scotland, for the references to the Town and Country Planning Act 1990, to Part III of that Act and to section 192 of that Act there shall be substituted references to the Town and Country Planning (Scotland) Act 1997, to Part III of that Act and to section 151 of that Act."

The Historic Buildings and Ancient Monuments Act 1953 (c. 49)

4.—(1) In section 5(2A)(a)(i) of the Historic Buildings and Ancient Monuments Act 1953, for "section 262 of the Town and Country Planning (Scotland) Act 1972" substitute "section 61 of the Planning (Listed Buildings and Conservation Areas) (Scotland) Act 1997".

(2) In section 6(1) of that Act, for "section thirty-eight of the Town and Country Planning (Scotland) Act 1947" substitute "section 42 of the Planning (Listed Buildings and Conservation Areas) (Scotland) Act 1997".

The Opencast Coal Act 1958 (c. 69)

5.—(1) In section 7(8) of the Opencast Coal Act 1958, for "the Town and Country Planning (Scotland) Act 1972" substitute "the Town and Country Planning (Scotland) Act 1997".

(2) In section 14A(2) of that Act, for "section 27A(2) of the Town and Country Planning (Scotland) Act 1972" substitute "paragraph 2(2) of Schedule 3 to the Act of 1997".

(3) In section 15(7) of that Act, for "the Town and Country Planning (Scotland) Act 1972" substitute "the Act of 1997".

(4) In section 32(2B)(b) of that Act, for "Part III of the Town and Country Planning (Scotland) Act 1972" substitute "Part III of the Town and Country Planning (Scotland) Act 1997".

(5) In section 52(2) of that Act—

(a) insert at the appropriate place—

""the Act of 1997" means the Town and Country Planning (Scotland) Act 1997"; and

(b) in the definition of "planning permission", for "Act of 1972" substitute "Act of 1997".

The Building (Scotland) Act 1959 (c. 24)

6.—(1) In section 2 of the Building (Scotland) Act 1959—

(a) in subsection (5)(b), for "subsection (2) of section ninety-eight of the Town and Country Planning (Scotland) Act, 1947" substitute "section 274(1) of the Town and Country Planning (Scotland) Act 1997"; and

(b) in subsection (6), for "Subsections (3) and (4) of the said section ninety-eight" substitute "Subsections (2) to (6) of the said section 274".

(2) In section 17(2) of that Act—

(a) in paragraph (b), for "section 56 of the Town and Country Planning (Scotland) Act 1972" substitute "section 3 of the Planning (Listed Buildings and Conservation Areas) (Scotland) Act 1997";

(b) in paragraph (bb), for "section 262A of the said Act of 1972" substitute "section 66 of the said Act of 1997;

(c) in paragraph (c), for "section 52 of the said Act of 1972" substitute "section 1 of the said Act of 1997"; and

(d) for "the said Act of 1972, the said Act of 1947" substitute "the said Act of 1997".

The Town and Country Planning (Scotland) Act 1959 (c. 70)

7.—(1) In section 27(5)(b) of the Town and Country Planning (Scotland) Act 1959, for "section 113 of the Town and Country Planning (Scotland) Act 1972" substitute "section 191 of the Town and Country Planning (Scotland) Act 1997".

(2) In paragraph 2 of Schedule 4 to that Act, for "The Town and Country Planning (Scotland) Act 1972" substitute—

"The Town and Country Planning (Scotland) Act 1997;

The Planning (Listed Buildings and Conservation Areas) (Scotland) Act 1997;".

The Flood Prevention (Scotland) Act 1961 (c. 41)

8.—(1) In section 3(3)(d) of the Flood Prevention (Scotland) Act 1961, for "Part II of the Town and Country Planning (Scotland) Act 1947" substitute "Part III of the Town and Country Planning (Scotland) Act 1997".

(2) In section 15(1) of that Act, in the definition of "statutory undertakers" and "statutory undertaking", for "1947" substitute "1997".

The Land Compensation (Scotland) Act 1963 (c. 51)

9.—(1) In section 15(6) of the Land Compensation (Scotland) Act 1963, for "Schedule 3 to the Town and Country Planning (Scotland) Act 1947" substitute "Schedule 11 to the Town and Country Planning (Scotland) Act 1997".

(2) In section 18 of that Act, for "1947" and "section 42(5)" substitute respectively "1997" and "section 233".

(3) In section 23 of that Act—

(a) in subsection (3), for "Schedule 16 to the Town and Country Planning (Scotland) Act 1972", "paragraph 1 of Schedule 6 to that Act" and "paragraph 2 of Schedule 6 to that Act" substitute respectively "Schedule 12 to the Town and Country Planning (Scotland) Act 1997", "paragraph 1 of Schedule 11 to that Act" and "paragraph 2 of Schedule 11 to that Act"; and

(b) in subsection (4)(c), for "section 24 of the said Act of 1947" and "section 25 of that Act" substitute respectively "section 71 of the said Act of 1997" and "section 83 of that Act".

(4) In section 28 of that Act, for "section 273(1)(c) of the Town and Country Planning (Scotland) Act 1972" substitute "section 275(1)(c) of the Town and Country Planning (Scotland) Act 1997".

(5) In section 31(3)(c) of that Act, for "section 107 of the Town and Country Planning (Scotland) Act 1972" substitute "section 45 of the Planning (Listed Buildings and Conservation Areas) (Scotland) Act 1997".

(6) In section 32(5) of that Act, for "section 34 of the Town and Country Planning (Scotland) Act 1972" substitute "section 47(2) of the Town and Country Planning (Scotland) Act 1997".

(7) In section 38(2) of that Act, for "section 113(1) of the Town and Country Planning (Scotland) Act 1947" substitute "section 277(1) of the Town and Country Planning (Scotland) Act 1997".

(8) In section 44 of that Act, for "Section 100 of the Town and Country Planning (Scotland) Act 1947" and "section 101" substitute respectively "Section 265 of the Town and Country Planning (Scotland) Act 1997" and "section 271".

(9) In section 45 of that Act—

(a) in subsection (1)—

(i) in the definition of "development", for "section 10 of the Town and Country Planning (Scotland) Act 1947" substitute "section 26 of the Town and Country Planning (Scotland) Act 1997";

(ii) in the definition of "development order", for "section 11(1) of the Town and Country Planning (Scotland) Act 1947" substitute "section 30 of the Town and Country Planning (Scotland) Act 1997";

(iii) for the definition of "development plan" substitute—

""development plan" shall be construed in accordance with section 24 of the Town and Country Planning (Scotland) Act 1997;";

(iv) in the definition of "planning authority", for "1947" substitute "1997";

(v) in the definition of "planning decision", for "Part II of the Town and Country Planning (Scotland) Act 1947" substitute "Part III of the Town and Country Planning (Scotland) Act 1997"; and

(vi) in the definition of "planning permission", for "Part II of the Town and Country Planning (Scotland) Act 1947" substitute "Part III of the Town and Country Planning (Scotland) Act 1997"; and

(b) in subsection (3)—

(i) in paragraph (c), for "section 14(3) of the Town and Country Planning (Scotland) Act 1947" substitute "section 47(2) of the Town and Country Planning (Scotland) Act 1997"; and

(ii) in paragraph (d), for "section 14(3) of the Town and Country Planning (Scotland) Act 1947" substitute "section 47(4) and (5) of the Town and Country Planning (Scotland) Act 1997".

(10) In Schedule 2 to that Act—

(a) in paragraph 1—

(i) in sub-paragraph (2)(a), for "Part VI of the Town and Country Planning (Scotland) Act 1972" substitute "Part VIII of the Town and Country Planning (Scotland) Act 1997 or sections 42 to 47 of the Planning (Listed Buildings and Conservation Areas) (Scotland) Act 1997"; and

(ii) in sub-paragraph (2)(c), for "Part IX of the Town and Country Planning (Scotland) Act 1972" substitute "Part V of the Town and Country Planning (Scotland) Act 1997 or sections 28 to 33 of the Planning (Listed Buildings and Conservation Areas) (Scotland) Act 1997"; and

(b) in paragraph 2(1)(b)—

(i) for "section 170 of the Town and Country Planning (Scotland) Act 1972" substitute "section 90 of the Town and Country Planning (Scotland) Act 1997"; and

(ii) for "section 182 of the Town and Country Planning (Scotland) Act 1972" substitute "section 101 of the Town and Country Planning (Scotland) Act 1997".

The Gas Act 1965 (c. 36)

10.—(1) In section 4(7) of the Gas Act 1965—

(a) for "the Town and Country Planning (Scotland) Act 1972" substitute "the Town and Country Planning (Scotland) Act 1997"; and

(b) for "section 37" substitute "section 57".

(2) In section 28(1) of that Act—

(a) in the definition of "planning authority", for "section 1 of the Town and Country Planning (Scotland) Act 1972" substitute "section 277(1) of the Town and Country Planning (Scotland) Act 1997"; and

(b) in the definition of "planning permission", for "Part III of the Town and Country Planning (Scotland) Act 1972" substitute "Part III of the Town and Country Planning (Scotland) Act 1997 (other than sections 55 and 56)".

(3) In Schedule 3 to that Act, in paragraph 7(2), for "the Town and Country Planning (Scotland) Act 1972" substitute "the Town and Country Planning (Scotland) Act 1997".

The Local Government (Scotland) Act 1966 (c. 51)

11.—(1) In section 35(1) of the Local Government (Scotland) Act 1966, for "section 113(1) of the Town and Country Planning (Scotland) Act 1947" substitute "section 277(1) of the Town and Country Planning (Scotland) Act 1997".

(2) In section 41 of that Act, for "the Town and Country Planning (Scotland) Act 1972" substitute "the Town and Country Planning (Scotland) Act 1997".

The Land Commission Act 1967 (c. 1)

12.—(1) In section 15 of the Land Commission Act 1967, for the words set out in the first column below (in each place where they occur in that section) substitute the words set out opposite them in the second column—

"of the Act of 1972"	"of the Act of 1997"
"section 117"	"section 196"
"sections 219 and 220"	"sections 224, 225 and 227"
"sections 226(2) and 227"	"sections 232(2) and 233"
"section 102"	"section 189 of that Act"
"section 219(1)"	"section 224(3) or 225(3)"

(2) In section 58(3) of that Act, for "section 275(1) of the Act of 1972" substitute "section 217 of the Act of 1997".

(3) In section 89(6)(b) of that Act, for "section 275(1) of the Act of 1972" substitute "section 217 of the Act of 1997".

(4) In section 99 of that Act—
(a) in subsection (1), for the definition of "the Act of 1972" substitute—
""the Act of 1997" means the Town and Country Planning (Scotland) Act 1997";
(b) in subsection (2)(b), for "any of paragraphs 1, 2, 3 and 5 to 9 of Schedule 6 to the Act of 1972, as read with Part III of that Schedule" substitute "paragraph 1 or 2 of Schedule 11 to the Act of 1997 as read with paragraphs 3 to 6 of that Schedule"; and
(c) in subsection (8), for "and section 275(1) (interpretation) of the Act of 1972" substitute "and section 277(1) (interpretation) of the Act of 1997".

(5) In Schedule 15 to that Act, in paragraph (viii), for "section 31 of the Town and Country Planning (Scotland) Act 1972" substitute "section 36 of the Town and Country Planning (Scotland) Act 1997".

(6) In Schedule 16 to that Act, in Part II, for "section 118 of the Act of 1972" and "said section 118" substitute respectively "section 197 of the Act of 1997" and "said section 196".

The Forestry Act 1967 (c. 10)

13.—(1) In section 9(4)(d) of the Forestry Act 1967, for "the Town and Country Planning (Scotland) Act 1972" substitute "the Town and Country Planning (Scotland) Act 1997".

(2) In section 35 of that Act, in the definition of "tree preservation order", for "section 58 of the Town and Country Planning (Scotland) Act 1972" substitute "section 160 of the Town and Country Planning (Scotland) Act 1997".

(3) In Schedule 3 to that Act—
(a) in paragraph 2, for "section 32 of the Town and Country Planning (Scotland) Act 1972" and "the said section 32" substitute respectively "section 46 of the Town and Country Planning (Scotland) Act 1997" and "the said section 46"; and
(b) in paragraph 3, for "the Town and Country Planning (Scotland) Act 1972" substitute "the Town and Country Planning (Scotland) Act 1997".

The Agriculture Act 1967 (c. 22)

14.—(1) In section 50(3)(b) of the Agriculture Act 1967, for "section 275(1) of the Town and Country Planning (Scotland) Act 1972" substitute "section 214 of the Town and Country Planning (Scotland) Act 1997".

(2) In section 52(2)(g) of that Act, for "the Town and Country Planning (Scotland) Act 1972" substitute "the Town and Country Planning (Scotland) Act 1997".

The Countryside (Scotland) Act 1967 (c. 86)

15.—(1) In the proviso to section 11(5) of the Countryside (Scotland) Act 1967, for "1947" substitute "1997".

(2) In section 38(6) of that Act, for "section 113(1) of the Act of 1947" substitute "section 217 of the Act of 1997".

(3) In section 73(5), for "section 83 of the Act of 1947" and "subsection (6)" substitute respectively "section 242 of the Act of 1997" and "subsection (3)".

(4) In section 76—

(a) in subsection (1), for "Section 50 of the Town and Country Planning (Scotland) Act 1945" substitute "section 265 of the Town and Country Planning (Scotland) Act 1997"; and

(b) in subsection (2), for "Section 101 of the Act of 1947" substitute "Section 271 of the Act of 1997".

(5) In section 78(1)—

(a) for the definition of "the Act of 1947" substitute—

""the Act of 1997" means the Town and Country Planning (Scotland) Act 1997;";

(b) in the definition of "enactment", for "the Act of 1947" substitute "the Act of 1997"; and

(c) in the definition of "statutory undertakers" and "statutory undertaking", for "section 113 of the Act of 1947" substitute "section 217 of the Act of 1997".

The Caravan Sites Act 1968 (c. 52)

16. In section 16 of the Caravan Sites Act 1968, as it applies in Scotland, in the definition of "planning permission", for "1972" substitute "1997".

The Transport Act 1968 (c. 73)

17.—(1) In section 108 of the Transport Act 1968—

(a) in subsection (2)—

(i) for paragraph (b) substitute—

"(b) land to which section 179 of the Town and Country Planning (Scotland) Act 1997 applies;"; and

(ii) for "the said Act of 1972" and "the said section 63" substitute respectively "the said Act of 1997" and "the said section 179"; and

(b) in subsection (3), for the words from "Part II" to "1947; and" substitute "Part II of the Town and Country Planning (Scotland) Act 1947; and".

(2) In section 112(3)(d) of that Act, for "section 63 of the Town and Country Planning (Scotland) Act 1972" substitute "section 179 of the Town and Country Planning (Scotland) Act 1997".

(3) In section 141(2) of that Act, for "section 275(1) of the Town and Country Planning (Scotland) Act 1972" substitute "section 214 of the Town and Country Planning (Scotland) Act 1997".

The Finance Act 1969 (c. 32)

18. In the Table in section 58(4)(c) of the Finance Act 1969, in the entry relating to the Town and Country Planning (Scotland) Act 1972—

(a) in the first column, for "section 172(3) of the Local Government (Scotland) Act 1973" substitute "section 1 of the Town and Country Planning (Scotland) Act 1997"; and

(b) in the second column, for "1972" substitute "1997".

The Post Office Act 1969 (c. 48)

19.—(1) In section 58(2) of the Post Office Act 1969—

(a) for "Sections 265(8) and 266(1) to (3) and (6) of the Town and Country Planning (Scotland) Act 1972" substitute "Sections 269(6) and 270(1) to (5), (8) and (9) of the Town and Country Planning (Scotland) Act 1997";

(b) for "the said section 265" substitute "the said section 269";

(c) in paragraph (a), for "section 266(1)" substitute "section 270(1)"; and

(d) in paragraph (b), for "section 265(8)" and "therein" substitute respectively "section 269(6)" and "in it".

(2) In Schedule 9 to that Act—

(a) in paragraph 27—

(i) in sub-paragraph (7) (as it applies in Scotland), for "Part XII of the Town and Country Planning (Scotland) Act 1972" substitute "Part XII of the Town and Country Planning (Scotland) Act 1997";

(ii) in sub-paragraph (9) (as it applies in Scotland), for "section 31 of the Town and Country Planning (Scotland) Act 1972" substitute "section 36 of the Town and Country Planning (Scotland) Act 1997";

(iii) in sub-paragraph (12)(a), for "the Town and Country Planning (Scotland) Act 1972" substitute "the Town and Country Planning (Scotland) Act 1997";

(iv) in sub-paragraph (14), for "sections 38 and 39 of the Town and Country Planning (Scotland) Act 1972" substitute "sections 58 and 59 of the Town and Country Planning (Scotland) Act 1997"; and

(v) in sub-paragraph (15) (as it applies in Scotland), for "Subsections (5) and (7) of section 40 of the Town and Country Planning (Scotland) Act 1972" and "sections 38 and 39 of that Act" substitute respectively "Subsections (2) and (4) of section 60 of the Town and Country Planning (Scotland) Act 1997" and "sections 58 and 59 of that Act";

(b) in paragraph 28—
    (i) in sub-paragraph (1), for "section 253 of the Town and Country Planning (Scotland) Act 1972" and "section 24 of the said Act of 1972" substitute respectively "section 245 of the Town and Country Planning (Scotland) Act 1997" and "section 35 of the Act of 1997"; and
    (ii) in sub-paragraph (2), for "the said Act of 1972" substitute "the said Act of 1997"; and

(c) in paragraph 29, for "paragraph 28 of Schedule 22 to the Town and Country Planning (Scotland) Act 1972" and "section 84 of the said Act of 1972" substitute respectively "paragraph 28 of Schedule 22 to the Town and Country Planning (Scotland) Act 1972 (as it continues in effect by virtue of Schedule 3 to the Planning (Consequential Provisions) (Scotland) Act 1997)" and "section 127 of the Town and Country Planning (Scotland) Act 1997".

The Employment and Training Act 1973 (c. 50)

20. In section 4 of the Employment and Training Act 1973—
(a) in subsection (3)(e), for "the Town and Country Planning (Scotland) Act 1972" substitute "a planning authority within the meaning of the Town and Country Planning (Scotland) Act 1997"; and
(b) in subsection (5)(d), for "1972" substitute "1997".

The Land Compensation (Scotland) Act 1973 (c. 56)

21.—(1) In section 2(6) of the Land Compensation (Scotland) Act 1973—
(a) for "section 181(4)(a) of the Town and Country Planning (Scotland) Act 1972" substitute "section 100(3)(a) of the Town and Country Planning (Scotland) Act 1997";
(b) for "section 196" substitute "section 122"; and
(c) for "section 182" substitute "section 101".
(2) In section 5 of that Act—
(a) in subsection (2)—
    (i) in paragraph (a), for "Schedule 16 to the Town and Country Planning (Scotland) Act 1972" and "paragraph 1 of Schedule 6" substitute respectively "Schedule 12 to the Town and Country Planning (Scotland) Act 1997" and "paragraph 1 of Schedule 11"; and
    (ii) in paragraph (b), for "paragraph 2 of Schedule 6" substitute "paragraph 2 of Schedule 11";
(b) in subsection (3)(c), for "section 49 of the said Act of 1972" and "section 159" substitute respectively "section 71 of or paragraph 1 of Schedule 8 to the said Act of 1997" and "section 83"; and
(c) in subsection (5), for "the said Act of 1972" substitute "the said Act of 1997".
(3) In section 24 of that Act—
(a) in subsection (2A), for the words from "subsections (3)" to "1972" substitute "section 100(2) (interests qualifying for protection under blight provisions) of the Town and Country Planning (Scotland) Act 1997";
(b) in subsection (2B), for "subsection (1) of the said section 181" substitute "Schedule 14 to the said Act of 1997"; and
(c) in subsection (6), for "section 275(1) of the Town and Country Planning (Scotland) Act 1972" substitute "section 214 of the Town and Country Planning (Scotland) Act 1997".
(4) In section 36(2) of that Act, for "section 181 of the Town and Country Planning (Scotland) Act 1972" substitute "section 100 of the Town and Country Planning (Scotland) Act 1997".
(5) In section 43(2) of that Act, for "section 181(4)(a) of the Town and Country Planning (Scotland) Act 1972", "section 196" and "section 182" substitute respectively "section 100(3)(a) of the Town and Country Planning (Scotland) Act 1997", "section 122" and "section 101".
(6) In section 46(4) of that Act, for "Schedule 24 to the Town and Country Planning (Scotland) Act 1972" substitute "Schedule 15 to the Town and Country Planning (Scotland) Act 1997".
(7) In section 47(6)(b) of that Act, for "the Town and Country Planning (Scotland) Act 1972" substitute "the Town and Country Planning (Scotland) Act 1997".

(8) In section 49 of that Act—

(a) in subsection (4), after "(3) above" insert "or such a notice is deemed to have been served by virtue of sections 88 to 95 of the Town and Country Planning (Scotland) Act 1997"; and

(b) in subsection (5)—

(i) omit the words from "sections 169" to "or"; and

(ii) for "Schedule 24 to the said Act of 1972" substitute "Schedule 15 to the Town and Country Planning (Scotland) Act 1997".

(9) In section 51(1) of that Act, for "paragraph 8 of Schedule 24 to the Town and Country Planning (Scotland) Act 1972" substitute "paragraph 15 of Schedule 15 to the Town and Country Planning (Scotland) Act 1997".

(10) In section 54(1) of that Act, for "section 191(2) of, or paragraph 26 of Schedule 24 to, the Town and Country Planning (Scotland) Act 1972" substitute "section 117(2) of, or paragraph 26 of Schedule 15 to, the Town and Country Planning (Scotland) Act 1997".

(11) In section 55(7) of that Act, for "section 253(7) of the Town and Country Planning (Scotland) Act 1972" substitute "section 242(1) of the Town and Country Planning (Scotland) Act 1997".

(12) In section 80(1) of that Act, in the definition of "agricultural unit", for "section 196(1) of the Town and Country Planning (Scotland) Act 1972" substitute "section 122 of the Town and Country Planning (Scotland) Act 1997".

The Local Government (Scotland) Act 1973 (c. 65)

22. In the definition of "protected informant" in paragraph 1(1) of Part III of Schedule 7A to the Local Government (Scotland) Act 1973, for "as defined in section 84(2) of the Town and Country Planning (Scotland) Act 1972" substitute "within the meaning of section 123(1) of the Town and Country Planning (Scotland) Act 1997".

The Control of Pollution Act 1974 (c. 40)

23.—(1) In section 5(2) of the Control of Pollution Act 1974, for "the Town and Country Planning (Scotland) Act 1972" substitute "the Town and Country Planning (Scotland) Act 1997".

2. In section 105(3) of that Act, for "subsection (7) of section 253 of the Town and Country Planning (Scotland) Act 1972" substitute "subsections (1) to (3) of section 242 of the Town and Country Planning (Scotland) Act 1997".

The Offshore Petroleum Development (Scotland) Act 1975 (c. 8)

24.—(1) In section 1(9) of the Offshore Petroleum Development (Scotland) Act 1975—

(a) in paragraph (a), for "Part III of the Town and Country Planning (Scotland) Act 1972" substitute "Part III of the Town and Country Planning (Scotland) Act 1997"; and

(b) in paragraph (b), for "section 21" substitute "section 30".

(2) In section 2 of that Act—

(a) in subsection (1)—

(i) for "section 108 of the Town and Country Planning (Scotland) Act 1972" substitute "section 194 of the Town and Country Planning (Scotland) Act 1997"; and

(ii) for "Part VI" in both places where those words occur substitute "Part VIII";

(b) in subsection (2)—

(i) for "the Town and Country Planning (Scotland) Act 1972" substitute "the Town and Country Planning (Scotland) Act 1997"; and

(ii) for "section 117 of the said Act of 1972" substitute "section 196 of the said Act of 1997";

(c) in subsection (3)—

(i) in paragraph (a), for "section 117 of the said Act of 1972" substitute "section 196 of the said Act of 1997";

(ii) in paragraph (b), for "section 118" substitute "section 197"; and

(iii) in paragraph (c), for "section 119" substitute "section 198"; and

(d) in subsection (4)—

(i) for "sections 219 and 220 of the said Act of 1972" substitute "sections 224 and 227 of the said Act of 1997";

(ii) for "sections 226(2) and 227" substitute "sections 232(2) and 233";

(iii) for "of sections 219 and 220" substitute "of sections 224 and 227"; and

(iv) for "the said section 219" substitute "the said section 224".

(3) In section 9(3)(b) of that Act, for "section 32 of the Town and Country Planning (Scotland) Act 1972" substitute "section 46 of the Town and Country Planning (Scotland) Act 1997".

(4) In section 15(2) of that Act, for "sections 265(8) and 266 of the Town and Country Planning (Scotland) Act 1972" and "section 265 of that Act" substitute respectively "sections 269(6) and 270 of the Town and Country Planning (Scotland) Act 1997" and "section 269".

(5) In section 16(3)(a) of that Act, for "Schedule 24 to the Town and Country Planning (Scotland) Act 1972" substitute "Schedule 15 to the Town and Country Planning (Scotland) Act 1997".

(6) In Schedule 2 to that Act—

(a) in paragraph 1(2), for "section 278 of the Town and Country Planning (Scotland) Act 1972 and Schedule 24" substitute "section 195 of the Town and Country Planning (Scotland) Act 1997 and Schedule 15";

(b) in paragraph 3(1)(b), for "Schedule 24 to the Town and Country Planning (Scotland) Act 1972" substitute "Schedule 15 to the Town and Country Planning (Scotland) Act 1997"; and

(c) in paragraph 4(1), for "Schedule 24 to the Town and Country Planning (Scotland) Act 1972" substitute "Schedule 15 to the Town and Country Planning (Scotland) Act 1997".

The House of Commons Disqualification Act 1975 (c. 24)

25. In Part II of Schedule 1 to the House of Commons Disqualification Act 1975, in the second entry relating to "A Planning Inquiry Commission", for "Part III of the Town and Country Planning (Scotland) Act 1972" substitute "Part III of the Town and Country Planning (Scotland) Act 1997".

The Race Relations Act 1976 (c. 74)

26. In section 19A(3)(b) of the Race Relations Act 1976, for "the Town and Country Planning (Scotland) Act 1972" substitute "the Town and Country Planning (Scotland) Act 1997, the Planning (Listed Buildings and Conservation Areas) (Scotland) Act 1997 and the Planning (Hazardous Substances) (Scotland) Act 1997".

The Refuse Disposal (Amenity) Act 1978 (c. 3)

27. In section 8 of the Refuse Disposal (Amenity) Act 1978—

(a) in subsection (2) as substituted by subsection (4)—

(i) for "Section 266(1) to (5) of the Town and Country Planning (Scotland) Act 1972" substitute "Section 270(1) to (7) of the Town and Country Planning (Scotland) Act 1997"; and

(ii) for "section 265", in both places where those words occur, substitute "section 269"; and

(b) in subsection (3), as substituted by subsection (4), for "Sections 267 to 270 of the said Act of 1972" substitute "Sections 265 to 268, 271 and 272 of the said Act of 1997".

The Estate Agents Act 1979 (c. 38)

28. In section 1(2)(e) of the Estate Agents Act 1979, for "the Town and Country Planning (Scotland) Act 1972" substitute "the Town and Country Planning (Scotland) Act 1997, the Planning (Listed Buildings and Conservation Areas) (Scotland) Act 1997, the Planning (Hazardous Substances) (Scotland) Act 1997".

The Ancient Monuments and Archaeological Areas Act 1979 (c. 46)

29.—(1) In section 32(1) of the Ancient Monuments and Archaeological Areas Act 1979—

(a) for "the Town and Country Planning (Scotland) Act 1972" substitute "the Town and Country Planning (Scotland) Act 1997 or the Planning (Listed Buildings and Conservation Areas) (Scotland) Act 1997"; and

(b) for "the said Act of 1972" substitute "the said Acts of 1997".

(2) In section 61 of that Act, in the definition of "works" in subsection (1) and in subsection (2)(b), for "the Town and Country Planning (Scotland) Act 1972" substitute "the Town and Country Planning (Scotland) Act 1997".

The Water (Scotland) Act 1980 (c. 45)

30.—(1) In section 10(5)(a) of the Water (Scotland) Act 1980, for "section 275(1) of the Town and Country Planning (Scotland) Act 1972" substitute "section 214 of the Town and Country Planning (Scotland) Act 1997".

(2) In section 110A of that Act—

(a) in subsection (7), in the definition of "the appropriate authority", for "section 253(7) of the Town and Country Planning (Scotland) Act 1972" substitute "section 242(2) of the Town and Country Planning (Scotland) Act 1997"; and

(b) in subsection (8), for "subsection (7) of section 253 of the Town and Country Planning (Scotland) Act 1972" substitute "subsection (3) of section 242 of the Town and Country Planning (Scotland) Act 1997".

The Local Government, Planning and Land Act 1980 (c. 65)

31.—(1) In section 3(5)(c) of the Local Government, Planning and Land Act 1980, for "the Town and Country Planning (Scotland) Act 1972" substitute "the Town and Country Planning (Scotland) Act 1997".

(2) In section 120(3) of that Act, in paragraph (b) of the definition of "statutory undertakers", for "the Town and Country Planning (Scotland) Act 1972" substitute "the Town and Country Planning (Scotland) Act 1997".

(3) In section 122 of that Act, in each of subsections (1), (2), (3), (6) and (8), for "sections" substitute "section".

(4) In section 141(4) of that Act, for "section 278 of the Town and Country Planning (Scotland) Act 1972" substitute "section 195 of the Town and Country Planning (Scotland) Act 1997".

(5) In section 148 of that Act—

(a) in subsection (2), for "section 21 of the 1972 Act" substitute "sections 30 and 31 of the 1997 Act"; and

(b) in subsection (3), for "section 52(1) of the 1972 Act" substitute "section 1 of the Planning (Listed Buildings and Conservation Areas) (Scotland) Act 1997".

(6) In section 149 of that Act—

(a) in subsection (6), for the words from "Part III" to "1973)" substitute "Part III of the 1997 Act";

(b) in subsection (8)(a), for "the 1972 Act" substitute "the 1997 Act and the Planning (Listed Buildings and Conservation Areas) (Scotland) Act 1997"; and

(c) in subsection (8)(b), for "the 1972 Act" substitute "those Acts".

(7) In section 170 of that Act—

(a) in subsection (1)(b), for "the 1972 Act" substitute "the 1997 Act"; and

(b) in subsection (3)(a), for "Part XI of the 1972 Act" and "the said Part XI" substitute respectively "Part X of the 1997 Act" and "the said Part X".

(8) In section 171 of that Act, for "1972" in both places where it occurs substitute "1997".

(9) In paragraph 15 of Schedule 27 to that Act, for "Schedule 24 to the Town and Country Planning (Scotland) Act 1972" substitute "Schedule 15 to the Town and Country Planning (Scotland) Act 1997".

(10) In Schedule 28 to that Act—

(a) in paragraph 8, for "Section 118 of the 1972 Act" substitute "Section 197 of the 1997 Act";

(b) in paragraph 11(2)(b)(i), for the words from "exercising" to "1973" substitute "within the meaning of section 1 of the 1997 Act";

(c) in paragraph 14(6), for "sections 227 and 229 of the 1972 Act" and "section 226(2) of the 1972 Act" substitute respectively "sections 233 and 235 of the 1997 Act" and "section 232(2) of the 1997 Act"; and

(d) in paragraph 16(8), for "sections 227 and 229 of the 1972 Act" and "section 226(3) of the 1972 Act" substitute respectively "sections 233 and 235 of the 1997 Act" and "section 232(4) of the 1997 Act".

(11) In Schedule 30 to that Act, for the enactments referred to in Part I substitute—

"Sections 125, 127 to 129, 135, 140, 141, 147, 159 to 161, 163, 167, 168, 170, 172, 174, 175, 179, 182 and 186 of the 1997 Act.

Sections 3, 4, 7, 9, 12 to 14, 20 to 24, 34, 38, 42, 43, 45, 48(1), 49, 61 to 64, 66, 73(2) to (4) and 77 of the Planning (Listed Buildings and Conservation Areas) (Scotland) Act 1997."

(12) For paragraphs 1 to 9 of Part II of that Schedule substitute—

"1. Section 90 of the 1997 Act shall have effect as if after "undertakers" there were inserted—

(a) in subsection (1)(b), "or an urban development corporation";

(b) in subsection (1)(c), "or any urban development corporation"; and

(c) in subsection (3), "or urban development corporation".

2. Section 91(2)(c) of that Act shall have effect as if, after "undertakers", there were inserted "or an urban development corporation".

3. Section 92(4) of that Act shall have effect as if, after "undertakers" in the first and second places where it occurs, there were inserted respectively "or an urban development corporation" and "or that corporation".

4. Section 94(1)(b) of that Act shall have effect as if, after "undertakers" in the first and second places where it occurs, there were inserted respectively "or an urban development corporation" and "or that corporation".

5. The definition of "relevant provisions" in section 99 of that Act shall have effect as if, after "undertaking", there were added "or, in the case of an urban development corporation, section 142 of the Local Government, Planning and Land Act 1980".

6. Section 203 of that Act shall have effect as if—

(a) in subsection (1), after "applies" there were inserted "subject to subsection (1A)"; and

(b) the following subsection were inserted after that subsection—

"(1A) Any reference in this section and in section 203 to a competent authority is to be construed as including a reference to an urban development corporation."

7. Section 205 of that Act shall have effect as if, after "authorities", there were inserted "and, in an urban development area, the urban development corporation".

8. Section 206 of that Act shall have effect as if—

(a) in subsection (1), for "Where" there were substituted "Subject to subsection (1A), where"; and

(b) the following subsection were inserted after that subsection—

"(1A) Where any land has been acquired by an urban development corporation or has vested in such a corporation and is for the time being held by them for the purpose of regenerating their area—

(a) the Secretary of State may by order extinguish any public right of way over the land if he is satisfied that an alternative right of way has been or will be provided or that the provision of an alternative right of way is not required;

(b) subject to paragraphs 4 and 5 of Schedule 16 to this Act, the urban development corporation may by order extinguish any such right over the land, being a footpath or bridleway, if they are so satisfied."

9. Section 272 of that Act shall have effect as if, in subsection (1), after "local authority" there were inserted "or an urban development corporation".

10. Section 29 of the Planning (Listed Buildings and Conservation Areas) (Scotland) Act 1997 shall have effect as if—

(a) in subsection (1)(b) and (c), after "undertakers" there were inserted "or an urban development corporation"; and

(b) in subsection (3), after "undertakers" there were inserted "or corporation",

11. Section 30 of that Act shall have effect as if—

(a) in subsection (2)(c), after "undertakers" there were inserted "or an urban development corporation"; and

(b) in each of subsections (3), (4) and (5), after "undertakers" there were inserted "or corporation".

12. Section 31(6) of that Act shall have effect as if after "undertakers" there were inserted "or an urban development corporation".

13. Section 32(4) of that Act shall have effect as if after "undertakers" in the first and second places where it occurs there were inserted respectively "or an urban development corporation" and "or that corporation".

14. Section 81(2) of that Act shall have effect as if "urban development corporation" were inserted in the appropriate place."

(13) In Schedule 32 to that Act—

(a) in paragraph 7(3), for "subsection (8) of section 265 and subsections (1) to (6) of section 266 of the 1972 Act" and "to section 265" substitute respectively "subsection (6) of section 269 and section 270 of the 1997 Act" and "to section 269";

(b) in paragraph 8, for "1972", in both places where it occurs, substitute "1997"; and

(c) in paragraph 26—

(i) in sub-paragraph (1), for "the 1972 Act", in the first place where those words occur, substitute "the 1997 Act, the Planning (Listed Buildings and Conservation Areas) (Scotland) Act 1997 or the Planning (Hazardous Substances) (Scotland) Act 1997";

(ii) in that sub-paragraph, for the definition of "the 1972 Act" substitute—

""the 1997 Act" means the Town and Country Planning (Scotland) Act 1997"; and

(iii) in sub-paragraph (2)(b), for "1972" substitute "1997".

The Zoo Licensing Act 1981 (c. 37)

32. In section 4(6) of the Zoo Licensing Act 1981, for "the Town and Country Planning (Scotland) Act 1972" and "1972" substitute respectively "the Town and Country Planning (Scotland) Act 1997" and "1997".

The Transport Act 1981 (c. 56)

33. In paragraph 9 of Schedule 4 to the Transport Act 1981, for "section 275(1) of the Town and Country Planning (Scotland) Act 1972" substitute "section 214 of the Town and Country Planning (Scotland) Act 1997".

The Wildlife and Countryside Act 1981 (c. 69)

34.—(1) In sections 28(8)(a), 29(9)(a) and 34(5) of the Wildlife and Countryside Act 1981, for "Part III of the Town and Country Planning (Scotland) Act 1972" substitute "Part III of the Town and Country Planning (Scotland) Act 1997".

(2) In section 70A(1) of that Act, for "section 269 of the Town and Country Planning (Scotland) Act 1972" substitute "section 271 of the Town and Country Planning (Scotland) Act 1997".

The Civil Aviation Act 1982 (c. 16)

35.—(1) In section 48(9) of the Civil Aviation Act 1982, for "subsections (1) and (2) of section 209 of the Town and Country Planning (Scotland) Act 1972" and "section 198 of the said Act of 1972" substitute respectively "subsections (1) to (4) of section 212 of the Town and Country Planning (Scotland) Act 1997" and "section 202 of the said Act of 1997".

(2) In section 51 of that Act—

(a) in subsection (2)(b), for "section 227(2), (3), (5) and (6) of the Town and Country Planning (Scotland) Act 1972" substitute "section 233(2) to (5), (7) and (8) of the Town and Country Planning (Scotland) Act 1997";

(b) in subsection (5)—

(i) for "subsections (2), (3), (5) and (6) of the said section 227" substitute "subsections (2) to (5), (7) and (8) of the said section 233";

(ii) in paragraph (a), for "section 227" and "section 226(2)" substitute respectively "section 233" and "section 232(2) or (3)"; and

(iii) in paragraph (c), for "subsection (6) of the said section 227" substitute "subsection (8) of the said section 233"; and

(c) in subsection (7), for "sections 222 to 224 of the Town and Country Planning (Scotland) Act 1972" substitute "sections 228 to 230 of the Town and Country Planning (Scotland) Act 1997".

(3) In section 53 of that Act—

(a) in subsection (1)—

(i) in paragraph (a), for "section 153, 154, 176(2) or 226(1) of the Town and Country Planning (Scotland) Act 1972" substitute "section 76, 77, 95(2) or 232(1) of the Town and Country Planning (Scotland) Act 1997"; and

(ii) in paragraph (b), for "the said section 153" and "section 42 of the said Act of 1972" substitute respectively "the said section 76" and "section 65 of the said Act of 1997";

(b) in subsection (2), for "section 157 of the said Act of 1972" substitute "section 82 of the said Act of 1997";

(c) in subsection (3), for "section 169 of the said Act of 1972" and "section 170(2) or 175(1) of the said Act of 1972" substitute respectively "section 88 of the said Act of 1997" and "section 90(3) or 94(1) of the said Act of 1997";

(d) in subsection (5), for "the said section 42" substitute "the said section 65"; and

(e) in subsection (6), for "the said Act of 1972" substitute "the said Act of 1997".

(4) In section 54 of that Act—

(a) in subsection (1), for "section 118 of the Town and Country Planning (Scotland) Act 1972" and "Part VI of the said Act of 1972" substitute respectively "section 197 of the Town and Country Planning (Scotland) Act 1997" and "Part VIII of the said Act of 1997"; and

(b) in subsection (2), for "and 118" and "Part VI of the said Act of 1972" substitute respectively "and 197" and "Part VIII of the said Act of 1997".

(5) In Schedule 10 to that Act—

(a) in paragraph 4—

(i) for "section 225 of the Town and Country Planning (Scotland) Act 1972" substitute "section 231 of the Town and Country Planning (Scotland) Act 1997";

        (ii) after sub-paragraph (a) insert "and"; and

        (iii) in sub-paragraph (b), for "section 225 to section 222 of the said Act of 1972" substitute "section 231 to section 228 of the said Act of 1997"; and

  (b) in paragraph 8—

        (i) for "section 225 of the Town and Country Planning (Scotland) Act 1972" substitute "section 231 of the Town and Country Planning (Scotland) Act 1997";

        (ii) after sub-paragraph (a) insert "and"; and

        (iii) in sub-paragraph (b), for "section 225 to section 224 of the said Act of 1972" substitute "section 231 to section 230 of the said Act of 1997".

The Mobile Homes Act 1983 (c. 34)

36. In the definition of "planning permission" in section 5(1) of the Mobile Homes Act 1983, for "Part III of the Town and Country Planning (Scotland) Act 1972" substitute "Part III of the Town and Country Planning (Scotland) Act 1997".

The Telecommunications Act 1984 (c. 12)

37.—(1) In section 35(4) of the Telecommunications Act 1984, for "the Town and Country Planning (Scotland) Act 1972", "section 118", "section 119" and "sections 219 to 221" substitute respectively "the Town and Country Planning (Scotland) Act 1997", "section 197", "section 198", and "sections 224 to 227".

(2) In section 38(2) of that Act, for "Sections 265(8) and 266(1) to (3) and (6) of the Town and Country Planning (Scotland) Act 1972", "the said section 265", "section 266(1)" and "section 265(8)" substitute respectively "Sections 269(6) and 270(1) to (5), (8) and (9) of the Town and Country Planning (Scotland) Act 1997", "the said section 269", "section 270(1)" and "section 269(6)".

The Roads (Scotland) Act 1984 (c. 54)

38.—(1) In section 12B(7) of the Roads (Scotland) Act 1984, for "Part III of the Town and Country Planning (Scotland) Act 1972" substitute "Part III of the Town and Country Planning (Scotland) Act 1997".

(2) In section 20A(5)(b) of that Act, for "the said Act of 1972" substitute "the Planning (Listed Buildings and Conservation Areas) (Scotland) Act 1997".

(3) In section 29(2)(c) of that Act, for "Part III of the Town and Country Planning (Scotland) Act 1972" substitute "Part III of the Town and Country Planning (Scotland) Act 1997".

(4) In section 53(5) of that Act, for "section 50 of the Town and Country Planning (Scotland) Act 1972" substitute "section 75 of the Town and Country Planning (Scotland) Act 1997".

(5) In section 83(10) of that Act, for "section 58(1) of the Town and Country Planning (Scotland) Act 1972" substitute "section 160(1) of the Town and Country Planning (Scotland) Act 1997".

(6) In section 91(8)(b)(ii) of that Act, for "section 58(1) of the Town and Country Planning (Scotland) Act 1972" substitute "section 160(1) of the Town and Country Planning (Scotland) Act 1997".

(7) In section 104(1)(b) of that Act, for "section 198, 198A or 201 of the Town and Country Planning (Scotland) Act 1972" and "section 203(1)(a) or (b)" substitute respectively "section 202, 203 or 207 of the Town and Country Planning (Scotland) Act 1997" and "section 206(1)(a) or (b)".

(8) In section 106 of that Act—

  (a) in subsection (2), for "section 181(3) to (5) of the Town and Country Planning (Scotland) Act 1972" and "section 182" substitute respectively "section 100(2) of the Town and Country Planning (Scotland) Act 1997" and "section 101";

  (b) in subsection (2A), for the words from "subsections (3)" to "1972" substitute "section 100(2) (interests qualifying for protection under blight provisions) of the Town and Country Planning (Scotland) Act 1997";

  (c) in subsection (2B), for "subsection (1) of the said section 181" substitute "Schedule 14 to the said Act of 1997";

  (d) in subsection (7), for "section 181(1)(e) of the Town and Country Planning (Scotland) Act 1972" substitute "paragraph 11 of Schedule 14 to the Town and Country Planning (Scotland) Act 1997"; and

  (e) in subsection (8), for "The said section 181" substitute "The said Schedule 14".

(9) In section 117(2) of that Act, for "Section 167(1) and (2) of the Town and Country Planning (Scotland) Act 1972", "Part VIII of that Act" and "the said Part VIII" substitute respectively "Section 87(1) and (2) of the Town and Country Planning (Scotland) Act 1997", "Part IV of that Act" and "the said Part IV".

(10) In section 118 of that Act, for "section 167 of the Town and Country Planning (Scotland) Act 1972" and "the said section 167" substitute respectively "section 87 of the Town and Country Planning (Scotland) Act 1997" and "the said section 87".

(11) In section 119(1) of that Act—

(a) in paragraph (b), for "section 169, 177 or 178 of the Town and Country Planning (Scotland) Act 1972" substitute "section 88 of the Town and Country Planning (Scotland) Act 1997"; and

(b) in paragraph (c), for "section 182 of the said Act of 1972" and "section 185 of the said Act of 1972" substitute respectively "section 101 of the said Act of 1997" and "section 105 of the said Act of 1997".

(12) In section 123 of that Act, for "section 20 of the Town and Country Planning (Scotland) Act 1972" substitute "section 28 of the Town and Country Planning (Scotland) Act 1997".

(13) In section 134 of that Act—

(a) in subsection (1)—

(i) for "section 219 of the Town and Country Planning (Scotland) Act 1972" substitute "section 224 of the Town and Country Planning (Scotland) Act 1997";

(ii) for "Part VI" in both places where it occurs substitute "Part VIII";

(iii) for "sections 220 and 222 to 225 of the said Act of 1972" substitute "sections 227 to 231 of the said Act of 1997"; and

(iv) for "the said section 219" substitute "the said section 224";

(b) in subsection (2), for "the said Act of 1972" substitute "the said Act of 1997"; and

(c) in subsection (3), for "the said section 219" substitute "the said section 224".

(14) In section 135 of that Act—

(a) in subsection (1), for "the Town and Country Planning (Scotland) Act 1972" substitute "the Town and Country Planning (Scotland) Act 1997";

(b) in subsection (2), for "the said Act of 1972" substitute "the said Act of 1997"; and

(c) in subsection (3), for "section 219 of the said Act of 1972" substitute "section 224 of the said Act of 1997".

(15) In section 151(1)—

(a) in the definition of "statutory undertakers", for "section 275 of the Town and Country Planning (Scotland) Act 1972" substitute "section 214 of the Town and Country Planning (Scotland) Act 1997"; and

(b) in the definition of "trunk road", for "section 198(2) of the Town and Country Planning (Scotland) Act 1972" substitute "section 202(3) of the Town and Country Planning (Scotland) Act 1997".

(16) In section 152(4), for "the Town and Country Planning (Scotland) Act 1972" substitute "the Town and Country Planning (Scotland) Act 1997".

The Airports Act 1986 (c. 31)

39.—(1) In section 59(6) of the Airports Act 1986, for "section 118 of the Town and Country Planning (Scotland) Act 1972" and "Part VI of that Act of 1972" substitute respectively "section 197 of the Town and Country Planning (Scotland) Act 1997" and "Part VIII of that Act of 1997".

(2) In section 61 of that Act—

(a) in subsection (1)—

(i) in paragraph (a), for "section 153, 154, 176(2) or 226(1) of the Town and Country Planning (Scotland) Act 1972 ("the 1972 Act")" substitute "section 76, 77, 95(2) or 232(1) of the Town and Country Planning (Scotland) Act 1997 ("the 1997 Act")"; and

(ii) in paragraph (b), for "section 153 of the 1972 Act" and "section 42 of the 1972 Act" substitute respectively "section 76 of the 1997 Act" and "section 65 of the 1997 Act";

(b) in subsection (2), for "section 157 of the 1972 Act" substitute "section 82 of the 1997 Act";

(c) in subsection (3), for "section 169 of the 1972 Act" and "section 170(2) or 175(1) of the 1972 Act" substitute respectively "section 88 of the 1997 Act" and "section 90(3) or 94(1) of the 1997 Act";

(d) in subsection (5), for "section 42 of the 1972 Act" substitute "section 65 of the 1997 Act"; and

(e) in subsection (6), for "the 1972 Act" substitute "the 1997 Act".

The Housing (Scotland) Act 1987 (c. 26)

40.—(1) In section 77(3) of the Housing (Scotland) Act 1987, for "section 278 of the Town and Country Planning (Scotland) Act 1972" substitute "section 195 of the Town and Country Planning (Scotland) Act 1997".

(2) In section 119 of that Act—

(a) in subsection (1), for "section 56 of the Town and Country Planning (Scotland) Act 1972" and "section 52(7)" substitute respectively "sections 3 to 5 of the Planning (Listed Buildings and Conservation Areas) (Scotland) Act 1997" and "section 1(4)"; and

(b) in subsection (2), for "the said section 56" and "the said section 52(7)" substitute respectively "the said sections 3 to 5" and "the said section 1(4)".

(3) In paragraph 3 of Schedule 2 to that Act, for "section 19 of the Town and Country Planning (Scotland) Act 1972" substitute "section 26 of the Town and Country Planning (Scotland) Act 1997".

(4) In Schedule 6 to that Act—

(a) for "*The Town and Country Planning (Scotland) Act 1972 (c. 52)*" substitute "*The Town and Country Planning (Scotland) Act 1997 (c. 8)*"; and

(b) in paragraph 1, for "Schedule 24" substitute "Schedule 15".

(5) In paragraph 1 of Schedule 7 to that Act—

(a) in sub-paragraph (2), for "section 52 of the Town and Country Planning (Scotland) Act 1972" and "section 53 of the said Act of 1972" substitute respectively "section 1 of the Planning (Listed Buildings and Conservation Areas) (Scotland) Act 1997" and "sections 6 to 8 of the said Act of 1997";

(b) in sub-paragraph (4)(a), for "the said section 53" substitute "the said sections 6 to 8";

(c) in sub-paragraph (7)(b), for "Part VI of the Town and Country Planning (Scotland) Act 1972" substitute "Part VIII of the Town and Country Planning (Scotland) Act 1997"; and

(d) in sub-paragraph (8)(b), for "Part VI of the said Act of 1972" substitute "Part VIII of the said Act of 1997".

(6) In paragraph 2 of that Schedule—

(a) in sub-paragraph (1), for "section 52 of the Town and Country Planning (Scotland) Act 1972" and "the said section 53" substitute respectively "section 1 of the Planning (Listed Buildings and Conservation Areas) (Scotland) Act 1997" and "the said sections 6 to 8"; and

(b) in sub-paragraph (3), for "the said section 53" and "Part VI of the Town and Country Planning (Scotland) Act 1972" substitute respectively "the said sections 6 to 8" and "Part VIII of the Town and Country Planning (Scotland) Act 1997".

(7) In paragraph 6 of that Schedule—

(a) in sub-paragraph (2)(b), for "Part VI of the Town and Country Planning (Scotland) Act 1972" substitute "Part VIII of the Town and Country Planning (Scotland) Act 1997"; and

(b) in sub-paragraph (3)(b), for "Part VI of the said Act of 1972" substitute "Part VIII of the said Act of 1997".

(8) In paragraph 13(1) of that Schedule, for "Part VI of the Town and Country Planning (Scotland) Act 1972" and "Part VI of the Act of 1972" substitute respectively "Part VIII of the Town and Country Planning (Scotland) Act 1997" and "Part VIII of the Act of 1997".

The Income and Corporation Taxes Act 1988 (c. 1)

41. In section 91A(7) of the Income and Corporation Taxes Act 1988, for "section 50 of the Town and Country Planning (Scotland) Act 1972" substitute "section 75 of the Town and Country Planning (Scotland) Act 1997".

The Housing (Scotland) Act 1988 (c. 43)

42. In section 2(7) of the Housing (Scotland) Act 1988, for "section 278 of the Town and Country Planning (Scotland) Act 1972" substitute "section 195 of the Town and Country Planning (Scotland) Act 1997".

The Road Traffic (Driver Licensing and Information Systems) Act 1989 (c. 22)

43. In Schedule 4 to the Road Traffic (Driver Licensing and Information Systems) Act 1989, in paragraph 2, for "Section 219 of the Town and Country Planning (Scotland) Act 1972" and "the 1972 Act" substitute respectively "Section 224 of the Town and Country Planning (Scotland) Act 1997" and "the 1997 Act".

The Electricity Act 1989 (c. 29)

44.—(1) In paragraph 2(5) of Schedule 3 to the Electricity Act 1989, for "the Town and Country Planning (Scotland) Act 1972" substitute "the Town and Country Planning (Scotland) Act 1997".

(2) In paragraph 12 of Schedule 4 to that Act, for "the Town and Country Planning (Scotland) Act 1972" substitute "the Town and Country Planning (Scotland) Act 1997".

The Capital Allowances Act 1990 (c. 1)

45. In section 121(1) of the Capital Allowances Act 1990, in the definition of "the relevant planning enactment", for "section 275(1) of the Town and Country Planning (Scotland) Act 1972" substitute "section 277(1) of the Town and Country Planning (Scotland) Act 1997".

The National Health Service and Community Care Act 1990 (c. 19)

46.—(1) In paragraph 24 of Schedule 6 to the National Health Service and Community Care Act 1990, for "section 118 of the Town and Country Planning (Scotland) Act 1972" substitute "section 197 of the Town and Country Planning (Scotland) Act 1997".

(2) In paragraph 17(2) and (3) of Schedule 8 to that Act, for "the Town and Country Planning (Scotland) Act 1972" in each place where those words occur substitute "the Town and Country Planning (Scotland) Act 1997".

The Enterprise and New Towns (Scotland) Act 1931 (c. 35)

47.—(1) In section 8(13) of the Enterprise and New Towns (Scotland) Act 1990, for "section 278 of the Town and Country Planning (Scotland) Act 1972" substitute "section 195 of the Town and Country Planning (Scotland) Act 1997".

(2) In section 9(5) of that Act, for the words from "sections 213" to the end substitute "sections 217 and 214 of the Town and Country Planning (Scotland) Act 1997".

(3) In section 12(5)(e) of that Act, for "the Town and Country Planning (Scotland) Act 1972" substitute "the Town and Country Planning (Scotland) Act 1997".

(4) In section 36(3) of that Act, for "section 278 of, and Schedule 24 to, the Town and Country Planning (Scotland) Act 1972" substitute "section 195 of, and Schedule 15 to, the Town and Country Planning (Scotland) Act 1997".

The Natural Heritage (Scotland) Act 1991 (c. 28)

48.—(1) In section 2(2) of the Natural Heritage (Scotland) Act 1991, for "the Town and Country Planning (Scotland) Act 1972" substitute "the Town and Country Planning (Scotland) Act 1997, the Planning (Listed Buildings and Conservation Areas) (Scotland) Act 1997 and the Planning (Hazardous Substances) (Scotland) Act 1997".

(2) In section 7(5A), for the words from "section 213(1)" to the end substitute "section 217 of the Town and Country Planning (Scotland) Act 1997".

The Planning and Compensation Act 1991 (c. 34)

49.—(1) In section 78(1)(b) of the Planning and Compensation Act 1991, for "Schedule 24 to the Town and Country Planning (Scotland) Act 1972" substitute "Schedule 15 to the Town and Country Planning (Scotland) Act 1997".

(2) In Part I of Schedule 18 to that Act, for the entries relating to the 1972 Act substitute the following—

"Section 76 of the Town and Country Planning (Scotland) Act 1997	Date of order under section 65
Section 77 of that Act	Date permission is refused or granted subject to conditions
Section 83 of that Act	Date damage suffered or expenses incurred
Section 95 of that Act	Date of direction under section 92(3)
Section 143 of that Act	Date of service of stop notice
Section 165 of that Act	Date consent required by tree preservation order is refused or granted subject to conditions
Section 166 of that Act	Date requirement is imposed by planning authority or Secretary of State
Section 185 of that Act	Date expenses incurred
Section 204(1) of that Act	Date on which order takes effect
Section 232 of that Act	Date planning permission refused or granted subject to conditions

Paragraph 1 of Schedule 13 to that Act	Date order made
Section 25 of the Planning (Listed Buildings and Conservation Areas) (Scotland) Act 1997	Date of order under section 21
Section 26 of that Act	Date building preservation notice served
Section 14 of the Planning (Hazardous Substances) (Scotland) Act 1997	Date of order revoking or modifying consent
Section 17 of that Act	Date of modification or revocation of consent".

The Coal Mining Subsidence Act 1991 (c. 45)

50. In section 19(1)(c) of the Coal Mining Subsidence Act 1991, for "section 52 of the Town and Country Planning (Scotland) Act 1972" substitute "section 1 of the Planning (Listed Buildings and Conservation Areas) (Scotland) Act 1997".

The Agricultural Holdings (Scotland) Act 1991 (c. 55)

51. In section 57(3) of the Agricultural Holdings (Scotland) Act 1991, for "section 102 or 110 of the Town and Country Planning (Scotland) Act 1972" substitute "section 189 of the Town and Country Planning (Scotland) Act 1997".

The Further and Higher Education (Scotland) Act 1992 (c. 37)

52. In section 31(7) of the Further and Higher Education (Scotland) Act 1992, for "section 278 of the Town and Country Planning (Scotland) Act 1972" substitute "section 195 of the Town and Country Planning (Scotland) Act 1997".

The Protection of Badgers Act 1992 (c. 51)

53. In section 10(1)(d) of the Protection of Badgers Act 1993, for "section 19(1) of the Town and Country Planning (Scotland) Act 1972" substitute "section 26(1) of the Town and Country Planning (Scotland) Act 1997".

The Radioactive Substances Act 1993 (c. 12)

54. For paragraph 14 of Schedule 3 to the Radioactive Substances Act 1993 substitute—
    "14. The Planning (Hazardous Substances) (Scotland) Act 1997."

The Crofters (Scotland) Act 1993 (c. 44)

55.—(1) In section 14(4) of the Crofters (Scotland) Act 1993, for "the 1972 Act" substitute "the 1997 Act".
    (2) In section 15(2)(b)(iv) of that Act, for "the 1972 Act" substitute "the 1997 Act".
    (3) In section 61(1) of that Act—
    (a) for the definition of "the 1972 Act" substitute—
        ""the 1997 Act" means the Town and Country Planning (Scotland) Act 1997;"; and
    (b) in the definition of "development", for "section 19 of the 1972 Act" substitute "section 26 of the 1997 Act".

The Coal Industry Act 1994 (c. 21)

56.—(1) In section 54(6) of the Coal Industry Act 1994, for "the Town and Country Planning (Scotland) Act 1972" and "that Act of 1972" substitute respectively "the Town and Country Planning (Scotland) Act 1997" and "that Act of 1997".
    (2) In paragraph 13(1) of Schedule 10 to that Act, for "those Acts" substitute "that Act".

The Value Added Tax Act 1994 (c. 23)

57. In Group 6 of Schedule 8 to the Value Added Tax Act 1994—
    (a) in Note (1)(a)(ii), for "the Town and Country Planning (Scotland) Act 1972" substitute "the Planning (Listed Buildings and Conservation Areas) (Scotland) Act 1997"; and

(b) in Note (4)(c)(ii), for "Part IV of the Town and Country Planning (Scotland) Act 1972" substitute "Part I of the Planning (Listed Buildings and Conservation Areas) (Scotland) Act 1997".

The Local Government etc. (Scotland) Act 1994 (c. 39)

58. In section 125A of the Local Government etc. (Scotland) Act 1994—
(a) in subsection (6), in the definition of "the appropriate authority", for "section 253(7) of the Town and Country Planning (Scotland) Act 1972" substitute "section 242(2) of the Town and Country Planning (Scotland) Act 1997"; and
(b) in subsection (7), for "subsection (7) of section 253 of the Town and Country Planning (Scotland) Act 1972" substitute "subsection (3) of section 242 of the Town and Country Planning (Scotland) Act 1997".

The Goods Vehicles (Licensing of Operators) Act 1995 (c. 23)

59.—(1) For section 12(12) of the Goods Vehicles (Licensing Operators) Act 1995, in paragraph (b) of the definition of "planning authority", for "1972" substitute "1997".
(2) For section 14(3)(b)(ii) of that Act substitute—
    "(ii) section 150 or 151 of the Town and Country Planning (Scotland) Act 1997;".
(3) For section 19(7)(b)(ii) of that Act substitute—
    "(ii) section 150 or 151 of the Town and Country Planning (Scotland) Act 1997;".

The Environment Act 1995 (c. 25)

60.—(1) In Schedule 13 to the Environment Act 1995—
(a) after paragraph 2(4)(b) insert "or"; and
(b) in paragraph 15(6), for "those sections" substitute "that section".
(2) In Schedule 14 to that Act, in paragraph 13(6), for "those sections" substitute "that section".

The Gas Act 1995 (c. 45)

61. In paragraph 2(1)(xxi) of Schedule 4 to the Gas Act 1995, for "sections 47 and 67" substitute "section 47".

Section 5   SCHEDULE 3

TRANSITIONAL PROVISIONS AND SAVINGS

1.—(1) The repeal by this Act of a provision relating to the coming into force of a provision reproduced in the consolidating Acts does not affect the operation of that provision, in so far as it is not specifically reproduced in the consolidating Acts but remains capable of having effect, in relation to the corresponding provision of the consolidating Acts.

(2) The repeal by this Act of a power to make provision or savings in preparation for or in connection with the coming into force of a provision reproduced in the consolidating Acts does not affect the power, in so far as it remains capable of having effect, in relation to the enactment reproducing the second provision.

2.—(1) The repeal by this Act of an enactment previously repealed subject to savings does not affect the continued operation of those savings.

(2) The repeal by this Act of a saving to which a previous repeal of an enactment is subject does not affect the operation of the saving in so far as it is not specifically reproduced in the consolidating Acts but remains capable of having effect.

3. Without prejudice to the generality of paragraphs 1 and 2, notwithstanding the repeal by this Act of Schedule 22 to the 1972 Act, the provisions of that Schedule shall continue to have effect, in so far as they are not specifically reproduced in this Schedule and remain capable of having effect, with any reference in those provisions to any provision of the repealed enactments which is reproduced in the consolidating Acts being taken, so far as the context permits, as including a reference to the corresponding provision of those Acts.

4. The repeal by this Act of an enactment which has effect as respects any provision of the repealed enactments (being a provision which is not reproduced in the consolidating Acts but continues in effect by virtue of this Schedule or the Interpretation Act 1978) does not affect its operation as respects that provison.

5. Any document made, served or issued after this Act comes into force which contains a reference to any of the repealed enactments shall be construed, except so far as a contrary intention appears, as referring or, as the context may require, including a reference to the corresponding provision of the consolidating Acts.

6. Where any provision of the repealed enactments amends an enactment (not being an enactment reproduced in the consolidating Acts) which is repealed or partly repealed by another enactment which is not in force when this Act comes into force, that provision shall continue to have effect, notwithstanding its repeal by this Act, but subject to section 2(4) of this Act.

7. In any regulations in force under section 88 of the 1972 Act (execution and cost of works required by enforcement notice) references to an enforcement notice, and an enforcement notice a copy of which has been served in respect of any breach of planning control, include a reference to a notice served under section 99 of that Act or section 168 of the principal Act (enforcement of duties as to replacement of trees).

8. The expressions "local authority" and "statutory undertakers" in any provision of the consolidating Acts shall, as respects any time when the corresponding provision in the repealed enactments (or any enactment replaced by them) was in force, have the same meanings as those expressions had at that time in that provision.

9. Notwithstanding the repeal by this Act of section 172 of the Local Government (Scotland) Act 1973, the amendments made by subsection (2) of that section (under which, in the term "local planning authority", wherever it occurs in any enactment or instrument made under or by virtue of an enactment, the word "local" is omitted) shall continue to have effect.

10.—(1) The repeal by this Act of section 1(8) of the Town and Country Planning Act 1984 (which validates certain permissions granted in respect of Crown land before 12th August 1984) shall not affect any permission to which that section applies immediately before the date on which the principal Act comes into force (and accordingly any such permission has effect and is deemed always to have had effect as provided in section 248(3) of the principal Act).

(2) The repeal by this Act of section 2(7) of that Act of 1984 (which makes similar provision as to tree preservation orders) shall not affect any order to which that section applies immediately before the date on which the principal Act comes into force (and accordingly any such order has effect and is deemed always to have had effect as provided in section 249(3) of the principal Act).

(3) The repeal by this Act of section 1(8) of that Act of 1984 (which makes similar provision as to listed building consents and conservation area consents) shall not affect any order to which that section applies immediately before the date on which the Planning (Listed Buildings and Conservation Areas) (Scotland) Act 1997 comes into force (and accordingly any such consent has effect and is deemed always to have had effect as provided in section 75(3) of the Planning (Listed Buildings and Conservation Areas) (Scotland) Act 1997).

11. In relation to any area which, on 1st April 1992, was designated as a National Scenic Area under section 262C of the 1972 Act, that section shall continue to apply as it had effect immediately prior to that date, and the area shall continue to be so designated until the designation is cancelled under subsection (1) of that section.

12. The repeal by this Act of section 4 of the Town and Country Planning (Costs of Inquiries etc.) Act 1995 (which validates certain payments etc. in connection with inquiries and hearings under section 8 of the Town and Country Planning (Scotland) Act 1969 and section 11 of the 1972 Act held before 8th November 1995) shall not affect the operation of that section in relation to any such inquiry or hearing.

13.—(1) Where the functions of a Minister under any enactment re-enacted or referred to in this Act have at any time been exercisable by another Minister or other Ministers, references in the relevant provision of this Act shall, as respects any such time, be construed as references to the other Minister or Ministers.

(2) In this paragraph "Minister" includes the Board of Trade and the Treasury.

14. Section 16 of, and paragraph 7(5) to (7) of Schedule 5 to, the principal Act shall have effect in relation to the performance of functions in relation to inquiries and hearings before as well as after 8th November 1995 (the date when the Town and Country Planning (Costs of Inquiries etc.) Act 1995 was passed).

INDEX

References are to sections and Schedules

CIVIL PROCEDURE ACT 1997*

(1997 c. 12)

An Act to amend the law about civil procedure in England and Wales; and for connected purposes. [27th February 1997]

PARLIAMENTARY DEBATES
Hansard, H.L. Vol. 575, cols. 21, 604, 1 (Moses Room); Vol. 576, cols. 872, 1276. H.C. Vol. 289, col. 543; Vol. 291, col. 212.

INTRODUCTION AND GENERAL NOTE
This Act is a paving measure following the Interim and Final Reports on Access to Justice by Lord Woolf. Despite its brevity, because it deals with the means of expression of the Rule of Law, it is of constitutional importance, see *R. v. Lord Chancellor, ex p. Witham, The Times,* March 13, 1997, discussing the right of access to the courts. The Act establishes a single Civil Court Rule Committee in place of the former Supreme Court Rules and County Court Committees. It also establishes an advisory Civil Justice Council. The intention underlying these changes is no less than a transformation in the culture of civil litigation. The opportunity has also been taken to place Anton Piller orders on a statutory footing and to regularise practice directions in the County Court.

The Parliamentary Secretary, Lord Chancellor's Department (Mr. Gary Streeter) set out the thinking behind the Act in these terms:
"The central messages underlying the reforms launched by the Bill are that civil litigation must become faster, cheaper and simpler. By 'faster', we mean that it is our aim that, once cases enter the litigation process, they should proceed along managed tracks to specified deadlines that are adhered to by all parties. We also mean that procedures should be in place to ensure that the real issues of a case are brought out into the open from the outset. By 'cheaper', we mean that the cost of litigation, both to individual litigants and to the public generally, must be reduced. It cannot be right that—as is true of too many cases in our system—the costs of taking or pursuing an action exceed the award made. Procedures must be proportionate to the claim.
By 'simpler', we mean that litigants should be in a position to know in advance how much a court case is likely to cost and how long it is likely to take. That must be supported by effective sanctions to ensure that the timetables and cost limits are met in all but the most

---

* Annotations by Joseph Jacob, London School of Economics.

exceptional cases. The civil justice system and all those involved in it must respond to the needs of litigants, not the other way around.

The key to the reforms is the emphasis placed on the court's proper role in encouraging fair settlement, efficient case management of contested cases and a greater sense of proportion in the resources involved in the litigation process. Judicial case management will empower the courts to take greater responsibility for each case in the system. Courts will have more power to make decisions on how cases should proceed, to flush out the central issues at an early stage, to encourage settlement and to minimise costly and time-wasting delay. Case management will be supported by well-defined litigation 'tracks' that will ensure that the appropriate level of court control is used to manage cases, and in the fast track by a new fixed-costs regime that will reward efficiency ...

In addition, it is proposed that protocols will be developed to promote good practice among litigants and their advisers both before and during the litigation process. Coupled with the greater emphasis on alternative dispute resolution, it is intended to foster an atmosphere in which litigation is truly seen as the last resort ...

To support these proposals, and to ensure that the civil justice system is truly accessible, it is our aim that procedures should be simple and easily comprehensible. The new procedures introduced under the reforms must be easily understood by all. Just as important, the new rules of court must facilitate such understanding ...

The reforms represent a challenging task for the courts. The judiciary, and the court staff who support them, will have to learn new techniques; they will have to adopt a far more proactive approach, and take far more responsibility for ensuring that cases progress as quickly and as efficiently as possible. To support this new role, a comprehensive training programme for the judiciary is being embarked on. New computer systems are also being developed to ensure that technical support is available." [*Hansard*, H.C., Vol. 289, cols. 543–4]

Thus behind the Act, lies a concern that also affected the Arbitration Act 1996 (c.23). It was that dispute resolution in England should be fair, speedy, and cost effective. As noted above, this Act paves the way for the implementation of the recommendations in Lord Woolf's report. The Arbitration Act 1996 was based on the Report of the Department of Trade and Industry's Departmental Advisory Committee chaired by Saville L.J., published in February 1996. It is instructive to note the similarities between the two Acts and the two reports. Both Acts contain purpose clauses. Both Acts emphasise the importance of non-litigated settlement. Both reports were influenced by the need for the English legal system to remain competitive in the world of increasingly globalised litigation. As the note in *Current Law Statutes* says of the 1996 Act it was passed "in order to increase the attractiveness and efficacy of arbitration as a method of dispute resolution and the attractiveness of London as a venue for international arbitration." Or, as Lord Woolf put it (Final Report, Sect. I, para. 5): "An efficient and cost effective justice system is ... of vital importance to the commercial, financial and industrial life of this country and I was anxious to improve this, especially because of the evidence I received that there was a substantial risk of the existing system changing our competitive position in relation to other jurisdictions."

Commenting on the timetable, the Parliamentary Secretary, Lord Chancellor's Department (Mr. Gary Streeter):

"The Government are working up the details of how to achieve the blueprint. In particular, the procedures necessary to support judicial case management—on the fast track and the multi-track—and the new costs regime need to be introduced carefully. We recognise the importance of consultation on the detail of the new procedural systems needed to ensure that cases are heard fairly and efficiently. In the next few months, we will meet interested bodies to discuss the procedures and will publish consultation papers later in the year ...
The Government remain fully committed to the October 1998 deadline for the introduction of the main aspects of the reforms, and the steps I have just outlined are a testament to that. A detailed plan of action has been drawn up to ensure that we keep on track." [*Hansard*, H.C., Vol. 291, col. 212]

The Opposition Front Bench spokesman, Mr. Paul Boateng committed his Party to a "rigorous cost-benefit analysis" of the civil justice system and civil legal aid as well as of the Woolf report and the Act. [*Hansard*, H.C., Vol. 289, col. 611]

The "Woolf" Reports are:—

Lord Woolf, *Access to Justice, Interim Report* to the Lord Chancellor on the civil justice system in England & Wales, June 1995.
The Issues Papers, January 1996: The proposed procedure for the new Fast Track, Multi-party actions; Medical Negligence Cases; Housing Cases; Expert Evidence; and, Costs.
Lord Woolf, *Access to Justice, Final Report*, July 1996.

The Woolf Report, *Access to Justice, Draft Civil Proceedings Rules*, July 1996, and see; *Access to Justice—'The Way Forward'*, The Lord Chancellor's strategy for implementing the review of the procedures of the civil courts.

These documents are available on two sites on the *World Wide Web* at:
http://www.law.warwick.ac.uk/Woolf/, and related sites and
http://www.open.gov.uk/lcd/justice/cjdnet.htm and related sites.

This last announced that it "will provide details of the Lord Chancellor's implementation strategy and regular progress reports. The site will also enable direct communication with those charged with taking forward the reforms, and will act as a source of information. It is anticipated that all consultation papers will be available on the site as they are published."

The first Bulletin (March 1, 1997) announced:

"The Lord Chancellor intends to appoint members to the new Civil Procedure Rule Committee in May, and the rule committee will begin its deliberations on the new draft rules in June 1997 ... The Lord Chancellor hopes to appoint members to the Civil Justice Council in July this year after consulting major organisations working in the civil justice field. The Lord Chancellor proposes that the number of Council members should be set at around 20 ... Formal consultation on the procedures and supporting rules for the [Fast and Multi-track, matters fundamental to the Woolf reforms but not mentioned in the legislation] should commence in July 1997 ... It is expected that Practice Directions will contain a lot of the detail of procedures which will no longer be in the rules. Variations in local practice have been a problem for practitioners. [The Lord Chancellor's Department is] working with the Vice-Chancellor and other members of the judiciary to develop the necessary practice directions to ensure the desirable consistency of practice [as to which see s.5 below]."

The Bulletin also contained further information about the costs regime, pre-action protocols, resources (including transitional costs for both the Judicial Studies Board and the Court Service), continuing costs, information technology and evaluation. It said:

"the reforms of housing and enforcement procedures will move forward on a slower timetable than those for the focus areas ... Judicial review procedures and rules are also the subject of consideration following the Law Commission's report. We aim to develop a timetable for the reform of this important area of business. It may be possible to join this with the focus areas to be achieved by October 1998 ... We will be in a position to assess the implementation of appeal procedures once the Review of the Court of Appeal (Civil Division) has reported in September 1997. However, we anticipate that we should be able to include at least some elements of the new appeal procedures in the October 1998 package ... Full evaluation of [Ombudsmen] has ... been postponed until the second stage of the reform process."

The Woolf proposals themselves followed much discussion including:

The Lord Chancellor's Department, *General Issues Paper*, 1987,

The Review Body on Civil Justice, *Final Report*, Cm.394, 1988, and

The Heilbron and Hodge Report, *Civil Justice on Trial—The case for change*, the Law Society and Bar Council, 1993.

A.A.S. Zuckerman and Ross Cranston, eds., *Reform of Civil Procedure: Essays on 'Access to Justice'*, 1995, and R. Smith, ed., *Achieving Civil Justice: Appropriate Dispute Resolution for the 1990s*, 1995, each offer a series of essays on various aspects of the Interim Report.

COMMENCEMENT

See s.11(2) and Introductory Note above.

ABBREVIATIONS

"J.A. 1925"   : Supreme Court of Judicature (Consolidation) Act 1925 (c.49)
"S.C.A. 1981" : Supreme Court Act 1981 (c.54)

Rules and directions

Civil Procedure Rules

1.—(1) There are to be rules of court (to be called "Civil Procedure Rules") governing the practice and procedure to be followed in—
  (a) the civil division of the Court of Appeal,

(b) the High Court, and

(c) county courts.

(2) Schedule 1 (which makes further provision about the extent of the power to make Civil Procedure Rules) is to have effect.

(3) The power to make Civil Procedure Rules is to be exercised with a view to securing that the civil justice system is accessible, fair and efficient.

DEFINITIONS

"Civil Procedure Rules": see subs. (1).

"court within the scope of the rules": see s.9(1).

"court outside the scope of the rules": see s.9(1).

GENERAL NOTE

This section provides power for a unified set of rules of court applying in the Supreme Court and county courts alike. It is supplemented by Sched. 1, which preserves and in some respects enlarges the broad scope of the existing rule-making powers. The section implements the central plank of the Woolf recommendations. It also continues the policy, seen most notably in the County Court Rules 1981 and the Courts and Legal Services Act 1990 (c.41), of permitting the assimilation of the procedures of the two courts. Henceforth, if Woolf is followed, the main distinctions will be between fast and multi-track cases. It will not be by the court or the mode of commencement.

Subs. (1)

The Supreme Court Practice summarised the history of the rules of the Supreme Court as follows (Vol. 1, para. 1/1/1):

"The first Rules of the Supreme Court were drafted by the Judges for the new High Court and Court of Appeal, and appeared as the First Schedule to the Judicature Act 1875. They were in part taken from pre-existing rules of the several Courts that were to be combined, and they have formed the basis of the Rules as subsequently developed. They were enlarged and re-issued in 1883 as the Rules of the Supreme Court 1883, and have subsequently been amended and enlarged many times; in later years usually several times a year. The task of undertaking an entire revision of the Rules was recommended by the Committee on Supreme Court Practice and Procedure in its Second Interim Report (1951, Cmd. 8176, para. 46). In 1962 the first stage of such general revision was effected by the R.S.C. (Revision) 1962, which came into force on January 1, 1964, together with amendments of those Rules made by the R.S.C. (No.1) 1963 (S.I. 1962 No.2145 and S.I. 1963 No.682) ... In 1965, the final stage of the revision of the R.S.C. was completed as an entire integral body of Rules which were made by the R.S.C. (Revision) 1965 (S.I. 1965 No.1776). By this Instrument, all the previous Rules and Orders made since 1883 were revoked ... and the provisions of nine Acts of Parliament were repealed (para. 1(2) and Sched. 2 thereto). The effect of the Instrument was therefore to provide a fresh starting point for the new Rules of the Supreme Court. The outstanding feature of the R.S.C. in their new form was and is their simple, logical arrangement, which involved the renumbering of most of the Orders and Rules, except those comprised in the 1962 Revision."

If the timetable set by the government is adhered to, October 1998 will be a second fresh starting point. In this connection it is instructive to recall what the *Supreme Court Practice* said about continuity of procedure in its general note to the 1981 Act (Vol. 2, para. 5104):

"Whereas J.A. 1925 contained an express provision for the saving of the former practice and procedure (see s.103 which replaced s.73 of J.A. 1873), S.C.A. 1981 omits this provision. Nevertheless, there are to be found scattered through the Act provisions which recall and reimpose those as to jurisdiction, practice and procedure which prevailed before the passing of the Act and which may, in some instances, refer back to the jurisdiction, practice and procedure prevailing before J.As. 1873–1875 (see, *e.g.* s.15(2)(b) (jurisdiction, civil and criminal of the Court of Appeal); s.19(2)(b) (jurisdiction, civil and criminal exercisable by the High Court); s.28(3)(b) (jurisdiction of the High Court to determine appeals from Crown Court and inferior courts); s.29(1) (orders of mandamus, prohibition and certiorari); s.44 (extraordinary functions of Judges of High Court); s.49(2) (jurisdiction as to the current administration of law and equity to be exercised 'as hitherto'); ... s.96(2) (business of the Central Office)). These provisions afford cogent evidence of the historical continuity of English procedural law and practice and the administration of civil justice. In this context, the rules enunciated by Brett L.J. in *Jackson v. Litchfield* (1882) 8 Q.B.D. 474, p.477 may provide useful guidelines:

'In all cases at common law, which are not provided for by the Judicature Acts (*i.e.* the Acts of 1873 and 1875), the proceedings are to be as they were before these Acts, and in all cases within the Judicature Acts, where no special steps in proceedings are provided, the proceedings are to be as nearly like as they can be to analogous proceedings before these Acts.'"

However, that may be, the fresh starting point of October 1998 will, if current plans go ahead, represent something of as big a break in the continuity as we have had. Nevertheless, many of the current reforms build upon ideas and institutions developed in the pre-transformation era. We can expect Brett L.J.'s *dictum* to be applied, if necessary, in the new system.

"*practice and procedure*". *The Supreme Court Practice* was at pains to define the scope of this phrase. Omitting words not affecting the current law, it said (Vol. 2, para. 5291):

"The overriding limitation on the powers of the ... Rule Committee to make Rules of ... Court is that such Rules must be made for the purpose of prescribing and regulating 'the practice and procedure' to be followed in the ... Court ... The term 'practice and procedure' is used in contrast to 'substantive law': on the one hand, substantive law comprises the body of rules of law which give or define legal rights and duties or create or confer legal status, and on the other hand, practice and procedure comprise the machinery by which such legal rights, duties and status are enforced or recognised, which is sometimes called 'adjective law.' The classic statement of this distinction is that expressed by Lush L.J. in *Poyser v. Minors* (1881) 7 Q.B.D. 329, pp.333, 334, C.A. when he said:

'Practice in its larger sense ... like "procedure" ... denotes the mode of proceeding by which a legal right is enforced as distinguished from the law which gives or defines the right and which by means of the proceeding the Court is to administer the machinery as distinguished from the product. "Practice" and "procedure" I take to be convertible terms.'

On the other hand, it may well be that the term 'procedure' is wider than the term 'practice,' since 'procedure' may be a generic term comprising the whole of adjective law, the whole legal machinery for the conduct of judicial proceedings, whether in a court, tribunal or other recognised judicial or decision-making body whereas the term 'practice' comprises the rules governing the steps to be taken in a particular piece of litigation (see *Att.-Gen. v. Sillem* (1864) 10 H.L.C. 704).

In any event, since the [rules] must be confined to matters of 'practice and procedure,' [By themselves] they cannot be made to confer or alter any existing jurisdiction or any existing legal rights and duties (see *Everett v. Griffiths* [1924] 1 K.B. 941; *Darlow v. Shuttleworth* [1902] 1 K.B. 721, p.730; *Guaranty Trust Co. of New York v. Hannay & Co.* [1915] 2 K.B. 536)."

For an extended account of the meaning of practice and procedure, see Halsbury's *Laws of England* (4th ed.), Vol. 37, para. 10.

As noted below, para. 3 of Sched. 1 has taken the opportunity to clarify and extend the rule making powers in relation to the law of evidence. And see s.4, which gives power to amend primary legislation "to facilitate the making of Civil Procedure Rules."

'*Procedural orders*'. In addition to the rules of court made under the former s.84 of the S.C.A. 1981, the *Supreme Court Practice* noted that the 1981 Act (Vol. 2, para. 5293) conferred a number of other powers. These remain in place. The *Supreme Court Practice* said the Act:

"confers powers on the Lord Chancellor to make 'orders' which may or will have the effect of regulating the practice and procedure in the Supreme Court. These orders, which may be called procedural orders, will also have the force of law, and must be made by a statutory instrument laid before Parliament. Among such procedural orders which the Lord Chancellor is empowered to make are those under the following provisions, s.40(4) (attachment of debts); s.54(4)(e) (Court of Appeal Civil Division); s.61(3) (distribution of business among Divisions); s.89(6) (Masters and Registrars); s.130(1) (fees to be taken in the Supreme Court with concurrence of Treasury); s.139(2) (attachment of National Savings Bank deposits). By virtue of s.149(1) and Sched. 3 to the 1981 Act, the Lord Chancellor has powers to make procedural orders under s.108(1) of the County Courts Act 1959 as to appeals from county courts.

These procedural orders should be distinguished from Orders and Direction which the Lord Chancellor is also empowered to make or give, *e.g.* s.63(2) (business assigned to specially nominated Judges); s.71(2) (directions as to sittings of the High Court in places outside London and the days and times of such sittings)."

Subs. (2)

This gives effect to Sched. 1. It restates the present broad powers of the previous rule committees and expands them in some respects. It deals, for example, with the power to make rules regarding the delegated exercise of jurisdiction and with the powers regarding modifications of rules of evidence.

Sched. 1, para. 1. The definition is recursive. As regards the Supreme Court, the previous power was contained in s.84 of the S.C.A. 1981. The matters about which Rules of Court could be made under that section included all matters of practice and procedure in the Supreme Court which were regulated or prescribed by Rules of Court immediately before the commencement of that Act. It enlarged the powers conferred by s.99 of J.A. 1925, which that section replaced. In relation to the former rules the *Supreme Court Practice* commented (Vol. 2, para. 5290):

"These Rules are a form of delegated or subordinate legislation, and they have the force of law (see for the earliest statement to this effect *per* Lord Denman C.J. in *Roffey v. Smith* (1834) 6 Car. & P. 662). Their function is to prescribe and regulate the practice and procedure to be followed in the Supreme Court ... Their validity may be challenged as being *ultra vires* the Rule Committee, see *e.g.* when the challenge was successful, *Grosvenor Hotel, London, Re (No.2)* [1965] Ch. 1210, C.A. (Crown privilege to withhold disclosure of documents) and *Ward v. James* [1966] 1 Q.B. 273, C.A. (extent of discretion to order trial by jury), and when the challenge was unsuccessful *Guaranty Trust Co. of New York v. Hannay & Co.* [1915] 2 K.B. 536, C.A. (power to order declarations of right), and *Rodriguez v. Parker* [1967] 1 Q.B. 116, and *Mitchell v. Harris Engineering Co.* [1967] 2 Q.B. 703, C.A. (powers to amend after expiry of limitation period)."

For an account of the history of such rule-making powers, see Halsbury's *Laws of England* (4th ed.), Vol. 37, para. 7.

Schedule 1, para. 2. "court within the scope of the rules": see s.1(1).

Schedule 1, para. 4. The Lord Chancellor said:

"The proposal that the rule-making powers should extend to the power to make civil procedure rules which impact on the rules of evidence attracted a large measure of support on consultation. I believe that the rules of evidence should facilitate and not hamper the early identification of the issues in the case and the evidence relevant to them. Recent developments in the field of civil justice have promoted relaxation of the strict rules of evidence in order to ensure that parties put their cards on the table at an early stage. This can be seen, for example, both in the provisions regarding the requirements for admissibility of witness statements, contained in Section 5 of the Courts and Legal Services Act 1990 and the further reform of the hearsay rule in the Civil Evidence Act 1995." [*Hansard*, H.L., Vol. 575, cols. 606–7]

He added:

"The Bill is about procedure and, although there are clearly blurred edges between the rules of procedure and the rules of evidence, it has always seemed to me that, in principle, the rules of evidence play a much more significant role in our law, particularly with respect to the protection of individual rights. That of course is perhaps much more dramatically demonstrated in the criminal process than in the civil process, but nevertheless there are occasions in a civil trial when the rules of evidence can make all the difference to the rights of the litigant." [*Hansard*, H.L., Vol. 575, col. CWH6]

And:

"the spill-over from procedure to evidence is a difficult boundary. Where is the boundary in a number of cases? I entirely agree that this is primarily concerned with giving the rule committee the power to make rules of procedure. But there are quite a number of examples in which the nature of the evidence required can have a considerable effect on the rules of procedure. For example, any attempt to limit the situation so far as the number of experts are concerned could well have an effect on the procedure to be adopted. It is at the heart of the proposals of my noble and learned friend Lord Woolf that that kind of thing should carefully be considered in relation to the overall procedure." [*Hansard*, H.L., Vol. 575, CWH6–7]

Schedule 1, para. 5. This paragraph should be read with the substituted and new subsections (5), (5A) and (6) of s.84 of the S.C.A. 1981.

Schedule 1, para. 6. This paragraph should be read together with s.5.

Schedule 1, para. 7. This paragraph enables rules to be made for piloting new procedures, that is, trying them out in only some areas or some courts or some types of cases.

Subs. (3)

This subsection sets out the purpose of any rules made by the Civil Procedure Rule Committee. It endeavours to give effect to the principles Lord Woolf had set out in his Interim and Final Reports. These were (Final Report, Sect.I, para. 1) that the system, "should: (a) be just in the results it delivers; (b) be fair in the way it treats litigants; (c) offer appropriate procedures at a reasonable cost; (d) deal with cases with reasonable speed; (e) be understandable to those who use it; (f) be responsive to the needs of those who use it; (g) provide as much certainty as the nature of particular cases allows; and (h) be effective, adequately resourced and organised." The subsection derives from the recommendation of the Select Committee on Delegated Powers that the Act should contain a purpose clause. The Renton Committee (Cmnd. 6053) had drawn a distinction between a statement of purpose which simply delimits and illuminates the legal effects of the Bill on the one hand and a statement of purpose which is a mere manifesto. This subsection is intended to be of the first kind.

The Lord Chancellor (Lord Mackay of Clashfern) said:

"I think that it is quite important that the statement of the aims should not give rise to any unintentional impression that some aims have higher priority than others, or that the stated aims are the only ones which have relevance. The phrase 'accessible, fair and efficient' brings together, I believe, the essence of what ... Lord Woolf has been emphasising; namely, accessibility (which covers the objective of keeping costs down, simplicity and clarity of rules and procedure), fairness (a synonym for justice) and efficiency (which covers, for example, speed and proper use of resources).

It is clear from [Lord Woolf's] report that he has taken great care to formulate his statement of justice so as to incorporate aspects other than the obvious one of fairness." [*Hansard*, H.L., Vol. 576, col. 873]

Rule Committee

2.—(1) Civil Procedure Rules are to be made by a committee known as the Civil Procedure Rule Committee, which is to consist of—
  (a) the Master of the Rolls,
  (b) the Vice-Chancellor, and
  (c) the persons currently appointed by the Lord Chancellor under subsection (2).
  (2) The Lord Chancellor must appoint—
  (a) one judge of the Supreme Court,
  (b) one Circuit judge,
  (c) one district judge,
  (d) one person who is a Master referred to in Part II of Schedule 2 to the Supreme Court Act 1981,
  (e) three persons who have a Supreme Court qualification (within the meaning of section 71 of the Courts and Legal Services Act 1990), including at least one with particular experience of practice in county courts,
  (f) three persons who have been granted by an authorised body, under Part II of that Act, the right to conduct litigation in relation to all proceedings in the Supreme Court, including at least one with particular experience of practice in county courts,
  (g) one person with experience in and knowledge of consumer affairs, and
  (h) one person with experience in and knowledge of the lay advice sector.
  (3) Before appointing a judge of the Supreme Court under subsection (2)(a), the Lord Chancellor must consult the Lord Chief Justice.
  (4) Before appointing a person under paragraph (e) or (f) of subsection (2), the Lord Chancellor must consult any body which—
  (a) has members who are eligible for appointment under that paragraph, and
  (b) is an authorised body for the purposes of section 27 or 28 of the Courts and Legal Services Act 1990.
  (5) The Lord Chancellor may reimburse the members of the Civil Procedure Rule Committee their travelling and out-of-pocket expenses.
  (6) The Civil Procedure Rule Committee must, before making or amending Civil Procedure Rules—
  (a) consult such persons as they consider appropriate, and
  (b) meet (unless it is inexpedient to do so).
  (7) The Civil Procedure Rule Committee must, when making Civil Procedure Rules, try to make rules which are both simple and simply expressed.
  (8) Rules made by the Civil Procedure Rule Committee must be signed by at least eight members of the Committee and be submitted to the Lord Chancellor, who may allow or disallow them.

DEFINITIONS
"Civil Procedure Rules": see s.1(1).

GENERAL NOTE
This section makes provision for the composition of the Civil Court Rule Committee. It is to have 14 members. The previous Supreme Court Rule Committee consisted of 11 members. There were seven judges and four others. The judges were the Lord Chief Justice, the Master of the Rolls, the President of the Family Division, the Vice-Chancellor, and three other judges of the Supreme Court. The other members were two persons with a Supreme Court qualification (that is, be qualified for appointment to a judge of the Supreme Court, mainly but not necessarily barristers) and two persons who had been granted by an authorised body the right to conduct litigation in relation to all proceedings in the Supreme Court (that is, mainly but not necessarily, solicitors). The previous County Rule Committee again consisted of 11 members. They were five judges of county courts, two district judges, two persons qualified for appointment to the Supreme Court and two persons who had been granted by an authorised body the right to conduct litigation in relation to all proceedings in the Supreme Court.

It is convenient here to summarise the changes. The most striking of these is the provision in subs. (2)(g) and (h) that "one person with experience in and knowledge of consumer affairs", and "one person with experience in and knowledge of the lay advice sector" shall be appointed. Their purpose was said to be to provide a counterbalance to the professional legal viewpoint. For a different perspective, see Sir Jack Jacob, "The Machinery of the Rule Committee of the Supreme Court" in *The Reform of Civil Procedural Law*, at p.325–6, where the point is taken that this may fail to "distinguish between the two distinct functions of rule-making and rule-reviewing." As to this second function, see s.6 below.

For the first time a Master of the Supreme Court is to be a member of the rule committee. This, at last, goes some way towards a recommendation of the 1951 Evershed Committee (Second Interim Report, Cmd. 8176, paras.132–39).

The numbers of advocates and solicitors are each increased from two to three, so as to allow appointments of those with experience in the Queen's Bench and Chancery Divisions and the county court. They are not representatives.

The Lord Chief Justice and the President of the Family Division have lost their places, although the Chief Justice must be consulted in relation to the appointment of the judge of the Supreme Court and, presumably, he can be appointed.

For a discussion of the operation of the former Supreme Court Rule Committee, see Sir Jack Jacob, "The Machinery of the Rule Committee of the Supreme Court" in *The Reform of Civil Procedural Law*, at pp.323–34.

Subs. (1)(b)
The Lord Chancellor said:
"Lord Woolf recommended that the head of civil justice should issue an annual report. The head of civil justice, as the Vice-Chancellor, will be a member of this committee. That report would be a more suitable medium for detailing the rules committee work than a stand-alone report. Once the main body of the rules is changed, there might not be a tremendous amount happening from time to time ... Lord Donaldson led the way in this by publishing an annual report for the Court of Appeal. That is an extremely useful and valuable method of drawing attention to its work, which has been carried on by his successors.
The head of civil justice will report. As I understand it, he will carry forward the recommendation. I believe it would be right to cover in that report any work that the rules committee is doing in the period covered by the report from time to time. I hope that will be an efficient way of dealing with this matter." [*Hansard*, H.L., Vol. 575, cols. CWH, 26]
It might be added that neither the office "the head of civil justice" nor its duties are defined in the legislation. Following the Woolf Interim Report, the Vice-Chancellor became the first holder. As noted below, it is anticipated that he will, among other things approve Practice Directions under the new s.74A of the County Courts Act 1984 (c.28) as inserted by s.5.

Subs. (2)(f)
This phrase includes, but is wider than, solicitors.

Subs. (6)(a)
This subsection requires the committee to consult. Lord Irvine of Lairg said:
"At present the position is that there is only consultation on proposed rule changes shortly before they are due to be introduced. After the rule committee has discussed in private the perceived problem and the options for solving it there must be early and meaningful consultation. It is perhaps unkind to mention it but the disaster of County Court Rule

17(11) would have been avoided by adequate consultation. That was the rule that provided for the automatic striking out of claims in the county court if the timetable provided for by the rules was not strictly followed. Poor rule drafting led to thousands of appeals and prolonged consequential litigation.

The new rule committee should really proceed democratically, as the Law Commission does. It should announce that a particular area of procedure is to be reviewed, invite ideas on that area and then consult in an open way on the options before—I emphasise the word 'before'—making any firm recommendations." [*Hansard*, H.L., Vol. 575, cols. CWH, 21]

The Lord Chancellor said; "strictly speaking, [the paragraph] is one which makes the matter subjective, but the overriding duty in performing a public law duty of this kind is to act reasonably." [*Hansard*, H.L., Vol. 576, col. 892]

Subs. (6)(b)

In the course of the debates it emerged that the Supreme Court rule committee does not meet, whereas the county court rule committee does. As Lord Irvine of Lairg put it: "the present Supreme Court Committee does not meet; it conducts its business solely by post. In effect, it is not a committee, but it may well be a group of individuals who are invited to endorse proposed rule changes put forward by others." [*Hansard*, H.L., Vol. 575, cols. 22, CWH]. It was described by Lord Thomas of Gresford as "a top-down culture ... whereby rules were handed down to the committee to approve" [*Hansard*, H.L. Vol. 575, col. 24, CWH]. It is intended that the new rule committee should follow the model of the county court rule committee. The Lord Chancellor said; "the working method of the committee is by meeting. The reservation regarding inexpediency would fall to be construed, if need be, as an objective requirement." [*Hansard*, H.L., Vol. 576, col. 1277]

Subs. (7)

On its face, this subsection would appear to suggest that if a simpler rule or a simpler expression of a rule can be found, the rule itself, if the committee is found not to have tried hard enough, may be *ultra vires*. The better view is that the subsection has no legal effect. So far as is known, it is unique in the delegation of rule-making powers.

Section 2: supplementary

3.—(1) Rules made and allowed under section 2 are to—
(a) come into force on such day as the Lord Chancellor may direct, and
(b) be contained in a statutory instrument to which the Statutory Instruments Act 1946 is to apply as if it contained rules made by a Minister of the Crown.

(2) A statutory instrument containing Civil Procedure Rules shall be subject to annulment in pursuance of a resolution of either House of Parliament.

DEFINITIONS
"Civil Procedure Rules": see s.1(1).

GENERAL NOTE
This section provides for the negative resolution of Parliament procedure to apply to the civil procedure rules. Under the previous legislation the rules of the Supreme Court were subject to parliamentary scrutiny under the negative resolution procedure. County court rules have not hitherto been subject to scrutiny. The section should be read together with s.4.

The Lord Chancellor undertook, "that when the rule committee has completed its deliberations on the substantial rules required to give effect to Lord Woolf's proposals, the Government will provide for debate in both Houses of Parliament so that the rule committee will have an opportunity of having the views of Members of Parliament in both Houses before finally adopting the rules". [*Hansard*, H.L., Vol. 575, col. 27, CWH]

Power to make consequential amendments

4.—(1) The Lord Chancellor may by order amend, repeal or revoke any enactment to the extent he considers necessary or desirable in consequence of—
(a) section 1 or 2, or
(b) Civil Procedure Rules.

(2) The Lord Chancellor may by order amend, repeal or revoke any enactment passed or made before the commencement of this section to the extent

he considers necessary or desirable in order to facilitate the making of Civil Procedure Rules.

(3) Any power to make an order under this section is exercisable by statutory instrument.

(4) A statutory instrument containing an order under subsection (1) shall be subject to annulment in pursuance of a resolution of either House of Parliament.

(5) No order may be made under subsection (2) unless a draft of it has been laid before and approved by resolution of each House of Parliament.

DEFINITIONS

"Civil Procedure Rules": see s.1(1).

GENERAL NOTE

The allocation of jurisdiction as between the county court and the High Court, is not a matter subject to the civil procedure rules. It is subject to orders made under s.1 of the Courts and Legal Services Act 1990 (c.41).

Subss. (1), (3) and (4)

The Lord Chancellor explained:

"the section deals with the need for power to make consequential amendments. This partly reflects the current rule-making provisions contained in the Supreme Court Act and the County Courts Act 1984. Your Lordships will understand that the powers conferred by this Bill will not be exercised until some time after it is enacted and it is important that there should be power to make alignments in other enactments reflecting the terms in which the rule committee's rules of procedure are made." [*Hansard*, H.L. Vol. 575, col. 607]

Subs. (2)

There appears to be a lacuna in this subsection. It only applies to enactments passed before its commencement. But, its purpose is to facilitate the making of Civil Procedure Rules. That is, where the Rules Committee finds that a statute hampers rules it wishes to make, it can apply to the Lord Chancellor for an order under the subsection. However, the time limitation means that the Committee cannot do so in respect of enactments passed after the subsection is in force. Clearly, there is an expectation that such statutes will be made after consultation with the Committee. On this basis, no problem would arise. The lacuna relates to enactments, if any, passed after the subsection is in force, but before the Committee has had time to consider the new rules. This is not however fatal because an order could be made under the subsection to amend the subsection itself, since it is an enactment passed before it comes into force.

Subss. (2) and (5)

The Lord Chancellor explained these subsections are:

"designed to give effect to ... the Government's response to the recommendations made by the Delegated Powers Scrutiny Committee ... If the rule committee is minded to make a rule which would override an enactment, the enactments would have to be identified and the necessary amendments made to those enactments. [The Lord Chancellor] would lay a draft order containing those amendments before the rules were made and that order would then be subject to the affirmative procedure. Once the order is approved, the rule committee would make the relevant rules.

The amendment builds on the order-making power ... contained in [s.4(1)] which provides for consequential amendments to be made via the negative resolution procedure ... subsection (2) then makes provision for an affirmative procedure to apply to amendments which are other than consequential. It will have the effect of ensuring ... that Parliament's approval is obtained before the committee makes the rule which overrides a statutory provision. The matters which would go into an affirmative order would include any rules flowing from paragraphs 2 to 4 of schedule [1] which overrides an enactment." [*Hansard*, H.L. Vol. 576, col. 896]

Practice directions

5.—(1) Practice directions may provide for any matter which, by virtue of paragraph 3 of Schedule 1, may be provided for by Civil Procedure Rules.

(2) After section 74 of the County Courts Act 1984 there is inserted—

"Practice directions

Practice directions

74A.—(1) Directions as to the practice and procedure of county courts may be made by the Lord Chancellor.

(2) Directions as to the practice and procedure of county courts may not be made by any other person without the approval of the Lord Chancellor.

(3) The power of the Lord Chancellor to make directions under subsection (1) includes power—

(a) to vary or revoke directions made by him or any other person, and

(b) to make different provision for different cases or different areas, including different provision—

(i) for a specific court, or

(ii) for specific proceedings, or a specific jurisdiction, specified in the directions.

(4) References in this section to the Lord Chancellor include any person authorised by him to act on his behalf."

DEFINITIONS
"Civil Procedure Rules": see s.1(1).

GENERAL NOTE

Subs. (1)

Practice directions may only be issued under this section if they deal with matters referred to in Sched. 1, para. 3. That paragraph is concerned with the removal of proceedings within the High Court and between county courts. Practice directions, notes, guidance, etc. dealing with other matters may continue to be issued within the Supreme Court in the usual way.

Subs. (2)

This subsection provides that county court practice directions should be subject to the approval of the Lord Chancellor, or someone authorised to act on his behalf. The Parliamentary Secretary, Lord Chancellor's Department (Mr. Gary Streeter) said, "It is intended that the Vice-Chancellor would fulfil that function." [*Hansard*, H.C., Vol. 289, col. 546]

Civil Justice Council

Civil Justice Council

6.—(1) The Lord Chancellor is to establish and maintain an advisory body, to be known as the Civil Justice Council.

(2) The Council must include—

(a) members of the judiciary,

(b) members of the legal professions,

(c) civil servants concerned with the administration of the courts,

(d) persons with experience in and knowledge of consumer affairs,

(e) persons with experience in and knowledge of the lay advice sector, and

(f) persons able to represent the interests of particular kinds of litigants (for example, businesses or employees).

(3) The functions of the Council are to include—

(a) keeping the civil justice system under review,

(b) considering how to make the civil justice system more accessible, fair and efficient,

(c) advising the Lord Chancellor and the judiciary on the development of the civil justice system,

(d) referring proposals for changes in the civil justice system to the Lord Chancellor and the Civil Procedure Rule committee, and

(e) making proposals for research.

(4) The Lord Chancellor may reimburse the members of the Council their travelling and out-of-pocket expenses.

DEFINITIONS
"Civil Procedure Rule Committee": see s.1.

GENERAL NOTE
This section establishes a Civil Justice Council whose functions are set out in subs. (3). The 1951 Evershed Committee (Second Interim Report Cmd.8176, paras.132–39), recommended the setting up of a body charged with the duty of keeping the rules of court under review. It is discussed in Sir Jack Jacob, "The Machinery of the Rule Committee of the Supreme Court" in *The Reform of Civil Procedural Law*, p.325. The section has now implemented the Evershed recommendation.

In his Interim Report, Lord Woolf recommended a Civil Justice Council (Sect.VI, Chap.27), and see the Final Report (Sect.I, para. 20). For suggested sub-committees, see Sect.VI, Chap.21, para. 34). In the debates Lord Woolf added:

"When I set out on the Inquiry which resulted in my Report, I was very conscious that since 1885 there had already been over 60 Reports each urging reform of the civil justice system yet the situation on which I had to report was one which many commentators described as being in crisis. Why should this be so? It is not because of any callous disregard of their responsibilities by those in charge of the system. It is my belief part of the cause is the absence of a broadly based body which has the clear responsibility for monitoring the justice system as a whole and identifying the areas which are in need of reform." [December 9, 1996, col. 877]

As to the reform of civil procedure, see generally A.S. Diamond, "The Summons for Directions", (1959) 75 *Law Quarterly Review* 43 and various writings of Sir Jack Jacob.

The Parliamentary Secretary, Lord Chancellor's Department (Mr. Gary Streeter) put the matter this way:

"The establishment of the Civil Justice Council is important to ensure that all those with an interest in the civil justice system can play their part in the reform process. Clearly, the reforms that we are introducing will have a significant impact on, and pose new challenges for, all those involved in the system. The Civil Justice Council will enable all groups to co-operate in the development of the reforms and ensure that they are prepared for the changes. We are firmly committed to carrying forward the reforms in partnership with all other participants in the system, and the council will provide a key forum for that. Our intention is for the council to be established by the summer, and our plans will be set out shortly." [*Hansard*, H.C., Vol. 291, col. 212]

There is no provision for, nor any prohibition on, the Council working through regional and subject sub-committees. The only limitation on its mode of work is that it is maintained by the Lord Chancellor.

The Lord Chancellor said; "If the Council wishes, and thinks it helpful to submit a report to the public through the Lord Chancellor, there is absolutely nothing to prevent it from doing so ... the head of the civil justice system intends to make an annual report of that character. The Master of the Rolls also now makes an annual report." [*Hansard*, H.L., Vol. 576, col. 1285]

In the course of the debates a number of justifications for such a Council were put forward. It is useful to record some of them. They are reflected in the composition and functions of the new Council.

Lord Irvine of Lairg said:

"It is behaviour on the ground that must change so as to make resolution of disputes less adversarial, speedier and cheaper. The function of the council would be to continue the co-operative method, by which Lord Woolf and his team worked, into the practical development of the new system. The function of the council would be to maintain a continuous overview of the system, to highlight the need for changes ... to put ideas to the new rule committee and the Lord Chancellor's Department, to assist the head of civil justice, to co-ordinate initiatives, both through practice directions and practice guides, and to monitor the impact of changes on the ground. An important area should be the development of pre-proceeding protocols, designed to help cases to settle before litigation has started, through the development of alternative dispute resolution approaches, in particular mediation, and through practice directions and guides.

The way ahead should be a permanent body specifically charged with monitoring and progressively improving the civil justice system. The council would be a vehicle for contributions from all interest groups. It could work with user groups in local courts and in Divisions of the High Court, to identify problems and to recommend reforms. It should provide a useful source of advice for the noble and learned Lord on the Woolsack, the senior judiciary and the rule committee." [*Hansard*, H.L., Vol. 575, cols. 9, CWH]

Lord Ackner argued:

"The monitoring ... might show that there are not enough judges. The monitoring ... might show that people of the wrong quality were being recruited, or that the training was inadequate. That may throw up problems about resources. There would be a greater prospect of those resources being provided if you had such a body going public and indicating in detail the deficiencies. It would enable the Lord Chancellor's Department, which would be represented on that body, to bring the necessary pressure to bear, if pressure was necessary, upon the Treasury to make sure those resources were provided." [*Hansard*, H.L., Vol. 575, cols. 11, CWH]

And later he said:

"What is overlooked is that the main thrust of the reform is to make access to justice more popular as a result of its being cheaper and quicker. If it becomes more popular, the case-load will inevitably increase ... What I anticipate may occur ... is that there will be resist-ance to providing adequate resources. After all, [the] proposal will involve shifting on to the public purse some of the expense hitherto borne by the litigant himself. If this occurs, it is essential for there to be a powerful statutory body which can state firmly and publicly that the system is falling behind its reasonable expectations because of being starved of the necessary funds." [*Hansard*, H.L., Vol. 576, col. 877]

Lord Thomas of Gresford added:

"[the] important function of the civil justice council would be to promote understanding of the system among the people who use it: to get rid of the mystique; to brush away the cobwebs which surround civil litigation and which make the experience of the civil courts such a nightmare for people who go to court to pursue their rights and remedies." [*Hansard*, H.L., Vol. 576, col. 880]

Subs. (2)

The obligation in subs. (1) on the Lord Chancellor "to establish and maintain" is presumably the authority needed for the appointment of members of the Council. It is to be noted that there is no limit other than the use of the plural in each of the six categories on the numbers who can be appointed, see Civil Procedure Review, Bulletin No.1, as mentioned in the Introduction and General Note above.

Subs. (2)(d)

See R. Thomas, "Civil Justice Review—Treating Litigants as Consumers", (1990) 9 C.J.Q. 51–60.

Subs. (3)

This subsection defines the functions of the Council. It is to be noted that whereas the Rules Committee under ss.1–4 is concerned with "practice and procedure", this Council has a wider remit. It includes that work, but encompasses all other matters which go to make the system. This presumably includes legal aid, court fees, the level and adequacy of resources and staffing (including judges and other staff). The Council is advisory only, see subs. (1) above.

Subs. (3)(b)

This paragraph is in similar terms to those in s.1(3).

Subs. (3)(e)

This paragraph only permits the making of proposals for research. It does not permit the Council to commission either research or pilot studies. The Council has no funds of its own.

Subs. (4)

This subsection is not wide enough to include payments for fees or loss of earnings, nor any payment to members of sub-committees who are not also members of the Council.

Court orders

Power of courts to make orders for preserving evidence, etc.

7.—(1) The court may make an order under this section for the purpose of securing, in the case of any existing or proposed proceedings in the court—

(a) the preservation of evidence which is or may be relevant, or

(b) the preservation of property which is or may be the subject-matter of the proceedings or as to which any question arises or may arise in the proceedings.

(2) A person who is, or appears to the court likely to be, a party to proceedings in the court may make an application for such an order.

(3) Such an order may direct any person to permit any person described in the order, or secure that any person so described is permitted—

(a) to enter premises in England and Wales, and

(b) while on the premises, to take in accordance with the terms of the order any of the following steps.

(4) Those steps are—

(a) to carry out a search for or inspection of anything described in the order, and

(b) to make or obtain a copy, photograph, sample or other record of anything so described.

(5) The order may also direct the person concerned—

(a) to provide any person described in the order, or secure that any person so described is provided, with any information or article described in the order, and

(b) to allow any person described in the order, or secure that any person so described is allowed, to retain for safe keeping anything described in the order.

(6) An order under this section is to have effect subject to such conditions as are specified in the order.

(7) This section does not affect any right of a person to refuse to do anything on the ground that to do so might tend to expose him or his spouse to proceedings for an offence or for the recovery of a penalty.

(8) In this section—

"court" means the High Court, and

"premises" includes any vehicle;

and an order under this section may describe anything generally, whether by reference to a class or otherwise.

DEFINITIONS

"court": see subs. (8).

"premises": see subs. (8).

GENERAL NOTE

This section deals with Anton Piller orders, see *Anton Piller KG v. Manufacturing Processes* [1976] Ch 55. These order a person to permit entry to premises for the purpose of finding or safeguarding evidence that is needed for civil proceedings. The section places them on a statutory footing. It arises from a recommendation made by the Judges Council, see the Consultation Paper of the Lord Chancellor's Department on Anton Piller orders prepared by a committee designated from the Judges' Council of July 20, 1992. The making of such an order in an appropriate case has been held by the European Court of Human Rights not to be in breach of Art. 8 of the European Convention on Human Rights (*Chappell v. U.K.* [1989] F.S.R. 617).

The Lord Chancellor explained that the purpose of the section "is certainly not to limit or reduce the jurisdiction which is currently being exercised under the Anton Piller order" [*Hansard*, H.L. Vol. 575, cols. 30, CWH]. See the Practice Direction (Mareva Injunctions and Anton Piller Orders) [1994] 1 W.L.R. 1233, [1994] 4 All E.R. 52; following the suggestions of Sir Donald Nicholls V.-C. in *Universal Thermosensors v. Hibben* [1992] 1 W.L.R. 840, 861, [1992] 3 All E.R. 257, 276, now governs applications as to the proper manner for execution of orders.

The Lord Chancellor said, "The Government believe, for reasons of principle, that powers which, in effect, amount to a right to require entry to premises should have the overt approval of Parliament, and should not solely rest on the footing of a court ordered requirement of consent. This ... [Act] provides the first opportunity since then to address the point." [*Hansard*, H.L., Vol. 575, col. 608]. He also added that: "This clause gives power to the court; in other words, it confers jurisdiction to make this order; but it does not exclude any other jurisdiction of the court to make any other order. If the court has jurisdiction to make two orders, there is no reason why we should not have a composite order with the two parts in it." [*Hansard*, H.L., Vol. 575, cols. 38,

CWH]. This would include, *e.g.* the interim delivery of goods to the applicant for immediate use by him, see s.4 of the Torts (Interference with Goods) Act 1977 (c.32) and R.S.C. Ord. 29, r. 2(a).

The Lord Chancellor said: "The main purpose of [the section is] to dispense with the fiction that the entry on the premises is with the consent of the owner/respondent. However, this clause will have the effect that in future it is more clearly the court order which is the basis of the requirement to permit entry, not the implied consent of the owner. It will no longer be desirable to imply that the execution of the Anton Piller order is dependent upon the consent of the owner or a person whom he might have authorised to give consent on his behalf." [*Hansard*, H.L., Vol. 576, col. 899]. The section thus solves the problem identified by Scott J. in *Bhimji v. Chatwani* [1991] 1 W.L.R. 989:

> "it is fundamental to the theory of Anton Piller type orders that a civil court in civil proceedings has no power to give one citizen the right to enter a house or premises of another citizen. These orders are *in personam* orders directed to the defendants. The defendants are ordered to allow entry and to allow search. The plaintiffs' right and their solicitors' right to enter and search is derived, on this theory of the law, from the defendants' permission given to them to do so. It is not derived from the power of the court to confer the right. The court does not have that power. Some might think that the subtlety of this distinction does little credit to the law and that a consent to enter given under threat of committal for contempt is not true consent at all, and not a consent upon which a right to enter and search can properly be based."

Subs. (3)

The Lord Chancellor explained that "it is not always the practice that all the persons who are authorised to enter the premises under the order will actually be named in the order. They will be described in some cases by their function—for example, the supervising solicitor—or by reference to the numbers of those who are authorised to enter." [*Hansard*, H.L., Vol. 576, col. 899]

Subs. (3)(a)

The reference to England and Wales presumably reverses the rule in *Cook Industries Inc. v. Galliher* [1979] Ch. 439 (inspection of flat in Paris) and maintains the rule in *Protector Alarms v. Maxim Alarms* [1978] F.S.R. 442 (no order for inspection of premises in Scotland).

Subs. (7)

As to self-incrimination, see *Rank Film Distributors v. Video Information Centre* [1982] A.C. 380 and *A. T. & T. Istel v. Tully* [1993] A.C. 45. The Lord Chancellor said: "the question [has been raised] of whether there was any intention through this clause of changing the law on privilege against self-incrimination. I took the view then, as I do now, that there was no such intention; indeed, I certainly never had such an intention." [*Hansard*, H.L., Vol. 576, col. 902]

Disclosure etc. of documents before action begun

8.—(1) The Lord Chancellor may by order amend the provisions of section 33(2) of the Supreme Court Act 1981, or section 52(2) of the County Courts Act 1984 (power of court to order disclosure etc. of documents where claim may be made in respect of personal injury or death), so as to extend the provisions—

(a) to circumstances where other claims may be made, or

(b) generally.

(2) The power to make an order under this section is exercisable by statutory instrument which shall be subject to annulment in pursuance of a resolution of either House of Parliament.

GENERAL NOTE

This section enables the Lord Chancellor to extend the circumstances in which the courts have power to order the disclosure of documents before legal proceedings. The clause is intended to give effect to Lord Woolf's recommendation that the power to order pre-action disclosure should be widened from the present power that applies only to claims in respect of personal injuries and death. (see Final Report, Chap. 10)

Lord Woolf had advocated the need for parties to adopt a co-operative approach from the earliest stages at which a potential claim begins to materialise. Under his proposals the primary tool for fostering this approach will be the development of pre-action protocols which identify the information which ought to be exchanged to put the parties in a position to consider settlement on a fair and well informed basis. The section therefore, takes power to widen the statutory powers regarding the disclosure of documents before proceedings commence. The government indicated it would wait and see how the pre-action protocols progress before activating this power. [*Hansard*, H.L., Vol. 575, col. 608]

General

Interpretation

9.—(1) A court the practice and procedure of which is governed by Civil Procedure Rules is referred to in this Act as being "within the scope" of the rules; and references to a court outside the scope of the rules are to be read accordingly.

(2) In this Act—
   "enactment" includes an enactment contained in subordinate legislation (within the meaning of the Interpretation Act 1978), and
   "practice directions" means directions as to the practice and procedure of any court within the scope of Civil Procedure Rules.

DEFINITIONS
   "Civil Procedure Rules": see s.1(1).
   "enactment": see subs. (2).
   "practice directions": see subs. (2).

Minor and consequential amendments

10.—Schedule 2 (which makes minor and consequential amendments) is to have effect.

DEFINITIONS
   "Civil Procedure Rules": see s.1(1).

GENERAL NOTE
   This section gives effect to Sched. 2.
   Sched. 2, para. 1(4): Section 84 of the S.C.A. 1981 was relevant both to rule-making powers for civil and criminal cases in the Supreme Court, and to other special rules applying to Supreme Court proceedings *i.e.* family proceeding rules made by other committees under other enactments. The power to make rules regarding civil cases is now contained in ss.1–4 of this Act. The amended paragraphs of s.84 contain the powers of the different rule authorities to apply rules made by other rule committees if so desired. See also Sched. 1, para. 5 of this Act. "Special rules" thus means rules which are made by an authority other than the Civil Court Rule Committee under any provision which confers on that authority power to make rules in relation to proceedings of that kind. See *e.g.* s.133 of S.C.A. 1981, which confers power on the Master of the Rolls to make regulation for the enrolment and engrossment of instruments and s.136 of S.C.A. 1981, which confers power on the Lord Chancellor and the Judges there specified to make rules as to the production of documents filed in or in the custody of the Supreme Court.
   Sched. 2, para. 2. This paragraph is consequential on the merger of the two previous rule committees.
   Sched. 2, para. 3. The Lord Chancellor explained:
      "the power to make rules of court in relation to family proceedings in the High Court and county courts is contained in Section 40 of the Matrimonial and Family Proceedings Act 1984. This [paragraph] inserts a new subsection into that section which provides that such rules may make different provision for different areas or for specific proceedings or specific courts. This would allow the rules to provide for future pilot projects and would bring them in line with the civil procedure rules in respect of which a similar power is contained in paragraph 7 of Schedule 1 to the [Act] . . . the President of the Family Division has indicated his support for such pilots. It is desirable to provide express power for such pilots." [*Hansard*, H.L., Vol. 576, col. 904]
   Sched. 2, para. 4. Previously, s.120(4) of the Courts and Legal Services Act 1990 had provided for positive resolution procedure to apply to the allocation of business between the High Court and county courts. Now the negative resolution procedure is to be used. The Lord Chancellor explained that amendments had been comparatively minor and attracted little attention since the big changes of 1990, and he "therefore felt that it was really no longer necessary to require Parliament's time to be taken up by an affirmative resolution procedure." [*Hansard*, H.L., Vol. 575, cols. 6, CWH]. Disingenuously, he added, "That does not seem a good use of Parliament's time. If people have questions, the negative resolution procedure is available."

[*Hansard*, H.L., Vol. 576, col. 905]. The Select Committee on Delegated Powers and Dereg-
ulation supported the justification for the change from affirmative to negative procedure.

The power to make orders regarding the allocation of business between the High Court and
county courts is vested in the Lord Chancellor, not the Rule Committee, and this change is not
therefore related to orders amending overriding enactments in s.4 *supra*. Presumably the
County Court limit is a matter on which the Civil Justice Council may advise under s.6.

Short title, commencement and extent

11.—(1) This Act may be cited as the Civil Procedure Act 1997.

(2) Sections 1 to 10 are to come into force on such day as the Lord Chancellor may by order made by statutory instrument appoint, and different days
may be appointed for different purposes.

(3) This Act extends to England and Wales only.

SCHEDULES

Section 1

SCHEDULE 1

CIVIL PROCEDURE RULES

Matters dealt with by the former rules

1. Among the matters which Civil Procedure Rules may be made about are any matters which
were governed by the former Rules of the Supreme Court or the former county court rules (that
is, the Rules of the Supreme Court (Revision) 1965 and the County Court Rules 1981).

Exercise of jurisdiction

2. Civil Procedure Rules may provide for the exercise of the jurisdiction of any court within
the scope of the rules by officers or other staff of the court.

Removal of proceedings

3.—(1) Civil Procedure Rules may provide for the removal of proceedings at any stage—
(a) within the High Court (for example, between different divisions or different district regis-
tries), or
(b) between county courts.
(2) In sub-paragraph (1)—
(a) "provide for the removal of proceedings" means—
(i) provide for transfer of proceedings, or
(ii) provide for any jurisdiction in any proceedings to be exercised (whether concurrently or not) elsewhere within the High Court or, as the case may be, by another
county court without the proceedings being transferred, and
(b) "proceedings" includes any part of proceedings.

Evidence

4. Civil Procedure Rules may modify the rules of evidence as they apply to proceedings in any
court within the scope of the rules.

Application of other rules

5.—(1) Civil Procedure Rules may apply any rules of court which relate to a court which is
outside the scope of Civil Procedure Rules.

(2) Any rules of court, not made by the Civil Procedure Rule Committee, which apply to
proceedings of a particular kind in a court within the scope of Civil Procedure Rules may be
applied by Civil Procedure Rules to other proceedings in such a court.

(3) In this paragraph "rules of court" includes any provision governing the practice and procedure of a court which is made by or under an enactment.

(4) Where Civil Procedure Rules may be made by applying other rules, the other rules may be applied—
(a) to any extent,
(b) with or without modification, and
(c) as amended from time to time.

Practice directions

6. Civil Procedure Rules may, instead of providing for any matter, refer to provision made or to be made about that matter by directions.

Different provision for different cases etc.

7. The power to make Civil Procedure Rules includes power to make different provision for different cases or different areas, including different provision—
(a) for a specific court or specific division of a court, or
(b) for specific proceedings, or a specific jurisdiction,
specified in the rules.

Section 10   SCHEDULE 2

MINOR AND CONSEQUENTIAL AMENDMENTS

Supreme Court Act 1981 (c. 54)

1.—(1) The Supreme Court Act 1981 is amended as follows.
(2) In section 18 (restrictions on appeals), in subsections (1A) and (1B)(a), for "Rules of the Supreme Court" there is substituted "rules of court".
(3) In section 68 (exercise of High Court jurisdiction otherwise than by judges)—
(a) in subsection (1), paragraph (c) and the word "or" immediately preceding it are omitted,
(b) in subsection (2)—
(i) paragraph (a) is omitted, and
(ii) in paragraph (b), for "any such person" there is substituted "a special referee",
(c) in subsection (3), for the words from "any" onwards there is substituted "a special referee or any officer or other staff of the court", and
(d) in subsection (4)—
(i) after "decision of" there is inserted "(a)", and
(ii) after "subsection (1)" there is inserted—
"or
(b) any officer or other staff of the court".
(4) In section 84 (power to make rules of court)—
(a) in subsection (1), for "Supreme Court" there is substituted "Crown Court and the criminal division of the Court of Appeal",
(b) subsection (4) is omitted,
(c) for subsections (5) and (6) there is substituted—
"(5) Special rules may apply—
(a) any rules made under this section, or
(b) Civil Procedure Rules,
to proceedings to which the special rules apply.
(5A) Rules made under this section may apply—
(a) any special rules, or
(b) Civil Procedure Rules,
to proceedings to which rules made under this section apply.
(6) Where rules may be applied under subsection (5) or (5A), they may be applied—
(a) to any extent,
(b) with or without modification, and
(c) as amended from time to time.", and
(d) in subsection (9), for "Supreme Court Rule Committee" there is substituted "Civil Procedure Rule Committee".
(5) Section 85 (Supreme Court Rule Committee) is omitted.
(6) In section 87 (particular matters for which rules of court may provide)—
(a) subsections (1) and (2) are omitted, and

(b) in subsection (3), for "Supreme Court" there is substituted "Crown Court or the criminal division of the Court of Appeal".

(7) In section 151 (interpretation)—

(a) in subsection (3), after the second "rules of court" there is inserted "in relation to the Supreme Court" and for "Supreme Court Rule Committee" there is substituted "Civil Procedure Rule Committee", and

(b) in subsection (4), the definition of "Rules of the Supreme Court" is omitted.

County Courts Act 1984 (c. 28)

2.—(1) The County Courts Act 1984 is amended as follows.

(2) For "county court rules", wherever occurring, there is substituted "rules of court".

(3) For "rule committee", wherever occurring, there is substituted "Civil Procedure Rule Committee".

(4) In section 1 (county courts to be held for districts), in subsection (1), for the words from "throughout" to "the district" there is substituted "each court".

(5) In section 3 (places and times of sittings of courts), subsection (3) is omitted.

(6) Section 75 (county court rules) is omitted.

(7) In section 77(1), for "the rules of the Supreme Court" there is substituted "Civil Procedure Rules".

(8) In section 81(2), for "any rules of the Supreme Court" there is substituted "Civil Procedure Rules".

(9) In section 147(1), the definitions of "county court rules" and "the rule committee" are omitted.

Matrimonial and Family Proceedings Act 1984 (c. 42)

3. In section 40 of the Matrimonial and Family Proceedings Act 1984 (family proceedings rules)—

(a) after subsection (3) there is inserted—

"(3A) Rules made under this section may make different provision for different cases or different areas, including different provision—

(a) for a specific court, or

(b) for specific proceedings, or a specific jurisdiction,

specified in the rules.",

and

(b) in subsection (4), the words from the first "in" to "and may" are omitted.

Courts and Legal Services Act 1990 (c. 41)

4. In section 120 of the Courts and Legal Services Act 1990 (regulations and orders), in subsection (4), "1(1)" is omitted.

INDEX

References are to sections and Schedules

UNITED NATIONS PERSONNEL ACT 1997

(1997 c. 13)

<small>ARRANGEMENT OF SECTIONS</small>

An Act to enable effect to be given to certain provisions of the Convention on the Safety of United Nations and Associated Personnel adopted by the General Assembly of the United Nations on 9th December 1994.

[27th February 1997]

PARLIAMENTARY DEBATES
Hansard, H.C. Vol. 285, col. 995; Vol. 288, col. 594. H.L. Vol. 577, cols. 446, 1812; Vol. 578, cols. 785, 1292.

INTRODUCTION
This Act enables the U.K. to ratify the Convention (defined in s.4(4)). Extraterritorial jurisdiction is created over offences committed in relation to attacks on UN workers and their premises and vehicles. A new offence is created by s.3 whereby a threat is made to commit attacks on UN workers with the objective of compelling a person to do or refrain from doing any act.

Attacks on UN workers

1.—(1) If a person does outside the United Kingdom any act to or in relation to a UN worker which, if he had done it in any part of the United Kingdom, would have made him guilty of any of the offences mentioned in subsection (2), he shall in that part of the United Kingdom be guilty of that offence.

(2) The offences referred to in subsection (1) are—

(a) murder, manslaughter, culpable homicide, rape, assault causing injury, kidnapping, abduction and false imprisonment;

(b) an offence under section 18, 20, 21, 22, 23, 24, 28, 29, 30 or 47 of the Offences against the Person Act 1861; and

(c) an offence under section 2 of the Explosive Substances Act 1883.

Attacks in connection with premises and vehicles

2.—(1) If a person does outside the United Kingdom any act, in connection with an attack on relevant premises or on a vehicle ordinarily used by a UN worker which is made when a UN worker is on or in the premises or vehicle, which, if he had done it in any part of the United Kingdom, would have made him guilty of any of the offences mentioned in subsection (2), he shall in that part of the United Kingdom be guilty of that offence.

(2) The offences referred to in subsection (1) are—

(a) an offence under section 2 of the Explosive Substances Act 1883;

(b) an offence under section 1 of the Criminal Damage Act 1971;

(c) an offence under article 3 of the Criminal Damage (Northern Ireland) Order 1977; and

(d) wilful fire-raising.

(3) In this section—

"relevant premises" means premises at which a UN worker resides or is staying or which a UN worker uses for the purpose of carrying out his functions as such a worker; and

"vehicle" includes any means of conveyance.

Threats of attacks on UN workers

3.—(1) If a person in the United Kingdom or elsewhere contravenes subsection (2) he shall be guilty of an offence.

(2) A person contravenes this subsection if, in order to compel a person to do or abstain from doing any act, he—

(a) makes to a person a threat that any person will do an act which is—

(i) an offence mentioned in section 1(2) against a UN worker, or

(ii) an offence mentioned in subsection (2) of section 2 in connection with such an attack as is mentioned in subsection (1) of that section, and

(b) intends that the person to whom he makes the threat shall fear that it will be carried out.

(3) A person guilty of an offence under this section shall be liable on conviction on indictment to imprisonment for a term—

(a) not exceeding ten years, and

(b) not exceeding the term of imprisonment to which a person would be liable for the offence constituted by doing the act threatened at the place where the conviction occurs and at the time of the offence to which the conviction relates.

Meaning of UN worker

4.—(1) For the purposes of this Act a person is a UN worker, in relation to an alleged offence, if at the time of the alleged offence—

(a) he is engaged or deployed by the Secretary-General of the United Nations as a member of the military, police or civilian component of a UN operation,

(b) he is, in his capacity as an official or expert on mission of the United Nations, a specialised agency of the United Nations or the International Atomic Energy Agency, present in an area where a UN operation is being conducted,

(c) he is assigned, with the agreement of an organ of the United Nations, by the Government of any State or by an international governmental organisation to carry out activities in support of the fulfilment of the mandate of a UN operation,

(d) he is engaged by the Secretary-General of the United Nations, a specialised agency or the International Atomic Energy Agency to carry out such activities, or

(e) he is deployed by a humanitarian non-governmental organisation or agency under an agreement with the Secretary-General of the United Nations, with a specialised agency or with the International Atomic Energy Agency to carry out such activities.

(2) Subject to subsection (3), in this section "UN operation" means an operation—

(a) which is established, in accordance with the Charter of the United Nations, by an organ of the United Nations,

(b) which is conducted under the authority and control of the United Nations, and

(c) which—

(i) has as its purpose the maintenance or restoration of international peace and security, or

(ii) has, for the purposes of the Convention, been declared by the Security Council or the General Assembly of the United Nations to be an operation where there exists an exceptional risk to the safety of the participating personnel.

(3) In this section "UN operation" does not include any operation—

(a) which is authorised by the Security Council of the United Nations as an enforcement action under Chapter VII of the Charter of the United Nations,

(b) in which UN workers are engaged as combatants against organised armed forces, and

(c) to which the law of international armed conflict applies.

(4) In this section—

"the Convention" means the Convention on the Safety of United Nations and Associated Personnel adopted by the General Assembly of the United Nations on 9th December 1994; and

"specialised agency" has the meaning assigned to it by Article 57 of the Charter of the United Nations.

(5) If, in any proceedings, a question arises as to whether—

(a) a person is or was a UN worker, or

(b) an operation is or was a UN operation,

a certificate issued by or under the authority of the Secretary of State and stating any fact relating to the question shall be conclusive evidence of that fact.

Provisions supplementary to sections 1 to 3

5.—(1) Proceedings for an offence which (disregarding the provisions of the Internationally Protected Persons Act 1978, the Suppression of Terrorism Act 1978 and the Nuclear Material (Offences) Act 1983) would not be an offence apart from section 1, 2 or 3 above shall not be begun—

(a) in England and Wales, except by or with the consent of the Attorney General;

(b) in Northern Ireland, except by or with the consent of the Attorney General for Northern Ireland.

(2) Without prejudice to any jurisdiction exercisable apart from this subsection, every sheriff court in Scotland shall have jurisdiction to entertain proceedings for an offence which (disregarding the provisions of the Internationally Protected Persons Act 1978, the Suppression of Terrorism Act 1978 and the Nuclear Material (Offences) Act 1983)) would not be an offence in Scotland apart from section 1, 2 or 3 above.

(3) A person is guilty of an offence under, or by virtue of, section 1, 2 or 3 regardless of his nationality.

(4) For the purposes of those sections, it is immaterial whether a person knows that another person is a UN worker.

Extradition

6.—(1) The offences to which an Order in Council under section 2 of the Extradition Act 1870 can apply shall include offences under section 3 of this Act.

(2) In section 22 of the Extradition Act 1989 (extension of purposes of extradition for offences under Acts giving effect to international Conventions)—

    (a) in subsection (2), after paragraph (k) there shall be inserted—

        "(l) the Convention on the Safety of United Nations and Associated Personnel adopted by the General Assembly of the United Nations on 9th December 1994 ("the UN Personnel Convention").", and

    (b) in subsection (4), after paragraph (k) there shall be inserted—

        "(l) in relation to the UN Personnel Convention—

            (i) an offence mentioned in section 1(2) of the United Nations Personnel Act 1997 which is committed against a UN worker within the meaning of that Act;

            (ii) an offence mentioned in subsection (2) of section 2 of that Act which is committed in connection with such an attack as is mentioned in subsection (1) of that section; and

            (iii) an offence under section 3 of that Act."

(3) In Schedule 1 to that Act (provisions deriving from Extradition Act 1870 and associated enactments), in paragraph 15 (deemed extension of jurisdiction of foreign states), after paragraph (m) there shall be inserted—

    "; or

    (n) an offence mentioned in section 1(2) of the United Nations Personnel Act 1997 which is committed against a UN worker within the meaning of that Act; or

    (o) an offence mentioned in subsection (2) of section 2 of that Act which is committed in connection with such an attack as is mentioned in subsection (1) of that section;

    (p) an offence under section 3 of that Act;

    (q) an attempt to commit an offence mentioned in paragraph (n), (o) or (p).".

Consequential amendments

7. The Schedule to this Act (consequential amendments) shall have effect.

Interpretation

8. In this Act—
    "act" includes omission; and
    "UN worker" has the meaning given in section 4.

Extent

9.—(1) This Act extends to Northern Ireland.

(2) Her Majesty may by Order in Council make provision for extending any of the provisions of this Act, with such exceptions, adaptations or modifications as may be specified in the Order, to any of the Channel Islands, the Isle of Man or any colony.

Short title and commencement

10.—(1) This Act may be cited as the United Nations Personnel Act 1997.

(2) This Act shall come into force at the end of the period of two months beginning with the day on which it is passed.

SCHEDULE

CONSEQUENTIAL AMENDMENTS

Visiting Forces Act 1952 (c. 67)

1.—(1) The Schedule to the Visiting Forces Act 1952 (which specifies the offences which are offences against the person and against property for the purposes of section 3 of that Act) shall be amended as follows.

(2) In paragraph 1, after sub-paragraph (d) there shall be inserted—

"(e) an offence of making such a threat as is mentioned in section 3 of the United Nations Personnel Act 1997 and any of the following offences against a UN worker within the meaning of that Act—

    (i) an offence of kidnapping;

    (ii) an offence of false imprisonment;

    (iii) an offence under section 2 of the Explosive Substances Act 1883 of causing an explosion likely to endanger life.";

(3) In paragraph 2, after sub-paragraph (d) there shall be inserted—

"(e) an offence of making such a threat as is mentioned in section 3 of the United Nations Personnel Act 1997 and an offence of causing an explosion likely to endanger life, committed against a UN worker (within the meaning of that Act), under section 2 of the Explosive Substances Act 1883.";

(4) In paragraph 3, after sub-paragraph (k) there shall be inserted—

"(l) an offence under section 2 of the Explosive Substances Act 1883 of causing an explosion likely to cause serious injury to property in connection with such an attack as is mentioned in section 2(1) of the United Nations Personnel Act 1997.";

(5) In paragraph 4, after sub-paragraph (d) there shall be inserted—

"(e) any of the following offences in connection with such an attack as is mentioned in section 2(1) of the United Nations Personnel Act 1997—

    (i) an offence of wilful fireraising;

    (ii) an offence under section 2 of the Explosive Substances Act 1883 of causing an explosion likely to cause serious injury to property.".

Internationally Protected Persons Act 1978 (c. 17)

2. In section 2 of the Internationally Protected Persons Act 1978 (supplementary provision about proceedings for offences under that Act), in subsections (1) and (2) for "and the Nuclear Material (Offences) Act 1983" there shall be substituted ", the Nuclear Material (Offences) Act 1983 and the United Nations Personnel Act 1997".

Suppression of Terrorism Act 1978 (c. 26)

3. In section 4 of the Suppression of Terrorism Act 1978 (jurisdiction in respect of certain offences committed outside the United Kingdom), in subsections (4) and (5) for "and the Nuclear Material (Offences) Act 1983" there shall be substituted ", the Nuclear Material (Offences) Act 1983 and the United Nations Personnel Act 1997".

Nuclear Material (Offences) Act 1983 (c. 18)

4. In section 3 of the Nuclear Material (Offences) Act 1983 (supplementary provision about proceedings for offences under that Act), in subsections (1) and (2) for "and the Suppression of Terrorism Act 1978" there shall be substituted ", the Suppression of Terrorism Act 1978 and the United Nations Personnel Act 1997".

INDEX

References are to sections and the Schedule

NATIONAL HERITAGE ACT 1997

(1997 c. 14)

An Act to extend the powers of the Trustees of the National Heritage
Memorial Fund.   [27th February 1997]

PARLIAMENTARY DEBATES
   Hansard, H.L. Vol. 575, cols. 21, 529, 1352; Vol. 576, cols. 782, 1190; Vol. 578, col. 1293. H.C.
Vol. 287, col. 989; Vol. 291, col. 198.

INTRODUCTION
   This Act allows financial assistance to be provided by the Trustees from the National Heritage
Memorial Fund for any project which appears to them to be of public benefit.

Financial assistance from the National Heritage Memorial Fund

   1.—(1) For section 3 of the National Heritage Act 1980 (grants and loans
from the fund) there is substituted—

"Financial assistance towards property, etc.

   3.—(1) The powers of the Trustees to give financial assistance under
this section are exercisable in the case of things of any kind which are of
scenic, historic, archaeological, aesthetic, architectural, engineering,
artistic or scientific interest, including animals and plants which are of
zoological or botanical interest.
   (2) The Trustees may, for the purpose of—
   (a) securing the preservation or enhancement of such things,
   (b) encouraging the study and understanding of them and the compi-
          lation and dissemination of information about them,
   (c) securing or improving access to them, or their display,
   (d) encouraging enjoyment of them, or
   (e) encouraging the maintenance and development of the skills
          required for their preservation or enhancement,
or for any purpose ancillary to those purposes, give financial assistance
for any project which appears to them to be of public benefit.
   (3) The projects for which financial assistance may be given under this
section for any of the purposes mentioned in subsection (2) above
include (among others) projects for any person to whom the assistance is
to be given to—
   (a) acquire property of any kind (including land),
   (b) construct or convert buildings,
   (c) carry out other works, or
   (d) provide education or training.
   (4) Before giving any financial assistance under this section for any
project, the Trustees—
   (a) shall obtain any expert advice about the project they consider
          appropriate, and
   (b) must be satisfied that the project is of importance to the national
          heritage.
   (5) Financial assistance under this section shall be given by way of
grant or loan out of the Fund, and in giving such assistance the Trustees
may impose any conditions they think fit.
   (6) The conditions that may be imposed in giving such assistance may
relate (among other things) to—
   (a) maintenance, repair, insurance and safe-keeping,
   (b) means of access or display,
   (c) disposal or lending, or
   (d) repayment of grant or loan.

(7) In giving any financial assistance under this section for any project for the preservation or enhancement of anything, or determining the conditions on which such assistance is to be given, the Trustees shall bear in mind the desirability of public access to, or the public display of, the thing in question and of its enjoyment by the public.

(8) The Secretary of State may, with the consent of the Treasury, apply sums received by him under this section as money provided by Parliament instead of paying them into the Consolidated Fund."

(2) After that section there is inserted—

"Financial assistance towards exhibitions, archives, etc.

3A.—(1) The Trustees may give financial assistance for any project within subsection (2) below which appears to them—

    (a) to relate to an important aspect of the history, natural history or landscape of the United Kingdom, and

    (b) to be of public benefit.

(2) The projects within this subsection are projects for any person to whom the assistance is to be given to—

    (a) set up and maintain a public exhibition,

    (b) compile and maintain an archive,

    (c) publish archive material, or

    (d) compile and publish a comprehensive work of reference (or publish a comprehensive work of reference that has previously been compiled),

or to do any ancillary thing.

(3) In subsection (2) above, "archive" includes any collection of sound recordings, images or other information, however stored.

(4) Before giving any financial assistance under this section for any project, the Trustees shall obtain any expert advice about the project they consider appropriate.

(5) Subsections (5), (6) and (8) of section 3 above apply for the purposes of this section as they apply for the purposes of that.

(6) In giving any financial assistance under this section for any project to compile or maintain an archive, or determining the conditions on which such assistance is to be given, the Trustees shall bear in mind the desirability of public access to the archive."

Remuneration and staff

2. In Schedule 1 to the National Heritage Act 1980 (the trustees of the fund)—

    (a) after paragraph 4 there is inserted—

"Remuneration

4A. There may be paid out of the Fund to a trustee such remuneration, on such terms and conditions, as the Secretary of State may approve.",

    (b) in paragraph 5(2) (allowances), for the words from "the Secretary of State" onwards there is substituted "the Trustees think fit", and

    (c) for paragraph 6 (staff) there is substituted—

"6. The Trustees may appoint such officers and servants as they think fit, on such terms (including terms as to remuneration and pensions) as they think fit."

Consequential amendments

3. The Schedule (which makes consequential amendments) shall have effect.

Short title, commencement and extent

4.—(1) This Act may be cited as the National Heritage Act 1997.

(2) The preceding sections of this Act shall come into force on such day as the Secretary of State may by order made by statutory instrument appoint and different days may be appointed for different purposes.

(3) This Act extends to Northern Ireland.

Section 3   SCHEDULE

CONSEQUENTIAL AMENDMENTS

PART I

ENACTMENTS

National Heritage Act 1980 (c. 17)

1.—(1) Section 4 of the National Heritage Act 1980 (other expenditure out of the fund) is amended as follows.

(2) In subsection (1), for "section 3(1) above" there is substituted "subsection (2) below".

(3) For subsection (2) there is substituted—

"(2) The property referred to in subsection (1) above is—

(a) any land, building or structure which in the opinion of the Trustees is of outstanding scenic, historic, archaeological, aesthetic, architectural, engineering or scientific interest;

(b) any object which in their opinion is of outstanding historic, artistic or scientific interest;

(c) any collection or group of objects, being a collection or group which taken as a whole is in their opinion of outstanding historic, artistic or scientific interest;

(d) any land or object not falling within paragraph (a), (b) or (c) above the acquisition, maintenance or preservation of which is in their opinion desirable by reason of its connection with land or a building or structure falling within paragraph (a) above; or

(e) any rights in or over land the acquisition of which is in their opinion desirable for the benefit of land or a building or structure falling within paragraph (a) or (d) above.

(2A) The Trustees shall not apply the Fund for any purpose under subsection (1) above in respect of any property unless they are of the opinion, after obtaining any expert advice they consider appropriate, that the property (or, in the case of land or an object falling within paragraph (d) of subsection (2) above, the land, building or structure with which it is connected, or in the case of rights falling within paragraph (e) of that subsection, the land, building or structure for whose benefit they are acquired) is of importance to the national heritage.

(2B) Notwithstanding that an object such as is mentioned in subsection (2)(b) above or a collection or group of objects such as is mentioned in subsection (2)(c) above is not of itself of importance to the national heritage, the Trustees may apply the Fund under subsection (1) above for any purpose connected with its acquisition if—

(a) they are satisfied that after the acquisition it will form part of a collection or group of objects such as is mentioned in subsection (2)(c) above, and

(b) after obtaining any expert advice they consider appropriate, they are of the opinion that that collection or group is of importance to the national heritage.

(2C) Subsection (7) of section 3 above shall have effect in relation to the application of any sums out of the Fund under this section as it has in relation to the making of a grant or loan under that section."

2.—(1) Section 9 of that Act (disposal of property accepted by Commissioners of Inland Revenue) is amended as follows.

(2) In subsection (2), for "section 3(6)(a), (b) or (c) above", there is substituted "subsection (2A) below".

(3) After subsection (2) there is inserted—

"(2A) The institutions or bodies referred to in subsection (2) above are—

(a) any museum, art gallery, library or other similar institution having as its purpose or one of its purposes the preservation for the public benefit of a collection of historic, artistic or scientific interest;

(b) any body having as its purpose or one of its purposes the provision, improvement or preservation of amenities enjoyed or to be enjoyed by the public or the acquisition of land to be used by the public; and

(c) any body having nature conservation as its purpose or one of its purposes."

3. In section 17 of that Act (expenses and receipts), for "section 3(6A)" there is substituted "section 3(8)".

The National Lottery etc. Act 1993 (c. 39)

4. In section 25 of the National Lottery etc. Act 1993 (application of money by distributing bodies), in subsection (4), for the words from "(acquisition" onwards there is substituted "(other expenditure out of the fund)".

5. In section 44 of that Act (interpretation)—

(a) in subsection (1), in the definition of "expenditure on or connected with the national heritage", for the words from "means" to the end there is substituted "means expenditure for any purpose for which expenditure may be incurred under section 3, 3A or 4 of the National Heritage Act 1980", and

(b) in subsection (2), after "section 3" there is inserted "3A or 4".

6. In Schedule 4 to that Act (amendments of the National Heritage Act 1980), paragraphs 3 and 4 are omitted.

Part II

Northern Ireland legislation

Planning (Northern Ireland) Order 1991 SI 1991/1220 (NI 11)

7. In the Planning (Northern Ireland) Order 1991, in Schedule 5, the amendment to section 3(6)(e) of the National Heritage Act 1980 is omitted.

Historic Monuments and Archaeological Objects (Northern Ireland) Order 1995 SI 1995/1625 (NI 9)

8. In the Historic Monuments and Archaeological Objects (Northern Ireland) Order 1995, paragraph 2 of Schedule 3 is omitted.

INDEX

References are to sections

CONSOLIDATED FUND ACT 1997

(1997 c. 15)

An Act to apply certain sums out of the Consolidated Fund to the service of the years ending on 31st March 1996 and 1997.   [19th March 1997]

PARLIAMENTARY DEBATES
  Hansard, H.C. Vol. 292, col. 468. H.L. Vol. 579, cols. 483, 788.

INTRODUCTION
    This Act makes provision for the application of £215,096,760.90 from the Consolidated Fund for the service of the year ending on March 31, 1996 and for the application of £1,554,472,000 for the service of the year ending on March 31, 1997.

Most Gracious Sovereign,

We, Your Majesty's most dutiful and loyal subjects, the Commons of the United Kingdom in Parliament assembled, towards making good the supply which we have cheerfully granted to Your Majesty in this Session of Parliament, have resolved to grant unto Your Majesty the sums hereinafter mentioned; and do therefore most humbly beseech Your Majesty that it may be enacted, and be it enacted by the Queen's most Excellent Majesty, by and with the advice and consent of the Lords Spiritual and Temporal, and Commons, in this present Parliament assembled, and by the authority of the same, as follows:—

Issue out of the Consolidated Fund for the year ended 31st March 1996

1. The Treasury may issue out of the Consolidated Fund of the United Kingdom and apply towards making good the supply granted to Her Majesty for the service of the year ended on 31st March 1996 the sum of £215,096,760.90.

Issue out of the Consolidated Fund for the year ending 31st March 1997

2. The Treasury may issue out of the Consolidated Fund of the United Kingdom and apply towards making good the supply granted to Her Majesty for the service of the year ending on 31st March 1997 the sum of £1,554,472,000.

Short title

3. This Act may be cited as the Consolidated Fund Act 1997.

INDEX

References are to sections

FINANCE ACT 1997*

(1997 c. 16)

ARRANGEMENT OF SECTIONS

PART I

EXCISE DUTIES

PART II

INSURANCE PREMIUM TAX

* Annotations by Ian Ferrier, Barrister.

An Act to grant certain duties, to alter other duties, and to amend the law relating to the National Debt and the Public Revenue, and to make further provision in connection with Finance.   [19th March 1997]

Parliamentary Debates
Hansard, H.C. Vol. 286, col. 932; Vol. 288, cols. 137, 976, 1089; Vol. 292, col. 152. H.L. Vol. 579, cols. 483, 903.

Introduction and General Note

This Act, only about half the length of its two predecessors, was passed just before the General Election. In view of the fact that the Government had lost its overall majority in the House of Commons, it contained little controversial material and nothing of an innovative nature.

The Act also marks the end of an era. The Government's heavy defeat in the General Election brings to a close 18 uninterrupted years of Conservative rule, a sequence without parallel in modern times. During that time the fiscal system was transformed. The top incremental rate of income tax was reduced from 98 per cent to 40 per cent and the main rate of corporation tax from 52 per cent to 33 per cent. On the other hand, the rate of value added tax was increased from 8 per cent to 17.5 per cent. The base date from which capital gains tax is calculated was moved from 1965 to 1982 and gains are subject to indexation for inflation. Capital transfer tax has been transformed into inheritance tax. Instead of a graduated scale reaching 75 per cent, there is a single rate of 40 per cent for amounts over the threshold. The introduction of relief for life-time gifts means that the tax is now closely equivalent to estate duty, whose shortcomings capital transfer tax was intended to remedy. Development land tax was abolished.

Unfortunately these changes have not been accompanied by a reduction in the volume of the legislation whose bulk and complication has continued to increase inexorably. As the result of a back-bench initiative, a project has now been put in hand to rewrite the tax legislation in simpler terms. It remains to be seen what this will achieve.

The national finances have passed through several phases during the 18 year period. An initial spell of recession, accompanied by high inflation and high interest rates, was followed by stabilisation and then by an economic boom characterised towards the end by a remarkable and unsustainable increase in property prices. The ensuing recession was severe and prolonged. Recovery has now lasted for several years, although unemployment and Government borrowing remain at high levels for this period of the economic cycle.

Many of the changes made by the Conservatives have been implicitly accepted by a reformed Labour party, but no doubt the new Government's first Budget, due in July, will signal a fresh approach to fiscal policy.

Part I

Excise Duties

Alcoholic liquor duties

Rates of duty on spirits and wines of equivalent strength

1.—(1) In section 5 of the Alcoholic Liquor Duties Act 1979 (spirits), for "£19.78" there shall be substituted "£18.99".

(2) In Part II of the Table of rates of duty in Schedule 1 to that Act (wine or made-wine of a strength exceeding 22 per cent), for "19.78" there shall be substituted "18.99".

(3) This section shall be deemed to have come into force at 6 o'clock in the evening of 26th November 1996.

General Note

The rate of duty on spirits and on wine (or made-wine) of a strength exceeding 22 per cent is reduced by 4 per cent. This repeats a similar reduction made last year.

Rates of duty on lower strengths of wine and made-wine

2.—(1) For Part I of the Table of rates of duty in Schedule 1 to the Alcoholic Liquor Duties Act 1979 (wine and made-wine of a strength not exceeding 22 per cent) there shall be substituted—

PART I

WINE OR MADE-WINE OF A STRENGTH NOT EXCEEDING 22 PER CENT

Description of wine or made-wine	*Rates of duty per hectolitre*
	£
Wine or made-wine of a strength not exceeding 4 per cent	43.28
Wine or made-wine of a strength exceeding 4 per cent but not exceeding 5.5 per cent	59.51
Wine or made-wine of a strength exceeding 5.5 per cent but not exceeding 15 per cent and not being sparkling	140.44
Sparkling wine or sparkling made-wine of a strength exceeding 5.5 per cent but less than 8.5 per cent	195.63
Sparkling wine or sparkling made-wine of a strength of 8.5 per cent or of a strength exceeding 8.5 per cent but not exceeding 15 per cent	200.64
Wine or made-wine of a strength exceeding 15 per cent but not exceeding 22 per cent	187.24

(2) This section shall be deemed to have come into force on 1st January 1997.

GENERAL NOTE

The section increases the rates of duty on wine (or made-wine) with a strength exceeding 1.2 per cent but not 4 per cent and between 4 per cent and 5.5 per cent. The purpose of this change is to bring the duty on "coolers" such as Alcopops and "FAB"s (flavoured alcoholic beverages) into line with beer duty.

Also, the existing sparkling wine duty band is divided into two and the duty on the range between 5.5 per cent and 8.5 per cent is reduced. This is to address the duty disadvantage suffered by low-strength sparkling wine as compared to sparkling cider (see further ss.3–5).

Duty on sparkling cider

3.—(1) In subsection (1A) of section 62 of the Alcoholic Liquor Duties Act 1979 (rates of excise duty on cider)—

    (a) in paragraph (a), after "exceeding 7.5 per cent" there shall be inserted "which is not sparkling cider"; and

    (b) immediately before the word "and" at the end of that paragraph there shall be inserted the following paragraph—

        "(aa) £36.45 per hectolitre in the case of sparkling cider of a strength exceeding 5.5 per cent;".

(2) After subsection (6) of that section there shall be inserted the following subsection—

    "(7) References in this section to making cider shall be construed as including references to producing sparkling cider by rendering cider sparkling; and references in this section to cider made in the United Kingdom, to makers of cider and to making cider for sale shall be construed accordingly."

(3) After that section there shall be inserted the following section—

"Meaning of "sparkling" etc. in section 62

62A.—(1) This section applies for the purposes of section 62 above.

(2) Cider which is for the time being in a closed bottle is sparkling if, due to the presence of carbon dioxide, the pressure in the bottle, measured at a temperature of 20 degrees C, is not less than 3 bars in excess of atmospheric pressure.

(3) Cider which is for the time being in a closed bottle is sparkling regardless of the pressure in the bottle if the bottle has a mushroom-

shaped stopper (whether solid or hollow) held in place by a tie or fastening.

(4) Cider which is not for the time being in a closed container is sparkling if it has characteristics similar to those of cider which has been removed from a closed bottle and which, before removal, fell within subsection (2) above.

(5) Cider shall be regarded as having been rendered sparkling if, as a result of aeration, fermentation or any other process, it either—

(a) falls within subsection (2) above; or

(b) takes on characteristics similar to those of cider which has been removed from a closed bottle and which, before removal, fell within subsection (2) above.

(6) Cider which has not previously been rendered sparkling by virtue of subsection (5) above shall be regarded as having been rendered sparkling if it is transferred into a closed bottle which has a mushroom-shaped stopper (whether solid or hollow) held in place by a tie or fastening.

(7) Cider which is in a closed bottle and has not previously been rendered sparkling by virtue of subsection (5) or (6) above shall be regarded as having been rendered sparkling if the stopper of its bottle is exchanged for a stopper of a kind mentioned in subsection (6) above."

(4) In section 64 of that Act (remission or repayment of duty on spoilt cider), after subsection (1) there shall be inserted the following subsection—

"(1A) In subsection (1) above the references to a maker of cider include references to any person who is taken for the purposes of section 62 above to be a maker of cider."

(5) This section shall be deemed to have come into force on 1st January 1997.

(6) Any order or regulations made under section 62 or 64 of the Alcoholic Liquor Duties Act 1979 before 1st January 1997—

(a) shall have effect (but only if and for so long as the order or regulations would be in force apart from this subsection) as if the amendments made to that Act by this section had been made before the making of the order or regulations, and

(b) shall be deemed at all times on or after that date so to have had effect.

GENERAL NOTE

A rate of £36.45 per hectolitre is introduced for sparkling cider (and perry) of a strength exceeding 5.5 per cent. Although sparkling cider accounts for less than 2 per cent of the total cider market, it was felt that the duty differential with sparkling wines of similar strength was anomalous.

New Alcoholic Liquor Duties Act 1979 (c. 4), s.62A provides a definition of "sparkling".

Cider labelled as strong cider

4.—(1) After the section 62A inserted into the Alcoholic Liquor Duties Act 1979 by section 3 above there shall be inserted the following section—

"Cider labelled as strong cider

62B.—(1) For the purposes of this Act, any liquor which would apart from this section be standard cider and which—

(a) is in an up-labelled container, or

(b) has, at any time after 31st December 1996 when it was in the United Kingdom, been in an up-labelled container,

shall be deemed to be strong cider, and not standard cider.

(2) Accordingly, references in this Act to making cider include references to—

(a) putting standard cider in an up-labelled container; or

(b) causing a container in which there is standard cider to be up-labelled.

(3) Where, by virtue of this section, any duty is charged under section 62 above on any cider, a rebate shall be allowed in respect of the amount of any duty charged on that cider under that section otherwise than by virtue of this section.

(4) For the purposes of this section—

(a) 'standard cider' means cider which is not sparkling and is of a strength not exceeding 7.5 per cent; and

(b) 'strong cider' means cider which is not sparkling and is of a strength exceeding 7.5 per cent.

(5) For the purposes of this section a container is up-labelled if there is anything on—

(a) the container itself,

(b) a label or leaflet attached to or used with the container, or

(c) any packaging used for or in association with the container,

which states or tends to suggest that the strength of any liquor in that container falls within the strong cider strength range.

(6) For the purposes of subsection (5) above, a strength falls within the strong cider strength range if it exceeds 7.5 per cent but is less than 8.5 per cent."

(2) This section shall be deemed to have come into force on 1st January 1997.

GENERAL NOTE

New Alcoholic Liquor Duties Act 1979, s.62B provides that strong cider (*i.e.* cider labelled as being within the range of 7.5 per cent to 8.5 per cent) shall be taxed at the rate applicable to the strength on the label.

Cider labelled as made-wine

5.—(1) After section 55A of the Alcoholic Liquor Duties Act 1979 there shall be inserted the following section—

"Cider labelled as made-wine

55B.—(1) For the purposes of this Act, any liquor which would apart from this section be cider and which—

(a) is in an up-labelled container, or

(b) has, at any time after 31st December 1996 when it was in the United Kingdom, been in an up-labelled container,

shall be deemed to be made-wine, and not cider.

(2) Accordingly, references in this Act to producing made-wine include references to—

(a) putting cider in an up-labelled container; or

(b) causing a container in which there is cider to be up-labelled.

(3) For the purposes of this Act, where any liquor is deemed by this section to be made-wine, it shall be deemed—

(a) if it is in an up-labelled container, to be made-wine of the strength that the labelling for the container states or tends to suggest; and

(b) if it is no longer in an up-labelled container, to be made-wine of the strength stated or suggested by the labelling for the up-labelled container in which it was contained when it was first deemed by this section to be made-wine.

(4) Subsection (3)(a) above has effect subject to any provision that may be made by regulations under section 2(3) above.

(5) Where, by virtue of this section, any duty is charged under section 55 above on any liquor, a rebate shall be allowed in respect of the amount of any duty charged on that liquor under section 62 below.

(6) For the purposes of this section a container is up-labelled if the labelling for the container states or tends to suggest that the strength of any liquor in that container is or exceeds 8.5 per cent.

(7) In this section references to the labelling for any container are references to anything on—

    (a) the container itself,

    (b) a label or leaflet attached to or used with the container, or

    (c) any packaging used for or in association with the container."

(2) In section 1 of that Act (interpretation)—

    (a) in subsection (5) (meaning of "made-wine"), after "subsection (10)" there shall be inserted "and section 55B(1)"; and

    (b) in subsection (6) (meaning of "cider"), after "means" there shall be inserted ", subject to section 55B(1) below,".

(3) In section 2(3A) of that Act (regulations may provide for duty to be charged by reference to strengths shown on bottle labels)—

    (a) after the word "beer,", in the first place where it occurs, there shall be inserted "cider,"; and

    (b) for the words "spirits, beer, wine or made-wine", in the second place where they occur, there shall be substituted "liquor in that bottle or other container".

(4) In section 56(1)(c) of that Act (restriction on use of wine in production of made-wine), after "of wine" there shall be inserted "or cider".

(5) Subsections (1) and (2) above shall be deemed to have come into force on 1st January 1997.

General Note

New Alcoholic Liquor Duties Act 1979, s.55B provides that cider in a container suggesting a strength of more than 8.5 per cent is to be taxed as made-wine.

Hydrocarbon oil duties

Rates of hydrocarbon oil duties and of rebates

6.—(1) In section 6(1) of the Hydrocarbon Oil Duties Act 1979, for "£0.3912" (duty on light oil) and "£0.3430" (duty on heavy oil) there shall be substituted "£0.4168" and "£0.3686", respectively.

(2) In section 8(3) of that Act (duty on road fuel gas), for "£0.2817" there shall be substituted "£0.2113".

(3) In section 11(1) of that Act (rebate on heavy oil), for "£0.0181" (fuel oil) and "£0.0233" (gas oil) there shall be substituted "£0.0194" and "£0.0250", respectively.

(4) In section 14(1) of that Act (rebate on light oil for use as furnace fuel), for "£0.0181" there shall be substituted "£0.0194".

(5) This section shall be deemed to have come into force at 6 o'clock in the evening of 26th November 1996.

General Note

Subs. (1)

The rate of excise duty on light and heavy oils is increased by 2.56p per litre.

Subs. (2)

The rate of duty on road fuel gas is reduced by 7.04p per kilogram.

Subs. (3)

The alteration in the duty rebates allowable on heavy oil result in an effective increase in excise duty of 0.17p per litre on gas oil and 0.13p per litre on fuel oil.

Subs. (4)
The alteration in the duty rebate on light oil used as furnace fuel results in an effective increase in excise duty of 0.13p per litre.

Ultra low sulphur diesel

7.—(1) In section 1 of the Hydrocarbon Oil Duties Act 1979 (definitions of oil)—
   (a) in subsection (1), for "(2) to (4)" there shall be substituted "(2) to (6)"; and
   (b) after subsection (4) there shall be inserted the following subsections—
      "(5) 'Gas oil' means heavy oil of which not more than 50 per cent by volume distils at a temperature not exceeding 240°C and of which more than 50 per cent by volume distils at a temperature not exceeding 340°C.
      (6) 'Ultra low sulphur diesel' means gas oil the sulphur content of which does not exceed 0.005 per cent by weight or is nil."
(2) In section 6 of that Act (excise duty on hydrocarbon oil), in subsection (1) (as amended by section 6 above), for the words from "the rate of £0.4168" to the end of the subsection there shall be substituted "the rates specified in subsection (1A) below."
(3) After subsection (1) of that section there shall be inserted the following subsection—
      "(1A) The rates at which the duty shall be charged are—
      (a) £0.4168 a litre in the case of light oil;
      (b) £0.3586 a litre in the case of ultra low sulphur diesel; and
      (c) £0.3686 a litre in the case of heavy oil which is not ultra low sulphur diesel."
(4) In subsection (3) of that section, for "that subsection" there shall be substituted "subsection (1A) above".
(5) In section 11(1) of that Act (rebate on heavy oil)—
   (a) in paragraph (b), after "gas oil" there shall be inserted "which is not ultra low sulphur diesel";
   (b) for the word "and" at the end of that paragraph there shall be substituted—
      "(ba) in the case of ultra low sulphur diesel, of £0.0250 a litre less than the rate at which the duty is for the time being chargeable; and";
      and
   (c) in paragraph (c), for "other than fuel oil and" there shall be substituted "which is neither fuel oil nor".
(6) In section 13AA(6) of that Act (rate for rebated gas oil), for "section 6(1) above in the case of heavy oil" there shall be substituted "section 6(1A) above in the case of heavy oil which is not ultra low sulphur diesel,".
(7) In subsection (1) of section 24 of that Act (control of use of duty-free and rebated oil), after "section 9(1) or (4)," there shall be inserted "section 11,".
(8) In section 27(1) of that Act (interpretation)—
   (a) after the definition of "aviation gasoline" there shall be inserted the following definition—
      " 'gas oil' has the meaning given by section 1(5) above;"
      and
   (b) after the definition of "road vehicle" there shall be inserted the following definition—
      " 'ultra low sulphur diesel' has the meaning given by section 1(6) above."
(9) In Schedule 2A to that Act (mixing of heavy oil)—
   (a) in paragraph 4(a), after "section 11(1)(b)" there shall be inserted "or (ba)";

(b) in paragraph 6(b), after "section 11(1)(b)" there shall be inserted "or (ba)";

(c) after paragraph 6 there shall be inserted—

"Mixing different types of partially rebated gas oil

6A. A mixture of heavy oils is produced in contravention of this paragraph if such a mixture is produced by mixing—
(a) ultra low sulphur diesel in respect of which a rebate has been allowed under section 11(1)(ba) of this Act; and
(b) gas oil in respect of which a rebate has been allowed under section 11(1)(b) of this Act.";

(d) in paragraph 7 (complex mixtures of heavy oils), for the words from "if such a mixture" to the end of the paragraph there shall be substituted "if the production of a mixture of two of the components of that mixture is a contravention of any of paragraphs 4 to 6A above.";

(e) in paragraph 8(4) (rate for light oil), for "section 6(1)" there shall be substituted "section 6(1A)";

(f) in paragraph 9(2) (rate for heavy oil), for "in the case of heavy oil by section 6(1) of this Act" there shall be substituted "by section 6(1A) of this Act in the case of heavy oil which is not ultra low sulphur diesel"; and

(g) in paragraph 11 (interpretation), for " 'fuel oil' and 'gas oil' have the same meanings" there shall be substituted " 'fuel oil' has the same meaning".

(10) This section shall come into force on such day as the Commissioners of Customs and Excise may by order made by statutory instrument appoint.

GENERAL NOTE
   The section provides for a new rate of duty on ultra low sulphur diesel ("ULSD") and for a rebate from that charge when ULSD is used as off-road fuel. It also provides for revenue safeguards against mixing ULSD and conventional diesel after duty has been paid at the differing rates. Since a derogation from E.C. regulations will be required, the section will take effect by statutory instrument subject to the negative resolution procedure.
   The duty rate for ULSD will be 35.86p per litre (1p less than the rate for heavy oil which includes ordinary diesel oil). When ULSD is used as off-road fuel there will be a rebate of 2.5p per litre.

Tobacco products duty

Rates of tobacco products duty

8.—(1) For the Table of rates of duty in Schedule 1 to the Tobacco Products Duty Act 1979 there shall be substituted—

TABLE

1. Cigarettes	An amount equal to 21 per cent of the retail price plus £65.97 per thousand cigarettes.
2. Cigars	£98.02 per kilogram.
3. Hand-rolling tobacco ...	£87.74 per kilogram.
4. Other smoking tobacco and chewing tobacco	£43.10 per kilogram.

(2) This section shall be deemed to have come into force at 6 o'clock in the evening of 26th November 1996.

GENERAL NOTE
   The rates of duty on tobacco products other than hand-rolling tobacco are increased by 7.1 per cent (*i.e.* the rate of inflation plus 5 per cent). For hand-rolling tobacco the increase is confined to

2.1 per cent. This reflects concern over the ease with which hand-rolling tobacco can be smuggled into the U.K.

Air passenger duty

Rates of air passenger duty

9.—(1) In subsection (2) of section 30 of the Finance Act 1994 (rate of duty for journeys ending in the U.K., another EEA State or certain territories for whose external relations either the U.K. or another member State is responsible), for "£5" there shall be substituted "£10".

(2) In subsection (4) of that section (rate of duty in other cases), for "£10" there shall be substituted "£20".

(3) This section applies in cases where, in accordance with section 28(2)(a) of that Act (duty becomes due when aircraft first takes off on passenger's flight), duty becomes due on or after 1st November 1997.

GENERAL NOTE
The rates of air passenger duty, introduced as from November 1, 1994 are increased from £5 to £10 in the case of internal flights, flights to members of the European Economic Area (the European Union plus Iceland and Norway), to Basle and Geneva and to certain overseas territories of European Union members, and from £10 to £20 for all other destinations.

The increased rates, effective from November 1, 1997 are expected to produce an additional £385 million in the first full year (1988/89).

Gaming duty

Gaming duty to replace gaming licence duty

10.—(1) A gaming licence shall not be required under section 13 of the Betting and Gaming Duties Act 1981 (gaming licence duty) for any gaming on or after 1st October 1997; but a duty of excise (to be known as "gaming duty") shall be charged in accordance with section 11 below on any premises in the United Kingdom where gaming to which this section applies ("dutiable gaming") takes place on or after that date.

(2) Subject to subsections (3) and (4) below, this section applies to gaming by way of any of the following games, that is to say, baccarat, punto banco, big six, blackjack, boule, casino stud poker, chemin de fer, chuck-a-luck, craps, crown and anchor, faro, faro bank, hazard, poker dice, pontoon, French roulette, American roulette, super pan 9, trente et quarante, vingt-et-un, and wheel of fortune.

(3) This section does not apply to any lawful gaming which is gaming to which any of the following provisions applies and takes place in accordance with the requirements of that provision, that is to say—

(a) section 2(2) of the Gaming Act 1968 or Article 55(2) of the Betting, Gaming, Lotteries and Amusements (Northern Ireland) Order 1985 (private parties);
(b) section 6 of that Act (premises licensed for the sale of liquor);
(c) section 34 of that Act or Article 108 of that Order (certain gaming machines);
(d) section 41 of that Act or Article 126 of that Order (gaming at entertainments not held for private gain);
(e) section 15 or 16 of the Lotteries and Amusements Act 1976 or Article 153 or 154 of that Order (amusements with prizes).

(4) This section does not apply to any gaming which takes place on premises in respect of which a club or miners' welfare institute is for the time being registered under Part II of the Gaming Act 1968.

(5) The Treasury may by order made by statutory instrument add to the games mentioned in subsection (2) above if it appears to them, having regard to the character of the game and the circumstances in which it is played, that it is appropriate to do so.

(6) Any reference in this section, or in an order under subsection (5) above, to a particular game shall be taken to include a reference to any game (by whatever name called) which is essentially similar to that game.

GENERAL NOTE

The section provides for a duty on premises where gaming takes place and replaces gaming licence duty. It restructures the duty currently levied on casinos to provide for registration rather than licensing and to remove some other regulatory measures.

Previously the duty was charged on the licence. In future it will be charged on the premises, but will be calculated in exactly the same way.

Rate of gaming duty

11.—(1) Gaming duty shall be charged on premises for every accounting period which contains a time when dutiable gaming takes place on those premises.

(2) Subject to subsection (3) below, the amount of gaming duty which is charged on any premises for any accounting period shall be calculated, in accordance with the following Table, by—

(a) applying the rates specified in that Table to the parts so specified of the gross gaming yield in that period from the premises; and

(b) aggregating the results.

TABLE

Part of gross gaming yield	*Rate*
The first £450,000	2½ per cent
The next £2,250,000	12½ per cent
The next £2,700,000	25 per cent
The remainder	33⅓ per cent

(3) Where, in an accounting period, unregistered gaming takes place on any premises, the amount of gaming duty which is charged on those premises for that period shall be equal to 33⅓ per cent of the gross gaming yield in that period from the premises.

(4) For the purposes of subsection (3) above, unregistered gaming takes place on premises in an accounting period if—

(a) dutiable gaming takes place on those premises at any time in that period, and

(b) at that time those premises are not specified in the entry on the gaming duty register for a person by whom at that time they are notifiable for the purposes of paragraph 6 of Schedule 1 to this Act.

(5) The Commissioners may by regulations—

(a) provide for the cases in which dutiable gaming is to be treated as taking place on any premises for part only of an accounting period; and

(b) in relation to such cases, provide for the parts of the gross gaming yield specified in the first column of the Table in subsection (2) above to be reduced in relation to those premises for that accounting period in such manner as may be determined in accordance with the regulations.

(6) Where the Commissioners are satisfied—

(a) that dutiable gaming is, has been or may be taking place in the course of any accounting period at different premises situated at the same location or in very close proximity to each other, and

(b) that the activities carried on at those premises are connected or form part of the same business or are, or are comprised in, connected businesses, the Commissioners may direct that for the purposes of gaming duty the different premises are to be treated as different parts of the same premises.

(7) Sections 14 to 16 of the Finance Act 1994 (review and appeals) shall have effect in relation to any decision of the Commissioners to make or vary a direction under subsection (6) above as if that decision were a decision of a description specified in Schedule 5 to that Act.

(8) For the purposes of this section the gross gaming yield from any premises in any accounting period shall consist of the aggregate of—

(a) the gaming receipts for that period from those premises; and

(b) where a provider of the premises (or a person acting on his behalf) is banker in relation to any dutiable gaming taking place on those premises in that period, the banker's profits for that period from that gaming.

(9) For the purposes of subsection (8) above the gaming receipts for an accounting period from any premises are the receipts in that period from charges made in connection with any dutiable gaming which has taken place on the premises other than—

(a) so much of any charge as represents value added tax, and

(b) any charge the payment of which confers no more than an entitlement to admission to the premises.

(10) In subsection (8) above the reference to the banker's profits from any gaming is a reference to the amount (if any) by which the value specified in paragraph (a) below exceeds the value specified in paragraph (b) below, that is to say—

(a) the value, in money or money's worth, of the stakes staked with the banker in any such gaming; and

(b) the value, in money or money's worth, of the winnings paid by the banker to those taking part in such gaming otherwise than on behalf of a provider of the premises.

(11) The Treasury may by order made by statutory instrument amend subsections (8) to (10) above.

GENERAL NOTE

The section establishes the charge to gaming duty. The rates are the same as for gaming licence duty, except that there is no advance payment of £10 every six months. For premises where dutiable gaming takes place but they are not registered the highest rate of charge will apply.

Liability to pay gaming duty

12.—(1) The liability to pay the gaming duty charged on any premises for any accounting period shall fall jointly and severally on—

(a) every person who is a provider of the premises at a time in that period when dutiable gaming takes place there;

(b) every person concerned in the organisation or management of any dutiable gaming taking place on those premises in that period;

(c) where any of the persons mentioned in paragraphs (a) and (b) above is a body corporate that is treated as a member of a group for the purposes of Part I of Schedule 1 to this Act, every body corporate that is treated as a member of that group for those purposes; and

(d) where any of the persons mentioned in paragraphs (a) to (c) above is a body corporate, every director of that body.

(2) A person shall for the purposes of this section be conclusively presumed to be a provider of premises at any time if at that time—

(a) he is registered on the gaming duty register, and

(b) those premises are specified in his entry on that register.

(3) The Commissioners may by regulations make provision—

(a) for apportioning the liability for any gaming duty charged on any premises for an accounting period between different persons; and

(b) for the amount of gaming duty charged on any premises for the different parts of a period for which an apportionment falls to be made to be computed (in accordance with regulations made by virtue of section 11(5)(b) above) as if each part of the period were the only part of the period during which dutiable gaming has taken place on those premises.

(4) The Commissioners may by regulations impose obligations on any of the persons mentioned in subsection (1) above requiring them to make payments on account of any gaming duty that is likely to be chargeable on any premises.

(5) Any failure by any person to pay any amount of gaming duty due from him—

(a) shall attract a penalty under section 9 of the Finance Act 1994 (civil penalties) which shall be calculated by reference to the amount that has not been paid; and

(b) shall also attract daily penalties.

(6) Where, in accordance with any regulations under subsection (4) above, any amount has become payable on account of gaming duty by any person, that amount shall be deemed—

(a) for the purposes of section 12 of the Finance Act 1994 (assessments to excise duty), to be an amount which has become due from that person in respect of gaming duty;

(b) for the purposes of section 116 of the Customs and Excise Management Act 1979 (time and place etc. for payment of excise duty), to be an amount of gaming duty that has become payable; and

(c) for the purposes of subsection (5) above, sections 51 and 52 below and section 137(1) of the Customs and Excise Management Act 1979 (recovery of duty), to be an amount of gaming duty due from that person;

and an amount paid on account of gaming duty shall be deemed for the purposes of section 137A of the Customs and Excise Management Act 1979 (recovery of overpaid duty) to be an amount paid by way of that duty.

GENERAL NOTE

The liability to pay gaming duty falls jointly and severally on persons providing the premises and persons concerned with the organisation or management of the gaming. A person is considered to be a provider of premises if he is on the gaming duty register and the premises are specified in his entry.

Provision is now made for the registration of groups of companies and the joint and several liability is extended to all members of the group and their directors.

The Customs and Excise are given power by regulation to apportion duty where there is a change of provider and to require payments on account.

Civil penalties under F.A. 1994 (c. 9), s.9 apply to failure to pay gaming duty.

Supplemental provisions relating to gaming duty

13.—(1) Schedule 1 to this Act (which makes supplemental provision with respect to gaming duty) shall have effect.

(2) Schedule 2 to this Act (which amends the Customs and Excise Management Act 1979 and contains other amendments) shall have effect.

GENERAL NOTE

The section introduces Scheds. 1 and 2, which provide respectively for the administration and enforcement of gaming duty and for consequential and incidental amendments to other legislation. See further the General Note to these Schedules.

Subordinate legislation relating to gaming duty

14.—(1) Any power conferred on the Commissioners by section 11 or 12 above or Schedule 1 to this Act to make regulations—

(a) shall be exercisable by statutory instrument subject to annulment in pursuance of a resolution of the House of Commons; and

(b) shall include power to make different provision for different cases.

(2) A statutory instrument containing an order under section 10(5) or 11(11) above—

(a) shall be laid before the House of Commons after being made; and

(b) shall cease to have effect (without prejudice to anything previously done under the order or to the making of a new order) at the end of the period of 28 days after the day on which it was made unless it has been approved, before the end of that period, by a resolution of that House.

(3) In reckoning the period of 28 days mentioned in subsection (2)(b) above, no account shall be taken of any time during which Parliament is dissolved or prorogued or during which the House of Commons is adjourned for more than four days.

GENERAL NOTE

Regulations made by the Customs and Excise are by statutory instrument subject to the negative resolution procedure. Orders made by the Treasury are also by statutory instrument, but subject to an affirmative resolution within 28 days. Treasury orders may add new games to those listed in s.10(2) and amend the provisions that specify gross gaming yield in s.11(8)–(10).

Interpretation of gaming duty provisions

15.—(1) This section shall have effect for the purposes of construing the gaming duty provisions of this Act, that is to say, sections 10 to 14 above, this section and Schedule 1 to this Act.

(2) The gaming duty provisions of this Act shall be construed as one with the Customs and Excise Management Act 1979.

(3) In the gaming duty provisions of this Act—

"accounting period" means, subject to the provisions of Schedule 1 to this Act, a period of six months beginning with 1st April or 1st October;

"dutiable gaming" means gaming to which section 10 above applies;

"gaming" means gaming within the meaning of the Gaming Act 1968 or the Betting, Gaming, Lotteries and Amusements (Northern Ireland) Order 1985;

"the gaming duty register" means the register maintained under paragraph 1 of Schedule 1 to this Act;

"premises" includes any place and any means of transport and shall be construed subject to section 11(6) above;

"provider", in relation to any premises where gaming takes place, means any person having a right to control the admission of persons to those premises, whether or not he has a right to control the admission of persons to the gaming.

(4) For the avoidance of doubt it is hereby declared that the imposition or payment of gaming duty does not make lawful any gaming which is otherwise unlawful.

GENERAL NOTE

This is the general interpretation section.

Subs. (4)

The payment of gaming duty does not legitimate unlawful gaming.

Vehicle excise duty

Increase in general rate

16.—(1) In Schedule 1 to the Vehicle Excise and Registration Act 1994 (annual rates of duty), in paragraph 1(2) (the general rate), for "£140" there shall be substituted "£145".

(2) This section applies in relation to licences taken out after 26th November 1996.

GENERAL NOTE
The general rate of vehicle excise duty is increased from £140 to £145, broadly in line with inflation. Other rates linked to the general rate under Vehicle Excise and Registration Act 1994 (c. 22) will also increase by £5 (£10 for trailers over 12 tonnes).

Exemption for vehicles for disabled persons

17. In paragraph 19 of Schedule 2 to the Vehicle Excise and Registration Act 1994 (exemption for vehicles for disabled persons), after sub-paragraph (2) there shall be inserted the following sub-paragraph—

"(2A) This paragraph shall have effect as if a person were in receipt of a disability living allowance by virtue of entitlement to the mobility component at the higher rate in any case where—

(a) he has ceased to be in receipt of it as a result of having ceased to satisfy a condition of receiving the allowance or of receiving the mobility component at that rate;

(b) that condition is either—

(i) a condition relating to circumstances in which he is undergoing medical or other treatment as an in-patient in a hospital or similar institution; or

(ii) a condition specified in regulations made by the Secretary of State;

and

(c) he would continue to be entitled to receive the mobility component of the allowance at the higher rate but for his failure to satisfy that condition."

GENERAL NOTE
The section legislates an extra-statutory concession which exempts from vehicle excise duty ("VED") certain disabled people undergoing long-term treatment in hospital. Beneficiaries of the higher rate mobility component of the disability living allowance are entitled to exemption from VED. This is now extended to cases where they lose this entitlement through being in hospital for more than 28 days.

Provisions applying to exempt vehicles

18. Schedule 3 to this Act (which contains provisions applying to exempt vehicles) shall have effect.

GENERAL NOTE
The section introduces Sched. 3, which strengthens the enforcement provisions relating to vehicles which are exempt from VED. See further the General Note to Sched. 3.

Issue of licences before payment of duty

19.—(1) After section 19A of the Vehicle Excise and Registration Act 1994 there shall be inserted the following section—

"Issue of licences before payment of duty
19B.—(1) The Secretary of State may, if he thinks fit, issue a vehicle licence or a trade licence to a person who has agreed with the Secretary of State to pay the duty payable on the licence in a manner provided for in the agreement.

(2) In a case where—

(a) a vehicle licence or a trade licence is issued to a person in accordance with subsection (1),

(b) the duty payable on the licence is not received by the Secretary of State in accordance with the agreement, and

(c) the Secretary of State sends a notice by post to the person inform-ing him that the licence is void as from the time when it was granted,

the licence shall be void as from the time when it was granted.

(3) In a case where—

(a) paragraphs (a) and (b) of subsection (2) apply,

(b) the Secretary of State sends a notice by post to the person requir-ing him to secure that the duty payable on the licence is paid within such reasonable period as is specified in the notice,

(c) the requirement in the notice is not complied with, and

(d) the Secretary of State sends a further notice by post to the person informing him that the licence is void as from the time when it was granted,

the licence shall be void as from the time when it was granted."

(2) In subsection (1)(a) of section 35A of that Act (dishonoured cheques)—

(a) after "19A(2)(b)" there shall be inserted "or 19B(2)(c)"; and

(b) after "19A(3)(d)" there shall be inserted "or 19B(3)(d)".

GENERAL NOTE

The Driver and Vehicle Licensing Agency ("DVLA") is to enable persons operating large vehicle fleets to re-license their vehicles via a computer link. VED will be paid by direct debit mandate. With the exception of payments made by cheque, Vehicle Excise and Registration Act 1994 does not provide for the issue of a licence before duty is received nor for the voiding or recovery of the licence or any outstanding duty where payment is dishonoured. The section provides the necessary legal framework.

Removal and disposal of vehicles

20.—(1) In paragraph 3 of Schedule 2A to the Vehicle Excise and Regis-tration Act 1994 (immobilisation, removal and disposal of vehicles), for sub-paragraph (1) there shall be substituted the following sub-paragraph—

"(1) The regulations may make provision with respect to any case where—

(a) an authorised person has reason to believe that an offence under section 29(1)—

(i) is being committed as regards a vehicle which is station-ary on a public road; or

(ii) was being committed as regards a vehicle at a time when an immobilisation device which is fixed to the vehicle was fixed to it in accordance with the regulations; and

(b) such conditions as may be prescribed are fulfilled."

(2) In sub-paragraph (2) of that paragraph, for "an authorised person, or a person acting under the direction of an authorised person" there shall be substituted "the authorised person, or a person acting under his direction".

(3) In sub-paragraph (6) of that paragraph, for "when the immobilisation device was fixed" there shall be substituted "when the vehicle was removed".

(4) This section shall come into force on such day as the Secretary of State may by order made by statutory instrument appoint.

GENERAL NOTE

Under current powers to wheelclamp unlicensed vehicles a vehicle cannot be removed from the road until it has been clamped and the vehicle keeper takes no action within 24 hours of clamping to pay charges and reclaim his vehicle. Under a recent pilot scheme, 6 per cent of wheelclamps were illegally removed. The section provides power to remove vehicles without first fixing a wheelclamp.

The power will be used where the vehicle concerned has previously been the subject of an illegal removal of a clamp, where there is strong reason to believe the clamp is likely to be removed and where an unlicensed motorcycle is detected. [Standing Committee B, February 4, 1996, col. 158.]

PART II

INSURANCE PREMIUM TAX

New rates of tax

Rate of tax

21.—(1) For section 51 of the Finance Act 1994 (rate of tax) there shall be substituted—

> **"Rate of tax**
> 51.—(1) Tax shall be charged—
>   (a) at the higher rate, in the case of a premium which is liable to tax at that rate; and
>   (b) at the standard rate, in any other case.
>   (2) For the purposes of this Part—
>   (a) the higher rate is 17.5 per cent; and
>   (b) the standard rate is 4 per cent."

(2) In section 73(1) of the Finance Act 1994 (general interpretation) there shall be inserted at the appropriate places—
    (a) " "the higher rate" shall be construed in accordance with section 51 above;"
    (b) " "the standard rate" shall be construed in accordance with section 51 above;".

GENERAL NOTE

The section introduces two rates of insurance premium tax ("IPT"). With effect from April 1, 1997 the existing single rate of 2.5 per cent is replaced with a standard rate of 4 per cent and a selective higher rate of 17.5 per cent.

The higher rate is being introduced to counter the problem of revenue lost when suppliers of goods and services also provide insurance, such as mechanical breakdown insurance for a television, and inflate the margin on the exempt insurance rather than on the goods and services which are liable to VAT.

Premiums liable to tax at the higher rate

22.—(1) After section 51 of the Finance Act 1994 (rate of tax) there shall be inserted—

> **"Premiums liable to tax at the higher rate**
> 51A.—(1) A premium received under a taxable insurance contract by an insurer is liable to tax at the higher rate if it falls within one or more of the paragraphs of Part II of Schedule 6A to this Act.
>   (2) Part I of Schedule 6A to this Act shall have effect with respect to the interpretation of that Schedule.
>   (3) Provision may be made by order amending Schedule 6A as it has effect for the time being.
>   (4) This section is subject to section 69 below."

(2) In section 74 of the Finance Act 1994 (regulations and orders)—
    (a) in subsection (4) (order under section 71 to be subject to affirmative procedure) after "An order under section" there shall be inserted "51A or"; and
    (b) in subsection (6) (regulations or orders, other than an order under section 71, to be subject to negative procedure) after "(other than an order under section" there shall be inserted "51A or".

(3) After Schedule 6 to the Finance Act 1994 there shall be inserted the Schedule set out in Schedule 4 to this Act.

GENERAL NOTE

The section, together with Sched. 4, describes those premiums liable at the new higher rate. The Treasury may by order amend the definition of premiums which are subject to the higher rate subject to the affirmative resolution procedure. Other orders are subject to the negative resolution procedure.

Charge to tax where different rates apply

23.—(1) For section 69 of the Finance Act 1994 (reduced chargeable amount) there shall be substituted—

"Charge to tax where different rates of tax apply

69.—(1) This section applies for the purpose of determining the chargeable amount in a case where a contract provides cover falling within any one of the following paragraphs, that is to say—

(a) cover for one or more exempt matters,

(b) cover for one or more standard rate matters, or

(c) cover for one or more higher rate matters,

and also provides cover falling within another of those paragraphs.

(2) In the following provisions of this section "the non-exempt premium" means the difference between—

(a) the amount of the premium; and

(b) such part of the premium as is attributable to any exempt matter or matters or, if no part is so attributable, nil.

(3) If the contract provides cover for one or more exempt matters and also provides cover for either—

(a) one or more standard rate matters, or

(b) one or more higher rate matters,

the chargeable amount is such amount as, with the addition of the tax chargeable at the standard rate or (as the case may be) the higher rate, is equal to the non-exempt premium.

(4) If the contract provides cover for both—

(a) one or more standard rate matters, and

(b) one or more higher rate matters,

the higher rate element and the standard rate element shall be found in accordance with the following provisions of this section.

(5) For the purposes of this section—

(a) "the higher rate element" is such portion of the non-exempt premium as is attributable to the higher rate matters (including tax at the higher rate); and

(b) "the standard rate element" is the difference between—

(i) the non-exempt premium; and

(ii) the higher rate element.

(6) In a case falling within subsection (4) above, tax shall be charged separately—

(a) at the standard rate, by reference to the standard rate chargeable amount, and

(b) at the higher rate, by reference to the higher rate chargeable amount,

and the tax chargeable in respect of the premium is the aggregate of those amounts of tax.

(7) For the purposes of this section—

"the higher rate chargeable amount" is such amount as, with the addition of the tax chargeable at the higher rate, is equal to the higher rate element;

"the standard rate chargeable amount" is such amount as, with the addition of the tax chargeable at the standard rate, is equal to the standard rate element.

(8) References in this Part to the chargeable amount shall, in a case falling within subsection (4) above, be taken as referring separately to the standard rate chargeable amount and the higher rate chargeable amount.

(9) In applying subsection (2)(b) above, any amount that is included in the premium as being referable to tax (whether or not the amount corresponds to the actual amount of tax payable in respect of the premium) shall be taken to be wholly attributable to the non-exempt matter or matters.

(10) In applying subsection (5)(a) above, any amount that is included in the premium as being referable to tax at the higher rate (whether or not the amount corresponds to the actual amount of tax payable at that rate in respect of the premium) shall be taken to be wholly attributable to the higher rate element.

(11) Subject to subsections (9) and (10) above, any attribution under subsection (2)(b) or (5)(a) above shall be made on such basis as is just and reasonable.

(12) For the purposes of this section—

    (a) an "exempt matter" is any matter such that, if it were the only matter for which the contract provided cover, the contract would not be a taxable insurance contract;

    (b) a "non-exempt matter" is a matter which is not an exempt matter;

    (c) a "standard rate matter" is any matter such that, if it were the only matter for which the contract provided cover, tax at the standard rate would be chargeable on the chargeable amount;

    (d) a "higher rate matter" is any matter such that, if it were the only matter for which the contract provided cover, tax at the higher rate would be chargeable on the chargeable amount.

(13) If the contract relates to a lifeboat and lifeboat equipment, the lifeboat and the equipment shall be taken together in applying this section.

(14) For the purposes of this section "lifeboat" and "lifeboat equipment" have the same meaning as in paragraph 6 of Schedule 7A to this Act."

(2) Accordingly, in section 50 of the Finance Act 1994 (chargeable amount) in subsection (3) (which provides that subsection (2) has effect subject to section 69) for "Subsection (2)" there shall be substituted "Subsections (1) and (2)".

GENERAL NOTE

    The section provides for the apportionment of the premium when cover is provided for matters which are taxable at different rates of IPT or for matters which are both taxable and exempt. It ensures that in these circumstances tax is only charged at the appropriate rate on that proportion of the premium which relates to non-exempt matters.

    The previous F.A. 1994, s.69, which this section replaces, was not designed to cope with more than one positive rate of tax. The new section gives only general guidelines about apportionment, rather than prescriptive formulae. The key requirement (under subs. (11)) is that any apportionment must be done on a just and reasonable basis.

Commencement of sections 21 to 23

24.—(1) Except as provided by subsection (2) below, sections 21 to 23 above have effect in relation to a premium which falls to be regarded for the purposes of Part III of the Finance Act 1994 as received under a taxable insurance contract by an insurer on or after 1st April 1997.

(2) Sections 21 to 23 above do not have effect in relation to a premium if the premium—

    (a) is in respect of a contract made before 1st April 1997; and

    (b) falls, by virtue of regulations under section 68 of the Finance Act 1994 (special accounting scheme), to be regarded for the purposes of Part III of that Act as received under the contract by the insurer on a date before 1st August 1997.

(3) Subsection (2) above does not apply in relation to a premium if the premium—

(a) is an additional premium under the contract;

(b) falls as mentioned in subsection (2)(b) above to be regarded as received under the contract by the insurer on or after 1st April 1997; and

(c) is in respect of a risk which was not covered by the contract before 1st April 1997.

(4) Without prejudice to the generality of subsections (1) to (3) above, those subsections shall be construed in accordance with sections 67A to 67C of the Finance Act 1994 (which are inserted by section 29 below).

GENERAL NOTE

This provides for a concessionary period during which certain premiums will be taxed at the 2.5 per cent rate rather than at the 4 per cent or 17.5 per cent rate. It also invokes provisions in s.29 designed to prevent tax avoidance by forestalling.

Most insurers use the special accounting scheme to account for IPT. Under F.A. 1994, s.68 they are allowed to treat the date they enter as the premium due date into their accounts (the "premium written date") as the date on which they actually receive the premium. For such insurers, if the premium written date falls before August 1, 1997 and the premium relates to a contract made before April 1, 1997 that premium may be taxed at 2.5 per cent.

However, additional premiums relating to a new risk added to a contract made before April 1, 1997 is excluded from relief.

Taxable intermediaries and their fees

Certain fees to be treated as premiums under higher rate contracts

25.—(1) After section 52 of the Finance Act 1994 there shall be inserted—

"Certain fees to be treated as premiums under higher rate contracts

52A.—(1) This section applies where—

(a) at or about the time when a higher rate contract is effected, and

(b) in connection with that contract,

a fee in respect of an insurance-related service is charged by a taxable intermediary to a person who is or becomes the insured (or one of the insured) under the contract or to a person who acts for or on behalf of such a person.

(2) Where this section applies—

(a) a payment in respect of the fee shall be treated for the purposes of this Part as a premium received under a taxable insurance contract by an insurer, and

(b) that premium—

(i) shall be treated for the purposes of this Part as so received at the time when the payment is made, and

(ii) shall be chargeable to tax at the higher rate.

(3) Tax charged by virtue of subsection (2) above shall be payable by the taxable intermediary as if he were the insurer under the contract mentioned in paragraph (a) of that subsection.

(4) For the purposes of this section, a contract of insurance is a "higher rate contract" if—

(a) it is a taxable insurance contract; and

(b) the whole or any part of a premium received under the contract by the insurer is (apart from this section) liable to tax at the higher rate.

(5) For the purposes of this Part a "taxable intermediary" is a person falling within subsection (6) below who—

(a) at or about the time when a higher rate contract is effected, and

(b) in connection with that contract,

charges a fee in respect of an insurance-related service to a person who is or becomes the insured (or one of the insured) under the contract or to a person who acts for or on behalf of such a person.

(6) A person falls within this subsection if—

  (a) he is a supplier of goods or services falling within subsection (7) below; or

  (b) he is connected with a supplier of goods or services falling within that subsection; or

  (c) he is a person who pays—

      (i) the whole or any part of the premium received under that contract, or

      (ii) a fee connected with the arranging of that contract,

to a supplier of goods or services falling within subsection (7) below or to a person who is connected with a supplier of goods or services falling within that subsection.

(7) A person is a supplier of goods or services falling within this subsection if—

  (a) he is a supplier of motor cars or motor cycles, within the meaning of paragraph 2 of Schedule 6A to this Act;

  (b) he is a supplier of relevant goods, within the meaning of paragraph 3 of that Schedule; or

  (c) he is a tour operator or travel agent.

(8) For the purposes of this section, any question whether a person is connected with another shall be determined in accordance with section 839 of the Taxes Act 1988.

(9) In this section—

"insurance-related service" means any service which is related to, or connected with, insurance;

"tour operator" and "travel agent" have the same meaning as in paragraph 4 of Schedule 6A to this Act."

(2) The amendment made by subsection (1) above has effect in relation to payments in respect of fees charged on or after the day on which this Act is passed.

GENERAL NOTE

New F.A. 1994, s.52A makes anti-avoidance provisions to ensure that premiums subject to the 17.5 per cent rate of IPT are not split into taxable and non-taxable elements to reduce the liability.

It is essentially a deterrent measure to ensure that a "taxable intermediary" (see subs. (5)) does not arrange affairs so that rather than being paid by commission derived from the taxable premium the intermediary would charge a fee separate to the contract of insurance on which no IPT (or VAT) was due. Such fees are brought within the scope of IPT.

Registration of taxable intermediaries

26. After section 53 of the Finance Act 1994 (registration of insurers) there shall be inserted—

"Registration of taxable intermediaries

53AA.—(1) A person who—

  (a) is a taxable intermediary, and

  (b) is not registered,

is liable to be registered.

(2) The register kept under this section may contain much information as the Commissioners think is required for the purposes of the care and management of the tax.

(3) A person who—

  (a) at any time forms the intention of charging taxable intermediary's fees, and

  (b) is not already charging such fees in the course of another business,

shall notify the Commissioners of those facts.

(4) A person who at any time—

(a) ceases to have the intention of charging taxable intermediary's fees in the course of his business, and

(b) has no intention of charging such fees in the course of another business of his,

shall notify the Commissioners of those facts.

(5) Where a person is liable to be registered by virtue of subsection (1) above, the Commissioners shall register him with effect from the time when he begins to charge taxable intermediary's fees in the course of the business concerned; and it is immaterial whether or not he notifies the Commissioners under subsection (3) above.

(6) Where a person—

(a) notifies the Commissioners under subsection (4) above, and

(b) satisfies them of the facts there mentioned,

the Commissioners shall cancel his registration with effect from the earliest practicable time after he ceases to charge taxable intermediary's fees in the course of any business of his.

(7) In a case where—

(a) the Commissioners are satisfied that a person has ceased to charge taxable intermediary's fees in the course of any business of his, but

(b) he has not notified them under subsection (4) above,

they may cancel his registration with effect from the earliest practicable time after he so ceased.

(8) For the purposes of this section regulations may make provision—

(a) as to the time within which a notification is to be made;

(b) as to the form and manner in which any notification is to be made and as to the information to be contained in or provided with it;

(c) requiring a person who has made a notification to notify the Commissioners if any information contained in or provided in connection with it is or becomes inaccurate;

(d) as to the correction of entries in the register.

(9) In this Part "taxable intermediary's fees" means fees which, to the extent of any payment in respect of them, are chargeable to tax by virtue of section 52A above."

GENERAL NOTE

New F.A. 1994, s.53AA deals with the registration of taxable intermediaries (see s.52A(5)) so that they account for the IPT on fees which they charge.

It is a necessary extension of the anti-avoidance measure provided for in s.25. If intermediaries are required to charge IPT, there must be some mechanism by which they bring it to account. The charging of fees is currently not usual practice, however, and few if any intermediaries are expected to have to register for IPT purposes.

Supplementary provisions

27.—(1) The Finance Act 1994 shall be amended in accordance with the following provisions of this section.

(2) In section 53A (information required to keep register up to date) in subsection (1)(b), after the words "register kept under section 53" there shall be inserted "or 53AA".

(3) In section 55 (credit)—

(a) after "insurer", wherever occurring other than in subsection (2), there shall be inserted "or taxable intermediary";

(b) in subsection (1), after "premium" there shall be inserted "or taxable intermediary's fee (as the case may be)";

(c) in subsection (3)(f), after "registrable" there shall be inserted "(whether under section 53 or section 53AA)";

(d) in subsection (5), after "insurer's" there shall be inserted "or taxable intermediary's"; and

(e) in subsection (8)(a), after "premium" there shall be inserted "or taxable intermediary's fee".

(4) In section 57 (tax representatives)—

(a) after "insurer", wherever occurring, there shall be inserted "or taxable intermediary";

(b) after "insurer's", wherever occurring, there shall be inserted "or taxable intermediary's"; and

(c) in subsection (1)(a), after "registered under section 53" there shall be inserted "or, as the case may be, section 53AA".

(5) In section 58 (rights and duties of tax representatives)—

(a) after "insurer", wherever occurring, there shall be inserted "or taxable intermediary"; and

(b) after "insurer's", wherever occurring, there shall be inserted "or taxable intermediary's".

(6) In section 59 (review of Commissioners' decisions) in subsection (1) (which specifies the kinds of decision to which the section applies) after paragraph (b) there shall be inserted—

"(bb) whether a payment falls to be treated under section 52A(2) above as a premium received under a taxable insurance contract by an insurer and chargeable to tax at the higher rate;".

(7) In section 62 (partnership, bankruptcy, transfer of business etc.) in subsections (1) and (5), after "insurer", wherever occurring, there shall be inserted "or taxable intermediary".

(8) In section 63(1) (which details the functions of representative members of groups of companies)—

(a) after paragraph (a) there shall be inserted—

"(aa) any business carried on by a member of the group who is a taxable intermediary shall be treated as carried on by the representative member,"; and

(b) after paragraph (b) there shall be inserted—

"(bb) the representative member shall be taken to be the taxable intermediary in relation to any taxable intermediary's fees as regards which a member of the group is the actual taxable intermediary,".

(9) In section 73 (interpretation) in subsection (1) there shall be inserted at the appropriate places—

(a) "taxable intermediary" shall be construed in accordance with section 52A above;"

(b) "taxable intermediary's fees" has the meaning given by section 53AA (9) above."

(10) At the beginning of subsection (3) of that section (meaning of "registrable person") there shall be inserted "Subject to subsection (3A) below," and after that subsection there shall be inserted—

"(3A) References in sections 53A and 54 above and paragraphs 1, 9 and 12 of Schedule 7 to this Act to a registrable person include a reference to a person who—

(a) is registered under section 53AA above; or

(b) is liable to be registered under that section."

(11) In Schedule 7, in paragraph 14 (penalty for failing to register under section 53)—

(a) in sub-paragraph (1), after "section 53(2)" there shall be inserted "or 53AA(3)"; and

(b) in sub-paragraph (2)(a), after "section 53" there shall be inserted "or, as the case may be, section 53AA".

GENERAL NOTE

The section makes various amendments to F.A. 1994 to ensure that most of the key rights and obligations of registered insurers apply to registered taxable intermediaries. The measures contained in the section are necessary to ensure that all the existing administrative machinery relating to IPT can be applied to taxable intermediaries.

Miscellaneous

Amounts charged by other intermediaries

28.—(1) In section 72 of the Finance Act 1994 (interpretation: premium) after subsection (1) there shall be inserted—

"(1A) Where an amount is charged to the insured by any person in connection with a taxable insurance contract, any payment in respect of that amount is to be regarded as a payment received under that contract by the insurer unless—

(a) the payment is chargeable to tax at the higher rate by virtue of section 52A above; or

(b) the amount is charged under a separate contract and is identified in writing to the insured as a separate amount so charged."

(2) The amendment made by subsection (1) above has effect in relation to payments received in respect of amounts charged on or after 1st April 1997.

GENERAL NOTE

The amendment to F.A. 1994, s.72 relates to the definition of "premium".

IPT is generally due on the gross premium charged under the contract of insurance, including any commission or mark up retained or added by an intermediary. In order for an amount charged in connection with a standard rate contract to be treated as outside the scope of IPT, the insured must be notified in writing of the existence of a separate fee contract and the amount of that fee. This is consistent with the insurance industry's Code of Practice.

Fees in relation to a contract subject to tax at the higher rate (see Sched. 4) are themselves subject to IPT at the higher rate (see s.25).

Prevention of pre-emption

29.—(1) After section 67 of the Finance Act 1994 there shall be inserted—

"Announced increase in rate of tax: certain premiums treated as received on date of increase

67A.—(1) This section applies in any case where a proposed increase is announced by a Minister of the Crown in the rate at which tax is to be charged on a premium if it is received by the insurer on or after a date specified in the announcement ("the date of the change").

(2) In a case where—

(a) a premium under a contract of insurance is received by the insurer on or after the date of the announcement but before the date of the change, and

(b) the period of cover for the risk begins on or after the date of the change,

for the purposes of this Part the premium shall be taken to be received on the date of the change.

(3) Subsection (4) below applies where—

(a) a premium under a contract of insurance is received by the insurer on or after the date of the announcement but before the date of the change;

(b) the period of cover for the risk begins before the date of the change and ends on or after the first anniversary of the date of the change; and

(c) the premium, or any part of it, is attributable to such of the period of cover as falls on or after the first anniversary of the date of the change.

(4) For the purposes of this Part—

(a) so much of the premium as is attributable to such of the period of cover as falls on or after the first anniversary of the date of the change shall be taken to be received on the date of the change; and

(b) so much as is so attributable shall be taken to be a separate premium.

(5) In determining whether the condition in subsection (2)(a) or (3)(a) above is satisfied, the provisions of regulations made by virtue of subsection (3) or (7) of section 68 below apply as they would apart from this section; but, subject to that, where subsection (2) or (4) above applies—

(a) that subsection shall have effect notwithstanding anything in section 68 below or regulations made under that section; and

(b) any regulations made under that section shall have effect as if the entry made in the accounts of the insurer showing the premium as due to him had been made as at the date of the change.

(6) Any attribution under this section shall be made on such basis as is just and reasonable.

(7) In this section—

"increase", in relation to the rate of tax, includes the imposition of a charge to tax by adding to the descriptions of contract which are taxable insurance contracts;

"Minister of the Crown" has the same meaning as in the Ministers of the Crown Act 1975.

Announced increase in rate of tax: certain contracts treated as made on date of increase

67B.—(1) This section applies in any case where—

(a) an announcement falling within section 67A(1) above is made; but

(b) a proposed exception from the increase in question is also announced by a Minister of the Crown; and

(c) the proposed exception is to apply in relation to a premium only if the conditions described in subsection (2) below are satisfied in respect of the premium.

(2) Those conditions are—

(a) that the premium is in respect of a contract made before the date of the change;

(b) that the premium falls, by virtue of regulations under section 68 below, to be regarded for the purposes of this Part as received under the contract by the insurer before such date ("the concessionary date") as is specified for the purpose in the announcement.

(3) In a case where—

(a) a premium under a contract of insurance is received by the insurer on or after the date of the announcement but before the concessionary date, and

(b) the period of cover for the risk begins on or after the date of the change,

the rate of tax applicable in relation to the premium shall be determined as if the contract had been made on the date of the change.

(4) Subsection (5) below applies where—

(a) a premium under a contract of insurance is received by the insurer on or after the date of the announcement but before the concessionary date;

(b) the period of cover for the risk begins before the date of the change and ends on or after the first anniversary of the date of the change; and

(c) the premium, or any part of it, is attributable to such of the period of cover as falls on or after the first anniversary of the date of the change.

(5) Where this subsection applies—

(a) the rate of tax applicable in relation to so much of the premium as is attributable to such of the period of cover as falls on or after the first anniversary of the date of the change shall be determined as if the contract had been made on the date of the change; and

(b) so much of the premium as is so attributable shall be taken to be a separate premium.

(6) Any attribution under this section shall be made on such basis as is just and reasonable.

(7) In this section—

"the date of the change" has the same meaning as in section 67A above;

"Minister of the Crown" has the same meaning as in section 67A above.

Announced increase in rate of tax: exceptions and apportionments

67C.—(1) Sections 67A(2) and 67B(3) above do not apply in relation to a premium if the risk to which that premium relates belongs to a class of risk as regards which the normal practice is for a premium to be received by or on behalf of the insurer before the date when cover begins.

(2) Sections 67A(3) and (4) and 67B(4) and (5) above do not apply in relation to a premium if the risk to which that premium relates belongs to a class of risk as regards which the normal practice is for cover to be provided for a period exceeding twelve months.

(3) If a contract relates to more than one risk, then, in the application of section 67A(2), 67A(3) and (4), 67B(3) or 67B(4) and (5) above—

(a) the reference in section 67A(2)(b) or (3)(b) or 67B(3)(b) or (4) (b), as the case may be, to the risk shall be taken as a reference to any given risk,

(b) so much of the premium as is attributable to any given risk shall be taken for the purposes of section 67A(2), 67A(3) and (4), 67B (3) or 67B(4) and (5) above, as the case may be, to be a separate premium relating to that risk,

(c) those provisions shall then apply separately in the case of each given risk and the separate premium relating to it, and

(d) any further attribution required by section 67A(3) and (4) or 67B (4) and (5) above shall be made accordingly,

and subsections (1) and (2) above shall apply accordingly.

(4) Any attribution under this section shall be made on such basis as is just and reasonable."

(2) In the application of sections 67A to 67C of the Finance Act 1994 in relation to the increases in insurance premium tax effected by this Part and the exceptions from those increases—

(a) the announcement relating to those increases, as described in section 67A(1), and to those exceptions, as described in section 67B(1), shall be taken to have been made on 26th November 1996;

(b) "the date of the change" is 1st April 1997; and

(c) "the concessionary date" is 1st August 1997.

(3) The amendment made by subsection (1) above has effect on and after 26th November 1996.

GENERAL NOTE

New F.A. 1994, ss.67A–C are designed to prevent avoidance of IPT by forestalling.

Where an attempt is made to avoid IPT by payment before the implementation of an announced increase or buying an extended period of insurance cover under a contract commencing before a rate rise, the premium is treated under s.67A as received or written on the date of the rate change and so liable to IPT at the new rate.

Section 67B removes the concessionary period from insurance premiums where an attempt to forestall has been made. The start date of the related insurance contract is moved so that for the purposes of the section, the contract is deemed to start on the date of the rate change. For example, an insurer using the special accounting schemes writes a premium on February 1, 1997 relating to a contract which started on March 1 and which covers risks beginning on April 1. The premium is caught by s.67A(2). However, the insurer could maintain that as the contract was made before the date of the rate rise, he can claim the benefit of the concessionary period (see s.24). The benefits of the concessionary period are removed by deeming the contract start to be April 1. [Standing Committee B, February 11, 1996, col. 248.]

Section 67C refines the anti-forestalling provisions so that separate risks under one insurance contract can be considered separately. For example, a premium relating to a contract of insurance is received on March 31, 1997 (*i.e.* before the date of the proposed rate change). The contract covers two risks, insurance cover for one commencing on March 31 and for the other on May 1. The anti-forestalling provisions relating to pre-payment will apply only to that proportion of the total premium which relates to the risk for which cover commences on May 1.

Tax point for payroll deductions

30.—(1) After subsection (7) of section 72 of the Finance Act 1994 (insurance premiums to be treated as received by the insurer when received by another person on his behalf) there shall be inserted—

"(7A) Where any person is authorised by or on behalf of an employee to deduct from anything due to the employee under his contract of employment an amount in respect of a payment due under a taxable insurance contract, subsection (7) above shall not apply to the receipt on behalf of the insurer by the person so authorised of the amount deducted."

(2) After subsection (8) of that section there shall be inserted—

"(8A) Where, by virtue of subsection (7A) above, subsection (7) above does not apply to the receipt of an amount by a person and the whole or part of the amount is referable to commission to which he is entitled—

(a) if the whole of the amount is so referable, the amount shall be treated as received by the insurer when it is deducted by that person; and

(b) otherwise, the part of the amount that is so referable shall be treated as received by the insurer when the remainder of the payment concerned is or is treated as received by him."

(3) This section applies in relation to amounts deducted on or after the day on which this Act is passed.

GENERAL NOTE

The section legislates an extra-statutory concession on the tax point for health insurance premiums which has applied since the introduction of IPT and widens it to include all premiums deducted from pay.

Under the cash method of accounting for IPT, the moment of deduction from an employee's pay of contributions for a healthcare scheme would constitute a tax point and an insurer would be required to account for tax at that date. This requirement would create administrative difficulties for the insurers involved who do not know the time when the premium was deducted.

The amendments to F.A. 1994, s.72 apply the concession to include all premiums deducted from pay and disregard the receipt of the premium by the employer for tax point purposes. The subsequent receipt by the insurer, or by an intermediary acting on his behalf, becomes the date at which IPT must be accounted for.

PART III

VALUE ADDED TAX

Registration

Aggregation of businesses

31.—(1) In Schedule 1 to the Value Added Tax Act 1994 (registration in respect of taxable supplies), after paragraph 1 there shall be inserted the following paragraph—

"1A.—(1) Paragraph 2 below is for the purpose of preventing the maintenance or creation of any artificial separation of business activities carried on by two or more persons from resulting in an avoidance of VAT.

(2) In determining for the purposes of sub-paragraph (1) above whether any separation of business activities is artificial, regard shall be had to the extent to which the different persons carrying on those activities are closely bound to one another by financial, economic and organisational links."

(2) In sub-paragraph (2) of paragraph 2 of that Schedule (power of Commissioners to make direction for aggregation of businesses)—

(a) in paragraph (b), the words from "which should properly" to "described in the direction" shall be omitted;

(b) in paragraph (c), for "that business" there shall be substituted "the business described in the direction"; and

(c) paragraph (d) (Commissioners to be satisfied before making direction for aggregation that avoidance is one of the main reasons for division) shall be omitted;

and, accordingly, in sub-paragraph (4) of that paragraph (power of Commissioners to make supplementary direction) the word "properly" shall be omitted.

(3) In section 84(7) of that Act (determination of appeals against directions), for the words from "as to the matters" onwards there shall be substituted "that there were grounds for making the direction."

(4) This section has effect in relation to the making of directions on or after the day on which this Act is passed.

GENERAL NOTE

The section is designed to counter avoidance of VAT in circumstances in which a business is artificially separated so that each part trades below the VAT registration threshold. Under the previous legislation, Customs and Excise required to be reasonably satisfied that one of the reasons for the separation was to avoid registration. The amendments to the Value Added Tax Act 1994 (c. 23) (VATA 1994), Sched. 1 include a clear statement of the purpose of the anti-avoidance provision, which is to prevent artificial arrangements resulting in loss of VAT, and are specifically aimed at separations which are clearly artificial, such as a series of limited companies running a pub, launderette or other retail outlet for only one month each year in order to keep the turnover of each company below the registration threshold (currently £48,000).

Voluntary registration

32. For sub-paragraph (2) of paragraph 10 of Schedule 1 to the Value Added Tax Act 1994 (non-taxable supplies in respect of which a person is entitled to be registered) there shall be substituted the following sub-paragraph—

"(2) A supply is within this sub-paragraph if—

(a) it is made outside the United Kingdom but would be a taxable supply if made in the United Kingdom; or

(b) it is specified for the purposes of subsection (2) of section 26 in an order made under paragraph (c) of that subsection."

GENERAL NOTE

The section legislates an extra-statutory concession allowing businesses which only make certain exempt financial supplies to register for VAT and recover the VAT incurred in making these supplies. It amends VATA 1994, Sched. 1, para. 10(2) to include supplies described in Value Added Tax (Input Tax) (Specified Supplies) Order 1992 (S.I. 1992 No. 3123).

Zero-rating

Sale of goods donated to charity

33.—(1) In Group 15 of Schedule 8 to the Value Added Tax Act 1994 (charities etc), for Note (1) there shall be substituted the following Note—
    "(1) Item 1 shall apply only if—
        (a) the supply is a sale of goods donated to that charity or taxable person;
        (b) the sale takes place as a result of the goods having been made available to the general public for purchase (whether in a shop or elsewhere); and
        (c) the sale does not take place as a result of any arrangements (whether legally binding or not) which related to the goods and were entered into by each of the parties to the sale before the goods were made available to the general public."
    (2) This section has effect in relation to supplies made on or after 26th November 1996.

GENERAL NOTE

The section provides that sales of donated goods by charities, or by bodies covenanted by deed to give all the profits of their sales to a charity, may be zero-rated only if they take place as a result of the goods having been made available to the general public for purchase and not as the result of a prior arrangement.

It is necessary to protect VAT revenue of £200 million per annum, which is at risk because of the development of tax avoidance schemes with the aim of enabling higher education institutions to purchase high-value items of equipment at the zero rate.

Charitable institutions providing care etc.

34.—(1) In Group 15 of Schedule 8 to the Value Added Tax Act 1994 (charities etc), after Note (4) there shall be inserted the following Notes—
    "(4A) Subject to Note (5B), a charitable institution shall not be regarded as providing care or medical or surgical treatment for handicapped persons unless—
        (a) it provides care or medical or surgical treatment in a relevant establishment; and
        (b) the majority of the persons who receive care or medical or surgical treatment in that establishment are handicapped persons.
    (4B) 'Relevant establishment' means—
        (a) a day-centre, other than a day-centre which exists primarily as a place for activities that are social or recreational or both; or
        (b) an institution which is—
            (i) approved, licensed or registered in accordance with the provisions of any enactment or Northern Ireland legislation; or
            (ii) exempted by or under the provisions of any enactment or Northern Ireland legislation from any requirement to be approved, licensed or registered;

and in paragraph (b) above the references to the provisions of any enactment or Northern Ireland legislation are references only to provisions which, so far as relating to England, Wales, Scotland or Northern Ireland, have the same effect in every locality within that part of the United Kingdom."

(2) After Note (5) to that Group there shall be inserted the following Notes—

"(5A) Subject to Note (5B), items 4 to 7 do not apply where the eligible body falls within Note (4)(f) unless the relevant goods are or are to be used in a relevant establishment in which that body provides care or medical or surgical treatment to persons the majority of whom are handicapped.

(5B) Nothing in Note (4A) or (5A) shall prevent a supply from falling within items 4 to 7 where—

(a) the eligible body provides medical care to handicapped persons in their own homes;

(b) the relevant goods fall within Note (3)(a) or are parts or accessories for use in or with goods described in Note (3)(a); and

(c) those goods are or are to be used in or in connection with the provision of that care."

(3) This section has effect in relation to supplies made on or after 26th November 1996.

GENERAL NOTE

The section amends the criteria for determining whether charitable care providers are eligible to purchase a specified range of equipment at the zero rate. A recent tribunal decision has extended the zero rate to bodies such as community transport groups or social centres for the elderly, because their services could be described as "care". The section replaces this difficult and highly subjective test with a set of clear criteria.

New VATA 1994, Sched. 8, Group 15, Notes (4A) and (4B) restrict the zero-rating to charities providing care in a "relevant establishment" where the majority of the recipients are handicapped (*i.e.* chronically sick or disabled).

New Notes (5A) and (5B) provides that institutional care providers will only qualify for zero-rating where the goods are actually used in a "relevant establishment" and that domiciliary care providers must provide medical care to handicapped people in their own homes with goods used in or in connection with that care.

Buildings and land

References to grants

35.—(1) Section 96 of the Value Added Tax Act 1994 (interpretation) shall have effect, and be deemed always to have had effect, with the following subsection inserted after subsection (10), namely—

"(10A) Where—

(a) the grant of any interest, right, licence or facilities gives rise for the purposes of this Act to supplies made at different times after the making of the grant, and

(b) a question whether any of those supplies is zero-rated or exempt falls to be determined according to whether or not the grant is a grant of a description specified in Schedule 8 or 9 or paragraph 2(2) or (3) of Schedule 10,

that question shall be determined according to whether the description is applicable as at the time of supply, rather than by reference to the time of the grant."

(2) Paragraph 3 of Schedule 10 to that Act (interpretation of the option to tax) shall have effect, and be deemed always to have had effect, with the following sub-paragraphs inserted after sub-paragraph (5)—

"(5A) Where—

  (a) an election under paragraph 2 above is made in relation to any land, and

  (b) apart from this sub-paragraph, a grant in relation to that land would be taken to have been made (whether in whole or in part) before the time when the election takes effect,

that paragraph shall have effect, in relation to any supplies to which the grant gives rise which are treated for the purposes of this Act as taking place after that time, as if the grant had been made after that time.

(5B) Accordingly, the references in paragraph 2(9) above and sub-paragraph (9) below to grants being exempt or taxable shall be construed as references to supplies to which a grant gives rise being exempt or, as the case may be, taxable."

(3) Amendments corresponding to those made by subsections (1) and (2) above shall be deemed to have had effect, for the purposes of the cases to which it applied, in relation to the Value Added Tax Act 1983; and any provisions about the coming into force of any amendment of that Act shall be deemed to have had effect accordingly.

(4) Nothing in this section shall be taken to affect the operation, in relation to times before its repeal took effect, of paragraph 4 of Schedule 10 to the Value Added Tax Act 1994 or of any enactment re-enacted in that paragraph.

GENERAL NOTE

The grant of an interest in property often results in a number of supplies over a period of time. When a lease is granted, for example, a supply is made each time that a payment of rent is received. The section seeks to put beyond doubt the long-standing treatment that the liability of each supply is determined at the time when the supply is made, rather than following the liability of the original grant, in cases where the liability of such a supply has changed.

Subs. (2)

An election to waive exemption applies to supplies made after the date of the election as if the grant had been made after the date of the election.

Subss. (3) and (4)

The provisions apply, where relevant, in relation to earlier enactments and amendments to them, but without prejudice to supplies whose time and liability were determined by previous special rules.

Buildings intended to be used as dwellings

36.—(1) After paragraph 2(2) of Schedule 10 to the Value Added Tax Act 1994 (under which the option to tax is not available in respect of buildings intended for use as dwellings), there shall be inserted the following sub-paragraphs—

"(2A) Subject to the following provisions of this paragraph, where—

  (a) an election has been made for the purposes of this paragraph in relation to any land, and

  (b) a supply is made that would fall, but for sub-paragraph (2)(a) above, to be treated as excluded by virtue of that election from Group 1 of Schedule 9,

then, notwithstanding sub-paragraph (2)(a) above, that supply shall be treated as so excluded if the conditions in sub-paragraph (2B) below are satisfied.

(2B) The conditions mentioned in sub-paragraph (2A) above are—

  (a) that an agreement in writing made, at or before the time of the grant, between—

    (i) the person making the grant, and

    (ii) the person to whom it is made,

declares that the election is to apply in relation to the grant; and
  (b) that the person to whom the supply is made intends, at the time when it is made, to use the land for the purpose only of making a supply which is zero-rated by virtue of paragraph (b) of item 1 of Group 5 of Schedule 8."

(2) This section has effect in relation to supplies made on or after the day on which this Act is passed.

GENERAL NOTE

The section legislates an extra-statutory concession allowing a person selling a non-residential property for conversion into dwellings to charge VAT on a sale that would otherwise be exempt.

When it was first introduced, the option to tax was not available for non-residential buildings sold to developers for conversion into dwellings for sale to the public. Such sales were at the time exempt from VAT, and the developers were unable to recover VAT paid in relation to the buildings. From March 1, 1995 sales of dwellings converted from other buildings became zero-rated (see VATA 1994, Sched. 8, Group 5) and so there was no longer any need to restrict the use of the option to tax.

The section requires that both the vendor and the purchaser must agree to the charge. This gives the purchaser a say in the matter and protects the vendor in the event of subsequent dispute.

Supplies to non-taxable persons etc.

37.—(1) Paragraphs 2(3A) and 3(8A) of Schedule 10 to the Value Added Tax Act 1994 (which relate to grants of land made to connected persons where they are not fully taxable) shall not have effect in relation to any supply made after 26th November 1996.

(2) In paragraph 2 of that Schedule (election to waive exemption), after sub-paragraph (3) there shall be inserted the following sub-paragraphs—

"(3AA) Where an election has been made under this paragraph in relation to any land, a supply shall not be taken by virtue of that election to be a taxable supply if—
  (a) the grant giving rise to the supply was made by a person ('the grantor') who was a developer of the land; and
  (b) at the time of the grant, it was the intention or expectation of—
    (i) the grantor, or
    (ii) a person responsible for financing the grantor's development of the land for exempt use,
  that the land would become exempt land (whether immediately or eventually and whether or not by virtue of the grant) or, as the case may be, would continue, for a period at least, to be such land."

(3) After paragraph 3 of that Schedule (construction of paragraph 2) there shall be inserted the following paragraph—

"3A.—(1) This paragraph shall have effect for the construction of paragraph 2(3AA) above.

(2) For the purposes of paragraph 2(3AA) above a grant made by any person in relation to any land is a grant made by a developer of that land if—
  (a) the land, or a building or part of a building on that land, is an asset falling in relation to that person to be treated as a capital item for the purposes of any regulations under section 26(3) and (4) providing for adjustments relating to the deduction of input tax; and
  (b) the grant was made at a time falling within the period over which such regulations allow adjustments relating to the deduction of input tax to be made as respects that item.

(3) In paragraph 2(3AA) above and this paragraph the references to a person's being responsible for financing the grantor's development of the land for exempt use are references to his being a person who, with

the intention or in the expectation that the land will become, or continue (for a period at least) to be, exempt land—
   (a) has provided finance for the grantor's development of the land; or
   (b) has entered into any agreement, arrangement or understanding (whether or not legally enforceable) to provide finance for the grantor's development of the land.
   (4) In sub-paragraph (3)(a) and (b) above the references to providing finance for the grantor's development of the land are references to doing any one or more of the following, that is to say—
   (a) directly or indirectly providing funds for meeting the whole or any part of the cost of the grantor's development of the land;
   (b) directly or indirectly procuring the provision of such funds by another;
   (c) directly or indirectly providing funds for discharging, in whole or in part, any liability that has been or may be incurred by any person for or in connection with the raising of funds to meet the cost of the grantor's development of the land;
   (d) directly or indirectly procuring that any such liability is or will be discharged, in whole or in part, by another.
   (5) The references in sub-paragraph (4) above to the provision of funds for a purpose referred to in that sub-paragraph include references to—
   (a) the making of a loan of funds that are or are to be used for that purpose;
   (b) the provision of any guarantee or other security in relation to such a loan;
   (c) the provision of any of the consideration for the issue of any shares or other securities issued wholly or partly for raising such funds; or
   (d) any other transfer of assets or value as a consequence of which any such funds are made available for that purpose.
   (6) In sub-paragraph (4) above the references to the grantor's development of the land are references to the acquisition by the grantor of the asset which—
   (a) consists in the land or a building or part of a building on the land, and
   (b) in relation to the grantor falls to be treated for the purposes mentioned in sub-paragraph (2)(a) above as a capital item;
and for the purposes of this sub-paragraph the acquisition of an asset shall be taken to include its construction or reconstruction and the carrying out in relation to that asset of any other works by reference to which it falls to be treated for the purposes mentioned in sub-paragraph (2)(a) above as a capital item.
   (7) For the purposes of paragraph 2(3AA) above and this paragraph land is exempt land if, at a time falling within the period mentioned in sub-paragraph (2)(b) above—
   (a) the grantor,
   (b) a person responsible for financing the grantor's development of the land for exempt use, or
   (c) a person connected with the grantor or with a person responsible for financing the grantor's development of the land for exempt use,
is in occupation of the land without being in occupation of it wholly or mainly for eligible purposes.
   (8) For the purposes of this paragraph, but subject to sub-paragraphs (10) and (12) below, a person's occupation at any time of any land is not capable of being occupation for eligible purposes unless he is a taxable person at that time.

(9) Subject to sub-paragraphs (10) to (12) below, a taxable person in occupation of any land shall be taken for the purposes of this paragraph to be in occupation of that land for eligible purposes to the extent only that his occupation of that land is for the purpose of making supplies which—
  (a) are or are to be made in the course or furtherance of a business carried on by him; and
  (b) are supplies of such a description that any input tax of his which was wholly attributable to those supplies would be input tax for which he would be entitled to a credit.
(10) For the purposes of this paragraph—
  (a) occupation of land by a body to which section 33 applies is occupation of the land for eligible purposes to the extent that the body occupies the land for purposes other than those of a business carried on by that body; and
  (b) any occupation of land by a Government department (within the meaning of section 41) is occupation of the land for eligible purposes.
(11) For the purposes of this paragraph, where land of which any person is in occupation—
  (a) is being held by that person in order to be put to use by him for particular purposes, and
  (b) is not land of which he is in occupation for any other purpose,
that person shall be deemed, for so long as the conditions in paragraphs (a) and (b) above are satisfied, to be in occupation of that land for the purposes for which he proposes to use it.
  (12) Sub-paragraphs (8) to (11) above shall have effect where land is in the occupation of a person who—
  (a) is not a taxable person, but
  (b) is a person whose supplies are treated for the purposes of this Act as supplies made by another person who is a taxable person,
as if the person in occupation of the land and that other person were a single taxable person.
  (13) For the purposes of this paragraph a person shall be taken to be in occupation of any land whether he occupies it alone or together with one or more other persons and whether he occupies all of that land or only part of it.
  (14) Any question for the purposes of this paragraph whether one person is connected with another shall be determined in accordance with section 839 of the Taxes Act."
(4) Subsections (2) and (3) above have effect in relation to any supply made on or after the day on which this Act is passed, other than a supply arising from a relevant pre-commencement grant.
(5) Subject to subsection (6) below, a grant is a relevant pre-commencement grant for the purposes of this section if it is either—
  (a) a grant made before 26th November 1996; or
  (b) a grant made on or after that date and before 30th November 1999 in pursuance of an agreement in writing entered into before 26th November 1996.
(6) For the purposes of this section a grant is not a relevant pre-commencement grant by virtue of paragraph (b) of subsection (5) above unless the terms on which the grant has been made are terms which, as terms for which provision was made by the agreement mentioned in that paragraph, were fixed before 26th November 1996.

GENERAL NOTE
  In 1989, VAT was charged on the construction and sale of new commercial buildings, following on the decision of the European Court of Justice in *E.C. Commission v. U.K.* [1988]

3 C.M.L.R. 169. Because the leasing and letting of commercial property in the EEC is exempt from VAT, developers and landlords could not then reclaim the VAT which they had incurred. To mitigate this situation, an "option to tax" was introduced, whereby developers were permitted to charge VAT on leases and rents and reclaim the VAT on the cost of their development.

This became abused by exempt businesses, typically financial services, banks and insurers, who created schemes which enabled input tax to be recovered although the building was not being used for a taxable purpose. An attempt to stop this in VATA 1994, Sched. 10, paras. 2(3A) and 3(8A) was not successful. It was accordingly announced on Budget day, November 26, 1996 that legislation would be introduced to prevent this abuse.

Clause 37 of the Finance Bill was heavily criticised by the British Property Federation and other interested parties and a new formulation was introduced at report stage.

Subs. (1)
The previous legislation is repealed as from Budget day.

Subs. (2)
New VATA 1994, Sched. 10, para. 2(3AA) removes the option to tax where a grant of land is made by a developer and it was the intention or expectation of the grantor or someone financing him that the land would be used for an exempt purpose.

Subs. (3)
New VATA 1994, Sched. 10, para. 3(3A) provides rules for construing para. 2(3AA).

Sub-para. (3A)(2)
This defines the circumstances in which a grantor is to be treated as a developer.

Sub-para. (3A)(3)
This defines the circumstances in which a person is to be treated as financing a developer.

Sub-para. (3A)(4)
This further explains the provision of finance.

Sub-para. (3A)(5)
This explains further the provision of funds.

Sub-para. (3A)(6)
This defines what is to be taken as development of land.

Sub-para. (3A)(7)
Land is to be taken as exempt land unless it is occupied wholly or mainly for eligible purposes.

Sub-para. (3A)(8)
Occupation is not for eligible purposes unless the occupier is a taxable person.

Sub-paras. (3A)(9)–(12)
These refine the definition of eligible purposes. Various public authorities and all Government departments are deemed to occupy property for eligible purposes.

Sub-para. (3A)(13)
Occupation includes joint or partial occupation.

Sub-para. (3A)(14)
"Connected persons" (see sub-para. (3A)(7)) is to be construed in accordance with ICTA 1988, s.839.

Subss. (4)–(6)
The new provisions generally apply from Budget day, although a three year grace period is allowed for grants made in pursuance of an agreement in writing whose terms were fixed before that date.

The new legislation is expected to save over £100m a year in tax. [Standing Committee B, February 11, 1997, cols. 278–294, February 13, 1997, cols. 1–16; *Hansard*, H.C. Vol. 292, cols. 239–244.]

Exempt insurance supplies

Exempt insurance supplies

38.—(1) In Schedule 9 to the Value Added Tax Act 1994 (exemptions), for Group 2 (insurance) there shall be substituted the following Group—

"GROUP 2—INSURANCE

Item No.

1.   The provision of insurance or reinsurance by a person who provides it in the course of—
   (a) any insurance business which he is authorised under section 3 or 4 of the Insurance Companies Act 1982 to carry on, or
   (b) any business in respect of which he is exempted under section 2 of that Act from the requirement to be so authorised.

2.   The provision by an insurer or reinsurer who belongs outside the United Kingdom of—
   (a) insurance against any of the risks or other things described in Schedules 1 and 2 to the Insurance Companies Act 1982, or
   (b) reinsurance relating to any of those risks or other things.

3.   The provision of insurance or reinsurance by the Export Credits Guarantee Department.

4.   The provision by an insurance broker or insurance agent of any of the services of an insurance intermediary in a case in which those services—
   (a) are related (whether or not a contract of insurance or reinsurance is finally concluded) to any such provision of insurance or reinsurance as falls, or would fall, within item 1, 2 or 3; and
   (b) are provided by that broker or agent in the course of his acting in an intermediary capacity.

Notes:

(1) For the purposes of item 4 services are services of an insurance intermediary if they fall within any of the following paragraphs—
   (a) the bringing together, with a view to the insurance or reinsurance of risks, of—
      (i) persons who are or may be seeking insurance or reinsurance, and
      (ii) persons who provide insurance or reinsurance;
   (b) the carrying out of work preparatory to the conclusion of contracts of insurance or reinsurance;
   (c) the provision of assistance in the administration and performance of such contracts, including the handling of claims;
   (d) the collection of premiums.

(2) For the purposes of item 4 an insurance broker or insurance agent is acting 'in an intermediary capacity' wherever he is acting as an intermediary, or one of the intermediaries, between—
   (a) a person who provides any insurance or reinsurance the provision of which falls within item 1, 2 or 3, and

    (b) a person who is or may be seeking insurance or reinsurance or is an insured person.

    (3) Where—

    (a) a person ('the supplier') makes a supply of goods or services to another ('the customer'),

    (b) the supply of the goods or services is a taxable supply and is not a zero-rated supply,

    (c) a transaction under which insurance is to be or may be arranged for the customer is entered into in connection with the supply of the goods or services,

    (d) a supply of services which are related (whether or not a contract of insurance is finally concluded) to the provision of insurance in pursuance of that transaction is made by—

        (i) the person by whom the supply of the goods or services is made, or

        (ii) a person who is connected with that person and, in connection with the provision of that insurance, deals directly with the customer,

    and

    (e) the related services do not consist in the handling of claims under the contract for that insurance,

those related services do not fall within item 4 unless the relevant requirements are fulfilled.

    (4) For the purposes of Note (3) the relevant requirements are—

    (a) that a document containing the statements specified in Note (5) is prepared;

    (b) that the matters that must be stated in the document have been disclosed to the customer at or before the time when the transaction mentioned in Note (3)(c) is entered into; and

    (c) that there is compliance with all such requirements (if any) as to—

        (i) the preparation and form of the document,

        (ii) the manner of disclosing to the customer the matters that must be stated in the document, and

        (iii) the delivery of a copy of the document to the customer,

as may be set out in a notice that has been published by the Commissioners and has not been withdrawn.

    (5) The statements referred to in Note (4) are—

    (a) a statement setting out the amount of the premium under any contract of insurance that is to be or may be entered into in pursuance of the transaction in question; and

    (b) a statement setting out every amount that the customer is, is to be or has been required to pay, otherwise than by way of such a premium, in connection with that transaction or anything that is to be, may be or has been done in pursuance of that transaction.

    (6) For the purposes of Note (3) any question whether a person is connected with another shall be determined in accordance with section 839 of the Taxes Act.

    (7) Item 4 does not include—

    (a) the supply of any market research, product design, advertising, promotional or similar services; or

    (b) the collection, collation and provision of information for use in connection with market research, product design, advertising, promotional or similar activities.

    (8) Item 4 does not include the supply of any valuation or inspection services.

(9) Item 4 does not include the supply of any services by loss adjusters, average adjusters, motor assessors, surveyors or other experts except where—
   (a) the services consist in the handling of a claim under a contract of insurance or reinsurance;
   (b) the person handling the claim is authorised when doing so to act on behalf of the insurer or reinsurer; and
   (c) that person's authority so to act includes written authority to determine whether to accept or reject the claim and, where accepting it in whole or in part, to settle the amount to be paid on the claim.

(10) Item 4 does not include the supply of any services which—
   (a) are supplied in pursuance of a contract of insurance or reinsurance or of any arrangements made in connection with such a contract; and
   (b) are so supplied either—
      (i) instead of the payment of the whole or any part of any indemnity for which the contract provides, or
      (ii) for the purpose, in any other manner, of satisfying any claim under that contract, whether in whole or in part."

(2) This section has effect in relation to supplies made on or after the day on which this Act is passed.

General Note

The amended VATA 1994, Sched. 9, Group 2 was the subject of public consultation exercises and discussions with the insurance industry. Only one change is made to the current VAT liability of supplies relating to insurance. Insurance related introductory services are now exempt from VAT.

The requirements of the anti-avoidance provisions in the section are consistent with the insurance industry code of practice. They are designed to deter suppliers from reducing the overall amount of tax due by reducing their margins on supplies of taxable goods and services and increasing their margins on associated supplies of exempt insurance. This supplements the main anti-avoidance provision in this area, the introduction of the selective higher rate of Insurance Premium Tax in ss.21–29 *supra*. For the anti-avoidance provisions see Notes (3)–(6).

Bad debt relief

Bad debt relief

39.—(1) In section 36 of the Value Added Tax Act 1994, paragraph (b) of subsection (4) (condition of bad debt relief that property in goods supplied has passed) shall not apply in the case of any claim made under that section in relation to a supply of goods made after the day on which this Act is passed.

(2) After that subsection there shall be inserted the following subsection—
   "(4A) Where—
   (a) a person is entitled under subsection (2) above to be refunded an amount of VAT, and
   (b) that VAT has at any time been included in the input tax of another person,
   that other person shall be taken, as from the time when the claim for the refund is made, not to have been entitled to any credit for input tax in respect of the VAT that has to be refunded on that claim."

(3) Subsection (2) above has effect in relation to any entitlement under section 36 of that Act of 1994 to a refund of VAT charged on a supply made after 26th November 1996.

(4) In subsection (5) of that section (regulations), after paragraph (e) there shall be inserted the following paragraph—
   "(ea) make provision, where there is a repayment by virtue of paragraph (e) above, for restoring the whole or any part of an entitlement to credit for input tax;".

(5) No claim for a refund may be made in accordance with section 22 of the Value Added Tax Act 1983 (old scheme for bad debt relief) at any time after the day on which this Act is passed.

GENERAL NOTE
   The changes to the bad debt relief scheme require debtors to repay to Customs and Excise any VAT which they have reclaimed on supplies for which no payment has been made and on which their supplier has claimed bad debt relief. Also, bad debt relief is permitted where the title in goods has not passed from the supplier to the debtor and the old scheme for bad debt relief which applied to supplies made before July 27, 1990 is withdrawn.
   The requirement for debtors to repay is expected to result in savings of £150m a year.

Groups of companies

Groups containing bodies of different descriptions

40.—(1) In section 43 of the Value Added Tax Act 1994 (groups of companies), after subsection (1) there shall be inserted the following subsections—
   "(1AA) Where—
    (a) it is material, for the purposes of any provision made by or under this Act ('the relevant provision'), whether the person by or to whom a supply is made, or the person by whom goods are acquired or imported, is a person of a particular description,
    (b) paragraph (b) or (c) of subsection (1) above applies to any supply, acquisition or importation, and
    (c) there is a difference that would be material for the purposes of the relevant provision between—
       (i) the description applicable to the representative member, and
       (ii) the description applicable to the body which (apart from this section) would be regarded for the purposes of this Act as making the supply, acquisition or importation or, as the case may be, as being the person to whom the supply is made,
the relevant provision shall have effect in relation to that supply, acquisition or importation as if the only description applicable to the representative member were the description in fact applicable to that body.
   (1AB) Subsection (1AA) above does not apply to the extent that what is material for the purposes of the relevant provision is whether a person is a taxable person."
   (2) In subsection (2) of that section (self supplies), at the end there shall be inserted "and may provide for that purpose that the representative member is to be treated as a person of such description as may be determined under the order."
   (3) Subsection (1) above has effect in relation to any supply made after 26th November 1996 and in relation to any acquisition or importation taking place after that date.

GENERAL NOTE
   Under VATA 1994, s.43 a member of a group of companies may be registered as its representative member and all intra-group transactions are disregarded for VAT purposes. It had been suggested that the status of the representative member (*e.g.* exempt or zero-rated) attached to the entire group and this view was upheld by the court in *Customs and Excise Commissioners v. Kingfisher plc* [1994] S.T.C. 63. The amendments to the section provide that the representative member retains its own status which does not apply to other members of the group. The change is to prevent tax avoidance. In some cases, groups may benefit.

Group supplies using an overseas member

41.—(1) In section 43 of the Value Added Tax Act 1994 (groups of companies), after subsection (2) there shall be inserted the following subsections—

"(2A) A supply made by a member of a group ('the supplier') to another member of the group ('the UK member') shall not be disregarded under subsection (1)(a) above if—

(a) it would (if there were no group) be a supply of services falling within Schedule 5 to a person belonging in the United Kingdom;

(b) those services are not within any of the descriptions specified in Schedule 9;

(c) the supplier has been supplied (whether or not by a person belonging in the United Kingdom) with services falling within any of paragraphs 1 to 8 of Schedule 5;

(d) the supplier belonged outside the United Kingdom when it was supplied with the services mentioned in paragraph (c) above; and

(e) the services so mentioned have been used by the supplier for making the supply to the UK member.

(2B) Subject to subsection (2C) below, where a supply is excluded by virtue of subsection (2A) above from the supplies that are disregarded in pursuance of subsection (1)(a) above, all the same consequences shall follow under this Act as if that supply—

(a) were a taxable supply in the United Kingdom by the representative member to itself, and

(b) without prejudice to that, were made by the representative member in the course or furtherance of its business.

(2C) A supply which is deemed by virtue of subsection (2B) above to be a supply by the representative member to itself—

(a) shall not be taken into account as a supply made by the representative member when determining any allowance of input tax under section 26(1) in the case of the representative member;

(b) shall be deemed for the purposes of paragraph 1 of Schedule 6 to be a supply in the case of which the person making the supply and the person supplied are connected within the meaning of section 839 of the Taxes Act (connected persons); and

(c) subject to paragraph (b) above, shall be taken to be a supply the value and time of which are determined as if it were a supply of services which is treated by virtue of section 8 as made by the person by whom the services are received.

(2D) For the purposes of subsection (2A) above where—

(a) there has been a supply of the assets of a business of a person ('the transferor') to a person to whom the whole or any part of that business was transferred as a going concern ('the transferee'),

(b) that supply is either—

(i) a supply falling to be treated, in accordance with an order under section 5(3), as being neither a supply of goods nor a supply of services, or

(ii) a supply that would have fallen to be so treated if it had taken place in the United Kingdom,

and

(c) the transferor was supplied with services falling within paragraphs 1 to 8 of Schedule 5 at a time before the transfer when the transferor belonged outside the United Kingdom,

those services, so far as they are used by the transferee for making any supply falling within that Schedule, shall be deemed to have been supplied to the transferee at a time when the transferee belonged outside the United Kingdom.

(2E) Where, in the case of a supply of assets falling within paragraphs (a) and (b) of subsection (2D) above—

(a) the transferor himself acquired any of the assets in question by way of a previous supply of assets falling within those paragraphs, and

(b) there are services falling within paragraphs 1 to 8 of Schedule 5 which, if used by the transferor for making supplies falling within that Schedule, would be deemed by virtue of that subsection to have been supplied to the transferor at a time when he belonged outside the United Kingdom,

that subsection shall have effect, notwithstanding that the services have not been so used by the transferor, as if the transferor were a person to whom those services were supplied and as if he were a person belonging outside the United Kingdom at the time of their deemed supply to him; and this subsection shall apply accordingly through any number of successive supplies of assets falling within paragraphs (a) and (b) of that subsection."

(2) Subject to subsection (3) below, subsection (1) above has effect in relation to supplies made on or after 26th November 1996.

(3) Section 43 of the Value Added Tax Act 1994 shall have effect in relation to supplies made after the day on which this Act is passed with the provisions inserted by subsection (1) above modified in accordance with subsections (4) and (5) below.

(4) In subsection (2A), in paragraph (c) for the words from "services" to the end of the paragraph there shall be substituted "any services falling within paragraphs 1 to 8 of Schedule 5 which do not fall within any of the descriptions specified in Schedule 9;".

(5) In subsection (2C), at the beginning there shall be inserted "Except in so far as the Commissioners may by regulations otherwise provide,".

GENERAL NOTE

This is an anti-avoidance measure to prevent businesses from receiving services free of VAT when the services are supplied by an overseas branch of a fellow member of a VAT group. In future such supplies of services must meet the criteria set out in new VATA 1994, s.43(2A).

Subs. (4)

The charge will not be triggered by the receipt of an exempt service.

Subs. (5)

The Customs and Excise are given power to make regulations varying the details of charges under the section. This is designed to ensure that the charge to tax made under the section is limited to the value of the services purchased overseas.

The possible revenue protected amounts to £800m per annum. [Standing Committee B, February 13, 1997, col. 19.]

Incidental and supplemental provisions etc.

Services subject to the reverse charge

42. In section 8 of the Value Added Tax Act 1994 (reverse charge on supplies falling within Schedule 5), after subsection (6) there shall be inserted the following subsections—

"(7) The power of the Treasury by order to add to or vary Schedule 5 shall include power to make such incidental, supplemental, consequential and transitional provision in connection with any addition to or variation of that Schedule as they think fit.

(8) Without prejudice to the generality of subsection (7) above, the provision that may be made under that subsection includes—

(a) provision making such modifications of section 43(2A) to (2E) as the Treasury may think fit in connection with any addition to or variation of that Schedule; and

(b) provision modifying the effect of any regulations under subsection (4) above in relation to any services added to the Schedule."

    Certain services received from abroad for business purposes are subject to VAT in the UK. The recipient charges himself and accounts for the VAT under a procedure known as the "reverse charge". Such services are specifically listed in VATA 1994, Sched. 5 (subject to Sched. 9) and the Treasury may by order add to, or vary, the list. There is currently no power for the Treasury to make transitional or other necessary provisions when such changes are made. This is likely to be necessary, particularly in view of the fact that telecommunications services may shortly be included in Sched. 5.

Payments on account: appeals

43. In section 28 of the Value Added Tax Act 1994 (payments on account), after subsection (2) there shall be inserted the following subsection—
    "(2AA) An order under this section may provide for the matters with respect to which an appeal under section 83 lies to a tribunal to include such decisions of the Commissioners under that or any other order under this section as may be specified in the order."

GENERAL NOTE
    An order will be made allowing businesses in the payments on account scheme to appeal to a tribunal against the revocation by the Customs and Excise of an option to pay the actual VAT liability as the payment on account.

PART IV

PAYMENTS AND OVERPAYMENTS IN RESPECT OF INDIRECT TAXES

Value added tax

Liability of Commissioners to interest

44.—(1) Section 78 of the Value Added Tax Act 1994 (interest) shall have effect, and be deemed always to have had effect, with the insertion of the following subsection after subsection (1)—
    "(1A) In subsection (1) above—
    (a) references to an amount which the Commissioners are liable in consequence of any matter to pay or repay to any person are references, where a claim for the payment or repayment has to be made, to only so much of that amount as is the subject of a claim that the Commissioners are required to satisfy or have satisfied; and
    (b) the amounts referred to in paragraph (d) do not include any amount payable under this section."
    (2) That section shall have effect in relation to any claim made on or after 18th July 1996, and shall be deemed always to have had effect in relation to such a claim, with the substitution of the following subsection for subsection (11)—
    "(11) A claim under this section shall not be made more than three years after the end of the applicable period to which it relates."
    (3) That section shall have effect, and be deemed always to have had effect, with the substitution of the following paragraph for paragraph (a) of subsection (12)—
    "(a) references to the authorisation by the Commissioners of the payment of any amount include references to the discharge by way of set-off (whether under section 81(3) or otherwise) of the Commissioners' liability to pay that amount; and".
    (4) For subsections (8) and (9) of that section (periods in respect of which the Commissioners are not liable to interest) there shall be substituted the following subsections—
    "(8) In determining in accordance with subsection (4), (6) or (7) above the applicable period for the purposes of subsection (1) above,

there shall be left out of account any period by which the Commissioners' authorisation of the payment of interest is delayed by the conduct of the person who claims the interest.

(8A) The reference in subsection (8) above to a period by which the Commissioners' authorisation of the payment of interest is delayed by the conduct of the person who claims it includes, in particular, any period which is referable to—

    (a) any unreasonable delay in the making of the claim for interest or in the making of any claim for the payment or repayment of the amount on which interest is claimed;

    (b) any failure by that person or a person acting on his behalf or under his influence to provide the Commissioners—

        (i) at or before the time of the making of a claim, or

        (ii) subsequently in response to a request for information by the Commissioners,

    with all the information required by them to enable the existence and amount of the claimant's entitlement to a payment or repayment, and to interest on that payment or repayment, to be determined; and

    (c) the making, as part of or in association with either—

        (i) the claim for interest, or

        (ii) any claim for the payment or repayment of the amount on which interest is claimed,

    of a claim to anything to which the claimant was not entitled.

(9) In determining for the purposes of subsection (8A) above whether any period of delay is referable to a failure by any person to provide information in response to a request by the Commissioners, there shall be taken to be so referable, except so far as may be prescribed, any period which—

    (a) begins with the date on which the Commissioners require that person to provide information which they reasonably consider relevant to the matter to be determined; and

    (b) ends with the earliest date on which it would be reasonable for the Commissioners to conclude—

        (i) that they have received a complete answer to their request for information;

        (ii) that they have received all that they need in answer to that request; or

        (iii) that it is unnecessary for them to be provided with any information in answer to that request."

(5) Subsection (4) above shall have effect for the purposes of determining whether any period beginning on or after the day on which this Act is passed is left out of account.

(6) Amendments corresponding to those made by subsections (1) and (3) above shall be deemed to have had effect, for the purposes of the cases to which the enactments applied, in relation to the enactments directly or indirectly re-enacted in section 78 of the Value Added Tax Act 1994.

GENERAL NOTE

    This section forms part of a package to introduce a three year limit for claims of amounts overpaid by way of VAT, other indirect taxes and related statutory interest and for assessments for underdeclaration of VAT and other indirect taxes. This is being done to limit the Government's current open-ended liability to repay claims dating as far back as the introduction of VAT in 1973. The three year limit became law on December 4, 1996, retrospectively to July 18, 1996, by virtue of a resolution of the House of Commons having statutory effect under Provisional Collection of Taxes Act 1968 (c. 2).

Subs. (1)

New VATA 1994, s.78(1A) limits statutory interest to that payable on amounts paid to the Customs and Excise by way of tax which they are liable to repay under s.80. It also provides that where there is a delay in paying statutory interest, further interest is not payable on the interest itself.

Subs. (2)

New s.78(11) applies the new provisions to any claim made on or after July 18, 1996 (when the change was announced) and imposes a three year time limit for claims.

Subs. (3)

New s.78(12)(a) limits statutory interest to that payable on the net amount repaid after set-off of any amounts due to Customs and Excise.

Subs. (4)

New s.78(8), (8A) and (9) exclude from entitlement to interest any period in which there were unreasonable delays by a claimant in making a claim or in providing information to establish the amount or validity. Particular examples of conduct constituting delay are given in new subs. (8A).

Subs. (5)

The amendments in subs. (4) take effect from Royal Assent (March 19, 1997).

Subs. (6)

The amendments in subss. (1) and (3) apply to claims pending under the previous provisions.

Assessment for overpayments of interest

45.—(1) After section 78 of the Value Added Tax Act 1994 there shall be inserted the following section—

"Assessment for interest overpayments

78A.—(1) Where—

(a) any amount has been paid to any person by way of interest under section 78, but

(b) that person was not entitled to that amount under that section, the Commissioners may, to the best of their judgement, assess the amount so paid to which that person was not entitled and notify it to him.

(2) An assessment made under subsection (1) above shall not be made more than two years after the time when evidence of facts sufficient in the opinion of the Commissioners to justify the making of the assessment comes to the knowledge of the Commissioners.

(3) Where an amount has been assessed and notified to any person under subsection (1) above, that amount shall be deemed (subject to the provisions of this Act as to appeals) to be an amount of VAT due from him and may be recovered accordingly.

(4) Subsection (3) above does not have effect if or to the extent that the assessment in question has been withdrawn or reduced.

(5) An assessment under subsection (1) above shall be a recovery assessment for the purposes of section 84(3A).

(6) Sections 74 and 77(6) apply in relation to assessments under subsection (1) above as they apply in relation to assessments under section 73 but as if the reference in subsection (1) of section 74 to the reckonable date were a reference to the date on which the assessment is notified.

(7) Where by virtue of subsection (6) above any person is liable to interest under section 74—

(a) section 76 shall have effect in relation to that liability with the omission of subsections (2) to (6); and

(b) section 77, except subsection (6), shall not apply to an assessment of the amount due by way of interest;

and (without prejudice to the power to make assessments for interest for later periods) the interest to which any assessment made under section

76 by virtue of paragraph (a) above may relate shall be confined to interest for a period of no more than two years ending with the time when the assessment to interest is made.

(8) For the purposes of this section notification to a personal representative, trustee in bankruptcy, interim or permanent trustee, receiver, liquidator or person otherwise acting in a representative capacity in relation to another shall be treated as notification to the person in relation to whom he so acts."

(2) In section 83 of that Act (matters subject to appeal), after paragraph (s) there shall be inserted the following paragraph—

"(sa) an assessment under section 78A(1) or the amount of such an assessment;".

(3) In section 84 of that Act (further provisions as to appeals), after subsection (3) there shall be inserted the following subsection—

"(3A) An appeal against an assessment which is a recovery assessment for the purposes of this subsection, or against the amount of such an assessment, shall not be entertained unless—

    (a) the amount notified by the assessment has been paid or deposited with the Commissioners; or

    (b) on being satisfied that the appellant would otherwise suffer hardship, the Commissioners agree, or the tribunal decides, that the appeal should be entertained notwithstanding that that amount has not been so paid or deposited."

(4) Subsection (1) above shall be deemed to have come into force on 4th December 1996 in relation to amounts paid by way of interest at any time on or after 18th July 1996.

(5) Subsections (2) and (3) above shall be deemed to have come into force on 4th December 1996 in relation to assessments made on or after that date.

(6) Section 76(10) of the Value Added Tax Act 1994 (notification to representative of person who made acquisition) shall have effect, and be deemed always to have had effect, as if for "the person who made the acquisition in question" there were substituted "another".

GENERAL NOTE

Currently Customs and Excise have to bring a civil action to recover overpaid statutory interest. New VATA 1994, s.78A introduces powers to assess to recover overpaid interest. Further consequential amendments to the Act are made in relation to such assessments.

Repayments of overpayments: unjust enrichment

46.—(1) In section 80 of the Value Added Tax Act 1994, after subsection (3) (defence of unjust enrichment to claim for repayment of an overpayment) there shall be inserted the following subsections—

"(3A) Subsection (3B) below applies for the purposes of subsection (3) above where—

    (a) there is an amount paid by way of VAT which (apart from subsection (3) above) would fall to be repaid under this section to any person ('the taxpayer'), and

    (b) the whole or a part of the cost of the payment of that amount to the Commissioners has, for practical purposes, been borne by a person other than the taxpayer.

(3B) Where, in a case to which this subsection applies, loss or damage has been or may be incurred by the taxpayer as a result of mistaken assumptions made in his case about the operation of any VAT provisions, that loss or damage shall be disregarded, except to the extent of the quantified amount, in the making of any determination—

    (a) of whether or to what extent the repayment of an amount to the taxpayer would enrich him; or

(b) of whether or to what extent any enrichment of the taxpayer would be unjust.

(3C) In subsection (3B) above—

'the quantified amount' means the amount (if any) which is shown by the taxpayer to constitute the amount that would appropriately compensate him for loss or damage shown by him to have resulted, for any business carried on by him, from the making of the mistaken assumptions; and

'VAT provisions' means the provisions of—

(a) any enactment, subordinate legislation or Community legislation (whether or not still in force) which relates to VAT or to any matter connected with VAT; or

(b) any notice published by the Commissioners under or for the purposes of any such enactment or subordinate legislation."

(2) After section 80 of that Act there shall be inserted the following sections—

"Arrangements for reimbursing customers

80A.—(1) The Commissioners may by regulations make provision for reimbursement arrangements made by any person to be disregarded for the purposes of section 80(3) except where the arrangements—

(a) contain such provision as may be required by the regulations; and

(b) are supported by such undertakings to comply with the provisions of the arrangements as may be required by the regulations to be given to the Commissioners.

(2) In this section 'reimbursement arrangements' means any arrangements for the purposes of a claim under section 80 which—

(a) are made by any person for the purpose of securing that he is not unjustly enriched by the repayment of any amount in pursuance of the claim; and

(b) provide for the reimbursement of persons who have for practical purposes borne the whole or any part of the cost of the original payment of that amount to the Commissioners.

(3) Without prejudice to the generality of subsection (1) above, the provision that may be required by regulations under this section to be contained in reimbursement arrangements includes—

(a) provision requiring a reimbursement for which the arrangements provide to be made within such period after the repayment to which it relates as may be specified in the regulations;

(b) provision for the repayment of amounts to the Commissioners where those amounts are not reimbursed in accordance with the arrangements;

(c) provision requiring interest paid by the Commissioners on any amount repaid by them to be treated in the same way as that amount for the purposes of any requirement under the arrangements to make reimbursement or to repay the Commissioners;

(d) provision requiring such records relating to the carrying out of the arrangements as may be described in the regulations to be kept and produced to the Commissioners, or to an officer of theirs.

(4) Regulations under this section may impose obligations on such persons as may be specified in the regulations—

(a) to make the repayments to the Commissioners that they are required to make in pursuance of any provisions contained in any reimbursement arrangements by virtue of subsection (3)(b) or (c) above;

(b) to comply with any requirements contained in any such arrangements by virtue of subsection (3)(d) above.

(5) Regulations under this section may make provision for the form and manner in which, and the times at which, undertakings are to be given to the Commissioners in accordance with the regulations; and any such provision may allow for those matters to be determined by the Commissioners in accordance with the regulations.

(6) Regulations under this section may—

(a) contain any such incidental, supplementary, consequential or transitional provision as appears to the Commissioners to be necessary or expedient; and

(b) make different provision for different circumstances.

(7) Regulations under this section may have effect (irrespective of when the claim for repayment was made) for the purposes of the making of any repayment by the Commissioners after the time when the regulations are made; and, accordingly, such regulations may apply to arrangements made before that time.

Assessments of amounts due under section 80A arrangements

80B.—(1) Where any person is liable to pay any amount to the Commissioners in pursuance of an obligation imposed by virtue of section 80A(4)(a), the Commissioners may, to the best of their judgement, assess the amount due from that person and notify it to him.

(2) Subsections (2) to (8) of section 78A apply in the case of an assessment under subsection (1) above as they apply in the case of an assessment under section 78A(1)."

(3) In section 83 of that Act (matters subject to appeal), after paragraph (t) there shall be inserted the following paragraph—

"(ta) an assessment under section 80B(1) or the amount of such an assessment;".

(4) Subsection (1) above has effect for the purposes of making any repayment on or after the day on which this Act is passed, even if the claim for that repayment was made before that day.

GENERAL NOTE

Under VATA 1994, s.80(3), the Customs and Excise could mount a defence of "unjust enrichment" to claims for refund of overpaid VAT. The defence was on the basis that the VAT reclaimed had been collected from customers and would not be refunded to them. However, some businesses argued that because of market pressures they absorbed the tax themselves and that the refund was compensation for lost profit.

The section refines the concept of "unjust enrichment", provides arrangements for reimbursement of tax refunds to customers and enables Customs and Excise to assess the taxpayer to recover refunds not reimbursed to customers.

Subs. (1)

New s.80(3A), (3B) and (3C), which were amended at committee stage to conform with Community law, applies the concept of "unjust enrichment" to cases where the customer has for practical purposes borne the VAT, except where the taxpayer can show a "quantified amount" which would appropriately compensate him for loss or damage resulting from mistaken assumptions about VAT.

Subs. (2)

New s.80A provides for regulations to be made by the Customs and Excise governing "reimbursement arrangements" to their customers by taxpayers who have received a refund and repayment to the Customs and Excise of amounts not reimbursed.

New s.80B provides for assessments to be raised in respect of such amounts. [Standing Committee B, February 13, 1997, col. 26.]

Repayments and assessments: time limits

47.—(1) For subsections (4) and (5) of section 80 of the Value Added Tax Act 1994 (time limit for making claim for a repayment of an overpayment) there shall be substituted the following subsection—

"(4) The Commissioners shall not be liable, on a claim made under this section, to repay any amount paid to them more than three years before the making of the claim."

(2) Subject to subsections (3) and (4) below, subsection (1) above shall be deemed to have come into force on 18th July 1996 as a provision applying, for the purposes of the making of any repayment on or after that date, to all claims under section 80 of the Value Added Tax Act 1994, including claims made before that date and claims relating to payments made before that date.

(3) Subsection (4) below applies as respects the making of any repayment on or after 18th July 1996 on a claim under section 80 of the Value Added Tax Act 1994 if—

(a) legal proceedings for questioning any decision ("the disputed decision") of the Commissioners, or of an officer of the Commissioners, were brought by any person at any time before that date,

(b) a determination has been or is made in those proceedings that the disputed decision was wrong or should be set aside,

(c) the claim is one made by that person at a time after the proceedings were brought (whether before or after the making of the determination), and

(d) the claim relates to—

(i) an amount paid by that person to the Commissioners on the basis of the disputed decision, or

(ii) an amount paid by that person to the Commissioners before the relevant date (including an amount paid before the making of the disputed decision) on grounds which, in all material respects, correspond to those on which that decision was made.

(4) Where this subsection applies in the case of any claim—

(a) subsection (4) of section 80 of the Value Added Tax Act 1994 (as inserted by this section) shall not apply, and shall be taken never to have applied, in relation to so much of that claim as relates to an amount falling within subsection (3)(d)(i) or (ii) above, but

(b) the Commissioners shall not be liable on that claim, and shall be taken never to have been liable on that claim, to repay any amount so falling which was paid to them more than three years before the proceedings mentioned in subsection (3)(a) above were brought.

(5) In subsection (3)(d) above—

(a) the reference to the relevant date is a reference to whichever is the earlier of 18th July 1996 and the date of the making of the determination in question; and

(b) the reference to an amount paid on the basis of a decision, or on any grounds, includes an amount so paid on terms (however expressed) which questioned the correctness of the decision or, as the case may be, of those grounds.

(6) After the subsection (4) inserted in section 80 of the Value Added Tax Act 1994 by this section there shall be inserted the following subsections—

"(4A) Where—

(a) any amount has been paid, at any time on or after 18th July 1996, to any person by way of a repayment under this section, and

(b) the amount paid exceeded the Commissioners' repayment liability to that person at that time,

the Commissioners may, to the best of their judgement, assess the excess paid to that person and notify it to him.

(4B) For the purposes of subsection (4A) above the Commissioners' repayment liability to a person at any time is—

    (a) in a case where any provision affecting the amount which they were liable to repay to that person at that time is subsequently deemed to have been in force at that time, the amount which the Commissioners are to be treated, in accordance with that provision, as having been liable at that time to repay to that person; and

    (b) in any other case, the amount which they were liable at that time to repay to that person.

(4C) Subsections (2) to (8) of section 78A apply in the case of an assessment under subsection (4A) above as they apply in the case of an assessment under section 78A(1)."

(7) In section 83 of that Act (matters subject to appeal), in paragraph (t), after "80" there shall be inserted ", an assessment under subsection (4A) of that section or the amount of such an assessment".

(8) Nothing contained in—

    (a) any regulations under section 25(1) of, or paragraph 2 of Schedule 11 to, that Act relating to the correction of errors or the making of adjustments, or

    (b) any requirement imposed under any such regulations,

shall be taken, in relation to any time on or after 18th July 1996, to have conferred an entitlement on any person to receive, by way of repayment, any amount to which he would not have had any entitlement on a claim under section 80 of that Act.

(9) Subsections (6) to (8) above shall be deemed to have come into force on 4th December 1996.

(10) Section 77 of the Value Added Tax Act 1994 (time limits etc. for assessments) shall have effect, and be deemed in relation to any assessment made on or after 18th July 1996 to have had effect, with the substitution in subsections (1) and (4), for the words "6 years", wherever they occur, of the words "3 years".

(11) In this section—

    "the Commissioners" means the Commissioners of Customs and Excise; and

    "legal proceedings" means any proceedings before a court or tribunal.

(12) Without prejudice to the generality of paragraph 1(2) of Schedule 13 to the Value Added Tax Act 1994 (transitional provisions), the references in this section, and in subsection (4) of section 80 of that Act (as inserted by this section), to a claim under that section include references to a claim first made under section 24 of the Finance Act 1989 (which was re-enacted in section 80).

GENERAL NOTE

The section introduces a three year time limit for claims for refunds of VAT, provides for assessments to be made to recover amounts repaid which were in excess of the Customs and Excise's liability to repay and provides a three year time limit for assessments of penalties and underdeclared VAT. This latter time limit, reduced from six years, meets business representations that while it was reasonable to impose a time limit on refunds of overpayments it was also reasonable to bring assessments for underpaid tax into line. It does not affect assessments where fraud or circumstances giving rise to a penalty under VATA 1994, s.67 are involved.

Where legal proceedings had begun before July 18, 1996 on a VAT matter, but no claim had been made, the three year limit runs from the start of the proceedings.

After July 18, 1996 the Customs and Excise deferred payments of any claims for refunds in excess of three years which had not been paid. This was held to be unlawful in *R. v. Customs and Excise Commissioners ex p. Kay and Co* [1996] S.T.C. 1500. They are now given powers to claw back repayments outside the limits set in the legislation. [Standing Committee B, February 13, 1997, cols. 31–43.]

Set-off of credits and debits

48.—(1) In section 81 of the Value Added Tax Act 1994 (which makes provision for the set-off of credits and debits), after subsection (3) there shall be inserted the following subsection—

"(3A) Where—
- (a) the Commissioners are liable to pay or repay any amount to any person under this Act,
- (b) that amount falls to be paid or repaid in consequence of a mistake previously made about whether or to what extent amounts were payable under this Act to or by that person, and
- (c) by reason of that mistake a liability of that person to pay a sum by way of VAT, penalty, interest or surcharge was not assessed, was not enforced or was not satisfied,

any limitation on the time within which the Commissioners are entitled to take steps for recovering that sum shall be disregarded in determining whether that sum is required by subsection (3) above to be set against the amount mentioned in paragraph (a) above."

(2) Subsection (1) above shall be deemed to have come into force on 18th July 1996 as a provision applying for determining the amount of any payment or repayment by the Commissioners on or after that date, including a payment or repayment in respect of a liability arising before that date.

GENERAL NOTE

The section allows the Customs and Excise to set off any tax, penalty, interest or surcharge due to them against a payment or repayment due to a taxpayer and to repay only the net amount (if any) due to the taxpayer. Previously, where a taxpayer overpaid tax but as a consequence simultaneously overclaimed input tax, the Customs could not set off the overclaimed input tax against the refund due if they were out of time to issue an assessment for the overclaimed input tax. It is not a general setting off provision. It will only apply to specific supplies where overclaims and overpayments have occurred as a result of the same mistake.

Transitional provision for set-offs etc.

49.—(1) Where—
- (a) at any time before 4th December 1996, any person ("the taxpayer") became liable to pay any sum ("the relevant sum") to the Commissioners by way of VAT, penalty, interest or surcharge,
- (b) at any time on or after 18th July 1996 and before 4th December 1996 an amount was set against the whole or any part of the relevant sum,
- (c) the amount set against that sum was an amount which is treated under section 47 above as not having been due from the Commissioners at the time when it was set against that sum, and
- (d) as a consequence, the taxpayer's liability to pay the whole or a part of the relevant sum falls to be treated as not having been discharged in accordance with section 81(3) of the 1994 Act,

the Commissioners may, to the best of their judgement, assess the amount of the continuing liability of the taxpayer and notify it to him.

(2) In subsection (1) above the reference to the continuing liability of the taxpayer is a reference to so much of the liability to pay the relevant sum as—
- (a) would have been discharged if the amount mentioned in subsection (1)(b) above had been required to be set against the relevant sum in accordance with section 81(3) of the 1994 Act, but
- (b) falls, by virtue of section 47 above, to be treated as not having been discharged in accordance with section 81(3) of that Act.

(3) The taxpayer's only liabilities under the 1994 Act in respect of his failure, on or after the time mentioned in subsection (1)(b) above, to pay an amount assessable under this section shall be—
- (a) his liability to be assessed for that amount under this section; and
- (b) liabilities arising under the following provisions of this section.

(4) Subsections (2) to (8) of section 78A of the 1994 Act apply in the case of an assessment under subsection (1) above as they apply in the case of an assessment under section 78A(1) of that Act.

(5) The 1994 Act shall have effect as if the matters specified in section 83 of that Act (matters subject to appeal) included an assessment under this section and the amount of such an assessment.

(6) Nothing contained in—

(a) any regulations under section 25(1) of, or paragraph 2 of Schedule 11 to, the 1994 Act relating to the correction of errors or the making of adjustments, or

(b) any requirement imposed under any such regulations,

shall be taken, in relation to any time on or after 18th July 1996, to have conferred on any person any entitlement, otherwise than in accordance with section 81(3) of that Act, to set any amount, as an amount due from the Commissioners, against any sum which that person was liable to pay to the Commissioners by way of VAT, penalty, interest or surcharge.

(7) In this section—

"the 1994 Act" means the Value Added Tax Act 1994; and

"the Commissioners" means the Commissioners of Customs and Excise.

(8) This section shall be deemed to have come into force on 4th December 1996.

(9) Where at any time on or after 4th December 1996 and before the day on which this Act is passed any assessment corresponding to an assessment under this section was made under a resolution of the House of Commons having effect in accordance with the provisions of the Provisional Collection of Taxes Act 1968, this section has effect, on and after the day on which this Act is passed, as if that assessment were an assessment under this section and as if any appeal brought under that resolution had been brought under this section.

GENERAL NOTE

The section covers the transitional position for set off between July 18, 1996 and December 4, 1996 where a taxpayer has recovered amounts which are no longer due to be repaid because of the three year time limit. It allows Customs and Excise to assess to recover the amount which was set off which is more than three years old. A taxpayer will only be assessed for the amount set off and any liabilities under the rest of the section. Penalties will not be payable in these circumstances.

Excise duties and other indirect taxes

Overpayments, interest, assessments, etc.

50.—(1) Schedule 5 to this Act (which makes provision in relation to excise duties, insurance premium tax and landfill tax which corresponds to that made for VAT by sections 44 to 48 above) shall have effect.

(2) Schedule 6 to this Act (which makes further provision for the assessment of amounts payable under enactments relating to excise duty) shall also have effect.

GENERAL NOTE

The section introduces Scheds. 5 and 6, which make provision for a three year time limit for payments and repayments for excise duties, insurance premium tax and landfill tax similar to those made for VAT by ss.44–48, and extend the excise assessment provisions to cover circumstances where there has been an underdeclaration, overclaim or other form of irregularity.

See further the General Note to these Schedules.

Enforcement of payment

Enforcement by distress

51.—(1) The Commissioners may by regulations make provision—
(a) for authorising distress to be levied on the goods and chattels of any person refusing or neglecting to pay—
    (i) any amount of relevant tax due from him, or
    (ii) any amount recoverable as if it were relevant tax due from him;
(b) for the disposal of any goods or chattels on which distress is levied in pursuance of the regulations; and
(c) for the imposition and recovery of costs, charges, expenses and fees in connection with anything done under the regulations.

(2) The provision that may be contained in regulations under this section shall include, in particular—
(a) provision for the levying of distress, by any person authorised to do so under the regulations, on goods or chattels located at any place whatever (including on a public highway); and
(b) provision authorising distress to be levied at any such time of the day or night, and on any such day of the week, as may be specified or described in the regulations.

(3) Regulations under this section may—
(a) make different provision for different cases, and
(b) contain any such incidental, supplemental, consequential or transitional provision as the Commissioners think fit;
and the transitional provision that may be contained in regulations under this section shall include transitional provision in connection with the coming into force of the repeal by this Act of any other power by regulations to make provision for or in connection with the levying of distress.

(4) The power to make regulations under this section shall be exercisable by statutory instrument subject to annulment in pursuance of a resolution of the House of Commons.

(5) The following are relevant taxes for the purposes of this section, that is to say—
(a) any duty of customs or excise, other than vehicle excise duty;
(b) value added tax;
(c) insurance premium tax;
(d) landfill tax;
(e) any agricultural levy of the European Community.

(6) In this section "the Commissioners" means the Commissioners of Customs and Excise.

(7) Regulations made under this section shall not have effect in Scotland.

GENERAL NOTE

The section provides for regulations to be made dealing with the recovery of tax through distraint on goods. The existing law covers VAT, insurance premium tax and landfill tax. The regulations will cover all taxes and duties administered by the Customs and Excise, other than vehicle excise duty. [Standing Committee B, February 13, 1997, col. 51.]

Enforcement by diligence

52.—(1) Where any amount of relevant tax or any amount recoverable as if it were relevant tax is due and has not been paid, the sheriff, on an application by the Commissioners accompanied by a certificate by them—
(a) stating that none of the persons specified in the application has paid the amount due from him;
(b) stating that payment of the amount due from each such person has been demanded from him; and
(c) specifying the amount due from and unpaid by each such person,

shall grant a summary warrant in a form prescribed by Act of Sederunt authorising the recovery, by any of the diligences mentioned in subsection (2) below, of the amount remaining due and unpaid.

(2) The diligences referred to in subsection (1) above are—

(a) a poinding and sale in accordance with Schedule 5 to the Debtors (Scotland) Act 1987;

(b) an earnings arrestment;

(c) an arrestment and action of furthcoming or sale.

(3) Subject to subsection (4) below and without prejudice to paragraphs 25 to 34 of Schedule 5 to the Debtors (Scotland) Act 1987 (expenses of poinding and sale) the sheriff officer's fees, together with the outlays necessarily incurred by him, in connection with the execution of a summary warrant shall be chargeable against the debtor.

(4) No fees shall be chargeable by the sheriff officer against the debtor for collecting, and accounting to the Commissioners for, sums paid to him by the debtor in respect of the amount owing.

(5) The following are relevant taxes for the purposes of this section, that is to say—

(a) any duty of customs or excise, other than vehicle excise duty;

(b) value added tax;

(c) insurance premium tax;

(d) landfill tax;

(e) any agricultural levy of the European Community.

(6) In this section "the Commissioners" means the Commissioners of Customs and Excise.

(7) This section shall come into force on such day as the Commissioners of Customs and Excise may by order made by statutory instrument appoint, and different days may be appointed under this subsection for different purposes.

(8) This section extends only to Scotland.

GENERAL NOTE

The section provides for the recovery of tax through diligence, the procedure in Scotland corresponding to distress in England. Again, the procedure is extended to cover taxes and duties administered by the Customs and Excise generally.

Subs. (1)

The sheriff is required to grant a summary warrant authorising the recovery of an amount of tax unpaid on an application by the Customs and Excise accompanied by an appropriate certificate.

Subs. (2)

The forms of diligence covered are listed.

Subss. (3) and (4)

The sheriff officer's fees are chargeable to the debtor. No fee is to be charged to him for collecting sums paid in respect of the amount owing.

Amendments consequential on sections 51 and 52

53.—(1) In section 117 of the Customs and Excise Management Act 1979 (execution and distress against revenue traders), after subsection (4) there shall be inserted the following subsection—

"(4A) This section does not apply for the purposes of levying distress in accordance with regulations under section 51 of the Finance Act 1997 or for the purposes of any execution under section 52 of that Act by diligence."

(2) In section 11(1)(a) of the Finance Act 1994 (walking possession agreements in connection with enforcement of excise duty)—

(a) for the words from "by virtue of" to "1981" there shall be substituted "in accordance with regulations under section 51 of the Finance Act 1997 (enforcement by distress)"; and

(b) after "default')" there shall be inserted "who has refused or neglected to pay any amount of relevant duty or any amount recoverable as if it were an amount of relevant duty due from him".

(3) In section 13(6) of the Finance Act 1994 (assessment for penalties), for the words "duty of excise", in each place where they occur, there shall be substituted "relevant duty".

(4) In section 18(8) of the Finance Act 1994 (saving relating to section 18(1), (2) and (4)), for ", (2) and (4)" there shall be substituted "and (2)".

(5) In paragraph 19(1)(a) of Schedule 7 to the Finance Act 1994 (walking possession agreements in connection with enforcement of insurance premium tax), for "paragraph 7(7) above" there shall be substituted "section 51 of the Finance Act 1997 (enforcement by distress)".

(6) In section 48 of the Value Added Tax Act 1994 (VAT representatives), after subsection (7) there shall be inserted the following subsection—

"(7A) A sum required by way of security under subsection (7) above shall be deemed for the purposes of—

(a) section 51 of the Finance Act 1997 (enforcement by distress) and any regulations under that section, and

(b) section 52 of that Act (enforcement by diligence),

to be recoverable as if it were VAT due from the person who is required to provide it."

(7) In section 68(1)(a) of the Value Added Tax Act 1994 (walking possession agreements), for "paragraph 5(4) of Schedule 11" there shall be substituted "section 51 of the Finance Act 1997 (enforcement by distress)".

(8) In paragraph 24(1)(a) of Schedule 5 to the Finance Act 1996 (walking possession agreements in connection with the enforcement of landfill tax), for "paragraph 13(1) above" there shall be substituted "section 51 of the Finance Act 1997 (enforcement by distress)".

(9) This section shall come into force on such day as the Commissioners of Customs and Excise may by order made by statutory instrument appoint, and different days may be appointed under this subsection for different purposes.

GENERAL NOTE

Various amendments are made to other statutes consequent on the enactment of ss.51 and 52.

PART V

INCOME TAX, CORPORATION TAX AND CAPITAL GAINS TAX

Income tax charge, rates and reliefs

Charge and rates of income tax for 1997–98

54.—(1) Income tax shall be charged for the year 1997–98, and for that year—

(a) the lower rate shall be 20 per cent;

(b) the basic rate shall be 23 per cent; and

(c) the higher rate shall be 40 per cent.

(2) For the year 1997–98 section 1(2) of the Taxes Act 1988 shall apply as if the amount specified in paragraph (aa) (the lower rate limit) were £4,100; and, accordingly, section 1(4) of that Act (indexation) shall apply for the year 1997–98 in relation only to the amount specified in section 1(2)(b) of that Act (the basic rate limit).

(3) In section 686(1A) of the Taxes Act 1988 (meaning of "the rate applicable to trusts"), for the words "for any year of assessment shall be the rate

equal to the sum of the basic rate and the additional rate in force for that year" there shall be substituted ", in relation to any year of assessment for which income tax is charged, shall be 34 per cent or such other rate as Parliament may determine".

(4) Subsection (3) above has effect in relation to the year 1997–98 and subsequent years of assessment.

(5) Section 559(4) of the Taxes Act 1988 (deductions from payments to sub-contractors in the construction industry) shall have effect—

(a) in relation to payments made on or after 1st July 1997 and before the appointed day (within the meaning of section 139 of the Finance Act 1995), with "23 per cent" substituted for "24 per cent"; and

(b) in relation to payments made on or after that appointed day, as if the substitution for which section 139(1) of the Finance Act 1995 provided were a substitution of "the relevant percentage" for "23 per cent".

GENERAL NOTE

The basic rate of income tax is reduced from 24 per cent to 23 per cent. The lower and higher rates remain at 20 per cent and 40 per cent respectively. The lower rate and basic rate limits are set at £4,100 and £26,100, increases of £200 and £600 respectively.

The tax rate for discretionary and accumulation trusts, previously expressed as the sum of the basic rate plus the additional rate, is set at 34 per cent. This is the same effective rate as the previous year.

The deduction rate for payments to sub-contractors in the construction industry is reduced from 24 per cent to 23 per cent.

Modification of indexed allowances

55.—(1) For the year 1997-98 the amounts specified in the provisions mentioned in subsection (2) below shall be taken to be as set out in that subsection; and, accordingly, section 257C(1) of the Taxes Act 1988 (indexation), so far as it relates to the amounts so specified, shall not apply for the year 1997-98.

(2) In section 257 of that Act (personal allowance)—

(a) the amount in subsection (1) (basic allowance) shall be £4,045;

(b) the amount in subsection (2) (allowance for persons aged 65 or more but not aged 75 or more) shall be £5,220; and

(c) the amount in subsection (3) (allowance for persons aged 75 or more) shall be £5,400.

GENERAL NOTE

The basic personal allowance, the allowance for over-65s and the allowance for over-75s are increased from £3,765 to £4,045, from £4,910 to £5,220 and from £5,090 to £5,400 respectively. Each is increased by £200 more than the amount required to index for inflation.

Blind person's allowance

56.—(1) In subsection (1) of section 265 of the Taxes Act 1988 (blind person's allowance), for "£1,250" there shall be substituted "£1,280".

(2) After that subsection there shall be inserted the following subsection—

"(1A) Section 257C (indexation) shall have effect (using the rounding up rule in subsection (1)(b) of that section) for the application of this section for the year 1998-99 and any subsequent year of assessment as it has effect for the application of sections 257 and 257A."

(3) Subsection (1) above shall apply for the year 1997-98 and, subject to subsection (2) above, for subsequent years of assessment.

GENERAL NOTE

The blind person's allowance is increased from £1,250 to £1,280. In future statutory indexation will apply, unless Parliament determines otherwise.

Limit on relief for interest

57. For the year 1997-98 the qualifying maximum defined in section 367(5) of the Taxes Act 1988 (limit on relief for interest on certain loans) shall be £30,000.

GENERAL NOTE
The limit on loans qualifying for mortgage interest and life annuity relief remains at £30,000, the level which has applied since 1983.

Corporation tax charge and rate

Charge and rate of corporation tax for 1997

58. Corporation tax shall be charged for the financial year 1997 at the rate of 33 per cent.

GENERAL NOTE
The main rate of corporation tax remains at 33 per cent.

Small companies

59. For the financial year 1997—
(a) the small companies' rate shall be 23 per cent; and
(b) the fraction mentioned in section 13(2) of the Taxes Act 1988 (marginal relief for small companies) shall be one fortieth.

GENERAL NOTE
The small companies' rate of corporation tax is reduced from 24 per cent to 23 per cent in line with the basic rate of income tax. The fraction providing marginal relief for profits between £300,000 and £1.5m is increased from nine four-hundredths to one fortieth, giving a marginal rate of 35.5 per cent.

Payments for wayleaves

Wayleaves for electricity cables, telephone lines, etc.

60.—(1) Section 120 of the Taxes Act 1988 (payments for wayleaves for electricity cables, telephone lines, etc.) shall be amended as follows.
(2) In subsection (1) (payments charged under Schedule D subject to deduction of tax)—
(a) at the beginning there shall be inserted "Subject to subsection (1A) below,"; and
(b) the words from "and, subject to" onwards (which provide for the deduction of tax) shall be omitted.
(3) After subsection (1) there shall be inserted the following subsection—
"(1A) If—
(a) the profits and gains arising to any person for any chargeable period include both rent in respect of any such easement as is mentioned in subsection (1) above and amounts which are charged to tax under Schedule A, and
(b) some or all of the land to which the easement relates is included in the land by reference to which the amounts charged under Schedule A arise,
then, for that period, that rent shall be charged to tax under Schedule A, instead of being charged under Schedule D."
(4) Subsections (2) to (4) and, in subsection (5), paragraph (c) and the word "and" immediately preceding it shall cease to have effect.
(5) This section has effect in relation to payments made on or after 6th April 1997.

GENERAL NOTE
The requirement to deduct tax at source from wayleave payments, *i.e.* extra payments in respect of electric, telegraphic or telephone wire and cableways, is abolished. Such payments

will continue to be chargeable under Sched. D, except where they arise to a landowner with Sched. A income in relation to the same land. In the latter case they will be charged under Sched. A.

Some special rules that were needed under the tax deduction scheme are abolished.

Schedule E

Phasing out of relief for profit-related pay

61.—(1) Chapter III of Part V of the Taxes Act 1988 (profit related pay) shall have effect as if, in section 171(4) (£4,000 limit on relief for profit period of twelve months), for "£4,000" there were substituted—

  (a) in relation to profit-related pay paid by reference to profit periods beginning on or after 1st January 1998 and before 1st January 1999, "£2,000"; and

  (b) in relation to profit-related pay paid by reference to profit periods beginning on or after 1st January 1999 and before 1st January 2000, "£1,000".

(2) That Chapter shall not have effect in relation to any payment made by reference to a profit period beginning on or after 1st January 2000.

(3) Accordingly—

  (a) a scheme shall not be registered under that Chapter if the only payments for which it provides are payments by reference to profit periods beginning on or after 1st January 2000; and

  (b) registration under that Chapter shall end on 31st December 2000.

GENERAL NOTE

The section provides for the phased withdrawal of the income tax relief for profit-related pay ("PRP") over a three to four year period. The present ceiling on the relief of £4,000 a year will remain unchanged until January 1, 1998. It will then be reduced over the following two years to £2,000 and £1,000 before disappearing completely from January 1, 2000.

PRP was introduced by F.(No. 2)A. 1987 (c. 51), following the publication of a Green Paper in 1986. There are currently some 14,000 registered PRP schemes, covering over 3.7 million employees.

Although generally welcomed when it was introduced, PRP proved open to abuse by schemes under which the main purpose was the saving of tax rather than the sharing of profits with employees. It was not in any case intended to be a permanent measure. Its abolition will save the Treasury more than £3bn in 2000–2001. [*Hansard*, H.C. Vol. 288, col. 997.]

Travelling expenses etc.

62.—(1) For subsection (1) of section 198 of the Taxes Act 1988 (relief for necessary expenses) there shall be substituted the following subsections—

  "(1) If the holder of an office or employment is obliged to incur and defray out of the emoluments of that office or employment—

    (a) any amount necessarily expended on travelling in the performance of the duties of the office or employment,

    (b) any other expenses of travelling which are not expenses of ordinary commuting but are attributable to the attendance of the holder of the office or employment at any place on an occasion when his attendance at that place is in the performance of the duties of the office or employment, or

    (c) any amount not comprised in expenses falling within paragraph (a) or (b) above but expended wholly, exclusively and necessarily in the performance of the duties of the office or employment,

then (subject to subsection (1A) below) there may be deducted from the emoluments to be assessed the amount which is so incurred and defrayed.

(1A) Where—
  (a) any person holding an office or employment undertakes any travelling the expenses of which fall within paragraph (a) or (b) of subsection (1) above, and
  (b) in consequence of his doing so, he does not incur expenses of ordinary commuting which it is likely he would have incurred had he not undertaken that travelling,
the amount (if any) which is deductible under subsection (1) above in respect of that travelling, or in respect of expenses incurred as mentioned in paragraph (c) of that subsection in connection with that travelling, shall be reduced by the amount of the expenses of ordinary commuting that have been saved.

(1B) For the purposes of subsection (1A) above the amount of any saving on ordinary commuting shall be calculated by using the same method for the expenses of the travelling comprised in ordinary commuting as would be used in the employee's case for calculating the deductible expenses of that travelling if it were not ordinary commuting."

(2) After section 198 of that Act there shall be inserted the following section—

"Interpretation of section 198

198A.—(1) For the purposes of section 198 and this section ordinary commuting, in relation to the holder of an office or employment, is—
  (a) travelling, in either direction, between a permanent workplace of his and a place mentioned in subsection (4) below (including any travel via another place so mentioned); or
  (b) travelling between two places in a case where, because of the proximity of one place to another, the journey in question is, for practical purposes, the same as a journey which would constitute ordinary commuting by virtue of paragraph (a) above.

(2) For the purposes of section 198 and this section a permanent workplace, in relation to the holder of an office or employment, is any place which—
  (a) he regularly attends in the performance of the duties of the office or employment and otherwise than for the purpose of performing a task of limited duration or for some other temporary purpose; and
  (b) is not a place falling within subsection (4)(a) below.

(3) The holder of an office or employment who does not have a permanent workplace apart from this subsection but is a person who—
  (a) in the performance of the duties of the office or employment, attends different places within a particular area, and
  (b) performs his duties at places in that area because his duties (except so far as requiring his attendance at places outside that area for the purpose of carrying out tasks of limited duration or for other temporary purposes) are defined by reference to that area,
shall be deemed for the purposes of section 198 and this section to have a permanent workplace comprising the whole area.

(4) The places referred to in subsection (1) above, in relation to the holder of an office or employment, are—
  (a) his home or any other place which he uses, otherwise than in the performance of the duties of that office or employment, as a permanent or temporary place of residence,
  (b) any place that he is visiting for social or personal reasons and otherwise than in the performance of the duties of that office or employment,

    (c) any place that he attends, otherwise than in the performance of the duties of that office or employment, for the purposes of any trade, profession or vocation carried on by him, and

    (d) any place that he attends in the performance of the duties of another office or employment held by him.

(5) For the purposes of this section attendance for limited purposes at—

    (a) a place which forms the base from which a person works in the performance of the duties of his office or employment, or

    (b) the place at which he is allocated the tasks that he is to carry out in the performance of those duties,

shall not be taken to involve attendance at that place to perform a task of limited duration or for a temporary purpose.

(6) For the purposes of this section, where on any occasion a person attends any place in the performance of the duties of any office or employment or performs those duties within a particular area—

    (a) the tasks which he carries out on that occasion at that place, or within that area, shall not be taken to be tasks of limited duration, and

    (b) the purposes for which, on that occasion, he attends that place or performs duties within that area shall not be taken to be temporary purposes,

if subsection (7) below applies to the place or area as respects that occasion.

(7) This subsection applies to a place or area as respects any occasion on which a task is carried out, or duties are performed, by a person holding an office or employment if—

    (a) the task is carried out, or the duties are performed—

        (i) in the course of a period of continuous work at that place or within that area; or

        (ii) at a time which it would be reasonable, on that occasion, to assume will be included in such a period;

    and

    (b) the period of continuous work is one of which more than twenty-four months has expired before that occasion or is one which it would be reasonable, on that occasion, to assume will in due course be either—

        (i) a period of more than twenty-four months; or

        (ii) a period comprising all or almost all of the period for which the person holding the office or employment is likely to continue to hold it after that occasion.

(8) The reference in subsection (7) above to a period of continuous work at a place or within an area is (subject to subsection (9) below) a reference to any continuous period throughout which the duties of the office or employment in question fall to be performed wholly or mainly at that place or, as the case may be, within that area.

(9) For the purposes of subsection (8) above any actual or contemplated modification of the place at which, or of the area within which, the duties of any office or employment fall to be performed shall be disregarded unless it is such that it has had, or would have, a significant effect on the expenses of any travel by the person holding the office or employment to or from the place or area where those duties fall wholly or mainly to be performed.

(10) For the purposes of this section, where a person holds any office or employment with a company, the reference in subsection (4)(d) above to another office or employment does not, in relation to that office or employment, include a reference to an office or employment with another company in the same group of companies.

(11) For the purposes of subsection (10) above two companies shall be taken to be members of the same group if, and only if, one of them is a 51 per cent subsidiary of the other or they are both 51 per cent subsidiaries of a third company."

(3) In section 158 of the Taxes Act 1988 (car fuel scales), in subsection (6) at the beginning there shall be inserted "Subject to subsection (7) below,"; and after that subsection there shall be inserted the following subsection—

"(7) Subsection (6) above does not apply in the relevant year unless the employee is required to make good, and does make good, to the person providing the fuel so much of the expenses incurred by him in or in connection with the provision of fuel for business travel as, for the purposes of section 198(1A), would be taken to represent expenses of ordinary commuting which (disregarding the requirement to make good) have been saved in consequence of the business travel having been undertaken."

(4) In subsections (5) and (5A) of section 168 of the Taxes Act 1988 (meaning of business travel), for paragraph (c) there shall be substituted, in each case, the following paragraph—

"(c) 'business travel', in relation to any employee, means any travelling the expenses of which, if incurred out of the emoluments of his employment, would be deductible under section 198;".

(5) This section has effect for the year 1998–99 and subsequent years of assessment.

GENERAL NOTE

The existing legislation allowing relief for expenses under Sched. E in ICTA 1988, s.198 is more than 150 years old. The new provisions attempt to make the basis of relief fairer and less complex. In particular, relief for business travel by employees who have no normal place of work is introduced. The changes are effective from the tax year 1998–99.

Subs. (1)

New ICTA 1988, s.198(1) replaces a classic formulation which included the expenses "of keeping and maintaining a horse". The horse is now gone (although it will still be allowed in appropriate circumstances) and is replaced by a fuller explanation of what constitutes travelling expenses allowable for tax in the modern era. The new subsection maintains a deduction for necessary expenditure on travel in the performance of duties. This includes the cost of business travel between an employee's normal place of work and the premises of one of the employer's clients, together with associated subsistence costs. The relief is extended to cover travel directly between an employee's home and a client's premises, but costs of "ordinary commuting" are excluded (see new ICTA 1988, s.198A(1) below).

New ICTA 1988, s.198(1A) introduces the concept of relief being available only for the "additional cost" element of any expenditure on travel. The relief in respect of travel under new s.198(1) is restricted by the amount of any savings realised on the cost of ordinary commuting.

New ICTA 1988, s.198(1B) requires a common approach to the calculation of travel costs and any off-set for ordinary commuting. For example, mileage rates for a particular vehicle will not vary depending on the nature or direction of the journey.

Subs. (2)

This introduces a new ICTA 1988, s.198A, which defines terms and sets parameters. Its length results from putting into legislative form existing case law and practice. (References are to subsections of new s.198A.)

New s.198A(1)

"Ordinary commuting" is defined as travel between a "permanent workplace" (see new s.198A(2)) and another place, as detailed in new s.198A(4). Ordinary commuting includes journeys between closely proximate premises.

New s.198A(2)

The "permanent workplace" is the place which the employee regularly attends in the performance of his duties except where such attendance is "for the performance of a task of limited duration or other temporary purpose" (see further new s.198A(6) and (7)). A taxpayer's home is excluded from the definition of permanent workplace, although it can qualify as a normal place of work, in which case travel between home and another place of work would qualify for relief.

New s.198A(3)

This covers individuals who have a particular area of work. The area is deemed to be their permanent workplace. It will affect very few employees. These will include social workers travelling a distance from home to their area of work and messengers distributing mail between neighbouring buildings.

New s.198A(4)

This completes the definition of "ordinary commuting" by dealing with the other end of the journey to a permanent workplace. The costs of travel from home are excluded from relief. Home includes any permanent or temporary place of residence, and also the homes of friends and relations. Travel between the office and a place of self-employment is also excluded, as is the cost of travel between two places of employment (but see s.198A(10) for travel within a group of companies).

New s.198A(5)

This covers employees such as bus drivers and delivery men operating from a depot who perform few duties at their permanent workplace. Their travel to work is nevertheless treated as ordinary commuting.

New s.198A(6)

This introduces subs. (7) which defines the exclusions from the scope of "for the purpose of performing a task of limited duration or for some other temporary purpose" (see subs. (2)).

New s.198A(7)

This refers to continuous attendance at a particular site. Any workplace attended for a continuous period in excess of 24 months or likely to be so attended is classified as a permanent workplace. Manipulation of the 24 month limit through recurring temporary appointments is prevented by taking these appointments together.

New s.198A(8)

Continuous work means work performed wholly or mainly at the site.

New s.198A(9)

A modified place or area of work is ignored unless it results in a significant effect on the cost of travel by the employee to that place.

New s.198A(10)

This puts on a statutory basis the first leg of Extra Statutory Concession A4 and extends it to allow relief for travel by anyone between employments or offices in two companies within a single group of companies.

New s.198A(11)

The 51 per cent rule applies for defining a group of companies (see ICTA 1988, s.838). (References below are to subsections of s.62.)

Subs. (3)

New ICTA 1988, s.158(7) excludes exemption from the fuel scale charge where an employee has been provided with and not made good the cost of, fuel in excess of the amount required to cover the additional cost of a business journey. The change ensures that there is no double charge and no failure to charge where a benefit arises.

Subs. (4)

The definition of "business travel" in ICTA 1988, s.168(5) and (5A) is linked directly to new s.139.

Subs. (5)
The new provisions come into effect from the next tax year.
[Standing Committee B, February 18, 1997, cols. 396–412.]

Work-related training

63.—(1) After section 200A of the Taxes Act 1988 there shall be inserted the following sections—

"Work-related training provided by employers

200B.—(1) This section applies for the purposes of Schedule E where any person ('the employer') incurs expenditure on providing work-related training for a person ('the employee') who holds an office or employment under him.

(2) Subject to section 200C, the emoluments of the employee from the office or employment shall not be taken to include—

(a) any amount in respect of that expenditure; or

(b) any amount in respect of the benefit of the work-related training provided by means of that expenditure.

(3) For the purposes of this section the employer shall be taken to incur expenditure on the provision of work-related training in so far only as he incurs expenditure in paying or reimbursing—

(a) the cost of providing any such training to the employee; or

(b) any related costs.

(4) In subsection (3) above 'related costs', in relation to any work-related training provided to the employee, means—

(a) any costs which are incidental to the employee's undertaking the training and are incurred wholly and exclusively as a result of his doing so;

(b) any expenses incurred in connection with an assessment (whether by examination or otherwise) of what the employee has gained from the training; and

(c) the cost of obtaining for the employee any qualification, registration or award to which he has or may become entitled as a result of undertaking the training or of undergoing such an assessment.

(5) In this section 'work-related training' means any training course or other activity which is designed to impart, instill, improve or reinforce any knowledge, skills or personal qualities which—

(a) is or, as the case may be, are likely to prove useful to the employee when performing the duties of any relevant employment; or

(b) will qualify him, or better qualify him—

(i) to undertake any relevant employment; or

(ii) to participate in any charitable or voluntary activities that are available to be undertaken in association with any relevant employment.

(6) In this section 'relevant employment', in relation to the employee, means—

(a) any office or employment which he holds under the employer or which he is to hold under the employer or a person connected with the employer;

(b) any office or employment under the employer or such a person to which he has a serious opportunity of being appointed; or

(c) any office or employment under the employer or such a person as respects which he can realistically expect to have such an opportunity in due course.

(7) Section 839 (meaning of 'connected person') applies for the purposes of this section.

Expenditure excluded from section 200B

200C.—(1) Section 200B shall not apply in the case of any expenditure to the extent that it is incurred in paying or reimbursing the cost of any facilities or other benefits provided or made available to the employee for one or more of the following purposes, that is to say—

    (a) enabling the employee to enjoy the facilities or benefits for entertainment or recreational purposes unconnected with the imparting, instilling, improvement or reinforcement of knowledge, skills or personal qualities falling within section 200B(5)(a) or (b);

    (b) rewarding the employee for the performance of the duties of his office or employment under the employer, or for the manner in which he has performed them;

    (c) providing the employee with an employment inducement which is unconnected with the imparting, instilling, improvement or reinforcement of knowledge, skills or personal qualities falling within section 200B(S)(a) or (b).

(2) Section 200B shall not apply in the case of any expenditure incurred in paying or reimbursing any expenses of travelling or subsistence, except to the extent that those expenses would be deductible under section 198 if the employee—

    (a) undertook the training in question in the performance of the duties of his office or employment under the employer; and

    (b) incurred those expenses out of the emoluments of that office or employment.

(3) Section 200B shall not apply in the case of any expenditure incurred in paying or reimbursing the cost of providing the employee with, or with the use of, any asset except where—

    (a) the asset is provided or made available for use only in the course of the training;

    (b) the asset is provided or made available for use in the course of the training and in the performance of the duties of the employee's office or employment but not for any other use;

    (c) the asset consists in training materials provided in the course of the training; or

    (d) the asset consists in something made by the employee in the course of the training or incorporated into something so made.

(4) Section 200B shall apply in the case of expenditure in connection with anything that is a qualifying course of training for the purposes of section 588 to the extent only that section 588(1) does not have effect.

(5) Section 200B shall not apply in the case of any expenditure incurred in enabling the employee to meet, or in reimbursing him for, any payment in respect of which there is an entitlement to relief under section 32 of the Finance Act 1991 (vocational training).

(6) In subsection (1) above the reference to enjoying facilities or benefits for entertainment or recreational purposes includes a reference to enjoying them in the course of any leisure activity.

(7) In this section—

    'employment inducement', in relation to the employee, means an inducement to remain in, or to accept, any office or employment with the employer or a person connected with the employer;

    'subsistence' includes food and drink and temporary living accommodation; and

    'training materials' means stationery, books or other written material, audio or video tapes, compact disks or floppy disks.

(8) Section 839 (meaning of 'connected person') applies for the purposes of this section.

Other work-related training

200D.—(1) For the purposes of Schedule E, where—

(a) any person ('the employee') who holds an office or employment under another ('the employer') is provided by reason of that office or employment with any benefit,

(b) that benefit consists in any work-related training or is provided in connection with any such training, and

(c) the amount which (apart from this section and sections 200B and 200C) would be included in respect of that benefit in the emoluments of the employee ('the chargeable amount') is or includes an amount that does not represent expenditure incurred by the employer,

the questions whether and to what extent those emoluments shall in fact be taken to include an amount in respect of that benefit shall be determined in accordance with those sections as if the benefit had been provided by means of a payment by the employer of an amount equal to the whole of the chargeable amount.

(2) In this section 'work-related training' has the same meaning as in section 200B."

(2) In section 200A(3)(b) of that Act (definition of a qualifying absence from home), the word "either" before sub-paragraph (i) shall be omitted and, at the end of sub-paragraph (ii), there shall be inserted "or

(iii) expenses the amount of which, having been paid or reimbursed by the person under whom he holds that office or employment, is excluded from his emoluments in pursuance of section 200B, or

(iv) expenses the amount of which would be so excluded if it were so paid or reimbursed."

(3) This section applies for the year 1997-98 and subsequent years of assessment.

GENERAL NOTE

This section enacts (at much greater length) Extra Statutory Concession A63, which exempts from tax as a benefit expenses borne by an employer for external training courses. The concession dates from 1986, but reflects a long standing practice. The section goes wider than the terms of the concession.

Subs. (1)

This introduces new ICTA 1988, ss.200B, 200C and 200D. Section 200B sets out the main rules. Section 200C gives definitions and exclusions from the exemption. Section 200D deals mainly with third-party training.

New section 200B confers the exemption for work-related training. It covers both direct expenditure by the employer and reimbursement of expenses incurred by the employee. The exemption includes related costs such as extra travel and additional childcare as well as examination expenses. The definition of "work-related training" is widely drawn and is designed to cover activities such as Outward Bound courses and those provided by the Prince's Trust and Raleigh International. Employee development schemes are also included. The exemption applies to training for the job currently held or for one that is planned and also training for a future job which an employee may stand a serious or realistic chance of holding under the employer. The section applies to training for jobs with the current employer or with an associate firm.

New section 200C denies exemption to the extent that the alleged training is actually for entertainment, recreation, reward or provided as an inducement. Where there is a dual purpose, the expenditure may be apportioned. Travelling and subsistence costs are allowable in line with the code under new ICTA 1988, s.198 (see s.62 above). Assets such as computers may be lent but not given to an employee but training materials (see s.200C(7)) may be provided. The new relief does not apply where it is already available under ICTA 1988, s.588, which covers retraining courses, or F.A. 1991, s.32, which covers vocational training.

New section 200D provides for work-related training funded by a third party to be exempt to the same extent as if the employer had incurred the expenditure. This would cover, for instance, training provided by a vacuum cleaner manufacturer to enable the staff of an electrical goods shop to demonstrate the operation of the vacuum cleaner.

Subs. (2)

ICTA 1988, s.200A is extended so that incidental overnight expenses paid to employees on training courses may be paid tax-free in the same way as incidental overnight expenses paid when an employee is away on business.

Subs. (3)

The new provisions operate from the tax year 1997–98. The concession will continue to apply in relation to new s.200C(2) which invokes new s.198; this does not come into force until the tax year 1998–99.

Relieved expenditure, losses etc.

Postponed company donations to charity

64.—(1) In section 339 of the Taxes Act 1988 (company donations to charity), after subsection (7) there shall be inserted the following subsections—

"(7AA) Where—

    (a) a covenanted donation to a charity is made by a company which is wholly owned by a charity,

    (b) the requirements of subsection (7) above for that donation to be regarded as a charge on income are satisfied,

    (c) the disposition or covenant under which the donation is made required it to be made in an accounting period of the company which ended before the time when it is in fact made, and

    (d) the donation is made within nine months of the end of that period,

the donation shall be deemed for the purposes of section 338 to be a charge on income paid in the accounting period in which it was required to be made, and not in any later period.

(7AB) For the purposes of this section a company is wholly owned by a charity if it is either—

    (a) a company with an ordinary share capital every part of which is owned by a charity (whether or not the same charity); or

    (b) a company limited by guarantee in whose case every person who—

        (i) is beneficially entitled to participate in the divisible profits of the company, or

        (ii) will be beneficially entitled to share in any net assets of the company available for distribution on its winding up,

    is or must be a charity or a company wholly owned by a charity.

(7AC) For the purposes of subsection (7AB) above ordinary share capital of a company shall be taken to be owned by a charity if there is a charity which—

    (a) within the meaning of section 838 directly or indirectly owns that share capital; or

    (b) would be taken so to own that share capital if references in that section to a body corporate included references to a charity which is not a body corporate."

(2) This section has effect in relation to donations made in accounting periods beginning on or after 1st April 1997.

GENERAL NOTE

A frequent method of operating trading activities by a charity is to set up a company which covenants its income to the charity. Under the current rules (which apply to all companies) the company must make the covenanted donation within the accounting period in which the profits arise if tax relief is to be given for that period. The section, which has effect in relation to donations made in accounting periods beginning on or after April 1, 1997, gives companies owned by charities nine months after the end of the accounting period in which the donation was due to make the covenanted payment and still receive tax relief in that accounting period.

New ICTA 1988, s.339(7AA) confers the relief, s.339(7AB) stipulates that all the ordinary share capital of the company in question must be owned by a charity (or in the case of a company limited by guarantee all the members must be charities or companies owned by charities) and s.339(7AC) extends the relief to indirect ownership and ownership by trusts.

National Insurance contributions

65.—(1) Section 617 of the Taxes Act 1988 (social security benefits and contributions) shall be amended as follows.

(2) In subsection (3) (which provides that, subject to subsection (4) and (5), no relief or deduction shall be given in respect of National Insurance contributions) the words "and (5)" shall be omitted in consequence of the repeal of subsection (5) by section 147 of the Finance Act 1996.

(3) For subsection (4) (exception from subsection (3) for secondary Class 1 contributions which are allowable as a deduction in certain computations) there shall be substituted—

"(4) Subsection (3) above shall not apply to a contribution if it is a secondary Class 1 contribution or Class 1A contribution (within the meaning of Part I of either of those Acts) and is allowable—

(a) as a deduction in computing profits or gains;

(b) as expenses of management deductible under section 75 or under that section as applied by section 76;

(c) as expenses of management or supervision deductible under section 121;

(d) as a deduction under section 198 from the emoluments of an office or employment; or

(e) as a deduction under section 332(3)(a) from the profits, fees or emoluments of the profession or vocation of a clergyman or minister of any religious denomination."

(4) Subsection (2) above has effect in relation to the year 1996-97 and subsequent years of assessment.

(5) Subsection (3) above has effect in relation to contributions paid on or after 26th November 1996.

GENERAL NOTE

The section makes amendments to ICTA 1988, s.617.

Subs. (2)

A consequential amendment is made to reflect the repeal of s.617(5) by F.A. 1996, s.147.

Subs. (3)

Under Extra Statutory Concession B48, published in May 1996, employers are entitled to relief for Class 1A National Insurance contributions, which are due when cars are provided for private use to directors and to employees earning more than £8,500 per annum. The concession is put in statutory form. Relief is also extended to cover the rare cases where an office-holder or a minister of religion has an employee and makes Class 1 or 1A contributions.

Expenditure on production wells etc.

66.—(1) After section 91B of the Taxes Act 1988 there shall be inserted the following section—

"Mineral exploration and access

91C. Where—

(a) a person carrying on a trade incurs expenditure on mineral exploration and access as defined in section 121(1) of the Capital Allowances Act 1990 in an area or group of sands in which the presence of mineral deposits in commercial quantities has already been established, and

(b) if the presence in that area or group of sands of mineral deposits in commercial quantities had not already been established, that expenditure would not have been allowed to be deducted in computing the profits or gains of the trade for the purposes of tax, that expenditure shall not be so deducted."

(2) In section 115 of the Capital Allowances Act 1990 (certain expenditure on purchased assets treated as expenditure on mineral exploration and access if attributable to previous trader's expenditure on mineral exploration and access), after subsection (2) there shall be inserted the following subsection—

"(2A) Expenditure incurred by the previous trader which is or has been deducted in computing, for the purposes of tax, the profits or gains of a trade carried on by him shall not be treated as expenditure on mineral exploration and access for the purposes of subsection (1)(b)."

(3) Subsection (1) above applies to expenditure which—
(a) is incurred on or after 26th November 1996; but
(b) is not incurred before 26th November 1997 in pursuance of a contract entered into before 26th November 1996.

(4) The reference in subsection (3) above to expenditure incurred in pursuance of a contract entered into before 26th November 1996 does not, in the case of a contract varied on or after that date, include a reference to so much of any expenditure of the sort described in section 91C of the Taxes Act 1988 as exceeds the amount of expenditure of that sort that would have been incurred if that contract had not been so varied.

(5) Subsection (2) above applies in relation to claims made on or after 26th November 1996.

GENERAL NOTE
The section provides that oil companies will no longer be entitled to an immediate 100 per cent deduction against corporation tax for the intangible costs of drilling production oil wells. This expenditure will now only qualify for mineral extraction capital allowances ("MEA") at a rate of 25 per cent per annum on a reducing balance basis. The change applies to expenditure incurred on or after November 26, 1996, except where it is incurred before November 26, 1997 under a contract entered into before November 26, 1996. Intangible costs are costs which do not result in the acquisition or creation of machinery and plant, such as the cost of hiring a drilling rig. The previous treatment reflected a decision by the Special Commissioners in 1920 that this expenditure was of a revenue nature.

The change does not affect intangible costs of the first production well in an area, which already qualify for MEA, but only to subsequent production wells, which enjoy the 100 per cent deduction. The 100 per cent Scientific Research Allowances available for expenditure on wells drilled to explore for oil or gas or to appraise discoveries are unaffected.

Subs. (1)
New ICTA 1988, s.91C implements the restriction.

Subs. (2)
This prevents the buyer of an interest in an oil field from claiming MEA on expenditure for which the seller has already claimed a 100 per cent revenue deduction.
[Standing Committee B, February 18, 1997, col. 413.]

Annuity business of insurance companies

67.—(1) In section 437 of the Taxes Act 1988 (extent to which payments in respect of new annuities are to be treated as charges on income), for subsections (1A) and (1B) there shall be substituted the following subsection—

"(1A) In the computation, otherwise than in accordance with the provisions applicable to Case I of Schedule D, of the profits for any accounting period of a company's life assurance business, new annuities paid by the company in that period shall be brought into account by treating an amount equal to the income limit for that period as a sum disbursed as expenses of management of the company for that period."

(2) In subsection (1C) of that section (interpretation of section), after "this section" there shall be inserted "(but subject to subsections (1CA) to (1CD)

below)"; and after that subsection there shall be inserted the following subsections—

"(1CA) Where a new annuity ('the actual annuity') is a steep-reduction annuity, the income limit for an accounting period of the company paying the annuity shall be computed for the purposes of this section as if—

(a) the contract providing for the actual annuity provided instead for the annuities identified by subsections (1CB) and (1CC) below; and

(b) the consideration for each of those annuities were to be determined by the making of a just and reasonable apportionment of the consideration for the actual annuity.

(1CB) The annuities mentioned in subsection (1CA)(a) above are—

(a) an annuity the payments in respect of which are confined to the payments in respect of the actual annuity that fall to be made before the earliest time for the making in respect of the actual annuity of a reduced payment such as is mentioned in section 437A(1)(c); and

(b) subject to subsection (1CC) below, an annuity the payments in respect of which are all the payments in respect of the actual annuity other than those mentioned in paragraph (a) above.

(1CC) Where an annuity identified by paragraph (b) of subsection (1CB) above ('the later annuity') would itself be a steep-reduction annuity, the annuities mentioned in subsection (1CA)(a) above—

(a) shall not include the later annuity; but

(b) shall include, instead, the annuities which would be identified by subsection (1CB) above (with as many further applications of this subsection as may be necessary for securing that none of the annuities mentioned in subsection (1CA)(a) above is a steep-reduction annuity) if references in that subsection to the actual annuity were references to the later annuity.

(1CD) Subsections (1CA) to (1CC) above shall be construed in accordance with section 437A."

(3) After that section there shall be inserted the following section—

"Meaning of 'steep-reduction annuity' etc.

437A.—(1) For the purposes of section 437 an annuity is a steep-reduction annuity if—

(a) the amount of any payment in respect of the annuity (but not the term of the annuity) depends on any contingency other than the duration of a human life or lives;

(b) the annuitant is entitled in respect of the annuity to payments of different amounts at different times; and

(c) those payments include a payment ('a reduced payment') of an amount which is substantially smaller than the amount of at least one of the earlier payments in respect of that annuity to which the annuitant is entitled.

(2) Where there are different intervals between payments to which an annuitant is entitled in respect of any annuity, the question whether or not the conditions in subsection (1)(b) and (c) above are satisfied in the case of that annuity shall be determined by assuming—

(a) that the annuitant's entitlement, after the first payment, to payments in respect of that annuity is an entitlement to payments at yearly intervals on the anniversary of the first payment; and

(b) that the amount to which the annuitant is assumed to be entitled on each such anniversary is equal to the annuitant's assumed entitlement for the year ending with that anniversary.

(3) For the purposes of subsection (2) above an annuitant's assumed entitlement for any year shall be determined as follows—

    (a) the annuitant's entitlement to each payment in respect of the annuity shall be taken to accrue at a constant rate during the interval between the previous payment and that payment; and

    (b) his assumed entitlement for any year shall be taken to be equal to the aggregate of the amounts which, in accordance with paragraph (a) above, are treated as accruing in that year.

(4) In the case of an annuity to which subsection (2) above applies, the reference in section 437(1CB)(a) to the making of a reduced payment shall be construed as if it were a reference to the making of a payment in respect of that annuity which (applying subsection (3)(a) above) is taken to accrue at a rate that is substantially less than the rate at which at least one of the earlier payments in respect of that annuity is taken to accrue.

(5) Where—

    (a) any question arises for the purposes of this section whether the amount of any payment in respect of any annuity—

        (i) is substantially smaller than the amount of, or

        (ii) accrues at a rate substantially less than,

    an earlier payment in respect of that annuity, and

    (b) the annuitant or, as the case may be, every annuitant is an individual who is beneficially entitled to all the rights conferred on him as such an annuitant,

that question shall be determined without regard to so much of the difference between the amounts or rates as is referable to a reduction falling to be made as a result of the occurrence of a death.

(6) Where the amount of any one or more of the payments to which an annuitant is entitled in respect of an annuity depends on any contingency, his entitlement to payments in respect of that annuity shall be determined for the purposes of section 437(1CA) to (1CC) and this section according to whatever (applying any relevant actuarial principles) is the most likely outcome in relation to that contingency.

(7) Where any agreement or arrangement has effect for varying the rights of an annuitant in relation to a payment in respect of any annuity, that payment shall be taken, for the purposes of section 437(1CA) to (1CC) and this section, to be a payment of the amount to which the annuitant is entitled in accordance with that agreement or arrangement.

(8) References in this section to a contingency include references to a contingency that consists wholly or partly in the exercise by any person of any option."

(4) Section 434B(2) of that Act (treatment of annuities paid by an insurance company) shall cease to have effect and accordingly—

    (a) in section 76(2A)(b) of that Act (limit on expenses of management of insurance companies), the word "and" shall be inserted at the end of sub-paragraph (ii), and sub-paragraph (iv) (together with the word "and" immediately preceding it) shall be omitted; and

    (b) in section 337(2B) of that Act, for "the references in sections 338(2) and 434B(2)" there shall be substituted "the reference in section 338(2)".

(5) In paragraph 9B of Schedule 19AC to that Act (subsection (3) inserted in section 434B in relation to overseas life insurance companies), for the words from the beginning to "An" there shall be substituted—

"9B. The following section shall be treated as inserted after section 434A—

     'Treatment of annuities

      434AA. An'.""

(6) In sub-paragraph (1) of paragraph 16 of Schedule 7 to the Finance Act 1991 (which makes transitional provision for annuities under contracts made in accounting periods beginning before 1st January 1992), for the words before paragraph (a) there shall be substituted—

> "(1) In the computation, otherwise than in accordance with the provisions applicable to Case I of Schedule D, of the profits for any accounting period of an insurance company's life assurance business, an amount equal to the lesser of the following amounts shall be treated (if it is not nil) as a sum disbursed as expenses of management of the company for that period, that is to say—".

(7) Subsections (1) and (4) to (6) above have effect in relation to accounting periods beginning after 5th March 1997.

(8) Subsections (2) and (3) above have effect in relation to accounting periods ending on or after 5th March 1997 but do not affect the computation of the capital elements contained in any annuity payments made before that date.

GENERAL NOTE

This section, introduced at report stage, is designed to prevent a recently discovered tax avoidance scheme. This involves a bank taking out annuities on employees. The annuities are so structured that substantial payments are made for short periods, followed by trivial amounts for a lengthy period. Under the existing rules, the insurance company paying the annuities is entitled to deduct from its profits large amounts in respect of the early years, although much of the payments are in truth a return of capital. The bank is unaffected, since it pays tax on the entire profit from the transaction.

The device is countered by dividing the annuity arrangement in two and limiting the deductible element for the short period as if the annuity were for that period. Excess annuities are treated as management expenses and so cannot be set against other non-life assurance profits or be surrendered to another group company.

Subs. (1)

New ICTA 1988, s.437(1A) introduces the concept of treating an amount equal to the income limit of a company taxed on the I minus E basis (see F.(No. 2)A. 1992 (c. 48), s.65) as management expenses.

Subs. (2)

New ICTA 1988, subss. (1CA)–(1CD) of s.437 provide for a just and reasonable apportionment of the consideration in the case of a "steep-reduction annuity".

Subs. (3)

New ICTA 1988, s.437A provides the definition of a "steep-reduction annuity". This applies to annuities where there is a payment of an amount which is substantially smaller than the amount of at least one of the earlier payments in respect of that annuity.

Subs. (4)

These amendments prevent annuities from being treated as a charge on income.

Subss. (5), (6)

These make consequential amendments to other provisions.

Subss. (7), (8)

The restriction on the treatment of excess annuities applies to accounting periods beginning after March 5, 1997 (when the Government announcement was made). Similarly, the limitation on the deductible element applies to payments on or after that date.

[*Hansard*, H.C. Vol. 292, col. 155.]

Consortium claims for group relief

68. In section 410 of the Taxes Act 1988 (group relief not available in certain cases including those where a person, either alone or with connected persons, controls 75 per cent or more of the voting rights in a company owned by a consortium), in the definition of "connected persons" in subsection (5) after "in accordance with section 839" there shall be inserted "but as if subsection (7) of that section (persons acting together to control a company are connected) were omitted".

GENERAL NOTE

This section, introduced at report stage in response to a back-bench initiative in standing committee, is designed to allay concerns following the Court of Appeal decision in *Steele v. EVC International NV* [1996] S.T.C. 785. Its effect is that shareholders' agreements concerning the governance of a company will not in themselves debar consortium relief for companies collaborating in joint ventures.

[Standing Committee B, February 25, 1997, col. 482; *Hansard*, H.C. Vol. 292, col. 158.]

Distributions etc.

Special treatment for certain distributions

69. Schedule 7 to this Act (which makes provision for the treatment of distributions arising on the purchase etc. by a company of its own shares and for cases where a distribution has a connection with a transaction in securities) shall have effect.

GENERAL NOTE

The section introduces Sched. 7, which is designed to end the loss of tax revenue arising from purchases of own shares by companies and special dividends where the recipient is able to reclaim the advance corporation tax. The method used is to treat such purchases and dividends as foreign income dividends, on which tax cannot be reclaimed.

See further the General Note to Schedule 7.

Distributions of exempt funds

70.—(1) In subsection (5) of section 236 of the Taxes Act 1988 (meaning of "relevant profits"
  (a) in paragraph (a), after "franked investment income" there shall be inserted "and foreign income dividends"; and
  (b) in paragraph (b), for "and franked investment income" there shall be substituted ", franked investment income and foreign income dividends".

(2) After subsection (7) of that section there shall be inserted the following subsection—

"(8) In this section 'foreign income dividends' shall be construed in accordance with Chapter VA of Part VI."

(3) This section has effect (subject to subsection (4) below) for the purposes of computing the relevant profits (within the meaning of section 236 of the Taxes Act 1988) arising to a company in any period falling wholly or partly after 7th October 1996.

(4) No foreign income dividend paid before 8th October 1996 shall be included or, as the case may be, excluded by virtue of this section from any such profits as are mentioned in subsection (3) above.

GENERAL NOTE

The amendments made by this section ensure that the provision in ICTA 1988, s.236 relating to the distributions of exempt funds will operate correctly, with effect from October 8, 1996. The anti-avoidance provision in ss.235–236 removes exemption from tax which would otherwise apply to the receipt of a distribution where the person entitled to the exemption owns more than 10 per cent of the paying company and the distribution represents profits arising before the shareholding was acquired. Foreign income dividends are now added to franked investment income for the purposes of the calculation under s.236.

Set-off against franked investment income

71. Section 242 of the Taxes Act 1988 (set-off of losses against surplus franked investment income) shall have effect, and be deemed always to have had effect, as if at the end of paragraph (c) of subsection (6) (power to carry set-off forward) there were inserted "and

(d) in relation to relief given in respect of amounts available to be set against profits under section 83 of the Finance Act 1996 or paragraph 4 of Schedule 11 to that Act or under section 131(4) of the Finance Act 1993 (which are provisions relating to deficits on loan relationships, foreign exchange losses and losses on certain financial instruments);".

GENERAL NOTE

The section is a relieving measure providing, with retrospective effect, that where franked payments made by a company exceed its franked investment income then any losses on loan relationships held or owed otherwise than for the purposes of a trade, foreign exchange movements, and financial instruments which were previously used to support a claim for payment of a tax credit are reinstated and available for set-off against profits of the company. This extends to such losses the treatment previously accorded to losses set against surplus franked investment income.

FIDs paid to unauthorised unit trusts

72.—(1) In section 246D(5) of the Taxes Act 1988 (section 233(1) and (1A) of that Act not to apply to FIDs paid to individuals, personal representatives or certain trustees), after "representatives" there shall be inserted ", a foreign income dividend paid to the trustees of a unit trust scheme to which section 469 applies".

(2) This section has effect in relation to distributions made on or after 26th November 1996.

GENERAL NOTE

This corrects a defect in the legislation applying to unauthorised unit trusts receiving foreign income dividends. It was possible for an exempt investor, such as a pension scheme, to obtain payment of tax treated as paid where a FID which is received by the trust in one tax year is not paid out to its unitholders until the following year. It is now provided that FIDs made to unauthorised units on or after November 26, 1996 will not be treated as having borne a notional lower rate income tax charge.

Tax advantages to include tax credits

73.—In section 709 of the Taxes Act 1988 (meaning of "tax advantage" etc. in Chapter I of Part XVII of that Act), after subsection (2) there shall be inserted the following subsection—

"(2A) In this Chapter references to a relief and to a repayment of tax include, respectively, references to a tax credit and to a payment of any amount in respect of a tax credit."

(2) This section—

(a) has effect for the purposes of the application of provisions of Chapter I of Part XVII of the Taxes Act 1988 in relation to chargeable periods ending at any time, including times before the passing of this Act, but

(b) without prejudice to the construction of that Chapter apart from this section, does not apply in the case of a tax credit in respect of a distribution made before 8th October 1996.

GENERAL NOTE

The anti-avoidance provisions of ICTA 1988, ss.703–709 are amended to include within the scope of "tax advantage" the payment of a tax credit. The amendment applies from October 8, 1996, but without prejudice to the application of the section prior to that date. In the recent case of *IRC v. Universities Superannuation Scheme Ltd* [1997] S.T.C. 1 it was held that the payment of a tax credit was caught by the existing legislation. The amendment is designed to catch cases which might not be covered by the new provisions in Sched. 7.

[Standing Committee B, February 18, 1997, col. 416.]

Investments etc.

Enterprise investment scheme

74. Schedule 8 to this Act (which amends the provisions in Chapter III of Part VII of the Taxes Act 1988 about the companies which are qualifying companies for the purposes of the enterprise investment scheme and makes related amendments to that Chapter) shall have effect.

GENERAL NOTE

The section introduces Sched. 8, which amends the provisions relating to the enterprise investment scheme ("EIS"). The changes, which will cost up to £5m in a full year, are designed to make the conditions for qualifying for tax relief more flexible.

See further the General Note to Sched. 8.

Venture capital trusts

75.—(1) Section 842AA of the Taxes Act 1988 (venture capital trusts) shall have effect, and be deemed always to have had effect, with the following subsections inserted after subsection (5)—

"(5A) Subsection (5B) below applies where—

(a) there has been an issue of ordinary share capital of a company ('the first issue'),

(b) an approval of that company for the purposes of this section has taken effect on or before the day of the making of the first issue, and

(c) a further issue of ordinary share capital of that company has been made since the making of the first issue.

(5B) Where this subsection applies, the use to which the money raised by the further issue is put, and the use of any money deriving from that use, shall be disregarded in determining whether any of the conditions specified in subsection (2)(b) and (c) above are, have been or will be fulfilled in relation to—

(a) the accounting period in which the further issue is made; or

(b) any later accounting period ending no more than three years after the making of the further issue."

(2) Subsection (6) of that section (withdrawal of approval) shall have effect, and be deemed always to have had effect, with the insertion of the following paragraph before the word "or" at the end of paragraph (c)—

"(ca) in a case where the use of any money falls to be disregarded for any accounting period in accordance with subsection (5B) above—

(i) that the first accounting period of the company for which the use of that money will not be disregarded will be a period in relation to which a condition specified in subsection (2) above will fail to be fulfilled; or

(ii) that the company has not fulfilled such other conditions as may be prescribed by regulations made by the Board in relation to, or to any part of, an accounting period for which the use of that money falls to be disregarded;".

(3) Schedule 9 to this Act (which amends the provisions of Schedule 28B to the Taxes Act 1988 defining "qualifying holdings") shall have effect.

GENERAL NOTE

This section, together with Sched. 9, relaxes the conditions governing a venture capital trust ("VCT"). The cost of the relaxations will be up to £5m in a full year.

Subs. (1)

New ICTA 1988, s.842(AA)(5A) and (5B) provide VCTs with additional time to invest funds raised by further share issues. The share issues concerned are issues of ordinary shares that follow an earlier issue of ordinary shares made on or after the day that approval of the company as a VCT has effect. Any investments funded by such an issue, and any later investments funded by money derived from those earlier investments, will be disregarded for a period of up to three years from the issue date when testing whether the VCT has a sufficient proportion of its investments in the types of shares and securities required by the scheme's rules. This allows a VCT separate periods of up to three years in which to invest capital from any share issues.

Subs. (2)

New ICTA 1988, s.842AA(6)(ca) applies the existing arrangements for withdrawal of approval from a VCT to cases where the additional time limits provided by s.842AA(5B) are operating.

Subs. (3)

This introduces Sched. 9, which amends the VCT rules for companies with subsidiaries. See further the General Note to Sched. 9.

[Standing Committee B, February 18, 1997, cols. 420–423.]

Stock lending and manufactured payments

76. Schedule 10 to this Act (which makes provision for the treatment for the purposes of income tax, corporation tax and capital gains tax of stock lending arrangements and manufactured payments) shall have effect.

GENERAL NOTE

This section introduces Sched. 10. It implements the Government's response to proposals from the London Stock Exchange for an order book trading system. At present, only market makers on the LSE and members of "LIFFE" (the London International Financial Futures and Options Exchange) can borrow U.K. equities. There are at present no tax restrictions on the borrowing or lending of securities other than U.K. equities. Removing the restrictions from U.K. equities means that the relevant legislative provisions can be repealed altogether. In turn, this change removes the need for manufactured payments to be categorised as either approved or unapproved. The opportunity is also being taken to rationalise the rules about manufactured payments on U.K. equities and securities. The new arrangements will come into effect from July 1, 1997.

See further the General Note to Sched. 10.

[Standing Committee B, February 18, 1997, cols. 423–426.]

Bond washing and repos

77.—(1) After subsection (2A) of section 731 of the Taxes Act 1988 (disapplication of bond washing rules where buyer has to make manufactured payment) there shall be inserted the following subsections—

"(2B) Subject to subsection (2E) below, where there is a repo agreement in relation to any securities—

(a) neither—

(i) the purchase of the securities by the interim holder from the original owner, nor

(ii) the repurchase of the securities by the original owner, shall be a purchase of those securities for the purposes of subsection (2) above; and

(b) neither—

(i) the sale of the securities by the original owner to the interim holder, nor

(ii) the sale by the interim holder under which the securities are bought back by the original owner, shall be taken for the purposes of subsection (2) above to be a subsequent sale of securities previously purchased by the seller.

(2C) Accordingly, where there is a repo agreement, the securities repurchased by the original owner shall be treated for the purposes of subsection (2) above (to the extent that that would not otherwise be the case) as if they were the same as, and were purchased by the original owner at the same time as, the securities sold by him to the interim holder.

(2D) For the purposes of subsections (2B) and (2C) above there is a repo agreement in relation to any securities if there is an agreement in pursuance of which a person ('the original owner') sells the securities to another ('the interim holder') and, in pursuance of that agreement or a related agreement, the original owner—

    (a) is required to buy back the securities;

    (b) will be required to buy them back on the exercise by the interim holder of an option conferred by the agreement or related agreement; or

    (c) is entitled, in pursuance of any obligation arising on a person's becoming entitled to receive an amount in respect of the redemption of those securities, to receive from the interim holder an amount equal to the amount of the entitlement.

(2E) Subsections (2B) and (2C) above do not apply if—

    (a) the agreement or agreements under which the arrangements are made for the sale and repurchase of the securities are not such as would be entered into by persons dealing with each other at arm's length; or

    (b) any of the benefits or risks arising from fluctuations, before the securities are repurchased, in the market value of the securities in question accrues to or falls on the interim holder.

(2F) Section 730B applies for the purposes of subsections (2B) to (2E) above as it applies for the purposes of section 730A."

(2) This section applies in relation to cases in which the interest becomes payable on or after the day on which this Act is passed.

GENERAL NOTE

This section prevents repos triggering the bond washing provisions in ICTA 1988, ss.731–735. The bond washing provisions impose a tax penalty on persons who buy dividends for tax reasons, by purchasing securities cum-dividend and then selling them ex-dividend shortly afterwards. They operate by reference to the timing of purchases and sales in relation to the date the securities concerned are first listed on an ex-div basis.

A repo is an arrangement under which securities are sold and later repurchased at a pre-arranged price but where the economic benefits and risks of holding the securities normally remain with the seller.

The purpose of the section is to ensure that tax issues do not hinder the development of a repo market in U.K. equities.

New s.731(2B–2F) excludes purchases and sales under repos from the bond washing provisions by ensuring that the person selling and repurchasing securities under the repo is treated as if the securities had not been repoed. The definition of repo is narrowly drawn, to prevent normal sales being disguised as repos.

National Savings Bank interest

78.—(1) In section 349(3) of the Taxes Act 1988 (cases where yearly interest may be paid without deduction of tax), after paragraph (b) there shall be inserted the following paragraph—

    "(ba) to interest paid on deposits with the National Savings Bank; or".

(2) This section applies to interest whenever paid (including interest paid before the day on which this Act is passed).

GENERAL NOTE

Doubts have recently been raised on the legal basis for the payment of interest by the National Savings Bank without deduction of tax. The section makes the position clear beyond doubt, retrospectively as well as for the future.

Payments under certain life insurance policies

79.—(1) In this section "relevant excepted benefit" means so much of any qualifying payment under a relevant life insurance policy as—

(a) is a sum falling, but for this section, to be treated for the purposes of the Tax Acts as an amount of interest or as an annual payment;

(b) is not a sum paid or falling to be paid by virtue of provisions of that policy which, taken alone, would constitute a different sort of policy; and

(c) does not represent interest for late payment on—

(i) any other part of that qualifying payment, or

(ii) the whole or any part of any other qualifying payment under the policy.

(2) For the purposes of subsection (1)(c) above, interest on the whole or any part of a qualifying payment under a policy ("the relevant amount") is interest for late payment if it is interest for a period beginning on or after the date of the occurrence of the event or contingency as a result of the occurrence of which the relevant amount falls to be paid.

(3) The Tax Acts shall have effect, and be deemed always to have had effect, as if—

(a) a relevant excepted benefit were neither an amount of interest nor an annual payment;

(b) the payments which are relevant capital payments for the purposes of section 541 of the Taxes Act 1988 (computation of gain in the case of life policies) included the payment of a relevant excepted benefit;

(c) on the payment of a relevant excepted benefit there were a surrender—

(i) except in a case falling within sub-paragraph (ii) below, of a part of the rights conferred by the policy in question; and

(ii) in a case where the payment of the benefit (or of that benefit together with any interest falling within subsection (1)(c) above) comprises the whole of the last payment to be made under the policy, of all of the remaining rights so conferred; and

(d) the value of the part or rights treated as surrendered on the payment of a relevant excepted benefit were equal to the amount of the payment.

(4) For the purposes of this section a qualifying payment under a relevant life insurance policy is any amount which has been or is to be paid under that policy by the insurer.

(5) In this section "relevant life insurance policy" means any contract of insurance (whenever effected) which—

(a) is of a description applying to contracts the effecting and carrying out of which falls within Class I or III of the classes of long term business specified in Schedule 1 to the Insurance Companies Act 1982; and

(b) is neither—

(i) an annuity contract, nor

(ii) a contract effected in the course of a company's pension business (within the meaning given by section 431B of the Taxes Act 1988 or the corresponding enactment in force when the contract was effected).

(6) In subsection (1)(b) above, the reference to a different sort of policy is a reference to any contract of a description applying to contracts the effecting and carrying out of which falls within any class of business specified in Schedule 1 or 2 to the Insurance Companies Act 1982 other than the Classes I and III specified in Schedule 1.

(7) This section shall be deemed to have had effect, for the purposes of the cases to which the enactments applied, in relation to enactments directly or indirectly re-enacted in the Tax Acts, as it has effect in relation to those Acts.

(8) For the purposes of subsection (7) above the reference in subsection (3)(b) above to section 541 of the Taxes Act 1988 shall be taken to include a reference to any corresponding provision contained in the enactments directly or indirectly re-enacted in the Tax Acts.

GENERAL NOTE

This section makes payments under certain life insurance policies taxable under the special rules for such policies, rather than as interest or annual payments. Many of the policies affected provide a series of regular payments and are commonly known as Guaranteed Income Bonds. The change removes uncertainty about the tax treatment of these payments and reflects the insurance industry's current practice. The change is retrospective, thus avoiding upsetting the expectations of those involved in these products.

Subs. (1)

This describes the payments affected by the section. These are payments from life insurance policies which, as a matter of law, are either interest or annual payments. There is an exception for interest added when benefits are paid late and for annual payments arising on the sickness of the insured.

Subs. (2)

The interest for late payment excluded from the operation of the section is described more fully. It is interest for any part of a period between the occurrence of an insured event, such as the death of the insured person, and the time when the payment of benefits is actually made.

Subs. (3)

This is the operative part of the section. It provides that the payments to which the section applies are not to be treated for any tax purposes as interest or annual payments. Instead they are treated as arising on a partial or full surrender of the life policy, as appropriate to the circumstances. The benefit is then taken into account in calculating any gain that may arise on the surrender under the special tax rules for life insurance policies. The provision is given full retrospective effect.

Subss. (4)–(6)

These provide definitions. In particular subs. (5) describes the life insurance policies affected by the section by reference to the regulatory classifications of insurance business and excludes annuity and pension contracts from the scope of the section, while subs. (6) links with the exclusion in subs. (1) of payments arising on the sickness of the insured. It also works by using the regulatory classification. Payments are excluded if, on the assumption that they were the only kind of benefit provided by the policy, it would not be a life policy. This mainly affects sickness benefits, because a free-standing policy that only provided such benefits would be classified as permanent health insurance rather than life insurance.

Subss. (7)–(8)

The retrospective effect of the section is extended to provisions in earlier legislation now consolidated in ICTA 1988 etc.

Futures and options: transactions with guaranteed returns

80.—(1) After section 127 of the Taxes Act 1988 there shall be inserted the following section—

> **"Futures and options: transactions with guaranteed returns**
>
> 127A. Schedule 5AA (which makes provision for the taxation of the profits and gains arising from transactions in futures and options that are designed to produce guaranteed returns) shall have effect."

(2) After Schedule 5 to that Act there shall be inserted, as Schedule 5AA to that Act, the Schedule set out in Schedule 11 to this Act.

(3) In section 128 of that Act (profits arising from commodity and financial futures etc. to be taxed only under the provisions relating to chargeable gains)—

(a) after the word "which", where it first occurs, there shall be inserted "is not chargeable to tax in accordance with Schedule 5AA and"; and

(b) for "that Schedule" there shall be substituted "Schedule D".

(4) In section 399 of that Act (withdrawal of loss relief for losses from dealing in futures etc.), after subsection (1) there shall be inserted the following subsection—

> "(1A) Subsection (1) above does not apply to a loss arising from a transaction to which Schedule 5AA applies."

(5) In section 469(9) of that Act (sections 686 and 687 disapplied in relation to unauthorised unit trusts), at the end there shall be inserted "except as respects income to which section 686 is treated as applying by virtue of paragraph 7 of Schedule 5AA."

(6) Subject to subsection (7) below, this section and Schedule 11 to this Act shall have effect, and be deemed to have had effect, for chargeable periods ending on or after 5th March 1997 in relation to profits and gains realised, and losses sustained, on or after that date.

(7) In relation to profits and gains realised, and losses sustained, on or after 5th March 1997, paragraph 1(6) and (7) of the Schedule 5AA to the Taxes Act 1988 (rule against double counting) inserted by this section shall be deemed to have had effect for chargeable periods beginning before that date (as well as for those beginning on or after that date).

GENERAL NOTE

This section, introduced at report stage along with Sched. 11, is designed to counteract the use of artificial transactions in derivatives for tax avoidance purposes. The schemes concerned are designed to turn what is effectively interest income into capital gains. The most popular variant is the "box spread" involving four linked options over, say, the FT-SE 100 index, constructed with mutually-cancelling exposures to the underlying index. The return to the investor is close to the ruling rate for a conventional term deposit, less a fee to the designer of the scheme.

Subs. (1)

This introduces ICTA 1988, s.127A, which itself introduces ibid. Sched. 5AA.

Subs. (2)

This introduces Sched. 11, which inserts Sched. 5AA into ICTA 1988. See further the General Note to Sched. 11.

Subss. (3)–(5)

Consequential amendments are made to ICTA 1988.

Subss. (6)–(7)

The changes apply generally from March 5, 1997, the date of a Government announcement, although a rule against double counting contained in Sched. 11, paras. 1(6) and (7) applied retrospectively.

[*Hansard*, H.C. Vol. 292, cols. 161–165.]

Transfer of assets abroad

Transfer of assets abroad

81.—(1) After section 739(1) of the Taxes Act 1988 (prevention of avoidance of income tax by means of transfer of assets with or without associated operations) there shall be inserted the following subsection—

"(1A) Nothing in subsection (1) above shall be taken to imply that the provisions of subsections (2) and (3) below apply only if—

(a) the individual in question was ordinarily resident in the United Kingdom at the time when the transfer was made; or

(b) the avoiding of liability to income tax is the purpose, or one of the purposes, for which the transfer was effected."

(2) This section applies irrespective of when the transfer or associated operations took place, but applies only to income arising on or after 26th November 1996.

GENERAL NOTE

The amendment to ICTA 1988, s.739 is of wide significance in relation to tax planning, particularly for individuals not domiciled in the U.K.

The first limb of new s.739(1A) reverses the decision in *IRC v. Willoughby* [1995] S.T.C. 1, currently under appeal to the House of Lords, in which the Court of Appeal held that the section did not apply to transfers of assets made by an individual when he is non-resident.

The second limb widens the ambit of the section to cover transfers of assets where the purpose of the transfer is to avoid capital gains tax or inheritance tax but has the effect of avoiding income tax as well.

The amendment applies irrespective of when the transfer took place, but only to income arising on or after November 26, 1996.

[Standing Committee B, February 18, 1997, cols. 426–428.]

Leasing and loan arrangements

Finance leases and loans

82. Schedule 12 to this Act (which makes provision about arrangements such as are treated for certain accounting purposes as finance leases or loans) shall have effect.

GENERAL NOTE

The section introduces Sched. 12, which seeks to prevent tax avoidance connected with finance leases. A finance lease is one where the economic benefits attached to the asset leased belong to the lessee rather than the lessor. The lease in economic and commercial substance is tantamount to a loan.

The first device attacked by the Schedule is one in which the lessor turns part of his return into a capital form by leasing the asset through a subsidiary company and then selling the company's shares rather than the asset itself.

The second is one in which lease rentals are concentrated towards the end of the rental period, so deferring the tax due.

The provisions are expected to save some £150m a year in tax.

[Standing Committee B, February 20, 1997, cols. 431–450.]

Loan relationships: transitions

83.—(1) Chapter II of Part IV of the Finance Act 1996 (loan relationships) shall be amended as follows.

(2) In subsection (5) of section 90 (changes in accounting methods), before the word "and" at the end of paragraph (a) there shall be inserted the following paragraph—

"(aa) the relationship is one to which the company in question is still a party at the end of the period or part of a period for which the accruals basis of accounting is used,".

(3) In that subsection for the words after paragraph (b) there shall be substituted—

"that amount shall be computed using for the closing value as at the end of that period or part of a period the amount specified in subsection (6) below."

(4) For subsection (6) of that section (amounts used for computations under subsection (5)) there shall be substituted the following subsection—

"(6) That amount is—

(a) in a case to which subsection (3) above applies, the amount taken for the purposes of subsection (3)(a)(ii) above to be the closing value as at the end of the period for which the accruals basis of accounting is used; and

(b) in a case to which subsection (2) above applies, the amount which, without the making of the assumptions mentioned in subsection (4) above, would be taken to be the closing value as at the end of the part of the period for which that basis is used."

(5) Subsections (2) to (4) above apply where the period or part of a period for which the superseded accounting method is or was used is a period ending on or after 14th November 1996.

(6) Schedule 13 to this Act (which contains amendments of the transitional provisions in Schedule 15 to the Finance Act 1996) shall have effect.

GENERAL NOTE

This section, together with Sched. 13, amends the legislation in F.A. 1996 relating to the taxation of corporate debt. The amendments ensure that the correct amount of profits and gains, including interest, is brought into account for corporation tax purposes. The section applies to cases where a company changes from one authorised method of accounting for its loan relationships to another. The Schedule amends various provisions relating to the transition to the loan relationship rules. The amendments apply where the relevant event occurs on or after November 14, 1996. Without the amendments, changes in the method of accounting for debt could have had the unintended effect of allowing amounts of interest to drop out of the charge to corporation tax altogether.

Subs. (2)

The provision relating to change from a market-to-market to an accruals basis applies only where the loan relationship has not ceased at the end of the first accounting period in which the accruals basis has been adopted.

Subss. (3) and (4)

The amendments adopt a simpler formula for calculating the amount to be brought into account on a change from a market-to-market to an accruals basis, ensure that the amount includes interest and expenses accruing from the date of the change to the end of the first accounting period in which the accruals basis has been adopted and make it clear how to find the closing value at the end of that period.

Subs. (6)

This introduces Sched. 13. See further the General Note to that Schedule.

[Standing Committee B, February 20, 1997, col. 454.]

Capital allowances

Writing-down allowances on long-life assets

84. Schedule 14 to this Act (which reduces the rate at which expenditure on long-life assets is written down for the purposes of writing-down allowances) shall have effect.

GENERAL NOTE

The section introduces Sched. 14, which implements a reduction in capital allowances for machinery and plant with a life of over 25 years from 25 per cent to 6 per cent on a reducing balance basis.

See further the General Note to Sched. 14.

Schedule A cases etc.

85. Schedule 15 to this Act (which makes provision in relation to capital allowances for cases where persons have income chargeable to tax under Schedule A or make lettings of furnished holiday accommodation in the United Kingdom) shall have effect.

GENERAL NOTE

The section introduces Sched. 15, which changes the rules for computing capital allowances on machinery and plant by bringing the rules for landlords, chargeable under Sched. A, into line with those for traders, chargeable under Sched. D, for both income tax and corporation tax purposes.

See further the General Note to Sched. 15.

Capital allowances on fixtures

86. Schedule 16 to this Act (which makes amendments relating to the provisions of the Capital Allowances Act 1990 about fixtures) shall have effect.

GENERAL NOTE

The section introduces Sched. 16, which makes various changes to the rules for giving capital allowances on fixtures. The main changes are:

(i) to limit the allowances that can be given overall to the original cost of the fixture;

(ii) to allow the purchaser and vendor to elect jointly to determine how much of the sale price of a building is apportioned to fixtures;

(iii) to prevent the acceleration of allowances on fixtures;

(iv) to debar allowances on fixtures leased to non-taxpayers if the lessor does not have an interest in the relevant land.

See further the General Note to Sched. 16.

Chargeable gains

Re-investment relief

87. Schedule 17 to this Act (which amends Chapter IA of Part V of the Taxation of Chargeable Gains Act 1992) shall have effect.

GENERAL NOTE

The section introduces Sched. 17, which makes two changes to the rules for capital gains tax reinvestment relief. The first will allow reinvestment relief for investment in groups of companies which have a member not resident in the U.K. However, relief will be given only where a company, or a group as a whole, carries on, or intends to carry on, its trade wholly or mainly in the U.K. New funds raised by a share issue will have to be applied to such a trade.

The second change will relax the way in which groups can structure their activities. At present, where a company has subsidiaries, no single subsidiary can carry on non-qualifying activities to any substantial extent. This company-by-company approach will be replaced by one which looks at the group as a whole.

See further the General Note to Sched. 17.

Conversion of securities: QCBs and debentures

88.—(1) The Taxation of Chargeable Gains Act 1992 shall be amended as follows.

(2) In paragraph (a) of subsection (3) of section 132 (meaning of conversion of securities)—

(a) after "includes" there shall be inserted "any of the following, whether effected by a transaction or occurring in consequence of the operation of the terms of any security or of any debenture which is not a security, that is to say";

(b) after sub-paragraph (i) there shall be inserted the following sub-paragraphs—

"(ia) a conversion of a security which is not a qualifying corporate bond into a security of the same company which is such a bond, and

(ib) a conversion of a qualifying corporate bond into a security which is a security of the same company but is not such a bond, and".

(3) After that subsection there shall be inserted the following subsections—

"(4) In subsection (3)(a)(ia) above the reference to the conversion of a security of a company into a qualifying corporate bond includes a reference to—

(a) any such conversion of a debenture of that company that is deemed to be a security for the purposes of section 251 as produces a security of that company which is a qualifying corporate bond; and

(b) any such conversion of a security of that company, or of a debenture that is deemed to be a security for those purposes, as produces a debenture of that company which, when deemed to be a security for those purposes, is such a bond.

(5) In subsection (3)(a)(ib) above the reference to the conversion of a qualifying corporate bond into a security of the same company which is not such a bond includes a reference to any conversion of a qualifying corporate bond which produces a debenture which—

(a) is not a security; and

(b) when deemed to be a security for the purposes of section 251, is not such a bond."

(4) In section 116(2) (qualifying corporate bonds), after the word "section", in the first place where it occurs, there shall be inserted "references to a transaction include references to any conversion of securities (whether or not effected by a transaction) within the meaning of section 132 and".

(5) In section 251(6) (deemed securities), after paragraph (d) there shall be inserted—

"and any debenture which results from a conversion of securities within the meaning of section 132, or is issued in pursuance of rights attached to such a debenture, shall be deemed for the purposes of this section to be a security (as defined in that section)."

(6) This section has effect for the purposes of the application of the Taxation of Chargeable Gains Act 1992 in relation to any disposal on or after 26th November 1996 and shall so have effect, where a conversion took place at a time before that date, as if it had come into force before that time.

GENERAL NOTE

The section counters attempts to avoid the charge on a capital gain where the terms of a security alter. A security may be outside the scope of capital gains tax if it satisfies the conditions to be a "qualifying corporate bond" ("QCB"). When a security changes from being a non-QCB into a QCB, the gain attaching to the non-QCB should remain chargeable when the QCBs are disposed of, even though QCBs themselves are exempt.

There was some doubt whether this result was achieved under the previous legislation. It had been suggested that where the terms of a security were altered, or its terms meant that it changed its status after it was issued, any capital gains on the security might not be chargeable when the security was disposed of. That gain might include a gain attributable to an earlier holding of shares which were exchanged for the securities. For example, if a security held by an individual has an option to convert into a non-sterling currency it will not be a QCB. If, however, the option lapses after a given time, the security may become a QCB. It was argued that in such cases, there would be no chargeable gain on the disposal of the security, nor would there be any disposal when the conversion right lapsed. To ensure that tax is not lost in these circumstances, the amendments to TCGA 1992 provide that the change of status of the security from a non-QCB to a QCB (and also a QCB into a non-QCB) is treated as a conversion of securities. This will ensure that the liability on any existing gain is preserved. Any capital gain resulting from the treatment of the change in status as a conversion of the security may still be deferred by the taxpayer, where existing rules allow for this, until the security is disposed of.

Subs. (2)

The amendments to s.132(3) ensure that a conversion of a non-QCB into a QCB, or a conversion of a QCB into a non-QCB, is included. The effect is to preserve the charge on a gain which is attributable to the non-QCB or QCB at the time of the conversion.

Subs. (3)

New s.132(4) and (5) ensure that the section includes as conversions that type of debt which is deemed to be a security because it was issued on a reorganisation of a company's capital or on a company take-over or a company reconstruction.

Subs. (4)

This amends s.116. That is the section on which s.132 relies to ensure that any capital gain up to the time of the conversion is preserved and brought into charge at the appropriate time. The amendment ensures that the extended definition of "conversion" is included in this provision.

Subs. (5)

This extends s.251(6) to ensure that any debt which results from a conversion of securities within s.132 is treated as a security, so that the extended conversion rules of s.132(4) and (5) inserted by subs. (3) above can apply to such debt.

Subs. (6)

The section applies to any disposal of a security on or after November 26, 1996, whenever the actual conversion from non-QCB to QCB status, or vice versa, took place.

Earn-out rights

89.—(1) After section 138 of the Taxation of Chargeable Gains Act 1992 there shall be inserted the following section—

"Use of earn-out rights for exchange of securities

138A.—(1) For the purposes of this section an earn-out right is so much of any right conferred on any person ('the seller') as—

(a) constitutes the whole or any part of the consideration for the transfer by him of shares in or debentures of a company ('the old securities');

(b) consists in a right to be issued with shares in or debentures of another company ('the new company');

(c) is such that the value or quantity of the shares or debentures to be issued in pursuance of the right ('the new securities') is unascertainable at the time when the right is conferred; and

(d) is not capable of being discharged in accordance with its terms otherwise than by the issue of the new securities.

(2) Where—

(a) there is an earn-out right,

(b) the exchange of the old securities for the earn-out right is an exchange to which section 135 would apply, in a manner unaffected by section 137, if the earn-out right were an ascertainable amount of shares in or debentures of the new company, and

(c) the seller elects under this section for the earn-out right to be treated as a security of the new company,

this Act shall have effect, in the case of the seller and every other person who from time to time has the earn-out right, in accordance with the assumptions specified in subsection (3) below.

(3) Those assumptions are—

(a) that the earn-out right is a security within the definition in section 132;

(b) that the security consisting in the earn-out right is a security of the new company and is incapable of being a qualifying corporate bond for the purposes of this Act;

(c) that references in this Act (including those in this section) to a debenture include references to a right that is assumed to be a security in accordance with paragraph (a) above; and

(d) that the issue of shares or debentures in pursuance of such a right constitutes the conversion of the right, in so far as it is discharged by the issue, into the shares or debentures that are issued.

(4) For the purposes of this section where—

(a) any right which is assumed, in accordance with this section, to be a security of a company ('the old right') is extinguished,

(b) the whole of the consideration for the extinguishment of the old right consists in another right ('the new right') to be issued with shares in or debentures of that company,

(c) the new right is such that the value or quantity of the shares or debentures to be issued in pursuance of the right ('the replacement securities') is unascertainable at the time when the old right is extinguished,

(d) the new right is not capable of being discharged in accordance with its terms otherwise than by the issue of the replacement securities, and

(e) the person on whom the new right is conferred elects under this section for it to be treated as a security of that company,

the assumptions specified in subsection (3) above shall have effect in relation to the new right, in the case of that person and every other person who from time to time has the new right, as they had effect in relation to the old right.

(5) An election under this section in respect of any right must be made, by a notice given to an officer of the Board—

    (a) in the case of an election by a company within the charge to corporation tax, within the period of two years from the end of the accounting period in which the right is conferred; and

    (b) in any other case, on or before the first anniversary of the 31st January next following the year of assessment in which that right is conferred.

(6) An election under this section shall be irrevocable.

(7) Subject to subsections (8) to (10) below, where any right to be issued with shares in or debentures of a company is conferred on any person, the value or quantity of the shares or debentures to be issued in pursuance of that right shall be taken for the purposes of this section to be unascertainable at a particular time if, and only if—

    (a) it is made referable to matters relating to any business or assets of one or more relevant companies; and

    (b) those matters are uncertain at that time on account of future business or future assets being included in the business or assets to which they relate.

(8) Where a right to be issued with shares or debentures is conferred wholly or partly in consideration for the transfer of other shares or debentures or the extinguishment of any right, the value and quantity of the shares or debentures to be issued shall not be taken for the purposes of this section to be unascertainable in any case where, if—

    (a) the transfer or extinguishment were a disposal, and

    (b) a gain on that disposal fell to be computed in accordance with this Act,

the shares or debentures to be issued would, in pursuance of section 48, be themselves regarded as, or as included in, the consideration for the disposal.

(9) Where any right to be issued with shares in or debentures of a company comprises an option to choose between shares in that company and debentures of that company, the existence of that option shall not, by itself, be taken for the purposes of this section either—

    (a) to make unascertainable the value or quantity of the shares or debentures to be issued; or

    (b) to prevent the requirements of subsection (1)(b) and (d) or (4)(b) and (d) above from being satisfied in relation to that right.

(10) For the purposes of this section the value or quantity of shares or debentures shall not be taken to be unascertainable by reason only that it has not been fixed if it will be fixed by reference to the other and the other is ascertainable.

(11) In subsection (7) above 'relevant company', in relation to any right to be issued with shares in or debentures of a company, means—

    (a) that company or any company which is in the same group of companies as that company; or

    (b) the company for whose shares or debentures that right was or was part of the consideration, or any company in the same group of companies as that company;

and in this subsection the reference to a group of companies shall be construed in accordance with section 170(2) to (14)."

(2) Subject to subsections (3) to (8) below—

(a) the section 138A inserted by subsection (1) above shall be deemed always to have been a section of the Taxation of Chargeable Gains Act 1992; and

(b) the enactments applying to chargeable periods beginning before 6th April 1992 shall be deemed always to have included a corresponding section.

(3) Subject to subsections (4) to (6) below, an election under section 138A of the Taxation of Chargeable Gains Act 1992 in respect of a right conferred on any person before 26th November 1996 may be made at any time before the end of the period for the making of such an election in respect of a right conferred on that person on that date.

(4) An election in respect of a right conferred on any person shall not be made by virtue of subsection (3) above at any time after the final determination of his liability to corporation tax or capital gains tax for the chargeable period in which the right was in fact conferred on him.

(5) A notice given to an officer of the Board before the day on which this Act is passed shall not have effect as an election under section 138A of the Taxation of Chargeable Gains Act 1992, or the corresponding provision applying to chargeable periods beginning before 6th April 1992, except in accordance with subsection (6) below.

(6) Where—

(a) any person has given a notification to an officer of the Board before the day on which this Act is passed, and

(b) that notification was given either—

    (i) in anticipation of the right to make an election under section 138A of the Taxation of Chargeable Gains Act 1992, or

    (ii) for the purposes of an extra-statutory concession available to be used by that person for purposes similar to those of that section,

that notification shall, unless the Board otherwise direct, be treated as if it were a valid and irrevocable election made by that person for the purposes of that section or, as the case may be, the corresponding provision.

(7) Where any notification given as mentioned in subsection (6)(b)(ii) above is treated as an election for the purposes of section 138A of the Taxation of Chargeable Gains Act 1992 or any corresponding provision, that section or, as the case may be, the corresponding provision shall be taken to have no effect by virtue of that election in relation to any disposal before 26th November 1996 of any asset which—

(a) was issued to any person in pursuance of an earn-out right;

(b) was issued to any person in pursuance of any such right as is mentioned in subsection (4) of that section; or

(c) falls for the purposes of that Act to be treated as the same as an asset issued at any time to any person in pursuance of such a right as is mentioned in paragraph (a) or (b) above but is not an asset first held by that person before that time.

(8) Subsection (7) above shall not prevent section 138A of the Taxation of Chargeable Gains Act 1992 from being taken, for the purposes of applying that Act to any disposal on or after 26th November 1996, to have had effect in relation to—

(a) any disposal before that date on which, by virtue of any of the enactments specified in section 35(3)(d) of that Act, neither a gain nor a loss accrued,

(b) any deemed disposal before that date by reference to which a gain or loss falls to be calculated in accordance with section 116(10)(a) of that Act, or

(c) any transaction before that date that would have fallen to be treated as a disposal but for section 127 of that Act.

GENERAL NOTE

The section puts on a legislative basis an existing extra-statutory concession (ESC D27) for the sale of shares in a company where part of the consideration is deferred and unascertainable. In certain circumstances, ESC D27, and now the section, allow the right to that consideration (commonly known as an "earn-out right") to be treated as a security for the purposes of the capital gains legislation. This allows the application of the rules on company take-overs and conversions of securities, which provide for deferral of the capital gain on the shares.

The earn-out right has been held by the courts to be an asset for CGT purposes (see *Marren v. Ingles* (1979) 54 T.C. 76). Treating the earn-out right as a security allows existing legislation on company take-overs and conversions of securities to have effect.

The earn-out right has to be satisfied by the issue of shares or debentures. Where debentures are issued and they are securities for CGT purposes, these securities may be outside the scope of CGT as a qualifying corporate bond (QCB) or within the scope of CGT as a non-QCB (see further the General Note to s.88 above). It had been contended that where the securities issued were QCBs the operation of the concession failed to preserve the gain in respect of the shares disposed of so that that gain could not be charged on the disposal of the QCBs. The Revenue did not accept this view, but since a resolution of the issue could take some time, it was decided to place the matter beyond doubt by the terms of this section.

Subs. (1)

New TCGA 1992, s.138A defines an earn-out right and provides that where the seller so elects and the share exchange provisions for company take-overs in s.135 would apply if the earn-out right was shares or debentures of the new company the earn-out right is treated as a security of the new company and as a non-QCB. The consequence is that the gain on the sale of shares of the old company can be deferred under the take-over rules. Where an earn-out right is extinguished and replaced by a new right to be issued with shares or debentures of the same company, then provided the new earn-out right would have qualified to be treated as a security had it been conferred in the first place, the holder can elect that it should be so treated.

An election, which is irrevocable, must be made by a company within two years after the end of the accounting period in which the right was conferred and for an individual within 22 months after the end of the year of assessment in which the right was conferred.

The value or quantity of shares to be issued in satisfaction of an earn-out right is treated as unascertainable where it is referable to the future business or assets of the acquired company where, in principle, it cannot be ascertained at the date of disposal.

The existing rules for deferred *ascertainable* consideration in s.48 are to be applied in priority to the rules in s.138A. A right to choose between shares in the new company or debentures of that company does not of itself make the consideration unascertainable but does not rule out an election being made in respect of that right. Deferred consideration is not unascertainable if, for example, the consideration is fixed in amount but, because it is to be satisfied by an issue of shares at their market value at the time of issue, the number of shares cannot be known until that point.

Subss. (2)–(8)

These set out the commencement provisions. New s.138A is to be treated as always having been part of TCGA and its predecessor legislation. An election may be made in respect of an earn-out right conferred before November 26, 1996, but with the time limit that would have applied if the right had been conferred on that date. Such an election cannot be made in cases where the tax liability of the seller has been finally agreed and determined.

A notification given in anticipation of a right to elect is to be treated as a valid election under the new section. A claim under ESC D27 is to be treated as an election under s.138A, but the effect of that section applies only where there is a disposal on or after November 26, 1996.

Where, prior to November 26, 1996 there are particular kinds of transfers of the securities of the new company, *e.g.* transfers which are treated as taking place on a no gain/no loss basis, followed by a disposal of the securities on or after that date, the effect of s.138A applies to the eventual disposal.

Double taxation relief

Restrictions of relief for underlying tax

90.—(1) After section 801 of the Taxes Act 1988 there shall be inserted the following section—

"Restriction of relief for underlying tax

801A.—(1) This section applies where—
(a) a company resident in the United Kingdom ('the United Kingdom company') makes a claim for an allowance by way of credit in accordance with this Part;

(b) the claim relates to underlying tax on a dividend paid to that company by a company resident outside the United Kingdom ('the overseas company');

(c) that underlying tax is or includes an amount in respect of tax ('the high rate tax') payable by—

    (i) the overseas company, or

    (ii) such a third, fourth or successive company as is mentioned in section 801;

at a rate in excess of the relievable rate; and

(d) the whole or any part of the amount in respect of the high rate tax which is or is included in the underlying tax would not be, or be included in, that underlying tax but for the existence of, or for there having been, an avoidance scheme.

(2) Where this section applies, the amount of the credit to which the United Kingdom company is entitled on the claim shall be determined as if the high rate tax had been tax at the relievable rate, instead of at a rate in excess of that rate.

(3) For the purposes of this section tax shall be taken to be payable at a rate in excess of the relievable rate if, and to the extent that, the amount of that tax exceeds the amount that would represent tax on the relevant profits at the relievable rate.

(4) In subsection (3) above 'the relevant profits', in relation to any tax, means the profits of the overseas company or, as the case may be, of the third, fourth or successive company which, for the purposes of this Part, are taken to bear that tax.

(5) In this section 'the relievable rate' means the rate of corporation tax in force when the dividend mentioned in subsection (1)(b) above was paid.

(6) In this section 'an avoidance scheme' means any scheme or arrangement which—

(a) falls within subsection (7) below; and

(b) is a scheme or arrangement the purpose, or one of the main purposes, of which is to have an amount of underlying tax taken into account on a claim for an allowance by way of credit in accordance with this Part.

(7) A scheme or arrangement falls within this subsection if the parties to it include both—

(a) the United Kingdom company, a company related to that company or a person connected with the United Kingdom company; and

(b) a person who was not under the control of the United Kingdom company at any time before the doing of anything as part of, or in pursuance of, the scheme or arrangement.

(8) In this section 'arrangement' means an arrangement of any kind, whether in writing or not.

(9) Section 839 (meaning of 'connected persons') applies for the purposes of this section.

(10) Subsection (5) of section 801 (meaning of 'related company') shall apply for the purposes of this section as it applies for the purposes of that section.

(11) For the purposes of this section a person who is a party to a scheme or arrangement shall be taken to have been under the control of the United Kingdom company at all the following times, namely—

(a) any time when that company would have been taken (in accordance with section 416) to have had control of that person for the purposes of Part XI;

(b) any time when that company would have been so taken if that section applied (with the necessary modifications) in the case of partnerships and unincorporated associations as it applies in the case of companies; and

(c) any time when that person acted in relation to that scheme or arrangement, or any proposal for it, either directly or indirectly under the direction of that company."

(2) This section has effect in relation to dividends paid to a company resident in the United Kingdom at any time on or after 26th November 1996.

GENERAL NOTE

The section introduces a limitation on the relief for foreign tax which a U.K. company may claim against U.K. tax when it receives a dividend from an overseas company in which it has a substantial interest. If a U.K. company receives such a dividend it can claim relief for the underlying tax, *i.e.* the tax which the overseas company has paid on the profits out of which it pays the dividend. The section provides that the foreign tax that is taken into account as underlying tax is to be restricted where, as a consequence of an avoidance scheme, a U.K. company has acquired highly taxed foreign income from a previously unconnected person.

New ICTA 1988, s.801A applies where a U.K. company claims credit for underlying tax in respect of a dividend from an overseas company; the underlying tax includes "high rate tax", payable in excess of the "relievable rate"; and the whole or part of the high rate tax would not have been included in the claim but for an avoidance scheme.

Tax is payable "at a rate in excess of the relievable rate" where the amount of tax payable exceeds the tax which would have been paid on the profits in question at the rate of corporation tax in force when the U.K. company received the dividend from the overseas company.

A scheme or arrangement is an avoidance scheme only where the parties to it include both a U.K. company, related companies or connected persons and a person who was not under the control of the U.K. company before anything was done as part of, or in pursuance of, the scheme.

[Standing Committee B, February 20, 1997, cols. 458–460.]

Disposals of loan relationships with or without interest

91.—(1) Section 807A of the Taxes Act 1988 (disposals and acquisitions of company loan relationships with or without interest) shall be amended as follows.

(2) At the beginning of subsection (2) there shall be inserted "Subject to subsection (2A) below,".

(3) After that subsection there shall be inserted the following subsection—

"(2A) Tax attributable to interest accruing to a company under a loan relationship does not fall within subsection (2) above if—

(a) at the time when the interest accrues, that company has ceased to be a party to that relationship by reason of having made the initial transfer under or in accordance with any repo or stock-lending arrangements relating to that relationship; and

(b) that time falls during the period for which those arrangements have effect."

(4) In subsection (3)(b), after "related transaction" there shall be inserted "other than the initial transfer under or in accordance with any repo or stock-lending arrangements relating to that relationship".

(5) After subsection (6) there shall be inserted the following subsection—

"(6A) In this section 'repo or stock-lending arrangements' has the same meaning as in paragraph 15 of Schedule 9 to the Finance Act 1996 (repo transactions and stock-lending); and, in relation to any such arrangements—

(a) a reference to the initial transfer is a reference to the transfer mentioned in sub-paragraph (3)(a) of that paragraph; and

(b) a reference to the period for which the arrangements have effect is a reference to the period from the making of the initial transfer until whichever is the earlier of the following—

(i) the discharge of the obligations arising by virtue of the entitlement or requirement mentioned in subparagraph (3)(b) of that paragraph; and

(ii) the time when it becomes apparent that the discharge mentioned in sub-paragraph (i) above will not take place."

(6) Subsections (2) and (3) above have effect in relation to interest accruing on or after 1st April 1996.

(7) Subsection (4) above has effect in relation to transactions made on or after 26th November 1996.

GENERAL NOTE

The section amends ICTA 1988, s.807A, inserted by F.A. 1996 (c. 8), Sched. 14, para. 46, which deals with relief against corporation tax for foreign tax paid on interest from overseas securities. It applies where the securities have been the subject of a transfer by way of repo or stock-lending arrangements.

Subs. (3)

New s.807(2A) effective from April 1, 1996, ensures that the transferring company which will continue to accrue interest on the security in its accounts, can claim relief for foreign tax paid on the interest during the period of the transfer.

Subs. (4)

The additional words inserted into s.807A(3)(b) deny companies the right to the automatic relief granted by the subsection where the "related transaction" mentioned there is the initial transfer of an overseas security under repo or stock-lending arrangements. Proof that tax has been paid on the interest will be required. The amendment is effective from November 26, 1996.

Subs. (5)

New s.807A(6A) provides that the terms "repo or stock-lending arrangements" and "initial transfer" have the same meaning as in F.A. 1996, Sched. 9, para. 15. It also defines the time period to which subs. (3) applies.

[Standing Committee B, February 20, 1997, cols. 460–461.]

Repayment supplement

Time from which entitlement runs

92.—(1) Section 824 of the Taxes Act 1988 (repayment supplements), where it has effect as amended by paragraph 41 of Schedule 19 to the Finance Act 1994, shall be amended in accordance with subsections (2) to (4) below.

(2) For paragraphs (a) and (b) of subsection (3) there shall be substituted the following paragraphs—

"(a) if the repayment is—

(i) the repayment of an amount paid in accordance with the requirements of section 59A of the Management Act on account of income tax for a year of assessment, or

(ii) the repayment of income tax for such a year which is not income tax deducted at source,

the relevant time is the date of the payment that is being repaid;

(b) if the repayment is of income tax deducted at source for a year of assessment, the relevant time is the 31st January next following that year; and".

(3) In paragraph (c) of that subsection, for the words from "the relevant time" to the end of that paragraph there shall be substituted "the relevant time is the date on which the penalty or surcharge was paid".

(4) For subsection (4) there shall be substituted the following subsections—

"(4) For the purposes of subsection (3) above, where a repayment in respect of income tax for a year of assessment is made to any person, that repayment—

(a) shall be attributed first to so much of any payment made by him under section 59B of the Management Act as is a payment in respect of income tax for that year;

(b) in so far as it exceeds the amount (if any) to which it is attributable under paragraph (a) above, shall be attributed in two equal parts to each of the payments made by him under section 59A of the Management Act on account of income tax for that year;

(c) in so far as it exceeds the amounts (if any) to which it is attributable under paragraphs (a) and (b) above, shall be attributed to income tax deducted at source for that year; and

(d) in so far as it is attributable to a payment made in instalments shall be attributed to a later instalment before being attributed to an earlier one.

(4A) In this section any reference to income tax deducted at source for a year of assessment is a reference to—

(a) income tax deducted or treated as deducted from any income, or treated as paid on any income, in respect of that year, and

(b) amounts which, in respect of that year, are tax credits to which section 231 applies,

but does not include a reference to amounts which, in that year, are deducted at source under section 203 in respect of previous years."

(5) In subsection (2) of section 283 of the Taxation of Chargeable Gains Act 1992 (repayment supplements), for the words from "the relevant time" to the end of that subsection there shall be substituted "the relevant time is the date on which the tax was paid".

(6) This section has effect as respects the year 1997–98 and subsequent years of assessment and shall be deemed to have had effect as respects the year 1996–97.

GENERAL NOTE

The original provisions regarding interest (repayment supplement) on amounts repaid to taxpayers under the self-assessment system were that this would run from the later of the statutory due date for payment or the date the payment was made. It will now run from the latter date only. The change will take effect from the start of the new system for self-assessment, the tax year 1996–97. Repayments of tax deducted at source, for example under PAYE, will not be affected. Interest on these will still run from January 31 after the end of the tax year. The provisions also apply to repayment of a penalty or surcharge.

For calculating interest, repayments of income tax will be attributed first to payments of tax under Taxes Management Act 1970 (c.9), s.59B (the balancing payment), next, equally to the two payments on account under s.59A and finally to tax deducted at source. Where payment has been made by instalments, the repayment is attributed to a later payment before being attributed to an earlier one.

The same provision applies for repayments of capital gains tax.

PART VI

INHERITANCE TAX

Rate bands

93.—(1) For the Table in Schedule 1 to the Inheritance Tax Act 1984 there shall be substituted—

TABLE OF RATES OF TAX

Portion of value		Rate of tax
Lower limit (£)	Upper limit (£)	Per cent
0	215,000	Nil
215,000	—	40

(2) Subsection (1) above shall apply to any chargeable transfer made on or after 6th April 1997; and section 8 of that Act (indexation of rate bands) shall not have effect as respects any difference between the retail prices index for the month of September 1995 and that for the month of September 1996.

Agricultural property relief

94. After section 124B of the Inheritance Tax Act 1984 there shall be inserted the following section—

"Land in habitat schemes

124C.—(1) For the purposes of this Chapter, where any land is in a habitat scheme—

(a) the land shall be regarded as agricultural land;

(b) the management of the land in accordance with the requirements of the scheme shall be regarded as agriculture; and

(c) buildings used in connection with such management shall be regarded as farm buildings.

(2) For the purposes of this section land is in a habitat scheme at any time if—

(a) an application for aid under one of the enactments listed in subsection (3) below has been accepted in respect of the land; and

(b) the undertakings to which the acceptance relates have neither been terminated by the expiry of the period to which they relate nor been treated as terminated.

(3) Those enactments are—

(a) regulation 3(1) of the Habitat (Water Fringe) Regulations 1994;

(b) the Habitat (Former Set-Aside Land) Regulations 1994;

(c) the Habitat (Salt-Marsh) Regulations 1994;

(d) the Habitats (Scotland) Regulations 1994, if undertakings in respect of the land have been given under regulation 3(2)(a) of those Regulations;

(e) the Habitat Improvement Regulations (Northern Ireland) 1995, if an undertaking in respect of the land has been given under regulation 3(1)(a) of those Regulations.

(4) The Treasury may by order made by statutory instrument amend the list of enactments in subsection (3) above.

(5) The power to make an order under subsection (4) above shall be exercisable by statutory instrument subject to annulment in pursuance of a resolution of the House of Commons.

(6) This section has effect—

(a) in relation to any transfer of value made on or after 26th November 1996; and

(b) in relation to transfers of value made before that date, for the purposes of any charge to tax, or to extra tax, which arises by reason of an event occurring on or after 26th November 1996."

PART VII

STAMP DUTY AND STAMP DUTY RESERVE TAX

Stamp duty

Mergers of authorised unit trusts

95.—(1) Stamp duty shall not be chargeable on an instrument transferring any property which is subject to the trusts of an authorised unit trust ("the target trust") to the trustees of another authorised unit trust ("the acquiring trust") if the conditions set out in subsection (2) below are fulfilled.

(2) Those conditions are that—

(a) the transfer forms part of an arrangement under which the whole of the available property of the target trust is transferred to the trustees of the acquiring trust;

(b) under the arrangement all the units in the target trust are extinguished;

(c) the consideration under the arrangement consists of or includes the issue of units ("the consideration units") in the acquiring trust to the persons who held the extinguished units;

(d) the consideration units are issued to those persons in proportion to their holdings of the extinguished units; and

(e) the consideration under the arrangement does not include anything else, other than the assumption or discharge by the trustees of the acquiring trust of liabilities of the trustees of the target trust.

(3) An instrument on which stamp duty is not chargeable by virtue only of this section shall not be taken to be duly stamped unless it is stamped with the duty to which it would be liable but for this section or it has, in accordance with section 12 of the Stamp Act 1891, been stamped with a particular stamp denoting that it is not chargeable with any duty.

(4) In this section—

"authorised unit trust" means a unit trust scheme in the case of which an order under section 78 of the Financial Services Act 1986 is in force;

"the whole of the available property of the target trust" means the whole of the property subject to the trusts of the target trust, other than any property which is retained for the purpose of discharging liabilities of the trustees of the target trust;

"unit" and "unit trust scheme" have the same meanings as in Part VII of the Finance Act 1946.

(5) Each of the parts of an umbrella scheme (and not the scheme as a whole) shall be regarded for the purposes of this section as an authorised unit trust; and in this section "umbrella scheme" has the same meaning as in section 468 of the Taxes Act 1988 and references to parts of an umbrella scheme shall be construed in accordance with that section.

(6) This section applies to any instrument which is executed—

(a) on or after the day on which this Act is passed; but

(b) before 1st July 1999.

GENERAL NOTE

The section exempts from stamp duty mergers between authorised unit trusts ("AUTs") from the date of Royal Assent (March 19, 1997) to June 30, 1999. The reason for introducing this exemption is to provide an opportunity for rationalisation of the unit trust industry, alongside the introduction of open-ended investment companies ("OEICs"). A similar exemption from stamp duty reserve tax is provided by ss.100–101 below.

The conditions for relief are:

(i) the whole of the property of the first AUT is transferred to the second AUT;

(ii) all the units in the first AUT are cancelled;

(iii) the unitholders in the first AUT receive units in the second AUT in proportion to their holding in the first;

(iv) no other financial consideration is involved, other than the liabilities of the first AUT being transferred to the second AUT.

The relevant documents must be stamped to indicate that stamp duty is not due.

Each part of an umbrella scheme (see ICTA 1988, s.468) is treated as a separate scheme. An umbrella unit trust scheme is one which consists of two or more sub-funds, which normally have different investment strategies.

The stamp duty treatment of conversions and mergers of AUTs into OEICs will be covered in regulations under F.A. 1995, s.152.

Demutualisation of insurance companies

96.—(1) This section applies where there is a relevant transfer, under a scheme, of the whole or any part of the business carried on by a mutual insurance company ("the mutual") to a company which has share capital ("the acquiring company").

(2) Stamp duty shall not be chargeable on an instrument executed for the purposes of or in connection with the transfer if the requirements of subsections (3) and (4) below are satisfied in relation to the shares of a company ("the issuing company") which is either—

(a) the acquiring company; or

(b) a company of which the acquiring company is a wholly-owned subsidiary.

(3) Shares in the issuing company must be offered, under the scheme, to at least 90 per cent of the persons who immediately before the transfer are members of the mutual.

(4) Under the scheme, all the shares in the issuing company which will be in issue immediately after the transfer has been made, other than shares which are to be or have been issued pursuant to an offer to the public, must be offered to the persons who (at the time of the offer) are—

(a) members of the mutual;

(b) persons who are entitled to become members of the mutual; or

(c) employees, former employees or pensioners of the mutual or of a company which is a wholly-owned subsidiary of the mutual.

(5) An instrument on which stamp duty is not chargeable by virtue only of subsection (2) above shall not be taken to be duly stamped unless it is stamped with the duty to which it would be liable but for that subsection or it has, in accordance with section 12 of the Stamp Act 1891, been stamped with a particular stamp denoting that it is not chargeable with any duty.

(6) For the purposes of this section, a company is a wholly-owned subsidiary of another person ("the parent") if it has no members except the parent and the parent's wholly-owned subsidiaries or persons acting on behalf of the parent or its wholly-owned subsidiaries.

(7) In this section "relevant transfer" means—

(a) a transfer to which Schedule 2C to the Insurance Companies Act 1982 (transfers of insurance business) applies; or

(b) a transfer to which that Schedule would apply but for section 15(1A) of that Act (provisions of Part II of that Act which do not apply to EC companies in certain circumstances).

(8) In this section—

"employee", in relation to a mutual insurance company or its wholly-owned subsidiary, includes any officer or director of the company or subsidiary and any other person taking part in the management of the affairs of the company or subsidiary;

"insurance company" has the meaning given in section 96 of the Insurance Companies Act 1982;

"mutual insurance company" means an insurance company carrying on business without having any share capital;

"pensioner", in relation to a mutual insurance company or its wholly-owned subsidiary, means a person entitled (whether presently or prospectively) to a pension, lump sum, gratuity or other like benefit referable to the service of any person as an employee of the company or subsidiary.

(9) The Treasury may by regulations amend subsection (3) above by substituting a lower percentage for the percentage there mentioned.

(10) The Treasury may by regulations provide that any or all of the references in subsections (3) and (4) above to members shall be construed as references to members of a class specified in the regulations; and different provision may be made for different cases.

(11) The power to make regulations under this section shall be exercisable by statutory instrument subject to annulment in pursuance of a resolution of the House of Commons.

(12) This section applies in relation to instruments executed on or after the day on which this Act is passed.

GENERAL NOTE

The section provides a stamp duty exemption for a transfer of business by a mutual insurance company to a company with share capital under a demutualisation scheme if certain conditions are satisfied.

The two main conditions are that at least 90 per cent of the members of the mutual must be offered shares in the new company and that any shares in the new company that are not offered to members are issued either to employees or pensioners of the mutual or are issued as the result of an offer to the public.

[Standing Committee B, February 20, 1997, cols. 461–462.]

Relief for intermediaries

97.—(1) Before section 81 of the Finance Act 1986 there shall be inserted the following sections—

"Sales to intermediaries

80A.—(1) Stamp duty shall not be chargeable on an instrument transferring stock of a particular kind on sale to a person or his nominee if—
(a) the person is a member of an EEA exchange, or a recognised foreign exchange, on which stock of that kind is regularly traded;
(b) the person is an intermediary and is recognised as an intermediary by the exchange in accordance with arrangements approved by the Commissioners; and
(c) the sale is effected on the exchange.

(2) Stamp duty shall not be chargeable on an instrument transferring stock of a particular kind on sale to a person or his nominee if—
(a) the person is a member of an EEA exchange or a recognised foreign options exchange;
(b) options to buy or sell stock of that kind are regularly traded on that exchange and are listed by or quoted on that exchange;
(c) the person is an options intermediary and is recognised as an options intermediary by that exchange in accordance with arrangements approved by the Commissioners; and
(d) the sale is effected on an EEA exchange, or a recognised foreign exchange, on which stock of that kind is regularly traded or subsection (3) below applies.

(3) This subsection applies if—
(a) the sale is effected on an EEA exchange, or a recognised foreign options exchange, pursuant to the exercise of a relevant option; and
(b) options to buy or sell stock of the kind concerned are regularly traded on that exchange and are listed by or quoted on that exchange.

(4) For the purposes of this section—

(a) an intermediary is a person who carries on a bona fide business of dealing in stock and does not carry on an excluded business; and

(b) an options intermediary is a person who carries on a bona fide business of dealing in quoted or listed options to buy or sell stock and does not carry on an excluded business.

(5) The excluded businesses are the following—

(a) any business which consists wholly or mainly in the making or managing of investments;

(b) any business which consists wholly or mainly in, or is carried on wholly or mainly for the purpose of, providing services to persons who are connected with the person carrying on the business;

(c) any business which consists in insurance business;

(d) any business which consists in managing or acting as trustee in relation to a pension scheme or which is carried on by the manager or trustee of such a scheme in connection with or for the purposes of the scheme;

(e) any business which consists in operating or acting as trustee in relation to a collective investment scheme or is carried on by the operator or trustee of such a scheme in connection with or for the purposes of the scheme.

(6) A sale is effected on an exchange for the purposes of subsection (1) or (2) above if (and only if)—

(a) it is subject to the rules of the exchange; and

(b) it is reported to the exchange in accordance with the rules of the exchange.

(7) An instrument on which stamp duty is not chargeable by virtue only of this section shall not be deemed to be duly stamped unless it has been stamped with a stamp denoting that it is not chargeable with any duty; and notwithstanding anything in section 122(1) of the Stamp Act 1891, the stamp may be a stamp of such kind as the Commissioners may prescribe.

Intermediaries: supplementary

80B.—(1) For the purposes of section 80A above the question whether a person is connected with another shall be determined in accordance with the provisions of section 839 of the Income and Corporation Taxes Act 1988.

(2) In section 80A above and this section—

"collective investment scheme" has the meaning given in section 75 of the Financial Services Act 1986;

"EEA exchange" means a market which appears on the list drawn up by an EEA State pursuant to Article 16 of European Communities Council Directive No. 93/22/EEC on investment services in the securities field;

"EEA State" means a State which is a contracting party to the agreement on the European Economic Area signed at Oporto on the 2nd May 1992 as adjusted by the Protocol signed at Brussels on the 17th March 1993;

"insurance business" means long term business or general business as defined in section 1 of the Insurance Companies Act 1982;

"quoted or listed options" means options which are quoted on or listed by an EEA exchange or a recognised foreign options exchange;

"stock" includes any marketable security;

"trustee" and "the operator" shall, in relation to a collective investment scheme, be construed in accordance with section 75(8) of the Financial Services Act 1986.

(3) In section 80A above "recognised foreign exchange" means a market which—

(a) is not in an EEA State; and

(b) is specified in regulations made by the Treasury under this subsection.

(4) In section 80A above and this section "recognised foreign options exchange" means a market which—

(a) is not in an EEA State; and

(b) is specified in regulations made by the Treasury under this subsection.

(5) In section 80A above "the exercise of a relevant option" means—

(a) the exercise by the options intermediary concerned of an option to buy stock; or

(b) the exercise of an option binding the options intermediary concerned to buy stock.

(6) The Treasury may by regulations provide that section 80A above shall not have effect in relation to instruments executed in pursuance of kinds of agreement specified in the regulations.

(7) The Treasury may by regulations provide that if—

(a) an instrument falls within subsection (1) or (2) of section 80A above, and

(b) stamp duty would be chargeable on the instrument apart from that section,

stamp duty shall be chargeable on the instrument at a rate, specified in the regulations, which shall not exceed 10p for every £100 or part of £100 of the consideration for the sale.

(8) The Treasury may by regulations change the meaning of "intermediary" or "options intermediary" for the purposes of section 80A above by amending subsection (4) or (5) of that section (as it has effect for the time being).

(9) The power to make regulations under subsections (3) to (8) above shall be exercisable by statutory instrument subject to annulment in pursuance of a resolution of the House of Commons."

(2) Section 81 of that Act (sales to market makers) shall be omitted.

(3) In section 88(1B)(b)(i) of that Act (which prevents repayment or cancellation of stamp duty reserve tax on certain agreements to transfer chargeable securities which were acquired by means of a transfer on which stamp duty was not chargeable by virtue of section 81) for "81" there shall be substituted "80A".

(4) Subsections (1) and (2) above apply to instruments executed on or after the commencement day.

(5) Subsection (3) above applies in relation to an agreement to transfer chargeable securities if the securities were acquired in a transaction which was given effect to by an instrument of transfer executed on or after the commencement day.

(6) For the purposes of this section the commencement day is such day as the Treasury may by order made by statutory instrument appoint.

GENERAL NOTE

The section provides a stamp duty relief for transactions in shares or options by intermediaries on a regulated market in the U.K. or elsewhere in the European Economic Area ("EEA") or a recognised foreign exchange on which shares of the relevant kind are regularly traded. The relief replaces the existing relief for sales to market makers under F.A. 1986, s.81. It is expected to be brought into force in September 1997 after adaptations have been made to the Crest system of paperless share transfers.

New s.80A provides the exemption, defines "intermediary" and lists five classes of business which are excluded from relief.

New s.80B provides definitions and confers power on the Treasury by regulation to exclude from relief instruments relating to specified kinds of agreement and to charge at a rate not to exceed 10p per £100 or part thereof instruments otherwise exempted under s.80A. This is a reserve power to prevent abuse of the relief.

Repurchases and stock lending

98.—(1) After section 80B of the Finance Act 1986 there shall be inserted the following section—

"**Repurchases and stock lending**

80C.—(1) This section applies where a person (A) has entered into an arrangement with another person (B) under which—

(a) B is to transfer stock of a particular kind to A or his nominee, and

(b) stock of the same kind and amount is to be transferred by A or his nominee to B or his nominee,

and the conditions set out in subsection (3) below are fulfilled.

(2) Stamp duty shall not be chargeable on an instrument transferring stock to B or his nominee or A or his nominee in accordance with the arrangement.

(3) The conditions are—

(a) that the arrangement is effected on an EEA exchange or a recognised foreign exchange; and

(b) that stock of the kind concerned is regularly traded on that exchange.

(4) An arrangement does not fall within subsection (1) above if—

(a) the arrangement is not such as would be entered into by persons dealing with each other at arm's length; or

(b) under the arrangement any of the benefits or risks arising from fluctuations, before the transfer to B or his nominee takes place, in the market value of the stock accrues to, or falls on, A.

(5) An instrument on which stamp duty is not chargeable by virtue only of subsection (2) above shall not be deemed to be duly stamped unless it has been stamped with a stamp denoting that it is not chargeable with any duty; and notwithstanding anything in section 122(1) of the Stamp Act 1891, the stamp may be a stamp of such kind as the Commissioners may prescribe.

(6) An arrangement is effected on an exchange for the purposes of subsection (3) above if (and only if)—

(a) it is subject to the rules of the exchange; and

(b) it is reported to the exchange in accordance with the rules of the exchange.

(7) In this section—

"EEA exchange" has the meaning given in section 80B(2) above; and

"recognised foreign exchange" has the meaning given in section 80B(3) above.

(8) The Treasury may by regulations provide that if stamp duty would be chargeable on an instrument but for subsection (2) above, stamp duty shall be chargeable on the instrument at a rate, specified in the regulations, which shall not exceed 10p for every £100 or part of £100 of the consideration for the transfer.

(9) The Treasury may by regulations amend this section (as it has effect for the time being) in order—

(a) to change the conditions for exemption from duty under this section; or

(b) to provide that this section does not apply in relation to kinds of arrangement specified in the regulations.

(10) The power to make regulations under subsection (8) or (9) above shall be exercisable by statutory instrument subject to annulment in pursuance of a resolution of the House of Commons."

(2) Section 82 of that Act (borrowing of stock by market makers) shall be omitted.

(3) This section applies to instruments executed on or after the commencement day.

(4) For the purposes of this section the commencement day is such day as the Treasury may by order made by statutory instrument appoint.

GENERAL NOTE

New F.A. 1986, s.80C, which replaces s.82 provides a stamp duty relief on stock borrowing and sale and repurchase (repo) arrangements effected on EEA or recognised foreign exchanges. It follows the lines of the relief conferred by s.97 above. The arrangement must be on an arm's length basis and the economic benefits and risks of holding the securities must remain with the seller.

[Standing Committee B, February 25, 1997, col. 465.]

Depositary receipts and clearing services

99.—(1) Subsection (4) of section 67 of the Finance Act 1986 (depositary receipts: reduced rate of stamp duty for qualified dealers other than market makers) shall be omitted.

(2) Accordingly—
(a) in subsection (3) of that section for "subsections (4) and" there shall be substituted "subsection"; and
(b) subsections (6) to (8) of section 69 of that Act (definition of "qualified dealer" and "market maker" for the purposes of section 67(4) and power to amend definition) shall be omitted.

(3) Subsection (4) of section 70 of that Act (clearance services: reduced rate of stamp duty for qualified dealers other than market makers) shall be omitted.

(4) Accordingly—
(a) in subsection (3) of that section for "subsections (4) and" there shall be substituted "subsection"; and
(b) section 72(4) of that Act (definition of "qualified dealer" and "market maker" for the purposes of section 70(4)) shall be omitted.

(5) This section applies to any instrument executed on or after the day which is the commencement day for the purposes of section 97 above, except an instrument which transfers relevant securities which were acquired by the transferor before that date.

GENERAL NOTE

The section removes provisions setting a one per cent rate of duty in certain cases where dealers who are not market makers transfer shares into depositary receipt schemes or clearance services. The introduction of the new relief for intermediaries under s.97 above will in practice make these provisions unnecessary.

Stamp duty reserve tax

Mergers of authorised unit trusts

100.—(1) Section 87 of the Finance Act 1986 shall not apply as regards an agreement to transfer securities which constitute property which is subject to the trusts of an authorised unit trust ("the target trust") to the trustees of another authorised unit trust ("the acquiring trust") if the conditions set out in subsection (2) below are fulfilled.

(2) Those conditions are that—
(a) the agreement forms part of an arrangement under which the whole of the available property of the target trust is transferred to the trustees of the acquiring trust;

(b) under the arrangement all the units in the target trust are extinguished;

(c) the consideration under the arrangement consists of or includes the issue of units ("the consideration units") in the acquiring trust to the persons who held the extinguished units;

(d) the consideration units are issued to those persons in proportion to their holdings of the extinguished units; and

(e) the consideration under the arrangement does not include anything else, other than the assumption or discharge by the trustees of the acquiring trust of liabilities of the trustees of the target trust.

(3) Where—

(a) stamp duty is not chargeable on an instrument by virtue of section 95(1) above, or

(b) section 87 of the Finance Act 1986 does not apply as regards an agreement by virtue of subsection (1) above,

section 87 of the Finance Act 1986 shall not apply as regards an agreement, or a deemed agreement, to transfer a unit to the managers of the target trust which is made in order that the unit may be extinguished under the arrangement mentioned in section 95(2)(a) or, as the case may be, subsection (2)(a) above.

(4) In this section—

"authorised unit trust" means a unit trust scheme in the case of which an order under section 78 of the Financial Services Act 1986 is in force;

"the whole of the available property of the target trust" means the whole of the property subject to the trusts of the target trust, other than any property which is retained for the purpose of discharging liabilities of the trustees of the target trust;

"unit" and "unit trust scheme" have the same meanings as in Part VII of the Finance Act 1946.

(5) Each of the parts of an umbrella scheme (and not the scheme as a whole) shall be regarded for the purposes of this section as an authorised unit trust; and in this section "umbrella scheme" has the same meaning as in section 468 of the Taxes Act 1988 and references to parts of an umbrella scheme shall be construed in accordance with that section.

(6) This section applies—

(a) to an agreement which is not conditional, if the agreement is made on or after the day on which this Act is passed but before 1st July 1999; and

(b) to a conditional agreement, if the condition is satisfied on or after the day on which this Act is passed but before 1st July 1999.

GENERAL NOTE

    The section temporarily exempts from stamp duty reserve tax ("SDRT") mergers between authorised unit trusts. It has the same purpose as and contains parallel provisions to s.95 above, which deals with stamp duty. See further the General Note to s.95.

Direction to hold trust property on other trusts

    101.—(1) Where an agreement to transfer securities constituting property subject to the trusts of an authorised unit trust ("the absorbed trust") is made by means of a direction by the holders of units in the absorbed trust ("the sellers") to the trustees of another trust ("the continuing trust") to hold the whole of the available property of the absorbed trust on the trusts of the continuing trust, section 87 of the Finance Act 1986 shall not apply as regards the agreement if the conditions set out in subsection (2) below are fulfilled.

    (2) Those conditions are that—

(a) the trustees of the absorbed trust are the same persons as the trustees of the continuing trust;

(b) the agreement forms part of an arrangement under which all the units in the absorbed trust are extinguished;

(c) the consideration for the direction by the sellers consists of or includes the issue of units ("the consideration units") in the continuing trust to the sellers;

(d) the consideration units are issued to the sellers in proportion to their holdings of the extinguished units; and

(e) the consideration for the direction by the sellers does not include anything else, other than the assumption or discharge by the trustees of the continuing trust of liabilities of the trustees of the absorbed trust.

(3) Where section 87 of the Finance Act 1986 does not apply as regards an agreement by virtue of subsection (1) above, that section shall not apply as regards an agreement, or a deemed agreement, to transfer a unit to the managers of the absorbed trust which is made in order that the unit may be extinguished under the arrangement mentioned in subsection (2)(b) above.

(4) In this section—

"authorised unit trust" and "unit" have the same meanings as in section 100 above (and section 100(5) applies for the purposes of this section as it applies for the purposes of section 100);

"the whole of the available property of the absorbed trust" means the whole of the property subject to the trusts of the absorbed trust, other than any property which is retained for the purpose of discharging liabilities of the trustees of the absorbed trust.

(5) This section applies—

(a) to an agreement which is not conditional, if the agreement is made on or after the day on which this Act is passed but before 1st July 1999; and

(b) to a conditional agreement, if the condition is satisfied on or after the day on which this Act is passed but before 1st July 1999.

GENERAL NOTE

This follows the previous section in giving an SDRT exemption for mergers between authorised unit trusts. It applies where the same trustees act for both trusts.

Relief for intermediaries

102.—(1) After section 88 of the Finance Act 1986 there shall be inserted the following sections—

"Section 87: exceptions for intermediaries

88A.—(1) Section 87 above shall not apply as regards an agreement to transfer securities of a particular kind to B or his nominee if—

(a) B is a member of an EEA exchange, or a recognised foreign exchange, on which securities of that kind are regularly traded;

(b) B is an intermediary and is recognised as an intermediary by the exchange in accordance with arrangements approved by the Board; and

(c) the agreement is effected on the exchange.

(2) Section 87 above shall not apply as regards an agreement to transfer securities of a particular kind to B or his nominee if—

(a) B is a member of an EEA exchange or a recognised foreign options exchange;

(b) options to buy or sell securities of that kind are regularly traded on that exchange and are listed by or quoted on that exchange;

(c) B is an options intermediary and is recognised as an options intermediary by that exchange in accordance with arrangements approved by the Board; and

(d) the agreement is effected on an EEA exchange, or a recognised foreign exchange, on which securities of that kind are regularly traded or subsection (3) below applies.

(3) This subsection applies if—

(a) the agreement is effected on an EEA exchange, or a recognised foreign options exchange, pursuant to the exercise of a relevant option; and

(b) options to buy or sell securities of the kind concerned are regularly traded on that exchange and are listed by or quoted on that exchange.

(4) For the purposes of this section—

(a) an intermediary is a person who carries on a bona fide business of dealing in chargeable securities and does not carry on an excluded business; and

(b) an options intermediary is a person who carries on a bona fide business of dealing in quoted or listed options to buy or sell chargeable securities and does not carry on an excluded business.

(5) The excluded businesses are the following—

(a) any business which consists wholly or mainly in the making or managing of investments;

(b) any business which consists wholly or mainly in, or is carried on wholly or mainly for the purpose of, providing services to persons who are connected with the person carrying on the business;

(c) any business which consists in insurance business;

(d) any business which consists in managing or acting as trustee in relation to a pension scheme or which is carried on by the manager or trustee of such a scheme in connection with or for the purposes of the scheme;

(e) any business which consists in operating or acting as trustee in relation to a collective investment scheme or is carried on by the operator or trustee of such a scheme in connection with or for the purposes of the scheme.

(6) An agreement is effected on an exchange for the purposes of subsection (1) or (2) above if (and only if)—

(a) it is subject to the rules of the exchange; and

(b) it is reported to the exchange in accordance with the rules of the exchange.

Intermediaries: supplementary

88B.—(1) For the purposes of section 88A above the question whether a person is connected with another shall be determined in accordance with the provisions of section 839 of the Income and Corporation Taxes Act 1988.

(2) In section 88A above and this section—

"collective investment scheme" has the meaning given in section 75 of the Financial Services Act 1986;

"EEA exchange" means a market which appears on the list drawn up by an EEA State pursuant to Article 16 of European Communities Council Directive No. 93/22/EEC on investment services in the securities field;

"EEA State" means a State which is a contracting party to the agreement on the European Economic Area signed at Oporto on the 2nd May 1992 as adjusted by the Protocol signed at Brussels on the 17th March 1993;

"insurance business" means long term business or general business as defined in section 1 of the Insurance Companies Act 1982;

"quoted or listed options" means options which are quoted on or listed by an EEA exchange or a recognised foreign options exchange;

"recognised foreign exchange" and "recognised foreign options exchange" have the meanings given, respectively, by subsections (3) and (4) of section 80B above;

"trustee" and "the operator" shall, in relation to a collective investment scheme, be construed in accordance with section 75(8) of the Financial Services Act 1986.

(3) In section 88A above "the exercise of a relevant option" means—

(a) the exercise by B of an option to buy securities; or

(b) the exercise of an option binding B to buy securities.

(4) The Treasury may by regulations provide that section 88A above shall not have effect in relation to kinds of agreement specified in the regulations.

(5) The Treasury may by regulations provide that if—

(a) an agreement falls within subsection (1) or (2) of section 88A above, and

(b) section 87 above would, apart from section 88A, apply to the agreement,

section 87 shall apply to the agreement but with the substitution of a rate of tax not exceeding 0.1 per cent for the rate specified in subsection (6) of that section.

(6) The Treasury may by regulations change the meaning of "intermediary" or "options intermediary" for the purposes of section 88A above by amending subsection (4) or (5) of that section (as it has effect for the time being).

(7) The power to make regulations under subsections (4) to (6) above shall be exercisable by statutory instrument subject to annulment in pursuance of a resolution of the House of Commons."

(2) Section 89 of that Act (exceptions for market makers etc.) shall be omitted.

(3) In section 88(1B)(b)(ii) of that Act (which prevents repayment or cancellation of stamp duty reserve tax on certain agreements to transfer property consisting of chargeable securities which were acquired in pursuance of an agreement on which tax was not chargeable by virtue of section 89) for "89" there shall be substituted "88A".

(4) Subsections (1) and (2) above apply to an agreement to transfer securities—

(a) in the case of an agreement which is not conditional, if the agreement is made on or after the commencement day; and

(b) in the case of a conditional agreement, if the condition is satisfied on or after the commencement day.

(5) Subsection (3) above applies in relation to property consisting of chargeable securities if the securities were acquired in pursuance of an agreement to which subsections (1) and (2) above apply (by virtue of subsection (4) above).

(6) For the purposes of this section the commencement day is such day as the Treasury may by order made by statutory instrument appoint.

GENERAL NOTE

The section provides for SDRT an exemption similar to that for stamp duty under s.97. See further the General Note to s.97.

New F.A. 1986, ss.88A and 88B replace the existing s.89.

Repurchases and stock lending

103.—(1) After section 89A of the Finance Act 1986 there shall be inserted the following section—

> **"Section 87: exception for repurchases and stock lending**
> 89AA.—(1) This section applies where a person (P) has entered into an arrangement with another person (Q) under which—
>> (a) Q is to transfer chargeable securities of a particular kind to P or his nominee, and
>> (b) chargeable securities of the same kind and amount are to be transferred by P or his nominee to Q or his nominee,
>
> and the conditions set out in subsection (3) below are fulfilled.
>
> (2) Section 87 above shall not apply as regards an agreement to transfer chargeable securities to P or his nominee or Q or his nominee in accordance with the arrangement.
>
> (3) The conditions are—
>> (a) that the agreement is effected on an EEA exchange or a recognised foreign exchange;
>> (b) that securities of the kind concerned are regularly traded on that exchange; and
>> (c) that chargeable securities are transferred to P or his nominee and Q or his nominee in pursuance of the arrangement.
>
> (4) An arrangement does not fall within subsection (1) above if—
>> (a) the arrangement is not such as would be entered into by persons dealing with each other at arm's length; or
>> (b) under the arrangement any of the benefits or risks arising from fluctuations, before the transfer to Q or his nominee takes place, in the market value of the chargeable securities accrues to, or falls on, P.
>
> (5) An agreement is effected on an exchange for the purposes of subsection (3) above if (and only if)—
>> (a) it is subject to the rules of the exchange; and
>> (b) it is reported to the exchange in accordance with the rules of the exchange.
>
> (6) In this section—
>> "EEA exchange" has the meaning given in section 88B(2) above;
>> "recognised foreign exchange" has the meaning given in section 80B(3) above.
>
> (7) The Treasury may by regulations provide that if section 87 would apply as regards an agreement but for subsection (2) above, section 87 shall apply as regards the agreement but with the substitution of a rate of tax not exceeding 0.1 per cent for the rate specified in subsection (6) of that section.
>
> (8) The Treasury may by regulations amend this section (as it has effect for the time being) in order—
>> (a) to change the conditions for exemption from tax under this section; or
>> (b) to provide that this section does not apply in relation to kinds of arrangement specified in the regulations.
>
> (9) The power to make regulations under subsection (7) or (8) above shall be exercisable by statutory instrument subject to annulment in pursuance of a resolution of the House of Commons."

(2) Section 89B of that Act (exceptions for stock lending and collateral security arrangements) shall be omitted.

(3) In consequence of subsections (1) and (2) above, for section 88(1)(1B)(b)(iia) of that Act (which is inserted by section 106(5)(c) below and which prevents repayment or cancellation of stamp duty reserve tax on

certain agreements to transfer property consisting of chargeable securities which were acquired in pursuance of an agreement on which tax was not chargeable by virtue of section 89B(1)(a)) there shall be substituted—

"(iia) in pursuance of an agreement to transfer securities which was made for the purpose of performing the obligation to transfer chargeable securities described in section 89AA(1)(a) below and as regards which section 87 above did not apply by virtue of section 89AA(2) below; or".

(4) After section 88(1B) of that Act there shall be inserted the following subsections—

"(1C) Where—

(a) there is an arrangement falling within subsection (1) of section 80C above (stamp duty relief for transfers in accordance with certain arrangements for B to transfer stock to A or his nominee and for A or his nominee to transfer stock of the same kind and amount back to B or his nominee), and

(b) under the arrangement stock is transferred to A or his nominee by an instrument on which stamp duty is not chargeable by virtue only of section 80C(2) above, but

(c) it becomes apparent that stock of the same kind or amount will not be transferred to B or his nominee by A or his nominee in accordance with the arrangement,

the instrument shall be disregarded in construing section 92(1A) and (1B) below.

(1D) Where—

(a) an instrument transferring stock in accordance with an arrangement is stamped under section 80C(5) above, but

(b) the instrument should not have been so stamped because the arrangement fell within section 80C(4)(a) or (b) above, and

(c) apart from section 80C above stamp duty would have been chargeable on the instrument,

the instrument shall be deemed to be duly stamped under section 80C(5) above, but shall be disregarded in construing section 92(1A) and (1B) below."

(5) Subsections (1) and (2) above apply to an agreement to transfer securities—

(a) in the case of an agreement which is not conditional, if the agreement is made on or after the commencement day; and

(b) in the case of a conditional agreement, if the condition is satisfied on or after the commencement day.

(6) Subsection (3) above applies in relation to property consisting of chargeable securities if the securities were acquired in pursuance of an agreement to which subsections (1) and (2) above apply (by virtue of subsection (5) above).

(7) Subsection (4) above applies to instruments executed on or after the commencement day.

(8) For the purposes of this section the commencement day is such day as the Treasury may by order made by statutory instrument appoint.

General Note

The section provides a relief from SDRT for stock borrowing and sale and repurchase arrangements (repos) parallel to the stamp duty relief under s.98 above. See further the General Notes to ss.97 and 98.

New F.A. 1986, s.89AA replaces s.89B.

Subs. (4)

New F.A. 1986, s.88(1C) and (1D) impose a charge to SDRT where stamp duty relief has been given but the stock borrowing or repurchase arrangement is not fully carried out, for example because the borrowed stock is not in fact returned to the lender, and also where an instrument has been stamped as not chargeable to duty and it subsequently becomes apparent that the conditions for stamp duty relief were not satisfied, for example because the arrangement was not on arm's length terms.

Depositary receipts and clearance services

104.—(1) Subsection (5) of section 93 of the Finance Act 1986 (depositary receipts: reduced rate of tax for qualified dealers other than market makers) shall be omitted.

(2) Accordingly—

(a) in subsection (4) of that section for "(5) to" there shall be substituted "(6) and";

(b) in subsection (7)(a) of that section for "subsections (4) to" there shall be substituted "subsections (4) and";

(c) subsections (5) to (7) of section 94 of that Act (definition of "qualified dealer" and "market maker" for the purposes of section 93(5) and power to substitute different definition) shall be omitted.

(3) Subsection (3) of section 96 of the Finance Act 1986 (clearance services: reduced rate of tax for qualified dealers other than market makers) shall be omitted.

(4) Accordingly—

(a) in subsection (2) of that section, for "(3) to" there shall be substituted "(4) and";

(b) in subsection (5)(a) of that section for "subsections (2) to" there shall be substituted "subsections (2) and";

(c) subsection (11) of that section (definition of "qualified dealer" and "market maker" for the purposes of that section) shall be omitted.

(5) This section applies where securities are transferred on or after the day which is the commencement day for the purposes of section 102 above, unless the securities were acquired by the transferor before that day.

<small>GENERAL NOTE</small>

The amendments to the SDRT provisions for depositary receipts and clearance services are parallel to the stamp duty amendments made by s.99. See further the General Note to that section.

Inland bearer instruments

105.—(1) Paragraph (b) of section 90(3) of the Finance Act 1986 (which provides that section 87 shall not apply as regards an agreement to transfer securities constituted by or transferable by means of an inland bearer instrument which does not fall within exemption 3 in the heading "Bearer Instrument" in Schedule 1 to the Stamp Act 1891) shall cease to have effect.

(2) After section 90(3) of that Act there shall be inserted—

"(3A) Section 87 above shall not apply as regards an agreement to transfer chargeable securities constituted by or transferable by means of an inland bearer instrument within the meaning of the heading "Bearer Instrument" in Schedule 1 to the Stamp Act 1891 unless subsection (3B), (3C) or (3E) below applies to the instrument.

(3B) This subsection applies to any instrument which falls within exemption 3 in the heading "Bearer Instrument" in Schedule 1 to the Stamp Act 1891 (renounceable letter of allotment etc. where rights are renounceable not later than six months after issue).

(3C) This subsection applies to an instrument if—

(a) the instrument was issued by a body corporate incorporated in the United Kingdom;

(b) stamp duty under the heading "Bearer Instrument" in Schedule 1 to the Stamp Act 1891 was not chargeable on the issue of the instrument by virtue only of—

(i) section 30 of the Finance Act 1967 (exemption for bearer instruments relating to stock in foreign currencies); or

(ii) section 7 of the Finance Act (Northern Ireland) 1967 (which makes similar provision for Northern Ireland); and

(c) the instrument is not exempt.

(3D) An instrument is exempt for the purposes of subsection (3C) above if—

(a) the chargeable securities in question are, or a depositary receipt for them is, listed on a recognised stock exchange; and

(b) the agreement to transfer those securities is not made in contemplation of, or as part of an arrangement for, a takeover of the body corporate which issued the instrument.

(3E) This subsection applies to an instrument if—

(a) the instrument was issued by a body corporate incorporated in the United Kingdom;

(b) stamp duty under the heading "Bearer Instrument" in Schedule 1 to the Stamp Act 1891 was not chargeable on the issue of the instrument—

(i) by virtue only of subsection (2) of section 79 above (exemption for bearer instruments relating to loan capital); or

(ii) by virtue only of that subsection and one or other of the provisions mentioned in subsection (3C)(b)(i) and (ii) above;

(c) by virtue of section 79(5) (convertible loan capital) or 79(6) (loan capital carrying special rights) above, stamp duty would be chargeable on an instrument transferring the loan capital to which the instrument relates; and

(d) the instrument is not exempt.

(3F) An instrument is exempt for the purposes of subsection (3E) above if—

(a) the chargeable securities in question are, or a depositary receipt for them is, listed on a recognised stock exchange;

(b) the agreement to transfer those securities is not made in contemplation of, or as part of an arrangement for, a takeover of the body corporate which issued the instrument; and

(c) those securities do not carry any right of the kind described in section 79(5) above (right of conversion into, or acquisition of, shares or other securities) by the exercise of which securities which are not listed on a recognised stock exchange may be obtained."

(3) At the end of that section there shall be added—

"(8) For the purposes of subsections (3D) and (3F) above—

(a) references to a depositary receipt for chargeable securities shall be construed in accordance with section 94(1) below;

(b) "recognised stock exchange" has same meaning as it has in the Tax Acts by virtue of section 841 of the Income and Corporation Taxes Act 1988;

(c) there is a takeover of a body corporate if a person, on his own or together with connected persons, loses or acquires control of it.

(9) For the purposes of subsection (8) above—

(a) any question whether a person is connected with another shall be determined in accordance with section 286 of the Taxation of Chargeable Gains Act 1992;

(b) "control" shall be construed in accordance with section 416 of the Income and Corporation Taxes Act 1988."

(4) This section applies to an agreement if the inland bearer instrument in question was issued on or after 26th November 1996 and—

(a) in the case of an agreement which is not conditional, the agreement is made on or after 26th November 1996; or

(b) in the case of a conditional agreement, the condition is satisfied on or after 26th November 1996.

GENERAL NOTE

The section is designed to prevent tax avoidance through the issue of bearer securities expressed in a foreign currency. Previously such securities were exempt from stamp duty under F.A. 1967, s.30. Avoidance schemes were developed whereby the target company on a takeover created new shares expressed in a foreign currency and issued them in bearer form. All or most of the value of the company was then transferred to these new shares, which the purchaser then acquired free of stamp duty.

The section as enacted replaced the original proposals in the Finance Bill, which were thought to be drawn too wide. It imposes a stamp duty reserve tax (SDRT) charge at 0.5 per cent on agreements to transfer the relevant kinds of bearer security, while continuing exemption for ordinary capital market transactions.

Subs. (1)

This removes the existing exemption from SDRT.

Subs. (2)

New s.90(3A) imposes a charge to SDRT unless any of the conditions set out below are satisfied.

New s.90(3B) takes out of the SDRT charge renounceable letters of allotment where the rights are renounceable not later than six months after issue.

New ss.90(3C) and (3D) take out of charge securities of a listed company where the agreement to transfer them is not part of a takeover deal.

New ss.90(3E) and (3F) take out of charge loan stock of a similar character. The loan stock must not carry rights of conversion into an unlisted security.

Subs. (3)

This contains consequential amendments and definitions.

Subs. (4)

Like the original proposals, the revised provisions apply from Budget day.
[Standing Committee B, February 25, 1997, cols. 466–470.]

Repayment or cancellation of tax

106.—(1) Section 87 of the Finance Act 1986 (the principal charge) shall be amended in accordance with subsections (2) and (3) below.

(2) For subsection (7A) (deemed separate agreements where there would be no charge to tax etc had there been such agreements) there shall be substituted—

"(7A) Where—
    (a) there would be no charge to tax under this section, or
    (b) there would, under section 92 below, be a repayment or cancellation of tax,

in relation to some of the chargeable securities to which the agreement between A and B relates if separate agreements had been made between them for the transfer of those securities and for the transfer of the remainder, this section and sections 88(5) and 92 below shall have effect as if such separate agreements had been made."

(3) Subsection (7B) (which, in consequence of the repeals made by section 188(1) of the Finance Act 1996, is of no further utility in relation to the charge to tax but whose effect is reproduced by subsection (8) below for the purposes of repayment or cancellation of tax) shall cease to have effect.

(4) Section 88 of the Finance Act 1986 (special cases) shall be amended in accordance with subsections (5) to (7) below.

(5) In subsection (1B) (certain instruments on which stamp duty is not chargeable to be disregarded in construing the conditions in section 92(1A) and (1B) for repayment or cancellation of tax)—

(a) in paragraph (a) (the property transferred by the instrument consists of chargeable securities) after "consists of" there shall be inserted "or includes";

(b) in paragraph (b) (which relates to the acquisition of the chargeable securities so transferred) for "the chargeable securities" there shall be substituted "any of those chargeable securities; and

(c) the word "or" at the end of sub-paragraph (ii) of that paragraph shall be omitted and after that sub-paragraph there shall be inserted—

"(iia) in pursuance of an agreement to transfer securities which was made for the purpose of performing the obligation to transfer chargeable securities described in paragraph (a) of subsection (1) of section 89B below and as regards which section 87 above did not apply by virtue of that subsection; or".

(6) For subsections (4) and (5) (identification of the securities in question and reduction of the charge in certain cases) there shall be substituted—

"(4) If chargeable securities cannot (apart from this subsection) be identified for the purposes of subsection (1B) above, securities shall be taken as follows, that is to say, securities of the same kind acquired later in the period of two years there mentioned (and not taken for the purposes of that subsection in relation to an earlier instrument) shall be taken before securities acquired earlier in that period.

(5) If, in the case of an agreement (or of two or more agreements between the same parties) to transfer chargeable securities—

(a) the conditions in section 92(1A) and (1B) below are not satisfied by virtue only of the application of subsection (1B) above in relation to the instrument (or any one or more of the two or more instruments) in question, but

(b) not all of the chargeable securities falling to be regarded for the purposes of that subsection as transferred by the instrument (or by the two or more instruments between them) were acquired as mentioned in paragraphs (a) and (b) of that subsection,

stamp duty reserve tax shall be repaid or cancelled under section 92 below in accordance with subsection (5A) below.

(5A) Any repayment or cancellation of tax falling to be made by virtue of subsection (5) above shall be determined as if (without prejudice to section 87(7A) above) there had, instead of the agreement (or the two or more agreements) in question been—

(a) a separate agreement (or two or more separate agreements) relating to such of the securities as were acquired as mentioned in paragraphs (a) and (b) of subsection (1B) above, and

(b) a single separate agreement relating to such of the securities as do not fall within those paragraphs,

and as if the instrument in question (or the two or more instruments in question between them) had related only to such of the securities as do not fall within those paragraphs."

(7) For the sidenote, there shall be substituted "Special cases."

(8) In section 92 of the Finance Act 1986 (repayment or cancellation of tax), after subsection (6) there shall be inserted—

"(7) This section shall have effect in relation to a person to whom the chargeable securities are transferred by way of security for a loan to B as it has effect in relation to a nominee of B."

(9) The amendments made by subsections (2), (3) and (8) above have effect in relation to an agreement to transfer securities if—

(a) the agreement is conditional and the condition is satisfied on or after 4th January 1997; or

(b) the agreement is not conditional and is made on or after that date.

(10) The amendments made by subsections (5) and (6) above have effect where the instrument on which stamp duty is not chargeable by virtue of

section 42 of the Finance Act 1930 or section 11 of the Finance Act (Northern Ireland) 1954 is executed on or after 4th January 1997 in pursuance of an agreement to transfer securities made on or after that date.

GENERAL NOTE
  The section makes a number of consequential amendments to the stamp duty reserve tax ("SDRT") provisions in F.A. 1996, which were designed to cater for the introduction of electronic share transfers. It also tightens up an anti-avoidance provision concerned with the case where, for example, a market maker buys shares with the benefit of the exemption for market makers and then transfers them to another company in its own group. The changes take effect from January 4, 1997.
  The amendments made by subss. (2), (3) and (8) complete the reorganisation of provisions made by F.A. 1996, s.192. That reorganisation was a consequence of the removal by s.188 of the two month period before a charge to SDRT arises on an agreement to transfer securities.
  Subsections (4)–(7) refine the provisions introduced by F.A. 1996, s.190 concerning transfers between associated bodies.

PART VIII

MISCELLANEOUS AND SUPPLEMENTAL

Miscellaneous

Petroleum revenue tax: non-field expenditure

  107.—(1) Section 113 of the Finance Act 1984 (restrictions on relief by reference to a qualifying date) shall be amended as follows.
  (2) In subsection (4) (meaning of "qualifying date"), after "means" there shall be inserted "(subject to subsection (6) below)".
  (3) In subsection (6) (old participator's qualifying date to be taken into account, in the case of a transfer, in determining as respects certain expenditure the date that is to be regarded as the new participator's qualifying date), for the words from "is an applicable date" onwards there shall be substituted ", rather than the date given by subsection (4) above, shall be taken to be the qualifying date in relation to the new participator."
  (4) This section has effect in relation to any expenditure in respect of which a claim is made on or after 23rd July 1996.

GENERAL NOTE
  The amendments to F.A. 1984, s.113 are designed to put it beyond doubt that oil companies cannot claim petroleum revenue tax ("PRT") relief on non-field expenditure (mainly expenditure on exploration for and appraisal of oil and gas reservoirs) originally incurred by an unrelated group of companies which continues to hold licence interests in the North Sea.
  It is provided that in such cases the qualifying date for claiming such expenditure will be that of the claimant, not that of the seller.
  The amendments, which take effect from July 23, 1996, the date of a Revenue announcement, could save £850m in PRT.
  [Standing Committee B, February 25, 1997, cols. 472–473.]

Payment of dividends on government stock

  108.—(1) For section 2 of the National Debt (Stockholders Relief) Act 1892 (date for striking balance for a dividend on government stock) there shall be substituted the following section—

"Effect of, and time for, striking balance

  2.—(1) Any person who, at the time of the balance being struck for a dividend on stock, is inscribed as a stockholder shall, as between himself and any transferee of the stock, be entitled to the then current half-year's or quarter's dividend.
  (2) Subject to subsections (3) and (4) below, the Bank may—
  (a) strike the balance for a dividend on stock before the day on which the dividend is payable, and

(b) strike the balances for dividends on stock at times such that the interval between—
> (i) the time at which the balance for a dividend is struck, and
> (ii) the day on which the dividend is payable,
is different in different cases.

(3) The balance for a dividend on any stock shall not be struck at different times for different holdings of that stock unless—

(a) the case is one where the use of different times for different holdings of the same stock is authorised by order made by the Treasury; and

(b) such requirements (if any) as may be imposed by an order so made are complied with in relation to the striking of that balance.

(4) The time at which the balance for a dividend on any stock is struck shall not fall before—

(a) the beginning of the tenth business day before the day on which the dividend is payable; or

(b) such later time (if any) as may be determined, in accordance with an order made by the Treasury, to be the earliest time at which that balance may be struck.

(5) In this section 'business day' means any day other than—

(a) a Saturday or Sunday;

(b) Good Friday or Christmas Day;

(c) a day which, in any part of the United Kingdom, is a bank holiday under the Banking and Financial Dealings Act 1971;

(d) a day specified in an order under section 2(1) of that Act (days on which financial dealings are suspended) and declared by that order to be a non-business day for the purposes of this section; or

(e) a day appointed by Royal proclamation as a public fast or thanksgiving day.

(6) An order made by the Treasury for the purposes of subsection (3) or (4) above—

(a) shall be made by statutory instrument subject to annulment in pursuance of a resolution of either House of Parliament; and

(b) may make different provision for different cases and contain such exceptions and exclusions, and such incidental, supplemental, consequential and transitional provision, as the Treasury may think fit."

(2) This section has effect in relation to dividends other than those for which the balance is struck on or before the day on which this Act is passed.

General Note
    The section, introduced at committee stage, opens the way for the abolition of the ex-dividend period for nearly all gilt-edged securities. The proposal, on which the Bank of England is consulting, would apply to gilts held in the Central Gilts Office (CGO) which represent over 90 per cent of the market. It would also enable the ex-div period to be shortened for certificated holdings on the National Savings Stock Register. A decision to proceed with the proposal and to introduce the necessary secondary legislation will be taken after consideration of the responses to the consultation.
    Currently, the ex-div period is seven working days, except for War Loan, where a ten working day period applies because of the large number of holders. In January 1996, the ex-div period was reduced from 37 days to seven working days to facilitate the introduction of the gilt repo market. Systems developments in both the settlement and registration processes for gilts open up the possibility of this further development. If a decision is taken to proceed, implementation would not be before the autumn, after the introduction of the upgraded CGO.

Nil levy on dwelling-house disposals

109. Section 136 of the Leasehold Reform, Housing and Urban Development Act 1993 (levy on local authorities in respect of dwelling-house disposals) shall have effect, and be deemed always to have had effect, with the following subsection inserted after subsection (4)—

"(4A) The power of the Secretary of State to determine a formula for the purposes of item D in subsection (3) shall include power to determine that, in such cases as he may determine, item D is to be taken to be equal to item CR."

GENERAL NOTE

The Leasehold Reform, Housing and Urban Development Act 1993 (c. 28) provides that a levy is payable on the receipts arising from certain disposals of council housing. The disposals affected are those comprising 500 or more units. The levy is currently 20 per cent of any amount by which the capital receipt ("CR") received by the authority exceeds the outstanding debt ("D") attributable to the buildings. To encourage authorities to transfer their housing stock, the Government announced as part of the Budget measures a three year holiday from this levy.

New s.136(4A) allows this to be implemented by permitting the Secretary of State to deem D to be equal to CR.

[Standing Committee B, February 25, 1997, cols. 473–475.]

Obtaining information from social security authorities

110.—(1) This section applies to—

(a) any information held by the Secretary of State or the Department of Health and Social Services for Northern Ireland for the purposes of any of his or its functions relating to social security; and

(b) any information held by a person in connection with the provision by him to the Secretary of State or that Department of any services which that person is providing for purposes connected with any of those functions.

(2) Subject to the following provisions of this section, the person holding any information to which this section applies shall be entitled to supply it to—

(a) the Commissioners of Customs and Excise or any person by whom services are being provided to those Commissioners for purposes connected with any of their functions; or

(b) the Commissioners of Inland Revenue or any person by whom services are being provided to those Commissioners for purposes connected with any of their functions.

(3) Information shall not be supplied to any person under this section except for one or more of the following uses—

(a) use in the prevention, detection, investigation or prosecution of criminal offences which it is a function of the Commissioners of Customs and Excise, or of the Commissioners of Inland Revenue, to prevent, detect, investigate or prosecute;

(b) use in the prevention, detection or investigation of conduct in respect of which penalties which are not criminal penalties are provided for by or under any enactment;

(c) use in connection with the assessment or determination of penalties which are not criminal penalties;

(d) use in checking the accuracy of information relating to, or provided for purposes connected with, any matter under the care and management of the Commissioners of Customs and Excise or the Commissioners of Inland Revenue;

(e) use (where appropriate) for amending or supplementing any such information; and

(f) use in connection with any legal or other proceedings relating to anything mentioned in paragraphs (a) to (e) above.

(4) An enactment authorising the disclosure of information by a person mentioned in subsection (2)(a) or (b) above shall not authorise the disclosure

by such a person of information supplied to him under this section except to the extent that the disclosure is also authorised by a general or specific permission granted by the Secretary of State or by the Department of Health and Social Services for Northern Ireland.

(5) In this section references to functions relating to social security include references to—

(a) functions in relation to social security contributions, social security benefits (whether contributory or not) or national insurance numbers; and

(b) functions under the Jobseekers Act 1995 or the Jobseekers (Northern Ireland) Order 1995.

(6) In this section "conduct" includes acts, omissions and statements.

(7) This section shall come into force on such day as the Treasury may by order made by statutory instrument appoint, and different days may be appointed under this subsection for different purposes.

GENERAL NOTE

The section provides for the Department of Social Security ("DSS") to be able to disclose information which is held for social security purposes to the Inland Revenue and the Customs and Excise. It mirrors a similar proposal to permit the disclosure of information to the DSS by the revenue departments.

There are two reasons for these proposals. The first is to assist in tackling tax evasion and fraud. If the DSS holds or obtains information which suggests that tax has been evaded, the section permits them to disclose this information to the Revenue or the Customs and Excise. At present, they can only do so in very limited circumstances. The second is to facilitate the joint working programme between the Inland Revenue, the Customs and Excise and the Contributions Agency. Greater sharing of information will allow, for example, more joint visits to businesses by officials of these departments, allowing a reduction in the number of separate visits and enquiries and thereby in the burdens on business.

[Standing Committee B, February 25, 1997, cols. 475–480.]

Report on VAT on energy saving materials

111. Within twelve months of this Act receiving Royal Assent the Treasury shall report to Parliament on the consequences to the Exchequer of reducing VAT on energy saving materials.

GENERAL NOTE

This section, introduced at report stage on the initiative of the opposition, reflects concern regarding home insulation and other energy saving measures.

[*Hansard*, H.C. Vol. 292, cols. 189–204.]

Supplemental

Interpretation

112. In this Act "the Taxes Act 1988" means the Income and Corporation Taxes Act 1988.

Repeals

113.—(1) The enactments mentioned in Schedule 18 to this Act (which include spent provisions) are hereby repealed to the extent specified in the third column of that Schedule.

(2) The repeals specified in that Schedule have effect subject to the commencement provisions and savings contained or referred to in the notes set out in that Schedule.

Short title

114. This Act may be cited as the Finance Act 1997.

SCHEDULES

                    SCHEDULE 1

GAMING DUTY: ADMINISTRATION, ENFORCEMENT ETC

PART I

THE GAMING DUTY REGISTER

The Register

1. The Commissioners shall establish and maintain a register of persons involved in the provision of dutiable gaming.

Interpretation

2.—(1) In this Part of this Schedule—
"the register" means the gaming duty register;
"registered person" means a person registered on the register; and
"registrable person" has the meaning given by paragraph 3 below.

(2) For the purposes of this Part of this Schedule premises in the United Kingdom are "unlicensed premises" unless they are premises in Great Britain—

(a) in respect of which a licence under the Gaming Act 1968 is for the time being in force, or

(b) in respect of which a club or miners' welfare institute is for the time being registered under Part II of that Act.

(3) References in this Part of this Schedule to being a member of a group and to being the representative member of a group shall be construed in accordance with paragraph 8 below.

Registration

3.—(1) The Commissioners shall, on receipt of a valid application made by—

(a) a registrable person, or

(b) a person who expects dutiable gaming to take place and to become a registrable person if it does,

add that person to the register.

(2) The following provisions of this paragraph have effect for the interpretation of sub-paragraph (1) above.

(3) A valid application is one which is made in such form and manner, and is accompanied by such information, as the Commissioners may require.

(4) Subject to sub-paragraph (5) below—

(a) the holder of a licence under the Gaming Act 1968 is a registrable person if and for so long as dutiable gaming takes place on the premises in respect of which the licence is for the time being in force;

(b) a provider of unlicensed premises is a registrable person if and for so long as dutiable gaming takes place on those premises;

(c) a person is a registrable person if and for so long as he is concerned in the organisation or management of dutiable gaming that takes place on unlicensed premises.

(5) A body corporate cannot be a registrable person if it—

(a) is a member of a group, but

(b) is not the representative member of that group.

(6) A body corporate which—

(a) is the representative member of a group, and

(b) is not a registrable person in its own right,

is a registrable person if another body corporate which is a member of that group would be a registrable person but for sub-paragraph (5) above.

Cancellation of registration

4.—(1) This paragraph has effect for determining when a registered person is to be removed by the Commissioners from the register.

(2) Where the Commissioners receive a valid notice from a registered person stating that he has ceased to be a registrable person, he shall be removed from the register.

(3) Where the Commissioners receive a valid notice from a registered person stating that he will, from a time specified in the notice, cease to be a registrable person, he shall be removed from the register with effect from that time.

(4) Where—

(a) a registered person has been added to the register on an application made under paragraph 3(1)(b) above, and

(b) the Commissioners receive a valid notice from him stating—

　(i) that the dutiable gaming which he expected to take place has not taken place, and

　(ii) that he no longer expects it to take place,

he shall be removed from the register.

(5) Where it appears to the Commissioners that a registered person has ceased to be a registrable person, he shall be removed from the register.

(6) A registered person shall be removed from the register if—

(a) he has been added to the register on an application made under paragraph 3(1)(b) above, and

(b) it appears to the Commissioners that the dutiable gaming which he expected to take place has not taken place and can no longer be expected to take place.

(7) For the purposes of this paragraph, a valid notice is one which is given in such form and manner, and accompanied by such information, as the Commissioners may require.

Penalties in connection with registration

5.—(1) There is a contravention of this sub-paragraph by every person who is a responsible person in relation to any premises if—

(a) dutiable gaming takes place on those premises on or after 1st October 1997; and

(b) at the time when the gaming takes place, no person by whom those premises are notifiable is registered on the register.

(2) For the purposes of this paragraph, a person is a responsible person in relation to any premises if—

(a) he is a registrable person; and

(b) those premises are notifiable by him.

(3) Where a person contravenes sub-paragraph (1) above, that contravention shall attract a penalty under section 9 of the Finance Act 1994 (civil penalties) and shall also attract daily penalties.

(4) References in this paragraph to premises being notifiable are references to them being notifiable for the purposes of paragraph 6 below.

Notification of premises

6.—(1) This paragraph has effect for determining the premises to be specified in a registered person's entry on the register.

(2) A person who makes an application under paragraph 3(1) above shall, on making that application, notify the Commissioners of all the premises which—

(a) are notifiable by him, or

(b) in a case where his application is made under paragraph 3(1)(b), will become notifiable by him if the expected gaming takes place;

and the Commissioners shall, on registering him on the register, cause those premises to be specified in his entry on the register.

(3) Where any premises not currently notified by a registered person become notifiable by him—

(a) he shall notify the Commissioners of those premises, and

(b) the Commissioners shall cause those premises to be specified in his entry on the register.

(4) Subject to sub-paragraph (5) below, where any premises currently notified by a registered person cease to be notifiable by him—

(a) he shall notify the Commissioners of that fact, and

(b) they shall cause those premises to be no longer specified in his entry on the register.

(5) A registered person is not required to notify the Commissioners as mentioned in sub-paragraph (4) above in a case where—

(a) he gives notice to the Commissioners under paragraph 4(2) above; or

(b) the premises ceasing to be notifiable by him so cease in accordance with a notification previously given by him to the Commissioners under sub-paragraph (6) below.

(6) Where—

(a) any premises are currently notified by a registered person, and

(b) he notifies the Commissioners of the date on which those premises will cease to be notifiable by him, the Commissioners shall ensure that those premises cease, with effect from that date, to be specified in his entry on the register.

(7) Subject to sub-paragraph (8) below, where—

(a) any premises are currently notified by a registered person,

(b) that person has been added to the register on an application made under paragraph 3(1)(b) above,

(c) any of the dutiable gaming which he expected to take place has not taken place,

(d) he no longer expects that gaming to take place, and

(e) in consequence of events turning out as mentioned in paragraphs (c) and (d) above, those premises have not and will not become notifiable by him,

he shall notify the Commissioners accordingly and they shall cause those premises to be no longer specified in his entry on the register.

(8) A registered person is not required to notify the Commissioners as mentioned in sub-paragraph (7) above in a case where he gives notice to the Commissioners under paragraph 4(4) above.

(9) For the purposes of this paragraph premises are currently notified by any person at any time if at that time they are specified in his entry on the register.

(10) For the purposes of this paragraph, in the case of a person who is not a body corporate, or who is a body corporate that is not a member of any group—

(a) premises in respect of which a licence under the Gaming Act 1968 is for the time being in force are notifiable by him if and for so long as—

(i) he is the holder of the licence, and

(ii) dutiable gaming takes place on those premises;

(b) unlicensed premises of which he is a provider are notifiable by him if and for so long as dutiable gaming takes place on those premises; and

(c) any unlicensed premises of which he is not a provider are notifiable by him if and for so long as—

(i) dutiable gaming takes place on those premises, and

(ii) he is concerned in the organisation or management of that gaming.

(11) For the purposes of this paragraph, in the case of a body corporate which is the representative member of a group—

(a) premises in respect of which a licence under the Gaming Act 1968 is for the time being in force are notifiable by the representative member if and for so long as—

(i) it, or another body corporate which is a member of that group, is the holder of the licence, and

(ii) dutiable gaming takes place on those premises;

(b) unlicensed premises of which the representative member or any such other body corporate is a provider are notifiable by the representative member if and for so long as dutiable gaming takes place on those premises; and

(c) unlicensed premises which are not notifiable by the representative member by virtue of paragraph (b) above are notifiable by it if and for so long as—

(i) dutiable gaming takes place on those premises, and

(ii) it or any such other body corporate is concerned in the organisation or management of that gaming.

Penalties in connection with notification

7.—(1) Where, in contravention of paragraph 6(2) above, a person fails to notify the Commissioners of any premises, that failure shall attract a penalty under section 9 of the Finance Act 1994 (civil penalties).

(2) Where—

(a) by virtue of paragraph 6(3), (4) or (7) above, a person at any time becomes subject to a requirement to notify the Commissioners of any premises or fact, and

(b) he fails to comply with that requirement before the end of the period of seven days beginning with the day on which that time falls,

that failure shall attract a penalty under section 9 of the Finance Act 1994 (civil penalties) and shall also attract daily penalties for every day after the end of that period on which the failure to notify continues.

Groups

8.—(1) Two or more bodies corporate are eligible to be treated as members of a group for the purposes of this Part of this Schedule if each is resident or has an established place of business in the United Kingdom and—

(a) one of them controls each of the others;

(b) one person (whether a body corporate or an individual) controls all of them; or

(c) two or more individuals carrying on a business in partnership control all of them.

(2) Subject to sub-paragraph (3) below, where an application for the purpose is made to the Commissioners with respect to two or more bodies corporate eligible to be treated as members of a group, then, from such date as may be specified in the application—

(a) they shall be so treated for the purposes of this Part of this Schedule; and

(b) such one of them as may be specified in the application shall be the representative member for those purposes.

(3) The Commissioners may refuse an application under sub-paragraph (2) above if, and only if, it appears to them necessary to do so for the protection of the revenue from gaming duty.

(4) Where any bodies corporate are treated as members of a group for the purposes of this Part of this Schedule and an application for the purpose is made to the Commissioners, then, from such time as may be specified in the application—

(a) a further body eligible to be so treated shall be included among the bodies so treated; or

(b) a body corporate shall be excluded from the bodies so treated; or

(c) another member of the group shall be substituted as the representative member; or

(d) the bodies corporate shall no longer be treated as members of a group.

(5) If it appears to the Commissioners necessary to do so for the protection of the revenue from gaming duty, they may—

(a) refuse any application made for the purpose mentioned in paragraph (a) or (c) of sub-paragraph (4) above; or

(b) refuse any application made for the purpose mentioned in paragraph (b) or (d) of that sub-paragraph in a case that does not appear to them to fall within sub-paragraph (6)(a) and (b) below.

(6) Where—

(a) a body corporate is treated as a member of a group for the purposes of this Part of this Schedule by virtue of being controlled by any person, and

(b) it appears to the Commissioners that it has ceased to be so controlled,

they shall, by notice given to that person, terminate that treatment from such date as may be specified in the notice.

(7) Where—

(a) a notice under sub-paragraph (6) above is given to a body corporate which is the representative member of a group,

(b) there are two or more other bodies corporate who will continue to be treated as members of the group after the time when that notice takes effect, and

(c) none of those bodies corporate is substituted from that time, or from before that time, as the representative member of the group in pursuance of an application under sub-paragraph (4)(c) above,

the Commissioners shall, by notice given to such one of the bodies corporate mentioned in paragraph (b) above as they think fit, substitute that body corporate as the representative member as from that time.

(8) Where a notice under sub-paragraph (6) above is given to one member of a group of which there is only one other member, then (subject to any further application under this paragraph) the other member shall also cease, from the time specified in the notice, to be treated for the purposes of this Part of this Schedule as a member of the group.

(9) An application under this paragraph with respect to any bodies corporate—

(a) must be made by one of those bodies or by the person controlling them; and

(b) must be made not less than 90 days before the date from which it is to take effect, or at such later time as the Commissioners may allow.

(10) For the purposes of this paragraph a body corporate shall be taken to control another body corporate if—

(a) it is empowered by statute to control that body's activities; or

(b) it is that body's holding company within the meaning of section 736 of the Companies Act 1985;

and an individual or individuals shall be taken to control a body corporate if (were he or they a company) he or they would be that body's holding company within the meaning of that Act.

(11) Sections 14 to 16 of the Finance Act 1994 (review and appeals) shall have effect in relation to any refusal by the Commissioners of an application under sub-paragraph (2) or (4) above as if that refusal were a decision of a description specified in Schedule 5 to that Act.

PART II

OTHER PROVISIONS

Accounting periods

9.—(1) Where, in the case of any premises, the Commissioners and every relevant person so agree, the provisions of sections 10 to 15 of this Act and this Schedule shall have effect in relation to those premises as if accounting periods for the purposes of those provisions were periods of six months beginning on such dates other than 1st October and 1st April as may be specified in the agreement.

(2) For the purposes of sub-paragraph (1) above, a person is a relevant person in relation to any premises if—

(a) he is registered on the gaming duty register, and

(b) the entry relating to him on the register specifies those premises.

(3) The Commissioners shall not enter into an agreement under this paragraph for a change in the date on which an accounting period begins in relation to any premises unless they are satisfied that appropriate transitional provision for the protection of the revenue is contained in the agreement.

(4) The provision which, for the purposes of sub-paragraph (3) above, may be contained in any agreement under this paragraph shall include any such provision as may be contained in regulations under section 11(5) of this Act.

(5) Sections 14 to 16 of the Finance Act 1994 (review and appeals) shall have effect in relation to any refusal of the Commissioners to enter into an agreement under this paragraph, or to enter into such an agreement on particular terms, as if that refusal were a decision of a description specified in Schedule 5 to that Act.

Directions as to the making of returns

10.—(1) The Commissioners may give directions as to the making of returns in connection with gaming duty by—

(a) persons registered on the gaming duty register;

(b) persons liable to pay any gaming duty.

(2) Directions under this paragraph may, in particular, make provision as to—

(a) when any returns are to be made;

(b) the persons by whom any returns are to be made;

(c) the form in which any returns are to be made;

(d) the information to be given in any returns;

(e) the declarations to be contained in returns and the manner in which returns are to be authenticated;

(f) returns being treated as not made until received by the Commissioners;

(g) the places to which returns are to be made.

(3) Where a person fails to comply with any provision of a direction given under this paragraph, that failure shall attract a penalty under section 9 of the Finance Act 1994 (civil penalties) and shall also attract daily penalties.

Regulations

11.—(1) The Commissioners may make regulations providing for any matter for which provision appears to them to be necessary or expedient for the administration or enforcement of gaming duty, or for the protection of the revenue from that duty.

(2) Regulations under this paragraph may, in particular, include provision as to the giving and operation of directions under section 11(6) of this Act.

(3) Where any person contravenes or fails to comply with any of the provisions of any regulations under this paragraph, his contravention or failure to comply shall attract a penalty under section 9 of the Finance Act 1994 (civil penalties).

Offences

12.—(1) Any person who obstructs any officer in the exercise of his functions in relation to gaming duty shall be guilty of an offence and liable, on summary conviction, to a penalty of level 5 on the standard scale.

(2) Any person who—

(a) in connection with gaming duty, makes any statement which he knows to be false in a material particular or recklessly makes any statement which is false in a material particular,

(b) in that connection, with intent to deceive, produces or makes use of any book, account, record, return or other document which is false in a material particular, or

(c) is knowingly concerned in, or in the taking of steps with a view to, the fraudulent evasion (by him or any other person) of any gaming duty or of any obligation to make a payment on account of gaming duty,

shall be guilty of an offence.

(3) A person guilty of an offence under subparagraph (2) above shall be liable—

(a) on summary conviction, to a penalty of—

    (i) the statutory maximum, or

    (ii) if greater, three times the duty or other amount which is unpaid or the payment of which is sought to be avoided,

or to imprisonment for a term not exceeding six months, or to both;

(b) on conviction on indictment, to a penalty of any amount, or to imprisonment for a term not exceeding—

    (i) two years in the case of an offence by virtue of sub-paragraph (2)(a) above, and

    (ii) seven years in any other case,

or to both.

(4) Section 27 of the Betting and Gaming Duties Act 1981 (offences by bodies corporate) shall have effect for the purposes of any offence under this paragraph as it has effect for the purposes of the offences mentioned in that section.

(5) Where a person has committed an offence under sub-paragraph (2) above, all designated items related to the relevant gaming shall be liable to forfeiture if—

(a) at the time the offence was committed that person was not registered on the gaming duty register; and

(b) the relevant gaming did not take place on premises which, at the time the offence was committed, were specified in any person's entry on that register.

(6) In sub-paragraph (5) above, "the relevant gaming" means—

(a) in relation to an offence under sub-paragraph (2)(a) or (b) above, any gaming to which the false statement or (as the case may be) the false document related; and

(b) in relation to an offence under sub-paragraph (2)(c) above, any gaming on the premises the gaming duty on which was, or was sought to be, fraudulently evaded.

(7) For the purposes of sub-paragraph (5) above, the designated items related to any gaming are—

(a) any furniture, machines and other articles and equipment which—

    (i) are on the premises where the gaming takes place; and

    (ii) have been or are being, or are capable of being, used for or in connection with gaming;

and

(b) any cash and gaming chips in the custody or under the control of any person who—

    (i) is a provider of the premises on which the gaming takes place, or

    (ii) is in any way concerned with the organisation or management of the gaming.

(8) For the purposes of sub-paragraph (7)(b) above the cash and gaming chips taken to be under the control of a person who is the provider of any premises or is concerned with the organisation or management of gaming on any premises shall include all cash and gaming chips in play or left on a gaming table on those premises.

Distress and poinding

13.—(1) Sections 28 and 29 of the Betting and Gaming Duties Act 1981 (recovery of duty) shall have effect as follows so as to apply in relation to gaming duty as they applied in relation to the duty on gaming licences—

(a) in subsection (1) of each section, for "or 14 above or of Schedule 2 to this Act" there shall be substituted "above or sections 10 to 15 of, and Schedule 1 to, the Finance Act 1997"; and

(b) in subsections (2) and (3) of each section, for the words "the duty on a gaming licence" there shall be substituted—

    (i) in the first place where they occur in subsection (2), the words "the gaming duty"; and

    (ii) in the other places where they occur, the words "gaming duty".

(2) Sub-paragraph (1) above shall cease to have effect on such day as the Commissioners may by order made by statutory instrument appoint, and different days may be appointed under this sub-paragraph for different purposes.

Disclosure of information

14.—(1) No obligation as to secrecy or other restriction on the disclosure of information imposed by statute or otherwise shall prevent—

  (a) the Commissioners or an authorised officer of the Commissioners from disclosing to the Gaming Board for Great Britain or to an authorised officer of that Board, or

  (b) that Board or an authorised officer of that Board from disclosing to the Commissioners or an authorised officer of the Commissioners,

information for the purpose of assisting the Commissioners in the carrying out of their functions with respect to gaming duty or, as the case may be, that Board in the carrying out of that Board's functions under the Gaming Act 1968.

(2) Information obtained by virtue of a disclosure authorised by this paragraph shall not be disclosed except—

  (a) to the Commissioners or the Gaming Board for Great Britain or to an authorised officer of the Commissioners or that Board; or

  (b) for the purposes of any proceedings connected with a matter in relation to which the Commissioners or that Board carry out the functions mentioned in sub-paragraph (1) above.

Evidence by certificate

15. Section 29A of the Betting and Gaming Duties Act 1981 (evidence by certificate) shall apply for the purposes of sections 10 to 15 of this Act and this Schedule as it applies for the purposes of that Act.

Protection of officers

16. Section 31 of the Betting and Gaming Duties Act 1981 (protection of officers) shall apply for the purposes of gaming duty as it applies for the purposes of general betting duty.

General Note

The Schedule provides the administrative framework for gaming duty, which replaces gaming licence duty. In future, duty will be imposed on premises rather than on licences.

Part I

This provides for the establishment of the gaming duty register.

Para. 3

Provision is made for additions to the register.

Para. 4

Provision is similarly made for the cancellation of registration.

Para. 5

Civil penalties under F.A. 1994, s.9 apply where a "responsible person" fails to register and dutiable gaming takes place on the premises. A responsible person is a registrable person (see para. 3(4)) where the premises are notifiable by him (see para. 6).

Para. 6

This paragraph determines which premises should be specified in a registered person's entry in the register.

Para. 7

Civil penalties under F.A. 1994, s.9 apply on a failure to notify premises under para. 6(2).

Para. 8

Provision is made for the registration of groups of companies in the name of a representative member.

Part II
Para. 9

Accounting periods in relation to premises will be six months long and may run by agreement from dates other than April 1 and October 1 specified in s.15(3).

Para. 10

The Customs and Excise can give directions with regard to the making of returns in connection with gaming duty.

Para. 11

They can also make regulations to administer or enforce gaming duty and for the protection of the revenue. Contravention of the regulations will attract a civil penalty.

Para. 12

A range of criminal offences is created in connection with gaming duty.

Para. 13

The recovery provisions for gaming licence duty are applied to gaming duty.

Para. 14

Information relevant to their functions may be exchanged between the Customs and Excise and the Gaming Board for Great Britain.

Paras. 15 and 16

Betting and Gaming Duties Act 1981 (c. 63), ss.29A and 31 are applied to gaming duty in the same way as they applied to gaming licence duty.

Section 13   SCHEDULE 2

Gaming duty: consequential and incidental amendments

Part I

Amendments of the Customs and Excise Management Act 1979

Introductory

1. The Customs and Excise Management Act 1979 shall be amended in accordance with the provisions of this Part of this Schedule.

Meaning of "revenue trade provisions" and "revenue trader"

2.—(1) This paragraph amends section 1(1) (interpretation).

(2) In the definition of "the revenue trade provisions of the customs and excise Acts", after paragraph (d) there shall be inserted the following paragraph—

"(e) the provisions of sections 10 to 15 of, and Schedule 1 to, the Finance Act 1997;".

(3) In paragraph (a) of the definition of "revenue trader", after sub-paragraph (ia) there shall be inserted the following sub-paragraphs—

"(ib) being (within the meaning of sections 10 to 15 of the Finance Act 1997) the provider of any premises for gaming;

(ic) the organisation, management or promotion of any gaming (within the meaning of the Gaming Act 1968 or the Betting, Gaming, Lotteries and Amusements (Northern Ireland) Order 1985); or".

(4) In sub-paragraph (ii) of that paragraph, for "or (ia)" there shall be substituted ", (ia), (ib) or (ic)".

Amendments of Part IXA

3. In section 118B (furnishing of information etc. by revenue traders)—

(a) in subsection (1)(a), after sub-paragraph (ii) there shall be inserted "or
(iii) any transaction or activity effected or taking place in the course or furtherance of a business,";

(b) in subsection (1)(b), at the end there shall be inserted "or to the transaction or activity"; and

(c) in subsection (3), after "any business" there shall be inserted ", or to any transaction or activity effected or taking place in the course or furtherance of any business,".

4.—(1) This paragraph amends section 118C (powers of entry and search).

(2) After subsection (2) there shall be inserted the following subsections—

"(2A) Where an officer has reasonable cause to believe that any premises are premises where gaming to which section 10 of the Finance Act 1997 (gaming duty) applies is taking place, has taken place or is about to take place, he may at any reasonable time enter and inspect those premises and inspect any relevant materials found on them.

(2B) In subsection (2A) above 'relevant materials' means—
(a) any accounts, records or other documents found on the premises in the custody or control of any person who is engaging, or whom the officer reasonably suspects of engaging—
     (i) in any such gaming, or
     (ii) in any activity by reason of which he is or may become liable to gaming duty, and
(b) any equipment which is being, or which the officer reasonably suspects of having been or of being intended to be, used on the premises for or in connection with any such gaming."

(3) In subsection (3) (justice's warrant for entry), after paragraph (b) there shall be inserted "or

     (c) that there is reasonable ground for suspecting—
         (i) that gaming to which section 10 of the Finance Act 1997 applies is taking place, has taken place or is about to take place on any premises, or
         (ii) that evidence of the commission of a gaming duty offence is to be found there,".

(4) In subsection (4)(b) (powers on entry under a warrant), after "of a serious nature" there shall be inserted "or in respect of a gaming duty offence".

(5) In subsection (5) (meaning of "fraud offence"), at the end there shall be inserted "and 'a gaming duty offence' means an offence under paragraph 12(2) of Schedule 1 to the Finance Act 1997 (offences in connection with gaming duty)".

PART II

OTHER AMENDMENTS

Licences under the Gaming Act 1968

5.—(1) Schedule 2 to the Gaming Act 1968 (grant etc. of licences) shall be amended in accordance with the provisions of this paragraph.

(2) In paragraph 20(1) (grounds for refusing to grant or renew a licence), after paragraph (f) there shall be inserted the following paragraph—

     "(g) that any gaming duty charged on the premises remains unpaid."

(3) In paragraph 48(1) (cancellation of licence on conviction for second or subsequent offence), after "the enactments consolidated by that Act)" there shall be inserted "or of an offence under paragraph 12 of Schedule 1 to the Finance Act 1997".

(4) In paragraph 60(c) (transfer of licence may be refused if duty unpaid), after "bingo duty" there shall be inserted "or gaming duty".

Preferential debts on insolvency

6. In paragraph 5(a) of Schedule 6 to the Insolvency Act 1986, paragraph 2(3)(a) of Schedule 3 to the Bankruptcy (Scotland) Act 1985 and paragraph 5(a) of Schedule 4 to the Insolvency (Northern Ireland) Order 1989 (preferential debts), for "or bingo duty" there shall, in each case, be substituted ", bingo duty or gaming duty".

Assessments to duty

7. In section 12(2)(c) of the Finance Act 1994 (duty may be assessed upon the occurrence of certain defaults in connection with betting duties and bingo duty), after "under Schedule 1 or 3 to the Betting and Gaming Duties Act 1981" there shall be inserted "or Schedule 1 to the Finance Act 1997".

GENERAL NOTE
    The Schedule amends references in other statutes to ensure that various provisions which applied to gaming licence duty continue to apply to gaming duty.

Para. 3
    The amendment to Customs and Excise Management Act 1979 (c. 2), s.118(B), coupled with the amendment to the definition of "revenue trades" in para. 2 is designed to ensure that adequate information-gathering powers are available in relation to gaming duty.

     SCHEDULE 3

VEHICLE EXCISE DUTY: EXEMPT VEHICLES

Interpretation

1. In this Schedule "the 1994 Act" means the Vehicle Excise and Registration Act 1994.

Registration of vehicle on issue of nil licence

2. In section 21 of the 1994 Act (registration of vehicles), for subsection (1) there shall be substituted the following subsection—

"(1) Subject to subsection (3), on the issue by the Secretary of State for a vehicle which is not registered under this section of either—

(a) a vehicle licence, or

(b) a nil licence,

the Secretary of State shall register the vehicle in such manner as he thinks fit without any further application by the person to whom the licence is issued."

Return of nil licence

3. In section 22 of the 1994 Act (registration regulations), after subsection (3) there shall be inserted the following subsection—

"(4) Regulations made by the Secretary of State may make provision for the return of any nil licence to the Secretary of State in such circumstances as may be prescribed by the regulations."

Offence of not exhibiting nil licence

4.—(1) In section 33 of the 1994 Act (not exhibiting licence), after subsection (1) there shall be inserted the following subsection—

"(1A) A person is guilty of an offence if—

(a) he uses, or keeps, on a public road an exempt vehicle,

(b) that vehicle is one in respect of which regulations under this Act require a nil licence to be in force, and

(c) there is not fixed to and exhibited on the vehicle in the manner prescribed by regulations made by the Secretary of State a nil licence for that vehicle which is for the time being in force."

(2) In subsection (2) of that section, after "(1)" there shall be inserted "or (1A)".

(3) For subsection (3) of that section there shall be substituted the following subsection—

"(3) Subsections (1) and (1A)—

(a) have effect subject to the provisions of regulations made by the Secretary of State, and

(b) are without prejudice to sections 29 and 43A."

(4) In subsection (4) of that section, for "in respect of which excise duty is chargeable" there shall be substituted "which is kept or used on a public road".

(5) After that subsection there shall be inserted the following subsection—

"(5) The reference to a licence in subsection (4) includes a reference to a nil licence."

Offence of failing to have nil licence for exempt vehicle

5. Immediately before section 44 of the 1994 Act there shall be inserted the following section—

"Failure to have nil licence for exempt vehicle

43A.—A person is guilty of an offence if—

(a) he uses, or keeps, on a public road an exempt vehicle,

(b) that vehicle is one in respect of which regulations under this Act require a nil licence to be in force, and

(c) a nil licence is not for the time being in force in respect of the vehicle.

(2) A person guilty of an offence under subsection (1) is liable on summary conviction to a fine not exceeding level 2 on the standard scale.

(3) Subsection (1) has effect subject to the provisions of regulations made by the Secretary of State.

(4) The Secretary of State may, if he thinks fit, compound any proceedings for an offence under this section."

Offence of forging or fraudulently using etc. nil licence

6. In subsection (2) of section 44 of the 1994 Act (forgery and fraud); for paragraph (c) there shall be substituted the following paragraph—

"(c) a nil licence,".

Supplemental provisions

7.—(1) In section 46 of the 1994 Act (duty to give information)—

(a) in subsection (1), for "or 37" there shall be substituted ", 37 or 43A";

(b) in subsections (2) and (3), after "section 29" there shall be inserted "or 43A".

(2) In subsection (1) of section 51 of that Act (admissions), for "or 34" there shall be substituted ", 34 or 43A".

(3) In subsection (1) of section 62 of that Act (other definitions), after the definition of "motor trader" there shall be inserted the following definition—

" 'nil licence' means a document which is in the form of a vehicle licence and is issued by the Secretary of State in pursuance of regulations under this Act in respect of a vehicle which is an exempt vehicle,".

(4) In paragraph 20 of Schedule 2 to that Act (exempt vehicles), sub-paragraph (4) shall cease to have effect.

Further amendments

8.—(1) In Schedule 3 to the Road Traffic Offenders Act 1988 (fixed penalty offences), in column 2 of the entry relating to section 33 of the 1994 Act, for "licence" there shall be substituted "vehicle licence, trade licence or nil licence".

(2) In Article 198 of the Road Traffic (Northern Ireland) Order 1981 (offences punishable without prosecution), in paragraph (1)(f) for "licence" there shall be substituted "vehicle licence, trade licence or nil licence".

Commencement

9. This Schedule shall come into force on such day as the Secretary of State may by order made by statutory instrument appoint; and different days may be appointed under this paragraph for different purposes.

GENERAL NOTE

The Schedule introduces provisions strengthening the enforcement of the law relating to vehicles which are exempt from VED.

Para. 2

This clarifies the law by requiring registration on the first issue of a nil licence, *i.e.* one indicating that no VED is payable, as on a vehicle licence.

Para. 3

The regulations under this paragraph may require a nil licence to be returned by the holder.

Paras. 4 and 5

These create offences of failing to take out and failing to display as required by regulations a nil licence, carrying a penalty of up to £500 and £200 respectively.

Para. 6

The offences of forging or fraudulently using a licence are extended to include a nil licence.

Para. 7

This extends the power to obtain information as to the identity of a person using or keeping an exempt vehicle in connection with an offence and also defines a "nil licence".

Para. 8

The police are empowered to apply fixed penalties to offences of failing to display a nil licence.

Section 22

SCHEDULE 4

INSURANCE PREMIUM TAX: THE HIGHER RATE

Schedule to be inserted into the Finance Act 1994

Section 51A

"SCHEDULE 6A

PREMIUMS LIABLE TO TAX AT THE HIGHER RATE

PART I

INTERPRETATION

1.—(1) In this Schedule—

"insurance-related service" means any service which is related to, or connected with, insurance;

"supply" includes all forms of supply; and "supplier" shall be construed accordingly.

(2) For the purposes of this Schedule, any question whether a person is connected with another shall be determined in accordance with section 839 of the Taxes Act 1988.

PART II

DESCRIPTIONS OF PREMIUM

Insurance relating to motor cars or motor cycles

2.—(1) A premium under a taxable insurance contract relating to a motor car or motor cycle falls within this paragraph if—

(a) the contract is arranged through a person falling within sub-paragraph (2) below, or

(b) the insurer under the contract is a person falling within that sub-paragraph,

unless the insurance is provided to the insured free of charge.

(2) A person falls within this sub-paragraph if—

(a) he is a supplier of motor cars or motor cycles;

(b) he is connected with a supplier of motor cars or motor cycles; or

(c) he pays—

(i) the whole or any part of the premium received under the taxable insurance contract, or

(ii) a fee connected with the arranging of that contract,

to a supplier of motor cars or motor cycles or to a person who is connected with a supplier of motor cars or motor cycles.

(3) Where a taxable insurance contract relating to a motor car or motor cycle is arranged through a person who is connected with a supplier of motor cars or motor cycles, the premium does not fall within this paragraph by virtue only of sub-paragraph (2)(b) above except to the extent that the premium is attributable to cover for a risk which relates to a motor car or motor cycle supplied by a supplier of motor cars or motor cycles with whom that person is connected.

(4) Where the insurer under a taxable insurance contract relating to a motor car or motor cycle is connected with a supplier of motor cars or motor cycles, the premium does not fall within this paragraph by virtue only of sub-paragraph (2)(b) above except to the extent that the premium is attributable to cover for a risk which relates to a motor car or motor cycle supplied by a supplier of motor cars or motor cycles with whom the insurer is connected.

(5) For the purposes of this paragraph, the cases where insurance is provided to the insured free of charge are those cases where no charge (whether by way of premium or otherwise) is made—

(a) in respect of the taxable insurance contract, or

(b) at or about the time when the taxable insurance contract is made and in connection with that contract, in respect of any insurance-related service,

by any person falling within sub-paragraph (2) above to any person who is or becomes the insured (or one of the insured) under the contract or to any person who acts, otherwise than in the course of a business, for or on behalf of such a person.

(6) In this paragraph—

"motor car" and "motor cycle" have the meaning given—

(a) by section 185(1) of the Road Traffic Act 1988; or

(b) in Northern Ireland, by Article 3(1) of the Road Traffic (Northern Ireland) Order 1995;

"supplier" does not include an insurer who supplies a car or motor cycle as a means of discharging liabilities arising by reason of a claim under an insurance contract.

Insurance relating to domestic appliances etc.

3.—(1) A premium under a taxable insurance contract relating to relevant goods falls within this paragraph if—

(a) the contract is arranged through a person falling within sub-paragraph (2) below, or

(b) the insurer under the contract is a person falling within that sub-paragraph,

unless the insurance is provided to the insured free of charge.

(2) A person falls within this sub-paragraph if—

(a) he is a supplier of relevant goods;

(b) he is connected with a supplier of relevant goods; or

(c) he pays—

(i) the whole or any part of the premium received under the taxable insurance contract, or

(ii) a fee connected with the arranging of that contract,

to a supplier of relevant goods or to a person who is connected with a supplier of relevant goods.

(3) Where a taxable insurance contract relating to relevant goods is arranged through a person who is connected with a supplier of relevant goods, the premium does not fall within this paragraph by virtue only of sub-paragraph (2)(b) above except to the extent that the premium is attributable to cover for a risk which relates to relevant goods supplied by a supplier of relevant goods with whom that person is connected.

(4) Where the insurer under a taxable insurance contract relating to relevant goods is connected with a supplier of relevant goods, the premium does not fall within this paragraph by virtue only of sub-paragraph (2)(b) above except to the extent that the premium is attributable to cover for a risk which relates to relevant goods supplied by a supplier of relevant goods with whom the insurer is connected.

(5) For the purposes of this paragraph, the cases where insurance is provided to the insured free of charge are those cases where no charge (whether by way of premium or otherwise) is made—

(a) in respect of the taxable insurance contract, or

(b) at or about the time when the taxable insurance contract is made and in connection with that contract, in respect of any insurance-related service,

by any person falling within sub-paragraph (2) above to any person who is or becomes the insured (or one of the insured) under the contract or to any person who acts, otherwise than in the course of a business, for or on behalf of such a person.

(6) In this paragraph—

"relevant goods" means any electrical or mechanical appliance of a kind—

(a) which is ordinarily used in or about the home; or

(b) which is ordinarily owned by private individuals and used by them for the purposes of leisure, amusement or entertainment;

"supplier" does not include an insurer who supplies relevant goods as a means of discharging liabilities arising by reason of a claim under an insurance contract.

(7) In sub-paragraph (6) above—

"appliance" includes any device, equipment or apparatus;

"the home" includes any private garden and any private garage or private workshop appurtenant to a dwelling.

Travel insurance

4.—(1) A premium under a taxable insurance contract relating to travel risks falls within this paragraph if—

(a) the contract is arranged through a person falling within sub-paragraph (2) below, or

(b) the insurer under the contract is a person falling within that sub-paragraph,

unless the insurance is provided to the insured free of charge.

(2) A person falls within this sub-paragraph if—

(a) he is a tour operator or travel agent;

(b) he is connected with a tour operator or travel agent; or

(c) he pays—

> (i) the whole or any part of the premium received under the contract, or
>
> (ii) a fee connected with the arranging of the contract,
>
> to a tour operator or travel agent or to a person who is connected with a tour operator or travel agent.

(3) Where a taxable insurance contract relating to travel risks is arranged through a person who is connected with a tour operator or travel agent, the premium does not fall within this paragraph by virtue only of sub-paragraph (2)(b) above except to the extent that the premium is attributable to cover for a risk which relates to services supplied by a tour operator or travel agent with whom that person is connected.

(4) Where the insurer under a taxable insurance contract relating to travel risks is connected with a tour operator or travel agent, the premium does not fall within this paragraph by virtue only of sub-paragraph (2)(b) above except to the extent that the premium is attributable to cover for a risk which relates to services supplied by a tour operator or travel agent with whom the insurer is connected.

(5) For the purposes of sub-paragraphs (3) and (4) above, a travel agent shall be treated as supplying any services whose provision he secures or arranges.

(6) For the purposes of this paragraph, the cases where insurance is provided to the insured free of charge are those cases where no charge (whether by way of premium or otherwise) is made—

> (a) in respect of the taxable insurance contract, or
>
> (b) at or about the time when the taxable insurance contract is made and in connection with that contract, in respect of any insurance-related service,

by any person falling within sub-paragraph (2) above to any person who is or becomes the insured (or one of the insured) under the contract or to any person who acts, otherwise than in the course of a business, for or on behalf of such a person.

(7) In this paragraph—

> "tour operator" includes any person who carries on a business which consists of or includes the provision, or the securing of the provision, of—
>
> > (a) services for the transport of travellers; or
> >
> > (b) accommodation for travellers;
>
> "travel agent" includes any person who carries on a business which consists of or includes the making of arrangements, whether directly or indirectly, with a tour operator for the transport or accommodation of travellers;
>
> "travel risks" means—
>
> > (a) risks associated with, or related to, travel or intended travel; or
> >
> > (b) risks to which a person travelling may be exposed at any place at which he may be in the course of his travel."

GENERAL NOTE

Suppliers of goods and services which are liable to VAT often arrange insurance, which is exempt from VAT, for some of their customers. Such suppliers often take a disproportionate margin on the insurance, rather than the taxable goods or services. To counter this an insurance premium tax ("IPT") charge of 17.5 per cent is introduced on such premiums, equivalent to the standard rate of VAT.

Para. 2

Insurance relating to cars and arranged by suppliers of cars is subject to the higher rate of IPT unless it is provided free.

Paras. 3 and 4

Similar treatment is applied to insurance relating to domestic appliances and arranged by suppliers of them and insurance relating to travel risks arranged by travel agents or tour operators.

The higher rate also extends to such insurance provided through or by persons connected within ICTA 1988, s.839 to the suppliers or arranged by or supplied by someone who passes a fee or commission relating to such insurance to one of the suppliers or someone connected to him.

SCHEDULE 5

INDIRECT TAXES: OVERPAYMENTS ETC.

PART I

UNJUST ENRICHMENT

Application of Part I

1.—(1) This Part of this Schedule has effect for the purposes of the following provisions (which make it a defence to a claim for repayment that the repayment would unjustly enrich the claimant), namely—

    (a) section 137A(3) of the Customs and Excise Management Act 1979 (excise duties);

    (b) paragraph 8(3) of Schedule 7 to the Finance Act 1994 (insurance premium tax); and

    (c) paragraph 14(3) of Schedule 5 to the Finance Act 1996 (landfill tax).

(2) Those provisions are referred to in this Part of this Schedule as unjust enrichment provisions.

(3) In this Part of this Schedule—

    "the Commissioners" means the Commissioners of Customs and Excise;

    "relevant repayment provision" means—

        (a) section 137A of the Customs and Excise Management Act 1979 (recovery of overpaid excise duty);

        (b) paragraph 8 of Schedule 7 to the Finance Act 1994 (recovery of overpaid insurance premium tax); or

        (c) paragraph 14 of Schedule 5 to the Finance Act 1996 (recovery of overpaid landfill tax);

    "relevant tax" means any duty of excise, insurance premium tax or landfill tax; and

    "subordinate legislation" has the same meaning as in the Interpretation Act 1978.

Disregard of business losses

2.—(1) This paragraph applies where—

    (a) there is an amount paid by way of relevant tax which (apart from an unjust enrichment provision) would fall to be repaid under a relevant repayment provision to any person ("the taxpayer"), and

    (b) the whole or a part of the cost of the payment of that amount to the Commissioners has, for practical purposes, been borne by a person other than the taxpayer.

(2) Where, in a case to which this paragraph applies, loss or damage has been or may be incurred by the taxpayer as a result of mistaken assumptions made in his case about the operation of any provisions relating to a relevant tax, that loss or damage shall be disregarded, except to the extent of the quantified amount, in the making of any determination—

    (a) of whether or to what extent the repayment of an amount to the taxpayer would enrich him; or

    (b) of whether or to what extent any enrichment of the taxpayer would be unjust.

(3) In sub-paragraph (2) above "the quantified amount" means the amount (if any) which is shown by the taxpayer to constitute the amount that would appropriately compensate him for loss or damage shown by him to have resulted, for any business carried on by him, from the making of the mistaken assumptions.

(4) The reference in sub-paragraph (2) above to provisions relating to a relevant tax is a reference to any provisions of—

    (a) any enactment, subordinate legislation or Community legislation (whether or not still in force) which relates to that tax or to any matter connected with it; or

    (b) any notice published by the Commissioners under or for the purposes of any such enactment or subordinate legislation.

(5) This paragraph has effect for the purposes of making any repayment on or after the day on which this Act is passed, even if the claim for that repayment was made before that day.

Reimbursement arrangements

3.—(1) The Commissioners may by regulations make provision for reimbursement arrangements made by any person to be disregarded for the purposes of any or all of the unjust enrichment provisions except where the arrangements—

(a) contain such provision as may be required by the regulations; and

(b) are supported by such undertakings to comply with the provisions of the arrangements as may be required by the regulations to be given to the Commissioners.

(2) In this paragraph "reimbursement arrangements" means any arrangements for the purposes of a claim under a relevant repayment provision which—

(a) are made by any person for the purpose of securing that he is not unjustly enriched by the repayment of any amount in pursuance of the claim; and

(b) provide for the reimbursement of persons who have for practical purposes borne the whole or any part of the cost of the original payment of that amount to the Commissioners.

(3) Without prejudice to the generality of sub-paragraph (1) above, the provision that may be required by regulations under this paragraph to be contained in reimbursement arrangements includes—

(a) provision requiring a reimbursement for which the arrangements provide to be made within such period after the repayment to which it relates as may be specified in the regulations;

(b) provision for the repayment of amounts to the Commissioners where those amounts are not reimbursed in accordance with the arrangements;

(c) provision requiring interest paid by the Commissioners on any amount repaid by them to be treated in the same way as that amount for the purposes of any requirement under the arrangements to make reimbursement or to repay the Commissioners;

(d) provision requiring such records relating to the carrying out of the arrangements as may be described in the regulations to be kept and produced to the Commissioners, or to an officer of theirs.

(4) Regulations under this paragraph may impose obligations on such persons as may be specified in the regulations—

(a) to make the repayments to the Commissioners that they are required to make in pursuance of any provisions contained in any reimbursement arrangements by virtue of sub-paragraph (3)(b) or (c) above;

(b) to comply with any requirements contained in any such arrangements by virtue of sub-paragraph (3)(d) above.

(5) Regulations under this paragraph may make provision for the form and manner in which, and the times at which, undertakings are to be given to the Commissioners in accordance with the regulations; and any such provision may allow for those matters to be determined by the Commissioners in accordance with the regulations.

(6) Regulations under this paragraph may—

(a) contain any such incidental, supplementary, consequential or transitional provision as appears to the Commissioners to be necessary or expedient; and

(b) make different provision for different circumstances.

(7) Regulations under this paragraph may have effect (irrespective of when the claim for repayment was made) for the purposes of the making of any repayment by the Commissioners after the time when the regulations are made; and, accordingly, such regulations may apply to arrangements made before that time.

(8) Regulations under this paragraph shall be made by statutory instrument subject to annulment in pursuance of a resolution of the House of Commons.

Contravention of requirement to repay Commissioners

4.—(1) Where any obligation is imposed by regulations made by virtue of paragraph 3(4) above, a contravention or failure to comply with that obligation shall, to the extent that it relates to amounts repaid under section 137A of the Customs and Excise Management Act 1979, attract a penalty under section 9 of the Finance Act 1994 (penalties in connection with excise duties).

(2) For the purposes of Schedule 7 to the Finance Act 1994 (insurance premium tax), a contravention or failure to comply with an obligation imposed by regulations made by virtue of paragraph 3(4) above shall be deemed, to the extent that it relates to amounts repaid under paragraph 8 of that Schedule (recovery of overpaid insurance premium tax), to be a failure to comply with a requirement falling within paragraph 17(1)(c) of that Schedule (breach of regulations).

(3) Paragraph 23 of Schedule 5 to the Finance Act 1996 (power to provide for penalty) shall have effect as if an obligation imposed by regulations made by virtue of paragraph 3(4) above were, to the extent that it relates to amounts repaid under paragraph 14 of that Schedule (recovery of overpaid landfill tax), a requirement imposed by regulations under Part III of that Act; and the provisions of that Schedule in relation to penalties under Part V of that Schedule shall have effect accordingly.

Repayments

5.—(1) For subsection (4) of section 137A of the Customs and Excise Management Act 1979 (time limit on recovery of overpaid excise duty) there shall be substituted the following subsection—

"(4) The Commissioners shall not be liable, on a claim made under this section, to repay any amount paid to them more than three years before the making of the claim."

(2) For sub-paragraphs (4) and (5) of paragraph 8 of Schedule 7 to the Finance Act 1994 (time limit on recovery of overpaid insurance premium tax) there shall be substituted the following sub-paragraph—

"(4) The Commissioners shall not be liable, on a claim made under this paragraph, to repay any amount paid to them more than three years before the making of the claim."

(3) For sub-paragraph (4) of paragraph 14 of Schedule 5 to the Finance Act 1996 (time limit on recovery of overpaid landfill tax) there shall be substituted the following sub-paragraph—

"(4) The Commissioners shall not be liable, on a claim made under this paragraph, to repay any amount paid to them more than three years before the making of the claim."

Assessments

6.—(1) In each of the enactments specified in sub-paragraph (2) below (which provide for the time limits applying to the making of assessments), for the words "six years", wherever they occur, there shall be substituted the words "three years".

(2) Those enactments are—

(a) section 12(4)(a) and (5) of the Finance Act 1994 (excise duties);

(b) paragraph 26(1) and (4) of Schedule 7 to that Act (insurance premium tax); and

(c) paragraph 33(1) and (4) of Schedule 5 to the Finance Act 1996 (landfill tax).

Part III

Interest

Interest on overpaid air passenger duty

7.—(1) Paragraph 9 of Schedule 6 to the Finance Act 1994 (interest payable by the Commissioners in connection with air passenger duty) shall have effect, and be deemed always to have had effect, with the amendments for which this paragraph provides.

(2) After sub-paragraph (1) there shall be inserted the following sub-paragraph—

"(1A) In sub-paragraph (1) above the reference to an amount which the Commissioners are liable to repay in consequence of the making of a payment that was not due is a reference to only so much of that amount as is the subject of a claim that the Commissioners are required to satisfy or have satisfied."

(3) For sub-paragraph (6) (claims for interest to be made within six years of discovery of error) there shall be substituted the following sub-paragraph—

"(6) A claim under this paragraph shall not be made more than three years after the end of the applicable period to which it relates;"

(4) For sub-paragraph (7) there shall be substituted the following sub-paragraph—

"(7) Any reference in this paragraph to the authorisation by the Commissioners of the payment of any amount includes a reference to the discharge by way of set-off of the Commissioners' liability to pay that amount."

8.—(1) In sub-paragraph (2) of that paragraph (applicable period), the words after paragraph (b) shall be omitted; and the following sub-paragraphs shall be substituted for sub-paragraphs (3) and (4)—

"(2A) In determining the applicable period for the purposes of this paragraph there shall be left out of account any period by which the Commissioners' authorisation of the payment of interest is delayed by the conduct of the person who claims the interest.

(2B) The reference in sub-paragraph (2A) above to a period by which the Commissioners' authorisation of the payment of interest is delayed by the conduct of the person who claims it includes, in particular, any period which is referable to—

(a) any unreasonable delay in the making of the claim for interest or in the making of any claim for the repayment of the amount on which interest is claimed;

   (b) any failure by that person or a person acting on his behalf or under his influence to provide the Commissioners—

      (i) at or before the time of the making of a claim, or

      (ii) subsequently in response to a request for information by the Commissioners,

   with all the information required by them to enable the existence and amount of the claimant's entitlement to a repayment, and to interest on the amount of that repayment, to be determined; and

   (c) the making, as part of or in association with either—

      (i) the claim for interest, or

      (ii) any claim for the payment or repayment of the amount on which interest is claimed,

   of a claim to anything to which the claimant was not entitled.

   (3) In determining for the purposes of sub-paragraph (2B) above whether any period of delay is referable to a failure by any person to provide information in response to a request by the Commissioners, there shall be taken to be so referable, except so far as may be prescribed, any period which—

   (a) begins with the date on which the Commissioners require that person to provide information which they reasonably consider relevant to the matter to be determined; and

   (b) ends with the earliest date on which it would be reasonable for the Commissioners to conclude—

      (i) that they have received a complete answer to their request for information;

      (ii) that they have received all that they need in answer to that request; or

      (iii) that it is unnecessary for them to be provided with any information in answer to that request."

   (2) Subparagraph (1) above shall have effect for the purposes of determining whether any period beginning on or after the day on which this Act is passed is left out of account.

Interest on overpaid insurance premium tax

   9.—(1) Paragraph 22 of Schedule 7 to the Finance Act 1994 (interest payable by the Commissioners in connection with insurance premium tax) shall have effect, and be deemed always to have had effect, with the amendments for which this paragraph provides.

   (2) After sub-paragraph (1) there shall be inserted the following sub-paragraph—

   "(1A) In sub-paragraph (1) above—

   (a) the reference in paragraph (a) to an amount which the Commissioners are liable to repay in consequence of the making of a payment that was not due is a reference to only so much of that amount as is the subject of a claim that the Commissioners are required to satisfy or have satisfied; and

   (b) the amounts referred to in paragraph (c) do not include any amount payable under this paragraph."

   (3) For sub-paragraph (9) of that paragraph (claims for interest to be made within six years of discovery of error) there shall be substituted the following sub-paragraph—

   "(9) A claim under this paragraph shall not be made more than three years after the end of the applicable period to which it relates."

   (4) For sub-paragraph (10) there shall be substituted the following sub-paragraph—

   "(10) References in this paragraph to the authorisation by the Commissioners of the payment of any amount include references to the discharge by way of set-off of the Commissioners' liability to pay that amount."

   10.—(1) For sub-paragraphs (5) to (7) of that paragraph (periods left out of account in computing periods for which the Commissioners are liable to interest) there shall be substituted the following sub-paragraphs—

   "(5) In determining the applicable period for the purposes of this paragraph there shall be left out of account any period by which the Commissioners' authorisation of the payment of interest is delayed by the conduct of the person who claims the interest.

   (5A) The reference in sub-paragraph (5) above to a period by which the Commissioners' authorisation of the payment of interest is delayed by the conduct of the person who claims it includes, in particular, any period which is referable to—

   (a) any unreasonable delay in the making of the claim for interest or in the making of any claim for the payment or repayment of the amount on which interest is claimed;

    (b) any failure by that person or a person acting on his behalf or under his influence to provide the Commissioners—
        (i) at or before the time of the making of a claim, or
        (ii) subsequently in response to a request for information by the Commissioners,
    with all the information required by them to enable the existence and amount of the claimant's entitlement to a payment or repayment, and to interest on that payment or repayment, to be determined; and

    (c) the making, as part of or in association with either—
        (i) the claim for interest, or
        (ii) any claim for the payment or repayment of the amount on which interest is claimed,
    of a claim to anything to which the claimant was not entitled.

    (6) In determining for the purposes of sub-paragraph (5A) above whether any period of delay is referable to a failure by any person to provide information in response to a request by the Commissioners, there shall be taken to be so referable, except so far as may be provided for by regulations, any period which—

    (a) begins with the date on which the Commissioners require that person to provide information which they reasonably consider relevant to the matter to be determined; and

    (b) ends with the earliest date on which it would be reasonable for the Commissioners to conclude—
        (i) that they have received a complete answer to their request for information;
        (ii) that they have received all that they need in answer to that request; or
        (iii) that it is unnecessary for them to be provided with any information in answer to that request."

    (2) Sub-paragraph (1) above shall have effect for the purposes of determining whether any period beginning on or after the day on which this Act is passed is left out of account.

Interest on overpaid landfill tax

    11.—(1) Paragraph 29 of Schedule 5 to the Finance Act 1996 (interest payable by the Commissioners in connection with landfill tax) shall have effect, and be deemed always to have had effect, with the amendments for which this paragraph provides.

    (2) After sub-paragraph (1) there shall be inserted the following sub-paragraph—
    "(1A) In sub-paragraph (1) above—

    (a) the reference in paragraph (a) to an amount which the Commissioners are liable to repay in consequence of the making of a payment that was not due is a reference to only so much of that amount as is the subject of a claim that the Commissioners are required to satisfy or have satisfied; and

    (b) the amounts referred to in paragraph (c) do not include any amount payable under this paragraph."

    (3) For sub-paragraph (8) (claims for interest to be made within six years of discovery of error) there shall be substituted the following sub-paragraph—
    "(8) A claim under this paragraph shall not be made more than three years after the end of the applicable period to which it relates."

    (4) For sub-paragraph (9) there shall be substituted the following sub-paragraph—
    "(9) References in this paragraph—
    (a) to receiving payment of any amount from the Commissioners, or
    (b) to the authorisation by the Commissioners of the payment of any amount,
    include references to the discharge by way of set-off (whether in accordance with regulations under paragraph 42 or 43 below or otherwise) of the Commissioners' liability to pay that amount."

    12.—(1) For sub-paragraphs (4) to (6) of that paragraph (periods left out of account in computing periods for which the Commissioners are liable to interest) there shall be substituted the following sub-paragraphs—
    "(4) In determining the applicable period for the purposes of this paragraph there shall be left out of account any period by which the Commissioners' authorisation of the payment of interest is delayed by the conduct of the person who claims the interest.

    (4A) The reference in sub-paragraph (4) above to a period by which the Commissioners' authorisation of the payment of interest is delayed by the conduct of the person who claims it includes, in particular, any period which is referable to—

    (a) any unreasonable delay in the making of the claim for interest or in the making of any claim for the payment or repayment of the amount on which interest is claimed;

(b) any failure by that person or a person acting on his behalf or under his influence to provide the Commissioners—

    (i) at or before the time of the making of a claim, or

    (ii) subsequently in response to a request for information by the Commissioners,

with all the information required by them to enable the existence and amount of the claimant's entitlement to a payment or repayment, and to interest on that payment or repayment, to be determined; and

(c) the making, as part of or in association with either—

    (i) the claim for interest, or

    (ii) any claim for the payment or repayment of the amount on which interest is claimed,

of a claim to anything to which the claimant was not entitled.

(5) In determining for the purposes of sub-paragraph (4A) above whether any period of delay is referable to a failure by any person to provide information in response to a request by the Commissioners, there shall be taken to be so referable, except so far as may be provided for by regulations, any period which—

(a) begins with the date on which the Commissioners require that person to provide information which they reasonably consider relevant to the matter to be determined; and

(b) ends with the earliest date on which it would be reasonable for the Commissioners to conclude—

    (i) that they have received a complete answer to their request for information;

    (ii) that they have received all that they need in answer to that request; or

    (iii) that it is unnecessary for them to be provided with any information in answer to that request."

(2) Sub-paragraph (1) above shall have effect for the purposes of determining whether any period beginning on or after the day on which this Act is passed is left out of account.

PART IV

SET-OFF INVOLVING LANDFILL TAX

13.—(1) In paragraph 42 of Schedule 5 to the Finance Act 1996 (set-off of amounts), after sub-paragraph (4) there shall be inserted the following sub-paragraph—

"(4A) The regulations may provide for any limitation on the time within which the Commissioners are entitled to take steps for recovering any amount due to them in respect of landfill tax to be disregarded, in such cases as may be described in the regulations, in determining whether any person is under such a duty to pay as is mentioned in sub-paragraph (1)(a) above."

(2) In paragraph 43 of that Schedule (set-off of amounts), after sub-paragraph (4) there shall be inserted the following sub-paragraph—

"(4A) The regulations may provide for any limitation on the time within which the Commissioners are entitled to take steps for recovering any amount due to them in respect of any of the taxes under their care and management to be disregarded, in such cases as may be described in the regulations, in determining whether any person is under such a duty to pay as is mentioned in sub-paragraph (1)(a) above."

PART V

RECOVERY OF EXCESS PAYMENTS BY THE COMMISSIONERS

Assessment for excessive repayment

14.—(1) Where—

(a) any amount has been paid at any time to any person by way of a repayment under a relevant repayment provision, and

(b) the amount paid exceeded the amount which the Commissioners were liable at that time to repay to that person,

the Commissioners may, to the best of their judgement, assess the excess paid to that person and notify it to him.

(2) Where any person is liable to pay any amount to the Commissioners in pursuance of an obligation imposed by virtue of paragraph 3(4)(a) above, the Commissioners may, to the best of their judgement, assess the amount due from that person and notify it to him.

(3) In this paragraph "relevant repayment provision" means—
(a) section 137A of the Customs and Excise Management Act 1979 (recovery of overpaid excise duty);
(b) paragraph 8 of Schedule 7 to the Finance Act 1994 (recovery of overpaid insurance premium tax); or
(c) paragraph 14 of Schedule 5 to the Finance Act 1996 (recovery of overpaid landfill tax).

Assessment for overpayments of interest

15.—(1) Where—
(a) any amount has been paid to any person by way of interest under a relevant interest provision, but
(b) that person was not entitled to that amount under that provision,
the Commissioners may, to the best of their judgement, assess the amount so paid to which that person was not entitled and notify it to him.
(2) In this paragraph "relevant interest provision" means—
(a) paragraph 9 of Schedule 6 to the Finance Act 1994 (interest payable by the Commissioners on overpayments of air passenger duty);
(b) paragraph 22 of Schedule 7 to that Act (interest payable by the Commissioners on overpayments etc. of insurance premium tax); or
(c) paragraph 29 of Schedule 5 to the Finance Act 1996 (interest payable by the Commissioners on overpayments etc. of landfill tax).

Assessments under paragraphs 14 and 15

16.—(1) An assessment under paragraph 14 or 15 above shall not be made more than two years after the time when evidence of facts sufficient in the opinion of the Commissioners to justify the making of the assessment comes to the knowledge of the Commissioners.
(2) Where an amount has been assessed and notified to any person under paragraph 14 or 15 above, it shall be recoverable (subject to any provision having effect in accordance with paragraph 19 below) as if it were relevant tax due from him.
(3) Sub-paragraph (2) above does not have effect if, or to the extent that, the assessment in question has been withdrawn or reduced.

Interest on amounts assessed

17.—(1) Where an assessment is made under paragraph 14 or 15 above, the whole of the amount assessed shall carry interest at the rate applicable under section 197 of the Finance Act 1996 from the date on which the assessment is notified until payment.
(2) Where any person is liable to interest under sub-paragraph (1) above the Commissioners may assess the amount due by way of interest and notify it to him.
(3) Without prejudice to the power to make assessments under this paragraph for later periods, the interest to which an assessment under this paragraph may relate shall be confined to interest for a period of no more than two years ending with the time when the assessment under this paragraph is made.
(4) Interest under this paragraph shall be paid without any deduction of income tax.
(5) A notice of assessment under this paragraph shall specify a date, being not later than the date of the notice, to which the amount of interest is calculated; and, if the interest continues to accrue after that date, a further assessment or assessments may be made under this paragraph in respect of amounts which so accrue.
(6) If, within such period as may be notified by the Commissioners to the person liable for interest under sub-paragraph (1) above, the amount referred to in that sub-paragraph is paid, it shall be treated for the purposes of that sub-paragraph as paid on the date specified as mentioned in sub-paragraph (5) above.
(7) Where an amount has been assessed and notified to any person under this paragraph it shall be recoverable as if it were relevant tax due from him.
(8) Sub-paragraph (7) above does not have effect if, or to the extent that, the assessment in question has been withdrawn or reduced.

Supplementary assessments

18. If it appears to the Commissioners that the amount which ought to have been assessed in an assessment under paragraph 14, 15 or 17 above exceeds the amount which was so assessed, then—
(a) under the same paragraph as that assessment was made, and
(b) on or before the last day on which that assessment could have been made,
the Commissioners may make a supplementary assessment of the amount of the excess and shall notify the person concerned accordingly.

Review of decisions and appeals

19.—(1) Sections 14 to 16 of the Finance Act 1994 (review and appeals) shall have effect in relation to any decision which—
(a) is contained in an assessment under paragraph 14, 15 or 17 above,
(b) is a decision about whether any amount is due to the Commissioners or about how much is due, and
(c) is made in a case in which the relevant repayment provision is section 137A of the Customs and Excise Management Act 1979 or the relevant interest provision is paragraph 9 of Schedule 6 to the Finance Act 1994,

as if that decision were such a decision as is mentioned in section 14(1)(b) of that Act of 1994.

(2) Sections 59 and 60 of that Act of 1994 (review and appeal in the case of insurance premium tax) shall have effect in relation to any decision which—
(a) is contained in an assessment under paragraph 14, 15 or 17 above,
(b) is a decision about whether any amount is due to the Commissioners or about how much is due, and
(c) is made in a case in which the relevant repayment provision is paragraph 8 of Schedule 7 to that Act or the relevant interest provision is paragraph 22 of that Schedule,

as if that decision were a decision to which section 59 of that Act applies.

(3) Sections 54 to 56 of the Finance Act 1996 (review and appeal in the case of landfill tax) shall have effect in relation to any decision which—
(a) is contained in an assessment under paragraph 14, 15 or 17 above,
(b) is a decision about whether any amount is due to the Commissioners or about how much is due, and
(c) is made in a case in which the relevant repayment provision is paragraph 14 of Schedule 5 to that Act or the relevant interest provision is paragraph 29 of that Schedule,

as if that decision were a decision to which section 54 of that Act applies.

Interpretation of Part V

20.—(1) In this Part of this Schedule "the Commissioners" means the Commissioners of Customs and Excise.

(2) In this Part of this Schedule "relevant tax", in relation to any assessment, mean—
(a) a duty of excise if the assessment relates to—
(i) a repayment of an amount paid by way of such a duty,
(ii) an overpayment of interest under paragraph 9 of Schedule 6 to the Finance Act 1994, or
(iii) interest on an amount specified in an assessment in relation to which the relevant tax is a duty of excise;
(b) insurance premium tax if the assessment relates to—
(i) a repayment of an amount paid by way of such tax,
(ii) an overpayment of interest under paragraph 22 of Schedule 7 to the Finance Act 1994, or
(iii) interest on an amount specified in an assessment in relation to which the relevant tax is insurance premium tax;
and
(c) landfill tax if the assessment relates to—
(i) a repayment of an amount paid by way of such tax,
(ii) an overpayment of interest under paragraph 29 of Schedule 5 to the Finance Act 1996, or
(iii) interest on an amount specified in an assessment in relation to which the relevant tax is landfill tax.

(3) For the purposes of this Part of this Schedule notification to a personal representative, trustee in bankruptcy, interim or permanent trustee, receiver, liquidator or person otherwise acting in a representative capacity in relation to another shall be treated as notification to the person in relation to whom he so acts.

Consequential amendment

21. In section 197(2) of the Finance Act 1996 (enactments for which interest rates are set under section 197), after paragraph (d) there shall be inserted "and
(e) paragraph 17 of Schedule 5 to the Finance Act 1997 (interest on amounts repayable in respect of overpayments by the Commissioners in connection with excise duties, insurance premium tax and landfill tax)."

GENERAL NOTE

The Schedule applies the new system of a three year time limit for assessment and repayment of tax to excise duties, insurance premium tax and landfill tax.

Part I

This deals with the restriction of repayments where it would unjustly enrich the taxpayer to repay him.

Para. 1

This sets out the application of the unjust enrichment provisions to excise duties, insurance premium tax and landfill tax and defines terms used in this part of the Schedule.

Para. 2

Where tax otherwise due to be repaid has been borne for practical purposes by a person other than the taxpayer, he must show a quantified amount to compensate him for loss or damage in order to escape the unjust enrichment provisions.

Para. 3

The Customs and Excise are authorised to make regulations to police reimbursement arrangements under which taxpayers refund to their customers overpaid tax which has been repaid to them.

Para. 4

Penalties apply to contravention of the regulations under para. 3.

Part II

This deals with the new system of time limits.

Para. 5

Taxpayers cannot reclaim amounts paid by way of excise duty, insurance premium tax and landfill tax which was overpaid more than three years before the claim was made.

Para. 6

Similarly, the six year time limit for making assessments is reduced to three years.

Part III

This part limits the Customs and Excise's liability to pay statutory interest on tax repaid. A claim for interest must be made within three years of the end of the period to which it relates. Interest is limited to that payable on the net amount after any set off. In calculating the period for which interest is payable account will be taken of unreasonable delays by a claimant in making a claim or in providing information to establish its amount or validity. Paragraphs 7 and 8 deal with air passenger duty, paras. 9 and 10 with insurance premium tax and paras. 11 and 12 with landfill tax.

Part IV
Para. 13

The Customs and Excise already have power to set off against an amount of landfill tax which they are liable to repay any sum due from the taxpayer, and to set off amounts due in respect of landfill tax against sums owed to the taxpayer in respect of other taxes. No time limit will apply to recovery of any amount by the Customs and Excise under these provisions.

Part V

This Part provides the machinery for recovering excess payments made by the Customs and Excise.

Para. 14

Assessments may be raised to recover excess repayments of excise duty, insurance premium tax and landfill tax, including unjust enrichment cases.

Para. 15

Similarly, assessments may be raised to recover overpaid interest in respect of air passenger duty, insurance premium tax and landfill tax.

Para. 16

A two year time limit applies to assessments under paras. 14 and 15.

Para. 17

Interest runs on assessments under paras. 14 and 15.

Para. 18

Supplementary assessments may be raised in relation to paras. 14, 15 and 17.

Para. 19

Taxpayers have a right of review and of appeal to the VAT and Duties Tribunal in relation to assessments under paras. 14, 15 and 17.

Para. 20

This is a general interpretation paragraph.

Para. 21

The rate of interest under para. 17 will be set by Treasury Order.

Section 50   SCHEDULE 6

ASSESSMENTS FOR EXCISE DUTY PURPOSES

Assessment of amounts payable to the Commissioners

1.—(1) After section 12 of the Finance Act 1994 there shall be inserted the following sections—

"Other assessments relating to excise duty matters

12A.—(1) This subsection applies where any relevant excise duty relief other than an excepted relief—

(a) has been given but ought not to have been given, or

(b) would not have been given had the facts been known or been as they later turn out to be.

(2) Where subsection (1) above applies, the Commissioners may assess the amount of the relief given as being excise duty due from the liable person and notify him or his representative accordingly.

(3) Where an amount has been assessed as due from any person under—

(a) subsection (2) above,

(b) section 94 or 96 of the Management Act, or

(c) section 10, 13, 14, 23 or 24 of the Hydrocarbon Oil Duties Act 1979,

and notice has been given accordingly, that amount shall, subject to any appeal under section 16 below, be deemed to be an amount of excise duty due from that person and may be recovered accordingly, unless, or except to the extent that, the assessment has subsequently been withdrawn or reduced.

(4) No assessment under any of the provisions referred to in subsection (3) above, or under section 61 or 167 of the Management Act, shall be made at any time after whichever is the earlier of the following times, that is to say—

(a) subject to subsection (6) below, the end of the period of three years beginning with the relevant time; and

(b) the end of the period of one year beginning with the day on which evidence of facts, sufficient in the opinion of the Commissioners to justify the making of the assessment, comes to their knowledge.

(5) Subsection (4) above shall be without prejudice, where further evidence comes to the knowledge of the Commissioners at any time after the making the assessment concerned, to the making of a further assessment within the period applicable by virtue of that subsection in relation to that further assessment.

(6) Subsection (4) above shall have effect as if the reference in paragraph (a) to three years were a reference to twenty years in any case where the assessment has been postponed or otherwise affected by, or the power to make the assessment arises out of, conduct

falling within subsection (5)(a) or (b) of section 12 above (construed in accordance with subsection (7) of that section).

Section 12A: supplementary provisions

12B.—(1) For the purposes of section 12A above and this section, relevant excise duty relief has been given if (and only if)—

(a) an amount of excise duty which a person is liable to pay has been remitted or payment of an amount of excise duty which a person is liable to pay has been waived;

(b) an amount of excise duty has been repaid to a person;

(c) an amount by way of drawback of excise duty has been paid to a person;

(d) an allowance of excise duty in any amount has been made to a person;

(e) an amount by way of rebate has been allowed to a person;

(f) the liability of a person to repay an amount paid by way of drawback of excise duty has been waived;

(g) an amount has been paid to a person under section 20(3) of the Hydrocarbon Oil Duties Act 1979 (payments in respect of contaminated or accidentally mixed oil); or

(h) an amount of relief has been allowed to a person by virtue of section 20AA of that Act (power to allow reliefs), or in accordance with paragraph 10 of Schedule 3 to that Act (power to make regulations for the purpose of relieving from excise duty oil intended for exportation or shipment as stores);

and the amount of the relief is the amount mentioned in relation to the relief in this subsection.

(2) For the purposes of section 12A above the relevant time is—

(a) in the case of an assessment under section 61 of the Management Act, the time when the ship or aircraft in question returned to a place within the United Kingdom;

(b) in the case of an assessment under section 94 of that Act, the time at which the goods in question were warehoused;

(c) in the case of an assessment under that section as it has effect by virtue of section 95 of that Act, the time when the goods in question were lawfully taken from the warehouse;

(d) in the case of an assessment under section 96 of that Act, the time when the goods in question were moved by pipe-line or notified as goods to be moved by pipe-line;

(e) in the case of an assessment under section 167 of that Act—

(i) if the assessment relates to unpaid duty, the time when the duty became payable or, if later, the time when the document in question was delivered or the statement in question was made; and

(ii) if the assessment relates to an overpayment, the time when the overpayment was made;

(f) in the case of an assessment under section 10, 13, 14 or 23 of the Hydrocarbon Oil Duties Act 1979, the time of the action which gave rise to the power to assess;

(g) in the case of an assessment under section 24(4A) or (4B) of that Act, the time when the rebate was allowed or the oil was delivered without payment of duty (as the case may be);

(h) in the case of an assessment under section 12A(2) above, the time when the relevant excise duty relief in question was given.

(3) In section 12A above "the liable person" means—

(a) in the case of excise duty which has been remitted or repaid under section 130 of the Management Act on the basis that goods were lost or destroyed while in a warehouse, the proprietor of the goods or the occupier of the warehouse;

(b) in the case of a rebate which has been allowed on any oil under section 11 of the Hydrocarbon Oil Duties Act 1979, the person to whom the rebate was allowed or the occupier of any warehouse from which the oil was delivered for home use;

(c) in the case of a rebate allowed on any petrol under section 13A of that Act, the person to whom the rebate was allowed or the occupier of any warehouse from which the petrol was delivered for home use;

(d) in any other case, the person mentioned in subsection (1) above to whom the relief in question was given.

(4) In section 12A above—

"excepted relief" means any relief which is given by the making of a repayment on a claim made under section 137A of the Management Act;

"representative", in relation to any person from whom the Commissioners assess an amount as being excise duty due, means his personal representative, trustee in bankruptcy or interim or permanent trustee, any receiver or liquidator appointed in relation to him or any of his property or any other person acting in a representative capacity in relation to him."

(2) After section 14(1)(b) of that Act there shall be inserted the following paragraph—

"(ba) any decision by the Commissioners to assess any person to excise duty under section 12A(2) above, section 61, 94, 96 or 167 of the Management Act or section 10, 13, 14, 23 or 24 of the Hydrocarbon Oil Duties Act 1979, or as to the amount of duty to which a person is to be assessed under any of those provisions;".

(3) In sections 12(8) and 13(7) of that Act (definition of "representative" for the purposes of sections 12 and 13), for "or trustee in bankruptcy," there shall be substituted ", trustee in bankruptcy or interim or permanent trustee,".

Assessments in cases of a deficiency in stores

2.—(1) After subsection (7) of section 61 of the Customs and Excise Management Act 1979 (duty payable where deficiency or excess deficiency discovered in goods on return of ship or aircraft to United Kingdom) there shall be inserted the following subsection—

"(7A) No amount of excise duty shall be payable under subsection (7) above unless the Commissioners have assessed that amount as being excise duty due from the master of the ship or the commander of the aircraft and notified him or his representative accordingly."

(2) In subsection (8) of that section (duty payable under subsection (7) recoverable as a civil debt) after "duty" there shall be inserted ", other than excise duty,".

(3) After that subsection there shall be inserted the following subsection—

"(8A) An amount of excise duty assessed as being due under subsection (7A) above shall, unless, or except to the extent that, the assessment has subsequently been withdrawn or reduced and subject to any appeal under section 16 of the Finance Act 1994, be recoverable summarily as a civil debt."

(4) In section 1(1) of that Act (interpretation), after the definition of "registered excise dealers and shippers regulations" there shall be inserted—

" "representative", in relation to any person from whom the Commissioners assess an amount as being excise duty due, means his personal representative, trustee in bankruptcy or interim or permanent trustee, any receiver or liquidator appointed in relation to him or any of his property or any other person acting in a representative capacity in relation to him;".

Assessments in cases of a deficiency in warehoused goods

3.—(1) Section 94 of the Customs and Excise Management Act 1979 shall be amended in accordance with sub-paragraphs (2) to (6) below.

(2) In subsection (3) (power to require payment of duty or repayment of drawback or allowance where warehoused goods are deficient), for the words from "require" to the end there shall be substituted the following paragraphs—

"(a) require the occupier of the warehouse or the proprietor of the goods to pay immediately any duty, other than excise duty, chargeable or deemed under warehousing regulations to be chargeable on the relevant goods or, in the case of goods warehoused on drawback which could not lawfully be entered for home use, an amount equal to any drawback or allowance of such duty paid in respect of the relevant goods;

(b) assess, as being excise duty due from the occupier of the warehouse or the proprietor of the goods, the excise duty chargeable or deemed under warehousing regulations to be chargeable on the relevant goods or, in the case of goods warehoused on drawback which could not lawfully be entered for home use, an amount equal to any drawback or allowance of excise duty paid in respect of the relevant goods."

(3) After subsection (3) there shall be inserted the following subsection—

"(3A) Where the Commissioners make an assessment under subsection (3)(b) above they shall notify the person assessed or his representative accordingly."

(4) In subsection (4) for "(3)" there shall be substituted "(3)(a)".

(5) After subsection (4) there shall be inserted the following subsections—

"(4A) If—

(a) the occupier of the warehouse or the proprietor of the goods refuses to pay any amount of excise duty to which he has been assessed under subsection (3)(b) above, and

(b) the conditions set out in subsection (4B) below are fulfilled, he shall be liable on summary conviction to a penalty of double that amount.

(4B) The conditions are that—

(a) the period of forty-five days referred to in section 14(3) of the Finance Act 1994 (period during which review may be required) has expired;

(b) on any review under Chapter II of Part I of that Act the Commissioners' decision ("the original decision") in relation to the assessment has been confirmed (or treated as confirmed by virtue of section 15(2) of that Act), or confirmed subject only to a reduction in the amount of duty due under the assessment; and

(c) the final result of any further appeal is that the original decision has been confirmed, subject only to any reduction in the amount of duty due under the assessment; and "final result" means the result of the last of any such appeals, against which no appeal may be made (whether because of expiry of time or for any other reason).

(4C) Where the amount of excise duty due under subsection (3)(b) above is reduced in consequence of a review or appeal, the penalty to which the person assessed is liable under subsection (4A) above shall be a penalty of double the reduced amount."

(6) After subsection (5) there shall be inserted the following subsection—

"(5A) In this section "the relevant goods" means the missing goods or the whole or any part of the deficiency, as the Commissioners see fit."

(7) In section 95 of that Act (application of section 94 to certain goods in the course of removal from warehouse), in subsection (2)(b) (section 94 to apply with the omission of references in subsections (3) and (4) to the occupier of the warehouse) for "and (4)" there shall be substituted ", (4) and (4A)".

Assessments in cases of a deficiency in goods moved by pipe-line

4.—(1) Section 96 of the Customs and Excise Management Act 1979 shall be amended in accordance with sub-paragraphs (2) to (6) below.

(2) In subsection (2) (power to require payment of unpaid or repaid duty, or repayment of drawback, where goods moved by pipe-line are deficient) for the words from "require" to the end there shall be substituted the following paragraphs—

"(a) require the owner of the pipe-line or the proprietor of the goods to pay immediately any duty, other than excise duty, unpaid or repaid on the relevant goods or, as the case may be, an amount equal to any drawback of such duty paid on the relevant goods;

(b) assess, as being excise duty due from the owner of the pipe-line or the proprietor of the goods, the excise duty unpaid or repaid on the relevant goods or, as the case may be, an amount equal to any drawback of excise duty paid on the relevant goods."

(3) After subsection (2) there shall be inserted the following subsection—

"(2A) Where the Commissioners make an assessment under subsection (2)(b) above they shall notify the person assessed or his representative accordingly."

(4) In subsection (3) for "(2)" there shall be substituted "(2)(a)".

(5) After subsection (3) there shall be inserted the following subsections—

"(3A) If—

(a) any person refuses to pay any amount of excise duty to which he has been assessed under subsection (2)(b) above, and

(b) the conditions set out in paragraphs (a) to (c) of section 94(4B) above (exhaustion of opportunities for review and appeal) are fulfilled,

he shall be liable on summary conviction to a penalty of double that amount.

(3B) Where the amount of excise duty due under subsection (2)(b) above is reduced in consequence of a review or appeal, the penalty to which the person assessed is liable under subsection (3A) above shall be a penalty of double the reduced amount."

(6) After subsection (5) there shall be inserted the following subsection—

"(5A) In this section "the relevant goods" means the missing goods or the whole or any part of the deficiency, as the Commissioners see fit."

Assessments in cases of untrue declarations etc.

5. After section 167(4) of the Customs and Excise Management Act 1979 (recovery as a debt due to the Crown or as a civil debt of amounts of duty not paid, and of overpayments in respect of drawback etc. made, by reason of untrue declaration etc.) there shall be inserted the following subsection—

"(5) An amount of excise duty, or the amount of an overpayment in respect of any drawback, allowance, rebate or repayment of any excise duty, shall not be recoverable as mentioned in subsection (4) above unless the Commissioners have assessed the amount of the duty or of the overpayment as being excise duty due from the person mentioned in subsection (1) or (3) above and notified him or his representative accordingly."

Assessments relating to hydrocarbon oil duty

6.—(1) In section 10(3) of the Hydrocarbon Oil Duties Act 1979 (power to recover excise duty where restrictions on use of duty-free oil infringed), for the words from "recover" to the end there shall be substituted "assess an amount equal to the excise duty on like oil at the rate in force at the time of the contravention as being excise duty due from him, and notify him or his representative accordingly.".

(2) In section 13(1) of that Act (power to recover rebate where heavy oil is misused), for the words from "recover" to the end there shall be substituted "assess an amount equal to the rebate on like oil at the rate in force at the time of the contravention as being excise duty due from him, and notify him or his representative accordingly."

(3) In section 14(4) of that Act (power to recover rebate where light oil delivered for use as furnace fuel is misused), for the words from "recover" to the end there shall be substituted "assess the amount of rebate allowed on the oil as being excise duty due from him, and notify him or his representative accordingly."

(4) After subsection (1A) of section 23 of that Act (prohibition on use of road fuel gas on which duty has not been paid) there shall be inserted the following subsection—

"(1B) Where any person—

(a) uses as fuel in, or

(b) takes as fuel into,

a road vehicle any road fuel gas on which the excise duty chargeable under section 8 above has not been paid, the Commissioners may assess the amount of that duty as being excise duty due from that person and notify him or his representative accordingly."

(5) In subsection (2) of that section, for "subsection (1)(b)" there shall be substituted "subsections (1)(b) and (1B)(b)".

(6) After subsection (4) of section 24 of that Act (control of use of duty-free and rebated oil) there shall be inserted the following subsections—

"(4A) Where—

(a) a rebate of duty is allowed on any oil, and

(b) a person contravenes or fails to comply with any requirement which, by virtue of any regulations made under this section, is a condition of allowing the rebate,

the Commissioners may assess an amount equal to the rebate as being excise duty due from that person, and notify him or his representative accordingly.

(4B) Where—

(a) any oil is delivered without payment of duty, and

(b) a person contravenes or fails to comply with any requirement which, by virtue of any regulations made under this section, is a condition of allowing the oil to be delivered without payment of duty,

the Commissioners may assess an amount equal to the excise duty on like oil at the rate in force at the time of the contravention or failure to comply as being excise duty due from that person, and notify him or his representative accordingly."

(7) In the Table set out in section 27(3) of that Act (interpretation), under the heading "Management Act" there shall be inserted at the appropriate place " "representative" ".

Commencement

7. This Schedule shall come into force on such day as the Commissioners of Customs and Excise may by order made by statutory instrument appoint; and different days may be appointed under this paragraph for different purposes.

GENERAL NOTE

Following a review of the modernisation of excise law, excise duty assessment provisions were introduced in F.A. 1994, s.12 in place of the various powers to estimate arrears of excise duty. This Schedule extends these assessment provisions to cover other circumstances where discrepancies arise. Rights of review of decisions and of appeal to the VAT and Duties Tribunal are similarly extended.

Para. 1

New F.A. 1994, ss.12A and 12B allow the Customs and Excise to raise assessments to recover excise duty relief (listed in s.12B(1)) which ought not to have been given.

Para. 2

New Customs and Excise Management Act 1979, s.61(7A) and (8A) allow the Customs and Excise to assess for amounts due as excise duty from the master of a ship or the commander of an aircraft where duty arising from a deficiency in stores is payable. The assessment is recoverable summarily as a civil debt, subject to any appeal.

Para. 3

The amendments to Customs and Excise Management Act 1979, ss.94 and 95 allow the Customs and Excise to assess to recover as excise duty amounts arising in relation to goods missing from warehouse, or going missing after lawful removal from warehouse.

Para. 4

The amendments to Customs and Excise Management Act 1979, s.96 allow the Customs and Excise to assess as excise duty amounts arising in relation to goods going missing in the course of a movement of the goods by pipe-line.

Para. 5

New Customs and Excise Management Act 1979, s.167(5) allows the Customs and Excise to assess as excise duty any amount due arising as the result of an untrue declaration and to recover it as a civil debt.

Para. 6

The amendments to Hydrocarbon Oil Duties Act 1979 (c. 5) allow the Customs and Excise to assess as excise duty amounts becoming due on the happening of certain irregularities relating to hydrocarbon oil.

Para. 7

The Customs and Excise are empowered to bring the provisions into effect by commencement order. Different days may be appointed for different purposes.

Section 69   SCHEDULE 7

SPECIAL TREATMENT FOR CERTAIN DISTRIBUTIONS

Distributions to which Schedule applies

1.—(1) Subject to paragraphs 4 to 7 below, this Schedule applies to any qualifying distribution which—
  (a) falls within either or both of sub-paragraphs (2) and (3) below; and
  (b) is a distribution made on or after 8th October 1996 by a company resident in the United Kingdom.

  (2) A qualifying distribution of a company falls within this sub-paragraph if it is a payment made by that company—
  (a) on the redemption, repayment or purchase of its own shares, or
  (b) on the purchase of rights to acquire its own shares.

  (3) A qualifying distribution of a company falls within this sub-paragraph if—
  (a) arrangements are or have been made by virtue of which any one or more of the specified matters is or was made referable (in some way and to any extent) to, or to the carrying out of, a transaction in securities; and
  (b) that transaction is a transaction completed on or after 8th October 1996, or some or all of those arrangements are arrangements made on or after that date.

  (4) For the purposes of this Schedule the specified matters, in relation to a qualifying distribution, are—
  (a) whether the distribution is made,
  (b) the time when it is made,
  (c) its form, and
  (d) its amount.

  (5) In this Schedule—
      "arrangements" means arrangements of any kind, whether in writing or not;
      "qualifying distribution" has the same meaning as in the Taxes Act 1988;
      "shares" has the same meaning as in sections 219 to 228 of that Act (purchase of own shares);
      "transaction in securities" has the same meaning as in Chapter I of Part XVII of that Act (cancellation of tax advantages from certain transactions in securities).

Distributions treated as FIDs

2.—(1) The Tax Acts shall have effect, and be deemed in relation to any time on or after 8th October 1996 to have had effect, as if a qualifying distribution to which this Schedule applies were a foreign income dividend within the meaning of Chapter VA of Part VI of the Taxes Act 1988 and, accordingly, as if the making of the distribution were the payment of a foreign income dividend.

(2) In section 246A of the Taxes Act 1988 (elections for dividends to be treated as foreign income dividends), after subsection (2) there shall be inserted the following subsection—

"(2A) An election under this section cannot be made as regards a distribution which already falls to be treated as a foreign income dividend by virtue of paragraph 2(1) of Schedule 7 to the Finance Act 1997."

(3) Sub-paragraph (1) above has effect subject to—

(a) section 95(1A)(b) of the Taxes Act 1988 (receipt of qualifying distribution by dealer not to be treated as FID for certain purposes); and

(b) section 247(5B) to (5D) of that Act (distributions that are subject to group income elections).

(4) Sub-paragraph (2) above has effect in relation to the making of elections on or after 8th October 1996.

Distributions treated as section 686 income of trustees

3.—(1) This paragraph applies where—

(a) a qualifying distribution to which this Schedule applies by virtue of its falling within paragraph 1(2) above is or has been made to trustees; and

(b) those trustees are not or, as the case may be, were not the trustees of a unit trust scheme within the meaning of section 469 of the Taxes Act 1988.

(2) The relevant part of that distribution (and, accordingly, the corresponding part of the foreign income dividend that paragraph 2(1) above deems the distribution to be) shall be treated for the purposes of the Tax Acts as if it were income to which section 686 of the Taxes Act 1988 (application of rate applicable to trusts to income of certain discretionary trusts) applies.

(3) In sub-paragraph (2) above the reference to the relevant part of the distribution is a reference to so much (if any) of that distribution as—

(a) is not income falling within paragraph (a) of section 686(2) of the Taxes Act 1988 (income which is to be accumulated or which is payable at any person's discretion);

(b) does not fall to be treated for the purposes of the Income Tax Acts as income of a settlor;

(c) is not income arising under a trust established for charitable purposes; and

(d) is not income from investments, deposits or other property held for any such purposes as are mentioned in sub-paragraph (i) or (ii) of section 686(2)(c) of the Taxes Act 1988 (property held for pension purposes).

(4) Subsection (6) of section 686 of the Taxes Act 1988 (meaning of "trustees" etc.) shall apply for the purpose of this paragraph as it applies for the purposes of that section.

(5) This paragraph has effect for the year 1997–98 and subsequent years of assessment and shall be deemed to have had effect for the year 1996–97 in relation to distributions made on or after 5th December 1996.

Stock options

4.—(1) A qualifying distribution does not fall within paragraph 1(3) above by reason only that it is made in consequence of the exercise of such an option as is mentioned in section 249(1)(a) of the Taxes Act 1988 (option to receive either a cash dividend or additional share capital).

(2) Section 251(1)(c) of the Taxes Act 1988 (interpretation of references to the exercise of an option to receive either a cash dividend or additional share capital) shall apply for the purposes of this paragraph as it applies for the purposes of sections 249 and 250 of that Act.

Dividends on fixed rate preference shares

5.—(1) A qualifying distribution consisting in a dividend on a fixed-rate preference share does not fall within paragraph 1(3) above by reason only that any of the specified matters is made referable to the terms on which the share was issued.

(2) In this paragraph "fixed-rate preference share" means—

(a) any fixed rate preference share within the meaning of section 95 of the Taxes Act 1988; or

(b) any share which would be such a share if the dividends mentioned in section 95(5)(c)(i) of that Act included dividends fixed by reference to a standard published rate of interest.

Pre-sale distributions

6.—(1) A qualifying distribution which is an excepted pre-sale distribution does not fall within paragraph 1(3) above if the only transactions in securities to which any of the specified matters are referable are relevant transactions.

(2) For the purposes of this paragraph, a qualifying distribution of a company is an excepted pre-sale distribution if, in the period beginning with the making of the distribution and ending with the fourteenth day after the day on which the distribution is made, there is a major change in the ownership of that company.

(3) For the purposes of sub-paragraph (2) above, there is a major change in the ownership of a company in any period if, in that period—

(a) a single person acquires a holding of 75 per cent or more of the ordinary share capital of the company; or

(b) each of two or more persons acquires a holding of ordinary share capital of the company, and the holdings together amount to 75 per cent or more of the ordinary share capital of the company.

(4) For the purposes of this paragraph a relevant transaction, in relation to any excepted pre-sale distribution, is any transaction in securities by which the holding or, as the case may be, any of the holdings mentioned in sub-paragraph (3) above is acquired.

(5) In applying sub-paragraph (3) above—

(a) the circumstances at any two points in time falling within the period in question may be compared, and a holder at the later time may be regarded as having acquired in that period whatever he did not hold at the earlier time, irrespective of what he has acquired or disposed of in between;

(b) to allow for any issue of shares or other reorganisation of capital, any such comparison may be made in terms of percentage holdings of the total ordinary share capital at the respective times, so that a person whose percentage holding is greater at the later time may be regarded as having acquired in the period a percentage holding equal to the increase;

(c) any acquisition of shares under the will or on the intestacy of a deceased person, and any gift of shares which is unsolicited and made without regard to the provisions of paragraphs 2 and 3 above, shall be left out of account.

(6) For the purposes of this paragraph, where—

(a) persons, whether company members or not, possess extraordinary rights or powers under the articles of association of a company or under any other document regulating the company, and

(b) because of that fact, ownership of the ordinary share capital may not be an appropriate test of whether there has been a major change in the ownership of the company,

then, in considering whether there has been a major change in the ownership of the company, holdings of all kinds of share capital, including preference shares, or of any particular kind of share capital, or voting power or any other special kind of power, shall be taken into account, and holdings of ordinary share capital shall be disregarded, to such extent as may be appropriate.

(7) For the purposes of this paragraph, references to ownership shall be construed as references to beneficial ownership, and references to acquisition shall be construed accordingly.

Manufactured payments

7.—(1) A manufactured dividend shall not be taken to be a qualifying distribution to which this Schedule applies except in pursuance of sub-paragraph (2) below.

(2) Where a payment is made which is representative of a qualifying distribution to which this Schedule applies, that payment shall be deemed to be such a distribution for all the purposes of the Tax Acts, except those for which Schedule 23A to the Taxes Act 1988 (manufactured payments) makes provision in relation to the payment which is different from the provision applying to distributions to which this Schedule applies.

(3) For the purposes of Schedule 23A to the Taxes Act 1988 a payment which is representative of a payment falling within paragraph 1(2) above shall be treated as if it were representative of a dividend on the shares redeemed, repaid or purchased or, as the case may be, on the shares to which the right relates.

(4) In this paragraph "manufactured dividend" has the same meaning as in Schedule 23A to the Taxes Act 1988.

Amendment of section 95 of the Taxes Act 1988

8.—(1) In section 95 of the Taxes Act 1988 (taxation of distributions received by dealers on purchase by a company of its own shares), for subsections (1) to (3) there shall be substituted the following subsections—

"(1) Each of the following, that is to say—

(a) any qualifying distribution to which Schedule 7 to the Finance Act 1997 (special treatment for certain distributions) applies which is received by a dealer, and

(b) any payment by a dealer which is representative of a qualifying distribution to which that Schedule applies,

shall be taken into account in computing the profits of the dealer which are chargeable to tax in accordance with the provisions of this Act applicable to Case I or II of Schedule D.

(1A) Accordingly, where a dealer receives a qualifying distribution to which Schedule 7 to the Finance Act 1997 applies—

(a) tax shall not be charged under Schedule F in respect of that distribution;

(b) that distribution shall not be treated for the purposes of sections 246D and 246F as a foreign income dividend received by the dealer;

(c) sections 208 and 234(1) shall not apply to that distribution; and

(d) paragraph 2A(2) of Schedule 23A shall not apply to the payment by the dealer of an amount which is representative of that distribution and is paid by him on or after the date appointed under paragraph 16(1) of Schedule 10 to the Finance Act 1997.

(1B) Where the result of any transaction is that a qualifying distribution to which Schedule 7 to the Finance Act 1997 applies is receivable by a dealer, that distribution shall not, in relation to that transaction, be treated as interest for the purposes of determining whether section 732 applies by virtue of section 731.

(2) For the purposes of this section a person is a dealer in relation to any qualifying distribution if—

(a) were there a sale by that person of the shares in respect of which the distribution is made, and

(b) the circumstances of that sale were such that the price would not fall to be treated as a qualifying distribution,

the price would be taken into account in computing the profits of that person which are chargeable to tax in accordance with the provisions of this Act applicable to Case I or II of Schedule D."

(2) In that Act—

(a) in section 20(1), in paragraph 1 of Schedule F, for "95(1)(a)" there shall be substituted "95(1A)(a)"; and

(b) in section 234(1) (information relating to distributions), for "95(1)(c)" there shall be substituted "95(1A)(c)".

(3) This paragraph has effect in relation to distributions made on or after 26th November 1996.

Information to be provided about deemed FID

9.—(1) In section 246G(1)(d) of that Act (information to be provided about a foreign income dividend), after "carries no entitlement to a tax credit" there shall be inserted "and, in the case of a qualifying distribution to which Schedule 7 to the Finance Act 1997 applies, that it is a foreign income dividend by virtue of paragraph 2(1) of that Schedule".

(2) This paragraph has effect in relation to distributions made on or after 26th November 1996.

Group income

10.—(1) In subsection (5A) of section 247 of that Act (under which the group income provisions do not apply to FIDs), at the beginning there shall be inserted the words "Subject to subsections (5B) to (5D) below,"; and after that subsection there shall be inserted the following subsections—

"(5B) Where—

(a) a company falling within subsection (5C) below and resident in the United Kingdom receives a dividend, and

(b) that dividend would, apart from subsection (5D) below, be a distribution to which Schedule 7 to the Finance Act 1997 (special treatment for certain distributions) applies,

the dividend shall be taken to be one in relation to which an election under subsection (1) above may have effect in accordance with this section.

(5C) The receiving company falls within this subsection if—

(a) it directly or indirectly owns all the ordinary share capital of the paying company, or

(b) all the ordinary share capital of the paying company is owned directly or indirectly by a company resident in the United Kingdom which also owns, directly or indirectly, all the ordinary share capital of the receiving company;

and section 838 shall apply for construing the references in this subsection to directly or indirectly owning ordinary share capital of a company.

(5D) If an election under subsection (1) above has effect in relation to such a distribution as is mentioned in subsection (5B) above, that distribution shall be deemed to be a distribution to which Schedule 7 to the Finance Act 1997 does not apply."

(2) This paragraph has effect in relation to distributions made on or after 26th November 1996.

Distribution accounts

11.—(1) In section 468I of that Act (distribution accounts of authorised unit trusts), after subsection (5) there shall be inserted the following subsection—

"(5A) The following amounts shown as available for distribution in the distribution accounts must be shown in those accounts as available for distribution as foreign income dividends—

(a) amounts deriving from qualifying distributions to which Schedule 7 to the Finance Act 1997 (special treatment for certain distributions) applies; and

(b) so much of any amounts not falling within paragraph (a) above as, if shown as available for distribution as dividends, would fall to be treated as distributions to which that Schedule applies."

(2) This paragraph applies to distribution accounts for any distribution period ending on or after 26th November 1996.

Amendments consequential on paragraph 3 above

12.—(1) In section 686 of that Act (application of rate applicable to trusts to income of certain discretionary trusts), paragraph (d) of subsection (2) shall be omitted; and after that subsection there shall be inserted the following subsection—

"(2AA) The rate at which income tax is chargeable on so much of any income arising to trustees in any year of assessment as—

(a) is income to which this section applies, and

(b) is treated in accordance with section 689B as applied in defraying the expenses of the trustees in that year which are properly chargeable to income (or would be so chargeable but for any express provisions of the trust),

shall be the rate at which it would be chargeable on that income apart from this section, instead of the rate applicable to trusts."

(2) In subsection (2A) of that section, for "subsection (2)(d)" there shall be substituted "subsection (2AA)".

(3) In section 233(1A)(a) of that Act (taxation of non-resident recipients of distributions), for sub-paragraph (ii) there shall be substituted—

"(ii) income to which section 686 applies,".

(4) This paragraph has effect for the year 1997–98 and subsequent years of assessment and shall be deemed to have had effect for the year 1996–97.

GENERAL NOTE

The Schedule is designed to prevent loss of tax revenue by arrangements involving the purchase of its own shares by a company or the payment of a special dividend where the recipient of the money is able to reclaim advance corporation tax ("ACT"). In defined circumstances the payment will be treated as a foreign income dividend ("FID") on which ACT cannot be reclaimed.

Para. 1

The scope of the payments caught by the Schedule are defined. These are a distribution on a purchase of its own shares by a company and a distribution where there are arrangements linking it to a transaction in shares or securities.

Para. 2

A distribution caught by para. 1 is treated as a FID.

Para. 3

Distributions arising in respect of purchases of own shares will be treated as income of trustee shareholders, chargeable at the rate applicable to trusts. A back-bench amendment was accepted confining the charge to distributions after December 5, 1996.

Para. 4

A dividend which might be linked to a transaction in securities only because it is a cash dividend alternative to a stock dividend under ICTA 1988, s.249 is exempted from the scope of the Schedule.

Para. 5

Exemption is also accorded to dividends on fixed rate preference shares, which might be caught because the amount or timing of the dividend was fixed at the time the shares were issued. The exemption includes shares where the dividend is tied to a standard published rate of interest.

Para. 6

Dividends or other distributions made in anticipation of the sale of a company are also exempted. The distribution must be made within 14 days before the change in ownership. The sale must involve 75 per cent or more of the ordinary share capital.

Para. 7

A manufactured dividend which represents a deemed FID will be treated as if it is itself a deemed FID, subject to the provisions of ICTA 1988, Sched. 23A.

Para. 8

This provides for special treatment of dealers in shares in respect of distributions which are within the scope of the Schedule. All distributions within the scope of the Schedule will be treated as receipts to be taken into account in computing the dealer's trading profit. This treatment already applies to distributions arising from purchases of own shares. The amendments to ICTA 1988, s.95 apply it to distributions linked to transactions in securities as well. The anti-avoidance provisions in *ibid.* s.732 are therefore disapplied from such distributions.

Para. 9

When a company supplies its normal voucher for shareholders in respect of a FID, this will have to show that any distribution which is a deemed FID is treated as a FID because it is within the scope of the new rules.

Para. 10

This allows, in certain circumstances, a dividend which would otherwise be within the new rules because it is linked to a transaction in securities, to be subject to a group income election. It applies where the company paying the dividend is a wholly owned subsidiary of another U.K. company. On an election being made, the dividend will not be treated as a deemed FID.

Para. 11

Two provisions are made applying to authorised unit trusts for distribution periods ending on or after November 26, 1996. First, deemed FIDs received by an authorised unit trust must not be included in amounts shown in the trust's distribution accounts as available for distribution in any form other than as foreign income dividends. Second, if an authorised unit trust makes a distribution which would itself be treated as a deemed FID under the new rules, the distribution must take the form of a foreign income dividend distribution.

Para. 12

Trustees will not be charged to tax under para. 3 at the rate applicable to trusts in respect of amounts which are applied in meeting trust management expenses.

[*Hansard*, H.C. Vol. 288, cols. 1096–1120.]

Section 74   SCHEDULE 8

ENTERPRISE INVESTMENT SCHEME: QUALIFYING COMPANIES

Introductory

1. Chapter III of Part VII of the Taxes Act 1988 (the enterprise investment scheme)—

  (a) in its application in relation to shares issued after 26th November 1996, and

  (b) in its application after 26th November 1996 in relation to shares which—

        (i) were issued on or after 1st January 1994 but before 27th November 1996, and

        (ii) immediately before 27th November 1996 were held by an individual and at that time were shares to which, within the meaning of that Chapter, any relief was attributable,

shall have effect with the following amendments.

Requirements to be satisfied by the company for whose business activity money is raised

2.—(1) In subsection (1) of section 289 (conditions for eligibility for relief), immediately before the word "and" at the end of paragraph (b) there shall be inserted the following paragraph—

"(ba) the requirements of subsection (1A) below are satisfied in relation to the company,".

(2) After that subsection there shall be inserted the following subsections—

"(1A) The requirements of this subsection are satisfied in relation to a qualifying company if throughout the relevant period the active company—

(a) is such a company as is mentioned in section 293(2)(a), or

(b) would be such a company if its purposes were disregarded to the extent that they consist in the carrying on of activities such as are mentioned in section 293(3D)(a) and (b) and (3E)(a), or

(c) is a subsidiary of the qualifying company and falls within subsection (1B) below.

(1B) A subsidiary of the qualifying company falls within this subsection if—

(a) apart from purposes capable of having no significant effect (other than in relation to incidental matters) on the extent of its activities, it exists wholly for the purpose of carrying on activities such as are mentioned in section 293(3D)(b); or

(b) it has no profits for the purposes of corporation tax and no part of its business consists in the making of investments.

(1C) In subsection (1A) above 'the active company' means the qualifying company or, where the qualifying business activity mentioned in subsection (1) above consists in a subsidiary of that company carrying on or preparing to carry on a qualifying trade, research and development or oil exploration, that subsidiary.

(1D) Subsection (6) of section 293 shall apply in relation to the requirements of subsection (1A) above as it applies in relation to subsection (2) of that section."

Limit on relief for trading groups which let or operate ships

3.—(1) In subsection (6) of section 290A (maximum sum eligible for relief in cases of trades involving the letting or operating of ships), for paragraphs (b) and (c) there shall be substituted "or

(aa) in the case of a company falling within subsection (2)(aa) of that section—

(i) it satisfies the requirements of subsection (6A) below, and

(ii) each of its subsidiaries is a shipping company,".

(2) After that subsection there shall be inserted the following subsections—

"(6A) A company satisfies the requirements of this subsection if, apart from purposes capable of having no significant effect (other than in relation to incidental matters) on the extent of its activities, the company exists wholly—

(a) for the purpose of carrying on activities such as are mentioned in section 293(3D)(a) and (b); or

(b) for the purpose of carrying on one or more qualifying trades which or each of which is a trade to which subsection (7) below applies; or

(c) for any combination of the purposes mentioned in paragraphs (a) and (b) above.

(6B) For the purposes of subsection (6) above a subsidiary of a company falling within section 293(2)(aa) is a shipping company if—

(a) that subsidiary satisfies the requirements of subsection (6A) above, or

(b) it would satisfy those requirements if the reference in subsection (6A)(a) above to section 293(3D)(a) and (b) included a reference to section 293(3E)(a), or

(c) it has no profits for the purposes of corporation tax and no part of its business consists in the making of investments."

Meaning of "qualifying company"

4.—(1) In subsection (2) of section 293 (meaning of "qualifying company"), for paragraph (b) there shall be substituted the following paragraph—

"(aa) the parent company of a trading group."

(2) After subsection (3) of that section there shall be inserted the following subsections—

"(3A) For the purposes of this section a company is the parent company of a trading group if—

(a) it has one or more subsidiaries;

(b) each of its subsidiaries is a qualifying subsidiary of the company; and

(c) the requirements of subsection (3B) below are fulfilled by what would be the business of the company and its subsidiaries if all the activities, taken together, of the company and its subsidiaries were regarded as one business.

(3B) A business fulfils the requirements of this subsection if neither the business nor a substantial part of it consists in, or in either of, the following, that is to say—

    (a) activities falling within section 297(2)(a) to (g) but not within subsection (3C) below; and

    (b) activities carried on otherwise than in the course of a trade.

(3C) The activities falling within this subsection are—

    (a) the receiving of royalties or licence fees in circumstances where the requirements mentioned in paragraphs (a) and (b) of section 297(4) or (5) are satisfied in relation to the company receiving them;

    (b) the letting of ships, other than oil rigs or pleasure craft, on charter in circumstances where the requirements mentioned in paragraphs (a) to (d) of section 297(6) are satisfied in relation to the company so letting them.

(3D) Activities of a company or of any of its subsidiaries shall be disregarded for the purposes of subsections (3A) to (3C) above to the extent that they consist in—

    (a) the holding of shares in or securities of, or the making of loans to, one or more of the company's subsidiaries; or

    (b) the holding and managing of property used by the company or any of its subsidiaries for the purposes of—

        (i) research and development from which it is intended that a qualifying trade to be carried on by the company or any of its subsidiaries will be derived; or

        (ii) one or more qualifying trades so carried on.

(3E) Activities of a subsidiary of a company shall also be disregarded for the purposes of subsections (3A) to (3C) above to the extent that they consist in—

    (a) the making of loans to the company; or

    (b) in the case of a mainly trading subsidiary, activities carried on otherwise than in pursuance of its main purpose.

(3F) For the purposes of subsection (3E) above—

    (a) 'mainly trading subsidiary' means a subsidiary which, apart from purposes capable of having no significant effect (other than in relation to incidental matters) on the extent of its activities, exists wholly for the purpose of carrying on one or more qualifying trades; and

    (b) that purpose shall be taken to be its main purpose."

Consequential amendments of section 297

5. In section 297(3)(c)(i), and in the words after paragraph (d) in section 297(6) (which refer to the activities falling within section 297(2)), for "(2)" there shall be substituted "(2)(a) to (g)".

Consequential repeals of provisions about subsidiaries

6. In section 308 (subsidiaries)—

    (a) paragraph (b) of subsection (1), and the word "and" immediately preceding that paragraph, and

    (b) paragraphs (a) and (b) of subsection (5),

shall be omitted.

GENERAL NOTE

The Schedule relaxes some of the conditions for investment in a company to qualify for relief under the enterprise investment scheme ("EIS").

Para. 1

The changes apply to new share issues made after November 26, 1996 and also, with effect from November 27, to shares issued before that date, provided they satisfied the conditions for EIS relief up to that point.

Para. 2

This deals with groups of companies.

New ICTA 1988, s.289(1A)–(1C) provide that for investment in a parent company to attract relief, the company using the money in its trade ("the active company") must satisfy one of two conditions. The first is that, ignoring certain intra-group activities, it exists solely for the purposes of carrying on a qualifying activity, or does so apart from purposes with insignificant effect. The second is that it exists wholly to hold or manage property for the group, or does so apart from having purposes with an insignificant effect on its activities, or has no corporation tax profits and does not make investments. The second condition preserves an existing relief.

New ICTA 1988, s.289(1D) provides that EIS relief will not be withdrawn from investment in a company qualifying under the first condition above where the company is wound up or dissolved for genuine commercial reasons and where its assets are distributed within a fixed time.

Para. 3

This amends the rules that determine which company which lets or operates ships qualifies for the higher maximum sum (£5m) eligible for relief under ICTA 1988, s.290(A)(6).

New s.290(A)(6A) provides that a parent company qualifies for the higher limit of relief if it exists wholly for the purpose of carrying on certain intra-group activities or of carrying on certain shipping operations or a combination of these purposes, and if each of its subsidiaries is a shipping company.

New s.290(A)(6B) defines "shipping company". This is a company which either satisfies the same conditions as its parent (or would do if activities arising from the making of loans to the parent were disregarded) or which has no corporation tax profits and does not make investments.

Para. 4

This contains provisions that replace the previous condition that every company in a group must have a qualifying activity.

New s.293(3A) and (3B) set out the conditions to be satisfied by the parent company of a trading group. These are that the company has one or more qualifying subsidiaries and that the business of the group as a whole does not consist to a substantial extent of non-qualifying activities and activities that are not trades.

New s.293(3C) leaves unchanged the scope of non-qualifying activities as listed in s.297(2)(a)–(g).

New s.293(3D)–(3F) provide for the following intra-group activities to be disregarded in establishing whether the business of the group as a whole qualifies:

(i) the holding of shares in or securities of subsidiary companies;

(ii) the making of loans by parent to subsidiary or vice versa;

(iii) the holding and managing of property used for the group's activities.

It is also provided that where qualifying subsidiaries exist wholly for the purposes of carrying on one or more qualifying trades, or do so apart from purposes with insignificant effect, activities resulting from such purposes will also be disregarded.

Para. 5

Two consequential amendments are made to references to the list of non-qualifying activities.

Para. 6

This repeals those parts of s.308 that restrict the types of activity which a qualifying subsidiary can carry on.

[Standing Committee B, February 18, 1997, cols. 418–420.]

Section 75   SCHEDULE 9

VENTURE CAPITAL TRUSTS: QUALIFYING HOLDINGS

Introductory

1. Schedule 28B to the Taxes Act 1988 (venture capital trusts: meaning of "qualifying holdings") shall be amended as follows.

Requirements as to business of company whose shares etc. are qualifying holdings

2.—(1) In paragraph 3 (requirements as to company's business), for paragraphs (b) and (c) of sub-paragraph (2) (company must be of one of the given descriptions) there shall be substituted "or

    (aa) the parent company of a trading group."

(2) After sub-paragraph (5) of that paragraph there shall be inserted the following sub-paragraphs—

    "(6) For the purposes of this paragraph a company is the parent company of a trading group if—

      (a) it has one or more subsidiaries;

      (b) each of its subsidiaries is a qualifying subsidiary of the company; and

(c) the requirements of sub-paragraph (7) below are fulfilled by what would be the business of the company and its qualifying subsidiaries if all the activities, taken together, of the company and its qualifying subsidiaries were regarded as one business.

(7) A business fulfils the requirements of this sub-paragraph if neither the business nor a substantial part of it consists in, or in either of, the following, that is to say—

(a) activities falling within paragraph 4(2)(a) to (f) below but not within sub-paragraph (8) below; and

(b) activities carried on otherwise than in the course of a trade.

(8) The activities falling within this sub-paragraph are—

(a) the receiving of royalties or licence fees in circumstances where the requirements mentioned in paragraphs (a) and (b) of paragraph 4(5) or (6) below are satisfied in relation to the company receiving them;

(b) the letting of ships, other than oil rigs or pleasure craft, on charter in circumstances where the requirements mentioned in paragraphs (a) to (d) of paragraph 4(7) below are satisfied in relation to the company so letting them.

(9) Activities of a company or of any of its qualifying subsidiaries shall be disregarded for the purposes of sub-paragraphs (6) to (8) above to the extent that they consist in—

(a) the holding of shares in or securities of, or the making of loans to, one or more of the company's qualifying subsidiaries; or

(b) the holding and managing of property used by the company or any of its qualifying subsidiaries for the purposes of—

(i) research and development from which it is intended that a qualifying trade to be carried on by the company or any of its qualifying subsidiaries will be derived; or

(ii) one or more qualifying trades so carried on.

(10) Activities of a qualifying subsidiary of a company shall also be disregarded for the purposes of sub-paragraphs (6) to (8) above to the extent that they consist in—

(a) the making of loans to the company; or

(b) in the case of a mainly trading subsidiary, activities carried on in pursuance of its insignificant purposes (within the meaning given by sub-paragraph (11) below).

(11) In sub-paragraph (10) above 'mainly trading subsidiary' means a qualifying subsidiary which, apart from purposes ('its insignificant purposes') which are capable of having no significant effect (other than in relation to incidental matters) on the extent of its activities, exists wholly for the purpose of carrying on one or more qualifying trades."

Consequential amendment of paragraph 4(7)

3. In paragraph 4(7), in the words after paragraph (d) (which contain a reference to activities of a kind falling within paragraph 4(2)) for "(2)" there shall be substituted "(2)(a) to (f)".

Application of investment

4. In paragraph 6 (requirements as to the money raised by the investment in question), after sub-paragraph (2) there shall be inserted the following sub-paragraphs—

"(2A) Where the relevant company is a company falling within paragraph 3(2)(aa) above, the requirements of this paragraph are not satisfied unless—

(a) the trader company is a company in relation to which the requirements of paragraph 3(2)(a) above are satisfied, or

(b) the trader company is a company in relation to which those requirements would be satisfied if its purposes were disregarded to the extent that they consist in the carrying on of activities such as are mentioned in paragraph 3(9)(a) and (b) and (10)(a) above, or

(c) the trader company is a qualifying subsidiary of the relevant company and falls within sub-paragraph (2B) below.

(2B) A qualifying subsidiary of the relevant company falls within this sub-paragraph if—

(a) apart from purposes capable of having no significant effect (other than in relation to incidental matters) on the extent of its activities, it exists wholly for the purpose of carrying on activities such as are mentioned in paragraph 3(9)(b) above; or

(b) it has no profits for the purposes of corporation tax and no part of its business consists in the making of investments.

(2C) In sub-paragraph (2A) above 'the trader company' means the company (whether the relevant company or a qualifying subsidiary of the relevant company) carrying on, or preparing to carry on, the trade by reference to which the requirements of paragraph 3(3) above are satisfied."

Qualifying subsidiaries

5.—(1) In sub-paragraph (1) of paragraph 10 (meaning of "qualifying subsidiary"), for "each of sub-paragraphs (2) and" there shall be substituted "sub-paragraph".

(2) Sub-paragraph (2) of that paragraph (requirements as to purposes for which subsidiaries exist) shall be omitted.

(3) In each of sub-paragraphs (4) and (5) of that paragraph (which contain references to companies falling within sub-paragraphs (2) and (3)), for "sub-paragraphs (2) and" there shall be substituted "sub-paragraph".

(4) In sub-paragraph (4)(a) of that paragraph, for "those sub-paragraphs" there shall be substituted "that sub-paragraph".

Commencement

6. This Schedule has effect for the purposes of determining whether shares or securities are, as at any time after 26th November 1996, to be regarded as comprised in a company's qualifying holdings.

GENERAL NOTE

The Schedule relaxes the conditions in the venture capital trust ("VCT") legislation dealing with investment in companies with subsidiaries.

Para. 1

This introduces amendments to ICTA 1988, Sched. 28B.

Para. 2

The previous condition that every company in a group must have a qualifying activity is replaced. The conditions to be satisfied by the parent company of a trading group are that the company has one or more qualifying subsidiaries and the business of the group as a whole does not consist to a substantial extent of non-qualifying activities and activities that are not trades. The scope of non-qualifying activities, listed in sub-para. 4(2)(a)–(f) is unchanged, but as now, does not include a limited range of trades, for example receiving licence fees from film production, that would otherwise be excluded but for some specific provisions (new sub-para. 3(8)).

New sub-paras. 3(9) and 3(10) provide for the following intra-group activities to be disregarded in establishing whether the business of the group as a whole qualifies:

(i) the holding of shares in, or securities of, subsidiary companies;
(ii) the making of loans by parent to subsidiary or vice versa;
(iii) the holding and managing of property used for the group's activities.

New sub-paras. 3(10) and 3(11) also provide that where qualifying subsidiaries exist wholly for the purposes of carrying on one or more qualifying trades, or so exist apart from purposes with insignificant effect, then activities resulting from such purposes will also be disregarded.

Para. 3

This introduces a consequential amendment to a reference to the list of non-qualifying activities.

Para. 4

This inserts new sub-paras. (2A)–(2C) into para. 6. The insertions are a consequence of the repeal of the parts of para. 10 dealing with the activities of qualifying subsidiaries. Their overall effect is to allow somewhat greater flexibility where activities that are wholly within the group are concerned, but otherwise to preserve the existing rules. For investment in the parent to attract relief, the company using the money in its trade ("the trader company") must satisfy one of two conditions. The first is that, ignoring certain intra-group activities, it exists wholly for the purposes of carrying on a qualifying activity, or does so apart from purposes with insignificant effect. The second is that, if a qualifying subsidiary, it is one that:

(i) exists wholly to hold or manage property used by the group, or does so apart from having purposes with an insignificant effect on its activities; or
(ii) has no corporation tax profits and does not make investments.

Para. 5

This removes those parts of para. 10 that restrict the types of activity a qualifying subsidiary can carry on.

Para. 6

The changes in Sched. 9 have effect after November 26, 1996.

SCHEDULE 10

STOCK LENDING ARRANGEMENTS AND MANUFACTURED PAYMENTS

PART I

STOCK LENDING

Approved stock lending arrangements: traders

1.—(1) Section 129 of the Taxes Act 1988 (treatment of approved stock lending arrangements when computing the profits of a trade) shall cease to have effect.

(2) Section 129A of, and Schedule 5A to, that Act (interest on cash collateral for approved stock lending arrangements) shall also cease to have effect.

Stock lending fees

2.—(1) In subsection (3) of section 129B of the Taxes Act 1988 (stock lending fees under approved stock lending arrangements), for "an approved" there shall be substituted "any".

(2) For subsection (4) of that section (meaning of approved stock lending arrangement) there shall be substituted the following subsection—

"(4) In this section 'stock lending arrangement' has the same meaning as in section 263B of the 1992 Act."

Stock lending agreements under which manufactured payments are not made

3. After section 736A of the Taxes Act 1988 (manufactured dividends and interest) there shall be inserted the following section—

"**Deemed manufactured payments in the case of stock lending arrangements**

736B.—(1) This section applies where—

(a) any interest on securities transferred by the lender under a stock lending arrangement is paid, as a consequence of the arrangement, to a person other than the lender; and

(b) no provision is made for securing that the lender receives payments representative of that interest.

(2) Where this section applies, Schedule 23A and the provisions for the time being contained in any regulations under that Schedule shall apply as if—

(a) the borrower were required under the stock lending arrangement to pay the lender an amount representative of the interest mentioned in subsection (1)(a) above;

(b) a payment were made by the borrower in discharge of that requirement; and

(c) that payment were made on the same date as the payment of the interest of which it is representative.

(3) In this section—

'interest' includes dividends; and

'stock lending arrangement' and 'securities' have the same meanings as in section 263B of the 1992 Act."

Manufactured payments in stock lending cases etc.

4. In Schedule 23A to the Taxes Act 1988 (manufactured payments)—

(a) paragraph 6 (unapproved manufactured payments) shall cease to have effect; and

(b) in paragraph 7(3)—

(i) in paragraph (a), the words "except where paragraph 6 above applies, and" shall be omitted;

(ii) paragraph (b) shall be omitted; and

(iii) for the words "3, 4 or 6" there shall be substituted "3 or 4".

Stock lending arrangements: capital gains

5.—(1) After section 263A of the Taxation of Chargeable Gains Act 1992 (agreements for sale and repurchase of securities) there shall be inserted the following sections—

"**Stock lending arrangements**

263B.—(1) In this section 'stock lending arrangement' means so much of any arrangements between two persons ('the borrower' and 'the lender') as are arrangements under which—

(a) the lender transfers securities to the borrower otherwise than by way of sale; and

(b) a requirement is imposed on the borrower to transfer those securities back to the lender otherwise than by way of sale.

(2) Subject to the following provisions of this section and section 263C(2), the disposals and acquisitions made in pursuance of any stock lending arrangement shall be disregarded for the purposes of capital gains tax.

(3) Where—

(a) the borrower under any stock lending arrangement disposes of any securities transferred to him under the arrangement,

(b) that disposal is made otherwise than in the discharge of the requirement for the transfer of securities back to the lender, and

(c) that requirement, so far as it relates to the securities disposed of, has been or will be discharged by the transfer of securities other than those transferred to the borrower,

any question relating to the acquisition of the securities disposed of shall be determined (without prejudice to the provisions of Chapter I of Part IV) as if the securities disposed of were the securities with which that requirement (so far as relating to the securities disposed of) has been or will be discharged.

(4) Where, in the case of any stock lending arrangement, it becomes apparent, at any time after the making of the transfer by the lender, that the requirement for the borrower to make a transfer back to the lender will not be complied with—

(a) the lender shall be deemed for the purposes of this Act to have made a disposal at that time of the securities transferred to the borrower;

(b) the borrower shall be deemed to have acquired them at that time; and

(c) subsection (3) above shall have effect in relation to any disposal before that time by the borrower of securities transferred to him by the lender as if the securities deemed to have been acquired by the borrower in accordance with paragraph (b) above were to be used for discharging a requirement to transfer securities back to the lender.

(5) References in this section, in relation to a person to whom securities are transferred, to the transfer of those securities back to another person shall be construed as if the cases where those securities are taken to be transferred back to that other person included any case where securities of the same description as those securities are transferred to that other person either—

(a) in accordance with a requirement to transfer securities of the same description; or

(b) in exercise of a power to substitute securities of the same description for the securities that are required to be transferred back.

(6) For the purposes of this section securities shall not be taken to be of the same description as other securities unless they are in the same quantities, give the same rights against the same persons and are of the same type and nominal value as the other securities.

(7) In this section—

'interest' includes dividends; and

'securities' means United Kingdom equities, United Kingdom securities or overseas securities (within the meaning, in each case, of Schedule 23A to the Taxes Act).

Stock lending involving redemption

263C.—(1) In section 263B references to the transfer back to a person of securities transferred by him shall be taken to include references to the payment to him, in pursuance of an obligation arising on any person's becoming entitled to receive an amount in respect of the redemption of those securities, of an amount equal to the amount of the entitlement.

(2) Where, in pursuance of any such obligation, the lender under any stock lending arrangement is paid any amount in respect of the redemption of any securities to which the arrangement relates—

(a) that lender shall be deemed for the purposes of this Act to have disposed, for that amount, of the securities in respect of whose redemption it is paid ('the relevant lent securities');

(b) the borrower shall not, in respect of the redemption, be taken for the purposes of this Act to have made any disposal of the relevant lent securities; and

(c) section 263B(3) shall have effect in relation to disposals of any of the relevant lent securities made by the borrower before the redemption as if—

(i) the amount paid to the lender were an amount paid for the acquisition of securities, and

(ii) the securities acquired were to be used by the borrower for discharging a requirement under the arrangement to transfer the relevant lent securities back to the lender.

(3) Expressions used in this section and section 263B have the same meanings in this section as in that section."

(2) Section 271(9) of that Act (treatment of approved stock lending arrangements) shall cease to have effect.

(3) In section 727(2) of the Taxes Act 1988 (stock lending and the accrued income scheme), for "section 271(9) of the 1992 Act" there shall be substituted "section 263B(2) of the 1992 Act".

Premiums trust funds of Lloyd's members

6. The following provisions of Chapter III of Part II of the Finance Act 1993 and Chapter V of Part IV of the Finance Act 1994 (Lloyd's members) shall cease to have effect—
  (a) section 174(4) and (5) and section 182(1)(ca)(i) of that Act of 1993 (stock lending arrangements applying to securities in the premiums trust funds of individual members); and
  (b) section 222(4) and (5) and section 229(ca)(i) of that Act of 1994 (which makes corresponding provision for the premiums trust funds of corporate members).

Commencement

7.—(1) This Part of this Schedule (except paragraph 4 above) has effect in relation to, and to transfers under, any arrangement made on or after such day as the Treasury may by order made by statutory instrument appoint.

(2) Paragraph 4 above has effect in relation to any manufactured payment made on or after the day appointed under sub-paragraph (1) above.

PART II

MANUFACTURED PAYMENTS

Repeal of section 737 of the Taxes Act 1988

8. Section 737 of the Taxes Act 1988 (manufactured dividends: treatment of tax deducted) shall cease to have effect.

Meaning of "foreign income dividend"

9. In paragraph 1(1) of Schedule 23A to that Act (interpretation of that Schedule), after the definition of "dividend manufacturing regulations" there shall be inserted the following definition—
  " 'foreign income dividend' shall be construed in accordance with Chapter VA of Part VI;".

Manufactured dividends on UK equities

10.—(1) For paragraph 2 of Schedule 23A to that Act (manufactured dividends on UK equities) there shall be substituted the following paragraphs—

"Manufactured dividends on UK equities: general

2.—(1) This paragraph applies in any case where, under a contract or other arrangements for the transfer of United Kingdom equities, one of the parties (a 'dividend manufacturer') is required to pay to the other ('the recipient') an amount (a 'manufactured dividend') which is representative of a dividend on the equities.

(2) A manufactured dividend paid by a dividend manufacturer who is a company resident in the United Kingdom shall be treated for the purposes of the Tax Acts as if the amount paid were a dividend of the dividend manufacturer.

(3) Where a manufactured dividend to which sub-paragraph (2) above does not apply is paid by any person—
  (a) an amount of tax representing the advance corporation tax that would have been payable in respect of the manufactured dividend if—
      (i) the dividend manufacturer were a company resident in the United Kingdom, and
      (ii) the manufactured dividend were a distribution by that company,
    shall be accounted for to the extent, and in the manner, specified in dividend manufacturing regulations;
  (b) the Tax Acts shall have effect in relation to the recipient, and persons claiming title through or under him, as if the manufactured dividend were a dividend on the United Kingdom equities in question; and
  (c) the Tax Acts shall have effect in relation to the dividend manufacturer subject to the provisions of paragraph 2A below.

(4) The persons who, under dividend manufacturing regulations, may be made liable to account for an amount of tax as mentioned in sub-paragraph (3)(a) above are—

(a) the dividend manufacturer, in the case of a manufactured dividend to which sub-paragraph (5) below applies; and

(b) the recipient, in the case of a manufactured dividend to which that sub-paragraph does not apply.

(5) This sub-paragraph applies to a manufactured dividend if—

(a) the dividend manufacturer is a person resident in the United Kingdom who is not a company; or

(b) the following two conditions are satisfied in the case of that manufactured dividend, that is to say—

(i) the dividend manufacturer is a company that is not so resident but carries on a trade in the United Kingdom through a branch or agency; and

(ii) the requirement to pay the manufactured dividend is attributable to the carrying on of a trade carried on through that branch or agency.

(6) Subject to paragraph 2B(2)(b) below, where—

(a) a dividend manufacturer pays a manufactured dividend, and

(b) that dividend manufacturer is, in respect of that dividend, required under dividend manufacturing regulations to account for an amount of tax such as is mentioned in sub-paragraph (3)(a) above,

the dividend manufacturer shall, on paying the manufactured dividend, provide the recipient with a statement in writing setting out the matters specified in sub-paragraph (7) below.

(7) Those matters are—

(a) the amount of the manufactured dividend;

(b) the date of the payment of the manufactured dividend; and

(c) the amount of the tax credit to which, by virtue of sub-paragraph (3)(b) above, the recipient or a person claiming title through or under him either—

(i) is entitled in respect of the manufactured dividend, or

(ii) would be so entitled were all the conditions of a right to a tax credit satisfied, in the case of the recipient or that person, as respects the dividend which the recipient is deemed to receive.

(8) The duty imposed by sub-paragraph (6) above shall be enforceable at the suit or instance of the recipient.

Deductibility of manufactured payment in the case of the manufacturer

2A.—(1) Where, in the case of a manufactured dividend, the dividend manufacturer—

(a) is resident in the United Kingdom, but

(b) is not a company,

the amount of the manufactured dividend actually paid (so far as is it is not otherwise deductible), together with an amount equal to the notional ACT, shall be allowable for the purposes of income tax as a deduction against the total income of the dividend manufacturer.

(2) Where, in the case of a manufactured dividend, the dividend manufacturer is a company which is not resident in the United Kingdom, no amount at all shall be deductible, in the case of that company, in respect of the payment of that manufactured dividend.

(3) The reference in sub-paragraph (1) above to an amount equal to the notional ACT is a reference to the amount equal to the advance corporation tax that would be payable in respect of the manufactured dividend if—

(a) the dividend manufacturer were a company resident in the United Kingdom, and

(b) the manufactured dividend were a distribution by that company.

(4) The references in this paragraph to an amount being deductible are references to its being either—

(a) deductible in computing the amount of any of the dividend manufacturer's profits or gains for the purposes of income tax or corporation tax; or

(b) deductible for those purposes from the total income or, as the case may be, total profits of the dividend manufacturer.

Manufactured dividends representative of foreign income dividends

2B.—(1) Where a manufactured dividend to which paragraph 2(2) above applies is representative of a foreign income dividend, the Tax Acts shall have effect for all purposes as if—

(a) the deemed dividend of the dividend manufacturer were itself a foreign income dividend; and

(b) that foreign income dividend were one in respect of which the dividend manufacturer is not liable to make any payment of advance corporation tax.

(2) Where a manufactured dividend to which paragraph 2(3) above applies is representative of a foreign income dividend—

(a) the Tax Acts shall have effect, in relation to the recipient and any persons claiming title through or under him, as if the dividend on the United Kingdom equities which the recipient is treated as having received were a foreign income dividend;

(b) there shall be no requirement for any person to account for tax in respect of that manufactured dividend by virtue of paragraph 2(3)(a) above;

(c) any deduction made in respect of the manufactured dividend under paragraph 2A(1) above shall be made without including an amount equal to the notional ACT in the deduction; and

(d) the dividend manufacturer, on paying the manufactured dividend in any case falling within sub-paragraph (3) below, shall provide the recipient with a statement in writing setting out the matters specified in sub-paragraph (4) below.

(3) A case falls within this sub-paragraph where, were it not for sub-paragraph (2)(a) and (b) above, the dividend manufacturer would be required to provide such a statement as is mentioned in paragraph 2(6) above.

(4) Those matters are—

(a) the amount of the manufactured dividend;

(b) the date on which it is paid;

(c) the fact that the dividend carries no entitlement to a tax credit; and

(d) in the case of a manufactured dividend which is representative of a qualifying distribution to which Schedule 7 to the Finance Act 1997 applies, the fact that the distribution is a foreign income dividend by virtue of paragraph 2(1) of that Schedule.

(5) The Board may give directions as to the form that must be taken by a statement provided for the purposes of sub-paragraph (2)(d) above.

(6) The duty imposed by sub-paragraph (2)(d) above shall be enforceable at the suit or instance of the recipient."

(2) In section 246F(4) of that Act (calculation of ACT where company receives foreign income dividend), for "paragraph 2(6)" there shall be substituted "paragraph 2B(1)".

(3) In paragraph 9A of Schedule 13 to that Act (exception for manufactured foreign income dividends), for "paragraph 2(2) and (6)" there shall be substituted "paragraphs 2(2) and 2B(1)".

Manufactured interest on UK securities

11.—(1) For paragraphs 3 and 3A of Schedule 23A to that Act (manufactured interest on UK securities) there shall be substituted the following paragraphs—

"Manufactured interest on UK securities: general

3.—(1) This paragraph applies (subject to paragraph 3A below) in any case where, under a contract or other arrangements for the transfer of United Kingdom securities, one of the parties (an 'interest manufacturer') is required to pay to the other ('the recipient') an amount ('the manufactured interest') which is representative of a periodical payment of interest on the securities.

(2) For the relevant purposes of the Tax Acts, in their application in relation to the interest manufacturer—

(a) the manufactured interest shall be treated, except in determining whether it is deductible, as if it—

(i) were an annual payment to the recipient, but

(ii) were neither yearly interest nor an amount payable wholly out of profits or gains brought into charge for income tax;

(b) the gross amount of that deemed annual payment shall be taken—

(i) to be equal to the gross amount of the interest of which the manufactured interest is representative; and

(ii) to constitute income of the recipient falling within section 1A; and

(c) an amount equal to so much of the gross amount of the manufactured interest as is not otherwise deductible shall be allowable as a deduction against the total income or, as the case may be, total profits of the interest manufacturer.

(3) For the relevant purposes of the Tax Acts, in their application in relation to the recipient and any persons claiming title through or under him—

(a) the manufactured interest shall be treated as if it were a periodical payment of interest on the securities in question; and

(b) the gross amount of that deemed periodical payment of interest shall be taken to be equal to the gross amount of the interest of which the manufactured interest is representative.

(4) Sub-paragraph (2) above shall not require any deduction of tax to be made by the interest manufacturer if—

(a) the interest manufacturer is not resident in the United Kingdom, and

(b) the manufactured interest is paid otherwise than in the course of a trade carried on by the interest manufacturer in the United Kingdom through a branch or agency.

(5) Where, in a case falling within sub-paragraph (4)(a) and (b) above, the recipient—

(a) is resident in the United Kingdom, or

(b) (without being so resident) receives the manufactured interest for the purposes of a trade carried on by him in the United Kingdom through a branch or agency,

the recipient shall be liable to account for income tax in respect of the manufactured interest.

(6) The amount of the income tax for which the recipient is liable to account under sub-paragraph (5) above is the amount equal to the income tax which the interest manufacturer, had he been resident in the United Kingdom, would have been required, in respect of the manufactured interest, to account for and pay by virtue of sub-paragraph (2) above.

(7) For the purposes of sub-paragraph (2) above, if the interest manufacturer is a company which—

(a) is not resident in the United Kingdom, but

(b) carries on a trade in the United Kingdom through a branch or agency,

Schedule 16 shall have effect in relation to the manufactured interest as it has effect in the case of a company which is resident in the United Kingdom but as if, in paragraph 7, the words 'section 11(3)' were substituted for the words 'section 7(2)'.

(8) Where sub-paragraph (2) above has effect in the case of any manufactured interest so as to require any amount to be deducted by way of tax from the gross amount of the manufactured interest, the interest manufacturer shall, on paying the manufactured interest, provide the recipient with a statement in writing setting out—

(a) the gross amount of the manufactured interest;

(b) the amount deducted by way of tax by the interest manufacturer;

(c) the amount actually paid by the interest manufacturer; and

(d) the date of the payment by the interest manufacturer.

(9) The duty imposed by sub-paragraph (8) above shall be enforceable at the suit or instance of the recipient.

(10) The references in this paragraph to an amount being deductible are references to its being either—

(a) deductible in computing the amount of any of the interest manufacturer's profits or gains for the purposes of income tax or corporation tax; or

(b) deductible for those purposes from the total income or, as the case may be, total profits of the interest manufacturer.

(11) For the purposes of this paragraph 'the relevant purposes of the Tax Acts' means all the purposes of those Acts except the purposes of Chapter II of Part IV of the Finance Act 1996 (loan relationships).

(12) Without prejudice to the generality of section 80(5) of the Finance Act 1996 (matters to be brought into account only under that Chapter), this paragraph does not have effect for determining how any manufactured interest falls to be treated for any purpose in relation to a company in relation to which that interest falls to be treated in accordance with section 97 of that Act.

(13) For the purposes of this paragraph references to the gross amount of any interest or payment are references to the amount of the interest or payment before the making of any deduction of income tax that is required to be deducted from it on its being paid or made.

Manufactured interest on gilt-edged securities etc.

3A.—(1) Where any manufactured interest is representative of interest on securities to which this paragraph applies—

(a) paragraph 3(2) above shall not require any deduction of tax to be made on the payment of that manufactured interest; and

(b) without prejudice to any other liability of his to income tax in respect of the manufactured interest, the recipient shall not by virtue of paragraph 3(5) above be liable to account for any income tax in respect of that manufactured interest.

(2) This paragraph applies to—

(a) gilt-edged securities (within the meaning of section 51A); and

  (b) securities not falling within paragraph (a) above on which the interest is payable without deduction of tax."

(2) In section 737C(8) of that Act, for paragraph (a) (amount of deemed manufactured interest) there shall be substituted the following paragraph—

    "(a) the amount which by virtue of section 737A(5) is taken to be the gross amount of the deemed manufactured payment for the purposes of paragraph 3 of Schedule 23A shall be taken to be the gross amount of the deemed manufactured interest for the purposes of this section;"

and in paragraph (b) for "paragraph 3 of Schedule 23A" there shall be substituted "that paragraph".

Repeal of paragraph 5 of Schedule 23A

12. Paragraph 5 of Schedule 23A to that Act (dividends and interest passing through the market) shall cease to have effect.

Consequential amendments in Schedule 23A

13.—(1) In sub-paragraph (1) of paragraph 8 of Schedule 23A to that Act (power to modify provisions of Schedule), for "paragraphs 2 to 5 above" there shall be substituted "paragraphs 2 to 4 above".

(2) In sub-paragraph (2) of that paragraph (powers with respect to accounts and records, returns, accounting for tax etc.), for the words after paragraph (d) there shall be substituted—

    "by persons by or to whom manufactured dividends, manufactured interest or manufactured overseas dividends are paid."

(3) After that sub-paragraph there shall be inserted the following sub-paragraph—

    "(2A) Dividend manufacturing regulations with respect to any liability to account for tax may contain any of the following, that is to say—

      (a) provision for computing the amounts to be accounted for;

      (b) provision, in relation to the determination of the amount to be paid on any occasion, for setting other amounts against the amounts to be accounted for;

      (c) provision as to the liabilities against which amounts accounted for are to be, or are not to be, set for the purposes of income tax or corporation tax;

      (d) provision modifying, or applying (with or without modifications), any enactments contained in the Tax Acts."

Amendments of Taxes Management Act 1970

14.—(1) Section 21 of the Taxes Management Act 1970 (information about a market maker's business) shall be amended as follows.

(2) For subsection (1) there shall be substituted the following subsection—

    "(1) The Board may exercise the powers conferred by this section as respects, and in connection with, any business consisting in or involving dealings in securities; and for the purposes of this section it shall be immaterial whether those dealings are or, as the case may be, were—

      (a) on behalf of persons other than the person carrying on the business;

      (b) by that person on his own behalf; or

      (c) a mixture of the two."

(3) In subsection (2)—

  (a) for the word "transactions", in the first place where it occurs, there shall be substituted "securities transactions"; and

  (b) for "market maker" there shall be substituted "person".

(4) In subsection (3), for "transactions in the course of" there shall be substituted "securities transactions in the course of any business of a person other than the broker which is".

(5) For subsection (4) there shall be substituted the following subsections—

    "(4) Where a person ('the recipient') who is not a broker has directly or indirectly received from another person any payment which—

      (a) is made by that other person in the course of a business within subsection (1) above, and

      (b) is a payment treated by that other person as made in respect of interest on securities,

the Board may by notice in writing require the recipient to state, within a time specified in the notice, whether the amount received is in whole or in part received on behalf of, or for payment on to, a third person and (if it is) to furnish the name and address of that third person.

(4A) Where a person ('the payer') has directly or indirectly paid to another person any sum which—

    (a) constitutes a receipt by that other person in the course of a business within subsection (1) above, and

    (b) is a receipt treated by that other person as accruing in respect of interest on securities, the Board may by notice in writing require the payer to state, within a time specified in the notice, whether the amount paid is in whole or in part received from, or paid on account of, a third person and (if it is) to furnish the name and address of that third person."

(6) In subsection (5)—

(a) for "whether brokers or market makers or not" there shall be substituted "at all"; and

(b) for "transactions" there shall be substituted "securities transactions".

(7) After that subsection there shall be inserted the following subsection—

    "(5A) Where it appears to the Board that a person may have incurred a liability to pay or account for tax under Schedule 23A to the principal Act (manufactured payments), the Board may by notice served on that person require him, within such period (not being less than 28 days) as may be specified in the notice, to provide the Board with information which—

    (a) is available to that person; and

    (b) is or may be relevant to whether that person has incurred such a liability, or to the extent of such a liability."

(8) For subsection (7) there shall be substituted the following subsection—

    "(7) In this section—

        'broker' means any person who is a member of a recognised investment exchange, within the meaning of the Financial Services Act 1986;

        'interest' includes dividends;

        'securities' includes shares and stock; and

        'securities transaction' means—

            (a) any transaction in securities;

            (b) any transaction under which a payment which is representative of any interest on a security has been, is to be or may be made; or

            (c) the making or receipt of such a payment."

Repeal of powers to modify information provisions

15. Paragraphs 7 and 9 of Schedule 18 to the Finance Act 1986 (which contain powers to modify section 21 of the Taxes Management Act 1970) shall cease to have effect.

Commencement

16.—(1) Subject to the following provisions of this paragraph, this Part of this Schedule has effect in relation to any payment of a manufactured dividend or manufactured interest which is a payment made on or after such day as the Treasury may by order made by statutory instrument appoint.

(2) Paragraph 14 above has effect (instead of in accordance with sub-paragraph (1) above but subject to sub-paragraph (3) below) for the purpose of conferring powers for obtaining information about—

(a) transactions entered into on or after such day as the Treasury may by order made by statutory instrument appoint; and

(b) payments made on or after that day (whether under such transactions or under transactions entered into before that day).

(3) Nothing in this Part of this Schedule shall affect the exercise, at any time on or after the day appointed under sub-paragraph (2) above, of the powers conferred apart from this Schedule by—

(a) section 21 of the Taxes Management Act 1970, or by any regulations modifying that section, or

(b) section 737(8) of the Taxes Act 1988,

for obtaining information about transactions entered into, or payments made, before that day.

GENERAL NOTE

The Schedule removes the existing income and capital gains tax restrictions from the borrowing and lending of U.K. equities and simplifies related legislation about manufactured payments, allowing about 70 pages of primary legislation and regulations to be repealed. These changes will assist the development of a repo market in U.K. equities.

Part I
This is concerned with stock lending.

Para. 1
ICTA 1988, ss.129 and 129A and Sched. 5A are repealed. These provisions relate to transfers of U.K. equities under approved stock lending arrangements and to the position where the collateral for the loan takes the form of cash. Their repeal aligns the position of stock lending with that of repos, repurchase agreements in which the seller of a gilt agrees with the buyer to repurchase it at an agreed time and price (see *ibid.*, ss.51A and 51B).

Para. 2
This makes a consequential amendment to *ibid.*, s.129, drawing on the definition in TCGA 1992, s.263B, inserted by para. 5.

Para. 3
New ICTA 1988, s.736B prevents stock lending being used to switch dividend income from one person to another for tax reasons. This is done by deeming manufactured payments (see *ibid.*, Sched. 23A) to be made in such circumstances.

Para. 4
Consequential changes are made to Sched. 23A.

Para. 5
This inserts new ss.263B and 263C into TCGA 1992 in place of s.271(9) and makes a consequential change to ICTA 1988, s.727(2). These changes ensure that transfers under stock loans do not trigger a capital gains charge.

Para. 6
Consequential repeals are made in the provisions about the Premium Trust Funds of Lloyd's members.

Para. 7
Provision is made regarding commencement. This is to be on July 1, 1997.

Part II
This deals with manufactured payments.

Para. 8
This repeals ICTA 1988, s.737, which is now subsumed into *ibid.* Sched. 23A, paras. 2–2B and 3–3A, inserted by paras. 10 and 11 below.

Para. 9
A definition of "foreign income dividend" is inserted into Sched. 23A.

Para. 10
This replaces Sched. 23A, para. 2 with new paras. 2, 2A and 2B, about manufactured dividends on U.K. equities. Where the manufacturer is a company resident in the U.K., the manufactured dividend is treated as if it were a dividend of the company itself. The general provisions in ICTA 1988 about companies paying dividends are applied, including the accounting arrangements in Sched. 13. Manufacturers not resident in the U.K. are treated in a broadly equivalent way. In particular, provision is made for an amount of tax to be accounted for equal to the ACT that would have been paid had the manufacturer been a company resident in the U.K. If the manufactured dividend is paid to a U.K. resident from abroad, the tax is to be accounted for by the U.K. recipient, rather than the manufacturer. Provision is made for the detailed accounting arrangements involved to be set out in new regulations, which will take the place of two existing sets of regulations.
Manufactured dividends paid by non-corporate taxpayers can be deducted in computing their income. Non-resident companies trading in the U.K. may not make such a deduction, in line with the treatment of resident companies. The treatment of the tax they account for on manufactured dividends they pay will mirror that of resident companies and will be set out in regulations.
Where the manufactured dividend is representative of a foreign income dividend ("FID"), the recipient is regarded as receiving a FID. Since the tax credit on such dividends is not payable, there is no obligation to account for tax on it.
Manufacturers are required to provide recipients with appropriate tax vouchers.

Para. 11

This replaces Sched. 23A, paras. 3 and 3A, with new paras. 3 and 3A, which deal with manufactured interest on U.K. securities.

In relation to the manufacturer, the same amount of tax is to be deducted as is deducted from the real interest of which it is representative. The manufactured interest is deductible in computing the manufacturer's income. In addition, as a result of deeming the payment to be an annual payment, the accounting arrangements in Sched. 16 apply in relation to companies resident in the U.K. The manufactured interest is treated in the hands of the recipient as if it were the interest of which it is representative.

There is no obligation on manufacturers who are neither resident nor trading in the U.K. to account for tax on manufactured interest. Where a manufactured payment made by such a manufacturer is received in the U.K., the U.K. recipient has to account for tax.

The accounting arrangements of Sched. 16 are applied to U.K. branches of non-resident companies.

Manufacturers must provide recipients with appropriate tax vouchers.

Provision is made for interaction with the loan relationship rules in F.A. 1996.

There is no obligation to deduct tax from manufactured interest on gilt-edged securities or on securities (such as those to which ICTA 1988, s.582 applies) the interest on which is always payable without deduction of tax.

Para. 12

Sched. 23A, para. 5, which deals with the previous treatment of dividends and interest passing through the market, is repealed.

Para. 13

This makes consequential amendments to Sched. 23A and provides the necessary additional regulation-making powers.

Para. 14

Amendments are made to the wording of Taxes Management Act 1970 (c. 9), s.21 to modernise it in the light of changes both in the markets and in tax legislation. These make no substantive change to the scope of the section.

Para. 15

This makes a consequential amendment regarding a power to modify s.21 which is no longer required.

Para. 16

Provision is made regarding commencement. The appointed date is July 1, 1997.

Section 80   SCHEDULE 11

FUTURES AND OPTIONS: TAXATION OF GUARANTEED RETURNS

Schedule to be inserted as Schedule 5AA to the Taxes Act 1988

"SCHEDULE 5AA

GUARANTEED RETURNS ON TRANSACTIONS IN FUTURES AND OPTIONS

Charge to tax etc.

1.—(1) Subject to sub-paragraph (2) below, profits and gains arising from a transaction to which this Schedule applies (including those which, apart from this sub-paragraph, would be taken to be of a capital nature) shall be treated, when realised—

(a) as income of the person by whom they are realised; and

(b) as chargeable to tax under Case VI of Schedule D for the chargeable period in which they are realised.

(2) Sub-paragraph (1) above does not apply to—

(a) so much of any profits or gains arising to a person from a transaction as are charged to tax in his case under Case I or V of Schedule D;

(b) any profits or gains arising to a company which is a qualifying company from a transaction which, as regards that company, is or is deemed to be a qualifying contract; or

(c) any profits or gains arising to an authorised unit trust (within the meaning of section 468).

(3) In sub-paragraph (2) above—

'qualifying company' means a qualifying company for the purposes of Chapter II of Part IV of the Finance Act 1994 (interest rate, currency and debt contracts); and

'qualifying contract' means a qualifying contract for those purposes.

(4) For the purposes of this Schedule the profits and gains arising from a transaction to which this Schedule applies are to be taken to be realised at the time when the disposal comprised in the transaction takes place.

(5) For the purposes of sections 392 and 396 any loss in a transaction to which this Schedule applies is to be taken to be sustained at the time when, in accordance with sub-paragraph (4) above, any profits or gains arising from that transaction would have been realised.

(6) Subject to sub-paragraph (7) below, the following, namely—

(a) profits and gains to which sub-paragraph (1) above applies, and

(b) losses in transactions the profits and gains from which (if there were any) would be profits and gains to which that sub-paragraph applies,

shall not be brought into account for the purposes of income tax, corporation tax or capital gains tax except by virtue of this Schedule and, in the case of losses, section 392 or 396.

(7) Nothing in sub-paragraph (6) above shall prevent any amount from being brought into account in accordance with section 83 of the Finance Act 1989 (receipts to be brought into account in any Case I computation made in respect of life insurance).

Transactions to which Schedule applies

2.—(1) This Schedule applies to a transaction if—

(a) it is a disposal of futures or options;

(b) it is one of two or more related transactions designed to produce a guaranteed return; and

(c) the guaranteed return comprises the return from that disposal or from a number of disposals of futures or options, of which that disposal is one, taken together.

(2) For the purposes of this Schedule two or more related transactions are transactions designed to produce a guaranteed return if, taking the transactions together, it would be reasonable to assume, from either or both of—

(a) the likely effect of the transactions, and

(b) the circumstances in which the transactions are entered into, or in which any of them is entered into,

that their main purpose, or one of their main purposes, is or was the production of a guaranteed return from one or more disposals of futures or options.

Production of guaranteed return

3.—(1) For the purposes of this Schedule a guaranteed return is produced from one or more disposals of futures or options wherever (taking all the disposals together where there is more than one) risks from fluctuations in the underlying subject matter are so eliminated or reduced as to produce a return from the disposal or disposals—

(a) the amount of which is not, to any significant extent, attributable (otherwise than incidentally) to any such fluctuations; and

(b) which equates, in substance, to the return on an investment of money at interest.

(2) For the purposes of sub-paragraph (1) above the cases where risks from fluctuations in the underlying subject matter are eliminated or reduced shall be deemed to include any case where the main reason, or one of the main reasons, for the choice of that subject matter is—

(a) that there appears to be no risk that it will fluctuate; or

(b) that the risk that it will fluctuate appears to be insignificant.

(3) In this paragraph the references, in relation to a disposal of futures or options, to the underlying subject matter are references to or to the value of the commodities, currencies, shares, stock or securities, interest rates, indices or other matters to which, or to the value of which, those futures or options are referable.

Disposals of futures or options

4.—(1) For the purposes of this Schedule a disposal is a disposal of futures or options if it consists in—

(a) the disposal of one or more futures;

(b) the disposal of one or more options; or

(c) the disposal of one or more futures together with one or more options.

(2) Subject to sub-paragraph (4) below, any question for the purposes of this Schedule as to whether there is a disposal falling within sub-paragraph (1)(a) to (c) above, or as to when such a

disposal is made, shall be determined, on the assumptions specified in sub-paragraph (3) below, in accordance with—

(a) section 143(5) and (6), 144 and 144A of the 1992 Act (closing out and settlement of futures contracts and rules in relation to options); and

(b) the other provisions having effect for determining for the purposes of that Act whether or when an asset is disposed of;

and references in this Schedule to entering into a transaction are references, in relation to a transaction consisting in a disposal, to the making of the disposal.

(3) Those assumptions are—

(a) that all futures are assets for the purposes of the 1992 Act;

(b) that the words "in the course of dealing in commodity or financial futures" are omitted in each place where they occur in section 143(5) and (6) of that Act; and

(c) that any reference in that Act to a financial option within the meaning given by section 144(8) of that Act is a reference to any option that is not a traded option.

(4) Subject to sub-paragraph (5) below, where—

(a) one of a number of related transactions designed to produce a guaranteed return is the grant of an option,

(b) at least one of the other transactions is a transaction entered into after the grant of the option, and

(c) the transaction or transactions entered into after the grant of the option is or include a disposal which is not itself the grant of an option,

the disposal consisting in the grant of the option shall be deemed for the purposes of this Schedule to be a disposal made on the first occasion after the grant of the option when one of the other transactions which is a disposal but is not itself the grant of an option is entered into.

(5) Nothing in sub-paragraph (4) above affects so much of sub-paragraph (2) above as (by applying section 144(2) or 144A(2) of the 1992 Act (cases where options are exercised))—

(a) requires the grant of an option and the transaction entered into by the grantor in fulfilment of his obligations under that option to be treated for the purposes of this Schedule as a single transaction; or

(b) determines the time at which such a single transaction is to be treated for the purposes of this Schedule as entered into.

(6) In this paragraph—

'future' means outstanding rights and obligations under a commodity or financial futures contract;

'option' means a traded option or an option which is not a traded option but is an option relating to—

(a) currency, shares, stock, securities or an interest rate; or

(b) rights under a commodity or financial futures contract;

'traded option' has the meaning given for the purposes of subsection (4) of section 144 of the 1992 Act by subsection (8) of that section.

The return from one or more disposals

5.—(1) In this Schedule references to the return from one or more disposals are references to the return on investment represented either—

(a) by the total net profits and gains arising from the disposal or disposals; or

(b) by all but an insignificant part of those net profits and gains.

(2) For the purposes of the references in sub-paragraph (1) above to the total net profits and gains from any two or more disposals, it shall be assumed that profits and gains realised, and losses sustained, by persons who are associated with each other are all realised or sustained by the same person.

(3) For the purposes of sub-paragraph (2) above persons are associated with each other in relation to any two or more disposals made in pursuance of the same scheme or arrangements if—

(a) each of those persons shares or is to share, to an extent determined for the purposes of or in accordance with the scheme or arrangements, in the net return represented by the aggregate of all the profits, gains and losses realised or sustained on those disposals;

(b) those persons are associated companies at the time when the last of those disposals is made; or

(c) those persons have been associated companies at an earlier time falling after the first occasion on which a transaction was entered into in pursuance of the scheme or arrangements.

(4) In this paragraph—

'associated company' shall be construed in accordance with section 416; and

'scheme or arrangements' shall be construed in accordance with paragraph 6(4) below.

Related transactions

6.—(1) For the purposes of this Schedule two or more transactions are related if all of them are entered into in pursuance of the same scheme or arrangements.

(2) Nothing in this Schedule shall be construed as preventing transactions with different parties, or transactions with parties different from the parties to the scheme or arrangements in pursuance of which they are entered into, from being related transactions.

(3) For the purposes of this paragraph the cases in which any two or more transactions are to be taken to be entered into in pursuance of the same scheme or arrangements shall include any case in which it would be reasonable to assume, from either or both of—

(a) the likely effect of the transactions, and
(b) the circumstances in which the transactions are entered into, or in which any of them is entered into,

that neither of them or, as the case may be, none of them would have been entered into independently of the other or others.

(4) In this paragraph 'scheme or arrangements' includes schemes, arrangements and understandings of any kind, whether or not legally enforceable.

Special rule for trusts

7.—(1) Where any profits or gains are treated, in accordance with paragraph 1 above, as income arising to trustees for any year of assessment, the relevant part of that income shall be treated for the purposes of the Tax Acts as if it were income to which section 686 applies (income taxable at the rate applicable to trusts).

(2) In sub-paragraph (1) above the reference to the relevant part of any income is a reference to so much (if any) of that income as—

(a) does not fall to be treated for the purposes of the Income Tax Acts as income of a settlor;
(b) is not income arising under a trust established for charitable purposes; and
(c) is not income from investments, deposits or other property held for any such purposes as are mentioned in sub-paragraph (i) or (ii) of section 686(2)(c) (property held for pension purposes).

(3) Subsection (6) of section 686 (meaning of 'trustees' etc.) shall apply for the purposes of this paragraph as it applies for the purposes of that section.

Transfer of assets abroad

8. For the purpose of determining whether an individual ordinarily resident in the United Kingdom has a liability for income tax in respect of any profit or gain which—

(a) is realised by a person resident or domiciled outside the United Kingdom, and
(b) arises from a transaction to which this Schedule applies,

sections 739 and 740 (transfer of assets abroad) shall have effect as if that profit or gain, when realised, constituted income becoming payable to the person resident or domiciled outside the United Kingdom.

Apportionment in the case of insurance companies

9. Section 432A (apportionment of insurance companies' income) shall have effect in the case of income and losses chargeable or relievable by virtue of this Schedule as if (where that would not otherwise be the case)—

(a) any such income were for the purposes of that section a gain accruing on the disposal of an asset; and
(b) any such loss were for the purposes of that section a loss accruing on the disposal of an asset."

General Note

This implements provisions to prevent tax avoidance through the use of artificial transactions in futures and options. It does so by inserting a new Sched. 5AA into ICTA 1988 (references below are to paragraphs in Sched. 5AA).

Para. 1

This brings into charge under Case VI of Sched. D transactions caught by the new provisions. Transactions already chargeable under Case I or Case V are excluded, as are profits arising to companies qualifying under F.A. 1994, Pt. IV, Chap. II and authorised unit trusts. The latter are excluded in the light of assurances from the unit trust industry.

Profits and gains are taken to be realised when the disposal comprised in the transaction takes place. The same rule applies to losses.

Such profits and gains, or losses, are taxable only under Sched. 5AA, except in relation to F.A. 1989, s.83, which deals with receipts to be brought into account in a Case I computation on the profits of a life insurance company.

Para. 2

The transactions to which the Schedule applies are those designed to produce a guaranteed return.

Para. 3

A guaranteed return is one which equates, in substance, to the return on an investment of money at interest. Insignificant risks of fluctuations in the return are to be ignored.

Para. 4

The provisions extend to packages including one or more futures, one or more options, or a mixture of both. The rules in TCGA 1992, ss.143, 144 and 144A relating to the closing out and settlement of futures contracts and to options apply, subject to appropriate assumptions. Where the grant of an option is linked with another transaction which is not the grant of an option the latter transaction is deemed to be a disposal. This is without prejudice to the rules in TCGA 1992, ss.144(2) or 144A(2), dealing with cases where options are exercised.

Para. 5

An insignificant part of profits and gains may be excluded in computing the return from one or more disposals. Profits and gains realised and losses sustained by associated persons are taken to be realised or sustained by the same person. Persons are taken to be associated if there is a pre-determined arrangement for sharing in the net return from the scheme or arrangements or if they are associated companies within ICTA 1988, s.416.

Para. 6

Further clarification is given on the meaning of "scheme or arrangements". The scope is fairly wide and includes understanding of any kind, whether or not legally enforceable.

Para. 7

Where the profits arise to trustees, they will generally be taxable at the rate applicable to trusts under ICTA 1988, s.686.

Para. 8

Any profits or gains arising to a person resident or domiciled outside the U.K. will be deemed to be income for the purposes of *ibid.*, ss.739–740.

Para. 9

For the purposes of *ibid.*, s.432A, dealing with the apportionment of insurance companies' income, income and losses chargeable or relievable as a result of the Schedule are treated as accruing on the disposal of an asset.

Section 82   SCHEDULE 12

LEASING ARRANGEMENTS: FINANCE LEASES AND LOANS

PART I

LEASING ARRANGEMENTS WHERE ANY OF THE RETURN ON INVESTMENT IS IN CAPITAL FORM

Purpose of this Part of this Schedule

1.—(1) This Part of this Schedule is concerned with arrangements—
(a) which involve the lease of an asset;
(b) which are or have been entered into by companies or other persons;
(c) which are of such a kind as, in the case of companies incorporated in any part of the United Kingdom, falls for the purposes of accounts of such companies to be treated in accordance with normal accountancy practice as finance leases or loans; and
(d) whose effect is that some or all of the return on investment in respect of the finance lease or loan—
      (i) is or may be in the form of a sum which is not rent; and
      (ii) would not, apart from this Schedule, be wholly brought into account for tax purposes as rent from the lease.

(2) The principal purpose of this Part of this Schedule is, in the case of any such arrangements—

   (a) to charge any person entitled to the lessor's interest under the lease of the asset to tax from time to time on amounts of income determined by reference to those which fall for accounting purposes to be treated in accordance with normal accountancy practice as the income return, on and after 26th November 1996, on investment in respect of the finance lease or loan (taking into account the substance of the matter as a whole, including in particular the state of affairs as between connected persons, or within a group of companies, as reflected or falling to be reflected in accounts of any of those persons or in consolidated group accounts);

   (b) where the sum mentioned in sub-paragraph (1)(d) above falls due, to recover by reference to that sum the whole or any part of any reliefs, allowances or deductions which are or have been allowed or made in respect of capital expenditure incurred in respect of the leased asset.

Application of this Part of this Schedule

2.—(1) This Part of this Schedule applies in any case where (whether before or after the passing of this Act)—

   (a) a lease of an asset is or has been granted; and

   (b) in the case of the lease, the conditions in paragraph 3 below are or have been satisfied at some time in a period of account of the current lessor.

(2) Where the conditions in paragraph 3 below have been satisfied at some time in a period of account of the person who was at that time the lessor, they shall be taken to continue to be satisfied for the purposes of this Part of this Schedule unless and until—

   (a) the asset ceases to be leased under the lease; or

   (b) the lessor's interest under the lease is assigned to a person who is not connected with any of the persons described in sub-paragraph (3) below.

(3) Those persons are—

   (a) the assignor;

   (b) any person who was the lessor at some time before the assignment; or

   (c) any person who at some time after the assignment becomes the lessor pursuant to arrangements made by a person who was the lessor, or was connected with the lessor, at some time before the assignment.

(4) Nothing in sub-paragraph (2) above prevents this Part of this Schedule from again applying in the case of the lease if the conditions for its application are satisfied after the assignment.

The conditions

3.—(1) The condition in this sub-paragraph is that at the relevant time the leasing arrangements are such as fall for accounting purposes to be treated in accordance with normal accountancy practice as a finance lease or a loan and—

   (a) the lessor, or a person connected with him, falls for accounting purposes to be treated in accordance with normal accountancy practice as the finance lessor in relation to the finance lease or loan, or

   (b) the finance lease or loan falls for accounting purposes to be treated, in accordance with normal accountancy practice, as subsisting for the purposes of consolidated group accounts of a group of companies of which the lessor is a member.

(2) The condition in this sub-paragraph is that, under the leasing arrangements, there is or may be payable to the lessor, or to a person connected with him, a sum (a "major lump sum") which is not rent but is a sum such as falls for accounting purposes to be treated in accordance with normal accountancy practice—

   (a) as to part, as repayment of some or all of the investment in respect of a finance lease or loan; and

   (b) as to part, as a return on investment in respect of a finance lease or loan.

(3) The condition in this sub-paragraph is that not all of that part of a major lump sum which falls within paragraph (b) of sub-paragraph (2) above would, apart from this Schedule, fall to be brought into account for tax purposes in chargeable periods of the lessor ending with the relevant chargeable period as the normal rent from the lease for periods of account of the lessor.

(4) The condition in this sub-paragraph is that, as respects the lessor at the relevant time—

   (a) the period of account of his in which the relevant time falls, or

   (b) an earlier period of account of his during which he was the lessor,

is a period of account for which the accountancy rental earnings in respect of the lease exceed the normal rent for the period.

(5) The condition in this sub-paragraph is that at the relevant time—

(a) arrangements falling within sub-paragraph (1) of paragraph 4 below exist; or

(b) if the condition in paragraph (a) above is not satisfied, circumstances falling within sub-paragraph (2) of that paragraph exist.

(6) In determining the normal rent for a period of account for the purpose of determining whether the condition in sub-paragraph (4) above is satisfied, rent which for the purposes of corporation tax under Schedule A falls to be brought into account as a person becomes entitled to it shall be treated—

(a) as if it accrued evenly throughout the period to which, in accordance with the terms of the lease, each payment to which the person becomes entitled relates, and

(b) as if he had become entitled to the rent as it so accrues,

unless any such payment falls due more than 12 months after the time at which any of the rent to which that payment relates is so treated as accruing.

(7) In determining the normal rent for a period of account for the purpose of determining whether the condition in sub-paragraph (4) above is satisfied, rent which falls to be brought into account for tax purposes as it falls due shall be treated—

(a) as accruing evenly throughout the period to which, in accordance with the terms of the lease, each payment falling due relates, and

(b) as falling due as it so accrues,

unless any such payment falls due more than 12 months after the time at which any of the rent to which that payment relates is so treated as accruing.

(8) In this paragraph—

"the relevant chargeable period", in the case of any major lump sum, means—

(a) the chargeable period of the lessor which is related to his period of account in which that major lump sum is or may be payable in accordance with the leasing arrangements; or

(b) if there are two or more such chargeable periods, the latest of them;

"the relevant time" means the time as at which it falls to be determined for the purposes of sub-paragraph (1) or (2) of paragraph 2 above whether the conditions in this paragraph are or, as the case may be, were satisfied.

The arrangements and circumstances in paragraph 3(5)

4.—(1) The arrangements mentioned in paragraph 3(5)(a) above are arrangements under which—

(a) the lessee or a person connected with him may acquire, whether directly or indirectly, the leased asset, or an asset representing the leased asset, from the lessor or a person connected with the lessor; and

(b) in connection with that acquisition, the lessor or a person connected with him may receive, whether directly or indirectly, a qualifying lump sum from the lessee or a person connected with the lessee.

(2) The circumstances mentioned in paragraph 3(5)(b) above are circumstances which make it more likely—

(a) that the events described in sub-paragraph (3) below will occur, than

(b) that the event described in sub-paragraph (4) below will occur.

(3) The events mentioned in sub-paragraph (2)(a) above are—

(a) that the lessee or a person connected with him will acquire, whether directly or indirectly, the leased asset or an asset representing the leased asset from the lessor or a person connected with the lessor; and

(b) that, in connection with that acquisition, the lessor or a person connected with him will receive, whether directly or indirectly, a qualifying lump sum from the lessee or a person connected with the lessee.

(4) The event mentioned in sub-paragraph (2)(b) above is that, before any such acquisition as is mentioned in sub-paragraph (3) above takes place, the leased asset or, as the case may be, the asset representing the leased asset, will have been acquired, in a sale on the open market, by a person who is not the lessor or the lessee and who is not connected with either of them.

(5) In this paragraph, "qualifying lump sum" means any sum which is not rent but at least part of which would, if the recipient were a company incorporated in the United Kingdom, fall for accounting purposes to be treated in accordance with normal accountancy practice as a return on investment in respect of a finance lease or loan.

Current lessor to be taxed by reference to accountancy rental earnings

5.—(1) Where, in the case of any period of account of the current lessor—

(a) this Part of this Schedule applies in the case of the lease, and

(b) the accountancy rental earnings in respect of the lease for that period of account exceed the normal rent for that period,

he shall be treated for tax purposes as if in that period of account he had been entitled to, and there had arisen to him, rent from the lease of an amount equal to those accountancy rental earnings (instead of the normal rent referred to in paragraph (b) above).

(2) Where a person is treated under sub-paragraph (1) above as if he had in a period of account been entitled to, and there had arisen to him, any rent from a lease of an asset, the rent shall be treated for tax purposes—

(a) as if it had accrued at an even rate throughout so much of the period of account as falls within the period for which the asset is leased; and

(b) as if that person had become entitled to it as it accrued.

Reduction of taxable rent by certain excesses

6.—(1) Subject to sub-paragraph (6)(b) below, if in the case of the lease—

(a) the normal rent for a period of account of the current lessor throughout which the leasing arrangements are such as fall for accounting purposes to be treated in accordance with normal accountancy practice as a finance lease or loan, exceeds

(b) the accountancy rental earnings for the period,

there is for the purposes of this paragraph a "normal rental excess" for that period of an amount equal to the excess.

(2) In this paragraph the "cumulative normal rental excess" in the case of the lease and a period of account of the current lessor means so much of the aggregate of the normal rental excesses for previous periods of account of his as (after taking account of any increases under paragraph 10 below) has not been—

(a) set off under this paragraph against the taxable rent for any such previous period; or

(b) reduced under paragraph 10 below.

(3) Subject to sub-paragraph (8)(b) below, if the taxable rent in the case of the lease for a period of account of the current lessor is, by virtue of paragraph 5 above, an amount equal to the accountancy rental earnings, there is for the purposes of this paragraph an "accountancy rental excess" for that period of an amount equal to the difference between—

(a) the accountancy rental earnings for the period of account; and

(b) the normal rent for the period.

(4) In this paragraph the "cumulative accountancy rental excess", in the case of the lease and a period of account of the current lessor, means so much of the aggregate of the accountancy rental excesses for previous periods of account of his as (after taking account of any increases under paragraph 9 below) has not been—

(a) set off under this paragraph against the taxable rent for any such previous period;

(b) reduced under paragraph 9 below; or

(c) set off under paragraph 12 below against the consideration for a disposal.

(5) If a period of account of the current lessor is one—

(a) for which the normal rent exceeds the accountancy rental earnings, and

(b) for which there is any cumulative accountancy rental excess,

sub-paragraph (6) below shall apply.

(6) Where this sub-paragraph applies—

(a) the taxable rent for the period of account shall be reduced (but not below the accountancy rental earnings) by setting against it the cumulative accountancy rental excess; and

(b) the normal rental excess for the period shall be the amount (if any) by which—

(i) the normal rent, reduced by an amount equal to the reduction under paragraph (a) above, exceeds

(ii) the accountancy rental earnings,

and if there is no such excess, there is no normal rental excess for the period.

(7) If a period of account of the current lessor is one—

(a) for which the taxable rent in the case of the lease is, by virtue of paragraph 5 above, an amount equal to the accountancy rental earnings, and

(b) there is any cumulative normal rental excess,

sub-paragraph (8) below shall apply.

(8) Where this sub-paragraph applies—

(a) the taxable rent for the period of account shall be reduced (but not below the normal rent) by setting against it the cumulative normal rental excess, and

(b) the accountancy rental excess for the period shall be the amount (if any) by which—

(i) the accountancy rental earnings, reduced by an amount equal to the reduction under paragraph (a) above, exceeds

(ii) the normal rent,

and if there is no such excess, there is no accountancy rental excess for the period.

(9) In this paragraph "the taxable rent", in the case of a period of account of the current lessor, means the amount which would, apart from this paragraph and paragraph 8(6) below, be treated for tax purposes as rent from the lease—

(a) which arises to him, and

(b) if rent arising to him from the lease is chargeable to corporation tax under Schedule A, to which he is entitled,

in that period of account for the purpose of determining his liability to tax for the related chargeable period or periods.

Assignments on which neither a gain nor a loss accrues

7.—(1) This paragraph applies in any case where—

(a) the current lessor assigns the lessor's interest under the lease; and

(b) the assignment is a disposal on which, by virtue of any of the enactments specified in section 35(3)(d) of the Taxation of Chargeable Gains Act 1992, neither a gain nor a loss accrues.

(2) Where this paragraph applies, this Schedule shall have effect as if—

(a) a period of account of the assignor ended, and

(b) a period of account of the assignee began,

with the assignment.

(3) Where this paragraph applies—

(a) any unused cumulative accountancy rental excess, or

(b) any unused cumulative normal rental excess,

of the assignor shall become the cumulative accountancy rental excess or the cumulative normal rental excess (as the case may be) for the period of account of the assignee which begins with the assignment.

(4) In sub-paragraph (3) above—

"unused cumulative accountancy rental excess", in relation to the assignor, means the aggregate of—

(a) any cumulative accountancy rental excess, and

(b) any accountancy rental excess,

for the period of account of his which ends with the assignment;

"unused cumulative normal rental excess", in relation to the assignor, means the aggregate of—

(a) any cumulative normal rental excess, and

(b) any normal rental excess,

for the period of account of his which ends with the assignment.

Relief for bad debts etc: corporation tax under Schedule A

8.—(1) Section 41 of the Taxes Act 1988 (which gives a person relief from corporation tax under Schedule A for rent etc not paid, by treating him as if he had never been entitled to the rent) shall be disregarded in determining for the purposes of this Part of this Schedule the amount of—

(a) the accountancy rental earnings in respect of the lease, or

(b) the normal rent from the lease,

for any period of account.

(2) Where for any period of account—

(a) a person is treated under paragraph 5 above as if he had been entitled to receive an amount of rent, and

(b) the amount is in respect of rents on the profits or gains arising from which that person is chargeable to corporation tax under Schedule A,

section 41 of the Taxes Act 1988 shall not have effect in relation to amounts in respect of rents from the lease of the asset for that or any subsequent period of account of his, or of any person to whom the lessor's interest under the lease is assigned, until the lease terminates or is assigned in circumstances such that paragraph 7 above does not apply.

(3) Where, by virtue of sub-paragraph (2) above, section 41 of the Taxes Act 1988 does not apply, sub-paragraph (4) below shall apply instead.

(4) In computing the profits or gains on which a person is chargeable to corporation tax under Schedule A in a case falling within sub-paragraph (2) above, any sums falling within sub-paragraph (i), (ii) or (iii) of section 74(1)(j) of the Taxes Act 1988 in respect of amounts in respect of rents from the lease of the asset shall be deductible in a period of account as an expense to the extent that they would be deductible in that period of account if—

(a) amounts in respect of rents from the lease of the asset fell to be taken into account as trading receipts in computing the profits or gains of a trade carried on by the person;

(b) the asset were leased in the course of that trade; and

(c) the charge to corporation tax under Schedule A were in respect of such annual profits or gains as are described in that Schedule arising from a trade.

(5) Any such expense as is mentioned in sub-paragraph (4) above shall be treated for the purposes of section 25 of the Taxes Act 1988 (deductions from rent for the purposes of corporation tax under Schedule A) as if that expense—

(a) were included among the permitted deductions, within the meaning of that section;

(b) were a payment made in respect of the premises comprised in the lease; and

(c) were a payment which became due, and was made, immediately before the end of the period of account mentioned in sub-paragraph (4) above.

(6) Where—

(a) a deduction has been made by virtue of sub-paragraph (4) above in respect of an amount, but

(b) subsequently an amount ("the relevant credit") is recovered or credited in respect of the amount in respect of which the deduction was made, and

(c) the relevant credit would, on the suppositions in paragraphs (a) to (c) of sub-paragraph (4) above, be brought into account for tax purposes as a trading receipt for a period of account of the current lessor,

the taxable rent for that period of account shall be increased by the amount of the relevant credit.

(7) In sub-paragraph (6) above, "the taxable rent", in the case of a period of account of the current lessor, means the amount which would, apart from that sub-paragraph, be treated for tax purposes as rent from the lease—

(a) which arises to him, and

(b) if rent arising to him from the lease is chargeable to corporation tax under Schedule A, to which he is entitled,

in that period of account for the purpose of determining his liability to tax for the related chargeable period or periods.

(8) After the time when the conditions in paragraph 3 above become satisfied as respects any particular lessor, no claim under section 41 of the Taxes Act 1988 shall be made in respect of any amount which that lessor was entitled to receive in respect of rents from the lease of the asset.

(9) Where—

(a) before the time at which the conditions in paragraph 3 above become satisfied as respects any particular lessor, a claim under section 41 of the Taxes Act 1988 in respect of an amount which he was entitled to receive in respect of any rents from the lease of the asset has been made, and

(b) the claim is to any extent allowed,

no amount shall be deductible under sub-paragraph (4) above in respect of that amount so far as so allowed.

Relief for bad debts etc: cumulative accountancy rental excess

9.—(1) If, in the case of the lease, for any period of account—

(a) the accountancy rental earnings exceed the normal rent,

(b) a bad debt deduction falls to be made in respect of rent from the lease,

(c) the amount of the bad debt deduction exceeds the amount of the accountancy rental earnings, and

(d) there is a cumulative accountancy rental excess,

the cumulative accountancy rental excess for the period of account shall be reduced (but not below nil) by the amount by which the bad debt deduction exceeds the accountancy rental earnings.

(2) If, in the case of the lease, for any period of account—

(a) the accountancy rental earnings do not exceed the normal rent,

(b) a bad debt deduction falls to be made in respect of rent from the lease, and

(c) there is a cumulative accountancy rental excess for that period of account,

sub-paragraph (3) below shall apply.

(3) Where this sub-paragraph applies, the amount of the cumulative accountancy rental excess which may be set against the taxable rent for the period of account shall not exceed the amount (if any) by which the normal rent exceeds the bad debt deduction (and, if the normal rent does not exceed the bad debt deduction, shall be nil).

(4) If, in a case where sub-paragraph (3) above applies, the bad debt deduction exceeds the normal rent for the period of account, the cumulative accountancy rental excess for the period of account shall be reduced (but not below nil) by the amount by which the bad debt deduction exceeds the normal rent.

(5) Where—

(a) the cumulative accountancy rental excess for any period of account of the current lessor has been reduced under sub-paragraph (1) or (4) above by reason of a bad debt deduction, but

(b) in a subsequent period of account of his, an amount ("the relevant credit") is recovered or credited in respect of the amount which constituted the bad debt deduction,

the cumulative accountancy rental excess (if any) for the period of account mentioned in paragraph (b) above shall, subject to sub-paragraph (6) below, be increased by the relevant credit.

(6) If, in a case falling within sub-paragraph (5) above—

(a) the relevant credit, exceeds

(b) the aggregate of the reductions falling within paragraph (a) of that sub-paragraph,

the amount of the increase under that sub-paragraph shall not exceed that aggregate.

(7) In this paragraph—

"bad debt deduction", in relation to a period of account, means the aggregate of any sums falling within sub-paragraph (i), (ii) or (iii) of section 74(1)(j) of the Taxes Act 1988 in respect of amounts in respect of rents from the lease of the asset which are deductible as expenses for that period, whether by virtue of paragraph 8(4) above or otherwise;

"taxable rent" has the same meaning as in paragraph 6 above.

Relief for bad debts etc: cumulative normal rental excess

10.—(1) If, in the case of the lease, for any period of account—

(a) the accountancy rental earnings do not exceed the normal rent,

(b) a bad debt deduction falls to be made in respect of rent from the lease,

(c) the amount of the bad debt deduction exceeds the amount of the normal rent, and

(d) there is a cumulative normal rental excess,

the cumulative normal rental excess for the period of account shall be reduced (but not below nil) by the amount by which the bad debt deduction exceeds the normal rent.

(2) If, in the case of the lease, for any period of account—

(a) the accountancy rental earnings exceed the normal rent,

(b) a bad debt deduction falls to be made in respect of rent from the lease, and

(c) there is a cumulative normal rental excess for that period of account,

sub-paragraph (3) below shall apply.

(3) Where this sub-paragraph applies, the amount of the cumulative normal rental excess which may be set against the taxable rent for the period of account shall not exceed the amount (if any) by which the accountancy rental earnings exceed the bad debt deduction (and, if the accountancy rental earnings do not exceed the bad debt deduction, shall be nil).

(4) If, in a case where sub-paragraph (3) above applies, the bad debt deduction exceeds the accountancy rental earnings for the period of account, the cumulative normal rental excess for the period of account shall be reduced (but not below nil) by the amount by which the bad debt deduction exceeds the accountancy rental earnings.

(5) Where—

(a) the cumulative normal rental excess for any period of account of the current lessor has been reduced under sub-paragraph (1) or (4) above by reason of a bad debt deduction, but

(b) in a subsequent period of account of his, an amount ("the relevant credit") is recovered or credited in respect of the amount which constituted the bad debt deduction,

the cumulative normal rental excess (if any) for the period of account mentioned in paragraph (b) above shall, subject to sub-paragraph (6) below, be increased by the relevant credit.

(6) If, in a case falling within sub-paragraph (5) above,—

(a) the relevant credit, exceeds

(b) the aggregate of the reductions falling within paragraph (a) of that sub-paragraph,

the amount of the increase under that sub-paragraph shall not exceed that aggregate.

(7) In this paragraph—

"bad debt deduction", in relation to a period of account, means the aggregate of any sums falling within sub-paragraph (i), (ii) or (iii) of section 74(1)(j) of the Taxes Act 1988 in respect of amounts in respect of rents from the lease of the asset which are deductible as expenses for that period, whether by virtue of paragraph 8(4) above or otherwise;

"taxable rent" has the same meaning as in paragraph 6 above.

Capital allowances

11.—(1) This paragraph applies in any case where an occasion occurs on or after 26th November 1996 on which a major lump sum falls to be paid in the case of the lease of the asset.

(2) In this paragraph "the relevant occasion" means the occasion mentioned in sub-paragraph (1) above.

(3) If capital expenditure incurred by the current lessor in respect of the leased asset is or has been taken into account for the purposes of any allowance or charge under any of the following groups of provisions, that is to say—

(a) sections 520 and 521 of the Taxes Act 1988 (patent rights),

(b) Part II of the Capital Allowances Act 1990 (machinery and plant), or

(c) Part IV of that Act (mineral extraction allowances),

the group of provisions in question ("the relevant provisions") shall have effect as if the relevant occasion were an event by reason of which a disposal value is to be brought into account of an amount equal (subject to any applicable limiting provision) to the amount or value of the major lump sum.

(4) In this paragraph "limiting provision" means a provision to the effect that the disposal value of the asset in question is not to exceed an amount ("the limit") described by reference to capital expenditure incurred in respect of the asset.

(5) Where—

(a) by virtue of sub-paragraph (3) above, a disposal value ("the relevant disposal value") falls or has fallen to be brought into account by a person in respect of the leased asset for the purposes of the relevant provisions, and

(b) a limiting provision has effect in the case of those provisions,

sub-paragraph (6) below shall apply.

(6) Where this sub-paragraph applies, the limiting provision shall have effect (if or to the extent that it would not otherwise do so)—

(a) in the case of the relevant disposal value, and

(b) in the case of any simultaneous or subsequent disposal value,

as if, instead of any particular disposal value, it were the aggregate amount of all the disposal values brought into account for the purposes of the relevant provisions by the current lessor in respect of the leased asset which is not to exceed the limit.

(7) In sub-paragraph (6) above "simultaneous or subsequent disposal value" means any disposal value which falls to be brought into account by the current lessor in respect of the leased asset by reason of any event occurring subsequent to, or at the same time as, the event by reason of which the relevant disposal value falls to be brought into account.

(8) If any allowance is or has been given in respect of capital expenditure incurred by the current lessor in respect of the leased asset under any provision of the Capital Allowances Acts other than those specified in sub-paragraph (3) above, an amount equal to the lesser of—

(a) the aggregate of the allowances so given (so far as not previously recovered or withdrawn),

(b) the amount or value of the major lump sum,

shall, in relation to the current lessor, be treated as if it were a balancing charge to be made on him for the chargeable period or its basis period in which falls the relevant occasion.

(9) If there is or has been allowed to the current lessor in respect of expenditure incurred in connection with the leased asset any deduction by virtue of—

(a) subsection (3) of section 68 of the Capital Allowances Act 1990 (films, tapes and discs), so far as relating to expenditure to which subsection (1) of that section applies, or

(b) section 42 of the Finance (No. 2) Act 1992 (production or acquisition expenditure on films),

sub-paragraph (10) below shall apply.

(10) Where this sub-paragraph applies, the current lessor shall be treated as if receipts of a revenue nature of an amount equal to the amount (if any) by which—

(a) the amount or value of the major lump sum, exceeds

(b) the amount or value of so much of the major lump sum as is treated as receipts of a revenue nature under section 68(8) of the Capital Allowances Act 1990,

arose to him from the trade or business in question on the relevant occasion.

(11) If there is or has been allowed to the current lesser in respect of capital expenditure incurred in connection with the leased asset any deduction by virtue of—

(a) section 91 of the Taxes Act 1988 (cemeteries etc), or

(b) section 91A or 91B of that Act (restoration and preparation expenditure in relation to a waste disposal site),

sub-paragraph (12) below shall apply.

(12) Where this sub-paragraph applies, the current lessor shall be treated as if trading receipts of an amount equal to the lesser of—

(a) the amount or value of the major lump sum,

(b) the deductions previously allowed,

arose to him from the trade in question on the relevant occasion.

(13) If, in a case where this paragraph applies, allowances are or have been made to a person ("the contributor") by virtue of section 154 of the Capital Allowances Act 1990 (allowances in respect of contributions to capital expenditure) in respect of his contribution of a capital sum to expenditure on the provision of the leased asset, the foregoing provisions of this paragraph shall have effect in relation to the contributor and allowances by virtue of that section in respect of the contribution as they have effect in relation to the current lessor and allowances in respect of capital expenditure incurred by him in respect of the leased asset.

(14) In sub-paragraph (8) above, "chargeable period or its basis period" shall be construed in accordance with the Capital Allowances Act 1990.

(15) In the application of sub-paragraph (8) above—

(a) in relation to a trade, profession or vocation set up and commenced on or after 6th April 1994, or

(b) as respects the year 1997-98 or any subsequent year of assessment in relation to a trade, profession or vocation set up and commenced before 6th April 1994,

that sub-paragraph shall have effect with the omission of the words "or its basis period" and sub-paragraph (14) above shall accordingly have effect with the same omission.

Chargeable gains

12.—(1) If, in the case of the lease—

(a) the current lessor or a person connected with him disposes of—

    (i) the lessor's interest under the lease, or

    (ii) the leased asset, or

    (iii) an asset representing the leased asset, and

(b) there is, for the period of account of the current lessor in which the disposal takes place, any cumulative accountancy rental excess,

then, in determining for the purposes of the Taxation of Chargeable Gains Act 1992 the amount of any gain accruing to the person making the disposal, the consideration for the disposal shall be treated as reduced (but not below nil) by setting against it the cumulative accountancy rental excess.

(2) If the disposal mentioned in sub-paragraph (1) above is, for the purposes of the Taxation of Chargeable Gains Act 1992, a part-disposal of an asset—

(a) the cumulative accountancy rental excess mentioned in sub-paragraph (1) above shall be apportioned between—

    (i) the property disposed of, and

    (ii) the property which remains undisposed of,

in the proportions in which the sums which under paragraph (a) or (b) of section 38(1) of that Act are attributable to the asset fall to be apportioned under section 42 of that Act; and

(b) only that portion of the cumulative accountancy rental excess which is so apportioned to the property disposed of shall be set against the consideration for the part-disposal in accordance with sub-paragraph (1) above.

(3) Sub-paragraph (1) above is without prejudice to section 37 of the Taxation of Chargeable Gains Act 1992 (deduction for money or money's worth charged to income tax etc) except as provided in sub-paragraph (4) below.

(4) Section 37 of that Act shall not apply if or to the extent that any money or money's worth which, apart from this sub-paragraph, would be excluded by virtue of that section from the consideration for a disposal is represented by any cumulative accountancy rental excess which in accordance with sub-paragraph (1) above—

(a) falls to be set against the consideration for the disposal; or

(b) has fallen to be set against the consideration for a previous disposal made by the person making the disposal in question or a person connected with him.

(5) Where the current lessor or a person connected with him disposes of—

(a) the lessor's interest under the lease, or

(b) the leased asset, or

(c) an asset representing the leased asset,

this Schedule shall have effect as if a period of account of the current lessor ended, and another period of account of his began, immediately before the disposal.

(6) If two or more disposals falling within sub-paragraph (1) above are made at the same time—

    (a) the cumulative accountancy rental excess mentioned in sub-paragraph (1) above shall, subject to sub-paragraph (2) above, be apportioned between them in such proportions as are just and reasonable; and

    (b) sub-paragraph (5) above shall have effect in relation to those disposals as if they together constituted a single disposal.

(7) In this paragraph "dispose" and "disposal" shall be construed in accordance with the Taxation of Chargeable Gains Act 1992.

Existing schemes where this Part does not at first apply

13.—(1) This paragraph applies in any case where—

    (a) the lease of the asset forms part of an existing scheme, but

    (b) the conditions in paragraph 3 above become satisfied after 26th November 1996.

(2) This Schedule shall have effect as if a period of account of the current lessor ended, and another period of account of his began—

    (a) immediately before the time at which the conditions in paragraph 3 above become satisfied as mentioned in sub-paragraph (1)(b) above; and

    (b) immediately after the time at which those conditions become so satisfied.

(3) If, on the assumption that this Part of this Schedule (other than this paragraph) had applied in the case of the lease at all times on or after 26th November 1996, there would be an amount of cumulative accountancy rental excess for the period of account of the current lessor in which the conditions in paragraph 3 above become satisfied, then—

    (a) that amount shall be the cumulative accountancy rental excess for that period of account; and

    (b) the current lessor shall be treated for tax purposes as if, in the immediately preceding period of account, he had been entitled to, and there had arisen to him, rent from the lease of an amount equal to that cumulative accountancy rental excess.

(4) If, on the assumption that this Part of this Schedule (other than this paragraph) had applied in the case of the lease at all times on or after 26th November 1996, there would be an amount of cumulative normal rental excess for the period of account of the current lessor in which the conditions in paragraph 3 above become satisfied, that amount shall be the cumulative normal rental excess for that period of account.

(5) The amount of rent mentioned in sub-paragraph (3)(b) above—

    (a) is in addition to any other rent from the lease for the period of account there mentioned; and

    (b) shall be left out of account for the purposes of paragraph 5 above.

(6) Where a person is treated under sub-paragraph (3)(b) above as if he had in a period of account been entitled to, and there had arisen to him, any rent, the rent shall be treated for tax purposes as if it had accrued, and he had become entitled to it, immediately before the end of that period of account.

(7) In determining for the purposes of this paragraph the amount which would, on the assumption in sub-paragraph (3) or (4) above, be the amount of—

    (a) the cumulative accountancy rental excess, or

    (b) the cumulative normal rental excess,

for the period of account of the current lessor in which the conditions in paragraph 3 above become satisfied, any amount of relief given for a period of account on a claim under section 41 of the Taxes Act 1988 shall be treated as if it had instead been given under paragraph 8(4) above for that period of account.

New schemes where this Part begins to apply after Part II has applied

14. If—

    (a) the conditions in paragraph 3 above become satisfied in the case of the lease of the asset, and

    (b) immediately before those conditions became so satisfied, Part II of this Schedule applied in the case of the lease,

then, in determining the cumulative accountancy rental excess or the cumulative normal rental excess for any period of account ending after those conditions become satisfied, this Schedule shall have effect as if this Part of this Schedule had applied in relation to the lease at any time when Part II of this Schedule applied in relation to it.

OTHER FINANCE LEASES

Purpose of this Part of this Schedule

15.—(1) This Part of this Schedule is concerned with arrangements (other than arrangements with which Part I of this Schedule is concerned)—

(a) which involve the lease of an asset;

(b) which are or have been entered into by companies or other persons; and

(c) which are of such a kind as, in the case of companies incorporated in any part of the United Kingdom, falls for the purposes of accounts of such companies to be treated in accordance with normal accountancy practice as finance leases or loans.

(2) The principal purpose of this Part of this Schedule is, in the case of any such arrangements, to charge any person entitled to the lessor's interest under the lease of the asset to tax from time to time on amounts of income determined by reference to those which fall for accounting purposes to be treated in accordance with normal accountancy practice as the income return, on and after 26th November 1996, on investment in respect of the finance lease or loan (taking into account the substance of the matter as a whole, including in particular the state of affairs as between connected persons, or within a group of companies, as reflected or falling to be reflected in accounts of any of those persons or in consolidated group accounts).

Application of this Part of this Schedule

16.—(1) This Part of this Schedule applies in any case where—

(a) a lease of an asset is or has been granted on or after 26th November 1996;

(b) the lease forms part of a new scheme;

(c) in the case of the lease, the condition in sub-paragraph (1) of paragraph 3 above is or has been satisfied at some time on or after 26th November 1996 in a period of account of the current lessor; and

(d) Part I of this Schedule does not apply in the case of the lease by reason of the conditions in sub-paragraphs (2) to (5) of that paragraph not all being, or having been, satisfied as mentioned in paragraph 2 above.

(2) Where the condition in paragraph 3(1) above has been satisfied at any time on or after 26th November 1996 in a period of account of the person who was at that time the lessor, it shall be taken to continue to be satisfied unless and until—

(a) the asset ceases to be leased under the lease; or

(b) the lessor's interest under the lease is assigned to a person who is not connected with any of the persons described in sub-paragraph (3) below.

(3) Those persons are—

(a) the assignor;

(b) any person who was the lessor at some time before the assignment; or

(c) any person who at some time after the assignment becomes the lessor pursuant to arrangements made by a person who was the lessor, or was connected with the lessor, at some time before the assignment.

(4) Nothing in sub-paragraph (2) above prevents this Part of this Schedule from again applying in the case of the lease if the conditions for its application are satisfied after the assignment.

Application of provisions of Part I for purposes of Part II

17. Paragraphs 5 to 10 and 12 above shall apply for the purposes of this Part of this Schedule as they apply for the purposes of Part I of this Schedule.

PART III

INSURANCE COMPANIES

Accounting purposes

18. In the application of this Schedule in relation to companies carrying on insurance business, "accounting purposes" does not include the purposes of accounts which Part II of the Insurance Companies Act 1982 (the Department of Trade and Industry rules) requires to be prepared.

Companies carrying on life assurance business

19.—(1) This paragraph applies if the current lessor is a company carrying on life assurance business.

(2) Where the leased asset is an asset of the company's long term business fund, no amount shall be brought into account by virtue of this Schedule in any computation of profits of life assurance business, or any class of life assurance business, carried on by the company where the computation is made in accordance with the provisions of the Taxes Act 1988 applicable to Case I of Schedule D.

(3) In determining whether the condition in sub-paragraph (3) or (4) of paragraph 3 above is satisfied in the case of the company, an amount shall not be regarded—

    (a) as falling to be brought into account for tax purposes as rent which arises to the company from the lease, or to which the company is entitled, in a period of account, or

    (b) as representing a portion of that part of a major lump sum which falls within paragraph 3(2)(b) above,

by reason only that it falls to be taken into account for any purpose by virtue of section 83(2) of the Finance Act 1989 (investment income from, and increases in value of, assets of long term business fund treated as receipts of period).

(4) Where—

    (a) under paragraph 5 or 13 above the company is treated for tax purposes as if in a period of account it had been entitled to, and there had arisen to it, any rent from the lease, and

    (b) the leased asset is an asset of the company's long term business fund or is linked to any category of insurance business, and

    (c) any question arises for the purposes of the Corporation Tax Acts as to the extent to which that rent is referable to any category of the company's long term business,

section 432A of the Taxes Act 1988 (apportionment of insurance companies' income) shall have effect in relation to the rent as it has effect in relation to the income arising from an asset.

PART IV

SUPPLEMENTARY PROVISIONS

Normal rent

20. For the purposes of this Schedule, the "normal rent" in respect of a lease for a period of account of the lessor is the amount which he would, apart from this Schedule, bring into account as rent from the lease—

    (a) which arises to him, and

    (b) if rent arising to him from the lease is chargeable to corporation tax under Schedule A, to which he is entitled,

in that period of account for the purpose of determining his liability to tax for the related chargeable period or periods.

Accountancy rental earnings

21.—(1) For the purposes of this Schedule, the "accountancy rental earnings" in respect of the lease for a period of account of the lessor is the greatest of the amounts specified in sub-paragraph (2) below.

(2) Those amounts are—

    (a) the rental earnings for the relevant period in respect of the lease, in the case of the lessor;

    (b) the rental earnings for the relevant period in respect of the lease, in the case of a person connected with the lessor;

    (c) the rental earnings for the relevant period in respect of the lease, for the purposes of consolidated group accounts of a group of companies of which the lessor is a member.

(3) In sub-paragraph (2) above, "the relevant period" means the period of account of the lessor which is mentioned in sub-paragraph (1) above.

Rental earnings

22. In this Schedule "the rental earnings" for any period in respect of the lease of the asset is, in the case of any person or any consolidated group accounts, the amount which falls for accounting purposes to be treated in accordance with normal accountancy practice as the gross return for that period on investment in respect of a finance lease or loan in respect of the leasing arrangements.

Periods of account which straddle 26th November 1996

23. This Schedule shall apply in relation to a period of account which begins before 26th November 1996 and ends on or after that date as if—

    (a) so much of the period as falls before 26th November 1996, and

(b) so much of the period as falls on or after that date,
were separate periods of account.

Time apportionment where periods do not coincide

24.—(1) This paragraph applies in any case where—
(a) a period of account of the lessor does not coincide with a period of account of a person connected with the lessor, or
(b) a period of account of the lessor does not coincide with a period for which consolidated group accounts of a group of companies of which the lessor is a member fall to be prepared.

(2) Where this paragraph applies, any amount which falls for the purposes of this Schedule to be found for the lessor's period of account but by reference to the connected person or, as the case may be, the consolidated group accounts shall be found by making such apportionments as may be necessary—
(a) between two or more periods of account of the connected person, or
(b) between two or more periods for which consolidated group accounts of the group fall to be prepared,
as the case may be.

(3) Any apportionment under sub-paragraph (2) above shall be made in proportion to the number of days in the respective periods which fall within the lessor's period of account.

Connected persons

25.—(1) If a person is connected with another at some time during the period which—
(a) begins at the earliest time at which any of the leasing arrangements were made, and
(b) ends when the current lessor finally ceases to have an interest in the asset or any arrangements relating to it,
he shall be treated for the purposes of this Schedule, in its application in consequence of those leasing arrangements, as being connected with that other throughout that period.

(2) Section 839 of the Taxes Act 1988 shall apply for the purposes of this Schedule.

Assets which represent the leased asset

26. For the purposes of this Schedule, the following assets shall be treated as representing the leased asset—
(a) any asset derived from, or created out of, the leased asset;
(b) any asset from or out of which the leased asset was derived or created;
(c) any asset derived from or created out of an asset from or out of which the leased asset was derived or created; or
(d) any asset which derives the whole or a substantial part of its value from the leased asset or from an asset which itself represents the leased asset.

Existing schemes and new schemes

27.—(1) For the purposes of this Schedule, a lease of an asset—
(a) forms part of an existing scheme if, and only if, the conditions in sub-paragraph (2) or (3) below are satisfied; and
(b) in any other case, forms part of a new scheme.

(2) The conditions in this sub-paragraph are that—
(a) a contract in writing for the lease of the asset has been made before 26th November 1996;
(b) either—
    (i) the contract is unconditional; or
    (ii) if the contract is conditional, the conditions have been satisfied before that date;
    and
(c) no terms remain to be agreed on or after that date.

(3) The conditions in this sub-paragraph are that—
(a) a contract in writing for the lease of the asset has been made before 26th November 1996;
(b) the condition in paragraph (b) or (c) of sub-paragraph (2) above is not satisfied in the case of the contract;
(c) either the contract is unconditional or, if it is conditional, the conditions are satisfied before the end of the finalisation period or within such further period as the Commissioners of Inland Revenue may allow in the particular case;
(d) no terms remain to be agreed after the end of the finalisation period or such further period as the Commissioners of Inland Revenue may allow in the particular case; and
(e) the contract in its final form is not materially different from the contract as it stood when it was made as mentioned in paragraph (a) above.

(4) In sub-paragraph (3) above, "the finalisation period" means the period which ends with the later of—

(a) 31st January 1997;

(b) the expiration of the period of six months next following the day on which the contract was made as mentioned in sub-paragraph (3)(a) above.

Accounting purposes and normal accountancy practice

28.—(1) In the application of any provisions of this Schedule which relate to accounting purposes or normal accountancy practice, it shall be assumed, if it is not the case, that the person who is at any time entitled to the lessor's interest under the lease of the asset, and any person connected with that person, is a company incorporated in a part of the United Kingdom.

(2) A person who is not in fact a body corporate shall not by virtue of sub-paragraph (1) above be treated as a member of a group of companies for any purpose of this Schedule.

(3) This Schedule shall have effect in relation to a person who, for accounting purposes, is not required to prepare accounts in accordance with normal accountancy practice as if he were required to do so.

(4) Nothing in sub-paragraph (3) above applies in relation to consolidated group accounts.

(5) This Schedule shall have effect in relation to a body corporate (wherever incorporated) which is a parent undertaking but which, for accounting purposes, is not required to prepare consolidated group accounts in accordance with normal accountancy practice as if the body corporate were required to do so.

(6) In sub-paragraph (5) above "parent undertaking" shall be construed in accordance with—

(a) section 258 of the Companies Act 1985, or

(b) in Northern Ireland, Article 266 of the Companies (Northern Ireland) Order 1986.

Assessments and adjustments

29. All such assessments and adjustments shall be made as are necessary to give effect to the provisions of this Schedule.

Interpretation

30.—(1) In this Schedule, unless the context otherwise requires—

"accountancy rental earnings" has the meaning given by paragraph 21(1) above;

"accountancy rental excess" shall be construed—

(a) for the purposes of Part I of this Schedule, in accordance with paragraph 6 above; and

(b) for the purposes of Part II of this Schedule, in accordance with paragraph 6 above as it has effect by virtue of paragraph 17 above;

"accounting purposes" means the purposes of—

(a) accounts of companies incorporated in any part of the United Kingdom, or

(b) consolidated group accounts for groups all the members of which are companies incorporated in any part of the United Kingdom;

"asset" means any form of property or rights;

"asset representing the leased asset" shall be construed in accordance with paragraph 26 above;

"assignment", in the application of this Schedule to Scotland, means assignation;

"consolidated group accounts" means group accounts which satisfy the requirements—

(a) of section 227 of the Companies Act 1985, or

(b) in Northern Ireland, of Article 235 of the Companies (Northern Ireland) Order 1986;

"cumulative accountancy rental excess" and "cumulative normal rental excess" shall be construed—

(a) for the purposes of Part I of this Schedule, in accordance with paragraph 6 above; and

(b) for the purposes of Part II of this Schedule, in accordance with paragraph 6 above as it has effect by virtue of paragraph 17 above;

"the current lessor", in the case of a lease of an asset, means the person who is for the time being entitled to the lessor's interest under the lease;

"existing scheme" shall be construed in accordance with paragraph 27(1)(a) above;

"finance lessor" means a person who for accounting purposes is treated in accordance with normal accountancy practice as the person with—

(i) the grantor's interest in relation to a finance lease; or

(ii) the lender's interest in relation to a loan;

"group of companies" means a group as defined—

    (a) in section 262(1) of the Companies Act 1985, or

    (b) in Northern Ireland, in Article 270(1) of the Companies (Northern Ireland) Order 1986,

and "member", in relation to a group of companies, means a company comprised in the group;

"lease"—

    (a) in relation to land, includes an underlease, sublease or any tenancy or licence, and any agreement for a lease, underlease, sublease or tenancy or licence and, in the case of land outside the United Kingdom, any interest corresponding to a lease as so defined; and

    (b) in relation to any form of property or right other than land, means any kind of agreement or arrangement under which payments are made for the use of, or otherwise in respect of, an asset;

and "rent" shall be construed accordingly;

"the leasing arrangements", in the case of a lease of an asset, means—

    (a) the lease of the asset,

    (b) any arrangements relating to or connected with the lease of the asset, and

    (c) any other arrangements of which the lease of the asset forms part,

and includes a reference to any of the leasing arrangements;

"the lessee", in the case of a lease of an asset, means (except in the expression "the lessee's interest under the lease") the person entitled to the lessee's interest under the lease;

"the lessor", in the case of a lease of an asset, means (except in the expression "the lessor's interest under the lease") the person entitled to the lessor's interest under the lease;

"major lump sum" shall be construed in accordance with paragraph 3(2) above;

"new scheme" shall be construed in accordance with paragraph 27(1)(b) above;

"normal rent" shall be construed in accordance with paragraph 20 above;

"normal rental excess" shall be construed—

    (a) for the purposes of Part I of this Schedule, in accordance with paragraph 6 above; and

    (b) for the purposes of Part II of this Schedule, in accordance with paragraph 6 above as it has effect by virtue of paragraph 17 above;

"period of account" means a period for which accounts are made up and, except for the purposes of paragraphs 2 to 4 and 23 above, means such a period which begins on or after 26th November 1996;

"related chargeable period" shall be construed in accordance with sub-paragraph (2) below;

"sum" includes any money or money's worth (and "pay" and cognate expressions shall be construed accordingly);

"the rental earnings", in relation to the lease of the asset and any period, has the meaning given by paragraph 22 above.

(2) For the purposes of this Schedule a chargeable period is related to a period of account (and a period of account is related to a chargeable period) if—

    (a) the chargeable period is an accounting period which consists of or includes the whole or any part of the period of account; or

    (b) the chargeable period is a year of assessment whose basis period for the purposes of Case I or Case II of Schedule D consists of or includes the whole or any part of the period of account.

GENERAL NOTE

The Schedule implements measures to prevent avoidance of tax through the use of certain finance leases.

Part I

This deals with cases where under a finance lease part of the rental income is turned into capital receipts.

Para. 1

Somewhat unusually, the purpose of Pt. I is set out. It is concerned with arrangements which under Standard Statement of Accounting Practice ("SSAP") 21 would be treated as finance leases and under which some of the return on the investment by the lessor might be in a form other than rent and not be wholly taxable apart from the Schedule.

The purpose of Pt. I is to align the tax treatment with normal accountancy practice, taking into account the state of affairs between connected persons or as reflected in consolidated group accounts and to claw back where appropriate capital allowances on the assets concerned.

Para. 2

This provides that Pt. I applies if a lease of an asset has been granted and all the five conditions in para. 3 are satisfied. The operation of Pt. I is retrospective.

Para. 3

The five conditions to be satisfied are:

(i) the arrangements would be treated as a finance lease in accordance with normal accounting practice;

(ii) the lessor may receive a "major lump sum" which is not rent;

(iii) the whole of the major lump sum would not be brought into charge to tax apart from the Schedule;

(iv) the "accountancy rental earnings" exceed the "normal rent" (see paras. 20 and 21);

(v) there must be some likelihood that the lessee or a connected person will buy out the lessor's interest in the leased asset for a lump sum.

Rent is to be treated as accruing evenly.

Para. 4

This expatiates further on condition (v) in para. 3.

Para. 5

The charge under the Schedule is equal to the accountancy rental earnings where these exceed the normal rent.

Para. 6

A running total is to be kept of aggregate differences between accountancy rental earnings and the normal rents. Any excess of the one can be set against the other, but only for periods of account beginning on or after Budget day.

Para. 7

Where a lease is assigned on a no gain/no loss basis, the assignee steps into the assignor's shoes for the purposes of para. 6 and para. 13, which deals with the tax consequences of a disposal of the lease otherwise than on such a basis.

Paras. 8–10

These are concerned with bad debts. Their purpose is to ensure that any bad debts are properly taken into account in computing taxable profits and excesses of accountancy rental earnings and normal rents. If the lease runs its course, the net rents taxed should equal the net rents payable after allowing for any bad debts.

Para. 11

This paragraph was substituted for paras. 11 and 12 in the Finance Bill at report stage. It was originally intended that finance leases involving capital payments entered into on or after Budget day should be denied capital allowances altogether, but this treatment was thought to be too draconian. Instead the same capital allowances treatment is accorded to new finance leases as to existing finance leases.

Where a major lump sum is received by a lessor it is brought into account for the purposes of a balancing charge.

Para. 12

On a disposal of the leased asset any unused cumulative excess of accountancy rental earnings is set against the disposal proceeds to ensure that the same sum is not taxed twice.

Para. 13

The leases affected by this paragraph are those which are not initially caught by the Schedule, but subsequently come within its scope. In such a case, the accumulated excess (if any) of the accountancy measure of income from the lease over the income actually taxed in earlier periods is brought into charge. Periods prior to Budget day are not subject to charge.

Para. 14

This provides continuity of reliefs where a lease initially subject to Pt. II of the Schedule becomes subject to Pt. I. Any cumulative excesses of accountancy rental earnings or of normal rent are carried forward.

Part II

This covers cases outside Pt. I where any assets are leased in such a way that, for accountancy purposes, they are a finance lease.

Para. 15

The paragraph provides an overview of the rules in Pt. II in the same way as para. 1 does for Pt. I. The purpose of Pt. II is to ensure that the taxable measure of earnings from the lease is not less than the accountancy measure. The rules take as the taxable earnings the measure under the existing law or the accountancy measure, whichever is higher. Unlike Pt. I, Pt. II contains no special rules relating to relief for capital expenditure.

Para. 16

The rules in this part apply to new schemes, *i.e.* leases which the lessor had not granted, or was not committed to grant, on Budget day. The rules continue to apply until the lease is assigned to an unconnected person and may be subsequently reapplied.

Para. 17

A number of the rules in Pt. I of the Schedule are applied for the purposes of Pt. II. These include para. 5 (the charge on accountancy rental earnings), para. 6 (cumulative excesses), para. 7 (assignment of a lease on no gain/no loss terms), paras. 8–10 (bad debts) and para. 12 (relief for cumulative accountancy rental excess against capital gains disposal proceeds). The provisions dealing with capital allowances (para. 11) or with the charge under para. 13 are not included.

Part III

This part applies the provisions of the Schedule to the special circumstances of insurance companies.

Para. 18

The Schedule refers not to the accounts which insurance companies are required to draw up under Insurance Companies Act 1982 (c. 50), but to those which they are required to prepare under the Companies Acts.

Para. 19

This sets out how the main rules in Pts. I and II are adapted to meet the case where the lessor is a company carrying on life assurance business. The rest of the Schedule is overridden where profits of any part of the life assurance business are computed in accordance with the rules applicable to Case I of Sched. D. However, the Schedule still applies even if some amounts have been brought into account under Case I of Sched. D.

Part IV

This sets out supplementary provisions, mainly defining the terms used earlier.

Para. 20

"Normal rent" is defined as the rent which would be brought into account for tax apart from the provisions of this Schedule.

Paras. 21 and 22

Between them, these define "accountancy rental earnings". These are the highest of the earnings, in accordance with normal accountancy practice, of the lessor, a connected person or the consolidated accounts of the group of which the lessor is a member.

Para. 23

Periods of account straddling Budget day are treated as separate.

Para. 24

Where a period of account of the lessor does not coincide with that of a connected person or of the group to which the lessor belongs, the figures are time apportioned as necessary.

Para. 25

The definition of "connected persons" in ICTA 1988, s.239 is adopted. Persons connected for any time during a period are treated as connected throughout the period.

Para. 26

Assets which represent leased assets include sub-leases, freeholds out of which leases are created, leases created out of the same freehold as the leased asset was created, and assets, such as shares in a property company, which derive at least a substantial part of their value from the leased asset.

Para. 27

For the distinction between new and existing leasing schemes, important for the provisions in Pt. II of the Schedule, the test is whether the lessor was substantially committed to the lease on Budget day and whether it was finalised reasonably quickly thereafter.

Para. 28

This sets out what is meant by "accountancy purposes" and "normal accountancy practice". In essence the approach is to determine what the accountancy treatment would be under the best U.K. commercial accounting practice.

Para. 29

All necessary assessments and adjustments may be made. This is particularly relevant in relation to the provisions dealing with capital allowances.

Para. 30

This provides sundry interpretative rules.

Section 83   SCHEDULE 13

LOAN RELATIONSHIPS: AMENDMENT OF TRANSITIONAL PROVISIONS

Introductory

1. Schedule 15 to the Finance Act 1996 (transitional provisions and savings for loan relationships) shall be amended as follows.

Transitional rules for transitional accounting periods

2. In paragraph 3 (basic transitional rules for transitional accounting periods), after sub-paragraph (5) there shall be inserted the following sub-paragraph—
 "(5A) Where—
 (a) sub-paragraph (5) above applies for determining the closing value of a continuing loan relationship of a company for a transitional accounting period ending on or after 14th November 1996, and
 (b) an opening valuation of that relationship falls to be made, as at the beginning of the immediately following accounting period, for the purpose of bringing amounts into account in that company's case on a mark to market basis of accounting,
 the opening value given by that opening valuation shall be taken to be the same as the closing value given in accordance with that sub-paragraph."

Opening valuations as at 1st April 1996

3. After paragraph 3 there shall be inserted the following paragraph—

 "*Adjustment of opening value where new accounting basis adopted as from an accounting period beginning on 1st April 1996*

 3A.—(1) This paragraph applies in the case of a continuing loan relationship of a company where—
 (a) the company's first relevant accounting period begins on 1st April 1996;
 (b) in that period amounts are brought into account for the purposes of this Chapter in respect of the relationship on a mark to market basis of accounting;
 (c) amounts falling to be brought into account in respect of the relationship for the purposes of corporation tax in the accounting period ending with 31st March 1996 were or (if there had been any) would have been so brought into account otherwise than on a mark to market basis of accounting; and
 (d) an opening valuation of the relationship falls to be made, as at the beginning of the accounting period immediately following the first relevant accounting period, for the purpose of bringing amounts into account on a mark to market basis of accounting.
 (2) Where this paragraph applies in the case of a continuing loan relationship of a company, the opening valuation mentioned in sub-paragraph (1)(d) above shall be made disregarding any amount of interest that has accrued in the company's first relevant accounting period or in any of its accounting periods preceding that period."

Adjustments in the case of pre-commencement trading relationships

4. In paragraph 5 (pre-commencement trading relationships), after sub-paragraph (4) there shall be inserted the following sub-paragraphs—

"(4A) In sub-paragraph (4) above the reference, in relation to a creditor relationship, to the amount deductible as representing the cost of a company's becoming a party to the relationship shall not, except where sub-paragraph (4B) or (4C) below applies, include a reference to so much of that amount as would represent the cost of acquiring any right to accrued interest under the loan relationship.

(4B) This sub-paragraph applies where—

(a) the company became a party to the relationship before the beginning of its first relevant accounting period,

(b) interest accruing under the relationship before the company became a party to it was paid to the company after it became a party to it but before the beginning of the company's first relevant accounting period, and

(c) the interest under the relationship which, in the case of that company, has been brought into account for the purposes of corporation tax has included interest accruing under the relationship before the company became a party to it but paid afterwards.

(4C) This sub-paragraph applies where—

(a) the company became a party to the loan relationship in a transitional accounting period, and

(b) in the case of that company, interest under the relationship which—

(i) accrued before the company became a party to the relationship, but

(ii) became due and payable afterwards,

is brought into account for the purposes of this Chapter in accordance with an authorised mark to market basis of accounting."

Chargeable assets held after commencement

5. In paragraph 8 (transitional provision for chargeable assets held after commencement), after sub-paragraph (5) there shall be inserted the following sub-paragraph—

"(5A) In any case where the relevant event has not occurred before 14th November 1996, the deemed chargeable gain or deemed allowable loss falling to be brought into account in accordance with sub-paragraph (3) above shall be computed without any account being taken of the provisions of section 119(6) and (7) of the 1992 Act (transfer of securities with or without accrued interest)."

Adjustments in the case of chargeable assets

6. In paragraph 11(adjustments in the case of chargeable assets), for sub-paragraphs (2) to (4) there shall be substituted the following sub-paragraphs—

"(2) Those amounts are—

(a) the notional closing value of the relationship as at 31st March 1996; and

(b) the amount which would be taken on a computation made—

(i) in accordance with an authorised accruals basis of accounting, and

(ii) on the assumption that such a basis of accounting had always been used as respects that relationship,

to represent the accrued value of the loan relationship in question on 1st April 1996.

(3) Where there is a difference between the amounts mentioned in sub-paragraph (2) above, that difference shall be brought into account—

(a) where the amount mentioned in paragraph (a) of that sub-paragraph is the smaller, as a credit given for the purposes of this Chapter for the accounting period in which the company ceases to be a party to the relationship; and

(b) in any other case, as a debit so given."

Commencement of Schedule

7.—(1) Subject to sub-paragraph (2) below, this Schedule has effect for the purpose of determining the credits and debits to be brought into account in any accounting period ending on or after 14th November 1996.

(2) Paragraphs 4 and 6 above do not apply in the case of a loan relationship to which the company in question has ceased to be a party before 14th November 1996 unless—

(a) that company ceased to be a party to the relationship as a result of being directly or indirectly replaced as a party to that relationship by another company, and

(b) the transaction, or series of transactions, by virtue of which the replacement took place fell within any of paragraphs (a) to (d) of paragraph 12(1) of Schedule 9 to the Finance Act

1996 (continuity of treatment in the case of groups and certain transfers of insurance business).

(3) A credit or debit a fraction of which falls to be brought into account under paragraph 6(4) of Schedule 15 to the Finance Act 1996 (election as to adjustments) in an accounting period ending on or after 14th November 1996 shall be determined, for the purposes mentioned in sub-paragraph (1) above, without applying sub-paragraph (2) above in relation to the relevant assumption.

GENERAL NOTE

This Schedule amends F.A. 1996, Sched. 15, which contains the transitional provisions for the new loan relationship rules.

Para. 2

This ensures that where a company uses a mark-to-market method of accounting in its transitional accounting period, all interest earned between the date of the latest interest period in the transitional accounting period and the end of that period is brought into account.

Para. 3

If a company changes its method of accounting on April 1, 1996, where this is the start of a new accounting period, to a mark-to-market basis of accounting, the valuation of the loan at the start of the next accounting period excludes any interest accrued up to that time.

Para. 4

In comparing the value of loan relationships under the old and new rules, no account is taken of accrued interest in arriving at the cost of the asset unless a first payment of interest has been received by the company in an accounting period before the company's first accounting period under the new rules and that interest payment was not effectively reduced for tax purposes by the amount of the accrued interest; or the company became a party to the loan relationship in the transitional accounting period and adopts a mark-to-market basis of accounting in that accounting period.

Para. 5

Where loan relationships which were previously subject to capital gains tax are treated as having been disposed of on March 31, 1996 at market value, the gain or loss is calculated without reference to TCGA 1992, s.119(6) or (7). This is to ensure symmetry of treatment.

Para. 6

This ensures that the adjustment for loan relationships which were previously chargeable assets is correctly calculated when a loan relationship ceases in the transitional accounting period and that interest accruing after March 31, 1996 is not included in the adjustment.

Para. 7

With certain exceptions, the Schedule applies to accounting periods ending on or after November 14, 1996.

Section 84   SCHEDULE 14

CAPITAL ALLOWANCES ON LONG-LIFE ASSETS

Introductory

1. The Capital Allowances Act 1990 shall be amended as follows.

New Chapter on long-life assets

2. In Part II (machinery and plant), the following new Chapter shall be inserted after Chapter IV (short-life assets)—

"CHAPTER IVA

LONG-LIFE ASSETS

Expenditure to which Chapter applies

Application of Chapter

38A.—(1) Subject to sections 38B to 38D and 38H, this Chapter applies to any capital expenditure incurred by a person on the provision of machinery or plant if that machinery or plant is a long-life asset.

(2) For the purposes of this Chapter machinery or plant is a long-life asset if—

(a) in the case of machinery or plant that is new, it is reasonable to expect that the machinery or plant will have a useful economic life of at least twenty-five years; or

(b) in any other case, it was reasonable, when the machinery or plant was new, to expect that it would have a useful economic life of at least twenty-five years.

(3) For the purposes of this section the useful economic life of machinery or plant is the period which—

(a) begins with the first occasion on which the machinery or plant is brought into use by any person for any purpose; and

(b) continues until the machinery or plant ceases to be machinery or plant that is or is likely to be used (whether or not by the person who first brought it into use and whether or not in a manner in which he used it) as a fixed asset of a business.

(4) Where, by virtue of any of the following provisions of this Chapter, this Chapter applies to part only of the expenditure incurred by any person on the provision of any long-life asset, this Act shall have effect in relation to that expenditure as if the part to which this Chapter applies and the part to which it does not were, in each case, expenditure on a separate item of machinery or plant.

(5) For the purposes of subsection (4) above all such apportionments shall be made as may be just and reasonable.

Expenditure excluded from the application of the Chapter

38B.—(1) This Chapter does not apply to expenditure on the provision of machinery or plant which is a fixture in, or is he provided for use in, any building used wholly or mainly—

(a) as a dwelling-house, retail shop, showroom, hotel or office; or

(b) for purposes ancillary to the purposes of a dwelling-house, retail shop, showroom, hotel or office.

(2) This Chapter does not apply to any expenditure on the provision of—

(a) a motor car; or

(b) a mechanically propelled road vehicle which would be a motor car but for section 36(1)(c).

(3) This Chapter does not apply to any expenditure incurred before 1st January 2011 on the provision of a ship of a sea-going kind if each of the following conditions is satisfied—

(a) that ship is not an offshore installation for the purposes of the Mineral Workings (Offshore Installations) Act 1971;

(b) that ship would not be such an installation if the activity for the carrying on of which it is or is to be established or maintained were carried on in or under controlled waters (within the meaning of that Act); and

(c) the primary use to which ships of the same kind as that ship are put by the persons to whom they belong (or, where their use is made available to others, by those others) is a use otherwise than for sport or recreation.

(4) This Chapter does not apply to any expenditure incurred before 1st January 2011 on the provision of a railway asset provided for use (whether by the person incurring the expenditure or by any other person) wholly and exclusively for the purposes of a railway business.

(5) In this section—

'fixture' has the same meaning as in Chapter VI of this Part;

'goods' has the same meaning as in Part I of the Railways Act 1993;

'light maintenance depot' means—

(a) any light maintenance depot within the meaning of Part I of the Railways Act 1993, or

(b) any land or other property which, in relation to anything which is a railway only where 'railway' has the wider meaning given by section 81(2) of that Act, is the equivalent of such a depot;

'railway' has the wider meaning given by section 81(2) of the Railways Act 1993 (which defines railway so as to include tramways and other systems of guided transport);

'railway asset' means any of the following—

(a) any locomotive, tram or other vehicle designed or adapted for use on a railway;

(b) any carriage, wagon or other rolling stock designed or adapted for such use;

(c) anything which is or is to be comprised in any railway track, railway station or light maintenance depot; and

(d) any apparatus falling to be installed in association with anything within paragraph (c) above;

'railway business' means so much of any business as is carried on for the provision of a service to the public for the carriage of goods or passengers by means of a railway in the United Kingdom or the Channel Tunnel;

'railway station' includes anything included in the definition of 'station' in section 83 of the Railways Act 1993 and anything that would be so included if, in that section, 'railway' had the wider meaning given by section 81(2) of that Act;

'railway track' includes anything included in the definition of 'track' in section 83 of the Railways Act 1993 and anything that would be so included if, in that section, 'railway' had the wider meaning given by section 81(2) of that Act;

'retail shop' includes any premises of a similar character where retail trade or business (including repair work) is carried on.

(6) For the purposes of subsection (4) above a railway asset falling within paragraph (a) or (b) of the definition in subsection (5) above shall not be treated as used otherwise than wholly and exclusively for the purposes of a railway business by reason only that it is used to carry goods or passengers from places in the United Kingdom to places outside the United Kingdom or vice versa.

Exclusion of Chapter where limit for individuals and partnerships not exceeded

38C.—(1) Subject to section 38F(3), this Chapter does not apply to any expenditure incurred by an individual, or by a partnership of which all the members are individuals, unless that expenditure is—

(a) expenditure incurred in a chargeable period the relevant limit for which is exceeded in the case of that individual or partnership; or

(b) expenditure which is not subject to that limit.

(2) For the purposes of this section the relevant limit for a chargeable period is exceeded in the case of an individual or partnership if the total amount of capital expenditure which—

(a) is incurred in that period by that individual or partnership,

(b) is subject to the limit, and

(c) is or, disregarding this section, would be expenditure to which this Chapter applies, exceeds the limit applying to that period.

(3) For the purposes of this section expenditure incurred by an individual is subject to the relevant limit for a chargeable period if—

(a) it was incurred by him for the purposes of a trade or profession carried on by him;

(b) that individual devotes substantially the whole of his time in that chargeable period to the carrying on of that trade or profession; and

(c) the expenditure is not excluded from the operation of the limit.

(4) For the purposes of this section expenditure incurred by a partnership is subject to the relevant limit for a chargeable period if—

(a) it was incurred by the partnership for the purposes of a trade or profession carried on by that partnership;

(b) at all times throughout that period at least half of the individuals who are for the time being members of the partnership are devoting substantially the whole of their time to the carrying on of that trade or profession; and

(c) the expenditure is not excluded from the operation of the limit.

(5) For the purposes of this section the expenditure which is excluded from the operation of the relevant limit for a chargeable period is any expenditure falling within any of the following paragraphs, that is to say—

(a) expenditure on the provision of a share in machinery or plant;

(b) expenditure which is treated as expenditure on the provision of machinery or plant by virtue of section 154 (contributions);

(c) expenditure incurred on the provision of machinery or plant for leasing (whether or not the leasing is in the course of a trade).

(6) The limit applying for the purposes of this section to a chargeable period of twelve months is £100,000.

(7) The limit applying for the purposes of this section to a chargeable period which is not twelve months is the amount given by a proportional reduction or, as the case may require, increase of £100,000.

(8) Where, in the case of any contract for the provision of machinery or plant, the capital expenditure which is or is to be incurred under that contract is or may fall to be treated for the purposes of this Act as incurred in different chargeable periods, all of the expenditure falling to be incurred under that contract on the provision of that machinery or plant shall

be treated for the purposes of this section as incurred in the first chargeable period in which any of that expenditure is incurred.

(9) This section does not apply for the purposes of corporation tax.

Exclusion of Chapter where company's limit not exceeded

38D.—(1) Subject to section 38F(3), this Chapter does not apply for the purposes of corporation tax to any expenditure by a company unless that expenditure is—

(a) expenditure incurred in a chargeable period the relevant limit for which is exceeded in relation to that company; or

(b) expenditure excluded from the operation of that limit.

(2) For the purposes of this section the relevant limit for a chargeable period is exceeded in relation to a company only if the total amount of capital expenditure which—

(a) is incurred by that company in that period,

(b) is not excluded from the operation of that limit, and

(c) is or, disregarding this section, would be expenditure to which this Chapter applies, exceeds the limit applying to that period.

(3) Subject to subsection (5) below, the limit applying for the purposes of this section to a chargeable period of twelve months is £100,000.

(4) Subject to subsection (5) below, the limit applying for the purposes of this section to a chargeable period of less than twelve months is the amount given by a proportional reduction of £100,000.

(5) Where, in a chargeable period, a company has one or more associated companies, the limit applying to that period for the purposes of this section shall be the amount produced by—

(a) taking the amount given for that period by subsection (3) or, as the case may be, subsection (4) above; and

(b) dividing that amount by one plus the number of those companies.

(6) Subsections (4) and (5) of section 13 of the principal Act (which identify the companies that are to count as associated companies for the purposes of section 13(3) of that Act) shall apply for the purposes of subsection (5) above as they apply for the purposes of subsection (3) of that section.

(7) Subsections (5) and (8) of section 38C apply for the purposes of this section as they apply for the purposes of that section.

Rules applying to expenditure on long-life assets

Separate pools for expenditure on long-life assets

38E.—(1) Where expenditure to which this Chapter applies has been incurred on the provision of machinery or plant wholly and exclusively for the purposes of a trade ('the actual trade'), the following provisions of this section shall have effect with respect to the allowances and charges to be made under section 24 in the case of the actual trade.

(2) It shall be assumed for the purposes of sections 24, 25 and 26—

(a) that the person carrying on the actual trade incurred the expenditure on the provision of the machinery or plant wholly and exclusively for the purposes of a trade carried on by him separately from the actual trade and from any other trade which he in fact carries on or is assumed for any purpose to carry on;

(b) that the purposes for which the machinery or plant is used (whether wholly or partly) are purposes of the separate trade if they are purposes of the actual trade, but not otherwise; and

(c) that the separate trade is permanently discontinued if the actual trade is or is treated as permanently discontinued, but not otherwise.

(3) Any allowance or charge under section 24 which, on those assumptions and having regard to subsection (4) below, would fall to be made for any chargeable period in the case of the separate trade shall be made for that period in the case of the actual trade.

(4) If an allowance under section 24 falling by virtue of this section to be made for any chargeable period ('the earlier period') in the case of the actual trade—

(a) is not claimed, or

(b) is reduced in amount in accordance with a requirement under subsection (3) of that section,

then, in determining the allowance or charge under that section which would fall to be made for any subsequent chargeable period in the case of the separate trade, any allowance falling to be made in the case of the separate trade for the earlier period shall be treated as not claimed or, as the case may require, as proportionately reduced.

(5) Where there is more than one item of machinery or plant to which subsection (2) above applies in the case of any person, this section shall have effect as if the separate trade for which, in that person's case, each of those items is treated as used were the same separate trade.

(6) The reference in subsection (1) above to expenditure incurred on the provision of machinery or plant wholly and exclusively for the purposes of a trade does not include a reference to any amount falling by virtue of section 31, 61, 79 or 80 to be treated as incurred on the provision of machinery or plant wholly and exclusively for the purposes of the separate trade mentioned in that section.

Modifications applying to pools for long-life assets

38F.—(1) Where sections 24, 25 and 26 apply, in any of the cases mentioned in subsection (2) below, to any expenditure to which this Chapter applies, they shall so apply as if the reference in section 24(2) to 25 per cent were a reference to 6 per cent.

(2) Those cases are—

(a) any case where sections 24, 25 and 26 apply in accordance with section 31, 38E, 79 or 80; and

(b) any case where the machinery or plant in question is machinery or plant to which section 61 applies.

(3) Where—

(a) any person entitled to do so has made a Part II claim in respect of expenditure incurred on the provision of any plant or machinery,

(b) that expenditure was expenditure falling to be treated for the purposes of that claim as expenditure to which this Chapter applies,

(c) at any time after the making of that claim, that person or another person makes a Part II claim in respect of any capital expenditure incurred at any time (including a time before the incurring of the expenditure to which the earlier claim relates) on the provision of the same machinery or plant,

(d) the expenditure to which the later claim relates would not (but for this subsection) be treated for the purposes of the later claim as expenditure to which this Chapter applies, and

(e) the expenditure to which the later claim relates does not fall within paragraph (d) above by virtue of being expenditure which is prevented by section 38B from being expenditure to which this Chapter applies,

this Part shall have effect in relation to the later claim as if the expenditure to which it relates were expenditure to which this Chapter applies.

(4) References in this section to the making of a Part II claim in respect of any expenditure are references to any of the following—

(a) the making of a return in which that expenditure is taken into account in determining a person's qualifying expenditure for the purposes of section 24;

(b) the giving of notice of any such amendment of a return as provides for the expenditure to be so taken into account;

(c) the making, in any other manner, of a claim for the expenditure to be so taken into account.

(5) In subsection (4) above 'return' means any return required to be made under the Taxes Management Act 1970 for income tax or corporation tax purposes.

(6) In the case of expenditure falling within subsection (1) of section 42, this section has effect subject to subsections (3) to (7) of that section.

Disposal value of long-life assets

38G.—(1) If, in a case where sections 24, 25 and 26 have had effect in accordance with section 38F(1) in relation to any expenditure incurred by a person ('the charged person')—

(a) an event occurs by reason of which a disposal value of that machinery or plant is to be brought into account by the charged person in accordance with section 24,

(b) the amount of the disposal value to be so brought into account would (but for this section) be less than the notional written-down value of the machinery or plant, and

(c) the event is comprised in, or occurs in pursuance of, any scheme or arrangement which has avoidance as its main object, or as one of its main objects,

this Part shall have effect in relation to the charged person as if the amount of the disposal value to be brought into account were equal to the notional written-down value of the machinery or plant.

(2) In this section 'the notional written-down value', in relation to any machinery or plant, means the amount which, if —
  (a) it were the disposal value falling to be brought into account as mentioned in subsection (1) above, and
  (b) the assumptions set out in subsection (3) below were made,
would give rise to neither a balancing allowance nor a balancing charge for the chargeable period for which that disposal value is to be brought into account.

(3) The assumptions mentioned in subsection (2) above are—
  (a) subject to paragraph (b) below, that expenditure on the provision of the machinery or plant were the only expenditure ever taken into account in determining the charged person's qualifying expenditure for the purposes of section 24;
  (b) that that expenditure were not, in the charged person's case, prevented by section 38C or 38D from being expenditure to which this Chapter applies; and
  (c) that the full amount of every allowance to which the charged person was entitled in respect of that expenditure had been made to him.

(4) The reference in subsection (1) above to avoidance is a reference to—
  (a) the obtaining under this Part for the charged person of an allowance or deduction or of a greater allowance or deduction, or
  (b) the avoidance or reduction of a charge under this Part on the charged person.

Transitional provisions

Transitional provisions

38H.—(1) This Chapter does not apply—
  (a) to any expenditure incurred before 26th November 1996; or
  (b) to any expenditure incurred before 1st January 2001 in pursuance of a contract entered into before 26th November 1996.

(2) This Chapter does not apply to expenditure incurred by any person ('the purchaser') on the acquisition of any long-life asset from another person ('the seller') in a case where—
  (a) the seller has made a Part II claim in respect of expenditure incurred on the provision of that asset ('the seller's expenditure'),
  (b) that claim is one which the seller was entitled to make,
  (c) the seller's expenditure was not expenditure falling for the purposes of that claim to be treated as expenditure to which this Chapter applies, and
  (d) the seller's expenditure would have fallen to be so treated if one or more of the assumptions specified in subsection (3) below were made.

(3) Those assumptions are—
  (a) that expenditure falling within paragraph (a) or (b) of subsection (1) above is not prevented by that paragraph from being expenditure to which this Chapter applies;
  (b) that the seller's expenditure was not prevented by subsection (2) above from being expenditure to which this Chapter applies; and
  (c) that this Chapter or, as the case may require, provision corresponding to it applied for chargeable periods ending before 26th November 1996.

(4) The reference in subsection (1) above to expenditure incurred in pursuance of a contract entered into before 26th November 1996 does not, in the case of a contract varied at any time on or after that date, include a reference to so much of the expenditure incurred under that contract as exceeds the amount of the expenditure that would have been incurred if that contract had not been so varied.

(5) Subsections (4) and (5) of section 38F have effect for the purposes of this section as they have effect for the purposes of that section."

Consequential amendments

3. In section 37(1), after paragraph (b) (election to treat assets as short-life assets), there shall be inserted the following paragraph—
  "(ba) the expenditure is not expenditure to which Chapter IVA of this Part applies; and".

4. For subsection (6) of section 41 (cases where the provision for separate pools for leased assets and inexpensive cars do not apply) there shall be substituted the following subsection—
  "(6) This section does not apply—
    (a) to machinery or plant in relation to which sections 24, 25 and 26 apply in accordance with section 34, 79 or 80; or
    (b) to machinery or plant the expenditure on which is expenditure to which Chapter IVA of this Part applies."

5. In section 42(2) (rate of writing down assets leased outside the United Kingdom), after "above" there shall be inserted "which is not expenditure to which Chapter IVA of this Part applies".

6. In section 43(3) (apportionments in leasing cases), after "26," there shall be inserted "38E,".

7. In section 46(7)(c) (leasing of ships to non-residents), for "section 41" there shall be inserted "whichever of sections 38E and 41 is applicable".

8. In section 50(3) (interpretation of Chapter V), in the definition of "normal writing down allowance", for "section 42(2)" there shall be substituted "sections 38F(1) and 42(2)".

9. In section 77(8) (provisions that do not apply where an election is made in the case of a connected person succeeding to a trade), after "Sections" there shall be inserted "38G,".

Commencement

10. This Schedule applies in relation to chargeable periods ending on or after 26th November 1996.

GENERAL NOTE

This Schedule implements a general reduction in capital allowances for machinery and plant with a life of over 25 years from 25 per cent to 6 per cent on a reducing balance basis.

Para. 2

This inserts new Chap. IVA (ss.38A–H) into Capital Allowances Act 1990 (c. 1) (CAA).

New s.38A

This provides for the Chapter to apply to capital expenditure on the provision of machinery and plant that is a long-life asset *i.e.* an asset with an expected useful economic life of at least 25 years. Where the new rules apply to part only of the expenditure on an asset, a just and reasonable apportionment may be made.

New s.38B

Various expenditure is excluded from the operation of the Chapter:

(i) machinery or plant which is a fixture in, or provided for use in, any building used wholly or mainly as, or for purposes ancillary to, a dwelling-house, retail shop, showroom, hotel or office;

(ii) motor cars, taxi cabs and other types of vehicles commonly used as private vehicles;

(iii) sea-going ships other than oil rigs, other offshore installations and ships primarily used for sport or recreation. A cruise liner is not a ship of a type primarily used for sport or recreation. This exclusion applies to expenditure incurred before January 1, 2011;

(iv) railway assets for use, whether by the person who incurs the expenditure or by another person, wholly and exclusively in a railway business. The exclusion also covers tramways and other such guided transport systems. Trains running through the Channel Tunnel or across the Irish border come within the exclusion. This exclusion also applies to expenditure incurred before January 1, 2011.

New s.38C

This applies a *de minimis* limit of £100,000 on expenditure incurred by an individual or partnership of individuals in a chargeable period on long-life assets. The limit applies to expenditure incurred for the purposes of a trade or profession carried on full time by the individual, or at least half the partners, throughout the chargeable period. Expenditure on a share in a long-life asset, a contribution to expenditure on a long-life asset and expenditure on the provision of a long-life asset for leasing are excluded. The *de minimis* limit is applied by treating all the expenditure incurred under a contract for the provision of a long-life asset as incurred in the first chargeable period in which any of the expenditure is incurred. The purpose of the latter two provisions is to prevent fragmentation of the *de minimis* limit and to ensure that expenditure on an asset will normally fall wholly inside or outside these rules.

New s.38D

A corresponding *de minimis* limit is provided for companies. It is applied to a group of companies by dividing the limit by one plus the number of associated companies. This matches the rules for small companies relief in ICTA 1988, s.13.

New ss.38E and F

These provide for expenditure to which Chap. IVA applies to go into a separate pool or, where other separate pooling provisions also apply, pools on which allowances are given at 6 per cent. Once an asset has been treated as long-life, it cannot be re-classified as non long-life by re-considering its expected life or through the operation of the *de minimis* rule. Allowances given on assets leased overseas at 10 per cent under CAA s.42 will continue at 6 per cent where Chap. IVA applies, subject to the provisions in s.42(3)–(7).

New s.38G

This counters avoidance of tax through the acceleration of allowances on long-life assets. It applies where a person who has claimed allowances on a long-life asset under Chap. IVA disposes of the asset for less than its notional written down value with the object of avoiding tax. It treats the person as having sold the asset for its notional written down value, computed by writing down the cost of the asset at 6 per cent a year. Avoidance is defined as the obtaining by a person of an allowance, for instance a balancing allowance, or the avoidance of a charge, for instance a balancing charge.

New s.38H

This provides that Chap. IVA applies to expenditure incurred on or after November 26, 1996, other than expenditure up to the end of the year 2000 under contracts entered into before November 26, 1996. Second hand assets are excluded where claims have been previously made under CAA Pt. II (machinery and plant). Where a contract is varied, only the pre-variation amount is allowable.

Paras. 3–10

These make consequential amendments and provide for commencement.

Section 85   SCHEDULE 15

CAPITAL ALLOWANCES: SCHEDULE A CASES ETC.

Repeal of existing rules

1. Section 32 of the Taxes Act 1988 (capital allowances in Schedule A cases) shall cease to have effect, both for the purposes of income tax and for the purposes of corporation tax.

Removal of restriction on set-off of losses

2.—(1) In section 379A(2) of the Taxes Act 1988 (cases in which Schedule A losses may be set against other income of the same year or the following year)—
   (a) in paragraph (a) (losses attributable to relevant capital allowances), the word "relevant" shall be omitted; and
   (b) the words after paragraph (b) (which define the relevant capital allowances) shall cease to have effect.

(2) In section 503 of that Act (letting of furnished holiday accommodation treated as trade), after subsection (1) there shall be inserted the following subsection—

   "(1A) In its application by virtue of subsection (1) above, section 384 shall have effect with the omission of subsections (6) to (8) and of the words after paragraph (b) in subsection (10) (restrictions on right to set off losses attributable to capital allowances)."

New general provision

3. In Chapter I of Part II of the Capital Allowances Act 1990 (general provisions about capital allowances in respect of machinery and plant), the following section shall be inserted after section 28—

"Schedule A cases

28A.—(1) Subject to subsection (3) below and section 29, where any person carries on a Schedule A business—
   (a) that person's Schedule A business shall be treated as a trade for the purposes of this Part and of the other provisions of the Tax Acts so far as relating to allowances or charges under this Part; and
   (b) that trade shall be treated for those purposes as one trade carried on separately from any other trade carried on by that person.

(2) For the purposes of the Corporation Tax Acts the reference in subsection (1) above to a Schedule A business is a reference, in relation to a company, to all the activities carried on by that company which—
   (a) would be treated as comprised in a Schedule A business if they were carried on by an individual, rather than by a company; and

(b) are not activities the profits and gains from which are treated for the purposes of the Corporation Tax Acts as chargeable to tax under Case VI of Schedule D.

(3) Expenditure incurred in providing machinery or plant for use in a dwelling-house shall not, by virtue of this section, be treated as incurred in providing that machinery or plant for the purposes of a trade.

(4) Where machinery or plant is provided partly for use in a dwelling-house and partly for other purposes, such apportionment of the expenditure incurred in providing that machinery or plant shall be made for the purposes of subsection (3) above as is just and reasonable."

4. In section 29 of that Act of 1990 (furnished holiday accommodation), for subsection (1), both as it applies for the purposes of income tax and as it applies for the purposes of corporation tax, there shall be substituted the following subsections—

"(1) Subject to subsection (1A) below, this Part and the other provisions of the Tax Acts so far as relating to allowances or charges under this Part shall have effect as if so much of the Schedule A business of any person as consists in the commercial letting of furnished holiday accommodation in the United Kingdom were a single trade carried on separately from both—

(a) the trade in which, in accordance with section 28A, the rest (if any) of that business is comprised; and

(b) any other trade carried on by that person.

(1A) Subsection (1) above does not apply for the purposes of the Corporation Tax Acts; but for those purposes this Part and the other provisions of those Acts so far as relating to allowances and charges under this Part shall have effect as if—

(a) the commercial letting of furnished holiday accommodation in the United Kingdom in respect of which profits or gains are chargeable under Case VI of Schedule D were a trade; and

(b) all such lettings made by the same person were a single trade carried on separately from any other trade which is, or under section 28A is treated as, carried on by that person."

Manner of making allowances and charges

5.—(1) In subsection (3) of section 67 of that Act of 1990 (manner of giving allowance on thermal insulation), the words from "shall be made" to "corporation tax," shall be omitted.

(2) After that subsection there shall be inserted the following subsection—

"(3A) Subsections (2) and (3) above have effect for the purposes of corporation tax only."

(3) After subsection (4) of that section there shall be inserted the following subsection—

"(4A) Where the letting of any industrial building or structure by any person is deemed by virtue of section 28A to be in the course of a trade, subsection (1) above shall have effect as if that person occupied that building or structure for the purposes of that trade throughout the period for which it is let by him."

6.—(1) In section 73 of that Act of 1990 (manner of making allowances and charges under Part II), in subsection (1), for "subsection (2)" there shall be substituted "subsections (1A) and (2)".

(2) After subsection (1) of that section there shall be inserted the following subsection—

"(1A) Any allowance or charge made to or on any company by virtue of section 28A shall be made for the purposes of corporation tax by way of discharge or repayment of tax and, for that purpose—

(a) any such allowance shall be available primarily against income chargeable to tax under Schedule A; and

(b) the amount on which any such charge is to be made shall be treated as income so chargeable."

Meaning of capital expenditure

7. In section 159 of that Act of 1990, after subsection (1) (capital expenditure and capital sums not to include trading expenses and receipts) there shall be inserted the following subsection—

"(1A) References in subsection (1) above to a trade include references to a Schedule A business or to any such activities as are mentioned in section 28A(2)."

Consequential amendment of section 434E of the Taxes Act 1988

8. In section 434E(2) of the Taxes Act 1988 (letting of investment assets of life assurance companies to be treated as letting otherwise than in the course of a trade), at the end there shall be inserted "except where it is a letting of machinery or plant that is deemed to be a letting in the course of a trade by virtue of section 28A of that Act (Schedule A businesses etc.)."

Commencement

9.—(1) Subject to sub-paragraph (2) below, this Schedule has effect—

(a) for the purposes of income tax, in relation to the year 1997–98 and subsequent years of assessment; and

(b) for the purposes of corporation tax, in relation to accounting periods ending on or after 1st April 1997.

(2) Paragraph 7 above has effect for any year of assessment or accounting period ending on or after 26th November 1996, but only in relation to expenditure incurred on or after that date and sums paid or received on or after that date.

GENERAL NOTE

The Schedule aligns the rules for capital allowances under Schedule A of ICTA 1988 with those applying under Sched. D.

Para. 1

ICTA 1988, s.32 is repealed.

Para. 2

Restrictions on the set-off against other income of excess capital allowances on machinery and plant used in a Sched. A business which are incompatible with pooling are removed.

Para. 3

This inserts new CAA s.28A.

New s.28A extends pooling to machinery and plant used in a Sched. A business. No capital allowances are given on machinery and plant provided for use in a dwelling-house, although wear and tear allowances may be due instead under Extra Statutory Concession B47.

Para. 4

This amends CAA s.29, which extends pooling to machinery and plant in furnished holidays lettings treated as a trade under ICTA 1988, s.503, to ensure that there are separate pools for furnished holiday lettings and the rest of the Sched. A business. This is necessary because the profits, losses and capital allowances are treated in different ways.

Para. 5

Consequential amendments are made to CAA s.67, which gives income tax relief for expenditure on thermal insulation, to ensure that it continues to work as before.

Para. 6

New CAA s.73(1A), which mirrors the rule for industrial buildings allowances in *ibid.* s.9, provides for allowances to be deducted from and charges treated as Sched. A profits for corporation tax purposes. Any allowances which cannot be relieved in this way can be carried forward and deducted from Sched. A profits or set off against other income of the same and the preceding accounting period under *ibid.* s.145.

Para. 7

New CAA s.159(1A) confirms that the prevention of double allowances or charges under s.159 by stopping amounts which are deducted or charged in computing the profits of a trade from also being allowed or charged under CAA, covers amounts deducted or charged in computing Sched. A profits for income tax and extends it to computations of Sched. A profit for corporation tax.

Para. 8

This makes a consequential amendment to ICTA 1988, s.434E to ensure that the rules in the Schedule apply to life assurance companies.

Para. 9

The Schedule applies for income tax from the year 1997/98 on and for corporation tax to accounting periods ending on or after April 1, 1997. Paragraph 7 applies to expenditure incurred and sums paid or received on or after November 26, 1996.

SCHEDULE 16

CAPITAL ALLOWANCES ON FIXTURES

PART I

AMENDMENTS OF THE CAPITAL ALLOWANCES ACT 1990

Introductory

1. The Capital Allowances Act 1990 shall be amended in accordance with the following provisions of this Part of this Schedule.

Interpretation of Chapter VI of Part II

2.—(1) In subsection (2) of section 51 (definitions), after the definition of "relevant land" there shall be inserted the following definition—

"'return' means (subject to section 59C(10)) any return required to be made under the Taxes Management Act 1970 for income tax or corporation tax purposes."

(2) In subsection (5) of that section—

(a) in paragraph (b), for "that expenditure is" there shall be substituted "that person is entitled to have that expenditure"; and

(b) in sub-paragraph (iii), for "he is required" there shall be substituted "he would be required (disregarding section 24(7))".

(3) After that subsection there shall be inserted the following subsection—

"(5A) In this Chapter references to making a claim for an allowance in respect of any expenditure include references—

(a) to making a return in which the expenditure is taken into account, as expenditure on the provision of a fixture, in determining a person's qualifying expenditure for the purposes of section 24, and

(b) to giving notice of any such amendment of a return as provides for that expenditure to be so taken into account."

(4) After subsection (6) of that subsection there shall be inserted the following subsection—

"(6A) Where a person who has made a return becomes aware that anything contained in that return has, after being made, become incorrect by reason of—

(a) the making an election under section 59B, or

(b) the operation, in his case, of section 56A(1), section 56B(1) or section 59C(3),

he shall, within three months of first becoming so aware, give notice to an officer of the Board of the amendments that are necessitated in his return in the light of the matter of which he has become aware."

(5) In subsection (8), paragraph (b) (expenditure under commitments made before 12th July 1984 not subject to the provisions of the Chapter) shall cease to have effect.

(6) Subject to sub-paragraphs (7) and (8) below, this paragraph has effect for chargeable periods ending on or after 24th July 1996.

(7) Where, but for this sub-paragraph, the latest time for the giving of a notice under subsection (6A) of section 51 would be before the end of the period of three months beginning with the day on which this Act is passed, that subsection shall have effect as if the latest time for the giving of that notice were the end of that period of three months.

(8) Section 59(10) shall not apply by virtue of sub-paragraph (5) above in any case where it would not have applied apart from that sub-paragraph and the fixture is treated as having ceased to belong to the former owner before 24th July 1996.

Allowances in respect of expenditure by equipment lessors

3.—(1) In subsection (1) of section 53 (cases where allowance may be made in respect of expenditure of an equipment lessor), at the beginning there shall be inserted "Subject to subsections (1A) to (1C) below,".

(2) In paragraph (b) of that subsection (agreement must be entered into for the purposes of a trade carried on by the equipment lessee etc.), after the word "trade", in the first place where it occurs, there shall be inserted "which is or is to be".

(3) After paragraph (b) of that subsection there shall be inserted the following paragraphs—

"(ba) that agreement is not an agreement for the lease of the machinery or plant for use in a dwelling-house, and

(bb) the equipment lessee is within the charge to tax in the United Kingdom on the profits of, as the case may be—

(i) the trade for the purposes of which he has entered into that agreement, or

(ii) the leasing of the machinery or plant by him to another, and".

(4) In paragraph (d) of that subsection, for the words from "the fixture" to the end of the paragraph there shall be substituted "the equipment lessee would, by virtue of section 52, have been entitled to an allowance in respect of the expenditure, as expenditure incurred on the provision of that fixture, and".

(5) After that subsection there shall be inserted the following subsections—

"(1A) Where the condition specified in paragraph (b) of subsection (1) above is satisfied in any case by reference to an agreement entered into for the purposes of a trade which the equipment lessee has not begun to carry on at the time of the agreement, that subsection shall have effect in that case as if the reference in the words after paragraph (e) to the time at which the expenditure is incurred were a reference to whichever is the later of that time and the time when the equipment lessee begins to carry on that trade.

(1B) Where the conditions set out in subsection (1C) below are satisfied in any case, subsection (1) above shall have effect in that case as if the following were omitted, that is to say—

(a) in paragraph (b), the words from 'for the purposes of' to 'course of a trade'; and

(b) paragraphs (bb) and (d).

(1C) Those conditions are as follows—

(a) that the machinery or plant becomes a fixture by virtue of being fixed to land that is neither a building nor part of a building;

(b) that the equipment lessee has an interest in that land at the time when he takes possession of the machinery or plant under the agreement for the lease of it;

(c) that, under the terms of that agreement, the equipment lessor is entitled to sever the machinery or plant, at the end of the period for which it is leased, from the land to which it is fixed at that time;

(d) that, under the terms of that agreement, the machinery or plant will belong to the equipment lessor on its severance from that land in accordance with that agreement;

(e) that the nature of the machinery or plant and the way in which it is fixed to land are such that its use on one set of premises does not, to any material extent, prevent it from being used, once severed, for the same purposes on a different set of premises; and

(f) that the agreement for the lease of the machinery or plant is such as falls, for the purposes of the accounts of equipment lessors who are companies incorporated in a part of the United Kingdom, to be treated, in accordance with normal accountancy practice, as an operating lease."

(6) Sub-paragraphs (1), (2) and (5) above have effect for chargeable periods ending on or after the day on which this Act is passed in relation to any case in which the agreement for the lease of the machinery or plant is entered into on or after that day.

(7) Sub-paragraphs (3) and (4) above have effect for chargeable periods ending on or after 24th July 1996 in relation to any case in which the expenditure incurred by the equipment lessor is expenditure incurred on or after that date.

Fixtures in respect of which more than one person gets an allowance

4.—(1) After section 56 there shall be inserted the following sections—

"Restrictions on duplicate allowances under sections 54 and 56

56A.—(1) Where the relevant conditions are satisfied in relation to any case in which the provisions of section 54(1) or action 56 would (but for this section) be treated as applying, those provisions shall not apply in that case, and shall be treated as never having applied in that case.

(2) The relevant conditions are as follows—

(a) that an interest in any land in which the whole or any part of the relevant land is comprised is held by any person immediately after the relevant time;

(b) that that interest is not the one which—

(i) in a case falling within section 54(1)(a), is acquired by the purchaser; or

(ii) in a case falling within section 56(a), is acquired by the lessee in consequence of the grant of the lease;

(c) that the person with that interest is a person falling to be treated for the purposes of this Part as a person to whom the fixture belonged immediately before the relevant time in consequence of the incurring by him of expenditure on the provision of the fixture;

(d) that that person does not fall to be so treated by virtue of section 154;

(e) that that person is entitled to an allowance in respect of that expenditure and makes or has made a claim for that allowance; and

(f) that the relevant time is on or after 24th July 1996.

(3) In this section 'the relevant time' means, as the case may be—

(a) the time when the purchaser acquires his interest in the relevant land; or

(b) the time of the grant of the lease.

Fixtures on which a former owner had an allowance

56B.—(1) Where—

(a) any machinery or plant falls to be treated for the purposes of this Part as a fixture belonging to any person ('the new claimant') in consequence of his incurring capital expenditure on the provision of that machinery or plant, and

(b) the requirements of subsection (2) below are satisfied in the case of that machinery or plant,

so much (if any) of that expenditure as exceeds the maximum allowable amount shall be disregarded for the purposes of this Part or, as the case may be, shall be taken to be expenditure that should never have been taken into account for those purposes.

(2) The requirements of this subsection are satisfied in the case of any machinery or plant where—

(a) it falls or has fallen, otherwise than by virtue of section 154, to be treated as having belonged at a relevant earlier time to any person ('the prior claimant') in consequence of his incurring expenditure ('the other expenditure') which is not the expenditure mentioned in subsection (1)(a) above;

(b) the prior claimant, as a consequence of having made a claim for an allowance in respect of the other expenditure, is or has been required to bring a disposal value of the machinery or plant into account; and

(c) the event by reason of which that disposal value has been or is to be brought into account is an event occurring on or after 24th July 1996.

(3) For the purposes of this section the new claimant and the prior claimant may be the same person.

(4) Subject to subsection (5) below, the maximum allowable amount for the purposes of this section is the sum of—

(a) the disposal value of the machinery or plant which the prior claimant has been or is required to bring into account; and

(b) so much (if any) of the expenditure mentioned in subsection (1)(a) above as is deemed by virtue of section 66 (installation costs) to be expenditure on the provision of the machinery or plant.

(5) Subsection (4) above shall have effect where the requirements of subsection (2) above are satisfied by reference to more than one such event as is mentioned in subsection (2)(c) above as if they were satisfied by reference only to the most recent of those events.

(6) In this section 'a relevant earlier time' means a time which—

(a) is before the time which is taken for the purposes of this Part to be the earliest time when the machinery or plant belonged to the new claimant in consequence of his incurring the expenditure mentioned in subsection (1)(a) above; and

(b) does not fall to be disregarded under subsection (7) below.

(7) For the purposes of subsection (6) above a time must be disregarded if—

(a) in consequence of any sale of the machinery or plant, it has ceased, at any time after that time and before the time mentioned in paragraph (a) of that subsection, to belong to any person;

(b) that person and the purchaser were not connected with each other, within the terms of section 839 of the principal Act, at the time of sale; and

(c) the sale was not a sale of the machinery or plant as a fixture.

Fixtures on which an allowance has been given under Part I

56C.—(1) Where—

(a) a person has at any time made a claim for an allowance to which he is entitled under Part I in respect of expenditure incurred on the construction of a building or structure,

(b) that expenditure was or included expenditure on the provision of machinery or plant,

(c) that person has made a transfer of the relevant interest in the building or structure ('the relevant transfer'),

(d) the person to whom the relevant transfer is made, or any person to whom for the purposes of this Part the machinery or plant is subsequently treated as belonging, makes a claim for an allowance under this Part, and

(e) that claim is for an allowance in respect of capital expenditure incurred, at a time on or after 24th July 1996 when it is a fixture in the building or structure, on the provision of the machinery or plant,

the amount taken for the purposes of the claim mentioned in paragraph (d) above to have been incurred on the provision of the fixture shall not exceed the relevant amount.

(2) In subsection (1) above 'the relevant amount' means the amount equal, on the relevant assumption, to the portion of the consideration for the relevant transfer which would have been attributable to the fixture.

(3) The relevant assumption for the purposes of subsection (2) above is that the relevant transfer was a sale of the relevant interest in the building or structure for the amount which immediately after that transfer represented the residue of the expenditure incurred on the construction of the building or structure.

(4) Expressions used both in this section and in Part I have the same meanings in this section as in that Part.

Fixtures on which an allowance has been given under Part VII

56D.—(1) Where—

(a) a person has at any time made a claim for an allowance to which he is entitled under Part VII in respect of any allowable scientific research expenditure of a capital nature ('the Part VII expenditure'),

(b) the Part VII expenditure was or included expenditure on the provision of machinery or plant,

(c) an asset representing the whole or any part of the Part VII expenditure ('the Part VII asset') has ceased, on any occasion, to belong to that person,

(d) the person who acquired the Part VII asset on that occasion, or any person to whom for the purposes of this Part the machinery or plant is subsequently treated as belonging, makes a claim for an allowance under this Part, and

(e) that claim is for an allowance in respect of capital expenditure incurred, at a time on or after 24th July 1996 when it is a fixture, on the provision of the machinery or plant,

the amount taken for the purposes of the claim mentioned in paragraph (d) above to have been incurred on the provision of the fixture shall not exceed the relevant amount.

(2) In subsection (1) above 'the relevant amount' means the amount equal, on the relevant assumption, to the portion of the consideration for the disposal of the Part VII asset which would have been attributable to the fixture.

(3) The relevant assumption for the purposes of subsection (2) above is that the occasion mentioned in subsection (1)(c) above was a disposal of the Part VII asset for the amount equal to whichever is the smaller of—

(a) the disposal value of the asset on that occasion; and

(b) so much of the Part VII expenditure as related to the provision of the Part VII asset.

(4) Expressions used both in subsection (1) above and in Part VII have the same meanings in that subsection as in that Part."

(2) In section 54(1)—

(a) paragraph (c) (cases where another person has had an entitlement), and the word "and" immediately preceding it, shall cease to have effect; and

(b) in the words after that paragraph, for "section 57" there shall be substituted "the following provisions of this Chapter".

(3) In section 56—

(a) paragraph (c) (cases where another person has had an entitlement) shall cease to have effect;

(b) in paragraph (d), for "that time" there shall be substituted "the time of the grant of the lease"; and

(c) in the words after paragraph (d), for "section 57" there shall be substituted "the following provisions of this Chapter".

(4) This paragraph has effect, subject to sub-paragraphs (5) and (6) below, for chargeable periods ending on or after 24th July 1996.

(5) Sub-paragraph (2)(a) above does not apply where the purchaser acquired the relevant interest before 24th July 1996.

(6) Sub-paragraph (3)(a) above does not apply where the lease was granted before 24th July 1996.

Disposal value in avoidance cases

5.—(1) In subsection (1) of section 59 (disposal value of fixtures determined in accordance with subsections (2) to (6)), after "determined" there shall be inserted "(subject to sections 59A and 59B)".

(2) In Chapter VI of Part II, after that section there shall be inserted the following section—

"Disposal values in avoidance cases

59A.—(1) If, in a case where machinery or plant has been treated by virtue of this Chapter as belonging to any person ('the charged person') in consequence of his incurring any expenditure—

    (a) an event occurs by reason of which a disposal value of that machinery or plant is to be brought into account by the charged person in accordance with section 24,

    (b) the amount of the disposal value to be so brought into account would (but for this section) be less than the notional written-down value of the machinery or plant, and

    (c) the event is comprised in, or occurs in pursuance of, any scheme or arrangement which has avoidance as its main object, or as one of its main objects,

this Part shall have effect in relation to the charged person as if the amount of the disposal value to be brought into account were equal to the notional written-down value of the machinery or plant.

(2) In this section 'the notional written-down value', in relation to any machinery or plant, means the amount which, if—

    (a) it were the disposal value falling to be brought into account as mentioned in subsection (1) above, and

    (b) the assumptions set out in subsection (3) below were made,

would give rise to neither a balancing allowance nor a balancing charge for the chargeable period for which that disposal value is to be brought into account.

(3) Those assumptions are—

    (a) that expenditure on the provision of the machinery or plant were the only expenditure ever taken into account in determining the charged person's qualifying expenditure for the purposes of section 24; and

    (b) that the full amount of every allowance to which that person was entitled in respect of that expenditure had been made to him.

(4) The reference in subsection (1) above to avoidance is a reference to—

    (a) the obtaining under this Part for the charged person of an allowance or deduction or of a greater allowance or deduction, or

    (b) the avoidance or reduction of a charge under this Part on the charged person."

(3) This paragraph has effect for chargeable periods ending on or after 24th July 1996 wherever the time of the occurrence of the event by virtue of which the disposal value falls to be brought into account is a time on or after that date.

Apportionment of expenditure by election

6.—(1) In Chapter VI of Part II, after the section 59A inserted by paragraph 5 above there shall be inserted the following sections—

"Election to use alternative apportionment

59B.—(1) This section applies where, in a case in which a disposal value of a fixture is required to be brought into account by the former owner, the price referred to in subsection (1) of section 59 falls to be determined in accordance with subsection (2) or (3) of that section.

(2) Subject to sections 56C, 56D and 59A and to the following provisions of this section, the purchaser and the former owner may jointly, by an election under this section, fix the amount which, for all the purposes of this Part, is to be taken—

    (a) in a case to which subsection (2) of section 59 applies, to be the portion of the sale price referred to in that subsection; or

    (b) in a case to which subsection (3) of that section applies, to be the portion of the capital sum referred to in section 55(1)(c) that falls to be treated as expenditure by the purchaser on the provision of the fixture.

(3) The amount fixed by an election under this section shall not exceed either of the following amounts, that is to say—

    (a) the amount of the capital expenditure which was taken for the purposes of this Part to have been incurred by the former owner on the provision of the fixture or of the machinery or plant which became the fixture; and

    (b) the actual amount of the sale price or capital sum referred to in section 59(2) or, as the case may be, section 55(1)(c).

(4) Where the portion of any amount which is to be taken as attributable to the provision of a fixture is fixed by an election under this section—

    (a) the remainder (if any) of that amount shall be taken for the purposes of this Act to be expenditure attributable to the acquisition of the property which is not the fixture but is acquired for that amount;

(b) if there is no remainder, the expenditure so attributable shall be taken for those purposes to be nil.

(5) An apportionment by virtue of an election under this section shall have effect in place of any apportionment that would otherwise be made under section 150.

(6) In this section—

'the former owner' shall be construed in accordance with subsection (1) of section 59; and

'the purchaser' means the purchaser or lessee referred to in subsection (2) or, as the case may be, subsection (3) of that section.

Elections under section 59B: supplemental

59C.—(1) A section 59B election must be made by notice given to an officer of the Board.

(2) A notice containing a section 59B election (in addition to specifying the amount fixed by the election) must contain the following information—

(a) the name of each of the persons making the election;

(b) information sufficient to identify the machinery or plant;

(c) information sufficient to identify the relevant land;

(d) particulars of the interest acquired by the purchaser or, as the case may be, of the lease granted to him; and

(e) the tax district references of each of the persons making the election.

(3) The amount specified as the amount fixed by a section 59B election must be quantified at the time when the election is made; but if, as a result of circumstances arising after the making of the election, the maximum amount which could be fixed by the election is reduced to an amount which is less than the amount specified in the election, that election shall be deemed for the purposes of this Act to have specified the amount to which the maximum is reduced.

(4) A section 59B election shall not be made more than two years after the time when the purchaser acquires the interest in question or, as the case may be, is granted the lease in question.

(5) Where a person who has joined in making a section 59B election subsequently makes a return for his relevant period, a copy of the notice containing the election must accompany the return.

(6) A section 59B election shall be irrevocable once made.

(7) Nothing in section 42 of, or Schedule 1A to, the Taxes Management Act 1970 (claims in returns and claims not included in returns) shall apply to a section 59B election.

(8) Where any question relating to a section 59B election falls to be determined by any body of Commissioners for the purposes of any proceedings before them—

(a) each of the persons who has joined in making the election shall be entitled to appear and be heard by the Commissioners, or to make representations to them in writing;

(b) the Commissioners shall determine that question separately from any other questions in those proceedings; and

(c) their determination on that question shall have effect as if made in an appeal to which each of those persons was a party.

(9) In this section—

'relevant period', in relation to any person who has joined in making a section 59B election, means the period for which a return is made by that person which is the first such period in which the election has an effect in his case for the purposes of income tax or corporation tax; and

'a section 59B election' means an election under section 59B;

and subsection (6) of section 59B applies for the purposes of this section as it applies for the purposes of that section.

(10) In the case of an election for the purposes of a trade, profession or business carried on by persons in partnership, the references in this section to a return shall be construed, in relation to those persons, as references to a return under section 12AA of the Taxes Management Act 1970 (partnership returns)."

(2) This paragraph has effect for chargeable periods ending on or after the day on which this Act is passed wherever the time when the fixture in question is or would be treated as ceasing to belong to the former owner is a time on or after that day.

Prohibition of double allowances

7.—(1) In section 147 (exclusion of double allowances), after subsection (2) there shall be inserted the following subsections—

"(2A) Subject to subsection (2B) below, where—

(a) a person entitled to do so has at any time made a claim for an allowance under any of the preceding Parts of this Act, other than Part II, and

(b) that claim is for an allowance in respect of capital expenditure relating, in whole or in part, to the construction, acquisition or provision of an asset,

no capital expenditure (whenever incurred) relating to the provision of that asset shall, by virtue of Chapter VI of Part II, be brought into account at any time after that time by any person at all.

(2B) Subsection (2A) above shall not prevent capital expenditure from being brought into account by virtue of Chapter VI of Part II where—

(a) the only claim made under a provision of this Act not contained in Part II is a claim under Part I or Part VII; and

(b) section 56C or 56D would apply by reference to that claim in relation to any claim for that expenditure to be so brought into account.

(2C) Where capital expenditure relating to the provision of any asset has at any time been brought into account by virtue of Chapter VI of Part II by any person entitled to do so, no capital expenditure (whenever incurred) relating to the construction, acquisition or provision of that asset shall, at any time after that time, be the subject of a claim made, by any person at all, for an allowance under any of the preceding Parts of this Act other than Part II.

(2D) For the purposes of subsections (2A) to (2C) above a person shall be taken to bring an amount of capital expenditure into account by virtue of Chapter VI of Part II if—

(a) he makes a claim for an allowance in respect of that expenditure, as expenditure on the provision of a fixture within the meaning of that Chapter,

(b) he makes a return in which that expenditure is taken into account, as expenditure on the provision of such a fixture, in determining his qualifying expenditure for the purpose of an allowance or charge under section 24, or

(c) he gives notice of any such amendment of a return as provides for that expenditure to be taken into account as mentioned in paragraph (b) above."

(2) In subsection (3) of that section after the definition of "capital expenditure" there shall be inserted "and

'return' means any return required to be made under the Taxes Management Act 1970 for income tax or corporation tax purposes,".

(3) This paragraph has effect for chargeable periods ending on or after 24th July 1996 but shall not be taken to prevent any allowance from being made, or any amount from being taken into account, in respect of expenditure incurred before that date.

Construction of amendments

8. Notwithstanding anything in subsection (1) of section 163 of the Capital Allowances Act 1990 (continuity of the law), subsection (2) of that section (under which references in that Act to provisions of that Act include references to repealed enactments) applies for construing that Act as amended by this Schedule as it applies for construing the provisions of that Act as originally enacted.

PART II

CONSEQUENTIAL AMENDMENT OF THE TAXES MANAGEMENT ACT 1970

9. In the second column of the Table in section 98 of the Taxes Management Act 1970 (penalties in respect of certain information provisions), in the entry relating to sections 23(2), 33F(4), 48 and 49(2) of the Capital Allowances Act 1990, for "and 49(2)" there shall be substituted ", 49(2) and 51(6A)".

GENERAL NOTE

The Schedule amends the provisions relating to capital allowances on fixtures. These are contained in Capital Allowances Act 1990 (CAA), Pt. II, Chap. VI, ss.51–59.

Para. 2

This makes various changes to CAA, s.51, which contains common definitions and provisions for Chap. VI. New s.51(6A) requires taxpayers who have claimed capital allowances on fixtures in amounts which subsequently become incorrect to amend the return accordingly. The repeal of s.51(8)(b) ensures that Chap. VI, as amended by the Schedule, provides a complete code for capital allowances on fixtures from July 24, 1996, when these changes were announced.

Para. 3

This amends the rules in s.53 for giving allowances to equipment lessors *i.e.* persons who lease out fixtures but have no interest in the land or building to which the fixture is attached.

Allowances are to be given to an equipment lessor on fixtures leased for the purposes of a trade to be carried on by the lessee when the lessee starts to trade.

Allowances may not be given to equipment lessors on fixtures in dwelling-houses.

No allowances are due on leases to non-taxpayers. This reverses the effect of the House of Lords decision in *Melluish v. BMI (No. 3)* [1995] S.T.C. 962.

New s.53(1A) treats a fixture as belonging to a lessor when the lessee starts to trade.

New ss.53(1B) and (1C) relax the conditions for certain leases in which affixation is incidental to the lease of the equipment. This lets allowances be given on fixtures leased to non-taxpayers in these cases. The following conditions must be satisfied:

(i) the equipment must be fixed to land, other than a building, in which the lessee has an interest;

(ii) the lessor must be able to remove the equipment at the end of the lease and re-use it;

(iii) the lease must fall to be treated in the accounts of the lessor as an operating lease, as opposed to a finance lease, under U.K. accounting standards.

The extension to agreements made before the lessee starts to trade and the relaxation for operating leases apply to agreements entered into on or after Royal Assent (March 19, 1997). The restrictions on fixtures in dwelling-houses and on leases to non-taxpayers apply to expenditure incurred by the lessor on or after July 24, 1996.

Para. 4

This imposes restrictions on allowances where more than one person receives an allowance on fixtures.

New s.56A prevents a fixture from being treated as belonging to two persons at the same time. It applies where the same or different persons could claim allowances by virtue of holding different interests in land and gives priority to whichever interest was held first. If no claim is made in respect of the interest held first, the holder of the other interest may claim.

New s.56B applies generally where allowances have been claimed in respect of a fixture by a previous owner and restricts the amount on which allowances can be claimed by the new owner to the disposal value of the last owner to claim allowances. Where the asset is installed by the new owner, he can also claim allowances on the installation costs.

New ss.56C and D limit the amount on which allowances can be claimed subsequently in cases where a previous owner has claimed industrial buildings allowance ("IBA") or scientific research allowance ("SRA"). In the IBA case, this is computed by apportioning the residue of the expenditure of the previous owner immediately after the disposal, as defined for IBA purposes, between the fixture and any other property included in the disposal. In the SRA case, it is the lower of the part of the disposal and the part of the cost of the previous owner attributable to the fixture, apportioning the disposal value and cost between the fixture and any other property included in the disposal or acquisition respectively.

Para. 5

New s.59A generalises the existing anti-avoidance rule in s.55(4)(b), which counters the acceleration of allowances on fixtures on the grant of a lease, to apply generally to disposals of fixtures. It treats the vendor as having disposed of a fixture for its notional written down value where it is disposed of for less than that amount as part of, or in pursuance of, a scheme or arrangement which has avoidance as its main, or one of its main, objects. The notional written down value is computed by writing down the cost of the asset at 25 per cent a year, or 6 per cent if it is a long-life asset (see Sched. 14 above). Avoidance is defined broadly as the obtaining by the vendor of an allowance, for instance a balancing allowance, or the avoidance of a charge, for instance a balancing charge.

Para. 6

Where an interest in land to which a fixture is attached is sold or acquired, CAA s.150 requires the overall sale price to be apportioned to determine the sale price of the fixture. To remove this burden, the purchaser and vendor are allowed to determine the amount apportioned to the fixtures by a joint election.

New s.59B authorises the election. The amount may not exceed either the cost of the fixture to the vendor or the amount to be apportioned.

New s.59C sets out the procedure for making the election, which is irrevocable, and must be made within two years of the disposal. The general rules for making claims and elections in TMA 1970, s.42 and Sched. 1A, which are replaced by these specific rules, do not apply.

Para. 7

This extends the rules in CAA s.147, which prevent a person from claiming allowances on the same expenditure under different parts of CAA, to prevent the same or different persons from claiming allowances on fixtures under CAA Pt. II and some other part of CAA.

New s.147(2A) prevents allowances from being given on a fixture under CAA Pt. II where allowances have been claimed by any person on the fixture under any other part of CAA.

New s.147(2B) relaxes this to let allowances be given under ss.56C and 56D (see para. 4 above) where industrial buildings allowances or scientific research allowances, which may be claimed in preference to CAA Pt. II as higher rates of allowance can apply, have been terminated through a disposal event.

New s.147(2C) prevent allowances from being given on a fixture under any part of CAA where they have been claimed by any person under CAA Pt. II.

New s.147(2D) explains what is meant by claiming allowances under Pt. II.

Para. 8

This provides for the changes to apply to all the provisions of CAA notwithstanding the consolidation in 1990.

Para. 9

This adds new s.51(6A) (see para. 2 above) to the list of provisions attracting penalties under TMA 1970, s.98 where statutory requirements are not met.

Section 87　　　　　　SCHEDULE 17

CHARGEABLE GAINS: RE-INVESTMENT RELIEF

Introductory

1. The Taxation of Chargeable Gains Act 1992 shall be amended in accordance with the provisions of this Schedule.

Qualifying investments

2.—(1) In subsection (8) of section 164A (cases where eligible shares are not a qualifying investment), after "in a qualifying company shall" there shall be inserted ", subject to subsection (8A) below,".

(2) After that subsection there shall be inserted the following subsections—

"(8A) Where the eligible shares acquired by any person in a qualifying company are shares which he acquires by their being issued to him, his acquisition of the shares shall not be regarded as the acquisition of a qualifying investment unless the qualifying company, or a qualifying subsidiary of that company, is intending to employ the money raised by the issue of the shares wholly for the purposes of a qualifying trade carried on by it.

(8B) For the purposes of subsection (8A) above—

(a) the purposes of a trade include the purpose of preparing for the carrying on of the trade; and

(b) 'qualifying subsidiary' has the same meaning as in section 164G."

Loss of relief

3.—(1) In subsection (1) of section 164F (failure of conditions of relief), after "or this section" there shall be inserted "or section 164FA".

(2) After that section there shall be inserted the following section—

"Loss of relief in cases where shares acquired on being issued

164FA.—(1) Subsection (5) below applies in any case falling cases where within any of subsections (2) to (4) below which is a case where—

(a) a person has acquired any eligible shares in a qualifying company ('the acquired holding') for a consideration which is treated as reduced, under section 164A or 164F or this section, by any amount ('the held-over gain'); and

(b) that person acquired those shares by their being issued to him.

(2) A case falls within this subsection if—

(a) the money raised by the issue of the shares comprised in the acquired holding was, at the time when those shares were acquired, intended to be employed for the purposes of a qualifying trade then being carried on; and

(b) that money has not been wholly employed for permissible purposes by the end of the initial utilisation period.

(3) A case falls within this subsection if—

(a) the money raised by the issue of the shares comprised in the acquired holding was, at the time when those shares were acquired, intended to be employed for the purposes of a qualifying trade not then being carried on;

(b) that trade begins to be carried on before the end of the period of 2 years from that time; and

(c) that money (apart from any part of it wholly employed for permissible purposes within the initial utilisation period) has not been wholly employed for the purposes of that trade by the end of the period of 1 year from the time when that trade begins to be carried on ('the first trading year').

(4) A case falls within this subsection if—

(a) the money raised by the issue of the shares comprised in the acquired holding was, at the time when those shares were acquired, intended to be employed for the purposes of a qualifying trade not then being carried on;

(b) that trade does not begin to be carried on before the end of the period of 2 years from that time; and

(c) that money has not been wholly employed for permissible purposes by the end of the initial utilisation period.

(5) In a case in which this subsection applies, but subject to the following provisions of this section, a chargeable gain equal to the appropriate portion of the held-over gain shall be treated as accruing to the person mentioned in subsection (1) above immediately before the utilisation time; and in this subsection 'the utilisation time' means—

(a) in relation to a case falling within subsection (2) above, the end of the initial utilisation period;

(b) in relation to a case falling within subsection (3) above, the end of the first trading year; and

(c) in relation to a case falling within subsection (4) above, the end of the period of 2 years mentioned in that subsection.

(6) If, in a case in which subsection (5) above applies, part (but only part) of the money raised by the issue of the shares comprised in the acquired holding has been permissibly employed, this Chapter shall have effect in relation to that holding—

(a) as if it were two separate holdings consisting of—

(i) a holding from which that part of the money was raised; and

(ii) a holding from which the remainder was raised;

and

(b) as if its value were to be apportioned accordingly between those two holdings;

but nothing in this subsection shall require any money whose use is disregarded by virtue of subsection (8)(e) below to be treated as raised by a different holding.

(7) For the purposes of subsection (6) above a part of the money raised by the issue of the shares comprised in the acquired holding shall be taken to have been permissibly employed if—

(a) in a case falling within subsection (2) or (4) above, that part has been wholly employed for permissible purposes within the initial utilisation period; or

(b) in a case falling within subsection (3) above that part has been wholly employed—

(i) for permissible purposes within the initial utilisation period, or

(ii) for the purposes of the trade mentioned in that subsection before the end of the first trading year.

(8) For the purposes of this section—

(a) the appropriate portion of the held-over gain is so much, if any, of that gain as has not already been charged on any disposal or under section 164F or this section;

(b) 'the initial utilisation period' means the period of 1 year from the time when the acquired holding was acquired;

(c) 'permissible purposes', in relation to a company, means the purposes of any qualifying trade carried on by it or by any of its qualifying subsidiaries;

(d) 'qualifying subsidiary' has the same meaning as in section 164G;

(e) money shall not be treated as employed otherwise than wholly for particular purposes if the only amount employed for other purposes is an amount which is not a significant amount; and

(f) the purposes of a qualifying trade shall be taken to include the purpose of preparing for the carrying on of the trade.

(9) Subsections (4) to (5) and (10A) to (11) of section 164F shall apply for the purposes of this section as they apply for the purposes of that section, but—

(a) subsection (5) of that section shall so apply—
     (i) with the omission of paragraphs (e) to (g), and
     (ii) as if the reference in paragraph (d) to any charge under subsection (2) of
      that section were a reference to any charge under subsection (5) of this section;
    and
(b) subsection (10A) of that section shall so apply as if the reference to subsection (2) of
    that section were a reference to subsection (5) of this section."

Meaning of "qualifying company"

4.—(1) For paragraphs (b) and (c) of subsection (2) of section 164G (company must be of one of the given descriptions) there shall be substituted "or
    (aa) an unquoted company which is the parent company of a trading group."

(2) For subsections (4) and (5) of that section (meaning of "qualifying subsidiary") there shall be substituted the following subsections—

"(4) In this section 'qualifying subsidiary', in relation to a company ('the holding company'), means any company which is a member of a group of companies of which the holding company is the principal company.

(4A) For the purposes of this section a company is the parent company of a trading group if—
    (a) it is the principal company of a group of companies; and
    (b) the requirements of subsection (4B) below are fulfilled by what would be the business of the company and its qualifying subsidiaries if all the activities, taken together, of the company and its qualifying subsidiaries were regarded as one business.

(4B) A business fulfils the requirements of this subsection if—
    (a) it is carried on wholly or mainly in the United Kingdom; and
    (b) neither the business nor a substantial part of it consists in, or in either of, the following, that is to say—
     (i) activities falling within section 164I(2) but not within subsection (4C) below; and
     (ii) activities carried on otherwise than in the course of a trade.

(4C) The activities falling within this subsection are—
    (a) the receiving of royalties or licence fees in circumstances where the requirements mentioned in paragraphs (a) and (b) of section 164I(5) or (6) are satisfied in relation to the company receiving them;
    (b) the letting of ships, other than oil rigs or pleasure craft, on charter in circumstances where the requirements mentioned in paragraphs (a) to (d) of section 164I(7) are satisfied in relation to the company so letting them.

(4D) Activities of a company or of any of its qualifying subsidiaries shall be disregarded for the purposes of subsections (4A) to (4C) above to the extent that they consist in—
    (a) the holding of shares in or securities of, or the making of loans to, one or more of the company's qualifying subsidiaries; or
    (b) the holding and managing of property used by the company or any of its qualifying subsidiaries for the purposes of—
     (i) research and development from which it is intended that a qualifying trade to be carried on by the company or any of its qualifying subsidiaries will be derived; or
     (ii) one or more qualifying trades so carried on.

(4E) Activities of a qualifying subsidiary of a company shall also be disregarded for the purposes of subsections (4A) to (4C) above to the extent that they consist in—
    (a) the making of loans to the company; or
    (b) in the case of a mainly trading subsidiary, activities carried on in pursuance of its insignificant purposes (within the meaning given by subsection (4F) below).

(4F) In subsection (4E) above 'mainly trading subsidiary' means a qualifying subsidiary which, apart from purposes ('its insignificant purposes') capable of having no significant effect (other than in relation to incidental matters) on the extent of its activities, exists wholly for the purpose of carrying on one or more qualifying trades."

Meaning of "qualifying trade"

5—(1) In paragraph (a) of subsection (1) of section 164I (meaning of "qualifying trade"), after "complies with the requirements of this section" there shall be inserted "and is carried on wholly or mainly in the United Kingdom".

(2) In paragraph (b) of that subsection—

(a) after the words "the carrying on" (where they first occur) there shall be inserted ", wholly or mainly in the United Kingdom,"; and

(b) after "complying with those requirements" there shall be inserted ", and to be carried on wholly or mainly in the United Kingdom,".

Interpretation of Chapter IA of Part V

6.—(1) For subsection (2) of section 164N (application of section 170 for the interpretation of sections 164G and 164I) there shall be substituted the following subsection—

"(2) Section 170 shall apply for the interpretation of sections 164G and 164I as it would apply for the interpretation of sections 171 to 181 if section 170(2)(a) together with the words '(although resident in the United Kingdom)' in section 170(9)(b) were omitted."

(2) In section 164N (interpretation of Chapter IA), after subsection (4) there shall be inserted the following subsection—

"(5) For the purposes of this Chapter, any allotment of shares before their issue shall be disregarded in determining whether and when a person acquires shares by their issue to him."

Commencement

7.—(1) This Schedule—

(a) applies in relation to shares acquired after 26th November 1996; and

(b) subject to sub-paragraph (3) below, applies after 26th November 1996 in relation to shares that fall within sub-paragraph (2) below.

(2) Shares fall within this sub-paragraph if—

(a) they were acquired by a person at any time on or before 26th November 1996;

(b) they were held by him throughout the period beginning with that time and ending with 26th November 1996; and

(c) at all times in that period they were, for the purposes of Chapter IA of Part V of the Taxation of Chargeable Gains Act 1992, eligible shares in a qualifying company.

(3) The application of the preceding provisions of this Schedule in relation to any shares falling within sub-paragraph (2) above shall not prevent those shares from being (or having been) shares in a qualifying company at any relevant time when those shares would have been shares in such a company if this Schedule had not been enacted.

(4) For the purposes of sub-paragraph (3) above a time is a relevant time in relation to any shares falling within sub-paragraph (2) above if it is a time after 26th November 1996 and within the period of 3 years after the acquisition of the shares.

GENERAL NOTE

This Schedule implements relaxations in the rules for reinvestment relief.

Para. 2

New TCGA 1992, s.164(8A) and (8B) ensure that relief on subscription for newly-issued shares will be given only where the company issuing the shares intends to employ the money raised wholly for the purposes of a qualifying trade which either it, or a qualifying subsidiary, carries on or is preparing to carry on.

Para. 3

New s.164FA sets out the time limits within which funds raised by a new share issue must be applied. Where it was to be applied to an existing trade this is one year; where it was raised for an intended trade, the trade must be begun within two years and the funds wholly applied to that trade within a further year; where it was raised for an intended trade, but the trade is not begun within two years, the money must be wholly used for other permissible purposes *i.e.* the purposes of a qualifying trade carried on by the company or its subsidiaries. Where these conditions are not met an appropriate proportion of the relief will be withdrawn.

Para. 4

The effect of the amendments made by this paragraph allows an investment in an unquoted parent company of a trading group to qualify for relief, where all the activities of the parent and its subsidiary companies, when taken together as a single business are carried on wholly or mainly in the U.K. and the business does not consist, to a substantial extent, of non-qualifying or non-trading activities. Certain intra-group activities are disregarded. The *de minimis* or specific exclusions that apply to a qualifying trade carried on by a single company are applied to the group's business.

Para. 5

The amendment to s.164I, which defines a qualifying trade, requires that the trade be carried on wholly or mainly in the U.K.

Para. 6

This contains the provision which allows groups with non-resident subsidiaries to qualify. It amends s.164N by modifying the extent to which it imports the definition of a group in s.170.

Para. 7

This deals with commencement of the new rules. The effect is that investment after Budget day will qualify if the company is within the new provisions. Relief for investment before then in a company which was eligible under the rules which prevailed at the earlier date will not be withdrawn. Relief will also continue if such a company subsequently changes its operations in a way which qualifies under the new rules.

[Standing Committee B, February 20, 1997, cols. 454–457.]

Section 113   SCHEDULE 18

Repeals

Part I

Hydrocarbon Oil Duty

Chapter	Short Title	Extent of repeal
1979 c. 5.	The Hydrocarbon Oil Duties Act 1979.	In section 11(2), the definition of "gas oil" and the word "and" immediately preceding that definition. In section 27(1), the word "and" immediately following the definition of "road fuel gas".

The power in subsection (10) of section 7 of this Act applies in relation to these repeals as it applies in relation to the provisions of that section.

Part II

Gaming Duty

Chapter	Short Title	Extent of repeal
1979 c. 2.	The Customs and Excise Management Act 1979.	In section 1(1)— (a) the word "and" at the end of paragraph (c) of the definition of "the revenue trade provisions of the customs and excise Acts"; and (b) the word "or" at the end of paragraph (a)(ia) of the definition of "revenue trader".
1981 c. 63.	The Betting and Gaming Duties Act 1981.	Sections 13 to 16. In section 27, the words "15 or" and "paragraph 7 of Schedule 2,". In section 31, the words "gaming licences or". In section 32— (a) in subsection (2), the words "Subject to subsection (3) below,"; and (b) subsection (3). In section 35(3), paragraphs (a) and (c) and the words after paragraph (d). Schedule 2.
1984 c. 60.	The Police and Criminal Evidence Act 1984.	In Schedule 6, paragraph 39(a).

Chapter	Short Title	Extent of repeal
1985 c. 66.	The Bankruptcy (Scotland) Act 1985.	In paragraph 2(3) of Schedule 3, paragraph (c) and the word "or" immediately preceding it.
1986 c. 45.	The Insolvency Act 1986.	In paragraph 5 of Schedule 6, paragraph (c) and the word "or" immediately preceding it.
1988 c. 39.	The Finance Act 1988.	In section 12(4), the words "and paragraph 7 of Schedule 2" and the word "each".
S.I. 1989/2405 (N.I. 19).	The Insolvency (Northern Ireland) Order 1989.	In paragraph 5 of Schedule 4, paragraph (c) and the word "or" immediately preceding it.
1991 c. 31.	The Finance Act 1991.	Section 6.
1994 c. 9.	The Finance Act 1994.	In section 12(7)(b), the words ", paragraph 7(3) of Schedule 2". In Schedule 4, paragraph 63.

1. The repeals in the Bankruptcy (Scotland) Act 1985, the Insolvency Act 1986 and the Insolvency (Northern Ireland) Order 1989 shall not apply in relation to any amount due in respect of duty chargeable for a period beginning before 1st October 1997.

2. The other repeals have effect in relation to any gaming on or after 1st October 1997.

PART III

VEHICLE EXCISE AND REGISTRATION: EXEMPT VEHICLES

Chapter	Short Title	Extent of repeal
1994 c. 22.	The Vehicle Excise and Registration Act 1994.	In Schedule 2, paragraph 20(4).

The power in paragraph 9 of Schedule 3 to this Act applies in relation to this repeal as it applies in relation to the provisions of that Schedule.

PART IV

VALUE ADDED TAX

(1) AGGREGATION OF BUSINESSES

Chapter	Short Title	Extent of repeal
1994 c. 23.	The Value Added Tax Act 1994.	In Schedule 1, in paragraph 2— (a) in sub-paragraph (2)(b), the words from "which should properly" to "described in the direction"; (b) paragraph (d) of sub-paragraph (2) and the word "and" immediately preceding it; and (c) in sub-paragraph (4), the word "properly".

These repeals have effect in relation to the making of directions on or after the day on which this Act is passed.

(2) THE OPTION TO TAX BUILDINGS AND LAND

Chapter	Short Title	Extent of repeal
1994 c. 23.	The Value Added Tax Act 1994.	In Schedule 10, paragraphs 2(3A) and 3(8A).

These repeals have effect in accordance with section 37(1) of this Act.

(3) BAD DEBT RELIEF

Chapter	Short Title	Extent of repeal
1994 c. 23.	The Value Added Tax Act 1994.	In section 36(4), paragraph (b) and the word "and" immediately preceding it. In Schedule 13, paragraph 9(1).

These repeals have effect in accordance with section 39 of this Act.

PART V

INDIRECT TAXES

(1) INTEREST REPAYMENTS

Chapter	Short Title	Extent of repeal
1994 c. 9.	The Finance Act 1994.	In Schedule 6, in paragraph 9(2), the words after paragraph (b).
1996 c. 8.	The Finance Act 1996.	In section 197(2), the word "and" at the end of paragraph (c).

The repeal in the Finance Act 1994 has effect in accordance with paragraph 8 of Schedule 5 to this Act.

(2) DISTRESS AND DILIGENCE

Chapter	Short Title	Extent of repeal
1979 c. 2.	The Customs and Excise Management Act 1979.	In section 117— (a) subsections (5) to (7A); (b) in subsection (9), paragraphs (c) to (f); and (c) subsection (10).
1981 c. 35.	The Finance Act 1981.	In Schedule 8, paragraph 8.
1981 c. 63.	The Betting and Gaming Duties Act 1981.	Sections 28 and 29.
1986 c. 41.	The Finance Act 1986.	In Schedule 4, paragraphs 8 and 9.
1987 c. 18.	The Debtors (Scotland) Act 1987.	In Schedule 6, paragraph 23.
1992 c. 48.	The Finance (No. 2) Act 1992.	In paragraph 5(a) of Schedule 2, the words "and (5)".
1994 c. 9.	The Finance Act 1994.	In section 18— (a) in subsection (2), paragraph (a), the words ", not being an amount in relation to which subsection (4) below applies," and the word "and"; (b) paragraph (b) of that subsection; and (c) subsection (4). In Schedule 7, paragraph 7(7) to (12).

Chapter	Short Title	Extent of repeal
1994 c. 23.	The Value Added Tax Act 1994.	In Schedule 11, paragraph 5(4) to (10).
1995 c. 4.	The Finance Act 1995.	In Schedule 5, paragraph 9.
1996 c. 8.	The Finance Act 1996.	In Schedule 5, paragraph 13.

These repeals come into force on such day as the Commissioners of Customs and Excise may by order made by statutory instrument appoint, and different days may be appointed for different purposes.

PART VI

INCOME TAX, CORPORATION TAX AND CAPITAL GAINS TAX

(1) ADDITIONAL RATE OF INCOME TAX

Chapter	Short Title	Extent of repeal
1988 c. 1.	The Income and Corporation Taxes Act 1988.	In section 832(1), the definition of "additional rate".
1988 c. 39.	The Finance Act 1988.	Section 24(4).

These repeals have effect in relation to the year 1997-98 and subsequent years of assessment.

(2) WAYLEAVES

Chapter	Short Title	Extent of repeal
1970 c. 9.	The Taxes Management Act 1970.	In section 42(7)(a) (as it has effect by virtue of section 196 of the Finance Act 1994), the words "120(2),".
1988 c. 1.	The Income and Corporation Taxes Act 1988.	In section 1A(2)(a)(ii), the words "or 120". In section 3, paragraph (c) and the word "or" immediately preceding it. Section 74(1)(q). In section 120— (a) in subsection (1), the words from "and, subject to" onwards; (b) subsections (2) to (4); and (c) in subsection (5), paragraph (c) and the word "and" immediately preceding it. In section 348(2), paragraph (b) and the word "or" immediately preceding it. In section 349(1), paragraph (c) and the word "or" immediately preceding it. Section 387(3)(c). In section 821(3), paragraph (c) and the word "and" immediately preceding it.

These repeals have effect in relation to payments made on or after 6th April 1997.

(3) PROFIT-RELATED PAY

Chapter	Short Title	Extent of repeal
1970 c. 9.	The Taxes Management Act 1970.	In section 98, in the Table— (a) in the first column, the entry relating to section 181(1) of the Taxes Act 1988; and (b) in the second column, the entry relating to section 180(1) of that Act.

Chapter	Short Title	Extent of repeal
1988 c. 1.	The Income and Corporation Taxes Act 1988.	Sections 169 to 184. Schedule 8.
1988 c. 39.	The Finance Act 1988.	In Schedule 13, paragraph 4.
1989 c. 26.	The Finance Act 1989.	Section 42(4). Section 61. Schedule 4. In Schedule 12, paragraph 18.
1989 c. 40.	The Companies Act 1989.	In Schedule 10, paragraph 38(2).
S.I. 1990/593 (N.I. 5).	The Companies (Northern Ireland) Order 1990.	In Schedule 10, paragraph 30(1).
1991 c. 31.	The Finance Act 1991.	Section 37.
1994 c. 9.	The Finance Act 1994.	Sections 98 and 99.
1995 c. 4.	The Finance Act 1995.	Section 136. Section 137(1) and (6).

1. These repeals have effect (subject to Notes 2 and 3 below) in accordance with section 61(2) and (3) of this Act.

2. These repeals do not affect the operation of any of the repealed provisions, or prevent the exercise of any power under those provisions, in relation to profit periods beginning before 1st January 2000 or for purposes connected with, or with the doing or not doing of anything in or in relation to, any such periods.

3. The repeal of Schedule 8 to the Taxes Act 1988 does not affect the application of any of the provisions of paragraph 7 of that Schedule by any of—

  (a) section 360A(5) and (7) of that Act;

  (b) paragraph 40(2) and (4) of Schedule 9 to that Act; and

  (c) paragraph 16(4) and (6) of Schedule 5 to the Finance Act 1989.

(4) WORK-RELATED TRAINING

Chapter	Short Title	Extent of repeal
1988 c. 1.	The Income and Corporation Taxes Act 1988.	In section 200A(3)(b), the word "either" before sub-paragraph (i).

This repeal has effect in accordance with section 63(3) of this Act.

(5) NATIONAL INSURANCE CONTRIBUTIONS

Chapter	Short Title	Extent of repeal
1988 c. 1.	The Income and Corporation Taxes Act 1988.	In section 617(3), the words "and (5)".

This repeal has effect in accordance with section 65 of this Act.

(6) ANNUITY BUSINESS OF INSURANCE COMPANIES

Chapter	Short Title	Extent of repeal
1988 c. 1.	The Income and Corporation Taxes Act 1988.	In section 76(2A)(b), sub-paragraph (iv) and the word "and" immediately preceding it. Section 434B(2). In section 490(2), the words from "but if" onwards.
1991 c. 31.	The Finance Act 1991.	In Schedule 7, paragraph 16(3) and (4).
1995 c. 4.	The Finance Act 1995.	In Schedule 8, paragraph 21(1).
1996 c. 8.	The Finance Act 1996.	Section 165(3).

These repeals have effect in relation to accounting periods beginning after 5th March 1997.

(7) Distributions treated as foreign income dividends

Chapter	Short Title	Extent of repeal
1988 c. 1.	The Income and Corporation Taxes Act 1988.	In section 118G(5)(a), the words "or applied in defraying expenses of the trustees". In section 231(1), the words "95(1)(b),". In section 481(4A), the words "or applied in defraying expenses of the trustees". In section 686(2), paragraph (d) and the word "and" immediately preceding it.
1992 c. 12.	The Taxation of Chargeable Gains Act 1992.	In section 5(2)— (a) paragraph (c); and (b) in paragraph (d), the words "or applied as mentioned in paragraph (c) above".

1. Subject to Note 2 below, these repeals have effect in accordance with paragraph 12(4) of Schedule 7 to this Act.

2. The repeal in section 231(1) of the Taxes Act 1988 has effect in accordance with paragraph 8(3) of that Schedule.

(8) Enterprise investment scheme

Chapter	Short Title	Extent of repeal
1988 c. 1.	The Income and Corporation Taxes Act 1988.	In section 308— (a) paragraph (b) of subsection (1), and the word "and" immediately preceding that paragraph; and (b) paragraphs (a) and (b) of subsection (5).

These repeals have effect in accordance with paragraph 1 of Schedule 8 to this Act.

(9) Venture capital trusts

Chapter	Short Title	Extent of repeal
1988 c. 1.	The Income and Corporation Taxes Act 1988.	In Schedule 28B, paragraph 10(2).

This repeal has effect in accordance with paragraph 6 of Schedule 9 to this Act.

(10) Stock lending and manufactured payments

Chapter	Short Title	Extent of repeal
1970 c. 9.	The Taxes and Management Act 1970.	In section 98, in the first column of the Table, the entry relating to section 737(8) of the Taxes Act 1988.
1986 c. 41.	The Finance Act 1986.	In Schedule 18, paragraphs 7 and 9.
1988 c. 1.	The Income and Corporation Taxes Act 1988.	Sections 129 and 129A. In section 387(3), paragraph (f) and the word "or" immediately preceding it. In section 715(6) the words "section 737 or". Section 727(1). Section 737.

Chapter	Short Title	Extent of repeal
		In section 737A(5), the words "section 737 and".
		In section 737C—
		(a) in subsection (2)(b), the words "section 737 and paragraph 2 of Schedule 23A apply, or";
		(b) subsections (5) and (6);
		(c) in subsection (7)(b), the words "(whether or not section 737 also applies in relation to that payment)";
		(d) in subsection (9), the words "subsections (6) and (8) above apply, or where"; and
		(e) subsection (11B).
		Section 738(3) and (4).
		Schedule 5A.
		In Schedule 23A—
		(a) in paragraph 1(1), the definitions of "approved stock lending arrangement", "market maker", "recognised clearing house", "recognised investment exchange", "unapproved manufactured payment" and "unapproved stock lending arrangement";
		(b) paragraph 1(2);
		(c) paragraph 5;
		(d) paragraph 6;
		(e) in paragraph 7(1), the words "Except where paragraph 5(2) or (4) above applies,";
		(f) paragraph 7(2); and
		(g) in paragraph 7(3) in paragraph (a), the words "except where paragraph 6 above applies, and", and paragraph (b).
1991 c. 31.	The Finance Act 1991.	Section 57.
		In Schedule 13, paragraphs 2 to 4.
1992 c. 12.	The Taxation of Chargeable Gains Act 1992.	Section 271(9).
		In Schedule 10, paragraph 14(8), (39) and (61).
1993 c. 34.	The Finance Act 1993.	Section 174(4) and (5).
		Section 182(1)(ca)(i).
		In Schedule 6, paragraphs 19 and 25(3) and (4).
1994 c. 9.	The Finance Act 1994.	Section 123(2) to (5) and (7).
		Section 222(4) and (5).
		Section 229(ca)(i).
		In Schedule 16, paragraphs 18 and 19.
1995 c. 4.	The Finance Act 1995.	Section 82.
		Sections 84 and 85.
		Schedule 19.
1996 c. 8.	The Finance Act 1996.	In section 97—
		(a) in subsection (4), the words "section 737 of, or"; and
		(b) subsection (5).
		In section 159—
		(a) subsections (2) and (3); and
		(b) in subsection (7), paragraph (b) and the word "and" immediately preceding it.
		In Schedule 6, paragraphs 18 and 19.
		In Schedule 14, paragraphs 38 and 52(2), (3), (5) and (6).

1. These repeals (except those to which Notes 2 to 6 below apply) have effect in relation to, and to transfers under, any arrangement made on or after such day as may be appointed by order under paragraph 7(1) of Schedule 10 to this Act.

2. The repeal of paragraph 6 of Schedule 23A to the Taxes Act 1988 and—
   (a) the repeals in paragraph 1(1) of that Schedule of the definitions of "unapproved manufactured payment" and "unapproved stock lending arrangement", and
   (b) the repeal of paragraph (b) of paragraph 1(2) of that Schedule, and
   (c) the repeals in paragraph 7(3) of that Schedule,

have effect in relation to manufactured payments made on or after such day as may be appointed by order under paragraph 7(1) of Schedule 10 to this Act.

3. Subject to Note 6 below, the repeals of the following provisions, that is to say—
   (a) sections 387(3)(f), 737, 737C(5), (6) and (11B) and 738(3) and (4) of the Taxes Act 1988,
   (b) paragraphs 5 and 7(2) of Schedule 23A to that Act, and
   (c) section 97(5) of the Finance Act 1996,

together with the repeals listed in Note 4 below, have effect in relation to payments made on or after such day as may be appointed by order under paragraph 16(1) of Schedule 10 to this Act.

4. The repeals mentioned in Note 3 above are—
   (a) any repeal of an enactment amending a provision specified in Note 3 above;
   (b) the repeal of the references to section 737 of the Taxes Act 1988 in sections 737A(5) and 737C(2)(b) and (7)(b) of that Act and in section 97(4) of the Finance Act 1996;
   (c) the repeal of the reference to section 737C(6) of the Taxes Act 1988 in section 737C(9) of that Act;
   (d) the repeal of the enactments amending paragraph 2 of Schedule 23A to that Act; and
   (e) the repeal in paragraph 7(1) of that Schedule.

5. The repeals of the provisions which amend, or authorise the amendment of, section 21 of the Taxes Management Act 1970 have effect in accordance with paragraph 16(2) and (3) of Schedule 10 to this Act.

6. The repeal of section 737(8) of the Taxes Act 1988 has effect subject to paragraph 16(3) of Schedule 10 to this Act; and the repeal of the entry relating to section 737(8) in the Table in section 98 of the Taxes Management Act 1970 has effect accordingly.

(11) Capital allowances: Schedule A cases

Chapter	Short Title	Extent of repeal
1988 c. 1.	The Income and Corporation Taxes Act 1988.	Section 32. In section 379A(2)— (a) in paragraph (a), the word "relevant"; and (b) the words after paragraph (b).
1990 c. 1.	The Capital Allowances Act 1990.	In section 67(3), the words from "shall be made" to "corporation tax,". Section 73(4). In section 141— (a) in subsection (2), the words "Subject to subsection (3) below,"; and (b) subsections (3), (4) and (6). In Schedule 1, paragraph 8(2).
1995 c. 4.	The Finance Act 1995.	In Schedule 6, paragraphs 8, 31 and 33.
1996 c. 8.	The Finance Act 1996.	In Schedule 21, paragraph 34.

These repeals have effect in accordance with paragraph 9(1) of Schedule 15 to this Act.

(12) Capital allowances: fixtures

Chapter	Short Title	Extent of repeal
1990 c. 1.	The Capital Allowances Act 1990.	In section 51(8), paragraph (b). In section 54(1), paragraph (c) and the word "and" immediately preceding it. In section 55(4), paragraph (b) and the word "or" immediately preceding it. In section 56, paragraph (c). Section 59(10).
1991 c. 31.	The Finance Act 1991.	In Schedule 14, paragraph 10.

1. These repeals have effect, subject to the following notes and paragraph 2(8) of Schedule 16 to this Act, for chargeable periods ending on or after 24th July 1996.

2. The repeal in section 54(1) of the Capital Allowances Act 1990 does not apply where the purchaser acquired the relevant interest before that date.

3. The repeals in sections 55(4) and 56 of that Act do not apply where the lease was granted before that date.

4. The repeal of section 59(10) of that Act does not apply where the fixture ceased to belong to the former owner before that date.

PART VII

STAMP DUTY AND STAMP DUTY RESERVE TAX

Chapter	Short Title	Extent of repeal
1986 c. 41.	The Finance Act 1986.	Section 67(4).
		Section 69(6) to (8).
		Section 70(4).
		Section 72(4).
		Sections 80A to 80C.
		Sections 81 and 82.
		Section 87(7B).
		In section 88(1B)(b), the word "or" at the end of sub-paragraph (ii).
		Sections 88A and 88B.
		Section 89.
		Section 89AA.
		Section 89B.
		Section 90(3)(b).
		Section 93(5).
		Section 94(5) to (7).
		Section 96(3) and (11).
1987 c. 16.	The Finance Act 1987.	Section 53.
		In Schedule 7, paragraph 4.
1988 c. 39.	The Finance Act 1988.	In Schedule 13, paragraph 23.
1996 c. 8.	The Finance Act 1996.	Section 191.
		Section 194(2)(b) and (4)(b).
1997 c. 16.	The Finance Act 1997.	Sections 97 to 106.

1. The repeals of sections 80A to 80C of the Finance Act 1986 and sections 97 to 99 of this Act have effect in accordance with section 108 of the Finance Act 1990.

2. The repeals in sections 67, 69, 70 and 72 of the Finance Act 1986 have effect in accordance with section 99 of this Act.

3. The repeal of section 81 of the Finance Act 1986 has effect in accordance with section 97 of this Act.

4. The repeals of section 82 of the Finance Act 1986 and section 53 of the Finance Act 1987 have effect in accordance with section 98 of this Act.

5. The repeals in sections 87 and 88 of the Finance Act 1986 have effect in accordance with section 106 of this Act.

6. The repeals of sections 88A, 88B and 89AA of the Finance Act 1986 and sections 100 to 106 of this Act have effect in accordance with section 110 of the Finance Act 1990.

7. The repeal of section 89 of the Finance Act 1986 and the repeal in Schedule 7 to the Finance Act 1987 have effect in accordance with section 102 of this Act.

8. The repeals of section 89B of the Finance Act 1986 and section 191 of the Finance Act 1996 have effect in accordance with section 103 of this Act.

9. The repeal of section 90(3)(b) of the Finance Act 1986 has effect in accordance with section 105 of this Act.

10. The repeals in sections 93, 94 and 96 of the Finance Act 1986, in Schedule 13 to the Finance Act 1988 and in section 194 of the Finance Act 1996 have effect in accordance with section 104 of this Act.

INDEX

CRIMINAL EVIDENCE (AMENDMENT) ACT 1997*

(1997 c. 17)

An Act to make provision extending the categories of persons from whom non-intimate body samples may be taken without consent under Part V of the Police and Criminal Evidence Act 1984; and to add a further time limit to those operating for the purposes of section 63A(4)(a) of that Act.

[19th March 1997]

PARLIAMENTARY DEBATES
Hansard, H.C. Vol. 285, col. 994; Vol. 288, col. 1230. H.L. Vol. 577, col. 1074; Vol. 578, cols. 105, 905, 1504.

GENERAL NOTE

The purpose of the Act is to allow the police to obtain body samples from persons serving sentences for sexual offences, crimes of violence and burglary. The "non-intimate" samples so taken will allow DNA extraction and screening against the National DNA database. In this way forensic samples from the scene of crimes can be matched against individual's DNA "fingerprints". This is seen as an important deterrence to these offenders committing further crime and a powerful detection tool for the police.

Although the original Bill appeared before Parliament as a Private Members' Bill, in truth it was a vehicle of the Home Office to remedy defects in earlier legislation which had been highlighted in a government consultation paper in 1996.

A serious weakness had been identified in the provisions covering the obtaining of body samples under the Police and Criminal Evidence Act 1984 (c.60) as amended by the Criminal Justice and Public Order Act 1994 (c.33). Certain categories of serious offenders, namely those convicted before April 10, 1995, were exempt from having samples taken. They avoided being registered and screened on the National DNA database. The 1997 Act sets out to close this gap in police powers and to extend the scope of the DNA database.

The regime governing the powers to take body samples first appeared in s.63 of the Police and Criminal Evidence Act 1984. A police officer could take "non-intimate" samples from a suspect while in police custody (by force if necessary) in order to prove or disprove that person's involvement in a serious crime.

Ten years later, when the Criminal Justice and Public Order Act 1994 came before Parliament, the concept of a National DNA database had taken root. This was intended to run on similar lines to the national fingerprint register which had been maintained by the police for many years.

The 1994 Act allowed the police to take non-intimate samples not only from suspects in police custody, but also from those charged with a recordable offence or convicted of such an offence.

---

*Annotations by Neil O'May, Bindman & Partners Solicitors.

In effect, it set up the machinery and raw material for the creation of the National DNA database.

Furthermore, since there has been some controversy over what constituted a "non-intimate sample", the 1994 Act made plain that a sample of hair (other than a pubic hair) was a non-intimate sample (by inserting s.63A(2) into PACE 1984), as was a mouth swab. Both body samples could now be taken without consent, and a DNA "fingerprint" could be used in a speculative search against the National DNA database.

However, the 1994 Act did not act retrospectively. Persons who had been convicted before the Act came into force on April 10, 1995 could not be the subjects of the new powers, and could not be registered on the national DNA database.

The DNA database is maintained at the Forensic Science Service in Birmingham. As it grew in size and power from April 1995, it became accepted dogma that persons convicted of sex offences, violence or burglary, not only tended to repeat their crimes (or to have been responsible for many more crimes than their record would suggest), but they were also more susceptible to being tracked down by a match on the DNA database. It was said that these categories of offenders would be either deterred from committing further offences, or would be more easily caught if they had been recorded on the DNA database.

The 1997 Act now extends the power of the police to obtain non-intimate bodily samples for use on the DNA database for prisoners convicted or detained (under the Mental Health Act 1993 for sexual offences, violent offences and burglary. It also allows the police to take such samples from those detained following an acquittal on grounds of insanity or on a finding of "unfitness to plead". In all cases, samples can be taken from the detained person in the prison or hospital where they are detained. Finally, there is a minor tidying up provision covering the time-limit for those persons required to attend the police station to have a sample taken after release under s.63A of the 1984 Act.

COMMENCEMENT

The changes introduced by the Act came into force on March 19, 1997, the date of Royal Assent. The Bill was originally presented to Parliament on November 20, 1996 and quickly passed all stages unopposed to its final reading on February 10, 1997.

Extension of power to take non-intimate body samples without consent

Persons imprisoned or detained by virtue of pre-existing conviction for sexual offence etc.

1.—(1) This section has effect for removing, in relation to persons to whom this section applies, the restriction on the operation of section 63(3B) of the Police and Criminal Evidence Act 1984 (power to take non-intimate samples without the appropriate consent from persons convicted of recordable offences)—

(a) which is imposed by the subsection (10) inserted in section 63 by section 55(6) of the Criminal Justice and Public Order Act 1994, and

(b) by virtue of which section 63(3B) does not apply to persons convicted before 10th April 1995.

(2) Accordingly, in section 63 of the 1984 Act, for the subsection (10) referred to in subsection (1) above there shall be substituted—

"(9A) Subsection (3B) above shall not apply to any person convicted before 10th April 1995 unless he is a person to whom section 1 of the Criminal Evidence (Amendment) Act 1997 applies (persons imprisoned or detained by virtue of pre-existing conviction for sexual offence etc.)."

(3) This section applies to a person who was convicted of a recordable offence before 10th April 1995 if—

(a) that offence was one of the offences listed in Schedule 1 to this Act (which lists certain sexual, violent and other offences), and

(b) at the relevant time he is serving a sentence of imprisonment in respect of that offence.

(4) This section also applies to a person who was convicted of a recordable offence before 10th April 1995 if—

(a) that offence was one of the offences listed in Schedule 1 to this Act, and

(b) at the relevant time he is detained under Part III of the Mental Health Act 1983 in pursuance of—

    (i) a hospital order or interim hospital order made following that conviction, or

    (ii) a transfer direction given at a time when he was serving a sentence of imprisonment in respect of that offence.

Expressions used in this subsection and in the Mental Health Act 1983 have the same meaning as in that Act.

(5) Where a person convicted of a recordable offence before 10th April 1995 was, following his conviction for that and any other offence or offences, sentenced to two or more terms of imprisonment (whether taking effect consecutively or concurrently), he shall be treated for the purposes of this section as serving a sentence of imprisonment in respect of that offence at any time when serving any of those terms.

(6) For the purposes of this section, references to a person serving a sentence of imprisonment include references—

(a) to his being detained in any institution to which the Prison Act 1952 applies in pursuance of any other sentence or order for detention imposed by a court in criminal proceedings, or

(b) to his being detained (otherwise than in any such institution) in pursuance of directions of the Secretary of State under section 53 of the Children and Young Persons Act 1933;

and any reference to a term of imprisonment shall be construed accordingly.

GENERAL NOTE

This section amends s.63 of the Police and Criminal Evidence Act 1984 (as amended by the Criminal Justice and Public Order Act 1994) by inserting a new subs. 9A. This allows a non-intimate sample to be taken without the appropriate consent from a person who has been convicted of a recordable offence provided:

(a) the offence is one listed in Sched. 1 to the 1997 Act (sexual, violent or "other" offence); and

(b) at the time the sample is taken he is serving a sentence of imprisonment for that offence (or detained under Pt. III of the Mental Health Act 1983) for that offence.

Accordingly, the powers cover a person convicted before or after April 1994 provided he is still serving a sentence for a Sched. 1 offence.

By subs. (4)(b), a person detained under Pt. III of the Mental Health Act 1983 is one detained in pursuance of a hospital order or interim hospital order following conviction, or detained by a transfer direction to a hospital given at a time when he was serving a sentence of imprisonment for that offence.

Subsection (5) empowers the police to take such samples from a person convicted of a recordable offence before April 10, 1995 who is serving two or more terms of imprisonment (consecutively or concurrently) provided one falls within Sched. 1 of the 1997 Act.

By subs. (6), the term "sentence of imprisonment" includes a young person detained pursuant to the directions of the Secretary of State under s.53 of the Children and Young Persons Act 1933 (c.12).

Persons detained following acquittal on grounds of insanity or finding of unfitness to plead

2.—(1) This section has effect for enabling non-intimate samples to be taken from persons under section 63 of the 1984 Act without the appropriate consent where they are persons to whom this section applies.

(2) Accordingly, in section 63 of the 1984 Act—

(a) after subsection (3B) there shall be inserted—

    "(3C) A non-intimate sample may also be taken from a person without the appropriate consent if he is a person to whom section 2 of the Criminal Evidence (Amendment) Act 1997 applies (persons detained following acquittal on grounds of insanity or finding of unfitness to plead)."; and

(b) in subsection (8A) (giving of reason for taking sample without appropriate consent), for "or (3B)" there shall be substituted ", (3B) or (3C) above".

(3) This section applies to a person if—

(a) at the relevant time he is detained under Part III of the Mental Health Act 1983 in pursuance of an order made under—

    (i) section 5(2)(a) of the Criminal Procedure (Insanity) Act 1964 or section 6 or 14 of the Criminal Appeal Act 1968 (findings of insanity or unfitness to plead), or

    (ii) section 37(3) of the Mental Health Act 1983 (power of magistrates' court to make hospital order without convicting accused); and

(b) that order was made on or after the date of the passing of this Act in respect of a recordable offence.

(4) This section also applies to a person if—

(a) at the relevant time he is detained under Part III of the Mental Health Act 1983 in pursuance of an order made under—

    (i) any of the provisions mentioned in subsection (3)(a), or

    (ii) section 5(1) of the Criminal Procedure (Insanity) Act 1964 as originally enacted; and

(b) that order was made before the date of the passing of this Act in respect of any offence listed in Schedule 1 to this Act.

(5) Subsection (4)(a)(i) does not apply to any order made under section 14(2) of the Criminal Appeal Act 1968 as originally enacted.

(6) For the purposes of this section an order falling within subsection (3) or (4) shall be treated as having been made in respect of an offence of a particular description—

(a) if, where the order was made following—

    (i) a finding of not guilty by reason of insanity, or

    (ii) a finding that the person in question was under a disability and did the act or made the omission charged against him, or

    (iii) a finding for the purposes of section 37(3) of the Mental Health Act 1983 that the person in question did the act or made the omission charged against him, or

    (iv) (in the case of an order made under section 5(1) of the Criminal Procedure (Insanity) Act 1964 as originally enacted) a finding that he was under a disability,

that finding was recorded in respect of an offence of that description; or

(b) if, where the order was made following the Court of Appeal forming such opinion as is mentioned in section 6(1) or 14(1) of the Criminal Appeal Act 1968, that opinion was formed on an appeal brought in respect of an offence of that description.

(7) In this section any reference to an Act "as originally enacted" is a reference to that Act as it had effect without any of the amendments made by the Criminal Procedure (Insanity and Unfitness to Plead) Act 1991.

GENERAL NOTE

These same powers can be used to take such samples from a person who is detained under Pt. III of the Mental Health Act 1983 pursuant to an order made under s.5(2)(a) of the Criminal Procedure (Insanity) Act 1964 (c.84), or ss.6 or 14 of the Criminal Appeal Act 1968 (c.19) (acquittal on grounds of insanity or a finding of unfitness to plead), or those detained under s.37(3) of the Mental Health Act 1983 (c.20) (a hospital order made by a Magistrates' Court without convicting the accused).

The power applies to any person who is the subject of such an order made before the passing of the 1997 Act in respect of any offence listed in Sched. 1. Where an order is made after the passing of this Act, the power applies to any recordable offence.

Taking of samples from detained persons at place where detained

3. In section 63A of the 1984 Act (supplementary provisions about finger-prints and samples), after subsection (3) there shall be inserted—

"(3A) Where—

  (a) the power to take a non-intimate sample under section 63(3B) above is exercisable in relation to any person who is detained under Part III of the Mental Health Act 1983 in pursuance of—

    (i) a hospital order or interim hospital order made following his conviction for the recordable offence in question, or

    (ii) a transfer direction given at a time when he was detained in pursuance of any sentence or order imposed following that conviction, or

  (b) the power to take a non-intimate sample under section 63(3C) above is exercisable in relation to any person,

the sample may be taken in the hospital in which he is detained under that Part of that Act.

Expressions used in this subsection and in the Mental Health Act 1983 have the same meaning as in that Act.

(3B) Where the power to take a non-intimate sample under section 63(3B) above is exercisable in relation to a person detained in pursuance of directions of the Secretary of State under section 53 of the Children and Young Persons Act 1933 the sample may be taken at the place where he is so detained."

GENERAL NOTE

This section inserts a new s.63A(3A) into PACE 1994. Where the 1997 Act empowers the police to take a non-intimate sample from a person, that sample can be taken from the person at the place where they are detained—whether a prison, a hospital or young offenders institution.

Additional time limit for purposes of 1984 Act

Time allowed for requiring person to attend police station to have sample taken

4. In section 63A of the 1984 Act, in subsection (5)(a) (time allowed, for the purposes of subsection (4)(a), for requiring person to attend police station to have sample taken) after "of the charge" there shall be inserted "or of his being informed as mentioned in that paragraph".

GENERAL NOTE

By s.63A(5) of Criminal Justice and Public Order Act 1994 (as amended) a constable can require a person who had been charged with a recordable offence to attend a police station for a sample to be taken in certain circumstances. The constable has to notify the person within one month from the date of charge or from the date when the officer is informed that a previous sample was not suitable.

A similar power exists where a person is informed that he will be reported for such an offence. However, by a legislative oversight, no time-limit was set in this case. Section 4 corrects this omission by amending s.63A(5)(a) and inserting the one month time-limit.

Supplementary

Interpretation

5. In this Act—

"the 1984 Act" means the Police and Criminal Evidence Act 1984;

"appropriate consent" has the meaning given by section 65 of the 1984 Act;

"non-intimate sample" has the meaning given by section 65 of the 1984 Act;

"recordable offence" means any offence to which regulations under section 27 of the 1984 Act (fingerprinting) apply;

"the relevant time" means, in relation to the exercise of any power to take a non-intimate sample from a person, the time when it is sought to take the sample.

Short title, repeal and extent

6.—(1) This Act may be cited as the Criminal Evidence (Amendment) Act 1997.

(2) For ease of reference sections 63 and 63A of the 1984 Act, as amended by sections 1 to 4 above, are set out in Schedule 2 to this Act.

(3) Section 55(6) of the Criminal Justice and Public Order Act 1994 is repealed.

(4) This Act extends to England and Wales only.

SCHEDULES

Section 1

SCHEDULE 1

LIST OF OFFENCES

Sexual offences and offences of indecency

1. Any offence under the Sexual Offences Act 1956, other than an offence under section 30, 31 or 33 to 36 of that Act.

2. Any offence under section 128 of the Mental Health Act 1959 (intercourse with mentally handicapped person by hospital staff etc.).

3. Any offence under section 1 of the Indecency with Children Act 1960 (indecent conduct towards young child).

4. Any offence under section 54 of the Criminal Law Act 1977 (incitement by man of his grand-daughter, daughter or sister under the age of 16 to commit incest with him).

5. Any offence under section 1 of the Protection of Children Act 1978.

Violent and other offences

6. Any of the following offences—
   (a) murder;
   (b) manslaughter;
   (c) false imprisonment; and
   (d) kidnapping.

7. Any offence under any of the following provisions of the Offences Against the Person Act 1861—
   (a) section 4 (conspiring or soliciting to commit nurder);
   (b) section 16 (threats to kill);
   (c) section 18 (wounding with intent to cause grievous bodily harm);
   (d) section 20 (causing grievous bodily harm);
   (e) section 21 (attempting to choke etc. in order to commit or assist in the committing of any indictable offence);
   (f) section 22 (using chloroform etc. to commit or assist in the committing of any indictable offence);
   (g) section 23 (maliciously administering poison etc. so as to endanger life or inflict grievous bodily harm);
   (h) section 24 (maliciously administering poison etc. with intent to injure etc.); and
   (i) section 47 (assault occasioning actual bodily harm).

8. Any offence under either of the following provisions of the Explosive Substances Act 1883—
   (a) section 2 (causing explosion likely to endanger life or property); and
   (b) section 3 (attempt to cause explosion, or making or keeping explosive with intent to endanger life or property).

9. Any offence under section 1 of the Children and Young Persons Act 1933 (cruelty to persons under 16).

10. Any offence under section 4(1) of the Criminal Law Act 1967 (assisting offender) committed in relation to the offence of murder.

11. Any offence under any of the following provisions of the Firearms Act 1968—
   (a) section 16 (possession of firearm with intent to injure);

(b) section 17 (use of firearm to resist arrest); and

(c) section 18 (carrying firearm with criminal intent).

12. Any offence under either of the following provisions of the Theft Act 1968—

(a) section 9 (burglary); and

(b) section 10 (aggravated burglary);

and any offence under section 12A of that Act (aggravated vehicle-taking) involving an accident which caused the death of any person.

13. Any offence under section 1 of the Criminal Damage Act 1971 (destroying or damaging property) required to be charged as arson.

14. Any offence under section 2 of the Child Abduction Act 1984 (abduction of child by person other than parent).

Conspiracy, incitement and attempts

15. Any offence under section 1 of the Criminal Law Act 1977 of conspiracy to commit any of the offences mentioned in paragraphs 1 to 14.

16. Any offence under section 1 of the Criminal Attempts Act 1981 of attempting to commit any of those offences.

17. Any offence of inciting another to commit any of those offences.

GENERAL NOTE

Non-intimate samples can only be taken from persons convicted or detained before April 10, 1995 if the offence is listed in Sched. 1 to the 1997 Act. Broadly, these cover sexual offences and offences of violence and burglary. The Schedule incorporates specific offences only, and persons convicted or detained before April 10, 1995 for offences which are not included in Sched. 1 are exempt.

This contrasts with the wider existing powers in the Police and Criminal Evidence Act 1984 (as amended) which enables the police to take a non-intimate sample from a person convicted of any recordable offence provided the conviction is after April 10, 1995.

Section 6 SCHEDULE 2

SECTIONS 63 AND 63A OF THE POLICE AND CRIMINAL EVIDENCE ACT 1984, AS AMENDED

Section 63

Other samples

63.—(1) Except as provided by this section, a non-intimate sample may not be taken from a person without the appropriate consent.

(2) Consent to the taking of a non-intimate sample must be given in writing.

(3) A non-intimate sample may be taken from a person without the appropriate consent if—

(a) he is in police detention or is being held in custody by the police on the authority of a court; and

(b) an officer of at least the rank of superintendent authorises it to be taken without the appropriate consent.

(3A) A non-intimate sample may be taken from a person (whether or not he falls within subsection (3)(a) above) without the appropriate consent if—

(a) he has been charged with a recordable offence or informed that he will be reported for such an offence; and

(b) either he has not had a non-intimate sample taken from him in the course of the investigation of the offence by the police or he has had a non-intimate sample taken from him but either it was not suitable for the same means of analysis or, though so suitable, the sample proved insufficient.

(3B) A non-intimate sample may be taken from a person without the appropriate consent if he has been convicted of a recordable offence.

(3C) A non-intimate sample may also be taken from a person without the appropriate consent if he is a person to whom section 2 of the Criminal Evidence (Amendment) Act 1997 applies (persons detained following acquittal on grounds of insanity or finding of unfitness to plead).

(4) An officer may only give an authorisation under subsection (3) above if he has reasonable grounds—

(a) for suspecting the involvement of the person from whom the sample is to be taken in a recordable offence; and

(b) for believing that the sample will tend to confirm or disprove his involvement.

(5) An officer may give an authorisation under subsection (3) above orally or in writing but, if he gives it orally, he shall confirm it in writing as soon as is practicable.

(6) Where—

(a) an authorisation has been given; and

(b) it is proposed that a non-intimate sample shall be taken in pursuance of the authorisation,

an officer shall inform the person from whom the sample is to be taken—

(i) of the giving of the authorisation; and

(ii) of the grounds for giving it.

(7) The duty imposed by subsection (6)(ii) above includes a duty to state the nature of the offence in which it is suspected that the person from whom the sample is to be taken has been involved.

(8) If a non-intimate sample is taken from a person by virtue of subsection (3) above—

(a) the authorisation by virtue of which it was taken; and

(b) the grounds for giving the authorisation,

shall be recorded as soon as is practicable after the sample is taken.

(8A) In a case where by virtue of subsection (3A), (3B) or (3C) above a sample is taken from a person without the appropriate consent—

(a) he shall be told the reason before the sample is taken; and

(b) the reason shall be recorded as soon as practicable after the sample is taken.

(8B) If a non-intimate sample is taken from a person at a police station, whether with or without the appropriate consent—

(a) before the sample is taken, an officer shall inform him that it may be the subject of a speculative search; and

(b) the fact that the person has been informed of this possibility shall be recorded as soon as practicable after the sample has been taken.

(9) If a non-intimate sample is taken from a person detained at a police station, the matters required to be recorded by subsection (8) or (8A) or (8B) above shall be recorded in his custody record.

(9A) Subsection (3B) above shall not apply to any person convicted before 10th April 1995 unless he is a person to whom section 1 of the Criminal Evidence (Amendment) Act 1997 applies (persons imprisoned or detained by virtue of pre-existing conviction for sexual offence etc.).

(10) Nothing in this section, except as provided in section 15(13) and (14) of, and paragraph 7(6C) and (6D) of Schedule 5 to, the Prevention of Terrorism (Temporary Provisions) Act 1989, applies to a person arrested or detained under the terrorism provisions.

Section 63A

Fingerprints and samples: supplementary provisions

63A.—(1) Where a person has been arrested on suspicion of being involved in a recordable offence or has been charged with such an offence or has been informed that he will be reported for such an offence, fingerprints or samples or the information derived from samples taken under any power conferred by this Part of this Act from the person may be checked against—

(a) other fingerprints or samples to which the person seeking to check has access and which are held by or on behalf of a police force (or police forces) falling within subsection (1A) below or are held in connection with or as a result of an investigation of an offence;

(b) information derived from other samples if the information is contained in records to which the person seeking to check has access and which are held as mentioned in paragraph (a) above.

(1A) Each of the following police forces falls within this subsection—

(a) a police force within the meaning given by section 62 of the Police Act 1964 (which relates to England and Wales);

(b) a police force within the meaning given by section 50 of the Police (Scotland) Act 1967;

(c) the Royal Ulster Constabulary and the Royal Ulster Constabulary Reserve;

(d) the States of Jersey Police Force;

(e) the salaried police force of the Island of Guernsey;

(f) the Isle of Man Constabulary.

(2) Where a sample of hair other than pubic hair is to be taken the sample may be taken either by cutting hairs or by plucking hairs with their roots so long as no more are plucked than the person taking the sample reasonably considers to be necessary for a sufficient sample.

(3) Where any power to take a sample is exercisable in relation to a person the sample may be taken in a prison or other institution to which the Prison Act 1952 applies.

(3A) Where—

(a) the power to take a non-intimate sample under section 63(3B) above is exercisable in relation to any person who is detained under Part III of the Mental Health Act 1983 in pursuance of—

   (i) a hospital order or interim hospital order made following his conviction for the recordable offence in question, or

   (ii) a transfer direction given at a time when he was detained in pursuance of any sentence or order imposed following that conviction, or

 (b) the power to take a non-intimate sample under section 63(3C) above is exercisable in relation to any person,

the sample may be taken in the hospital in which he is detained under that Part of that Act.

 Expressions used in this subsection and in the Mental Health Act 1983 have the same meaning as in that Act.

 (3B) Where the power to take a non-intimate sample under section 63(3B) above is exercisable in relation to a person detained in pursuance of directions of the Secretary of State under section 53 of the Children and Young Persons Act 1933 the sample may be taken at the place where he is so detained.

 (4) Any constable may, within the allowed period, require a person who is neither in police detention nor held in custody by the police on the authority of a court to attend a police station in order to have a sample taken where—

 (a) the person has been charged with a recordable offence or informed that he will be reported for such an offence and either he has not had a sample taken from him in the course of the investigation of the offence by the police or he has had a sample so taken from him but either it was not suitable for the same means of analysis or, though so suitable, the sample proved insufficient; or

 (b) the person has been convicted of a recordable offence and either he has not had a sample taken from him since the conviction or he has had a sample taken from him (before or after his conviction) but either it was not suitable for the same means of analysis or, though so suitable, the sample proved insufficient.

 (5) The period allowed for requiring a person to attend a police station for the purpose specified in subsection (4) above is—

 (a) in the case of a person falling within paragraph (a), one month beginning with the date of the charge or of his being informed as mentioned in that paragraph or one month beginning with the date on which the appropriate officer is informed of the fact that the sample is not suitable for the same means of analysis or has proved insufficient, as the case may be;

 (b) in the case of a person falling within paragraph (b), one month beginning with the date of the conviction or one month beginning with the date on which the appropriate officer is informed of the fact that the sample is not suitable for the same means of analysis or has proved insufficient, as the case may be.

 (6) A requirement under subsection (4) above—

 (a) shall give the person at least 7 days within which he must so attend; and

 (b) may direct him to attend at a specified time of day or between specified times of day.

 (7) Any constable may arrest without a warrant a person who has failed to comply with a requirement under subsection (4) above.

 (8) In this section "the appropriate officer" is—

 (a) in the case of a person falling within subsection (4)(a), the officer investigating the offence with which that person has been charged or as to which he was informed that he would be reported;

 (b) in the case of a person falling within subsection (4)(b), the officer in charge of the police station from which the investigation of the offence of which he was convicted was conducted.

INDEX

References are to sections and Schedules

POLICYHOLDERS PROTECTION ACT 1997

(1997 c. 18)

ARRANGEMENT OF SECTIONS

General scope of the Board's functions

Companies in financial difficulties

Levies on insurance companies

Intermediaries

Miscellaneous other amendments of the 1975 Act

Interpretation of the 1975 Act

Friendly societies

Supplementary

An Act to amend the Policyholders Protection Act 1975; and for connected
purposes.   [19th March 1997]

PARLIAMENTARY DEBATES
    Hansard, H.C. Vol. 285, col. 996; Vol. 288, col. 1237. H.L. Vol. 577, col. 1074; Vol. 578, cols.
312, 1292; Vol. 579, col. 9.

INTRODUCTION
    This Act makes amendments to the Policyholders Protection Act 1975. Section 1 redefines
those insurance companies to which the 1975 Act applies, so as to include EC companies which

provide insurance in the U.K. through an establishment elsewhere in the European Economic Area. Boundaries of protection are redefined, as are the persons who may benefit from measures taken by the Policyholders Protection Board under s.16 of the 1975 Act. Further amendments and insertions to the 1975 Act relate, *inter alia*, to companies in financial difficulties and levies on insurance companies.

General scope of the Board's functions

Insurance companies to which the 1975 Act applies

1.—(1) For section 3 of the 1975 Act there shall be substituted—

"Insurance companies to which this Act applies

3.—(1) The functions of the Board under this Act shall be exercisable in relation to policyholders and others who have been or may be prejudiced in consequence of the inability of insurance companies to meet their liabilities under policies issued or securities given by them only in cases where the insurance companies in question are insurance companies to which this Act applies.

(2) An insurance company is one to which this Act applies if it is—

(a) authorised under section 3 or 4 of the Insurance Companies Act 1982 to carry on insurance business of any class in the United Kingdom,

(b) an EC company which is lawfully carrying on insurance business of any class in the United Kingdom, or

(c) an EC Company not falling within paragraph (b) above which provides general insurance or long term insurance in the United Kingdom."

(2) Schedule 1 to this Act (consequential amendments) shall have effect.

Eligibility of policyholders for protection

2.—(1) For section 4 of the 1975 Act there shall be substituted—

"Protection confined to insurance under qualifying policies of protected risks or commitments

4.—(1) A policyholder is eligible for the assistance or protection of the Board in accordance with any provision of sections 6 to 16 below only in respect of the insurance under a qualifying policy of a protected risk or commitment.

(2) The following are qualifying policies for the purposes of this Act—

(a) a policy of insurance issued by an insurance company authorised under section 3 or 4 of the Insurance Companies Act 1982 through an establishment in—

(i) the United Kingdom,

(ii) another EEA State, or

(iii) the Channel Islands or the Isle of Man, and

(b) a policy of insurance issued by an EC company through an establishment in an EEA State.

(3) A risk or commitment is a protected risk or commitment for the purposes of this Act—

(a) in the case of a policy falling within subsection (2)(a)(i) above, if it is situated in an EEA State, the Channel Islands or the Isle of Man;

(b) in the case of a policy falling within subsection (2)(a)(ii) or (2)(b) above, if it is situated in the United Kingdom;

(c) in the case of a policy falling within subsection (2)(a)(iii) above, if it is situated in the United Kingdom, the Channel Islands or the Isle of Man."

(2) Schedule 2 to this Act (consequential amendments) shall have effect.

(3) This section shall not have effect in relation to a policy, or security, where the contract which the policy evidences, or which governs the security, was entered into before the day on which this section comes into force.

(4) For the purposes of subsection (3) above, where a contract for a term of more than one year—

(a) was entered into before the day on which this section comes into force, and

(b) continues in force beyond an anniversary of its inception which falls on or after the day on which this section comes into force,

the contract shall be treated as having been entered into on that anniversary, unless the effecting of the contract constituted the carrying on of long term business (within the meaning of the Insurance Companies Act 1982).

Companies in financial difficulties

Persons qualifying for protection

3.—(1) Section 16 of the 1975 Act (which enables the Board to take measures to protect policyholders of companies in financial difficulties) shall be amended as follows.

(2) In subsection (2) (under which the Board's powers are exercisable for the purpose of safeguarding policyholders of a company in financial difficulties who are eligible for protection under the section)—

(a) for "policyholders of a company in financial difficulties who are eligible for protection under this section" there shall be substituted "those who are qualifying persons in relation to a company in financial difficulties", and

(b) for "such policyholders" there shall be substituted "such persons".

(3) In subsection (3) (power to secure or facilitate transfer of business of company in financial difficulties on terms including reducing liabilities or benefits under any policies), for the words from "the liabilities" to "policies)" there shall be substituted "any of the things to which any of those who are qualifying persons in relation to the company in financial difficulties are entitled in their capacity as such)".

(4) In subsection (5) (power to assist company in financial difficulties conditionally on reduction of liabilities or benefits under any of its policies), for the words from "any liabilities" to "the company" there shall be substituted "of the things to which any of those who are qualifying persons in relation to the company are entitled in their capacity as such".

(5) In subsection (8) (restriction on exercise of powers)—

(a) for "any policyholders of" there shall be substituted "any of those who are qualifying persons in relation to", and

(b) for "the policyholders" there shall be substituted "the persons".

(6) After subsection (8B) there shall be inserted—

"(8C) For the purposes of this section, a person is a qualifying person in relation to a company in financial difficulties if—

(a) he is a policyholder of the company who is eligible for protection under this section,

(b) he is a security holder in respect of a security given by the company who is eligible for protection under this section, or

(c) he is a person to whom the company is liable to pay any sum in respect of his entitlement to the benefit of a judgment under the provisions mentioned in paragraphs (a) and (b) of section 7 above."

(7) After subsection (9) there shall be inserted—

"(9A) A security holder in respect of a security given by a company in financial difficulties is eligible for protection under this section if—

(a) it is a security to which section 6 above applies, and

    (b) it would have been a United Kingdom policy at the relevant time if it had been an insurance policy and the contract governing the security had been a contract of insurance."

Deferment of payment

4.—(1) Section 16 of the 1975 Act shall be amended as follows.

(2) In subsection (1) (definition of company in financial difficulties), in paragraph (c) (application made for sanctioning compromise or arrangement providing for reducing liabilities or benefits under company's policies), after "reducing" there shall be inserted ", or deferring payment of,".

(3) In subsection (3) (power to secure or facilitate transfer of business of company in financial difficulties on terms including reducing entitlements of qualifying persons), after "reducing" there shall be inserted ", or deferring payment of,".

(4) In subsection (5) (power to assist company in financial difficulties conditionally on reduction of entitlements of qualifying persons), after "reduction of" there shall be inserted ", or the deferment of the payment of,".

Operation of the "cost test"

5. In section 16 of the 1975 Act, after subsection (8) (which prevents the Board taking measures under subsection (3) or (4) if it appears to them that it would cost them less if the company went into liquidation) there shall be inserted—

    "(8A) In making any calculation for the purposes of subsection (8) above, the Board shall—
        (a) discount future costs to a present value using such rates of interest as appear to them to be appropriate, and
        (b) in evaluating contingent costs, make such assumptions, and use such statistical and other methods, as appear to them to be reasonable.

    (8B) If in pursuance of subsection (3) or (4) above the Board have entered into an obligation to do anything, subsection (8) above shall not apply in relation to anything done in pursuance of the obligation."

Schemes of arrangement, etc.: power of Secretary of State to intervene

6.—(1) In the 1975 Act, after section 17 there shall be inserted—

    "Schemes of arrangement, etc.: power of Secretary of State to intervene
    17A.—(1) This section applies where a company is a company in financial difficulties for the purposes of section 16 above by virtue of subsection (1)(c) of that section.

    (2) The Secretary of State may, after consultation with the Board, exercise any power conferred on him by subsection (3) or (4) below for the purpose of safeguarding those who are qualifying persons in relation to the company, or any class or description of such persons, to any extent appearing to the Secretary of State to be appropriate, against relevant loss arising from the financial difficulties of the company.

    (3) The Secretary of State may by notice in writing direct the Board to take any measures appearing to him to be necessary for securing or facilitating the transfer of all or any part of the insurance business carried on by the company to another insurance company to which this Act applies or an authorised friendly society, on terms (including terms reducing, or deferring payment of, any of the things to which any of those who are qualifying persons in relation to the company in financial difficulties are entitled in their capacity as such) appearing to him to be appropriate.

    (4) In any case where it appears to the Secretary of State that it would be practicable to secure the purpose mentioned in subsection (2) above

by the Board giving assistance to the company to enable it to continue to carry on insurance business, the Secretary of State may by notice in writing direct the Board to take such measures as appear to the Secretary of State to be necessary for giving such assistance.

(5) Without prejudice to the generality of subsection (4) above, a direction under that subsection may require the Board to make the giving of any assistance to the company conditional on the reduction of, or the deferment of the payment of, any of the things to which any of those who are qualifying persons in relation to the company are entitled in their capacity as such to any extent appearing to the Secretary of State to be appropriate.

(6) The Secretary of State shall send a copy of any notice under subsection (3) or (4) above to the company.

(7) A direction under subsection (3) or (4) above shall not have effect to require the Board to take any measures which, by virtue of section 16(6) or (8) or 17(1) above, they would be prevented from taking under section 16(3) or (4) above.

(8) Where it appears to the Board that a direction under subsection (3) or (4) above is affected by subsection (7) above, they shall—

    (a) notify the Secretary of State in writing of that fact and of the reasons for their opinion, and

    (b) send a copy of the notice to the company.

(9) In subsection (2) above, "relevant loss" means loss in connection with a matter by virtue of which a person is a qualifying person in relation to the company.

(10) Subsection (8C) of section 16 above shall apply for the purposes of this section as it applies for the purposes of that."

(2) Schedule 3 to this Act (consequential amendments of the 1975 Act) shall have effect.

Levies on insurance companies

Extension of levies

7.—(1) Section 21 of the 1975 Act (power to impose levies) shall be amended as set out in subsections (2) to (9) below.

(2) In subsection (1) (general business levy), for the words from "authorised" to "United Kingdom" there shall be substituted "insurance companies to which this Act applies which are—

    (a) carrying on general business in the United Kingdom, or

    (b) providing general insurance in United Kingdom,".

(3) In subsection (2) (long term business levy), for the words from "authorised" to "United Kingdom" there shall be substituted "insurance companies to which this Act applies which are—

    (a) carrying on long term business in the United Kingdom, or

    (b) providing long term insurance in United Kingdom,".

(4) In subsection (3) (income by reference to which general business levy calculated)—

    (a) for "net premium income" there shall be substituted "relevant net premium income", and

    (b) the words from "in respect of" to "relevant time" shall be omitted.

(5) After that subsection there shall be inserted—

"(3A) In the case of a company falling within subsection (1)(a) above which is authorised under section 3 or 4 of the Insurance Companies Act 1982, the reference in subsection (3) above to relevant net premium income is to the net premium income of the company in respect of—

    (a) general policies which were United Kingdom policies at the relevant time,

(b) the insurance through an establishment in the Channel Islands or the Isle of Man, under general policies, of risks situated in the United Kingdom, the Channel Islands or the Isle of Man, and

(c) the insurance through an establishment in an EEA State other than the United Kingdom, under general policies, of risks situated in the United Kingdom.

(3B) In the case of a company falling within subsection (1)(a) above which is not authorised under section 3 or 4 of the Insurance Companies Act 1982, the reference in subsection (3) above to relevant net premium income is to the net premium income of the company in respect of—

(a) general policies which were United Kingdom policies at the relevant time, and

(b) the insurance through an establishment in an EEA State other than the United Kingdom, under general policies, of risks situated in the United Kingdom.

(3C) In the case of a company falling within subsection (1)(b) above, other than a company to which subsection (3A) or (3B) above applies, the reference in subsection (3) above to relevant net premium income is to the net premium income of the company in respect of the insurance through an establishment in an EEA State other than the United Kingdom, under general policies, of risks situated in the United Kingdom."

(6) In subsection (4) (income by reference to which long term business levy calculated)—

(a) for "net premium income" there shall be substituted "relevant net premium income", and

(b) the words from "in respect of" to "relevant time" shall be omitted.

(7) After that subsection there shall be inserted—

"(4A) In the case of a company falling within subsection (2)(a) above which is authorised under section 3 or 4 of the Insurance Companies Act 1982, the reference in subsection (4) above to relevant net premium income is to the net premium income of the company in respect of—

(a) long term policies affected after 31st December 1974 which were United Kingdom policies at the relevant time,

(b) the insurance through an establishment in the Channel Islands or the Isle of Man, under long term policies effected on or after the relevant day, of commitments situated in the United Kingdom, the Channel Islands or the Isle of Man, and

(c) the insurance through an establishment in an EEA State other than the United Kingdom, under long term policies effected on or after the relevant day, of commitments situated in the United Kingdom.

(4B) In the case of a company falling within subsection (2)(a) above which is not authorised under section 3 or 4 of the Insurance Companies Act 1982, the reference in subsection (4) above to relevant net premium income is to the net premium income of the company in respect of—

(a) long term policies effected after 31st December 1974 which were United Kingdom policies at the relevant time, and

(b) the insurance through an establishment in an EEA State other than the United Kingdom, under long term policies effected on or after the relevant day, of commitments situated in the United Kingdom.

(4C) In the case of a company falling within subsection (2)(b) above, other than a company to which subsection (4A) or (4B) above applies, the reference in subsection (4) above to relevant net premium income is to the net premium income of the company in respect of the insurance through an establishment in an EEA State other than United Kingdom, under long term policies effected on or after the relevant day, of commitments situated in the United Kingdom."

(8) After subsection (7) there shall be inserted—

"(7A) In this section, references to the net premium income of a company for any year in respect of insurance of any description means the gross amounts recorded in the company's accounts during that year as paid or due to the company by way of premiums in respect of insurance of that description, less any amounts deductible for that year in respect of insurance of that description in accordance with subsection (7B) below.

(7B) In calculating a company's net premium income for any year in respect of insurance of any description, any rebates or refunds recorded in the company's accounts during that year as allowed or given in respect of any amounts so recorded during that or any previous year as paid or due to the company by way of premiums in respect of insurance of that description shall be deductible."

(9) After subsection (9) there shall be inserted—

"(9A) For the purposes of this section, a policy of insurance is a United Kingdom policy at any time when the performance by the insurer of any of his obligations under the contract evidenced by the policy would constitute the carrying on by the insurer of insurance business of any class in the United Kingdom.

(9B) In this section, "relevant day" means the day on which section 7 of the Policyholders Protection Act 1997 came into force."

(10) In section 25(1) of the 1975 Act (application of surplus funds by the Board), for "authorised insurance companies carrying on business in the United Kingdom" there shall be substituted "insurance companies to which this Act applies".

(11) In Schedule 3 to that Act (additional provisions with respect to levies), in paragraph 4, for "authorised insurance company", in each place, there shall be substituted "insurance company to which this Act applies".

(12) In that Schedule, at the end there shall be inserted—

"8A.—(1) The Secretary of State may by regulations made by statutory instrument—

(a) make provision for the purpose of securing, in relation to a company which at any time—

(i) is an insurance company to which this Act applies, and

(ii) does not have any business establishment or other fixed establishment in the United Kingdom,

that another person is the company's levy representative at that time, and

(b) make provision with respect to the functions of a person who is a company's levy representative under paragraph (a) above.

(2) Regulations under paragraph (b) of sub-paragraph (1) above may, in particular, impose on a person who is a company's levy representative under paragraph (a) of that sub-paragraph obligations and liabilities relating to the company's obligations and liabilities under this Schedule.

(3) Regulations under this paragraph may contain such supplementary, incidental and consequential provisions as the Secretary of State thinks fit.

(4) In sub-paragraph (2) above, references to obligations include obligations enforceable under the criminal law and references to liabilities include criminal penalties."

Restriction of leviable income

8.—(1) Section 21 of the 1975 Act shall be amended as follows.

(2) In subsection (3A), for paragraph (a) there shall be substituted—

"(a) the insurance through an establishment in the United Kingdom, under general policies, of risks situated in an EEA State, the Channel Islands or the Isle of Man,".

(3) In subsection (3B)—

(a) paragraph (a), and the word "and" at the end of that paragraph, shall be omitted, and

(b) in paragraph (b), the words "other than the United Kingdom" shall be omitted.

(4) In subsection (4A), for paragraph (a) there shall be substituted—

"(a) the insurance through an establishment in the United Kingdom, under long term policies effected after 31st December 1974, of commitments situated in an EEA State, the Channel Islands or the Isle of Man,".

(5) In subsection (4B)—

(a) paragraph (a), and the word "and" at the end of that paragraph, shall be omitted, and

(b) in paragraph (b), the words "other than the United Kingdom" shall be omitted.

Calculation of payment under general business levies

9.—(1) Section 21(7) of the 1975 Act (which provides for the deduction of reinsurance premiums in determining net premium income for the purposes of calculating amount payable under the general business levies) shall cease to have effect.

(2) In paragraph 2(1) of Schedule 3 to that Act (which provides for general business levies in any financial year not to exceed specified percentage of company's income), for "one per cent." there shall be substituted "0.8 per cent.".

Exemption from payment

10.—(1) Schedule 3 to the 1975 Act (which makes provision as to the imposition and enforcement of general and long term business levies) shall be amended as follows.

(2) After paragraph 6(2) there shall be inserted—

"(2A) If there is for the time being in force a limit under paragraph 7(1) below, sub-paragraph (2) above shall not require the Board to send notice to a company in relation to which the Board believe that its income liable to the levy for the year ending last before the financial year in which the levy is imposed does not exceed the limit."

(3) In paragraph 7, at the end of sub-paragraph (1) there shall be inserted ", except where that income does not exceed such amount as the Secretary of State may specify for the purposes of this provision by regulations made by statutory instrument."

Payment by instalments

11.—(1) In Schedule 3 to the 1975 Act, in paragraph 7 (liability following notification of levy), in sub-paragraph (1), for "pay to the Board within one month of the date of the notice" there shall be substituted "be liable to pay to the Board in accordance with sub-paragraph (1A) below", and after that sub-paragraph there shall be inserted—

"(1A) The amount which an insurance company is liable to pay under sub-paragraph (1) above shall be payable—

(a) on such date, or

(b) in such instalments on such dates,

as the Board may require by notice given to the company.

(1B) The power conferred by sub-paragraph (1A) above may not be exercised so as to require any payment to be made earlier than one month after the date of the notice under paragraph 6 above."

(2) In that Schedule, in paragraph 8 (service of notices), for "or 6" there shall be substituted ", 6 or 7".

Intermediaries

Payment of levies by instalments

12.—(1) In Schedule 2 to the 1975 Act (levies on intermediaries), in paragraph 6 (liability following notification of levy), in sub-paragraph (1), for "pay to the Board within one month of the date of the notice" there shall be substituted "be liable to pay to the Board in accordance with sub-paragraph (1A) below", and after that sub-paragraph there shall be inserted—

"(1A) The amount which an intermediary is liable to pay under sub-paragraph (1) above shall be payable—
  (a) on such date, or
  (b) in such instalments on such dates,
as the Board may require by notice given to the intermediary.

(1B) The power conferred by sub-paragraph (1A) above may not be exercised so as to require any payment to be made earlier than one month after the date of the notice under paragraph 5 above."

(2) In that Schedule, in paragraph 7 (service of notices), for "or 5" there shall be substituted ", 5 or 6".

Right to reimbursement by the Board

13. After section 23 of the 1975 Act there shall be inserted—

"Reimbursement by Board of payments by intermediaries

23A.—(1) If—
  (a) a payment is treated because of section 14(1) above as reducing a sum payable in accordance with section 6 or 8 above,
  (b) the payment is made with the consent of the holder of the policy or security under which the liability to which the payment is referable arises, and
  (c) at the time of the payment, that policy or security is one in relation to which the person by whom the payment is made ("the payer") is the holder's intermediary,
it shall be the duty of the Board to secure that a sum equal to the full amount of the reduction is paid to the payer as soon as reasonably practicable after the beginning of the liquidation to which the Board's liability under that section was attributable.

(2) The Board may secure the payment of any sum payable under subsection (1) above by either or both of the following methods, that is to say—
  (a) by themselves making payments in respect of the sum in question; or
  (b) by securing by any measures appearing to them to be appropriate that such payments are made by any other person.

(3) Section 13(3) above shall apply in relation to subsection (1) above as it applies in relation to any provision of sections 6 to 11 above.

(4) For the purposes of this section, a person is another's intermediary in relation to a policy or security at any time when he is engaged by the other to assist in its administration and performance."

Miscellaneous other amendments of the 1975 Act

Increase in the Board's borrowing limit

14.—(1) Section 1 of the 1975 Act (which makes provision for the financing of the Board's expenditure in performing their functions) shall be amended as follows.

(2) In subsection (4) (limit on amount outstanding in respect of principal of money borrowed by the Board), for "£10 million" there shall be substituted "£40 million".

(3) After that subsection there shall be inserted—

"(4A) The Secretary of State may by order made by statutory instrument amend subsection (4) above by substituting a different figure for the figure for the time being specified there.

(4B) An order made under this section may be revoked by a subsequent order so made.

(4C) Any statutory instrument containing an order under this section shall be subject to annulment in pursuance of a resolution of either House of Parliament."

Transfer of insurance business to authorised friendly society

15.—(1) In section 11(5)(a) of the 1975 Act (powers of the Board in relation to the transfer of the long term business of a company in liquidation), after "another insurance company to which this Act applies" there shall be inserted "or an authorised friendly society".

(2) In section 16(3) of that Act (corresponding provision in relation to companies in financial difficulties), after "another insurance company to which this Act applies" there shall be inserted "or an authorised friendly society".

Interpretation of the 1975 Act

Extension of definition of "policy holder"

16.—(1) In section 32 of the 1975 Act (interpretation), in subsection (2) (which provides that expressions used in that Act have the same meaning as in the Insurance Companies Act 1982), after "above," there shall be inserted "but subject to subsection (2ZA) below".

(2) After that subsection there shall be inserted—

"(2ZA) In its application by virtue of subsection (2) above, the definition of the expression "policy holder" (in section 96(1) of the Insurance Companies Act 1982) shall have effect as if the reference in paragraph (b) of the definition to a person to whom a sum is due included a person to whom a sum is contingently due."

Situation of risks and commitments

17.—(1) In section 32 of the 1975 Act (interpretation), after subsection (2ZA) there shall be inserted—

"(2A) Subject to subsection (2C) below, the situation of a risk for the purposes of this Act shall be determined as follows—

(a) in the case of insurance relating to buildings or to buildings and their contents (in so far as the contents are covered by the same policy), the risk shall be treated as situated where the property is situated;

(b) in the case of insurance relating to vehicles of any type, the risk shall be treated as situated where the vehicle is registered;

(c) in the case of policies of a duration of four months or less covering travel or holiday risks (whatever the class concerned), the risk shall be treated as situated where the policyholder took out the policy;

    (d) in a case not covered by paragraphs (a) to (c) above—

        (i) where the policyholder is an individual, the risk shall be treated as situated where he has his habitual residence at the date when the contract is entered into;

        (ii) where the policyholder is not an individual, the risk shall be treated as situated where the establishment of the policyholder to which the risk relates is situated at that date.

(2B) Subject to subsection (2C) below, the situation of a commitment for the purposes of this Act shall be determined as follows—

    (a) in the case of a policy where the policyholder is an individual, the commitment shall be treated as situated where the individual has his habitual residence at the date when the commitment is entered into;

    (b) in the case of a policy where the policyholder is not an individual, the commitment shall be treated as situated where the establishment to which the commitment relates is situated at that date.

(2C) The Secretary of State may by regulations made by statutory instrument make such provision as he thinks fit about how the situation of a risk or commitment is to be determined for the purposes of this Act; but no regulations shall be made under this subsection unless a draft of the regulations has been laid before and approved by a resolution of each House of Parliament."

(2) In section 31 of that Act (regulations), in subsection (1) (which provides for negative resolution procedure), after "any provision of this Act" there shall be inserted ", except section 32(2C) below,".

Miscellaneous

18.—(1) In section 32 of the 1975 Act, in subsection (1), at the appropriate places in alphabetical order, there shall be inserted—

" "authorised friendly society" means a society authorised under section 32 of the Friendly Societies Act 1992 to carry on in the United Kingdom insurance business such as is mentioned in section 31 of that Act;"

" "EC company" and "EEA State" have the same meanings as in the Insurance Companies Act 1982;"

" "establishment" has the same meaning as in the Insurance Companies Act 1982;".

(2) In that section, after subsection (2C) there shall be inserted—

"(2D) For the purposes of this Act—

    (a) a company shall be taken to provide general insurance in the United Kingdom if it covers (otherwise than by reinsurance) a risk situated there through an establishment in another EEA State, and

    (b) a company shall be taken to provide long term insurance in the United Kingdom if it covers (otherwise than by reinsurance) a commitment situated there through an establishment in another EEA State."

Friendly societies

Application of levy provisions

19. In section 21 of the 1975 Act, at the end there shall be inserted—

"(10) Subject to subsections (11) and (12) below, this section and Schedule 3 to this Act apply to qualifying friendly societies carrying on general business or long term business in the United Kingdom as they apply to insurance companies authorised under section 3 or 4 of the Insurance Companies Act 1982 carrying on such business there.

(11) In the application of subsections (4), (7A) and (7B) above by virtue of subsection (10) above, contributions in respect of discretionary benefits shall be disregarded.

(12) No levy under subsection (1) or (2) above may be imposed on a friendly society for the purpose of financing any expenditure in pursuance of a function which arose before the day on which section 19 of the Policyholders Protection Act 1997 came into force."

Consequential amendments

20.—(1) Schedule 17 to the Friendly Societies Act 1992 (which prospectively amends the 1975 Act for the purpose of extending it to contracts of insurance with friendly societies) shall have effect subject to the amendments in Part I of Schedule 4 to this Act (which are consequential on the other provisions of this Act).

(2) The 1975 Act, in its application to contracts of insurance with friendly societies entered into before the day on which section 2 above comes into force, shall have effect subject to the amendments in Part II of Schedule 4 to this Act (which have the effect that eligibility for protection in relation to such contracts is determined without regard to the amendments made by section 2 above).

(3) In this section, "friendly society" has the same meaning as in the Friendly Societies Act 1992.

Supplementary

Interpretation

21. In this Act—

"the Board" means the Policyholders Protection Board; and

"the 1975 Act" means the Policyholders Protection Act 1975.

Repeals

22. The enactments mentioned in Schedule 5 to this Act are hereby repealed to the extent specified in the third column of that Schedule.

Short title, commencement and extent

23.—(1) This Act may be cited as the Policyholders Protection Act 1997.

(2) Section 20(1) and (3) above, section 22 above, so far as relating to the Friendly Societies Act 1992, and this section shall come into force on the day on which this Act is passed.

(3) The remaining provisions of this Act shall come into force on such day as the Secretary of State may by order made by statutory instrument appoint; and different days may be so appointed for different purposes.

(4) An order under subsection (3) above may contain such transitional provisions and savings as the Secretary of State thinks fit.

(5) This Act extends to Northern Ireland.

SCHEDULES

SCHEDULE 1

SECTION 1: CONSEQUENTIAL AMENDMENTS

1. The 1975 Act shall be amended as follows.

2. In section 5(1) and (4), for "authorised insurance company" there shall be substituted "insurance company to which this Act applies".

3. In section 6(2), for "authorised insurance company" there shall be substituted "insurance company to which this Act applies".

4. In section 9(1), for "authorised insurance company" there shall be substituted "insurance company to which this Act applies".

5. In section 11(5), for "authorised insurance company", in both places, there shall be substituted "insurance company to which this Act applies".

6. In section 15(1), for "authorised insurance company" there shall be substituted "insurance company to which this Act applies".

7.—(1) Section 16 shall be amended as follows.

(2) In subsection (1), for "authorised insurance company" there shall be substituted "insurance company to which this Act applies".

(3) In subsection (3), for "authorised insurance company" there shall be substituted "insurance company to which this Act applies".

8. In section 23(1), for "authorised insurance company" there shall be substituted "insurance company to which this Act applies".

9. In section 26(1), for "authorised insurance company" there shall be substituted "insurance company to which this Act applies".

10. In section 32, after subsection (1) there shall be inserted—

"(1A) In this Act, references to an insurance company to which this Act applies shall be construed in accordance with section 3(2) above."

11.—(1) In Schedule 1, paragraph 1 shall be amended as follows.

(2) In sub-paragraph (2), for "authorised insurance companies", in both places, there shall be substituted "insurance companies to which this Act applies".

(3) In sub-paragraph (4), for "authorised insurance company" there shall be substituted "insurance company to which this Act applies".

(4) In sub-paragraph (5)—

(a) for "authorised insurance companies" there shall be substituted "insurance companies to which this Act applies", and

(b) for "authorised insurance company" there shall be substituted "insurance company to which this Act applies".

SCHEDULE 2

SECTION 2: CONSEQUENTIAL AMENDMENTS

1. The 1975 Act shall be amended as follows.

2.—(1) Section 6 shall be amended as follows.

(2) In subsection (6), for "subsection (8)" there shall be substituted "subsections (8) and (8A)".

(3) In subsection (8)—

(a) in paragraph (a), for "was a United Kingdom policy at the beginning of the liquidation" there shall be substituted "is a qualifying policy", and

(b) in paragraph (b), for "United Kingdom policy at the beginning of the liquidation" there shall be substituted "qualifying policy".

(4) After that subsection there shall be inserted—

"(8A) The duty of the Board under subsection (6) above shall not apply unless the liability is in respect of a protected risk."

(5) In subsection (9)—

(a) for "were United Kingdom policies at any time" there shall be substituted "are qualifying policies", and

(b) in paragraph (a), for "United Kingdom policies at the time in question" there shall be substituted "qualifying policies".

3.—(1) Section 8 shall be amended as follows.

(2) In subsection (2)—

(a) after "14" there shall be inserted "and subsection (2A)", and

(b) for the words "was a United Kingdom policy at the beginning of the liquidation" there shall be substituted "is a qualifying policy".

(3) After that subsection there shall be inserted—

"(2A) The duty of the Board under subsection (2) above shall not apply unless the liability is in respect of a protected risk."

4.—(1) Section 9 shall be amended as follows.

(2) In subsection (1), for "was a United Kingdom policy at the beginning of the liquidation" there shall be substituted "is a qualifying policy".

(3) In subsection (2), for "was a United Kingdom policy at the beginning of the first-mentioned company's liquidation" there shall be substituted "is a qualifying policy".

5.—(1) Section 10 shall be amended as follows.

(2) In subsection (2)—

(a) after "14" there shall be inserted "and subsection (2A)", and

(b) for "was a United Kingdom policy at the beginning of the liquidation" there shall be substituted "is a qualifying policy".

(3) After that subsection there shall be inserted—

"(2A) The duty of the Board under subsection (2) above shall not apply unless the liability is in respect of a protected commitment."

6.—(1) Section 11 shall be amended as follows.

(2) In subsection (3)—

(a) after "14" there shall be inserted "and subsection (3A)", and

(b) for "was a United Kingdom policy at the beginning of the liquidation" there shall be substituted "is a qualifying policy".

(3) After that subsection there shall be inserted—

"(3A) The duty of the Board under subsection (3) above shall not apply in relation to a commitment which is not a protected commitment."

7.—(1) Section 12 shall be amended as follows.

(2) In subsection (1)—

(a) at the beginning there shall be inserted "Subject to subsection (1A) below,", and

(b) for "was a United Kingdom policy at the beginning of the liquidation" there shall be substituted "is a qualifying policy".

(3) After that subsection there shall be inserted—

"(1A) The duty of the Board under subsection (1) above shall not apply if the policy does not relate to a protected commitment."

8.—(1) Section 15 shall be amended as follows.

(2) In subsection (2), for paragraphs (a) and (b) there shall be substituted "if he is a policyholder in respect of a general policy or a long term policy of a company in liquidation or provisional liquidation which—

(a) is a qualifying policy, and

(b) relates to the insurance of a protected risk or commitment."

(3) In subsection (3), after "may" there shall be inserted ", in relation to the insurance of a protected risk or commitment".

9.—(1) Section 16 shall be amended as follows.

(2) In subsection (2), after "arising" there shall be inserted "in relation to matters by virtue of which they are such persons".

(3) In subsection (9), for "was a United Kingdom policy at the relevant time" there shall be substituted "is a qualifying policy and insures a protected risk or commitment".

(4) In subsection (9A), for "United Kingdom policy at the relevant time" there shall be substituted "qualifying policy".

10.—(1) Section 17 shall be amended as follows.

(2) In subsection (4)—

(a) at the beginning there shall be inserted "Subject to subsection (4A) below,", and

(b) for "was a United Kingdom policy at the relevant time as defined by section 16(6) above" there shall be substituted "is a qualifying policy".

(3) After that subsection there shall be inserted—

"(4A) The duty of the Board under subsection (4) above shall not apply if the policy does not relate to a protected commitment."

11. In section 32(1), after the definition of the expression "long term policy" there shall be inserted—

""protected commitment" and "protected risk" have the meanings given by section 4(3) above;

"qualifying policy" has the meaning given by section 4(2) above;".

Section 6   SCHEDULE 3

<small>SECTION 6: CONSEQUENTIAL AMENDMENTS</small>

1. The 1975 Act shall be amended as follows.

2. In section 1(2), after paragraph (a) there shall be inserted—

"(za) to comply with any directions under section 17A below; and".

3. In section 18(3)(a), for "or 16" there shall be substituted ", 16 or 17A".

4.—(1) Section 28 shall be amended as follows.

(2) In subsection (1)—

(a) after paragraph (b) there shall be inserted "; or

(c) which is a company in financial difficulties within the meaning of section 16 above in relation to which the Board have taken any measures in pursuance of a direction under section 17A above;", and

(b) after "paragraph (b)" there shall be inserted "or (c)".

(3) In subsection (2), there shall be inserted at the end "; and

(c) in a case falling within paragraph (c) of that subsection, the period of six months beginning with the date on which the Secretary of State receives written notification from the Board that they have taken measures in relation to the company in question in pursuance of a direction under section 17A above."

(4) In subsection (3), after "paragraph (b)" there shall be inserted "or (c)".

Section 20   SCHEDULE 4

<small>FRIENDLY SOCIETIES: CONSEQUENTIAL AMENDMENTS</small>

<small>PART I</small>

<small>AMENDMENTS OF SCHEDULE 17 TO THE FRIENDLY SOCIETIES ACT 1992</small>

1. In paragraph 1(1), in the inserted section 1(2)(aa), for sub-paragraph (i) there shall be substituted—

"(i) members of friendly societies who have entered into contracts of insurance with societies of which they are members;".

2. For paragraph 3 there shall be substituted—

"3.—(1) Section 4 (protection confined to insurance under qualifying policies of protected risks or commitments) shall be amended as follows.

(2) In subsection (2), at the end there shall be inserted ", and

(c) a contract of insurance with a friendly society entered into through an establishment in—

(i) the United Kingdom,

(ii) another EEA State, or

(iii) the Channel Islands or the Isle of Man."

(3) In subsection (3)—

(a) in paragraph (a), after "above" there shall be inserted ", or a contract falling within subsection (2)(c)(i) above",

(b) in paragraph (b), after "above" there shall be inserted ", or a contract falling within subsection (2)(c)(ii) above", and

(c) in paragraph (c), after "above" there shall be inserted "or a contract falling within subsection (2)(c)(iii) above"."

3.—(1) Paragraph 6 shall be amended as follows.

(2) In sub-paragraph (1), in the words inserted in subsection (1) of section 8 of the 1975 Act, for "authorised insurance company" there shall be substituted "insurance company to which this Act applies".

(3) In sub-paragraph (2), in the words inserted in subsection (4) of that section, for "authorised insurance companies" there shall be substituted "insurance companies which are not friendly societies".

4.—(1) In paragraph 7, the inserted section 8A shall be amended as follows.

(2) The existing provision shall become subsection (1) and, in that subsection—

(a) after "14" there shall be inserted "and subsection (2)", and

(b) for "was a United Kingdom policy at the beginning of the liquidation" there shall be substituted "is a qualifying policy".

(3) After that subsection there shall be inserted—

"(2) The duty of the Board under subsection (1) above shall only apply if the liability is in respect of a protected risk".

5. In paragraph 9—

(a) for "subsection (3)" there shall be substituted "subsection (3A)",

(b) the subsection inserted in section 11 of the 1975 Act shall be renumbered "(3B)" and, in that subsection, for paragraph (b) there shall be substituted—

"(b) in subsection (5)(b) below, with the insertion after the words "this Act applies" of the words "or authorised friendly society",", and

(c) at the end there shall be inserted "and in subsection (5)(a) for "another" there shall be substituted "an" ".

6. In paragraph 11, in the subsection inserted in section 16 of the 1975 Act, after paragraph (a) there shall be inserted—

"(aa) with, in subsection (3), the substitution for "another" of "an";.

7. For paragraph 16 there shall be substituted—

"16. In section 25 (application of surplus funds by the Board), in subsection (1), after the word "applies", there shall be inserted "and to qualifying friendly societies carrying on business in the United Kingdom"."

8.—(1) Paragraph 18 shall be amended as follows.

(2) For sub-paragraph (3) there shall be substituted—

"(3) In subsection (2), for "subsection (2ZA)" there shall be substituted "subsections (2ZA) to (2ZC)".

(3) In sub-paragraph (4)—

(a) for "subsection (2)" there shall be substituted "subsection (2ZA)", and

(b) the subsections inserted in section 32 of the 1975 Act shall be renumbered "(2ZB)" and "(2ZC)" respectively.

(4) After that sub-paragraph there shall be inserted—

"(4A) In subsection (2A), in paragraph (c)—

(a) after "policies" there shall be inserted ", or contracts,", and

(b) at the end there shall be inserted ", or entered into the contract".

(4B) In subsection (2B), after "policy", in both places, there shall be inserted "or contract"."

PART II

APPLICATION OF THE 1975 ACT TO EXISTING CONTRACTS

9. For section 4 there shall be substituted—

"Protection confined to United Kingdom policies

4.—(1) A policyholder is eligible for the assistance or protection of the Board in accordance with any provision of sections 8A to 16 below only in respect of a policy of insurance which was a United Kingdom policy for the purposes of this Act at the material time for the purposes of the provision in question.

(2) A contract of insurance with a friendly society is a United Kingdom policy for the purposes of this Act at any time when the performance by the society of any of its obligations under the contract would constitute the carrying on by the society in the United Kingdom of insurance business of any class."

10. In section 8A—

(a) in subsection (1)—

(i) the words "and subsection (2)" shall be omitted, and

(ii) for "is a qualifying policy" there shall be substituted "was a United Kingdom policy at the beginning of the liquidation", and

(b) subsection (2) shall be omitted.

11. In section 10—

(a) in subsection (2)—

(i) the words "and subsection (2A)" shall be omitted, and

(ii) for "is a qualifying policy" there shall be substituted "was a United Kingdom policy at the beginning of the liquidation", and

(b) subsection (2A) shall be omitted.

12. In section 11—

(a) in subsection (3)—

(i) the words "and subsection (3A)" shall be omitted, and

(ii) for "is a qualifying policy" there shall be substituted "was a United Kingdom policy at the beginning of the liquidation", and

(b) subsection (3A) shall be omitted.

13. In section 12—

(a) in subsection (1)—

    (i) the words "Subject to subsection (1A) below," shall be omitted, and

    (ii) for "is a qualifying policy" there shall be substituted "was a United Kingdom policy at the beginning of the liquidation", and

(b) subsection (1A) shall be omitted.

14. In section 15—

(a) in subsection (2), for the words from "if" to the end there shall be substituted—

    "(a) if he is a policyholder in respect of a general policy or a long term policy of a company in liquidation which was a United Kingdom policy at the beginning of the liquidation; or

    (b) if he is a policyholder in respect of a general policy or a long term policy of a company in provisional liquidation which was a United Kingdom policy at the time when the provisional liquidator was appointed.", and

(b) in subsection (3), the words ", in relation to the insurance of a protected risk or commitment" shall be omitted.

15. In section 16—

(a) in subsection (6), after "In this subsection" there shall be inserted "and in the following provisions of this section", and

(b) in subsection (9), for "is a qualifying policy and insures a protected risk or commitment" there shall be substituted "was a United Kingdom policy at the relevant time".

16. In section 17—

(a) in subsection (4)—

    (i) the words "Subject to subsection (4A) below," shall be omitted, and

    (ii) for "is a qualifying policy" there shall be substituted "was a United Kingdom policy at the relevant time as defined by section 16(6) above", and

(b) subsection (4A) shall be omitted.

17. In section 21, subsection (9A) shall be omitted.

18. In section 32(1), at the end there shall be inserted "and references to United Kingdom policies shall be construed in accordance with section 4 above".

Section 22   SCHEDULE 5

REPEALS

Chapter	Short title	Extent of repeal
1975 c. 75.	The Policyholders Protection Act 1975.	In section 1(2), in paragraph (a), the words "carrying on business in the United Kingdom", and, in paragraph (b), the words "in the United Kingdom".
		In section 16(6), the words "and in the following provisions of this section".
		In section 21, in subsection (2B), the definition of the expression "EC company", in subsection (3), the words from "in respect of" to "relevant time", in subsection (3B), paragraph (a), and the word "and" at the end of that paragraph, in paragraph (b), the words "other than the United Kingdom", in subsection (4), the words from "in respect of" to "relevant time", in subsection (4B), paragraph (a), and the word "and" at the end of that paragraph, and, in paragraph (b), the words "other than the United Kingdom", and subsections (5) to (7) and (9A).
		In section 32(1), the definition of the expression "authorised insurance company", and the words from "and references" to the end.
		In Schedule 3, in paragraph 6(1) and (2), the words "authorised insurance", and, in paragraph 8, the words "in the United Kingdom".

Chapter	Short title	Extent of repeal
1980 c. 25.	The Insurance Companies Act 1980.	In Schedule 3, paragraph 9.
1981 c. 31.	The Insurance Companies Act 1981.	In Schedule 4, paragraph 25(2).
1982 c. 50.	The Insurance Companies Act 1982.	In Schedule 5, paragraph 16(a).
1992 c. 40.	The Friendly Societies Act 1992.	In Schedule 17, paragraph 15 and, in paragraph 18(2), the definition of "authorised friendly society".

INDEX

References are to sections and Schedules

PHARMACISTS (FITNESS TO PRACTISE) ACT 1997*

(1997 c. 19)

An Act to make provision about finding registered pharmaceutical chemists unfit to practise due to ill health; and for connected purposes.

[19th March 1997]

PARLIAMENTARY DEBATES

Hansard, H.C. Vol. 285, col. 996; Vol. 288, col. 594. H.L. Vol. 577, cols. 446, 1510; Vol. 578, col. 1504; Vol. 579, col. 9.

INTRODUCTION AND GENERAL NOTE

The Pharmacists (Fitness to Practise) Act 1997 (c. 19) amends the Pharmacy Act 1954 (c. 61) so as to extend the powers of the Royal Pharmaceutical Society of Great Britain to protect the public from pharmacists who are unfit to practise due to physical or mental ill-health, including drink or drug related illnesses. Procedures already existed to deal with cases of misconduct rendering a pharmaceutical chemist unfit to have his or her name on the register.

The Act establishes a new Health Committee to consider allegations and cases referred to the Council of the Society (new s.13A of and Sched. 2 to the 1954 Act). It creates two new orders to deal with cases; suspension orders (which may sometimes be imposed on an interim basis) and conditions of practice orders (new s.13C and 13F)). It should be noted that suspension from the register prevents pharmaceutical chemists working as such, and that this may make it unlawful to carry on businesses under their control (see the amendment to s.69 of the Medicines Act 1968 (c. 67) made by para. 5 of the Schedule to the 1997 Act). Appeals against a decision of the Health Committee can be made to an appeal tribunal established by the Privy Council (new s.13J and Sched. 1C). The Act provides for detailed procedures to be drawn up by the Council of the Society within the framework set out in ss.13G (for the Health Committee) and 13K (for the appeals tribunals). The criterion governing the exercise of the Health Committee's powers is set out in s.13E. It requires the Committee or appeal tribunal to impose the minimum restrictions on the practice of pharmaceutical chemists that it considers protects the public.

The effect of this Act is to bring the regulation of pharmacists in line with that of a number of other health professions. Procedures for dealing with practitioners who are ill already exist under the Medical Act 1983 (c. 54), the Dentists Act 1984 (c. 24), and the Nurses, Midwives and Health Visitors Act 1997 (c. 24). This pattern is not yet uniform, and there are no "health procedures" under the Professions Supplementary to Medicine Act 1960 (c. 66), the Hearing Aid Council Act 1968 (c. 50) and the Opticians Act 1989 (c. 44). Under the Osteopaths Act 1993 (c. 21) and the Chiropractors Act 1994 (c. 17) health matters are dealt with under the same procedures as disciplinary ones, although the power to make orders is based on serious impairments of health rather than misconduct or incompetence (which provide other bases for jurisdiction). However, in contrast with other health professions, the new Act does not provide procedures for the transfer of cases between the disciplinary and health jurisdictions.

COMMENCEMENT

The Act is to be brought into force on a day to be appointed (s.2).

ABBREVIATIONS

"the 1954 Act": Pharmacy Act 1954 (c.61).

Fitness to practise

1.—(1) The Schedule (which amends the Pharmacy Act 1954 for the purposes mentioned below and makes consequential amendments) is to have effect.

(2) Those purposes are—

(a) establishing a new committee of the Royal Pharmaceutical Society of Great Britain,

(b) enabling the committee to consider allegations against registered pharmaceutical chemists of unfitness to practise due to ill health, and

(c) enabling the committee to impose practising conditions on, or suspend from registration, registered pharmaceutical chemists whose ability to practise it finds to be seriously impaired due to ill health.

---

*Annotations by Jonathan Montgomery B.A. LL.M., Senior Lecturer in Law, University of Southampton.

DEFINITIONS
"registered pharmaceutical chemist": ss.2, 24 of the 1954 Act.

GENERAL NOTE
This section spells out in general terms the impact of the amendments introduced by the Act. The details of the new provisions are set out in the sections inserted by the Schedule to the Act. These are annotated separately below, with cross-references to the sections of the Pharmacy Act 1954.

Subs. (2)
Royal Pharmaceutical Society of Great Britain. The Society is incorporated by Royal Charter and is governed by its own bye-laws. The Pharmacy Act 1954 confers upon the Council of the Society duties and powers in respect of the keeping of a professional register. These include powers relating to entry on the register, required qualifications and certificates of entry. They also include powers relating to removal from the register for non-payment of fees and for misconduct. The 1954 Act establishes a Committee of the Council, known as the Statutory Committee, in order to carry out these latter functions.
new committee. The Health Committee established under s.13A. The constitution and powers are set out in Sched. 1B to the 1954 Act.
unfitness to practise. The new s.13B refers to a chemist's "ability" to practise being seriously impaired by their physical or mental condition. This indicates that "unfitness" in this context refers to ill-health rather than to a moral judgment about the appropriateness of the person to continue to practise. Such judgments are to be made by the Statutory Committee not the Health Committee.

Commencement

2.—(1) Section 1 and the Schedule are to come into force on such day as the Secretary of State may by order made by statutory instrument appoint.

(2) Different days may be appointed for different purposes.

Short title and extent

3.—(1) This Act may be cited as the Pharmacists (Fitness to Practise) Act 1997.

(2) This Act (except paragraph 5 of the Schedule) does not extend to Northern Ireland.

Section 1   SCHEDULE

FITNESS TO PRACTISE OF REGISTERED PHARMACEUTICAL CHEMISTS

Pharmacy Act 1954 (c. 61)

1. The Pharmacy Act 1954 is amended as follows.
2. After section 13 there is inserted—

"Imposition of practising conditions and suspension from the register

The Health Committee
13A.—(1) There shall be appointed a committee of the Society, to be known as the Health Committee.
(2) The provisions of Schedule 1B to this Act shall have effect in relation to the Health Committee.

GENERAL NOTE
Under Sched. 1B, the Health Committee will consist of a chairman and deputy chairman (who will be registered medical practitioners appointed to the Committee by the Privy Council), and six members of the Council of the Royal Pharmaceutical Committee of Great Britain (at least

three of whom must be registered pharmaceutical chemists). Three members of the committee, the chairman or deputy chairman and at least one registered chemist, will hear each case. There is no requirement for a lay person to be a member of the Committee. Decisions may be taken by a majority (para. 4(3)). The Committee will be advised by a legal assessor (para. 6).

Preliminary investigation by the Council
13B.—(1) This section applies to an allegation to the effect that the ability of a registered pharmaceutical chemist to practise as a pharmaceutical chemist is seriously impaired because of his physical or mental condition.

(2) Where such an allegation is made or referred to the Council, they shall—
- (a) notify the pharmaceutical chemist of the allegation and invite him to give them his observations before the end of the permitted period,
- (b) take such steps as are reasonably practicable to obtain as much information as possible about the case, and
- (c) consider, in the light of the information which they have been able to obtain and any observations duly made to them by the pharmaceutical chemist, whether in their opinion there is a case to answer.

(3) In subsection (2)(a) of this section "the permitted period" means—
- (a) the period of 28 days beginning with the day on which notice of the allegation is sent to the pharmaceutical chemist, or
- (b) where the Council consider that, were the allegation to be well founded, it would be necessary for members of the public to be protected without delay, such shorter period as may be specified by the Council in regulations.

(4) Where the Council conclude that there is a case to answer, they shall—
- (a) notify the pharmaceutical chemist of their conclusion, and
- (b) refer the allegation, as formulated by them, to the Health Committee.

(5) Where the Council conclude that there is no case to answer, they shall notify the pharmaceutical chemist of their conclusion.

(6) The Council may make regulations with respect to the procedure to be followed on an investigation under this section.

DEFINITIONS
"Council": s.24.
"Health Committee": s.13A, Sched. 1B.
"registered pharmaceutical chemist": ss.2, 24.

GENERAL NOTE
This section outlines the procedure to be followed when an allegation is made to the Council of the Royal Pharmaceutical Society of Great Britain that a chemist's ability to practise is seriously impaired by ill-health. It makes it mandatory for the Council to follow up such allegations by taking reasonably practicable steps to obtain full information about the case, including obtaining the comments of the pharmacist in question (subs. (2)). However, it provides for the Council to make preliminary enquiries to ascertain whether there is a case to answer before referring it to the Health Committee for a full hearing.

A similar screening process is found in the regulation of other professions (see *e.g.* Nurses, Midwives and Health Visitors (Professional Conduct) Rules 1993, (S.I. 1993 No. 893); General Medical Council Health Committee (Procedure) Rules 1987, (S.I. 1987 No. 2174)). In those procedures, it is usual to invite the practitioner who is alleged to be unfit to practise to undergo a medical examination (with provisions dealing with cases where such an invitation is declined). No such provisions are included in the case of pharmacists, nor is there explicit provision for the pharmacist to be told what steps are being taken to obtain information about the allegations. The Council has the power to make regulations in respect of procedure at the screening stage (subs. (6)), which may clarify these points.

The Council must notify the chemist of the results of the screening process (subss. (4),(5)). However, there is no provision in the Act for notification of the informant who made the allegation that the chemist was unfit to practise, or referred such an allegation to the Council.

There is no power to make an interim suspension order in order to protect the public pending a full hearing. Where the safety of the public is thought to be immediately at risk, the time taken by the screening process can be reduced (subs. (3)) and the case referred quickly to the Health Committee. However, that Committee's power to make interim orders only arises when a full order is made, see the annotations to s.13F.

Conditions of practice orders and suspension orders
13C.—(1) The Health Committee shall consider an allegation against a pharmaceutical chemist referred to them under section 13B of this Act.

(2) If, having considered the allegation, the Committee is satisfied that it is well founded, the Committee shall—

    (a) make an order imposing conditions with which the pharmaceutical chemist must comply while practising as a pharmaceutical chemist (a "conditions of practice order"), or

    (b) make an order directing the registrar to suspend the pharmaceutical chemist's registration for the period specified in the order (a "suspension order").

(3) Any condition in a conditions of practice order shall have effect for the period specified in the order.

(4) The period specified in a conditions of practice order or a suspension order shall not exceed three years.

(5) An order under this section shall have effect—

    (a) if there is no appeal against it under section 13J of this Act, when the period for making such an appeal expires, or

    (b) if there is an appeal against it under that section, when the appeal is withdrawn or otherwise disposed of.

DEFINITIONS

  "Health Committee": s.13A, Sched. 1B.
  "registered pharmaceutical chemist": ss.2, 24.
  "Registrar": s.1.

GENERAL NOTE

  This section defines the orders available to the Health Committee if they find the allegations against a pharmaceutical chemist proven. The criterion governing the exercise of the Health Committee's powers is set out in s.13E. It requires the Committee or appeal tribunal to impose the minimum restrictions on the practice of pharmaceutical chemists that it considers protects the public. There appears to be no limit expressed for the type of condition that may be imposed under a conditions of practice order. Orders may not be for longer than three years (subs. (4)). There is provision in s.13D(1) for extending the order further in cases where a chemist continues to be unable to practise due to ill-health, provided that the Health Committee reviews the case before the expiry of the existing order.

Subs. (2)

  well founded. This phrase does not provide a clear statement of the burden of proof. It will be necessary for the appeal tribunals and possibly the courts to establish the standard of proof required.

Subs. (5)

  This subsection provides that orders will not take effect until the chemist's right of appeal has been exhausted, either through an appeal being withdrawn or rejected or by being out of time (see s.13J). Where the Health Committee believes that it should make a suspension order with immediate effect, recourse can be had to the power to make interim orders under s.13F.

Review of orders

    13D.—(1) The Health Committee may review a conditions of practice order or a suspension order made with respect to a pharmaceutical chemist at any time while the order has effect.

    (2) The Committee shall review such an order on the written application of the pharmaceutical chemist.

    (3) The Committee shall not consider an application under subsection (2) of this section for a review of an order if—

    (a) the pharmaceutical chemist has made an earlier application under that subsection for a review of the order,

    (b) the earlier application was made within the period of twelve months ending with the date on which the Committee received the application, and

    (c) the order was not varied on the earlier review.

    (4) On a review under subsection (1) of this section of a conditions of practice order, the Committee may—

    (a) confirm the order,

    (b) revoke the order,

    (c) vary the order, or

    (d) replace the order with a suspension order.

    (5) On a review under subsection (1) of this section of a suspension order, the Committee may—

(a) confirm the order,

(b) revoke the order,

(c) vary the order,

(d) replace the order with a conditions of practice order, or

(e) make a conditions of practice order with which the pharmaceutical chemist must comply if he resumes practice as a pharmaceutical chemist after the end of his period of suspension.

(6) On a review under subsection (1) of this section, an order may be varied by—

(a) extending (or further extending) or reducing the period specified in the order, or

(b) in the case of a conditions of practice order, imposing additional conditions or removing or altering any of the existing conditions,

but the period specified in the order may not be extended (or further extended) by more than three years.

(7) On a review under subsection (2) of this section, the Committee may—

(a) confirm the order,

(b) revoke the order, or

(c) vary the order.

(8) On such a review, an order may be varied by—

(a) reducing the period specified in the order, or

(b) in the case of a conditions of practice order, removing or altering any of the conditions.

(9) If an order is revoked on a review under this section without being replaced by another order, the revocation shall have immediate effect.

(10) Any other decision on a review under this section shall have effect—

(a) if there is no appeal against it under section 13J of this Act, when the period for making such an appeal expires, or

(b) if there is an appeal against it under that section, when the appeal is withdrawn or otherwise disposed of.

DEFINITIONS

"conditions of practice order": s.13C.

"Health Committee": s.13A, Sched. 1B.

"registered pharmaceutical chemist": ss.2, 24.

"suspension order": s.13C.

GENERAL NOTE

This section provides the Health Committee with the power to review orders at any time while they still have effect (subs. (1)). This provides for their extension beyond the three year maximum period if it is necessary to protect the public (subs. (6)). Orders can also be varied, and a suspension order can be substituted for a conditions or practice order, and vice versa (subss. (4),(5)).

Under subs. (2), a chemist subject to an order may apply in writing for a review. The Health Committee will be bound to carry out such a review unless there has been an earlier application for review, within the previous 12 months, that did not result in a variation of the order. In such cases a review cannot take place under subs. (2), see subs. (3). However, the Committee could still exercise its discretion to review cases at any time under subs. (1).

Where a review is held upon the application from the chemist, there is no power to extend the period of suspension or conditions, only to reduce it (subs. (8)). If the Committee believes that such an extension is necessary, it would need to instigate a review under subs. (1). The criterion governing the exercise of the Health Committee's powers is set out in s.13E. It requires the Committee or appeal tribunal to impose the minimum restrictions on the practice of pharmaceutical chemists that it considers protects the public.

Exercise by Health Committee of its powers

13E. In exercising any power to make, confirm, vary or revoke a conditions of practice order or a suspension order, the Health Committee shall ensure that any conditions imposed on the pharmaceutical chemist are, or any period of suspension imposed on him is, the minimum which it considers necessary for the protection of members of the public.

DEFINITIONS

"conditions of practice order": s.13C.

"Health Committee": s.13A, Sched. 1B.

"registered pharmaceutical chemist": ss.2, 24.

"suspension order": s.13C.

GENERAL NOTE

This section establishes the criterion governing the exercise of the Health Committee's powers. It requires the Committee to impose the minimum restrictions on the practice of pharmaceutical chemists that it considers protects the public.

Interim suspension orders

13F.—(1) Where the Health Committee makes a suspension order with respect to a pharmaceutical chemist, it may make an order directing the registrar to suspend the pharmaceutical chemist's registration with immediate effect (an "interim suspension order").

(2) The Committee may only make an interim suspension order if it is satisfied that it is necessary to do so in order to protect members of the public.

(3) If there is no appeal against the suspension order under section 13J of this Act, an interim suspension order shall cease to have effect when the period for making such an appeal expires.

(4) If there is an appeal against the suspension order under that section, an interim suspension order shall cease to have effect—

(a) when the appeal is withdrawn or otherwise disposed of, or

(b) (if sooner) at the end of the period of 12 weeks beginning with the day on which the interim suspension order is made.

DEFINITIONS

"Health Committee": s.13A, Sched. 1B.

"registered pharmaceutical chemist": ss.2, 24.

"Registrar": s.1.

"suspension order": s.13C.

GENERAL NOTE

The power to make interim suspension orders is necessary because the full suspension order does not take effect until the period for making an appeal has expired, or any appeal has been dismissed. This section does not permit the Health Committee to suspend a chemist pending the outcome of hearings. The power to make an interim suspension order only arises when a full suspension order is made.

Procedural regulations

13G.—(1) The Council shall make regulations as to the procedure to be followed—

(a) on the consideration of an allegation against a pharmaceutical chemist under section 13C of this Act, and

(b) on a review under section 13D of this Act of an order made with respect to a pharmaceutical chemist.

(2) The regulations shall, in particular, include provision—

(a) requiring the pharmaceutical chemist to be given notice of the allegation or review,

(b) giving the pharmaceutical chemist an opportunity to put his case at a hearing,

(c) entitling the pharmaceutical chemist to be legally represented at any hearing in respect of the allegation or review,

(d) enabling such a hearing to be held in the absence of the pharmaceutical chemist if the requirements of regulations made by virtue of paragraphs (a) to (c) of this subsection have been met,

(e) securing that such a hearing is held in private unless—

(i) the pharmaceutical chemist requires the hearing or any part of it to be held in public, or

(ii) the Health Committee considers that it is appropriate to hold the hearing or any part of it in public,

(f) requiring the pharmaceutical chemist to be notified by the Committee of its decision, its reasons for reaching that decision and of his right of appeal,

(g) giving the Committee power to require persons to attend and give evidence or to produce documents,

(h) about the admissibility of evidence, and

(i) enabling the Committee to administer oaths.

(3) No person shall be required by any regulations made under this section to give any evidence or produce any document or other material at a hearing in respect of the allegation or review which he could not be compelled to give or produce in civil proceedings in any court in the part of Great Britain in which the hearing takes place.

"Council": s.24.
"Health Committee": s.13A, Sched. 1B.
"registered pharmaceutical chemist": ss.2, 24.

GENERAL NOTE
Procedure will be governed by regulations that the Council of the Royal Pharmaceutical Committee of Great Britain are required to produce by this section. Subsection (2) outlines the content of those regulations, making it clear that hearings will usually be in private and that chemists will be entitled to be legally represented at hearings.

Duties of registrar in relation to orders, etc.

13H.—(1) Where a conditions of practice order is made, the registrar shall enter in the register a note of—
  (a) the conditions imposed, and
  (b) the period for which each condition is to have effect.
(2) Where a suspension order is made, the registrar shall enter in the register a note of—
  (a) the suspension, and
  (b) the period of the suspension.
(3) Where a conditions of practice order or a suspension order is revoked or varied on a review under section 13D of this Act or an appeal under section 13J of this Act, the registrar shall delete, or make the necessary alterations to, any note entered in the register under subsection (1) or (2) of this section.
(4) Where an interim suspension order is made, the registrar shall enter in the register a note of the suspension.
(5) When an interim suspension order ceases to have effect, the registrar shall delete the note entered in the register under subsection (4) of this section.

DEFINITIONS
"conditions of practice order": s.13C.
"interim suspension order": s.13F.
"Register": s.2.
"Registrar": s.1.
"suspension order": s.13C.

GENERAL NOTE
Under s.2(1) of the Pharmacy Act 1954 the Register is to be published annually.

Effect of suspension of registration

13I.—(1) A pharmaceutical chemist who is subject to a suspension order or an interim suspension order shall be treated as if his name was not registered for the purposes of—
  (a) sections 2, 5 and 14 of, and paragraphs 2(3) of Schedule 1B and 3(2) of Schedule 1C to, this Act,
  (b) sections 10, 23, 31, 33 and 52 of the Medicines Act 1968,
  (c) section 7 of the Misuse of Drugs Act 1971,
  (d) the Poisons Act 1972,
  (e) paragraph 1 of Schedule 9 to the National Health Service Act 1977, and
  (f) paragraph 1 of Schedule 8 to the National Health Service (Scotland) Act 1978.
(2) For the purposes of this section a pharmaceutical chemist is subject to an order during the period for which the order has effect.

DEFINITIONS
"interim suspension order": s.13F.
"registered pharmaceutical chemist": ss.2, 24.
"suspension order": s.13C.

GENERAL NOTE
Registered pharmaceutical chemists have certain legal privileges in relation to the possession and supply of medicines whose availability is controlled. This section ensures that they cannot be exercised by a chemist who is subject to a suspension order.

Appeals against decisions of the Health Committee

13J.—(1) A pharmaceutical chemist with respect to whom an appealable decision is made by the Health Committee may appeal against the decision.

(2) In subsection (1) of this section "appealable decision" means—

(a) a conditions of practice order,

(b) a suspension order,

(c) variation of an order on a review under section 13D of this Act, or

(d) replacement of an order with another order on such a review.

(3) An appeal under this section may not be made after the end of the period of 28 days beginning with the date on which notification of the decision is sent to the pharmaceutical chemist.

(4) An appeal under this section lies to an appeal tribunal established for the purpose of the appeal by the Privy Council.

(5) The provisions of Schedule 1C to this Act shall have effect in relation to appeal tribunals established under this section.

DEFINITIONS

"conditions of practice order": s.13C.

"Health Committee": s.13A, Sched. 1B.

"registered pharmaceutical chemist": ss.2, 24.

"suspension order": s.13C.

GENERAL NOTE

This section provides for an appeal against a decision of the Health Committee to impose orders. Appeals must be made within 28 days of the decision. Usually the order will not take effect until this period has expired or until the appeal is resolved, if one is made (see s.13C(5)). In certain cases, an interim suspension order can be made under s.13F, which will have immediate effect.

The constitution of the appeals tribunals is governed by Sched. 1C. A panel of persons eligible for membership of tribunals shall be constituted, consisting of a chairman and deputy chairman (who must be lawyers of five years' standing), two registered doctors and two registered pharmaceutical chemists. An appeal tribunal will consist of three persons, one from each of these categories.

Procedure will be governed by regulations to be made under s.13K.

The powers of appeal tribunals are set out in s.13L.

Procedure on appeals

13K.—(1) In this section "an appeal" means an appeal made by a pharmaceutical chemist under section 13J of this Act to an appeal tribunal established under that section.

(2) An appeal shall be by way of a rehearing of the case.

(3) The Council shall be the respondent to an appeal.

(4) The Council shall make regulations as to the procedure to be followed on an appeal.

(5) The regulations shall, in particular, include provision—

(a) as to the manner in which the appeal is to be made,

(b) giving the pharmaceutical chemist an opportunity to put his case at a hearing,

(c) entitling the pharmaceutical chemist to be legally represented at any hearing in respect of the appeal,

(d) enabling such a hearing to be held in the absence of the pharmaceutical chemist if the requirements of regulations made by virtue of paragraphs (a) to (c) of this subsection have been met,

(e) securing that such a hearing is held in private unless the pharmaceutical chemist or the Council require it to be held in public,

(f) requiring the pharmaceutical chemist to be notified by the appeal tribunal of its decision and its reasons for reaching that decision,

(g) giving the appeal tribunal power to require persons to attend and give evidence or to produce documents,

(h) about the admissibility of evidence, and

(i) enabling the appeal tribunal to administer oaths.

(6) No person shall be required by any regulations made under subsection (4) of this section to give any evidence or produce any document or other material at a hearing in respect of an appeal which he could not be compelled to give or produce in civil proceedings in any court in the part of Great Britain in which the hearing takes place.

DEFINITIONS

"appeal tribunal": s.13J, Sched. 1C.

"Council": s.24.
"registered pharmaceutical chemist": ss.2, 24.

GENERAL NOTE
Procedure on appeals will be governed by regulations that the Council of the Royal Pharmaceutical Committee of Great Britain are required to produce by this section. Subsection (5) outlines the content of those regulations, making it clear that hearings will usually be in private and that chemists will be entitled to be legally represented at hearings. Appeals will be by way of a full rehearing (subs. (2)).

Decisions of appeal tribunals

13L.—(1) This section applies where an appeal is made by a pharmaceutical chemist under section 13J of this Act to an appeal tribunal established under that section.

(2)
The appeal tribunal may—
   (a) confirm a conditions of practice order or suspension order,
   (b) revoke such an order,
   (c) vary such an order,
   (d) replace a conditions of practice order with a suspension order,
   (e) replace a suspension order with a conditions of practice order, or
   (f) make a conditions of practice order with which the pharmaceutical chemist must comply if he resumes practice as a pharmaceutical chemist after the end of his period of suspension.

(3) An order may be varied by—
   (a) extending or reducing the period specified in the order, or
   (b) in the case of a conditions of practice order, imposing additional conditions or removing or altering any of the existing conditions,
but the period specified in the order may not be extended by more than three years.

(4) Section 13E of this Act shall apply to an appeal tribunal as it applies to the Health Committee.

(5) The appeal tribunal may award costs or expenses.

(6) Any decision of the appeal tribunal may be made by a majority of its members.

(7) A decision of the tribunal on an appeal shall have effect when notification of it is sent to the pharmaceutical chemist.

DEFINITIONS
"appeal tribunal": s.13J, Sched. 1C.
"conditions of practice order": s.13C.
"Council": s.24.
"Health Committee": s.13A, Sched. 1B.
"registered pharmaceutical chemist": ss.2, 24.
"suspension order": s.13C.

GENERAL NOTE
This section sets out the powers of the appeal tribunal. The decision of the tribunal is governed by the criterion set out in s.13E, that the minimum restrictions on the practice of pharmaceutical chemists should be imposed that the tribunal considers necessary to protect the public. Decisions may be made by a majority (subs. (6)).

Approval of regulations

13M.—(1) No regulations made under section 13B, 13G or 13K of this Act shall come into operation until they are approved by the Privy Council by order made by statutory instrument.

(2) Any statutory instrument made under this section shall be subject to annulment in pursuance of a resolution of either House of Parliament."

3. In section 24 (interpretation)—
   (a) after the definition of "byelaws" there is inserted—
      " "conditions of practice order" has the meaning given by section 13C(2)(a) of this Act",
   (b) after the definition of "the Council" there is inserted—
      " "interim suspension order" has the meaning given by section 13F(1) of this Act", and
   (c) after the definition of "the Society" there is inserted—
      " "suspension order" has the meaning given by section 13C(2)(b) of this Act".

4. After Schedule 1A there is inserted—

"SCHEDULE 1B

THE HEALTH COMMITTEE

Interpretation

1. In this Schedule—
   "the Committee" means the Health Committee, and
   "member" (except in paragraph 6(5) of this Schedule) means a member of the
   Committee.

Constitution

2.—(1) The Committee shall consist of—
(a) a chairman and deputy chairman appointed by the Privy Council, and
(b) six other members appointed by the Council.
(2) The members appointed by the Privy Council shall be registered medical practitioners at the time of their appointment.
(3) At least three of the members appointed by the Council shall be registered pharmaceutical chemists at the time of their appointment.

Term of office and resignation

3.—(1) A member appointed by the Privy Council—
(a) shall hold office for a period of five years, and
(b) (unless he holds office by virtue of being re-appointed under this paragraph) shall be
    eligible for re-appointment at the end of his period of office.
(2) A member appointed by the Council shall hold office for such period as may be determined by the Council.
(3) Subject to sub-paragraph (1)(b) of this paragraph, a person shall not be prevented
from being a member merely because he has previously been a member.
(4) Any member may at any time resign his office by giving notice in writing to the
Council.
(5) If a conditions of practice order or a suspension order is made with respect to a member, he shall cease to be a member on the date on which the order has effect.

Procedure

4.—(1) In any case, the functions of the Committee shall be performed by three members, of whom—
(a) one shall be the chairman or (if the chairman is not available) the deputy chairman,
    and
(b) the other two shall be selected by the chairman or (as the case may be) the deputy
    chairman from the members appointed by the Council.
(2) At least one of the members selected by the chairman or deputy chairman shall be a
registered pharmaceutical chemist.
(3) The Committee may act by a majority of the members performing its functions in any
case.

Expenses

5. The Council may pay to any member such expenses and fees as they consider appropriate in connection with the performance of any functions of the Committee.

Legal assessors

6.—(1) The Council shall appoint persons to be legal assessors.
(2) The legal assessors shall have the function of giving advice to the Committee on questions of law arising in connection with any matter which the Committee is considering.
(3) To be qualified for appointment under this paragraph as a legal assessor, a person
must—
(a) have a five year general qualification (within the meaning of section 71 of the Courts
    and Legal Services Act 1990), or
(b) be an advocate or solicitor in Scotland of at least five years' standing.
(4) The Council may pay such fees, allowances and expenses to the legal assessors as they
consider appropriate.

(5) If a legal assessor appointed under this paragraph is also a member of the Committee or the Statutory Committee, any payment made to him in his capacity as a legal assessor shall be in addition to any to which he is entitled as such a member.

SCHEDULE 1C

Appeal Tribunals

Interpretation

1. In this Schedule—
   "appeal tribunal" means an appeal tribunal estabnlished under section 13J of this Act, and
   "the panel" means the panel appointed under paragraph 3 of this Schedule.

Constitution

2. An appeal tribunal shall consist of three members of the panel, of whom—
(a) one shall be the chairman or (if the chairman is not available) the deputy chairman,
(b) one shall be a registered medical practitioner, and
(c) one shall be a registered pharmaceutical chemist.

Appeal tribunals panel

3.—(1) There shall be a panel of persons eligible for membership of appeal tribunals, appointed by the Privy Council.
   (2) The panel shall consist of—
(a) a chairman and deputy chairman,
(b) two persons who, at the time of their appointment, are registered medical practitioners, and
(c) two persons who, at the time of their appointment, are registered pharmaceutical chemists.
   (3) A person shall not be appointed a member of the panel if—
(a) he is a member of the Council or the Statutory Committee,
(b) he holds any office in the Society, or
(c) he is employed by, or provides any service to, the Society.
   (4) A person shall not be appointed as the chairman or deputy chairman unless—
(a) he is qualified for the appointment, and
(b) his appointment has been approved by the Lord Chancellor and the Lord Advocate.
   (5) To be qualified for appointment as the chairman or deputy chairman, a person must—
(a) have a five year general qualification (within the meaning of section 71 of the Courts and Legal Services Act 1990), or
(b) be an advocate or solicitor in Scotland of at least five years' standing.

Term of office and resignation

4.—(1) A member of the panel—
(a) shall hold office for a period of five years, and
(b) (unless he holds office by virtue of being re-appointed under this paragraph) shall be eligible for re-appointment at the end of his period of office.
   (2) Subject to sub-paragraph (1)(b) of this paragraph, a person shall not be prevented from being a member of the panel merely because he has previously been a member.
   (3) Any member of the panel may at any time resign his office by giving notice in writing to the Privy Council.
   (4) If a conditions of practice order or a suspension order is made with respect to a member of the panel, he shall cease to be a member on the date on which the order has effect.
   (5) The Privy Council may remove any member of the panel from office for inability to perform his duties or for misbehaviour.

Clerks of tribunals

5. The chairman or deputy chairman may appoint a person approved by the other members of an appeal tribunal to act as clerk of the tribunal.

Expenses

6. Any expenses reasonably incurred by an appeal tribunal, including any incurred in connection with the appointment of a clerk, shall be met by the Council."

Medicines Act 1968 (c. 67)

5. In section 69 of the Medicines Act 1968 (general provisions as to when a person is lawfully conducting a retail pharmacy business)—

  (a) in subsection (1), after "Subject to" there is inserted "subsection (1A) below and", and

  (b) after subsection (1) there is inserted—

     "(1A) A person carrying on a retail pharmacy business shall not be taken to be a person lawfully conducting such a business if—

        (a) (in any case) the business is under the personal control of a pharmacist who is subject to a suspension order or an interim suspension order, or

        (b) (in the case of a body corporate) the business is under the management of a superintendent who is subject to such an order.

     (1B) For the purposes of subsection (1A) of this section—

        (a) a person is subject to an order during the period for which the order has effect, and

        (b) "suspension order" and "interim suspension order" have the same meaning as in the Pharmacy Act 1954."

National Health Service Act 1977 (c. 49)

6. In section 43 of the National Health Service Act 1977 (persons authorised to provide pharmaceutical services), after subsection (3) there is added—

  "(4) Where—

     (a) arrangements for the provision of pharmaceutical services have been made with a registered pharmacist, and

     (b) a suspension order or an interim suspension order is made with respect to him,

he shall not provide pharmaceutical services in person during the period of suspension.

  (5) In subsection (4) above, "suspension order" and "interim suspension order" have the same meaning as in the Pharmacy Act 1954."

National Health Service (Scotland) Act 1978 (c. 29)

7. In section 28 of the National Health Service (Scotland) Act 1978 (persons authorised to provide pharmaceutical services), after subsection (2) there is added—

  "(3) Where—

     (a) arrangements for the provision of pharmaceutical services have been made with a registered pharmacist, and

     (b) a suspension order or an interim suspension order is made with respect to him,

he shall not provide pharmaceutical services in person during the period of suspension.

  (4) In subsection (3), "suspension order" and "interim suspension order" have the same meaning as in the Pharmacy Act 1954."

INDEX

References are to sections and the Schedule

BRITISH NATIONALITY (HONG KONG) ACT 1997*

(1997 c. 20)

An Act to provide for the acquisition of British citizenship by certain British nationals in Hong Kong. [19th March 1997]

PARLIAMENTARY DEBATES

Hansard, H.L. Vol. 575, col. 1350; Vol. 576, col. 1211; Vol. 577, cols. 91, 560, 1211. H.C. Vol. 290, cols. 592, 719; Vol. 291, col. 594

INTRODUCTION AND GENERAL NOTE

The British Nationality (Hong Kong) Act 1997 may well go down in history as the last example of legislation resulting from a private member's Bill, introduced in the Upper House by an hereditary peer, Lord Willoughby de Broke—the twenty-first holder of that title.

The Hong Kong Act 1985 (c.15) created a new form of British nationality to replace British Dependent Territories citizenship which would come to an end for inhabitants of the Colony formerly entitled to it on the cessation of British jurisdiction. At the heart of the debates on the 1997 Act lay a difference of opinion on the value of the new status—that of British National (Overseas)—to those inhabitants of Hong Kong (estimates varied between 5,000 and 8,000) who hold no other nationality and will not acquire Chinese nationality because of their non-Chinese ethnic origins. Proponents of the legislation objected that the new status gives no more than a right to a passport with no right of abode. That, it was argued, was not a nationality but merely a qualification for a travel document. The U.K. was seen as owing a particular obligation to them because they are largely descendants of immigrants who had settled in Hong Kong in the service of the Crown as soldiers and civil servants from other parts of the Empire, particularly India. The Government's view was that the right to a British National (Overseas) passport was a valuable right. Under the Joint Declaration the ethnic minorities retained a right of abode in Hong Kong and, if for any reason they had to leave Hong Kong they had an assurance of admission to the U.K., given by the Prime Minister in March 1996. [*Hansard,* H.L. Vol. 576, cols. 1228–1231 (*per* Baroness Blatch, Minister of State, Home Office).]

The 1997 Act was the third, and presumably final, statutory variation in the terms of the 1985 scheme. The British Nationality (Hong Kong) Act 1990 (c.34) authorised the Secretary of State to register up to 50,000 persons and their dependants recommended by the Governor of Hong Kong as British citizens. It was hoped that the granting of full British citizenship would encourage those registered to stay in Hong Kong. The Hong Kong (War Wives and Widows) Act 1996 (c.41) provided for the conferment of British citizenship on a group estimated to number, at most 50. The 1997 Act, as noted above, extends to something like 8,000 people. The Secretary of State retains a wide but not unlimited power under the British Nationality Act 1981 (c.61), s.4, to confer British citizenship on British Dependent Territories citizens by registration.

In the light of the strength of support for Lord Willoughby de Broke's Bill, the Government withdrew its opposition to the principle of the legislation, but secured its comprehensive redrafting in the Commons.

Acquisition of British citizenship

1.—(1) Subject to the provisions of this section, the Secretary of State shall, on an application made for the purpose, register as a British citizen any person who—

(a) is ordinarily resident in Hong Kong at the time of the application; and
(b) satisfies the requirements of subsection (2) or (3) below.

(2) The requirements of this subsection are that, immediately before 4th February 1997 ("the relevant date"), the person—

(a) was ordinarily resident in Hong Kong;
(b) was a British Dependent Territories citizen by virtue only of his having a connection with Hong Kong (within the meaning given by the Schedule to this Act); and
(c) would have been a stateless person if he had not been such a citizen, or such a citizen and a British National (Overseas).

(3) The requirements of this subsection are that, immediately before the relevant date, the person—

---

*Annotations by Professor Paul Jackson, University of Reading.

(a) was ordinarily resident in Hong Kong;

(b) was a British Overseas citizen, a British subject or a British protected person; and

(c) would have been a stateless person if he had not been such a citizen, subject or person.

(4) Subsections (2) and (3) above shall each have effect, in relation to a person who is or was born at any time on or after the relevant date, as if the reference to immediately before that date were a reference to that time.

(5) Paragraphs (b) and (c) of each of those subsections shall have effect, in relation to a person who, at any time on or after the relevant date, becomes or became—

(a) in the case of subsection (2) above, a British Dependent Territories citizen; or

(b) in the case of subsection (3) above, a British Overseas citizen, a British subject or a British protected person,

as if the reference to immediately before that date were a reference to that time.

(6) A person shall not be registered under subsection (1) above if, on or after the relevant date, he renounces or renounced, or otherwise gives or gave up of his own volition, the status of a national or citizen of a country or territory outside the United Kingdom.

(7) A person shall not be registered under subsection (1) above before 1st July 1997.

(8) In this section expressions which are also used in the British Nationality Act 1981 ("the principal Act") have the same meanings as in that Act.

DEFINITIONS

"British citizen": British Nationality Act 1981, ss.1–11, 14, 36 and 39.

"British Dependent Territories citizen": British Nationality Act 1981, ss.15–25 and Sched. 6.

"British National (Overseas)": Hong Kong Act 1985, s.2(2) and Sched.

"British protected person": British Nationality Act 1981, s.38.

"British subject": British Nationality Act 1981, ss.30–35.

"Hong Kong": that is the island of Hong Kong, Kowloon and Stonecutters Island, and the New Territories.

"Secretary of State": Interpretation Act 1978 (c.30), s.5 and Sched. 1.

GENERAL NOTE

The object of the section is to provide for the acquisition by registration of British citizenship on the part of any person who is linked to Hong Kong by *ordinary residence* and has no nationality apart from the status of British Dependent Territories citizenship arising from connection with Hong Kong or British National (Overseas) citizenship.

The Government saw no reason to allow applications for registration from persons within the categories above if they had in fact acquired residence outside Hong Kong and therefore introduced the requirement of a link with the colony in the form of *ordinary residence*. Although this phrase was criticised in Standing Committee as unduly vague, Miss Widdecombe, Minister of State, Home Office, defended it as referring to "a concept [which] is well understood in law" (Standing Committee E, col. 20).

In *R. v. Barnet L.B.C. ex p. Shah* [1983] 2 A.C. 309, at 340, Lord Scarman said,

"Ordinary residence is not a term of art in English law. But it embodies an idea of which Parliament has made increasing use in the statute law of the United Kingdom since the beginning of the 19th century. The words have been a feature of the Income Tax Acts since 1806.

The words "ordinary residence" were considered by this House in two tax cases reported in 1928. In each, the House saw itself as seeking the natural and ordinary meaning of the words. In *Levene v. Inland Revenue Commissioners* [1928] A.C. 217, 225 Viscount Cave L.C. said:

"I think that [ordinary residence] connotes residence in a place with some degree of continuity and apart from accidental or temporary absences."

In *Inland Revenue Commissioners v. Lysaght* [1928] A.C. 234, 243 Viscount Sumner said:

"I think the converse to 'ordinarily' is 'extraordinarily' and that part of the regular order of a man's life, adopted voluntarily and for settled purposes, is not 'extraordinary.'

In *Levene's* case Lord Warrington of Clyffe said, at p.232:

"I do not attempt to give any definition of the word 'resident'. In my opinion it has no technical or special meaning for the purposes of the Income Tax Act. 'Ordinarily resident' also seems to me to have no such technical or special meaning. In particular it is in my opinion impossible to restrict its connotation to its duration. A member of this House may well be said to be ordinarily resident in London during the Parliamentary session and in the country during the recess. If it has any definite meaning I should say it means according to the way in which a man's life is usually ordered." "

(See too, *R. v. Eastleigh Borough Council ex p. Betts* [1983] 2 A.C. 613 where, however, the House of Lords was concerned with the phrase "local connection".)

Subs. (1)

Register. For relevant provisions on acquisition of citizenship by registration, see British Nationality Act 1981, ss.4, 41 and 42.

Hong Kong. See the Definitions section above for meaning.

Subs. (2)

February 4, 1997. This is the date by which the legislation had concluded its passage through the House of Lords.

Subs. (6)

This subsection prevents an inhabitant of Hong Kong from renouncing any nationality to which he may be entitled with a view to applying for British nationality as a stateless person under subss. (2) or (3).

Subs. (7)

July 1, 1997. "As from 1st July 1997 Her Majesty shall no longer have sovereignty or jurisdiction over any part of Hong Kong": Hong Kong Act 1985, s.1(1).

Supplementary

2.—(1) A person who is registered as a British citizen under subsection (1) of section 1 above, and satisfies the requirements of subsection (2) of that section, shall be treated for the purposes of the principal Act as—

(a) a British citizen by descent; or

(b) a British citizen otherwise than by descent,

according as, immediately before becoming a British citizen, he was for the purposes of that Act a British Dependent Territories citizen by descent or a British Dependent Territories citizen otherwise than by descent.

(2) A person who is registered as a British citizen under subsection (1) of section 1 above, and satisfies the requirements of subsection (3) of that section, shall be treated for the purposes of the principal Act as a British citizen by descent.

(3) The following provisions of the principal Act shall have effect as if this Act were included in that Act, namely—

> section 37 (Commonwealth citizenship);
> section 40 (deprivation of citizenship);
> section 41 (regulations);
> section 42 (general provisions about registration etc.);
> section 45 (evidence);
> section 46 (offences);
> section 47 (legitimated children);
> section 48 (posthumous children);
> section 50 (interpretation);
> section 51(3) (meaning of "citizen of the United Kingdom and Colonies" in other Acts and instruments).

DEFINITIONS

"British citizen by descent": British Nationality Act 1981, s.14.

Short title and extent

3.—(1) This Act may be cited as the British Nationality (Hong Kong) Act 1997.

(2) This Act has the same extent as the provisions of the principal Act mentioned in section 2(3) above.

         SCHEDULE

PERSONS HAVING A CONNECTION WITH HONG KONG

1.—(1) A person shall be taken to have a connection with Hong Kong for the purposes of section 1(2) of this Act if—

  (a) subject to paragraph 2 below, he, his father or his mother was born, naturalised or registered in Hong Kong or found abandoned there as a new-born infant;

  (b) he, his father or his mother was adopted (whether or not in Hong Kong) and the adopter or, in the case of a joint adoption, one of the adopters was at the time of the adoption a British Dependent Territories citizen by virtue of his having a connection with Hong Kong as specified in this Schedule;

  (c) he, his father or his mother ("the registered person") was registered outside Hong Kong on an application based (wholly or partly) on any of the following—

    (i) residence in Hong Kong;

    (ii) descent from a person born in Hong Kong;

    (iii) descent from a person naturalised, registered or settled in Hong Kong (whether before or after the birth of the registered person);

    (iv) descent from a person adopted (whether or not in Hong Kong) in the circumstances specified in sub-paragraph (b) above;

    (v) marriage to a person who is a British Dependent Territories citizen by virtue of his having a connection with Hong Kong as specified in this Schedule or would, but for his death or renunciation of citizenship, be such a citizen by virtue of his having such a connection;

    (vi) Crown service under the government of Hong Kong;

    (vii) where the registered person had previously renounced citizenship of the United Kingdom and Colonies, or British Dependent Territories citizenship, birth, naturalisation or registration in Hong Kong;

  (d) at the time of his birth his father or mother was settled in Hong Kong;

  (e) his father or mother was born to a parent who at the time of the birth was a citizen of the United Kingdom and Colonies by virtue of his having a connection with Hong Kong as specified in this Schedule; or

  (f) being a woman, she was married before 1st January 1983 to a man who is a British Dependent Territories citizen by virtue of his having a connection with Hong Kong as specified in this Schedule or would, but for his death or renunciation of citizenship, be such a citizen by virtue of his having such a connection.

(2) In sub-paragraph (1) above "registered" means registered—

  (a) as a British Dependent Territories citizen, or

  (b) before 1st January 1983, as a citizen of the United Kingdom and Colonies;

and "registration" shall be construed accordingly.

2. A person born in Hong Kong on or after 1st January 1983 shall not be taken to have a connection with Hong Kong as specified in paragraph 1(1)(a) above by virtue of his birth there unless, at the time of his birth, one of his parents was—

  (a) settled in Hong Kong; or

  (b) a British Dependent Territories citizen by virtue of his having a connection with Hong Kong as specified in this Schedule.

INDEX

References are to sections and the Schedule

KNIVES ACT 1997*

(1997 c. 21)

An Act to create new criminal offences in relation to the possession or marketing of, and publications relating to, knives; to confer powers on the police to stop and search people or vehicles for knives and other offensive weapons and to seize items found; and for connected purposes.

[19th March 1997]

PARLIAMENTARY DEBATES
Hansard, H.C. Vol. 285, col. 993; Vol. 287, col. 515; Vol. 288, col. 1237. H.L. Vol. 577, col. 1074; Vol. 578, col. 970; Vol. 579, cols. 9, 654.

INTRODUCTION AND GENERAL NOTE
   This short Act started as a Private Member's Bill, introduced by Mr Jimmy Wray, who had won first place in the ballot. It received Government support, and had a very easy passage through Parliament. Indeed, no member spoke against the Bill on its second reading, and the Commons Committee stage was completed in one meeting of less than 30 minutes. There was no debate of its provisions in the House of Lords.
   The purpose of the Act is to control the distribution, and possession in public, of what the Act calls knives "suitable for combat". These are knives, swords, machetes, and other bladed implements, sold under names such as "Rambo shortsword", "SAS shoulder holster knife", or "Terminator Terror sword", and marketed in such a way as to emphasise their use for fighting, and causing personal injury. There was much concern expressed in the second reading debate about the perceived growth of a "knife culture" amongst young people. Mr Wray, opening the debate referred to statistics showing that in 1995
      "in England and Wales, 2,559 people were convicted of carrying an article with a blade or a
      point in a public place; 3,190 people were prosecuted and convicted of carrying an offensive
      weapon without reasonable excuse in a public place. In Scotland in 1994, 53 per cent of
      homicide victims were killed with a sharp instrument; in 1993, knives were used in 13 per
      cent of all incidents of violence." (*Hansard*, H.C. Vol. 287, cols. 515–516)
   The particular event, however, which gave impetus to the passage of the Bill, and probably reduced any possibility of opposition to it, was the murder in December 1995 of the headmaster Philip Lawrence. Mr Lawrence was killed outside his school by a young man carrying a knife. His

---

* Annotations by Professor Richard Stone, Nottingham Trent University.

murder unsurprisingly attracted massive media attention, and in itself created a debate about the carrying of knives in public. Mr Lawrence's widow, Frances subsequently produced a "manifesto for the nation" in which she wrote:

> "It is shocking to discover how easy it is to acquire battlefield blades which can have no function other than to be flourished by the inadequate and cowardly."

Mr Wray quoted this passage at the beginning of his speech on the second reading (*Hansard*, H.C. Vol. 287, col. 515). Many references were made to the Lawrence case by other speakers, and the horror which this crime produced clearly affected the tenor of the debate. In particular, it may explain why there was no opposition to the extension of the law proposed by the Bill. The Government had been reluctant to act on the basis that the problems of defining the particular type of knives to be attacked was too difficult. The distinction between a combat knife and a carving knife was one which, it was argued, was not susceptible to legal definition. This objection was not accepted by the proponents of reform, and the Government in the end agreed that the approach taken by the Bill, focusing on the descriptions attached to knives, rather than the weapons themselves, was workable.

The provisions of the Knives Act need to be considered in the context of other legislation dealing with the possession, or distribution, of knives. The Prevention of Crime Act 1953 (c.14), for example, makes it an offence to be in possession of an "offensive weapon" in a public place. "Offensive weapon" is defined as "any article made or adapted for use for causing injury to the person, or intended by the person having it with him for such use by him or by some other person" (s.1(4)). This is clearly wide enough to cover "combat knives" of the kind at which the 1997 Act is addressed, or indeed any knife if carried with the required intention. A power of stop and search in relation to such offensive weapons was given by s.1 of the Police and Criminal Evidence Act 1984 (c.60). The Restriction of Offensive Weapons Act 1959 (c.37), however, is directed at the specific problem of "flick knives" and "gravity knives" (as defined in s.1(1)). It makes it an offence to manufacture or distribute such knives. The Criminal Justice Act 1988 (c.33), s.139, makes it an offence to be in possession in a public place of "any article which has a blade or is sharply pointed except a folding pocket-knife." And, by virtue of the Offensive Weapons Act 1996 (c.26), s.139A of the Criminal Justice Act 1988 makes special provision in relation to the possession of such articles, or other offensive weapons, on school premises.

There is, therefore, a range of statutory control over knives, apart from the Knives Act 1997. The particular focus of the 1997 Act is the marketing of knives as "suitable for combat". In other words, it does not make it an offence to manufacture, sell, distribute or possess any particular type of knife. Rather it criminalises the advertisement, sale or hire, of knives with a particular type of description attached. This is done by ss.1 and 2. Sections 3 and 4 then provide certain defences, and ss.5–7 give supplementary powers of entry, search, seizure and forfeiture.

The second main change in the law is contained in s.8. This provides for the extension of the grounds for the authorisation of random stop and search powers given to the police in particular situations by s.60 of the Criminal Justice and Public Order Act 1994 (c.33) in relation to "dangerous instruments or offensive weapons".

The remaining sections (ss.9–11) deal with offences by corporations, interpretation, commencement and extent.

COMMENCEMENT

Section 11 (short title, commencement, extent, etc.) of the Act came into force on the date of Royal Assent, which was March 19, 1997. The rest of the Act will come into force on a date, or dates, appointed by the Secretary of State. At the time of writing, no such dates have been announced. The power to make the commencement order, which is exercisable by statutory instrument, includes the power to make transitional provisions or savings as thought appropriate by the Secretary of State.

The offences

Unlawful marketing of knives

1.—(1) A person is guilty of an offence if he markets a knife in a way which—

(a) indicates, or suggests, that it is suitable for combat; or

(b) is otherwise likely to stimulate or encourage violent behaviour involving the use of the knife as a weapon.

(2) "Suitable for combat" and "violent behaviour" are defined in section 10.

(3) For the purposes of this Act, an indication or suggestion that a knife is suitable for combat may, in particular, be given or made by a name or description—

(a) applied to the knife;

(b) on the knife or on any packaging in which it is contained; or

(c) included in any advertisement which, expressly or by implication, relates to the knife.

(4) For the purposes of this Act, a person markets a knife if—

(a) he sells or hires it;

(b) he offers, or exposes, it for sale or hire; or

(c) he has it in his possession for the purpose of sale or hire.

(5) A person who is guilty of an offence under this section is liable—

(a) on summary conviction to imprisonment for a term not exceeding six months or to a fine not exceeding the statutory maximum, or to both;

(b) on conviction on indictment to imprisonment for a term not exceeding two years or to a fine, or to both.

DEFINITIONS

"knife": s.10.

"markets": s.1(4).

"suitable for combat": s.10.

"violent behaviour": s.10.

GENERAL NOTE

This section contains the main innovation introduced by the Act. It sets out the offence of "unlawful marketing of knives". "Marketing", as defined by s.1(4) means in effect engaging in transactions involving commercial distribution, or indicating a willingness to engage in such transactions. The definition of "knife" in s.10 makes it clear that the Act is concerned with all bladed or pointed instruments. Swords, machetes, axes, scissors, shears, scythes and sickles, for example, will all potentially fall within the Act's scope.

Subs. (1)

There are two ways in which a person marketing a knife may commit an offence. One is by "indicating" or "suggesting" that the knife is "suitable for combat". The way in which this may be done is further explained by subs. (3). The other method is by "stimulating" or "encouraging" violent behaviour involving the use of the knife. It is not clear how this might be done, other than by giving descriptions in packaging, or advertisements, of how the knife might be used.

There is no mens rea requirement as to this element of the offence. The prosecution does not have to prove that the offending manner of marketing the knife was intentional or reckless. There are, however, various defences available under ss.3 and 4, which involve the defendant proving lack of knowledge or intention.

Subs. (2)

The definitions of "suitable for combat" and "violent behaviour" are discussed in the annotations to s.10.

Subs. (3)

The list of ways in which "indications or suggestions" of a knife's suitability for combat may be demonstrated is not exhaustive. It is open to the prosecutor to prove in some other way that the knife was being marketed (or was going to be marketed) in a way which would offend subs. (1).

Subs. (4)

offers for sale: Note that the offence of "offering for sale" will probably not be committed by a display in a shop or shop window (*Pharmaceutical Society of Britain v. Boots Cash Chemists (Southern)* [1953] 1 Q.B. 401; *Fisher v. Bell* [1961] 1 Q.B. 394), or an advertisement in a magazine (*Partridge v. Crittenden* [1968] 2 All ER 421). In such cases the appropriate charge will be "exposing for sale" in relation to a shop display, and the "publication" offence under s.2 in relation to the advertisement.

possession: simple possession of a knife is not an offence, even if there is an intention to sell or hire it. It must be possession for the purpose of selling or hiring *in a way* which is prohibited by subs. (1), *e.g.* with a particular description attached. The wholesaler of combat knives or other weapons who is found in possession of them will not commit an offence under the Act unless the packaging indicates that they will be marketed in a way which contravenes subs. (1), or there is other extrinsic evidence suggesting that this is the case. (Examples of such evidence are given in subs. (3)).

Subs. (5)
The offence is triable either way.

Publications

2.—(1) A person is guilty of an offence if he publishes any written, pictorial or other material in connection with the marketing of any knife and that material—
    (a) indicates, or suggests, that the knife is suitable for combat; or
    (b) is otherwise likely to stimulate or encourage violent behaviour involving the use of the knife as a weapon.
    (2) A person who is guilty of an offence under this section is liable—
    (a) on summary conviction to imprisonment for a term not exceeding six months or to a fine not exceeding the statutory maximum, or to both;
    (b) on conviction on indictment to imprisonment for a term not exceeding two years or to a fine, or to both.

DEFINITIONS
    "knife": s.10.
    "marketing": s.1(4).
    "publication": s.10.
    "suitable for combat": s.10.
    "violent behaviour": s.10.

GENERAL NOTE
    The second main offence created by the Act is the publication of material in a form which contravenes subs. (1). The publication has to be "in connection" with the marketing of a knife, but clearly does not have to be by the person doing the marketing. The publisher of a magazine or newspaper carrying an advertisement which fell within this section would commit an offence. It was with such advertisements that much of the second reading debate was concerned, and they must be regarded as one of the Act's prime targets. The definition of "publication" in s.10 includes electronic publication. Advertisements on the internet will therefore be covered, though the general issue of whether everyone who is involved in the provision of internet services is also the "publisher" of the content, and therefore of such advertisements, is as yet unresolved. The supply of offending material on computer disks, or CD-ROM would clearly fall within the section.
    No mens rea needs to be proved in relation to this offence, but there are defences under ss.3 and 4 which involve the defendant proving lack of knowledge or intention.

The defences

Exempt trades

3.—(1) It is a defence for a person charged with an offence under section 1 to prove that—
    (a) the knife was marketed—
        (i) for use by the armed forces of any country;
        (ii) as an antique or curio; or
        (iii) as falling within such other category (if any) as may be prescribed;
    (b) it was reasonable for the knife to be marketed in that way; and
    (c) there were no reasonable grounds for suspecting that a person into whose possession the knife might come in consequence of the way in which it was marketed would use it for an unlawful purpose.
    (2) It is a defence for a person charged with an offence under section 2 to prove that—
    (a) the material was published in connection with marketing a knife—
        (i) for use by the armed forces of any country;
        (ii) as an antique or curio; or

        (iii) as falling within such other category (if any) as may be prescribed;

  (b) it was reasonable for the knife to be marketed in that way; and

  (c) there were no reasonable grounds for suspecting that a person into whose possession the knife might come in consequence of the publishing of the material would use it for an unlawful purpose.

(3) In this section "prescribed" means prescribed by regulations made by the Secretary of State.

DEFINITIONS
  "knife": s.10.
  "marketed": s.1(4).
  "prescribed": s.3(3).
  "publication": s.10.

GENERAL NOTE

The defences in this section relate to the permitted marketing of "combat knives". The two defences in subss. (1) and (2) use almost identical language, and place the burden of proof on the defence (on the balance of probabilities). Subsection (1) is concerned with the s.1 offence of "marketing"; subs. (2) with the s.2 offence of "publication". In both cases there are three elements ((a), (b) and (c)) to the defence, which are cumulative. In other words, the defence has to prove all three to succeed. The first element (subss. (1)(a) and (2)(a)) relates to the uses for which the knife is marketed. In addition to the two specified uses, the Secretary of State has the power to prescribe other uses by regulation. At the time of writing, no such regulations had been issued. The words "antique" and "curio" are not defined, and so it will be up to the courts to decide what they mean. During the second reading debate Mr Richard Spring referred to the fact that he owned two "Omani khunjas" which were "framed and behind glass" (*Hansard*, H.C. Vol. 287, col. 523); and Mr John McWilliam mentioned that he had been presented with a "kukri" by the brigade of Gurkhas, which he kept "safely locked away" (*Hansard*, H.C. Vol. 287, col. 542). These are examples of the kind of items which would presumably be covered by the s.3 exemption.

The other two elements of the offence use objective tests of "reasonableness". It will be irrelevant what the defendant thought about the reasonableness of the marketing, or whether he genuinely did not suspect that the knife was likely to be used for an "unlawful purpose". If there were objectively reasonable grounds for thinking otherwise, then the defence will fail. "Unlawful purpose" is undefined; it presumably means the commission of any crime or tort involving violence, or the threat of violence. It is not clear whether violence against property would be sufficient. The whole thrust of the Act is concerned with violence against the person; the phrase "unlawful purpose", however is not necessarily limited in that way.

Other defences

4.—(1) It is a defence for a person charged with an offence under section 1 to prove that he did not know or suspect, and had no reasonable grounds for suspecting, that the way in which the knife was marketed—

  (a) amounted to an indication or suggestion that the knife was suitable for combat; or

  (b) was likely to stimulate or encourage violent behaviour involving the use of the knife as a weapon.

(2) It is a defence for a person charged with an offence under section 2 to prove that he did not know or suspect, and had no reasonable grounds for suspecting, that the material—

  (a) amounted to an indication or suggestion that the knife was suitable for combat; or

  (b) was likely to stimulate or encourage violent behaviour involving the use of the knife as a weapon.

(3) It is a defence for a person charged with an offence under section 1 or 2 to prove that he took all reasonable precautions and exercised all due diligence to avoid committing the offence.

DEFINITIONS
  "knife": s.10.
  "marketed": s.1(4).

"suitable for combat": s.10.
"violent behaviour": s.10.

GENERAL NOTE

The defences contained in this section provide protection for the "innocent" marketer or publisher. It arises where the defendant has committed the actus reus of one of the offences under ss.1 or 2. There are two types of defence available. In relation to the first, contained in subss. (1) and (2), the burden of proof is on the defence to establish that the defendant was unaware of, and had no reasonable grounds to suspect, the way in which a knife was being marketed, or the nature of the publication. This defence might protect, for example, the seller of a consignment of goods, containing knives, who is unaware that the packaging indicates that the knives are suitable for combat. Subsection (2) might cover the distributor or retailer of a newspaper or magazine who is unaware of the content of an advertisement contained in it. They would probably be regarded as "publishing" the advertisement, but would be likely to be able to use this defence.

The second defence, contained in subs. (3), is based on "due diligence". Mr Wray, in the second reading debate, suggested that it might apply where a shopkeeper

"issued instructions to all his staff not to market knives in an aggressive way, only to discover that one of his staff had flouted those instructions without his knowledge or authority." (*Hansard*, H.C. Vol. 287, col. 519)

The burden of proof is again on the defence.

It is important to note that subs. (3) contains an entirely separate defence. There is no need for a person relying on the defence under subss. (1) or (2) to prove the use of "reasonable precautions" or "due diligence".

Supplementary powers

Supplementary powers of entry, seizure and retention

5.—(1) If, on an application made by a constable, a justice of the peace or sheriff is satisfied that there are reasonable grounds for suspecting—

(a) that a person ("the suspect") has committed an offence under section 1 in relation to knives of a particular description, and

(b) that knives of that description and in the suspect's possession or under his control are to be found on particular premises,

the justice or sheriff may issue a warrant authorising a constable to enter those premises, search for the knives and seize and remove any that he finds.

(2) If, on an application made by a constable, a justice of the peace or sheriff is satisfied that there are reasonable grounds for suspecting—

(a) that a person ("the suspect") has committed an offence under section 2 in relation to particular material, and

(b) that publications consisting of or containing that material and in the suspect's possession or under his control are to be found on particular premises,

the justice or sheriff may issue a warrant authorising a constable to enter those premises, search for the publications and seize and remove any that he finds.

(3) A constable, in the exercise of his powers under a warrant issued under this section, may if necessary use reasonable force.

(4) Any knives or publications which have been seized and removed by a constable under a warrant issued under this section may be retained until the conclusion of proceedings against the suspect.

(5) For the purposes of this section, proceedings in relation to a suspect are concluded if—

(a) he is found guilty and sentenced or otherwise dealt with for the offence;

(b) he is acquitted;

(c) proceedings for the offence are discontinued; or

(d) it is decided not to prosecute him.

(6) In this section "premises" includes any place and, in particular, any vehicle, vessel, aircraft or hovercraft and any tent or movable structure.

Definitions
"conclusion of proceedings": s.5(5).
"knife": s.10.
"premises": s.5(6).
"publication": s.10.

General Note

Subss. (1) and (2)
These subsections contain powers in standard form enabling a police officer to obtain a warrant to enter and search specified premises. The power only arises where there are reasonable grounds for believing that an offence under s.1 or s.2 *has been* committed, and that the items sought are in the possession of the suspect. It is not sufficient, for example, that material intended for publication is in a person's possession, but has not yet been published. Nor would the power arise where knives falling within the Act are in the possession of someone who bought them from the suspect.

The procedures for obtaining and exercising a warrant issued under this section will be governed by ss.15 and 16 of the Police and Criminal Evidence Act 1984 ("PACE"), and its accompanying Code (*i.e.* Code B). The protective provisions governing access to legally privileged, excluded and special procedure material will not, however, apply (PACE, ss.9–14). Such material can be obtained with an ordinary warrant issued under this section. In practice, the only items which might possibly fall within one of the protected categories, are publications which might constitute or include "journalistic" material (PACE, s.13), and therefore be either excluded or special procedure material (PACE, ss.11 and 14).

Subss. (4) and (5)
The specific regulations contained in these subsections concerning the retention of items seized will operate in place of the provisions contained in s.22 of PACE. The provisions of s.21 of PACE, relating to access and copying, would, however, appear to apply to items seized under the Knives Act.

Forfeiture of knives and publications

6.—(1) If a person is convicted of an offence under section 1 in relation to a knife of a particular description, the court may make an order for forfeiture in respect of any knives of that description—
   (a) seized under a warrant issued under section 5; or
   (b) in the offender's possession or under his control at the relevant time.
   (2) If a person is convicted of an offence under section 2 in relation to particular material, the court may make an order for forfeiture in respect of any publications consisting of or containing that material which—
   (a) have been seized under a warrant issued under section 5; or
   (b) were in the offender's possession or under his control at the relevant time.
   (3) The court may make an order under subsection (1) or (2)—
   (a) whether or not it also deals with the offender in respect of the offence in any other way; and
   (b) without regard to any restrictions on forfeiture in any enactment.
   (4) In considering whether to make an order, the court must have regard—
   (a) to the value of the property; and
   (b) to the likely financial and other effects on the offender of the making of the order (taken together with any other order that the court contemplates making).
   (5) In this section "relevant time"—
   (a) in relation to a person convicted in England and Wales or Northern Ireland of an offence under section 1 or 2, means the time of his arrest for the offence or of the issue of a summons in respect of it;
   (b) in relation to a person so convicted in Scotland, means the time of his arrest for the offence or of his being cited as an accused in respect of it.

<small>DEFINITIONS</small>
"knife": s.10.
"publication": s.10.
"relevant time": s.6(5).
"the court": s.10.

<small>GENERAL NOTE</small>

Subss. (1) and (2)

A power of forfeiture is given in relation to both knives and publications, following conviction. It applies to items seized under a warrant, or in the possession or under the control of the
person convicted at the time of arrest or summons. The conviction must relate to items of the
kind which are to be forfeited. If, for example, a person is charged with offences under both ss.1
and 2, but is only convicted under s.1, there is no power to forfeit any publications seized. On the
other hand, knives to be forfeited need not have been before the court, as long as they are of the
same description as those in relation to which the conviction has been obtained. Similarly, any
publication containing material which has been the subject of a conviction can be forfeited, even
if the publication itself was not before the court.

Possession. The state of mind required for possession of an article has been considered in
various cases concerning drugs (see, in particular, *Warner v. Metropolitan Police Commissioner*
[1969] 2 A.C. 256, *R. v. Lewis (Gareth)* (1988) 87 Cr. App. R. 270, and *R. v. McNamara* (1988) 87
Cr. App. R. 246). The position seems to be that some knowledge is required for possession, but
that a person may possess the contents of a container if he knows that there is *something* in it,
even if he is unaware of the precise nature of the contents.

Subss. (3) and (4)

The court may impose a forfeiture order independently of any other penalty (subs. (3)). On
the other hand, it should, by virtue of subs. (4), consider the totality of the penalties imposed on
the offender, so as not to risk "overdoing the punishment" (*per* Park J. in *R. v. Buddo* (1982) 4
Cr. App. R. (S.) 268, discussing the similar provision in s.43(1A) of the Powers of Criminal
Courts Act 1973 (c.62). See also *Archbold: Criminal Pleading and Practice*, 1997 Ed., paras.
5.403–5.409). Mr Wray, in the Commons Second Reading debate, cited the situation where the
offence is

"only of a very marginal kind but forfeiture of all the property would have a very serious
effect on that person's livelihood". (*Hansard*, H.C. Vol. 287, col. 519)

Effect of a forfeiture order

7.—(1) An order under section 6 (a "forfeiture order") operates to deprive
the offender of his rights, if any, in the property to which it relates.

(2) The property to which a forfeiture order relates must be taken into the
possession of the police (if it is not already in their possession).

(3) The court may, on an application made by a person who—
(a) claims property to which a forfeiture order applies, but
(b) is not the offender from whom it was forfeited,
make an order (a "recovery order") for delivery of the property to the applicant if it appears to the court that he owns it.

(4) An application to a sheriff must be made in such manner as may be
prescribed by act of adjournal.

(5) No application may be made after the end of the period of 6 months
beginning with the date on which the forfeiture order was made.

(6) No application may succeed unless the claimant satisfies the court—
(a) that he had not consented to the offender having possession of the
property; or
(b) that he did not know, and had no reason to suspect, that the offence
was likely to be committed.

(7) If a person has a right to recover property which is in the possession of
another in pursuance of a recovery order, that right—
(a) is not affected by the making of the recovery order at any time before
the end of the period of 6 months beginning with the date on which the
order is made; but
(b) is lost at the end of that period.

(8) The Secretary of State may make regulations, in relation to property forfeited under this section, for disposing of the property and dealing with the proceeds in cases where—

(a) no application has been made before the end of the period of 6 months beginning with the date on which the forfeiture order was made; or

(b) no such application has succeeded.

(9) The regulations may also provide for investing money and auditing accounts.

(10) In this section, "application" means an application under subsection (3).

DEFINITIONS

"application": s.7(10).
"forfeiture order": s.7(1).
"recovery order": s.7(3).
"the court": s.10.

GENERAL NOTE

This section does two things. First it makes provision for dealing with forfeited items (subss. (1), (2), (8) and (9)). Secondly, it provides a procedure whereby the owner of forfeited items, not being the offender from whom they were forfeited, may recover them (subss. (3)–(7)).

The normal procedure for forfeited items will be for them to be taken into, or remain in, police possession, and then disposed of in accordance with regulations made by the Secretary of State under subs. (8). At the time of writing no such regulations have been made.

A person claiming ownership of forfeited items has six months from the date of forfeiture to seek a "recovery order". He will have to establish his innocence in relation to the possession by the offender, or the possibility of an offence being committed: subs. (6).

Subs. (7)

This is a convoluted provision, the effect of which is not easy to comprehend at first reading. It seems to be dealing with the situation where more than one person is claiming a right to property which has been the subject of a forfeiture order. Its effect appears to be as follows. The property is in the possession of one person as a result of ("in pursuance of") a recovery order. The other claimant does not lose his rights over the property until six months after the date of the recovery order. At that point, however, all rights over the property are lost. This assumes that the word "order" in the final line of subs. 7(a) means a "recovery order", and not a "forfeiture order". The meaning is not helped by the use of the phrase "at any time before" in lines 2–3 of the subsection, where the word "until" might have been clearer.

Subss. (8) and (9)

At the time of writing, no regulations have been made under these subsections.

Stopping and searching

Powers to stop and search for knives or offensive weapons

8.—(1) Section 60 of the Criminal Justice and Public Order Act 1994 (powers to stop and search in anticipation of violence) is amended as follows.

(2) For subsection (1) substitute—

"(1) If a police officer of or above the rank of inspector reasonably believes—

(a) that incidents involving serious violence may take place in any locality in his police area, and that it is expedient to give an authorisation under this section to prevent their occurrence, or

(b) that persons are carrying dangerous instruments or offensive weapons in any locality in his police area without good reason,

he may give an authorisation that the powers conferred by this section are to be exercisable at any place within that locality for a specified period not exceeding 24 hours."

(3) Subsection (2) (exercise by chief inspector or inspector of power to give authorisation) is repealed.

(4) In subsection (3) (continuation of authorisation)—

(a) for "the officer who gave the authorisation or to a" substitute "an officer of or above the rank of";

(b) for "incident" substitute "activity";

(c) for "six" substitute "24".

(5) After subsection (3) insert—

"(3A) If an inspector gives an authorisation under subsection (1) he must, as soon as it is practicable to do so, cause an officer of or above the rank of superintendent to be informed."

(6) In subsection (9) (matters to be specified in authorisations) after "specify" insert "the grounds on which it is given and".

(7) In subsection (10), the words from "and similarly" to the end of the subsection are repealed.

(8) After subsection (10) insert—

"(10A) A person who is searched by a constable under this section shall be entitled to obtain a written statement that he was searched under the powers conferred by this section if he applies for such a statement not later than the end of the period of twelve months from the day on which he was searched."

(9) In subsection (11), in the definition of "offensive weapon", after "Act 1984" insert "or, in relation to Scotland, section 47(4) of the Criminal Law (Consolidation) (Scotland) Act 1995".

(10) After subsection (11) insert—

"(11A) For the purposes of this section, a person carries a dangerous instrument or an offensive weapon if he has it in his possession."

(11) Section 60 of the Act of 1994 is to extend to Scotland; and accordingly in section 172(8) of that Act (list of provisions that extend to Scotland), for "61 to 67" substitute "60 to 67".

GENERAL NOTE

The stop and search powers contained in s.60 of the Criminal Justice and Public Order Act 1994 are amended by this section. Section 60 allows for random stops and searches of pedestrians and vehicles for a limited period, and in a limited area, following an authorisation by a senior police officer. The amendments contained in this section, *inter alia,* add to the grounds on which an authorisation can be granted, reduce the minimum rank of the officer who may give an authorisation, and lengthen the period for which an authorisation may be extended.

Subs. (2)

Section 60 of the Criminal Justice and Public Order Act 1994 as originally drafted referred only to "incidents involving serious violence". The amended section extends the basis on which an authorisation may be issued to the situation where there are reasonable grounds to believe that "dangerous instruments" (defined in the same way as "knives" in s.10 of the Knives Act) or "offensive weapons" are being carried in a particular area. It thus links to the concerns expressed in the debates on the Act about a growing "knife culture", in which young people in particular routinely carry knives.

The subsection also has the effect of reducing the minimum rank of an officer required to give authorisation from superintendent to inspector. The Home Office Minister, Mr David Maclean, explained this as part of a general "devolution of police powers" (*Hansard*, H.C. Standing Committee C, January 22, 1997, col. 4). The inspector must, however, inform a superintendent as soon as practicable (subs. (5)).

Subs. (4)

The period for which an initial authorisation may be extended is increased from six hours to 24 hours. The extension must, however, be authorised by a superintendent, rather than an inspector.

Subs. (8)

This subsection clarifies the right of a pedestrian who has been searched under these powers to obtain a written statement to this effect. Under the existing provisions of s.60 the right is tagged on to the similar right given by s.60(10) to the driver of a vehicle which is stopped.

Subs. (10)
For the meaning of "possession", see the General Note to s.6.

Miscellaneous

Offences by bodies corporate

9.—(1) If an offence under this Act committed by a body corporate is proved—
    (a) to have been committed with the consent or connivance of an officer, or
    (b) to be attributable to any neglect on his part,
he as well as the body corporate is guilty of the offence and liable to be proceeded against and punished accordingly.

(2) In subsection (1) "officer", in relation to a body corporate, means a director, manager, secretary or other similar officer of the body, or a person purporting to act in any such capacity.

(3) If the affairs of a body corporate are managed by its members, subsection (1) applies in relation to the acts and defaults of a member in connection with his functions of management as if he were a director of the body corporate.

(4) If an offence under this Act committed by a partnership in Scotland is proved—
    (a) to have been committed with the consent or connivance of a partner, or
    (b) to be attributable to any neglect on his part,
he as well as the partnership is guilty of the offence and liable to be proceeded against and punished accordingly.

DEFINITIONS
"officer": s.9(2).

GENERAL NOTE
This is a standard provision, appearing in similar terms in many statutes. Its object is to ensure that where an offence is committed by a corporation, the officers of the corporation may also be liable. Thus, where a company is guilty of the offence of "marketing" under s.1, for example because, in legal terms, it has "sold" a knife under a description which indicates that it is suitable for combat, any director who consented to the sale will similarly be guilty of the offence.

Interpretation

10. In this Act—
"the court" means—
       (a) in relation to England and Wales or Northern Ireland, the Crown Court or a magistrate's court;
       (b) in relation to Scotland, the sheriff;
"knife" means an instrument which has a blade or is sharply pointed;
"marketing" and related expressions are to be read with section 1(4);
"publication" includes a publication in electronic form and, in the case of a publication which is, or may be, produced from electronic data, any medium on which the data are stored;
"suitable for combat" means suitable for use as a weapon for inflicting injury on a person or causing a person to fear injury;
"violent behaviour" means an unlawful act inflicting injury on a person or causing a person to fear injury.

DEFINITIONS
"marketing": s.1(4).

GENERAL NOTE
Knife. The definition is the same as that used in s.139 of the Criminal Justice Act 1988 (c.33) in relation to articles which it is an offence to possess in a public place, and in s.60 of the Criminal

Justice and Public Order Act 1994 (c.33) in relation to "dangerous instruments". It is a very wide definition, and if taken literally will cover not only knives, swords, machetes, etc., but also many garden implements (spades, hoes, scythes), other hand tools (chisels, saws, screwdrivers), and items of kitchen equipment. The limiting factor in this Act is that the instrument must be marketed in a way that suggests that it is suitable for combat, or which will encourage violent behaviour. Only a limited range of items falling within the definition are likely to be marketed in such a way.

Suitable for combat; violent behaviour. The definitions of these two phrases in terms of "inflicting injury" and "causing fear" of injury, are closely related to the general criminal law offences of battery and assault. The difference is that although battery involves personal physical contact, and assault the causing of fear of harm, neither offence requires "injury". It is presumed that "injury" implies something equivalent to at least "actual bodily harm", under s.47 of the Offences Against the Person Act 1861 (c.100).

The requirement of an "unlawful act" in relation to violent behaviour means that actions taken in self-defence will not be covered. If, therefore, a knife is marketed purely as a means of protecting oneself against attacks from others, this might not constitute an offence under the Act.

Short title, commencement, extent etc.

11.—(1) This Act may be cited as the Knives Act 1997.

(2) This section comes into force on the passing of this Act.

(3) The other provisions of this Act come into force on such date as may be appointed by order made by the Secretary of State; but different dates may be appointed for different provisions and for different purposes.

(4) Any such order may include such transitional provisions or savings as the Secretary of State considers appropriate.

(5) The power—

(a) to make regulations under section 3 or 7, or

(b) to make an order under this section,

is exercisable by statutory instrument.

(6) A statutory instrument made under section 3 or 7 shall be subject to annulment in pursuance of a resolution of either House of Parliament.

(7) Except for section 8, this Act extends to Northern Ireland.

GENERAL NOTE

Subs. (2)
Royal Assent was granted on March 19, 1997.

Subss. (3)–(6)
At the time of writing, no regulations have been made under these subsections.

INDEX

References are to sections

ARCHITECTS ACT 1997*

(1997 c. 22)

[A Table showing the derivation of the provisions of this consolidation Act will be found at the end of the Act. The Act has no official status.]

ARRANGEMENT OF SECTIONS

Part I

THE ARCHITECTS REGISTRATION BOARD

Part II

REGISTRATION ETC.

The Registrar and the Register

Registration

Removal from Register etc.

List of visiting EEA architects

Part III

DISCIPLINE

Professional standards

Disciplinary orders

Visiting EEA architects

Part IV

USE OF TITLE "ARCHITECT"

* Annotations by Charles Gardner LL.B., M.Sc., F.C.I.Arb., Partner at Reynolds Porter Chamberlain.

An Act to consolidate the enactments relating to architects.

[19th March 1997]

PARLIAMENTARY DEBATES
Hansard, H.L. Vol. 576, col. 1394; Vol. 577, col. 384; Vol. 578, cols. 785, 1503. H.C. Vol. 292, col. 696.

INTRODUCTION

The Architects Act 1997 (c.22) ("the 1997 Act") has been enacted to consolidate the law relating to the registration of architects, which was already revised by the Housing Grants, Construction and Regeneration Act (c.53) ("the 1996 Act") last year. Part III of the 1996 Act amended the Architects (Registration) Act 1931 (c.33), the Architects Registration Act 1934 (c.38) and repealed the Architects Registration (Amendment) Act 1969 (c.42). The pre-war legislation was retained by the 1996 Act but extensive textual changes were made involving many consequential amendments and repeals. In consequence, Pt. III of the 1996 Act had to be read together with both the 1931 and 1938 Acts, a situation which made consolidation highly desirable.

The 1997 Act was introduced into the House of Lords by the then Lord Chancellor, Lord Mackay of Clashfern, on January 20, 1997 and received the Royal Assent on March 19, 1997 following its third reading in the House of Commons on March 17, 1997. It is now the sole statutory source on the subject of the registration of architects. The Act includes all the new legislation and replaces all the earlier Acts (including the 1996 Act, ss.118 to 125 and Sched. 2).

The 1997 Act retains the spirit of the 1996 Act and preserves all the changes which that Act introduced. The Architects Registration Board, the Register of Architects and the Professional Conduct Committee have the same functions with which they were invested by the 1996 Act (which functions replaced those of the former Board of Architectural Education, the Admission Committee, the Discipline Committee and the Architects Registration Council of the U.K., previously established under the 1931 Act).

The 1997 Act also restates many of the sections in the 1931 and the 1938 Acts, as amended by the 1996 Act including those amended sections which dealt with the recognition of European and other qualifications. It follows closely the Council of the European Communities Directive of June 10, 1985 on the mutual recognition of formal qualifications in architecture and sets out the rights of registration of foreign architects.

COMMENCEMENT

This United Kingdom Act will come into force in accordance with the provisions of s.28(2) upon such day as may be appointed by the Secretary of State. The Act is also applicable to Northern Ireland (s.28(3)).

ABBREVIATIONS
  "1931 Act"   : Architects (Registration) Act 1931 (c.33).
  "1934 Act"   : Architects Registration Act 1934 (c.38).

"1996 Act"	: Housing Grants, Construction and Regeneration Act 1996 (c.53).
"1985 Council Directive"	: Council Directive 85/384/EEC on the mutual recognition of diplomas, certificates and other evidence of formal qualifications in architecture, as amended.
"ARB; the"	: Architects Registration Board.
"ARCUK"	: Architects Registration Council of the U.K.

PART I

THE ARCHITECTS REGISTRATION BOARD

The Board

1.—(1) There shall continue to be a body corporate known as the Architects Registration Board.

(2) There shall continue to be a Professional Conduct Committee of the Board.

(3) Part I of Schedule 1 makes provision about the Board.

(4) Part II of that Schedule makes provision about the Professional Conduct Committee.

(5) Part III of that Schedule gives the Board power to establish other committees and makes provision about committees established by the Board.

(6) Part IV of that Schedule makes general provision about the Board and its committees.

DEFINITIONS

"Architects Registration Board": s.1(1), Sched.1, Pt. I.

"Board, the": ss.25, 1(1), Sched.1, Pts. I, III and IV.

"Professional Conduct Committee": s.1(4), Sched.1, Pt. II.

GENERAL NOTE

Subsection (1) confirms the continued existence of the Architects Registration Board ("ARB"), which was given that name by the 1996 Act in replacement of the former Architects Registration Council of the U.K. ("ARCUK"), itself originally established under the 1931 Act. It is worth noting that in 1996 the Government changed its mind at least twice on the question of whether to retain any form of statutory registration board, initially taking the view that ARCUK should be abolished and that other arrangements should be made to secure the continued integrity of the architectural profession (see *Hansard*, H.L. Vol. 569, col. 980). The Government ultimately decided that ARCUK should be reformed in order to make it more efficient and gave statutory effect to those reforms in the 1996 Act. This reformed body is now preserved by the Act.

Under Sched. 1, Pt. I, provision is maintained for the ARB to consist of a total of 15 members, seven of whom are to be elected and eight appointed. The elected members represent bodies who are deemed to be representative of architects in accordance with a scheme to be prepared by the ARB and approved by the Privy Council. The appointed members represent consumer and public interests and are to be appointed by the Privy Council. A major change from ARCUK's constitution is preserved – that the majority of the members (eight) are to be lay members and not architects. The profession is not therefore self-regulating. This is unusual as in most professions the governing or disciplinary body is composed of members of the profession itself. The aim of 1996 reforms now enshrined in this Act was to strike a balance between the interests of architects generally and those of the general public.

The Board of Architectural Education, the Admission Committee and the Discipline Committee, bodies established under the 1931 Act, were swept away by the 1996 Act and their powers and duties were at the same time conferred upon the ARB: whilst the Board is given power by the Act to establish other committees (subs.(5)), provision is specifically made under subs.(2) for the creation of a Professional Conduct Committee whose constitution and regulation are set out in Sched.1, Pt. II repeating the same provisions of the 1996 Act. The ARB is not expected to spawn several new, large or expensive committees (see *Hansard*, H.L. Vol. 571, col. 45). Though members of any additional committees need not be members of the ARB, the majority must be ARB members (s.19, Sched. 1, Pt. III) and the ARB can only discharge its statutory functions through its own members (s.18, Sched. 1, Pt. III) (see also *Hansard*, H.L. Vol. 571, col.45). The aim of the 1996 Act to reduce the members of ARCUK from 73 to the 15 required for the ARB and ensure a minimalist organisation is therefore also retained.

PART II

REGISTRATION ETC.

The Registrar and the Register

The Registrar

2.—(1) The Board shall appoint a person to be known as the Registrar of Architects.

(2) The Board shall decide the period for which, and the terms on which, the Registrar is appointed.

(3) The Registrar shall have the functions provided by or by virtue of this Act and any other functions which the Board directs.

(4) The Board may, in addition to paying to the Registrar a salary or fees, pay pensions to or in respect of him, or make contributions to the payment of such pensions, and pay him allowances, expenses and gratuities.

DEFINITIONS
"Board, the": ss.25, 1(1), Sched.1, Pts. I, III and IV.
"Registrar of Architects": s.2(1).

GENERAL NOTE
The post of Registrar of Architects which was created by the 1996 Act has been preserved. The Registrar is appointed and paid by the ARB and his functions are to exercise the responsibilities set out in ss.3 and 4 of the Act, together with such other functions as the ARB may decide. The ARB's powers to remunerate the Registrar are expressly set out in subs.(4) but these limitations on the ARB's discretion are widely set and it may make payments not only of salary but also of such fees, pensions, allowances, expenses and gratuities as it thinks fit.

The Register

3.—(1) The Registrar shall maintain the Register of Architects in which there shall be entered the name of every person entitled to be registered under this Act.

(2) The Register shall show the regular business address of each registered person.

(3) The Registrar shall make any necessary alterations to the Register and, in particular, shall remove from the Register the name of any registered person who has died or has applied in the prescribed manner requesting the removal of his name.

(4) The Board shall publish the current version of the Register annually and a copy of the most recently published version shall be provided to any person who requests one on payment of a reasonable charge decided by the Board.

(5) A copy of the Register purporting to be published by the Board shall be evidence (and, in Scotland, sufficient evidence) of any matter mentioned in it.

(6) A certificate purporting to be signed by the Registrar which states that a person—

   (a) is registered;
   (b) is not registered;
   (c) was registered on a specified date or during a specified period;
   (d) was not registered on a specified date or during a specified period; or
   (e) has never been registered,

shall be evidence (and, in Scotland, sufficient evidence) of any matter stated.

DEFINITIONS
"Board, the": ss.25, 1(1), Sched.1, Pts. I, III and IV.
"Register of Architects; the": s.3(1).

"Register, the": s.3.
"Registrar of Architects": s.2(1).
"registered person": s.3(1).

GENERAL NOTE
    This section follows s.120 of the 1996 Act and requires the Registrar of Architects to maintain a Register of Architects, containing the name of every person entitled to be registered and showing the regular business address of each such registered person. The Registrar of Architects is required to make the necessary alterations to the Register in order to keep it up-to-date and also to publish it annually, providing a copy to anyone requiring one, on payment of a reasonable fee which shall be determined by the ARB. A copy of the Register or a Certificate extracted from the Register and purporting to be signed by the Registrar of Architects shall amount to formal evidence of the details set out in the certificate (Evidence Act 1845 (c.113), s.1) (or in Scotland, sufficient evidence).

Registration

Registration: general

    4.—(1) A person who has applied to the Registrar in the prescribed manner for registration in pursuance of this section is entitled to be registered if—
  (a) he holds such qualifications and has gained such practical experience as may be prescribed; or
  (b) he has a standard of competence which, in the opinion of the Board, is equivalent to that demonstrated by satisfying paragraph (a).
    (2) The Board may require a person who applies for registration on the ground that he satisfies subsection (1)(b) to pass a prescribed examination in architecture.
    (3) Before prescribing—
  (a) qualifications or practical experience for the purposes of subsection (1)(a); or
  (b) any examination for the purposes of subsection (2),
the Board shall consult the bodies representative of architects which are incorporated by royal charter and such other professional and educational bodies as it thinks appropriate.
    (4) Where a person has duly applied for registration in pursuance of this section—
  (a) if the Registrar is satisfied that the person is entitled to be registered, he shall enter his name in the Register; but
  (b) if the Registrar is not so satisfied, he shall refer the application to the Board.
    (5) The Registrar shall not consider an application for registration in pursuance of this section in any case in which it is inappropriate for him to do so (for instance because he is in any way connected with the applicant) but in such a case he shall refer the application to the Board.
    (6) Where a person's application is referred to the Board under subsection (4) or (5), the Board shall direct the Registrar to enter the person's name in the Register if it is satisfied that he is entitled to be registered.

DEFINITIONS
  "Board, the": ss.25, 1(1), Sched.1, Pts. I, III and IV.
  "Register, the": s.3(1).
  "Registrar, the": s.2(1).
  "registered person": s.3(1).

GENERAL NOTE
    This section, by reproducing most of s.120(2) of the 1996 Act, deals specifically with the requirements for registration. An architect has the right to be registered, providing he holds such qualifications and practical experience as the ARB shall prescribe or has satisfied the ARB that he has achieved an equivalent standard of competence. The requirements for any examination or any alternative qualification will be set by the ARB after consultation with relevant

professional and educational bodies. In this context, the Board must consult the chartered bodies, that is to say the Royal Institute of British Architects and its equivalents in Scotland and Northern Ireland, but it may also consult such other professional and educational bodies as it thinks appropriate.

Other powers of the Registrar conferred by the 1996 Act are not removed. The Registrar is himself entitled to enter the applicant's name on the Register (s.4(4)(a)), if he is properly satisfied that the person is entitled to be registered but otherwise shall refer the application to the ARB (s.4(4)(b)). The Registrar must refer the application to the Board if in any case it is inappropriate for him to register the applicant himself and, although the Act gives the example of a case where the Registrar is in any way connected with the applicant (s.4(5)), this stricture would also seem to apply where the Registrar had special knowledge of the applicant which was relevant to the application.

Registration: EEA qualifications

5.—(1) A national of an EEA State who has applied to the Registrar in the prescribed manner for registration in pursuance of this section is entitled to be registered if he holds—

(a) a recognised EEA qualification;

(b) an established EEA qualification; or

(c) a relevant EEA certificate.

(2) A qualification is a recognised EEA qualification for the purposes of this section if it is required to be recognised under Article 2 of the Directive (recognition of qualifications satisfying the requirements of Articles 3 and 4 of the Directive which are included in a list published in the Official Journal in accordance with Article 7).

(3) A qualification is an established EEA qualification for the purposes of this section if it is required to be recognised under Article 10 or 14 of the Directive (recognition of established qualifications set out in Article 11 and certain equivalent qualifications).

(4) A certificate is a relevant EEA certificate for the purposes of this section if it is issued by a competent authority of an EEA State in accordance with Article 5 or 12 of the Directive and states—

(a) in the case of a certificate issued in accordance with Article 5 of the Directive, that the person concerned is, by reason of his distinguished achievements in the field of architecture, entitled to use the title of architect; or

(b) in the case of a certificate issued in accordance with Article 12 of the Directive, that the person concerned has been, no later than the date on which that State implemented the Directive, authorised in that State to use the title of architect and that he has pursued activities in the field of architecture effectively for at least three consecutive years during the five years preceding the issue of the certificate.

(5) A recognised EEA qualification or an established EEA qualification shall be accompanied by—

(a) a certificate issued by a competent authority of an EEA State, in accordance with Article 23(2) of the Directive, stating that the person concerned has gained at least two years' practical training experience in that State under the supervision of a person established as an architect in that State; or

(b) a certificate issued by a competent authority of the Federal Republic of Germany, in accordance with Article 4(1) of the Directive, stating that the person concerned has gained at least four years' appropriate professional experience in the Federal Republic of Germany.

(6) An application by a person for registration in pursuance of this section may be refused if there is a disqualifying decision in another EEA State in force in respect of that person.

(7) A person who is registered in pursuance of this section shall, when using his academic title or any abbreviation of it, express the title or abbreviation in the language or one of the languages of the EEA State in which the

body conferring the title is located and shall follow the title or abbreviation with the name and location of the body conferring the title.

Definitions
DEFINITIONS
"Registrar, the": s.2(1).
"recognised EEA qualification": s.5(1)(2).
"established EEA qualification": s.5(1)(3).
"relevant EEA certificate": s.5(4).
"Directive, the": s.5(2).

GENERAL NOTE
This section inserts a provision complying with the European Council Directive of June 10, 1985 which dealt with the mutual recognition of diplomas, certificates and other evidence of formal qualifications in architecture. This Directive was adopted in accordance with Art. 57 of the Treaty of Rome, which in particular provides that directives be issued for the mutual recognition of diplomas. The 1985 Directive provides that qualifications acquired in one of the Member States shall be recognised by other Member States on a mutual basis.

The problem of recognising European qualifications had previously been dealt with in an amendment to the 1931 Act, which inserted the Architects' Qualification (EEC) Recognition Order 1987, last modified in 1988. The 1996 Act did not repeal those provisions and the Act remained effective in its amended form. The 1997 Act has now repealed all these instruments and directly integrated the Directive into this Consolidation Act. In the process, the previous law has been broadened and whilst s.6 of the 1931 Act referred solely the case of those persons who being nationals held one of the qualifications listed in Sched. 4 of that Act, the new Act has introduced more general provisions which however remain closely related to the Directive.

A national of an EEA State is now entitled to be registered if he holds a recognised EEA qualification, an established EEA qualification or a relevant EEA certificate. Definitions of these qualifications and certificates are given by precise reference to provisions of the Directive (Arts. 3, 4, 10, 14).

Pursuant to Art. 23(2) of the Directive, the EEA qualifications must be certified by certificates issued by competent authority of the EEA States. As under the previous law (s.7A of the 1931 Act), a disqualification in any one of the EEA States remains a valid reason for refusing an application.

Section 5(7) provides that the recognised academic titles must be expressed in the language of the country in which they were conferred. A distinction must still be made between local and foreign titles.

Registration: further procedural requirements

6.—(1) The Board may require an applicant for registration in pursuance of section 4 or 5 to pay a fee of a prescribed amount.

(2) The Board may require a candidate for any examination under section 4(2) to pay a fee of a prescribed amount.

(3) The Board may prescribe the information and evidence to be provided to the Registrar in connection with an application for registration in pursuance of section 4 or 5.

(4) The Registrar shall serve on an applicant for registration in pursuance of section 4 or 5 written notice of the decision on his application—

(a) where the application is made on the ground that he satisfies section 4(1)(a) or in pursuance of section 5, within three months of his application being duly made; and

(b) where the application is made on the ground that he satisfies section 4(1)(b), within six months of his application being duly made.

(5) If, in pursuance of Article 17(4) or 18(2) of the Directive, the Board consults an EEA State in respect of an application for registration in pursuance of section 5, the period mentioned in subsection (4)(a) shall be extended by such period as may elapse between initiating the consultation and the receipt by the Board of a final reply from that State.

DEFINITIONS
"Board, the": ss.1(1), 25, Sched.1, Pts. I, III and IV.
"Register; the": s.3(1).

"Registrar, the": s.2(1).

Following s.120(2) of the 1996 Act, power is given to the ARB to require an applicant for registration or a candidate for any examination prescribed under s.4(2) of the Act to pay such fees as the ARB shall determine. Applicants for registration may be required to provide such information and evidence as the ARB may require in connection with the application for registration (s.6(1)(2)).

As provided by the 1996 Act, all decisions of the Registrar on applications should be made within three months of the application and shall be notified to the applicant, save where the applicant is not applying on the grounds of established qualifications and practical experience but on the grounds of an acceptable standard of competence, when the period shall be six months. This period can be extended if the Board consults an EEA State in respect of the application for registration of a national of another EEA state by such period as may elapse between the start of that consultation process and the receipt of a final reply. In practical terms, such an extension will last as long as there is enthusiasm on both sides to continue the consultation process. However, the delay concession is drafted with reference to Arts. 17(4) and 18(2) of the Directive and as these only refer to the case where a host Member State has detailed knowledge of a serious matter which has occurred outside its territory prior to the establishment of the person concerned in that state which is likely to affect the pursuit of the activity concerned in that state, the general progress of routine registration of EEA recognised architects will usually be complete within six months.

Penalty for obtaining registration by false representation

7.—(1) A person commits an offence if he intentionally becomes or attempts to become registered under this Act by making or producing, or causing to be made or produced, any false or fraudulent representation or declaration (whether oral or written).

(2) A person guilty of an offence under this section is liable on summary conviction to a fine not exceeding level 3 on the standard scale.

This section incorporates in the new Act and in more modern wording, the principles of s.12 of the 1931 Act, making it an offence punishable by a fine not exceeding Level 3 on the standard scale (currently £1,000) for any person intentionally to make or produce any false or fraudulent declaration whether oral or written in connection with an actual or attempted registration under the Act.

Removal from Register etc.

Retention of name in Register

8.—(1) The Board may require a registered person to pay a retention fee of a prescribed amount if he wishes his name to be retained in the Register in any calendar year after that in which it was entered.

(2) Where, after the Registrar has sent a registered person who is liable to pay a retention fee a written demand for the payment of the fee, the person fails to pay the fee within the prescribed period, the Registrar may remove the person's name from the Register.

(3) Where a person whose name has been removed from the Register under subsection (2) pays the retention fee, together with any further prescribed fee, before the end of the calendar year for which the retention fee is payable or such longer period as the Board may allow—

(a) his name shall be re-entered in the Register (without his having to make an application under section 4 or 5); and

(b) if the Board so directs, it shall be treated as having been re-entered on the date on which it was removed.

"Board, the": ss.1(1), 25, Sched.1, Pts. I, III and IV.
"registered person": s.4(1).

"retention fee": s.8(1).
"Register, the": s.3.
"Registrar, the": s.2.

<small>GENERAL NOTE</small>
Under this section, which repeats the first part of s.120(3) of the 1996 Act, a retention fee to be assessed by the Board may be annually charged to any registered person who wishes to retain his name on the Register. Provision is made for the removal of a registered person's name for failure to pay after a written demand has been sent by the Registrar (subs.(2)) and for reinstatement on the Register if subsequently, the defaulter pays the retention fee before the end of the relevant calendar year or such longer period as the Board may permit.

Competence to practise

9.—(1) Where the Board is not satisfied that a person who—
(a) applies for registration in pursuance of section 4 or 5;
(b) wishes his name to be retained or re-entered in the Register under section 8; or
(c) applies for his name to be re-entered in the Register under section 18, has gained such recent practical experience as the Board may prescribe, his name shall not be entered or re-entered in the Register, or shall be removed from it, unless he satisfies the Board of his competence to practise.

(2) Where the Board decides that the name of a person to whom paragraph (b) of subsection (1) applies is by virtue of that subsection to be removed from, or not to be re-entered in, the Register, the Registrar shall serve written notice of the decision on him within the prescribed period after the date of the decision.

<small>DEFINITIONS</small>
"Board; the": ss.1(1), 25, Sched.1, Pts. I, III and IV.
"Register; the": s.3.

<small>GENERAL NOTE</small>
This section follows the second part of s.120(3) of the 1996 Act and sets out the requirements for Registration when the Board is not satisfied that an applicant for Registration or indeed a person already registered, has had an adequate level of practical experience. The Board will have power to remove from the Register a person who has not maintained an adequate level of practical experience. This power is to be exercised by notice under subs.(2).

Disqualification in an EEA State

10.—(1) The Board may order the Registrar to remove a person's name from the Register if—
(a) it was entered in the Register in pursuance of section 5 at a time when there was a disqualifying decision in another EEA State in force in respect of the person;
(b) at that time the Board was unaware of that fact; and
(c) the Board is satisfied that the person was at that time and is still subject to that disqualifying decision.

(2) Where the Board orders the Registrar to remove a person's name from the Register under this section, the Registrar shall serve written notice of the removal on him as soon as is reasonably practicable.

<small>DEFINITIONS</small>
"Board; the": ss.1(2), 25, Sched.1, Pts. I, III and IV.
"Register; the": s.3.
"Registrar of Architects": s.2.

<small>GENERAL NOTE</small>
This section follows s.7A(1) of the 1931 Act and confirms that a national of an EEA state who may have applied for registration under s.5 may be removed from the Register in any case where a disqualifying decision has been made in respect in another EEA state, unless of course the

Board was aware of that decision at the time of registration. The Board must also be satisfied (subs.(2)) that both at the time of registration and at the date of intended removal, he remained subject to the disqualifying decision.

A new provision states that such a decision of removal from the Register or a refusal to re-enter a name in the Register must be served by written notice to the foreign national.

Failure to notify change of address

11. Where the Registrar serves notice in writing on a registered person asking if he has changed his regular business address—

(a) if no answer is received within six months from the sending of the notice, the Registrar shall serve further written notice on him; and

(b) if no answer is received within three months from the sending of the further notice, the Registrar may remove his name from the Register.

DEFINITIONS
"Register, the": s.3.
"Registrar of Architects": s.2.

GENERAL NOTE
This section follows s.11 of the 1931 Act and requires the architects to respond to written notices they may receive from the Registrar under this section requesting whether they have changed their regular business address. Failure to respond to such notices (after six months a second notice shall be served requesting a response within three months) will enable the Registrar to remove the name from the Register.

List of visiting EEA architects

Visiting EEA architects

12.—(1) The Registrar shall maintain, in addition to the Register, a list of visiting EEA architects and shall permit any person to inspect it during normal working hours.

(2) The list of visiting EEA architects shall show the name and qualifications of each person enrolled on it and the period or periods for which and services in respect of which each enrolment is effective.

(3) A national of an EEA State established as an architect in an EEA State other than the United Kingdom who has applied to the Registrar in the manner specified in subsection (4) is entitled to be enrolled on the list of visiting EEA architects.

(4) An application is made by supplying—

(a) a declaration in writing giving particulars of the services to be provided by the person while visiting the United Kingdom and the period or periods for which he expects to provide them; and

(b) a certificate (or certificates) issued not more than twelve months previously by the competent authority of an EEA State in which he is established as an architect showing that he is lawfully pursuing activities in the field of architecture in an EEA State other than the United Kingdom and holds a qualification or certificate specified in section 5(1).

(5) Enrolment on the list of visiting EEA architects shall be for such period or periods and in respect of such services as the Registrar considers appropriate having regard to the particulars given in the declaration made under subsection (4)(a).

(6) No fee shall be charged for enrolment on the list of visiting EEA architects.

(7) A person shall not be enrolled on the list of visiting EEA architects at a time when—

(a) he is subject to a disqualifying decision in another EEA State;

(b) he is required under section 9(1) to satisfy the Board of his competence to practise but has not done so; or

(c) his name has been removed from the Register because of a suspension order or an erasure order and has not been re-entered.

(8) A person's name shall be removed from the list of visiting EEA architects if—

(a) he becomes established as an architect in the United Kingdom;

(b) he renders services in the United Kingdom otherwise than in accordance with a declaration supplied by him under subsection (4)(a); or

(c) he may no longer lawfully pursue activities in the field of architecture in the EEA State in which the certificate supplied under subsection (4)(b) showed he was lawfully pursuing such activities.

(9) A person enrolled on the list of visiting EEA architects shall, when using his title or any abbreviation of it, express the title or abbreviation in the language or one of the languages of the EEA State in which the body conferring the title is located and shall follow the title or abbreviation with the name and location of the body conferring the title.

DEFINITIONS

"Register, the": s.3.
"Registrar of Architects": s.2.
"qualifications": s.5(1)(2)(3).
"certificates": s.5(1)(4).

GENERAL NOTE

This section maintains the obligation upon the Registrar to keep a list of visiting EEA architects originally inserted as s.1A in the 1938 Act by the Architect's Qualifications (EEC Recognition) Order 1987.

This list is to be open for inspection by any person during normal working hours. Inclusion on the list primarily concerns those EEA architects (who must also be EEA nationals) who may be visiting the U.K. to carry out specific services for specific periods of time (subs. 4(a)) under their foreign title (s.12(9)).

As the entitlement to be enrolled (there is no fee (subs.(6)) is only for such periods and in respect of such services as the Registrar considers appropriate, given the terms of the application provided by the applicant, it is unlikely to permit an EEA architect to practice in the U.K. for long without formal registration. A certificate issued not more than 12 months previously by a competent authority in the concerned EEA State must also be provided (s.12(4)(b)).

Of course, enrolment on the list remains subject to there being no disqualifying decision in another member state and to proof of competence. Removal from the list is automatic (subs.(8) (a)) once an architect becomes a registered architect in the U.K. under the Act.

PART III

DISCIPLINE

Professional standards

Code of practice

13.—(1) The Board shall issue a code laying down standards of professional conduct and practice expected of registered persons.

(2) The Board shall keep the code under review and vary its provisions whenever it considers it appropriate to do so.

(3) Before issuing or varying the code, the Board shall—

(a) consult such professional bodies and such other persons with an interest in architecture as it considers appropriate; and

(b) publish in such manner as it considers appropriate notice that it proposes to issue or vary the code, stating where copies of the proposals can be obtained.

(4) Failure by a registered person to comply with the provisions of the code—

(a) shall not be taken of itself to constitute unacceptable professional conduct or serious professional incompetence on his part; but

(b) shall be taken into account in any proceedings against him under section 14.

(5) The Board shall provide a copy of the code to any person who requests one on payment of a reasonable charge decided by the Board (and may provide a copy free of charge whenever it considers appropriate).

DEFINITIONS
   "Board, the": s.1(2), Sched.1, Pts. I, III, IV.
   "registered person": s.1(2), Sched.1, Pts. I, III, IV.

GENERAL NOTE
   This section re-enacts s.122 of the 1996 Act, which created a new statutory obligation upon the ARB to lay down a code of professional conduct and practice setting the standards to be expected of registered persons. The code will be kept under continuous review and will be produced after consultation with such professional bodies and such other persons with an interest in architecture as it considers appropriate (subs.(3)). The object of the code appears to be to establish a general standard which the public can expect architects to observe and to provide guidelines by which registered persons may avoid committing unacceptable acts which may lead to disciplinary proceedings under s.15. Copies of the code will be available upon request to the ARB.

Professional misconduct and incompetence

14.—(1) Where an allegation is made that a registered person is guilty of—
   (a) unacceptable professional conduct (that is, conduct which falls short of the standard required of a registered person); or
   (b) serious professional incompetence,
or it appears to the Registrar that a registered person may be so guilty, the case shall be investigated by persons appointed in accordance with rules made by the Board.

(2) Where persons investigating a case under subsection (1) find that a registered person has a case to answer, they shall report their findings to the Professional Conduct Committee.

(3) Where the Professional Conduct Committee receives a report under subsection (2) in relation to a registered person, the Committee shall consider whether he is guilty of unacceptable professional conduct or serious professional incompetence.

(4) Before considering whether a registered person is guilty of unacceptable professional conduct or serious professional incompetence the Professional Conduct Committee shall—
   (a) serve written notice on him outlining the case against him; and
   (b) give him the opportunity to appear before the Committee to argue his case.

(5) At any such hearing the registered person is entitled to be legally represented.

(6) The Board may make rules as to the procedure to be followed by the Professional Conduct Committee in any proceedings under this section.

(7) If the Board does not make rules for the appointment of persons to investigate whether registered persons have been guilty of unacceptable professional conduct or serious professional incompetence, the Professional Conduct Committee shall consider such questions without any prior investigation.

DEFINITIONS
   "Board, the": s.1(2), Sched.1, Pts. I, III, IV.
   "Professional Conduct Committee": s.1(2), (4), Sched.1, Pt. II.
   "the Registrar of Architects": s.2.
   "registered person": s.4(1).

GENERAL NOTE
This section re-enacts s.121 of the 1996 Act (in turn replacing s.7 of the 1931 Act). The powers and obligations of the 1996 Professional Conduct Committee are much more extensive than those of the old Discipline Committee set up under the 1931 Act.

Whereas the 1931 Act as originally amended, provided that a registered person was liable to be removed from the Register if he had been guilty of a criminal offence or of disgraceful conduct, the new provisions in this section define the basis for disciplinary action as either any "unacceptable professional conduct" or "serious professional incompetence".

The provision in old s.7 of the 1931 Act which subjected a registered person to removal from the Register if he had been convicted of any criminal offence is modified. Only those criminal offences which have a material relevance to his fitness to practise as an architect will now be taken into account (s.15(1)(b)). Concern that professional incompetence alone might lead to some Architects being unjustly penalised, led to a late amendment to the 1996 Act (preserved by the 1997 Act) requiring that the professional incompetence must be serious. Judicial interpretation of this word may initially give rise to problems, since it is likely to be wholly a matter for subjective assessment and therefore variable judicial opinion until some legal precedent is set.

As provided by the 1996 Act, the Registrar of Architects is of his own volition entitled to refer a registered person for investigation (subs.(1)) and, if it is found that a registered Architect has a case to answer, the Professional Conduct Committee must consider the issue. It should be noted that as in 1996, subs.(3) requires the Professional Conduct Committee to consider any case where there has been an allegation of either of the two kinds of offences and, since the Committee has no option but to pursue the matter, this may well lead to an increase in its administrative activities and may impair its efficiency.

Disciplinary orders

Disciplinary orders

15.—(1) The Professional Conduct Committee may make a disciplinary order in relation to a registered person if—

    (a) it is satisfied, after considering his case, that he is guilty of unacceptable professional conduct or serious professional incompetence; or

    (b) he has been convicted of a criminal offence other than an offence which has no material relevance to his fitness to practise as an architect.

(2) In this Act "disciplinary order" means—

    (a) a reprimand;

    (b) a penalty order;

    (c) a suspension order; or

    (d) an erasure order.

(3) Where the Professional Conduct Committee makes a disciplinary order in relation to a person, the Registrar shall serve written notice of the order on him as soon as is reasonably practicable.

(4) The Professional Conduct Committee shall, at appropriate intervals and in such manner as it considers appropriate, publish—

    (a) the names of persons whom it has found guilty of unacceptable professional conduct or serious professional incompetence or in relation to whom it has made a disciplinary order under subsection (1)(b); and

    (b) in the case of each person a description of the conduct, incompetence or offence concerned and the nature of any disciplinary order made.

(5) Where, after considering the case of a registered person, the Professional Conduct Committee is not satisfied that he is guilty of unacceptable professional conduct or serious professional incompetence, it shall, if he so requests, publish a statement of that fact in such manner as it considers appropriate.

(6) If a person who is registered in pursuance of section 5 becomes subject to a disqualifying decision in another EEA State expressed to be made on the ground that he has committed a criminal offence, he shall be deemed for the purposes of subsection (1) to have been convicted of that offence.

Penalty orders

16.—(1) Where a penalty order is made in relation to a registered person, he shall pay to the Board the sum specified in the order.

(2) A penalty order may not specify a sum exceeding the amount which, at the relevant time, is the amount specified as level 4 on the standard scale of fines for summary offences.

In this subsection "the relevant time" means—

(a) in a case within subsection (1)(a) of section 15, the time of the conduct or incompetence of which the registered person is found guilty; and

(b) in a case within subsection (1)(b) of that section, the time when he committed the criminal offence of which he has been convicted.

(3) A penalty order shall specify the period within which the sum specified in it is to be paid.

(4) If the person in relation to whom a penalty order is made does not pay the sum specified in the order within the period so specified, the Professional Conduct Committee may make a suspension order or an erasure order in relation to him.

(5) The Board shall pay into the Consolidated Fund any sum paid under a penalty order.

Suspension orders

17. Where a suspension order is made in relation to a registered person, the Registrar shall remove his name from the Register but shall re-enter it in the Register at the end of such period not exceeding two years as is specified in the order.

Erasure orders

18.—(1) Where an erasure order is made in relation to a registered person, the Registrar shall remove his name from the Register and it shall not be re-entered in the Register unless the Board so directs.

(2) No application shall be made for the name of a person in relation to whom an erasure order has been made to be re-entered in the Register—

(a) before the end of the period of two years beginning with the date of the erasure order or such longer period specified in the erasure order as the Professional Conduct Committee considers appropriate in a particular case; or

(b) where he has made a previous application for his name to be re-entered in the Register, before the end of the prescribed period beginning with the date of the decision of the Board on that application.

(3) The Registrar shall serve on a person who applies for his name to be re-entered in the Register under this section written notice of the decision on his application within the prescribed period after the date of the decision.

(4) The Board may require a person whose name is re-entered in the Register under this section to pay a fee of a prescribed amount.

DEFINITIONS
"disciplinary order": s.15(2).
"Professional Conduct Committee": s.1(4), Sched.1, Pt. II.
"registered person": s.4(1).
"Registrar; the": s.2.
"relevant time; the": s.16(2).

GENERAL NOTE
The 1996 Act gave the Professional Conduct Committee a wide range of penalties which it could impose once satisfied that a registered person was guilty of the offences now defined by s.14 of the Act. These are preserved by ss.15, 16, 17 and 18 of the 1997 Act. Whereas previously the only option was the removal from the Register of a registered person, the Professional Conduct Committee now has discretionary power to make a disciplinary order (s.15(2)) which may

be either a reprimand or it may impose financial penalties (s.16) or it may impose suspension (s.17) or erasure from the Register of Architects (s.18). The period of suspension which may be imposed by the Professional Conduct Committee may not exceed a period of two years, after which the Registrar must reinstate the architect (s.17), whereas the previous legislation provided only that any period of disqualification from registration was discretionary. In common with similar procedures for other professions, the Professional Conduct Committee is also entitled to publish the names of persons against whom it has been made a disciplinary order (s.15(4)), together with a description of the person's conduct giving rise to the offence and the nature of the disciplinary order that may be made. If a person is not found guilty of a disciplinary offence, he may require a statement to be published to that purpose (s.15(5)).

Visiting EEA architects

Application of discipline provisions to visiting EEA architects

19. The provisions of, and of rules under, this Act relating to disciplinary proceedings shall apply to a person who is or has been enrolled on the list of visiting EEA architects as if that person had been registered in pursuance of section 4; and references in those provisions to the Register shall be construed accordingly.

DEFINITIONS
 "list of visiting architects": s.12.
 "disciplinary proceedings": ss.15 to 18.

GENERAL NOTE
 This section makes the powers to apply disciplinary proceedings against registered persons also fully applicable to the EEA nationals enrolled on the list of visiting architects created by s.12. As a result, any foreign architect carrying on temporary business in the U.K. will be subject to the same discipline of the Professional Conduct Committee if he behaves with "unacceptable professional conduct" or displays "serious professional incompetence".

PART IV

USE OF TITLE "ARCHITECT"

Use of title "architect"

20.—(1) A person shall not practise or carry on business under any name, style or title containing the word "architect" unless he is a person registered under this Act.

(2) Subsection (1) does not prevent any use of the designation "naval architect", "landscape architect" or "golf-course architect".

(3) Subsection (1) does not prevent a body corporate, firm or partnership from carrying on business under a name, style or title containing the word "architect" if—

(a) the business of the body corporate, firm or partnership so far as it relates to architecture is under the control and management of a registered person who does not act at the same time in a similar capacity for any other body corporate, firm or partnership; and

(b) in all premises where its business relating to architecture is carried on it is carried on by or under the supervision of a registered person.

(4) The Board may by rules provide that subsection (3) shall not apply in relation to a body corporate, firm or partnership unless it has provided to the Board such information necessary for determining whether that subsection applies as may be prescribed.

(5) A person enrolled on the list of visiting EEA architects may practise or carry on business under a name, style or title containing the word "architect" while visiting the United Kingdom without being a person registered under this Act during the period, and in respect of the services, for which his enrolment is effective.

(6) For the purposes of this section a person is not treated as not practising by reason only of his being in the employment of another person.

(7) In this section "business" includes any undertaking which is carried on for gain or reward or in the course of which services are provided otherwise than free of charge.

(8) Nothing in this section affects the validity of any building contract in customary form.

DEFINITIONS
    "architect": s.20(1).
    "Board, the": s.1(2), Sched.1, Pts. I, III, IV.
    "list of visiting EEA architects": s.12.
    "registered person": s.4(1).

GENERAL NOTE
    This section re-enacts the offence of practising while not registered, which was introduced by s.1 of the 1938 Act.

    The 1996 Act provided that the offence arises when an attempt is made to practise or carry on the business of an architect under any name, style or title containing the word "architect". In consequence, since any person using the title "architect" has to be registered, it was thought that the general public should not be misled by those who might seek to offer themselves as architects in any commercial venture or in any undertaking where architectural services are not free but are provided for a consideration. It would appear that a mere reference to holding professional qualifications such as FRIBA or RIBA does not necessarily infringe these provisions providing there is no specific holding out of a willingness to practise the profession of architect.

    As under s.1 of the 1938 Act it will not be considered an offence to use the designations "Naval Architect", "Landscape architect", "Golf-course architect" and the provision does not prevent a body corporate, firm, or partnership from carrying on a business under a name containing the word "architect" if the business is under the control and management of a registered person, or is under the supervision of a registered person.

    In accordance with the 1985 Council Directive, EEA architects must also be able to use their title or any abbreviation of it in the language of the EEA country where the title was conferred (s.12(9)). Subsection (5) therefore provides that the persons enrolled on the list of visiting EEA architects may practise under a name containing the word "architect" without being registered.

    The Act also clearly states that any person practising in the employment of another person is subject to this provision (subs. (6)).

Offence

21.—(1) If any person contravenes section 20(1) he commits an offence and is liable on summary conviction to a fine not exceeding level 4 on the standard scale.

(2) A person is not guilty of an offence by reason of contravening section 20(1) on any particular date if—

    (a) the contravention is occasioned by the fact that an application on his part for registration under this Act has not been granted; and

    (b) notice of the decision not to grant the application had not been duly served under this Act before that date.

(3) A person is not guilty of an offence by reason of contravening section 20(1) on any particular date if the contravention is occasioned by the removal of his name from the Register in circumstances in which notice is required to be served on him and—

    (a) the notice had not been duly served before that date;

    (b) the time for bringing an appeal against the removal had not expired at that date; or

    (c) such an appeal had been duly brought, but had not been determined, before that date.

(4) In relation to an offence under subsection (1)—

    (a) section 127(1) of the Magistrates' Courts Act 1980 (information to be laid within six months of offence);

    (b) Article 19(1) of the Magistrates' Courts (Northern Ireland) Order 1981 (complaint to be made within that time); and

   (c) section 136(1) of the Criminal Procedure (Scotland) Act 1995 (pro-
      ceedings to be commenced within that time),
shall have effect as if for the references in them to six months there were
substituted references to two years.

   The maximum penalty for practising whilst not registered is now also applicable in Northern
Ireland upon the same basis as for the rest of the U.K. The maximum penalty is a fine not exceeding Level 4 on the standard scale (currently £2,500, s.143 of the Magistrates' Courts Act 1980
(c.43) as amended).
   The Act introduces certain situations when contravention of s.20 is not to be considered an
offence. These are cases where the Registrar has not served proper notice that a registration has
not been granted or that a name has been removed from the Register, or that the time allowed
for bringing an appeal from such removal had not expired.

PART V

GENERAL AND SUPPLEMENTARY

General

Appeals
   22. Any person aggrieved by—
     (a) his name not being re-entered in, or being removed from, the Register
        by virtue of section 9;
     (b) the Board ordering the Registrar to remove his name from the Regis-
        ter under section 10; or
     (c) the making of a disciplinary order in relation to him,
may appeal to the High Court or the Court of Session within three months
from the date on which notice of the decision or order concerned is served on
him; and on an appeal under this section the Court may make any order
which appears appropriate, and no appeal shall lie from any decision of the
Court on such an appeal.

   This section sets out detailed provisions regarding the appeal proceedings from decisions of
the Registrar and Professional Conduct Committee. A similar appeals procedure was in place
under the 1931 Act in the case of a removal from the register or disqualification. The procedure
is now extended towards all disciplinary orders. The appeal must be made within three months
from the date on which notice of the decision or order concerned is served on the person.

Rules
   23.—(1) The Board may make rules generally for carrying out or facilitating the purposes of this Act.
   (2) The Board shall, before making any rules under this Act, publish a
draft of the rules and give those to whom the rules would be applicable an
opportunity of making representations to the Board.
   (3) The Registrar shall on payment of the prescribed charges supply a copy
of any rules made under this Act and of any forms prescribed by such rules to
any person applying for them.

   "Board; the": s.1(2), Sched.1, Pts. I, III, IV.

   This section sets out details of the way in which rules may be drafted by the ARB. The ARB
must first publish a draft of any rules and give people concerned by the rules a chance to make
representations to the ARB. Any person may apply for a copy of rules enacted by the ARB. The
provision has obviously been incorporated to protect the interests of architects who no longer
constitute the majority of the ARB and it would seem likely to create a better balance between
the interests of architects and those of both the consumer and the public.

Service of documents

24.—(1) Any notice or document required to be served by or for the purposes of this Act may be sent by post, and when sent to any registered person shall be deemed to be properly addressed if addressed to him at his address in the Register.

(2) Any notice relating to the refusal to register any person or required to be served by section 9(2), 10(2), 11(a), 14(4)(a) or 15(3) shall be sent by post as a registered letter.

GENERAL NOTE

This section concerns the service of documents. Documents are usually required to be sent by post. Registered post is required for notice of refusal of admission to the Register.

The documents must be sent to the last current address indicated in the Register and notices to registered architects will be regularly sent by the Registrar to obtain confirmation as to whether there has been a change of address (s.11).

Supplementary

Interpretation

25. In this Act—
"the Board" means the Architects Registration Board;
"competent authority", in relation to an EEA State, means an authority or body designated by the State in accordance with the Directive;
"the Directive" means Council Directive 85/384/EEC on the mutual recognition of diplomas, certificates and other evidence of formal qualifications in architecture, as amended;
"disciplinary order" has the meaning given by section 15;
"disqualifying decision in another EEA State", in relation to any person, means a decision made by a competent authority of an EEA State other than the United Kingdom which—
    (a) is expressed to be made on the ground that he has committed a criminal offence or has misconducted himself in a professional respect; and
    (b) has the effect in that State that he is no longer registered or otherwise officially recognised as an architect or that he is prohibited from practising as an architect there;
"EEA State" means any State which is a Contracting Party to the Agreement on the European Economic Area signed at Oporto on 2nd May 1992, as adjusted by the Protocol signed at Brussels on 17th March 1993;
"erasure order" shall be construed in accordance with section 18;
"list of visiting EEA architects" means the list maintained under section 12;
"national" does not include a person who, by virtue of Article 2 of Protocol No. 3 (Channel Islands and Isle of Man) to the Treaty of Accession, is not to benefit from Community provisions relating to the free movement of persons and services;
"penalty order" shall be construed in accordance with section 16;
"prescribed" means prescribed by rules made by the Board and "prescribe" means prescribe by rules;
"the Register" means the Register of Architects;
"registered person" means a person whose name is in the Register;
"the Registrar" means the Registrar of Architects;
"suspension order" shall be construed in accordance with section 17; and
"unacceptable professional conduct" has the meaning given by section 14.

Consequential amendments

26. In—

(a) section 6 of the Inspection of Churches Measure 1955, in the definition of "qualified person";

(b) section 52(1) of the Cathedrals Measure 1963, in the definition of "architect"; and

(c) section 20(1) of the Care of Cathedrals Measure 1990, in the definition of "architect",

for "Architects Acts 1931 to 1996" substitute "Architects Act 1997".

Transitionals, repeals etc.

27. Schedule 2 (transitional provisions and savings) and Schedule 3 (repeals and revocations) have effect.

Short title, commencement and extent

28.—(1) This Act may be cited as the Architects Act 1997.

(2) This Act (apart from this section) shall come into force on such day as the Secretary of State may by order made by statutory instrument appoint.

(3) This Act extends to Northern Ireland.

SCHEDULES

Section 1

SCHEDULE 1

THE BOARD AND ITS COMMITTEES

PART I

THE BOARD

Membership

1. The Board shall consist of—

(a) seven elected members; and

(b) eight appointed members.

Elected members

2.—(1) The elected members shall be elected in accordance with an electoral scheme made by the Board, with the approval of the Privy Council, after consultation with such bodies as appear to the Board to be representative of architects.

(2) An electoral scheme under sub-paragraph (1) may be amended by the Board with the approval of the Privy Council and after consultation with such bodies as are mentioned in that sub-paragraph.

(3) The persons qualified—

(a) to elect the elected members; and

(b) to be elected as elected members,

are all those who are registered persons when the election is held.

Appointed members

3.—(1) The appointed members shall be appointed by the Privy Council, after consultation with the Secretary of State and such other persons or bodies as the Privy Council thinks fit, to represent the interests of users of architectural services and the general public.

(2) No registered person shall be eligible for appointment as an appointed member.

Term of office

4.—(1) Subject to sub-paragraphs (2) and (3), the term of office of a member of the Board is three years.

(2) A member may resign at any time by notice in writing addressed to the Registrar.

(3) The Board may prescribe grounds (such as repeated absence from meetings or unacceptable professional conduct) on which any member may be removed from office and the procedure for removal.

5. A person who has held office as a member of the Board for a continuous period of six years may not be elected or appointed as a member until at least three years have elapsed since he last held office.

Casual vacancies

6.—(1) Where a vacancy occurs among the members of the Board otherwise than by the expiry of a member's term of office—

    (a) if the vacancy is among the elected members, the Board shall appoint a registered person to fill it; and

    (b) if the vacancy is among the appointed members, the Privy Council shall appoint a person to fill it.

(2) Subject to paragraph 4(2) and (3), a person appointed under sub-paragraph (1) to fill a vacancy holds office until the date on which the term of office of the member whose vacancy he fills would have expired.

(3) A person appointed under sub-paragraph (1)(a) shall be regarded as an elected member and a person appointed under sub-paragraph (1)(b) shall be regarded as an appointed member.

Chairman

7.—(1) The members of the Board shall elect a chairman from among themselves.

(2) The chairman—

    (a) may resign by notice in writing addressed to the Registrar; and

    (b) may be removed by a majority vote of the other members of the Board.

(3) Rules made by the Board may make provision for the appointment of a person to act as chairman in the event of a vacancy in the office of chairman or in such other circumstances as may be prescribed.

8. In the event of a tie in any vote of the Board the chairman shall have an additional casting vote.

Procedure

9. The quorum of the Board shall be nine, of whom at least four shall be elected members and at least four shall be appointed members.

10. The Board may make rules governing its meetings and procedure.

Staff

11.—(1) The Board may appoint staff.

(2) The Board shall determine the period for which, and the terms on which, its staff are appointed.

(3) Staff appointed by the Board shall have the duties which the Board directs.

(4) The Board may, in addition to paying salaries to its staff, pay pensions to or in respect of them, or make contributions to the payment of such pensions, and pay them allowances, expenses and gratuities.

Seal

12. The Board shall have a common seal which shall be authenticated in the prescribed manner; and any document purporting to be sealed with the seal authenticated in that manner shall be receivable as evidence of the particulars stated in it.

PART II

THE PROFESSIONAL CONDUCT COMMITTEE

13. The Professional Conduct Committee shall consist of—

    (a) four elected members of the Board, including at least one whose address in the Register is in Scotland, or (if there is no elected member whose address in the Register is in Scotland or no such elected member who is willing to act) three elected members and one registered person whose address in the Register is in Scotland;

    (b) three appointed members of the Board; and

    (c) two persons nominated by the President of the Law Society.

14.—(1) The members of the Professional Conduct Committee shall elect a chairman from among themselves.

(2) The chairman—

(a) may resign by notice in writing addressed to the Registrar; and

(b) may be removed by a majority vote of the other members of the Professional Conduct Committee.

(3) Rules made by the Board may make provision for the appointment of a person to act as chairman in the event of a vacancy in the office of chairman or in such other circumstances as may be prescribed.

15.—(1) The quorum of the Professional Conduct Committee shall be one elected member of the Board, one appointed member of the Board and one person nominated by the President of the Law Society.

(2) Where the Committee is considering the case of a person whose address in the Register is in Scotland, the Committee is not quorate unless there is present a member of the Committee who is a registered person and whose address in the Register is in Scotland.

16. In the event of a tie in any vote of the Professional Conduct Committee the chairman shall have an additional casting vote; and in any proceedings relating to a registered person the additional vote shall be cast in favour of that person.

17. The Board may make rules governing the selection and term of office of members of the Professional Conduct Committee (including casual vacancies).

Part III

Other committees

18.—(1) The Board may establish such committees as it considers appropriate—

(a) to discharge any of its functions under this Act other than those to which sub-paragraph (2) applies; or

(b) to assist the Board in the discharge by the Board of any of its functions.

(2) This sub-paragraph applies to the following functions—

(a) prescribing fees under section 6(1) or (2), 8(1) or (3) or 18(4); and

(b) acting under section 4(1) or (2), 5(1), 6(3), 9(1) or 13(1), (2) or (3).

19.—(1) Any committee established by the Board may include persons who are not members of the Board; but if a committee is established to discharge any function of the Board, the majority of the members of the committee must be members of the Board.

(2) Subject to that, the membership of any committee established by the Board shall be determined by the Board.

20. No vote of any committee established by the Board for the discharge of any of its functions shall be valid unless the majority of those voting are members of the Board.

21. The Board may make rules governing the term of office of members of any committee established by the Board (including casual vacancies) and the meetings and procedure (including chairmanship and quorum) of any committee established by the Board.

Part IV

General

22.—(1) The Board, the Professional Conduct Committee and any committee established by the Board may exercise its functions even though there is a vacancy among its members.

(2) No proceedings of the Board, the Professional Conduct Committee or any committee established by the Board are invalidated by any defect in the election or appointment of a member.

23. The Board may by rules provide for the payment to members of the Board, the Professional Conduct Committee or any committee established by the Board of—

(a) fees for attendance at meetings of the Board or committee; and

(b) travelling and subsistence allowances in respect of attendance at such meetings or the conduct of business of the Board or committee.

24.—(1) The Secretary of State may, after consultation with the Board and such other persons or bodies as he thinks fit, by order amend the provisions of this Schedule.

(2) An order under sub-paragraph (1) shall be made by statutory instrument which shall be subject to annulment in pursuance of a resolution of either House of Parliament.

Section 27   SCHEDULE 2

Transitional provisions and savings

General transitionals and savings

1. The substitution of this Act for the provisions repealed or revoked by this Act does not affect the continuity of the law.

2. Anything done, or having effect as if done, (including the making of rules) under or for the purposes of any provision repealed or revoked by this Act has effect as if done under or for the purposes of any corresponding provision of this Act.

3. Any reference (express or implied) in this Act or any other enactment, or in any instrument or document, to a provision of this Act is (so far as the context permits) to be read as (according to the context) being or including in relation to times, circumstances and purposes before this Act comes into force a reference to the corresponding provision repealed or revoked by this Act.

4.—(1) Any reference (express or implied) in any enactment, or in any instrument or document, to a provision repealed or revoked by this Act is (so far as the context permits) to be read as (according to the context) being or including in relation to times, circumstances and purposes after this Act comes into force a reference to the corresponding provision of this Act.

(2) In particular, where a power conferred by an Act is expressed to be exercisable in relation to enactments contained in an Act passed before or in the same Session as the Act conferring the power, the power is also exercisable in relation to provisions of this Act which reproduce such enactments.

5. Paragraphs 1 to 4 have effect in place of section 17(2) of the Interpretation Act 1978 (but are without prejudice to any other provision of that Act).

First appointments to the Board

6. The term of office of the members of the Board who were appointed by the Privy Council to take office on the day on which Part III of the 1996 Act came into force (and who remain members of the Board when this Act comes into force)—

 (a) is one year beginning with that day in the case of three of those members;
 (b) is two years beginning with that day in the case of another three of those members; and
 (c) is three years beginning with that day in the case of the remaining two members.

Registration

7. If—
 (a) a person duly applied for registration under the 1931 Act before Part III of the 1996 Act came into force; but
 (b) no decision on the application has been made before this Act comes into force,
the application shall be dealt with in the same way as an application duly made after this Act comes into force (except that no further fee may be required to be paid).

8. Examinations in architecture which immediately before the day on which Part III of the 1996 Act came into force were recognised by the Council for the purposes of section 6(1)(c) of the 1931 Act (as it had effect before Part III of the 1996 Act came into force) shall (subject to rules made by the Board) be treated as qualifications prescribed under section 4(1)(a).

9. The reference in subsection (3) of section 8 to a person whose name has been removed from the Register under subsection (2) of that section shall be treated as including a reference to a person whose name was removed from the Register under section 13(5) of the 1931 Act before Part III of the 1996 Act came into force.

10. The reference to the Board in section 10(1)(b) shall be construed, in relation to the entry of a name in the Register before Part III of the 1996 Act came into force, as a reference to the Council.

Discipline

11. If—
 (a) before Part III of the 1996 Act came into force, the Discipline Committee began an inquiry into any case in which it was alleged that a registered person had been guilty of conduct disgraceful to him in his capacity as an architect; but
 (b) the case has not been decided or referred to the Professional Conduct Committee before this Act comes into force,
the case shall be referred to the Professional Conduct Committee which shall consider whether he is guilty of unacceptable professional conduct or serious professional incompetence.

12.—(1) Subject to sub-paragraph (2), sections 14 to 18 have effect in relation to anything done or omitted to be done before this Act comes into force (including anything done before Part III of the 1996 Act came into force) as in relation to anything done or omitted to be done after this Act comes into force.

(2) The Professional Conduct Committee—
 (a) may only make a disciplinary order in respect of anything done or omitted to be done by a person before Part III of the 1996 Act came into force if the Council could have removed his name from the Register under section 7 of the 1931 Act (as it had effect before Part III of the 1996 Act came into force); and

(b) may not make a reprimand or penalty order in respect of anything done or omitted to be done before Part III of the 1996 Act came into force.

13.—(1) If a person's name was removed from the Register under section 7 of the 1931 Act before Part III of the 1996 Act came into force, he may at any time apply to the Board for his name to be re-entered in the Register.

(2) If he does so, the Board may direct that his name shall be re-entered in the Register.

(3) The Registrar shall serve on a person who applies for his name to be re-entered in the Register under this paragraph written notice of the decision on his application within the prescribed period after the date of the decision.

(4) The Board may require a person whose name is re-entered in the Register under this paragraph to pay a fee of such amount, not exceeding the fee then payable by an applicant for registration in pursuance of section 4, as may be prescribed.

14. If—

(a) a person's name was removed from the Register, or the Council determined that a person be disqualified for registration during any period, before Part III of the 1996 Act came into force; and

(b) the period of three months from the date on which notice of the removal or determination was served on him has not ended before this Act comes into force,

he may appeal under section 22 against the removal or determination at any time before the end of that period.

15. Section 12(7)(c) shall have effect as if it included a reference to a period of disqualification imposed by the Council.

Offence of practising while not registered

16. The repeal by this Act of Schedule 2 to the 1996 Act does not affect the continued operation of paragraphs 31 and 32 of that Schedule in relation to an offence committed before Part III of the 1996 Act came into force.

The Education Fund

17.—(1) This paragraph applies if when this Act comes into force the assets of the Architects' Registration Council Education Fund have not been transferred by the Board.

(2) The Board may transfer the assets of the Fund to such person and on such terms as may be approved by the Secretary of State.

(3) The repeal by the 1996 Act of sections 1(1) and (4) to (6), 3 and 4 of the 1969 Act shall not come into force until the transfer is made; and until the transfer references in those provisions to the Council shall have effect as references to the Board.

18. A person to whom the assets of the Fund are transferred (whether under section 124 of the 1996 Act or paragraph 17) shall apply the assets, and all income arising from the assets, for the purposes authorised in subsection (4) of section 1 of the 1969 Act (assuming for this purpose that the reference in that subsection to the Council were a reference to the person to whom the assets of the Fund are transferred).

19.—(1) In this Schedule—

(a) "the 1931 Act" means the Architects (Registration) Act 1931;

(b) "the 1969 Act" means the Architects Registration (Amendment) Act 1969; and

(c) "the 1996 Act" means the Housing Grants, Construction and Regeneration Act 1996.

(2) In this Schedule—

(a) "the Council" means the Architects' Registration Council of the United Kingdom established under the 1931 Act, which was renamed as the Board by section 118(1) of the 1996 Act; and

(b) "the Discipline Committee" means the Discipline Committee constituted under the 1931 Act, which was abolished by section 118(2) of the 1996 Act.

SCHEDULE 3

REPEALS AND REVOCATIONS

Chapter or number	Short title or title	Extent of repeal or revocation
21 & 22 Geo. 5 c. 33.	The Architects (Registration) Act 1931.	The whole Act.
1 & 2 Geo. 6 c. 54.	The Architects Registration Act 1938.	The whole Act.
S.I. 1987/1824.	The Architects' Qualifications (EEC Recognition) Order 1987.	The whole instrument.
S.I. 1988/2241.	The Architects' Qualifications (EC Recognition) Order 1988.	The whole instrument.
1996 c. 53.	The Housing Grants, Construction and Regeneration Act 1996.	Sections 118 to 125. In section 148, in subsection (2), the words "Part III (architects)," and, in subsection (3), the words "Part III (architects), and". Schedule 2.

TABLE OF DERIVATIONS

Notes:

1. This Table shows the derivation of the provisions of the consolidation.
2. The following abbreviations are used in the Table—

1931	= Architects (Registration) Act 1931 (c. 33)
1938	= Architects Registration Act 1938 (c. 54)
1987	= Architects' Qualifications (EEC Recognition) Order 1987 (S.I. 1987/1824)
1988	= Architects' Qualifications (EC Recognition) Order 1988 (S.I. 1988/2241)
1993	= European Economic Area Act 1993 (c. 51)
1996	= Housing Grants, Construction and Regeneration Act 1996 (c. 53)

Provision	Derivation
1(1)	1931 s.3(1); 1996 s.118(1), Sch. 2 para. 3(2).
(2)	1931 s.3(2B); 1996 s.118(3).
(3)	—
(4)	—
(5)	—
(6)	—
2	1931 s.4; 1996 s.119.
3	1931 s.5A; 1996 s.120(1).
4(1) to (3)	1931 s.6(1) to (3); 1996 s.120(2).
(4) to (6)	1931 s.6(6) to (8); 1996 s.120(2).
5(1)	1931 s.6A(1), (2); 1988 art. 2; 1993 s.2(1); 1996 Sch. 2 para. 4(2).
(2)	1931 s.6A(2)(a); 1988 art. 2.
(3)	1931 s.6A(2)(a), (5), (6); 1988 art. 2.
(4)	1931 s.6A(2)(b), (c); 1988 art. 2; 1993 s.2(1).
(5)	1931 s.6A(3), (4); 1988 art. 2; 1993 s.2(1).
(6)	1931 s.6A(7); 1988 art. 2; 1993 s.2(1); 1996 Sch. 2 para. 4(4).
(7)	1931 s.6A(10); 1988 art. 2; 1993 s.2(1).
6(1)	1931 ss.6(4)(a), 6A(1A); 1996 s.120(2), Sch. 2 para. 4(3).
(2)	1931 s.6(4)(b); 1996 s.120(2).
(3)	1931 ss.6(5), 6A(1B); 1996 s.120(2), Sch. 2 para. 4(3).
(4)	1931 ss.6(9), 6A(8); 1988 art. 2; 1996 s.120(2), Sch. 2 para. 4(5).
(5)	1931 s.6A(9); 1988 art. 2; 1993 s.2(1); 1996 Sch. 2 para. 4(6).

Provision	Derivation
7	1931 s.12; Criminal Justice Act 1982 (c. 48) ss.38, 46; Fines and Penalties (Northern Ireland) Order 1984 (S.I. 1984/703 (N.I. 3)) arts. 5, 6; Criminal Procedure (Consequential Provisions) (Scotland) Act 1995 (c. 40) Sch. 1 paras. 5, 6; 1996 Sch. 2 para. 8.
8	1931 s.6B; 1996 s.120(3).
9	1931 s.6C; 1996 s.120(3).
10(1)	1931 s.7A(1); 1987 art. 7; 1993 s.2(1); 1996 Sch. 2 para. 5(2).
(2)	1931 s.7A(3); 1996 Sch. 2 para. 5(4).
11	1931 s.11; 1996 Sch. 2 para. 7.
12(1)	1938 s.1A(4); 1987 art. 8; 1993 s.2(1); 1996 Sch. 2 para. 14(2).
(2)	1938 s.1A(4); 1987 art. 8; 1993 s.2(1).
(3)	1938 s.1A(1) to (3); 1987 art. 8; 1993 s.2(1); 1996 Sch. 2 para. 14(2).
(4)	1938 s.1A(2); 1987 art. 8; 1993 s.2(1).
(5)	1938 s.1A(3); 1987 art. 8; 1993 s.2(1); 1996 Sch. 2 para. 14(3).
(6)	1938 s.1A(5); 1987 art. 8; 1993 s.2(1).
(7)	1938 s.1A(6); 1987 art. 8; 1993 s.2(1); 1996 Sch. 2 para. 14(4).
(8)	1938 s.1A(7); 1987 art. 8; 1993 s.2(1).
(9)	1938 s.1A(9); 1987 art. 8; 1993 s.2(1).
13	1931 s.7ZE; 1996 s.122.
14	1931 s.7; 1996 s.121.
15(1) to (5)	1931 s.7ZA; 1996 s.121.
(6)	1931 s.7A(2); 1987 art. 7; 1993 s.2(1); 1996 Sch. 2 para. 5(3).
16	1931 s.7ZB; 1996 s.121.
17	1931 s.7ZC; 1996 s.121.
18	1931 s.7ZD; 1996 s.121.
19	1938 s.1A(8); 1987 art. 8; 1993 s.2(1); 1996 Sch. 2 para. 14(5).
20(1)	1938 s.1(1).
(2)	1938 s.1(1) proviso.
(3)	1931 s.17(1); 1938 s.1(3); 1996 s.123(4), Sch. 2 para. 12(2), (3).
(4)	1931 s.17(2); 1996 s.123(4).
(5)	1938 s.1A(1); 1987 art. 8; 1993 s.2(1).
(6)	1938 s.4(2).
(7)	1938 s.1(1A); 1996 s.123(1).
(8)	1938 s.1(1) proviso.
21(1)	1938 s.3(1); 1996 s.123(2), (3).
(2)	1938 s.3(1) proviso.
(3)	1938 s.3(1) proviso; 1996 Sch. 2 para. 15(b).
(4)	1938 s.3(2); 1996 s.123(3).
22	1931 s.9; 1996 Sch. 2 para. 6(2).
23(1), (2)	1931 s.13(1), (2); 1996 Sch. 2 para. 9.
(3)	1931 s.15; 1996 Sch. 2 para. 10.
24(1)	1931 s.16(1); 1996 Sch. 2 para. 11(2).
(2)	1931 ss.11, 16(2); 1996 Sch. 2 para. 11(3).
25	
"the Board"	1931 s.2; 1996 Sch. 2 para. 2(2).
"competent authority"	1931 s.2; 1987 art. 3; 1993 s.2(1).
"the Directive"	1931 s.2; 1987 art. 3.
"disciplinary order"	1931 s.2; 1996 Sch. 2 para. 2(6).
"disqualifying decision in another EEA State"	1931 s.2; 1987 art. 3; 1993 s.2(1).
"EEA State"	—
"erasure order"	1931 s.2; 1996 Sch. 2 para. 2(6).
"list of visiting EEA architects"	—
"national"	1931 s.2; 1987 art. 3.

Provision	Derivation
"penalty order"	1931 s.2; 1996 Sch. 2 para. 2(6).
"prescribed"	1931 s.2; 1996 Sch. 2 para. 2(4).
"prescribe"	1931 ss.6(5), 6A(1B), 6C(1); 1996 s.120(2), (3), Sch. 2 para. 4(3).
"the Register"	1931 s.2; 1996 Sch. 2 para. 2(5).
"the Registrar"	1931 s.2; 1996 Sch. 2 para. 2(6).
"registered person"	1931 s.2; 1996 Sch. 2 para. 2(3).
"suspension order"	1931 s.2; 1996 Sch. 2 para. 2(6).
"unacceptable professional conduct"	—
26	—
27	—
28(1)	—
(2)	—
(3)	1931 s.18(2); 1938 s.6(1); 1996 Sch. 2 paras. 13, 17.
Sch. 1	
paras. 1 to 10	1931 1st Sch. paras. 1 to 10; 1996 Sch. 2 para. 1.
11	1931 s.4A; 1996 s.119.
12	1931 s.3(1), (2); 1996 Sch. 2 para. 3(3)(b).
13 to 24	1931 1st Sch. paras. 11 to 22; 1996 Sch. 2 para. 1.
Sch. 2	—
Sch. 3	—

TABLE OF DESTINATIONS

ARCHITECTS (REGISTRATION) ACT 1931
(C.33)

1931	1997	1931	1997	1931	1997
s.2 .... s.25,		s.3(2B) .... s.1(2)		s.6B s.8	
"the Board"		4 2		6C 9	
"competent		4A .... Sched. 1,		(1) 25	
authority"			para. 11		"prescribe"
"the		5A s.3		7 14	
Directive"		6(1)–(3) ..... 4(1)–(3)		7A(1) ...... 10(1)	
"disciplinary		(4)(a) ...... 6(1)		(2) ...... 15(6)	
order"		(4)(b) ...... 6(2)		(3) ...... 10(2)	
"disqualifying		(5) .... ss.6(3), 25		7ZA .... 15(1)–(5)	
decision in			"prescribe"	7ZB 16	
other EEA		(6)–(8) ..... s.4(4)–(6)		7ZC 17	
states"		(9) .... 6(4)		7ZD 18	
"erasure		6A(1) .... 5(1)		7ZE 13	
order"		(1A) ..... 6(1)		9 22	
"national"		(1B) ..... 6(3), 25		11 .... ss.11, 24(2)	
"penalty			"prescribe"	12 .... s.7	
order"		(2) .... 5(1)		13(1), (2).... 23(1), (2)	
"prescribed"		(2)(a) .... 5(2), (3)		15 .... 23(3)	
"the Register"		(2)(b) .... 5(4)		16(1) .... 24(1)	
"the		(2)(c) .... 5(4)		(2) .... 24(2)	
Registrar"		(3) ...... 5(5)		17(1) .... 20(3)	
"registered		(4) ...... 5(5)		(2) .... 20(4)	
person"		(5) ...... 5(3)		18(2) .... 28(3)	
"suspension		(6) ...... 5(3)		Sched. 1,	
order"		(7) ...... 5(6)		paras. 1–10 .. Sched. 1,	
3(1) .... 1(1), Sched. 1,		(8) ...... 6(4)			paras. 1–10
	para. 12	(9) ...... 6(5)		paras. 11–22 . Sched. 1,	
(2) .... Sched. 1,		(10) ..... 5(7)			paras. 13–24
	para. 12				

ARCHITECTS REGISTRATION ACT 1938
(C.54)

1938	1997
s.1(1) .... s.20(1), (2), (8)	
(1A) .... 20(5), (7)	
(3) .... 20(3)	
1A(1) ...... 12(3)	
(2) ...... 12(3), (4)	
(3) ...... 12(3), (5)	
(4) ...... 12(1), (2)	
(5) ...... 12(6)	
(6) ...... 12(7)	
(7) ...... 12(8)	
(8) 19	
(9) ...... 12(9)	
3(1) .... 21(1)–(3)	
(2) .... 21(4)	
4(2) .... 20(6)	
6(1) .... 28(3)	

CRIMINAL JUSTICE ACT 1982
(C.48)

1982	1997
s.38 .... s.7	
46 7	

TABLE OF DESTINATIONS

EUROPEAN ECONOMIC AREA ACT 1993
(C.51)

1993	1997
s.2(1).........	ss.5(1), (4), (5), (6), (7), 6(5), 10(1), 12(1), (2), (3), (4), (5), (6), (7), (8), (9), 15(6), 19, 20(5), s.25, "competent authority" "disqualifying decision in another EEA State"

CRIMINAL PROCEDURE (CONSEQUENTIAL PROVISIONS) (SCOTLAND) ACT 1995
(C.40)

1995	1997
Sched. 1,	
para. 5	s.7
para. 6	7

HOUSING GRANTS, CONSTRUCTION AND REGENERATION ACT 1996
(C.53)

1996	1997	1996	1997	1996	1997
s.118(1)	s.1(1)	Sched. 2—cont.		Sched. 2—cont.	
(3)	1(2)	para. 2(3)....	s.25, "registered person"	para. 4(4)....	s.5(6)
119	2, Sched. 1, para. 11	para. 2(4)....	25, "prescribed"	para. 4(5)....	6(4)
120(1)	3	para. 2(5)....	25, "the Register"	para. 4(6)....	6(5)
(2)	ss.4(1)–(3), (4)–(6), 6(2), (3), (4), 25, "prescribe"	para. 2(6)....	25, "disciplinary order" "erasure order" "penalty order" "the Registrar" "suspension order"	para. 5(2)....	10(1)
(3)	8, 9, 25, "prescribe"			para. 5(3)....	15(6)
121	14, 15(1)–(5), 16, 17, 18			para. 5(4)....	10(2)
122	s.13			para. 6(2)....	22
123(1)	20(7)			para. 7	11
(2)	21(1)			para. 8	7
(3)	21(1), (4)			para. 9	23(1), (2)
(4)	20(3), (4)			para. 10	23(3)
Sched. 2,		para. 3(2)....	1(1)	para. 11(2)...	24(1)
para. 1	Sched. 1, paras. 1–10, 13–24	para. 3(3)(b).	Sched. 1, para. 12	para. 11(3)...	24(2)
para. 2(2)....	s.25, "the Board"	para. 4(2)....	s.5(1)	para. 12(2)...	20(3)
		para. 4(3)....	ss.6(1), (3), 25, "prescribe"	para. 12(3)...	20(3)
				para. 13	28(3)
				para. 14(2)...	12(1), (3)
				para. 14(3)...	12(5)
				para. 14(4)...	12(7)
				para. 14(5)...	19
				para. 15(b) ..	21(3)
				para. 17	28(3)

FINES AND PENALTIES (NORTHERN IRELAND) ORDER 1984
(S.I. 1984 No. 703)
(N.I. 3)

1984	1997
art. 5	s.7
art. 6	7

TABLE OF DESTINATIONS

ARCHITECTS' QUALIFICATIONS (EEC RECOGNITION) ORDER 1987
(S.I. 1987 No. 1824)

1987	1997
art. 3	s.25,
	"competent authority"
	"the Directive"
	"disqualifying decision in another EEA State"
	"national"
art. 7	ss.10(1), 15(6)
art. 8	12(1), (2), (3), (4), (5), (6), (7), (8), (9), 19, 20(5)

ARCHITECTS' QUALIFICATIONS (EC RECOGNITION) ORDER 1988
(S.I. 1988 No. 2241)

1988	1997
art. 2	ss.5(1), (2), (3), (4), (5), (6), (7), 6(4), (5)

INDEX

References are to sections and Schedules

LIEUTENANCIES ACT 1997

(1997 c. 23)

An Act to consolidate certain enactments relating to the lieutenancies in Great Britain.   [19th March 1997]

PARLIAMENTARY DEBATES
   Hansard, H.L. Vol. 577, cols. 19, 384; Vol. 578, cols. 785, 1503. H.C. Vol. 292, col. 696.

INTRODUCTION
   This Act consolidates provisions relating to lieutenancies in Great Britain. It allows for the appointment of lord-lieutenants, deputy lieutenants and vice lord-lieutenants for each county in England and Wales, and each area in Scotland (other than the cities of Aberdeen, Dundee, Edinburgh and Glasgow, where the Lord Provost is lord-lieutenant by virtue of his office).

Lieutenancies in Great Britain

   1.—(1) A lord-lieutenant shall be appointed by Her Majesty for each county in England, each county in Wales and each area in Scotland (other than the cities of Aberdeen, Dundee, Edinburgh and Glasgow).

   (2) The Lord Provost of each of the cities of Aberdeen, Dundee, Edinburgh and Glasgow is, by virtue of his office, lord-lieutenant for that city.

   (3) Her Majesty may appoint lieutenants (in addition to the lord-lieutenant) for any county or area.

   (4) Schedule 1 to this Act (which identifies the areas which are counties in England and Wales and areas in Scotland for the purposes of the lieutenancies) shall have effect; and in this Act "county" and "area" shall be construed accordingly.

Deputy lieutenants

   2.—(1) The lord-lieutenant of a county or area shall appoint such persons as he thinks fit to be his deputy lieutenants.

   (2) A person may only be appointed as a deputy lieutenant of a county or area if—
   (a) he is shown to have rendered appropriate service; and
   (b) he has a place of residence in, or within 7 miles from the boundary of, that county or area.

   (3) In subsection (2) "appropriate service" means either worthy service as a member of, or in a civil capacity in connection with, Her Majesty's naval, military or air forces or such other service as makes a person suitable for appointment as a deputy lieutenant.

   (4) The lord-lieutenant of a county or area shall notify to Her Majesty the name of any person whom he proposes to appoint as a deputy lieutenant; and

a commission as deputy lieutenant shall not be granted to that person until the lord-lieutenant has been informed by the Secretary of State that Her Majesty does not disapprove of the granting of the commission.

(5) A commission as deputy lieutenant of a county or area is not vacated by reason that the person who granted it dies or otherwise ceases to hold office as lord-lieutenant.

(6) A commission as deputy lieutenant of a county or area may be revoked by the lord-lieutenant of that county or area; and the lord-lieutenant shall revoke the commission forthwith on being informed of Her Majesty's pleasure that it be revoked.

(7) The clerk of the lieutenancy of a county or area shall arrange for the publication in the London Gazette or, as the case may be, the Edinburgh Gazette of the names of the persons appointed deputy lieutenants for that county or area, with the dates of their commissions.

Vice lord-lieutenants

3.—(1) The lord-lieutenant of a county or area may, with Her Majesty's approval, appoint a lieutenant or deputy lieutenant of that county or area as his vice lord-lieutenant.

(2) If a lord-lieutenant who has appointed a vice lord-lieutenant dies or otherwise ceases to hold office, the commission of the vice lord-lieutenant is vacated on the appointment of a new lord-lieutenant for the county or area concerned.

(3) A commission as vice lord-lieutenant of a county or area may, with the approval of Her Majesty, be revoked by the lord-lieutenant who granted it; and the lord-lieutenant shall revoke the commission forthwith on being informed of Her Majesty's pleasure that it be revoked.

(4) Without prejudice to Her Majesty's power to make other provision under section 4, if—

(a) the lord-lieutenant of a county or area is absent from the county or area, sick or otherwise unable to act; or

(b) there is a vacancy in the office of lord-lieutenant for a county or area,

the vice lord-lieutenant of that county or area shall stand for all purposes in the lord-lieutenant's place and, accordingly, may do anything which may be done by the lord-lieutenant.

Absence, etc. of lord-lieutenant

4.—(1) If—

(a) the lord-lieutenant of a county or area is absent from the United Kingdom, sick or otherwise unable to act; or

(b) there is a vacancy in the office of lord-lieutenant of a county or area,

Her Majesty may authorise any three deputy lieutenants or lieutenants of that county or area to act as its lord-lieutenant.

(2) During the period for which they are authorised to act, the persons authorised under this section shall stand for all purposes in the lord-lieutenant's place and, accordingly, may do anything which may be done by the lord-lieutenant.

Appointment of clerks of lieutenancies

5.—(1) There shall be a clerk of the lieutenancy for each county or area, appointed by the lord-lieutenant.

(2) The lord-lieutenant of a county or area may revoke the appointment of the clerk of the lieutenancy.

Functions of lord-lieutenant, lieutenants and deputy lieutenants

6. The lord-lieutenant, lieutenants (if any) and deputy lieutenants of a county or area shall have such functions and privileges (whether provided for under any enactment or otherwise) as are for the time being exercisable by or vested in the lord-lieutenant, lieutenants and deputy lieutenants respectively of that county or area.

Commissioners of lieutenancy for the City of London

7.—(1) Her Majesty may issue commissions of lieutenancy in respect of the City of London to such persons as She thinks fit to be the Commissioners of Lieutenancy for the City of London (in this section referred to as "the commissioners").

(2) For the purposes of the application of sections 5 and 6 to the City of London, the commissioners shall be treated as if they were the lord-lieutenant of a county.

(3) Nothing in this Act affects the raising and levying of the Trophy Tax in the City or any other functions or privileges of the commissioners (whether provided for under any enactment or otherwise).

(4) The proceeds of the Trophy Tax may be applied by the commissioners (if they see fit to do so) for any of the purposes of a territorial and volunteer reserve association established under Part XI of the Reserve Forces Act 1996 for an area including the City of London.

(5) For the purposes of the law relating to, or to matters connected with, the lieutenancies the City of London includes the Inner Temple and the Middle Temple.

Consequential amendments, transitional provisions, repeals and revocation

8.—(1) In section 61 of the Local Government (Wales) Act 1994 (lieutenancies)—

(a) in subsection (2), for the words "section 130 of the Act of 1980" there shall be substituted the words "section 1 of, and Schedule 1 to, the Lieutenancies Act 1997"; and

(b) in subsection (3), for the words "Act of 1980" there shall be substituted the words "Lieutenancies Act 1997".

(2) In section 9 of the Reserve Forces Act 1996 (enlistment) for the words "Part VI of the Reserve Forces Act 1980" there shall be substituted the words "the Lieutenancies Act 1997".

(3) Schedule 2 to this Act (which contains transitional provisions and savings) shall have effect.

(4) The enactments mentioned in Schedule 3 to this Act (which include some spent enactments) are repealed to the extent specified in the third column of that Schedule.

(5) Regulation 9 of the Local Government Changes for England (Miscellaneous Provision) Regulations 1995 is hereby revoked.

Short title, commencement and extent

9.—(1) This Act may be cited as the Lieutenancies Act 1997.

(2) This Act shall come into force on 1st July 1997.

(3) Any amendment, repeal or revocation made by this Act has the same extent as the provision amended, repealed or revoked.

(4) Subject to subsection (3), this Act does not extend to Northern Ireland.

SCHEDULES

SCHEDULE 1

COUNTIES AND AREAS FOR THE PURPOSES OF THE LIEUTENANCIES IN GREAT BRITAIN

Preliminary

1. The provisions of this Schedule identify the areas which constitute counties in England, counties in Wales or areas in Scotland for the purposes of the lieutenancies in Great Britain.

Counties in England

2. The counties in England for the purposes of this Act are—
(a) Greater London (excluding the City of London);
(b) the areas which are to be regarded as counties for those purposes by virtue of paragraph 3; and
(c) any other areas in England which are counties for the purposes of the Local Government Act 1972.

3. The local government areas (or parts of local government areas) described in each entry in the second column of the following Table shall be regarded for the purposes of this Act as one county to be known by the name specified in the first column.

TABLE

County for the purposes of this Act	Local government areas
Bedfordshire	Bedfordshire and Luton
Buckinghamshire	Buckinghamshire and Milton Keynes
Derbyshire	Derbyshire and Derby
Dorset	Dorset, Bournemouth and Poole
Durham	Durham, Darlington, Hartlepool and so much of Stockton-on-Tees as lies north of the line for the time being of the centre of the River Tees
The East Riding of Yorkshire	The East Riding of Yorkshire and Kingston upon Hull (City of)
East Sussex	East Sussex and Brighton and Hove
Gloucestershire	Gloucestershire and South Gloucestershire
Hampshire	Hampshire, Portsmouth and Southampton
Leicestershire	Leicestershire and Leicester
Lincolnshire	Lincolnshire, North Lincolnshire and North East Lincolnshire
North Yorkshire	North Yorkshire, Middlesbrough, Redcar and Cleveland, York and so much of Stockton-on-Tees as lies south of the line for the time being of the centre of the River Tees
Somerset	Somerset, Bath and North East Somerset and North Somerset
Staffordshire	Staffordshire and Stoke-on-Trent
Wiltshire	Wiltshire and Thamesdown

4. The City of London shall be treated as a county for the purposes of sections 5 and 6.
5. The Isles of Scilly shall be treated as part of the county of Cornwall for the purposes of this Act.

Counties in Wales

6. The counties in Wales for the purposes of this Act are the preserved counties, that is to say, the counties in Wales as they stood immediately before the passing of the Local Government (Wales) Act 1994 (but subject to any redrawing of their boundaries by or under that Act or the Local Government Act 1972).

Areas in Scotland

7. The areas in Scotland for the purposes of this Act are—
(a) the cities of Aberdeen, Dundee, Edinburgh and Glasgow; and
(b) the areas specified in an Order in Council under paragraph 8.

8. Her Majesty may by Order in Council divide Scotland (apart from the cities of Aberdeen, Dundee, Edinburgh and Glasgow) into such areas for the purposes of this Act as She thinks fit.

9. Any deputy lieutenant who, immediately before the date on which an Order in Council under paragraph 8 is made, holds office for an area affected by the Order shall (without prejudice to any power of removal or directing removal from any office) continue to hold office on and after that date as deputy lieutenant for the area in which he resides or for such other area as may be specified in the Order.

Section 8(3)   SCHEDULE 2

TRANSITIONAL AND SAVING PROVISIONS

General

1. The substitution of this Act for the enactments repealed or revoked by this Act does not affect the continuity of the law.

2. Anything done (including subordinate legislation made) or having effect as done under a provision reproduced in this Act has effect as if done under the corresponding provision of this Act.

3. References (express or implied) in this Act or any other enactment, instrument or document to a provision of this Act shall, so far as the context permits, be construed as including, in relation to times, circumstances and purposes before the commencement of this Act, a reference to corresponding earlier provisions.

4. A reference (express or implied) in any enactment, instrument or document to a provision reproduced in this Act shall be construed, so far as is required for continuing its effect, as being or, as the case may require, including a reference to the corresponding provision of this Act.

5. Any document made, served or issued on or after the commencement of this Act which contains a reference to any provision reproduced by this Act shall be construed, except so far as a contrary intention appears, as referring or, as the case may require, including a reference to the corresponding provision of this Act.

Continuation in office of current office-holders

6. Nothing in this Act prevents the continuation in office of a lord-lieutenant, lieutenant or deputy lieutenant of a county or area who is in office immediately before the commencement of this Act.

This paragraph is without prejudice to any power of removal or directing removal from any office.

7. The repeal by this Act of paragraphs 13(2) and 14(2) of Schedule 8 to the Reserve Forces Act 1980 does not affect the operation of any Order in Council or order having effect as made under either of those paragraphs in relation to any person to whom that paragraph applied immediately before the commencement of this Act.

Old references to the lieutenant of a county

8. Any reference to a lieutenant of a county or Greater London—
(a) in any enactment passed before the end of the session in which the Local Government Act 1972 was passed, or
(b) in any instrument made before 26th October 1972 (the date of the passing of that Act),
shall continue to be construed as a reference to the lord-lieutenant of a county or of Greater London (as the case may be).

9. Any reference to a lieutenant of a county in Scotland—
(a) in any enactment passed before the end of the session in which the Local Government (Scotland) Act 1973 was passed, or
(b) in any instrument made before 25th October 1973 (the date of the passing of that Act),
shall continue to be construed as a reference to the lord-lieutenant holding office for an area in Scotland.

SCHEDULE 3

REPEALS

Chapter	Short title	Extent of repeal
1964 c. 42.	Administration of Justice Act 1964.	In section 26, the word "lieutenants".
1980 c. 9.	Reserve Forces Act 1980.	Sections 130 to 137. In section 138, subsection (1), in subsection (2), the words "the lieutenancies and" and from "and so" to the end, and subsections (3) to (5). In section 156(1), the definition of "area". In Schedule 8, paragraphs 13 and 14.
1994 c. 19.	Local Government (Wales) Act 1994.	Section 61(1) and (5).
1994 c. 39.	Local Government etc. (Scotland) Act 1994.	In Schedule 13, paragraph 116.
1996 c. 14.	Reserve Forces Act 1996.	Section 121. Schedule 6.

TABLE OF DERIVATIONS

Note: The following abbreviations are used in this Table:—

SA 1887	=	The Sheriffs Act 1887
RFA80	=	The Reserve Forces Act 1980 (c. 9)
LGWA	=	The Local Government (Wales) Act 1994 (c. 19)
LGSA	=	The Local Government etc. (Scotland) Act 1994 (c. 39)
RFA96	=	The Reserve Forces Act 1996 (c. 14)
SI 1995/1748	=	The Local Government Changes for England (Miscellaneous Provision) Regulations 1995
SI 1996/2009	=	The Local Government Changes for England (Sheriffs) Order 1996

Provision of Bill	Derivation
1(1)	RFA80 ss.130(1)(a), 131(1)(a); LGSA Sch. 13, para. 116(2)(a).
(2)	RFA80 s.131(2); LGSA Sch. 13, para. 116(2)(b).
(3)	RFA80 ss.130(1)(b), 131(1)(b), (2); LGSA Sch. 13, para. 116(2)(a).
(4)	Drafting.
2(1)	RFA80 s.133(1).
(2)	RFA80 s.133(2); drafting.
(3)	RFA80 s.133(2)(b).
(4)	RFA80 s.133(3).
(5)	RFA80 s.133(4).
(6)	RFA80 s.133(4), 136; RFA96 Sch. 6, para. 2(b).
(7)	RFA80 s.133(5); RFA96 Sch. 6, para. 2(c).
3(1)	RFA80 s.135(1).
(2)	RFA80 s.135(1B); RFA96 Sch. 6, para. 3.
(3)	RFA80 ss.135(1A), 136; RFA96 Sch. 6, para. 3.
(4)	RFA80 s.135(1), (2); drafting.
4(1), (2)	RFA80 s.134.
5(1), (2)	RFA80 s.137(2).
6	RFA80 s.137(1); RFA96 Sch. 6, para. 5.
7(1)	RFA80 s.138(1); drafting.
(2)	RFA80 s.138(2), (3).
(3)	RFA80 s.138(2), (4).
(4)	RFA80 s.138(5).
(5)	Administration of Justice Act 1964 (c. 42) s.26.

Provision of Bill	Derivation
8	Drafting.
9(1), (2), (3)	Drafting.
(4)	RFA80 s.132; drafting.
Schedule 1	
para. 1	Drafting.
para. 2(a)	RFA80 s.130(1), (2)(a).
(b), (c)	RFA80 s.130(1A); SA 1887 s.38 ("county"); SI 1995/1748 Regs. 8, 9.
para. 3	RFA80 s.130(1A); SA 1887 Sch. 2A; SI 1995/1748 Regs. 8, 9; SI 1996/2009.
para. 4	RFA80 s.138(2), (3).
para. 5	RFA80 s.130(2)(b).
para. 6	RFA80 s.130(4); LGWA ss.61(1), 64(1) ("preserved county").
para. 7	RFA80 ss.131(1A), (2), 156(1) ("area"); LGSA Sch. 13, para. 116(2)(a).
para. 8	RFA80 s.131(1A)(a), (5); LGSA Sch. 13, para. 116(2)(a), (4).
para. 9	RFA80 s.131(1B); LGSA Sch. 13, para. 116(2)(a), (d).
Schedule 2	*transitional and saving provisions*
Schedule 3	*repeals*

TABLE OF DESTINATIONS

SHERIFFS ACT 1887
(c.55)

1887	1997
s.38 "county"	Sched. 1, para. 2(b), (c)
Sched. 2A	Sched. 1, para. 3

ADMINISTRATION OF JUSTICE ACT 1964
(c.42)

1964	1997
s.26	s.7(5)

RESERVE FORCES ACT 1980
(c.9)

1980	1997	1980	1997	1980	1997
s.130(1)	Sched. 1, para. 2(a)	s.131(1A)(a)	Sched. 1, para. 8	s.135(1)	3(1), (4)
(1)(a)	s.1(1)	(1B)	Sched. 1, para. 9	(1A)	3(3)
(b)	1(3)	(2)	1(2), (3), Sched. 1, para. 7	(1B)	3(2)
(1A)	Sched. 1, paras. 2(b), (c), 3	(5)	Sched. 1, para. 8	(2)	3(4)
(2)(a)	Sched. 1, para. 2(a)	132	9(4)	136	ss.2(6), 3(3)
(2)(b)	Sched. 1, para. 5	133(1)	2(1)	137(1)	s.6
(4)	Sched. 1, para. 6	(2)	2(2)	(2)	5(1), (2)
131(1)(a)	s.1(1)	(b)	2(3)	138(1)	7(1)
(b)	1(3)	(3)	2(4)	(2)	7(2), (3), Sched. 1, para. 4
(1A)	Sched. 1, para. 7	(4)	2(5), (6)	(3)	7(2), Sched. 1, para. 4
		(5)	2(7)	(4)	7(3)
		134	4(1), (2)	(5)	7(4)
				156(1) "area"	Sched. 1, para. 7

LOCAL GOVERNMENT (WALES) ACT 1994
(c.19)

1994	1997
s.61(1)	Sched. 1, para. 6
64(1) "preserved county"	Sched. 1, para. 6

LOCAL GOVERNMENT ETC. (SCOTLAND) ACT 1994
(c.39)

1994	1997
Sched. 13, para. 116 (2)(a)	s.1(1), (3), Sched. 1, paras. 7, 8, 9
para. 116(2)(b)	s.1(2)
para. 116(2)(d)	Sched. 1, para. 9
para. 116(4)	Sched. 1, para. 8

TABLE OF DESTINATIONS

RESERVE FORCES ACT 1996
(c.14)

LOCAL GOVERNMENT CHANGES FOR ENGLAND (MISCELLANEOUS PROVISION) REGULATIONS 1995
(S.I. 1995 No. 1748)

LOCAL GOVERNMENT CHANGES FOR ENGLAND (SHERIFFS) ORDER 1996
(S.I. 1996 No. 2009)

INDEX

References are to sections and Schedules

NURSES, MIDWIVES AND HEALTH VISITORS ACT 1997*

(1997 c. 24)

[A Table showing the derivation of the provisions of this consolidation Act will be found at the end of the Act. The Table has no official status.]

ARRANGEMENT OF SECTIONS

The Central Council

An Act to consolidate the Nurses, Midwives and Health Visitors Act 1979 and the enactments amending it. [19th March 1997]

PARLIAMENTARY DEBATES
Hansard, H.L. Vol. 577, cols. 19, 385; Vol. 578, cols. 785, 1504. H.C. Vol. 292, col. 696.

INTRODUCTION AND GENERAL NOTE

This Act sets out the regulatory framework for the professions of Nursing, Midwifery and Health Visiting. It establishes a register of professionals, defining admission requirements and providing powers to remove names from that register in cases of unfitness to practise (ss.7–12).

---

* Annotations by Jonathan Montgomery B.A., LL.M., Senior Lecturer in Law, University of Southampton.

Appeals against removal are permitted by s.12. The Act continues the existence of the United Kingdom Central Council for Nursing, Midwifery and Health Visiting to oversee the professions, with its statutory committees and functions (ss.1–4, 19). It also continues the role of the four National Boards in relation to education (ss.5–6). Special provisions are continued in relation to midwifery (ss.14–16). The position of practitioners visiting from elsewhere in the European Economic Area is clarified (ss.20–21). Section 13 makes it an offence to make a false claim of professional registration or qualifications.

The Origins of the Statute

The Act consolidates amendments made to the Nurses, Midwives and Health Visitors Act 1979 (c.36) deriving principally from three instruments.

First the Nursing and Midwifery (EEC Recognition) Order 1983 (S.I. 1983 No. 884). These amendments should be read in conjunction with the EEC Nursing and Midwifery Qualifications Designation Order 1983 (S.I. 1983 No. 921). This Order made provision in accord with the First and Second Midwifery Directives (Nos. 80/154/EEC, [1980] O.J. L33/1, and 80/155/EEC, [1980] O.J. L33/8) and the Second Nursing Directive (77/453/EEC, [1977] O.J. L176/8).

The Order is now superseded by the European Nursing and Midwifery Qualifications Designation Order 1996 (S.I. 1996 No. 3102).

Secondly, the Nurses, Midwives and Health Visitors Act 1992 (c.16) (the 1992 Act) which implemented reforms to the regulatory structure of the professions following the *Review of the UKCC and Four National Boards for Nursing, Midwifery and Health Visiting* (1989) carried out for the Department of Health, the Scottish Home and Health Department, the Welsh Office and the Department of Health and Social Services (Northern Ireland). The 1992 Act altered the constitution of the United Kingdom Central Council for Nursing, Midwifery and Health Visiting to become more democratic and to take on disciplinary functions that were previously performed by National Boards established for each country. Those National Boards also ceased to be responsible for providing courses of training, adopting a supervisory jurisdiction instead. Some changes were also made to the powers available in disciplinary proceedings.

Thirdly, the Nurses, Midwives and Health Visitors Act 1979 (Amendment) Regulations 1996 (S.I. 1996 No. 3101). These Regulations regularised references to the EEC to become EEA and incorporated developments in European law.

Existing regulations

As the Act is a consolidating statute, many of the Regulations expressed to be made under its provisions are already in existence. Although these were originally made under the superseded Acts, they continue to have force (Sched. 5 superseding the effect of the Interpretation Act 1978 (c.30), s.17(2)). These regulations are therefore noted in the annotations to the relevant sections.

COMMENCEMENT

The Act came into force on June 19, 1997 (s.24(2)).

EXTENT

The Act extends to Northern Ireland as well as to England, Scotland and Wales (s.24(6)).

ABBREVIATIONS

"the 1979 Act": Nurses, Midwives and Health Visitors Act 1979 (c.36).
"the 1992 Act": Nurses, Midwives and Health Visitors Act 1992 (c.16).
"PPC": Preliminary Proceedings Committee.
"UKCC": United Kingdom Central Council for Nursing, Midwifery and Health Visiting.

The Central Council

Constitution of Central Council

1.—(1) There shall continue to be a corporate body known as the United Kingdom Central Council for Nursing, Midwifery and Health Visiting.

(2) Subject to any order under paragraph 1 of Schedule 1 to this Act, the Council shall consist of sixty members.

(3) Two-thirds of the members of the Council ("elected members") shall be appointed by the Secretary of State on being elected under the electoral

scheme, that is to say, the scheme having effect under the United Kingdom Central Council for Nursing, Midwifery and Health Visiting (Electoral Scheme) Order 1992 (with any variations under paragraph 2 of Schedule 1 to this Act).

(4) Appointments otherwise than for the purposes of subsection (3) shall be made by the Secretary of State from among persons who—

   (a) are registered nurses, midwives, health visitors or medical practitioners; or

   (b) have such qualifications and experience in education or other fields as, in the opinion of the Secretary of State, will be of value to the Council in the performance of its functions.

(5) In making appointments for the purposes of subsection (4) the Secretary of State shall have especially in mind—

   (a) the need to secure that the members of the Council include registered nurses, midwives and health visitors and persons living or working in each part of the United Kingdom; and

   (b) the need to secure that qualifications and experience in the teaching of nursing, midwifery and health visiting are adequately represented on the Council.

(6) The Council shall have a president and a vice-president appointed by the Council from among its members.

(7) Schedule 1 to this Act shall have effect with respect to the constitution and administration etc. of the Council.

(8) For the purposes of subsection (3), a person appointed as a replacement for an elected member shall be treated as an elected member.

DEFINITIONS

   "registered health visitor": s.7.
   "registered medical practitioner": Medical Act 1983 (c.54), s.2.
   "registered midwife": s.7.
   "registered nurse": s.7.

GENERAL NOTE

   The UKCC was originally established under the 1979 Act. Its jurisdiction began in July 1983 when it took over from the previous authorities. Its functions are set out in s.2, and a number of statutory committees are prescribed. Under s.3 there must be a Finance Committee and a Midwifery Committee (on the latter see s.4). Three further Committees exist to deal with questions of fitness to remain on the register, established by the Nurses, Midwives and Health Visitors (Professional Conduct) Rules 1993 (S.I. 1993 No. 893). These are the Preliminary Proceedings Committee, the Professional Conduct Committee and the Health Committee. Further standing committees may be prescribed by the Secretary of State at the Council's request under s.3(3).

   The rules on membership of the Central Council are set out in the UKCC (Membership Proposal) Approval Order 1992 (S.I. 1992 No. 2160). Under these rules, the UKCC consists of 60 members of which 40 are elected under the scheme set out in the UKCC (Electoral Scheme) Order 1992 (S.I. 1992 No. 2159) as amended (see subs. (2)). That scheme ensures that at least seven nurses, two midwives and one health visitor are returned for each of England, Scotland, Wales and Northern Ireland. The remaining 20 persons are appointed by the Secretary of State, see subs. (4). The factors that the Secretary of State is required to take into account when exercising these powers are set out in subs. (5). There is no requirement that there be any lay members, nor that other health professions are represented. In practice the Secretary of State has used this power to appoint lay people and also doctors to the Council.

   Members of the UKCC are appointed for five years under the UKCC (Term of Office for Members) Order 1993 (S.I. 1993 No. 590).

Functions of the Council

   2.—(1) The principal functions of the Central Council shall be to establish and improve standards of training and professional conduct for nurses, midwives and health visitors.

   (2) The Council shall ensure that the standards of training it establishes are such as to meet any Community obligation of the United Kingdom.

(3) The Council shall by means of rules determine the conditions of a person's being admitted to training, and the kind, content and standard of training to be undertaken, with a view to registration.

(4) The rules may also make provision with respect to the kind, content and standard of further training available to persons who are already registered.

(5) The powers of the Council shall include that of providing, in such manner as it thinks fit, advice for nurses, midwives and health visitors on standards of professional conduct.

(6) In the discharge of its functions the Council shall have proper regard for the interests of all groups within the professions, including those with minority representation.

DEFINITIONS
    "Central Council": ss.1, 22.
    "Council": ss.1, 22.

GENERAL NOTE
    This section sets out the functions of the UKCC, which must be discharged with proper regard for the interests of all groups within the professions (subs. (6)). The rules governing training are found in the Nurses, Midwives and Health Visitors Rules 1983 (S.I. 1983 No. 873), as amended.

Community obligation
    See the First and Second Nursing Directive (77/452/EEC, [1977] O.J. L176/1, and 77/453/EEC, [1977] O.J. L176/8) and the First and Second Midwifery Directives (Nos. 80/154/EEC, [1980] O.J. L33/1, and 80/155/EEC, [1980] O.J. L33/8). In addition to establishing mutual recognition of qualifications, Community law outlines the content of training required for nurses and midwives (see the Second Directives in respect of each profession).

Subs. (5)
    The most important documents that the Council has issued exercising this power are the *Code of Professional Conduct for the Nurse, Midwife and Health Visitor* (3rd ed. 1992), the *Midwife's Code of Practice* (2nd ed. 1989) and *Guidelines for Professional Practice* (1996). See also *The Scope of Professional Practice* (1992), *Standards for the Administration of Medicines* (1992), *Standards for Records and Record Keeping* (1993). An Ethics Advisory Panel has also been established.

Standing committees of Council

3.—(1) The Secretary of State shall by order constitute as standing committees of the Council a Midwifery Committee and a Finance Committee.

(2) The Council shall consult the Finance Committee on all financial matters.

(3) If the Council (having regard to the duty imposed by section 2(6)) requests the Secretary of State to do so, he may by order constitute other standing committees of the Council and (to the extent prescribed by the order) require the Council to consult them on, or empower them to discharge functions of the Council with respect to, other matters.

(4) An order constituting a standing committee of the Council—
    (a) may provide for persons who are not members of the Council to be appointed as members of that committee; and
    (b) shall provide for a majority on the committee to be persons who work or have worked in the professional field with which it is primarily concerned.

DEFINITIONS
    "Council": ss.1, 22.
    "Midwifery Committee": s.4.

GENERAL NOTE

Subs. (1)

See the Nurses, Midwives and Health Visitors (Finance Committee of the Central Council) Order 1982 (S.I. 1982 No. 1566), and the Nurses, Midwives and Health Visitors (Midwifery Committee of the Central Council) Order 1982 (S.I. 1982 No. 1567).

Subs. (3)

See the Nurses, Midwives and Health Visitors (Educational Policy Advisory Committee) Order 1983 (S.I. 1983 No. 726).

The Midwifery Committee

4.—(1) Of the members of the Council's Midwifery Committee the majority shall be practising midwives.

(2) The Council shall consult the Committee on all matters relating to midwifery and the Committee shall, on behalf of the Council, discharge such of the Council's functions as are assigned to the Committee either by the Council or by the Secretary of State by order.

(3) The Council shall assign to the Committee any matter involving a proposal to make, amend or revoke rules under section 14 below; and the Committee shall consider the proposal and report on it to the Council.

(4) The Secretary of State shall not approve rules relating to midwifery practice unless satisfied that they are framed in accordance with recommendations of the Council's Midwifery Committee.

(5) Any matter which is assigned to the Midwifery Committee otherwise than under subsection (3) shall be finally dealt with by the Committee on behalf of the Council so far as the Council expressly authorises the Committee to deal finally with it; and the Committee shall make a report to the Council as to the way in which it has dealt with the matter.

DEFINITIONS

"Council": ss.1, 22.

GENERAL NOTE

This section ensures that there is a separate voice within the UKCC for midwives. It reflects concern amongst midwives that the distinctive nature of their profession is lost within the common regulatory structure. Other distinctive features of the regulation of midwifery in the statute are the restrictions on attendance in childbirth set out in s.16 and the provision of local supervision of midwifery practice (see s.14). The Council is also required to produce Midwives Rules by s.14. These are contained in the Nurses, Midwives, and Health Visitors Rules 1983 (S.I. 1983 No. 873) (as amended).

'practising midwives'

Under s.22 of the Act, a person is 'practising' if she or he is working in some capacity by virtue of a professional qualification. However the phrase 'practising midwife' is defined more precisely in r.27 of the Nurses, Midwives, and Health Visitors Rules 1983 (S.I. 1983 No. 873) (as amended). There, it means 'a midwife who attends professionally upon a woman during the antenatal, intranatal and/or postnatal period or who holds a post for which a midwifery qualification is essential and who notifies her intention to practise to the local supervising authority'. Such notification has to be given annually (r.36). It would seem that midwives would only qualify as 'practising' if they have given such notice in the year in question. See s.14 of this Act for the parent provision for this rule.

'in accordance with'

This phrase does not necessarily require rules to be made in the precise terms in which the Midwifery Committee recommends them.

The National Boards and their relationship to the Central Council

Constitution of National Boards

5.—(1) England, Wales, Scotland and Northern Ireland shall each continue to have a National Board for Nursing, Midwifery and Health Visiting, and the Boards shall be corporate bodies.

(2) A National Board shall consist of—

(a) a chairman appointed by the Secretary of State from among persons who are registered nurses, midwives or health visitors;

(b) such number of other members appointed by the Secretary of State as he may specify by order;

(c) the person for the time being appointed in pursuance of subsection (7)(a) to be the chief executive officer of the Board; and

(d) any person for the time being appointed in pursuance of subsection (7)(b) to an office under the Board which is specified for the purposes of this paragraph by the Secretary of State by order.

(3) Appointments to a National Board for the purposes of subsection (2)(b) shall be made from among persons who—

(a) are registered nurses, midwives or health visitors; or

(b) have such qualifications and experience in education or other fields as, in the opinion of the Secretary of State, will be of value to the Board in the performance of its functions.

(4) The Secretary of State shall so exercise his powers under this section as to secure in relation to a National Board that a majority of the members of the Board are registered nurses, midwives or health visitors.

(5) The Secretary of State may, with the consent of the Treasury—

(a) pay such remuneration as he thinks fit to any person who is a member of a National Board by virtue of appointment by the Secretary of State; and

(b) make such provision as he thinks fit for the payment to or in respect of any such person of pensions, allowances or gratuities.

(6) A National Board may pay to its chairman and members and to other persons appointed to serve on its standing and other committees, such travelling and other allowances as the Secretary of State may determine with the approval of the Treasury.

(7) A National Board shall have—

(a) a chief executive officer, and

(b) such other officers as the Secretary of State may by order specify for the purposes of this paragraph,

appointed by the Board.

(8) The Secretary of State may by order make such further provision with respect to the constitution and administration of a National Board as he thinks fit.

(9) Without prejudice to the generality of subsection (8), provision under that subsection may include provision—

(a) with respect to qualification for membership;

(b) for the appointment of a deputy chairman and with respect to his powers;

(c) with respect to the tenure of office of the chairman, deputy chairman and other members;

(d) with respect to the appointment of officers;

(e) requiring payments to employees, and provision for the payment of pensions, allowances or gratuities to or in respect of them, to be such as the Secretary of State may, with the consent of the Treasury, approve;

(f) requiring powers with respect to the employment of staff to be exercised in accordance with written directions of the Secretary of State;

(g) with respect to procedure, including the constitution of committees;
(h) authorising the appointment of persons who are not Board members to committees of the Board.

(10) Orders under subsection (8) may include provision with respect to proof of documents.

(11) Orders under this section may make different provision in relation to different Boards.

DEFINITIONS
"registered health visitor": s.7.
"registered midwife": s.7.
"registered nurse": s.7.

GENERAL NOTE
With the implementation of the 1992 Act, the National Boards became executive bodies, with members appointed rather than elected as was the case under the unamended 1979 Act. The section provides that the Boards must have professional chairmen, and must have a professional majority, but not explicitly that it contain representatives of each of the professional groups (subss. (2)–(4)).

The National Board for Nursing, Midwifery and Health Visiting for England (Constitution and Administration) Order 1993 (S.I. 1993 No. 629), has been made and amended under this section. It provides that the Board comprises a chair, chief executive, a finance officer, a professional officer, and six appointed members. Of the appointed members, one must be from each of the three professions and one must have educational experience and qualifications. Equivalent provisions have been made in the National Board for Nursing, Midwifery and Health Visiting for Scotland Order 1993 (S.I. 1993 No. 637) and the National Board for Nursing, Midwifery and Health Visiting for Wales (Constitution and Administration) Order 1993 (S.I. 1993 No. 614).

The functions of the National Boards established under this section are set out in s.6.

Adaptations are made to the provisions of this section for the National Board for Nursing, Midwifery and Health Visiting for Northern Ireland by Sched. 3 to the Act. See also the National Board for Nursing, Midwifery and Health Visiting for Northern Ireland Order 1993 (S.I. 1993 No. 115).

Subs. (6)
The Secretary of State may cause this subsection to cease to have effect, by order under s.24(4).

Functions of Boards

6.—(1) The National Boards shall in England, Wales, Scotland and Northern Ireland respectively—
(a) approve institutions in relation to the provision of—
  (i) courses of training with a view to enabling persons to qualify for registration as nurses, midwives or health visitors or for the recording of additional qualifications in the register; and
  (ii) courses of further training for those already registered;
(b) ensure that such courses meet the requirements of the Central Council as to their kind, content and standard;
(c) hold, or arrange for others to hold, such examinations as are necessary to enable persons to satisfy requirements for registration or to obtain additional qualifications;
(d) collaborate with the Council in the promotion of improved training methods; and
(e) perform such other functions relating to nurses, midwives or health visitors as the Secretary of State may by order prescribe.

(2) The National Boards shall discharge their functions subject to and in accordance with any applicable rules of the Council and shall take account of any difference in the considerations applying to the different professions.

<small>DEFINITIONS</small>
   "Council": ss.1, 22.
   "National Boards": s.5.
   "registration": ss.7, 22.
   "training": s.22.

<small>GENERAL NOTE</small>
   The National Boards are executive bodies, charged with supervising professional training, which includes education, in accordance with the requirements of the UKCC as to kind, content and standard. They are thus executive rather than policy making bodies.
   Prior to the implementation of the 1992 Act the Boards had more extensive functions, embracing the formulation of policy, the direct provision of courses (rather than the accreditation of institutions as now) and also investigations into disciplinary matters.

Registration

The professional register

   7.—(1) The Central Council shall continue to maintain a register of qualified nurses, midwives and health visitors.

   (2) The register shall be divided into such parts as the Secretary of State may by order determine, the parts being indicative of different qualifications and different kinds and standards of training, and in this Act references to parts of the register are to the parts so determined.

   (3) The Council may by rules make provision—

   (a) as to the documentary and other evidence to be produced, and the fees to be paid, by those applying for registration or for additional qualifications to be recorded, or for any entry in the register to be altered or restored;

   (b) as to the keeping of the register and the means of obtaining access to, and copies of extracts from, the register;

   (c) for a person's registration to remain effective without limitation of time (subject to removal from the register for misconduct or otherwise) or to lapse after a specified period or in specified cases, or to be subject to renewal as and when provided by the rules.

   (4) The Secretary of State may by order provide—

   (a) for persons to be registered in one or more parts of the register by virtue of having been included in one or more of the registers, rolls or lists maintained under enactments repealed by the Nurses, Midwives and Health Visitors Act 1979, or having been certified under any of those enactments;

   (b) for a specified part of the register to be closed, as from a date specified by the order, so that on or after that date no further persons can become registered in that part;

   (c) for a specified part of the register to be sub-divided into two or more parts, or for two or more parts to be combined into one.

   (5) The Secretary of State shall consult the Central Council before making, varying or revoking any order under this section.

   (6) A certificate issued and duly authenticated by the Council stating that a person is, or was at any date, or is not, or was not at any date, registered shall be evidence in all courts of law of the fact stated in the certificate.

   (7) In any enactment or instrument (past or future, and including this Act) "registered", in relation to nurses, midwives and health visitors, means registered in the register maintained under this section by virtue of qualifications in nursing, midwifery or health visiting, as the case may be.

   (8) Orders under subsection (2) may, by reference to the part or parts in which a person is registered, prescribe the more advanced qualifications which he must have in order to be treated as a qualified nurse for the purposes of any particular enactment or instrument.

"Central Council": ss.1, 22.
"Council": ss.1, 22.
"training": s.22.

GENERAL NOTE
This section establishes the register of nurses qualified to practise. Admission to the register is governed by s.8. Special provisions in relation to nurses visiting from other EEA countries are made in ss.9 and 21. Removal from the register is governed by s.10 and the rules made under it, other than removal for failure to renew registration (which is governed by the Nurses, Midwives and Health Visitors Rules 1983 (S.I. 1983 No. 873), as amended).

Subs. (2)
Under the Nurses, Midwives and Health Visitors (Parts of the Register) Order 1983 (S.I. 1983 No. 667) as amended, there are currently 15 different categories on the register. There are separate parts for midwifery and health visiting. The nursing register is subdivided according to the specialities of general, mental illness, mental health, mental handicap, adult and children's nursing. There are also subdivisions in relation to nursing differentiating between first level (sometimes known as registered nurses) and second level (sometimes known as enrolled nurses). This complexity reflects the changing historical pattern of nurse training and the need to continue to register those who have undergone categories of training that are no longer available as well as the current subdivisions.

Subs. (3)
Part II of the Nurses, Midwives and Health Visitors Rules 1983 (S.I. 1983 No. 873) as amended, sets out the provisions under this subsection.

Admission to register

8.—(1) A person seeking admission to a part of the register must make application to the Central Council in accordance with the Council's rules.

(2) Subject to subsection (6) below, the applicant shall be registered in that part (on payment of such fee as may be required by the rules) if he satisfies the Council that he is of good character and has the appropriate professional qualifications.

(3) He is to be regarded as having those qualifications if—
   (a) he has in the United Kingdom undergone the training, and passed the examinations, required by the Council's rules for admission to that part of the register; or
   (b) being a national of any EEA State, he has professional qualifications, obtained in an EEA State other than the United Kingdom, which the Secretary of State has by order designated as having Community equivalence for the purposes of registration in that part; or
   (c) he has, elsewhere than in the United Kingdom, undergone training in nursing, midwifery or health visiting (as the case may be) and either—
      (i) that training is recognised by the Central Council as being to a standard sufficient for registration in that part; or
      (ii) it is not so recognised, but the applicant has undergone in the United Kingdom or elsewhere such additional training as the Council may require.

(4) An order under subsection (3)(b) may provide that a professional qualification designated by the order is to be regarded as having Community equivalence for the purposes of registration in a part of the register only if prescribed conditions required by a directive issued by the Council of the European Communities are fulfilled; and different conditions may be prescribed with respect to the same qualification for different circumstances.

(5) Any person who—

(a) is not a national of an EEA State, but

(b) is, by virtue of a right conferred by Article 11 of Council Regulation (EEC) No. 1612/68 or any other enforceable Community right, entitled to be treated, for the purposes of access to the nursing profession, or the profession of midwifery, no less favourably than a national of such a State,

shall be treated for the purposes of subsection (3)(b) as if he were such a national.

(6) In the case of an applicant within subsection (3)(c), the rules may either—

(a) make it an additional condition of his being registered that he has the necessary knowledge of English; or

(b) require him to have that knowledge within a period specified by the rules (failing which his registration will lapse at the end of the period).

(7) In any case where—

(a) an application for admission to a part of the register is made by an applicant within subsection (3)(b), and

(b) the Central Council has received all the documentary evidence as to his character and qualifications required to enable him to be registered,

he shall be registered in that part within three months of the date on which the Council was in receipt of that evidence or such longer period as may be permitted in his case by Article 10 of the Nursing Directive or Article 11 of the Midwifery Directive.

(8) In this Act—

"EEA State" means a Contracting Party to the EEA Agreement;

"EEA Agreement" means the Agreement on the European Economic Area signed at Oporto on 2nd May 1992 as adjusted by the Protocol signed at Brussels on 17th March 1993;

"national", in relation to an EEA State, means the same as it does for the purposes of the Community Treaties.

DEFINITIONS

"Central Council": ss.1, 22.
"Council": ss.1, 22.
"register": s.7.
"training": s.22.

GENERAL NOTE

This section sets out the requirements needed before nurses, midwives and health visitors can have their names entered on the professional register. Applicants must possess the appropriate qualifications, be of good character, and pay the appropriate fee (subs. (2)). The qualifications that are required depend on which of three categories the practitioner comes within.

Applicants who have trained in the U.K. must have passed a qualification complying with UKCC requirements (subs. (3)(a)). These are set out in the Nurses, Midwives and Health Visitors Rules 1983 (S.I. 1983 No. 873), as amended.

Those nationals of EEA states who qualify in an EEA state other than the U.K. must have a designated qualification conforming with the nursing and midwifery directives (subs. (3)(b)). The order referred to in subss. (3)(b) and (4) is the European Nursing and Midwifery Qualifications Designation Order 1996 (S.I. 1996 No. 3102), which made provision in accord with the First and Second Midwifery Directives (Nos. 80/154/EEC, [1980] O.J. L33/1, and 80/155/EEC, [1980] O.J. L33/8) and the Second Nursing Directive (77/453/EEC, [1977] O.J. L176/8). The First Nursing Directive was 77/452/EEC ([1977] O.J. L176/1). EEA practitioners visiting temporarily will be given deemed registration under s.9, to be read in conjunction with s.21.

Applicants who trained outside the U.K. and are not EEA nationals falling within the previous provision may register if their training is recognised by the UKCC, or if they undergo such additional training as the UKCC requires (subs. (3)(c)). Applicants in this category may also be required to show a satisfactory knowledge of English (subs. (6)).

Deemed registration of visiting EEA nurses and midwives

9.—(1) A visiting EEA nurse may practise as a nurse responsible for general care during the period specified in his relevant documents in pursuance of section 21(5)(a)(ii), and while he is so practising he shall be deemed to be registered as a nurse responsible for general care.

(2) A visiting EEA midwife shall be deemed to be registered as a midwife during the period specified in her relevant documents in pursuance of section 21(5)(a)(ii).

DEFINITIONS
"visiting EEA nurse": s.21.
"visiting EEA midwife": s.21.

GENERAL NOTE
This section provides for deemed registration for EEA practitioners visiting on a temporary basis. Those visiting permanently need to apply for registration under s.8.

Relevant documents
See s.21(5). Visiting practitioners are required to supply a declaration of the intention to practise, including the address where they intend to do so and the period of intended practice. They are also required to produce a recent certificate that they hold appropriate qualifications and are currently lawfully practising in another EEA state.

Removal from, and restoration to, register

10.—(1) The Central Council shall by rules determine circumstances in which, and the means by which—

(a) a person may, for misconduct or otherwise, be removed from the register or a part of it, whether or not for a specified period;

(b) a person who has been removed from the register or a part of it may be restored to it;

(c) a person's registration in the register or a part of it may be directed to be suspended, that is to say, not to have effect during such period as may be specified in the direction;

(d) the suspension of a person's registration in the register or a part of it may be terminated; and

(e) an entry in the register may be removed, altered or restored.

(2) Committees of the Council shall be constituted by the rules to deal with proceedings for a person's removal from, or restoration to, the register, for the suspension, or termination of the suspension, of a person's registration in the register or for the removal, alteration or restoration of any entry.

(3) The Council may bring proceedings before a committee constituted in pursuance of subsection (2) in respect of a visiting EEA nurse or midwife for the purpose of determining whether by reason of his misconduct or otherwise the provisions of this Act (except this section) relating to visiting EEA nurses or midwives should cease to apply to him; and the provisions of this section and of rules made under this section shall apply, with any necessary modifications, in relation to any such proceedings as they apply in relation to proceedings relating to a person's removal from the register.

(4) In any case where it is determined that those provisions should cease to apply to any person he shall thereupon cease to be a visiting EEA nurse or, as the case may be, a visiting EEA midwife for the purposes of this Act and accordingly shall also cease to be deemed to be registered; and he shall not be entitled to be treated as such a nurse or midwife before the expiry of such period (if any) as may be specified in the determination, or if no such period is specified, without the written consent of the Council.

(5) The committees need not be constituted exclusively from members of the Council, but the rules shall provide, in relation to committees constituted by them, that there shall be a quorum only if a majority of those present are members of the Council.

(6) The rules shall so provide that the members of a committee constituted to adjudicate upon the conduct of any person are selected with due regard to the professional field in which that person works.

(7) The rules shall make provision as to the procedure to be followed, and the rules of evidence to be observed, in such proceedings, whether before the Council itself or before any committee so constituted, and for the proceedings to be in public except in such cases (if any) as the rules may specify.

(8) Schedule 2 to this Act has effect with respect to the conduct of proceedings to which this section applies.

(9) Where a person's registration in the register or a part of it is suspended under subsection (1)(c), he shall be treated as not being registered in the register or part notwithstanding that his name still appears in it.

Definitions
"Central Council": ss.1, 22.
"Council": ss.1, 22.
"register": s.7.
"visiting EEA nurse": s.21.
"visiting EEA midwife": s.21.

General Note
The constitutions and procedural rules of the committees set up to perform the functions governed by this section are found in the Nurses, Midwives and Health Visitors (Professional Conduct) Rules 1993 (S.I. 1993 No. 893). These establish a Health Committee to deal with cases where a practitioner is alleged to be unfit to practise due to ill-health, and two committees to deal with allegations of misconduct. The Preliminary Proceedings Committee (PPC) considers whether a full hearing is required because there is a case to be answered. The Professional Conduct Committee hears cases referred by the PPC at a full hearing with the examination and cross-examination of witnesses. Schedule 2 to this Act provides a power to take oaths and *subpoena* witnesses. It also ensures that the Professional Conduct Committee will have a legal assessor, of at least 10 years' standing in the legal profession.

There is no power to make registration conditional on compliance with directions as to practice, as is available to the General Medical Council.

Subs. (1)(a)
The definition of 'misconduct' is found in r.1(2)(k) of the Nurses, Midwives and Health Visitors (Professional Conduct) Rules 1993 (S.I. 1993 No. 893). That defines 'professional misconduct' as 'conduct unworthy of a nurse, midwife or health visitor, as the case may be, and includes obtaining registration by fraud'. There is no need for misconduct to be 'serious' before the UKCC has jurisdiction to take action against a practitioner, as there is under the Medical Act 1983 (c.54), s.36. In 1990 the UKCC issued a booklet called '... *with a view to removal from the register...?'* indicating a number of common reasons for removal from the register. These include 'reckless and wilfully unskilled practice', concealing mishaps, failing to keep records, falsifying records, abuse of patients, failing to act when a colleague is abusing patients, and breach of confidentiality. Examples of the practice of the UKCC can also be found in R. Pyne, *Professional Discipline in Nursing, Midwifery and Health Visiting* (2nd ed., Blackwell Scientific, 1992). It is probable that misconduct would now be taken to be limited to conduct in a professional respect, but in *Stock v. Central Midwives Board* [1915] 3 K.B. 756 a midwife was struck off for extra-marital cohabitation on the basis that her immorality made her unfit to be a midwife.

Subs. (1)(c)
The intended purpose for the power of suspension was to deal with health cases (see the discussion in the debates on the 1992 Act, *Hansard*, H.L. Vol. 532, col. 508). However, there is nothing in the wording of the Act that prevents it being used as a sanction (as under s.36(1) of the Medical Act 1983).

Cautions

11.—(1) Without prejudice to the generality of section 10, rules under that section may make provision with respect to the giving, in the course of disciplinary proceedings, of cautions as to future conduct.

(2) Rules under section 10 may also make provision with respect to the keeping by the Council of a record of any caution as to future conduct given in the course of disciplinary proceedings.

(3) For the purposes of this section, "disciplinary proceedings" means proceedings for removal from the register or a part of it for misconduct.

DEFINITIONS
"Council": ss.1, 22.

GENERAL NOTE
The power to caution was added by the 1992 Act after the UKCC had been advised that it had no power to caution practitioners. It was intended to prevent the unnecessary pursuit of less serious cases before the Professional Conduct Committee, which had caused a considerable backlog of cases pending a hearing.

The power to keep a record of cautions (subs. (2)) is intended to enable the UKCC to identify and consider actions against practitioners who are persistently guilty of relatively minor misconduct.

Appeals

12.—(1) A person aggrieved by a decision to remove him from the register or to direct that his registration in the register be suspended or to remove or alter any entry in respect of him, or by any decision under section 10(3) or (4), may, within three months after the date on which notice of the decision is given to him by the Council, appeal to the appropriate court; and on the appeal—

(a) the court may give such directions in the matter as it thinks proper, including directions as to the costs of the appeal; and

(b) the order of the court shall be final.

(2) The appropriate court for the purposes of this section is the High Court, the Court of Session or the High Court in Northern Ireland, according as the appellant's ordinary place of residence is in England and Wales, Scotland or Northern Ireland at the time when notice of the decision is given.

DEFINITIONS
"Council": ss.1, 22.

GENERAL NOTE
The court is entitled to hear fresh evidence on an appeal if it is necessary to do justice; *Hefferon v. Professional Conduct Committee of U.K. Central Council for Nursing, Midwifery and Health Visiting* (1988) 10 BMLR 1, *Stock v. Central Midwives Board* [1915] 3 K.B. 756. The courts have been reluctant to challenge the Professional Conduct Committee's decisions on the meaning of misconduct and on what sanction is appropriate. However, they have overturned decisions where there was an error of law, no admissible evidence to support the finding, or where there were procedural irregularities that rendered the hearing unfair. On these points, see *Stock v. Central Midwives Board,* above, *Hefferon v. Professional Conduct Committee of U.K. Central Council for Nursing, Midwifery and Health Visiting* (1988) 10 BMLR 1, *Smith v. Professional Conduct Committee of U.K. Central Council for Nursing, Midwifery and Health Visiting,* unreported, April 14, 1988 and *Sinclair v. Professional Conduct Committee of U.K. Central Council for Nursing, Midwifery and Health Visiting,* unreported, June 28, 1988.

False claim of professional qualification

13.—(1) A person commits an offence if, with intent to deceive (whether by words or in writing or by the assumption of any name or description, or by the wearing of any uniform or badge or by any other kind of conduct)—

(a) he falsely represents himself to possess qualifications in nursing, midwifery or health visiting; or

(b) he falsely represents himself to be registered in the register, or in a particular part of it.

(2) A person commits an offence if—

(a) with intent that any person shall be deceived, he causes or permits another person to make any representation about himself which, if made by himself with intent to deceive, would be an offence by him under subsection (1); or

(b) with intent to deceive, he makes with regard to another person any representation which—

(i) is false to his own knowledge, and

(ii) if made by the other with that intent would be an offence by the other under that subsection.

(3) A person guilty of an offence under this section shall be liable on summary conviction to a fine not exceeding level 4 on the standard scale.

DEFINITIONS
"register": s.7.

GENERAL NOTE
This section creates offences that serve to protect the status of both professional qualifications and registration. Strictly speaking, it is not an offence to use the title 'nurse', 'midwife', or 'health visitor'. However, the use of those titles would usually be taken to be a representation of either registration or professional qualification (see the parenthesis in subs. (1)). Thus, in effect, the titles are protected. The false representations must be made with intent to deceive before an offence is committed.

Miscellaneous provisions about midwifery

Rules as to midwifery practice

14.—(1) The Council shall make rules regulating the practice of midwives and these rules may in particular—

(a) determine the circumstances in which, and the procedure by means of which, midwives may be suspended from practice;

(b) require midwives to give notice of their intention to practise to the local supervising authority for the area in which they intend to practise; and

(c) require registered midwives to attend courses of instruction in accordance with the rules.

(2) If rules are made requiring midwives to give the notice referred to in subsection (1)(b), it is then the duty of the local supervising authority to inform the Council of any notices given to the authority in compliance with the rules.

DEFINITIONS
"Council": ss.1, 22.
"local supervising authorities": s.15.
"registered midwife": s.7.

GENERAL NOTE
The rules in question are to be found in the Nurses, Midwives and Health Visitors Rules 1983 (S.I. 1983 No. 873), as amended. They require midwives to notify their intention to practise annually to the supervisors for each area in which they intend to work. Suspension from practice may be as a result of misconduct or because there is a risk that the midwife may spread an infection (see r.38 of the above Rules).

Local supervision of midwifery practice

15.—(1) The following bodies shall be local supervising authorities for midwives—

(a) in England and Wales, Health Authorities;

(b) in Scotland, Health Boards; and

(c) in Northern Ireland, Health and Social Services Boards.

(2) Each local supervising authority shall—

(a) exercise general supervision, in accordance with rules under section 14, over all midwives practising within its area;

(b) report any prima facie case of misconduct on the part of a midwife which arises in its area to the Council;

(c) have power in accordance with the Council's rules to suspend a midwife from practice.

(3) The Council may by rules prescribe the qualifications of persons who may be appointed by a local supervising authority to exercise supervision over midwives within its area, and no person shall be so appointed who is not qualified in accordance with the rules.

(4) The National Boards are responsible for providing the authorities with advice and guidance in respect of the exercise of their functions under this section.

(5) The Council may by rules prescribe standards to be observed with respect to advice and guidance provided under subsection (4).

DEFINITIONS
"Council": ss.1, 22.
"National Boards": s.5.

GENERAL NOTE
Prior to the abolition of Regional Health Authorities by the Health Authorities Act 1995 (c.17), it was those authorities who were the supervising bodies. Supervision is carried out by experienced midwives, appointed by the supervising authorities to do the task, who have undergone prescribed training (see r.44 of the Nurses, Midwives and Health Visitors Rules 1983 (S.I. 1983 No. 873), as amended).

Attendance by unqualified persons at childbirth

16.—(1) A person other than a registered midwife or a registered medical practitioner shall not attend a woman in childbirth.

(2) Subsection (1) does not apply—

(a) where the attention is given in a case of sudden or urgent necessity; or

(b) in the case of a person who, while undergoing training with a view to becoming a medical practitioner or to becoming a midwife, attends a woman in childbirth as part of a course of practical instruction in midwifery recognised by the General Medical Council or one of the National Boards.

(3) A person who contravenes subsection (1) shall be liable on summary conviction to a fine not exceeding level 4 on the standard scale.

DEFINITIONS
"General Medical Council": Medical Act 1983 (c.54), s.1.
"National Boards": s.5.
"registered medical practitioner": Medical Act 1983 (c.54), s.2.
"registered midwife": s.7.

GENERAL NOTE
This section creates an occupational monopoly for doctors and midwives over attending women in childbirth. There is a view that the section only applies where someone "attends" in a professional capacity or for financial gain (see J. Eekelaar and R. Dingwall, "Some Legal Issues in Obstetric Practice" [1984] JSWL 258). However, it is clear that at least one father has been prosecuted for delivering his own baby. The case was decided in 1982 and is unreported, although it is discussed in J. Finch, "Paternalism and Professionalism in Childbirth" (1982) 132 NLJ 995, 1011.

Financial provisions

Finances of Council and Boards

17.—(1) The Central Council and the National Boards may each charge such fees, in respect of such matters, as are determined by them respectively with the approval of the Secretary of State, including fees in connection with the training, qualification, examination and certification of nurses, midwives and health visitors.

(2) Fees received by the Council and Boards shall be applied to defray the expenses of the Council and Boards respectively.

(3) The Secretary of State may make grants to the Council and the Boards towards expenses incurred, or to be incurred, by them with the approval of the Secretary of State in connection with—

(a) the promotion by the Council and Boards of improvements in the education and training of nurses, midwives and health visitors;

(b) the performance by the National Boards of their duties under section 6(1)(a) and (b) above;

(c) the coming into force (whether in whole or part) of any provision of the Nurses, Midwives and Health Visitors Act 1992.

(4) Any sums required by the Secretary of State for making grants under subsection (3) shall be paid out of money provided by Parliament.

DEFINITIONS
"Central Council": ss.1, 22.
"Council": ss.1, 22.
"National Boards": s.5.

Accounts of Council and Boards

18.—(1) The Central Council and each of the National Boards shall—

(a) keep proper accounts, and such records in relation to the accounts, as the Secretary of State may direct; and

(b) in respect of each financial year, prepare a statement of accounts in such form as the Secretary of State may with the approval of the Treasury direct.

(2) The accounts of the Council and of each of the Boards shall be audited in such manner and by such persons as the Secretary of State may direct; and copies of the statements of account, together with the auditors' reports, shall be sent to the Secretary of State who shall send them to the Comptroller and Auditor General not later than 30th November in the year following that for which the accounts are made up.

(3) A person shall not be appointed as auditor under subsection (2) unless he is eligible for appointment as a company auditor under section 25 of the Companies Act 1989.

(4) The Comptroller and Auditor General shall examine the statements of account and auditors' reports, certify the statements and prepare a report on the results of his examination.

(5) For the purposes of his examination, the Comptroller and Auditor General may inspect the accounts of the Council and Boards and any records relating to them.

(6) The Council and each of the Boards shall annually, within such time as may be limited by the Secretary of State, submit a report to him on the performance of their respective functions during the period since their last such report, and a report under this subsection shall, in the case of a report by any of the Boards, be in such form as the Secretary of State may require.

(7) The Secretary of State shall lay before each House of Parliament—

(a) copies of the statements of account certified by the Comptroller and Auditor General, and the auditors' reports in respect of the Council and each of the Boards, together with copies of the report made by the Comptroller and Auditor General under subsection (4); and

(b) copies of the reports submitted by the Council and each of the Boards under subsection (6).

DEFINITIONS
"Central Council": ss.1, 22.
"Council": ss.1, 22.
"National Boards": s.5.

Miscellaneous and general

Central Council rules

19.—(1) The Council may make rules for the purpose of giving effect to this Act, and in particular with respect to anything which by this Act is required or authorised to be determined by rules.

(2) Rules under this Act may make different provision in relation to England, Wales, Scotland and Northern Ireland respectively.

(3) Before making any rules under this Act, the Council shall consult—

(a) representatives of any group of persons who appear likely to be affected by the proposed rules; and

(b) the National Boards for the parts of the United Kingdom to which the proposed rules are to extend.

(4) Subsection (3)(b) shall not require the Council to consult a National Board if the proposed rules do not appear to the Council to be relevant to the Board's functions.

(5) Rules under section 10 shall not come into force until approved by order by the Lord Chancellor and, in the case of rules which apply to proceedings in Scotland, the Lord Advocate; otherwise, rules come into force only when approved by the Secretary of State by order.

DEFINITIONS
"Council": ss.1, 22.
"National Boards": s.5.

Community documents

20. A registered nurse or midwife who—

(a) wishes to practise as a nurse or midwife in any EEA State, and

(b) requires for that purpose any such documentary evidence relating to his qualification as is referred to in the Nursing Directive or, as the case may be, the Midwifery Directive,

may apply to the Council for, and the Council shall provide, the necessary documents.

DEFINITIONS
"Council": ss.1, 22.
"EEA State": s.8(8).
"Midwifery Directive": s.21(6).
"Nursing Directive": s.21(6).
"registered midwife": s.7.
"registered nurse": s.7.

Visiting EEA nurses and midwives

21.—(1) In this Act "visiting EEA nurse" and "visiting EEA midwife" means a person who—

(a) is a national of any EEA State;

(b) is lawfully practising in an EEA State other than the United Kingdom as a nurse responsible for general care or, as the case may be, as a midwife;

(c) holds the appropriate diploma;

(d) is temporarily in the United Kingdom as a visitor; and

(e) provides the Council with the relevant documents.

(2) Any person who—

(a) is not a national of an EEA State, but

(b) is, by virtue of a right conferred by Article 11 of Council Regulation (EEC) No. 1612/68 or any other enforceable Community right, entitled to be treated, for the purposes of access to the nursing profession, or the profession of midwifery, no less favourably than a national of such a State,

shall be treated for the purposes of subsection (1) as if he were such a national.

(3) A visiting EEA nurse and a visiting EEA midwife shall provide the Council with the relevant documents before he provides any services as a nurse or midwife in the United Kingdom except that, in a case of sudden or urgent necessity, a nurse may provide the documents as soon as possible after he has provided his services as a nurse.

This subsection is without prejudice to section 16(2)(a).

(4) For the purposes of this Act "the appropriate diploma" means a diploma, certificate or other evidence of formal qualifications which EEA States are required to recognise in the case of a nurse, by the Nursing Directive or, in the case of a midwife, by the Midwifery Directive.

(5) For the purposes of this Act "relevant documents", in relation to any person means—

(a) a written declaration stating—

　　(i) that he is intending to practise in the United Kingdom as a nurse responsible for general care or, as the case may be, as a midwife; and

　　(ii) the address of the place where and the period during which he intends so to practise; and

(b) a certificate or certificates issued, not more than twelve months before the date on which the Council is provided with the relevant documents, by the competent authority of the EEA State in which he is practising as mentioned in subsection (1)(b) certifying—

　　(i) that he is lawfully practising as a nurse responsible for general care or, as the case may be, as a midwife in that State; and

　　(ii) that he holds an appropriate diploma.

(6) For the purposes of this Act—

"competent authority", in relation to an EEA State, means the authority or body designated by that State as competent for the purposes of the Nursing Directive or, as the case may be, the Midwifery Directive;

"Nursing Directive" means Council Directive No. 77/452/EEC, concerning the mutual recognition of diplomas, certificates and other evidence of the formal qualifications of nurses responsible for general care, as adapted, amended or extended by the Accession of Greece Act, Council Directive No. 81/1057/EEC, the Accession of Spain and Portugal Act, Council Directives Nos. 89/594/EEC, 89/595/EEC and 90/658/EEC, the EEA Agreement and the Accession of Austria, Finland and Sweden Act; and

"Midwifery Directive" means Council Directive No. 80/154/EEC, concerning the mutual recognition of diplomas, certificates and other evidence of the formal qualifications in midwifery, as adapted, amended or extended by Council Directive No. 80/1273/EEC, the Accession of Spain and Portugal Act, Council Directives Nos. 89/594/EEC and 90/658/EEC, the EEA Agreement and the Accession of Austria, Finland and Sweden Act;

and "EEA Agreement", "EEA State" and "national" shall be construed in accordance with section 8(8).

(7) For the purposes of this section—

"the Accession of Greece Act" means the Act annexed to the Treaty relating to the accession of the Hellenic Republic to the European Community signed at Athens on 28th May 1979;

"the Accession of Spain and Portugal Act" means the Act annexed to the Treaty relating to the accession of the Kingdom of Spain and the Portuguese Republic to the European Community signed at Madrid and Lisbon on 12th June 1985;

"the Accession of Austria, Finland and Sweden Act" means the Act annexed to the Treaty relating to the accession of the Kingdom of Norway, the Republic of Austria, the Republic of Finland and the Kingdom of Sweden to the European Union, signed at Corfu on 24th June 1994, as adjusted by the Decision of the Council of the European Union of 1st January 1995 adjusting the instruments concerning the accession of new member States to the European Union.

DEFINITIONS
"Council": ss.1, 22.

GENERAL NOTE
This section meets the U.K.'s obligations in respect of the free movement of persons from other EEA states. It provides for the lawful practice, on a temporary basis, of nurses and midwives from such countries provided that they furnish the UKCC with prescribed documents. There is no requirement for actual registration of temporary visitors from this category, as they are deemed to be registered under s.9. If such practitioners wish to work in the U.K. permanently, then they should seek registration under s.8(2)(b).

Interpretation and supplementary

22.—(1) In this Act—

"by order" means by order in a statutory instrument;

"the Central Council" and "the Council" mean the body mentioned in section 1(1);

"elected members" and "electoral scheme" have the meaning given by section 1(3);

"the National Boards" and "the Boards" mean the bodies mentioned in section 5(1);

"prescribed" means prescribed by the Secretary of State by order;

"the professional register" means the register maintained by the Council under section 7(1), and "registration" and "register" shall be construed accordingly;

"rules" means rules made by the Council;

"training" includes education;

and for a person to be treated as "practising" he must be working in some capacity by virtue of a qualification in nursing, midwifery or health visiting as the case may be.

(2) Orders under this Act shall be subject to annulment in pursuance of a resolution of either House of Parliament; but this does not apply to orders under section 19(5) or 24(3) or (4) or under Schedule 2.

(3) Schedule 3 to this Act has effect for adapting the provisions of this Act there mentioned in their application to Northern Ireland and to the National Board for Nursing, Midwifery and Health Visiting for Northern Ireland.

GENERAL NOTE
For discussion of the application of the definition of 'practising' in respect of midwives, see the annotations to s.4.

Consequential amendments, transitionals, repeals etc.

23.—(1) The enactments mentioned in Schedule 4 to this Act shall be amended in accordance with that Schedule.

(2) Schedule 5 to this Act which contains transitional provisions and savings has effect.

(3) The enactments and instruments mentioned in Schedule 6 to this Act are repealed or revoked to the extent specified in the third column of that Schedule.

GENERAL NOTE
The principal effect of the transitional provisions in Sched. 5 is to ensure the continuity of the subordinate legislation made under the Acts that are consolidated.

Short title, commencement, extent etc.

24.—(1) This Act may be cited as the Nurses, Midwives and Health Visitors Act 1997.

(2) Subject to subsection (3) below, this Act shall come into force at the end of the period of three months beginning with the day on which it is passed.

(3) Until such day as the Secretary of State may by order appoint, section 6(1)(a) shall apply to Northern Ireland with the substitution for the words preceding sub-paragraph (i) of the words "provide, or arrange for others to provide, at institutions approved by the Board".

(4) Section 5(6) shall cease to have effect from such day as the Secretary of State may appoint by order.

(5) Different days may be appointed under subsection (3) or (4) in relation to different purposes.

(6) This Act extends to Northern Ireland.

SCHEDULES

Section 1   SCHEDULE 1

CONSTITUTION ETC. OF CENTRAL COUNCIL

Variation of membership

1.—(1) If the Secretary of State approves a proposal submitted to him by the Council with respect to the number of its members, he shall by order amend section 1 as he thinks fit for the purpose of giving effect to the proposal.

(2) The Secretary of State may not approve a proposal under this paragraph if the number proposed—
(a) is greater than sixty, or
(b) is not a multiple of three.

Variation of electoral scheme

2.—(1) The Council may vary the electoral scheme with the approval of the Secretary of State.

(2) The Secretary of State may not approve a variation under this paragraph if it would have the effect of making anyone other than a registered nurse, midwife or health visitor living or working in the United Kingdom eligible to be elected in an election held under the scheme.

(3) The Secretary of State shall signify his approval of a variation under this paragraph by order.

Tenure of office of members and president etc.

3.—(1) Appointment as a member of the Council shall be for a period prescribed by the Secretary of State by order.

(2) The period prescribed by the Secretary of State for the purposes of sub-paragraph (1) above shall not be less than three nor more than five years.

4.—(1) This paragraph applies where a person ("the former member") ceases to be a member of the Council before the end of the period for which he was appointed.

(2) The vacancy left by the former member shall be filled by a person appointed by the Secretary of State for the remainder of the period for which the former member was appointed.

(3) If the former member was an elected member, the Secretary of State shall appoint under sub-paragraph (2) above a person nominated by the Council who shall have the same qualification for election under the electoral scheme as the former member had at the time of his appointment.

(4) If the former member was not an elected member, the Secretary of State shall, in making an appointment under sub-paragraph (2) above, have regard to the qualification by virtue of which the former member was appointed.

(5) In sub-paragraphs (3) and (4) above, references to an elected member include a replacement for such a member.

5.—(1) Where a member of the Council or any of its committees is absent from meetings for more than six months consecutively or is disqualified from practising as a nurse, midwife or health visitor, the Council may by resolution declare that he has ceased to be a member.

(2) An elected member shall cease to be a member if he ceases to hold any qualification by virtue of which he was elected.

(3) A person appointed as a replacement for an elected member shall cease to be a member if he ceases to hold any qualification by virtue of which he was appointed.

6. If the president or vice-president ceases to be a member of the Council he shall also cease to be president or vice-president.

Procedure

7.—(1) The Council may act notwithstanding—
(a) any vacancy among its members; or
(b) that by reason of one or more vacancies, less than two-thirds of the members of the Council are elected members (or their replacements).

(2) At any meeting of the Council the quorum shall be twenty members including, in the case of each part of the United Kingdom, at least one member living or working in that part.

(3) The Council may constitute committees of itself for the purpose of transacting particular business of the Council.

(4) Persons who are not members of the Council may be appointed by it as members of such committees; but not more than one-third of the members of such a committee shall be persons appointed by virtue of this sub-paragraph.

(5) The Council may, by means of standing orders, regulate its own procedure, that of its standing committees and that of any committees constituted under sub-paragraph (3) above, and may, to such extent and in such cases as may be permitted or required by orders of the Secretary of State or by its rules and standing orders, act through those standing and other committees.

(6) No defect in the appointment of any member shall invalidate any proceedings of the Council or of its committees.

Remuneration, allowances and pensions

8.—(1) The Council may pay to its president such remuneration, and make such provision for the payment of pensions, allowances or gratuities to or in respect of him, as it thinks fit.

(2) The Council may pay to its members and to other persons appointed to serve on its committees such travelling and other allowances as it thinks fit.

Documents

9. A document purporting to be duly executed under the seal of the Council or to be signed on its behalf shall be received in evidence and shall be deemed to be so executed or signed unless the contrary is proved.

Section 10(8)   SCHEDULE 2

PROCEEDINGS BEFORE COUNCIL AND COMMITTEES

1. For purposes of proceedings under section 10 before the Council or a committee in England and Wales—
(a) the Council or committee may administer oaths;
(b) a solicitor to the Council, and any person entitled to appear at the proceedings, may sue out writs of subpoena ad testificandum and duces tecum (but not so as to compel a person to produce a document which he could not be compelled to produce on the trial of an action); and
(c) section 36 of the Supreme Court Act 1981 (subpoena valid throughout United Kingdom) applies as in relation to causes or matters in the High Court.

2.—(1) For purposes of proceedings under section 10 before the Council or a committee in Scotland—

(a) the Council or committee may administer oaths; and

(b) the Court of Session shall, on the application of any party to the proceedings, have the same such powers as are mentioned in sub-paragraph (2) below as it has in an action in that court.

(2) The powers mentioned above are—

(a) to grant warrant for the citation of witnesses and havers to give evidence or to produce documents before the Council or committee, and for the issue of second diligence against any witness or haver failing to appear after due citation;

(b) to grant warrant for the recovery of documents; and

(c) to grant commissions to persons to take the evidence of witnesses or to examine havers and receive their exhibits and productions.

3.—(1) The Central Council shall appoint assessors (either generally or for any particular proceedings or class of proceedings) to advise the Council or committees on questions of law arising in the proceedings.

(2) Assessors shall be—

(a) persons who have a ten year general qualification within the meaning of section 71 of the Courts and Legal Services Act 1990;

(b) advocates or solicitors in Scotland of at least ten years' standing; or

(c) members of the Bar of Northern Ireland or solicitors of the Supreme Court of Northern Ireland of at least ten years' standing.

(3) The Council shall pay to assessors such remuneration as it may determine.

4.—(1) The Lord Chancellor and, for proceedings in Scotland, the Lord Advocate may by order make provision with regard to the functions of assessors.

(2) In particular, provision may be made—

(a) requiring assessors, when advising the Council or any of its committees, to do so in the presence of the parties or, where advice is given in private, requiring the parties to be notified of the advice tendered by the assessors; and

(b) requiring the parties to be informed in cases where the assessors' advice is not accepted.

Section 22(3)   SCHEDULE 3

ADAPTATIONS FOR NORTHERN IRELAND AND ITS NATIONAL BOARD

1. In sections 5, 6, 17, 18, 19 and 22 and Schedule 2, as they apply to Northern Ireland and to the National Board for Nursing, Midwifery and Health Visiting for Northern Ireland, there are made the adaptations provided for by this Schedule.

2. Subject to the following provisions of this Schedule, in the provisions of this Act specified in column 1 of the Table set out below, for any reference specified in column 2 substitute the reference specified in column 3.

TABLE

Provision	*Reference*	*Substituted reference*
Sections 5(9)(e) and (f) and 18(6) and (7)	The Secretary of State	The Head of the Department of Health and Social Services for Northern Ireland.
Sections 6(1)(e), 17(1) and (3) and 18(1) and (2)	The Secretary of State	The Department of Health and Social Services for Northern Ireland.
Sections 5(9)(e) and 18(1)(b)	The Treasury	The Department of Finance and Personnel in Northern Ireland.
Section 18	The Comptroller and Auditor General	The Comptroller and Auditor General for Northern Ireland.
Section 18(3)	Section 25 of the Companies Act 1989	Article 28 of the Companies (Northern Ireland) Order 1990.
Section 18(7)	Each House of Parliament	The Northern Ireland Assembly.
Section 19(5) and Schedule 2, paragraph 4	The Lord Chancellor	The Lord Chief Justice of Northern Ireland.

3. In section 5, for subsections (2) to (8) substitute—

"(2) The National Board for Nursing, Midwifery and Health Visiting for Northern Ireland shall consist of—

    (a) a chairman appointed by the Head of the Department of Health and Social Services for Northern Ireland from among persons who are registered nurses, midwives or health visitors;

    (b) such number of other members appointed by the Head of the Department of Health and Social Services for Northern Ireland as that Department may specify by order;

    (c) the person for the time being appointed in pursuance of subsection (7)(a) to be the chief executive officer of the Board; and

    (d) any person for the time being appointed in pursuance of subsection (7)(b) to an office under the Board which is specified for the purposes of this paragraph by the Department of Health and Social Services for Northern Ireland by order.

(3) Appointments to the Board for the purposes of subsection (2)(b) shall be made from among persons who—

    (a) are registered nurses, midwives or health visitors; or

    (b) have such qualifications and experience in education or other fields as, in the opinion of the Head of the Department of Health and Social Services for Northern Ireland, will be of value to the Board in the performance of its functions.

(4) The powers conferred by this section shall be so exercised as to secure that a majority of the members of the Board are registered nurses, midwives or health visitors.

(5) The Department of Health and Social Services for Northern Ireland may, with the consent of the Department of Finance and Personnel in Northern Ireland—

    (a) pay such remuneration as the Department of Health and Social Services for Northern Ireland thinks fit to any person who is a member of the Board by virtue of appointment by the Head of that Department; and

    (b) make such provision as the Department of Health and Social Services for Northern Ireland thinks fit for the payment to or in respect of any person who is a member of the Board by virtue of such appointment of pensions, allowances or gratuities.

(6) A National Board may pay to its chairman and members and to other persons appointed to serve on its standing and other committees, such travelling and other allowances as the Department of Health and Social Services for Northern Ireland may determine with the consent of the Department of Finance and Personnel in Northern Ireland.

(7) The Board shall have—

    (a) a chief executive officer; and

    (b) such other officers as the Department of Health and Social Services for Northern Ireland may by order specify for the purposes of this paragraph,

appointed by the Board.

(8) The Department of Health and Social Services for Northern Ireland may by order make such further provision with respect to the constitution and administration of the Board as it thinks fit."

4. In section 22(1)—

    (a) in the definition of "by order", at the end add the words "or, in the case of an order under section 5 or 6 made by the Department of Health and Social Services for Northern Ireland or an order under section 19(5) or paragraph 4 of Schedule 2 made by the Lord Chief Justice of Northern Ireland, means by order made by statutory rule for the purposes of the Statutory Rules (Northern Ireland) Order 1979";

    (b) in the definition of "prescribed" after the words "Secretary of State" insert the words "or, as the case may be, the Department of Health and Social Services for Northern Ireland".

5. In section 22(2) at the end add the words "or orders made by the Department of Health and Social Services for Northern Ireland under section 5 or 6; and the orders made by that Department under those sections shall be subject to negative resolution as defined by section 41(6) of the Interpretation Act (Northern Ireland) 1954 as if they were statutory instruments within the meaning of that Act."

6. In paragraph 1 of Schedule 2 for "in England and Wales" substitute "in Northern Ireland" and for sub-paragraph (c) substitute—

    "(c) section 67 of the Judicature (Northern Ireland) Act 1978 (subpoena valid throughout United Kingdom) applies as in relation to causes or matters in the High Court in Northern Ireland".

Section 23(1) SCHEDULE 4

CONSEQUENTIAL AMENDMENTS

The House of Commons Disqualification Act 1975 (c. 24)

1. In Part III of Schedule 1 to the House of Commons Disqualification Act 1975 in the entry relating to the National Boards constituted under section 5 of the Nurses, Midwives and Health Visitors Act 1979 for "constituted under section 5 of the Nurses, Midwives and Health Visitors Act 1979" substitute "mentioned in section 5 of the Nurses, Midwives and Health Visitors Act 1997".

The Northern Ireland Assembly Disqualification Act 1975 (c. 25)

2. In Part III of Schedule 1 to the Northern Ireland Assembly Disqualification Act 1975 there shall continue to be an entry as follows—
"Chairman of the National Board for Nursing, Midwifery and Health Visiting for Northern Ireland or member of that Board appointed at a salary".

The Registered Homes Act 1984 (c. 23)

3. In section 42(4)(a) of the Registered Homes Act 1984, for "the Nurses, Midwives and Health Visitors Act 1979" substitute "the Nurses, Midwives and Health Visitors Act 1997".

The Video Recordings Act 1984 (c. 39)

4. In section 3(11) of the Video Recordings Act 1984, for "the Nurses, Midwives and Health Visitors Act 1979" substitute "the Nurses, Midwives and Health Visitors Act 1997".

The Registered Homes (Northern Ireland) Order 1992 (S.I. 1992/3204 (N.I. 20))

5. In Article 32(2)(b) of the Registered Homes (Northern Ireland) Order 1992 for "section 10 of the Nurses, Midwives and Health Visitors Act 1979" substitute "section 7 of the Nurses, Midwives and Health Visitors Act 1997".

The Value Added Tax Act 1994 (c. 23)

6. In Part II of Schedule 9 to the Value Added Tax Act 1994, in item 1(d) in Group 7, for "section 10 of the Nurses, Midwives and Health Visitors Act 1979" substitute "section 7 of the Nurses, Midwives and Health Visitors Act 1997".

Section 23(2) SCHEDULE 5

TRANSITIONAL PROVISIONS AND SAVINGS

General

1. The substitution of this Act for the provisions repealed by it does not affect the continuity of the law.

2. Anything done (including subordinate legislation made) under or otherwise by reference to a provision repealed by this Act has effect as if done under or by reference to any corresponding provision of this Act.

3. Any reference, express or implied, in this Act, another enactment or an instrument or document, to a provision of this Act is, subject to its context, to be read as being or including a reference to the corresponding provision repealed by this Act, in relation to times, circumstances or purposes in relation to which the repealed provision had effect.

4.—(1) Any reference, express or implied, in any enactment, instrument or document, to a provision repealed by this Act is, subject to its context, to be read as being or including a reference to the corresponding provision of this Act, in relation to times, circumstances or purposes in relation to which that provision has effect.

(2) In particular, where a power conferred by an Act is expressed to be exercisable in relation to enactments contained in Acts passed before or in the same Session as that Act, the power is also exercisable in relation to any corresponding provision of this Act.

5. Any reference to an enactment repealed by this Act which is contained in a document made, served or issued after the repeal has come into force is, subject to its context, to be read as being or including a reference to the corresponding provision of this Act.

6. Paragraphs 1 to 5 are in place of section 17(2) of the Interpretation Act 1978 but do not otherwise affect the application of that Act.

Claims against pre-1979 bodies

7.—(1) Where a person formerly employed by any of the bodies dissolved by virtue of section 21(1) of the Nurses, Midwives and Health Visitors Act 1979 claims to have a right of action against that body arising from his employment by it but is unable to pursue his claim because of the dissolution of the body, he may bring his claim—

(a) if he was transferred to the employment of the Central Council or one of the National Boards, against the body to whose employment he was transferred; or

(b) in any other case, against the Central Council.

(2) The body against whom a claim is brought by virtue of sub-paragraph (1) shall be liable in the same manner and to the same extent as the body dissolved would have been liable if it had not been dissolved.

Section 23(3) SCHEDULE 6

REPEALS AND REVOCATIONS

Chapter or number	Short title or title	Extent of repeal or revocation
1979 c. 36.	The Nurses, Midwives and Health Visitors Act 1979.	The whole Act so far as unrepealed except sections 23(4) and 24 and Schedule 7.
S.I. 1983/884.	The Nursing and Midwifery Qualifications (EEC Recognition) Order 1983.	The whole instrument.
S.I. 1984/1975.	The Nursing and Midwifery Qualifications (EEC Recognition) Amendment Order 1984.	The whole instrument.
1985 c. 9.	The Companies Consolidation (Consequential Provisions) Act 1985.	In Schedule 2, the entry relating to the Nurses, Midwives and Health Visitors Act 1979.
1990 c. 41.	The Courts and Legal Services Act 1990.	In Schedule 10, paragraph 43.
1992 c. 16.	The Nurses, Midwives and Health Visitors Act 1992.	The whole Act.
1995 c. 17.	The Health Authorities Act 1995.	In Schedule 1, paragraph 104.
S.I. 1996/3101.	The Nurses, Midwives and Health Visitors Act 1979 (Amendment) Regulations 1996.	The whole instrument.

TABLE OF DERIVATIONS

Notes:

1. This Table shows the derivation of the provisions of the Act.
2. The following abbreviations are used in the Table—

Acts of Parliament

1979	= Nurses, Midwives and Health Visitors Act 1979 (c. 36)
1992	= Nurses, Midwives and Health Visitors Act 1992 (c. 16)

Subordinate Legislation

S.I. 1983/884 = Nursing and Midwifery Qualifications (EEC Recognition) Order 1983

S.I. 1996/3101 = Nurses, Midwives and Health Visitors Act 1979 (Amendment) Regulations 1996

Provision	Derivation
1(1)	1979 s.1(1).
(2) to (8)	1979 s.1(2) to (8); 1992 ss.1(1), 2, Sch. 2 para. 8(3); United Kingdom Central Council for Nursing, Midwifery and Health Visiting (Membership Proposal) Approval Order 1992 (S.I. 1992/2160); United Kingdom Central Council for Nursing, Midwifery and Health Visiting (Electoral Scheme) Order 1992 (S.I. 1992/2159).
2(1), (2)	1979 s.2(1), (2).
(3)	1979 s.2(3); 1992 Sch. 2 para. 3.
(4) to (6)	1979 s.2(4) to (6).
3(1), (2)	1979 s.3(1), (2).
(3)	1979 s.3(3); 1992 s.3.
(4)	1979 s.3(4).
4	1979 s.4.
5(1)	1979 s.5(1).
(2) to (5)	1979 s.5(2) to (5); 1992 s.4.
(6)	1979 Sch. 2 para. 7(b); Transfer of Functions (Minister for the Civil Service and Treasury) Order 1981 (S.I. 1981/1670) Arts. 2 and 3(5).
(7) to (11)	1979 s.5(6) to (10); 1992 s.4.
6(1)(a)	1979 s.6(1)(a); 1992 s.5(2).
(b)	1979 s.6(1)(b); 1992 Sch. 2 para. 4.
(c), (d)	1979 s.6(1)(c), (d).
(e)	1979 s.6(1)(da); 1992 s.5(3).
(2)	1979 s.6(2); 1992 s.5(5).
7	1979 s.10.
8(1), (2)	1979 s.11(1), (2).
(3)	1979 s.11(3); S.I. 1996/3101 Reg. 2(1).
(4)	1979 s.11(3A); S.I. 1983/884 Art. 3(a); Nursing and Midwifery Qualifications (EEC Recognition) Amendment Order 1984 (S.I. 1984/1975) Art. 2.
(5)	1979 s.11(3B); S.I. 1996/3101 Reg. 2(2).
(6)	1979 s.11(4); European Communities (Medical, Dental and Nursing Professions) (Linguistic Knowledge) Order 1981 (S.I. 1981/432) Art. 2(1)(f).
(7)	1979 s.11(4A); S.I. 1983/884 Art. 3(b); S.I. 1996/3101 Reg. 2(3).
(8)	1979 s.11(5); S.I. 1996/3101 Reg. 2(4).
9	1979 s.11A; S.I. 1983/884 Art. 4; S.I. 1996/3101 Reg. 4(1).
10(1)(a)	1979 s.12(1)(a).
(b)	1979 s.12(1)(b).
(c), (d)	1979 s.12(1)(ba), (bb); 1992 s.7(2).
(e)	1979 s.12(1)(c).
(2)	1979 s.12(2); 1992 ss.7(3), 8(2).
(3), (4)	1979 s.12(2A), (2B); S.I. 1983/884 Art. 5(1); S.I. 1996/3101 Reg. 4(2).
(5), (6)	1979 s.12(3), (3A); 1992 s.8(3)(a), (b).
(7), (8)	1979 s.12(4), (5).
(9)	1979 s.12(6); 1992 s.7(4).
11	1979 s.12A; 1992 s.9.
12(1)	1979 s.13(1); 1992 s.7(5); S.I. 1983/884 Art. 5(2).
(2)	1979 s.13(2).
13(1), (2)	1979 s.14(1), (2).
(3)	1979 s.14(3); Criminal Justice Act 1982 (c. 48) s.46; Criminal Justice (Scotland) Act 1975 (c. 21) s.289G; Fines and Penalties (Northern Ireland) Order 1984 (S.I. 1984/703 (N.I. 3)) Art. 5.
14(1)	1979 s.15(1).
(2)	1979 s.15(2); 1992 s.11.
15(1)(a)	1979 s.16(1)(a); Health Authorities Act 1995 (c. 17) Sch. 1 para. 104.
(b), (c)	1979 s.16(1)(c), (d).
(2)(a)	1979 s.16(2)(a).
(b)	1979 s.16(2)(b); 1992 Sch. 2 para. 5.
(c)	1979 s.16(2)(c).

Provision	Derivation
15(3), (4)	1979 s.16(3), (4).
(5)	1979 s.16(5); 1992 s.12.
16(1)	1979 s.17(1).
(2)	1979 s.17(3); 1992 Sch. 2 para. 6.
(3)	1979 s.17(4); Criminal Justice Act 1982 (c. 48) s.46; Criminal Justice (Scotland) Act 1975 (c. 21) s.289G; Fines and Penalties (Northern Ireland) Order 1984 (S.I. 1984/703 (N.I. 3)) Art. 5.
17	1979 s.19; 1992 s.13(2)(b).
18(1), (2)	1979 s.20(1), (2).
(3)	1979 s.20(2A); Companies Act 1989 (Eligibility for Appointment as Company Auditor) (Consequential Amendments) Regulations 1991 (S.I. 1991/1997) Sch. para. 32.
(4), (5)	1979 s.20(3), (4).
(6)	1979 s.20(5); 1992 Sch. 2 para. 7.
(7)	1979 s.20(6).
19(1) to (3)	1979 s.22(1) to (3).
(4)	1979 s.22(3A); 1992 s.14.
(5)	1979 s.22(4).
20	1979 s.22A; S.I. 1983/884 Art. 6; S.I. 1996/3101 Reg. 4(3).
21(1)	1979 s.22B(1); S.I. 1983/884 Art. 6; S.I. 1996/3101 Reg. 3(1).
(2)	1979 s.22B(1A); S.I. 1996/3101 Reg. 3(2).
(3) to (5)	1979 s.22B(2) to (4); S.I. 1983/884 Art. 6; S.I. 1996/3101 Reg. 3(3), (4).
(6), (7)	1979 s.22B(5), (6); S.I. 1996/3101 Reg. 3(5).
22(1)	1979 s.23(1); 1992 Sch. 2 para. 8.
(2), (3)	1979 s.23(2), (3).
23	—
24(1), (2)	—
(3)	See Nurses, Midwives and Health Visitors Act 1992 (Commencement No. 1) Order 1993 (S.I. 1993/588 (C. 11)) and 1979 s.6(1)(a).
(4)	See Nurses, Midwives and Health Visitors Act 1992 (Commencement No. 1) Order 1993 (S.I. 1993/588 (C. 11)) and 1992 Sch. 3.
(5)	1992 s.17(3).
(6)	1979 s.24(3); 1992 s.17(4).
Sch. 1	1979 Sch. 1; 1992 s.1(2), Sch. 1.
Sch. 2.	
para. 1	1979 Sch. 3 para. 1; Interpretation Act 1978 (c. 30) s.17(2)(a) and Supreme Court Act 1981 (c. 54) s.36.
para. 2	1979 Sch. 3 para. 2.
para. 3(1)	1979 Sch. 3 para. 3(1).
para. 3(2)	1979 Sch. 3 para. 3(2); Courts and Legal Services Act 1990 (c. 41) Sch. 10 para. 43.
para. 3(3)	1979 Sch. 3 para. 3(3).
para. 4	1979 Sch. 3 para. 4.
Sch. 3	
para. 1	1979 Sch. 6 para. 1; 1992 Sch. 2 para. 9(2).
para. 2	1979 Sch. 6 para. 2; 1992 Sch. 2 para. 9(3); Departments (Northern Ireland) Order 1982 (S.I. 1982/338 (N.I. 6)) Art. 3; Companies (1990 Order) (Eligibility for Appointment as Company Auditor) (Consequential Amendments) Regulations (Northern Ireland) 1993 (S.I. 1993/67) Sch. para. 8.
para. 3	1979 Sch. 6 para. 2A; 1992 Sch. 2 para. 9(4); as to s.5(6), 1979 Sch. 2 para. 7(b) and Sch. 6 para. 2, and Departments (Northern Ireland) Order 1982 (S.I. 1982/338 (N.I. 6)) Arts. 4 and 7.
para. 4	1979 Sch. 6 para. 3; 1992 Sch. 2 para. 9(5); Statutory Rules (Northern Ireland) Order 1979 (S.I. 1979/1573 (N.I. 12)) Sch. 4 para. 28.
para. 5	1979 Sch. 6 para. 4; 1992 Sch. 2 para. 9(6).
para. 6	1979 Sch. 6 para. 5.
Sch. 4	
para. 1	—

Provision	Derivation
Sch. 4—*cont.*	
para. 2	1979 Sch. 2 para. 5(2); 1992 Sch. 2 para. 2.
Sch. 5	
paras. 1 to 6	—
para. 7	1979 Sch. 5 para. 6.
Sch. 6	—

TABLE OF DESTINATIONS

CRIMINAL JUSTICE (SCOTLAND) ACT 1975
(C.21)

1975	1997
s.289G	ss.13(3), 16(3)

INTERPRETATION ACT 1978
(C.30)

1978	1997
s.17(2)(a)	Sched. 2, para. 1

NURSES, MIDWIVES AND HEALTH VISITORS ACT 1979
(C.36)

1979	1997	1979	1997	1979	1997
s.1(1)	s.1(1)	s.12(3A)	s.10(5), (6)	s.24(3)	s.24(6)
(2)–(8)	1(2)–(8)	(4), (5)	10(7), (8)	Sched. 1	Sched. 1
2(1), (2)	2(1), (2)	(6)	10(9)	Sched. 2,	
(3)	2(3)	12A	11	para. 5(2)	Sched. 4, para. 2
(4)–(6)	2(4)–(6)	13(1)	12(1)	para. 7(b)	s.5(6), Sched. 3, para. 3
3(1)	3(1), (2)	(2)	12(2)	Sched. 3,	
(2)	3(1), (2)	14(1), (2)	13(1), (2)	para. 1	Sched. 2, para. 1
(3)	3(3)	(3)	13(3)	para. 2	Sched. 2, para. 2
(4)	3(4)	15(1)	14(1)	para. 3(1)	Sched. 2, para. 3(1)
4	4	(2)	14(2)	para. 3(2)	Sched. 2, para. 3(2)
5(1)	5(1)	16(1)(a)	15(1)(a)	para. 3(3)	Sched. 2, para. 3(3)
5(2)–(5)	5(2)–(5)	(1)(c), (d)	15(1)(b), (c)	para. 4	Sched. 2, para. 4
5(6)–(10)	5(7)–(11)	(2)(a)	15(2)(a)	Sched. 5,	
6(1)(a)	ss.6(1)(a), 24(3)	(2)(b)	15(2)(b)	para. 6	Sched. 5, para. 7
(1)(b)	s.6(1)(b)	(2)(c)	15(2)(c)	Sched. 6,	
(1)(c), (d)	6(1)(c), (d)	(3), (4)	15(3), (4)	para. 1	Sched. 3, para. 1
(1)(da)	6(1)(e)	(5)	15(5)	para. 2	Sched. 3, paras. 2, 3
(2)	6(2)	17(1)	16(1)	para. 2A	Sched. 3, para. 3
10	7	(3)	16(2)	para. 3	Sched. 3, para. 4
11(1), (2)	8(1), (2)	(4)	16(3)	para. 4	Sched. 3, para. 5
(3)	8(3)	19	17	para. 5	Sched. 3, para. 6
(3A)	8(4)	20(1), (2)	18(1), (2)		
(3B)	8(5)	(2A)	18(3)		
(4)	8(6)	(3), (4)	18(4), (5)		
(4A)	8(7)	(5)	18(6)		
(5)	8(8)	(6)	18(7)		
11A	9	22(1)–(3)	19(1)–(3)		
12(1)(a)	10(1)(a)	(3A)	19(4)		
(1)(b)	10(1)(b)	(4)	19(5)		
(1)(ba)	10(1)(c), (d)	22A	20		
(1)(bb)	10(1)(c), (d)	22B(1)	21(1)		
(1)(c)	10(1)(e)	(1A)	21(2)		
(2)	10(2)	(2)–(4)	21(3)–(5)		
(2A), (2B)	10(3), (4)	(5), (6)	21(6), (7)		
(3)	10(5), (6)	23(1)	22(1)		
		(2), (3)	22(2), (3)		

SUPREME COURT ACT 1981
(C.54)

1981	1997
s.36	Sched. 2, para. 1

24–29

TABLE OF DESTINATIONS

CRIMINAL JUSTICE ACT 1982
(c.48)

1982	1997
s.46	ss.13(3), 16(3)

COURTS AND LEGAL SERVICES ACT 1990
(c.41)

1990	1997
Sched. 10,	
para. 43	Sched. 2,
	para. 3(2)

NURSES, MIDWIVES AND HEALTH VISITORS ACT 1992
(c.16)

1992	1997	1992	1997	1992	1997
s.1(1).........	s.1(2)–(8)	s.9	s.11	Sched. 2—cont.	
(2).........	1(2)–(8),	11	14(2)	para. 7	s.18(6)
	Sched. 1	12	15(5)	para. 8	22(1)
3	3(3)	13(2)(b).....	17	para. 8(3)....	1(2)–(8)
4	5(2)–(5),	14	19(4)	para. 9(2)....	Sched. 3,
	(7)–(11)	17(3).......	24(5)		para. 1
5(2)........	6(1)(a)	(4).......	24(6)	para. 9(3)....	Sched. 3,
(3)........	6(1)(e)	Sched. 1	Sched. 1		para. 2
(5)........	6(2)	Sched. 2,		para. 9(4)....	Sched. 3,
7(2)........	10(1)(c), (d)	para. 2	Sched. 4,		para. 3
(3)........	10(2)		para. 2	para. 9(5)....	Sched. 3,
(4)........	10(9)	para. 3	s.2(3)		para. 4
(5)........	12(1)	para. 4	6(1)(b)	para. 9(6)....	Sched. 3,
8(2)........	10(2)	para. 5	15(2)(b)		para. 5
(3)(a), (b)..	10(5), (6)	para. 6	16(2)	Sched. 3	s.24(4)

HEALTH AUTHORITIES ACT 1995
(c.17)

1995	1997
Sched. 1,	
para. 104	s.15(1)(a)

STATUTORY RULES (NORTHERN IRELAND) ORDER 1979
(S.I. 1979 No. 1573)
(N.I. 12)

1979	1997
Sched. 4,	
para. 28	Sched. 3,
	para. 4

EUROPEAN COMMUNITIES (MEDICAL, DENTAL AND NURSING PROFESSIONS) (LINGUISTIC KNOWLEDGE) ORDER 1981
(S.I. 1981 No. 432)

1981	1997
art. 2(1)(f)	s.8(6)

TRANSFER OF FUNCTIONS (MINISTER FOR THE CIVIL SERVICE AND TREASURY) ORDER 1981
(S.I. 1981 No. 1670)

1981	1997
art. 2	s.5(6)
art. 3(5)	5(6)

TABLE OF DESTINATIONS

DEPARTMENTS (NORTHERN IRELAND) ORDER 1982
(S.I. 1982 No. 338)
(N.I. 6)

1982	1997
art. 3	Sched. 3, para. 2
art. 4	Sched. 3, para. 3
art. 7	Sched. 3, para. 3

NURSING AND MIDWIFERY QUALIFICATIONS (EEC RECOGNITION) ORDER 1983
(S.I. 1983 No. 884)

1983	1997
art. 3(a)	s.8(4)
art. 3(b)	8(7)
art. 4	9
art. 5(1)	10(3), (4)
art. 5(2)	12(1)
art. 6	ss.20, 21(1), (3)–(5)

FINES AND PENALTIES (NORTHERN IRELAND) ORDER 1984
(S.I. 1984 No. 703)
(N.I. 3)

1984	1997
art. 5	ss.13(3), 16(3)

NURSING AND MIDWIFERY QUALIFICATIONS (EEC RECOGNITION) AMENDMENT ORDER 1984
(S.I. 1984 No. 1975)

1984	1997
art. 2	s.8(4)

COMPANIES ACT 1989 (ELIGIBILITY FOR APPOINTMENT AS COMPANY AUDITOR) (CONSEQUENTIAL AMENDMENTS) REGULATIONS 1991
(S.I. 1991 No. 1997)

1991	1997
Sched., para. 32	s.18(3)

UNITED KINGDOM CENTRAL COUNCIL FOR NURSING, MIDWIFERY AND HEALTH VISITING (ELECTORAL SCHEME) ORDER 1992
(S.I. 1992 No. 2159)

1992	1997
S.I. 1992 No. 2159	s.1(2)–(8)

TABLE OF DESTINATIONS

UNITED KINGDOM CENTRAL COUNCIL FOR NURSING, MIDWIFERY AND HEALTH VISITING (MEMBERSHIP PROPOSAL) APPROVAL ORDER 1992
(S.I. 1992 No. 2160)

1992	1997
S.I. 1992 No.	
2160	s.1(2)–(8)

COMPANIES (1990 ORDER) (ELIGIBILITY FOR APPOINTMENT AS COMPANY AUDITOR) (CONSEQUENTIAL AMENDMENTS) REGULATIONS (NORTHERN IRELAND) 1993
(S.I. 1993 No. 67)

1993	1997
Sched.,	
para. 8	Sched. 3,
	para. 2

NURSES, MIDWIVES AND HEALTH VISITORS ACT 1992
(COMMENCEMENT NO. 1) ORDER 1993
(S.I. 1993 No. 588 (C.11))

1993	1997
S.I. 1993 No.	
588	s.24(3), (4)

NURSES AND MIDWIFERY AND HEALTH VISITORS ACT 1979
(AMENDMENT) REGULATIONS 1996
(S.I. 1996 No. 3101)

1996	1997
reg. 2(1)	s.8(3)
reg. 2(2)	8(5)
reg. 2(3)	8(7)
reg. 2(4)	8(8)
reg. 3(1)	21(1)
reg. 3(2)	21(2)
reg. 3(3), (4) ..	21(3)–(5)
reg. 3(5)	21(6), (7)
reg. 4(1)	9
reg. 4(2)	10(3), (4)
reg. 4(3)	20

INDEX

References are to sections and Schedules

JUSTICES OF THE PEACE ACT 1997

(1997 c. 25)

ARRANGEMENT OF SECTIONS

PART I

COMMISSIONS OF THE PEACE AND PETTY SESSIONS AREAS

PART II

JUSTICES OF THE PEACE

Justices other than stipendiary magistrates

Stipendiary magistrates

Metropolitan stipendiary magistrates

City of London magistrates

General provisions

PART III

MAGISTRATES' COURTS COMMITTEES

An Act to consolidate the Justices of the Peace Act 1979 and provisions of Part IV of the Police and Magistrates' Courts Act 1994.

[19th March 1997]

PARLIAMENTARY DEBATES
Hansard, H.L. Vol. 577, cols. 1081, 1535; Vol. 578, col. 1504; Vol. 579, col. 9. H.C. Vol. 292, col. 696.

INTRODUCTION

This Act consolidates, together with several amendments, revocations and repeals, the Justices of the Peace Act 1979 and provisions of the Police and Magistrates' Courts Act 1994. The Act covers the appointment and removal of justices of the peace and magistrates, provisions as to magistrates' courts committees, justices' chief executives, justices' clerks and staff. Miscellaneous provisions covered by the Act include training and disqualification.

PART I

COMMISSIONS OF THE PEACE AND PETTY SESSIONS AREAS

Commission areas

1.—(1) There shall in England be a commission of the peace for each of the following areas—
    (a) every metropolitan county;
    (b) every retained county;
    (c) every London commission area; and
    (d) the City of London.
    (2) There shall in Wales be a commission of the peace for each of the following areas—
    (a) every commission area specified in Schedule 1 to this Act; and
    (b) every retained county no part of which falls within a commission area so specified.
    (3) In this Act "commission area" means an area for which there is a commission of the peace.

London commission areas

2.—(1) In this Act "London commission area" means, subject to the provisions of subsections (3) to (5) below, any of the areas specified in Schedule 2 to this Act.
    (2) The area specified in Part I of that Schedule is the inner London area; and the areas whose names are listed in Part II of that Schedule are in this Act referred to as the "outer London areas".
    (3) Her Majesty may by Order in Council substitute for any one or more of the areas specified in that Schedule any other area or areas comprising the whole or part of Greater London, or alter the boundaries of any area so

specified; but the City of London shall not by virtue of any such Order be included in a London commission area.

(4) An Order in Council made under this section may contain such incidental, consequential, transitional or supplementary provisions as may be necessary or expedient for the purposes of the Order (including provisions amending this Act or any other enactment).

(5) Any statutory instrument made by virtue of this section shall be subject to annulment in pursuance of a resolution of either House of Parliament.

General form of commissions of the peace

3. The commission of the peace for any commission area shall be a commission under the Great Seal addressed generally, and not by name, to all such persons as may from time to time hold office as justices of the peace for the commission area.

Petty sessions areas

4.—(1) The following areas are petty sessions areas—
(a) any specified area which is not divided into petty sessional divisions;
(b) any petty sessional division of a specified area; and
(c) the City of London.
(2) For the purposes of subsection (1)(a) and (b) above "specified area" means—
(a) a retained county;
(b) a metropolitan district;
(c) the inner London area; or
(d) an outer London borough.

PART II

JUSTICES OF THE PEACE

Justices other than stipendiary magistrates

Appointment and removal of justices of the peace

5.—(1) Subject to the following provisions of this Act, justices of the peace for any commission area shall be appointed by the Lord Chancellor by instrument on behalf and in the name of Her Majesty and a justice so appointed may be removed from office in like manner.
(2) Subsection (1) above—
(a) does not apply to stipendiary magistrates; and
(b) is without prejudice to the position of the Lord Mayor and aldermen as justices for the City of London by virtue of the charters of the City.

Residence qualification

6.—(1) Subject to the provisions of this section, a person shall not be appointed as a justice of the peace for a commission area in accordance with section 5 above, nor act as a justice of the peace by virtue of any such appointment, unless he resides in or within 15 miles of that area.

(2) If the Lord Chancellor is of the opinion that it is in the public interest for a person to act as a justice of the peace for a particular area though not qualified to do so under subsection (1) above, he may direct that, so long as any conditions specified in the direction are satisfied, that subsection shall not apply in relation to that person's appointment as a justice of the peace for the area so specified.

(3) Where a person appointed as a justice of the peace for a commission area in accordance with section 5 above is not qualified under the preceding

provisions of this section to act by virtue of the appointment, he shall be removed from office as a justice of the peace in accordance with that section if the Lord Chancellor is of the opinion that the appointment ought not to continue having regard to the probable duration and other circumstances of the lack of qualification.

(4) No act or appointment shall be invalidated by reason only of the disqualification or lack of qualification under this section of the person acting or appointed.

Supplemental list for England and Wales

7.—(1) There shall be kept in the office of the Clerk of the Crown in Chancery a supplemental list for England and Wales as provided for by this Act (in this Act referred to as "the supplemental list").

(2) Subject to the following provisions of this section, there shall be entered in the supplemental list—

(a) the name of any justice of the peace who has attained the age of 70 and neither holds nor has held high judicial office within the meaning of the Appellate Jurisdiction Act 1876; and

(b) the name of any justice of the peace who holds or has held such office and has attained the age of 75.

(3) A person who, on the date when his name falls to be entered in the supplemental list in accordance with subsection (2) above, holds office as chairman of the justices for a petty sessions area (whether by an election under section 22 below, or, in the City of London, as Chief Magistrate or acting Chief Magistrate) shall have his name so entered on the expiry or earlier determination of the term for which he holds office on that date.

(4) The Lord Chancellor may direct that the name of a justice of the peace for any area shall be entered in the supplemental list if the Lord Chancellor is satisfied either—

(a) that by reason of the justice's age or infirmity or other similar cause it is expedient that he should cease to exercise judicial functions as a justice for that area; or

(b) that the justice declines or neglects to take a proper part in the exercise of those functions.

(5) On a person's appointment as a justice of the peace for any area the Lord Chancellor may direct that his name shall be entered in the supplemental list if that person is appointed a justice for that area on ceasing to be a justice for some other area.

(6) The name of a justice of the peace shall be entered in the supplemental list if he applies for it to be so entered and the application is approved by the Lord Chancellor.

(7) Nothing in this section applies to a person holding office as stipendiary magistrate.

Removal of name from supplemental list

8.—(1) A person's name shall be removed from the supplemental list if—
(a) he ceases to be a justice of the peace; or
(b) the Lord Chancellor so directs.

(2) Subsection (1)(b) above does not apply where the person's name is required to be entered in the supplemental list by section 7(2) or (3) above.

Effect of entry of name in supplemental list

9.—(1) Subject to the provisions of this section, a justice of the peace for any area, while his name is entered in the supplemental list, shall not by reason of being a justice for that area be qualified as a justice to do any act or to be a member of any committee or other body.

(2) Subsection (1) above does not preclude a justice from doing all or any of the following acts as a justice, namely—

   (a) signing any document for the purpose of authenticating another person's signature;

   (b) taking and authenticating by his signature any written declaration not made on oath; and

   (c) giving a certificate of facts within his knowledge or of his opinion as to any matter.

(3) The entry of a person's name in the supplemental list does not preclude him, if so authorised by the Lord Chancellor, from acting as a judge of the Crown Court so long as he has not attained the age of 72.

(4) No act or appointment shall be invalidated by reason of the disqualification under this section of the person acting or appointed.

Travelling, subsistence and financial loss allowances

10.—(1) Subject to the provisions of this section, a justice of the peace shall be entitled—

   (a) to receive payments by way of travelling allowance or subsistence allowance where expenditure on travelling or, as the case may be, on subsistence is necessarily incurred by him for the purpose of enabling him to perform any of his duties as a justice; and

   (b) to receive payments by way of financial loss allowance where for that performance he incurs any other expenditure to which he would not otherwise be subject or he suffers any loss of earnings or of benefit under the enactments relating to social security which he would otherwise have made or received.

(2) For the purposes of this section a justice following a training course under a scheme made in accordance with arrangements approved by the Lord Chancellor, or a training course provided by the Lord Chancellor, shall be treated as acting in the performance of his duties as a justice.

(3) A justice shall not be entitled to any payment under this section in respect of any duties if—

   (a) in respect of those duties a payment of the like nature may be paid to him under arrangements made apart from this section; or

   (b) regulations provide that this section shall not apply.

(4) A stipendiary magistrate shall not be entitled to any payment under this section in respect of his duties as such.

(5) Allowances payable under this section shall be paid at rates determined by the Lord Chancellor with the consent of the Treasury.

(6) An allowance payable under this section shall be paid—

   (a) in the case of an allowance payable in respect of duties as a justice in the Crown Court, by the Lord Chancellor; and

   (b) in the case of an allowance otherwise payable to a justice for any commission area in respect of his duties as such, by the appropriate authority.

(7) In subsection (6)(b) above, "the appropriate authority" means—

   (a) in relation to a justice for the City of London, the Common Council;

   (b) in relation to a justice for any of the outer London areas, the council of the outer London borough which is or includes the petty sessions area for which he acts;

   (c) in relation to a justice for a metropolitan county, the council of the metropolitan district which is or includes the petty sessions area for which he acts;

   (d) in relation to a justice for any other commission area—

      (i) the council of the local government area which is or includes the petty sessions area for which he acts; or

(ii) where he acts for a petty sessions area which is partly included in two or more local government areas, the councils of those local government areas.

(8) In subsection (7)(d) above, "local government area" means—

(a) in relation to the inner London area, an inner London borough;

(b) in relation to Wales, a county or a county borough; and

(c) otherwise, a county for which there is a council or a unitary district.

(9) Where by virtue of subsection (7)(d)(ii) above an allowance under this section is payable jointly by two or more councils the manner in which it is to be borne by each of them shall be determined by agreement between them or, in default of agreement, by the Lord Chancellor.

(10) Regulations may make provision as to the manner in which this section is to be administered, and in particular—

(a) for prescribing the forms to be used and the particulars to be provided for the purpose of claiming payment of allowances; and

(b) for avoiding duplication between payments under this section and under other arrangements where expenditure is incurred for more than one purpose, and otherwise for preventing abuses.

(11) Regulations for the purposes of this section shall be made by the Lord Chancellor by statutory instrument.

(12) A statutory instrument containing (whether alone or with other provisions) regulations made by virtue of this section shall be subject to annulment in pursuance of a resolution of either House of Parliament.

Stipendiary magistrates

Appointment and removal of stipendiary magistrates

11.—(1) Her Majesty may appoint a person who has a 7 year general qualification (within the meaning of section 71 of the Courts and Legal Services Act 1990) to be, during Her Majesty's pleasure, a whole-time stipendiary magistrate in any commission area or areas outside the inner London area and the City of London, and may appoint more than one such magistrate in the same area or areas.

(2) A person so appointed to be a stipendiary magistrate in any commission area shall by virtue of his office be a justice of the peace for that area.

(3) Any stipendiary magistrate appointed under this section—

(a) shall be a person recommended to Her Majesty by the Lord Chancellor; and

(b) shall not be removed from office except on the Lord Chancellor's recommendation.

(4) The number of stipendiary magistrates appointed under this section shall not at any time exceed 50 or such other number (which is not less than 40) as Her Majesty may from time to time by Order in Council specify.

(5) No Order in Council may be made under subsection (4) above unless a draft of the Order has been laid before Parliament and approved by resolution of each House.

Retirement of stipendiary magistrates

12.—(1) A stipendiary magistrate appointed on or after 31st March 1995 shall vacate his office on the day on which he attains the age of 70.

(2) A stipendiary magistrate appointed before 31st March 1995 shall vacate his office at the end of the completed year of service in the course of which he attains the age of 70.

(3) Subsections (1) and (2) above are subject to section 26(4) to (6) of the Judicial Pensions and Retirement Act 1993 (Lord Chancellor's power to authorise continuance in office up to the age of 75) and to section 27 of that Act (completion of proceedings) and Schedule 7 to that Act (transitional provisions).

Acting stipendiary magistrate

13.—(1) Where it appears to the Lord Chancellor that it is expedient to do so in order to avoid delays in the administration of justice in any commission area in which a stipendiary magistrate can be appointed under section 11 above, the Lord Chancellor—

     (a) may authorise any person qualified to be so appointed to act as a stipendiary magistrate in that area during such period (not exceeding three months at one time) as the Lord Chancellor thinks fit; or

     (b) may require so to act any stipendiary magistrate appointed under that section in another commission area.

(2) While acting as a stipendiary magistrate in any commission area under subsection (1) above, a person shall have the same jurisdiction, powers and duties as if he had been appointed stipendiary magistrate in that area and were a justice of the peace for that area.

(3) Part V of this Act applies to a person acting as a stipendiary magistrate under subsection (1) above as it applies to a stipendiary magistrate.

(4) The Lord Chancellor may pay to any person who is authorised to act under this section and is not a stipendiary magistrate such remuneration as he may, with the approval of the Treasury, determine.

Place of sitting and powers of stipendiary magistrates

14.—(1) A stipendiary magistrate appointed under section 11 above in any commission area shall sit at such court-houses in the area, on such days and at such times as may be determined by, or in accordance with, directions given by the Lord Chancellor from time to time.

(2) A stipendiary magistrate appointed under section 11 above, sitting in a place appointed for the purpose, shall have power—

     (a) to do any act; and

     (b) to exercise alone any jurisdiction,

which can be done or exercised by two justices, including any act or jurisdiction expressly required to be done or exercised by justices sitting or acting in petty sessions.

(3) Subsection (2) above does not apply where the law under which the act or jurisdiction can be done or exercised was made after 2nd August 1858 and contains express provision contrary to that subsection.

(4) Any statutory provision auxiliary to the jurisdiction exercisable by two justices of the peace shall apply also the jurisdiction of such a stipendiary magistrate.

(5) Subsections (2) and (4) above do not apply where the act or jurisdiction relates to the grant or transfer of any licence.

(6) Any authority or requirement in any enactment for persons to be summoned or to appear at petty sessions in any case shall include authority or a requirement in such a case for persons to be summoned or to appear before such a stipendiary magistrate at the place appointed for his sitting.

(7) Nothing in this section applies to the hearing or determination of family proceedings within the meaning of section 65 of the Magistrates' Courts Act 1980.

Certain restrictions on magistrates' courts not to apply to stipendiary magistrates

15.—(1) Subject to subsection (2) below, nothing in the Magistrates' Courts Act 1980—

     (a) requiring a magistrates' court—

         (i) to be composed of two or more justices; or

         (ii) to sit in a petty sessional court-house or an occasional court-house; or

     (b) limiting the powers of a magistrates' court—

(i) when composed of a single justice; or

(ii) when sitting elsewhere than in a petty sessional court-house,

shall apply to any stipendiary magistrate sitting in a place appointed for the purpose.

(2) Subsection (1) above does not apply to the hearing or determination of family proceedings within the meaning of section 65 of the Magistrates' Courts Act 1980.

Metropolitan stipendiary magistrates

Appointment, removal and retirement of metropolitan stipendiary magistrates

16.—(1) Metropolitan stipendiary magistrates shall be appointed by Her Majesty, and Her Majesty shall from time to time appoint such number of persons as is necessary; but the number of metropolitan stipendiary magistrates shall not at any time exceed 60 or such larger number as Her Majesty may from time to time by Order in Council specify.

(2) A person shall not be qualified to be appointed a metropolitan stipendiary magistrate unless he has a 7 year general qualification (within the meaning of section 71 of the Courts and Legal Services Act 1990).

(3) The Lord Chancellor shall designate one of the metropolitan stipendiary magistrates to be the chief metropolitan stipendiary magistrate.

(4) Each metropolitan stipendiary magistrate—

(a) shall by virtue of his office be a justice of the peace for each of the London commission areas and for the retained counties of Essex, Hertfordshire, Kent and Surrey; and

(b) may be removed from office by the Lord Chancellor for inability or misbehaviour.

(5) Section 12 above applies to metropolitan stipendiary magistrates as well as other stipendiary magistrates in England or Wales.

(6) No Order in Council shall be made under subsection (1) above unless a draft of the Order has been laid before Parliament and approved by resolution of each House.

Metropolitan stipendiary magistrates: allocation and sittings etc.

17.—(1) The Lord Chancellor may assign metropolitan stipendiary magistrates to petty sessional divisions of the inner London area and may alter any assignment under this subsection; but the assignment of a magistrate to a particular division shall not preclude him from exercising jurisdiction for any other division of the inner London area.

(2) Metropolitan stipendiary magistrates shall sit at such court-houses provided for the inner London area under the following provisions of this Act on such days and at such times as may be determined by, or in accordance with, directions given by the Lord Chancellor from time to time.

(3) The chief metropolitan stipendiary magistrate shall—

(a) cause a meeting of all the metropolitan stipendiary magistrates (or such of them as are able to attend) to be held at least once in every three months; and

(b) if present, preside over the meeting.

Jurisdiction of metropolitan stipendiary magistrates and lay justices for inner London area

18.—(1) Metropolitan stipendiary magistrates shall hold magistrates' courts for the inner London area.

(2) In the inner London area the jurisdiction conferred on justices of the peace by any enactment, by their commission or by the common law shall be exercisable both—

   (a) by metropolitan stipendiary magistrates; and
   (b) by justices of the peace for that area who are not metropolitan stipen-
      diary magistrates (in this Part of this Act referred to as "lay justices").
   (3) Subject to subsections (4) and (5) below, the jurisdiction conferred on
metropolitan stipendiary magistrates as such by any enactment shall be exercisable both—
   (a) by metropolitan stipendiary magistrates; and
   (b) by lay justices for the inner London area.
   (4) Subsection (3)(b) above does not apply to the jurisdiction conferred on
metropolitan stipendiary magistrates by—
   (a) section 25 of the Children and Young Persons Act 1933 (restrictions
      on persons under 18 going abroad for the purpose of performing for
      profit); or
   (b) the Extradition Act 1989.
   (5) A magistrates' court consisting of lay justices for the inner London area
shall not by virtue of subsection (3) above try an information summarily or
hear a complaint except when composed of at least two justices.
   (6) Without prejudice to subsection (2) above, subsections (2) to (7) of
section 14 above apply to a metropolitan stipendiary magistrate as they apply
to a stipendiary magistrate appointed under section 11 above.
   (7) Section 15 above applies to metropolitan stipendiary magistrates as
well as other stipendiary magistrates in England or Wales.

Acting metropolitan stipendiary magistrate

   19.—(1) If it appears to the Lord Chancellor that it is expedient to do so in
order to avoid delays in the administration of justice in the inner London
area, he may authorise any person who has a 7 year general qualification
(within the meaning of section 71 of the Courts and Legal Services Act 1990)
to act as a metropolitan stipendiary magistrate during such period (not
exceeding three months at one time) as the Lord Chancellor thinks fit.
   (2) Anything required or authorised by law to be done by, to or before a
metropolitan stipendiary magistrate may be done by, to or before any person
acting as a metropolitan stipendiary magistrate under subsection (1) above.
   (3) Part V of this Act applies to a person acting as a metropolitan stipendiary magistrate under subsection (1) above as it applies to a metropolitan
stipendiary magistrate.
   (4) The Lord Chancellor may pay to any person authorised to act under
this section such remuneration as he may, with the approval of the Treasury,
determine.

Division of work in inner London area

   20.—(1) There shall be a committee established for the purposes mentioned in subsection (6) below.
   (2) The committee shall consist of the following members—
   (a) the chief metropolitan stipendiary magistrate;
   (b) six lay justices appointed by the chairmen of the petty sessional div-
      isions of the inner London area; and
   (c) six metropolitan stipendiary magistrates appointed by the chief
      metropolitan stipendiary magistrate.
   (3) The lay justices eligible for appointment under paragraph (b) of subsection (2) above include any of the chairmen referred to in that paragraph.
   (4) The members of the committee shall hold office for a period of twelve
months, but shall be eligible for re-appointment.
   (5) The chief metropolitan stipendiary magistrate shall be the chairman of
the committee.
   (6) It shall be the duty of the committee—

(a) to keep under consideration the division of work in the inner London area between the metropolitan stipendiary magistrates and the lay justices; and

(b) to give general directions to any magistrates' courts committee for any area which consists of or includes the whole or any part of the inner London area as to the division of the work.

City of London magistrates

Ex officio and appointed justices

21.—(1) The Lord Mayor and aldermen of the City of London shall by virtue of the charter granted by His late Majesty King George II dated 25th August 1741 continue to be justices of the peace for the City but any of them may be excluded by the Lord Chancellor from the exercise of his functions as a justice.

(2) The persons holding office as justices of the peace for the City shall constitute a single body of justices, without distinction between those holding office by virtue of the charter and those appointed; and the jurisdiction and powers of the Lord Mayor and aldermen as justices by virtue of the charter are the same in all respects as those of appointed justices.

(3) The jurisdiction and powers of the justices of the peace for the City are in continuation of those which, before the issue of a commission of the peace for the City, belonged exclusively to the justices holding office by virtue of the charter.

General provisions

Chairman and deputy chairmen of justices

22.—(1) For any petty sessions area there shall be a chairman and one or more deputy chairmen of the justices chosen from amongst themselves by the magistrates for the area; and any contested election for the purpose of this section shall be held by secret ballot.

(2) Subject to subsections (3) and (4) below, if the chairman or a deputy chairman of the justices for a petty sessions area is present at a meeting of those justices, he shall preside unless he requests another justice to preside in accordance with rules made under section 24 below.

(3) Subsection (2) above does not confer on any chairman or deputy chairman of the justices the right to preside in court if, under rules made under section 24 below, he is ineligible to preside in court.

(4) Subsection (2) above does not confer on any chairman or deputy chairman of the justices the right to preside—

(a) in a youth court or family proceedings court;

(b) at meetings of a committee or other body of justices having its own chairman; or

(c) at meetings when any stipendiary magistrate is engaged as such in administering justice.

(5) A metropolitan stipendiary magistrate who is by virtue of his office a justice of the peace for any area mentioned in section 16(4) above shall not, by reason only of his being a justice of the peace for that area by virtue of that office, be qualified—

(a) to be chosen under subsection (1) above as chairman or deputy chairman of the justices for a petty sessional division of that area; or

(b) to vote under that subsection at the election of any such chairman or deputy chairman.

Chairman and deputy chairmen of justices in the City of London

23.—(1) In the City of London, the Lord Mayor for the time being, if not disqualified, shall be chairman of the justices, with the style of Chief Magistrate, instead of a chairman being elected under section 22(1) above; and, subject to subsection (3) below, the aldermen who have been Lord Mayor and are not disqualified (or, if there are more than eight such aldermen, the eight who were last Lord Mayor) shall be deputy chairmen in addition to any deputy chairmen elected under section 22(1) above.

(2) For the purposes of this section a Lord Mayor or alderman is disqualified at any time while his name is entered in the supplemental list.

(3) If the Lord Mayor is disqualified, then during his mayoralty the senior of the aldermen designated as deputy chairmen in subsection (1) above shall, instead of being a deputy chairman, be chairman of the justices as acting Chief Magistrate.

(4) Subsections (2) and (4) of section 22 above apply to any Lord Mayor or alderman as chairman or deputy chairman of the justices as they apply to a chairman or deputy chairman elected under subsection (1) of that section.

Rules as to chairmanship and size of bench

24.—(1) The number of justices (other than metropolitan stipendiary magistrates) sitting to deal with a case as a magistrates' court shall not be greater than the number prescribed by rules made under this section.

(2) Rules made under this section may make provision as to the manner in which section 22 above and this section are to be administered, and in particular—

(a) as to the arrangements to be made for securing the presence on the bench of enough, but not more than enough, justices;

(b) as to the term of office and the procedure at an election of the chairman or a deputy chairman of the justices for a petty sessions area (including any procedure for nominating candidates at any such election), and the number of deputy chairmen to be elected for any such area;

(c) as to training courses to be completed by justices before they may preside in court;

(d) as to the approval of justices, by committees of justices constituted in accordance with the rules, before they may preside in court, as to the justices who may be so approved and as to the courts to which the approval relates; and

(e) as to circumstances in which a justice may preside in court even though requirements imposed by virtue of paragraph (c) or (d) above are not satisfied in relation to him.

(3) The right of magistrates to vote at an election of the chairman or a deputy chairman of the justices for a petty sessions area may, by rules made under this section, be restricted with a view to securing that the election is made by magistrates experienced as such in the area.

(4) No rules shall be made under this section except on the advice of, or after consultation with, the rule committee established under section 144 of the Magistrates' Courts Act 1980.

(5) Rules under this section shall be made by the Lord Chancellor by statutory instrument, which shall be subject to annulment in pursuance of a resolution of either House of Parliament.

Records of justices of the peace

25.—(1) In each commission area, other than the City of London, such one of the justices as may be designated by the Lord Chancellor shall be keeper of the rolls.

(2) There shall be transmitted to the keeper of the rolls for each commission area, and be enrolled in the records of the justices for that area, a copy of any instrument appointing or removing a justice of the peace in that area in accordance with section 5 above; and the keeper of the rolls shall be

notified, in such manner as the Lord Chancellor may direct, of any resignation or death of a justice so appointed, and shall cause to be kept, and from time to time rectified, a record of those for the time being holding office by virtue of any such appointment.

(3) Subsection (2) above has effect in relation to the City of London as if for each reference to the keeper of the rolls there were substituted a reference to the Lord Mayor.

(4) There shall be kept in the office of the Clerk of the Crown in Chancery a record of all persons for the time being holding office as justices of the peace by virtue of appointments made in accordance with section 5 above, together with the instruments of appointment or removal.

Greater Manchester, Merseyside and Lancashire

26.—(1) Sections 5(1), 6 and 25 above have effect in relation to the counties of Greater Manchester and Merseyside and the retained county of Lancashire with the substitution, for any reference to the Lord Chancellor, of a reference to the Chancellor of the Duchy of Lancaster.

(2) In relation to the entry in or removal from the supplemental list of the name of a person who is a justice of the peace only for any of—

(a) the counties of Greater Manchester and Merseyside; and

(b) the retained county of Lancashire,

sections 7(4) to (6) and 8 above have effect with the substitution, for any reference to the Lord Chancellor, of a reference to the Chancellor of the Duchy of Lancaster.

PART III

MAGISTRATES' COURTS COMMITTEES

General provisions as to magistrates' courts committees

27.—(1) There shall be committees (known as "magistrates' courts committees") set up in accordance with the provisions of this Part of this Act, with such functions as are or may be conferred on them by or under this or any other Act and such other functions relating to matters of an administrative character as they may be authorised by the Lord Chancellor to undertake.

(2) Subject to section 32 below and to any order made under section 69 of the Police and Magistrates' Courts Act 1994 before the commencement of this Act, there shall in England be a magistrates' courts committee for each of the following areas—

(a) every retained county;

(b) every metropolitan district;

(c) every outer London borough;

(d) the inner London area; and

(e) the City of London.

(3) Subject to section 32 below and to any order made under section 69 of the Police and Magistrates' Courts Act 1994 before the commencement of this Act, there shall in Wales be a magistrates' courts committee for every retained county.

Constitution of magistrates' courts committees

28.—(1) A magistrates' courts committee shall, subject to subsections (2) to (4) below, be composed of magistrates for the area to which the committee relates, chosen in accordance with regulations under section 29 below.

(2) Not more than two other members, who need not be justices of the peace, may be either—

(a) co-opted by a magistrates' courts committee to the committee with the approval of the Lord Chancellor; or

(b) appointed by the Lord Chancellor to the committee.

(3) The chief metropolitan stipendiary magistrate shall by virtue of his office be a member of the inner London magistrates' courts committee.

(4) Until such day as the Lord Chancellor may by order made by statutory instrument appoint, two members of the inner London magistrates' courts committee shall be other metropolitan stipendiary magistrates appointed by the chief metropolitan stipendiary magistrate.

(5) In subsections (3) and (4) above "the inner London magistrates' courts committee" means the magistrates' courts committee for an area consisting of or including the whole of the inner London area or, if there is no such committee, every magistrates' courts committee for any area which consists of or includes any part of the inner London area.

Powers of Lord Chancellor in relation to magistrates' courts committees

29.—(1) The Lord Chancellor may by statutory instrument make general regulations about the constitution, procedure and quorum of magistrates' courts committees; but any such regulations shall have effect subject to the provisions of section 28 above.

(2) The regulations shall provide for the members referred to in section 28(1) above to be chosen by a selection panel constituted in accordance with the regulations.

(3) The regulations may—

(a) lay down an upper limit for the number of members of a magistrates' courts committee (inclusive of the members referred to in subsections (2), (3) and (4) of section 28 above); and

(b) enable the Lord Chancellor to direct that, in relation to any magistrates' courts committee to which the direction is given, any members co-opted or appointed under subsection (2) of that section are to be left out of account in applying the upper limit.

(4) The regulations may also make different provision in relation to the magistrates' courts committees for areas which consist of or include the whole or any part of the inner London area from that made in relation to other committees.

(5) The regulations may also make provision with respect to the persons (other than the members, clerks and officers of the committee) who may be entitled to attend the meetings of a magistrates' courts committee and the rights of such persons to make representations to the committee.

(6) A statutory instrument containing (whether alone or with other provisions) regulations made by virtue of this section shall be subject to annulment in pursuance of a resolution of either House of Parliament.

(7) The Lord Chancellor may give general or special directions with respect to convening the first meeting of magistrates' courts committees.

Supplementary provisions as to magistrates' courts committees

30.—(1) Subject to subsection (2) below, a magistrates' courts committee shall appoint one of their members to be chairman of the committee.

(2) Until such day as the Lord Chancellor may by order made by statutory instrument appoint, the chief metropolitan stipendiary magistrate shall by virtue of his office be the chairman of any magistrates' courts committee for an area which consists of or includes the whole of the inner London area.

(3) Where the magistrates for a petty sessions area are required to meet for the purpose of carrying out any functions under section 29 above, a meeting shall be convened by the magistrates' courts committee or, if there is no such committee or the Lord Chancellor considers it appropriate, by the Lord Chancellor.

(4) A magistrates' courts committee may act through sub-committees appointed by them which, if they include at least one member of the committee, may also include persons who are not members.

(5) A magistrates' courts committee may also arrange for the discharge of any of their functions—

(a) by the chairman of the committee; or

(b) by the justices' chief executive.

(6) Subject to the provisions of this Act, a magistrates' courts committee shall have power to regulate their own procedure, including quorum.

(7) The proceedings of a magistrates' courts committee shall not be invalidated by reason of any vacancy among the members or of any defect in the appointment of a member.

(8) A magistrates' courts committee shall be a body corporate.

(9) A magistrates' courts committee shall, on at least one occasion in every calendar year, admit members of the public to a meeting of the committee.

(10) The minutes of proceedings of every meeting of a magistrates' courts committee shall be open to inspection by members of the public at the offices of the committee, except to the extent that the committee determine that the minutes disclose information of a confidential nature.

(11) Copies of any minutes which are open to inspection under subsection (10) above shall be made available to the public on payment of such reasonable fee as the magistrates' courts committee may in any case determine.

(12) A magistrates' courts committee making a determination under subsection (10) above shall state their reasons for regarding the information in question as being of a confidential nature.

General powers and duties of magistrates' courts committees

31.—(1) A magistrates' courts committee shall be responsible for the efficient and effective administration of the magistrates' courts for their area.

(2) A magistrates' courts committee may, in particular—

(a) allocate administrative responsibilities among the justices' chief executive, the justices' clerks and the staff of the committee; and

(b) determine the administrative procedures to be followed by any of the persons mentioned in paragraph (a) above.

(3) It shall be the duty of every magistrates' courts committee to provide training courses for justices' clerks and for staff of the committee.

(4) The Lord Chancellor may give directions to magistrates' courts committees requiring each of them, in discharging their responsibilities under subsection (1) above, to meet specified standards of performance.

(5) The Lord Chancellor may also give directions to magistrates' courts committees requiring each of them to take specified steps, at such intervals as may be specified—

(a) for the purpose of keeping the magistrates for their area informed as to the activities of the committee; or

(b) for the purpose of ascertaining the views of those magistrates on particular matters related to the functions of the committee.

(6) In discharging their responsibilities under subsection (1) above, a magistrates' courts committee shall have regard to the needs of court users who are disabled; and so long as any direction under subsection (4) above is in force the standards of performance required under that subsection must include standards relating to the provision made for such court users.

(7) A direction under this section may be given to all magistrates' courts committees or to one or more particular committees.

(8) The Lord Chancellor shall arrange for any direction given under this section to be published in such manner as he thinks fit.

Alteration of magistrates' courts committee areas

32.—(1) A magistrates' courts committee may at any time submit to the Lord Chancellor written proposals—

(a) for the replacement of two or more magistrates' courts committees (including the committee submitting the proposals) with a single magistrates' courts committee or with two or more magistrates' courts committees in relation to areas different from the existing magistrates' courts committee areas; or

(b) for the replacement of the committee submitting the proposals with two or more magistrates' courts committees.

(2) Before submitting such proposals, the magistrates' courts committee shall consult—

(a) the magistrates for their area or any other existing magistrates' courts committee area to which the proposal relates;

(b) any other magistrates' courts committee to which the proposal relates; and

(c) every interested authority.

(3) Whether or not proposals have been submitted to him under subsection (1) above, the Lord Chancellor may by order made by statutory instrument provide—

(a) for the replacement of two or more magistrates' courts committees with a single magistrates' courts committee or with two or more magistrates' courts committees relating to areas which are different from the existing magistrates' courts committee areas; or

(b) for the replacement of a magistrates' courts committee with two or more magistrates' courts committees.

(4) The Lord Chancellor shall not make an order under subsection (3) above unless he is satisfied that the making of the order is likely to contribute to an overall increase in the efficiency of the administration of the magistrates' courts for the magistrates' courts committee area or areas to which the order relates.

(5) Before making an order under subsection (3) above, other than an order which implements proposals submitted to him under subsection (1) above, the Lord Chancellor shall consult—

(a) the magistrates for each of the existing magistrates' courts committee areas to which the order relates;

(b) the magistrates' courts committees to which the proposal relates; and

(c) every interested authority.

(6) For the purposes of subsection (5) above, an order shall be taken to implement proposals if it implements them without alteration or any departures from the proposals do not, in the opinion of the Lord Chancellor, effect important alterations in the proposals.

(7) Where proposals under subsection (1) above or an order under subsection (3) above would (apart from this subsection) divide a petty sessions area between the areas of two or more magistrates' courts committees, the proposals or order shall provide for a consequential alteration of petty sessions areas.

(8) An order under subsection (3) above may contain such consequential and transitional provisions as appear to the Lord Chancellor to be necessary or expedient, including—

(a) provision for the transfer of property, rights and liabilities;

(b) provision for the management or custody of transferred property (whether real or personal); and

(c) provision for any magistrates' courts committee coming into existence by virtue of the order to be constituted under section 30 above as a body corporate, and to incur liabilities, before the date on which the functions of any existing magistrates' courts committee are transferred to it.

(9) A statutory instrument containing an order under subsection (3) above shall be subject to annulment in pursuance of a resolution of either House of Parliament.

(10) In this section—

"existing magistrates' courts committee area" means a magistrates' courts committee area existing by virtue of—

    (a) section 27(2) or (3) above;

    (b) an order made under section 69 of the Police and Magistrates' Courts Act 1994 before the commencement of this Act; or

    (c) a previous order under subsection (3) above;

"interested authority", in relation to a proposal or order, means any relevant authority whose area includes all or any part of any of the existing magistrates' courts committee areas to which the proposal or order relates; and

"relevant authority" means—

    (a) a county council;

    (b) a county borough council;

    (c) the council of a unitary district;

    (d) a London borough council; or

    (e) the Common Council of the City of London.

Powers and duties of committee as to petty sessional divisions

33.—(1) Subject to the provisions of this section and section 34 below, a magistrates' courts committee may at any time submit to the Lord Chancellor a draft order making such provision about the division of their area or any part of their area into petty sessional divisions as the committee think fit.

(2) It shall be the duty of a magistrates' courts committee, if directed to do so by the Lord Chancellor, to review the division of their area or any part of their area into petty sessional divisions and, on completion of the review, to submit to the Lord Chancellor either a draft order under subsection (1) above or a report giving reasons for making no change.

(3) Subject to the provisions of this section and section 34 below—

(a) where a magistrates' courts committee submit a draft order to the Lord Chancellor under this section, he may by statutory instrument make the order either in the terms of the draft or with such modifications as he thinks fit; and

(b) where a magistrates' courts committee fail to comply within six months with a direction of the Lord Chancellor under subsection (2) above, or the Lord Chancellor is dissatisfied with the draft order or report submitted in pursuance of such a direction, he may by statutory instrument make such order as he thinks fit about the division into petty sessional divisions of the area to which the direction related.

(4) An order under this section may provide for an area ceasing to be divided into petty sessional divisions, and a direction under subsection (2) above may be given with respect to the division of an area which is not for the time being so divided.

(5) No order may be made under this section for the division of the City of London into petty sessional divisions.

(6) Any order under this section may contain transitional and other consequential provisions.

Procedure relating to s.33

34.—(1) Before submitting to the Lord Chancellor a draft order or a report under section 33 above about any area, a magistrates' courts committee—

(a) shall consult—

    (i) every relevant council; and

    (ii) the magistrates for any existing petty sessional division in the area; and

(b) in the case of a draft order which relates to any district which is not a unitary district, after complying with paragraph (a) above, shall send a copy of their proposals to every relevant district council and take into consideration any objections made in the prescribed manner and within the prescribed time.

(2) A magistrates' courts committee submitting to the Lord Chancellor a draft order or a report under section 33 above shall comply with such requirements (if any) as to notice as may be prescribed.

(3) Before making an order under section 33 above about any area otherwise than in accordance with a draft submitted to him by the magistrates' courts committee, the Lord Chancellor shall send a copy of his proposals to—

(a) the magistrates' courts committee;
(b) every relevant council;
(c) the magistrates for any existing petty sessional division in the area; and
(d) if the proposals relate to any district which is not a unitary district, every relevant district council.

(4) Before making any order under section 33 above the Lord Chancellor shall take into consideration any objections made in the prescribed manner and within the prescribed time, and may cause a local inquiry to be held.

(5) For the purposes of this section—

(a) "relevant council", in relation to an order, a draft order or a report, means any council of—

(i) a county;
(ii) a county borough;
(iii) a unitary district; or
(iv) a London borough,

which includes all or part of the area to which the order, draft order or report relates;

(b) "relevant district council", in relation to an order or draft order about any area, means any council of a district, other than a unitary district, which includes all or part of the area;

(c) "prescribed" means prescribed by regulations made by the Lord Chancellor by statutory instrument; and

(d) an order shall be taken to be made in accordance with a draft order if it is made in terms of the draft order or any departures from the draft order do not, in the opinion of the Lord Chancellor, effect important alterations in the draft order.

Alteration of names of petty sessions areas outside the City of London

35.—(1) Subject to the provisions of this section and section 36 below, a magistrates' courts committee may at any time submit to the Lord Chancellor a draft order altering the name of the petty sessions area for which they are the committee or, if they are the committee for more than one petty sessions area, the name of any of those areas.

(2) Subject to the provisions of this section and section 36 below, where a magistrates' courts committee submit a draft order to the Lord Chancellor under this section, he may by statutory instrument make the order either in the terms of the draft or with such modifications as he thinks fit.

(3) Nothing in this section authorises the name of the petty sessions area consisting of the City of London to be altered.

(4) Any order under this section may contain transitional and other consequential provisions.

Procedure relating to s.35

36.—(1) Before submitting to the Lord Chancellor a draft order under section 35 above, a magistrates' courts committee—

(a) shall consult—

(i) every relevant council; and

(ii) the magistrates for the petty sessions area to which their proposals relate; and

(b) if the order relates to any district which is not a unitary district, after complying with paragraph (a) above, shall send a copy of their proposals to every relevant district council and take into consideration any objections made in the prescribed manner and within the prescribed time.

(2) A magistrates' courts committee submitting to the Lord Chancellor a draft order under section 35 above shall comply with such requirements (if any) as to notice as may be prescribed.

(3) Before making an order under section 35 above otherwise than in accordance with a draft submitted to him by the magistrates' courts committee, the Lord Chancellor shall send a copy of his proposals to—

(a) the magistrates' courts committee;

(b) every relevant council; and

(c) if the proposals relate to any district which is not a unitary district, every relevant district council.

(4) Before making any order under section 35 above the Lord Chancellor shall take into consideration any objections made in the prescribed manner and within the prescribed time, and may cause a local inquiry to be held.

(5) For the purposes of this section—

(a) "relevant council", in relation to an order or a draft order, means any council of—

(i) a county;

(ii) a county borough;

(iii) a unitary district; or

(iv) a London borough,

which includes all or part of the petty sessions area to which the order or draft order relates;

(b) "relevant district council", in relation to an order or draft order, means any council of a district, other than a unitary district, which includes all or part of the petty sessions area to which the order or draft order relates;

(c) "prescribed" means prescribed by regulations made by the Lord Chancellor by statutory instrument; and

(d) an order shall be taken to be made in accordance with a draft order if it is made in terms of the draft order or any departures from the draft order do not, in the opinion of the Lord Chancellor, effect important alterations in the draft order.

Reports and plans

37.—(1) The Lord Chancellor may by regulations made by statutory instrument require magistrates' courts committees to submit to him such reports and plans, in relation to matters for which they are responsible, as may be prescribed.

(2) Any report or plan required by regulations under this section—

(a) shall be prepared in the prescribed manner, after such consultation as may be prescribed, and within such time as may be prescribed;

(b) shall be in the prescribed form;

(c) shall be sent to such persons as may be prescribed; and

(d) shall be made available to the public on payment of such reasonable fee as the magistrates' courts committee may in any case determine.

(3) The Lord Chancellor may direct any one or more magistrates' courts committees to produce such additional reports or plans in relation to matters for which they are responsible as may be specified in the direction.

(4) In this section "prescribed" means prescribed by regulations made by the Lord Chancellor by statutory instrument; and a statutory instrument con-

taining (whether alone or with other provisions) regulations made by virtue of this section shall be subject to annulment in pursuance of a resolution of either House of Parliament.

Default powers

38.—(1) The Lord Chancellor may make an order under subsection (3) below if he is of the opinion that, without reasonable excuse, a magistrates' courts committee—

(a) are failing properly to discharge any duty imposed on them by or under any enactment; or

(b) have so failed and are likely to do so again.

(2) Before making an order under subsection (3) below, the Lord Chancellor shall give a written warning to the magistrates' courts committee specifying the default or defaults to which the order relates.

(3) An order under this subsection shall—

(a) state that the Lord Chancellor is of the opinion mentioned in subsection (1) above; and

(b) provide either or both of the following—

(i) that, on the making of the order, the chairman of the committee is to vacate his office as chairman; or

(ii) that, on the making of the order, one or more specified members of the committee (who may include the chairman but may not consist of all the members of the committee) are to vacate their office.

(4) If, after making an order under subsection (3) above, the Lord Chancellor remains of the opinion mentioned in subsection (1) above, he may make an order—

(a) stating that he remains of that opinion; and

(b) providing—

(i) that all the members of the committee are to vacate their office on the making of the order; and

(ii) that for a specified period, not exceeding three months, beginning with the making of the order the committee is to consist of persons nominated by the Lord Chancellor (who need not be justices of the peace).

(5) An order under subsection (4) above shall provide for new members of the committee to be chosen, in accordance with regulations under section 29 above, to take office at the end of the specified period.

(6) In relation to the magistrates' courts committee for an area which consists of or includes the whole or any part of the inner London area, the reference in subsection (3)(b)(ii) above to members of the committee does not include the chief metropolitan stipendiary magistrate; and where an order under subsection (4) above is made in relation to any such committee, section 28(3) and (4) above shall not apply in relation to the committee during the period specified in the order.

Studies by Audit Commission

39.—(1) The Audit Commission may, at the request of a magistrates' courts committee, undertake or promote comparative and other studies—

(a) designed to enable the Commission to make recommendations for improving economy, efficiency and effectiveness in the performance of the committee's functions; and

(b) for improving the financial or other management of the committee.

(2) Any magistrates' courts committee which has requested a study in accordance with subsection (1) above, and any officer or member of such a committee, shall provide the Audit Commission, or any person authorised by

it, with such information as it or he may reasonably require for the carrying out of the study.

(3) The Audit Commission shall charge the magistrates' courts committee concerned such fees for any study carried out under subsection (1) above as will cover the full cost of carrying it out.

(4) In this section "the Audit Commission" means the Audit Commission for Local Authorities and the National Health Service in England and Wales.

PART IV

JUSTICES' CHIEF EXECUTIVES, JUSTICES' CLERKS AND STAFF

Appointment of justices' chief executive

40.—(1) Every magistrates' courts committee shall appoint a justices' chief executive.

(2) A person may not be appointed as justices' chief executive unless—

(a) the magistrates' courts committee have submitted to the Lord Chancellor, in accordance with regulations, an application for approval of one or more persons offering themselves for appointment;

(b) the Lord Chancellor has approved one or more of those persons; and

(c) the person appointed is a person so approved.

(3) Where a person employed as a justices' chief executive under a contract for a fixed term is re-appointed on the expiry of that term, subsection (2) above does not apply in relation to the re-appointment.

(4) Where the Lord Chancellor declines to approve any person who is named in an application under subsection (2)(a) above, he shall inform the magistrates' courts committee of the reasons for his decision.

(5) A person may not be appointed as justices' chief executive unless he is eligible under section 43 below for appointment as justices' clerk.

(6) A person may not be appointed both as justices' chief executive and as justices' clerk for a petty sessions area unless the Lord Chancellor has agreed that he may hold both appointments.

(7) Where, in accordance with subsection (6) above, a person holds an appointment as justices' chief executive with an appointment as justices' clerk for a petty sessions area, he shall not exercise any functions as justices' clerk for the petty sessions area unless authorised to do so (either generally or in any particular case) by the magistrates' courts committee for the area which includes that petty sessions area.

(8) In this section "regulations" means regulations made by the Lord Chancellor by statutory instrument; and a statutory instrument containing (whether alone or with other provisions) regulations made by virtue of this section shall be subject to annulment in pursuance of a resolution of either House of Parliament.

Functions of justices' chief executive

41.—(1) The justices' chief executive in relation to any magistrates' courts committee shall—

(a) act as clerk to the committee; and

(b) subject to and in accordance with any directions given by the committee, carry on the day to day administration of the magistrates' courts for the area to which the committee relates.

(2) A justices' chief executive may arrange for his functions under subsection (1)(a) above to be exercised by any member of the staff of the magistrates' courts committee.

(3) It shall be the duty of the justices' chief executive to make arrangements for discussions relating to law, practice and procedure among the justices' clerks for petty sessions areas within the area of the committee.

Appointment and removal of justices' clerks

42.—(1) Justices' clerks shall be appointed by the magistrates' courts committee; and a magistrates' courts committee may appoint more than one justices' clerk for any petty sessions area.

(2) A person may not be appointed as justices' clerk unless—

(a) the magistrates' courts committee have submitted to the Lord Chancellor, in accordance with regulations, an application for approval of one or more persons offering themselves for the appointment;

(b) the Lord Chancellor has approved one or more of those persons; and

(c) the person appointed is a person so approved.

(3) Where a person employed as a justices' clerk under a contract for a fixed term is re-appointed on the expiry of that term, subsection (2) above does not apply in relation to the re-appointment.

(4) Where the Lord Chancellor declines to approve any person who is named in an application under subsection (2)(a) above, he shall inform the magistrates' courts committee of the reasons for his decision.

(5) The approval of the Lord Chancellor shall be required—

(a) for any decision to increase the number of justices' clerks for a petty sessions area or to have more than one justices' clerk for a new petty sessions area; or

(b) for the removal of the justices' clerk for a petty sessions area where the magistrates for the area do not consent to the removal.

(6) A magistrates' courts committee shall consult the magistrates for any petty sessions area—

(a) on the appointment of a justices' clerk for the area, except in the case of a re-appointment on the expiry of a fixed term; or

(b) on the removal of a justices' clerk for the area.

(7) Before—

(a) approving any person under subsection (2) above; or

(b) approving the removal of a justices' clerk,

the Lord Chancellor shall consider any representations made to him by the magistrates for the petty sessions area concerned; and before approving the removal of a justices' clerk the Lord Chancellor shall also consider any representations made to him by the clerk.

(8) Where a person is employed as a justices' clerk under a contract for a fixed term, the expiry of that term without renewal shall be treated for the purposes of subsections (5) to (7) above as his removal as justices' clerk, unless he has consented to the failure to renew.

(9) In this section "regulations" means regulations made by the Lord Chancellor by statutory instrument; and a statutory instrument containing (whether alone or with other provisions) regulations made by virtue of this section shall be subject to annulment in pursuance of a resolution of either House of Parliament.

Qualifications for appointment as justices' clerk

43. No person shall be appointed as justices' clerk unless either—

(a) at the time of appointment—

(i) he has a 5 year magistrates' courts qualification (within the meaning of section 71 of the Courts and Legal Services Act 1990); or

(ii) he is a barrister or solicitor and has served for not less than five years as assistant to a justices' clerk; or

(b) he then is or has previously been a justices' clerk.

Terms of employment of justices' chief executives, justices' clerks and staff

44.—(1) Except as provided by this Act, a justices' chief executive or justices' clerk—

(a) shall be employed by the magistrates' courts committee on such terms as they may determine; and

(b) shall hold and vacate office in accordance with the terms of his contract of service.

(2) A magistrates' courts committee may employ staff on such terms as they think fit.

(3) Without prejudice to the generality of subsection (1) of section 144 of the Magistrates' Courts Act 1980, the power conferred by that section to make rules for regulating and prescribing the procedure and practice to be followed by justices' clerks includes power to provide that, subject to any exceptions prescribed by the rules, persons—

(a) shall not be employed to assist a justices' clerk in any capacity so prescribed; or

(b) shall not be permitted to do on behalf of a justices' clerk any such acts as may be so prescribed,

unless those persons are qualified to be appointed justices' clerk or have such other qualifications as may for any purpose be allowed by the rules or approved by the Lord Chancellor in accordance with the rules.

General powers and duties of justices' clerks

45.—(1) Rules made in accordance with section 144 of the Magistrates' Courts Act 1980 may (except to the extent that any enactment passed after this Act otherwise directs) make provision enabling things authorised to be done by, to or before a single justice of the peace to be done instead by, to or before a justices' clerk.

(2) Such rules may also make provision enabling things authorised to be done by, to or before a justices' clerk (whether by virtue of subsection (1) above or otherwise) to be done instead by, to or before a person appointed by a magistrates' courts committee to assist him.

(3) Any enactment (including any enactment contained in this Act) or any rule of law which—

(a) regulates the exercise of any jurisdiction or powers of justices of the peace; or

(b) relates to things done in the exercise or purported exercise of any such jurisdiction or powers,

shall apply in relation to the exercise or purported exercise of any such jurisdiction or powers by the clerk to any justices by virtue of subsection (1) above as if he were one of those justices.

(4) The functions of a justices' clerk include giving advice to the justices to whom he is clerk, at their request, about law, practice or procedure on questions arising in connection with the discharge of their functions, including questions arising when the clerk is not personally attending on them.

(5) The powers of a justices' clerk include, at any time when he thinks he should do so, bringing to the attention of those justices any point of law, practice or procedure that is or may be involved in any question so arising.

(6) For the purposes of subsections (4) and (5) above the functions of justices of the peace do not include functions as a judge of the Crown Court.

(7) Subsections (4) and (5) above—

(a) apply in relation to any of the justices to whom the justices' clerk is clerk as they apply in relation to all of them; and

(b) do not define or in any respect limit—

(i) the powers and duties of a justices' clerk; or

(ii) the matters on which justices may obtain assistance from their clerk.

Functions of justices' clerk as collecting officer

46. Without prejudice to the provisions of sections 59 and 59A of the

Magistrates' Courts Act 1980 (periodical payments through justices' clerk and proceedings by the clerk etc.) or section 62 of that Act (payments required to be made to a child), a justices' clerk—

    (a) shall, by virtue of his office, be collecting officer of any magistrates' court of which he is the clerk; and

    (b) in that capacity shall act under any order directing the payment of money to him which was made by any court under section 30 of the Criminal Justice Administration Act 1914 (which provided for periodical payments under court orders to be made through an officer of the court or other third party) and which continues to have effect in accordance with the provisions of paragraph 18 of Schedule 4 to this Act.

Person acting as substitute clerk to justices

    47.—(1) Subject to any rules made under section 144 of the Magistrates' Courts Act 1980, where a person who is not the justices' clerk (or one of the justices' clerks) for a petty sessions area acts as clerk to the justices for that petty sessions area—

    (a) he shall be treated as acting as deputy to the justices' clerk; and

    (b) he shall make a return to the justices' clerk of—

        (i) all matters done before the justices; and

        (ii) all matters that the clerk to the justices is required to register or record.

    (2) Where there are two or more justices' clerks for the petty sessions area, any reference in subsection (1) above to the justices' clerk is a reference to such one of them as may be designated for the purpose by the magistrates' courts committee.

Independence of justices' clerk and staff in relation to legal functions

    48.—(1) When exercising the functions specified in subsection (2) below or giving advice to justices of the peace in an individual case—

    (a) a justices' clerk shall not be subject to the direction of the magistrates' courts committee, the justices' chief executive or any other person; and

    (b) any member of the staff of a magistrates' courts committee shall not be subject to the direction of that committee or of the justices' chief executive (when acting as such).

    (2) The functions referred to in subsection (1) above are functions conferred by rules made in accordance with section 144 of the Magistrates' Courts Act 1980 by virtue of section 45(1) or (2) above.

Appointment of justices' clerks for youth courts and family proceedings courts

    49.—(1) The inner London magistrates' courts committee shall appoint one or more justices' clerks for the youth courts and family proceedings courts for the metropolitan area.

    (2) Subsections (2) to (4), (5)(b), (6) and (7) of section 42 above apply to any justices' clerk appointed under subsection (1) above as they apply to a justices' clerk for a petty sessions area, but with the substitution for any reference to the magistrates for a petty sessions area of a reference to the justices of the peace who are members of the youth court panel for the metropolitan area or (as the case may be) of a family panel for that area, other than any such justice whose name is for the time being entered on the supplemental list.

(3) In this section—

"the inner London magistrates' courts committee" means the magistrates' courts committee for an area consisting of or including the whole of the inner London area or, if there is no such committee, all the magistrates courts' committees for areas which consist of or include any part of the inner London area acting jointly; and

"the metropolitan area" means the inner London area and the City of London.

Pensions etc. of justices' chief executive, justices' clerks and staff in inner London area

50.—(1) Schedule 3 to this Act (which re-enacts certain provisions relating to the functions of the Receiver for the Metropolitan Police District with respect to pensions etc. of court staff) shall have effect.

(2) The Lord Chancellor may by order make provision with respect to pensions, allowances or gratuities payable to or in respect of inner London court staff, or any class of inner London court staff.

(3) An order under subsection (2) above may—

(a) itself make provision with respect to the pensions, allowances or gratuities which, subject to the fulfilment of such requirements and conditions as may be prescribed by the order, are to be or may be paid to or in respect of inner London court staff, or any class of inner London court staff; or

(b) provide that the civil service provisions are to have effect, with such modifications as may be prescribed by the order, in relation to the payment by such persons as may be so prescribed, out of such funds as may be so prescribed, of pensions, allowances and gratuities to or in respect of inner London court staff, or any class of inner London court staff.

(4) Without prejudice to the generality of subsections (2) and (3) above, an order under subsection (2)—

(a) may include all or any of the provisions referred to in paragraphs 1 to 11 of Schedule 3 to the Superannuation Act 1972; and

(b) may make different provision as respects different classes of persons and different circumstances.

(5) Paragraphs 1 to 11 of Schedule 3 to the Superannuation Act 1972 shall have effect, in their application for the purposes of this section, as if references to regulations were references to an order under this section and references to the Secretary of State were references to the Lord Chancellor.

(6) Subsections (3) and (4) of section 7 of the Superannuation Act 1972 (which relate to increases under the Pensions (Increase) Act 1971) shall have effect in relation to an order under subsection (2) above as they have effect in relation to regulations under that section.

(7) The Lord Chancellor may by order repeal or amend any of the relevant enactments, whether or not he makes provision under subsection (2) above.

(8) An order under subsection (2) or (7) above may make such consequential, transitional, incidental or supplemental provision (including provision amending or repealing any provision of this Act or any other enactment) as the Lord Chancellor thinks necessary or expedient.

(9) Before making an order under subsection (2) or (7) above the Lord Chancellor shall consult—

(a) the inner London magistrates' courts committee;

(b) such local authorities as appear to him to be concerned;

(c) the Receiver for the Metropolitan Police District; and

(d) such representatives of other persons likely to be affected by the proposed order as appear to him to be appropriate.

(10) An order under subsection (2) or (7) above shall be made by statutory instrument which shall be subject to annulment in pursuance of a resolution of either House of Parliament.

(11) In this section—

"the civil service provisions" has the meaning given by section 15(1) of the Superannuation (Miscellaneous Provisions) Act 1967;

"inner London court staff" means the justices' chief executive employed by the inner London magistrates' courts committee, any justices' clerk for the inner London area and staff of the inner London magistrates' courts committee;

"the inner London magistrates' courts committee" means the magistrates' courts committee for an area consisting of or including the inner London area or, if there is no such committee, every magistrates' courts committee for any area which consists of or includes any part of the inner London area; and

"the relevant enactments" means—

(a) Schedule 3 to this Act; and

(b) section 15 of the Superannuation (Miscellaneous Provisions) Act 1967 (superannuation of metropolitan civil staffs) so far as it relates to the persons mentioned in subsection (1)(a)(ii) of that section.

PART V

PROTECTION AND INDEMNIFICATION OF JUSTICES AND JUSTICES' CLERKS

Immunity for acts within jurisdiction

51. No action shall lie against any justice of the peace or justices' clerk in respect of any act or omission of his—

(a) in the execution of his duty—

(i) as such a justice; or

(ii) as such a clerk exercising, by virtue of any statutory provision, any of the functions of a single justice; and

(b) with respect to any matter within his jurisdiction.

Immunity for certain acts beyond jurisdiction

52. An action shall lie against any justice of the peace or justices' clerk in respect of any act or omission of his—

(a) in the purported execution of his duty—

(i) as such a justice; or

(ii) as such a clerk exercising, by virtue of any statutory provision, any of the functions of a single justice; but

(b) with respect to a matter which is not within his jurisdiction,

if, but only if, it is proved that he acted in bad faith.

Where action prohibited, proceedings may be set aside

53. If any action is brought in circumstances in which this Part of this Act provides that no action is to lie, a judge of the court in which the action is brought may, on the application of the defendant and upon an affidavit as to the facts, set aside the proceedings in the action, with or without costs, as the judge thinks fit.

Indemnification of justices and justices' clerks

54.—(1) For the purposes of subsection (2) below, the following amounts are "relevant amounts" in relation to a justice of the peace or justices' clerk—

(a) any costs which he reasonably incurs—

(i) in or in connection with proceedings against him in respect of anything done or omitted in the exercise (or purported exercise) of his duty as a justice of the peace or justices' clerk; or

(ii) in taking steps to dispute any claim which might be made in such proceedings;

(b) any damages awarded against him or costs ordered to be paid by him in any such proceedings; and

(c) any sums payable by him in connection with a reasonable settlement of any such proceedings or claim,

and relevant amounts relate to criminal matters if the duty mentioned in paragraph (a)(i) above relates to criminal matters.

(2) Subject to the provisions of this section, a justice of the peace or justices' clerk—

(a) shall be indemnified out of local funds in respect of relevant amounts which relate to criminal matters unless it is proved, in respect of the matters giving rise to the proceedings or claim, that he acted in bad faith; and

(b) in respect of other relevant amounts—

(i) may be indemnified out of local funds; and

(ii) shall be so indemnified if, in respect of the matters giving rise to the proceedings or claim, he acted reasonably and in good faith.

(3) Any question whether, or to what extent, a person is to be indemnified under this section shall be determined by the magistrates' courts committee for the area for which he acted at the material time.

(4) A determination under subsection (3) above with respect to any such costs or sums as are mentioned in subsection (1)(a) or (c) above may, if the person claiming to be indemnified so requests, be made in advance before those costs are incurred or the settlement made, as the case may be.

(5) Any such determination in advance for indemnity in respect of costs to be incurred shall be subject to such limitations, if any, as the committee think proper and to the subsequent determination of the amount of the costs reasonably incurred and shall not affect any other determination which may fall to be made in connection with the proceedings or claim in question.

(6) An appeal shall lie to a person appointed for the purpose by the Lord Chancellor—

(a) on the part of the person claiming to be indemnified, from any decision of the magistrates' courts committee under subsection (3) or (4) above, other than a decision to postpone until after the conclusion of the proceedings any determination with respect to his own costs or to impose limitations on making a determination in advance for indemnity in respect of such costs;

(b) on the part of any paying authority, from any determination of the magistrates' courts committee under subsection (3) above other than a determination in advance for indemnity in respect of costs to be incurred by the person claiming to be indemnified.

(7) Where there are two or more paying authorities in relation to any justice or justices' clerk, any question as to the extent to which the funds required to indemnify him are to be provided by each authority shall be determined by agreement between those authorities and the magistrates' courts committee concerned or, in default of such agreement, shall be determined by the Lord Chancellor.

(8) The Lord Chancellor may by statutory instrument make rules prescribing the procedure to be followed in any appeal under subsection (6) above; and any statutory instrument made by virtue of this subsection shall be subject to annulment in pursuance of a resolution of either House of Parliament.

(9) In this section—

"justices' clerk" includes any person appointed by a magistrates' courts committee to assist a justices' clerk;

"local funds", in relation to a justice or justices' clerk, means funds out of which the expenses of the magistrates' courts committee for the area for which he acted at the material time are payable; and

"paying authority", in relation to a justice or justices' clerk, means any authority which is a paying authority for the purposes of section 55 below in relation to the magistrates' courts committee for the area for which he acted at the material time.

PART VI

ADMINISTRATIVE AND FINANCIAL ARRANGEMENTS

Duties of local authorities

55.—(1) Subject to the provisions of this Act, the paying authority or authorities in relation to any magistrates' courts committee shall provide the petty sessional court-houses and other accommodation, and the goods and services, proper for the performance of the functions of—

(a) the magistrates for the magistrates' courts committee area;

(b) the magistrates' courts committee;

(c) any other committee of the magistrates for that area; or

(d) the justices' clerks for any part of the magistrates' courts committee area.

(2) Subsection (1) above shall not require the paying authority or authorities to provide any current item or class of current items if the magistrates' courts committee have notified the authority or authorities that they intend to obtain that item or class of items otherwise than from that authority or any of those authorities.

(3) For the purposes of subsection (2) above "current item" means any goods or services which are of such a kind that expenditure incurred by a paying authority on providing them would not be capital expenditure.

(4) Where there is one paying authority in relation to a magistrates' courts committee, that authority shall pay the expenses of the committee.

(5) Where there are two or more paying authorities in relation to a magistrates' courts committee, each of those authorities shall pay a proper proportion of those expenses.

(6) For the purposes of subsections (4) and (5) above the expenses of a magistrates' courts committee shall be taken to include—

(a) expenses incurred by them in obtaining goods and services which are proper for the purposes mentioned in subsection (1) above but which by virtue of subsection (2) above the paying authority or authorities are not required to provide;

(b) the sums payable under Part IV of this Act on account of a person's salary or expenses as justices' chief executive or as justices' clerk for any part of the magistrates' courts committee area, the remuneration of any staff employed by the committee and the remuneration of any court security officers employed (whether by the committee or a paying authority) under section 76(2)(a) of the Criminal Justice Act 1991 in relation to petty sessions areas within the magistrates' courts committee area together with—

(i) secondary Class I contributions payable in respect of any such person, staff or officers under Part I of the Social Security Contributions and Benefits Act 1992; and

(ii) contributions equivalent premiums so payable under Chapter III of Part III of the Pension Schemes Act 1993;

(c) the sums payable under any contract entered into (whether by any such magistrates' courts committee or a paying authority) under section 76(2)(b) of the Criminal Justice Act 1991; and

(d) so far as they are not otherwise provided for, all other costs incurred, with the general or special authority of the magistrates' courts committee, by the justices for the magistrates' courts committee area.

(7) Nothing in subsection (1), (4) or (5) above requires any paying authority to incur any expenditure or make any payment which would—

(a) cause the net cost to it in any year of the matters mentioned in subsection (1) of section 57 below to exceed the amount which, in relation to that authority and that year, is for the time being determined by the Lord Chancellor under subsection (3)(b) of that section; or

(b) cause its capital expenditure in any year in pursuance of functions under this Part of this Act to exceed the amount which, in relation to that authority and that year, is for the time being determined by the Lord Chancellor under subsection (4)(b) of that section;

and in determining any such net cost as is mentioned in paragraph (a) above there shall be disregarded any such capital expenditure as is mentioned in paragraph (b) above.

(8) Subject to section 14(1) above, any accommodation provided under this section for any justice, justices' clerk or justices' chief executive may be outside the area for which the justices act and, in the case of a petty sessional court-house, shall be treated as being in that area for the purposes of the jurisdiction of the justices when acting in the court-house.

(9) Two or more paying authorities may arrange for accommodation, goods or services provided for the purposes of this section by one of them to be used also as if provided for those purposes by the other or each of the others.

(10) In this section—

"paying authority" in relation to a magistrates' courts committee, means any responsible authority whose area comprises all or part of the area to which the committee relates; and

"responsible authority" means any council of—

(a) a county;

(b) a county borough;

(c) a unitary district; or

(d) a London borough,

or the Common Council of the City of London.

Provisions supplementary to s.55

56.—(1) Subject to the provisions of this section—

(a) the petty sessional court-houses and other accommodation, goods and services to be provided by the paying authority, or each of the paying authorities, under section 55 above;

(b) the salary to be paid to a justices' clerk or justices' chief executive and to staff of a magistrates' courts committee; and

(c) the nature and amount of the expenses which a magistrates' courts committee may incur in the discharge of any functions or may authorise to be incurred,

shall be such as may from time to time be determined by the magistrates' courts committee after consultation with the paying authority or authorities.

(2) Where the expenses of a magistrates' courts committee (including any sums which, by virtue of section 55(6) above, are to be taken to be such expenses) fall to be borne by more than one paying authority, any question as to the manner in which they are to be borne by the authorities concerned shall be determined by agreement between those authorities and the magistrates' courts committee concerned or, in default of such agreement, shall be determined by the Lord Chancellor.

(3) Any paying authority which is aggrieved by a determination of a magistrates' courts committee under subsection (1) above may, within one month

from the receipt by the authority of written notice of the determination, appeal to the Lord Chancellor, whose decision shall be binding upon the magistrates' courts committee and any authority concerned.

(4) The approval of the Lord Chancellor shall be required for any determination under subsection (1) above reducing the salary of a justices' clerk or justices' chief executive, unless the justices' clerk or justices' chief executive concerned consents to the reduction.

(5) In this section "paying authority" has the same meaning as in section 55 above.

Grants by Lord Chancellor to responsible authorities

57.—(1) The Lord Chancellor may pay to the responsible authorities grants towards the net cost to them in any year—

(a) of their functions under this Part of this Act;

(b) of their functions under any regulations made, or having effect as if made, under section 7 or 24 of the Superannuation Act 1972 with respect to court staff;

(c) of their functions under any regulations having effect by virtue of paragraph 20(1)(a) or (2) of Schedule 4 to this Act; and

(d) of making payments under section 10 or 54 above;

and in determining any such net cost as is mentioned above there shall be disregarded any such capital expenditure as is mentioned in subsection (2) below.

(2) The Lord Chancellor may also pay to the responsible authorities grants towards their capital expenditure in any year in pursuance of their functions under this Part of this Act.

(3) The amount of any grant under subsection (1) above towards the net cost to a responsible authority in any year of the matters mentioned in that subsection shall not exceed 80 per cent of whichever of the following is the less—

(a) that net cost; and

(b) the amount which, in relation to the authority and that year, is for the time being determined by the Lord Chancellor.

(4) The amount of any grant under subsection (2) above towards the capital expenditure in any year of a responsible authority in pursuance of its functions under this Part of this Act shall not exceed 80 per cent of whichever of the following is the less—

(a) that capital expenditure; and

(b) the amount which, in relation to the authority and that year, is for the time being determined by the Lord Chancellor.

(5) The Lord Chancellor, with the concurrence of the Treasury, may by statutory instrument make regulations as to the manner in which—

(a) income and expenditure of responsible authorities are to be taken into account in determining the net cost to them in any year of the matters mentioned in subsection (1) above; or

(b) expenditure of such authorities is to be taken into account in determining their capital expenditure in any year in pursuance of their functions under this Part of this Act;

and for the purposes of this section any question as to that net cost or that capital expenditure shall (subject to the regulations) be determined by the Lord Chancellor.

(6) The Lord Chancellor may direct that, in determining—

(a) the net cost to a responsible authority in any year of the matters mentioned in subsection (1) above; or

(b) the capital expenditure of such an authority in any year in pursuance of its functions under this Part of this Act, there shall be taken into account or disregarded, to such extent as may be specified in the direction, such items as may be so specified.

(7) Grants under this section shall be paid at such times, in such manner and subject to such conditions as the Lord Chancellor may with the approval of the Treasury determine.

(8) In this section—

"court staff" means justices' chief executives, justices' clerks and staff of magistrates' courts committees;

"responsible authority" has the same meaning as in section 55 above.

Local authority land appropriated to magistrates' courts purposes

58.—(1) Where on or after 1st April 1995 a responsible authority appropriate any land owned by them to magistrates' courts purposes, the authority shall be taken for the purposes of section 57(2) above to incur, in the year in which the appropriation is made, capital expenditure in pursuance of their functions under this Part of this Act of an amount equal to the open market value of the land at the time of the appropriation.

(2) In subsection (1) above—

"magistrates' courts purposes" means the purposes of being provided under section 55(1) above as a petty sessional court-house or other accommodation; and

"responsible authority" has the same meaning as in section 55 above.

Regulations as to accounts and audit

59.—(1) The Lord Chancellor may by regulations made by statutory instrument require magistrates' courts committees—

(a) to keep prescribed accounts and prescribed records in relation to those accounts; and

(b) to cause any such accounts to be audited in accordance with the regulations.

(2) In subsection (1) above "prescribed" means prescribed by the regulations; and a statutory instrument containing (whether alone or with other provisions) regulations made by virtue of this section shall be subject to annulment in pursuance of a resolution of either House of Parliament.

Application of fines and fees

60.—(1) Subject to paragraphs (a) and (b) of section 139 of the Magistrates Courts Act 1980 (which relates to the disposal of sums adjudged to be paid by a summary conviction) and to the following provisions of this section, there shall be paid to the Lord Chancellor—

(a) all fines imposed by a magistrates' court and all sums which become payable by virtue of an order of such a court and are by any enactment made applicable as fines so imposed or any class or description of such fines; and

(b) all other sums received by a justices' clerk by reason of his office except—

(i) sums to which a person other than the Lord Chancellor is by law entitled and which are paid to that person; and

(ii) sums paid into court in pursuance of orders under section 35 of the Powers of Criminal Courts Act 1973 (compensation orders).

(2) The sums payable to the Lord Chancellor by virtue of subsection (1)(a) above do not include—

(a) any sums which by or in pursuance of any provision in the enactments relating to those sums are directed to be paid to the Commissioners of

Customs and Excise or to any officer of theirs or person appointed by
them;

(b) any sums which by or in pursuance of any such provision are directed
to be paid—

(i) to or for the benefit of the party aggrieved, party injured or a
person described in similar terms; or

(ii) to or for the benefit of the family or relatives of a person
described in any such terms or of a person dying in consequence of
an act or event which constituted or was the occasion of an offence;

(c) any sums which by or in pursuance of any such provision are directed
to be applied in making good any default or repairing any damage or
paying or reimbursing any expenses (other than those of the prosecution); or

(d) any sums which are directed to be paid to any person by or in pursuance of any such provision referring in terms to awarding or reimbursing a loss, or to damages, compensation or satisfaction for loss,
damage, injury or wrong.

(3) Paragraph (b) of subsection (1) above does not apply to sums received
by a justices' clerk on account of his salary or expenses as such; and any sum
paid to the Lord Chancellor by virtue of that paragraph shall be paid to him
subject to its being repaid to any person establishing his title to it.

(4) The Lord Chancellor, with the concurrence of the Treasury, may by
statutory instrument make regulations as to the times at which, and the manner in which, justices' clerks shall account for and pay the sums payable to
him under this section, and as to the keeping, inspection and audit of
accounts of justices' clerks, whether for the purposes of this section or
otherwise.

(5) For the purposes of this section anything done by the Crown Court on
appeal from a magistrates' court shall be treated as done by the magistrates'
court.

(6) In this section "fine" includes—

(a) any pecuniary penalty, pecuniary forfeiture or pecuniary compensation payable under a conviction; and

(b) any non-pecuniary forfeiture on conviction by, or under any order of,
a magistrates' court so far as the forfeiture is converted into or consists
of money.

Defaults of justices' clerks etc.

61. The Lord Chancellor may, if he thinks fit, pay to any person any money
due to that person which he has not received because of the default of a
justices' clerk or of any staff of a magistrates' courts committee.

PART VII

INSPECTION OF MAGISTRATES' COURTS SERVICE

Inspectors of the magistrates' courts service

62.—(1) The Lord Chancellor may appoint such number of inspectors of
the magistrates' courts service (to be known collectively as "Her Majesty's
Magistrates' Courts Service Inspectorate") as he may consider appropriate.

(2) The Lord Chancellor shall appoint one of the persons so appointed to
be Her Majesty's Chief Inspector of the Magistrates' Courts Service.

(3) It shall be the duty of inspectors of the magistrates' courts service—

(a) to inspect and report to the Lord Chancellor on the organisation and
administration of magistrates' courts for each magistrates' courts
committee area; and

(b) to discharge such other functions in connection with the organisation and administration of magistrates' courts as the Lord Chancellor may from time to time direct.

(4) Her Majesty's Chief Inspector of the Magistrates' Courts Service shall make an annual report to the Lord Chancellor as to the discharge of the functions of the Inspectorate; and the Lord Chancellor shall, within one month of receiving the report, lay a copy of it before each House of Parliament.

(5) The Lord Chancellor shall make to or in respect of inspectors of the magistrates' courts service such payments by way of remuneration, allowances or otherwise as he may with the approval of the Treasury determine.

Powers of inspectors

63.—(1) Subject to subsection (2) below, an inspector of the magistrates' courts service exercising his functions under section 62 above shall have at all reasonable times—

(a) a right of entry to any court-house or other premises occupied by a magistrates' courts committee; and

(b) a right to inspect, and take copies of, any records kept by a magistrates' courts committee, and any other documents containing information relating to the administration of the magistrates' courts for their area, which he considers relevant to the discharge of his functions.

(2) Subsection (1) above does not entitle an inspector—

(a) to be present when a magistrates' court is hearing proceedings in private; or

(b) to attend any private deliberations of the justices of the peace.

(3) The records referred to in paragraph (b) of subsection (1) above include records kept by means of a computer; and an inspector exercising the power to inspect records conferred by that subsection—

(a) shall be entitled at any reasonable time to have access to, and inspect and check the operation of, any computer and associated apparatus or material which is or has been in use in connection with the records in question; and

(b) may require—

(i) the person by whom or on whose behalf the computer is or has been so used; or

(ii) any person having charge of, or otherwise concerned with the operation of, the computer, apparatus or material,

to afford him such reasonable assistance as he may require.

PART VIII

MISCELLANEOUS AND SUPPLEMENTARY PROVISIONS

Training courses

64.—(1) It shall be the duty of every magistrates' courts committee, in accordance with arrangements approved by the Lord Chancellor, to make and administer schemes providing for training courses for justices of the peace of their area.

(2) If training courses are not provided for justices of the peace of any area as required by subsection (1) above, the Lord Chancellor may recover from the magistrates' courts committee in default any expenses which he incurs in providing training courses to make good the default.

(3) The Lord Chancellor may provide training courses for justices' clerks and for staff of magistrates' courts committees.

Disqualification in case of bankruptcy

65.—(1) A person who is adjudged bankrupt shall be disqualified for being appointed or acting as a justice of the peace.

(2) Where a person is disqualified under this section, the disqualification shall cease—

(a) on his discharge from bankruptcy; or

(b) if the bankruptcy order is previously annulled, on the date of its annulment.

Disqualification in certain cases of justices who are members of local authorities

66.—(1) A justice of the peace who is a member of a local authority shall not act as a member of the Crown Court or of a magistrates' court in any proceedings brought by or against, or by way of appeal from a decision of, the authority or any committee or officer of the authority.

(2) For the purposes of subsection (1) above—

(a) any reference to a committee of a local authority includes a joint committee, joint board, joint authority or other combined body of which that authority is a member or on which it is represented; and

(b) any reference to an officer of a local authority refers to a person employed or appointed by the authority, or by a committee of the authority, in the capacity in which he is employed or appointed to act.

(3) A justice of the peace who is a member of the Common Council of the City of London shall not act as a member of the Crown Court or of a magistrates' court in any proceedings brought by or against, or by way of appeal from a decision of, the Corporation of the City or the Common Council or any committee or officer of the Corporation or Common Council.

(4) Subsection (2) above applies for the purposes of subsection (3) above with the substitution, for references to a local authority, of references to the Corporation or the Common Council.

(5) Nothing in this section prevents a justice from acting in any proceedings by reason only of their being brought by a police officer.

(6) No act shall be invalidated by reason only of the disqualification under this section of the person acting.

(7) In this section "local authority" means—

(a) a local authority within the meaning of the Local Government Act 1972 or the Local Government (Scotland) Act 1973;

(b) a police authority established under section 3 of the Police Act 1996;

(c) a joint authority established by Part IV of the Local Government Act 1985;

(d) a housing action trust established under Part III of the Housing Act 1988;

(e) the Broads Authority; and

(f) a National Park authority.

Justices not disqualified by reason of liability to local taxation

67. A justice of the peace may perform any act in the execution of his office as such a justice in relation to the laws concerning—

(a) rates leviable by a rating authority;

(b) community charges of a charging authority;

(c) council tax set by a billing authority; or

(d) the non-domestic rate of a special authority within the meaning of section 144(6) of the Local Government Finance Act 1988,

even though he is rated to or chargeable with any rates falling within paragraph (a) above or is liable, or would but for any enactment or anything provided or done under any enactment be liable, to pay an amount in respect of any charge, tax or rate falling within paragraphs (b) to (d) above in the area affected by the act in question.

Acts done by justices outside their commission area

68.—(1) A justice of the peace for any commission area may act as a justice for that area in any commission area which adjoins the commission area for which he is a justice.

(2) Justices for the retained county of Surrey or the retained county of Kent may hold special or petty sessions for any division of their retained county at any place in Greater London; and for all purposes relating to sessions so held the place at which they are held shall be treated as being within the retained county and the division for which the justices holding them are justices.

Promissory oaths of certain justices

69.—(1) Subject to the provisions of this section, any person who, under this Act, is a justice of the peace for any area by virtue of any other office held by him shall, before acting as such a justice, take the oath of allegiance and judicial oath in accordance with the Promissory Oaths Acts.

(2) A person shall not be required by virtue of subsection (1) above to take those oaths as a justice of the peace by reason only of his being appointed under this Act to act temporarily as deputy for, or as if he were, the holder of another office to which that subsection applies; but those oaths may be taken by and administered to any such person despite anything in the Promissory Oaths Act or any other enactment.

(3) A person shall not be required, on becoming a justice of the peace for any area, to take the oath of allegiance and judicial oath in accordance with the Promissory Oaths Acts if he has at any time done so as justice of the peace for that or any other area.

(4) The oaths required by law to be taken by a metropolitan stipendiary magistrate may, in the case of a person authorised to act as such under section 19 above, be taken before any of the metropolitan stipendiary magistrates.

(5) In this section "the Promissory Oaths Acts" means the Promissory Oaths Act 1868 and the Promissory Oaths Act 1871.

Application of enactments to the City of London

70.—(1) Subject to the provisions of sections 21, 23, 25(3), 33(5) and 35(3) above, in any enactment relating to justices of the peace, magistrates' courts, justices' clerks or matters connected therewith (including, except to the extent that it otherwise expressly provides, any such enactment passed after the passing of this Act)—

    (a) any reference to a county or to county justices shall be taken to include the City of London or justices for the City; and

    (b) any reference to a county council shall be taken to include the Corporation of the City acting through the Common Council, and references to a county fund shall be taken to include the City fund;

but in any such enactment which refers in the same context both to a non-metropolitan county and to a metropolitan district, the reference to a non-metropolitan county shall be taken to include the City.

(2) Where any such enactment (including any enactment contained in this Act) expressly refers in the same context both—

    (a) to a county or non-metropolitan county or to justices or magistrates for a county or non-metropolitan county; and

    (b) to the City or to justices or magistrates for the City,

the operation of that enactment shall not be affected by, and shall be without prejudice to the generality of, subsection (1) above.

Isles of Scilly

71. For the purposes of this Act the Isles of Scilly shall be treated as forming part of the county and the retained county of Cornwall.

Interpretation

72.—(1) In this Act, except to the extent that the context otherwise requires—

"capital expenditure" means expenditure for capital purposes (construed in accordance with section 40 of the Local Government and Housing Act 1989);

"commission area" has the meaning given by section 1 above;

"justices' clerk" means a clerk to the justices for a petty sessions area;

"London commission areas", "inner London area" and "outer London areas" have the meanings given by section 2 above;

"magistrate"—

(a) in relation to a commission area, means a justice of the peace for the commission area, other than a justice whose name is for the time being entered in the supplemental list;

(b) in relation to a part of a commission area, means a person who (in accordance with paragraph (a) of this definition) is a magistrate for that area and ordinarily acts in and for that part of it; and

(c) in relation to a magistrates' courts committee area, means a person who (in accordance with paragraphs (a) and (b) of this definition) is a magistrate for that area or any part of that area;

"magistrates' courts committee area" means the area to which a magistrates' courts committee relates;

"officer" includes the holder of any place, situation or employment, and "office" shall be construed accordingly;

"petty sessional court-house" means—

(a) a court-house or place at which justices are accustomed to assemble for holding special or petty sessions or for the time being appointed as a substitute for such a court-house or place (including, where justices are accustomed to assemble for either special or petty sessions at more than one court-house or place in a petty sessional division, any such court-house or place); or

(b) a court-house or place at which a stipendiary magistrate is authorised by law to do alone any act authorised to be done by more than one justice of the peace:

"petty sessions area" has the meaning given by section 4 above;

"preserved county" has the meaning given by section 64 of the Local Government (Wales) Act 1994;

"retained county"—

(a) in relation to England, means the area of a non-metropolitan county created by Part I of the Local Government Act 1972, as it stood immediately before 1st April 1995; and

(b) in relation to Wales, means preserved county;

"stipendiary magistrate" includes a metropolitan stipendiary magistrate;

"the supplemental list" has the meaning given by section 7 above; and

"unitary district" means a district comprised in an area for which there is no county council.

(2) Any reference in this Act to a retained county by name, where the name is that of a non-metropolitan county in England, is a reference to that county as it stood immediately before 1st April 1995.

Transitional provisions, consequential amendments and repeals

73.—(1) The transitional provisions and savings in Schedule 4 to this Act shall have effect.

(2) The enactments and instruments mentioned in Schedule 5 to this Act shall be amended in accordance with that Schedule.

(3) The enactments mentioned in Schedule 6 to this Act shall be repealed, and the instruments mentioned in that Schedule shall be revoked, to the extent specified in the third column of that Schedule.

Commencement

74.—(1) Subject to—

(a) subsection (2) below; and

(b) paragraphs 7(2)(f) and 8 of Schedule 4 to this Act,

this Act shall come into force at the end of the period of three months beginning with the day on which it is passed (and any reference in this Act to the commencement of this Act is a reference to its coming into force at the end of that period).

(2) If section 82 of and Schedule 7 to the Police and Magistrates' Courts Act 1994 have not come into force before the commencement of this Act, then section 50 of and Schedule 3 to this Act shall come into force on the relevant commencement date.

(3) In subsection (2) above "relevant commencement date" means—

(a) if before the commencement of this Act a date on or after the date of that commencement has been appointed by an order under section 94 of the Police and Magistrates' Courts Act 1994 (commencement and transitional provisions) as the date on which section 82 of and Schedule 7 to that Act are to come into force, the date so appointed; and

(b) otherwise, such date as the Lord Chancellor may by order appoint.

(4) Subsections (4), (5), (7) and (8) of section 94 of the Police and Magistrates' Courts Act 1994 shall apply to an order under subsection (3)(b) above as they would apply to an order under subsection (2) of that section.

Short title and extent

75.—(1) This Act may be cited as the Justices of the Peace Act 1997.

(2) Subject to subsections (3) and (4) below, any amendment, repeal or revocation contained in Schedule 5 or 6 to this Act has the same extent as the provision it amends, repeals or revokes.

(3) In Schedule 5 to this Act—

(a) paragraphs 2 and 5 extend to England and Wales only; and

(b) paragraph 9 extends to the United Kingdom.

(4) In Schedule 6 to this Act, the repeal of section 70 of the Criminal Procedure and Investigations Act 1996 extends to England and Wales only.

(5) Subject to subsections (2) to (4) above, this Act extends to England and Wales only.

SCHEDULES

Section 1

SCHEDULE 1

COMMISSION AREAS IN WALES

Name	Area
Gwent commission area (or, in Welsh, ardal comisiwn Gwent)	The preserved county of Gwent, together with so much of the preserved county of Mid Glamorgan as falls within the county borough of Caerphilly.
South Wales commission area (or, in Welsh, ardal comisiwn De Cymru)	The preserved counties of Mid Glamorgan and South Glamorgan, but excluding so much of the preserved county of Mid Glamorgan as falls within the county borough of Caerphilly.

Section 2

SCHEDULE 2

LONDON COMMISSION AREAS

PART I

INNER LONDON AREA

Name	Area
Inner London area	The inner London boroughs

PART II

OUTER LONDON AREAS

Name	Area
North-east London area	The London boroughs of Barking, Havering, Newham, Redbridge and Waltham Forest.
South-east London area	The London boroughs of Bexley, Bromley and Croydon.
South-west London area	The London boroughs of Kingston upon Thames, Merton, Richmond upon Thames and Sutton.
Middlesex area	The London boroughs of Barnet, Brent, Ealing, Enfield, Haringey, Harrow, Hillingdon and Hounslow.

Section 50

SCHEDULE 3

CONTINUING FUNCTIONS OF RECEIVER FOR THE METROPOLITAN POLICE DISTRICT IN RELATION TO PENSIONS ETC. OF COURT STAFF

1. In this Schedule—
   "the committee of magistrates" means the committee which until 1st April 1995 existed for the inner London area under section 35 of the Justices of the Peace Act 1979;
   "court staff" has the same meaning as in section 57 of this Act;
   "the inner London magistrates' courts committee" has the same meaning as in section 50 of this Act;
   "the Receiver" means the Receiver for the Metropolitan Police District; and
   "responsible authority" has the same meaning as in section 55 of this Act.
2. The Receiver shall pay out of the metropolitan police fund any superannuation benefits payable in respect of justices' clerks and other officers employed by the committee of magistrates or the inner London magistrates' courts committee under any enactment or instrument

applied to those clerks or other officers by regulations having effect in accordance with section 15(9) of the Superannuation (Miscellaneous Provisions) Act 1967, other than benefits payable by the London Residuary Body, and any superannuation contributions and other payments for which the inner London magistrates' courts committee may be liable as their employer under any such enactment or instrument.

3. Nothing in paragraph 2 above shall require the Receiver to incur any expenditure or make any payment which would cause the net cost to him in any year of the matters mentioned in paragraph 4 below to exceed the amount which, in relation to that year, is for the time being determined by the Lord Chancellor under paragraph 5(b) below.

4. The Lord Chancellor may out of money provided by Parliament pay to the Receiver grants towards the net cost to the Receiver in any year—

    (a) of the Receiver's functions under paragraph 2 above; and

    (b) of the Receiver's functions corresponding to those of responsible authorities under regulations made, or having effect as if made, under section 7 of the Superannuation Act 1972 with respect to court staff.

5. The amount of any grant under paragraph 4 above towards the net cost to the Receiver in any year of the matters mentioned in that paragraph shall not exceed 80 per cent of whichever of the following is the less, namely—

    (a) that net cost; and

    (b) the amount which, in relation to that year, is for the time being determined for the purposes of this paragraph by the Lord Chancellor.

6. In subsections (5), (6) and (7) of section 57 of this Act (grants by Lord Chancellor to responsible authorities)—

    (a) references to that section include references to this Schedule; and

    (b) references to the matters mentioned in subsection (1) of that section include references to the matters mentioned in paragraph 4 above.

Section 73(1)   SCHEDULE 4

TRANSITIONAL PROVISIONS AND SAVINGS

PART I

GENERAL PROVISIONS

Continuity of the law

1.—(1) The repeal (or revocation) and re-enactment of provisions by this Act does not affect the continuity of the law.

(2) Any subordinate legislation made or other thing done, or having effect as if made or done, under or for the purposes of any provision repealed (or revoked) and re-enacted by this Act shall, if in force or effective immediately before the commencement of the corresponding provision of this Act, have effect thereafter as if made or done under or for the purposes of that corresponding provision.

(3) Any reference (express or implied) in this Act or any other enactment or in any instrument or document—

    (a) to any provision of this Act; or

    (b) to things done or falling to be done under or for the purposes of any provision of this Act,

shall (so far as the context permits) be construed as including, in relation to times, circumstances or purposes in relation to which the corresponding provision repealed (or revoked) by this Act had effect, a reference—

    (i) to that corresponding provision; or

    (ii) to things done or falling to be done under or for the purposes of that corresponding provision,

as the case may be.

(4) Any reference (express or implied) in any enactment or in any instrument or document—

    (a) to any provision repealed (or revoked) and re-enacted by this Act; or

    (b) to things done or falling to be done under or for the purposes of any such provision,

shall (so far as the context permits) be construed as including, in relation to times, circumstances or purposes in relation to which the corresponding provision of this Act has effect, a reference—

    (i) to that corresponding provision; or

    (ii) to things done or falling to be done under or for the purposes of that corresponding provision,

as the case may be.

(5) Without prejudice to the generality of sub-paragraph (4) above, where a power conferred by an Act is expressed to be exercisable in relation to enactments contained in Acts passed

before or in the same Session as the Act conferring the power, the power is also exercisable in relation to provisions of this Act which reproduce such enactments.

(6) Sub-paragraphs (1) to (5) above have effect instead of section 17(2) of the Interpretation Act 1978 (but are without prejudice to any other provision of that Act).

General saving for old transitional provisions and savings

2. The repeal (or revocation) by this Act of any transitional provision or saving relating to the coming into force of a provision reproduced in this Act does not affect the operation of the transitional provision or saving in so far as it is not specifically reproduced in this Act but remains capable of having effect in relation to the corresponding provision of this Act or otherwise.

3. The repeal by this Act of an enactment previously repealed subject to savings does not affect the continued operation of those savings.

Use of existing forms, etc.

4. Any reference to an enactment repealed (or revoked) by this Act which is contained in a document made, served or issued on or after the commencement of that repeal (or revocation) shall be construed, except so far as a contrary intention appears, as a reference or, as the context may require, as including a reference to the corresponding provision of this Act.

PART II

PROVISIONS RELATING TO PARTICULAR ENACTMENTS

Interpretation

5. In this Part of this Schedule—
(a) the "1979 Act" means the Justices of the Peace Act 1979;
(b) the "1994 Act" means the Police and Magistrates' Courts Act 1994; and
(c) any reference to the commencement of this Act shall be construed in accordance with section 74(1) of this Act.

Petty sessions areas

6. The repeal by this Act of—
(a) paragraph 9 of Schedule 1 to the 1979 Act (saving for petty sessional divisions); or
(b) section 91(3) of the 1994 Act (saving for petty sessional divisions of inner London area), does not affect the continued existence of any petty sessions area.

Inner London area

7.—(1) If section 83(1) of the 1994 Act (administrative and financial arrangements for magistrates' courts) has not come into force in relation to the inner London area before the commencement of this Act then, until the relevant commencement date, sections 55 and 56 of this Act shall not apply in relation to that area.

(2) If section 83(2) of the 1994 Act (repeal of sections 57 and 58 of 1979 Act), so far as it relates to section 58 of the 1979 Act (duties of Receiver in relation to inner London area), and the repeal of section 58 of the 1979 Act by Part II of Schedule 9 to the 1994 Act have not come into force before the commencement of this Act then, until the relevant commencement date—
(a) notwithstanding the repeal of the 1979 Act by this Act—
    (i) section 58 of the 1979 Act shall continue to have effect; and
    (ii) section 70 of the 1979 Act (interpretation) shall continue to have effect for the purpose of interpreting section 58 of that Act;
(b) section 54 of this Act shall have effect as if the Receiver for the Metropolitan Police District were the paying authority for the purposes of that section in respect of a justice or justices' clerk acting for the inner London area;
(c) any reference in any enactment to Part VI of this Act (including the reference in section 57(1)(a) of this Act) shall have effect as if it included a reference to section 58 of the 1979 Act;
(d) the Receiver for the Metropolitan Police District shall be—

(i) the paying authority and the responsible authority for the purposes of section 82 of the Road Traffic Offenders Act 1988 (accounting for fixed penalties); and

(ii) the paying authority for the purposes of section 76 of the Criminal Justice Act 1991 (provision of court security officers)

in relation to the magistrates' courts committee for the inner London area;

(e) the provisions of subsections (3) and (4) of section 76 of the Criminal Justice Act 1991 shall not apply in relation to the magistrates' courts committee for the inner London area; and

(f) the repeals by this Act of—

(i) section 60(6) of the Local Government Act 1985;

(ii) paragraph 7 of Schedule 11 to the Children Act 1989, so far as that repeal relates to paragraph (c) of that paragraph; and

(iii) paragraph 40(2)(k) of Schedule 11 to the Criminal Justice Act 1991,

shall not come into force.

(3) If paragraph 1 of Schedule 8 to the 1994 Act has not come into force before the commencement of this Act then, until the relevant commencement date, section 10 of this Act shall have effect—

(a) as if in subsection (7), after paragraph (a), there were inserted—

"(aa) in relation to a justice for the inner London area, the Receiver for the Metropolitan Police District;"; and

(b) with the omission of subsections (8)(a) and (9).

(4) If paragraph 19(3) of Schedule 8 to the 1994 Act has not come into force in relation to the inner London area before the commencement of this Act then, until the relevant commencement date, section 57 of this Act shall have effect in relation to the inner London area as if the Receiver for the Metropolitan Police District were the responsible authority for the purposes of that section.

(5) If paragraph 23 of Schedule 8 to the 1994 Act has not come into force before the commencement of this Act then, until the relevant commencement date, paragraph 27(2) below shall have effect as if the reference to sections 55 and 56 of this Act included a reference to section 58 of the 1979 Act.

(6) If the repeal by Part II of Schedule 9 to the 1994 Act of words in section 59(1)(b) of the 1979 Act has not come into force before the commencement of this Act then, until the relevant commencement date, section 57 of this Act shall have effect as if, at the end of subsection (1)(b), there were inserted the words "or, in the case of the Receiver for the Metropolitan Police District, his corresponding functions".

(7) "Relevant commencement date", in relation to any of sub-paragraphs (1) to (6) above, means—

(a) if before the commencement of this Act a date on or after the date of that commencement has been appointed by an order under section 94 of the 1994 Act (commencement and transitional provisions) as the date on which the provision (or provisions) of the 1994 Act mentioned in that sub-paragraph is (or are) to come into force (or is to come into force in relation to the area, or for the purpose, so mentioned), the date so appointed; and

(b) otherwise, such date as the Lord Chancellor may by order appoint.

(8) Subsections (4), (5), (7) and (8) of section 94 of the 1994 Act shall apply to an order under sub-paragraph (7)(b) above as they would apply to an order under subsection (2) of that section.

8.—(1) If paragraph 24 of Schedule 8 to the 1994 Act has not come into force before the commencement of this Act, then paragraph 4 of Schedule 5 to this Act shall not come into force until immediately after that provision of the 1994 Act has come into force.

(2) If paragraph 35 of Schedule 8 to the 1994 Act has not come into force before the commencement of this Act, then paragraph 30(a) of Schedule 5 to this Act shall not come into force until immediately after that provision of the 1994 Act has come into force.

9. The committee established for the purposes of section 34A of the 1979 Act (division of work in inner London area) shall after the commencement of this Act continue in existence as the committee established for the purposes of section 20 of this Act and each person who immediately before the commencement of this Act holds office as a member of the committee shall continue to hold office as a member until the expiry of the period for which he was appointed under section 34A(3) of the 1979 Act.

10. Subject to any order made under section 32 of this Act—

(a) any reference in any document to the committee of magistrates shall have effect, in relation to any time on or after 1 April 1995, as a reference to the magistrates' courts committee for the inner London area; and

(b) without prejudice to the generality of paragraph 1 above or 13 below, the body corporate formerly constituted under section 35 of the 1979 Act (committee of magistrates for inner

London area) which, by virtue of section 79(2) of the 1994 Act (savings), is the magistrates' courts committee for that area shall continue to be that magistrates' courts committee.

11.—(1) Sub-paragraph (2) below applies to any person who, immediately before the commencement of this Act is treated by virtue of section 80(2) or (3) of the 1994 Act (abolition of offices of principal chief clerk and chief clerk: savings) as having been appointed by the magistrates' courts committee for the inner London area—

(a) under section 24D of the 1979 Act, as justices' chief executive; or

(b) as a justices' clerk—

    (i) under section 25 of that Act, for any petty sessional division of the inner London area; or

    (ii) under section 34B of that Act, for the youth courts or family proceedings courts for that area and the City of London.

(2) Subject to section 42(5) to (7) of this Act, any person to whom this sub-paragraph applies shall hold and vacate office—

(a) in accordance with the terms of his appointment; or

(b) if he has entered into a contract of service, in accordance with the terms of his contract of service.

(3) Where, immediately before the commencement of this Act, a person is employed under a contract of service to which subsection (5) of section 80 of the 1994 Act (abolition of offices of senior deputy chief clerk and deputy chief clerk: savings for contract of service) applies—

(a) the repeal by this Act of that subsection shall not affect the continuation of that person's contract of service;

(b) he shall not be dismissed from his employment without the approval of the Lord Chancellor; and

(c) before approving his dismissal the Lord Chancellor shall consider any representations made by him.

(4) Any reference in any instrument or document to the chief clerk for any petty sessional division of the inner London area or for the youth courts or family proceedings courts for that area and the City of London shall have effect, in relation to any time on or after 1st April 1995, as a reference to the justices' clerk for that petty sessional division or, as the case may be, for those courts.

Stipendiary magistrates

12.—(1) This paragraph applies where immediately before the commencement of this Act a stipendiary magistrate who holds office in any commission area or commission areas is treated by virtue of paragraph 7(b) of Schedule 1 to the 1979 Act (stipendiary magistrates appointed under section 29 of the Justices of the Peace Act 1949 who held office immediately before 1st April 1974) as having been appointed under section 13 of the 1979 Act.

(2) The stipendiary magistrate shall continue to hold office in that commission area or those commission areas as if appointed under section 11 of this Act.

(3) His salary shall not be less than that payable to him immediately before 1st April 1974.

(4) For the purposes of section 12 of this Act he shall be treated as having been appointed on the date on which he was appointed to the office which he held immediately before 1st April 1974.

(5) Sub-paragraph (2) above is without prejudice to the generality of paragraph 1(2) above.

Magistrates' courts committees

13. Any magistrates' courts committee which was set up in accordance with the provisions of Part II of the 1979 Act for any area and is in existence immediately before the commencement of this Act shall after that commencement be treated as having been set up in accordance with the provisions of Part III of this Act as the magistrates' courts committee for that area.

14. Without prejudice to the generality of paragraph 1(2) above, the repeal by this Act of section 69 of the 1994 Act does not affect the continued operation of any order made under that section before the commencement of this Act.

Justices' chief executives

15.—(1) If, before the commencement of this Act, section 75 of the 1994 Act has not come into force, so far as it inserts section 24D(5) in the 1979 Act, in relation to the appointment of a justices' chief executive by the magistrates' courts committee for Hampshire, Kent or Lincolnshire, then, until the relevant commencement date, section 40 of this Act shall have effect in relation to such an appointment with the omission of subsection (5).

(2) In sub-paragraph (1) above, "relevant commencement date" means, in relation to such an appointment—

(a) if before the commencement of this Act a date on or after the date of that commencement has been appointed by an order under section 94 of the 1994 Act (commencement and transitional provisions) as the date on which section 75 of that Act, so far as it inserts section 24D(5) in the 1979 Act, is to come into force in relation to such an appointment, the date so appointed; and

(b) otherwise, such date as the Lord Chancellor may by order appoint.

(3) Subsections (4), (5), (7) and (8) of section 94 of the 1994 Act shall apply to an order under sub-paragraph (2)(b) above as they would apply to an order under subsection (2) of that section.

(4) The references to Hampshire, Kent and Lincolnshire in sub-paragraph (1) above are to those counties as they stood on 1st April 1995.

16. A person who, immediately before the commencement of this Act, continues to hold office as clerk to a magistrates' courts committee by virtue of Article 6(1) of the Police and Magistrates' Courts Act 1994 (Commencement No. 8 and Transitional Provisions) Order 1995 may continue in that appointment until the magistrates' courts committee have appointed a justices' chief executive in accordance with section 40(1) of this Act.

Justices' clerks etc.

17.—(1) Section 44(1) of this Act shall not have effect in relation to any person appointed by a magistrates' courts committee before 1st April 1995 as justices' clerk for a petty sessions area so long as he—

(a) continues to hold office as a justices' clerk for that area or for any one or more petty sessions areas including any part of that area; and

(b) has not entered into a contract of service on or after that date.

(2) Any justices' clerk in relation to whom, by virtue of sub-paragraph (1) above, section 44(1) of this Act does not have effect shall hold office during the pleasure of the magistrates' courts committee concerned.

(3) Any such justices' clerk shall be paid a salary for his personal remuneration, and the salary shall be taken to be remuneration for all business which he may by reason of his office as justices' clerk be called upon to perform, other than any duties as secretary to a licensing planning committee under Part VII of the Licensing Act 1964.

(4) Any such justices' clerk may be paid a single salary in respect of two or more clerkships.

(5) Any such justices' clerk shall, in addition to his salary, be paid the amount of any expenses of a description specified when his salary is determined, being expenses incurred by him with the general or special authority of the magistrates' courts committee.

18. Any order made before 1st April 1953 under—

(a) section 30 of the Criminal Justice Administration Act 1914; or

(b) section 1 of the Affiliation Orders Act 1914,

which is in force immediately before the commencement of this Act and, by virtue of paragraph 14 of Schedule 1 to the 1979 Act, has effect as if it required payments under it to be made to a justices' clerk in his capacity as collecting officer of a magistrates' court shall, so long as the order remains in force, continue to have that effect by virtue of this paragraph.

19. So far as, immediately before the commencement of this Act—

(a) section 23(7) of the Justices of the Peace Act 1949 (terms and conditions of employment of persons transferred to magistrates' courts committee on 1st April 1953); or

(b) paragraph 15 of Schedule 3 to the Justices of the Peace Act 1968 (terms and conditions of employment of persons transferred to certain magistrates' courts committees on 10th November 1969),

has effect in relation to any person by virtue of paragraph 11 or 12 of Schedule 1 to the 1979 Act, it shall continue to have effect in relation to him.

20.—(1) Any regulations made under—

(a) section 42 of the Justices of the Peace Act 1949 (compensation in connection with Parts II and III of that Act); or

(b) paragraph 16 of Schedule 3 to the Justices of the Peace Act 1968 (compensation in connection with section 1 of that Act),

which are in force immediately before the commencement of this Act by virtue of paragraph 13 of Schedule 1 to the 1979 Act shall continue to have effect and may be revoked or varied notwithstanding the repeal by the 1979 Act of the provisions under which they were made.

(2) The reference in sub-paragraph (1)(a) above to section 42 of the Justices of the Peace Act 1949 includes a reference to that section as extended by section 32 of the Administration of

Justice Act 1964 (extension for persons not qualified at date of enactment of the Justices of the Peace Act 1949).

(3) The functions of a responsible authority mentioned in paragraphs (b) and (c) of section 57(1) of this Act do not include their functions in respect of decisions made by a determining authority before 3rd February 1995 under the Justices of the Peace Act 1949 (Compensation) Regulations 1978.

Immunity and indemnification of justices and justices' clerks

21. Subject to paragraphs 22 and 23 below, the provisions of Part V of this Act shall have effect in relation to anything done, or omitted, before the commencement of this Act as they would have effect in relation to any corresponding thing done, or omitted, after the commencement of this Act.

22. The repeal by this Act of the 1979 Act is subject to paragraph 16(1) of Schedule 19 to the Courts and Legal Services Act 1990 (1979 Act to continue to apply in relation to matters arising before 1st January 1991 as if section 108 of that Act of 1990 (liability of magistrates for damages and costs) had not been enacted).

23. In section 54(2) of this Act—

(a) paragraph (a) shall have effect only in relation to things done or omitted on or after 1st October 1996; and

(b) in relation to things done or omitted before that date, paragraph (b) shall have effect with the omission of the word "other".

Pensions Act 1995

24.—(1) If before the commencement of this Act paragraph 8 of Schedule 5 to the Pensions Act 1995 has not come into force then, until the relevant commencement date, section 55(6)(b)(ii) of this Act shall have effect with the substitution, for the words "contributions equivalent premiums", of the words "state scheme premiums".

(2) In sub-paragraph (1) above, "relevant commencement date" means—

(a) if before the commencement of this Act the Secretary of State has made an order under section 180 of the Pensions Act 1995 (commencement) appointing a date on or after the date of that commencement as the date on which paragraph 8 of Schedule 5 to that Act is to come into force, the date so appointed; and

(b) otherwise, such date as the Secretary of State may by order appoint.

(3) Sections 174 (orders and regulations) and 180(4) of the Pensions Act 1995 shall apply to an order under sub-paragraph (2)(b) above as they would apply to an order under section 180(1) of that Act.

Enactments passed before 18th April 1973

25.—(1) This paragraph applies where, immediately before the commencement of this Act, any enactment passed or instrument made before the 18th April 1973 has effect by virtue of section 71(3) of the 1979 Act (modifications of certain enactments and instruments) as if it referred to—

(a) a person being appointed or removed from office as a justice of the peace in accordance with section 6 of the 1979 Act; or

(b) the supplemental list for England and Wales kept under section 8 of the 1979 Act.

(2) After the commencement of this Act the enactment or instrument shall have effect as if—

(a) any reference to a person appointed justice by a commission of the peace or to a person being removed from a commission of the peace were a reference to his being appointed or removed from office as a justice of the peace in accordance with section 5 of this Act; and

(b) any reference to a supplemental list kept by virtue of section 4 of the Justices of the Peace Act 1949 in connection with the commission of the peace for any area were a reference to the supplemental list for England and Wales kept under section 7 of this Act.

Justices of the Peace Act 1949, Schedule 2

26.—(1) This paragraph applies where, immediately before the commencement of this Act, any reference in Schedule 1 to the 1979 Act to any enactment under which a person held or was treated as holding any office or employment is to be construed by virtue of paragraph 15 of that Schedule as including a reference to any provision of Schedule 2 to the Justices of the Peace Act 1949.

(2) Any reference in this Schedule which corresponds to that reference in Schedule 1 to the 1979 Act shall be construed as including a reference to that provision of Schedule 2 to the Justices of the Peace Act 1949.

Saving for superannuation provisions

27.—(1) Nothing in this Act shall affect any pension rights or other superannuation benefits or the person by whom or the manner in which any pension or other superannuation benefit is to be paid or borne.

(2) Sub-paragraph (1) above is subject to sections 55 and 56 of this Act.

Saving for amendment of Local Government Act 1974

28. The repeal by this Act of the 1979 Act does not affect the amendment made by paragraph 28 of Schedule 2 to that Act to section 1(6)(a) of the Local Government Act 1974 (rate support grants).

Provision made by subordinate legislation

29. Any power which, immediately before the commencement of this Act, is exercisable by order to amend or revoke any provision reproduced in this Schedule of an order made under section 94 of the 1994 Act shall be so exercisable in relation to the corresponding provision of this Schedule.

Section 73(2) SCHEDULE 5

CONSEQUENTIAL AMENDMENTS

The Sheriffs Act 1887 (c. 55)

1. In section 38 of the Sheriffs Act 1887 (definitions), for "(as defined in section 1 of the Justices of the Peace Act 1979)" there shall be substituted "(within the meaning of the Justices of the Peace Act 1997)".

The Maintenance Orders (Facilities for Enforcement) Act 1920 (c. 33)

2. In section 3 of the Maintenance Orders (Facilities for Enforcement) Act 1920 (provisional orders against persons resident in dominions), in subsection (4), for "the Justices of the Peace Act 1979" there shall be substituted "the Justices of the Peace Act 1997".

The Children and Young Persons Act 1933 (c. 12)

3. In Schedule 2 to the Children and Young Persons Act 1933 (constitution of youth courts), in paragraph 8A, for "section 2 of the Justices of the Peace Act 1979" there shall be substituted "the Justices of the Peace Act 1997".

The London Building Acts (Amendment) Act 1939 (c. xcvii)

4. In section 151 of the London Building Acts (Amendment) Act 1939 (Crown exemptions), in subsection (1), in paragraph (bb), for "the Justices of the Peace Act 1979" there shall be substituted "the Justices of the Peace Act 1997".

The National Assistance Act 1948 (c. 29)

5. In section 43 of the National Assistance Act 1948 (recovery of cost of assistance from persons liable to maintenance), in subsection (4), for "the Justices of the Peace Act 1979" there shall be substituted "the Justices of the Peace Act 1997".

The Marriage Act 1949 (c. 76)

6. In section 3 of the Marriage Act 1949 (marriage of a child), in subsection (5), for "the Justices of the Peace Act 1979" there shall be substituted "the Justices of the Peace Act 1997".

The Licensing Act 1964 (c. 26)

7.—(1) The Licensing Act 1964 shall be amended as follows.

(2) In section 2 (licensing justices and districts), in subsection (2A), for "section 2 of the Justices of the Peace Act 1979" there shall be substituted "the Justices of the Peace Act 1997".

(3) In section 201 (interpretation), in subsection (1), in the definition of "the metropolis", for "the Justices of the Peace Act 1979" there shall be substituted "the Justices of the Peace Act 1997".

The Administration of Justice Act 1964 (c. 42)

8. In section 38 of the Administration of Justice Act 1964 (interpretation), in subsection (1), for the entry beginning "London commission areas" there shall be substituted—

" "London commission areas", "inner London area" and "outer London areas" have
the same meanings as in the Justices of the Peace Act 1997;".

The Backing of Warrants (Republic of Ireland) Act 1965 (c. 45)

9. In the Schedule to the Backing of Warrants (Republic of Ireland) Act 1965 (proceedings
before magistrates' court: supplementary provisions), for the proviso to paragraph 2 there shall
be substituted—
    "2A. Section 15 of the Justices of the Peace Act 1997 (which exempts stipendiary magis-
    trates from certain restrictions imposed by the Magistrates' Courts Act 1980) shall apply as
    if paragraph 2 of this Schedule were contained in the Magistrates' Courts Act 1980."
and, in paragraph 3, for "paragraph 2" there shall be substituted "paragraphs 2 and 2A".

The Immigration Act 1971 (c. 77)

10. In Schedule 2 to the Immigration Act 1971 (control on entry: administrative provisions), in
paragraphs 23(3) and 31(4), for the words from "purposes" to "being" there shall be substituted
"purposes of the Justices of the Peace Act 1997 and, in particular, section 60 of that Act, as
being".

The Local Government Act 1972 (c. 70)

11. In Schedule 12A to the Local Government Act 1972 (access to information: exempt information), in paragraph 2(a), for "section 19 of the Justices of the Peace Act 1979" there shall be
substituted "section 27 of the Justices of the Peace Act 1997".

The Criminal Justice Act 1972 (c. 71)

12. In section 51 of the Criminal Justice Act 1972 (execution of process between England and
Wales and Scotland), in subsection (4), for the words from "by virtue" to "it has" there shall be
substituted "by virtue of section 45(1) of the Justices of the Peace Act 1997, as it has".

The Administration of Justice Act 1973 (c. 15)

13.—(1) The Administration of Justice Act 1973 shall be amended as follows.
(2) For section 5 there shall be substituted—

    "Consequential
      5. Paragraph 7 of Schedule 1 to this Act shall have effect; and the enactments specified in
    paragraph 10 of that Schedule shall have effect subject to the amendments specified in that
    paragraph."
(3) In section 9 (judicial salaries), in paragraph (f) of subsection (1), for the words from
"appointed" to the end of that paragraph there shall be substituted "appointed, or treated as
appointed, under section 11 of the Justices of the Peace Act 1997;".
    (4) In Schedule 1 (consequential provisions), in paragraph 7, for "section 10(2)(a) to (c) of the
Justices of the Peace Act 1979" there shall be substituted "section 9(2)(a) to (c) of the Justices of
the Peace Act 1997".

The Matrimonial Causes Act 1973 (c. 18)

14. In section 35 of the Matrimonial Causes Act 1973 (alteration of maintenance agreements
by courts), in subsection (3), for "the Justices of the Peace Act 1979" there shall be substituted
"the Justices of the Peace Act 1997".

The Powers of Criminal Courts Act 1973 (c. 62)

15. In section 32 of the Powers of Criminal Courts Act 1973 (enforcement etc. where fine or
other sum imposed or forfeited by Crown Court), in subsection (6), for "Justices of the Peace
Act 1979 and, in particular, section 61 thereof (application of fines and fees)" there shall be
substituted "Justices of the Peace Act 1997 and, in particular, section 60 of that Act (application
of fines and fees)".

The Solicitors Act 1974 (c. 47)

16. In section 38 of the Solicitors Act 1974 (solicitor who is a justice of the peace not to act in
certain proceedings)—
    (a) in subsection (3), for "section 8 of the Justices of the Peace Act 1979" there shall be substi-
        tuted "section 7 of the Justices of the Peace Act 1997"; and
    (b) in subsection (4), for "the proviso to section 39(1) of the Justices of the Peace Act 1979"
        there shall be substituted "section 21(1) of the Justices of the Peace Act 1997".

The House of Commons Disqualification Act 1975 (c. 24)

17. In Part I of Schedule 1 to the House of Commons Disqualification Act 1975 (judicial offices disqualifying for membership of the House of Commons), for "Stipendiary Magistrate within the meaning of the Justices of the Peace Act 1979." there shall be substituted "Stipendiary Magistrate within the meaning of the Justices of the Peace Act 1997.".

The Domestic Proceedings and Magistrates' Courts Act 1978 (c. 22)

18. In section 88 of the Domestic Proceedings and Magistrates' Courts Act 1978 (interpretation), in subsection (1)—
    (a) in the definition of "commission area", for "the Justices of the Peace Act 1979" there shall be substituted "the Justices of the Peace Act 1997"; and
    (b) for the definition of "petty sessions area" there shall be substituted—
        " "petty sessions area" has the same meaning as in the Justices of the Peace Act 1997;".

The Magistrates' Courts Act 1980 (c. 43)

19.—(1) The Magistrates' Courts Act 1980 shall be amended as follows.
(2) In each of the provisions of that Act specified in sub-paragraph (3) below, for "the Justices of the Peace Act 1979" there shall be substituted "the Justices of the Peace Act 1997".
(3) The provisions mentioned in sub-paragraph (2) above are—
    (a) section 52 (jurisdiction to deal with complaints);
    (b) in section 67 (family proceedings courts and panels), subsection (4);
    (c) in section 87 (enforcement of payment of fines by High Court and county court), subsection (4); and
    (d) in section 87A (fines imposed on companies), subsection (2).
(4) In section 139 (disposal of sums adjudged to be paid by conviction), in paragraph (c), for "section 61 of the Justices of the Peace Act 1979" there shall be substituted "section 60 of the Justices of the Peace Act 1997".
(5) In section 150 (interpretation), in subsection (1)—
    (a) in the definitions of—
        (i) "commission area"; and
        (ii) "London commission area",
    for "the Justices of the Peace Act 1979" there shall be substituted "the Justices of the Peace Act 1997"; and
    (b) for the definition of "petty sessions area" there shall be substituted—
    " "petty sessions area" has the same meaning as in the Justices of the Peace Act 1997;".

The Child Abduction Act 1984 (c. 37)

20. In the Schedule to the Child Abduction Act 1984 (abduction of child by parent: particular cases), in paragraph 5(b), for "the Justices of the Peace Act 1979" there shall be substituted "the Justices of the Peace Act 1997".

The Prosecution of Offences Act 1985 (c. 23)

21. In section 20 of the Prosecution of Offences Act 1985 (regulations), in subsection (5), for "section 61 of the Justices of the Peace Act 1979" there shall be substituted "section 60 of the Justices of the Peace Act 1997".

The Local Government Act 1985 (c. 51)

22.—(1) The Local Government Act 1985 shall be amended as follows.
(2) In section 99 (disqualification of justices), for "Section 64 of the Justices of the Peace Act 1979" there shall be substituted "Section 66 of the Justices of the Peace Act 1997".
(3) In Schedule 13 (residuary bodies), in paragraph 13, for paragraph (i) there shall be substituted—
    "(i) section 66 of the Justices of the Peace Act 1997;".

The Criminal Justice Act 1988 (c. 33)

23. In section 81 of the Criminal Justice Act 1988 (confiscation orders: application of proceeds of realisation etc.)—
    (a) in subsections (8) and (9)(d), for "section 61 of the Justices of the Peace Act 1979" there shall be substituted "section 60 of the Justices of the Peace Act 1997"; and
    (b) in subsection (10), for "the Justices of the Peace Act 1979" there shall be substituted "the Justices of the Peace Act 1997".

The Legal Aid Act 1988 (c. 34)

24. In Schedule 3 to the Legal Aid Act 1988 (criminal proceedings: enforcement of contribution orders), in paragraph 4—
  (a) in sub-paragraph (1), for "the Justices of the Peace Act 1979" there shall be substituted "the Justices of the Peace Act 1997"; and
  (b) in sub-paragraph (2), for "section 61(4) of the Justices of the Peace Act 1979" there shall be substituted "section 60(4) of the Justices of the Peace Act 1997".

The Road Traffic Offenders Act 1988 (c. 53)

25. In section 82 of the Road Traffic Offenders Act 1988 (accounting for fixed penalties)—
  (a) in subsection (1), for "section 61 (application of fines and fees) of the Justices of the Peace Act 1979" there shall be substituted "section 60 of the Justices of the Peace Act 1997 (application of fines and fees)";
  (b) in subsection (2)(b), for "section 59 of the Justices of the Peace Act 1979" there shall be substituted "section 57 of the Justices of the Peace Act 1997"; and
  (c) in subsection (2A), for "the Justices of the Peace Act 1979" there shall be substituted "the Justices of the Peace Act 1997".

The Prevention of Terrorism (Temporary Provisions) Act 1989 (c. 4)

26. In Schedule 4 to the Prevention of Terrorism (Temporary Provisions) Act 1989 (forfeiture orders), in paragraph 1(3), for "section 61 of the Justices of the Peace Act 1979" there shall be substituted "section 60 of the Justices of the Peace Act 1997".

The Children Act 1989 (c. 41)

27. In Schedule 1 to the Children Act 1989 (financial provision for children), in paragraph 10(6), for "the Justices of the Peace Act 1979" there shall be substituted "the Justices of the Peace Act 1997".

The Computer Misuse Act 1990 (c. 18)

28. In section 11 of the Computer Misuse Act 1990 (proceedings for offence of unauthorised access to computer material), in subsection (6), for "the Justices of the Peace Act 1979" there shall be substituted "the Justices of the Peace Act 1997".

The Criminal Justice Act 1991 (c. 53)

29.—(1) The Criminal Justice Act 1991 shall be amended as follows.
  (2) In section 76 (provision of court security officers), in subsection (6), in the definition of "paying authority", for "the 1979 Act" there shall be substituted "the Justices of the Peace Act 1997".
  (3) In section 92 (interpretation of Part IV), in subsection (2), for "the 1979 Act" there shall be substituted "the Justices of the Peace Act 1997".

The Local Government Finance Act 1992 (c. 14)

30. In section 46 of the Local Government Finance Act 1992 (special items relating to part of area)—
  (a) in subsection (2)(d), for "Schedule 7 to the Police and Magistrates' Courts Act 1994" there shall be substituted "Schedule 3 to the Justices of the Peace Act 1997"; and
  (b) in subsection (4), in the definition of "inner London area", for "the Justices of the Peace Act 1979" there shall be substituted "the Justices of the Peace Act 1997".

The Local Government Act 1992 (c. 19)

31. In section 19 of the Local Government Act 1992 (regulations of general application), in subsection (2)(d)(i), for "the Justices of the Peace Act 1979" there shall be substituted "the Justices of the Peace Act 1997".

The Tribunals and Inquiries Act 1992 (c. 53)

32. In Part I of Schedule 1 to the Tribunals and Inquiries Act 1992 (tribunals under direct supervision of Council on Tribunals), in paragraph 23, for "section 53(3) of the Justices of the Peace Act 1979 (c. 55)" there shall be substituted "section 54(6) of the Justices of the Peace Act 1997 (c. 25)".

The Prisoners and Criminal Proceedings (Scotland) Act 1993 (c. 9)

33. In section 27 of the Prisoners and Criminal Proceedings (Scotland) Act 1993 (interpretation of Part I), in subsection (1), in the definition of "petty sessions area", for "the Justices of the Peace Act 1979" there shall be substituted "the Justices of the Peace Act 1997".

The Probation Service Act 1993 (c. 47)

34.—(1) The Probation Service Act 1993 shall be amended as follows.

(2) In section 30 (interpretation), in subsection (1), in the definition of "inner London area", for "the Justices of the Peace Act 1979" there shall be substituted "the Justices of the Peace Act 1997".

(3) In Schedule 1 (probation committees and probation liaison committees), in paragraph 6, for sub-paragraph (4) there shall be substituted—

"(4) In sub-paragraph (3) "commission area" has the same meaning as in the Justices of the Peace Act 1997."

The Local Government (Wales) Act 1994 (c. 19)

35.—(1) The Local Government (Wales) Act 1994 shall be amended as follows.

(2) In section 55 (orders making provision about justices of the peace)—

(a) in subsection (2)(a), for "the Justices of the Peace Act 1979" there shall be substituted "the Justices of the Peace Act 1997";

(b) in subsection (3)—

(i) in paragraph (a), for "section 1 of the Act of 1979" there shall be substituted "section 1 of (or Schedule 1 to) the Act of 1997"; and

(ii) in paragraph (c), for "section 19 of" there shall be substituted "section 27 of".

(3) In Schedule 13 (the Residuary Body for Wales), in paragraph 20(h), for "section 64 of the Justices of the Peace Act 1979 (c. 55)" there shall be substituted "section 66 of the Justices of the Peace Act 1997 (c. 25)".

The Drug Trafficking Act 1994 (c. 37)

36. In section 30 of the Drug Trafficking Act 1994 (confiscation orders: application of proceeds etc.)—

(a) in subsection (8), for "section 61 of the Justices of the Peace Act 1979" there shall be substituted "section 60 of the Justices of the Peace Act 1997"; and

(b) in subsection (9), for "the Justices of the Peace Act 1979" there shall be substituted "the Justices of the Peace Act 1997".

The Police Act 1996 (c. 16)

37.—(1) The Police Act 1997 shall be amended as follows.

(2) In section 5 (reductions in size of police authorities), in subsection (2)(c), for "section 21(1A) of the Justices of the Peace Act 1979" there shall be substituted "section 29(2) of the Justices of the Peace Act 1997".

(3) In Schedule 2 (police authorities)—

(a) in paragraph 7, for "section 21(1A) of the Justices of the Peace Act 1979" there shall be substituted "section 29(2) of the Justices of the Peace Act 1997"; and

(b) in paragraph 27, for "the Justices of the Peace Act 1979" there shall be substituted "the Justices of the Peace Act 1997".

Section 73(3)   SCHEDULE 6

Repeals and Revocations

Part I

Repeals

Chapter	Short title	Extent of repeal
1973 c. 15.	The Administration of Justice Act 1973.	In Schedule 1, paragraph 3.
1979 c. 55.	The Justices of the Peace Act 1979.	The whole Act.

Chapter	Short title	Extent of repeal
1980 c. 43.	The Magistrates' Courts Act 1980.	In Schedule 7, paragraphs 55 and 191 to 197.
1982 c. 53.	The Administration of Justice Act 1982.	Section 65.
1985 c. 51.	The Local Government Act 1985.	Section 12. Section 60(6). In Schedule 14, paragraph 57.
1988 c. 4.	The Norfolk and Suffolk Broads Act 1988.	In Schedule 6, paragraph 20.
1988 c. 33.	The Criminal Justice Act 1988.	Section 164. In Schedule 15, paragraph 63.
1988 c. 41.	The Local Government Finance Act 1988.	In Schedule 12, paragraph 2.
1988 c. 50.	The Housing Act 1988.	In Schedule 17, paragraph 27.
1989 c. 41.	The Children Act 1989.	In Schedule 11, paragraph 7.
1989 c. 43.	The Statute Law (Repeals) Act 1989.	In Schedule 2, paragraph 3.
1990 c. 41.	The Courts and Legal Services Act 1990.	Section 108. Section 117. In Schedule 10, paragraphs 44 and 45.
1991 c. 17.	The Maintenance Enforcement Act 1991.	In Schedule 2, paragraph 4.
1991 c. 53.	The Criminal Justice Act 1991.	Section 93(3) and (4). In section 99(1), the definition of "the 1979 Act". In Schedule 11, paragraph 40(2)(k).
1992 c. 14.	The Local Government Finance Act 1992.	In Schedule 13, paragraph 48.
1993 c. 8.	The Judicial Pensions and Retirement Act 1993.	In Schedule 6, paragraph 19.
1994 c. 19.	The Local Government (Wales) Act 1994.	In Schedule 2, paragraph 10.
1994 c. 29.	The Police and Magistrates' Courts Act 1994.	Sections 69 to 90 and 91(2) and (3). In Schedule 4, paragraph 54. Schedule 7. In Schedule 8, Part I.
1995 c. 25.	The Environment Act 1995.	In Schedule 10, paragraph 19.
1995 c. 26.	The Pensions Act 1995.	In Schedule 5, paragraph 8.
1996 c. 16.	The Police Act 1996.	In Schedule 7, paragraph 1(2)(o).
1996 c. 25.	The Criminal Procedure and Investigations Act 1996.	Section 70.

PART II

REVOCATIONS

Chapter	Short title	Extent of repeal
S.I. 1985/1383.	The Local Government (Magistrates' Courts etc.) Order 1985.	In the Schedule, paragraph 3.
S.I. 1990/531.	The Justices of the Peace Act 1979 (Amendment) Order 1990.	The whole order.
S.I. 1994/2594.	The Police and Magistrates' Courts Act 1994 (Commencement No. 3 and Transitional Provisions) Order 1994.	The whole order.

Chapter	Short title	Extent of repeal
S.I. 1995/42.	The Police and Magistrates' Courts Act 1994 (Commencement No. 6 and Transitional Provisions) Order 1995.	The whole order.
S.I 1995/685.	The Police and Magistrates' Courts Act 1994 (Commencement No. 8 and Transitional Provisions) Order 1995.	The whole order.
S.I. 1996/674.	The Local Government Changes for England (Magistrates' Courts) Regulations 1996.	In the Schedule, paragraphs 1 and 4(2).
S.I. 1996/675.	The Magistrates' Courts (Wales) (Consequences of Local Government Changes) Order 1996.	In the Schedule, paragraph 1.
S.I. 1996/676.	The Commission Areas (Gwent, Mid Glamorgan and South Glamorgan) Order 1996.	The whole order.
S.I. 1996/1924.	The Maximum Number of Stipendiary Magistrates Order 1996.	The whole Order.

TABLE OF DERIVATIONS

Notes:

1. This Table shows the derivation of the provisions of the Act.
2. The following abbreviations are used in the Table:—

Acts of Parliament

1979	=	Justices of the Peace Act 1979 (c. 55)
1994	=	Police and Magistrates' Courts Act 1994 (c. 29)

Subordinate legislation

1996/674	=	Local Government Changes for England (Magistrates' Courts) Regulations 1996 (S.I. 1996/674)
1996/675	=	Magistrates' Courts (Wales) (Consequences of Local Government Changes) Order 1996 (S.I. 1996/675)

3. The functions of the Secretary of State under 1979 were transferred to the Lord Chancellor by the Transfer of Functions (Magistrates' Courts and Family Law) Order 1992 (S.I. 1992/709) Art. 2(1)(a).

Provision	Derivation
1(1)	1979 s.1(a), (b), (c); 1996/674 Sch. para. 1(1)(c).
(2)(a)	Drafting.
(b)	1979 s.1(aa); Local Government (Wales) Act 1994 (c.19) Sch. 2 para. 10(1); drafting.

Provision	Derivation
(3)	1979 s.1; 1996/674 Sch. para. 1(1)(d).
2(1), (2)	1979 s.2(1).
(3) to (5)	1979 s.3.
3	1979 s.5(1).
4(1)(a)	1979 s.4(1)(a), (c), (1A), (2)(b), (d); Local Government Act 1985 (c.51) s.12(2); Local Government (Wales) Act 1994 (c.19) Sch. 2 para. 10(2); 1996/674 Sch. para. 1(2).
(b)	1979 s.4(1)(b), (d), (1A), (2)(c), (e); Local Government Act 1985 (c.51) s.12(2); Local Government (Wales) Act 1994 (c.19) Sch. 2 para. 10(2); 1996/674 Sch. para. 1(2).
(c)	1979 s.4(2)(f); Local Government Act 1985 (c.51) s.12(2).
(2)	1979 s.4(1), (1A), (2)(b) to (e), Local Government Act 1985 (c.51) s.12(2); Local Government (Wales) Act 1994 (c.19) Sch. 2 para. 10(2); 1996/674 Sch. para. 1(2).
5(1)	1979 s.6(1); Administration of Justice Act 1982 (c.53) s.65.
(2)	1979 s.6(2).
6	1979 s.7.
7	1979 s.8.
8(1)(a)	1979 s.9(1).
(b)	1979 s.9(2).
(2)	1979 s.9(2).
9	1979 s.10.
10(1), (2)	1979 s.12(1), (2).
(3)	1979 s.12(3).
(4)	1979 s.12(3).
(5)	1979 s.12(4); Transfer of Functions (Minister for the Civil Service and Treasury) Order 1981 (S.I. 1981/1670).
(6)	1979 s.12(5).
(7)(a)	1979 s.12(5)(a).
(b)	1979 s.12(5)(c); Local Government Act 1985 (c.51) s.12(3).
(c)	1979 s.12(5)(e).
(d)	1979 s.12(5)(b), (d), (f); 1994 Sch. 8 para. 1(2); 1996/674 Sch. para. 1(3)(b); 1996/675 Sch. para. 1(2).
(8)	1979 s.12(5)(b), (d), (f); 1994 Sch. 8 para. 1(2); 1996/674 Sch. para. 1(3)(b); 1996/675 Sch. para. 1(2).
(9)	1979 s.12(5A); 1994 Sch. 8 para. 1(3); 1996/674 Sch. para. 1(3)(c).
(10)	1979 s.12(6).
(11)	1979 s.12(7).
(12)	1979 s.69A; 1994 s.90.
11(1)	1979 s.13(1); Courts and Legal Services Act 1990 (c.41) Sch. 10 para. 44(1).
(2), (3)	1979 s.13(2), (3).
(4)	1979 s.13(4); Maximum Number of Stipendiary Magistrates Order 1996 (S.I. 1996/1924) Art. 2.
(5)	1979 s.13(5).
12(1)	1979 s.14(1A); Judicial Pensions and Retirement Act 1993 (c.8) Sch. 6 para. 19(2); Judicial Pensions and Retirement Act 1993 (Commencement) Order 1995 (S.I. 1995/631) Art. 2.
(2)	1979 s.14(1); Judicial Pensions and Retirement Act 1993 (c.8) Sch. 6 para. 19(3)(a); Judicial Pensions and Retirement Act 1993 (Commencement) Order 1995 (S.I. 1995/631) Art. 2.
(3)	1979 s.14(3); Judicial Pensions and Retirement Act 1993 (c.8) s.26(10), Sch. 6 para. 19(5).
13(1), (2)	1979 s.15(1), (2).
(3)	1979 s.15(2A); Courts and Legal Services Act 1990 (c.41) s.108(4); drafting.
(4)	1979 s.15(3); Transfer of Functions (Minister for the Civil Service and Treasury) Order 1981 (S.I. 1981/1670).
14(1)	1979 s.16(2).
(2)	1979 s.16(3), (4).

Provision	Derivation
(3)	1979 s.16(3).
(4)	1979 s.16(3).
(5)	1979 s.16(5).
(6)	1979 s.16(4).
(7)	1979 s.16(5); Magistrates' Courts Act 1980 (c.43) Sch. 7 para. 191(b); Children Act 1989 (c.41) Sch. 11 para. 7(a).
15(1)	1979 s.16(1); Magistrates' Courts Act 1980 (c.43) Sch. 7 para. 191(a).
(2)	1979 s.16(5); Magistrates' Courts Act 1980 (c.43) Sch. 7 para. 191(b); Children Act 1989 (c.41) Sch. 11 para. 7(a).
16(1)	1979 s.31(1).
(2)	1979 s.31(2); Courts and Legal Services Act 1990 (c.41) Sch. 10 para. 44(2).
(3)	1979 s.31(3).
(4)	1979 s.31(4); drafting.
(5)	1979 s.31(6).
(6)	1979 s.31(7).
17(1)	1979 s.32(1); 1994 Sch. 8 para. 14.
(2), (3)	1979 s.32(2), (3).
18(1)	1979 s.33(2).
(2)	1979 s.33(1).
(3)(a)	1979 s.33(2).
(b)	1979 s.33(3).
(4)	1979 s.33(3); drafting.
(5)	1979 s.33(3).
(6)	1979 s.33(4).
(7)	Drafting.
19(1)	1979 s.34(1); Courts and Legal Services Act 1990 (c.41) Sch. 10 para. 44(2).
(2)	1979 s.34(2).
(3)	1979 s.34(2A); Courts and Legal Services Act 1990 (c.41) s.108(5); drafting.
(4)	1979 s.34(3); Transfer of Functions (Minister for the Civil Service and Treasury) Order 1981 (S.I. 1981/1670).
20(1)	1979 s.34A(1); 1994 s.81.
(2)	1979 s.34A(1); 1994 s.81.
(3) to (6)	1979 s.34A(2) to (5); 1994 s.81.
21(1), (2)	1979 s.39(1), (2).
(3)	1979 s.39(3).
22(1)	1979 s.17(1); 1994 Sch. 8 para. 2(2).
(2)	1979 s.17(2); 1994 Sch. 8 para. 2(3).
(3)	1979 s.17(2A); 1994 Sch. 8 para. 2(4).
(4)	1979 s.17(3); Children Act 1989 (c.41) Sch. 11 para. 7(b); Criminal Justice Act 1991 (c.53) s.70.
(5)	1979 s.31(5).
23	1979 s.40.
24(1)	1979 s.18(1).
(2)(a)	1979 s.18(2)(a).
(b)	1979 s.18(2)(b); 1994 Sch. 8 para. 3(a).
(c) to (e)	1979 s.18(2)(c) to (e); 1994 Sch. 8 para. 3(b).
(3)	1979 s.18(3).
(4)	1979 s.18(4); Magistrates' Courts Act 1980 (c.43) Sch. 7 para. 192.
(5)	1979 s.18(5).
25(1), (2)	1979 s.11(1), (2).
(3)	1979 s.43; drafting.
(4)	1979 s.11(3).
26	1979 s.68; drafting.
27(1)	1979 s.19(1); 1994 Sch. 8 para. 4(2).
(2)	1979 s.19(2); 1994 Sch. 8 para. 4(3); drafting.
(a)	1979 s.19(2)(a); Local Government (Wales) Act 1994 (c.19) Sch. 2 para. 10(3); 1996/674 Sch. para. 1(4).
(b)	1979 s.19(2)(b).
(c)	1979 s.19(2)(c); Local Government Act 1985 (c.51) s.12(4)(b).

Provision	Derivation
(d)	1979 s.19(2)(cc); 1994 s.79(4).
(e)	1979 s.19(2)(d).
(3)	1979 s.19(2)(bb); Local Government (Wales) Act 1994 (c.19) Sch. 2 para. 10(3); 1994 Sch. 8 para. 4(3); drafting.
28	1979 s.20; 1994 s.70.
29(1)	1979 s.21(1).
(2)	1979 s.21(1A); 1994 s.71(2).
(3), (4)	1979 s.21(2), (2A); 1994 s.71(3).
(5)	1979 s.21(3).
(6)	1979 s.69A; 1994 s.90.
(7)	1979 s.21(4).
30(1), (2)	1979 s.22(1), (1A); 1994 s.72(2).
(3)	1979 s.22(3); 1994 Sch. 8 para. 5.
(4)	1979 s.22(4); 1994 s.72(4).
(5)	1979 s.22(4A); 1994 s.72(5).
(6) to (8)	1979 s.22(5) to (7).
(9) to (12)	1979 s.22(8) to (11); 1994 s.72(6).
31	1979 s.22A; 1994 s.73.
32(1) to (9)	1994 s.69(1) to (9).
(10)	1994 s.69(10); drafting.
33(1)	1979 s.23(1); 1994 Sch. 8 para. 6(2).
(2)	1979 s.23(2); 1994 Sch. 8 para. 6(3).
(3)	1979 s.23(3).
(4)	1979 s.23(4); 1994 Sch. 8 para. 6(4).
(5)	1979 s.42; 1994 Sch. 8 para. 17; drafting.
(6)	1979 s.23(5).
34(1)(a)	1979 s.24(1)(a); Local Government Act 1985 (c.51) s.12(8)(a)(i); 1994 Sch. 8 para. 7(2)(a), (c); 1996/674 Sch. para. 1(5)(a); 1996/675 Sch. para. 1(3).
(b)	1979 s.24(1)(b); Local Government Act 1985 (c.51) s.12(8)(a)(ii); 1996/675 Sch. para. 1(3); drafting.
(2)	1979 s.24(2).
(3)	1979 s.24(2); Local Government Act 1985 (c.51) s.12(8)(b); 1994 Sch. 8 para. 7(3)(a), (c); 1996/674 Sch. para. 1(5)(a); 1996/675 Sch. para. 1(3); drafting.
(4)	1979 s.24(3).
(5)(a)	1979 s.24(1)(a), (2); Local Government Act 1985 (c.51) s.12(8); 1994 Sch. 8 para. 7(2), (3); 1996/674 Sch. para. 1(5)(a); 1996/675 Sch. para. 1(3).
(b)	1979 s.24(6)(a); Local Government Act 1985 (c.51) s.12(8)(d); 1996/674 Sch. para. 1(5)(b).
(c)	1979 s.70 ("prescribed").
(d)	1979 s.24(6)(b).
35(1), (2)	1979 s.24A(1), (2); Criminal Justice Act 1988 (c.33) s.164(2).
(3)	1979 s.24A(2A); 1994 Sch. 8 para. 8(3).
(4)	1979 s.24A(3); Criminal Justice Act 1988 (c.33) s.164(2).
36(1)(a)	1979 s.24B(1)(a); Criminal Justice Act 1988 (c.33) s.164(2); 1994 Sch. 8 para. 9; 1996/674 Sch. para. 1(6)(a); 1996/675 Sch. para. 1(4).
(b)	1979 s.24B(1)(b); Criminal Justice Act 1988 (c.33) s.164(2); drafting.
(2)	1979 s.24B(2); Criminal Justice Act 1988 (c.33) s.164(2).
(3)	1979 s.24B(2); Criminal Justice Act 1988 (c.33) s.164(2); 1994 Sch. 8 para. 9; 1996/674 Sch. para. 1(6)(a); 1996/675 Sch. para. 1(4).
(4)	1979 s.24B(3); Criminal Justice Act 1988 (c.33) s.164(2).
(5)(a)	1979 s.24B(1)(a), (2); Criminal Justice Act 1988 (c.33) s.164(2); 1994 Sch. 8 para. 9; 1996/674 Sch. para. 1(6)(a); 1996/675 Sch. para. 1(4).
(b)	1979 s.24B(4)(a); Criminal Justice Act 1988 (c.33) s.164(2); 1996/674 Sch. para. 1(6)(b).
(c)	1979 s.70 ("prescribed").
(d)	1979 s.24B(4)(b); Criminal Justice Act 1988 (c.33) s.164(2).
37(1) to (3)	1979 s.24C; 1994 s.74.
(4)	1979 ss.69A, 70 ("prescribed"); 1994 s.90.

Provision	Derivation
38	1994 s.88.
39	1994 s.89.
40(1) to (7)	1979 s.24D(1) to (7); 1994 s.75.
(8)	1979 ss.24D(8), 69A; 1994 ss.75, 90.
41	1979 s.24E; 1994 s.75.
42(1) to (8)	1979 s.25(1) to (8); 1994 s.76.
(9)	1979 ss.25(9), 69A; 1994 ss.76, 90.
43(a)	1979 s.26(1)(a), (3); Courts and Legal Services Act 1990 (c.41) Sch. 10 para. 45; 1994 Sch. 8 para. 10(3).
(b)	1979 s.26(1)(b).
44(1)	1979 s.26A(1); 1994 s.77.
(2)	1979 s.27(6); 1994 Sch. 8 para. 11(3).
(3)	1979 s.27(8); Magistrates' Courts Act 1980 (c.43) Sch. 7 para. 193; 1994 Sch. 8 para. 11(4).
45(1)	1979 s.28(1); Magistrates' Courts Act 1980 (c.43) Sch. 7 para. 194; drafting.
(2)	1979 s.28(1A); Courts and Legal Services Act 1990 (c.41) s.117.
(3)	1979 s.28(2).
(4)	1979 s.28(3).
(5)	1979 s.28(3).
(6)	1979 s.28(3).
(7)(a)	1979 s.28(3).
(b)	1979 s.28(4).
46	1979 s.29(1), (2)(b), (3); Magistrates' Courts Act 1980 (c.43) Sch. 7 para. 195; Maintenance Enforcement Act 1991 (c.17) Sch. 2 para. 4.
47(1)	1979 s.30(1), (2); Magistrates' Courts Act 1980 (c.43) Sch. 7 para. 196.
(2)	1979 s.30(3).
48	1979 s.30A; 1994 s.78.
49	1979 s.34B; 1994 Sch. 8 para. 15.
50	1994 s.82.
51	1979 s.44; Courts and Legal Services Act 1990 (c.41) s.108(2).
52	1979 s.45; Courts and Legal Services Act 1990 (c.41) s.108(3).
53	1979 s.50.
54(1)	1979 s.53(1), (1A); Criminal Procedure and Investigations Act 1996 (c.25) s.70(1); drafting.
(2)(a)	1979 s.53(1), (1A); Criminal Procedure and Investigations Act 1996 (c.25) s.70(1).
(b)	1979 s.53(1).
(3) to (5)	1979 s.53(2).
(6)	1979 s.53(3); 1994 Sch. 8 para. 18(2).
(7)	1979 s.53(3A); 1994 Sch. 8 para. 18(3).
(8)	1979 s.53(4); 1994 Sch. 8 para. 18(4).
(9)	1979 s.53(5); 1994 Sch. 8 para. 18(5).
55(1) to (5)	1979 s.55(1) to (5); 1994 s.83(1).
(6)	1979 s.55(6); 1994 s.83(1); Pensions Act 1995 (c.26) Sch. 5 para. 8.
(7) to (9)	1979 s.55(7) to (9); 1994 s.83(1).
(10)	1979 s.55(10); 1994 s.83(1); drafting.
56	1979 s.56; 1994 s.83(1).
57(1)	1979 s.59(1); Criminal Justice Act 1991 (c.53) s.93(3); 1994 Sch. 8 para. 19(2).
(2) to (7)	1979 s.59(2) to (7); Criminal Justice Act 1991 (c.53) s.93(3).
(8)	1979 s.59(8); 1994 Sch. 8 para. 19(3).
58(1)	1979 s.59A(1); 1994 s.84; Police and Magistrates' Courts Act 1994 (Commencement No. 8 and Transitional Provisions) Order 1995 (S.I. 1995/685) Art. 4(j).
(2)	1979 s.59A(2); 1994 s.84.
59(1)	1979 s.62A(1); 1994 s.85.
(2)	1979 ss.62A(2), 69A; 1994 ss.85, 90.
60(1)	1979 s.61(1); Magistrates' Courts Act 1980 (c.43) Sch. 7 para. 197; Criminal Justice Act 1988 (c.33) Sch. 15 para. 63.

Provision	Derivation
(2) to (5)	1979 s.61(2) to (5).
(6)	1979 s.61(7).
61	1979 s.62(1); 1994 Sch. 8 para. 20.
62	1994 s.86(1) to (5).
63	1994 s.87.
64(1)	1979 s.63(1).
(2)	1979 s.63(4).
(3)	1979 s.63(5); 1994 Sch. 8 para. 21.
65	1979 s.63A; Statute Law (Repeals) Act 1989 (c.43) Sch. 2 para. 3.
66(1), (2)	1979 s.64(1), (2).
(3), (4)	1979 s.64(3).
(5), (6)	1979 s.64(4), (5).
(7)	1979 s.64(2A), (6); Local Government Act 1985 (c.51) Sch. 14 para. 57(b); Norfolk and Suffolk Broads Act 1988 (c.4) Sch. 6 para. 20; Housing Act 1988 (c.50) Sch. 17 para. 27; 1994 Sch. 4 para. 54; Environment Act 1995 (c.25) Sch. 10 para. 19; Police Act 1996 (c.16) Sch. 7 para. 1(1), (2)(o).
67	1979 s.65; Justices of the Peace Act 1979 (Amendment) Order 1990 (S.I. 1990/531) Art. 2(2); Local Government Finance Act 1992 (c.14) Sch. 13 para. 48; drafting.
68(1)	1979 s.66(1).
(2)	1979 s.66(2); drafting.
69	1979 s.67.
70(1)	1979 ss.24A(2A), 41(1); Local Government Finance Act 1988 (c.41) Sch. 12 para. 2; 1994 Sch. 8 para. 8(3); drafting.
(2)	1979 s.41(2).
71	1979 s.69; drafting.
72(1)	"capital expenditure": 1979 s.70 ("capital expenditure"); Criminal Justice Act 1991 (c.53) s.93(4).
	"commission area", "justices' clerk": 1979 s.70 ("commission area", "justices' clerk").
	"London commission areas", "inner London area" and "outer London area": 1979 s.70 ("London commission areas", "inner London area" and "outer London areas").
	"magistrate", "magistrates' courts committee area": 1979 s.70 ("magistrate", "magistrates' courts committee area"); 1994 Sch. 8 para. 22.
	"officer", "petty sessional court-house", "petty sessions area": 1979 s.70 ("officer", "petty sessional court-house", "petty sessions area").
	"preserved county": 1979 s.70 ("preserved county"); Local Government (Wales) Act 1994 (c.19) Sch. 2 para. 10(4).
	"retained county": 1979 s.70 ("relevant area"); 1996/674 Sch. para. 1(7)(a); drafting.
	"stipendiary magistrate", "the supplemental list": 1979 s.70 ("stipendiary magistrate", "the supplemental list").
	"unitary district": 1979 s.70 ("unitary district"); 1996/674 Sch. para. 1(7)(b).
(2)	Drafting.
73	—
74	—
75(1) to (4)	—
(5)	1979 s.72(3); 1994 s.96(1).
Sch. 1	Commission Areas (Gwent, Mid Glamorgan and South Glamorgan) Order 1996 (S.I. 1996/676) Arts. 4, 5.
Sch. 2 Part I	1979 s.2(1)(a).
Part II	1979 s.2(1)(b) to (e).
Sch. 3, 1	1994 Sch. 7 para. 1; drafting.
2 to 6	1994 Sch. 7 para. 2 to 6.
Sch. 4, 1 to 5	—
6	1979 Sch. 1 para. 9; drafting.

Provision	Derivation
7(1)	—
(2)(a)	—
(b)	Police and Magistrates' Courts Act 1994 (Commencement No. 8 and Transitional Provisions) Order 1995 (S.I. 1995/685) Art. 6(2)(a).
(c)	—
(d)	Police and Magistrates' Courts Act 1994 (Commencement No. 8 and Transitional Provisions) Order 1995 (S.I. 1995/685) Art. 6(2)(b), (c).
(e)	Police and Magistrates' Courts Act 1994 (Commencement No. 8 and Transitional Provisions) Order 1995 (S.I. 1995/685) Art. 6(2)(c).
(f)	—
(3) to (8)	—
8, 9	—
10	1994 s.79(2), (3).
11(1), (2)	1994 s.80(2) to (4).
(3)	1994 s.80(5), (6); drafting.
(4)	1994 s.80(7); Police and Magistrates' Courts (Commencement No. 8 and Transitional Provisions) Order 1995 (S.I. 1995/685) Art. 4(f).
12(1), (2)	—
(3), (4)	1979 Sch. 1 para. 8; drafting.
(5)	—
13, 14	—
15	Police and Magistrates' Courts Act 1994 (Commencement No. 8 and Transitional Provisions) Order 1995 (S.I. 1995/685) Art. 5(4); drafting.
16	Police and Magistrates' Courts Act 1994 (Commencement No. 8 and Transitional Provisions) Order 1995 (S.I. 1995/685) Art. 6(1); drafting.
17(1)	1979 s.26A(2); 1994 s.77; Police and Magistrates' Courts Act 1994 (Commencement No. 8 and Transitional Provisions) Order 1995 (S.I. 1995/685) Art. 4(e).
(2)	1979 s.26A(3); 1994 s.77.
(3) to (5)	1979 s.27(1), (2), (4); 1994 s.91(2).
18	1979 Sch. 1 para. 14; drafting.
19	1979 Sch. 1 para. 11, 12; drafting.
20(1), (2)	1979 Sch. 1 para. 13; drafting.
(3)	Police and Magistrates' Courts Act 1994 (Commencement No. 6 and Transitional Provisions) Order 1995 (S.I. 1995/42) Art. 3.
21, 22	—
23	Criminal Procedure and Investigations Act 1996 (c.25) s.70(2); Criminal Procedure and Investigations Act 1996 (Appointed Day No. 1) Order 1996 (S.I. 1996/2343) Art. 2.
24	—
25	1979 s.71(3); drafting.
26	1979 Sch. 1 para. 15; drafting.
27	1979 Sch. 1 para. 17; 1994 Sch. 8 para. 23.
28, 29	—
Sch. 5	—
Sch. 6	—

TABLE OF DESTINATIONS

MAGISTRATES' COURTS ACT 1980
(c.43)

TABLE OF DESTINATIONS

TABLE OF DESTINATIONS

STATUTE LAW (REPEALS) ACT 1989
(c.43)

1989	1997
Sched. 2,	
para. 3 ..... s.65	

COURTS AND LEGAL SERVICES ACT 1990
(c.41)

1990	1997
s.108(2) s.51	
(3) 52	
(4) ...... 13(3)	
(5) ...... 19(3)	
117 .... 45(2)	
Sched. 10,	
para. 44(1) . 11(1)	
(2) . ss.16(2), 19(1)	
para. 45 .... s.43(a)	

MAINTENANCE ENFORCEMENT ACT 1991
(c.17)

1991	1997
Sched. 2,	
para. 4 ..... s.46	

CRIMINAL JUSTICE ACT 1991
(c.53)

1991	1997
s.70 .... s.22(4)	
93(3)........ 57(1), (2) to	
(7)	
(4)........ 72(1)	

JUDICIAL PENSIONS AND RETIREMENT ACT 1993
(c.8)

1993	1997
s.26(10) ...... s.12(3)	
Sched. 6,	
para. 19(2)... 12(1)	
(3)(a) 12(2)	
(5)... 12(3)	

LOCAL GOVERNMENT (WALES) ACT 1994
(c.19)

1994	1997
Sched. 2,	
para. 10(1) . s.1(2)(b)	
(2) . 4(1)(a), (b),	
(2)	
(3) . 27(2)(a), (3)	
(4) . 72(1)	

POLICE AND MAGISTRATES' COURTS ACT 1994
(c.29)

ENVIRONMENT ACT 1995
(c.25)

PENSIONS ACT 1995
(c.26)

POLICE ACT 1996
(c.16)

TABLE OF DESTINATIONS

CRIMINAL PROCEDURE AND INVESTIGATIONS ACT 1996
(c.25)

1996	1997
s.70(1).......	s.54(1), (2)(a)
(2).......	Sched. 4, para. 23

TRANSFER OF FUNCTIONS (MINISTER FOR THE CIVIL SERVICE AND TREASURY) ORDER 1981
(S.I. 1981 No. 1670)

1981	1997
S.I. 1981 No. 1670	ss.10(5), 13(4), 19(4)

JUSTICES OF THE PEACE ACT 1979 (AMENDMENT) ORDER 1990
(S.I. 1990 No. 531)

1990	1997
Art. 2(2)......	s.67

JUDICIAL PENSIONS AND RETIREMENT ACT 1993 (COMMENCEMENT) ORDER 1993
(S.I. 1993 No. 631)

1993	1997
Art. 2	s.12(1), (2)

POLICE AND MAGISTRATES' COURTS ACT 1994
(COMMENCEMENT NO. 6 AND TRANSITIONAL PROVISIONS) ORDER 1995
(S.I. 1995 No. 42)

1995	1997
Art. 3	Sched. 4, para. 20(3)

POLICE AND MAGISTRATES' COURTS ACT 1994
(COMMENCEMENT NO. 8 AND TRANSITIONAL PROVISIONS) ORDER 1995
(S.I. 1995 No. 685)

1995	1997
Art. 4(e)......	Sched. 4, para. 17(1)
(f)......	Sched. 4, para. 11(4)
(j)......	s.58(1)
Art. 5(4)......	Sched. 4, para. 15
Art. 6(1)......	Sched. 4, para. 16
(2)(a)...	Sched. 4, para. 7(2)(b)
(b)...	Sched. 4, para. 7(2)(d)
(c)...	Sched. 4, para. 7(2)(d), (e)

TABLE OF DESTINATIONS

INDEX

TRANSFER OF CROFTING ESTATES (SCOTLAND) ACT 1997*

(1997 c. 26)

Arrangement of Sections

An Act to enable the Secretary of State to dispose of his crofting estates and certain other property of his in the crofting counties to approved crofting bodies; and for connected purposes. [19th March 1997]

Parliamentary Debates

Hansard, H.L. Vol. 575, cols. 22, 870, 894, 1351; Vol. 577, cols. CWH1, 1470; Vol. 578, col. 121. H.C. Vol. 292, col. 729.

Introduction and General Note

In February 1996 the then Secretary of State for Scotland issued a consultation paper on the disposal of his crofting estates to crofting trusts. In that consultation paper he suggested that ownership of his crofting estates in the Highlands and Islands might be transferred to local crofting or community trusts. Any such transfers would be on a voluntary basis and he would be prepared to consider the possibility of transfers at no consideration where that was necessary to make sure that the Trust got off to a good start.

The estates owned by the Secretary of State were acquired by the Scottish Office in the early years of this century to facilitate land settlement mostly after the First World War often for returning soldiers and sailors. The Estates vary considerably in size and extent, from the very large Estates in Skye with hundreds of tenants to very small pockets in other areas, especially on the East Coast. Altogether there are almost 1,400 crofting lets over some 105,000 hectares of land. There are 55 tenanted crofting estates but only 30 have common grazings. The Secretary of State's Department currently owns and receives income from the sporting rights on 18 estates and mineral rights on 27 estates.

In the consultation paper it was suggested that a crofting trust would own all the land on a particular estate or group of estates on behalf of the local communities concerned. It would own all the common grazings and the tenanted inbye land. The existing crofting tenants would become tenants of the Crofting Trusts and the protection, rights and obligations given to crofters under the Crofters (Scotland) Act 1993 (c. 44) would continue to apply including security of tenure, fair rents and the right to compensation for tenant's improvements; eligibility to apply for assistance under the various crofting grants schemes; the right to acquire the house site and inbye land from the landlord *i.e.* the Crofting Trust and the obligation on tenants to continue to pay rent for their crofts to the Trust. There are various mechanisms for establishing a Trust, for example, as a company limited by guarantee or as a co-operative. It would be for the crofters to decide whether membership of the Trust should be restricted to local crofters or also include other local community representatives. The consultation paper gives three examples of existing Croft Trusts at Assynt, Borve and Annishadder and the Stornoway Trust.

It is stated in the consultation paper that the benefits of a Crofting Trust would allow local communities to own the land and, therefore, exercise control and choice over the management of the estate as a whole and ownership of the land might include any associated sporting and mineral rights depending on the terms in which the land is transferred to the Trust. In general, however, ownership of the land should allow the local community to exploit potential development opportunities in both the short and long term. The creation of a Crofting Trust would ensure that the day to day management of the Estate and use of the land is sympathetic to local needs. It is difficult to be specific about the type of development opportunity that might arise, since each community will have its own priorities and each township its own characteristics. Nevertheless some examples of the opportunities and projects that might be developed include

---

* Annotations by Keith Graham, Principal Clerk of the Scottish Land Court.

forestry development schemes; the development of fisheries on land and sea; the exploitation of natural resources for windpower or hydro electricity schemes; the development of recreational, cultural and tourist projects and the setting aside of land for housing for local people or small scale industries on crofts.

The Transfer of Crofting Estates (Scotland) Act 1997 (c. 26) gives the Secretary of State power to dispose of his crofting estates to bodies which he believes are representative of the crofters on the estate. The Act also gives the Secretary of State power to provide financial assistance in establishing such bodies and removes any rights of pre-emption over the estates.

ABBREVIATIONS

the 1993 Act: the Crofters (Scotland) Act 1993 (c. 44).

DEFINITIONS

These words are used throughout this Act:

"Crofting counties": The former counties of Argyll, Caithness, Inverness, Orkney, Ross and Cromarty, Sutherland and Shetland—see s.61 of the Crofters (Scotland) Act 1993.
"Crofting interests": s.7(1).
"Crofting property": s.1(3).
"relevant property": s.6(5).
"right of pre-emption": s.5(8).

Disposal of crofting property

1.—(1) The Secretary of State may dispose of any of his crofting property in accordance with this Act.

(2) The power of the Secretary of State under subsection (1) may be exercised by him notwithstanding any restriction contained in any other enactment or rule of law which affects the right of—

(a) the Secretary of State in particular; or

(b) the owner of any interest in such property,

to dispose of such property.

(3) In this Act any reference, however expressed, to the crofting property of the Secretary of State shall include any property in which he has an interest as owner—

(a) which is held subject to the 1993 Act;

(b) which comprises fishermen's dwellings and holdings for the purposes of section 4(1)(e) of the Congested Districts (Scotland) Act 1897; or

(c) which is situated in the crofting counties and is held as part of the Secretary of State's crofting estate but is not held subject to the 1993 Act.

(4) The disposal of property under this Act shall be on such terms as the Secretary of State, with the consent of the Treasury, may agree with the body acquiring the property.

(5) Where the Secretary of State disposes of any crofting property under this Act the disposal may include the disposal of any interest he has in the mineral, sporting or other rights effeiring to the property.

(6) Where the Secretary of State disposes of crofting property under this Act—

(a) no body or person acquiring such property; and

(b) no body or person who acquires any such property under any subsequent disposal,

shall be entitled to require proof of consent of the Treasury to the disposal or shall be affected by any failure or omission to obtain such consent.

(7) Any sums received by the Secretary of State in pursuance of this section shall be paid into the Consolidated Fund.

DEFINITIONS

"Crofting property": s.1(3).
"Crofting counties": see s.61(1) of the Crofters (Scotland) Act 1993.
"the 1993 Act": Crofters (Scotland) Act 1993.

GENERAL NOTE
Subsections (1) and (2) of s.1 give the Secretary of State power to dispose of his crofting property.

Subsection (3) defines crofting property with reference to property held subject to the 1993 Act which must include crofts, common grazings and cottar subjects. Also included in the definition of crofting property are fishermen's dwellings and holdings created by the Commissioners of the Congested Districts Board in terms of the Congested Districts (Scotland) Act 1897 (c. 53). The definition of crofting property also includes properties situated in the crofting counties (the former counties of Argyll, Caithness, Inverness, Orkney, Ross and Cromarty, Sutherland and Shetland) which are part of the Secretary of State's crofting estate but not subject to the 1993 Act. Presumably this would include any agricultural holdings situated in these counties.

Subsection (4) states that the disposal of property shall be subject to such terms as the Secretary of State and the body acquiring the property may agree. There is no mechanism in the Act to have such terms determined by any third party should the Secretary of State and the acquiring body fail to agree. The phrase "terms" must include the question of a consideration payable for the property, for subs. (7) obliges the Secretary of State to pay any sums received in pursuance of subs. (1) into the Consolidated Fund. Again there is no mechanism in the Act to enable a third party to determine the consideration payable should the Secretary of State and the acquiring body fail to agree on the amount of the consideration. In the House of Lords, the Parliamentary Under-Secretary of State (the Earl of Lindsay) said that the Government "envisage that the vast majority of land will be transferred free of charge, but exceptions may be necessary to protect the public interest and on the grounds of equity." [*Hansard*, Vol. 577, col. CWH5.]

Subsection (5) allows the Secretary of State to include in the disposal of any crofting property, interest he has in mineral, sporting or other rights. These rights could in certain circumstances be of considerable value to the acquiring authority and indeed could make the acquiring authority a viable proposition.

Restrictions on disposal

2.—(1) The Secretary of State may dispose of crofting property under this Act only to a body, corporate or unincorporated, which has been approved by him, after consultation with the Commission, as a body which—
   (a) is representative of the crofting interests in the property to be disposed of; and
   (b) has the promotion of the interests of persons residing on such property as its primary objective.

(2) For the purposes of responding to the consultation, the Commission shall have regard to—
   (a) the general interests of the crofting community in the district in which the property is situated;
   (b) the views of crofters in that district; and
   (c) any other matter which they consider to be relevant.

(3) In the application of this section to property mentioned in paragraph (b) or (c) of section 1(3)—
   (a) in each place where it occurs, the word "crofting" shall be omitted; and
   (b) in paragraph (b) of subsection (2) for the word "crofters" there shall be substituted the word "tenants".

DEFINITIONS
   "Crofting property": s.1(3).

GENERAL NOTE
This section in effect restricts the Secretary of State's powers to dispose of crofting property by allowing him to dispose of the property only to organisations which he deems to be representative of the crofting interests in the property and has as one of its primary objectives the promotion of the interests of people residing in the property. The Secretary of State is required to consult with the Commission—presumably the Crofters Commission in Inverness.

Consultation is all that is required with the Commission and presumably therefore the Secretary of State could over-rule a recommendation of the Commission, say, to refuse to dispose of his property to a Crofting Trust. There is no right of appeal should the Secretary of State refuse to approve a Crofting Trust.

Financial assistance by Secretary of State

3. The Secretary of State may provide such assistance as he considers appropriate by way of grant or loan to any body to which he proposes to dispose of crofting property under section 1—
  (a) for the purpose of establishing the body; and
  (b) to defray expenditure incurred by the body by way of legal fees and other costs in connection with the transfer of the property to it.

DEFINITIONS
  "Crofting property": s.1(3).

GENERAL NOTE
  This section allows the Secretary of State to provide financial assistance towards the start up costs of a body to whom property is to be transferred including the legal expenses of the transfer of the property. It should be noted that the section does not empower the Secretary of State to give financial assistance towards the payment of any consideration which he may require in respect of the transfer of the property to the Trust.

Disapplication of the 1897 Act

4. Section 7 of the Congested Districts (Scotland) Act 1897 does not apply to any disposal of crofting property under this Act.

DEFINITIONS
  "crofting property": s.1(3).

GENERAL NOTE
  This section disapplies s.7 of the Congested Districts (Scotland) Act 1897 (c. 53) which would require the Scottish Office to prepare and register all deeds necessary to complete the title to the crofting property in favour of a Crofting Trust.

Rights of pre-emption

5.—(1) Where the Secretary of State disposes of any property under this Act, any right of pre-emption in respect of the property shall, by virtue of this section, be extinguished for all time coming.
  (2) Where the Secretary of State has disposed of any property under this Act he shall advertise the disposal in such manner as appears to him to be appropriate.
  (3) Where, within four months of the publication of an advertisement under subsection (2), no claim for compensation has been intimated to the Secretary of State by a person who is entitled to exercise a right of pre-emption in respect of the property, no compensation shall be payable in respect of the extinction of the right.
  (4) Where a claim for compensation is made within the period of four months the Secretary of State shall notify the claimant that he accepts or rejects the claim; and where the Secretary of State rejects a claim, the claimant may, within a period of six weeks from the date of notification of the rejection, apply to the Scottish Land Court for a determination that the claim is valid.
  (5) Where a claim for compensation is accepted by the Secretary of State or held to be valid by the Scottish Land Court the claimant shall be entitled to compensation of such amount—
  (a) as may be agreed between him and the Secretary of State; or, failing such agreement,
  (b) as may be found to be just by the Scottish Land Court on an application made by the claimant or the Secretary of State.

(6) Subject to subsection (7), the Scottish Land Court shall have jurisdiction to determine all questions arising under this section.

(7) No failure or omission of the Secretary of State or any other person to comply with any provision of this section shall affect the title to any property disposed of by the Secretary of State under this Act.

(8) In this section "right of pre-emption" includes any such right created by any enactment, rule of law or in any document.

DEFINITIONS
"Right of pre-emption": s.5(8).

GENERAL NOTE
This section extinguishes all rights of pre-emption in respect of crofting property which is to be disposed to a Crofting Trust. Such rights of pre-emption may arise from the original conveyance of the Estate in favour of the Secretary of State or indeed in terms of s.6(5) of the Land Settlement (Scotland) Act 1919 (c. 97) which requires the Board (now the Scottish Office Agriculture Environment and Fisheries Department) before selling any land which is not required for the purposes of that Act, to offer the land to the person from whom it was purchased or his successor in title at a price to be determined, failing agreement, by the Scottish Land Court.

The Secretary of State is required to advertise the disposal of any of his property and a period of four months from the publication of the advertisement is allowed for any person claiming to be entitled to exercise a right of pre-emption to notify the Secretary of State. If such a claim is lodged, the Secretary of State must notify the claimant as to whether he accepts or rejects the claim and in the event of the claim being rejected the claimant may apply to the Scottish Land Court for a determination that the claim is valid. If a claim for compensation is accepted by the Secretary of State the claimant is then entitled to compensation, which, failing agreement may be determined by the Scottish Land Court.

In the event of a claimant being notified that the Secretary of State rejects his claim then an application should be submitted to the Scottish Land Court (1 Grosvenor Crescent, Edinburgh, EH12 5ER). Such an application could contain two craves, the first asking the Court to determine the claimant's entitlement to exercise a right of pre-emption and in the event of him being successful in that crave and negotiations on the question of compensation with the Secretary of State failing, then to assess the amount of compensation. No guidelines are laid down as to how the Court are to assess the amount of compensation.

Subsection (6) confers jurisdiction on the Court to determine all questions arising from the section. As the Scottish Land Court is a statutory body this subsection is necessary to confer jurisdiction. Even where parties agree to refer a particular matter to the Court for decision that is not sufficient to confer jurisdiction and any jurisdiction must be conferred by Act of Parliament—see *McCallum v. Arthur*, 1956 S.L.C.R. 3 at p. 13.

Continuation of tenant's entitlement to buy holding

6.—(1) Where relevant property is disposed of by the Secretary of State under this Act, section 6(3) and (4) of the Land Settlement (Scotland) Act 1919 shall apply to the tenant of that property as if for the references to "the Board" or, as the case may be, "the Secretary of State" there were substituted references to the body to whom the Secretary of State disposes of the relevant property and any successor in title to such body.

(2) A tenant's period of occupation shall continue to run for the purposes of section 6(3) of the Land Settlement (Scotland) Act 1919 notwithstanding that the relevant property has been disposed of by the Secretary of State to a body under this Act or to any successor in title.

(3) In this section "relevant property" means property to which section 6(3) of the Land Settlement (Scotland) Act 1919 applies.

DEFINITIONS
"relevant property": s.6(3).

GENERAL NOTE
This section ensures the continuation of the right of tenants of land not subject to crofting tenure, as conferred by the Land Settlement (Scotland) Act 1919, to buy their holdings if they have been in occupation for six years or more.

Interpretation

7.—(1) In this Act—

"crofting interests" in relation to any property, means the persons with an interest in the property—

(a) as tenants; or

(b) by virtue of rights to use any common grazings forming part of the property;

"crofting property of the Secretary of State" and cognate expressions shall be construed in accordance with section 1(3);

"the 1993 Act" means the Crofters (Scotland) Act 1993.

(2) Expression used in this Act and in the 1993 Act shall, unless the context otherwise requires, have the same meaning as in that Act.

Short title, commencement and extent

8.—(1) This Act may be cited as the Transfer of Crofting Estates (Scotland) Act 1997.

(2) This Act shall come into force on such day as the Secretary of State may, by order made by statutory instrument, appoint.

(3) This Act extends to Scotland only.

GENERAL NOTE

The Act is to come into effect on a date to be determined by the Secretary of State by Statutory Instrument.

INDEX

References are to sections

SOCIAL SECURITY (RECOVERY OF BENEFITS) ACT 1997

(1997 c. 27)

ARRANGEMENT OF SECTIONS

An Act to re-state, with amendments, Part IV of the Social Security Administration Act 1992. [19th March 1997]

PARLIAMENTARY DEBATES
Hansard, H.L. Vol. 575, cols. 731, 1200, 1215; Vol. 576, cols. 672, 941, 968; Vol. 577, cols. 110, 628. H.C. Vol. 291, col. 170; Vol. 292, col. 749.

INTRODUCTION
This Act creates a revised scheme whereby the Secretary of State can recover benefits paid in respect of an accident, injury or disease where the person claiming the benefits also receives compensation from a third party. The compensator will be liable to repay to the Secretary of State the full amount of certain benefits paid to the injured person, and will then be entitled to reduce the payment to the injured person.

Introductory

Cases in which this Act applies

1.—(1) This Act applies in cases where—
(a) a person makes a payment (whether on his own behalf or not) to or in respect of any other person in consequence of any accident, injury or disease suffered by the other, and
(b) any listed benefits have been, or are likely to be, paid to or for the other during the relevant period in respect of the accident, injury or disease.
(2) The reference above to a payment in consequence of any accident, injury or disease is to a payment made—
(a) by or on behalf of a person who is, or is alleged to be, liable to any extent in respect of the accident, injury or disease, or
(b) in pursuance of a compensation scheme for motor accidents;
but does not include a payment mentioned in Part I of Schedule 1.
(3) Subsection (1)(a) applies to a payment made—
(a) voluntarily, or in pursuance of a court order or an agreement, or otherwise, and
(b) in the United Kingdom or elsewhere.
(4) In a case where this Act applies—
(a) the "injured person" is the person who suffered the accident, injury or disease,
(b) the "compensation payment" is the payment within subsection (1)(a), and
(c) "recoverable benefit" is any listed benefit which has been or is likely to be paid as mentioned in subsection (1)(b).

Compensation payments to which this Act applies

2. This Act applies in relation to compensation payments made on or after the day on which this section comes into force, unless they are made in pursuance of a court order or agreement made before that day.

"The relevant period"

3.—(1) In relation to a person ("the claimant") who has suffered any accident, injury or disease, "the relevant period" has the meaning given by the following subsections.

(2) Subject to subsection (4), if it is a case of accident or injury, the relevant period is the period of five years immediately following the day on which the accident or injury in question occurred.

(3) Subject to subsection (4), if it is a case of disease, the relevant period is the period of five years beginning with the date on which the claimant first claims a listed benefit in consequence of the disease.

(4) If at any time before the end of the period referred to in subsection (2) or (3)—

(a) a person makes a compensation payment in final discharge of any claim made by or in respect of the claimant and arising out of the accident, injury or disease, or

(b) an agreement is made under which an earlier compensation payment is treated as having been made in final discharge of any such claim,

the relevant period ends at that time.

Certificates of recoverable benefits

Applications for certificates of recoverable benefits

4.—(1) Before a person ("the compensator") makes a compensation payment he must apply to the Secretary of State for a certificate of recoverable benefits.

(2) Where the compensator applies for a certificate of recoverable benefits, the Secretary of State must—

(a) send to him a written acknowledgement of receipt of his application, and

(b) subject to subsection (7), issue the certificate before the end of the following period.

(3) The period is—

(a) the prescribed period, or

(b) if there is no prescribed period, the period of four weeks,

which begins with the day following the day on which the application is received.

(4) The certificate is to remain in force until the date specified in it for that purpose.

(5) The compensator may apply for fresh certificates from time to time.

(6) Where a certificate of recoverable benefits ceases to be in force, the Secretary of State may issue a fresh certificate without an application for one being made.

(7) Where the compensator applies for a fresh certificate while a certificate ("the existing certificate") remains in force, the Secretary of State must issue the fresh certificate before the end of the following period.

(8) The period is—

(a) the prescribed period, or

(b) if there is no prescribed period, the period of four weeks,

which begins with the day following the day on which the existing certificate ceases to be in force.

(9) For the purposes of this Act, regulations may provide for the day on which an application for a certificate of recoverable benefits is to be treated as received.

Information contained in certificates

5.—(1) A certificate of recoverable benefits must specify, for each recoverable benefit—

(a) the amount which has been or is likely to have been paid on or before a specified date, and

(b) if the benefit is paid or likely to be paid after the specified date, the rate and period for which, and the intervals at which, it is or is likely to be so paid.

(2) In a case where the relevant period has ended before the day on which the Secretary of State receives the application for the certificate, the date specified in the certificate for the purposes of subsection (1) must be the day on which the relevant period ended.

(3) In any other case, the date specified for those purposes must not be earlier than the day on which the Secretary of State received the application.

(4) The Secretary of State may estimate, in such manner as he thinks fit, any of the amounts, rates or periods specified in the certificate.

(5) Where the Secretary of State issues a certificate of recoverable benefits, he must provide the information contained in the certificate to—

(a) the person who appears to him to be the injured person, or

(b) any person who he thinks will receive a compensation payment in respect of the injured person.

(6) A person to whom a certificate of recoverable benefits is issued or who is provided with information under subsection (5) is entitled to particulars of the manner in which any amount, rate or period specified in the certificate has been determined, if he applies to the Secretary of State for those particulars.

Liability of person paying compensation

Liability to pay Secretary of State amount of benefits

6.—(1) A person who makes a compensation payment in any case is liable to pay to the Secretary of State an amount equal to the total amount of the recoverable benefits.

(2) The liability referred to in subsection (1) arises immediately before the compensation payment or, if there is more than one, the first of them is made.

(3) No amount becomes payable under this section before the end of the period of 14 days following the day on which the liability arises.

(4) Subject to subsection (3), an amount becomes payable under this section at the end of the period of 14 days beginning with the day on which a certificate of recoverable benefits is first issued showing that the amount of recoverable benefit to which it relates has been or is likely to have been paid before a specified date.

Recovery of payments due under section 6

7.—(1) This section applies where a person has made a compensation payment but—

(a) has not applied for a certificate of recoverable benefits, or

(b) has not made a payment to the Secretary of State under section 6 before the end of the period allowed under that section.

(2) The Secretary of State may—

(a) issue the person who made the compensation payment with a certificate of recoverable benefits, if none has been issued, or

(b) issue him with a copy of the certificate of recoverable benefits or (if more than one has been issued) the most recent one,

and (in either case) issue him with a demand that payment of any amount due under section 6 be made immediately.

(3) The Secretary of State may, in accordance with subsections (4) and (5), recover the amount for which a demand for payment is made under subsection (2) from the person who made the compensation payment.

(4) If the person who made the compensation payment resides or carries on business in England and Wales and a county court so orders, any amount recoverable under subsection (3) is recoverable by execution issued from the county court or otherwise as if it were payable under an order of that court.

(5) If the person who made the payment resides or carries on business in Scotland, any amount recoverable under subsection (3) may be enforced in like manner as an extract registered decree arbitral bearing a warrant for execution issued by the sheriff court of any sheriffdom in Scotland.

(6) A document bearing a certificate which—

(a) is signed by a person authorised to do so by the Secretary of State, and

(b) states that the document, apart from the certificate, is a record of the amount recoverable under subsection (3),

is conclusive evidence that that amount is so recoverable.

(7) A certificate under subsection (6) purporting to be signed by a person authorised to do so by the Secretary of State is to be treated as so signed unless the contrary is proved.

Reduction of compensation payment

Reduction of compensation payment

8.—(1) This section applies in a case where, in relation to any head of compensation listed in column 1 of Schedule 2—

(a) any of the compensation payment is attributable to that head, and

(b) any recoverable benefit is shown against that head in column 2 of the Schedule.

(2) In such a case, any claim of a person to receive the compensation payment is to be treated for all purposes as discharged if—

(a) he is paid the amount (if any) of the compensation payment calculated in accordance with this section, and

(b) if the amount of the compensation payment so calculated is nil, he is given a statement saying so by the person who (apart from this section) would have paid the gross amount of the compensation payment.

(3) For each head of compensation listed in column 1 of the Schedule for which paragraphs (a) and (b) of subsection (1) are met, so much of the gross amount of the compensation payment as is attributable to that head is to be reduced (to nil, if necessary) by deducting the amount of the recoverable benefit or, as the case may be, the aggregate amount of the recoverable benefits shown against it.

(4) Subsection (3) is to have effect as if a requirement to reduce a payment by deducting an amount which exceeds that payment were a requirement to reduce that payment to nil.

(5) The amount of the compensation payment calculated in accordance with this section is—

(a) the gross amount of the compensation payment,

less

(b) the sum of the reductions made under subsection (3),

(and, accordingly, the amount may be nil).

Section 8: supplementary

9.—(1) A person who makes a compensation payment calculated in accordance with section 8 must inform the person to whom the payment is made—

(a) that the payment has been so calculated, and

(b) of the date for payment by reference to which the calculation has been made.

(2) If the amount of a compensation payment calculated in accordance with section 8 is nil, a person giving a statement saying so is to be treated for the purposes of this Act as making a payment within section 1(1)(a) on the day on which he gives the statement.

(3) Where a person—

(a) makes a compensation payment calculated in accordance with section 8, and

(b) if the amount of the compensation payment so calculated is nil, gives a statement saying so,

he is to be treated, for the purpose of determining any rights and liabilities in respect of contribution or indemnity, as having paid the gross amount of the compensation payment.

(4) For the purposes of this Act—

(a) the gross amount of the compensation payment is the amount of the compensation payment apart from section 8, and

(b) the amount of any recoverable benefit is the amount determined in accordance with the certificate of recoverable benefits.

Reviews and appeals

Review of certificates of recoverable benefits

10.—(1) The Secretary of State may review any certificate of recoverable benefits if he is satisfied—

(a) that it was issued in ignorance of, or was based on a mistake as to, a material fact, or

(b) that a mistake (whether in computation or otherwise) has occurred in its preparation.

(2) On a review under this section the Secretary of State may either—

(a) confirm the certificate, or

(b) (subject to subsection (3)) issue a fresh certificate containing such variations as he considers appropriate.

(3) The Secretary of State may not vary the certificate so as to increase the total amount of the recoverable benefits unless it appears to him that the variation is required as a result of the person who applied for the certificate supplying him with incorrect or insufficient information.

Appeals against certificates of recoverable benefits

11.—(1) An appeal against a certificate of recoverable benefits may be made on the ground—

(a) that any amount, rate or period specified in the certificate is incorrect, or

(b) that listed benefits which have been, or are likely to be, paid otherwise than in respect of the accident, injury or disease in question have been brought into account.

(2) An appeal under this section may be made by—

(a) the person who applied for the certificate of recoverable benefits, or

(b) (in a case where the amount of the compensation payment has been calculated under section 8) the injured person or other person to whom the payment is made.

(3) No appeal may be made under this section until—

(a) the claim giving rise to the compensation payment has been finally disposed of, and

(b) the liability under section 6 has been discharged.

(4) For the purposes of subsection (3)(a), if an award of damages in respect of a claim has been made under or by virtue of—

(a) section 32A(2)(a) of the Supreme Court Act 1981,

(b) section 12(2)(a) of the Administration of Justice Act 1982, or

(c) section 51(2)(a) of the County Courts Act 1984,

(orders for provisional damages in personal injury cases), the claim is to be treated as having been finally disposed of.

(5) Regulations may make provision—

(a) as to the manner in which, and the time within which, appeals under this section may be made,

(b) as to the procedure to be followed where such an appeal is made, and

(c) for the purpose of enabling any such appeal to be treated as an application for review under section 10.

(6) Regulations under subsection (5)(c) may (among other things) provide that the circumstances in which a review may be carried out are not to be restricted to those specified in section 10(1).

Reference of questions to medical appeal tribunal

12.—(1) The Secretary of State must refer to a medical appeal tribunal any question mentioned in subsection (2) arising for determination on an appeal under section 11.

(2) The questions are any concerning—

(a) any amount, rate or period specified in the certificate of recoverable benefits, or

(b) whether listed benefits which have been, or are likely to be, paid otherwise than in respect of the accident, injury or disease in question have been brought into account.

(3) In determining any question referred to it under subsection (1), the tribunal must take into account any decision of a court relating to the same, or any similar, issue arising in connection with the accident, injury or disease in question.

(4) On a reference under subsection (1) a medical appeal tribunal may either—

(a) confirm the amounts, rates and periods specified in the certificate of recoverable benefits, or

(b) specify any variations which are to be made on the issue of a fresh certificate under subsection (5).

(5) When the Secretary of State has received the decisions of the tribunal on the questions referred to it under subsection (1), he must in accordance with those decisions either—

(a) confirm the certificate against which the appeal was brought, or

(b) issue a fresh certificate.

(6) Regulations may make provision—

(a) as to the manner in which, and the time within which, a reference under subsection (1) is to be made, and

(b) as to the procedure to be followed where such a reference is made.

(7) Regulations under subsection (6)(b) may (among other things) provide for the non-disclosure of medical advice or medical evidence given or submitted following a reference under subsection (1).

(8) In this section "medical appeal tribunal" means a medical appeal tribunal constituted under section 50 of the Social Security Administration Act 1992.

Appeal to Social Security Commissioner

13.—(1) An appeal may be made to a Commissioner against any decision of a medical appeal tribunal under section 12 on the ground that the decision was erroneous in point of law.

(2) An appeal under this section may be made by—

(a) the Secretary of State,

(b) the person who applied for the certificate of recoverable benefits, or

(c) (in a case where the amount of the compensation payment has been calculated in accordance with section 8) the injured person or other person to whom the payment is made.

(3) Subsections (7) to (10) of section 23 of the Social Security Administration Act 1992 apply to appeals under this section as they apply to appeals under that section.

(4) In this section "Commissioner" has the same meaning as in the Social Security Administration Act 1992 (see section 191).

Reviews and appeals: supplementary

14.—(1) This section applies in cases where a fresh certificate of recoverable benefits is issued as a result of a review under section 10 or an appeal under section 11.

(2) If—

(a) a person has made one or more payments to the Secretary of State under section 6, and

(b) in consequence of the review or appeal, it appears that the total amount paid is more than the amount that ought to have been paid,

regulations may provide for the Secretary of State to pay the difference to that person, or to the person to whom the compensation payment is made, or partly to one and partly to the other.

(3) If—

(a) a person has made one or more payments to the Secretary of State under section 6, and

(b) in consequence of the review or appeal, it appears that the total amount paid is less than the amount that ought to have been paid,

regulations may provide for that person to pay the difference to the Secretary of State.

(4) Regulations under this section may provide—

(a) for the re-calculation in accordance with section 8 of the amount of any compensation payment,

(b) for giving credit for amounts already paid, and

(c) for the payment by any person of any balance or the recovery from any person of any excess,

and may provide for any matter by modifying this Act.

Courts

Court orders

15.—(1) This section applies where a court makes an order for a compensation payment to be made in any case, unless the order is made with the consent of the injured person and the person by whom the payment is to be made.

(2) The court must, in the case of each head of compensation listed in column 1 of Schedule 2 to which any of the compensation payment is attributable, specify in the order the amount of the compensation payment which is attributable to that head.

Payments into court

16.—(1) Regulations may make provision (including provision modifying this Act) for any case in which a payment into court is made.

(2) The regulations may (among other things) provide—

(a) for the making of a payment into court to be treated in prescribed circumstances as the making of a compensation payment,

(b) for application for, and issue of, certificates of recoverable benefits, and

(c) for the relevant period to be treated as ending on a date determined in accordance with the regulations.

(3) Rules of court may make provision governing practice and procedure in such cases.

(4) This section does not extend to Scotland.

Benefits irrelevant to assessment of damages

17. In assessing damages in respect of any accident, injury or disease, the amount of any listed benefits paid or likely to be paid is to be disregarded.

Reduction of compensation: complex cases

Lump sum and periodical payments

18.—(1) Regulations may make provision (including provision modifying this Act) for any case in which two or more compensation payments in the form of lump sums are made by the same person to or in respect of the injured person in consequence of the same accident, injury or disease.

(2) The regulations may (among other things) provide—

(a) for the re-calculation in accordance with section 8 of the amount of any compensation payment,

(b) for giving credit for amounts already paid, and

(c) for the payment by any person of any balance or the recovery from any person of any excess.

(3) For the purposes of subsection (2), the regulations may provide for the gross amounts of the compensation payments to be aggregated and for—

(a) the aggregate amount to be taken to be the gross amount of the compensation payment for the purposes of section 8,

(b) so much of the aggregate amount as is attributable to a head of compensation listed in column 1 of Schedule 2 to be taken to be the part of the gross amount which is attributable to that head;

and for the amount of any recoverable benefit shown against any head in column 2 of that Schedule to be taken to be the amount determined in accordance with the most recent certificate of recoverable benefits.

(4) Regulations may make provision (including provision modifying this Act) for any case in which, in final settlement of the injured person's claim, an agreement is entered into for the making of—

(a) periodical compensation payments (whether of an income or capital nature), or

(b) periodical compensation payments and lump sum compensation payments.

(5) Regulations made by virtue of subsection (4) may (among other things) provide—

(a) for the relevant period to be treated as ending at a prescribed time,

(b) for the person who is to make the payments under the agreement to be treated for the purposes of this Act as if he had made a single compensation payment on a prescribed date.

(6) A periodical payment may be a compensation payment for the purposes of this section even though it is a small payment (as defined in Part II of Schedule 1).

Payments by more than one person

19.—(1) Regulations may make provision (including provision modifying this Act) for any case in which two or more persons ("the compensators") make compensation payments to or in respect of the same injured person in consequence of the same accident, injury or disease.

(2) In such a case, the sum of the liabilities of the compensators under section 6 is not to exceed the total amount of the recoverable benefits, and the regulations may provide for determining the respective liabilities under that section of each of the compensators.

(3) The regulations may (among other things) provide in the case of each compensator—

(a) for determining or re-determining the part of the recoverable benefits which may be taken into account in his case,

(b) for calculating or re-calculating in accordance with section 8 the amount of any compensation payment,

(c) for giving credit for amounts already paid, and

(d) for the payment by any person of any balance or the recovery from any person of any excess.

Miscellaneous

Amounts overpaid under section 6

20.—(1) Regulations may make provision (including provision modifying this Act) for cases where a person has paid to the Secretary of State under section 6 any amount ("the amount of the overpayment") which he was not liable to pay.

(2) The regulations may provide—

(a) for the Secretary of State to pay the amount of the overpayment to that person, or to the person to whom the compensation payment is made, or partly to one and partly to the other, or

(b) for the receipt by the Secretary of State of the amount of the overpayment to be treated as the recovery of that amount.

(3) Regulations made by virtue of subsection (2)(b) are to have effect in spite of anything in section 71 of the Social Security Administration Act 1992 (overpayments - general).

(4) The regulations may also (among other things) provide—

(a) for the re-calculation in accordance with section 8 of the amount of any compensation payment,

(b) for giving credit for amounts already paid, and

(c) for the payment by any person of any balance or the recovery from any person of any excess.

(5) This section does not apply in a case where section 14 applies.

Compensation payments to be disregarded

21.—(1) If, when a compensation payment is made, the first and second conditions are met, the payment is to be disregarded for the purposes of sections 6 and 8.

(2) The first condition is that the person making the payment—

(a) has made an application for a certificate of recoverable benefits which complies with subsection (3), and

(b) has in his possession a written acknowledgment of the receipt of his application.

(3) An application complies with this subsection if it—

(a) accurately states the prescribed particulars relating to the injured person and the accident, injury or disease in question, and

(b) specifies the name and address of the person to whom the certificate is to be sent.

(4) The second condition is that the Secretary of State has not sent the certificate to the person, at the address, specified in the application, before the end of the period allowed under section 4.

(5) In any case where—

(a) by virtue of subsection (1), a compensation payment is disregarded for the purposes of sections 6 and 8, but

(b) the person who made the compensation payment nevertheless makes a payment to the Secretary of State for which (but for subsection (1)) he would be liable under section 6,

subsection (1) is to cease to apply in relation to the compensation payment.

(6) If, in the opinion of the Secretary of State, circumstances have arisen which adversely affect normal methods of communication—

(a) he may by order provide that subsection (1) is not to apply during a specified period not exceeding three months, and

(b) he may continue any such order in force for further periods not exceeding three months at a time.

Liability of insurers

22.—(1) If a compensation payment is made in a case where—

(a) a person is liable to any extent in respect of the accident, injury or disease, and

(b) the liability is covered to any extent by a policy of insurance,

the policy is also to be treated as covering any liability of that person under section 6.

(2) Liability imposed on the insurer by subsection (1) cannot be excluded or restricted.

(3) For that purpose excluding or restricting liability includes—

(a) making the liability or its enforcement subject to restrictive or onerous conditions,

(b) excluding or restricting any right or remedy in respect of the liability, or subjecting a person to any prejudice in consequence of his pursuing any such right or remedy, or

(c) excluding or restricting rules of evidence or procedure.

(4) Regulations may in prescribed cases limit the amount of the liability imposed on the insurer by subsection (1).

(5) This section applies to policies of insurance issued before (as well as those issued after) its coming into force.

(6) References in this section to policies of insurance and their issue include references to contracts of insurance and their making.

Provision of information

23.—(1) Where compensation is sought in respect of any accident, injury or disease suffered by any person ("the injured person"), the following persons must give the Secretary of State the prescribed information about the injured person—

(a) anyone who is, or is alleged to be, liable in respect of the accident, injury or disease, and

(b) anyone acting on behalf of such a person.

(2) A person who receives or claims a listed benefit which is or is likely to be paid in respect of an accident, injury or disease suffered by him, must give the Secretary of State the prescribed information about the accident, injury or disease.

(3) Where a person who has received a listed benefit dies, the duty in subsection (2) is imposed on his personal representative.

(4) Any person who makes a payment (whether on his own behalf or not)—

(a) in consequence of, or

(b) which is referable to any costs (in Scotland, expenses) incurred by reason of,

any accident, injury or disease, or any damage to property, must, if the Secretary of State requests him in writing to do so, give the Secretary of State such particulars relating to the size and composition of the payment as are specified in the request.

(5) The employer of a person who suffers or has suffered an accident, injury or disease, and anyone who has been the employer of such a person at any time during the relevant period, must give the Secretary of State the prescribed information about the payment of statutory sick pay in respect of that person.

(6) In subsection (5) "employer" has the same meaning as it has in Part XI of the Social Security Contributions and Benefits Act 1992.

(7) A person who is required to give information under this section must do so in the prescribed manner, at the prescribed place and within the prescribed time.

(8) Section 1 does not apply in relation to this section.

Power to amend Schedule 2

24.—(1) The Secretary of State may by regulations amend Schedule 2.

(2) A statutory instrument which contains such regulations shall not be made unless a draft of the instrument has been laid before and approved by resolution of each House of Parliament.

Provisions relating to Northern Ireland

Corresponding provision for Northern Ireland

25. An Order in Council made under paragraph 1(1)(b) of Schedule 1 to the Northern Ireland Act 1974 which contains a statement that it is made only for purposes corresponding to those of the provisions of this Act—
- (a) shall not be subject to sub-paragraphs (4) and (5) of paragraph 1 of that Schedule (affirmative resolution of both Houses of Parliament), but
- (b) shall be subject to annulment in pursuance of a resolution of either House of Parliament.

Residence of the injured person

26.—(1) In a case where this Act applies, if the injured person's address is in Northern Ireland—
- (a) the person making the compensation payment must apply for a certificate under the Northern Ireland provisions, and may not make any separate application for a certificate of recoverable benefits,
- (b) any certificate issued as a result under the Northern Ireland provisions—
  - (i) is to be treated as including a certificate of recoverable benefits,
  - (ii) must state that it is to be so treated, and
  - (iii) must state that any payment required to be made to the Secretary of State under this Act is to be made to the Northern Ireland Department as his agent, and
- (c) any payment made pursuant to a certificate so issued is to be applied—
  - (i) first towards discharging the liability of the person making the compensation payment under the Northern Ireland provisions, and
  - (ii) then, as respects any remaining balance, towards discharging his liability under section 6.

(2) In a case where the Northern Ireland provisions apply, if the injured person's address is in any part of Great Britain—
- (a) the person making the compensation payment must apply for a certificate of recoverable benefits, and may not make any separate application for a certificate under the Northern Ireland provisions,

(b) any certificate of recoverable benefits issued as a result—
     (i) is to be treated as including a certificate under the Northern Ireland provisions,
     (ii) must state that it is to be so treated, and
     (iii) must state that any payment required to be made to the Northern Ireland Department under the Northern Ireland provisions is to be made to the Secretary of State as its agent, and
(c) any payment made pursuant to a certificate of recoverable benefits so issued is to be applied—
     (i) first towards discharging the liability of the person making the compensation payment under section 6, and
     (ii) then, as respects any remaining balance, towards discharging his liability under the Northern Ireland provisions.

(3) In this section—
(a) "the injured person's address" is the address first notified in writing to the person making the payment by or on behalf of the injured person as his residence (or, if he has died, by or on behalf of the person entitled to receive the compensation payment as the injured person's last residence),
(b) "Northern Ireland Department" means the Department of Health and Social Services for Northern Ireland,
(c) "the Northern Ireland provisions" means—
     (i) any legislation corresponding to this Act (other than this section and section 27) and having effect in Northern Ireland, and
     (ii) this section and section 27,
and
(d) any reference in relation to the Northern Ireland provisions to—
     (i) the injured person, means the injured person within the meaning of those provisions,
     (ii) a certificate, means a certificate under those provisions corresponding to the certificate of recoverable benefits, and
     (iii) a compensation payment, means a compensation payment within the meaning of those provisions.

Jurisdiction of courts

27.—(1) In a case where this Act applies, if immediately before making a compensation payment a person—
(a) is not resident and does not have a place of business in Great Britain, but
(b) is resident or has a place of business in Northern Ireland,
subsections (4) and (5) of section 7 apply in relation to him as if at that time he were resident or had a place of business in the relevant part of Great Britain.

(2) In a case where the Northern Ireland provisions apply, if immediately before making a compensation payment a person—
(a) is not resident and does not have a place of business in Northern Ireland, but
(b) is resident or has a place of business in any part of Great Britain,
any provision of the Northern Ireland provisions corresponding to subsection (4) or (5) of section 7 applies in relation to him as if at that time he were resident or had a place of business in Northern Ireland.

(3) In this section—
(a) "the relevant part of Great Britain" means—
     (i) the part of Great Britain in which the injured person is or was most recently resident (as determined by any written statement given to the person making the payment by or on behalf of the injured person or, if he has died, by or on behalf of the person entitled to receive the compensation payment), or

(ii) if no such statement has been given, such part of Great Britain as may be prescribed, and

(b) "the Northern Ireland provisions" and references to compensation payments in relation to such provisions have the same meaning as in section 26.

General

The Crown

28. This Act applies to the Crown.

General interpretation

29. In this Act—

"benefit" means any benefit under the Social Security Contributions and Benefits Act 1992, a jobseeker's allowance or mobility allowance,

"compensation scheme for motor accidents" means any scheme or arrangement under which funds are available for the payment of compensation in respect of motor accidents caused, or alleged to have been caused, by uninsured or unidentified persons,

"listed benefit" means a benefit listed in column 2 of Schedule 2,

"payment" means payment in money or money's worth, and related expressions are to be interpreted accordingly,

"prescribed" means prescribed by regulations, and

"regulations" means regulations made by the Secretary of State.

Regulations and orders

30.—(1) Any power under this Act to make regulations or an order is exercisable by statutory instrument.

(2) A statutory instrument containing regulations or an order under this Act (other than regulations under section 24 or an order under section 34) shall be subject to annulment in pursuance of a resolution of either House of Parliament.

(3) Regulations under section 20, under section 24 amending the list of benefits in column 2 of Schedule 2 or under paragraph 9 of Schedule 1 may not be made without the consent of the Treasury.

(4) Subsections (4), (5), (6) and (9) of section 189 of the Social Security Administration Act 1992 (regulations and orders - general) apply for the purposes of this Act as they apply for the purposes of that.

Financial arrangements

31.—(1) There are to be paid out of the National Insurance Fund any expenses of the Secretary of State in making payments under section 14 or 20 to the extent that he estimates that those payments relate to sums paid out of that Fund.

(2) There are to be paid out of money provided by Parliament—

(a) any expenses of the Secretary of State in making payments under section 14 or 20 to the extent that he estimates that those payments relate to sums paid out of the Consolidated Fund, and

(b) (subject to subsection (1)) any other expenses of the Secretary of State incurred in consequence of this Act.

(3) Any sums paid to the Secretary of State under section 6 or 14 are to be paid—

(a) into the Consolidated Fund, to the extent that the Secretary of State estimates that the sums relate to payments out of money provided by Parliament, and

(b) into the National Insurance Fund, to the extent that he estimates that they relate to payments out of that Fund.

Power to make transitional, consequential etc. provisions

32.—(1) Regulations may make such transitional and consequential provisions, and such savings, as the Secretary of State considers necessary or expedient in preparation for, in connection with, or in consequence of—

(a) the coming into force of any provision of this Act, or

(b) the operation of any enactment repealed or amended by a provision of this Act during any period when the repeal or amendment is not wholly in force.

(2) Regulations under this section may (among other things) provide—

(a) for compensation payments in relation to which, by virtue of section 2, this Act does not apply to be treated as payments in relation to which this Act applies,

(b) for compensation payments in relation to which, by virtue of section 2, this Act applies to be treated as payments in relation to which this Act does not apply, and

(c) for the modification of any enactment contained in this Act or referred to in subsection (1)(b) in its application to any compensation payment.

Consequential amendments and repeals

33.—(1) Schedule 3 (which makes consequential amendments) is to have effect.

(2) The enactments shown in Schedule 4 are repealed to the extent specified in the third column.

Short title, commencement and extent

34.—(1) This Act may be cited as the Social Security (Recovery of Benefits) Act 1997.

(2) Sections 1 to 24, 26 to 28 and 33 are to come into force on such day as the Secretary of State may by order appoint, and different days may be appointed for different purposes.

(3) Apart from sections 25 to 27, section 33 so far as it relates to any enactment which extends to Northern Ireland, and this section this Act does not extend to Northern Ireland.

SCHEDULES

Section 1

SCHEDULE 1

COMPENSATION PAYMENTS

PART I

EXEMPTED PAYMENTS

1. Any small payment (defined in Part II of this Schedule).

2. Any payment made to or for the injured person under section 35 of the Powers of Criminal Courts Act 1973 or section 249 of the Criminal Procedure (Scotland) Act 1995 (compensation orders against convicted persons).

3. Any payment made in the exercise of a discretion out of property held subject to a trust in a case where no more than 50 per cent. by value of the capital contributed to the trust was directly or indirectly provided by persons who are, or are alleged to be, liable in respect of—

(a) the accident, injury or disease suffered by the injured person, or

(b) the same or any connected accident, injury or disease suffered by another.

4. Any payment made out of property held for the purposes of any prescribed trust (whether the payment also falls within paragraph 3 or not).

5. Any payment made to the injured person by an insurance company within the meaning of the Insurance Companies Act 1982 under the terms of any contract of insurance entered into between the injured person and the company before—

(a) the date on which the injured person first claims a listed benefit in consequence of the disease in question, or

(b) the occurrence of the accident or injury in question.

6. Any redundancy payment falling to be taken into account in the assessment of damages in respect of an accident, injury or disease.

7. So much of any payment as is referable to costs.

8. Any prescribed payment.

PART II

POWER TO DISREGARD SMALL PAYMENTS

9.—(1) Regulations may make provision for compensation payments to be disregarded for the purposes of sections 6 and 8 in prescribed cases where the amount of the compensation payment, or the aggregate amount of two or more connected compensation payments, does not exceed the prescribed sum.

(2) A compensation payment disregarded by virtue of this paragraph is referred to in paragraph 1 as a "small payment".

(3) For the purposes of this paragraph—

(a) two or more compensation payments are "connected" if each is made to or in respect of the same injured person and in respect of the same accident, injury or disease, and

(b) any reference to a compensation payment is a reference to a payment which would be such a payment apart from paragraph 1.

Section 8   SCHEDULE 2

CALCULATION OF COMPENSATION PAYMENT

(1) *Head of compensation*	(2) *Benefit*
1. Compensation for earnings lost during the relevant period	Disability working allowance Disablement pension payable under section 103 of the 1992 Act Incapacity benefit Income support Invalidity pension and allowance Jobseeker's allowance Reduced earnings allowance Severe disablement allowance Sickness benefit Statutory sick pay Unemployability supplement Unemployment benefit
2. Compensation for cost of care incurred during the relevant period	Attendance allowance Care component of disability living allowance Disablement pension increase payable under section 104 or 105 of the 1992 Act
3. Compensation for loss of mobility during the relevant period	Mobility allowance Mobility component of disability living allowance

NOTES

1.—(1) References to incapacity benefit, invalidity pension and allowance, severe disablement allowance, sickness benefit and unemployment benefit also include any income support paid with each of those benefits on the same instrument of payment or paid concurrently with each of those benefits by means of an instrument for benefit payment.

(2) For the purpose of this Note, income support includes personal expenses addition, special transitional additions and transitional addition as defined in the Income Support (Transitional) Regulations 1987.

2. Any reference to statutory sick pay—

(a) includes only 80 per cent. of payments made between 6th April 1991 and 5th April 1994, and

(b) does not include payments made on or after 6th April 1994.

3. In this Schedule "the 1992 Act" means the Social Security Contributions and Benefits Act 1992.

Section 33(1)   SCHEDULE 3

CONSEQUENTIAL AMENDMENTS

Law Reform (Personal Injuries) Act 1948 (c. 41)

1. In section 2 of the Law Reform (Personal Injuries) Act 1948 (assessment of damages in personal injuries actions) subsections (1), (1A), (3) and (6) are omitted.

Social Security Administration Act 1992 (c. 5)

2. The Social Security Administration Act 1992 is amended as follows.

3. Part IV is omitted.

4.—(1) Section 110 (appointment and powers of inspectors) is amended as follows.

(2) In subsection (2)(b)(ii), for "relevant" there is substituted "listed".

(3) In subsections (2)(c)(iii), (6)(a)(iii) and (7)(e)(ii), for "relevant payment" there is substituted "payment to the Secretary of State under section 6 of the Social Security (Recovery of Benefits) Act 1997".

(4) In subsection (3)(d)—

(a) in sub-paragraph (i), for "is the compensator in relation to" there is substituted "makes a compensation payment in consequence of", and

(b) in sub-paragraph (ii), for the words from "any" to the end there is substituted "such a compensation payment has been, may have been, or may be, made".

(5) In subsection (8), the word "and" immediately preceding paragraph (e) is omitted and after that paragraph there is inserted—

"(f) the Social Security (Recovery of Benefits) Act 1997".

(6) For subsection (9) there is substituted—

"(9) In this section "compensation payment" and "listed benefit" have the same meaning as in the Social Security (Recovery of Benefits) Act 1997".

5. In section 125(1) (regulations as to notification of deaths), after "1995" there is inserted "the Social Security (Recovery of Benefits) Act 1997".

6. In section 163 (general financial arrangements), subsections (1)(e) and (2)(i) are omitted.

7. In section 164(6) (destination of repayments), the words from "or paid" to "82 above" are omitted.

8. In section 170(5) (the Social Security Advisory Committee)—

(a) in the definition of "the relevant enactments", after paragraph (ab) there is inserted—

"(ac) the provisions of the Social Security (Recovery of Benefits) Act 1997; and", and

(b) in the definition of "the relevant Northern Ireland enactments", after paragraph (ab) there is inserted—

"(ac) any provisions in Northern Ireland which correspond to provisions of the Social Security (Recovery of Benefits) Act 1997; and".

9. In section 180 (payment of travelling expenses by the Secretary of State), after "1995" (in both places) there is inserted ", the Social Security (Recovery of Benefits) Act 1997".

10. In section 189(8) (Treasury approval to regulations and orders), the words from "and" to "85 above" are omitted.

11. In section 190 (parliamentary control of orders and regulations), in subsection (1)(b), "102(2) or" is omitted.

12. In section 191 (interpretation), the definitions of "compensation payment" and "compensator" are omitted.

13. In section 192(5) (extent), "section 101" is omitted.

SCHEDULE 4

Repeals

Chapter	Short title	Extent of repeal
1948 c. 41.	The Law Reform (Personal Injuries) Act 1948.	In section 2, subsections (1), (1A), (3) and (6).
1985 c. 66.	The Bankruptcy (Scotland) Act 1985.	In section 31(8), the words "and to section 89(2) of the Social Security Administration Act 1992".
1992 c. 5.	The Social Security Administration Act 1992.	Part IV. In section 110(8), the word "and" immediately preceding paragraph (e). In section 163, subsections (1)(e) and (2)(i). In section 164(6), the words from "or paid" to "82 above". In section 189(8), the words from "and" to "85 above". In section 190(1)(b), "102(2) or". In section 191, the definitions of "compensation payment" and "compensator". In section 192(5), "section 101".
1995 c. 18.	The Jobseekers Act 1995.	In Schedule 2, paragraphs 52 and 54.

INDEX

References are to sections and Schedules